Stephans' Railroad Directory

Volume 1

Model Railroader 1934–1985

Trains 1940–1985

COMPILED BY EARL STEPHANS

TIOGA PUBLICATIONS   NEW YORK

Copyright (C) ~~1985~~ 1986 by Earl Stephans

All Rights Reserved

Reproduction or translation of any part of this work beyond that permitted by Sections 107 and 108 of the 1976 United States Copyright Act without the permission of the copyright owner is unlawful. Requests for permission or further information should be addressed to the Permissions Department, Tioga Publications 101 N. Fenton Road Chenango Forks, NY 13746.

Stephans'
Railroad
Directory

Volume 1
Model Railroader
Trains

Library of Congress Cataloging in Publications Data:

Stephans, Earl
    Stephans' Railroad Directory Volume 1
    Model Railroader 1934-1985
    Trains 1940-1985

    1: Index to "Model Railroader" Magazine
    2: Index to "Trains" Magazine
    3: Model Railroads
    4: Prototype Railroads
    5: Railroad History
    6: Railroad Drawings-Plans-Specifications
    7: Model Building Techniques
Library of Congress Catalog Number 86-90268
ISBN 0-9616890-0-5

CONSIST	1ST SEC MR	2ND SEC T	3RD SEC ADM
---------------------------------	---	---	---
DETAILED CONSIST	---	---	4
OPERATING INSTRUCTION UBRI-100	---	---	12
THE SOURCE (HISTORY)	14	240	---
LOCOMOTIVES	16	242	---
PASSENGER CARS	64	282	---
FREIGHT CARS	82	292	---
NON-REVENUE EQUIPMENT	112	298	---
TRACTION	126	302	---
STRUCTURES & SIGNALS	134	304	---
VEHICLES	172	---	---
PROTOTYPE MODELING IDEAS	174	310	---
RAILROAD HISTORIES	178	314	---
MODEL LAYOUTS	180	---	---
ELECTRICAL & ELECTRONICS	200	---	---
TOOLS & MATERIALS	208	---	---
TECHNIQUES	212	---	---
TOY & TINPLATE TRAINS	218	---	---
RAIL ROSTERS	218	324	---
RAIL LITERATURE REVIEWS	220	328	---
GENERAL RAILROADING	230	336	---
APPENDIX A - ROADNAMES	---	---	350
APPENDIX B - BUILDERS	---	---	374
APPENDIX C - MANUFACTURERS	---	---	378
CATEGORY INDEX	---	---	386
DISPATCHERS REPORT	---	---	394
THE OFFICIALS	---	---	396
FREIGHT ORDERS	---	397	399

NOTE: SEE PAGE 400

DETAILED CONSIST	1ST SEC MR	2ND SEC T	3RD SEC ADM
DETAILED CONSIST	---	---	4
OPERATING INSTRUCTION UBRI-100	---	---	12
THE SOURCE (HISTORY)	14	240	---
LOCOMOTIVES	16	242	---
STEAM LOCOMOTIVES	18	244	---
STEAM LOCOMOTIVE PROTOTYPE DATA	18	244	---
STEAM LOCO PROTOTYPE DATA BY ROAD	20	250	---
STEAM LOCOMOTIVE PLANS	21	255	---
STEAM LOCOMOTIVE PLANS BY ROAD	24	255	---
STEAM LOCOMOTIVE PHOTOS	28	256	---
STEAM LOCOMOTIVE PHOTOS BY ROAD	---	261	---
STEAM LOCOMOTIVE MODELS	28	---	---
STEAM LOCOMOTIVE MODEL REVIEWS	34	---	---
STEAM LOCO MODEL REVIEWS BY MFG.	37	---	---
STEAM LOCO MODEL REVIEWS BY ROAD	41	---	---
TENDERS	44	266	---
TENDER PROTOTYPE DATA	44	266	---
TENDER PROTOTYPE DATA BY ROAD	---	266	---
TENDER PLANS	44	266	---
TENDER PLANS BY ROAD	44	---	---
TENDER PHOTOS	44	266	---
TENDER PHOTOS BY ROAD	---	266	---
TENDER MODELS	44	---	---
TENDER MODEL REVIEWS	44	---	---
DIESEL LOCOMOTIVES	46	266	---
DIESEL LOCOMOTIVE PROTOTYPE DATA	46	266	---
DIESEL LOCO PROTOTYPE DATA BY ROAD	47	268	---
DIESEL LOCOMOTIVE PHOTOS	48	269	---
DIESEL LOCOMOTIVE PHOTOS BY ROAD	---	274	---
DIESEL LOCOMOTIVE PLANS	48	278	---
DIESEL LOCOMOTIVE PLANS BY ROAD	49	278	---
DIESEL LOCOMOTIVE MODELS	51	---	---
DIESEL LOCOMOTIVE MODEL REVIEWS	54	---	---
DIESEL LOCO MODEL REVIEWS BY MFG.	56	---	---
DIESEL LOCO MODEL REVIEWS BY ROAD	58	---	---
ELECTRIC LOCOMOTIVES	58	278	---
ELECTRIC LOCOMOTIVE PROTOTYPE DATA	58	278	---
ELEC LOCO PROTOTYPE DATA BY ROAD	58	279	---
ELECTRIC LOCOMOTIVE PLANS	59	279	---
ELECTRIC LOCOMOTIVE PLANS BY ROAD	59	---	---
ELECTRIC LOCOMOTIVE PHOTOS	59	280	---
ELECTRIC LOCOMOTIVE PHOTOS BY ROAD	---	280	---
ELECTRIC LOCOMOTIVE MODELS	60	---	---
ELECTRIC LOCOMOTIVE MODEL REVIEWS	60	---	---
ELEC LOCO MODEL REVIEWS BY MFG.	61	---	---
ELEC LOCO MODEL REVIEWS BY ROAD	61	---	---
GENERAL LOCOMOTIVES	62	281	---
GENERAL LOCOMOTIVE PROTOTYPE DATA	62	281	---
GENERAL LOCO PROTOTYPE DATA BY ROAD	---	281	---
GENERAL LOCOMOTIVE MODELING	62	---	---
GENERAL LOCOMOTIVE MODEL REVIEWS	63	---	---
PASSENGER EQUIPMENT	64	282	---
BAGGAGE CARS	66	284	---
BAGGAGE CAR PROTOTYPE DATA	66	284	---
BAGGAGE CAR PLANS	66	---	---

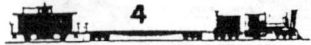

DETAILED CONSIST	1ST SEC MR	2ND SEC T	3RD SEC ADM
BAGGAGE CAR PLANS BY ROAD	66	---	---
BAGGAGE CAR MODELS	66	---	---
BAGGAGE CAR MODEL REVIEWS	66	---	---
BAGGAGE CAR MODEL REVIEWS BY MFG.	66	---	---
COMBINES	67	---	---
COMBINE PROTOTYPE DATA	67	---	---
COMBINE PLANS	67	---	---
COMBINE PLANS BY ROAD	67	---	---
COMBINE PHOTOS	67	---	---
COMBINE MODELS	68	---	---
COMBINE MODEL REVIEWS	68	---	---
COMBINE MODEL REVIEWS BY MFG.	68	---	---
EXPRESS CARS	68	284	---
EXPRESS CAR PROTOTYPE DATA	---	284	---
EXPRESS CAR PLANS	68	---	---
EXPRESS CAR PLANS BY ROAD	68	---	---
EXPRESS CAR MODELS	68	---	---
EXPRESS CAR MODEL REVIEWS	69	---	---
EXPRESS CAR MODEL REVIEWS BY MFG.	69	---	---
DINERS	69	284	---
DINER PROTOTYPE DATA	69	284	---
DINER PLANS	69	---	---
DINER PLANS BY ROAD	69	---	---
DINER PHOTOS	---	284	---
DINER PHOTOS BY ROAD	---	284	---
DINER RECIPES	---	284	---
DINER MODELS	69	---	---
DINER MODEL REVIEWS	69	---	---
DINER MODEL REVIEWS BY MFG.	69	---	---
RPO CARS	70	284	---
RPO PROTOTYPE DATA	70	284	---
RPO PLANS	70	---	---
RPO PLANS BY ROAD	70	---	---
RPO PHOTOS	---	284	---
RPO MODELS	70	---	---
RPO MODEL REVIEWS	70	---	---
RPO MODEL REVIEWS BY MFG.	70	---	---
SLEEPERS	70	285	---
SLEEPER PROTOTYPE DATA	70	285	---
SLEEPER PROTOTYPE DATA BY ROAD	---	285	---
SLEEPER PLANS	70	---	---
SLEEPER PLANS BY ROAD	70	---	---
SLEEPER PHOTOS	---	285	---
SLEEPER PHOTOS BY ROAD	---	285	---
SLEEPER MODELS	71	---	---
SLEEPER MODEL REVIEWS	71	---	---
SLEEPER MODEL REVIEWS BY MFG.	71	---	---
COACHES	71	284	---
COACH PROTOTYPE DATA	71	284	---
COACH PROTOTYPE DATA BY ROAD	---	284	---
COACH PLANS	71	284	---
COACH PLANS BY ROAD	72	---	---
COACH PHOTOS	72	284	---
COACH PHOTOS BY ROAD	---	284	---
COACH MODELS	73	---	---

DETAILED CONSIST	1ST SEC MR	2ND SEC T	3RD SEC ADM
COACH MODEL REVIEWS	73	---	---
COACH MODEL REVIEWS BY ROAD	74	---	---
COACH MODEL REVIEWS BY MFG.	75	---	---
DOME CARS	75	285	---
DOME CAR PROTOTYPE DATA	75	285	---
DOME CAR PROTOTYPE DATA BY ROAD	---	285	---
DOME CAR PLANS	75	---	---
DOME CAR PLANS BY ROAD	75	---	---
DOME CAR PHOTOS	---	285	---
DOME CAR PHOTOS BY ROAD	---	285	---
DOME CAR MODELS	76	---	---
DOME CAR MODEL REVIEWS	76	---	---
DOME CAR MODEL REVIEWS BY MFG.	76	---	---
OBSERVATION CARS	76	285	---
OBSERVATION CAR PROTOTYPE DATA	76	285	---
OBSERVATION CAR PLANS	76	---	---
OBSERVATION CAR PLANS BY ROAD	76	---	---
OBSERVATION CAR PHOTOS	---	285	---
OBSERVATION CAR PHOTOS BY ROAD	---	286	---
OBSERVATION CAR MODELS	76	---	---
OBSERVATION CAR MODEL REVIEWS	76	---	---
OBSERVATION CAR MODEL REVIEWS BY MFG.	76	---	---
RAILCARS	77	286	---
RAILCAR PROTOTYPE DATA	77	286	---
RAILCAR PROTOTYPE DATA BY ROAD	---	286	---
RAILCAR PLANS	77	286	---
RAILCAR PLANS BY ROAD	77	---	---
RAILCAR PHOTOS	77	286	---
RAILCAR PHOTOS BY ROAD	---	287	---
RAILCAR MODELS	77	---	---
RAILCAR MODEL REVIEWS	77	---	---
RAILCAR MODEL REVIEWS BY MFG.	77	---	---
GENERAL PASSENGER CARS	78	287	---
GENERAL PASSENGER CAR PROTOTYPE DATA	78	287	---
GENERAL PASS CAR PROTOTYPE DATA BY ROAD	---	289	---
GENERAL PASSENGER CAR PLANS	78	287	---
GENERAL PASSENGER CAR PLANS BY ROAD	78	---	---
GENERAL PASSENGER CAR PHOTOS	78	287	---
GENERAL PASSENGER CAR PHOTOS BY ROAD	---	287	---
GENERAL PASSENGER CAR MODELS	79	---	---
GENERAL PASSENGER CAR MODEL REVIEWS	80	---	---
GENERAL PASS CAR MODEL REVIEWS BY MFG.	80	---	---
FREIGHT CARS	82	292	---
BOX CARS	84	294	---
BOX CAR PROTOTYPE DATA	84	294	---
BOX CAR PROTOTYPE DATA BY ROAD	84	294	---
BOX CAR PLANS	84	---	---
BOX CAR PLANS BY ROAD	85	---	---
BOX CAR PHOTOS	85	294	---
BOX CAR PHOTOS BY ROAD	---	294	---
BOX CAR MODELS	86	---	---
BOX CAR MODEL REVIEWS	87	---	---
BOX CAR MODEL REVIEWS BY ROAD	89	---	---
BOX CAR MODEL REVIEWS BY MFG.	89	---	---
FLAT CARS	91	294	---

DETAILED CONSIST	1ST SEC MR	2ND SEC T	3RD SEC ADM
FLAT CAR PROTOTYPE DATA	91	294	---
FLAT CAR PROTOTYPE DATA BY ROAD	91	---	---
FLAT CAR PLANS	91	295	---
FLAT CAR PLANS BY ROAD	92	---	---
FLAT CAR PHOTOS	---	295	---
FLAT CAR PHOTOS BY ROAD	---	295	---
FLAT CAR MODELS	92	---	---
FLAT CAR MODEL REVIEWS	93	---	---
FLAT CAR MODEL REVIEWS BY ROAD	93	---	---
FLAT CAR MODEL REVIEWS BY MFG.	94	---	---
GONDOLAS	94	295	---
GONDOLA PROTOTYPE DATA	94	295	---
GONDOLA PROTOTYPE DATA BY ROAD	94	295	---
GONDOLA PLANS	95	---	---
GONDOLA PLANS BY ROAD	95	---	---
GONDOLA MODELS	96	---	---
GONDOLA MODEL REVIEWS	96	---	---
GONDOLA MODEL REVIEWS BY ROAD	97	---	---
GONDOLA MODEL REVIEWS BY MFG.	97	---	---
HOPPERS	98	295	---
HOPPER PROTOTYPE DATA	98	295	---
HOPPER PROTOTYPE DATA BY ROAD	98	295	---
HOPPER PLANS	98	---	---
HOPPER PLANS BY ROAD	99	---	---
HOPPER PHOTOS	99	295	---
HOPPER PHOTOS BY ROAD	---	296	---
HOPPER MODELS	100	---	---
HOPPER MODEL REVIEWS	101	---	---
HOPPER MODEL REVIEWS BY ROAD	101	---	---
HOPPER MODEL REVIEWS BY MFG.	102	---	---
REFRIGERATOR CARS	102	296	---
REFRIGERATOR CAR PROTOTYPE DATA	102	296	---
REFRIGERATOR PROTOTYPE DATA BY ROAD	102	---	---
REFRIGERATOR CAR PLANS	103	---	---
REFRIGERATOR PLANS BY ROAD	103	---	---
REFRIGERATOR CAR PHOTOS	103	296	---
REFRIGERATOR CAR MODELS	103	---	---
REFRIGERATOR CAR MODEL REVIEWS	104	---	---
REFRIGERATOR MODEL REVIEWS BY ROAD	104	---	---
REFRIGERATOR MODEL REVIEWS BY MFG.	105	---	---
STOCK CARS	105	296	---
STOCK CAR PROTOTYPE DATA	105	---	---
STOCK CAR PLANS	105	---	---
STOCK CAR PLANS BY ROAD	106	---	---
STOCK CAR PHOTOS	106	296	---
STOCK CAR MODELS	106	---	---
STOCK CAR MODEL REVIEWS	106	---	---
STOCK CAR MODEL REVIEWS BY ROAD	106	---	---
STOCK CAR MODEL REVIEWS BY MFG.	106	---	---
TANK CARS	107	296	---
TANK CAR PROTOTYPE DATA	107	296	---
TANK CAR PROTOTYPE DATA BY ROAD	---	296	---
TANK CAR PLANS	107	---	---
TANK CAR PLANS BY ROAD	107	---	---
TANK CAR PHOTOS	107	296	---

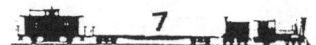

DETAILED CONSIST	1ST SEC MR	2ND SEC T	3RD SEC ADM
TANK CAR MODELS	107	---	---
TANK CAR MODEL REVIEWS	108	---	---
TANK CAR MODEL REVIEWS BY ROAD	108	---	---
TANK CAR MODEL REVIEWS BY MFG.	109	---	---
GENERAL FREIGHT CARS	109	297	---
GENERAL FREIGHT PROTOTYPE DATA	109	297	---
GENERAL FRT PROTOTYPE DATA BY ROAD	---	297	---
GENERAL FREIGHT PLANS	109	---	---
GENERAL FREIGHT MODELS	110	---	---
GENERAL FREIGHT MODEL REVIEWS	110	---	---
GENERAL FREIGHT MODEL REVIEWS BY MFG.	111	---	---
NON-REVENUE EQUIPMENT	112	298	---
CABOOSES	114	300	---
CABOOSE PROTOTYPE DATA	114	300	---
CABOOSE PROTOTYPE DATA BY ROAD	---	300	---
CABOOSE PLANS	114	---	---
CABOOSE PLANS BY ROAD	115	---	---
CABOOSE PHOTOS	116	300	---
CABOOSE PHOTOS BY ROAD	---	300	---
CABOOSE MODELS	117	---	---
CABOOSE MODEL REVIEWS	118	---	---
CABOOSE MODEL REVIEWS BY ROAD	119	---	---
CABOOSE MODEL REVIEWS BY MFG.	119	---	---
MOW EQUIPMENT	120	300	---
MOW PROTOTYPE DATA	120	300	---
MOW PROTOTYPE DATA BY ROAD	---	300	---
MOW PLANS	120	---	---
MOW PLANS BY ROAD	121	---	---
MOW PHOTOS	121	301	---
MOW PHOTOS BY ROAD	---	301	---
MOW MODELS	121	---	---
MOW MODEL REVIEWS	122	---	---
MOW MODEL REVIEWS BY ROAD	123	---	---
MOW MODEL REVIEWS BY MFG.	123	---	---
TRACTION	126	302	---
TRACTION PROTOTYPE DATA	128	303	---
TRACTION PROTOTYPE DATA BY ROAD	---	303	---
TRACTION PLANS	128	---	---
TRACTION PLANS BY ROAD	129	---	---
TRACTION PHOTOS	---	303	---
TRACTION PHOTOS BY ROAD	---	303	---
TRACTION MODELS	130	---	---
TRACTION MODEL REVIEWS	131	---	---
TRACTION MODEL REVIEWS BY ROAD	132	---	---
TRACTION MODEL REVIEWS BY MFG.	133	---	---
TRACTION IN GENERAL	---	303	---
STRUCTURES & SIGNALS	134	304	---
BRIDGES & TUNNELS	136	306	---
BRIDGE & TUNNEL PROTOTYPE DATA	136	306	---
BRIDGE & TUNNEL PROTOTYPE DATA BY ROAD	---	306	---
BRIDGE & TUNNEL PLANS	136	306	---
BRIDGE & TUNNEL PLANS BY ROAD	137	---	---
BRIDGE & TUNNEL PHOTOS	137	306	---
BRIDGE & TUNNEL PHOTOS BY ROAD	---	306	---
BRIDGE & TUNNEL MODELS	137	---	---

DETAILED CONSIST	1ST SEC MR	2ND SEC T	3RD SEC ADM
BRIDGE & TUNNEL MODEL REVIEWS	138	---	---
BRIDGE & TUNNEL MODEL REVIEWS BY MFG	139	---	---
COMMERCIAL STRUCTURES	140	306	---
COMMERCIAL BUILDING PROTOTYPE DATA	140	---	---
COMMERCIAL BUILDING PLANS	141	---	---
COMMERCIAL BUILDING PLANS BY ROAD	142	---	---
COMMERCIAL BUILDING PHOTOS	142	306	---
COMMERCIAL BUILDING MODELS	143	---	---
COMMERCIAL BUILDING MODEL REVIEWS	145	---	---
COMMERCIAL BUILDING MODEL REV BY MFG.	148	---	---
DEPOTS	150	307	---
DEPOT PROTOTYPE DATA	150	307	---
DEPOT PROTOTYPE DATA BY ROAD	---	307	---
DEPOT PLANS	151	307	---
DEPOT PLANS BY ROAD	152	---	---
DEPOT PHOTOS	---	307	---
DEPOT PHOTOS BY ROAD	---	307	---
DEPOT MODELS	153	---	---
DEPOT MODEL REVIEWS	154	---	---
DEPOT MODEL REVIEWS BY MFG.	154	---	---
RAILROAD STRUCTURES	155	307	---
RAILROAD STRUCTURE PROTOTYPE DATA	155	307	---
RAILROAD STRUCTURE PROTOTYPE DATA BY RD	---	308	---
RAILROAD STRUCTURE PLANS	156	---	---
RAILROAD STRUCTURE PLANS BY ROAD	158	---	---
RAILROAD STRUCTURE PHOTOS	---	308	---
RAILROAD STRUCTURE PHOTOS BY ROAD	---	308	---
RAILROAD STRUCTURE MODELS	159	---	---
RAILROAD STRUCTURE MODEL REVIEWS	162	---	---
RAILROAD STRUCTURE MODEL REV BY MFG.	164	---	---
RAILROAD STRUCTURE MODEL REV BY ROAD	165	---	---
SIGNALS	166	308	---
SIGNAL PROTOTYPE DATA	166	308	---
SIGNAL PROTOTYPE DATA BY ROAD	---	308	---
SIGNAL PLANS	166	---	---
SIGNAL PLANS BY ROAD	166	---	---
SIGNAL PHOTOS	166	308	---
SIGNAL PHOTOS BY ROAD	---	308	---
SIGNAL MODELS	167	---	---
SIGNAL MODEL REVIEWS	167	---	---
SIGNAL MODEL REVIEWS BY MFG.	168	---	---
GENERAL STRUCTURES	168	---	---
GENERAL STRUCTURE PROTOTYPE DATA	168	---	---
GENERAL STRUCTURE PLANS	168	---	---
GENERAL STRUCTURE PLANS BY ROAD	168	---	---
GENERAL STRUCTURE MODELS	169	---	---
GENERAL STRUCTURE MODEL REVIEWS	170	---	---
GENERAL STRUCTURE MODEL REV BY MFG.	170	---	---
VEHICLES	172	---	---
VEHICLE PLANS	173	---	---
VEHICLE PHOTOS	---	311	---
VEHICLE MODELS	173	---	---
VEHICLE MODEL REVIEWS	173	---	---
PROTOTYPE MODELING IDEAS	174	310	---
RAILROADS YOU CAN MODEL	175	---	---

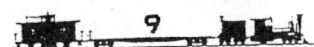

DETAILED CONSIST	1ST SEC MR	2ND SEC T	3RD SEC ADM
PROTOTYPE TRACKWORK	175	311	---
PROTOTYPE EXAMPLES	176	311	---
WRECKS	---	311	---
PROTOTYPE SPEED	---	312	---
SPECIAL TRAINS	---	312	---
RAILROAD HISTORIES	178	314	---
MODEL LAYOUTS	180	---	---
LAYOUT DESIGN	181	---	---
LAYOUT PLANS	182	---	---
LAYOUT BUILDING	183	---	---
MODEL TRACKWORK	185	---	---
SCENERY	188	---	---
LAYOUT OPERATION	190	---	---
LAYOUT VISITS	192	---	---
ELECTRICAL & ELECTRONICS	200	---	---
COMPUTERS	201	---	---
GENERAL ELECTRONICS	201	---	---
TOOLS & MATERIALS	208	---	---
TOOLS	209	---	---
MATERIALS	210	---	---
TECHNIQUES	212	---	---
MODELING TECHNIQUES	213	---	---
PAINTING TECHNIQUES	215	---	---
WEATHERING TECHNIQUES	216	---	---
PHOTOGRAPHY	216	311	---
TOY & TINPLATE TRAINS	218	---	---
RAIL ROSTERS	218	324	---
RAIL LITERATURE REVIEWS	220	328	---
PROTOTYPE BOOKS	221	329	---
MODELING BOOKS	227	---	---
VIDEOS	229	---	---
GENERAL RAILROADING	230	336	---
GENERAL RAILROADING FICTION	---	338	---
GENERAL RAILROADING NON-FICTION	---	337	---
GENERAL RAILROADING	231	338	---
APPENDIX A - ROADNAMES	---	---	350
ROADNAME-ABBREVIATION	---	---	351
ABBREVIATION-ROADNAME	---	---	362
APPENDIX B - BUILDERS	---	---	374
BUILDER-ABBREVIATION	---	---	375
ABBREVIATION-BUILDER	---	---	376
APPENDIX C - MANUFACTURERS	---	---	378
MANUFACTURER-ABBREVIATION	---	---	379
ABBREVIATION-MANUFACTURER	---	---	382
CATEGORY INDEX	---	---	386
DISPATCHERS REPORT	---	---	394
THE OFFICIALS	---	---	396
FREIGHT ORDERS	---	397	399

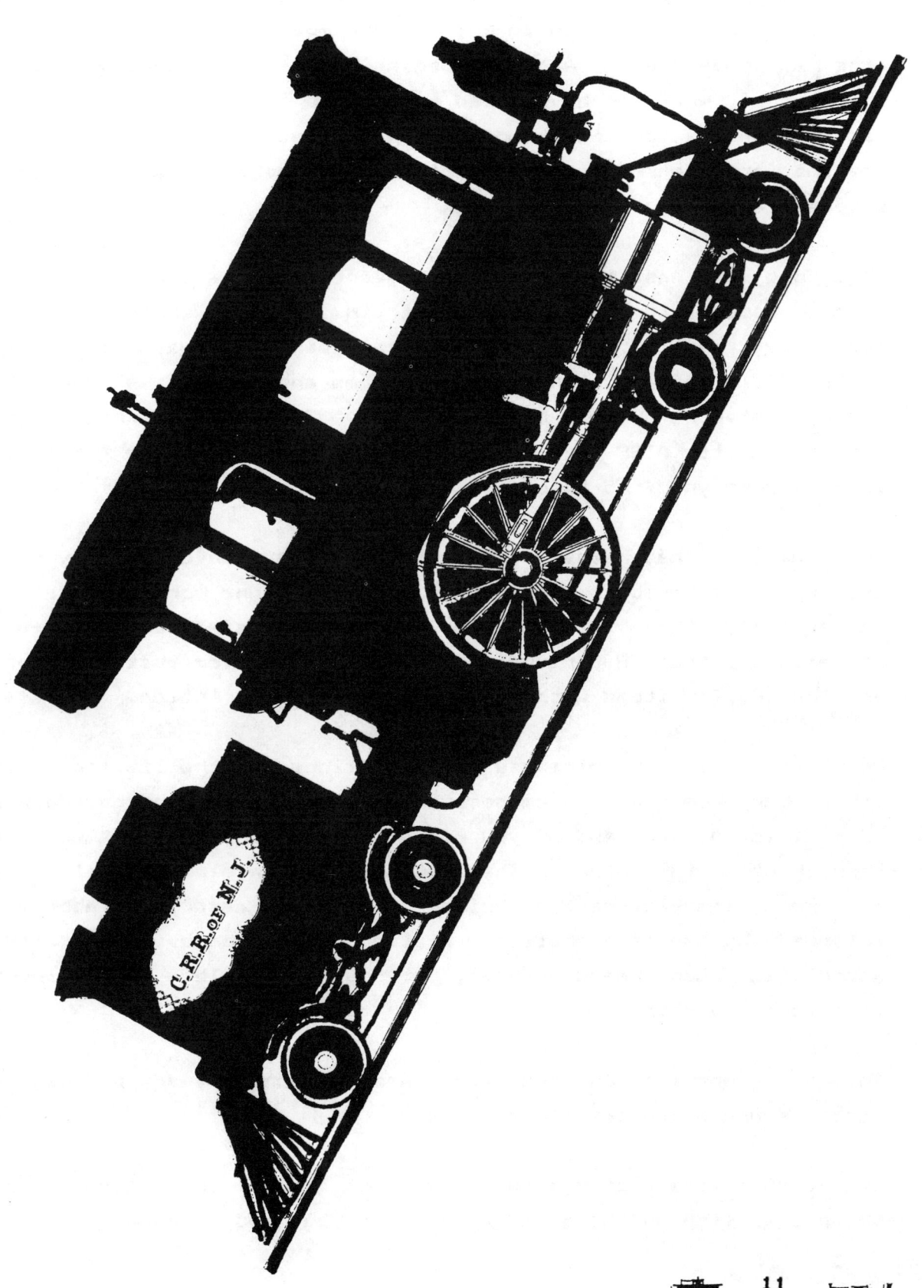

OPERATING INSTRUCTION   UBRI-100

YOU'D BETTER READ IT-100

This index was made to be read as well as a method of looking up your favorite project. The format has a brief description of the item listed. We have tried to put as much meaningful information in this line as possible. At the beginning of each section there is an outline of what we have tried to include in the description for that section and a continuation of the consist showing more detail. The entries are generally by subject only. Some entries may appear under several categories.

This project has taken several years and as a result some slight format inconsistencies have crept in. As an example in the steam locomotive section: The wheel arrangement is always first. This is followed in some instances by road name and locomotive number, and in other instances by road classification. Consequently when looking for your favorite ATSF 4-8-4 you should read down all the 4-8-4 listings to make sure you find them all.

Our computer has helped us with this volume. Unfortunately computers are kind of dumb. They only look at one character at a time. Consequently they think a 2-10-2 should be listed before a 2-8-2. (1 is smaller than 8 in their book.) So watch for that quirk when you are looking for items with numbers in their description.

We have tried to minimize abbreviations in the listings. This at times has been a problem because of the line length constraints. In Appendixes A, B, and C you will find the abbreviations we have used throughout this volume. The listing shows an alphabetical listing of the road, manufacturer, or builder with their associated abbreviation, followed by an alphabetical listing of the abbreviations with their associated road, manufacturer, or builder. This will allow you to find your favorites.

The next entries on the line are the month, year, and page of the magazine where the article resides.

By scanning the listings in the subject area of your interest you will be able to find anything and everything you need to know.

We have tabulated, verified and corrected this data by going through all magazines page by page a minimum of three times. I am sure we still have a few errors. If you find any a card noting them will be greatly appreciated.

Many of the issues listed in this directory are out of print. Tioga Publications maintains a complete library of all issues listed. We will allow research by appointment in this library. We also have duplicate copies of about 80% of these issues. They are available at a nominal cost. You will receive our 6 page list of these and other Railroad titles by sending a Large Self-Addressed Stamped Envelope to:

TIOGA PUBLICATIONS 101 N. Fenton Road Chenango Forks, NY 13746

Magazines are also available from:

WINSTON DALLMAN 332 Brownell Street Fall River, Mass. 02720 who carries a large stock of the most popular Prototype, Railfan and Model Railroading titles. He has a selection of annual reports, employee magazines, and general paper railroadiana. Send a Self-Addressed Stamp Envelope for his list.

C.N. VALLETTE Box 447 Bethayres, PA 19006 has over 50 different railroad oriented titles in stock. Specify interests and send a Large Self-Addressed Stamp Envelope for his current list.

JOHN W. ALKER 1054 Mayflower Court Martinsville, NJ 08836 tries to maintain a stock of back issues of Model Railroader, Railroad Model Craftsman, Trains, and Railroad Magazine from the 1940's to date. Other less long running similar periodicals are also in stock. Quality is guaranteed. Send a Self-Addressed Stamped Envelope for a current list of available magazine issues. Send your want list also. He will notify you when the items you want become available. Phone inquiries are welcome. Call 201-356-5099.

In addition watch the classified ads in the various rail publications for other sources.

NOTE: SEE PAGE 400

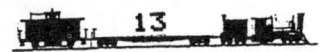

Model Railroader

BILL OF LADING   THE SOURCE (HISTORY)

Model Railroader was conceived in 1933 by Al Kalmbach. It was born in January of 1934 when its first issue was released. This publication has been issued monthly without interruption to date. Over the years it has merged with various other magazines of the hobby and added their highpoints to make a bigger and better Model Railroader. The publisher does have some back issues available. The current subscription rate is $25.00 a year. For back issues and subscription write:

    Model Railroader
    1027 N. Seventh Street
    Milwaukee, Wi 53233

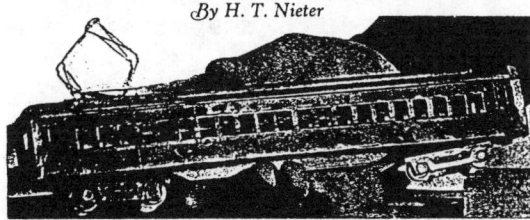

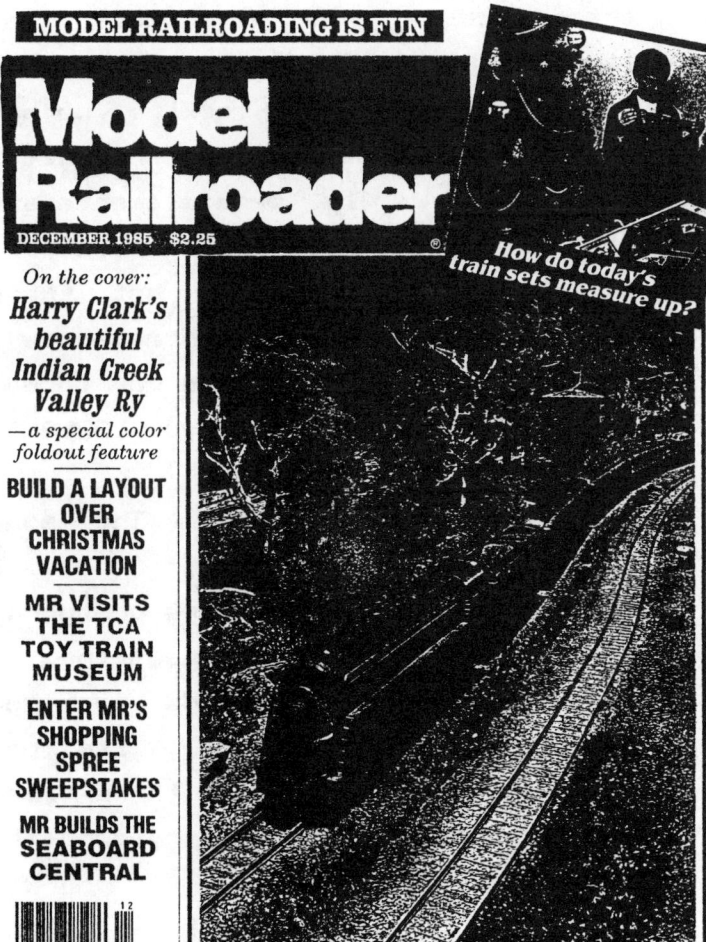

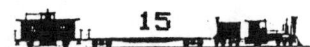

BILL OF LADING LOCOMOTIVES

The locomotive section is broken down into five categories. Steam Locomotives, Tenders, Diesel Locomotives, Electric Locomotives and the catch-all of General Locomotives. Each of these categories is then broken into the five sub categories. Prototype Data, Plans and Drawings, Photos, Models, and Model Reviews.

The prototype data section contains articles on the specific prototype, tables that list prototype specifications and other listings of information of interest. The descriptor line contains the definition of the locomotive, the class, road and road number when available, the builder, and on occasion the year built. All of this information is taken from the article as written. We have made no attempt to research further when the information is not provided. The plans and drawings section lists just that. Again the type of locomotive is followed by class, road, road number, builder, and date. Over the years plans and drawings have improved in quality and detail tremendously. We have tried to specify a plan as a less detailed layout than a drawing. While this is a general practice it is not a rule. Photos come next. We have not tried to list all photos but rather only photos that show detail that would be of interest to the researcher. The same elements are included in the descriptor. Look at the "Prototype Data" section too as many times photographs accompany those entries but those photos did not get billing in the photo section. The three above are presented twice. Once in their alphabetical listing and for those associated with a specific road by road. This should help you LOP&G fans.

Now to models. The model section is generally how to build/kitbash/rebuild/power those little beauties we all know and love. Also included are photographs of exceptional models that have been highlighted in the magazines. As an example, "MOM" in the Model Railroader listing stands for Model of the Month. The model review section lists the model, its road, its scale, and its manufacturer. This section is listed three times: once in alphabetical order, once by road name, and finally by manufacturer.

Hopefully this overall format will become as easy for you to use as it has for us. If you can suggest improvements please drop us a line.

MANIFEST LOCOMOTIVES

	PAGE
LOCOMOTIVES	16
STEAM LOCOMOTIVES	18
STEAM LOCOMOTIVE PROTOTYPE DATA	18
STEAM LOCO PROTOTYPE DATA BY ROAD	20
STEAM LOCOMOTIVE PLANS	21
STEAM LOCOMOTIVE PLANS BY ROAD	24
STEAM LOCOMOTIVE PHOTOS	28
STEAM LOCOMOTIVE MODELS	28
STEAM LOCOMOTIVE MODEL REVIEWS	34
STEAM LOCO MODEL REVIEWS BY MFG.	37
STEAM LOCO MODEL REVIEWS BY ROAD	41
TENDERS	44
TENDER PROTOTYPE DATA	44
TENDER PLANS	44
TENDER PLANS BY ROAD	44
TENDER PHOTOS	44
TENDER MODELS	44
TENDER MODEL REVIEWS	44
DIESEL LOCOMOTIVES	46
DIESEL LOCOMOTIVE PROTOTYPE DATA	46
DIESEL LOCO PROTOTYPE DATA BY ROAD	47
DIESEL LOCOMOTIVE PHOTOS	48
DIESEL LOCOMOTIVE PLANS	48
DIESEL LOCOMOTIVE PLANS BY ROAD	49
DIESEL LOCOMOTIVE MODELS	51
DIESEL LOCOMOTIVE MODEL REVIEWS	54
DIESEL LOCO MODEL REVIEWS BY MFG.	56
DIESEL LOCO MODEL REVIEWS BY ROAD	58
ELECTRIC LOCOMOTIVES	58
ELECTRIC LOCOMOTIVE PROTOTYPE DATA	58
ELEC LOCO PROTOTYPE DATA BY ROAD	58
ELECTRIC LOCOMOTIVE PLANS	59
ELECTRIC LOCOMOTIVE PLANS BY ROAD	59
ELECTRIC LOCOMOTIVE PHOTOS	59
ELECTRIC LOCOMOTIVE MODELS	60
ELECTRIC LOCOMOTIVE MODEL REVIEWS	60
ELEC LOCO MODEL REVIEWS BY MFG.	61
ELEC LOCO MODEL REVIEWS BY ROAD	61
GENERAL LOCOMOTIVES	62
GENERAL LOCOMOTIVE PROTOTYPE DATA	62
GENERAL LOCOMOTIVE MODELING	62
GENERAL LOCOMOTIVE MODEL REVIEWS	63

NOTE: SEE PAGE 400

LOCOMOTIVES

STEAM LOCOMOTIVE PROTOTYPE DATA

	M	Y	P
0-10-2 DM&IR CLASS S7 KING OF SWITCHERS	08	63	30
0-4-0 CLASS C16A OF 1912 BALDWIN B&O #99	12	40	667
0-4-0 FIRELESS LOCOMOTIVE OPC #2	04	81	96
0-4-0 PRR CLASS A-5S LOCOMOTIVES	10	73	46
0-6-0 BALDWIN #3 OPC #3 1920	06	80	77
0-6-0 BALDWIN BUILT SWITCHERS	03	78	74
0-6-0 CLASS M-1 C&NW #2094 1917	07	77	58
0-6-0 MILW SWITCHER UNUSUAL HEADLIGHT	04	71	74
0-6-0 TAYLOR ROUNDHOUSE GOAT #567 SP	09	46	584
0-6-0T B&CH GRANITE LOCOMOTIVES 1916 B	11	83	164
0-8-0 USRA ON MP 1918	01	79	88
2-10-0 LIGHT DECAPODS OF BALDWIN	03	69	42
2-10-0 WM CLASS I2 DECAPODS 1922	06	85	74
2-10-2 LOCOMOTIVES ON ACL 1925 B	07	62	32
2-10-2 LOCOMOTIVES ON C&IM 1925 B	07	62	32
2-10-4 TEXAS C&O CLASS T-1 LIMA 1930	01	77	61
2-10-4 TEXAS TYPE CB&Q CLASS M4 BALDWIN	10	61	36
2-10-4 TEXAS TYPE CLASS E-7 DM&IR BALDWI	10	61	36
2-10-4 TEXAS TYPE CLASS H-1 B&LE BALDWIN	10	61	36
2-4-0 BALDWIN INDUSTRIAL LOCOMOTIVE 1907	11	81	82
2-4-2 COLUMBIA BY BALDWIN	12	63	80
2-4-4T ENGINE #7 B&SR PROTOTYPE DATA	01	78	66
2-6-2 CLASS K1 PRAIRIES MILW #5588 1907	04	37	145
2-8-0 CLASS H-9 CONSOLIDATED WM #810	09	36	263
2-8-0 CLASS H9 OF WM	11	72	48
2-8-0 CLASS I-5C PRR 1892 B	09	45	371
2-8-0 CONSOLIDATION CMI CLASS 115 1886	09	81	78
2-8-0 READER INFORMATION MP	07	75	15
2-8-2 CAMELBACKS LV CLASS N-1 1903 B	02	79	89
2-8-2 CLASS MS-4 MIKADOS OF SOUTHERN	01	82	76
2-8-2 D&RGW CLASS K-37 1928 D&RGW SHOPS	10	79	70
2-8-2 IN BRASS CONST QUESTIONS & ANSWERS	05	83	24
2-8-2 MIKADO CLASS K-27 RGS 1	05	73	61
2-8-2 MIKADO CLASS K-27 RGS DETAILS	06	73	38
2-8-2 MIKADO CLASS K-3A C&O	04	36	102
2-8-2 MIKADO NARROW GAUGE WP&Y	06	74	52
2-8-2 MIKADOS CN CLASS S-2	11	80	93
2-8-2 NARROW GAUGE MIKADO D&RGW #478	07	42	335
2-8-2 NARROW GAUGE MIKADO D&RGW DETAILS	06	73	38
2-8-2 NARROW GAUGE MIKADO D&RGW VAUCLAIN	03	73	61
2-8-2 STD GAUGE MIKADOS OF D&RGW	03	78	80
2-8-2 USRA B&O CLASS Q3 1918 B	10	82	82
2-8-4 C&O CLASS K4 STATISTICS 1946 LIMA	01	76	65
2-8-4 CLASS J-4 BERKSHIRE C&NW#2804 ALCO	01	38	29
2-8-4 CLASS L-63 BERKSHIRE OF IC	12	35	318
2-8-4 OBIQUITOUS NKP BERKSHIRE 1949 L	03	69	30
2-8-4 V CLASS BA STATISTICS 1946 LIMA	01	76	65
2-8-8-2 AC-2 CAB FORWARD DETAILS	01	71	72
2-8-8-2 ARTICULATED CLASS AC-2 SP	11	70	57
2-8-8-2 ARTICULATED DM&IR	07	75	57
26 TON SHAY M-CL 1903	01	85	82
4-14-4 RUSSIAN BUILT LOCOMOTIVE	12	35	337
4-4-0 1873 GRANT LOCOMOTIVES	03	85	114
4-4-0 AMERICAN WM MASON 1856 B&O #25	09	43	405
4-4-0 CAMELBACK CLASS D8C ON READING	12	82	103

STEAM LOCOMOTIVE PROTOTYPE DATA

	M	Y	P
4-4-0 CLASS D-11 READING #419 1914	02	38	68
4-4-0 EIGHT WHEELERS	05	36	125
4-4-2 CLASS D ATLANTICS OF C&NW 1904 SLW	06	81	76
4-4-2 CLASS E6 ATLANTICS PRR	09	78	91
4-4-2 CLASS E6 HISTORY PRR #460	03	34	11
4-4-2 MILWAUKEE TYPE HIAWATHA MILW	09	35	237
4-4-4 TYPES ON CP	12	35	337
4-4-4-4 LOCOMOTIVE ANNOUNCED PRR	07	37	264
4-6-0 CLASS F-1 SOUTHERN LOCOMOTIVES	11	75	64
4-6-0 CLASS P TEN WHEELERS PF 1901 NP	03	37	105
4-6-0 IC 5000 SERIES LOCOMOTIVES	12	81	96
4-6-0 TEN WHEELERS OF SP 1924 SP SHOPS	05	83	64
4-6-2 CLASS E PACIFICS OF C&NW	12	78	76
4-6-2 CLASS E PACIFICS OF C&NW	11	35	289
4-6-2 CLASS F-3 PACIFIC MILW #6105 1913	06	38	240
4-6-2 CLASS J1 OF WABASH	02	70	45
4-6-2 K-4 PACIFIC PRR #5495 1914	07	36	185
4-6-2 L&N K4 & K4A PACIFICS	09	83	78
4-6-2 PACIFIC EVOLUTION	07	78	68
4-6-2 PACIFIC POPPET VALVE CL P-1 D&H653	02	75	52
4-6-2 PACIFICS OF MKT	11	85	92
4-6-2 F6 CLASS HUDSON MILW #6414	01	36	10
4-6-4 HDSN CLASS DIFFERENCE NYC J1A TO E	03	36	66
4-6-4 HUDSON ATSF BALDWIN 1938	05	39	251
4-6-4 HUDSON OF 1927 NYC #5212	02	37	54
4-6-4 VARIATIONS ON NYC	10	78	58
4-6-6-4 "CHALLENGER" UNION PACIFIC	11	39	579
4-6-6T CLASS D1A BOSTON & ALBANY #400	12	37	456
4-8-0'S OF MONON	08	80	77
4-8-2 CLASS M-1A MOUNTAIN LIMA PRR #6707	09	38	368
4-8-2 CLASS M75 OF D&RGW 1926 BALDWIN	06	84	80
4-8-2 MOUNTAIN CLASS K-1 N&W #105	02	63	42
4-8-2 MOUNTAIN N&W K CLASS N&O 1916	11	74	52
4-8-2 MUCH TRAVELED K3 MOUNTAINS ON N&W	12	77	70
4-8-4 C&NW #3006 CLASS H 1929 BALDWIN	06	36	146
4-8-4 CLASS S-2 MILW #206 1940	02	40	95
4-8-4 D&H CLASS 300	04	57	41
4-8-4 MILW CLASS S-3	04	57	41
4-8-4 NORTHERNS OF NP	03	77	60
4-8-4 NORTHERNS OF NP CORRECTION	05	77	23
4-8-4 NYC NIAGARA CLASS	04	57	41
4-8-8-2 SP CLASS AC-9 NON CAB FOWARD	10	63	26
6-4-4-6 CLASS S1 PRR#6100 PRR SHOPS 1939	05	93	93
AIR BRAKE VALVE ACTION	08	68	40
BABY SHAYS POWER AT CONSTRUCT PROJECTS	09	85	103
BALDWIN'S 2-4-4-2	03	62	48
BARCO POWER REVERSE AN UNUSUAL TYPE	01	70	86
BEYER-GARRAT CLASS AD60 NSWG DETAILS	05	66	32
BOOSTERS ENGINES FOR STEAM LOCOMOTIVES	12	65	79
CAMELBACK LOCOMOTIVES	09	85	134
CLASS E2 #578 OF N&W PART 1 1910	08	77	62
CLASS E2 #578 OF N&W PART 2	12	77	38
CLASSIFICATION AND WHEEL ARRANGEMENT	04	34	8
CLASSIFICATION AND WHEEL ARRANGEMENT	04	47	291
CLASSIFICATION AND WHEEL ARRANGEMENT.	02	46	103

LOCOMOTIVES

STEAM LOCOMOTIVE PROTOTYPE DATA

Title	M	Y	P
COAL TURBINE CLASS M-1 LOCOMOTIVE C&O	02	71	47
COMPONENTS OF MODEL STEAM LOCOS B. PETE	02	41	65
CONTINUOUS TRAIN CONTROL ON LOCOMOTIVES	11	83	163
COWLES LOCOMOTIVE 1886-FLAT DRIVE WHEELS	08	51	56
CROSS COMPOUND AIR COMPRESSOR	10	37	365
CYLINDER DRAIN COCKS	05	37	180
CYLINDERS WITH POPET VALVES	08	69	78
DEWITT CLINTON OF MOHAWK & HUDSON	05	79	76
DIFFERENT SIZE CYLINDERS ON MALLETS	01	74	89
DOUBLE HEADERS	05	52	26
DRIVING WHEELS ON STEAM LOCOMOTIVES	02	46	94
DRY ICE COLD STEAM LOCOMOTIVES	10	49	10
DUAL GENERATORS ON SHAYS	08	83	128
ENGINE #6 OF MCCLOUD RIVER RAILROAD	03	78	64
EQUALIZING THE LOCOMOTIVE	09	36	264
FEEDWATER HEATERS	09	53	55
FEEDWATER HEATERS (COFFIN TYPE)	03	68	67
FILER AND STOWELL LOGGING LOCOMOTIVES	05	76	46
FREELANCING ENGINES AN ART VISITED	12	48	908
GRANT 4-4-0 OF 1870 GLW	02	43	77
HOW A STEAM LOCOMOTIVE WORKS	10	82	80
HOW A STEAM LOCOMOTIVE WORKS CORRECTION	11	82	170
INSIDE-OUTSIDE ADMISSION STEAM LOCOS	08	73	76
JAWN HENRY STEAM TURBINE 1950 N&W	10	75	98
JOHNSON BAR CONTROL FOR STEAM LOCOMOTIVE	03	70	64
LARGEST OF THE SHAYS WM LAST ORDER	05	71	43
LARGEST SHAY CORRECTION GC&E #12 1921 L	12	71	88
LE CHATELIER WATER BREAKS	07	65	56
LEADING TRUCKS	08	36	228
LIBERATION MIKADO (FRENCH)	07	73	48
LITTLE JOE IS NO MORE	12	51	44
LOCOMOTIVE AND TENDER DETAILS BLUEBOOK	01	57	67
LOCOMOTIVE CLASS SYMBOLS OF VARIOUS RDS	11	36	323
LOCOMOTIVE CLASSES VS ROAD	10	53	49
LOCOMOTIVE PIPING	11	37	397
LOCOMOTIVE PIPING CLASSIFICATIONS	03	49	30
LOCOMOTIVE RUNNING GEAR BOOMER PETE	11	43	490
LOCOMOTIVE SMOKEBOX COLORS	12	84	165
LOCOMOTIVE TO TENDER CONNECTIONS	03	47	204
LOCOMOTIVE TYPES BLUEBOOK	12	55	73
LOCOMOTIVE WHISTLES	09	36	248
LOCOMOTIVES AND THEIR GADGETS B. PETE	05	43	212
LONGEST SMOKESTACK LONG BELL LUMBER #803	06	80	125
MASON BOGIE VALVE GEAR	11	71	84
MCARTHUR VS MIKADO FOR 2-8-2'S	01	83	165
MIKADO'S SKYLINE DM&IR CLASS N	06	62	27
MILW HIAWATHA 1936	01	84	112
MILW ROAD TRAIN OF '90'S	12	70	47
OVERFIRE JETS ON STEAM LOCOMOTIVES	11	67	71
PARTS DIAGRAM OF A STEAM LOCOMOTIVE	05	70	72
PILOT PLOWS	09	60	26
PILOTS & COWCATCHERS	12	53	88
PILOTS AND COWCATCHERS	04	69	66
POLING AND HOW USED	02	74	83
POPPET VALVES HOW THEY WORK	04	83	142
PORTER MOGUL LOCOMOTIVES	08	65	51
POWER REVERSE WHAT & WHERE	12	63	78
PRESENTING THE ACE 3000	06	82	77
PROTOTYPE LOCOMOTIVE KITBASHING	06	66	58
RAIL SANDING DEVICES	06	37	217
RUSSIANS & YELLOW JACKETS OF NC&SL	02	78	94
SAFETY PLUGS FOR STEAM LOCOMOTIVES	01	45	28
SHAY LOCOMOTIVE OPERATIONS	05	71	30
SHAY SUPERDETAILING PC WEALTH OF INFO	07	83	50
SIAMESE TWIN BALDWIN LOCOMOTIVES	03	78	64
SMOKE LIFTERS	01	73	90A
SMOKESTACKS FOR STEAM LOCOMOTIVES	10	68	79
SP CLASS GS 4-8-4'S	04	72	42
STEAM ENGINE BRAKE RIGGING	08	71	61
STEAM LOCO DETAILS SAFETY APPLIANCES	01	59	95
STEAM LOCO INFOMATION FOR THE NOVICE	12	79	174
STEAM LOCOMOTIVE DESIGN CHARACTERISTICS	12	37	454
STEAM LOCOMOTIVE DETAILS #46	02	59	71
STEAM LOCOMOTIVE DETAILS #48	03	59	67
STEAM LOCOMOTIVE DETAILS #50	04	59	63
STEAM LOCOMOTIVE DETAILS #52	05	59	63
STEAM LOCOMOTIVE DETAILS #54	06	59	63
STEAM LOCOMOTIVE DETAILS #56	07	59	63
STEAM LOCOMOTIVE DETAILS #58	08	59	63
STEAM LOCOMOTIVE SERVICING & FACILITIES	04	82	68
STEAM LOCOMOTIVE SERVICING FACILITIES 1	07	63	59
STEAM LOCOMOTIVE SERVICING FACILITIES 2	08	63	61
STEAM LOCOMOTIVES WHAT, WHY WHEN CORRECT	11	82	170
STEAM LOCOMOTIVES WHAT, WHY, WHEN	10	82	70
STEAM LOCOMOTIVES WHAT, WHY, WHEN ADDEND	12	82	23
STEAM TURBINE LOCOMOTIVE BY GE FOR UP	02	39	100
T3A CLASS NYC ELECTRICS	10	72	43
TAKING WATER ON THE FLY	09	36	264
THREE CYLINDER LOCOMOTIVE RUNNING GEAR	10	64	67
THROTTLE VALVE	12	36	353
TRAILER TRUCK BOOSTER ENGINES	05	82	134
TRIPEX LOCOMOTIVE INFORMATION	06	72	76
VALVE GEAR A.J. STEVENS	10	73	82
VALVE GEAR BAKER	03	38	113
VALVE GEAR BLUEBOOK 5 TYPES	04	56	57
VALVE GEAR CAPROTTI TYPE	08	63	64
VALVE GEAR POSITIONS	09	67	62
VALVE GEAR SOUTHERN	10	36	296
VALVE GEAR STEPHENSON	04	36	89
VALVE GEAR WALSCHAERTS	06	36	147
WHISTLE SIGNALS	02	37	70
WHISTLE SIGNALS.	04	72	71
WHYTE'S CLASSIFICATION OF LOCOMOTIVES	12	42	562

LOCOMOTIVES

STEAM LOCO PROTOTYPE DATA BY ROAD

RD		M	Y	P
ACL	2-10-2 LOCOMOTIVES ON ACL 1925 B	07	62	32
ATSF	4-6-4 HUDSON ATSF BALDWIN 1938	05	39	251
B&A	4-6-6T CLASS D1A BOSTON & ALBANY #400	12	37	456
B&CH	0-6-0T B&CH GRANITE LOCOMOTIVES 1916 B	11	83	164
B&LE	2-10-4 TEXAS TYPE CLASS H-1 B&LE BALDWIN	10	61	36
B&O	2-8-2 USRA B&O CLASS Q3 1918 B	10	82	82
	0-4-0 CLASS C16A OF 1912 BALDWIN B&O #99	12	40	667
	4-4-0 AMERICAN WM MASON 1856 B&O #25	09	43	405
B&SR	2-4-4T ENGINE #7 B&SR PROTOTYPE DATA	01	78	66
C&IM	2-10-2 LOCOMOTIVES ON C&IM 1925 B	07	62	32
C&NW	4-6-2 CLASS E PACIFICS OF C&NW	12	78	76
	4-4-2 CLASS D ATLANTICS OF C&NW 1904 SLW	06	81	76
	4-6-2 CLASS E PACIFICS OF C&NW	11	35	289
	4-8-4 C&NW #3006 CLASS H 1929 BALDWIN	06	36	146
	2-8-4 CLASS J-4 BERKSHIRE C&NW#2804 ALCO	01	38	29
	0-6-0 CLASS M-1 C&NW #2094 1917	07	77	58
C&O	2-8-4 C&O CLASS K4 STATISTICS 1946 LIMA	01	76	65
	2-8-2 MIKADO CLASS K-3A C&O	04	36	102
	2-10-4 TEXAS C&O CLASS T-1 LIMA 1930	01	77	61
	COAL TURBINE CLASS M-1 LOCOMOTIVE C&O	02	71	47
CB&Q	2-10-4 TEXAS TYPE CB&Q CLASS M4 BALDWIN	10	61	36
CMI	2-8-0 CONSOLIDATION CMI CLASS 115 1886	09	81	78
CN	2-8-2 MIKADOS CN CLASS S-2	11	80	93
CP	4-4-4 TYPES ON CP	12	35	337
D&H	4-8-4 D&H CLASS 300	04	57	41
	4-6-2 PACIFIC POPPET VALVE CL P-1 D&H653	02	75	52
D&RGW	2-8-2 D&RGW CLASS K-37 1928 D&RGW SHOPS	10	79	70
	2-8-2 STD GAUGE MIKADOS OF D&RGW	03	78	80
	4-8-2 CLASS M75 OF D&GRW 1926 BALDWIN	06	84	80
	2-8-2 NARROW GAUGE MIKADO D&RGW #478	07	42	335
	2-8-2 NARROW GAUGE MIKADO D&RGW DETAILS	06	73	38
	2-8-2 NARROW GAUGE MIKADO D&RGW VAUCLAIN	03	73	61
DM&IR	0-10-2 DM&IR CLASS S7 KING OF SWITCHERS	08	63	30
	MIKADO'S SKYLINE DM&IR CLASS N	06	62	27
	2-8-8-2 ARTICULATED DM&IR	07	75	57
	2-10-4 TEXAS TYPE CLASS E-7 DM&IR BALDWI	10	61	36
GC&E	LARGEST SHAY CORRECTION GC&E #12 1921 L	12	71	88
IC	4-6-0 IC 5000 SERIES LOCOMOTIVES	12	81	96
	2-8-4 CLASS L-63 BERKSHIRE OF IC	12	35	318
L&N	CONTINUOUS TRAIN CONTROL ON LOCOMOTIVES	11	83	163
	4-6-2 L&N K4 & K4A PACIFICS	09	83	78
LV	2-8-2 CAMELBACKS LV CLASS N-1 1903 B	02	79	89
M	4-8-0'S OF MONON	08	80	77
M&HR	DEWITT CLINTON OF MOHAWK & HUDSON	05	79	76
M-CL	26 TON SHAY M-CL 1903	01	85	82
MCRI	ENGINE #6 OF MCCLOUD RIVER RAILROAD	03	78	64
MILW	MILW HIAWATHA 1936	01	84	112
	4-4-2 MILWAUKEE TYPE HIAWATHA MILW	09	35	237
	4-6-2 F6 CLASS HUDSON MILW #6414	01	36	10
	2-6-2 CLASS K1 PRAIRIES MILW #5588 1907	04	37	145
	4-8-4 CLASS S-2 MILW #206 1940	02	40	95
	4-6-2 CLASS F-3 PACIFIC MILW #6105 1913	06	38	240
	MILW ROAD TRAIN OF '90'S	12	70	47
	0-6-0 MILW SWITCHER UNUSUAL HEADLIGHT	04	71	74
	4-8-4 MILW CLASS S-3	04	57	41
MKT	4-6-2 PACIFICS OF MKT	11	85	92
MP	0-8-0 USRA ON MP 1918	01	79	88
	2-8-0 READER INFORMATION MP	07	75	15
N&W	4-8-2 MOUNTAIN N&W K CLASS N&O 1916	11	74	52
	4-8-2 MOUNTAIN CLASS K-1 N&W #105	02	63	42
	CLASS E2 #578 OF N&W PART 2	12	77	38
	JAWN HENRY STEAM TURBINE 1950 N&W	10	75	98
	CLASS E2 #578 OF N&W PART 1 1910	08	77	62
	4-8-2 MUCH TRAVELED K3 MOUNTAINS ON N&W	12	77	70
NC&SL	RUSSIANS & YELLOW JACKETS OF NC&SL	02	78	94
NKP	2-8-4 OBIQUITOUS NKP BERKSHIRE 1949 L	03	69	30
NP	4-6-0 CLASS P TEN WHEELERS PF 1901 NP	03	37	105
	4-8-4 NORTHERNS OF NP	03	77	60
	4-8-4 NORTHERNS OF NP CORRECTION	05	77	23
NSWG	BEYER-GARRAT CLASS AD60 NSWG DETAILS	05	66	32
NYC	4-6-4 VARIATIONS ON NYC	10	78	58
	4-6-4 HDSN CLASS DIFFERENCE NYC JIA TO E	03	36	66
	4-6-4 HUDSON OF 1927 NYC #5212	02	37	54
	T3A CLASS NYC ELECTRICS	10	72	43
	4-8-4 NYC NIAGARA CLASS	04	57	41
OPC	0-6-0 BALDWIN #3 OPC #3 1920	06	80	77
	0-4-0 FIRELESS LOCOMOTIVE OPC #2	04	81	96
P&R	2-8-0 CLASS I-5C PRR 1892 B	09	45	371
PC	SHAY SUPERDETAILING PC WEALTH OF INFO	07	83	50
PRR	6-4-4-6 CLASS S1 PRR#6100 PRR SHOPS 1939	05	93	93
	4-4-2 CLASS E6 ATLANTICS PRR	09	78	91
	4-6-2 K-4 PACIFIC PRR #5495 1914	07	36	185
	4-4-4-4 LOCOMOTIVE ANNOUNCED PRR	07	37	264
	4-8-2 CLASS M-1A MOUNTAIN LIMA PRR #6707	09	38	368
	4-4-2 CLASS E6 HISTORY PRR #460	03	34	11
	0-4-0 PRR CLASS A-5S LOCOMOTIVES	10	73	46
R	4-4-0 CAMELBACK CLASS D8C ON READING	12	82	103
	4-4-0 CLASS D-11 READING #419 1914	02	38	68
RGS	2-8-2 MIKADO CLASS K-27 RGS DETAILS	06	73	38
	2-8-2 MIKADO CLASS K-27 RGS 1	05	73	61
S	2-8-2 CLASS MS-4 MIKADOS OF SOUTHERN	01	82	76
	4-6-0 CLASS F-1 SOUTHERN LOCOMOTIVES	11	75	64
SP	4-6-0 TEN WHEELERS OF SP 1924 SP SHOPS	05	83	64
	4-8-8-2 SP CLASS AC-9 NON CAB FOWARD	10	63	26
	SP CLASS GS 4-8-4'S	04	72	42
	2-8-8-2 ARTICULATED CLASS AC-2 SP	11	70	57
UP	STEAM TURBINE LOCOMOTIVE BY GE FOR UP	02	39	100
	4-6-6-4 "CHALLENGER" UNION PACIFIC	11	39	579
V	2-8-4 V CLASS BA STATISTICS 1946 LIMA	01	76	65
W	4-6-2 CLASS J1 OF WABASH	02	70	45
WM	2-8-0 CLASS H-9 CONSOLIDATED WM #810	09	36	263
	2-8-0 CLASS H9 OF WM	11	72	48
	LARGEST OF THE SHAYS WM LAST ORDER	05	71	43
	2-10-0 WM CLASS I2 DECAPODS 1922	06	85	74
WP&Y	2-8-2 MIKADO NARROW GAUGE WP&Y	06	74	52

LOCOMOTIVES

STEAM LOCOMOTIVE PLANS

	M	Y	P
0-10-0T SCTC #598 PLANS BALDWIN 1891	08	73	46
0-10-2 SWITCHER PLNS DM&IR#601 CLSS S7 B	08	63	32
0-4-0 CAMELBACK CLASS A4A PLANS R #1196	07	74	58
0-4-0 CAMELBACK CLASS A4B PLANS R #1192	07	74	59
0-4-0 CLASS A-5S PLANS PRR #1288	01	74	75
0-4-0 CLASS A-5S PLANS PRR #1289 1916	10	73	48
0-4-0 CLASS A3 PRR #1591 PLANS	12	52	52
0-4-0 CLASS A3A PRR #310 PLANS	12	52	53
0-4-0 CLASS C16 SADDLE TANK PLNS B&O #97	01	39	23
0-4-0 CLASS C16A B&O #96 PLANS	04	51	16
0-4-0 CLASS C16A B&O #99 PLANS BALDWIN	12	40	666
0-4-0 CRAB LOCO MEZEPPA PLANS B&O #17	07	76	83
0-4-0 DEWITT CLINTON OF M&HR PLANS	05	79	78
0-4-0 FIRELESS PLANS OPC #2 1945 POR	04	81	96
0-4-0 MONONGAHELA CONNECTING #3 PLANS	06	63	48
0-4-0 SANS PAREIL OF 1829 PLANS	03	35	76
0-4-0 YORK OF 1831 B&O	07	76	82
0-4-0T CLASS 4-11C NAR GA PLANS BALDWIN	10	71	42
0-4-0T COMMUNIPAW GOAT PLANS CNJ#840 B	11	62	64
0-4-0T DOCKSIDE PLANS B&O #98	03	47	216
0-4-0T KNICKERBOCKER LIME #4 PLAN 1900 K	07	51	33
0-4-0T PORTER PLANS 1910	10	63	46
0-4-2T VULCAN CL A-4 TANK N-W #12 PLAN	02	37	48
0-6-0 BALDWIN OPC #3 PLANS 1920	06	80	78
0-6-0 BALDWIN SWITCHER PLANS	03	78	74
0-6-0 CAMELBACK CLASS B8A R #1343 PLANS	02	56	39
0-6-0 CLASS B-4A PLANS PRR #101 AS 1893	07	68	42
0-6-0 CLASS F-10 CSPM&O #23 PLANS	01	54	108
0-6-0 CLASS M-1 PLANS C&NW #2094 1917	07	77	60
0-6-0 CLASS M1 SWITCHER PLAN C&NW	10	43	450
0-6-0 CLASS S PLAN UP #4474 LIMA OF 1920	12	58	48
0-6-0 CLASS S-12 SP #126 PLANS	04	38	154
0-6-0 CLASS S-5 PLANS SP #71 BALDWIN	07	61	34
0-6-0 ILLINOIS CENTRAL #216 PLANS	07	37	252
0-6-0 INDUSTRIAL LOCO OIM #86 PLANS	03	52	36
0-6-0 NCC #101 PLANS ALCO OF 1916	05	57	38
0-6-0 PLANS CMI #101 1887 SLW	04	66	36
0-6-0 SWITCHER PLANS NOPB #11 1908 B	07	56	34
0-6-0 USRA #210 PLANS	05	50	38
0-6-0 USRA SWITCHER PLANS	11	36	321
0-6-0 USRA SWITCHER PLN CLSS D30 B&O#350	09	39	457
0-6-0T LEETONIA & CHERRY VALLEY #1 PLANS	05	58	49
0-6-4T GODCHAUX SUGAR #7 PLANS PO 1906	04	56	35
0-8-0 CLASS C-1 PLAN PRR #6556	01	35	12
0-8-0 CLASS M-4 #2636 C&NW PLAN	08	36	216
0-8-0 CLASS S-57 RI #307 1925 ALCO PLANS	04	60	44
0-8-0 INDIANAPOLIS UNION #9 PLANS B	06	53	38
0-8-0 USRA PLANS MP #9777 1918	01	79	90
2-10-0 "RUSSIAN DECAPOD" PLAN FRIS #1618	10	58	38
2-10-0 BALDWIN CLASS 12-45-2 GW #90 PLAN	03	69	42
2-10-0 BR&P PLANS	09	49	12
2-10-0 CLASS I-1 PLANS PRR #4638	02	53	46
2-10-0 CLASS I2 DEPACOD PLANS WM #1112	06	85	78
2-10-10-2 VIRGINIAN #802 ALCO 1913 PLAN	08	67	36
2-10-2 CLASS 3600 ATSF #3876 PLANS	09	54	65

STEAM LOCOMOTIVE PLANS

	M	Y	P
2-10-2 CLASS H-2 PLANS CM&I #757 BALDWIN	07	62	33
2-10-2 CLASS N-1S PLANS PRR #7344 ALCO	11	69	48
2-10-2 CLASS N1 PLANS PRR #7344 1919	10	79	117
2-10-2 CLASS Q1 PLANS ACL B 1925	07	62	33
2-10-2 CLASS S-1 PLANS B&O #6115	05	60	38
2-10-2 IC #2952 SANTA FE TYPE PLAN	07	38	294
2-10-4 CLASS 5011 PLANS ATSF #5012	07	49	34
2-10-4 PLANS B&LE CLASS H-1	10	61	42
2-10-4 PLANS CB&Q CLASS M-4	10	61	42
2-10-4 PLANS DM&IR #716 CLASS E7	10	61	42
2-10-4 T&P #609 PLANS LIMA 1925	10	57	38
2-10-4 TEXAS CLASS T1 C&O #3004 PLANS L	01	77	58
2-10-4 TEXAS PLANS ATSF #5012	04	47	303
2-4-0 INDUSTRIAL LOCO PLANS CLE #2 1907B	11	81	82
2-4-4-2 MALLET PLANS LITRI #126 BALDWIN	03	62	48
2-4-4T #7 PLANS B&SR	01	78	68
2-4-4T SR&RL #9 PLANS 1909 BALDWIN	06	57	51
2-4-4T SUBURBAN PLANS IC #1420	12	65	34
2-6-0 1920 BALDWIN PLANS B&S #112	02	60	64
2-6-0 CLASS 541 PLANS IC #555 1893	03	40	162
2-6-0 CLASS E10A PLANS CN #96 1910	08	62	50
2-6-0 CLASS F-3 PENNSYLVANIA #2063 PLANS	11	44	496
2-6-0 CLASS F4 W #573 PLANS	01	59	42
2-6-0 CLASS M-21 SP #520 PLANS 1928	12	55	68
2-6-0 GREEN BAY & WESTERN #56 PLANS	02	55	42
2-6-0 LOCOMOTIVE OF 1883 PLANS BROOKS	05	58	36
2-6-0 MOGUL BALDWIN 1870 SKETCHES	03	47	226
2-6-0 MOGUL PLANS C&WI #213 LIMA 1925	09	60	36
2-6-0 MOGUL PLANS CNO&TP #230 1884	01	62	34
2-6-0 MOGUL PLANS PANAMA RR #704	12	47	980
2-6-0 MOGUL PLANS VANDALIA	04	49	19
2-6-0 MOGUL SP #1658 CLASS M-4 PLAN	03	35	65
2-6-0 NARROW GAUGE PLANS MWC #6 1891 BAL	08	70	54
2-6-0 NARROW GUAGE PLANS NB&W #2 1904	02	66	52
2-6-0 NYC&H #798 PLANS	11	53	50
2-6-0 OF 1884 PLANS DSP&P #71 CLW	06	60	36
2-6-2 CLASS K-1 MILW #5588 PRAIRIE PLAN	04	37	144
2-6-2 CLASS R-1 PLANS CB&Q #1700 1900	09	69	42
2-6-2 DOUBLE ENDED SWITCHER PL CS&CC#102	09	72	34
2-6-2 NARROW GUAGE PLANS EN #7 PORTER	05	62	24
2-6-6-2 CLASS H-6 C&O #1304 PLANS 1949 B	01	57	42
2-6-6-2 GN 1906 PLANS B	10	53	84
2-6-6-4 MALLET SAL #250 CLASS R-1 PLAN	03	36	62*
2-6-6-6 CLASS H-8 PLANS C&O #1603	02	47	127
2-6-6-T MASON BOGIE CL DH-1 DSP&P#42 PLN	09	60	48
2-8-0 B&O CONSOLIDATION PLANS	11	41	568
2-8-0 BALDWIN PLANS 1914 NCN #9	11	49	30
2-8-0 CAMELBACK CLASS I5C R#952 1892 PLN	03	49	66
2-8-0 CAMELBACK P&R CLASS I-5C 1892 PLAN	09	45	370
2-8-0 CLASS C-2 MILW #7624 PLANS	03	39	138
2-8-0 CLASS H-1 PLANS PRR #369 1875	02	59	40
2-8-0 CLASS H-3 CONSOL PLAN PRR #1187	02	44	78
2-8-0 CLASS H-6SB PLANS PRR #1	01	74	76
2-8-0 CLASS H-6SB PLANS PRR #1 1910	02	61	52
2-8-0 CLASS H-9 CONSOLIDATION WM#810 PLN	09	36	262

LOCOMOTIVES

STEAM LOCOMOTIVE PLANS

	M	Y	P
2-8-0 CLASS H-95 PRR #3506 PLANS	09	48	632
2-8-0 CLASS H9 PLANS WM #830	11	72	50
2-8-0 CLASS I-10 R #2017 PLANS	10	53	50
2-8-0 CLASS I8SA CAMELBACK PLANS R #1504	06	72	56
2-8-0 CLASS Z PLANS C&NW #1712 1910 BALD	04	70	44
2-8-0 CONSOL CLASS H9S PRR #1731 PLANS	12	45	550
2-8-0 CONSOL PLANS B&O #2715 CLASS E27	10	45	418
2-8-0 CONSOLIDATION PLANS CMI CL 115 #1	09	81	78
2-8-0 CONSOLIDATION PLANS IC #908 B 1909	04	58	38
2-8-0 CONSOLIDATION PLANS MA&PA #43	10	59	38
2-8-0 CONSOLIDATION PLANS MA&PA #43 1925	05	72	56
2-8-0 CONSOLIDATION PLANS NCBT #2 1911	04	84	64
2-8-0 CONSOLIDATION PLANS NP #485 B 1889	11	58	46
2-8-0 CONSOLIDATION PLANS UP #6201 (201)	09	58	36
2-8-0 FREELANCE LOCOMOTIVE PLANS	07	40	372
2-8-0 KS7 CLASS S #588 PLANS ALCO 1906	11	56	44
2-8-0 NARROW GAUGE CONSOL D&RGW#223 PLNS	06	44	264
2-8-0 NARROW GAUGE PLANS ET&WNC #5	12	68	70
2-8-0 PLANS MA&PA #26	09	52	42
2-8-0 PLANS MP #152 1910	10	74	50
2-8-0 READING PLAN	01	37	18
2-8-2 "LIBERATION" FRENCH RAILROAD PLANS	07	73	53
2-8-2 ATSF #3283 PLANS	12	53	95
2-8-2 CAMELBACKS LV #220 CLASS N-1 PLANS	02	79	90
2-8-2 CLASS H-10B MIKADO PLANS NYC #2390	01	47	35
2-8-2 CLASS J-2A PLANS L&N #1491	07	64	34
2-8-2 CLASS J-A MIKADO C&NW #2504 PLANS	10	47	815
2-8-2 CLASS K-27 PLANS RGS #461	06	73	44
2-8-2 CLASS K-37 PLANS D&RGW #490 1928	10	79	72
2-8-2 CLASS K3A #2318 C&O PLAN	04	36	102
2-8-2 CLASS L-1S PRR #843 PLANS 1914	06	52	34
2-8-2 CLASS O-8 PLANS GN #3388 1945	08	58	34
2-8-2 CLASS S2C PLANS CN #3546 1923 MLW	11	80	90
2-8-2 CLASS W PLANS NP #1592 1907 BROOKS	09	76	62
2-8-2 MIKADO CLASS 3160 PLANS ATSF 1917	06	40	325
2-8-2 MIKADO CLASS JA C&NW #2504 PLANS	02	49	44
2-8-2 MIKADO PLANS ATSF #3283	06	47	486
2-8-2 MIKADO PLANS EBT #16 BALDWIN 1916	09	61	42
2-8-2 NARROW G CLASS K-27 PLAN D&RGW#453	06	73	44
2-8-2 NARROW G CLASS K-27 PLN D&RGW #450	03	73	58
2-8-2 NARROW GAUGE MIKADO PLNS D&RGW#478	07	42	334
2-8-2 NARROW GAUGE PLANS WP&Y #70 B 1938	06	74	50
2-8-2 PLANS BW&GF #3 1902 BALDWIN	09	65	38
2-8-2 PLANS GNO #105 1929 BALDWIN	06	66	28
2-8-2 USRA B&O #4500 CLASS Q3 PLANS 1918	10	82	82
2-8-2 USRA HEAVY MIKADO PLANS	06	50	38
2-8-2 USRA HEAVY PLANS	02	36	41
2-8-2 USRA LIGHT MIKADO PLANS	06	41	310
2-8-2 USRA MODIFIED PLAN KO&G #602	05	56	34
2-8-2CLASS MS-4 MIKADO PLANS S#4843 1923	01	82	79
2-8-4 CLASS BA PLANS V #507 1946 LIMA	01	76	62
2-8-4 CLASS J-4 PLANS C&NW #2812	01	70	70
2-8-4 CLASS J4 BERKSHIRE C&NW #2804 PLAN	01	38	28
2-8-4 CLASS K2 PLANS C&O #2754 1947 ALCO	01	65	42
2-8-4 CLASS K4 C&O #2771 PLANS	07	67	41

STEAM LOCOMOTIVE PLANS

	M	Y	P
2-8-4 CLASS L-63 PLANS ALCO 1924 IC#7049	12	35	318S
2-8-4 CLASS M-1 PLANS L&N #1967 1942 B	09	59	38
2-8-4 CLASS S-3 PLANS NKP #777 LIMA 1945	07	57	38
2-8-4 CLASS S-4 ERIE #3389 PLANS	08	44	354
2-8-8-2 CAB FORW CLASS AC-2 PLAN SP#4024	11	70	61
2-8-8-2 MALLET PLANS DM&IR #202 1910 B	07	75	54
2-8-8-4 CLASS M-4 PLANS DM&IR #229	03	58	22
4-12-2 PLANS UP #9017 ALCO OF 1926	02	58	40
4-14-4 TYPE RUSSIAN LOCO DRAWING	01	36	14
4-2-0 "PIONEER" C&NW PLANS 1838	06	48	398
4-2-0 LAFAYETTE PLANS B&O #13 1837 NLW	07	76	82
4-4-0 "GENOA" V&T PLANS	07	50	38
4-4-0 1873 GRANT PLANS	03	85	114
4-4-0 1888 DM&IR PLANS 1888	08	38	315
4-4-0 BALDWIN 1880'S PLAN	02	35	34
4-4-0 BOSTON & MAINE #1011 PLANS	11	45	470
4-4-0 BOSTON & MAINE #1011 PLANS	11	48	814
4-4-0 CAMELBACK R #408 CLASS D8C PLANS	12	82	103
4-4-0 CLASS B-3 PLANS KCS #143 1895 PCLW	12	56	64
4-4-0 CLASS D-13C PRR #6013 PLANS 1893	03	56	38
4-4-0 CLASS D-16SB PLANS PRR #6235	09	40	498
4-4-0 CLASS D-3 PENNSYLVANIA PLANS	09	44	388
4-4-0 CLASS H-5 PLANS CMSP #315 1890	11	70	64
4-4-0 CO&L #12 PLANS NARROW GAUGE	04	52	34
4-4-0 D&IR #24 PLAN	12	82	91
4-4-0 GRANT AMERICAN STD DRAWINGS 1870	02	43	78
4-4-0 MA&PA #6 1901 RLW PLANS	03	65	36
4-4-0 NARROW GAUGE CLASS 42 PLANS D&RG	03	44	126
4-4-0 NYC #999 PLANS	05	36	126
4-4-0 NYC #999 PLANS 1893	11	57	44
4-4-0 OF 1852 PLANS B&O #107	12	46	825
4-4-0 OF 1924 PLANS CORNWALL #14	04	61	38
4-4-0 ORIGINAL "WM CROOKS" SP&P #1 PLAN	06	67	36
4-4-0 PLANS B&O #853	12	52	32
4-4-0 PLANS D&IR #24 BALDWIN 1888	09	67	34
4-4-0 PLANS NYNH&H #1213	05	36	126
4-4-0 PLANS W&N OF 1911 B	10	52	46
4-4-0 READING #419 PLANS CLASS D-11 1914	02	38	66
4-4-0 SAM HILL PLANS A&G	08	41	414
4-4-2 "HIAWATHA" MILW TYPE CMSP&P PLAN	09	35	238
4-4-2 ATLANTIC #395 C&NW PLAN	06	35	156
4-4-2 ATLANTIC B&O CLASS A-1 #1472 PLANS	05	38	198
4-4-2 ATLANTIC CLASS 1480 ATSF#1491 PLNS	04	49	50
4-4-2 ATLANTIC PLANS ATSF #1491	02	51	64
4-4-2 ATLANTIC PLANS RI	04	35	89
4-4-2 ATLANTIC PLANS SP #3000	01	50	49
4-4-2 CLASS 1480 ATSF #1493 PLANS	10	40	549
4-4-2 CLASS A-6 #3003 PLANS SP	07	37	245
4-4-2 CLASS A-79 IC #1006 PLANS	09	37	328
4-4-2 CLASS A-9 B&SQ #1485 PLAN 1904 BLW	02	57	44
4-4-2 CLASS D C&NW #126 PLANS	08	40	437
4-4-2 CLASS D PLANS C&NW #493 1904 SLW	06	81	77
4-4-2 CLASS E-1 CBELT #605 PLANS 1909 B	12	54	48
4-4-2 CLASS E-6 PLANS PRR #13 1910	09	62	52
4-4-2 CLASS E-6 PRR PLANS	03	34	10

LOCOMOTIVES

STEAM LOCOMOTIVE PLANS

	M	Y	P
4-4-2 CLASS E3 ATLANTIC PLANS PRR	03	41	160
4-4-2 CLASS E6 ATLANTIC PLAN PRR #13	09	78	92
4-4-2 CLASS P-5E CAMELBACK READING PLANS	12	38	526
4-4-2 FREELANCE LOCOMOTIVE PLANS	07	40	372
4-4-2 HARRIMAN CLASS A81 PLANS C&A #554	01	58	44
4-4-2 HIAWATHA DRAWING MILW	01	84	114
4-4-2 INSPECTION LOCO PLAN P&R #100 1913	02	42	73
4-4-4 CLASS F-1A PLANS CP #2925 1937	12	63	38
4-4-4 CLASS F-2A CP #3001 PLANS	01	40	30
4-4-4 FREE LANCE LOCOMOTIVE PLAN	08	37	279
4-4-4-4 CLASS T-1 PLANS PRR #6110	10	46	660
4-6-0 "CASEY JONES" PLANS IC #382 1898	12	57	48
4-6-0 1863 B&O #9 PLANS (PERKINS) 1863	09	50	24
4-6-0 B&M #763 TEN WHEELER PLANS	10	38	428
4-6-0 BALDWIN MA&PA #28 PLANS 1910	10	54	42
4-6-0 BALTIMORE & OHIO # 2024 PLANS	04	40	220
4-6-0 CAMELBACK 1852 PLANS B&O #158	04	49	8
4-6-0 CAMELBACK CLASS L PLANS CNJ #754	05	59	40
4-6-0 CAMELBACK DL&W #1032 PLANS	01	45	26
4-6-0 CAMELBACK DL&W #1032 PLANS	12	48	924
4-6-0 CLASS D-22 L&A #394 PLANS 1913 B	04	54	42
4-6-0 CLASS D-4G PLANS CP #419 1912 MLW	05	63	36
4-6-0 CLASS D-8 T&P #252 PLANS 1899	09	56	38
4-6-0 CLASS F-1 PLANS S #949 1893 B	11	75	66
4-6-0 CLASS G-5S PENNSYLVANIA PLANS	06	39	308
4-6-0 CLASS I-1 PLANS CSPM&O #303	10	68	48
4-6-0 CLASS I-1 PLANS CSPM&O #303 ALCO	07	60	34
4-6-0 CLASS K-2 PLANS CB&Q #630 1892 R	01	61	42
4-6-0 CLASS P-2 1901 ALCO NP #240 PLANS	03	37	106
4-6-0 DRAWING SYLVANIA CENTRAL #103	07	59	38
4-6-0 G-5S CLASS PRR #5720 PLANS 1923	11	52	50
4-6-0 LS&MC #602 PLANS BROOKS 1899	12	53	54
4-6-0 NARROW GAUGE PLANS D&RGW #167 1883	07	48	466
4-6-0 NARROW GAUGE PLANS NCO #11 1907 B	09	70	44
4-6-0 PLANS A&LM #1 BLADWIN OF 1920	01	60	44
4-6-0 PLANS CMI #25 SLW 1887	02	64	42
4-6-0 PLANS ET&WNC #11 1907 B	07	81	64
4-6-0 PLANS IC #5012 1901 ROG	12	81	98
4-6-0 TEN WHEELER CGW PLANS	10	34	6
4-6-0 TEN WHEELER PLANS B&O CLASS B-8	01	48	10
4-6-0 TEN WHEELER PLANS NYC #2146	08	48	550
4-6-0 TEN WHEELERS PLANS SP #12 SP SHOPS	05	83	65
4-6-2 "ROYAL BLUE" 1896 B&O #1300 PLAN B	06	37	216
4-6-2 BOSTON & MAINE #3712 PLANS	05	50	60
4-6-2 CLASS E #1648 C&NW PLAN	11	35	286S
4-6-2 CLASS E PACIFIC PLANS C&NW #1589	12	78	78
4-6-2 CLASS E-3 PLANS CSPM&O #602 ALCO	06	76	62
4-6-2 CLASS E2 PLANS N&W #578 ALCO	08	77	62
4-6-2 CLASS E2A C&NW #2903 PLANS	09	51	36
4-6-2 CLASS F3 PACIFIC MILW #6105 PLANS	06	38	242
4-6-2 CLASS G-2SA PLANS R #175 1926 B	06	56	34
4-6-2 CLASS G-3C PLANS CP #2322 MLW 1919	04	64	36
4-6-2 CLASS G4 OR P-51 CNJ #814 PLANS B	08	66	34
4-6-2 CLASS H3A PACIFIC PLAN MKT #378	11	85	93
4-6-2 CLASS I4 PACIFIC PLANS NYNH&H	08	37	271S

STEAM LOCOMOTIVE PLANS

	M	Y	P
4-6-2 CLASS J-1 PLANS W #675	02	70	46
4-6-2 CLASS J-4E PLANS CN #5127 1920 CNS	08	59	40
4-6-2 CLASS K-3 NYC #3267 PLANS	10	39	517
4-6-2 CLASS K-4 1914 PLAN PRR #5495 1914	07	36	186
4-6-2 CLASS K-4 PACIFIC PLANS PRR #5494	10	49	17
4-6-2 CLASS K-4S PACIFIC PLANS PRR #3768	07	43	316
4-6-2 CLASS K-5 PACIFIC #2937 PLNS ERROR	10	35	271
4-6-2 CLASS K-5 PACIFIC E #2937 PLANS	07	35	182
4-6-2 CLASS K4 PACIFIC PLANS PRR #5495	07	43	318
4-6-2 CLASS K4 PLANS L&N #235 1914	09	83	78
4-6-2 CLASS P-1 PLANS D&H #653 1929 D&H	02	75	54
4-6-2 CLASS P-13 SOUTHERN PACIFIC PLANS	05	37	173
4-6-2 CLASS P-5 PLANS SP #2440 B 1912	06	55	34
4-6-2 CLASS P-7 BALTIMORE & OHIO PLAN	10	37	376
4-6-2 CLASS P-73 MISSOURI PACIFIC PLANS	01	42	26
4-6-2 CLASS PS4 PLANS S #1400 ALCO 1923	01	59	38
4-6-2 CLASS PS4 SOUTHERN DRAWING	08	64	40
4-6-2 GREAT NORTHERN #1445 PLANS	01	49	99
4-6-2 PACIFIC CLASS K5A ERIE #2936 PLANS	03	49	50
4-6-2 PACIFIC PLANS B&M #3712	04	46	266
4-6-2 PACIFIC PLANS GN #1445	06	45	248
4-6-2 PACIFIC PLANS ATSF #3448	07	53	68
4-6-2 PLANS DL&W #1119 ALCO 1922	05	64	36
4-6-2 REBUILD PLAN IC #1000 OF 1907	03	57	40
4-6-2 USRA HEAVY PACIFIC PLANS	12	36	354
4-6-2 USRA PLANS B&O CLASS P-5 #5207	05	40	260
4-6-4 BOSTON & ALBANY #605 CLASS J2S PLAN	02	48	118
4-6-4 CLASS 3460 ATSF #3462 PLANS	05	48	346
4-6-4 CLASS F-6A BALTIC PLANS MILW #6414	12	46	843
4-6-4 CLASS F-6A PLANS MILW #6414	01	36	11
4-6-4 CLASS J-3A PLANS NYC #5405 ALCO	11	60	46
4-6-4 CLASS K-5A PLANS CN #5703 1930 MLW	10	64	38
4-6-4 CLASS L-2 PLANS C&O #307 BALDWIN	10	44	448
4-6-4 CLASS L-2 PLANS C&O #313 1948 B	06	58	34
4-6-4 CLASS P-1 PLANS W #700	03	51	38
4-6-4 CLASS S-4 HUDSON PLANS CB&Q #3000	01	44	26
4-6-4 HUDSON CONVENTIONAL PLAN ATSF#3462	05	39	251
4-6-4 HUDSON OF 1927 PLANS NYC #5212	02	37	54S
4-6-4 HUDSON PLANS IC # 2499	11	47	907
4-6-4 HUDSON STREAMLINE PLANS ATSF #3460	05	39	251
4-6-4 T CLASS H1 SUBURBAN CNJ #229 PLAN	11	34	9
4-6-4T SUBURBAN CLASS H1 CNJ #227 PLANS	11	66	65
4-6-6-4 "CHALLENGER" PLANS UP #3939	11	39	580
4-6-6-4 "CHALLENGER" PLANS UP #3950	11	59	28
4-6-6-4 CLASS M-2 PLANS WM #1201 B 1940	10	60	42
4-6-6-4 CLASS Z-8 PLANS NP #5141	05	74	55
4-6-6-4 CLASS Z8 NP #5141 PLAN 1936 ALCO	05	70	34
4-6-6T SUBURBAN B&A #400 CLASS DIA PLANS	12	37	456
4-8-0 12 WHEELER PLANS GN #410	03	53	42
4-8-0 CLASS E1B PLANS M #230 1926 BLW	08	80	78
4-8-2 CLASS K-1 PLANS N&W #105 1916 N&W	02	63	46
4-8-2 CLASS K2 PLANS N&W #118	11	74	61
4-8-2 CLASS L-3A NYC PLANS ALCO 1940	01	41	19
4-8-2 CLASS M-1 MOUNTAIN PRR 8800 SERIES	05	35	128
4-8-2 CLASS M-1A PLANS PRR #6749 1930	03	68	40

LOCOMOTIVES

STEAM LOCOMOTIVE PLANS

Title	M	Y	P
4-8-2 CLASS M-1A PRR #6707 PLANS L 1926	09	38	369
4-8-2 CLASS M1 PLANS W #2810 1929 B	07	71	51
4-8-2 CLASS M75 PLANS D&RGW #1604 1926	06	84	77
4-8-2 CLASS MT-3 PLANS SP #4328 1925	08	39	402
4-8-2 CLASS R-3A NYNH&H #3553 PLANS	02	39	87
4-8-2 CLASS U1F CN #6060 PLANS 1944	06	54	38
4-8-2 MOUNTAIN PLANS SOUTHERN #1470	02	45	76
4-8-2 MOUNTIAN NYC #2569 PLAN	08	35	203
4-8-2 PACIFIC PLANS WP #176	08	47	636
4-8-2 PLANS B&M #4112	08	52	38
4-8-2 USRA HEAVY C&O #133 PLANS 1918	08	53	38
4-8-2 USRA NYNH&H #3300 PLANS	04	51	34
4-8-2 WESTERN PACIFIC #176 PLANS	10	53	84
4-8-4 "GOVERNORS" PLANS RF&P #610/#613	11	67	42
4-8-4 5100 CLASS RI #5100 PLAN 1944 ALCO	04	57	39
4-8-4 CLASS A-5 PLANS NP #2680 BALDWIN	07	58	34
4-8-4 CLASS E-1 PLANS SP&S #701	05	74	54
4-8-4 CLASS GS-2 SP DAYLIGHT 4410 PLANS	04	42	182
4-8-4 CLASS GS-4 PLANS SP #4454 1941	04	72	46
4-8-4 CLASS H PLANS OF 1929 C&NW #3006	06	36	146
4-8-4 CLASS J-4 PLAN C&NW#2812 1927 ALCO	07	69	49
4-8-4 CLASS K PLANS CG #456 LIMA OF 1943	09	57	38
4-8-4 CLASS K-62 PLAN D&H #308 ALCO 1943	05	61	36
4-8-4 CLASS M68 OF 1938 D&RGW #1804 B	12	51	42
4-8-4 CLASS O-5A PLANS CB&Q #5629 1940 B	07	70	44
4-8-4 CLASS S-2 MILW #206 1940	02	40	92
4-8-4 DAYLIGHT PLANS SP	10	48	711
4-8-4 FREE LANCE PLANS 3 CYL TANK TYPE	11	36	335
4-8-4 NIAGAR PLANS NYC #6025 1945 ALCO	11	46	751
4-8-4 NIAGARA PLANS NYC #6025	03	49	14
4-8-4 NORTHERN CLASS A5 PLANS NP #2680	03	77	65
4-8-4 PLANS ACL #1808 BLADWIN OF 1935	08	60	34
4-8-4 PLANS MP #2212 BALDWIN OF 1943	12	60	35
4-8-8-2 CAB FWD CLASS AC-11 SP#4272 PLAN	06	48	414
4-8-8-4 "BIG BOY" UP #4002 PLANS 1941	03	54	46
48,000 LOCOMOTIVES FROM ONE PLAN	12	36	366S
6-8-6 STEAM TURBINE PRR #6200 PLANS	03	48	198
ACE 3000 PLANS	06	82	78
BEYER-GARRATT AD60 CLASS NSWG#6007 PLANS	05	66	35
CLIMAX NARROW GAUGE PLANS CH&N #2	09	64	34
COAL TURBINE LOCO CLASS M-1 C&O #500 PLN	02	71	48
GEARED 2 TRUCK LOCOMTIVE PLANS	01	45	12
HEISLER GEARED LOCO PLANS	02	49	32
LARGEST 3 TRUCK SHAY PLANS WM #6	05	71	44
LOGGING LOCO FILER & STOWELL PLANS	05	76	48
RACK LOCOMOTIVE PLANS M&PP	03	58	54
SHAY 13T 2' CLASS A PLANS CWN #1	09	85	106
SHAY 2 TRUCK PLANS SCPA #3 LIMA 1906	05	71	58
SHAY 26 TON PLANS M-CL #5	01	85	84
SHAY 3 TRUCK B&SQ PLANS	05	43	234
STEAM DUMMY PLANS HTR #1 BALDWIN 1898	03	67	52
TWO TRUCK SHAY PLAN LIMA OF 1880	01	57	48
WM MASON 1856 B&O #25 PLANS	09	43	406

STEAM LOCOMOTIVE PLANS BY ROAD

RD	Title	M	Y	P
A&G	4-4-0 SAM HILL PLANS A&G	08	41	414
A&LM	4-6-0 PLANS A&LM #1 BLADWIN OF 1920	01	60	44
ACL	2-10-2 CLASS Q1 PLANS ACL B 1925	07	62	33
	4-8-4 PLANS ACL #1808 BLADWIN OF 1935	08	60	34
ATSF	2-8-2 MIKADO PLANS ATSF #3283	06	47	486
	4-6-2 PACIFIC PLANS ATSF #3448	07	53	68
	2-10-2 CLASS 3600 ATSF #3876 PLANS	09	54	65
	2-8-2 ATSF #3283 PLANS	12	53	95
	4-6-4 CLASS 3460 ATSF #3462 PLANS	05	48	346
	2-10-4 TEXAS PLANS ATSF #5012	04	47	303
	4-4-2 ATLANTIC PLANS ATSF #1491	02	51	64
	4-4-2 ATLANTIC CLASS 1480 ATSF#1491 PLNS	04	49	50
	2-10-4 CLASS 5011 PLANS ATSF #5012	07	49	34
	2-8-2 MIKADO CLASS 3160 PLANS ATSF 1917	06	40	325
	4-6-4 HUDSON CONVENTIONAL PLAN ATSF#3462	05	39	251
	4-6-4 HUDSON STREAMLINE PLANS ATSF #3460	05	39	251
	4-4-2 CLASS 1480 ATSF #1493 PLANS	10	40	549
B&A	4-6-4 BOSTON & ALBANY#605 CLASS J2S PLAN	02	48	118
	4-6-6T SUBURBAN B&A #400 CLASS DIA PLANS	12	37	456
B&LE	2-10-4 PLANS B&LE CLASS H-1	10	61	42
B&M	4-6-2 PACIFIC PLANS B&M #3712	04	46	266
	4-4-0 BOSTON & MAINE #1011 PLANS	11	48	814
	4-6-2 BOSTON & MAINE #3712 PLANS	05	50	60
	4-8-2 PLANS B&M #4112	08	52	38
	4-6-0 B&M #763 TEN WHEELER PLANS	10	38	428
	4-4-0 BOSTON & MAINE #1011 PLANS	11	45	470
B&O	0-4-0 YORK OF 1831 B&O	07	76	82
	4-2-0 LAFAYETTE PLANS B&O #13 1837 NLW	07	76	82
	0-4-0 CRAB LOCO MEZEPPA PLANS B&O #17	07	76	83
	2-8-2 USRA B&O #4500 CLASS Q3 PLANS 1918	10	82	82
	2-10-2 CLASS S-1 PLANS B&O #6115	05	60	38
	4-4-0 OF 1852 PLANS B&O #107	12	46	825
	0-4-0T DOCKSIDE PLANS B&O #98	03	47	216
	4-6-0 TEN WHEELER PLANS B&O CLASS B-8	01	48	10

LOCOMOTIVES

STEAM LOCOMOTIVE PLANS BY ROAD

RD		M	Y	P
	0-4-0 CLASS C16A B&O #96 PLANS	04	51	16
	4-6-0 1863 B&O #9 PLANS (PERKINS) 1863	09	50	24
	4-4-0 PLANS B&O #853	12	52	32
	2-8-0 CONSOL PLANS B&O #2715 CLASS E27	10	45	418
	WM MASON 1856 B&O #25 PLANS	09	43	406
	4-6-0 CAMELBACK 1852 PLANS B&O #158	04	49	8
	2-8-0 B&O CONSOLIDATION PLANS	11	41	568
	0-6-0 USRA SWITCHER PLN CLSS D30 B&O#350	09	39	457
	0-4-0 CLASS C16 SADDLE TANK PLNS B&O #97	01	39	23
	4-4-2 ATLANTIC B&O CLASS A-1 #1472 PLANS	05	38	198
	4-6-2 USRA PLANS B&O CLASS P-5 #5207	05	40	260
	4-6-0 BALTIMORE & OHIO # 2024 PLANS	04	40	220
	0-4-0 CLASS C16A B&O #99 PLANS BALDWIN	12	40	666
	4-6-2 CLASS P-7 BALTIMORE & OHIO PLAN	10	37	376
	4-6-2 "ROYAL BLUE" 1896 B&O #1300 PLAN B	06	37	216
B&S	2-6-0 1920 BALDWIN PLANS B&S #112	02	60	64
B&SQ	4-4-2 CLASS A-9 B&SQ #1485 PLAN 1904 BLW	02	57	44
	SHAY 3 TRUCK B&SQ PLANS	05	43	234
B&SR	2-4-4T #7 PLANS B&SR	01	78	68
BR&P	2-10-0 BR&P PLANS	09	49	12
BW&GF	2-8-2 PLANS BW&GF #3 1902 BALDWIN	09	65	38
C&A	4-4-2 HARRIMAN CLASS A81 PLANS C&A #554	01	58	44
C&IM	2-10-2 CLASS H-2 PLANS CM&I #757 BALDWIN	07	62	33
C&NW	4-4-2 CLASS D PLANS C&NW #493 1904 SLW	06	81	77
	0-6-0 CLASS M-1 PLANS C&NW #2094 1917	07	77	60
	4-6-2 CLASS E PACIFIC PLANS C&NW #1589	12	78	78
	4-8-4 CLASS J-4 PLAN C&NW#2812 1927 ALCO	07	69	49
	2-8-4 CLASS J-4 PLANS C&NW #2812	01	70	70
	2-8-0 CLASS Z PLANS C&NW #1712 1910 BALD	04	70	44
	4-2-0 "PIONEER" C&NW PLANS 1838	06	48	398
	2-8-2 CLASS J-A MIKADO C&NW #2504 PLANS	10	47	815
	4-6-2 CLASS E2A C&NW #2903 PLANS	09	51	36
	0-6-0 CLASS M1 SWITCHER PLAN C&NW	10	43	450
	2-8-2 MIKADO CLASS JA C&NW #2504 PLANS	02	49	44
	2-8-4 CLASS J4 BERKSHIRE C&NW #2804 PLAN	01	38	28
	4-4-2 CLASS D C&NW #126 PLANS	08	40	437
	4-8-4 CLASS H PLANS OF 1929 C&NW #3006	06	36	146
	4-6-2 CLASS E #1648 C&NW PLAN	11	35	286S
	4-4-2 ATLANTIC #395 C&NW PLAN	06	35	156
	0-8-0 CLASS M-4 #2636 C&NW PLAN	08	36	216
C&O	2-10-4 TEXAS CLASS T1 C&O #3004 PLANS L	01	77	58
	COAL TURBINE LOCO CLASS M-1 C&O #500 PLN	02	71	48
	2-8-4 CLASS K4 C&O #2771 PLANS	07	67	41
	2-6-6-2 CLASS H-6 C&O #1304 PLANS 1949 B	01	57	42
	2-8-4 CLASS K2 PLANS C&O #2754 1947 ALCO	01	65	42
	4-6-4 CLASS L-2 PLANS C&O #313 1948 B	06	58	34
	2-6-6-6 CLASS H-8 PLANS C&O #1603	02	47	127
	4-8-2 USRA HEAVY C&O #133 PLANS 1918	08	53	38
	4-6-4 CLASS L-2 PLANS C&O #307 BALDWIN	10	44	448
	2-8-2 CLASS K3A #2318 C&O PLAN	04	36	102
C&WI	2-6-0 MOGUL PLANS C&WI #213 LIMA 1925	09	60	36
CB&Q	2-6-2 CLASS R-1 PLANS CB&Q #1700 1900	09	69	42
	4-8-4 CLASS O-5A PLANS CB&Q #5629 1940 B	07	70	44
	2-10-4 PLANS CB&Q CLASS M-4	10	61	42
	4-6-0 CLASS K-2 PLANS CB&Q #630 1892 R	01	61	42
	4-6-4 CLASS S-4 HUDSON PLANS CB&Q #3000	01	44	26
CBELT	4-4-2 CLASS E-1 CBELT #605 PLANS 1909 B	12	54	48
CG	4-8-4 CLASS K PLANS CG #456 LIMA OF 1943	09	57	38
CGW	4-6-0 TEN WHEELER CGW PLANS	10	34	6
CH&N	CLIMAX NARROW GAUGE PLANS CH&N #2	09	64	34
CLE	2-4-0 INDUSTRIAL LOCO PLANS CLE #2 1907B	11	81	82
CMI	2-8-0 CONSOLIDATION PLANS CMI CL 115 #1	09	81	78
	0-6-0 PLANS CMI #101 1887 SLW	04	66	36
	4-6-0 PLANS CMI #25 SLW 1887	02	64	42
CMSP	4-4-0 CLASS H-5 PLANS CMSP #315 1890	11	70	64
CN	2-8-2 CLASS S2C PLANS CN #3546 1923 MLW	11	80	90
	2-6-0 CLASS E10A PLANS CN #96 1910	08	62	50
	4-6-0 CLASS D-46 PLANS CP #419 1912 MLW	05	63	36
	4-6-4 CLASS K-5A PLANS CN #5703 1930 MLW	10	64	38
	4-6-2 CLASS J-4E PLANS CN #5127 1920 CNS	08	59	40
	4-8-2 CLASS U1F CN #6060 PLANS 1944	06	54	38
CNJ	0-4-0T COMMUNIPAW GOAT PLANS CNJ#840 B	11	62	64
	4-6-4T SUBURBAN CLASS H1 CNJ #227 PLANS	11	66	65
	4-6-2 CLASS G4 OR P-51 CNJ #814 PLANS B	08	66	34
	4-6-0 CAMELBACK CLASS L PLANS CNJ #754	05	59	40
	4-6-4 T CLASS H1 SUBURBAN CNJ #229 PLAN	11	34	9
CNO&TP	2-6-0 MOGUL PLANS CNO&TP #230 1884	01	62	34
CO&L	4-4-0 CO&L #12 PLANS NARROW GAUGE	04	52	34
CORN	4-4-0 OF 1924 PLANS CORNWALL #14	04	61	38
CP	4-4-4 CLASS F-1A PLANS CP #2925 1937	12	63	38
	4-6-2 CLASS G-3C PLANS CP #2322 MLW 1919	04	64	36
	4-4-4 CLASS F-2A CP #3001 PLANS	01	40	30
CS&CC	2-6-2 DOUBLE ENDED SWITCHER PL CS&CC#102	09	72	34
CSPM&O	4-6-2 CLASS E-3 PLANS CSPM&O #602 ALCO	06	76	62
	4-6-0 CLASS I-1 PLANS CSPM&O #303	10	68	48
	4-6-0 CLASS I-1 PLANS CSPM&O #303 ALCO	07	60	34
	0-6-0 CLASS F-10 CSPM&O #23 PLANS	01	54	108
CWN	SHAY 13T 2' CLASS A PLANS CWN #1	09	85	106
D&H	4-6-2 CLASS P-1 PLANS D&H #653 1929 D&H	02	75	54
	4-8-4 CLASS K-62 PLAN D&H #308 ALCO 1943	05	61	36
D&IR	4-4-0 D&IR #24 PLAN	12	82	91
	4-4-0 PLANS D&IR #24 BALDWIN 1888	09	67	34
D&RG	4-4-0 NARROW GAUGE CLASS 42 PLANS D&RG	03	44	126
D&RGW	4-8-2 CLASS M75 PLANS D&RGW #1604 1926	06	84	77
	2-8-2 NARROW G CLASS K-27 PLN D&RGW #450	03	73	58
	2-8-2 NARROW G CLASS K-27 PLAN D&RGW#453	06	73	44
	2-8-2 CLASS K-37 PLANS D&RGW #490 1928	10	79	72
	4-6-0 NARROW GAUGE PLANS D&RGW #167 1883	07	48	466
	4-8-4 CLASS M68 OF 1938 D&RGW #1804 B	12	51	42
	2-8-0 NARROW GAUGE CONSOL D&RGW#223 PLNS	06	44	264
	2-8-2 NARROW GAUGE MIKADO PLNS D&RGW#478	07	42	334
DL&W	4-6-2 PLANS DL&W #1119 ALCO 1922	05	64	36
	4-6-0 CAMELBACK DL&W #1032 PLANS	12	48	924
	4-6-0 CAMELBACK DL&W #1032 PLANS	01	45	26
DM&IR	0-10-2 SWITCHER PLNS DM&IR#601 CLSS S7 B	08	63	32
	2-8-8-2 MALLET PLANS DM&IR #202 1910 B	07	75	54
	2-10-4 PLANS DM&IR #716 CLASS E7	10	61	42
	2-8-8-4 CLASS M-4 PLANS DM&IR #229	03	58	22
	4-4-0 1888 DM&IR PLANS 1888	08	38	315
DSP&P	2-6-6-T MASON BOGIE CL DH-1 DSP&P#42 PLN	09	60	48

LOCOMOTIVES

STEAM LOCOMOTIVE PLANS BY ROAD

RD		M Y P
	2-6-0 OF 1884 PLANS DSP&P #71 CLW	06 60 36
E	2-8-4 CLASS S-4 ERIE #3389 PLANS	08 44 354
	4-6-2 PACIFIC CLASS K5A ERIE #2936 PLANS	03 49 50
	4-6-2 CLASS K-5 PACIFIC E #2937 PLANS	07 35 182
EBT	2-8-2 MIKADO PLANS EBT #16 BALDWIN 1916	09 61 42
EN	2-6-2 NARROW GUAGE PLANS EN #7 PORTER	05 62 24
ET&WNC	4-6-0 PLANS ET&WNC #11 1907 B	07 81 64
	2-8-0 NARROW GAUGE PLANS ET&WNC #5	12 68 70
FRIS	2-10-0 "RUSSIAN DECAPOD" PLAN FRIS #1618	10 58 38
GB&W	2-6-0 GREEN BAY & WESTERN #56 PLANS	02 55 42
GN	2-8-2 CLASS O-8 PLANS GN #3388 1945	08 58 34
	4-8-0 12 WHEELER PLANS GN #410	03 53 42
	2-6-6-2 GN 1906 PLANS B	10 53 84
	4-6-2 GREAT NORTHERN #1445 PLANS	01 49 99
	4-6-2 PACIFIC PLANS GN #1445	06 45 248
GNO	2-8-2 PLANS GNO #105 1929 BALDWIN	06 66 28
GS	0-6-4T GODCHAUX SUGAR #7 PLANS PO 1906	04 56 35
GW	2-10-0 BALDWIN CLASS 12-45-2 GW #90 PLAN	03 69 42
HTR	STEAM DUMMY PLANS HTR #1 BALDWIN 1898	03 67 52
IC	4-6-0 PLANS IC #5012 1901 ROG	12 81 98
	4-6-0 "CASEY JONES" PLANS IC #382 1898	12 57 48
	4-6-2 REBUILD PLAN IC #1000 OF 1907	03 57 40
	2-4-4T SUBURBAN PLANS IC #1420	12 65 34
	2-8-0 CONSOLIDATION PLANS IC #908 B 1909	04 58 38
	4-6-4 HUDSON PLANS IC # 2499	11 47 907
	2-10-2 IC #2952 SANTA FE TYPE PLAN	07 38 294
	2-6-0 CLASS 541 PLANS IC #555 1893	03 40 162
	4-4-2 CLASS A-79 IC #1006 PLANS	09 37 328
	2-8-4 CLASS L-63 PLANS ALCO 1924 IC#7049	12 35 318S
	0-6-0 ILLINOIS CENTRAL #216 PLANS	07 37 252
IU	0-8-0 INDIANAPOLIS UNION #9 PLANS B	06 53 38
KCS	4-4-0 CLASS B-3 PLANS KCS #143 1895 PCLW	12 56 64
KL	0-4-0T KNICKERBOCKER LIME #4 PLAN 1900 K	07 51 33
KO&G	2-8-2 USRA MODIFIED PLAN KO&G #602	05 56 34
L&A	4-6-0 CLASS D-22 L&A #394 PLANS 1913 B	04 54 42
L&CV	0-6-0T LEETONIA & CHERRY VALLEY #1 PLANS	05 58 49
L&N	4-6-2 CLASS K4 PLANS L&N #235 1914	09 83 78
	2-8-2 CLASS J-2A PLANS L&N #1491	07 64 34
	2-8-4 CLASS M-1 PLANS L&N #1967 1942 B	09 59 38
LITRI	2-4-4-2 MALLET PLANS LITRI #126 BALDWIN	03 62 48
LS&MC	4-6-0 LS&MC #602 PLANS BROOKS 1899	12 53 54
LV	2-8-2 CAMELBACKS LV #220 CLASS N-1 PLANS	02 79 90
M	4-8-0 CLASS E1B PLANS M #230 1926 BLW	08 80 78
M&HR	0-4-0 DEWITT CLINTON OF M&HR PLANS	05 79 78
M&PP	RACK LOCOMOTIVE PLANS M&PP	03 58 54
M-CL	SHAY 26 TON PLANS M-CL #5	01 85 84
MA&PA	2-8-0 CONSOLIDATION PLANS MA&PA #43 1925	05 72 56
	4-4-0 MA&PA #6 1901 RLW PLANS	03 65 36
	2-8-0 CONSOLIDATION PLANS MA&PA #43	10 59 38
	4-6-0 BALDWIN MA&PA #28 PLANS 1910	10 54 42
	2-8-0 PLANS MA&PA #26	09 52 42
MCO	0-4-0 MONONGAHELA CONNECTING #3 PLANS	06 63 48
MILW	4-4-2 HIAWATHA DRAWING MILW	01 84 114
	4-6-4 CLASS F-6A BALTIC PLANS MILW #6414	12 46 843
	2-8-0 CLASS C-2 MILW #7624 PLANS	03 39 138

STEAM LOCOMOTIVE PLANS BY ROAD

RD		M Y P
	4-6-2 CLASS F3 PACIFIC MILW #6105 PLANS	06 38 242
	4-8-4 CLASS S-2 MILW #206 1940	02 40 92
	4-6-4 CLASS F-6A PLANS MILW #6414	01 36 11
	4-4-2 "HIAWATHA" MILW TYPE CMSP&P PLAN	09 35 238
	2-6-2 CLASS K-1 MILW #5588 PRAIRIE PLAN	04 37 144
MISC	0-4-0T PORTER PLANS 1910	10 63 46
MKT	4-6-2 CLASS H3A PACIFIC PLAN MKT #378	11 85 93
MP	0-8-0 USRA PLANS MP #9777 1918	01 79 90
	4-8-4 PLANS MP #2212 BALDWIN OF 1943	12 60 35
	2-8-0 PLANS MP #152 1910	10 74 50
	4-6-2 CLASS P-73 MISSOURI PACIFIC PLANS	01 42 26
MWC	2-6-0 NARROW GAUGE PLANS MWC #6 1891 BAL	08 70 54
N&W	4-6-2 CLASS E2 PLANS N&W #578 ALCO	08 77 62
	4-8-2 CLASS K-1 PLANS N&W #105 1916 N&W	02 63 46
	4-8-2 CLASS K2 PLANS N&W #118	11 74 61
N-W	0-4-2T VULCAN CL A-4 TANK N-W #12 PLAN	02 37 48
NB&W	2-6-0 NARROW GUAGE PLANS NB&W #2 1904	02 66 52
NCBT	2-8-0 CONSOLIDATION PLANS NCBT #2 1911	04 84 64
NCC	0-6-0 NCC #101 PLANS ALCO OF 1916	05 57 38
NCN	2-8-0 BALDWIN PLANS 1914 NCN #9	11 49 30
NCO	4-6-0 NARROW GAUGE PLANS NCO #11 1907 B	09 70 44
NKP	2-8-4 CLASS S-3 PLANS NKP #777 LIMA 1945	07 57 38
NOPB	0-6-0 SWITCHER PLANS NOPB #11 1908 B	07 56 34
NP	2-8-2 CLASS W PLANS NP #1592 1907 BROOKS	09 76 62
	4-8-4 NORTHERN CLASS A5 PLANS NP #2680	03 77 65
	4-6-6-4 CLASS Z8 NP #5141 PLAN 1936 ALCO	05 70 34
	2-8-0 CONSOLIDATION PLANS NP #485 B 1889	11 58 46
	4-8-4 CLASS A-5 PLANS NP #2680 BALDWIN	07 58 34
	4-6-6-4 CLASS Z-8 PLANS NP #5141	05 74 55
	4-6-0 CLASS P-2 1901 ALCO NP #240 PLANS	03 37 106
NSWG	BEYER-GARRATT AD60 CLASS NSWG#6007 PLANS	05 66 35
NYC	4-4-0 NYC #999 PLANS 1893	11 57 44
	4-6-4 CLASS J-3A PLANS NYC #5405 ALCO	11 60 46
	4-8-4 NIAGAR PLANS NYC #6025 1945 ALCO	11 46 751
	4-6-0 TEN WHEELER PLANS NYC #2146	08 48 550
	2-8-2 CLASS H-10B MIKADO PLANS NYC #2390	01 47 35
	4-8-4 NIAGARA PLANS NYC #6025	03 49 14
	4-6-2 CLASS K-3 NYC #3267 PLANS	10 39 517
	4-8-2 CLASS L-3A NYC PLANS ALCO 1940	01 41 19
	4-4-0 NYC #999 PLANS	05 36 126
	4-8-2 MOUNTIAN NYC #2569 PLAN	08 35 203
	4-6-4 HUDSON OF 1927 PLANS NYC #5212	02 37 54S
NYC&H	2-6-0 NYC&H #798 PLANS	11 53 50
NYNH&H	4-8-2 USRA NYNH&H #3300 PLANS	04 51 34
	4-8-2 CLASS R-3A NYNH&H #3553 PLANS	02 39 87
	4-4-0 PLANS NYNH&H #1213	05 36 126
	4-6-2 CLASS I4 PACIFIC PLANS NYNH&H	08 37 271S
OIM	0-6-0 INDUSTRIAL LOCO OIM #86 PLANS	03 52 36
OPC	0-6-0 BALDWIN OPC #3 PLANS 1920	06 80 78
	0-4-0 FIRELESS PLANS OPC #2 1945 POR	04 81 96
P&R	2-8-0 CAMELBACK P&R CLASS 1-5C 1892 PLAN	09 45 370
	4-4-2 INSPECTION LOCO PLAN P&R #100 1913	02 42 73
PAN	2-6-0 MOGUL PLANS PANAMA RR #704	12 47 980
PRR	0-4-0 CLASS A-5S PLANS PRR #1289 1916	10 73 48
	4-4-2 CLASS E6 ATLANTIC PLAN PRR #13	09 78 92

LOCOMOTIVES

STEAM LOCOMOTIVE PLANS BY ROAD

RD		M	Y	P
	2-10-2 CLASS N1 PLANS PRR #7344 1919	10	79	117
	0-6-0 CLASS B-4A PLANS PRR #101 AS 1893	07	68	42
	4-8-2 CLASS M-1A PLANS PRR #6749 1930	03	68	40
	2-10-2 CLASS N-1S PLANS PRR #7344 ALCO	11	69	48
	4-4-2 CLASS E-6 PLANS PRR #13 1910	09	62	52
	2-8-0 CLASS H-6SB PLANS PRR #1 1910	02	61	52
	4-4-0 CLASS D-13C PRR #6013 PLANS 1893	03	56	38
	4-4-4-4 CLASS T-1 PLANS PRR #6110	10	46	660
	2-8-0 CLASS H-1 PLANS PRR #369 1875	02	59	40
	6-8-6 STEAM TURBINE PRR #6200 PLANS	03	48	198
	2-8-0 CLASS H-95 PRR #3506 PLANS	09	48	632
	2-10-0 CLASS I-1 PLANS PRR #4638	02	53	46
	4-6-2 CLASS K-4 PACIFIC PLANS PRR #5494	10	49	17
	2-8-0 CLASS H-6SB PRR #1	01	74	76
	0-4-0 CLASS A-5S PLANS PRR #1288	01	74	75
	4-6-0 G-5S CLASS PRR #5720 PLANS 1923	11	52	50
	2-8-2 CLASS L-1S PRR #843 PLANS 1914	06	52	34
	0-4-0 CLASS A3 PRR #1591 PLANS	12	52	52
	0-4-0 CLASS A3A PRR #310 PLANS	12	52	53
	2-8-0 CONSOL CLASS H9S PRR #1731 PLANS	12	45	550
	4-6-2 CLASS K4 PACIFIC PLANS PRR #5495	07	43	318
	2-6-0 CLASS F-3 PENNSYLVANIA #2063 PLANS	11	44	496
	2-8-0 CLASS H-3 CONSOL PLAN PRR #1187	02	44	78
	4-4-0 CLASS D-3 PENNSYLVANIA PLANS	09	44	388
	4-6-2 CLASS K-4S PACIFIC PLANS PRR #3768	07	43	316
	4-4-2 CLASS E3 ATLANTIC PLANS PRR	03	41	160
	4-4-0 CLASS D-16SB PRR #6235	09	40	498
	4-8-2 CLASS M-1A PRR #6707 PLANS L 1926	09	38	369
	4-6-0 CLASS G-5S PENNSYLVANIA PLANS	06	39	308
	4-8-2 CLASS M-1 MOUNTAIN PRR 8800 SERIES	05	35	128
	4-6-2 CLASS K-4 1914 PLAN PRR #5495 1914	07	36	186
	4-4-2 CLASS E-6 PRR PLANS	03	34	10
	0-8-0 CLASS C-1 PLAN PRR #6556	01	35	12
R	4-4-0 CAMELBACK R #408 CLASS D8C PLANS	12	82	103
	2-8-0 CLASS I8SA CAMELBACK PLANS R #1504	06	72	56
	0-6-0 CAMELBACK CLASS B8A R #1343 PLANS	02	56	39
	4-6-2 CLASS G-2SA PLANS R #175 1926 B	06	56	34
	2-8-0 CLASS I-10 R #2017 PLANS	10	53	50
	2-8-0 CAMELBACK CLASS I5C R#952 1892 PLN	03	49	66
	0-4-0 CAMELBACK CLASS A4B PLANS R #1192	07	74	59
	0-4-0 CAMELBACK CLASS A4A PLANS R #1196	07	74	58
	4-4-2 CLASS P-5E CAMELBACK READING PLANS	12	38	526
	4-4-0 READING #419 PLANS CLASS D-11 1914	02	38	66
	2-8-0 READING PLAN	01	37	18
RF&P	4-8-4 "GOVERNORS" PLANS RF&P #610/#613	11	67	42
RGS	2-8-2 CLASS K-27 PLANS RGS #461	06	73	44
RI	4-8-4 5100 CLASS RI #5100 PLAN 1944 ALCO	04	57	39
	0-8-0 CLASS S-57 RI #307 1925 ALCO PLANS	04	60	44
	4-4-2 ATLANTIC PLANS RI	04	35	89
S	2-8-2 CLASS MS-4 MIKADO PLANS S#4843 1923	01	82	79
	4-6-0 CLASS F-1 PLANS S #949 1893 B	11	75	66
	4-6-2 CLASS PS4 SOUTHERN DRAWING	08	64	40
	2-8-0 KS7 CLASS S #588 PLANS ALCO 1906	11	56	44
	4-6-0 DRAWING SYLVANIA CENTRAL #103	07	59	38
	4-6-2 CLASS PS4 PLANS S #1400 ALCO 1923	01	59	38

STEAM LOCOMOTIVE PLANS BY ROAD

RD		M	Y	P
	4-8-2 MOUNTAIN PLANS SOUTHERN #1470	02	45	76
SAL	2-6-6-4 MALLET SAL #250 CLASS R-1 PLAN	03	36	62*
SCPA	SHAY 2 TRUCK PLANS SCPA #3 LIMA 1906	05	71	58
SCT	0-10-0T SCTC #598 PLANS BALDWIN 1891	08	73	46
SP	4-6-0 TEN WHEELERS PLANS SP #12 SP SHOPS	05	83	65
	4-8-4 CLASS GS-4 PLANS SP #4454 1941	04	72	46
	2-8-8-2 CAB FORW CLASS AC-2 PLAN SP#4024	11	70	61
	0-6-0 CLASS S-5 PLANS SP #71 BALDWIN	07	61	34
	4-8-4 DAYLIGHT PLANS SP	10	48	711
	4-8-8-2 CAB FWD CLASS AC-11 SP#4272 PLAN	06	48	414
	4-4-2 ATLANTIC PLANS SP #3000	01	50	49
	4-6-2 CLASS P-5 PLANS SP #2440 B 1912	06	55	34
	2-6-0 CLASS M-21 SP #520 PLANS 1928	12	55	68
	4-8-4 CLASS GS-2 SP DAYLIGHT 4410 PLANS	04	42	182
	4-8-2 CLASS MT-3 PLANS SP #4328 1925	08	39	402
	0-6-0 CLASS S-12 SP #126 PLANS	04	38	154
	2-6-0 MOGUL SP #1658 CLASS M-4 PLAN	03	35	65
	4-6-2 CLASS P-13 SOUTHERN PACIFIC PLANS	05	37	173
	4-4-2 CLASS A-6 #3003 PLANS SP	07	37	245
SP&P	4-4-0 ORIGINAL "WM CROOKS" SP&P #1 PLAN	06	67	36
SP&S	4-8-4 CLASS E-1 PLANS SP&S #701	05	74	54
SR&RL	2-4-4T SR&RL #9 PLANS 1909 BALDWIN	06	57	51
T&P	2-10-4 T&P #609 PLANS LIMA 1925	10	57	38
	4-6-0 CLASS D-8 T&P #252 PLANS 1899	09	56	38
UP	4-6-6-4 "CHALLENGER" PLANS UP #3950	11	59	28
	0-6-0 CLASS S PLAN UP #4474 LIMA OF 1920	12	58	48
	2-8-0 CONSOLIDATION PLANS UP #6201 (201)	09	58	36
	4-12-2 PLANS UP #9017 ALCO OF 1926	02	58	40
	4-8-8-4 "BIG BOY" UP #4002 PLANS 1941	03	54	46
	4-6-6-4 "CHALLENGER" PLANS UP #3939	11	39	580
USRA	2-8-2 USRA HEAVY MIKADO PLANS	06	50	38
	0-6-0 USRA #210 PLANS	05	50	38
	2-8-2 USRA LIGHT MIKADO PLANS	06	41	310
	0-6-0 USRA SWITCHER PLANS	11	36	321
	4-6-2 USRA HEAVY PACIFIC PLANS	12	36	354
	2-8-2 USRA HEAVY PLANS	02	36	41
V	2-8-4 CLASS BA PLANS V #507 1946 LIMA	01	76	62
	2-10-10-2 VIRGINIAN #802 ALCO 1913 PLAN	08	67	36
V&T	4-4-0 "GENOA" V&T PLANS	07	50	38
VA	2-6-0 MOGUL PLANS VANDALIA	04	49	19
W	4-8-2 CLASS M1 PLANS W #2810 1929 B	07	71	51
	4-6-2 CLASS J-1 PLANS W #675	02	70	46
	2-6-0 CLASS F4 W #573 PLANS	01	59	42
	4-6-4 CLASS P-1 PLANS W #700	03	51	38
W&N	4-4-0 PLANS W&N OF 1911 B	10	52	46
WM	2-8-0 CLASS H9 PLANS WM #830	11	72	50
	LARGEST 3 TRUCK SHAY PLANS WM #6	05	71	44
	2-10-0 CLASS I2 DEPACOD PLANS WM #1112	06	85	78
	4-6-6-4 CLASS M-2 PLANS WM #1201 B 1940	10	60	42
	2-8-0 CLASS H-9 CONSOLIDATION WM#810 PLN	09	36	262
WP	4-8-2 PACIFIC PLANS WP #176	08	47	636
	4-8-2 WESTERN PACIFIC #176 PLANS	10	53	84
WP&Y	2-8-2 NARROW GAUGE PLANS WP&Y #70 B 1938	06	74	50

LOCOMOTIVES

STEAM LOCOMOTIVE PHOTOS	M	Y	P
0-6-6-0 DOUBLE ENDER T&B PHOTO	06	48	426
2-8-0 MP PHOTO ESSAY	10	74	48
4-4-0 "MONKEY BOX" LOCO PHOTO C&WM #130	07	56	9
4-4-2 CLASS P5E READING LOCOMOTIVE #343	12	38	527
4-6-0 C&NW CLASS R-1 #470/#344 PORTRAITS	01	69	80
4-6-0 C&NW CLASS R1 PHOTOS	12	64	40
4-6-2 CAST FRAME TRAILING TRUCK MKT #403	11	85	92
4-6-2 CLASS H3A PACIFIC MKT #380 PHOTO	11	85	93
4-6-2 CLASS H3B PACIFIC MKT #395 PHOTO	11	85	92
B&O CLASS S1 CAB W/BRAKEMAN SEAT PHOTO	12	42	571
CAMELBACK PHOTO ESSAY READING	07	74	56
HEADLIGHT FROM OLD DOME PROTO MILW #185	01	55	24
SHAY PHOTO NYC #7189 UNUSUAL	08	71	69

STEAM LOCOMOTIVE MODELS	M	Y	P
0-4-0 CLASS C-16A CONST "O"	04	51	16
0-4-0 CLASS C-16A CONST ASH PAN "O"	07	51	36
0-4-0 CLASS C-16A CONST BOILER "O"	06	51	38
0-4-0 CLASS C-16A CONST CYLINDERS "O"	05	51	37
0-4-0 CLASS C-16A CONST FINISHING "O"	08	51	44
0-4-0 CLASS C-16A CONST TENDER "O"	09	51	42
0-4-0 CLS A5S FROM 0-6-0 CLS B6SB PRR	01	74	72
0-4-0 FREELANCE TEA KETTLE CONSTRUCTION	01	49	30
0-4-0 LIGHTS FOR LI'L JOE	08	52	29
0-4-0 MANTUA "GOAT" KIT ASSEMBLY	08	48	529
0-4-0 SADDLE TANK SWITCH B&O#97 CLSS C16	01	39	22
0-4-0 SUPERDETAILED YARD BIRD SWITCHER	06	50	20
0-4-0 SWITCHER ASSEMBLY "O" THOMAS IND.	12	48	915
0-4-0T DOCKSIDE DETAILING VARNEY	03	47	216
0-4-0T UPGRADING VARNEY DOCKSIDE	02	81	70
0-4-4T INDUSTRIAL LOCOMOTIVE DETAILING	07	56	20
0-6-0 B-6SB SWITCHER "O"	03	37	103
0-6-0 CLASS M-1 SWITCHER C&NW BEGIN CONS	10	43	450
0-6-0 CLASS M-1 SWITCHER C&NW CAB/SUPER	12	43	542
0-6-0 CLASS M-1 SWITCHER C&NW VALVE/BOIL	11	43	485
0-6-0 FREELANCE SWITCHER CONSTRUCTION	06	71	34
0-6-0 KITCHEN TABLE SWITCHER CONST 1	11	53	34
0-6-0 KITCHEN TABLE SWITCHER CONST 2	12	53	56
0-6-0 KITCHEN TABLE SWITCHER CONST 3	02	54	54
0-6-0 MANTUA SHIFTER DETAILING	09	51	20
0-6-0 SWITCHER C&NW TENDER CONSTRUCTION	01	44	28
0-6-0 SWITCHER DETAILING ROUNDHOUSE	01	51	32
0-6-0 SWITCHER USRA BOILER/CAB CONSTRUCT	11	39	572
0-6-0 SWITCHER USRA CONSTRUCTION B&O#350	09	39	457
0-6-0 SWITCHER USRA CYLINDER/ROD CONSTRU	10	39	511
0-6-0 SWITCHER USRA FITTING CONSTRUCTION	12	39	622
0-6-0 SWITCHER USRA STACK DOME CONSTRUCT	01	40	24
0-6-0 SWITCHER USRA TENDER CONSTRUCTION	02	40	79
0-8-0 FROM 2-8-0 CONVERSION "O" PEARCE	08	56	32
0-8-0 HO SWITCHER CONSTRUCTION BOILER	08	50	28
0-8-0 HO SWITCHER CONSTRUCTION FRAME	07	50	24
0-8-0 HO SWITCHER CONSTRUCTION TENDER	09	50	36
0-8-0 IHB MODIFICATION	09	71	36
0-8-0 NH Y4B FROM IHB 0-8-0	04	73	59
1000 MILE LOCOMOTIVE CHECKUPS	06	65	36
2 NARROW GAUGE LOCOS FOR UNDER $100.00	10	79	79
2-10-2 CLASS N1 PRR "N" KITBASH	10	79	116
2-4-0 BOWKER "O" CLEMENT	01	41	18
2-4-2 COLUMBIA CONVERSION CB&Q 1895 BALD	12	50	24
2-4-4T "MUDHEN" FREELANCED CROSS KIT	09	63	32
2-6-0 "O" MODEL PHOTOS BEASLEY	10	61	22
2-6-0 BACKDATING THE MANTUA PRAIRIE	08	58	36
2-6-0 CONST BRAKE & BOILER DETAILS	03	59	52
2-6-0 CONST CAB & SUPERSTRUCTURE WABASH	05	59	53
2-6-0 CONST DETAILING BACKHEAD/SMOKE BOX	04	59	55
2-6-0 CONST MOTOR & RUNNING GEAR WABASH	02	59	56
2-6-0 CONST TENDER WITH MOGUL WABASH	06	59	54
2-6-0 CONST WABASH CLASS FX FRAME	01	59	41
2-6-0 MODERNIZING THE MANTUA MOGUL	11	48	792
2-6-0 ON3 NARROW GAUGE MASTERPEICE PHOTO	12	60	37

LOCOMOTIVES

STEAM LOCOMOTIVE MODELS	M	Y	P
2-6-0 PORTER MOGUL-VERSATILE RASCAL CONS	07	62	58
2-6-2 PRAIRIE FROM SWITCHER BASH	04	67	45
2-6-6-2 C&O CLASS H-2 MALLET MODEL PHOTO	04	61	24
2-6-6-2 HOME BUILT 12 WHEELS POWERED	04	55	20
2-6-6-2 SP CABFORWARD FROM SIERRA KBASH1	10	60	46
2-6-6-2 SP CABFORWARD FROM SIERRA KBASH2	11	60	60
2-6-6-2 SP CABFORWARD FROM SIERRA KBASH3	12	60	76
2-6-6T BOGIE FROM LIONEL 4-6-2 B&A LIO	02	42	80
2-8-0 CLASS C-18 D&RGW CONSTRUCTION	10	79	79
2-8-0 CLASS C-25 D&RGW CONSTRUCTION	10	79	79
2-8-0 CLASS H10 CONSOLIDATION KBASH PRR	12	75	50
2-8-0 CLS H6SB FROM 0-6-0 CLS B6SB PRR	01	74	72
2-8-0 COMPOUND CONST DOMES & STACK	03	60	52
2-8-0 COMPOUND CONST RUNNING GEAR	01	60	68
2-8-0 COMPOUND CONST SUPERSTRUCTURE	02	60	76
2-8-0 COMPOUND CONST TENDER	04	60	54
2-8-0 COMPOUND SCRATCH CONST STARTING	12	59	42
2-8-0 CONSOLIDATION BOILER/ASH CAN CONST	12	45	534
2-8-0 CONSOLIDATION CAB/DOME CONSTRUCT	02	46	98
2-8-0 CONSOLIDATION CONSTRUCTION 1 "O"	01	54	46
2-8-0 CONSOLIDATION CONSTRUCTION 2 "O"	02	54	46
2-8-0 CONSOLIDATION CONSTRUCTION 3 "O"	03	54	66
2-8-0 CONSOLIDATION CONSTRUCTION 4 "O"	04	54	49
2-8-0 CONSOLIDATION CONSTRUCTION 5 "O"	05	54	45
2-8-0 CONSOLIDATION CONSTRUCTION 7	08	54	44
2-8-0 CONSOLIDATION CONSTRUCTION B&O	10	45	416
2-8-0 CONSOLIDATION CONSTRUCTION TENDER	06	54	41
2-8-0 CONSOLIDATION CYLINDER/ROD CONST	11	45	458
2-8-0 CONSOLIDATION FREELANCED "O"	04	50	12
2-8-0 CONSOLIDATION FROM ATLAS 0-8-0	04	72	41
2-8-0 CONSOLIDATION FROM MDC 0-6-0	10	55	34
2-8-0 CONSOLIDATION KIT ASSEMBLY "O" TH	11	49	68
2-8-0 CONSOLIDATION MA&PA ALTERATIONS	04	61	26
2-8-0 CONSOLIDATION SMOKE BOX CONSTRUCT	01	46	22
2-8-0 CONSOLIDATION TENDER CONSTRUCTION	03	46	174
2-8-0 PENNLINE CONSOLIDATION FREELANCED	11	56	40
2-8-0 SP CLASS C-3 CONSOLIDATION CONST	04	78	64
2-8-2 CLASS K-28 MIKADO DETAILING PFM	06	58	32
2-8-2 CLASS L-1 MIKADO DETAILING PENLINE	07	53	14
2-8-2 FROM BALBOA SP TO UP	06	68	41
2-8-2 GN "GLACIER" PARK COLORS MOD & PT	08	85	111
2-8-2 GN GLACIER PARK MOD & PT	12	84	162
2-8-2 IN BRASS CONST BEARINGS/GEARBOX	01	83	72
2-8-2 IN BRASS CONST BOILER & CAB	05	83	92
2-8-2 IN BRASS CONST BOILER DETAILS	07	83	76
2-8-2 IN BRASS CONST ENG TRUCKS/COUPLERS	03	83	80
2-8-2 IN BRASS CONST FRAME & DRIVERS	11	82	114
2-8-2 IN BRASS CONST RUNNING GEAR/FRAME	09	83	84
2-8-2 IN BRASS CONST TENDER & PAINTING	11	83	102
2-8-2 IN BRASS CONSTRUCTION TOOLS NEEDED	10	82	74
2-8-2 KITCHEN TABLE MIKADO CAB DOME DETA	01	55	68
2-8-2 KITCHEN TABLE MIKADO PART 1	11	54	48
2-8-2 KITCHEN TABLE MIKADO PART 2 BOILER	12	54	72
2-8-2 KITCHEN TABLE MIKADO TENDER	02	55	64
2-8-2 LIGHT MIKADO USRA BRAKE RIGGING	08	41	416

STEAM LOCOMOTIVE MODELS	M	Y	P
2-8-2 LIGHT MIKADO USRA CAB CONSTRUCTION	09	41	468
2-8-2 LIGHT MIKADO USRA CYLINDER/VALVE	07	41	356
2-8-2 LIGHT MIKADO USRA FRAME CONSTRUCT	06	41	308
2-8-2 LIGHT MIKADO USRA SMOKE BOX CONSTR	10	41	512
2-8-2 LIGHT MIKADO USRA TENDER CONSTRUCT	11	41	576
2-8-2 MANTUA MIKADO - OTHER VERSIONS	10	50	32
2-8-2 MANTUA MIKADO DETAILING	10	50	26
2-8-2 MIKADO ENGLISH TO B&O	09	52	25
2-8-2 MIKADO OF 1910 CONSTRUCTION "O"	02	52	18
2-8-2 PRECISELY DETAILED 1/2" MODEL PHOT	05	61	28
2-8-2 STD GAUGE MIKADO CONST D&RGW	03	78	80
2-8-2 USRA LIGHT MIKADO KITBASH	09	77	75
2-8-4 BERKSHIRE FROM MANTUA 2-8-2 (1)	10	51	8
2-8-4 BERKSHIRE FROM MANTUA 2-8-2 (2)	11	51	26
2-8-4 BERKSHIRE FROM PFM C&O 2-8-4 V	01	76	67
2-8-4 BERKSHIRE FROM TYCO 2-8-2 C&NW 1	01	70	70
2-8-4 BERKSHIRE FROM TYCO 2-8-2 C&NW 2	02	70	62
2-8-4 FREELANCE BERKSHIRE KIT PARTS 1	02	50	34
2-8-4 FREELANCE BERKSHIRE KIT PARTS 2	03	50	31
2-8-4 FREELANCE BERKSHIRE KIT PARTS 3	04	50	52
2-8-8-0 GN CLASS N-3 MODEL PHOTOS "HO"	12	59	48
2-8-8-2 FROM KIT PARTS "O" PART 1	10	52	22
2-8-8-2 FROM KIT PARTS "O" PART 2	11	52	46
4-2-4T POWERING THE "C P HUNTINGTON" SP	08	51	41
4-4-0 1852 BALTIMORE & OHIO CONSTRUCTION	12	46	824
4-4-0 AMERICAN CONSTRUCTION 1 MKT MODERN	02	57	24
4-4-0 AMERICAN CONSTRUCTION 2 MKT	03	57	42
4-4-0 AMERICAN SCALE FROM MARKLIN TINPLA	09	38	357
4-4-0 AMERICAN TYPE OF 1910 CONST 1	12	52	32
4-4-0 AMERICAN TYPE OF 1910 CONST 2	01	53	36
4-4-0 AMERICAN TYPE OF 1910 CONST BOILER	02	53	33
4-4-0 AMERICAN TYPE OF 1910 CONST CAB	03	53	53
4-4-0 AMERICAN TYPE OF 1910 CONST TENDER	04	53	40
4-4-0 FRENCH FROM ALL-NATION KIT	04	70	35
4-4-0 FROM 4-6-0 "CASEY JONES"	05	75	44
4-4-0 KITCHEN TABLE AMERICAN 1	02	51	12
4-4-0 KITCHEN TABLE AMERICAN 2 SUPERSTRU	03	51	40
4-4-0 KITCHEN TABLE AMERICAN 3	04	51	36
4-4-0 MANTUA "BELL OF THE 80S" DETAILING	01	58	54
4-4-0 MDC/MANTUA KITBASH	12	82	90
4-4-0 REDETAILING A PFM RENO LOCO	01	63	63
4-4-0 UPDATED OLDTIMER MODEL 1915	12	54	40
4-4-2 ATLANTIC BOILER & CAB CONSTRUCTION	07	38	288
4-4-2 ATLANTIC CAB & AIR TANK CONSTRUCTI	09	38	378
4-4-2 ATLANTIC COAL FIRED MODEL "3/4"	09	34	9
4-4-2 ATLANTIC CONSTRUCTION	05	38	196
4-4-2 ATLANTIC CYLINDERS & MOTION CONSTR	06	38	244
4-4-2 ATLANTIC SMOKEBOX & RIVET CONSTRUC	08	38	328
4-4-2 ATLANTIC TENDER CONSTRUCTION	10	38	423
4-4-2 CLASS E3SD ATLANTIC PRR CONSTRUCT	08	74	43
4-4-2 CLASS E6 ATLANTIC CONST PRR "HO"	09	78	91
4-4-2 KIT ASSEMBLY "HO" M	09	49	33
4-4-2 LIVE STEAM "1 1/2" MODEL	07	74	50
4-4-2 PENNLINE ATLANTIC FREELANCED	11	56	40
4-4-2 SCALE LOCO FROM 4-4-2 AMER FLYER	12	38	516

LOCOMOTIVES

STEAM LOCOMOTIVE MODELS		M	Y	P
4-4-4-4 KIT ASSEMBLY PRR T1	PL	08	49	27
4-6-0 "HON3" FROM MDC 2-8-0		07	81	85
4-6-0 CAMELBACK OF 1852 B&O #158 CONST		04	49	8
4-6-0 CIVIL WAR LOCO B&O #9 CONST 1863		09	50	22
4-6-0 HOME BUILT 10 WHEEL BOIL/CAB/F BOX		02	41	74
4-6-0 HOME BUILT 10 WHEEL LOCOMOTIVE		12	40	652
4-6-0 HOME BUILT 10 WHEEL TENDER CONSTRU		03	41	142
4-6-0 HOME BUILT 10 WHEEL VALVE MOT/ROD		01	41	25
4-6-0 LOCO CONVERSION TO C&NW CLASS R1		12	64	39
4-6-0 TEN WHEELER BOILER FITTINGS CONST		05	48	340
4-6-0 TEN WHEELER BOILER/CAB CONSTRUCT		03	48	180
4-6-0 TEN WHEELER CAB FITTING CONSTRUCT		04	48	268
4-6-0 TEN WHEELER CYLINDER/ROD CONSTRUCT		02	48	88
4-6-0 TEN WHEELER FRAME CONSTRUCTION		01	48	8
4-6-0 TEN WHEELER TENDER CONSTRUCTION		06	48	418
4-6-2 ACL PACIFIC	MOD & PT	01	82	130
4-6-2 ASSEMBLY PRR K-5 KIT "S" MIDGAGE		11	48	810
4-6-2 BOWSER NYC PACIFIC TO SOO 4-6-2		05	70	60
4-6-2 BOWSER PACIFIC TO B&M 3600 CLASS		05	51	28
4-6-2 CLASS K-4 CONSTRUCTION 4 SUPERSTUR		01	50	67
4-6-2 CLASS K-4 CONSTRUCTION 5 TENDER		02	50	59
4-6-2 CLASS K-4 CONSTRUCTION CHASSIS		11	49	39
4-6-2 CLASS K-4 CONSTRUCTION PRR "HO"		10	49	16
4-6-2 CLASS K-4 CONSTRUCTION SUPERSTRUCT		12	49	42
4-6-2 CN #5250 KITBASH 1918 MLW		03	80	70
4-6-2 HOMEMADE PACIFIC "O"		10	34	4
4-6-2 LIGHT PACIFIC USRA BOILER/FIREBOX		07	40	384
4-6-2 LIGHT PACIFIC USRA CONSTRUCTION		05	40	256
4-6-2 LIGHT PACIFIC USRA EXTERIOR PIPING		09	40	488
4-6-2 LIGHT PACIFIC USRA RUNNING GEAR		06	40	330
4-6-2 LIGHT PACIFIC USRA SMOKEBOX/DETAIL		08	40	444
4-6-2 LIGHT PACIFIC USRA TENDER CONSTRUC		10	40	551
4-6-2 LIVE STEAM SOUTHERN #1410		06	72	46
4-6-2 MANTUA TO B&O "PRESIDENT"		03	83	63
4-6-2 PACIFIC CONSTRUCION SUPERST/DETAIL		10	37	366
4-6-2 PACIFIC CONSTRUCT FINISHING PIPES		09	37	331
4-6-2 PACIFIC CONSTRUCTION CAB/FIRE DOOR		06	37	210
4-6-2 PACIFIC CONSTRUCTION CONTINUED		01	37	5
4-6-2 PACIFIC CONSTRUCTION DOMES & STACK		07	37	248
4-6-2 PACIFIC CONSTRUCTION FINISHING		11	37	407
4-6-2 PACIFIC CONSTRUCTION FRAME		12	36	355
4-6-2 PACIFIC CONSTRUCTION MAT/RESCALE		04	37	147
4-6-2 PACIFIC CONSTRUCTION MOTORS & RODS		08	37	288
4-6-2 PACIFIC CONSTRUCTION PILOT TRUCK		03	37	97
4-6-2 PACIFIC CONSTRUCTION TENDER		12	37	441
4-6-2 PACIFIC CONSTRUCTION THE BEGINNING		11	36	329
4-6-2 PACIFIC CONSTRUCTION VALVE/CHEAD		02	37	58
4-6-2 PACIFIC EVOLUTION CONSTRUCTION		07	78	68
4-6-2 PACIFIC KIT ASSEMBLY "O" GM		02	49	20
4-6-2 PACIFICS TIPS ON MODELING N&W		08	77	90
4-6-2 SCRATCHBUILT IN BRASS		11	70	48
4-6-2-2-6-4 BEYER-GARRATT MODEL PHOTOS		09	64	30
4-6-4 AIMEE LIVE STEAM LOCOMOTIVE		03	65	50
4-6-4 HUDSON FREELANCED CONSTRUCTION		05	54	32
4-6-4 HUDSON FROM MANTUA 4-6-2		08	56	24

STEAM LOCOMOTIVE MODELS		M	Y	P
4-6-4 J3 NYC BRASS HUDSON	MOD & PT	08	84	108
4-6-4 VARIATIONS CONSTRUCTION NYC		10	78	58
4-6-6-4 CAMERA STUDY "O"	SCHMIDT	09	57	22
4-6-6-4 CONSTRUCTION "OO"		11	50	36
4-6-6T FROM AMERICAN FLYER 4-6-4		03	46	182
4-6-6T SUPER DETAILED LOCOMOTIVE		02	45	79
4-8-0 KITBASH FROM 0-8-0		08	81	84
4-8-2 CLASS R NH PRIZE WINNING PHOTOS		08	65	21
4-8-2 MOUNTAIN ASSSEMBLY "HO" BOW		10	49	41
4-8-4 CANADIAN NATIONALS NORTHERNS		03	79	71
4-8-4 CS&W	MOD & PT	11	76	121
4-8-4 LOCOMOTIVE UNDER MAGIFYING GLASS		12	63	28
4-8-4 NORTHERN ASSEMBLY HO SCALE V		01	49	27
4-8-4 SOO CLASS O-20	MOD & PT	04	82	119
4-8-8-2 1/4 SCALE CAB FOWARD MODEL		05	57	44
4-8-8-2 SP 1/4 SCALE PHOTOS	TEABY	11	61	26
4-8-8-4 BIG BOY SUPER DETAILING COMPLETE		04	62	53
4-8-8-4 BIG BOY SUPERSTRUCTRE SUPRDETAIL		03	62	54
ADDING DETAIL TO STEAM LOCOMOTIVES		02	40	72
ADJUSTING FLANGE DEPTH		06	64	38
ALL WEATHER CAB MODERNIZATION		03	63	57
AMAZING 4-8-4 SIMULATES SOUND & MOTIONS		07	85	84
AMERICANIZE EGGER-BAHN INDUSTRIAL LOCO		07	65	48
AN ADVENTURE IN FREELANCING		11	51	44
ASSEMBLING AND MAINTAINING KIT LOCOS		07	52	16
AXLE SPRINGING IN STEAM LOCOMOTIVES		06	70	34
BACKDATING SUNSETS BULL MOOSE 2-8-8-0		05	81	64
BENT LOCOMOTIVE FRAME CORRECTION		08	51	50
BETTER TRACKING FOR TRAILING TRUCKS		03	65	44
BILL LENOIRS ENGINES		08	52	22
BOILER CONSTRUCTION MADE EASY		11	57	56
BOILER CONSTRUCTION-ROLL YOUR OWN		06	51	30
BOILER FRAME AND CYLINDER FASTEN METHODS		01	72	81
BOILER WEIGHT INSTALLATION		10	77	134
BRASS LOCOMOTIVES BASICS		08	85	76
BRASS-BASHING REDETAILING WITH BRASS		05	74	52
BUILD A BRASS STEAM STEAM DOME		11	50	40
BUILD A HO ARTICULATED FROM STOCK PARTS1		05	49	8
BUILD A HO ARTICULATED FROM STOCK PARTS2		06	49	17
BUILD A HO ARTICULATED FROM STOCK PARTS3		07	49	24
BUILDING IN BRASS BOILER CAB FITTING		10	68	49
BUILDING IN BRASS THE FRAME		09	68	44
BUILDING IN BRASS THE TENDER		12	68	64
BUILDING LOCOMOTIVES FROM KITS & PARTS		12	72	50
BURLINGTON LOCOMOTIVES OF B. CORBIN "O"		05	58	23
CAMELBACK PACIFIC/MIKADO MODIFICATION LV		08	84	68
CHALLENGER MODEL PHOTO STUDY		12	58	38
CHANGING A KIT LOCO TO A DIFFERENT TYPE		01	52	61
CLOSE COUPLING STEAM LOCO TENDERS		07	68	40
COMPLETE BUILT UP LOCOMOTIVE		01	37	18
CONVERSION IDEAS HO TO ON 2 1/2		11	83	126
CONVERT ROUNDHOUSE 0-6-0 TO 2-6-0		11	46	724
COWCATCHERS IN "HO"		03	35	69
DESIGN OF GOOD STEAM RUNNING GEAR		02	62	39
DETAILING 4-4-0 NEW LIFE FOR OLD AMERICA		05	77	56

STEPHANS" RAILROAD DIRECTORY

LOCOMOTIVES

STEAM LOCOMOTIVE MODELS	M	Y	P
DETAILING A PC SHAY BOILER & TENDER	08	83	88
DIE-CAST LOCOMOTIVE DETAILING	11	70	45
DOUBLE CHAIN DRIVE LOCOMOTIVE	10	71	68
DRILLING LOCOMOTIVE FRAMES	04	46	234
DRIVE WHEEL MACHINING & QUARTERING	12	46	820
DRIVE WHEEL SIZES AND APPLICATIONS	03	36	67
DUAL DRIVE FOR POCKET SIZE MALLET	01	64	61
DUAL DRIVE FOR RIVEROSSI ARTICULATED	09	70	58
DUMMY SPRINGS FOR LOCOMOTIVES	11	42	511
EARLY TRAILING TRUCK CONSTRUCTION $1	11	73	80
EQUALIZING LOCOMOTIVE DRIVERS	09	72	62
FILL UNSIGHTLY LOCO-TENDER GAP	11	79	148
FLYWHEEL DRIVE FOR STEAM LCOOMTOIVES	11	45	450
FLYWHEELS IN STEAM LOCOMOTIVES	06	51	28
FREE LANCE LOCOMOTIVES THEN & NOW	08	36	211
FREE ROLLING STEAM LOCOMOTIVE DRIVE	11	85	90
FREELANCE FORNEY	10	68	70
FREELANCE LOCOMOTIVE DESIGN	01	76	83
GEARED 2 TRUCK LOCO INCENSE FIRED CONSTR	01	45	12
GENERAL 4-4-0 IN 1" SCALE PHOTOS	08	60	44
GG1 TWO MOTOR MODEL	06	38	252
GIVE YOUR LOCOS A FAMILY LOOK	07	66	36
GOOD LOCO PERFORMANCE THROUGH ADJUSTMENT	09	44	405
HALF SCRATCHBUILDING W/NO MACHINE TOOLS	10	74	40
HEADLIGHT (WORKING) CONSTRUCTION	07	51	16
HEISLER ARIZONA CENTRAL MOD & PT	04	79	127
HEISLER DETAIL MODIFICATION	02	73	66
HELPER ENGINE COUPLERS	12	53	33
HO KIT LOCOMOTIVE CONVERSIONS	06	56	20
IMPROVED PERFORMANCE FROM MDC SHAY	08	85	84
INSTALLING LOCOMOTIVE DETAIL HINTS	12	49	28
INSULATING DRIVE WHEELS	03	42	112
KADEE COUPLERS ON AHM Y6B & CHALLENGER	05	79	135
KIT LOCOMOTIVE DETAILING	02	56	23
LAGGED BOILER CONSTRUCTION	09	67	43
LEAD TRUCK IMPROVEMENT FOR STEAM LOCOS	07	63	50
LENOIRS LOCOMOTIVES	01	42	16
LIFE OF A LIVE STEMAER	11	48	800
LIVE STEAM 4-6-2 PACIFIC BOILER/FIREBOX	12	35	322
LIVE STEAM 4-6-2 PACIFIC CROSSHEADS	08	35	212
LIVE STEAM 4-6-2 PACIFIC CYLINDERS/VALVE	06	35	152
LIVE STEAM 4-6-2 PACIFIC DRIVERS & RODS	05	35	119
LIVE STEAM 4-6-2 PACIFIC FRAME CONSTRUCT	04	35	92
LIVE STEAM 4-6-2 PACIFIC SMOKE BX SADDLE	07	35	178
LIVE STEAM 4-6-2 PACIFIC V GEAR/EX PIPE	10	35	257
LIVE STEAM IN FRANCE	03	70	42
LOCO UPGRADING, REWORKING OLDER BRASS	02	79	85
LOCOMOTIVE AIR PUMPS CONSTRUCTION	07	45	291
LOCOMOTIVE BOILER CONSTRUCTION	10	48	743
LOCOMOTIVE BUILT TO 1/305 SCALE	10	70	68
LOCOMOTIVE CROSSHEAD & GUIDES CONSTRUCT	08	45	329
LOCOMOTIVE PILOT CONSTRUCTION	03	46	158
LOCOMOTIVES OF THE UNADILLA VALLEY	10	48	714
LOCOMOTIVES OF WALTER SARDINHA	07	65	32
LOCOMOTIVES WITH CHARACTER EXAMPLES	01	64	48

STEAM LOCOMOTIVE MODELS	M	Y	P
LOST HUDSON MODEL	02	74	48
LOW WHEELED PACIFIC	05	40	249
MACHINING DRIVE WHEELS	04	45	152
MAKE LOCOMOTIVE DRIVERS	08	62	54
MAKE YOUR LOCOMOTIVE SMOKE WITH DRY ICE	09	45	356
MALLET LOCOMOTIVES (0-4-0 TYPE) SPOOF	03	39	148
MANTUA "GOAT" CONVERSION	03	49	8
MANTUA 8 DRIVE WHEEL MECHANISM REV "HO"M	07	40	410
MESCAL LINES CONSOLIDATION #12 CONSTRUCT	01	79	82
MODEL LOCOMOTIVES OF JACK BRAMBLE	02	49	8
MODELERS WORKBENCH STEAM DOME	11	50	40
MODELING A PRR T-1	01	47	22
MODELING LOCOMOTIVE BOILERS	11	47	909
MODELS IN NEW LIMITEDS	07	38	274
MODIFYING A MODERATELY PRICED LOCOMOTIVE	12	67	65
MODIFYING THE TYCO 4-6-0	08	81	102
MODLERS WORKBENCH LOCO AIRTANK	10	50	44
MOM 0-4-0 IRON PONY "1/4AAR" COFFEY	10	68	41
MOM 0-4-0T PORTER "HO" GROTH	06	72	51
MOM 0-6-0 C&NW "0" KISTEN	03	43	135
MOM 0-6-0 FRENCH LOCOMOTIVE "O" ALLENDEN	01	69	63
MOM 0-6-0 SWITCHER "HO" HOWELL	06	71	34
MOM 0-8-0 PRR CLASS C-1 "17/64" HUEBNER	06	36	153
MOM 0-8-0 SWITCHER "HO" KJELLANDER	04	69	49
MOM 0-8-0 THREE CYLINDER SWITCH MERIDITH	07	39	366
MOM 2 FOOT SHAY "O" EDGELL	08	84	83
MOM 2 TRUCK SHAY "1/4AARN3" BROWN	01	70	69
MOM 2-10-0 CP DECAPOD "HO" SMALTZ	05	79	75
MOM 2-10-0 DECAPOD ATSF 2565 CLASS	01	77	52
MOM 2-10-10-2 "HO" LIVE STEAMER SHERWOOD	06	51	17
MOM 2-10-2 CP CLASS S-2 "HO" SMALTZ	03	74	50
MOM 2-10-4 C&O T1 "1/4" EUDALY	03	73	48
MOM 2-10-4 TEXAS C&O CLASS T-1 SPANAGEL	08	77	50
MOM 2-6-0 CLASS J2 CP "HO" SMALTZ	12	75	85
MOM 2-6-0 FREELANCE "HO" KING	08	69	56
MOM 2-6-2 MILW CLASS K1 "HO" LARSON	01	76	79
MOM 2-6-2 SR&RL "1/4 FS" 1919 COLLINS	09	73	34
MOM 2-6-6-4 SUPERDETAIL LOCO "O" HUEBNER	04	39	175
MOM 2-6-6-6 & 2-8-4 "1/4" MARTIN	10	62	44
MOM 2-6-6-6 C&O "O" MARTIN	01	49	34
MOM 2-8-0 CLASS 25 D&RGW "ON3" MORRIS	04	79	61
MOM 2-8-0 CLASS C-16 RGS #15 "ON3" KOCH	01	82	67
MOM 2-8-0 CONSOLIDATED CLASS C-16 D&RGW	02	77	88
MOM 2-8-0 CONSOLIDATED D&RGW CLASS C-11	07	77	57
MOM 2-8-0 CONSOLIDATION "ON3" MARTY	02	76	77
MOM 2-8-0 CONSOLIDATION M #273 "HO" SWAN	04	83	65
MOM 2-8-0 D&RGW #268 "SN3" BOOTH	02	85	67
MOM 2-8-0 D&RGW CLASS C-16 "HO" FREELAND	02	74	54
MOM 2-8-0 DSP&P #63 "HON3" EATON	02	80	81
MOM 2-8-0 MOTHER HUBBARB "#2" VAUGHAN	03	36	64
MOM 2-8-2 C&O CLASS K-3A BRANCH	04	74	39
MOM 2-8-2 CLASS K-27 RGS "ON3" BARTIG	02	82	102
MOM 2-8-2 FRIS CLASS 1350 MIKADO "HO"	12	82	89
MOM 2-8-2 MICHC CLASS H-10B "HO" MOXLEY	05	62	20
MOM 2-8-8-0 PRR HC1 "HO" SAVERS	08	78	88

LOCOMOTIVES

STEAM LOCOMOTIVE MODELS		M	Y	P
MOM 2-8-8-2 N&W #2201 "HO"	DRESSLER	02	71	46
MOM 2-8-8-4 B&O CLASS EM-1 "HO"	KURILEC	07	80	81
MOM 3 TRUCK SHAY "O"	POLI	08	72	57
MOM 3 TRUCK WM SHAY "HO"	COLLIER	04	73	70
MOM 4-4-0 "3/8"	VAUGHAN	05	34	5
MOM 4-4-0 AMERICAN "HO" 1910	BRISKMAN	03	71	39
MOM 4-4-0 AMERICAN OF 1860 "O"	HOLT	05	77	72
MOM 4-4-0 B&O OF 1910 "HO"	BRISKMAN	01	85	81
MOM 4-4-0 FRENCH LOCOMOTIVE "O"	ALLERTON	03	70	72
MOM 4-4-0 LOCOMOTIVE 3.5MM	LANGE	04	38	153
MOM 4-4-2 CB&Q #1591 CLASS P1C	CORBIN	06	69	56
MOM 4-4-2 PRR E6 "O"	STEPEK	01	79	86
MOM 4-6-0 B&O CLASS B18CA "O"	STEPEK	09	62	42
MOM 4-6-0 ROGERS "O"	NAGEL	03	81	69
MOM 4-6-2 B&O CLASS P5A "O"	WHELOVE	02	55	40
MOM 4-6-2 CN CLASS J-4E "HO"	WOODWARD	12	68	63
MOM 4-6-2 ERIE K-5 "O"	RUSSELL	10	36	286
MOM 4-6-2 LIVE STEAM LOCO "2 1/2"	HOPKINS	01	35	2
MOM 4-6-2 NH CLASS J-2 "HO"	ALDRICH	04	72	33
MOM 4-6-2 P-1D B&O "O"	KLOPPENBURG	07	51	34
MOM 4-6-2 PACIFIC "HO"	WARD	08	42	358
MOM 4-6-2 PRR #384 CLASS K-4 "O"	STRAYER	09	70	38
MOM 4-6-2 PRR A5 #5678 "O"	RICHARDS	01	43	9
MOM 4-6-2 PS4 SOUTHERN "1/4"	BOYD	03	75	62
MOM 4-6-2 USRA "O"	HUGHES	01	50	39
MOM 4-6-4 ATSF CLASS 3450 "HO"	KJELLANDER	08	73	38
MOM 4-6-4 C&O "O"	HARLEY	10	85	73
MOM 4-6-4 CLASS H-1-E CP #2844 "HO"		12	84	130
MOM 4-6-4 CLASS S-4 CB&Q "O"	CORBIN	09	76	68
MOM 4-6-4T CNJ TANKER "O"	NOLDE	02	37	72
MOM 4-6-6-4 UP CLASS 3950 "HO"	COSGROVE	07	75	65
MOM 4-8-2 N&W #124 CLASS K2 "O"	DRESSLER	07	70	36
MOM 4-8-2 WP "S"	SCHUSTER	03	69	37
MOM 4-8-4 CLASS O CB&Q "HO"	MIDDLETON	10	76	61
MOM 4-8-4 CLASS O5A BURL #5631 "HO"		02	53	30
MOM 4-8-4 D&RGW "O"	MCDERMOTT	10	39	505
MOM 4-8-4 FEF-3 CLASS UP "1/4"	LEIDER	09	75	77
MOM 4-8-4 UP FEF-3 "HO"	CADARET	04	81	73
MOM 4-8-8-2 SP ARTICULATED "O"	ASHLEY	06	37	2123
MOM CLIMAX "1/4"	CANNON	05	69	49
MOM COMPOUND 0-4-0 "HO"	LATHROP	04	70	65
MOM D&RGW #491 K-37 MIKADO "HON3"	FRANCIS	07	68	49
MOM F&S LOGGING 0-6-0	BILODEAU	11	77	63
MOM HEISELER "HO"	MCKOWN	07	71	38
MOM HEISELER MODEL "O"	CLEMENT	02	50	24
MOM LOCOMOTIVE CRANE "HO"	KJELLANDER	09	71	43
MOM NYC #999		01	37	16
MOM PAIR OF NYC LOCOS 4-8-2/2-8-2	CARTER	12	39	619
MOM SHAY "HO"	MURRAY	10	69	69
MOM SHAY "ON3" MICH-CAL #6	FERRELL	05	71	47
MOM SHAY 150T 4 TRUCK "HO"	MURRAY	10	77	60
MOM SHAY LOCOMOTIVE "ON3"	FREY	11	78	72
MOM SP CLASS MM-2 2-6-6-2 "HO"	QUEYREL	01	75	80
MOM UP 4-6-6-4 "HO"	RIDLEY	11	70	78
MOM WM THREE TRUCK SHAY "3/16"	BILODEAU	07	74	33

STEAM LOCOMOTIVE MODELS	M	Y	P
MOMENTUM IN BRASS STEAM LOCOS	12	69	64
MORE DETAIL FOR YOUR LOCOMOTIVES	02	50	18
N&W MODELER GOES WESTERN	09	75	78
NARROW GAUGE LIVE STEAMER	03	41	146
NEW RUNNING GEAR FOR DAMAGED BRASS PACIF	10	85	96
NEW ZEALAND K88 SCRATCHBUILD (2-4-2)	02	85	68
ONE MANS ROSTER FREEDMAN	01	65	46
ONE MANS ROSTER JAMES EUDALY	03	64	56
ONE MANS ROSTER---EARLY LOCOS--THENBURGH	09	69	46
OPERATING CLASS LIGHTS WITH FIBER OPTICS	07	70	68
OVERHAUL OF BRASS FROM STORAGE	03	85	134
PAINTING SHAY TIPS	12	85	161
PENNSY BOILER CONSTRUCTION PRR	06	47	474
PIECE-PART APPROACH TO SCRATCHBUILDING	09	74	67
PILOT CONSTRUCTION	04	50	26
PILOT CONSTRUCTION	09	56	36
PILOT MODELING	05	69	66
PIPE CONNECTORS SQUARE FLANGE CONSTRUCTI	10	70	52
PORTFOLIO OF STEAM LOCOS TRACKSIDE PHOTO	04	61	28
PRECISION MOTORS FOR STEAM LOCOMOTIVES 1	02	76	66
PRECISION MOTORS FOR STEAM LOCOMOTIVES 2	03	76	42
PRR CLASS Q-2 TO CLASS Q-1 4-6-4-4	03	73	34
QUARTERING A LOCOMOTIVE BOILER	03	51	63
QUARTERING THE DRIVERS	09	83	139
REBUILT LIMA SHAY	10	79	82
REDETAILING A GARRATT	12	68	72
REGEARING MANTUA STEAM LOCOMOTIVES	08	80	90
REJUVENATING OLD DIE CAST LOCOMOTIVES	06	79	102
REMOTORING AHM HEISLER	10	85	134
REMOTORING FOR BETTER PERFORMANCE	12	85	94
REPOWERING MANTUAS CAMELBACK MIKADO	07	83	86
REPOWERING WSM D&RGW K36	04	79	86
REVERSIBLE VALVE GEAR	12	49	35
RIGIDIZING LOCOMOTIVES AND WHY	09	64	27
RON CRANDALL'S 2-6-2 "O" MODEL PHOTOS	12	69	40
ROSTER OF A&P LOCOS LIONEL MODIFICATIONS	06	41	298
RUSSIANS & YELLOW JACKET DETAILING NC&SL	02	78	94
SANS PAREIL LOCOMOTIVE OF 1829	03	35	75
SCIOTO VALLEY SOUTHERN MIKADOS "ON3"	01	80	84
SCRATCHBUILD A LOCOMOTIVE FRAME	01	67	48
SCRATCHBUILDERS LOCOMOTIVE KINKS & HINTS	03	74	48
SCRATCHBUILDING IN BRASS 4-8-4	02	68	58
SIAMESE TWIN BALDWIN LOCOS CONSTRUCTION	03	78	64
SIMPLE REBUILT LOCOMOTIVE	12	37	465
SMOKEBOX FRONTS	09	46	568
SMOOTH & QUIET DRIVE MODIFICATIONS F/LOC	08	66	30
SNOWPLOW PILOT CONSTRUCTION	11	64	42
SOLDERING DETAIL ONTO BRASS	08	69	36
SOLDERLESS DOME PIPING	10	48	750
SPRINGING DRIVER TECHNIQUES	09	70	72
SPRINGING LOCOMOTIVES BOOMER PETE	10	41	522
STEAM LOCO PAINTING RESEARCH	04	75	18B
STEAM LOCOMOTIVE DRIVERS	09	68	63
STEAM TYPE CYLINDERS OF WOOD	10	35	261
SUPER SCRATCH BLDR LIVE ST R. MCALLISTER	06	76	88

LOCOMOTIVES

STEAM LOCOMOTIVE MODELS	M	Y	P
SUPERDETAILED REBUILDING	07	64	26
SUPERDETAILING A C&O CLASS K4 2-8-4 LOCO	07	67	38
SUPERDETAILING A PC SHAY CAB INT/SOUND	10	83	76
SUPERDETAILING PC SHAY WEALTH OF INFO	07	83	50
SUPERDETAILING STEAM LOCOMOTIVES 1 TOOLS	11	61	48
SUPERDETAILING STEAM LOCOMOTIVES 3	02	62	39
SUPERDETAILING STEAM LOCOMOTIVES 4	03	62	54
SUPERDETAILING STEAM LOCOMOTIVES 5	04	62	53
SUPERDETAILING STEAM LOCOS 2 METALWORKNG	12	61	71
TAPERED BOILER SECTION FROMATION	02	52	34
TAPERED BOILER SECTIONS	06	69	72
TENDER FROM OIL TO COAL CONVERSION	04	63	52
TENDER LOCOMOTIVE WIRE CONNECTION	07	59	67
TENDER TO LOCO DRIVES	10	69	88
TENDER-HOUSED LOCOMOTIVE DRIVE	07	67	28
THIS IS AN N SCALE SHAY!	03	70	34
TINPLATE LOCOS TO SCALE ELEC CONTROL	03	52	50
TOM DRESSLER'S N&W LOCOMOTIVEWS	11	69	55
TOM THUMB IN "O" GAUGE	10	53	27
TOP PERFORMANCE & SOUND IN A SHAY (PFM)	11	73	46
TOP PERFORMANCE FROM LOCOMOTIVES	02	63	52
TORQUE ARM DRIVE FOR STEAM LOCOMOTIVES	11	80	116
TOUCH OF REALISM FOR MDC CLIMAX	12	82	114
TRUCK CENTERING SPRINGS FOR STEAM LOCOS	03	71	40
UNPOWERED STEAM POWER & ILLUSION	03	79	88
UPGRADE AHM CHALLENGER DETAILS/WEATHERIN	02	84	78
UPGRADING RIVAROSSI PACIFICS & MIKADOS	06	82	80
VALVE GEAR SET FOR A TYCO 0-4-0	12	78	187
WAHLOP PACKING COMPANY DRAWINGS	03	65	54
WOOD AND CARD MATERIALS IN LOCO BUILDING	05	72	48
WOOD CARVED LOCOS OF ERNEST WARTHER	04	70	60
WOODEN FIREBOX CONVERSION	07	74	60
WORKING BOOSTER INCREASES LOCO PULL	06	66	50
WORKING COUPLERS UP FRONT	11	66	38
WORKING STEPHENSON VALVE GEAR	01	75	68
WORLD'S LARGEST LOCOMOTIVE ROSTER LOWRY	09	55	22
WORTHINGTON TYPE S FEEDWATER HEATER CONS	12	63	66
YOUR LOCOS CLEAN THE TRACK-THIS DOES IT	05	49	13

LOCOMOTIVES

STEAM LOCOMOTIVE MODEL REVIEWS

	M	Y	P
0-2-2 LIVE STEAM "ROCKET" LOCO "HO" LSL	12	79	38
0-4-0 B&O DOCKSIDE REVIEW "HO" PFM 1912	07	63	8
0-4-0 CAMELBACK REVIEW "HO" MANTUA	07	39	374
0-4-0 CB&Q SWITCHER REVIEW "HO" ARISTO	01	63	25
0-4-0 CLASS A3 PRR LISTING "HO" AHM	01	78	50
0-4-0 DEWITT CLINT M&HR "HO" B 1831 WPF	05	83	46
0-4-0 DOCKSIDE REVIEW "HO" VARNEY	01	42	48
0-4-0 DOCKSIDE REVIEW "S" REX	06	52	36
0-4-0 INDUSTRIAL SWITCHER REV "HO" INT	09	50	53
0-4-0 LISTING "G" LGB	04	77	46
0-4-0 MOTHER HUB R CLASS A-5A REV "HO" G	01	69	16
0-4-0 SEITCHER REVIEW "N" AT 1921 B	05	73	25
0-4-0 SWITCHER REVIEW "HO" RIV	11	62	14
0-4-0 SWITCHER REVIEW "HO" M	08	67	11
0-4-0 SWITHCER REVIEW "HO" M	09	50	52
0-4-0T CLASS A3A PRR REVIEW "HO" AM 1895	01	82	46
0-4-0T DOCKSIDE B&O REVIEW "HO" PCO B	05	81	38
0-4-0T DOCKSIDE SWITCHER B&O REV "N" B	03	71	23
0-4-0T PORTER CLASS B-S REVIEW "ON3" GL	01	81	39
0-4-0T SWITCHER KIT REVIEW "HO" M	12	49	81
0-4-2T LIVE STEAM REVIEW "NO 1" SPPR	03	81	41
0-4-2T PLANTATION REVIEW "HON3" KK	11	67	13
0-4-4-0T OF 1913 REV "HO" HD	09	64	10
0-6-0 ATSF #2100 SWITCHER REV "HO" BAL	09	67	12
0-6-0 C&NW CLASS M2 REVIEW "HO" TI	07	67	13
0-6-0 CLASS O18A CN REVIEW "HO" PFM 1920	11	76	37
0-6-0 CMI SWITCHER REVIEW "HO" MEW 1887	10	66	11
0-6-0 CN CLASS O-12A REV "HO" F&G	12	62	16
0-6-0 LOCOMOTIVE REVIEW "N" RAPIDO	01	66	12
0-6-0 LOCOMOTIVE REVIEW "O" WALTERS	01	41	56
0-6-0 SP 1200 CLASS REVIEW "HO" PAR	02	59	12
0-6-0 SP CALSS S9 REVIEW "HO" MDC 1912 B	03	73	20
0-6-0 SP CLASS S-12 REVIEW "HO" MBA	07	60	9
0-6-0 SP CLASS S-2 REVIEW "TT" SRA	05	59	16
0-6-0 SP SWITCHER REVIEW "HO" MDC	10	53	14
0-6-0 SWITCHER KIT REVIEW "HO" MDC	12	49	80
0-6-0 SWITCHER KIT REVIEW "TT" HP	02	48	149
0-6-0 SWITCHER REVIEW "3/16" CMS	03	38	130
0-6-0 SWITCHER REVIEW "HO" MKL	02	50	75
0-6-0 SWITCHER REVIEW "HO" GIL	08	50	50
0-6-0 SWITCHER REVIEW "HO" GEORGE STOCK	08	39	424
0-6-0 SWITCHER REVIEW "N" RAP	04	67	16
0-6-0 USRA REVIEW "HO" NWSL 1918	11	76	41
0-6-0 USRA REVIEW "O" KM 1918	02	68	12
0-6-0 USRA SWITCHER REVIEW "HO" ATH	08	62	11
0-6-0 USRA SWITCHER REVIEW "HO" RIV 1918	10	71	21
0-6-0T BR80 GERMAN LOCO REV "1/45" AHM	09	72	25
0-6-0T D&RG #105 REVIEW "HON3" PS 1881 B	12	80	52
0-6-0T INDUSTRIAL SWITCHER REV "HO" AHM	06	72	20
0-6-0T KIT REVIEW "HO" MDC	05	53	52
0-6-2T REVIEW "1/22.5" GM LGB	12	73	30
0-6-6-0T MALLET REVIEW "G" LGB	10	84	47
0-8-0 B&O CAMELBACK REVIEW "O" MB 1960	03	64	6
0-8-0 CLASS C-15A C&O SWITCHER HO REV L	02	77	32
0-8-0 IHB CLASS U-42 REVIEW "HO" AHM	01	62	16

STEAM LOCOMOTIVE MODEL REVIEWS

	M	Y	P
0-8-0 IHB SWITCHER REV "HO" IMPROVED AHM	12	71	28
0-8-0 IHB SWITCHER REVIEW "1/4" AHM 1927	04	71	21
0-8-0 IHB SWITCHER REVIEW "HO" 1937 AHM	08	77	31
0-8-0 IHB SWITCHER REVIEW "N" AT 1927	06	68	14
0-8-0 SWITCHER AC&I REVIEW "HO" ARISTO	03	62	18
0-8-0 SWITCHER KIT REVIEW "HO" ABJ	10	35	275
0-8-0 USRA REVIEW "O" PTO	01	54	22
0-8-0 USRA SWITCHER REVIEW "HO" PFM	09	56	10
0-8-0T SWITCHER REVIEW "HO" NWSL	12	66	20
2-10-0 92000 CLASS "HO" USAI 1960	01	77	43
2-10-0 BOILER REVIEW "HO" CLW	06	60	11
2-10-0 BRITISH LOCO REV "OO" RK	03	61	11
2-10-0 CLASS D-1 SP REVIEW "HO" SUN	08	76	27
2-10-0 PRR CLASS I REVIEW "N" MTX	08	79	43
2-10-0 PRR I-1 CLASS KIT REVIEW "HO" PL	02	55	10
2-10-2 ATSF 3800 CLASS REV "HO" KEY 1923	10	79	52
2-10-2 B&O CLASS S-1A REVIEW "HO" RIV	12	67	10
2-10-2 B&O CLASS S1 REVIEW "HO" LMB	10	62	14
2-10-2 SANTA FE TYPE PRR REV "HO" G 1918	05	75	23
2-10-4 CLASS J4 PRR REV "HO" AHM BRASS	10	66	16
2-10-4 CLASS T1 C&O REVIEW "HO" AM	12	83	54
2-10-4 CP CLASS 5900 REV "HO" F&G MLW	07	61	12
2-10-4 REVIEW "HO" LMB	05	64	10
2-10-4 T&P TEXAS REVIEW "HO" LMB 1925 L	04	60	10
2-4-0 V&T BOWKER REVIEW "HO" AHM 1875	06	67	12
2-4-0 V&T LISTING "HO" AHM	01	77	48
2-4-4 SUBURBAN REVIEW "S" REX	11	53	15
2-4-4-2 BALDWIN MALLET REVIEW "HO" G	11	63	12
2-4-4T FORNEY REVIEW "HO" DM	07	64	6
2-6-0 C&S MOGUL REVIEW "NN3" ROSL	01	84	68
2-6-0 CLASS M-21 SP REVIEW "HO" M 1928	04	82	39
2-6-0 CLASS M4 SP REVIEW "HO" PCO	05	81	38
2-6-0 GM DSP&P REVIEW "GM" LGB	12	85	58
2-6-0 MOGUL KIT REVIEW "HO" ACI	12	55	14
2-6-0 MOGUL KIT REVIEW "O" LOB	08	55	8
2-6-0 MOGUL REVIEW "S" S&P	07	64	7
2-6-0 MOGUL SP CLASS M-21 REV "HO" MBA	12	58	23
2-6-0 MOGUL W REVIEW "O" KEM	09	59	10
2-6-0 PORTER MOGUL KIT REVIEW "S" KK	01	65	10
2-6-0 PORTER MOGUL REVIEW "HO" KK 1888	12	61	16
2-6-0 PORTER MOGUL REVIEW "O" MB 1880	06	59	10
2-6-0 PORTER REVIEW "HON3" DM	05	65	9
2-6-0 SP MOGUL CLASS M-1 REV "HO" G 1928	03	64	9
2-6-0 WABASH CLASS F4 REVIEW "HO" AHM	08	66	8
2-6-2 BALDWIN REVIEW "HO" PFM	06	57	10
2-6-2 CONVERTIBLE TANK LOCO REV "O" LMB	10	62	16
2-6-2 NP CLASS T-1 REVIEW "HO" PFM 1906	09	68	9
2-6-2 PRAIRIE ATSF REVIEW "HO" MDC	06	59	10
2-6-2 PRAIRIE MILW REVIEW "HO" NWSL 1908	06	77	36
2-6-2 PRAIRIE REVIEW "HO" M	06	67	9
2-6-2 PRAIRIE REVIEW "HO" MBA 1907	12	59	17
2-6-6 MASON BOGIE DSP&P REV "HON3" PFM	08	66	10
2-6-6-2 LOGGER REVIEW "HO" NWSL	09	60	10
2-6-6-2 SIERRA REVIEW WTC "HO" PFM	03	59	10
2-6-6-2T LOGGER CWP REVIEW "HO" NWSL B	12	59	13

LOCOMOTIVES

STEAM LOCOMOTIVE MODEL REVIEWS

	M	Y	P
2-6-6-2T LOGGING LOCOMOTIVE REV "HO" M	05	82	35
2-6-6-6 CLASS H-8 KIT REVIEW "HO" W	10	50	48
2-8-0 B&O CLASS E24A REVIEW "HO" L	01	78	38
2-8-0 BALDWIN CONSOLIDATION REV "HO" MDC	08	77	28
2-8-0 C&S REVIEW "HON3" PS 1898 BLW	06	83	37
2-8-0 CLASS C-16 D&RG REVIEW "SN3" TOM	10	68	11
2-8-0 CLASS C-16 REV D&RGW"ON3" SUN 1882	03	77	31
2-8-0 CLASS C-18 D&RGW REVIEW "HON3" KEY	05	79	49
2-8-0 CLASS H-10 PRR REVIEW "O" CLWO B	07	59	12
2-8-0 CLASS I 10SA R REV "HO" G 1923 B	11	81	41
2-8-0 CLASS I-10SA R REVIEW "HO" BACHMAN	01	77	35
2-8-0 CLASS Z NKP REVIEW "HO" NPP 1910 B	11	83	57
2-8-0 CONSOLIDATION REVIEW "HO" MANTUA	03	38	130
2-8-0 CONSOLIDATION REVIEW "HO" V	05	56	10
2-8-0 CONSOLIDATION REVIEW "HON3" WSM B	09	71	21
2-8-0 CP CLASS N2A REV "HO" F&G 1912	08	64	7
2-8-0 D&RGW CLASS C48 REVIEW "1/4" PFM	12	71	36
2-8-0 KIT REVIEW "TT" HP	06	48	433
2-8-0 KIT REVIEW PRR "O" SPM	08	40	460
2-8-0 LOCOS OF D&RGW REVIEW "SN3" PBLW	08	85	42
2-8-0 MA&PA #126 REVIEW "1/4" IH	06	78	36
2-8-0 NP OF 1889 REVIEW "HO" G	04	65	12
2-8-0 PRR CLASS H6 REV "HO" L 1899 B	12	73	25
2-8-0 PRR H-9 REVIEW "HO" PL	09	52	52
2-8-0 PRR H9 KIT REVIEW "HO" BOWSER 1907	03	71	23
2-8-0 REVIEW "HO" LOCOMOTIVE COMPANY	10	78	44
2-8-0 REVIEW "HON3" MDC	04	78	37
2-8-0 UP CLASS 6200 REV "HO" PFM 1904 B	11	61	12
2-8-2 ATSF 3129 CLASS REV "HO" H 1916 B	11	82	51
2-8-2 ATSF CLASS 3160 REV "HO" HFW 1917	01	60	18
2-8-2 B&O CLASS Q-4B REV "HO" AK 1922 B	03	62	12
2-8-2 BOILER REVIEW CARY LOCO BOILER WKS	05	59	12
2-8-2 CLASS H10B NYC REVIEW "O" USH 1920	10	76	38
2-8-2 CLASS J-4 L&N REV "HO" OM 1918 BLW	07	81	35
2-8-2 CLASS K-27 D&RGW REVIEW "ON3" PFM	12	76	41
2-8-2 D&RGW CLASS K-27 MUDHEN REVIEW PFM	09	77	31
2-8-2 D&RGW CLASS K-37 REVIEW "SN3" MISM	08	80	36
2-8-2 D&RGW K-27 REVIEW "HON3" PFM 1897	06	63	6
2-8-2 FRIS 4000 CLASS REV "HO" KEY 1919	10	82	48
2-8-2 K28 D&RGW REVIEW "ON3" SUN	07	78	37
2-8-2 MIKADO D&RGW K27 "HON3" REVIEW PS	11	85	41
2-8-2 MIKADO KIT REVIEW "HO" M	05	50	43
2-8-2 MIKADO REVIEW "O" WAL	02	38	86
2-8-2 NH CLASS J-1 REV "HO" KEY 1916	10	82	48
2-8-2 NKP CLASS H6D REV "HO" KEY 1922 L	10	82	48
2-8-2 NP CLASS W-3 REVIEW "HO" NWSL	04	62	15
2-8-2 NYC CLASS H10 REV "N" KEY 1922	02	85	49
2-8-2 PRR CLASS L-1 REVIEW "HO" PL	02	53	65
2-8-2 S MIKADO REVIEW "HO" EMP 1911 B	01	79	46
2-8-2 SP CLASS MK-5 REVIEW "HO" BAL	04	65	9
2-8-2 USRA CLASS H6A MIKADO REV "HO" KEY	12	77	42
2-8-2 USRA HEAVY MIKADO REV "N" CC 1918	03	85	42
2-8-2 USRA LIGHT MIKADO REVIEW "HO" OE	05	61	12
2-8-2 USRA MIKADO REVIEW "N" AT 1918	02	70	14
2-8-2 WABASH KIT REVIEW "HO" TYCO	01	75	32

STEAM LOCOMOTIVE MODEL REVIEWS

	M	Y	P
2-8-2 WP #327 REVIEW "HO" PFM 1926 ALCO	04	68	10
2-8-2T LOGGER REVIEW "HO" NWSL	03	66	11
2-8-4 B&A CLASS A-1 REVIEW "HO" LMB 1926	02	64	10
2-8-4 B&M CLASS T-1 REVIEW "HO" LMB 1928	02	64	10
2-8-4 BERKSHIRE CLASS A1B B&A REVIEW NKP	11	77	35
2-8-4 BERKSHIRE REVIEW "HO" V	03	58	11
2-8-4 BERKSHIRE REVIEW C&NW "O" LOB	06	47	515
2-8-4 BERKSHIRE REVIEW C&NW "O" LOB	11	39	608
2-8-4 C&NW BOILER REVIEW "HO" CLW	07	65	8
2-8-4 C&NW CLASS J-4 REVIEW "HO" NPP	07	80	38
2-8-4 C&NW DETAIL KIT REVIEW "HO" CLW	07	65	9
2-8-4 CLASS 4100 ATSF REV "HO" PFM 1927	04	58	10
2-8-4 CLASS S NKP REVIEW "N" MRC ALCO	05	69	8
2-8-4 NKP CLASS S3 REVIEW "HO" RIV	11	65	8
2-8-4 NKP REVIEW "S" SLS LIMA	12	66	10
2-8-8-0 GN CLASS N-3 REVIEW "HO" PFM	05	68	12
2-8-8-2 CLASS L-125 D&RGW REV "HO" PFM	08	61	10
2-8-8-2 N&W CLASS Y6B REVIEW "N" MRC	05	70	13
2-8-8-2 N&W Y6B REVIEW "HO" RIV	03	65	9
2-8-8-2 USRA OF 1920 REVIEW "HO" G	04	65	13
2-8-8-2 Y6B N&W LISTING "HO" AHM	07	78	50
2-8-8-4 SP CLASS AC-9 REVIEW "HO" G 1939	09	64	7
4-10-2 SP CLASS SP1 REV "HO" KEY 1926	06	84	33
4-10-2 UP 3 CYLINDER LOCO REV "HO" WSM	10	71	24
4-2-4 HUNTINGTON STATIC MODEL REVIEW SS	02	51	57
4-2-4 LV INSPECTION LOCO REVIEW "HO" HD	05	65	8
4-4-0 AMERICAN CP #60 REVIEW "N" B	04	80	29
4-4-0 AMERICAN UP #119 REVIEW "N" B	04	80	29
4-4-0 B&M CLASS A-41 "HO" PFM 1900 ALCO	05	80	44
4-4-0 BALDWIN REV "ON3" BASE FOR FINISHG	10	77	38
4-4-0 BRITISH LIVE STEAM REVIEW CI	09	76	38
4-4-0 CONVERSION KIT REVIEW "HO" CLW	07	66	9
4-4-0 ENGLISH LOCOMOTIVE REVIEW "TT" GEM	11	71	35
4-4-0 GENERAL KIT REVIEW "HO" M	08	51	54
4-4-0 GENOA REVIEW "HO" KK	09	58	10
4-4-0 KIT REVIEW "O" GW	12	47	1040
4-4-0 LOCOMOTIVE KIT REVIEW "HO" COMI	05	38	216
4-4-0 LOCOMOTIVE REVIEW "O" WALTERS	01	41	56
4-4-0 NEW HAVEN REVIEW "O" LOB	04	41	227
4-4-0 NYC #999 REVIEW "HO" GEM MODELS	02	60	12
4-4-0 NYC REVIEW "HO" KK 1890	01	64	6
4-4-0 RENO V&T LISTING "1/28" LIVE STEAM	07	77	42
4-4-0 REVIEW "O" AN	11	54	18
4-4-0 V&T GENOA REVIEW "HO" AHM POCHER	02	65	9
4-4-0 V&T GENOA REVIEW "O" RIV 1873 B	10	73	22
4-4-2 ATLANTIC ATSF REVIEW "HO" MDC	02	54	15
4-4-2 ATLANTIC KIT PRR E-6 REVIEW"HO" GS	12	35	334
4-4-2 ATLANTIC KIT REVIEW "HO" M	09	48	674
4-4-2 ATLANTIC REVIEW "OO" SCK	04	37	159
4-4-2 ATSF CLASS 1480 REV "HO" BAL	10	64	9
4-4-2 CLASS E6 PRR REVIEW "HO" MDC 1914	07	75	20
4-4-2 SP CLASS A6 REVIEW "HO" MBA 1904 B	02	62	20
4-6-0 1/4 SCALE MOTORIZING REVIEW AHM	12	69	14
4-6-0 CASEY JONES REV "HO" HD 1898	04	63	7
4-6-0 CLASS B-18 B&O REV "HO" AHM 1901	03	60	16

LOCOMOTIVES

STEAM LOCOMOTIVE MODEL REVIEWS

	M	Y	P
4-6-0 CLASS K-2 CB&Q REV "HO" NPP 1892	06	75	23
4-6-0 CLASS L CNJ CAMELBACK REV "HO" AHM	08	60	11
4-6-0 CMI CLASS 93 REV "HO" MEW 1893 SLW	12	64	6
4-6-0 D&RG CLASS T-12 REV "ON3" PFM 1883	08	73	15
4-6-0 F&CC REVIEW "ON3" PFM 1899	10	59	13
4-6-0 IC CASEY JONES REVIEW "HO" AHM	10	71	26
4-6-0 LOCOMOTIVE REVIEW "O" CMS	02	38	86
4-6-0 LS&MC REVIEW "HO" PM 1899 BLW	02	61	14
4-6-0 PRR CLASS G-5 REVIEW "O" MAX GRAY	12	63	10
4-6-0 PRR CLASS G5 REVIEW "HO" BOW 1923	07	84	35
4-6-0 PRR CLASS G5S REVIEW "HO" LL	02	72	19
4-6-0 REVIEW "HO" LOCOMOTIVE COMPANY	10	78	44
4-6-0 REVIEW SIERRA RR REVIEW "HO" ARB	09	78	40
4-6-0 SIERRA #3 REVIEW "HO" M 1891	01	66	11
4-6-0 SP CLASS T-28 REVIEW "HO" WSM	02	65	9
4-6-0 STATIC CASEY JONES REVIEW "O" AHM	04	69	11
4-6-0 T&P CLASS D8 REVIEW "HO" G	05	66	14
4-6-0 TEN WHEELER KIT REVIEW "O" V	10	46	702
4-6-0 TEN WHEELER REVIEW "HO" V	05	51	51
4-6-0 TEN WHEELER REVIEW "N" RM	09	72	20
4-6-0 UP NYC REVIEW "HO" SUNSET MODELS	09	78	34
4-6-0 V&T #26 REVIEW "HO" WSM 1907 B	11	68	11
4-6-0 V&T REVIEW "HO" PFM B	11	56	11
4-6-2 ATSF 3400 CLASS REVIEW "N" JAM	09	69	8
4-6-2 ATSF CLASS 3400 REV "HO" MG 1930 B	05	62	12
4-6-2 B&M CLASS P-4B REVIEW "HO" ATH	01	63	22
4-6-2 BATTLE OF BRITIAN "HO" USAI 1947	01	77	43
4-6-2 C&NW CLASS E REVIEW "HO" NPP 1909	08	83	41
4-6-2 CLASS 3400 ATSF REVIEW "HO" AHM B	04	75	23
4-6-2 CLASS K-4S PRR REVIEW "HO" PFM	04	61	18
4-6-2 CLASS PS-4 S REVIEW "HO" PFM	11	60	14
4-6-2 ERIE CLASS K-5A REV "HO" MG 1923	05	63	10
4-6-2 ERIE CLASS K5A REVIEW "HO" KEY	07	82	30
4-6-2 ERIE K5 REVIEW "HO" AK 1919	06	63	13
4-6-2 K5 PACIFIC REVIEW NYC "HO" SUN	08	78	36
4-6-2 MP 2" GAUGE REVIEW SRM	11	34	18
4-6-2 NP CLASS Q6 REVIEW "HO" NWSL	05	66	11
4-6-2 NYC CLASS K-11 REVIEW "HO" BOW	01	62	12
4-6-2 PACIFIC KIT REVIEW "HO" M	09	48	674
4-6-2 PACIFIC KIT REVIEW "HO" M	04	48	300
4-6-2 PACIFIC KIT REVIEW "HO" M	06	52	36
4-6-2 PACIFIC REVIEW "HO" V	10	47	857
4-6-2 PACIFIC REVIEW "HO" PL	02	51	52
4-6-2 PACIFIC REVIEW "TT" HP	11	62	23
4-6-2 SP CLAS P-5 REV "HO" MBA 1912 B	09	60	16
4-6-2 USRA PACIFIC REVIEW "HO" RIV 1919	02	73	29
4-6-2 USRA PACIFIC REVIEW "N" RAP	05	69	14
4-6-2 USRA REVIEW "N" AT 1919	11	68	16
4-6-2 WABASH J-1 REVIEW "HO" NPP	04	76	25
4-6-4 CLASS J-3A NYC STATIC REV "HO" RK	08	62	16
4-6-4 CLASS L2 C&O REV "HO" RIV 1941 B	04	79	38
4-6-4 HUDSON REVIEW "O" LIONEL	11	37	432
4-6-4 J-1E HUDSON REVIEW NYC "HO" WSM	08	78	37
4-6-4 MILW CLASS F6A REVIEW "HO" AHM	08	67	10
4-6-4 MILW CLASS F6A REVIEW "HO" PFM	09	67	9

STEAM LOCOMOTIVE MODEL REVIEWS

	M	Y	P
4-6-4 NYC CLASS J-3A REVIEW "HO" LMB	12	62	19
4-6-4 NYC CLASS J-3A REVIEW "N" CC	06	69	15
4-6-4 NYC CLASS J3 REVIEW "HO" RIV 1938	03	72	21
4-6-4 NYC CLASS J3A REVIEW "HO" RIV	09	66	9
4-6-4 SL HUDSON ATSF LISTING "HO" AHM	01	77	48
4-6-6-4 ARTICULATED KIT REVIEW "TT" HP	08	50	44
4-6-6-4 CHALLENGER REVIEW "O" LOB	04	56	15
4-6-6-4 CHALLENGER UP REVIEW "HO" AHM	06	77	41
4-6-6-4 D&RGW 3700 CLASS REV "HO" MG	06	62	11
4-6-6-4 D&RGW CLASS L-105 REVIEW "HO" PS	10	85	48
4-6-6-4 UP SERIES 3900 REVIEW "HO" BOW	11	51	55
4-8-0 N&W CLASS M REVIEW "HO" LMB 1906	12	63	6
4-8-2 2500 CLASS IC REVIEW HO H 1937 IC	10	76	33
4-8-2 BIA CB&Q REVIEW "HO" OM	12	78	46
4-8-2 C&O SANTA FE TYPE 3 REVIEW "HO" SUN	04	77	33
4-8-2 CLASS M-1A REVIEW PRR "O" HH	09	50	53
4-8-2 CLASS M-2 T&P REV "HO" H 1925 ALCO	03	82	35
4-8-2 MOUNTAIN KIT REVIEW "TT" HP	10	49	68
4-8-2 MOHAWK NYC REVIEW "HO" PFM	11	58	10
4-8-4 ATSF CLASS 3776 REVIEW "HO" B 1941	01	80	52
4-8-4 ATSF NORTHERN REVIEW "N" B 1941 B	05	72	25
4-8-4 ATSF REVIEW "O" MG	01	57	18
4-8-4 C&O GREENBRIER KIT REV "O" LOB	06	55	14
4-8-4 CLASS FEF-3 UP REV "HO" AHM 1944	03	81	39
4-8-4 CLASS H C&NW REVIEW "OO" SCC	11	50	60
4-8-4 CLASS S1 GN REVIEW "HO" PFM 1929	04	59	18
4-8-4 CLASS U2G CN REVIEW "HO" PFM MLW	02	73	22
4-8-4 GS 64-77 WP REV "HO" WSM 1947 L	10	81	48
4-8-4 N&W CLASS J REVIEW "HO" B 1941	05	85	35
4-8-4 NORTHERN KIT REVIEW "O" CLWO	10	58	12
4-8-4 SP CLASS GS-1 REVIEW "HO" PFM 1930	06	68	12
4-8-4 SP CLASS GS-4 REVIEW "HO" B 1941	01	80	52
4-8-4-4-8-4 BEYER-GARRAT REVIEW "HO" PFM	03	67	10
4-8-8-2 SP CLASS AC-5&6 REVIEW "HO" SUN	07	85	41
4-8-8-2 SP CLASS AC11 REVIEW "HO" RIV	06	66	9
4-8-8-4 BIG BOY REVIEW "O" MG	01	59	14
4-8-8-4 UP BIG BOY REV "N" RIV ALCO 1941	08	80	35
4-8-8-4 UP BIGBOY REVIEW "HO" RIV	07	67	10
BELLE OF 80'S REVIEW "HO" M	09	40	520
BLUE COMET TRAIN CNJ LISTING "HO" AHM	12	78	65
CHALLENGER SET UP "HO" AHM	10	78	55
CLIMAX REVIEW "HO" PFM	08	56	10
DEWITT CLINTON KIT LISTING "1/4" EPA	11	77	54
DIECAST SWITCHER REVIEW "HO" ROUNDHOUSE	03	39	160
DIESEL SWITCHER REVIEW "S" SSM	12	47	1039
GERMAN 4-6-4 05 SERIES REVIEW "HO" LIL	10	77	44
HEISLER 2 TRUCK WSL REVIEW "O/ON3" WSM	11	71	27
HEISLER REVIEW "HO" AHM	08	78	40
HEISLER REVIEW "HO" PFM	10	57	17
HUDSON REVIEW "HO" AC GILBERT	10	38	452
ICKEN LOCOMOTIVES REVIEW "O" IMC	03	42	151
LIGHT MIKADO BOILER REVIEW "HO" CLW	11	59	12
LOCOMOTIVE GN REVIEW "HO" RD DENISE	02	40	120
OLD TIME BELLE OF THE 80'S REVIEW "HO" M	04	40	240
PRR A-5 SWITCHER KIT REVIEW "HO" JE	10	49	70

STEPHANS' RAILROAD DIRECTORY

LOCOMOTIVES

STEAM LOCOMOTIVE MODEL REVIEWS

	M	Y	P
SHAY 13 TON LISTING "1/4"" US HOBBIES	03	77	44
SHAY 13 TON REVIEW "HON3" NWSL 1884 L	10	82	35
SHAY 162T 3 TRUCK WM REVIEW "HO" PS 1945	09	84	42
SHAY 3 TRUCK STATIC REVIEW "HO/HON3" KLW	09	77	40
SHAY 42 TON CLASS B REVIEW "HO" MDC	11	83	41
SHAY CLASS B REVIEW "O" MG	07	55	8
SHAY ENGINE REVIEW "1/4" BACK SHOP	01	77	33
SHAY HARRINGTON REVIEW "HO" PFM	11	82	45
SHAY REVIEW "HON3/HON2 1/2" F2	10	85	52
SHAY THREE TRUCK REVIEW "N" L	01	84	80
SHAY TWO TRUCK P&WE REVIEW "HO" NWSL L	11	73	28
SHAY TWO TRUCK REVIEW "HO" PFM	10	55	14
SHAY WILLAMETTE REVIEW "HO" PFM 1922	01	82	39
SHAY WSL #12 REVIEW "SN3" MISM 1928	02	84	44
STEPHENSON ROCKET REVIEW "OO" IHC 1829	01	84	74
SWITCHER KIT REVIEW "O" HIL	01	48	64
SWITCHER PILOT REVIEW SP "HO" PETERBUILT	05	77	37
SWITCHER REVIEW "O" AMERICAN FLYER	03	39	160
UP STREAMLINED TRAIN REVIEW "O" LIONEL	11	34	18

STEAM LOCO MODEL REVIEWS BY MFG.

MFG		M	Y	P
ABJ	0-8-0 SWITCHER KIT REVIEW "HO" ABJ	10	35	275
ACI	2-6-0 MOGUL KIT REVIEW "HO" ACI	12	55	14
AF	SWITCHER REVIEW "O" AMERICAN FLYER	03	39	160
AHM	0-4-0 CLASS A3 PRR LISTING "HO" AHM	01	78	50
	0-6-0T BR80 GERMAN LOCO REV "1/45" AHM	09	72	25
	0-6-0T INDUSTRIAL SWITCHER REV "HO" AHM	06	72	20
	0-8-0 IHB CLASS U-42 REVIEW "HO" AHM	01	62	16
	0-8-0 IHB SWITCHER REV "HO" IMPROVED AHM	12	71	28
	0-8-0 IHB SWITCHER REVIEW "1/4" AHM 1927	04	71	21
	0-8-0 IHB SWITCHER REVIEW "HO" 1937 AHM	08	77	31
	2-10-4 CLASS J4 PRR REV "HO" AHM BRASS	10	66	16
	2-4-0 V&T BOWKER REVIEW "HO" AHM 1875	06	67	12
	2-4-0 V&T LISTING "HO" AHM	01	77	48
	2-6-0 WABASH CLASS F4 REVIEW "HO" AHM	08	66	8
	2-8-8-2 Y6B N&W LISTING "HO" AHM	07	78	50
	4-4-0 V&T GENOA REVIEW "HO" AHM POCHER	02	65	9
	4-6-0 1/4 SCALE MOTORIZING REVIEW AHM	12	69	14
	4-6-0 CLASS B-18 B&O REV "HO" AHM 1901	03	60	16
	4-6-0 CLASS L CNJ CAMELBACK REV "HO" AHM	08	60	11
	4-6-0 IC CASEY JONES REVIEW "HO" AHM	10	71	26
	4-6-0 STATIC CASEY JONES REVIEW "O" AHM	04	69	11
	4-6-2 CLASS 3400 ATSF REVIEW "HO" AHM B	04	75	23
	4-6-4 MILW CLASS F6A REVIEW "HO" AHM	08	67	10
	4-6-4 SL HUDSON ATSF LISTING "HO" AHM	01	77	48
	4-6-6-4 CHALLENGER UP REVIEW "HO" AHM	06	77	41
	4-8-4 CLASS FEF-3 UP REV "HO" AHM 1944	03	81	39
	BLUE COMET TRAIN CNJ LISTING "HO" AHM	12	78	65
	CHALLENGER SET UP "HO" AHM	10	78	55
	HEISLER REVIEW "HO" AHM	08	78	40
AK	2-8-2 B&O CLASS Q-4B REV "HO" AK 1922 B	03	62	12
	4-6-2 ERIE K5 REVIEW "HO" AK 1919	06	63	13
AM	0-4-0T CLASS A3A PRR REVIEW "HO" AM 1895	01	82	46
	2-10-4 CLASS T1 C&O REVIEW "HO" AM	12	83	54
AN	4-4-0 REVIEW "O" AN	11	54	18
ARB	4-6-0 REVIEW SIERRA RR REVIEW "HO" ARB	09	78	40
ARISTO	0-4-0 CB&Q SWITCHER REVIEW "HO" ARISTO	01	63	25
	0-8-0 SWITCHER AC&I REVIEW "HO" ARISTO	03	62	18
AST	4-4-0 RENO V&T LISTING "1/28" LIVE STEAM	07	77	42
AT	0-4-0 SEITCHER REVIEW "N" AT 1921 B	05	73	25
	0-8-0 IHB SWITCHER REVIEW "N" AT 1927	06	68	14
	2-8-2 USRA MIKADO REVIEW "N" AT 1918	02	70	14
	4-6-2 USRA REVIEW "N" AT 1919	11	68	16
ATH	0-6-0 USRA SWITCHER REVIEW "HO" ATH	08	62	11
	4-6-2 B&M CLASS P-4B REVIEW "HO" ATH	01	63	22
B	0-4-0 DEWITT CLINT M&HR "HO" B 1831 WPF	05	83	46
	0-4-0T DOCKSIDE SWITCHER B&O REV "N" B	03	71	23
	2-8-0 CLASS I-10SA R REVIEW "HO" BACHMAN	01	77	35

LOCOMOTIVES

STEAM LOCO MODEL REVIEWS BY MFG.

MFG		M	Y	P
	4-4-0 AMERICAN CP #60 REVIEW "N" B	04	80	29
	4-4-0 AMERICAN UP #119 REVIEW "N" B	04	80	29
	4-8-4 ATSF CLASS 3776 REVIEW "HO" B 1941	01	80	52
	4-8-4 ATSF NORTHERN REVIEW "N" B 1941 B	05	72	25
	4-8-4 N&W CLASS J REVIEW "HO" B 1941	05	85	35
	4-8-4 SP CLASS GS-4 REVIEW "HO" B 1941	01	80	52
BAL	0-6-0 ATSF #2100 SWITCHER REV "HO" BAL	09	67	12
	2-8-2 SP CLASS MK-5 REVIEW "HO" BAL	04	65	9
	4-4-2 ATSF CLASS 1480 REV "HO" BAL	10	64	9
BOW	2-8-0 PRR H9 KIT REVIEW "HO" BOWSER 1907	03	71	23
	4-6-0 PRR CLASS G5 REVIEW "HO" BOW 1923	07	84	35
	4-6-2 NYC CLASS K-11 REVIEW "HO" BOW	01	62	12
	4-6-6-4 UP SERIES 3900 REVIEW "HO" BOW	11	51	55
BS	SHAY ENGINE REVIEW "1/4" BACK SHOP	01	77	33
CC	2-8-2 USRA HEAVY MIKADO REV "N" CC 1918	03	85	42
	4-6-4 NYC CLASS J-3A REVIEW "N" CC	06	69	15
CI	4-4-0 BRITISH LIVE STEAM REVIEW CI	09	76	38
CLW	2-10-0 BOILER REVIEW "HO" CLW	06	60	11
	2-8-2 BOILER REVIEW CARY LOCO BOILER WKS	05	59	12
	2-8-4 C&NW BOILER REVIEW "HO" CLW	07	65	8
	2-8-4 C&NW DETAIL KIT REVIEW "HO" CLW	07	65	9
	4-4-0 CONVERSION KIT REVIEW "HO" CLW	07	66	9
	LIGHT MIKADO BOILER REVIEW "HO" CLW	11	59	12
CLWO	2-8-0 CLASS H-10 PRR REVIEW "O" CLWO B	07	59	12
	4-8-4 NORTHERN KIT REVIEW "O" CLWO	10	58	12
CMS	0-6-0 SWITCHER REVIEW "3/16" CMS	03	38	130
	4-6-0 LOCOMOTIVE REVIEW "O" CMS	02	38	86
COMI	4-4-0 LOCOMOTIVE KIT REVIEW "HO" COMI	05	38	216
DM	2-4-4T FORNEY REVIEW "HO" DM	07	64	6
	2-6-0 PORTER REVIEW "HON3" DM	05	65	9
EMP	2-8-2 S MIKADO REVIEW "HO" EMP 1911 B	01	79	46
EPA	DEWITT CLINTON KIT LISTING "1/4" EPA	11	77	54
F&G	0-6-0 CN CLASS O-12A REV "HO" F&G	12	62	16
	2-10-4 CP CLASS 5900 REV "HO" F&G MLW	07	61	12
	2-8-0 CP CLASS N2A REV "HO" F&G 1912	08	64	7
F2	SHAY REVIEW "HON3/HON2 1/2" F2	10	85	52
G	0-4-0 MOTHER HUB R CLASS A-5A REV "HO" G	01	69	16
	2-10-2 SANTA FE TYPE PRR REV "HO" G 1918	05	75	23
	2-4-4-2 BALDWIN MALLET REVIEW "HO" G	11	63	12
	2-6-0 SP MOGUL CLASS M-1 REV "HO" G 1928	03	64	9
	2-8-0 CLASS I 10SA R REV "HO" G 1923 B	11	81	41
	2-8-0 NP OF 1889 REVIEW "HO" G	04	65	12
	2-8-8-2 USRA OF 1920 REVIEW "HO" G	04	65	13
	2-8-8-4 SP CLASS AC-9 REVIEW "HO" G 1939	09	64	7
	4-4-0 NYC #999 REVIEW "HO" GEM MODELS	02	60	12
	4-6-0 T&P CLASS D8 REVIEW "HO" G	05	66	14

STEAM LOCO MODEL REVIEWS BY MFG.

MFG		M	Y	P
GEM	4-4-0 ENGLISH LOCOMOTIVE REVIEW "TT" GEM	11	71	35
GIL	0-6-0 SWITCHER REVIEW "HO" GIL	08	50	50
	HUDSON REVIEW "HO" AC GILBERT	10	38	452
GL	0-4-0T PORTER CLASS B-S REVIEW "ON3" GL	01	81	39
GS	0-6-0 SWITCHER REVIEW "HO" GEORGE STOCK	08	39	424
	4-4-2 ATLANTIC KIT PRR E-6 REVIEW "HO" GS	12	35	334
GW	4-4-0 KIT REVIEW "O" GW	12	47	1040
H	2-8-2 ATSF 3129 CLASS REV "HO" H 1916 B	11	82	51
	4-8-2 2500 CLASS IC REVIEW HO H 1937 IC	10	76	33
	4-8-2 CLASS M-2 T&P REV "HO" H 1925 ALCO	03	82	35
HD	0-4-4-0T OF 1913 REV "HO" HD	09	64	10
	4-2-4 LV INSPECTION LOCO REVIEW "HO" HD	05	65	8
	4-6-0 CASEY JONES REV "HO" HD 1898	04	63	7
HFW	2-8-2 ATSF CLASS 3160 REV "HO" HFW 1917	01	60	18
HH	4-8-2 CLASS M-1A REVIEW PRR "O" HH	09	50	53
HIL	SWITCHER KIT REVIEW "O" HIL	01	48	64
HP	0-6-0 SWITCHER KIT REVIEW "TT" HP	02	48	149
	2-8-0 KIT REVIEW "TT" HP	06	48	433
	4-6-2 PACIFIC REVIEW "TT" HP	11	62	23
	4-6-6-4 ARTICULATED KIT REVIEW "TT" HP	08	50	44
	4-8-2 MOUNTAIN KIT REVIEW "TT" HP	10	49	68
ICM	ICKEN LOCOMOTIVES REVIEW "O" IMC	03	42	151
IH	2-8-0 MA&PA #126 REVIEW "1/4" IH	06	78	36
IHC	STEPHENSON ROCKET REVIEW "OO" IHC 1829	01	84	74
INT	0-4-0 INDUSTRIAL SWITCHER REV "HO" INT	09	50	53
JAM	4-6-2 ATSF 3400 CLASS REVIEW "N" JAM	09	69	8
JE	PRR A-5 SWITCHER KIT REVIEW "HO" JE	10	49	70
KEM	2-6-0 MOGUL W REVIEW "O" KEM	09	59	10
KEY	2-10-2 ATSF 3800 CLASS REV "HO" KEY 1923	10	79	52
	2-8-0 CLASS C-18 D&RGW REVIEW "HON3" KEY	05	79	49
	2-8-2 FRIS 4000 CLASS REV "HO" KEY 1919	10	82	48
	2-8-2 NH CLASS J-1 REV "HO" KEY 1916	10	82	48
	2-8-2 NKP CLASS H6D REV "HO" KEY 1922 L	10	82	48
	2-8-2 NYC CLASS H10 REV "N" KEY 1922	02	85	49
	2-8-2 USRA CLASS H6A MIKADO REV "HO" KEY	12	77	42
	4-10-2 SP CLASS SP1 REV "HO" KEY 1926	06	84	33
	4-6-2 ERIE CLASS K5A REVIEW "HO" KEY	07	82	30
KK	0-4-2T PLANTATION REVIEW "HON3" KK	11	67	13
	2-6-0 PORTER MOGUL KIT REVIEW "S" KK	01	65	10
	2-6-0 PORTER MOGUL REVIEW "HO" KK 1888	12	61	16
	4-4-0 GENOA REVIEW "HO" KK	09	58	10
	4-4-0 NYC REVIEW "HO" KK 1890	01	64	6
KLW	SHAY 3 TRUCK STATIC REVIEW "HO/HON3" KLW	09	77	40
KM	0-6-0 USRA REVIEW "O" KM 1918	02	68	12
L	0-8-0 CLASS C-15A C&O SWITCHER HO REV L	02	77	32
	2-8-0 B&O CLASS E24A REVIEW "HO" L	01	78	38
	2-8-0 PRR CLASS H6 REV "HO" L 1899 B	12	73	25
	SHAY THREE TRUCK REVIEW "N" L	01	84	80

LOCOMOTIVES

STEAM LOCO MODEL REVIEWS BY MFG.

MFG		M Y P
LGB	0-4-0 LISTING "G" LGB	04 77 46
	0-6-2T REVIEW "1/22.5" GM LGB	12 73 30
	0-6-6-0T MALLET REVIEW "G" LGB	10 84 47
	2-6-0 GM DSP&P REVIEW "GM" LGB	12 85 58
LIL	GERMAN 4-6-4 05 SERIES REVIEW "HO" LIL	10 77 44
LIO	4-6-4 HUDSON REVIEW "O" LIONEL	11 37 432
	UP STREAMLINED TRAIN REVIEW "O" LIONEL	11 34 18
LL	4-6-0 PRR CLASS G5S REVIEW "HO" LL	02 72 19
LMB	2-10-2 B&O CLASS S1 REVIEW "HO" LMB	10 62 14
	2-10-4 REVIEW "HO" LMB	05 64 10
	2-10-4 T&P TEXAS REVIEW "HO" LMB 1925 L	04 60 10
	2-6-2 CONVERTIBLE TANK LOCO REV "O" LMB	10 62 16
	2-8-4 B&A CLASS A-1 REVIEW "HO" LMB 1926	02 64 10
	2-8-4 B&M CLASS T-1 REVIEW "HO" LMB 1928	02 64 10
	4-6-4 NYC CLASS J-3A REVIEW "HO" LMB	12 62 19
	4-8-0 N&W CLASS M REVIEW "HO" LMB 1906	12 63 6
LOB	2-6-0 MOGUL KIT REVIEW "O" LOB	08 55 8
	2-8-4 BERKSHIRE REVIEW C&NW "O" LOB	06 47 515
	2-8-4 BERKSHIRE REVIEW C&NW "O" LOB	11 39 608
	4-4-0 NEW HAVEN REVIEW "O" LOB	04 41 227
	4-6-6-4 CHALLENGER REVIEW "O" LOB	04 56 15
	4-8-4 C&O GREENBRIER KIT REV "O" LOB	06 55 14
LOC	2-8-0 REVIEW "HO" LOCOMOTIVE COMPANY	10 78 44
	4-6-0 REVIEW "HO" LOCOMOTIVE COMPANY	10 78 44
LSL	0-2-2 LIVE STEAM "ROCKET" LOCO "HO" LSL	12 79 38
M	0-4-0 CAMELBACK REVIEW "HO" MANTUA	07 39 374
	0-4-0 SWITCHER REVIEW "HO" M	08 67 11
	0-4-0 SWITHCER REVIEW "HO" M	09 50 52
	0-4-0T SWITCHER KIT REVIEW "HO" M	12 49 81
	2-6-0 CLASS M-21 SP REVIEW "HO" M 1928	04 82 39
	2-6-2 PRAIRIE REVIEW "HO" M	06 67 9
	2-6-6-2T LOGGING LOCOMOTIVE REV "HO" M	05 82 35
	2-8-0 CONSOLIDATION REVIEW "HO" MANTUA	03 38 130
	2-8-2 MIKADO KIT REVIEW "HO" M	05 50 43
	4-4-0 GENERAL KIT REVIEW "HO" M	08 51 54
	4-4-2 ATLANTIC KIT REVIEW "HO" M	09 48 674
	4-6-0 SIERRA #3 REVIEW "HO" M 1891	01 66 11
	4-6-2 PACIFIC KIT REVIEW "HO" M	09 48 674
	4-6-2 PACIFIC KIT REVIEW "HO" M	04 48 300
	4-6-2 PACIFIC KIT REVIEW "HO" M	06 52 36
	BELLE OF 80'S REVIEW "HO" M	09 40 520
	OLD TIME BELLE OF THE 80'S REVIEW "HO" M	04 40 240
MBA	0-6-0 SP CLASS S-12 REVIEW "HO" MBA	07 60 9
	2-6-0 MOGUL SP CLASS M-21 REV "HO" MBA	12 58 23
	2-6-2 PRAIRIE REVIEW "HO" MBA 1907	12 59 17
	4-4-2 SP CLASS A6 REVIEW "HO" MBA 1904 B	02 62 20
	4-6-2 SP CLAS P-5 REV "HO" MBA 1912 B	09 60 16
MDC	0-6-0 SP CALSS S9 REVIEW "HO" MDC 1912 B	03 73 20

STEAM LOCO MODEL REVIEWS BY MFG.

MFG		M Y P
	0-6-0 SP SWITCHER REVIEW "HO" MDC	10 53 14
	0-6-0 SWITCHER KIT REVIEW "HO" MDC	12 49 80
	0-6-0T KIT REVIEW "HO" MDC	05 53 52
	2-6-2 PRAIRIE ATSF REVIEW "HO" MDC	06 59 10
	2-8-0 BALDWIN CONSOLIDATION REV "HO" MDC	08 77 28
	2-8-0 REVIEW "HON3" MDC	04 78 37
	4-4-2 ATLANIC ATSF REVIEW "HO" MDC	02 54 15
	4-4-2 CLASS E6 PRR REVIEW "HO" MDC 1914	07 75 20
	SHAY 42 TON CLASS B REVIEW "HO" MDC	11 83 41
MEW	0-6-0 CMI SWITCHER REVIEW "HO" MEW 1887	10 66 11
	4-6-0 CMI CLASS 93 REV "HO" MEW 1893 SLW	12 64 6
MG	0-8-0 B&O CAMELBACK REVIEW "O" MG 1860	03 64 6
	2-6-0 PORTER MOGUL REVIEW "O" MG 1880	06 59 10
	4-6-0 PRR CLASS G-5 REVIEW "O" MAX GRAY	12 63 10
	4-6-2 ATSF CLASS 3400 REV "HO" MG 1930 B	05 62 12
	4-6-2 ERIE CLASS K-5A REV "HO" MG 1923	05 63 10
	4-6-6-4 D&RGW 3700 CLASS REV "HO" MG	06 62 11
	4-8-4 ATSF REVIEW "O" MG	01 57 18
	4-8-8-4 BIG BOY REVIEW "O" MG	01 59 14
	SHAY CLASS B REVIEW "O" MG	07 55 8
MISM	2-8-2 D&RGW CLASS K-37 REVIEW "SN3" MISM	08 80 36
	SHAY WSL #12 REVIEW "SN3" MISM 1928	02 84 44
MKL	0-6-0 SWITCHER REVIEW "HO" MKL	02 50 75
MRC	2-8-4 CLASS S NKP REVIEW "N" MRC ALCO	05 69 8
	2-8-8-2 N&W CLASS Y6B REVIEW "N" MRC	05 70 13
MTX	2-10-0 PRR CLASS I REVIEW "N" MTX	08 79 43
NKP	2-8-4 BERKSHIRE CLASS A1B B&A REVIEW NKP	11 77 35
NPP	2-8-0 CLASS Z NKP REVIEW "HO" NPP 1910 B	11 83 57
	2-8-4 C&NW CLASS J-4 REVIEW "HO" NPP	07 80 38
	4-6-0 CLASS K-2 CB&Q REV "HO" NPP 1892	06 75 23
	4-6-2 C&NW CLASS E REVIEW "HO" NPP 1909	08 83 41
	4-6-2 WABASH J-1 REVIEW "HO" NPP	04 76 25
NWSL	0-6-0 USRA REVIEW "HO" NWSL 1918	11 76 41
	0-8-0T SWITCHER REVIEW "HO" NWSL	12 66 20
	2-6-2 PRAIRIE MILW REVIEW "HO" NWSL 1908	06 77 36
	2-6-6-2 LOGGER REVIEW "HO" NWSL	09 60 10
	2-6-6-2T LOGGER CMP REVIEW "HO" NWSL B	12 59 13
	2-8-2 NP CLASS W-3 REVIEW "HO" NWSL	04 62 15
	2-8-2T LOGGER REVIEW "HO" NWSL	03 66 11
	4-6-2 NP CLASS Q6 REVIEW "HO" NWSL	05 66 11
	SHAY 13 TON REVIEW "HON3" NWSL 1884 L	10 82 35
	SHAY TWO TRUCK P&WE REVIEW "HO" NWSL L	11 73 28
OE	2-8-2 USRA LIGHT MIKADO REVIEW "HO" OE	05 61 12
OM	2-8-2 CLASS J-4 L&N REV "HO" OM 1918 BLW	07 81 35
	4-8-2 B1A CB&Q REVIEW "HO" OM	12 78 46
PAR	0-6-0 SP 1200 CLASS REVIEW "HO" PAR	02 59 12
PBLW	2-8-0 LOCOS OF D&RGW REVIEW "SN3" PBLW	08 85 42

LOCOMOTIVES

STEAM LOCO MODEL REVIEWS BY MFG.

MFG		M	Y	P
	SWITCHER PILOT REVIEW SP "HO" PETERBUILT	05	77	37
PCO	0-4-0T DOCKSIDE B&O REVIEW "HO" PCO B	05	81	38
	2-6-0 CLASS M4 SP REVIEW "HO" PCO	05	81	38
PFM	0-4-0 B&O DOCKSIDE REVIEW "HO" PFM 1912	07	63	8
	0-6-0 CLASS 018A CN REVIEW "HO" PFM 1920	11	76	37
	0-8-0 USRA SWITCHER REVIEW "HO" PFM	09	56	10
	2-6-2 BALDWIN REVIEW "HO" PFM	06	57	10
	2-6-2 NP CLASS T-1 REVIEW "HO" PFM 1906	09	68	9
	2-6-6 MASON BOGIE DSP&P REV "HON3" PFM	08	66	10
	2-6-6-2 SIERRA REVIEW WTC "HO" PFM	03	59	10
	2-8-0 D&RGW CLASS C48 REVIEW "1/4" PFM	12	71	36
	2-8-0 UP CLASS 6200 REV "HO" PFM 1904 B	11	61	12
	2-8-2 CLASS K-27 D&RGW REVIEW "ON3" PFM	12	76	41
	2-8-2 D&RGW CLASS K-27 MUDHEN REVIEW PFM	09	77	31
	2-8-2 D&RGW K-27 REVIEW "HON3" PFM 1897	06	63	6
	2-8-2 WP #327 REVIEW "HO" PFM 1926 ALCO	04	68	10
	2-8-4 CLASS 4100 ATSF REV "HO" PFM 1927	04	58	10
	2-8-8-0 GN CLASS N-3 REVIEW "HO" PFM	05	68	12
	2-8-8-2 CLASS L-125 D&RGW REV "HO" PFM	08	61	10
	4-4-0 B&M CLASS A-41 "HO" PFM 1900 ALCO	05	80	44
	4-6-0 D&RG CLASS T-12 REV "ON3" PFM 1883	08	73	15
	4-6-0 F&CC REVIEW "ON3" PFM 1899	10	59	13
	4-6-0 V&T REVIEW "HO" PFM B	11	56	11
	4-6-2 CLASS K-4S PRR REVIEW "HO" PFM	04	61	18
	4-6-2 CLASS PS-4 S REVIEW "HO" PFM	11	60	14
	4-6-4 MILW CLASS F6A REVIEW "HO" PFM	09	67	9
	4-8-2 MOHAWK NYC REVIEW "HO" PFM	11	58	10
	4-8-4 CLASS S1 GN REVIEW "HO" PFM 1929	04	59	18
	4-8-4 CLASS U2G CN REVIEW "HO" PFM MLW	02	73	22
	4-8-4 SP CLASS GS-1 REVIEW "HO" PFM 1930	06	68	12
	4-8-4-4-8-4 BEYER-GARRAT REVIEW "HO" PFM	03	67	10
	CLIMAX REVIEW "HO" PFM	08	56	10
	HEISLER REVIEW "HO" PFM	10	57	17
	SHAY HARRINGTON REVIEW "HO" PFM	11	82	45
	SHAY TWO TRUCK REVIEW "HO" PFM	10	55	14
	SHAY WILLAMETTE REVIEW "HO" PFM 1922	01	82	39
PL	2-10-0 PRR I-1 CLASS KIT REVIEW "HO" PL	02	55	10
	2-8-0 PRR H-9 REVIEW "HO" PL	09	52	52
	2-8-2 PRR CLASS L-1 REVIEW "HO" PL	02	53	65
	4-6-2 PACIFIC REVIEW "HO" PL	02	51	52
PM	4-6-0 LS&MC REVIEW "HO" PM 1899 BLW	02	61	14
PS	0-6-0T D&RG #105 REVIEW "HON3" PS 1881 B	12	80	52
	2-8-0 C&S REVIEW "HON3" PS 1898 BLW	06	83	37
	2-8-2 MIKADO D&RGW K27 "HON3" REVIEW PS	11	85	41
	4-6-6-4 D&RGW CLASS L-105 REVIEW "HO" PS	10	85	48
	SHAY 162T 3 TRUCK WM REVIEW "HO" PS 1945	09	84	42
PTO	0-8-0 USRA REVIEW "O" PTO	01	54	22
RAP	0-6-0 LOCOMOTIVE REVIEW "N" RAPIDO	01	66	12
	0-6-0 SWITCHER REVIEW "N" RAP	04	67	16
	4-6-2 USRA PACIFIC REVIEW "N" RAP	05	69	14

STEAM LOCO MODEL REVIEWS BY MFG.

MFG		M	Y	P
RD	DIECAST SWITCHER REVIEW "HO" ROUNDHOUSE	03	39	160
RDD	LOCOMOTIVE GN REVIEW "HO" RD DENISE	02	40	120
REX	0-4-0 DOCKSIDE REVIEW "S" REX	06	52	36
	2-4-4 SUBURBAN REVIEW "S" REX	11	53	15
RIV	0-4-0 SWITCHER REVIEW "HO" RIV	11	62	14
	0-6-0 USRA SWITCHER REVIEW "HO" RIV 1918	10	71	21
	2-10-2 B&O CLASS S-1A REVIEW "HO" RIV	12	67	10
	2-8-4 NKP CLASS S3 REVIEW "HO" RIV	11	65	8
	2-8-8-2 N&W Y6B REVIEW "HO" RIV	03	65	9
	4-4-0 V&T GENOA REVIEW "O" RIV 1873 B	10	73	22
	4-6-2 USRA PACIFIC REVIEW "HO" RIV 1919	02	73	29
	4-6-4 CLASS L2 C&O REV "HO" RIV 1941 B	04	79	38
	4-6-4 NYC CLASS J3 REVIEW "HO" RIV 1938	03	72	21
	4-6-4 NYC CLASS J3A REVIEW "HO" RIV	09	66	9
	4-8-8-2 SP CLASS AC11 REVIEW "HO" RIV	06	66	9
	4-8-8-4 UP BIG BOY REV "N" RIV ALCO 1941	08	80	35
	4-8-8-4 UP BIGBOY REVIEW "HO" RIV	07	67	10
RK	2-10-0 BRITISH LOCO REV "OO" RK	03	61	11
	4-6-4 CLASS J-3A NYC STATIC REV "HO" RK	08	62	16
RM	4-6-0 TEN WHEELER REVIEW "N" RM	09	72	20
ROSL	2-6-0 C&S MOGUL REVIEW "NN3" ROSL	01	84	68
S&P	2-6-0 MOGUL REVIEW "S" S&P	07	64	7
SCC	4-8-4 CLASS H C&NW REVIEW "OO" SCC	11	50	60
SCK	4-4-2 ATLANTIC REVIEW "OO" SCK	04	37	159
SLS	2-8-4 NKP REVIEW "S" SLS LIMA	12	66	10
SPM	2-8-0 KIT REVIEW PRR "O" SPM	08	40	460
SPPR	0-4-2T LIVE STEAM REVIEW "NO 1" SPPR	03	81	41
SRA	0-6-0 SP CLASS S-2 REVIEW "TT" SRA	05	59	16
SRM	4-6-2 MP 2" GAUGE REVIEW SRM	11	34	18
SS	4-2-4 HUNTINGTON STATIC MODEL REVIEW SS	02	51	57
SSM	DIESEL SWITCHER REVIEW "S" SSM	12	47	1039
SUN	2-10-0 CLASS D-1 SP REVIEW "HO" SUN	08	76	27
	2-8-0 CLASS C-16 REV D&RGW"ON3" SUN 1882	03	77	31
	2-8-2 K28 D&RGW REVIEW "ON3" SUN	07	78	37
	4-6-0 UP NYC REVIEW "HO" SUNSET MODELS	09	78	34
	4-6-2 K5 PACIFIC REVIEW NYC "HO" SUN	08	78	36
	4-8-2 C&O SANTA FE TYPE 3 REVIEW "HO"SUN	04	77	33
	4-8-8-2 SP CLASS AC-5&6 REVIEW "HO" SUN	07	85	41
T	2-8-2 WABASH KIT REVIEW "HO" TYCO	01	75	32
TI	0-6-0 C&NW CLASS M2 REVIEW "HO" TI	07	67	13
TOM	2-8-0 CLASS C-16 D&RG REVIEW "SN3" TOM	10	68	11
USAI	2-10-0 92000 CLASS "HO" USAI 1960	01	77	43
	4-6-2 BATTLE OF BRITIAN "HO" USAI 1947	01	77	43
USH	2-8-2 CLASS H10B NYC REVIEW "O" USH 1920	10	76	38
	SHAY 13 TON LISTING "1/4"" US HOBBIES	03	77	44
V	0-4-0 DOCKSIDE REVIEW "HO" VARNEY	01	42	48
	2-8-0 CONSOLIDATION REVIEW "HO" V	05	56	10
	2-8-4 BERKSHIRE REVIEW "HO" V	03	58	11
	4-6-0 TEN WHEELER KIT REVIEW "O" V	10	46	702

LOCOMOTIVES

STEAM LOCO MODEL REVIEWS BY MFG.

MFG		M	Y	P
	4-6-0 TEN WHEELER REVIEW "HO" V	05	51	51
	4-6-2 PACIFIC REVIEW "HO" V	10	47	857
W	2-6-6-6 CLASS H-8 KIT REVIEW "HO" W	10	50	48
WAL	0-6-0 LOCOMOTIVE REVIEW "O" WALTERS	01	41	56
	2-8-2 MIKADO REVIEW "O" WAL	02	38	86
	4-4-0 LOCOMOTIVE REVIEW "O" WALTERS	01	41	56
WSM	2-8-0 CONSOLIDATION REVIEW "HON3" WSM B	09	71	21
	4-10-2 UP 3 CYLINDER LOCO REV "HO" WSM	10	71	24
	4-6-0 SP CLASS T-28 REVIEW "HO" WSM	02	65	9
	4-6-0 V&T #26 REVIEW "HO" WSM 1907 B	11	68	11
	4-6-4 J-1E HUDSON REVIEW NYC "HO" WSM	08	78	37
	4-8-4 GS 64-77 WP REVIEW "HO" WSM 1947 L	10	81	48
	HEISLER 2 TRUCK WSL REVIEW "O/ON3" WSM	11	71	27

STEAM LOCOMOTIVE MODEL REVIEWS BY ROAD

RD		M	Y	P
AC&I	0-8-0 SWITCHER AC&I REVIEW "HO" ARISTO	03	62	18
ATSF	2-10-2 ATSF 3800 CLASS REV "HO" KEY 1923	10	79	52
	2-6-2 PRAIRIE ATSF REVIEW "HO" MDC	06	59	10
	2-8-2 ATSF 3129 CLASS REV "HO" H 1916 B	11	82	51
	2-8-2 ATSF CLASS 3160 REV "HO" HFW 1917	01	60	18
	2-8-4 CLASS 4100 ATSF REV "HO" PFM 1927	04	58	10
	4-4-2 ATSF CLASS 1480 REV "HO" BAL	10	64	9
	4-6-2 ATSF 3400 CLASS REVIEW "N" JAM	09	69	8
	4-6-2 ATSF 3400 REV "HO" MG 1930 B	05	62	12
	4-6-2 CLASS 3400 ATSF REVIEW "HO" AHM B	04	75	23
	4-6-4 SL HUDSON ATSF LISTING "HO" AHM	01	77	48
	4-8-4 ATSF CLASS 3776 REVIEW "HO" B 1941	01	80	52
	4-8-4 ATSF NORTHERN REVIEW "N" B 1941 B	05	72	25
B&A	2-8-4 B&A CLASS A-1 REVIEW "HO" LMB 1926	02	64	10
	2-8-4 BERKSHIRE CLASS A1B B&A REVIEW NKP	11	77	35
B&M	2-8-4 B&M CLASS T-1 REVIEW "HO" LMB 1928	02	64	10
	4-4-0 B&M CLASS A-41 "HO" PFM 1900 ALCO	05	80	44
	4-6-2 B&M CLASS P-4B REVIEW "HO" ATH	01	63	22
B&O	0-4-0 B&O DOCKSIDE REVIEW "HO" PFM 1912	07	63	8

STEAM LOCOMOTIVE MODEL REVIEWS BY ROAD

RD		M	Y	P
	0-4-0 SWITCHER REVIEW "HO" RIV	11	62	14
	0-4-0T DOCKSIDE B&O REVIEW "HO" PCO B	05	81	38
	0-4-0T DOCKSIDE SWITCHER B&O REV "N" B	03	71	23
	0-8-0 B&O CAMELBACK REVIEW "O" MG	03	64	6
	2-10-2 B&O CLASS S-1A REVIEW "HO" RIV	12	67	10
	2-10-2 B&O CLASS S1 REVIEW "HO" LMB	10	62	14
	2-8-0 B&O CLASS E24A REVIEW "HO" L	01	78	38
	2-8-2 B&O CLASS Q-4B REV "HO" AK 1922 B	03	62	12
	4-6-0 CLASS B-18 B&O REV "HO" AHM 1901	03	60	16
C&NW	0-6-0 C&NW CLASS M2 REVIEW "HO" TI	07	67	13
	2-8-4 BERKSHIRE REVIEW C&NW "O" LOB	06	47	515
	2-8-4 BERKSHIRE REVIEW C&NW "O" LOB	11	39	608
	2-8-4 C&NW CLASS J-4 REVIEW "HO" NPP	07	80	38
	4-6-2 C&NW CLASS E REVIEW "HO" NPP 1909	08	83	41
C&O	0-8-0 CLASS C-15A C&O SWITCHER HO REV L	02	77	32
	2-10-4 CLASS T1 C&O REVIEW "HO" AM	12	83	54
	4-6-4 CLASS L2 C&O REV "HO" RIV 1941 B	04	79	38
	4-8-2 C&O SANTA FE TYPE 3 REVIEW "HO" SUN	04	77	33
	4-8-4 C&O GREENBRIER KIT REV "O" LOB	06	55	14
C&S	2-6-0 C&S MOGUL REVIEW "NN3" ROSL	01	84	68
	2-8-0 C&S REVIEW "HON3" PS 1898 BLW	06	83	37
CB&Q	0-4-0 CB&Q SWITCHER REVIEW "HO" ARISTO	01	63	25
	4-6-0 CLASS K-2 CB&Q REV "HO" NPP 1892	06	75	23
	4-8-2 B1A CB&Q REVIEW "HO" OM	12	78	46
CMI	0-6-0 CMI SWITCHER REVIEW "HO" MEW 1887	10	66	11
	4-6-0 CMI CLASS 93 REV "HO" MEW 1893 SLW	12	64	6
CN	0-6-0 CLASS O18A CN REVIEW "HO" PFM 1920	11	76	37
	0-6-0 CN CLASS O-12A REV "HO" F&G	12	62	16
	4-8-4 CLASS U2G CN REVIEW "HO" PFM MLW	02	73	22
CNJ	4-6-0 CLASS L CNJ CAMELBACK REV "HO" AHM	08	60	11
	BLUE COMET TRAIN CNJ LISTING "HO" AHM	12	78	65
CP	2-10-4 CP CLASS 5900 REV "HO" F&G MLW	07	61	12
	2-8-0 CP CLASS N2A REV "HO" F&G 1912	08	64	7
	4-4-0 AMERICAN CP #60 REVIEW "N" B	04	80	29
CWP	2-6-6-2T LOGGER CWP REVIEW "HO" NWSL B	12	59	13
D&RG	0-6-0T D&RG #105 REVIEW "HON3" PS 1881 B	12	80	52
	2-8-0 CLASS C-16 D&RG REVIEW "SN3" TOM	10	68	11
	4-6-0 D&RG CLASS T-12 REV "ON3" PFM 1883	08	73	15
D&RGW	2-8-0 CLASS C-16 REV D&RGW"ON3" SUN 1882	03	77	31
	2-8-0 D&RGW CLASS C48 REVIEW "1/4" PFM	12	71	36
	2-8-0 LOCOS OF D&RGW REVIEW "SN3" PBLW	08	85	42
	2-8-2 CLASS K-27 D&RGW REVIEW "ON3" PFM	12	76	41
	2-8-2 D&RGW CLASS K-27 MUDHEN REVIEW PFM	09	77	31
	2-8-2 D&RGW CLASS K-37 REVIEW "SN3" MISM	08	80	36
	2-8-2 D&RGW K-27 REVIEW "HON3" PFM 1897	06	63	6

LOCOMOTIVES

STEAM LOCOMOTIVE MODEL REVIEWS BY ROAD

RD		M	Y	P
	2-8-2 K28 D&RGW REVIEW "ON3" SUN	07	78	37
	2-8-8-2 CLASS L-125 D&RGW REV "HO" PFM	08	61	10
	4-6-6-4 D&RGW 3700 CLASS REV "HO" MG	06	62	11
	4-6-6-4 D&RGW CLASS L-105 REVIEW "HO" PS	10	85	48
DSP&P	2-6-0 GM DSP&P REVIEW "GM" LGB	12	85	58
	2-6-6 MASON BOGIE DSP&P REV "HON3" PFM	08	66	10
E	4-6-2 ERIE CLASS K-5A REV "HO" MG 1923	05	63	10
	4-6-2 ERIE CLASS K5A REVIEW "HO" KEY	07	82	30
	4-6-2 ERIE K5 REVIEW "HO" AK 1919	06	63	13
F&CC	4-6-0 F&CC REVIEW "ON3" PFM 1899	10	59	13
FRIS	2-8-2 FRIS 4000 CLASS REV "HO" KEY 1919	10	82	48
GN	2-8-8-0 GN CLASS N-3 REVIEW "HO" PFM	05	68	12
	4-8-4 CLASS S1 GN REVIEW "HO" PFM 1929	04	59	18
IC	4-6-0 CASEY JONES REV "HO" HD 1898	04	63	7
	4-6-0 IC CASEY JONES REVIEW "HO" AHM	10	71	26
	4-6-0 STATIC CASEY JONES REVIEW "O" AHM	04	69	11
	4-8-2 2500 CLASS IC REVIEW HO H 1937 IC	10	76	33
IHB	0-8-0 IHB CLASS U-42 REVIEW "HO" AHM	01	62	16
	0-8-0 IHB SWITCHER REV "HO" IMPROVED AHM	12	71	28
	0-8-0 IHB SWITCHER REVIEW "1/4" AHM 1927	04	71	21
	0-8-0 IHB SWITCHER REVIEW "HO" 1937 AHM	08	77	31
	0-8-0 IHB SWITCHER REVIEW "N" AT 1927	06	68	14
L&N	2-8-2 CLASS J-4 L&N REV "HO" OM 1918 BLW	07	81	35
LITRI	2-4-4-2 BALDWIN MALLET REVIEW "HO" G	11	63	12
LS&MC	4-6-0 LS&MC REVIEW "HO" PM 1899 BLW	02	61	14
LV	4-2-4 LV INSPECTION LOCO REVIEW "HO" HD	05	65	8
M&HR	0-4-0 DEWITT CLINT M&HR "HO" B 1831 WPF	05	83	46
	DEWITT CLINTON KIT LISTING "1/4" EPA	11	77	54
MA&PA	2-8-0 MA&PA #126 REVIEW "1/4" IH	06	78	36
MILW	2-6-2 PRAIRIE MILW REVIEW "HO" NWSL 1908	06	77	36
	4-6-4 MILW CLASS F6A REVIEW "HO" AHM	08	67	10
	4-6-4 MILW CLASS F6A REVIEW "HO" PFM	09	67	9
MP	4-6-2 MP 2" GAUGE REVIEW SRM	11	34	18
N&W	2-8-8-2 N&W CLASS Y6B REVIEW "N" MRC	05	70	13
	2-8-8-2 N&W Y6B REVIEW "HO" RIV	03	65	9
	2-8-8-2 Y6B N&W LISTING "HO" AHM	07	78	50
	4-8-0 N&W CLASS M REVIEW "HO" LMB 1906	12	63	6
	4-8-4 N&W CLASS J REVIEW "HO" B 1941	05	85	35
NH	2-8-2 NH CLASS J-1 REV "HO" KEY 1916	10	82	48
	4-4-0 NEW HAVEN REVIEW "O" LOB	04	41	227
NKP	2-8-0 CLASS Z NKP REVIEW "HO" NPP 1910 B	11	83	57
	2-8-2 NKP CLASS H6D REV "HO" KEY 1922 L	10	82	48
	2-8-4 CLASS S NKP REVIEW "N" MRC ALCO	05	69	8
	2-8-4 NKP CLASS S3 REVIEW "HO" RIV	11	65	8
	2-8-4 NKP REVIEW "S" SLS LIMA	12	66	10
NP	2-6-2 NP CLASS T-1 REVIEW "HO" PFM 1906	09	68	9
	2-8-0 NP OF 1889 REVIEW "HO" G	04	65	12
	2-8-2 NP CLASS W-3 REVIEW "HO" NWSL	04	62	15
	4-6-2 NP CLASS Q6 REVIEW "HO" NWSL	05	66	11
NSWG	4-8-4-4-8-4 BEYER-GARRAT REVIEW "HO" PFM	03	67	10
NWSL	4-4-0 BALDWIN REV "ON3" BASE FOR FINISHG	10	77	38
NYC	2-8-2 CLASS H10B NYC REVIEW "O" USH 1920	10	76	38
	2-8-2 NYC CLASS H10 REV "N" KEY 1922	02	85	49
	4-4-0 NYC #999 REVIEW "HO" GEM MODELS	02	60	12
	4-4-0 NYC REVIEW "HO" KK 1890	01	64	6
	4-6-0 UP NYC REVIEW "HO" SUNSET MODELS	09	78	34
	4-6-2 K5 PACIFIC REVIEW NYC "HO" SUN	08	78	36
	4-6-2 NYC CLASS K-11 REVIEW "HO" BOW	01	62	12
	4-6-4 CLASS J-3A NYC STATIC REV "HO" RK	08	62	16
	4-6-4 J-1E HUDSON REVIEW NYC "HO" WSM	08	78	37
	4-6-4 NYC CLASS J-3A REVIEW "HO" LMB	12	62	19
	4-6-4 NYC CLASS J3 REVIEW "HO" RIV 1938	03	72	21
	4-6-4 NYC CLASS J3A REVIEW "HO" RIV	09	66	9
	4-8-2 MOHAWK NYC REVIEW "HO" PFM	11	58	10
ORTC	2-6-6-2 LOGGER REVIEW "HO" NWSL	09	60	10
P&WE	SHAY TWO TRUCK P&WE REVIEW "HO" NWSL L	11	73	28
PRR	0-4-0 CLASS A3 PRR LISTING "HO" AHM	01	78	50
	0-4-0T CLASS A3A PRR REVIEW "HO" AM 1895	01	82	46
	2-10-0 PRR CLASS I REVIEW "N" MTX	08	79	43
	2-10-2 SANTA FE TYPE PRR REV "HO" G 1918	05	75	23
	2-10-4 CLASS J4 PRR REV "HO" AHM BRASS	10	66	16
	2-8-0 CLASS H-10 PRR REVIEW "O" CLWO B	07	59	12
	2-8-0 KIT REVIEW PRR "O" SPM	08	40	460
	2-8-0 PRR CLASS H6 REV "HO" L 1899 B	12	73	25
	2-8-0 PRR H9 KIT REVIEW "HO" BOWSER 1907	03	71	23
	2-8-2 PRR CLASS L-1 REVIEW "HO" PL	02	53	65
	4-4-2 ATLANTIC KIT PRR E-6 REVIEW"HO" GS	12	35	334
	4-4-2 CLASS E6 PRR REVIEW "HO" MDC 1914	07	75	20
	4-6-0 PRR CLASS G-5 REVIEW "O" MAX GRAY	12	63	10
	4-6-0 PRR CLASS G5 REVIEW "HO" BOW 1923	07	84	35
	4-6-0 PRR CLASS G5S REVIEW "HO" LL	02	72	19
	4-6-2 CLASS K-4S PRR REVIEW "HO" PFM	04	61	18
	4-8-2 CLASS M-1A REVIEW PRR "O" HH	09	50	53
R	0-4-0 MOTHER HUB R CLASS A-5A REV "HO" G	01	69	16
	2-8-0 CLASS I 10SA R REV "HO" G 1923 B	11	81	41
	2-8-0 CLASS I-10SA R REVIEW "HO" BACHMAN	01	77	35
S	2-8-2 S MIKADO REVIEW "HO" EMP 1911 B	01	79	46
	4-6-2 CLASS PS-4 S REVIEW "HO" PFM	11	60	14
SIE	4-6-0 SIERRA #3 REVIEW "HO" M 1891	01	66	11
SIER	4-6-0 REVIEW SIERRA RR REVIEW "HO" ARB	09	78	40
SP	0-6-0 SP CALSS S9 REVIEW "HO" MDC 1912 B	03	73	20
	0-6-0 SP CLASS S-12 REVIEW "HO" MBA	07	60	9
	0-6-0 SP CLASS S-2 REVIEW "TT" SRA	05	59	16
	0-6-0 SP SWITCHER REVIEW "HO" MDC	10	53	14
	2-10-0 CLASS D-1 SP REVIEW "HO" SUN	08	76	27

42

LOCOMOTIVES

```
STEAM LOCOMOTIVE MODEL REVIEWS BY ROAD
  RD                                             M  Y  P
  --- -------------------------------------      -- -- ----
      2-6-0 CLASS M-21 SP REVIEW "HO" M    1928  04 82 39
      2-6-0 MOGUL SP CLASS M-21 REV "HO" MBA     12 58 23
      2-6-0 SP MOGUL CLASS M-1 REV "HO" G  1928  03 64 9
      2-8-2 SP CLASS MK-5 REVIEW "HO" BAL        04 65 9
      2-8-8-4 SP CLASS AC-9 REVIEW "HO" G  1939  09 64 7
      4-10-2 SP CLASS SP1 REV "HO" KEY  1926     06 84 33
      4-4-2 SP CLASS A6 REVIEW "HO" MBA 1904 B   02 62 20
      4-6-0 SP CLASS T-28 REVIEW "HO" WSM        02 65 9
      4-6-2 SP CLAS P-5 REV "HO" MBA 1912   B    09 60 16
      4-8-4 SP CLASS GS-1 REVIEW "HO" PFM 1930   06 68 12
      4-8-4 SP CLASS GS-4 REVIEW "HO" B 1941     01 80 52
      4-8-8-2 SP CLASS AC-5&6 REVIEW "HO" SUN    07 85 41
      4-8-8-2 SP CLASS AC11 REVIEW "HO" RIV      06 66 9
      SWITCHER PILOT REVIEW SP "HO" PETERBUILT   05 77 37

  SUP 4-10-2 UP 3 CYLINDER LOCO REV "HO"   WSM   10 71 24
  T&P 2-10-4 T&P TEXAS REVIEW "HO" LMB 1925 L    04 60 10
      4-6-0 T&P CLASS D8 REVIEW "HO" G           05 66 14
      4-8-2 CLASS M-2 T&P REV "HO" H 1925 ALCO   03 82 35

  UP  2-8-0 UP CLASS 6200 REV "HO" PFM 1904 B    11 61 12
      4-4-0 AMERICAN UP #119 REVIEW "N" B        04 80 29
      4-6-6-4 CHALLENGER UP REVIEW "HO" AHM      06 77 41
      4-8-4 CLASS FEF-3 UP REV "HO" AHM 1944     03 81 39
      4-8-8-4 UP BIG BOY REV "N" RIV ALCO 1941   08 80 35
      4-8-8-4 UP BIGBOY REVIEW "HO" RIV          07 67 10
      UP STREAMLINED TRAIN REVIEW "O" LIONEL     11 34 18

  USRA 2-8-2 USRA CLASS H6A MIKADO REV "HO" KEY  12 77 42
       2-8-2 USRA LIGHT MIKADO REVIEW "HO"  OE   05 61 12
       2-8-8-2 USRA OF 1920 REVIEW "HO" G        04 65 13
       4-6-2 USRA PACIFIC REVIEW "HO" RIV 1919   02 73 29
       4-6-2 USRA REVIEW "N"  AT 1919            11 68 16
       4-8-2 MOUNTAIN KIT REVIEW "TT"   HP       10 49 68

  V&T  2-4-0 V&T BOWKER REVIEW "HO" AHM 1875     06 67 12
       2-4-0 V&T LISTING    "HO"     AHM         01 77 48
       4-4-0 RENO V&T LISTING "1/28" LIVE STEAM  07 77 42
       4-4-0 V&T GENOA REVIEW "HO" AHM POCHER    02 65 9
       4-4-0 V&T GENOA REVIEW "O" RIV 1873 B     10 73 22
       4-6-0 V&T #26 REVIEW "HO" WSM 1907 B      11 68 11
       4-6-0 V&T REVIEW "HO" PFM   B             11 56 11

  W    2-6-0 MOGUL W REVIEW "O"  KEM             09 59 10
       2-6-0 WABASH CLASS F4 REVIEW "HO" AHM     08 66 8
       2-8-2 WABASH KIT REVIEW "HO" TYCO         01 75 32

  WM   SHAY 162T 3 TRUCK WM REVIEW "HO" PS 1945  09 84 42
  WP   2-8-2 WP #327 REVIEW "HO" PFM 1926 ALCO   04 68 10
       4-8-4 GS 64-77 WP REVIEW "HO" WSM 1947 L  10 81 48

  WSL  HEISLER 2 TRUCK WSL REVIEW "O/ON3" WSM    11 71 27
       SHAY WSL #12 REVIEW "SN3" MISM 1928       02 84 44

  WTC  2-6-6-2 SIERRA REVIEW WTC "HO" PFM        03 59 10
```

LOCOMOTIVES

TENDER PROTOTYPE DATA

	M	Y	P
ANOTHER USE FOR OLD TENDERS	11	62	62
AUXILIARY TENDERS	03	67	67
AUXILIARY TENDERS	05	78	130
CENTIPEDE TENDERS WHAT THEY ARE	01	70	89
CENTIPEDE TENDERS-MORE	04	70	26
LOCOMOTIVE AND TENDER DETAILS BLUEBOOK	01	57	67
TENDER CAPACITY	10	73	78
TENDER DETAILS	08	59	63
TENDER DOG HOUSES	06	81	139
TENDERS FOR DIESEL LOCOMOTIVES	10	84	148
VANDERBUILT TENDER HISTORY	10	83	161

TENDER PLANS

	M	Y	P
BALDWIN 5000 GM SLOPE BACK TENDER PLAN	04	36	94
DAYLIGHT TENDER PLANS	10	48	708
SINGLE TRUCK CLIMAX TENDER PLANS CH&N	09	64	34
STANDARD B&O TEFDER2NCL0P			419
SWITCH ENGINE TENDERS PLANS	05	50	40
TENDER CLASS 160-C-2 PLANS SP	08	39	405
TENDER DRAWING B&O #853	04	53	40
TENDER FOR 0-4-0 CLASS C16A B&O PLAN "O"	09	51	42
TENDER FOR 2-8-0 DRAWING B&O	03	46	175
TENDER OF 1893 PLANS B&O	06	48	419
TENDER PLANS FOR C&NW 0-6-0	01	44	29
TENDER PLN 4-6-0 CLASS P-2/5C/12C/13C NP	03	37	104
VANDERBUILT TENDER PLANS SP	05	37	172
VANDERBUILT TENDER ROCK ISLAND #2504 PLN	10	46	644

TENDER PLANS BY ROAD

RD		M	Y	P
B&O	TENDER DRAWING B&O #853	04	53	40
	TENDER FOR 2-8-0 DRAWING B&O	03	46	175
	TENDER OF 1893 PLANS B&O	06	48	419
	TENDER FOR 0-4-0 CLASS C16A B&O PLAN "O"	09	51	42
C&NW	TENDER PLANS FOR C&NW 0-6-0	01	44	29
CH&N	SINGLE TRUCK CLIMAX TENDER PLANS CH&N	09	64	34
NP	TENDER PLN 4-6-0 CLASS P-2/5C/12C/13C NP	03	37	104
RI	VANDERBUILT TENDER ROCK ISLAND #2504 PLN	10	46	644
SP	TENDER CLASS 160-C-2 PLANS SP	08	39	405
	VANDERBUILT TENDER PLANS SP	05	37	172

TENDER MODELS

	M	Y	P
2-8-0 COMPOUND CONST TENDER	04	60	54
2-8-0 CONSOLIDATION CONSTRUCTION TENDER	06	54	41
2-8-2 IN BRASS CONST TENDER & PAINTING	11	83	102
2-8-2 KITCHEN TABLE MIKADO TENDER	02	55	64
4-6-2 CLASS K-4 CONSTRUCTION 5 TENDER	02	50	59
4-6-2 PACIFIC TENDER CONSTRUCTION	12	37	441
ARTICULATED TENDERS	05	40	269
BUILDING IN BRASS THE TENDER	12	68	64
CHANGING REAR SECTIONS OF TENDERS	05	66	62
COAL OR WOOD LOADS FOR A TENDER $1	01	68	54
CUSTOM BUILDING TENDERS	06	64	23
CYLINDRICAL TYPE TENDER FOR BULL MOOSE	01	83	124
FILL UNSIGHTLY LOCO-TENDER GAP	11	79	148
IMPROVING BRASS LOCOMOTIVE TENDERS	04	82	143
LOWERING A PRR STANDARD TENDER	06	81	86
TENDER CONSTRUCT 2-8-2 LT MIKADO USRA	11	41	576
TENDER CONSTRUCT 4-6-2 LT PACIFIC USRA	10	40	551
TENDER CONSTRUCTION 0-6-0 C&NW SWITCHER	01	44	28
TENDER CONSTRUCTION 0-6-0 USRA SWITCHER	02	40	79
TENDER CONSTRUCTION FOR 4-4-2 ATLANTIC	10	38	423
TENDER CONSTRUCTION FOR 4-6-0	03	41	142
TENDER DETAILING	09	73	48
TENDER FOR 0-8-0 CONSTRUCTION	09	50	36
TENDER FOR 2-6-0 CONSTRCUTION WABASH	06	59	54
TENDER FOR 4-6-0 TEN WHEELER CONSTRUCT	06	48	418
TENDER FOR B&O CLASS C16A CONSTRUCTION	09	51	42
TENDER PROPULSION	11	49	92
TENDER SHELL CONSTRUCTION	04	50	38
TENDER SPEAKER FOR NOISE EFFECTS	01	71	62
VANDERBUILT TENDER KITBASH IN "N"	01	80	104

TENDER PHOTOS

	M	Y	P
DOGHOUSE PHOTOS KELLY CRK & NWESTERN RR	10	71	18

TENDER MODEL REVIEWS

	M	Y	P
14 WHEEL TENDER REVIEW "HO" KENTRON	06	53	56
CLEAR VISION TENDER REVIEW "HO" PFM	01	58	12
S.DETAILED VANDERBUILT TENDER REV"HO"KEM	08	57	10
SEMI VANDERBILT TENDER REVIEW "HO" BOW	02	54	25
TENDER KIT REVIEW "HO" V	06	49	57
TENDER KIT REVIEW "HO" PL	12	50	59
TENDER REVIEW "HO" V	02	41	116
VANDERBUILT TENDER REVIEW "HO" USH 1905	07	73	19

LOCOMOTIVES

DIESEL LOCOMOTIVE PROTOTYPE DATA

	M	Y	P
16 CYLINDER CONSTANT TORQUE LOCO B&O	11	37	410
23 TON INDUSTRIAL LOCOMOTIVE	06	81	72
44 TONNERS PROTOTYPE DATA 1 A&A GE	09	78	80
44 TONNERS PROTOTYPE DATA A&A GE	09	78	112
45 TON DIESEL SWITCHER 1942 VULCAN	08	82	81
45 TON GE DIESEL ELECTRIC SWITCHER	10	80	84
85 TON CSS&SB #1013	03	38	105
ALCO ROAD SWITCHER COLOR CHART GN	10	61	73
ALCO ROAD SWITCHER COLOR CHART LI	06	61	64
ALCO ROAD SWITCHER COLOR CHART LV	05	61	63
ALCO ROAD SWITCHERS	09	59	63
ALCO SWITCHER COLOR CHART MILW	08	61	57
ALL WEATHER CAB WINDOW EXTENSIONS	03	77	117
BQ23-7 GE ROAD DIESEL SCL 1978	07	83	72
C420 CENTURY ALCO ROAD SWITCHER 1963	02	85	84
C630 MASTER & SLAVE OF N&W 1971	12	80	98
CENTURY 628 ALCO UNIT	11	65	41
CLASSIFICATION LIGHTS ON DIESELS	12	84	192
DETAILS ON MILWAUKEE ROAD DIESELS	09	65	35
DIESEL AIR & ELECTRICAL CONNECTIONS	04	62	61
DIESEL CLASSIFICATION LIGHTS	12	84	192
DIESEL COLOR CHART ATSF	03	61	62
DIESEL COLOR CHART E	01	61	78
DIESEL COLOR CHART FEC	03	61	61
DIESEL LOCO BASICS CHOOSE RIGHT UNITS	09	84	79
DIESEL LOCOMOTIVE COLOR CHART SP	01	61	77
DIESEL LOCOMOTIVE MILESTONES PHOTO FEAT	09	84	82
DIESEL LOCOMOTIVE QUIZ	07	82	112
DIESEL LOCOMOTIVE SERVICING	06	82	59
DIESEL SPOTTER CHART (SILHOUETTS)	05	52	18
DL-109 ALCO GE UNITS	03	71	51
E UNIT COLOR CHART C&EI	01	59	98
E UNIT COLOR CHART C&NW	08	60	58
E UNIT COLOR CHART C&O	06	59	66
E UNIT COLOR CHART CB&Q	11	59	78
E UNIT COLOR CHART FRIS	05	61	64
E UNIT COLOR CHART PRR	06	59	65
E UNIT COLOR CHART S	04	60	66
E UNIT COLOR CHART SP	12	59	90
E UNITS OF EMD	07	60	57
E2 EMD PASSENGER LOCOMOTIVES 1937	09	73	43
E8 COLOR CHART IC	01	58	74
ELECTRO-MOTIVE FT: FIRST FREIGHT DIESEL	04	75	48
EMD ROAD SWITCHER COLOR CHART C&IM	06	61	63
EMD YARD SWITCHER COLOR CHART ACL	07	61	57
EMD YARD SWITCHER COLOR CHART CB&Q	10	61	74
EVOLUTION OF THE EMD DIESEL TRUCK	06	77	65
F AND FP DIFFERENCES	03	64	64
F UNIT COLOR CHART UP	10	58	75
F UNIT COLOR CHART ACL	07	58	56
F UNIT COLOR CHART B&LE	06	58	58
F UNIT COLOR CHART B&M	10	59	78
F UNIT COLOR CHART B&O	05	59	66
F UNIT COLOR CHART C&O.	12	59	89
F UNIT COLOR CHART CB	07	61	58

DIESEL LOCOMOTIVE PROTOTYPE DATA

	M	Y	P
F UNIT COLOR CHART CN	04	59	66
F UNIT COLOR CHART D&RGW	09	58	64
F UNIT COLOR CHART FEC	03	60	66
F UNIT COLOR CHART FRIS	08	58	56
F UNIT COLOR CHART GN	11	59	77
F UNIT COLOR CHART KCS	11	58	78
F UNIT COLOR CHART L&N	05	60	62
F UNIT COLOR CHART MILW	08	62	57
F UNIT COLOR CHART MKT	03	60	65
F UNIT COLOR CHART MP	06	58	57
F UNIT COLOR CHART NP	01	59	97
F UNIT COLOR CHART PRR	08	58	55
F UNIT COLOR CHART R	08	60	57
F UNIT COLOR CHART SOO	03	59	70
F UNIT COLOR CHART SP	07	59	66
F UNIT COLOR CHART T&P	08	62	58
F UNIT COLOR CHART W	06	60	57
F UNIT COLOR CHART WM	06	60	58
F UNIT COLOR CHART WP	09	62	56
F40PH EARLY & LATE DIFFERENCES A	09	82	135
F45 EMD LOCOMOTIVES 1968	12	75	69
F7 COLOR CHART CB&Q	04	58	66
F7 COLOR CHART NYC	05	58	58
F7 COLOR CHART S	01	58	73
FL-9 COLOR CHART NH	08	61	58
FP45 COWL DESIGN REASONS	07	72	12
FP45 UNITS EMD 1967	02	72	47
GP COLOR CHART SP	05	60	61
GP COLOR CHART ACL	07	59	65
GP COLOR CHART B&O	02	59	74
GP COLOR CHART DL&W	10	58	76
GP COLOR CHART FEC	02	59	73
GP COLOR CHART FRIS	04	59	65
GP COLOR CHART IC	08	59	66
GP COLOR CHART L&N	09	58	63
GP COLOR CHART MKT	05	59	65
GP COLOR CHART MP	08	59	65
GP COLOR CHART NKP	03	59	69
GP COLOR CHART PRR	10	59	77
GP COLOR CHART S	01	60	82
GP COLOR CHART SOO	01	60	81
GP COLOR CHART UP	04	60	65
GP COLOR CHART WP	11	58	77
GP35 PROTOTYPE INFORMATION EMD	05	78	72
GP38-2 PROTOTYPE INFORMATION EMD 1966	02	80	84
GP50 FIRST OF THE EMD 50 SERIES 1953	01	83	91
GP7 COLOR CHART W	02	58	69
GP7 & GP9 ATSF REBUILDS	01	84	236
GP9 COLOR CHART B&M	12	57	80
GP9 COLOR CHART C&NW	03	58	65
GP9 COLOR CHART C&O	07	58	55
GP9 COLOR CHART GN	05	58	57
GP9 COLOR CHART GTW	12	57	81
GP9 COLOR CHART NP	02	58	70
GP9 COLOR CHART R	04	58	65

LOCOMOTIVES

DIESEL LOCOMOTIVE PROTOTYPE DATA

	M	Y	P
GP9 COLOR CHART WM	03	58	66
GP9 AND GP7 DIFFERENCES	03	82	148
H-16-44 GENERAL PURPOSE LOCOS OF FM	03	70	46
H24-66 TRAINMASTER DEMONSTRATOR COLORS	12	82	185
HOW A DIESEL WORKS	09	84	84
KRAUSS-MAFFEI DIESELS 1961	12	83	176
MILWAUKEE ROAD DIESEL COLORS	12	78	184
MP15 & MP15AC OF EMD	10	78	86
NOTES ON DIESELS FOR MODEL RAILROADS	03	72	34
NW3 EMD LOCOMOTIVES OF GN 1931 EMD	06	83	146
ORIGINAL ROCKET STREAMLINERS RI	05	80	52
PAINT & LETTERING SCL DIESELS	07	68	34
ROAD SWITCHER COLOR CHART L&HR #8	07	63	51
ROAD SWITCHERS EMD	12	58	87
RS-3 PROTOTYPE DATA ALCO	02	78	79
SD40-2 UNITS EMD STATE OF THE ART	07	76	63
SD50 EMD'S NEWEST 6 AXLE 6 MOTOR 1982	01	84	132
SD50 PREDECEASORS SD40X-SD50S	01	84	146
SERVICING FACILITIES FOR DIESELS	10	65	45
SP BLACK WIDOW UNITS	10	83	156
SPARK ARRESTERS ON DIESEL LOCOMOTIVES	02	68	72
SW1500 UNITS EMD	12	76	77
SWAPPING DIESEL TRUCKS	08	75	83
SWITCHER COLOR CHART C&W #214	07	63	51
SWITCHER COLOR CHART NSO #1501 AND #661	07	63	52
SWITCHER COLOR CHART RI	09	62	55
TURBINE FEVER ALCO 1948	04	81	58
U25B GE LOCOMOTIVES	09	71	44
U33C EMD ROAD DIESELS 1968	08	82	72
WHITCOMB 44 T DIESEL ELECTRICS 1941	07	80	68
WHITCOMB INDUSTRIAL LOCOMOTIVES	02	78	115
WHO SAYS ALL AMTRAK DIESELS ARE ALIKE?	12	75	98
YARD SWITCHER IDENTIFICATION EMD BLUE BK	11	57	71

DIESEL LOCO PROTOTYPE DATA BY ROAD

RD		M	Y	P
A	F40PH EARLY & LATE DIFFERENCES A	09	82	135
	WHO SAYS ALL AMTRAK DIESELS ARE ALIKE?	12	75	98
A&A	44 TONNERS PROTOTYPE DATA A&A GE	09	78	112
	44 TONNERS PROTOTYPE DATA 1 A&A GE	09	78	80
ACL	F UNIT COLOR CHART ACL	07	58	56
	EMD YARD SWITCHER COLOR CHART ACL	07	61	57
	GP COLOR CHART ACL	07	59	65
ATSF	GP7 & GP9 ATSF REBUILDS	01	84	236
	DIESEL COLOR CHART ATSF	03	61	62
B&LE	F UNIT COLOR CHART B&LE	06	58	58
B&M	GP9 COLOR CHART B&M	12	57	80
	F UNIT COLOR CHART B&M	10	59	78
B&O	16 CYLINDER CONSTANT TORQUE LOCO B&O	11	37	410
	GP COLOR CHART B&O	02	59	74
	F UNIT COLOR CHART B&O	05	59	66
C&EI	E UNIT COLOR CHART C&EI	01	59	98
C&IM	EMD ROAD SWITCHER COLOR CHART C&IM	06	61	63
C&NW	GP9 COLOR CHART C&NW	03	58	65
	E UNIT COLOR CHART C&NW	08	60	58
C&O	GP9 COLOR CHART C&O	07	58	55
	E UNIT COLOR CHART C&O	06	59	66
	F UNIT COLOR CHART C&O.	12	59	89
C&W	SWITCHER COLOR CHART C&W #214	07	63	51
CB&Q	EMD YARD SWITCHER COLOR CHART CB&Q	10	61	74
	E UNIT COLOR CHART CB&Q	11	59	78
	F7 COLOR CHART CB&Q	04	58	66
CG	F UNIT COLOR CHART CG	07	61	58
CN	F UNIT COLOR CHART CN	04	59	66
CSS&SB	85 TON CSS&SB #1013	03	38	105
D&RGW	F UNIT COLOR CHART D&RGW	09	58	64
DL&W	GP COLOR CHART DL&W	10	58	76
E	DIESEL COLOR CHART E	01	61	78
FEC	F UNIT COLOR CHART FEC	03	60	66
	DIESEL COLOR CHART FEC	03	61	61
	GP COLOR CHART FEC	02	59	73
FRIS	E UNIT COLOR CHART FRIS	05	61	64
	GP COLOR CHART FRIS	04	59	65
	F UNIT COLOR CHART FRIS	08	58	56
GN	NW3 EMD LOCOMOTIVES OF GN 1931 EMD	06	83	146
	ALCO ROAD SWITCHER COLOR CHART GN	10	61	73
	F UNIT COLOR CHART GN	11	59	77
	GP9 COLOR CHART GN	05	58	57
GTW	GP9 COLOR CHART GTW	12	57	81
IC	GP COLOR CHART IC	08	59	66
	E8 COLOR CHART IC	01	58	74
KCS	F UNIT COLOR CHART KCS	11	58	78
L&HR	ROAD SWITCHER COLOR CHART L&HR #8	07	63	51
L&N	F UNIT COLOR CHART L&N	05	60	62
	GP COLOR CHART L&N	09	58	63
LI	ALCO ROAD SWITCHER COLOR CHART LI	06	61	64
LV	ALCO ROAD SWITCHER COLOR CHART LV	05	61	63
MILW	MILWAUKEE ROAD DIESEL COLORS	12	78	184
	F UNIT COLOR CHART MILW	08	62	57
	DETAILS ON MILWAUKEE ROAD DIESELS	09	65	35
	ALCO SWITCHER COLOR CHART MILW	08	61	57
MKT	F UNIT COLOR CHART MKT	03	60	65
	GP COLOR CHART MKT	05	59	65
MP	GP COLOR CHART MP	08	59	65
	F UNIT COLOR CHART MP	06	58	57
N&W	C630 MASTER & SLAVE OF N&W 1971	12	80	98

LOCOMOTIVES

DIESEL LOCO PROTOTYPE DATA BY ROAD

RD		M	Y	P
NH	FL-9 COLOR CHART NH	08	61	58
NKP	GP COLOR CHART NKP	03	59	69
NP	F UNIT COLOR CHART NP	01	59	97
	GP9 COLOR CHART NP	02	58	70
NSO	SWITCHER COLOR CHART NSO #1501 AND #661	07	63	52
NYC	F7 COLOR CHART NYC	05	58	58
PRR	E UNIT COLOR CHART PRR	06	59	65
	GP COLOR CHART PRR	10	59	77
	F UNIT COLOR CHART PRR	08	58	55
R	F UNIT COLOR CHART R	08	60	57
	GP9 COLOR CHART R	04	58	65
RI	ORIGINAL ROCKET STREAMLINERS RI	05	80	52
	SWITCHER COLOR CHART RI	09	62	55
S	GP COLOR CHART S	01	60	82
	E UNIT COLOR CHART S	04	60	66
	F7 COLOR CHART S	01	58	73
SCL	BQ23-7 GE ROAD DIESEL SCL 1978	07	83	72
	PAINT & LETTERING SCL DIESELS	07	68	34
SOO	GP COLOR CHART SOO	01	60	81
	F UNIT COLOR CHART SOO	03	59	70
SP	GP COLOR CHART SP	05	60	61
	DIESEL LOCOMOTIVE COLOR CHART SP	01	61	77
	F UNIT COLOR CHART SP	07	59	66
	E UNIT COLOR CHART SP	12	59	90
T&P	F UNIT COLOR CHART T&P	08	62	58
UP	GP COLOR CHART UP	04	60	65
	F UNIT COLOR CHART UP	10	58	75
W	GP7 COLOR CHART W	02	58	69
	F UNIT COLOR CHART W	06	60	57
WM	GP9 COLOR CHART WM	03	58	66
	F UNIT COLOR CHART WM	06	60	58
WP	F UNIT COLOR CHART WP	09	62	56
	GP COLOR CHART WP	11	58	77

DIESEL LOCOMOTIVE PLANS

	M	Y	P
1000 HP ALCO SWITCHER PLAN D&H #3000	02	46	114
1500 HP BALDWIN SHARKNOSE PLANS BALDWIN	10	66	38
1500 HP CLASS DS-14 B ROAD SWITCHER PLAN	07	60	53
16 CYL CONSTANT-TORQUE LOC B&O PLANS	11	37	410
1600 ALL PURPOSE FM UNITS ATSF #3010 PLN	10	55	40
1600 HP ALCO ALL-PURPOSE LOCO PLANS	05	53	18
1600 HP BALDWIN PLANS	12	67	57
23 TON INDUSTRIAL LOCOMOTIVE PLANS	06	81	73
44 TON GE SWITCHER PLANS	04	73	50
44 TON GE SWITCHER PLANS 380 HP	05	55	34
44 TONNER PLANS GE	09	78	80
45 TON DIESEL SWITCHER PLANS VULCAN 1942	08	82	81
45 TON GE DIESEL ELECTRIC SWITCHER PLANS	10	80	84
600 HP EMD SWITCHER PLANS	11	40	618
600 HP GE SWITCHER PLANS	01	56	27
70 TON GE BRANCHLINE UNIT PLANS	10	69	38
A & B ALCO FREIGHT UNITS PLANS 6000 HP	06	49	38
A & B EMD FREIGHT UNIT PLANS S	08	46	513
ALCO ROAD SWITCHER PLANS SES #233	04	48	274
AS616 BALDWIN ROAD SWITCHER PLANS	07	75	40
BALDWIN SWITCHER ATSF #2207 PLANS	12	48	954
BL-2 EMD UNIT PLANS	10	50	33
BL-2 EMD UNIT PLANS	06	62	42
BOXCAB 1925 CNJ #1000 ALCO OF 1925 PLAN	12	61	36
BOXCAB 300 HP CNJ #1000 PLANS 1925	04	56	34
BP-20 PRR PASENGER UNIT PLAN BALDWIN	03	61	38
BQ23-7 GE ROAD DIESEL PLAN SCL#5131 1978	07	83	74
C+C TRANSFER UNIT PLANS PRR #5621 LHN	10	56	40
C-630 SLUG PLANS N&W #9917	12	80	98
C420 CENTURY ALCO RAOD SWITCHER PLN 1963	02	85	86
CENTURY 628 ALCO UNIT PLANS	11	65	41
CITY OF SAN FRANCISCO 1937 EMD PLANS UP	03	55	38
CN PIONEER DIESEL #9000 PLANS	03	66	36
CONSOLIDATION FM DIESEL PLANS 1950	05	53	38
CUMMINS 90 TON SWITCHER PLANS FW&DC	05	57	50
DD-40 EMD UNIT PLANS	08	65	34
DD-40 EMD UNIT PLANS	05	66	52
DD-40X EMD UNIT PLANS UP #6900 1969 EMD	08	69	44
DIESEL SWITCHER PLANS	09	47	712
DL-109 ALCO-GE UNIT PLANS	04	71	52
DL-640 ALCO ROAD SWITCHER OF 1960 PLANS	06	60	52
DRS 6-6-15 PLANS BALDWINS REPOWERED	04	82	75
E-2 A&B EMD PLANS FOR "CITIES OF LA & SF	09	73	46
E-6 EMD UNIT CITY OF SAN FRANCISCO PLANS	06	46	391
E-9A EMD UNIT PLANS 1954	03	63	38
E7 DIESEL PLANS C&NW "400"	12	49	51
EMD DIESEL TRUCK DRAWINGS	06	77	65
EMD TRUCK DRAWING CORRECTION	02	69	77
F-3A & F-3B EMD UNIT PLANS	10	70	48
F45 EMD LOCOMOTIVE PLANS 1960	12	75	70
FA-1 FB-1 ALCO UNITS PLANS 1945	02	69	50
FAIRBANKS-MORSE A&B UNIT PLANS	02	49	50
FL-9 THIRD RAIL DIESEL-ELECTRIC NH PLAN	08	61	34
FLEXOMOTIVE INDUSTRIAL SWITCHER PLANS	02	51	35
FP-45 EMD UNIT PLANS	02	72	48

DIESEL LOCOMOTIVE PHOTOS

	M	Y	P
SW-600 PHOTOS CL #100	06	64	43
SW-900 PHOTOS CNW #1281	06	64	42
SW-900 PHOTS GTW #7265	06	64	41

LOCOMOTIVES

DIESEL LOCOMOTIVE PLANS

Title	M	Y	P
FP-9 EMD UNIT PLANS 1956	11	63	46
FT EMD A&B UNITS PLANS	04	75	50
GAS TURBINE LOCO PLANS UP #51	09	53	44
GAS TURBINE LOCO PLANS WESTINGHOUSE	06	51	34
GM NARROW GAUGE UNIT CLASS GR12A CN PLAN	02	67	60
GP-20 EMD UNIT PLANS 1959	07	63	36
GP-30 EMD UNIT PLANS & PHOTOS	05	62	40
GP-7 ATSF #2655 EMD UNIT PLANS	02	54	50
GP22 PLANS SOO #2554 1978	10	80	95
GP35 PLANS EMD	05	78	72
GP38-2 DRAWING EMD 1966	02	80	87
GP50 EMD PLANS 1953	01	83	94
H-16-44 FM UNIT PLANS	03	70	46
HALF-BREED DIESEL DRAWING	10	64	54
INGALLS-DIESEL-ELECTRIC 1946 PLANS GM&O	11	51	43
JEEP 30 TON DIESEL DRAWING B	05	47	379
LIMA-HAMILTON SWITCHER #1000 PLANS	11	49	56
MODEL 40 EMD SWITCHER PLANS EMD 1940	04	62	42
MP15 PLANS EMD	10	78	86
NW-5 EMD ROAD SWITCHER PLANS 1946	06	68	38
NW2 EMD SWITCHER PLANS 1939	12	79	74
RS-1 ALCO ROAD SWITCHER PLANS	05	69	40
RS-1325 EMD ROAD SWITCHER PLAN C&IM #31	06	61	36
RS-2 PLANS ALCO	02	78	82
S-5 & S-6 ALCO SWITCHER PLANS 1954	04	76	56
SC600 EMD SWITCHER OF 1936 PLANS	07	67	34
SD-7 EMD UNIT DRAWINGS	02	55	34
SD40-2 EMD PLANS 1972	07	76	66
SD45 EMD N&W #1700 PLANS 1966	10	75	73
SD45 PLANS EMD ATSF #1819 1967	10	67	32
SD45T2 EMD UNIT PLANS 1972	07	72	62
SD50 EMD PLANS SEA #8510 1982	01	84	136
SW-1200 EMD UNIT PLANS "HO" 1937	10	62	37
SW-1500 EMD UNIT PLANS 1966	12	76	78
SW-900 EMD UNIT PLANS	06	64	43
TA CLASS STREAMLINED ROCKET PLANS RI	05	80	55
THREE POWER LOCO NYC #1528 CLS DES-3 PLN	11	37	416
TR-1 COW & CALF TRANSFER UNIT PLAN IC	03	64	38
TRAIN MASTER FM UNIT PLANS TM-4	11	54	46
U25B GE PLANS 1959	09	71	44
U33C EMD ROAD DIESEL PLANS	08	82	73
WHITCOMB 44 T DIESEL ELECTRICS PLANS	07	80	69
WHITCOMB INDUSTRIAL DIESEL PLANS	02	78	114

DIESEL LOCOMOTIVE PLANS BY ROAD

RD	Title	M	Y	P
ATSF	SD45 PLANS EMD ATSF #1819 1967	10	67	32
	BALDWIN SWITCHER ATSF #2207 PLANS	12	48	954
	GP-7 ATSF #2655 EMD UNIT PLANS	02	54	50
	1600 ALL PURPOSE FM UNITS ATSF #3010 PLN	10	55	40
B&O	16 CYL CONSTANT-TORQUE LOC B&O PLANS	11	37	410
C&IM	RS-1325 EMD ROAD SWITCHER PLAN C&IM #31	06	61	36
C&NW	E7 DIESEL PLANS C&NW "400"	12	49	51
CN	GM NARROW GAUGE UNIT CLASS GR12A CN PLAN	02	67	60
	CN PIONEER DIESEL #9000 PLANS	03	66	36
CNJ	BOXCAB 1925 CNJ #1000 ALCO OF 1925 PLAN	12	61	36
	BOXCAB 300 HP CNJ #1000 PLANS 1925	04	56	34
D&H	1000 HP ALCO SWITCHER PLAN D&H #3000	02	46	114
FW&DC	CUMMINS 90 TON SWITCHER PLANS FW&DC	05	57	50
GM&O	INGALLS-DIESEL-ELECTRIC 1946 PLANS GM&O	11	51	43
IC	TR-1 COW & CALF TRANSFER UNIT PLAN IC	03	64	38
N&W	C-630 SLUG PLANS N&W #9917	12	80	98
	SD45 EMD N&W #1700 PLANS 1966	10	75	73
NYC	THREE POWER LOCO NYC #1528 CLS DES-3 PLN	11	37	416
NYNH&H	FL-9 THIRD RAIL DIESEL-ELECTRIC NH PLAN	08	61	34
PRR	BP-20 PRR PASENGER UNIT PLAN BALDWIN	03	61	38
	C+C TRANSFER UNIT PLANS PRR #5621 LHW	10	56	40
RI	TA CLASS STREAMLINED ROCKET PLANS RI	05	80	55
S	A & B EMD FREIGHT UNIT PLANS S	08	46	513
SCL	BQ23-7 GE ROAD DIESEL PLAN SCL#5131 1978	07	83	74
SEA	SD50 EMD PLANS SEA #8510 1982	01	84	136
SES	ALCO ROAD SWITCHER PLANS SES #233	04	48	274
SOO	GP22 PLANS SOO #2554 1978	10	80	95
UP	DD-40X EMD UNIT PLANS UP #6900 1969 EMD	08	69	44
	GAS TURBINE LOCO PLANS UP #51	09	53	44
	CITY OF SAN FRANCISCO 1937 EMD PLANS UP	03	55	38

STEPHANS' RAILROAD DIRECTORY

50

LOCOMOTIVES

DIESEL LOCOMOTIVE MODELS	M	Y	P
100 TON BOXCAB FROM MDC 60 TON CONSTRUCT	09	81	59
1600 HP ALL PURPOSE LOCO ALCO CONST 1	05	53	18
1600 HP ALL PURPOSE LOCO ALCO CONST 2	06	53	20
1600 HP ALL PURPOSE LOCO ALCO CONST 3	07	53	28
44 TON GE SWITCHER CONST SUPERSTRUCTURE	06	55	40
44 TON GE SWITCHER CONSTRUCT CONCLUSION	07	55	40
44 TON GE SWITCHER CONSTRUCTION 1	05	55	20
50 TON BOXCAB CONSTRUCTION	05	80	92
ALCO B UNIT CONVERSION FROM A UNIT	07	70	62
ALCO ROAD DIESEL CONSTRUCTION 1	08	53	20
ALCO ROAD DIESEL CONSTRUCTION 2	09	53	36
AS616 BALDWIN UNIT KITBASHED	07	75	40
ATHEARN FLYWHEEL CONVERSIONS	07	78	132
AUTO TRAIN SWITCHER MOD & PT	12	74	23
B30-7A GE BURLINGTON NORTHERN MOD & PT	01	83	146
BALDWIN DIESEL IN STYRENE CONSTRUCT $1	12	67	56
BALDWIN QUARTET KITBASH	04	84	74
BARR-NIXON SWITCHER	04	49	28
BOXCAB OIL/ELECTRIC FROM ATHEARN CABOOSE	03	83	75
BUILD CLINCH ROLLING STOCK	07	79	58
BUILDING A BABY TRAINMASTER	01	80	98
BURLINGTON NORTHERN EMD SWITCH MOD & PT	09	74	17
C&O DIESEL SWITCHERS MOD & PT	04	76	88
C30-7 GE GN #5501 1976 MOD & PT	04	85	118
C32-8 GE KITBASH	01	85	88
C420 CENTURY ALCO KITBASH 1963	02	85	88
C424 CENTURY ALCO KITBASH 1963	02	85	88
C425 CENTURY ALCO KITBASH 1963	02	85	88
C628 CENTURY HIGH NOSE KITBASH	09	83	70
C630 MASTER & SLAVE N&W CONSTRCUTION	12	80	90
CASE FOR PAINTING BRASS DIESELS	04	77	97
CP ROAD SWITCHER MOD & PT	11	74	27
D&H #5015 EXPERIMENTAL PAINT SCHEME	01	78	127
DD40 EMD UNIT SCRATCHBUILT	05	66	51
DEMONSTRATOR LOCOMOTIVES MOD & PT	12	76	115
DIAPHRAGMS ON DIESEL UNITS	07	70	74
DIESEL LOCOMOTIVE PERFORMANCE IMPROVEMNT	06	68	66
DIESEL SWITCHER CINEBAR WESTERN MOD & PT	06	78	105
DIESEL SWITCHER CONSTRUCTION	09	47	712
DIESEL SWITCHER MODIFICATIONS "HON30"	07	82	84
DIESELS I LIKE 'EM	11	63	48
DOME FLASHER FOR DIESELS	04	73	72
DOUBLE YOUR DIESELS POWER	09	49	10
DS 4-4-10 6 CYL BALDWIN KITBASH	04	84	74
DS 4-4-10 8 CYL BALDWIN KITBASH	04	84	74
DS 4-4-6 6 CYL BALDWIN KITBASH	04	84	74
E1A & B ATSF LOCOMOTIVE MOD & PT	06	75	18
E6 PASSENGER DIESEL ROCK ISLAND MOD & PT	08	79	110
E7 FEC #1018 EXPERIMENTAL PAINT SCHEME	01	78	126
E7 MISSOURI PACIFIC EAGLE MOD & PT	12	85	155
E7 NYC #4003 EXPERIMENTAL PAINT SCHEME	01	78	128
E7B NYC MOD & PT	10	75	84
E7C HELPER AL&W 1970 MOD & PT	10	81	122
E8 B&M MOD & PT	12	79	158
E8 EMD UNITS REMODELING RIVAROSSI UNITS	06	70	62

LOCOMOTIVES

DIESEL LOCOMOTIVE MODELS

Title		M	Y	P
E8 NYC #4083 EXPERIMENTAL PAINT SCHEME		01	78	127
E8 PASSENGER DIESEL RI	MOD & PT	12	83	167
E9 EMD BUILT FROM F7 PARTS		01	59	68
EMD COW AND CALF UNIT CONSTRUCTION		07	57	40
EMD GEEP B UNIT CONSTRUCTION		03	58	42
EMD HISTORY IN MODELS		10	72	51
ERASTZ "N" SCALE COOLING FAN CONSTRUCTIO		03	80	114
F3 GEORGIA	MOD & PT	10	77	99
F40PH WITH ATLAS POWER EMD		01	81	84
F7 EMD CONVERTED FROM F3 VARNEY		02	53	12
F7 EMD FACE-LIFTING UP LATEST VERSION		04	59	31
F7 HEADLIGHTS MOVE TO CORRECT LOCATION		12	82	175
F7 MAROON B&M	MOD & PT	05	75	20
F7 SP #631 EXPERIMENTAL PAINT SCHEME		01	78	127
F7A ERIE LACKAWANNA	MOD & PT	03	79	115
F9 EMD MODIFYING ATLAS "O"		06	76	48
FA'S SHARKS & KADEE COUPLERS		02	79	126
FA1, FB2 ALCO DIESELS OF NH	MOD & PT	02	83	126
FA2 ANN ARBOR 1950	MOD & PT	07	75	34
FA2, FB2 NYC "LIGHTNING STRIPE"	MOD & PT	11	82	155
FL-9 THIRD RAIL DIESEL-ELECTRIC CONST NH		08	61	37
FLYWHEEL DRIVE ADVANTAGES & MOUNTING		10	70	84
FLYWHEEL DRIVE LOCOMOTIVES		08	46	508
FLYWHEEL MECHANICS FOR N GAUGE		12	69	62
FM 1000 KIT ASSEMBLY HO BARR NIXON		00	00	00
FP45 AMTRAK	MOD & PT	03	80	128
FP45 DIESEL MILW	MOD & PT	09	78	105
FP7 CONVERSION FROM F7		04	72	40
FP7 EXPERIMENTAL PAINT SCHEME C&O #8000		01	78	127
FP7 FRISCO EMD	MOD & PT	10	83	142
FP7 OSO	MOD & PT	06	78	103
FP7 SOUTHERN EMD	MOD & PT	10	83	142
FP7 WP	MOD & PT	10	77	100
FREELANCE BRANCHLINE DIESEL CONSTRUCTION		09	50	60
FT EMD UNIT KITBASHED		04	75	44
GEARLESS DRIVE FOR MULTITRUCK LOCOS		05	65	47
GP20 COW & CALF EMD LOW HOOD		11	60	32
GP22 SOO KITBASH		10	80	94
GP30 DETAILING FOR S		07	79	66
GP30 C&EI	MOD & PT	11	79	158
GP30 CONVERTED FROM GP35		01	75	66
GP35 UP	MOD & PT	11	79	155
GP35 AA #385 NEW IMAGE	MOD & PT	06	80	111
GP35 DT&I #355 1980	MOD & PT	12	81	147
GP35 GM&O #640 OF 1965 MOD & PT EMD		02	76	82
GP35 OSO #17	MOD & PT	09	75	34
GP35 WESTMINSTERS 1776	MOD & PT	09	75	34
GP35 WP ORANGE & GREEN	MOD & PT	09	84	106
GP38 CHOPPING THE ATLAS SHORT HOOD		04	76	80
GP38 FAM #4021	MOD & PT	11	78	118
GP38 OF SOUTHERN	MOD & PT	07	79	108
GP38-2 DT&I #228 1980	MOD & PT	12	81	147
GP38AC NORFOLK SOUTHERN	MOD & PT	10	84	134
GP39-2 EMD KITBASH FROM ATHEARN GP35		12	84	80
GP40 B&O TRADITIONAL BLUE	MOD & PT	01	81	126

DIESEL LOCOMOTIVE MODELS

Title		M	Y	P
GP40 DRESSING UP A PLAIN JANE		07	85	62
GP40 FRIS SERIES	MOD & PT	04	78	118
GP40X KITBASH FROM SD40-2 EMD 1972		10	85	110
GP50 IN SANTA FE COLORS (BRASS)	MOD & PT	04	84	114
GP50 KITBASH FROM SD40-2 1980 EMD		10	85	112
GP50 KITBASHING		01	83	86
GP7 CB&Q	MOD & PT	03	80	127
GP7 ATSF ZEBRA STRIPED UNITS	MOD & PT	11	85	134
GP7 DETAILING ATSF 2650 CLASS ZEBRA#2707		11	85	134
GP7 MC #567	MOD & PT	12	79	159
GP7 MC #575	MOD & PT	12	79	158
GP7 NKP ROAD DIESEL	MOD & PT	05	85	130
GP7 NW SNOOT GEEP EMD 1953		07	84	110
GP7 PRECISION NATIONAL CORD#970	MOD & PT	12	75	96
GP7 PT	MOD & PT	12	79	159
GP7 ROAD SWITCHER ROCK ISLAND	MOD & PT	08	79	114
GP7 TH&B	MOD & PT	02	80	126
GP9 TH&B	MOD & PT	02	80	126
GP9 EMD SUPERDETAILING ATHEARN UNITS		09	57	34
GP9 PAINTING C&O		01	78	129
GYRATING WARNING LIGHTS		01	66	72
HALF-BREED DIESEL CONSTRUCTION		10	64	54
HH1000 ALCO SWITCHER MILW	MOD & PT	02	77	108
HYBRID ALCO-EMD RD SWITCHER CONST RI#453		12	57	41
ICG NEW DIESEL IMAGE	MOD & PT	07	82	82
IMPROVED DIESEL LOCOMOTIVE APPEARANCE		11	75	83
IMPROVED TURBINE LOCOMOTIVE PERFORMANCE		03	70	64
IMPROVING ATHEARN RUBBER BAND DRIVE		11	82	171
IMPROVING KMT DIESEL PERFORMANCE		02	83	128
JEEP 30 TON DIESEL CONSTRUCTION		05	47	378
KADEE COUPLER MOUNTING ATH DIESEL SWITCH		05	85	120
KADEES FOR ATLAS HO DIESELS		07	78	130
KITBASH A REBUILT BALDWIN VO-1000		04	83	58
KITBASH FP9 FROM ATLAS F9		06	78	139
KITBASH UP VERANDA TURBINE 1948 ALCO		04	81	58
KITBASHING "ON2" DIESELS		02	80	76
MARS LIGHTS THAT OPERATE CONSTRUCTION		01	50	19
MATCHING DIESEL SPEEDS		07	84	133
MOM 1200 HP LIGHT SWITCH NYC "HO" HANSEN		10	83	105
MOM 44T GE SWITCHER 1/26.5 HUGHES		12	73	61
MOM B&O F7 ABA EMD "O" POWELL		11	80	73
MOM C&NW GP7 "HO" FEDDERSON		11	84	88
MOM FREE LANCED DIESEL SWITCH 'ON3'ALLEN		12	80	86
MOM GP38AC GTW #5808 "HO" PAPP		07	85	70
MOM H-24-66 FM TRAINMASTER "HO" CALLAHAN		11	75	57
MOM HIGH HOOD SD40 "HO" CALLAHAN		01	73	48
MOM SD45-2 ATSF BICENTENNIAL #5701		03	76	51
MOM SP F7A-B COMBINATION "O" NEUBERT		07	83	71
MOM UP 8500 HP GAS TURBINE "HO"ALBERTSON		04	68	47
MONON THOROUGHBRED LOCO	MOD & PT	05	78	112
NORTHWESTERNS REPOWERED BALDWIN MODIFICA		04	82	74
NW2 KITBASH FROM ATHEARN SW1500		12	79	72
OTHER BODY SHELLS ON MTX "N" U28C CHASIS		01	81	74
PA-1 & PB-1 PASS DIESELS ATSF	MOD & PT	07	83	115
PAINT & LETTERING AA ALCO FA2		07	75	34

LOCOMOTIVES

DIESEL LOCOMOTIVE MODELS		M	Y	P
PAINT & LETTERING GUIDE FOR L&N		06	69	30
PAINTING DIESEL SWITCHERS		07	74	36
PIONEER DIESEL UNIT CONST 1 CNJ #1000		04	56	20
PIONEER DIESEL UNIT CONST 2 CNJ #1000		05	56	47
PLYMOUTH SWITCHER CONVERSION TO HON3		02	66	42
POSSIBILITIES OF LIVE DIESEL-ELEC LOCO		07	78	95
PROTOTYPE DIESEL CAB CONSTRUCTION		11	76	99
PS1 DYNATROL RRL RECEIVER FOR ATLAS RS-3		09	85	116
REBUILDING ALCO 420 & 424 SWITCHERS		07	81	86
REPOWERING A BRASS SWITCHER ALCO S1		06	84	132
REPOWERING ATHEARN DIESELS		10	76	58
REPOWERING POPULAR ATHEARN DIESELS		04	80	85
RS-2 LONG ISLAND	MOD & PT	10	78	125
RSD-15 FROM U28 CONVERSION		01	83	171
SD20 ICG #2000 1979	MOD & PT	07	85	118
SD24 EMD	MOD & PT	02	77	106
SD38-2 KITBASH FROM SD40-2 1972 EMD		10	85	109
SD40 WM #7474 1966	MOD & PT	12	75	95
SD40-2 (ATHEARN) KITBASHERS GOLD MINE		10	85	108
SD40-2 EMD KITBASH		07	76	59
SD40-2 MODELING FOR SOUTHERN		10	84	75
SD40T-2 MODELING EMD D&RGW		04	79	58
SD40T-2 SNOOT DETAILING CBELT #8326 EMD		01	85	100
SD45 EMD MODELING N&W		10	75	70
SD45 UP	MOD & PT	08	79	112
SD45-2 KITBASH EMD 1972		11	82	75
SD45-2 KITBASH FROM SD40-2 EMD 1972		10	85	111
SD50 EMD KITBASH FROM ATHEARN SD40-2		01	84	138
SD60 DEMONSTRATOR	MOD & PT	10	85	124
SD7 EMD CONSTRUCTION 1		02	55	34
SD7 EMD CONSTRUCTION FINISHING		03	55	54
SD9 BN #6156	MOD & PT	10	76	87
SD9 CONVERTED FROM PLASTIC LOCO		12	62	40
SD9 DM&IR #129	MOD & PT	10	76	87
SD9 MILW #539	MOD & PT	10	76	89
SD9 RIO GRANDE #5302 MOD & PT		10	76	88
SD9 SP #5319	MOD & PT	10	76	89
SD9 SP #5327	MOD & PT	10	76	90
SLUG UNIT CONVERTED FROM 2 ATHEARN GP35S		08	75	66
SOUTHEASTERN RAILROADS CAB UNIT MOD & PT		01	80	140
SPECIAL CP DSA-DSSB SWITCHERS	MOD & PT	10	77	98
SPUD POWER TRUCKS FROM PFM		06	81	67
SUPER DETAILING DIESEL LOCOMOTIVES		09	84	142
SW1200 AD&N #1205	MOD & PT	03	81	78
SW1200 AD&N #174	MOD & PT	03	81	78
SW1200 RS CN	MOD & PT	08	81	110
SW1500 EMD SWITCHER YOUNGSTOWN STEEL		09	82	116
SW1500 GM DEMONSTRATOR	MOD & PT	12	76	116
SW1500 MN&S	MOD & PT	08	75	21
SW1500 SEATTLE & NORTH COAST	MOD & PT	01	83	138
SW1500 WESTMINSTER	MOD & PT	08	75	20
SW9 HB&T SWITCHER	MOD & PT	11	77	130
TESTING PDT UNDER FLOOR TRUCK		08	83	59
TRAINMASTER SP	MOD & PT	09	81	128
TRIO OF NARROW GAUGE DIESEL CONVERSIONS		10	80	74

DIESEL LOCOMOTIVE MODELS		M	Y	P
TT DIESEL SWITCHER CONVERSIONS		10	64	41
U18B MAINE CENTRAL GE KITBASH 1975		03	84	98
U30C MP OF 1974	MOD & PT	01	76	26
U30C SOO PAINT SCHEME	MOD & PT	03	78	113
VARIETY OF EMD HOOD UNITS KITBASHED		09	84	74
VO 1000 8 CYL BALDWIN KITBASH		04	84	74
WINDSHIELD WIPERS FOR DIESELS		07	77	109
WORKING MARS LIGHTS		03	75	74

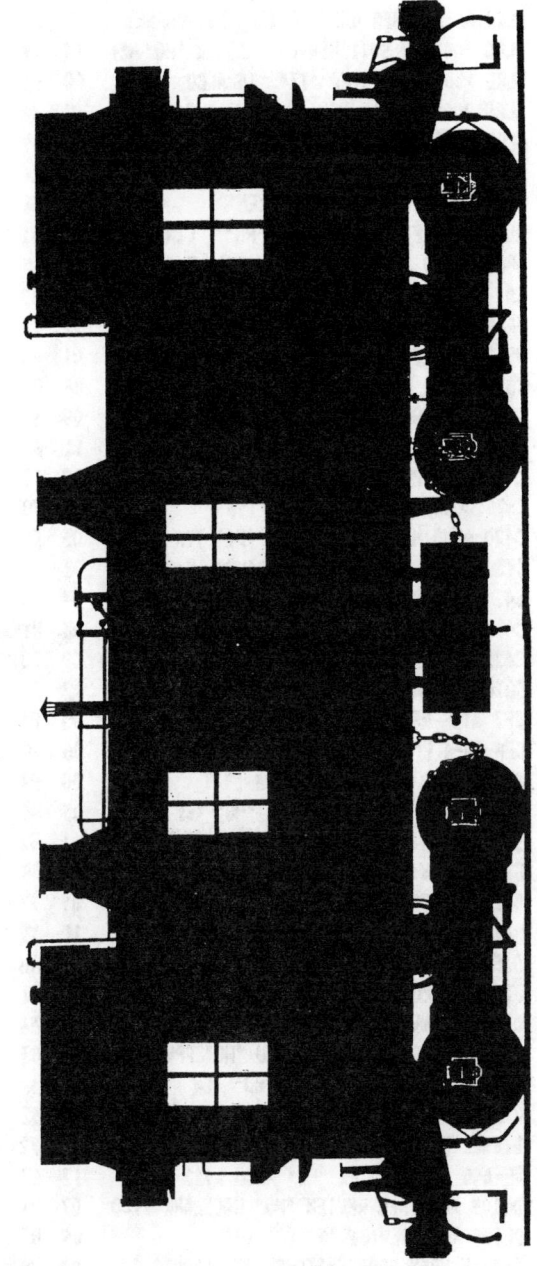

LOCOMOTIVES

DIESEL LOCOMOTIVE MODEL REVIEWS

Title	M	Y	P
1600 HP ALCO ROAD SWITCHER REV "HO" HOB	08	57	15
2000 HP ALCO PASSENGER REVIEW "N" CC	03	68	14
2000 HP ALCO REVIEW "HO" HOB	05	53	53
2000 HP ALCO REVIEW "O" CLWO	02	64	6
25 TON BOX CAB REVIEW GE "HON3" GL	11	78	46
35 TON DIESEL LISTING "HO/ON3/S" AHM	05	78	52
4 WHEEL SWITCHER KIT REVIEW "O" KWR	01	50	77
44 TON GE SWITCHER REVIEW "HO" KLW 1937	06	81	27
44 TON SWITCHER REVIEW "HO" MEW	02	57	11
60 TON BOXCAB REVIEW "HO" MDC 1927 ALCO	06	72	19
70 TON DIESEL ELCTRIC REVIEW "O" SUN GE	09	81	36
AEROTRAIN POWER UNIT REVIEW "HO" VARNEY	07	56	10
ALCO 1000 HP SWITCHER KIT REVIEW "HO" WM	04	48	303
ALCO 1500 HP REVIEW "TT" TOMALCO	08	65	8
ALCO 2000 HP A&B REVIEW "HO" CA	01	48	67
ALCO PASSENGER BODY REV "HO" HOBBIES INC	11	49	95
ALCO ROAD SWITCHER REVIEW "HO" HOB	01	54	20
ALCO-GE 1600 REVIEW "O" KEN	09	54	10
ALCO-GE DIESEL REVIEW "HO" LIN	06	51	50
AS616 ROAD SWITCHER REVIEW "HO" H 1950 B	10	75	33
BALDWIN JEEP REVIEW "HO" PMO	07	49	52
BALDWIN-WESTINGHOUSE 1000 HP REV "HO" HG	10	47	861
BL-2 EMD REVIEW "HO" AHM 1949	01	64	10
BOXCAB EMD ATSF #1 REVIEW "HO" H 1935	06	82	31
C415 ALCO REVIEW "HO" ATI 1960 ALCO	08	69	6
C415 ALCO REVIEW "HO" PSM	11	69	12
C420 ALCO CENTURY REVIEW "N" MP	02	77	34
C420 ALCO REVIEW "N" MRC 1963	08	70	13
C420 ALCO SWITCHER REVIEW "HO" TVM	05	82	31
C430 ALCO CENTURY REVIEW "HO" M 1967	02	67	10
C430 ALCO ROAD SWITCHER REVIEW "HO" ALCO	04	74	19
C430 CENTURY ALCO REVIEW "HO" PCO	05	81	38
C628 ALCO REVIEW "HO" LIFELIKE 1963	08	73	16
CATERPILLAR INDUST SWITCHER REV "HO" WSM	12	71	34
CF7 ATSF REVIEW "HO" H	05	81	42
CFA-20-4 FM REVIEW "O" RIV 1950	06	70	21
DD40AX EMD UP REVIEW "N" B 1969	08	84	37
DD40AX EMD UP ROAD DIESEL "HO" KEY 1969	05	84	32
DDA40X EMD UP CENTENNIAL REV "HO" B 1969	11	82	42
DIESEL CONVERSIONS REVIEW "HO" PPW	08	79	48
DIESEL DETAIL LISTING "HO" DETAILS WEST	09	77	45
DIESEL ELECTRIC REVIEW "HO" DMC	11	45	504
DIESEL KIT REVIEW "HO" V	03	48	225
DIESEL PILOT LISTING "HO" JSM	09	77	45
DIESEL POWER CHASSIS REVIEW "HO" HOB	12	64	10
DIESEL REPOWER UNIT REVIEW "HO" PPW	03	85	52
DIESEL SWITCHER REVIEW "HO" BN	12	48	991
DIESEL SWITCHER WOOD REVIEW "O" WAL	09	42	440
DIESEL-MECHANICAL D&RGW REVIEW "ON3" PFM	03	72	28
DL-640 ALCO REVIEW "HO" ALCO 1960	12	67	14
DL109 ALCO A&B REVIEW "HO" HALLMARK 1940	07	71	20
DL109 ALCO REVIEW "N" CC 1942	06	82	40
DL535E WP&Y ROAD SWITCHER REV "HON3" PS	03	79	52
DL702 ALCO REVIEW "HO" 1956 ALCO	06	74	20
DR-4-4-15 SHARKNOSE REV "HO" MP 1949 B	08	72	22

DIESEL LOCOMOTIVE MODEL REVIEWS

Title	M	Y	P
E6 BODY CASTING REVIEW "HO" CLW	08	71	20
E7 LOCOMOTIVE REVIEW "HO" HOB	01	51	58
E7 POWER UNIT REVIEW "HO" HOB	07	65	8
E7 DIESEL LISTING "N" ATLAS	06	77	48
E8 EMD PASSENGER LOCO REVIEW "HO" AHM	08	74	19
E8 EMD PASSENGER REVIEW "N" AT	02	68	13
E8 PASSENGER DIESEL REVIEW "N" CC	01	85	58
E8 PASSENGER REVIEW "HO" RIV	01	67	14
E9 A&B EMD UNITS REVIEW "HO" TI	04	68	14
EMC A&B LOCOMOTIVE REVIEW "HO" HOB	06	48	437
EMC DIESEL KIT REVIEW "HO" WAL	01	49	95
EMC LOCOMOTIVE KIT REVIEW "HO" CMP	03	48	222
EMC PASSENGER DIESEL KIT REVIEW "O" WAL	05	48	372
EMD SWITCHER REVIEW "HO" LIN	11	49	93
F3 EMD A&B REVIEW "N" CC	06	80	43
F3 EMD REVIEW "N" CC 1945	04	75	28
F3A & F3B DIESEL REVIEW "O" WAL	07	47	597
F40PH EMD REVIEW "N" MP	02	82	31
F40PH EMD REVIEW "HO" LIFELIKE	12	78	48
F7 DIESEL REVIEW "O" AN	08	54	9
F7 DUAL DRIVE REVIEW "HO" OE	10	60	14
F7 DUMMY REVIEW "HO" GLOBE MODELS	10	54	12
F7 HIFI DRIVE REVIEW "HO" ATH	12	56	12
F7 CHASSIS REVIEW "HO" HOBBYTOWN BOSTON	03	55	14
F7 EMD DIESEL REVIEW "HO" M	10	82	45
F7 EMD DIESEL REVIEW "Z" MKL 1947	03	85	35
F7 EMD REVIEW "O" AN	12	69	18
F7 EMD ROAD DIESEL REVIEW "HO" LL	07	77	38
F7 REVIEW "Z" KD	02	85	39
F9 TWIN POWERED REVIEW "HO" M	07	60	13
F9 EMD REVIEW "N" MTX	01	69	10
F9 EMD REVIEW "1/4" AT	07	72	18
F9 TRACK CLEANING DIESEL REV "HO" BAU	12	60	18
FA-1 ALCO REVIEW "N" AT	05	78	36
FA-1 ALCO REVIEW "O" CLWO 1946	11	73	36
FA-2 ALCO REVIEW "N" MRC 1950	01	70	16
FA-2 ALCO REVIEW "N" RAP 1950	11	69	20
FA1 ALCO REVIEW "HO" LIO 1946	08	75	24
FA1 ALCO ROAD DIESEL REVIEW "HO" TMI	02	83	39
FA2 ALCO REVIEW "HO" MER 1950	01	72	26
FM 1600 HP ROAD SWITCHER REV "HO" PAM	01	57	10
FM 2000 HP SWITCHER KIT REVIEW "O" WAL	04	49	73
FM B UNIT REVIEW "HO" RIV	03	63	9
FM C-LINER REVIEW "HO" AHM 1950	04	63	10
FM POWER UNIT REVIEW "O" AHM	11	73	31
FP45 & F45 EMD DIESEL REVIEW "HO" ATH	03	74	20
FP45 AMTRACK LISTING "HO" AHM	11	77	54
FP7 EMD ROAD DIESEL REVIEW "S" AMI 1949	12	82	60
FP9 EMD REVIEW "N" RAP	11	67	12
FREIGHT DIESEL KIT REVIEW "O" WPM	05	48	370
FT EMD DIESEL REVIEW "HO" AHM 1942	02	75	29
FT EMD OF 1939 REVIEW "HO" H	02	69	10
GE EXPORT DIESEL REVIEW "N" JMC	05	79	42
GERMAN DIESEL REVIEW "1/32" MKL	08	82	35
GP-7 LOCOMOTIVE REVIEW "HO" LLA	01	51	60

LOCOMOTIVES

DIESEL LOCOMOTIVE MODEL REVIEWS

```
                                                  M  Y   P
                                                  -- -- ----
GP20  EMD REVIEW "HO" T       1960                04 62  12
GP20  EMD ROAD SWITCHER REVIEW "O" KEM            07 76  34
GP30  EMD REVIEW "N" RAP 1963                     02 69  10
GP30  POWER CHASSIS REVIEW "HO" HOB               02 64  14
GP30  DIESEL REVIEW "HO"    FR                    06 84  44
GP30  EMD REVIEW "N" AT 1961                      05 75  30
GP38  LISTING "HO"    ATLAS                       03 77  44
GP38-2 EMD LISTING "HO"  LIFELIKE                 12 78  69
GP40  3000 HP REVIEW "HO" G 1965                  12 72  31
GP40  EMD LOCOMOTIVE REVIEW "HO" B 1965           05 71  17
GP40  EMD REVIEW "N" B 1965                       09 69  14
GP40  EMD REVIEW CN "HO" LPD                      11 78  52
GP50  EMD REVIEW "HO" H                           01 83  48
GP7   EMD 1500 HP REVIEW "HO" H 1953 EMD          09 68  12
GP7   EMD REVIEW "HO" LIO                         09 75  30
GP7   ROAD SWITCHER REVIEW "O"  KEM               12 54  22
GP9   GEAR OR HIFI DRIVE REVIEW "HO" ATH          05 57  11
GP9   REVIEW "HO" PFM                             08 56  12
GP9   ROAD SWITCHER REVIEW "HO" PFM               03 56  13
GP9 & F7 POWER CHASSIS REVIEW "HO" HOB            01 58  10
GP9   DIESEL DRIVE REVIEW "HO" PPW                06 84  41
GP9   EMD DIESEL REVIEW "N" AT  1954              02 75  27
GP9   EMD REVIEW "N" RAP 1954                     09 69  18
GP9   EMD ROAD SWITCHER REVIEW HO ATH 1949        05 84  29
H-12-44 FM DIESEL REVIEW "HO"  JE                 03 53  63
H-12-44 FM SWITCHER REVIEW "N" MTX 1950           09 74  24
H-16-44 FM BABY TRAINMASTER REV "HO" HD           10 69  15
H-24-66 FM TRAINMASTER REV "HO" ATH 1953          10 79  43
H-24-66 FM TRAINMASTER REVIEW "HO" HD             12 69  26
HUSTLER REPOWER UNIT REVIEW "HO" NWSL             08 84  45
INDUSTRIAL DIESEL LISTING "N"    ATLAS            12 77  62
INDUSTRIAL SWITCHER KIT REVIEW "HO"  PL           09 49  54
INDUSTRIAL SWITCHER REVIEW "HO"  G                01 61  14
KM DIESEL HYDROLIC REVIEW "HO" AHM                11 64   7
M-10000 STREAMLIN TRAIN UP REV HO NPP             02 79  42
M-10000 STREAMLINE TRAIN UP REV HO AHM            02 79  42
MP15AC EMD SWITCHER REVIEW "HO" ALCO              02 82  27
PA-1 ALCO DIESEL REVIEW "HO" CC                   03 70  15
PA-1 ALCO REVIEW "HO" ATH   1949                  10 70  14
PLANETARY CLUTCH REVIEW "HO" W&T MODELS           12 57  12
PLYMOUTH SWITCHER REVIEW "HO" M                   03 62  20
PLYMOUTH WDT REVIEW "N"  AT                       04 73  29
PLYMOUTH WDT REVIEW "O"  AT                       04 73  30
RF16 "SHARK NOSE" DIESEL REVIEW "HO" M            11 53  14
RF16  BALDWIN SHARKNOSE CAB REV "HO" MP           12 76  30
RS-11 ALCO LISTING "HO" MODEL POWER               12 78  65
RS1  ALCO ROAD SWITCHER REVIEW N H 1941           09 83  33
RS1  ALCO REVIEW "O" NJI 1941                     03 81  54
RS1  ALCO SWITCHER REVIEW "HO" ALCO               05 68  15
RS11 ALCO ROAD SWITCHER REVIEW "HO" MP            03 77  34
RS2  ALCO REVIEW "HO" AHM                         09 69  11
RS3  ALCO REVIEW "HO" AT 1950                     01 85  47
RS3  1600HP ALCO REVIEW "N" AT 1950               01 84  58
RS3  ALCO RAOD SWITCHER REV "HO" KUM 1950         11 84  54D
RS3  ALCO REVIEW "HO"    STEW 1950                05 85  38
```

DIESEL LOCOMOTIVE MODEL REVIEWS

```
                                                  M  Y   P
                                                  -- -- ----
RS3 ALCO REVIEW "N"   OL 1950                     12 84  52
RSD-15 ALCO REVIEW "N" MRC 1956                   08 70  15
S1   SP ALCO REVIEW "G"  MAGN                     02 84  39
S1,S2,S3,S4 ALCO SWITCHER REVIEW "N" KEY          03 84  33
S12  BALDWIN SWITCHER REV "HO" ATH 1951           07 74  16
S2   ALCO LISTING "HO"  AHM                       06 78  52
S2/S4 ALCO SWITCHER BODY REV "HO" CLW             11 82  38
SD24 EMD ROAD SWITCHER REVIEW "HO" AT             04 75  26
SD35 EMD REVIEW  "HO"  PCO                        05 81  38
SD35 EMD ROAD DIESEL REVIEW "HO" AT 1964          05 75  24
SD38-2 EMD REVIEW "HO" ALCO 1978                  09 82  31
SD40 EMD 1966 REVIEW "HO" AHM                     03 80  33
SD40 EMD ROAD SWITCHER REV "O" LIO 1966           02 83  50
SD40-2 EMD REVIEW "HO" ATH  1972                  04 83  35
SD40-2 EMD REVIEW "N"  H  1972                    01 83  41
SD40-2 EMD REVIEW "N" CC 1972                     08 84  44
SD40-2 EMD ROAD DIESEL REVIEW "HO" GSB            05 83  35
SD40T-2 EMD D&RGW REVIEW "N" KEY  1974            01 84  62
SD40T-2 EMD SP REVIEW "N" KEY EMD 1974            01 84  62
SD45  DIESEL REVIEW "HO"  ATH                     05 66  13
SD45 EMD REVIEW "N"  CC 1966                      04 72  21
SD45 REPOWERED DIESEL REVIEW "HO" H 1979          04 84  38
SD9  ROAD SWITCHER REVIEW "HO" PFM                03 56  13
SDP40F EMD A REVIEW "HO" G  1973                  10 74  18D
SIX WHEEL DIESEL DRIVE REVIEW "HO" CMP            01 50  88
SPUD POWER TRUCKS FROM PFM                        06 81  67
SW 1500 EMD SWITCHER REVIEW "HO" ALCO             01 72  25
SW1 EMD YARD SWITCHER REVIEW "HO" AHM             11 76  46
SW1500 EMD COW & CALF REVIEW "N" AT               05 71  24
SW1500 EMD SWITCHER BODY REV "HO" CLW             11 80  54
SW7 EMD SWITCHER REVIEW "HO" CC                   04 84  45
TOKAIDO EXPRESS REVIEW "HO"    TI                 04 67  14
TR6 EMD COW & CALF REVIEW "HO" TI                 01 67  10
TRACK CLEANING BOXCAB REVIEW "HO" IH              04 81  49
U25B EMD REVIEW "HO"  OL   1960                   11 81  45
U25C GE REVIEW "HO"   AHM                         06 66  10
U28C GE REVIEW "N" TRIX                           08 70  10
U30B EMD REVIEW "HO" ATH   1972                   03 72  28
U36B SCL #1776 REVIEW "HO" ATH 1970 EMD           01 73  25
U50 GE ROAD SWITCHER REVIEW "N" CC 1963           01 74  22
ZEPHYR 9900 CB&Q REV "HO" NPP BUDD 1934           10 72  28
```

LOCOMOTIVES

DIESEL LOCO MODEL REVIEWS BY MFG.

MFG		M Y P
AHM	35 TON DIESEL LISTING "HO/ON3/S" AHM	05 78 52
	BL-2 EMD REVIEW "HO" AHM 1949	01 64 10
	E8 EMD PASSENGER LOCO REVIEW "HO" AHM	08 74 19
	FM C-LINER REVIEW "HO" AHM 1950	04 63 10
	FM POWER UNIT REVIEW "O" AHM	11 73 31
	FP45 AMTRACK LISTING "HO" AHM	11 77 54
	FT EMD DIESEL REVIEW "HO" AHM 1942	02 75 29
	KM DIESEL HYDROLIC REVIEW "HO" AHM	11 64 7
	M-10000 STREAMLINE TRAIN UP REV HO AHM	02 79 42
	RS2 ALCO REVIEW "HO" AHM	09 69 11
	S2 ALCO LISTING "HO" AHM	06 78 52
	SD40 EMD 1966 REVIEW "HO" AHM	03 80 33
	SW1 EMD YARD SWITCHER REVIEW "HO" AHM	11 76 46
	U25C GE REVIEW "HO" AHM	06 66 10
ALCO	C430 ALCO ROAD SWITCHER REVIEW "HO" ALCO	04 74 19
	DL-640 ALCO REVIEW "HO" ALCO 1960	12 67 14
	DL702 ALCO REVIEW "HO" 1956 ALCO	06 74 20
	MP15AC EMD SWITCHER REVIEW "HO" ALCO	02 82 27
	RS1 ALCO SWITCHER REVIEW "HO" ALCO	05 68 15
	SD38-2 EMD REVIEW "HO" ALCO 1978	09 82 31
	SW 1500 EMD SWITCHER REVIEW "HO" ALCO	01 72 25
AMI	FP7 EMD ROAD DIESEL REVIEW "S" AMI 1949	12 82 60
AN	F7 DIESEL REVIEW "O" AN	08 54 9
	F7 EMD REVIEW "O" AN	12 69 18
AT	E7 DIESEL LISTING "N" ATLAS	06 77 48
	E8 EMD PASSENGER REVIEW "N" AT	02 68 13
	F9 EMD REVIEW "1/4" AT	07 72 18
	FA-1 ALCO REVIEW "N" AT	05 78 36
	GP30 EMD REVIEW "N" AT 1961	05 75 30
	GP38 LISTING "HO" ATLAS	03 77 44
	GP9 EMD DIESEL REVIEW "N" AT 1954	02 75 27
	INDUSTRIAL DIESEL LISTING "N" ATLAS	12 77 62
	PLYMOUTH WDT REVIEW "N" AT	04 73 29
	PLYMOUTH WDT REVIEW "O" AT	04 73 30
	RS3 ALCO REVIEW "HO" AT 1950	01 85 47
	RS3 1600HP ALCO REVIEW "N" AT 1950	01 84 58
	SD24 EMD ROAD SWITCHER REVIEW "HO" AT	04 75 26
	SD35 EMD ROAD DIESEL REVIEW "HO" AT 1964	05 75 24
	SW1500 EMD COW & CALF REVIEW "N" AT	05 71 24
ATH	F7 HIFI DRIVE REVIEW "HO" ATH	12 56 12
	FP45 & F45 EMD DIESEL REVIEW "HO" ATH	03 74 20
	GP9 GEAR OR HIFI DRIVE REVIEW "HO" ATH	05 57 11
	GP9 EMD ROAD SWITCHER REVIEW HO ATH 1949	05 84 29
	H-24-66 FM TRAINMASTER REV "HO" ATH 1953	10 79 43
	PA-1 ALCO REVIEW "HO" ATH 1949	10 70 14
	S12 BALDWIN SWITCHER REV "HO" ATH 1951	07 74 16
	SD40-2 EMD REVIEW "HO" ATH 1972	04 83 35
	SD45 DIESEL REVIEW "HO" ATH	05 66 13
	U30B EMD REVIEW "HO" ATH 1972	03 72 28
	U36B SCL #1776 REVIEW "HO" ATH 1970 EMD	01 73 25
ATT	C415 ALCO REVIEW "HO" ATT 1960 ALCO	08 69 6

DIESEL LOCO MODEL REVIEWS BY MFG.

MFG		M Y P
B	DD40AX EMD UP REVIEW "N" B 1969	08 84 37
	DDA40X EMD UP CENTENNIAL REV "HO" B 1969	11 82 42
	GP40 EMD LOCOMOTIVE REVIEW "HO" B 1965	05 71 17
	GP40 EMD REVIEW "N" B 1965	09 69 14
BAU	F9 TRACK CLEANING DIESEL REV "HO" BAU	12 60 18
BN	DIESEL SWITCHER REVIEW "HO" BN	12 48 991
CA	ALCO 2000 HP A&B REVIEW "HO" CA	01 48 67
CC	2000 HP ALCO PASSENGER REVIEW "N" CC	03 68 14
	DL109 ALCO REVIEW "N" CC 1942	06 82 40
	E8 PASSENGER DIESEL REVIEW "N" CC	01 85 58
	F3 EMD A&B REVIEW "N" CC	06 80 43
	F3 EMD REVIEW "N" CC 1945	04 75 28
	PA-1 ALCO DIESEL REVIEW "HO" CC	03 70 15
	SD40-2 EMD REVIEW "N" CC 1972	08 84 44
	SD45 EMD REVIEW "N" CC 1966	04 72 21
	SW7 EMD SWITCHER REVIEW "HO" CC	04 84 45
	U50 GE ROAD SWITCHER REVIEW "N" CC 1963	01 74 22
CLW	E6 BODY CASTING REVIEW "HO" CLW	08 71 20
	S2/S4 ALCO SWITCHER BODY REV "HO" CLW	11 82 38
	SW1500 EMD SWITCHER BODY REV "HO" CLW	11 80 54
CLWO	2000 HP ALCO REVIEW "O" CLWO	02 64 6
	FA-1 ALCO REVIEW "O" CLWO 1946	11 73 36
CMP	EMC LOCOMOTIVE KIT REVIEW "HO" CMP	03 48 222
	SIX WHEEL DIESEL DRIVE REVIEW "HO" CMP	01 50 88
DMC	DIESEL ELECTRIC REVIEW "HO" DMC	11 45 504
DW	DIESEL DETAIL LISTING "HO" DETAILS WEST	09 77 45
FR	GP30 DIESEL REVIEW "HO" FR	06 84 44
G	GP40 3000 HP REVIEW "HO" G 1965	12 72 31
	INDUSTRIAL SWITCHER REVIEW "HO" G	01 61 14
	SDP40F EMD A REVIEW "HO" G 1973	10 74 18D
GL	25 TON BOX CAB REVIEW GE "HON3" GL	11 78 46
GLO	F7 DUMMY REVIEW "HO" GLOBE MODELS	10 54 12
GSB	SD40-2 EMD ROAD DIESEL REVIEW "HO" GSB	05 83 35
H	AS616 ROAD SWITCHER REVIEW "HO" H 1950 B	10 75 33
	BOXCAB EMD ATSF #1 REVIEW "HO" H 1935	06 82 31
	CF7 ATSF REVIEW "HO" H	05 81 42
	DL109 ALCO A&B REVIEW "HO" HALLMARK 1940	07 71 20
	FT EMD OF 1939 REVIEW "HO" H	02 69 10
	GP50 EMD REVIEW "HO" H	01 83 48
	GP7 EMD 1500 HP REVIEW "HO" H 1953 EMD	09 68 12
	RS1 ALCO ROAD SWITCHER REVIEW N H 1941	09 83 33
	SD40-2 EMD REVIEW "N" H 1972	01 83 41
	SD45 REPOWERED DIESEL REVIEW "HO" H 1979	04 84 38
HD	H-16-44 FM BABY TRAINMASTER REV "HO" HD	10 69 15
	H-24-66 FM TRAINMASTER REVIEW "HO" HD	12 69 26
HG	BALDWIN-WESTINGHOUSE 1000 HP REV "HO" HG	10 47 861
HI	ALCO PASSENGER BODY REV "HO" HOBBIES INC	11 49 95

56

LOCOMOTIVES

DIESEL LOCO MODEL REVIEWS BY MFG.

MFG		M Y P
HOB	1600 HP ALCO ROAD SWITCHER REV "HO" HOB	08 57 15
	2000 HP ALCO REVIEW "HO" HOB	05 53 53
	ALCO ROAD SWITCHER REVIEW "HO" HOB	01 54 20
	DIESEL POWER CHASSIS REVIEW "HO" HOB	12 64 10
	E7 LOCOMOTIVE REVIEW "HO" HOB	01 51 58
	E7 POWER UNIT REVIEW "HO" HOB	07 65 8
	EMC A&B LOCOMOTIVE REVIEW "HO" HOB	06 48 437
	F7 CHASSIS REVIEW "HO" HOBBYTOWN BOSTON	03 55 14
	GP30 POWER CHASSIS REVIEW "HO" HOB	02 64 14
	GP9 & F7 POWER CHASSIS REVIEW "HO" HOB	01 58 10
IH	TRACK CLEANING BOXCAB REVIEW "HO" IH	04 81 49
JE	H-12-44 FM DIESEL REVIEW "HO" JE	03 53 63
JMC	GE EXPORT DIESEL REVIEW "N" JMC	05 79 42
JSM	DIESEL PILOT LISTING "HO" JSM	09 77 45
KD	F7 REVIEW "Z" KD	02 85 39
KEM	ALCO-GE 1600 REVIEW "O" KEM	09 54 10
	GP20 EMD ROAD SWITCHER REVIEW "O" KEM	07 76 34
	GP7 ROAD SWITCHER REVIEW "O" KEM	12 54 22
KEY	DD40AX EMD UP ROAD DIESEL "HO" KEY 1969	05 84 32
	S1,S2,S3,S4 ALCO SWITCHER REVIEW "N" KEY	03 84 33
	SD40T-2 EMD D&RGW REVIEW "N" KEY 1974	01 84 62
	SD40T-2 EMD SP REVIEW "N" KEY EMD 1974	01 84 62
KLW	44 TON GE SWITCHER REVIEW "HO" KLW 1937	06 81 27
KUM	RS3 ALCO RAOD SWITCHER REV "HO" KUM 1950	11 84 54D
KWR	4 WHEEL SWITCHER KIT REVIEW "O" KWR	01 50 77
LIN	ALCO-GE DIESEL REVIEW "HO" LIN	06 51 50
	EMD SWITCHER REVIEW "HO" LIN	11 49 93
LIO	FA1 ALCO REVIEW "HO" LIO 1946	08 75 24
	GP7 EMD REVIEW "HO" LIO	09 75 30
	SD40 EMD ROAD SWITCHER REV "O" LIO 1966	02 83 50
LL	C628 ALCO REVIEW "HO" LIFELIKE 1963	08 73 16
	F40PH EMD REVIEW "HO" LIFELIKE	12 78 48
	F7 EMD ROAD DIESEL REVIEW "HO" LL	07 77 38
	GP38-2 EMD LISTING "HO" LIFELIKE	12 78 69
LLA	GP-7 LOCOMOTIVE REVIEW "HO" LLA	01 51 60
LPD	GP40 EMD REVIEW CN "HO" LPD	11 78 52
M	C430 ALCO CENTURY REVIEW "HO" M 1967	02 67 10
	F7 EMD DIESEL REVIEW "HO" M	10 82 45
	F9 TWIN POWERED REVIEW "HO" M	07 60 13
	PLYMOUTH SWITCHER REVIEW "HO" M	03 62 20
	RF16 "SHARK NOSE" DIESEL REVIEW "HO" M	11 53 14
MAGN	S1 SP ALCO REVIEW "G" MAGN	02 84 39
MDC	60 TON BOXCAB REVIEW "HO" MDC 1927 ALCO	06 72 19
MER	FA2 ALCO REVIEW "HO" MER 1950	01 72 26
MEW	44 TON SWITCHER REVIEW "HO" MEW	02 57 11
MKL	F7 EMD DIESEL REVIEW "Z" MKL 1947	03 85 35
	GERMAN DIESEL REVIEW "1/32" MKL	08 82 35
MP	C420 ALCO CENTURY REVIEW "N" MP	02 77 34

DIESEL LOCO MODEL REVIEWS BY MFG.

MFG		M Y P
	DR-4-4-15 SHARKNOSE REV "HO" MP 1949 B	08 72 22
	F40PH EMD REVIEW "N" MP	02 82 31
	RF16 BALDWIN SHARKNOSE CAB REV "HO" MP	12 76 30
	RS-11 ALCO LISTING "HO" MODEL POWER	12 78 65
	RS11 ALCO ROAD SWITCHER REVIEW "HO" MP	03 77 34
MRC	C420 ALCO REVIEW "N" MRC 1963	08 70 13
	FA-2 ALCO REVIEW "N" MRC 1950	01 70 16
	RSD-15 ALCO REVIEW "N" MRC 1956	08 70 15
MTX	F9 EMD REVIEW "N" MTX	01 69 10
	H-12-44 FM SWITCHER REVIEW "N" MTX 1950	09 74 24
NJI	RS1 ALCO REVIEW "O" NJI 1941	03 81 54
NPP	M-10000 STREAMLIN TRAIN UP REV HO NPP	02 79 42
	ZEPHYR 9900 CB&Q REV "HO" NPP BUDD 1934	10 72 28
NWSL	HUSTLER REPOWER UNIT REVIEW "HO" NWSL	08 84 45
OE	F7 DUAL DRIVE REVIEW "HO" OE	10 60 14
OL	RS3 ALCO REVIEW "N" OL 1950	12 84 52
	U25B EMD REVIEW "HO" OL 1960	11 81 45
PAM	FM 1600 HP ROAD SWITCHER REV "HO" PAM	01 57 10
PCO	C430 CENTURY ALCO REVIEW "HO" PCO	05 81 38
	SD35 EMD REVIEW "HO" PCO	05 81 38
PFM	DIESEL-MECHANICAL D&RGW REVIEW "ON3" PFM	03 72 28
	GP9 REVIEW "HO" PFM	08 56 12
	GP9 ROAD SWITCHER REVIEW "HO" PFM	03 56 13
	SD9 ROAD SWITCHER REVIEW "HO" PFM	03 56 13
	SPUD POWER TRUCKS FROM PFM	06 81 67
PL	INDUSTRIAL SWITCHER KIT REVIEW "HO" PL	09 49 54
PMO	BALDWIN JEEP REVIEW "HO" PMO	07 49 52
PPW	DIESEL CONVERSIONS REVIEW "HO" PPW	08 79 48
	DIESEL REPOWER UNIT REVIEW "HO" PPW	03 85 52
	GP9 DIESEL DRIVE REVIEW "HO" PPW	06 84 41
PS	DL535E WP&Y ROAD SWITCHER REV "HON3" PS	03 79 52
PSM	C415 ALCO REVIEW "HO" PSM	11 69 12
RAP	FA-2 ALCO REVIEW "N" RAP 1950	11 69 20
	FP9 EMD REVIEW "N" RAP	11 67 12
	GP30 EMD REVIEW "N" RAP 1963	02 69 10
	GP9 EMD REVIEW "N" RAP 1954	09 69 18
RIV	CFA-20-4 FM REVIEW "O" RIV 1950	06 70 21
	E8 PASSENGER REVIEW "HO" RIV	01 67 14
	FM B UNIT REVIEW "HO" RIV	03 65 9
STEW	RS3 ALCO REVIEW "HO" STEW 1950	05 85 38
SUN	70 TON DIESEL ELCTRIC REVIEW "O" SUN GE	09 81 36
T	GP20 EMD REVIEW "HO" T 1960	04 62 12
TI	E9 A&B EMD UNITS REVIEW "HO" TI	04 68 14
	TOKAIDO EXPRESS REVIEW "HO" TI	04 67 14
	TR6 EMD COW & CALF REVIEW "HO" TI	01 67 10

LOCOMOTIVES

DIESEL LOCO MODEL REVIEWS BY MFG.

MFG		M	Y	P
TMI	FA1 ALCO ROAD DIESEL REVIEW "HO" TMI	02	83	39
TOM	ALCO 1500 HP REVIEW "TT" TOMALCO	08	65	8
TRIX	U28C GE REVIEW "N" TRIX	08	70	10
TVM	C420 ALCO SWITCHER REVIEW "HO" TVM	05	82	31
V	AEROTRAIN POWER UNIT REVIEW "HO" VARNEY	07	56	10
	DIESEL KIT REVIEW "HO" V	03	48	225
W&T	PLANETARY CLUTCH REVIEW "HO" W&T MODELS	12	57	12
WAL	DIESEL SWITCHER WOOD REVIEW "O" WAL	09	42	440
	EMC DIESEL KIT REVIEW "HO" WAL	01	49	95
	EMC PASSENGER DIESEL KIT REVIEW "O" WAL	05	48	372
	F3A & F3B DIESEL REVIEW "O" WAL	07	47	597
	FM 2000 HP SWITCHER KIT REVIEW "O" WAL	04	49	73
WM	ALCO 1000 HP SWITCHER KIT REVIEW "HO" WM	04	48	303
WPM	FREIGHT DIESEL KIT REVIEW "O" WPM	05	48	370
WSM	CATERPILLAR INDUST SWITCHER REV "HO" WSM	12	71	34

ELECTRIC LOCOMOTIVE PROTOTYPE DATA

	M	Y	P
62 TON GE STEEPLE CAB SN # 650 1923	09	77	64
63 TON BOXCAB ELECTRICS P&N 1914 GE	02	82	82
CLASS C ELECTRICS OF IT	08	45	325
DD-1 PRR CLASS ELECTRICAL LOCOMOTIVES	03	71	48
ELECTRIC INDUSTRIAL RAILROAD IDEAS	01	50	48
ELECTRIC LOCOMOTIVE CLASSIFICATION	04	36	95
FOUR TRUCK FREIGHT ELECTRICS P&N 1917	04	84	82
FRICK STANDARD ELECTRIC COKE LARRY	06	81	107
GE 25 TON STEEPLE CAB LOCOMOTIVE	02	77	72
IN THE CAB ON AN ELECTRIC LOCO	03	35	71
LITTLE JOE 2-D+D-2 CSS&SB #801	08	56	34
PENNSY'S NEW O-1 & P-5 ELECTRIC LOCOS	01	34	5
PENNSYLVANIA ELECTRIC EQUIP GGA MP54-E	10	35	265
SOUTH SHORES INHERITED NYC BOXCARS	08	71	44

DIESEL LOCOMOTIVE MODEL REVIEWS BY ROAD

RD		M	Y	P
A	FP45 AMTRACK LISTING "HO" AHM	11	77	54
	SDP40F EMD A REVIEW "HO" G 1973	10	74	18D
ATSF	BOXCAB EMD ATSF #1 REVIEW "HO" H 1935	06	82	31
	CF7 ATSF REVIEW "HO" H	05	81	42
CB&Q	ZEPHYR 9900 CB&Q REV "HO" NPP BUDD 1934	10	72	28
CN	GP40 EMD REVIEW CN "HO" LPD	11	78	52
D&RGW	DIESEL-MECHANICAL D&RGW REVIEW "ON3" PFM	03	72	28
	SD40T-2 EMD D&RGW REVIEW "N" KEY 1974	01	84	62
SCL	U36B SCL #1776 REVIEW "HO" ATH 1970 EMD	01	73	25
SP	S1 SP ALCO REVIEW "G" MAGN	02	84	39
	SD40T-2 EMD SP REVIEW "N" KEY EMD 1974	01	84	62
UP	DD40AX EMD UP REVIEW "N" B 1969	08	84	37
	DD40AX EMD UP ROAD DIESEL "HO" KEY 1969	05	84	32
	DDA40X EMD UP CENTENNIAL REV "HO" B 1969	11	82	42
	M-10000 STREAMLIN TRAIN UP REV HO NPP	02	79	42
	M-10000 STREAMLINE TRAIN UP REV HO AHM	02	79	42
WP&Y	DL535E WP&Y ROAD SWITCHER REV "HON3" PS	03	79	52

ELEC LOCO PROTOTYPE DATA BY ROAD

RD		M	Y	P
CSS&SB	SOUTH SHORES INHERITED NYC BOXCARS	08	71	44
	LITTLE JOE 2-D+D-2 CSS&SB #801	08	56	34
IT	CLASS C ELECTRICS OF IT	08	45	325
P&N	FOUR TRUCK FREIGHT ELECTRICS P&N 1917	04	84	82
	63 TON BOXCAB ELECTRICS P&N 1914 GE	02	82	82
PRR	PENNSY'S NEW O-1 & P-5 ELECTRIC LOCOS	01	34	5
SN	62 TON GE STEEPLE CAB SN # 650 1923	09	77	64

LOCOMOTIVES

ELECTRIC LOCOMOTIVE PLANS

	M	Y	P
"ELECTRA" UNIT PLANS PE #1544 1902	08	58	57
2-4-2 CLASS A-1 FREELANCE STEEPLE CAB PL	05	34	6
40 TON STEEPLE CAB GE LOCOMOTIVE PLANS	01	60	58
62 TON GE STEEPLE CAB PLAN SN #650	09	77	66
63 TON BOXCAB PLANS P&N #5100 1914 GE	02	82	83
85 TON CSS&SB #1013 PLANS	03	38	107
85 TON STEEPLECAB PLANS CSS&B #1012 1929	04	74	48
ALCO-GE UNIT PLAN FOR BA&P #65	09	46	560
B CLASS LOCO PLANS IT #1569 1919	12	57	60
BALDWIN CLASS B-1 STEEPLECAB PLANS ST#15	12	62	42
BALDWIN-WESTINGHOUSE CLASS D LOCO PLAN	02	46	108
BOXCAB PLANS CSS&SB #706 1930 GE	08	71	44
C CLASS ELECTRIC LOCO PLANS IT	08	45	324
C CLASS LOCO ILLINOIS TERMINAL #1595 PLN	04	60	62
C CLASS LOCO PLANS IT #1596 1924 IT	05	65	46
DD-1 CLASS DRAWINGS PRR #3980	03	71	48
E-2B CLASS PLANS PRR #4941	10	68	46
EA-1 CLASS NYNH&H #0200 SWITCHER PLANS	12	34	12
ELECTRIC 2-6-6-2 LOCOMOTIVE PLANS GN	09	36	250
ELECTRIC LOCO #753 THI&E PLANS	03	48	172
FL-9 THIRD RAIL DIESEL-ELECTRIC NH PLAN	08	61	34
FOUR TRUCK FREIGHT ELECTRIC PLN P&N#5610	04	84	82
FREE LANCE SWITCH MOTOR PLANS	10	66	57
FREE LANCED BOXCAB PLANS	09	79	81
FREIGHT MOTOR PLANS S&IE #M1	05	59	48
FRICK STANDARD ELECTRIC COKE LARRY PLANS	06	81	107
GE 25 TON STEEPLE CAB LOCOMOTIVE PLANS	02	77	73
GG-1 CLASS ELECTRIC LOCO PLANS PRR #4801	10	35	266
GG-1 CLASS PLANS PRR #4929 1933	09	54	38
INDUSTRIAL LOCOMOTIVE PLANS IL&S #3	01	50	48
LITTLE JOE 2-D+D-2 PLAN MILW #E-70	08	56	34
O-1 CLASS ELECTRIC LOCO PRR PLANS	01	34	7
O-1A CLASS PLANS PRR #7850 1930	05	54	38
OIL ELECTRIC LOCOMOTIVE PLANS CN #7700	08	74	44
P-5 CLASS ELECTRIC LOCO PRR PLANS	01	34	7
P-5A CLASS PLANS PRR #4760 1930	05	54	38
PANTOGRAPH PLANS	02	70	81
S-1 CLASS PLANS NYC&H #6000	02	49	26
STEEPLECAB 45 TON PLANS KCKV&W #503	08	60	52
SWITCHING LOCO CLASS 0440 E209-A PLANS	01	43	33
T-3A CLASS BOXCAB PLANS NYC #1173	12	39	646
T-3A CLASS UNIT PLANS NYC #1173 1913	10	72	47
THREE TRUCK ELECTRIC SWITCHER PLAN	03	35	70
TROLLEY-BATTERY LOCO PLANS CNS&M #456	01	47	11

ELECTRIC LOCOMOTIVE PLANS BY ROAD

RD		M	Y	P
BA&P	ALCO-GE UNIT PLAN FOR BA&P #65	09	46	560
CN	OIL ELECTRIC LOCOMOTIVE PLANS CN #7700	08	74	44
CNS&M	TROLLEY-BATTERY LOCO PLANS CNS&M #456	01	47	11
CSS&SB	BOXCAB PLANS CSS&SB #706 1930 GE	08	71	44
	85 TON STEEPLECAB PLANS CSS&B #1012 1929	04	74	48
	85 TON CSS&SB #1013 PLANS	03	38	107
GN	ELECTRIC 2-6-6-2 LOCOMOTIVE PLANS GN	09	36	250
IL&S	INDUSTRIAL LOCOMOTIVE PLANS IL&S #3	01	50	48
IT	B CLASS LOCO PLANS IT #1569 1919	12	57	60
	C CLASS LOCO PLANS IT #1596 1924 IT	05	65	46
	C CLASS LOCO ILLINOIS TERMINAL #1595 PLN	04	60	62
	C CLASS ELECTRIC LOCO PLANS IT	08	45	324
KCKV&W	STEEPLECAB 45 TON PLANS KCKV&W #503	08	60	52
MILW	LITTLE JOE 2-D+D-2 PLAN MILW #E-70	08	56	34
NH	FL-9 THIRD RAIL DIESEL-ELECTRIC NH PLAN	08	61	34
NYC	T-3A CLASS UNIT PLANS NYC #1173 1913	10	72	47
	T-3A CLASS BOXCAB PLANS NYC #1173	12	39	646
NYC&H	S-1 CLASS PLANS NYC&H #6000	02	49	26
NYNH&H	EA-1 CLASS NYNH&H #0200 SWITCHER PLANS	12	34	12
P&N	FOUR TRUCK FREIGHT ELECTRIC PLN P&N#5610	04	84	82
	63 TON BOXCAB PLANS P&N #5100 1914 GE	02	82	83
PE	"ELECTRA" UNIT PLANS PE #1544 1902	08	58	57
PRR	E-2B CLASS PLANS PRR #4941	10	68	46
	DD-1 CLASS DRAWINGS PRR #3980	03	71	48
	GG-1 CLASS PLANS PRR #4929 1933	09	54	38
	O-1A CLASS PLANS PRR #7850 1930	05	54	38
	P-5A CLASS PLANS PRR #4760 1930	05	54	38
	GG-1 CLASS ELECTRIC LOCO PLANS PRR #4801	10	35	266
	O-1 CLASS ELECTRIC LOCO PRR PLANS	01	34	7
	P-5 CLASS ELECTRIC LOCO PRR PLANS	01	34	7
S&IE	FREIGHT MOTOR PLANS S&IE #M1	05	59	48
SN	62 TON GE STEEPLE CAB PLAN SN #650	09	77	66
ST	BALDWIN CLASS B-1 STEEPLECAB PLANS ST#15	12	62	42
THI&E	ELECTRIC LOCO #753 THI&E PLANS	03	48	172

ELECTRIC LOCOMOTIVE PHOTOS

	M	Y	P
85 TON ELECTRIC LOCO PHOTO CSS&SB #1013	03	38	106
85 TON STEEPLECAB PHOTO ESSAY CSS&SB	04	74	47
P-5 ELECTRIC #4760 PRR PHOTO	01	34	6
SWITCHING LOCO CLASS 0440 E209-A PHOTO	01	43	33

LOCOMOTIVES

ELECTRIC LOCOMOTIVE MODELS

```
                                            M  Y   P
-----------------------------------------  -- --  ----
82 TON BOX CAB ELECTRIC LOCO CONST         05 76   59
BOXCAB ELECTRIC CONSTRUCTION               09 79   82
ELECTRIC SWITCHING LOCO CONSTRUCTION       05 34    7
FL-9 THIRD RAIL DIESEL-ELECTRIC CONST NH   08 61   37
HEAVY ELECTRIC LOCOS FROM DIESEL BODIES    11 57   48
HEAVY ELECTRIC NORTH SHORE #459 MOD & PT   08 82  106
MOM 4-6-6-4 NYC HEAVY ELECT LOCOS "O"      08 51   34
MOM BI POLAR ELECT MILW E1 "HO"RADEBAUGH   11 52   16
MOM ELECTRIC 2-6-6-2 LOCO GN "O" WALKER    09 36  250
MOM ELECTRIC LOCOMOTIVE EF4 LITTLE JOE O   03 77   49
MOM IT CLASS B LOCOMOTIVE "HO"   BRONSKY   08 81   66
MOM UP ELECTRIC E-100 "1/48"         MIX   02 73   42
PANTOGRAPH CONSTRUCTION.                   06 44  248
PANTOGRAPHS MADE BY JIGS                   05 69   43
POWERING A STEEPLE-CAB ELEC LOCOMOTIVE     01 42    8
STEEPLE-CAB SWITCH MOTOR CONSTRUCTION      10 66   56
T-3A CLASS BOXCAB CONSTRUCTION NYC #1173   12 39  642
THIRD RAIL SHOE CONSTRUCTION               04 45  161
THREE POWER CLASS DES-3 NYC #1528 CONST    11 37  417
```

ELECTRIC LOCOMOTIVE MODEL REVIEWS

```
                                            M  Y   P
-----------------------------------------  -- --  ----
2-C & C-2 CUT REVIEW MEW                   11 68   11
2-D+D-2 MILW LITTLE JOE REV "HO" NWSL GE   06 73   25
49T BOXCAB REVIEW "HO" MMP  BW             02 74   32
40 TON STEEPLE CAB REV "HO" MEW 1915 GE    06 60   14
B-1 ELECTRIC LOCOMOTIVE REVIEW "HO" CAPL   03 48  227
BOX CAB BA&P REVIEW "HO"  S                02 58   10
BOXCAB FREIGHT MOTOR S&IE REV "HO" KK      08 61   11
BOXCAB GN CLASS Z-1 REV "HO"  S 1928 BW    03 60   12
BRILL GAS ELECTRIC ATSF REVIEW HO 1931 H   11 76   36
C+C CUT LOCOMOTIVE REVIEW "HO" NPP ALCO    05 74   18
DD-1 PRR BOXCAB REVIEW "HO" ALCO           04 71   22
E60C GE LOCOMOTIVE REVIEW "HO" WAL 1972    07 85   31
E60CP LOCOMOTIVE A REVIEW "HO" AGK         04 77   38
ELECTRIC LOCOMOTIVE REVIEW "HO" MFI        09 71   21
ELECTRIC LOCOMOTIVE REVIEW "N" KD          04 85   47
ELECTRIC LOCOMOTIVE REVIEW "O"   IMC       11 39  610
GAS-ELECTRIC ATSF M-190 REVIEW "O" MG      08 60   10
GG1 LIONEL REPRODUCTION REVIEW "O" WRL     07 82   29
GG1 PRR REVIEW "HO"  AHM  1937             05 70   19
GG1 PRR REVIEW "HO" PENN LINE              04 57   11
GG1 PRR REVIEW "N"  RAP  1935              12 71   38
GG1 SPECIAL RELEASE LISTING "HO"    AHM    08 78   48
GG1 TWIN MOTOR REVIEW "HO"  GEORGE STOCK   06 37  228
HEAVY ELECTRIC CNS&M REV "HO" MCW  1948    03 82   46
INDUSTRIAL SWITCHER REVIEW "HO"  G         01 61   14
MINE LOCO & DUMP CAR REVIEW "HO" RHM       10 62   16
MINE LOCOMOTIVE REVIEW "ON3"   GL          04 78   42
NEW HAVEN ELECTRIC REVIEW  "O"   PST       01 40   54
NYC CLASS S 1-D-1 LOCO REVIEW "HO" KAW     02 66   10
NYC CLASS T1 ELECTRIC REV "HO" MEW 1913    04 61   12
NYC OIL-ELECTRIC REVIEW "HO" CB  1928      06 72   20
NYNH&H CLASS EF-1 REVIEW "HO"  MEW 1912    11 66   12
SOUTH SHORE ELECTRIC REVIEW "HO" KK        11 65   12
STEEPLE CAB LOCOMOTIVE REVIEW "HO" KK      10 57   12
STEEPLE CAB REVIEW "O"  NWSL  1920  BW     09 80   48
```

LOCOMOTIVES

ELEC LOCO MODEL REVIEWS BY MFG.

MFG		M Y P
AGK	E60CP LOCOMOTIVE A REVIEW "HO" AGK	04 77 38
AHM	GG1 PRR REVIEW "HO" AHM 1937	05 70 19
	GG1 SPECIAL RELEASE LISTING "HO" AHM	08 78 48
ALCO	DD-1 PRR BOXCAB REVIEW "HO" ALCO	04 71 22
CAPL	B-1 ELECTRIC LOCOMOTIVE REVIEW "HO" CAPL	03 48 227
CB	NYC OIL-ELECTRIC REVIEW "HO" CB 1928	06 72 20
G	INDUSTRIAL SWITCHER REVIEW "HO" G	01 61 14
GL	MINE LOCOMOTIVE REVIEW "ON3" GL	04 78 42
H	BRILL GAS ELECTRIC ATSF REVIEW HO 1931 H	11 76 36
IMC	ELECTRIC LOCOMOTIVE REVIEW "O" IMC	11 39 610
KAW	NYC CLASS S 1-D-1 LOCO REVIEW "HO" KAW	02 66 10
KD	ELECTRIC LOCOMOTIVE REVIEW "N" KD	04 85 47
KK	BOXCAB FREIGHT MOTOR S&IE REV "HO" KK	08 61 11
	SOUTH SHORE ELECTRIC REVIEW "HO" KK	11 65 12
	STEEPLE CAB LOCOMOTIVE REVIEW "HO" KK	10 57 12
MCW	HEAVY ELECTRIC CNS&M REV "HO" MCW 1948	03 82 46
MEW	2-C & C-2 CUT REVIEW MEW	11 68 11
	40 TON STEEPLE CAB REV "HO" MEW 1915 GE	06 60 14
	NYC CLASS T1 ELECTRIC REV "HO" MEW 1913	04 61 12
	NYNH&H CLASS EF-1 REVIEW "HO" MEW 1912	11 66 12
MFI	ELECTRIC LOCOMOTIVE REVIEW "HO" MFI	09 71 21
MG	GAS-ELECTRIC ATSF M-190 REVIEW "O" MG	08 60 10
MMP	49T BOXCAB REVIEW "HO" MMP BW	02 74 32
NPP	C+C CUT LOCOMOTIVE REVIEW "HO" NPP ALCO	05 74 18
NWSL	2-D+D-2 MILW LITTLE JOE REV "HO" NWSL GE	06 73 25
	STEEPLE CAB REVIEW "O" NWSL 1920 BW	09 80 48
PL	GG1 PRR REVIEW "HO" PENN LINE	04 57 11
PST	NEW HAVEN ELECTRIC REVIEW "O" PST	01 40 54
RAP	GG1 PRR REVIEW "N" RAP 1935	12 71 38
RHM	MINE LOCO & DUMP CAR REVIEW "HO" RHM	10 62 16
S	BOX CAB BA&P REVIEW "HO" S	02 58 10
	BOXCAB GN CLASS Z-1 REV "HO" S 1928 BW	03 60 12
WAL	E60C GE LOCOMOTIVE REVIEW "HO" WAL 1972	07 85 31
WRL	GG1 LIONEL REPRODUCTION REVIEW "O" WRL	07 82 29

ELEC LOCOMOTIVE MODEL REVIEWS BY ROAD

RD		M Y P
ATSF	BRILL GAS ELECTRIC ATSF REVIEW HO 1931 H	11 76 36
	GAS-ELECTRIC ATSF M-190 REVIEW "O" MG	08 60 10
BA&P	BOX CAB BA&P REVIEW "HO" S	02 58 10
CNS&M	HEAVY ELECTRIC CNS&M REV "HO" MCW 1948	03 82 46
CSS&SB	SOUTH SHORE ELECTRIC REVIEW "HO" KK	11 65 12
CUT	2-C & C-2 CUT REVIEW MEW	11 68 11
	C+C CUT LOCOMOTIVE REVIEW "HO" NPP ALCO	05 74 18
GN	BOXCAB GN CLASS Z-1 REV "HO" S 1928 BW	03 60 12
MILW	2-D+D-2 MILW LITTLE JOE REV "HO" NWSL GE	06 73 25
NH	NEW HAVEN ELECTRIC REVIEW "O" PST	01 40 54
NYC	NYC CLASS S 1-D-1 LOCO REVIEW "HO" KAW	02 66 10
	NYC CLASS T1 ELECTRIC REV "HO" MEW 1913	04 61 12
	NYC OIL-ELECTRIC REVIEW "HO" CB 1928	06 72 20
NYNH&H	NYNH&H CLASS EF-1 REVIEW "HO" MEW 1912	11 66 12
PRR	B-1 ELECTRIC LOCOMOTIVE REVIEW "HO" CAPL	03 48 227
	DD-1 PRR BOXCAB REVIEW "HO" ALCO	04 71 22
	GG1 PRR REVIEW "N" RAP 1935	12 71 38
S&IE	BOXCAB FREIGHT MOTOR S&IE REV "HO" KK	08 61 11

LOCOMOTIVES

GENERAL LOCOMOTIVE PROTOTYPE DATA

	M	Y	P
AUTO CAR IDENTIFICATION MARKING LOCATION	12	83	171
CLASSIFICATION & MARKER LIGHTS	08	57	66
CLASSIFICATION LIGHTS ON MA&PA	09	82	138
CLASSIFICATION OF DIES/ELECT LOCO EXPLAN	10	75	105
COCOONING FOR LOCOMOTIVE STORAGE	10	81	90
HORSEPOWER AND DRAW BAR PULL	11	36	333
IMPROVE TENDER DRIVES	03	71	76
KH-6 BRAKESTAND OF 1949	08	68	46
MARKER LIGHTS	03	38	91
MARKERS FOR YOUR TRAINS	08	38	337
MIX & MATCH MOTIVE POWER	03	63	43
MOTIVE POWER EXPERIENCES	01	37	23
SVS MOTIVE POWER UPDATE	03	81	138
WHAT DIESELS REPLACED WHAT STEAM ENGINES	03	72	39

GENERAL LOCOMOTIVE MODELING

	M	Y	P
ADAPTING LOCOMOTIVES TO TWO RAIL SYSTEM	02	36	37
ASH-CAN MODEL 4-2-4 TRAMP ART	08	40	441
AUTHENTIC SOUND IN LOCOMOTIVES	05	59	33
BALANCING BRASS LOCOMOTIVES	04	81	94
BASIC DRIVE OF "N" LOCOS ASSEMBLY	10	75	99
BETTER CONTACT FOR SMOOTH PERFORMANCE	01	64	36
CARE AND FEEDING OF LOCOMOTIVES	06	46	385
COCOONING MODEL LOCOMITVES	10	81	90
CONTINENTAL LOCOMOTIVES MODEL DESIGN	01	68	55
DEVELOPING A MOTIVE POWER THEME MOD & PT	06	79	106
DIFFERENCE BETWEEN CAN & MICRO MOTORS	05	79	138
ELECTRICAL DEVICES 2 LOCOMOTIVE MOTORS	05	57	66
FLUID DRIVE REVIEW "HO/O/S" W	11	51	50
FLUID DRIVES FOR LOCOS	12	50	50
FLYWHEELS FOR MOTORS	10	61	33
HANDMADE BRASS FROM JAPAN	03	73	64
HO GAUGE LOCOMOTIVE HINTS	10	36	281
HOLLOW KINGPIN MOTOR TRUCK CONSTRUCTION	08	45	312
IMPROVED LOCOMOTIVE PULLING POWER	08	79	134
IMPROVING ATHEARN RUBBER BAND DRIVE	11	82	171
IMPROVING LOCOMOTIVE TRACTION	12	78	187
IMPROVING RTR LOCOMOTIVE PERFORMANCE	06	74	66
INSTALLING LOCOMOTIVE LIGHTS	03	78	130
INSULATING LOCOMOTIVES AND TENDERS	11	52	30
LOCO BUILDERS PLATE CONSTRUCTION	01	52	52
LOCO CONTROL PROBLEM W/SELECT POWER PACK	05	82	138
LOCOMOTIVE AIR OPERATED WHISTLE CONST	09	76	74
LOCOMOTIVE BALANCING	09	49	42
LOCOMOTIVE DOCTORING BOOMER PETE	05	38	195
LOCOMOTIVE MAINTENANCE	04	48	276
LOCOMOTIVE MOTOR MAINTENANCE	04	62	63
LOCOMOTIVE PERFORMANCE	09	70	39
LOCOMOTIVE PERFORMANCE CHART	07	58	53
LOCOMOTIVE SPEED AND GEARING	05	47	382
LOCOMOTIVE TEST RACKS	08	71	66
LOCOMOTIVE WEIGHTING	06	53	63
LOCOMOTIVES BY MINTON CRONKHITE	06	66	44
LOCOMOTIVES WON'T RUN SLOW	12	78	184
MAINTAINING & TROUBLESHOOTING LOCOS	06	80	90
MAINTAINING LOCOMOTIVES CLEAN/LUB/REPAIR	02	85	75
MAXIMUM POWER FORM YOUR LOCOMOTIVES	11	48	847
MORE POWER TO YOUR WHEELS 1	08	39	408
MORE POWER TO YOUR WHEELS 2	11	39	559
MORE POWER TO YOUR WHEELS 3	12	39	620
NO PRIORITY MOTOR TRUCK CONSTRUCTION	03	44	123
PICKUP SHOES FOR SHORT LOCOMOTIVES	02	77	123
POWER TRUCKS	09	45	362
REBUILDING MOTORS	07	37	239
REPAIRING SHORTED DRIVERS	11	55	32
SAFE WEIGHTING LOCOMOTIVES	09	56	30
SIDE ROD BIND CORRECTIONS SIX CAUSES	02	71	67
SLOW DOWN RUSHING FREIGHT TRAINS	11	62	76
SMOOTH LOCOMOTIVE OPERATION	06	37	199
SUPERDETAILING LOCOS IN "N" SCALE	12	78	122
TIN PLATE MOTORS FOR SCALE LOCOMOTIVES	04	35	100

LOCOMOTIVES

GENERAL LOCOMOTIVE MODELING

	M	Y	P
TUNEUP OF LOCOMOTIVES	01	76	53
TUNING AND BREAKING IN RTR LOCOMOTIVES	12	69	80
TORQUE ARMS FOR KTM GEAR BOXES	09	83	80
VARIETY OF PEOPLE IN THE CAB	03	77	96
WORM AND GEAR SETS	05	78	131
WORM GEAR DRIVE TROUBLESHOOTING	12	52	77

GENERAL LOCOMOTIVE MODEL REVIEWS

	M	Y	P
CENTRIFUGAL CLUTCH CHASSIS REV "HO" ARR	03	52	55
INDUSTRIAL EQUIPMENT REVIEW "HO2 1/2" AHM	09	65	12
RACK RAILWAY REVIEW "1/45" MRC	10	85	37
ROKAL "TT" EQUIPMENT REVIEW	06	63	7
SHAY DRIVE REVIEW "HO/HON3" NWSL	01	78	45
TOMHAR FLUID DRIVE REVIEW "HO" TOMH	05	52	54
TT GAUGE EQUIPMENT REVIEW "TT" ROKAL	11	64	10

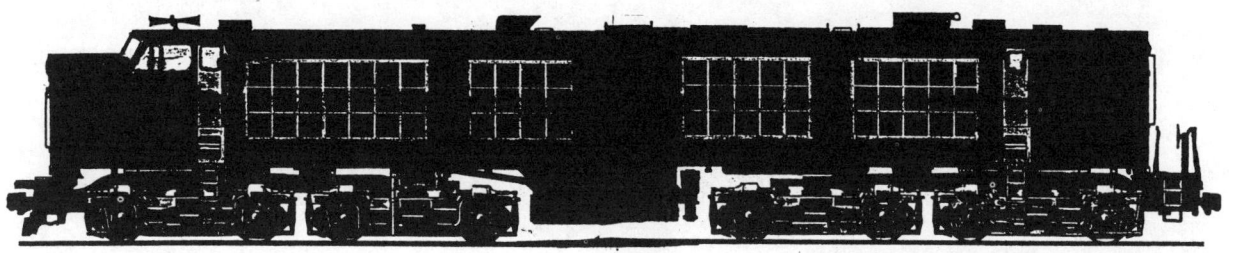

BILL OF LADING — PASSENGER EQUIPMENT

The passenger equipment section is broken down into eleven categories: Baggage Cars, RPO's, Express Cars, Combines, Coaches, Diners, Sleepers, Dome Cars, Observation Cars, Self Motorized Cars, and General Passenger Equipment. These eleven have the following five subject areas:

Prototype data includes articles and specifications on the real thing. In many instances there are photographs with these articles that did not get special billing in the photograph section. The plans and drawings are just that. Generally by our convention a drawing is more detailed than a plan, but this is not a hard and fast rule. The plans are listed twice: once alphabetically and once by road. The photo section shows details or unusual photos of interest to the researcher. Obviously we did not list all photos that appear in these magazines. The model section highlights exceptional models and tells how to build/kitbash/rebuild your own "gems". Finally the model review section list those items that have a chance of surviving as a recognizable entity. Included is the description, scale, and manufacturer. These are listed three ways: alphabetically, by road, and by manufacturer.

The passenger descriptor line includes the description of the car, its road, number, class, builder, and date built. As much of this information that is available or that will fit is included.

MANIFEST   PASSENGER CARS

	PAGE		PAGE
PASSENGER EQUIPMENT	64	SLEEPER MODEL REVIEWS	71
BAGGAGE CARS	66	SLEEPER MODEL REVIEWS BY MFG.	71
BAGGAGE CAR PROTOTYPE DATA	66	COACHES	71
BAGGAGE CAR PLANS	66	COACH PROTOTYPE DATA	71
BAGGAGE CAR PLANS BY ROAD	66	COACH PLANS	71
BAGGAGE CAR MODELS	66	COACH PLANS BY ROAD	72
BAGGAGE CAR MODEL REVIEWS	66	COACH PHOTOS	72
BAGGAGE CAR MODEL REVIEWS BY MFG.	66	COACH MODELS	73
COMBINES	67	COACH MODEL REVIEWS	73
COMBINE PROTOTYPE DATA	67	COACH MODEL REVIEWS BY ROAD	74
COMBINE PLANS	67	COACH MODEL REVIEWS BY MFG.	75
COMBINE PLANS BY ROAD	67	DOME CARS	75
COMBINE PHOTOS	67	DOME CAR PROTOTYPE DATA	75
COMBINE MODELS	68	DOME CAR PLANS	75
COMBINE MODEL REVIEWS	68	DOME CAR PLANS BY ROAD	75
COMBINE MODEL REVIEWS BY MFG.	68	DOME CAR MODELS	76
EXPRESS CARS	68	DOME CAR MODEL REVIEWS	76
EXPRESS CAR PLANS	68	DOME CAR MODEL REVIEWS BY MFG.	76
EXPRESS CAR PLANS BY ROAD	68	OBSERVATION CARS	76
EXPRESS CAR MODELS	68	OBSERVATION CAR PROTOTYPE DATA	76
EXPRESS CAR MODEL REVIEWS	69	OBSERVATION CAR PLANS	76
EXPRESS CAR MODEL REVIEWS BY MFG.	69	OBSERVATION CAR PLANS BY ROAD	76
DINERS	69	OBSERVATION CAR MODELS	76
DINER PROTOTYPE DATA	69	OBSERVATION CAR MODEL REVIEWS	76
DINER PLANS	69	OBSERVATION CAR MODEL REVIEWS BY MFG.	76
DINER PLANS BY ROAD	69	RAILCARS	77
DINER MODELS	69	RAILCAR PROTOTYPE DATA	77
DINER MODEL REVIEWS	69	RAILCAR PLANS	77
DINER MODEL REVIEWS BY MFG.	69	RAILCAR PLANS BY ROAD	77
RPO CARS	70	RAILCAR PHOTOS	77
RPO PROTOTYPE DATA	70	RAILCAR MODELS	77
RPO PLANS	70	RAILCAR MODEL REVIEWS	77
RPO PLANS BY ROAD	70	RAILCAR MODEL REVIEWS BY MFG.	77
RPO MODELS	70	GENERAL PASSENGER CARS	78
RPO MODEL REVIEWS	70	GENERAL PASSENGER CAR PROTOTYPE DATA	78
RPO MODEL REVIEWS BY MFG.	70	GENERAL PASSENGER CAR PLANS	78
SLEEPERS	70	GENERAL PASSENGER CAR PLANS BY ROAD	78
SLEEPER PROTOTYPE DATA	70	GENERAL PASSENGER CAR PHOTOS	78
SLEEPER PLANS	70	GENERAL PASSENGER CAR MODELS	79
SLEEPER PLANS BY ROAD	70	GENERAL PASSENGER CAR MODEL REVIEWS	80
SLEEPER MODELS	71	GENERAL PASS CAR MODEL REVIEWS BY MFG.	80

NOTE: SEE PAGE 400

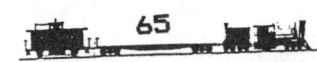

PASSENGER EQUIPMENT

BAGGAGE CAR PROTOTYPE DATA

	M	Y	P
BAGGAGE EXPRESS CARS OF 1880 ATSF	12	83	102
WOODEN BAGGAGE CARS B&O #6142	04	78	69
WOODEN BAGGAGE CARS OF B&O CAR 6142	07	78	18

BAGGAGE CAR PLANS

	M	Y	P
63' BAGGAGE CAR HEAVY WEIGHT NYC PLANS	10	38	430
BAGGAGE CAR DRAWINGS GN	08	60	49
BAGGAGE CAR OLD TIME PLANS SP&P #1	06	67	38
BAGGAGE CAR PLANS MA&PA #42	09	52	44
BAGGAGE CAR PLANS USRA	01	37	18
BAGGAGE CARRAGE PLANS B&O 1836	07	76	84
BAGGAGE CARS OF STEEL PLANS	09	46	582
BAGGAGE EXPRESS 60' PLANS CP	06	59	40
BAGGAGE EXPRESS CARS PLANS ATSF #29 1880	12	83	102
BAGGAGE HEAVY WEIGHT 40' SP	02	50	46
BAGGAGE HEAVY WEIGHT PLANS 2 SP	10	52	68
BAGGAGE NARROW-GAUGE PLANS D&RGW #125	02	47	119
HEAVY WEIGHT 72' BAG CAR ATSF #1793 PLNS	08	42	378
HEAVY WEIGHT BAGGAGE CARS PLAN ATSF #204	08	57	49
THROUGH-BAGGAGE CAR CP #4941 PLANS	04	50	42
TURTLEBACK ROOF BAGGAGE CAR PLAN UP	02	37	62
WOOD BAGGGE CAR PLANS B&O #6142	04	78	69
WOOD SHEATED BAGGAGE CAR PLANS $1	06	54	18
WOODEN BAGGAGE CAR PLANS OF 1870 PRR	11	48	842

BAGGAGE CAR PLANS BY ROAD

RD		M	Y	P
ATSF	BAGGAGE EXPRESS CARS PLANS ATSF #29 1880	12	83	102
	HEAVY WEIGHT BAGGAGE CARS PLAN ATSF #204	08	57	49
	HEAVY WEIGHT 72' BAG CAR ATSF #1793 PLNS	08	42	378
B&O	WOOD BAGGGE CAR PLANS B&O #6142	04	78	69
	BAGGAGE CARRAGE PLANS B&O 1836	07	76	84
CP	THROUGH-BAGGAGE CAR CP #4941 PLANS	04	50	42
	BAGGAGE EXPRESS 60' PLANS CP	06	59	40
D&RGW	BAGGAGE NARROW-GAUGE PLANS D&RGW #125	02	47	119
GN	BAGGAGE CAR DRAWINGS GN	08	60	49
MA&PA	BAGGAGE CAR PLANS MA&PA #42	09	52	44
NYC	63' BAGGAGE CAR HEAVY WEIGHT NYC PLANS	10	38	430
PRR	WOODEN BAGGAGE CAR PLANS OF 1870 PRR	11	48	842
SP	BAGGAGE HEAVY WEIGHT PLANS 2 SP	10	52	68
	BAGGAGE HEAVY WEIGHT 40' SP	02	50	46
SP&P	BAGGAGE CAR OLD TIME PLANS SP&P #1	06	67	38
UP	TURTLEBACK ROOF BAGGAGE CAR PLAN UP	02	37	62
USRA	BAGGAGE CAR PLANS USRA	01	37	18

BAGGAGE CAR MODELS

	M	Y	P
ALTERING ATHEARN BAGGAGE CARS	11	79	104
BAGGAGE CAR SOUTHERN MOD & PT	09	78	104
BAGGAGE CAR MILW MOD & PT	05	79	108
END DOOR BAGGAGE CAR CONSTRUCTION	01	80	115
WEATHERING A COMBINE BRINGS IT TO LIFE	12	79	79
WOOD SHEATHED BAGGAGE CAR CONST GN#03292	08	60	46

BAGGAGE CAR MODEL REVIEWS

	M	Y	P
60' HARRIMAN BAGGAGE REVIEW "HO" KK	05	60	14
64' BAGGAGE NYO&W REV "HO" NPP OB 1922	04	74	24
BAGGAGE LISTING "N" RIVEROSSI	08	78	48
BAGGAGE OF 1905 REVIEW "HO" LA	08	60	12
F&CC BAGGAGE CAR REVIEW "HO" LA	09	61	12
STREAMLINED BAGGE REVIEW "HO" M	07	56	14

BAGGAGE CAR MODEL REVIEWS BY MFG.

MFG		M	Y	P
KK	60' HARRIMAN BAGGAGE REVIEW "HO" KK	05	60	14
LA	BAGGAGE OF 1905 REVIEW "HO" LA	08	60	12
	F&CC BAGGAGE CAR REVIEW "HO" LA	09	61	12
M	STREAMLINED BAGGE REVIEW "HO" M	07	56	14
NPP	64' BAGGAGE NYO&W REV "HO" NPP OB 1922	04	74	24
RIV	BAGGAGE LISTING "N" RIVEROSSI	08	78	48

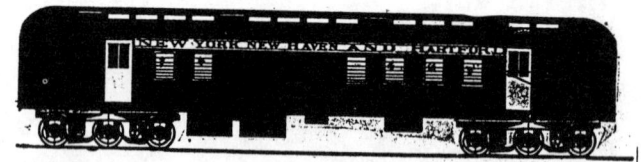

PASSENGER EQUIPMENT

COMBINE PROTOTYPE DATA	M	Y	P
COMBINES OF THE NINETIES PRR	11	73	58

COMBINE PLANS	M	Y	P
68' BAGGAGE MAIL COMBINE PLANS P&R	07	48	482
71' COMBINE POSTAL-BAGGAGE HW KCS PLANS	10	44	438
BAG/COACH COMBINE CLASS CVI R #408 PLANS	11	84	96
BAG/EXPRESS COMBINE CLASS BAA R#1757 PLN	11	84	94
BAG/EXPRESS COMBINE CLASS BAT R#1691 PLN	11	84	93
BAG/EXPRESS COMBINE CLASS BAU R#1562 PLN	11	84	95
BAG/EXPRESS COMBINE CLASS BAV R#1629 PLN	11	84	94
BAG/RPO COMBINE CLASS MBP R #1730 PLAN	11	84	92
BAGGAGE-COACH COMBINE HW NYC #201 PLANS	09	49	38
BAGGAGE-TAVERN-LOUNGE PLANS LW C&NW "400	12	49	50
COACH-BAGGAGE COMBINE PLANS PRR #4639	11	73	56
COMBINE #14 PLANS SR&RL	11	78	67
COMBINE BAGGAGE COACH PLANS D&IR #5 1885	09	67	36
COMBINE BAGGAGE DYNAMO 1882 PLN MILW#195	12	70	46
COMBINE BAGGAGE MAIL H WT CLS MB SOO#549	09	35	238
COMBINE BAGGAGE-BUFFET 1893 PLN MILW#270	12	70	48
COMBINE BAGGAGE-POSTAL PLANS D&IR #7	09	67	35
COMBINE BAGGAGE-RPO 1921 H&BTM #16 PLAN	04	69	46
COMBINE BAGGAGE-SMOKING PLANS C&NW #7408	08	71	48
COMBINE CABOOSE-BAG-COACH N.G. D&RGW PLN	10	47	803
COMBINE CAFE-OBSERVATION PLANS D&IR #26	09	67	37
COMBINE COACH BAGGAGE HV N&W #601 PLAN	04	36	98
COMBINE MU HVYWT CLASS PB54 PRR#4546 PLN	10	69	78
COMBINE NARROW GAUGE PLANS D&RGW #210	11	46	727
COMBINE OLD-TIME DM&IR PLANS 1887	08	38	314
COMBINE OLD-TIME RPO-BAG PLANS CS&CC #50	08	64	26
COMBINE PLANS	01	39	29
COMBINE PLANS BI&B OF 1877	06	57	50
COMBINE PLANS MA&PA #34	09	52	44
COMBINE PLANS OF 1900 B&O #341	05	52	10
COMBINE POSTAL BAGGAGE MU PLAN PRSL#5458	02	69	42
COMBINE RPO-BAG PLANS FC&GU #8 CLASS ND	07	52	40
COMBINE RPO/COACH OLD TIME PLANS NYLE&W	09	59	51
DAYLIGHT BAGGAGE-COACH COMBINE PLANS SP	10	48	709
HEAVY WEIGHT COMBINE ATSF #2602 PLAN	05	47	402
MAIL BAGGAGE COMBINE 1860 PLAN PRR #482	04	69	46
NARROW VESTIBULE COMBINE PLANS KCP&G	03	58	40
OLD TIME COMBINE PRR #4532 PLANS 1880	07	44	310
PANAMA LIMITED BAGGAGE-DORM LW PLANS IC	05	65	34
PULLMAN SMOKING BAGGAGE COMBINE PLN 1893	04	63	40
RPO-BAG-COACH MPB70 COMBINE PLN PRR#5202	08	63	36
STANDARD PASSENGER BAGGAGE COMB PLANS SP	02	40	68
SUPERLINER COACH-BAGGAGE PLANS A PS	11	82	87
SUPERLINER LOUNGE-CAFE PLAN A PS	11	82	90

RD	COMBINE PLANS BY ROAD	M	Y	P
*P	PULLMAN SMOKING BAGGAGE COMBINE PLN 1893	04	63	40
A	SUPERLINER COACH-BAGGAGE PLANS A PS	11	82	87
	SUPERLINER LOUNGE-CAFE PLAN A PS	11	82	90
ATSF	HEAVY WEIGHT COMBINE ATSF #2602 PLAN	05	47	402
B&O	COMBINE PLANS OF 1900 B&O #341	05	52	10
BI&B	COMBINE PLANS BI&B OF 1877	06	57	50
C&NW	COMBINE BAGGAGE-SMOKING PLANS C&NW #7408	08	71	48
	BAGGAGE-TAVERN-LOUNGE PLANS LW C&NW "400	12	49	50
CS&CC	COMBINE OLD-TIME RPO-BAG PLANS CS&CC #50	08	64	26
D&IR	COMBINE BAGGAGE COACH PLANS D&IR #5 1885	09	67	36
	COMBINE BAGGAGE-POSTAL PLANS D&IR #7	09	67	35
	COMBINE CAFE-OBSERVATION PLANS D&IR #26	09	67	37
D&RGW	COMBINE CABOOSE-BAG-COACH N.G. D&RGW PLN	10	47	803
	COMBINE NARROW GAUGE PLANS D&RGW #210	11	46	727
DM&IR	COMBINE OLD-TIME DM&IR PLANS 1887	08	38	314
FC&GU	COMBINE RPO-BAG PLANS FC&GU #8 CLASS ND	07	52	40
H&BTM	COMBINE BAGGAGE-RPO 1921 H&BTM #16 PLAN	04	69	46
IC	PANAMA LIMITED BAGGAGE-DORM LW PLANS IC	05	65	34
KCP&G	NARROW VESTIBULE COMBINE PLANS KCP&G	03	58	40
KCS	71' COMBINE POSTAL-BAGGAGE HW KCS PLANS	10	44	438
MA&PA	COMBINE PLANS MA&PA #34	09	52	44
MILW	COMBINE BAGGAGE-BUFFET 1893 PLN MILW#270	12	70	48
	COMBINE BAGGAGE DYNAMO 1882 PLN MILW#195	12	70	46
N&W	COMBINE COACH BAGGAGE HV N&W #601 PLAN	04	36	98
NYC	BAGGAGE-COACH COMBINE HW NYC #201 PLANS	09	49	38
NYLE&W	COMBINE RPO/COACH OLD TIME PLANS NYLE&W	09	59	51
P&R	68' BAGGAGE MAIL COMBINE PLANS P&R	07	48	482
PRR	COMBINE MU HVYWT CLASS PB54 PRR#4546 PLN	10	69	78
	MAIL BAGGAGE COMBINE 1860 PLAN PRR #482	04	69	46
	RPO-BAG-COACH MPB70 COMBINE PLN PRR#5202	08	63	36
	COACH-BAGGAGE COMBINE PLANS PRR #4639	11	73	56
	OLD TIME COMBINE PRR #4532 PLANS 1880	07	44	310
PRSL	COMBINE POSTAL BAGGAGE MU PLAN PRSL#5458	02	69	42
R	BAG/RPO COMBINE CLASS MBP R #1730 PLAN	11	84	92
	BAG/EXPRESS COMBINE CLASS BAT R#1691 PLN	11	84	93
	BAG/EXPRESS COMBINE CLASS BAA R#1757 PLN	11	84	94
	BAG/EXPRESS COMBINE CLASS BAV R#1629 PLN	11	84	94
	BAG/EXPRESS COMBINE CLASS BAU R#1562 PLN	11	84	95
	BAG/COACH COMBINE CLASS CVI R #408 PLANS	11	84	96
SOO	COMBINE BAGGAGE MAIL H WT CLS MB SOO#549	09	35	238
SP	DAYLIGHT BAGGAGE-COACH COMBINE PLANS SP	10	48	709
	STANDARD PASSENGER BAGGAGE COMB PLANS SP	02	40	68
SR&RL	COMBINE #14 PLANS SR&RL	11	78	67

COMBINE PHOTOS	M	Y	P
47' COMBINE CB&Q "003" PHOTO 1911	02	67	53

PASSENGER EQUIPMENT

COMBINE MODELS

	M	Y	P
CAFE PARLOR OBS COMBINE CONSTRUCTION CP	09	66	34
COMBINE MOD & PT	05	76	90
COMBINE CONSTRUCTION	02	40	66
OPEN VESTIBULE COMBINE KITBASH	05	85	84
RPO/COACH OLD TIME COMBINE CONST NYLE&W	09	59	50
SCRATCHBUILT NARROW GAUGE COMBINE	11	78	66

COMBINE MODEL REVIEWS

	M	Y	P
1860 COMBINE REVIEW "HO" M	10	58	16
85' MAIL BAGGAE COMBINE GN REV "HO" ABL	06	60	9
BAGGAGE CHAIR COMBINE REVIEW "HO" WE	11	67	20
BAGGAGE COACH COMBINE OF 1905 REV "HO LA	08	60	12
BAGGAGE COACH COMBINE REV "HO" LA 1900	10	73	31
BAGGAGE-COACH D&RGW REVIEW "SN3" TOM	05	72	21
BAGGAGE-COACH KIT REVIEW "HO" JC	08	50	43
BAGGAGE-MAIL COMBINE REVIEW "HO" KK	12	61	24
BAGGAGE-MAIL COMBINE REVIEW "O" JC	11	53	18
COACH BAGGAGE SP COMBINE REVIEW "HO" KK	03	61	13
COACH COMBINE KIT 1890 REVIEW "O" RCH	01	48	65
COACH-BAGGAGE COMBINE REVIEW "HO" LA	04	63	14
COMBINE SIE #5 REVIEW "O" WAL 1960	11	75	25
F&CC BAGGAGE COACH COMBINE REV "HO" LA	09	61	12
RPO BAGGAGE LISTING CNJ "S" TRAIN STUFF	06	78	54
SIERRA COMBINE REVIEW "HO" LAC	07	53	5
STREAMLINED COMBINE REVIEW "HO" M	07	56	14

COMBINE MODEL REVIEWS BY MFG.

MFG		M	Y	P
ABL	85' MAIL BAGGAE COMBINE GN REV "HO" ABL	06	60	9
JC	BAGGAGE-MAIL COMBINE REVIEW "O" JC	11	53	18
	BAGGAGE-COACH KIT REVIEW "HO" JC	08	50	43
KK	BAGGAGE-MAIL COMBINE REVIEW "HO" KK	12	61	24
	COACH BAGGAGE SP COMBINE REVIEW "HO" KK	03	61	13
LA	BAGGAGE COACH COMBINE REV "HO" LA 1900	10	73	31
	COACH-BAGGAGE COMBINE REVIEW "HO" LA	04	63	14
	BAGGAGE COACH COMBINE OF 1905 REV "HO LA	08	60	12
	F&CC BAGGAGE COACH COMBINE REV "HO" LA	09	61	12
LAC	SIERRA COMBINE REVIEW "HO" LAC	07	53	5
M	STREAMLINED COMBINE REVIEW "HO" M	07	56	14
	1860 COMBINE REVIEW "HO" M	10	58	16
RCH	COACH COMBINE KIT 1890 REVIEW "O" RCH	01	48	65
TOM	BAGGAGE-COACH D&RGW REVIEW "SN3" TOM	05	72	21
TRS	RPO BAGGAGE LISTING CNJ "S" TRAIN STUFF	06	78	54
WAL	COMBINE SIE #5 REVIEW "O" WAL 1960	11	75	25
WE	BAGGAGE CHAIR COMBINE REVIEW "HO" WE	11	67	20

EXPRESS CAR PLANS

	M	Y	P
EXPRESS BOXCAR CLASS BXMU PLANS R #1866	11	84	91
EXPRESS HEAVY WEIGHT PRR PLANS	10	51	38
EXPRESS REEFER CAR PLANS P&R #1587 1910	06	58	27
EXPRESS REEFER CAR PLANS WELLS FARGO#160	10	55	40
EXPRESS REEFER CLASS RS SP#35461 PFE PLN	04	35	90
EXPRESS REEFER MILK CAR PLANS NYC #6427	07	53	45
EXPRESS REEFER MP #3153 PLANS	05	36	130
EXPRESS REEFER PLANS	09	49	32
EXPRESS REEFER PLANS GN	01	40	14
EXPRESS REEFER PLANS *MDT #8320 1900	08	57	49
EXPRESS REFRIGERATOR CAR PLAN 44' CMSP&P	06	34	12
EXPRESS REFRIGERATOR CAR PRR #2699 PLANS	03	45	130
EXPRESS REFRIGERATOR MILW #3300	04	60	38
SILK AND TEA CAR SP #6920	02	65	44

EXPRESS CAR PLANS BY ROAD

RD		M	Y	P
*MDT	EXPRESS REEFER PLANS *MDT #8320 1900	08	57	49
GN	EXPRESS REEFER PLANS GN	01	40	14
MILW	EXPRESS REFRIGERATOR MILW #3300	04	60	38
	EXPRESS REFRIGERATOR CAR PLAN 44' CMSP&P	06	34	12
MP	EXPRESS REEFER MP #3153 PLANS	05	36	130
NYC	EXPRESS REEFER MILK CAR PLANS NYC #6427	07	53	45
P&R	EXPRESS REEFER CAR PLANS P&R #1587 1910	06	58	27
PRR	EXPRESS HEAVY WEIGHT PRR PLANS	10	51	38
	EXPRESS REFRIGERATOR CAR PRR #2699 PLANS	03	45	130
R	EXPRESS BOXCAR CLASS BXMU PLANS R #1866	11	84	91
SP	SILK AND TEA CAR SP #6920	02	65	44
	EXPRESS REEFER CLASS RS SP#35461 PFE PLN	04	35	90

EXPRESS CAR MODELS

	M	Y	P
EXPRESS BAGGAGE ATSF #1849 MOD & PT	04	80	119
EXPRESS BOXCAR GN MOD & PT	06	75	22
EXPRESS BOXCARS PRR CLASS X29 MOD & PT	01	85	140
EXPRESS REEFER CAR CONSTRUCTION READING	06	58	25
EXPRESS REEFER CONSTRUCTION	01	40	11
EXPRESS REEFER CONSTRUCTION $1	04	54	22
EXPRESS REEFER CONSTRUCTION TINPLATE	09	49	30
MILK CAR WESTMINSTER MOD & PT	03	82	127
MOM MILK EXPRESS "HO" KUNZELMANN	06	73	62
SILK EXPRESS CAR CONSTRUCTION SP $1	02	65	42

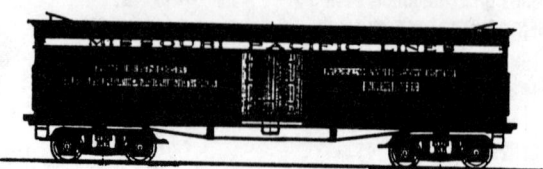

PASSENGER EQUIPMENT

EXPRESS CAR MODEL REVIEWS

	M	Y	P
1900 EXPRESS CAR MILW REV "HO" LA 1901	03	62	12
50' EXPRESS REEFER REVIEW "HO" MLI	08	57	11
50' EXPRESS REEFER REVIEW "HO" MDC	02	71	22
52' REA EXPRESS REEVER REVIEW "O" MLI	06	59	12
60' UP BAGGAGE EXPRESS CAR REV "HO" AMB	02	72	24
EXPRESS REEFER GN REVIEW "HO" EH BESSEY	04	41	226
EXPRESS REEFER KIT REVIEW "HO" AMB	10	54	08
EXPRESS REEFER REVIEW "HO" TI 1910	07	68	12
HORSE EXPRESS CAR PRR REVIEW "HO" WAL	04	62	13
REA EXPRESS REEFER REVIEW "HO" AMB	07	70	18
REA EXPRESS REEFER REVIEW "HO" MDC	02	67	14

EXPRESS CAR MODEL REVIEWS BY MFG.

MFG		M	Y	P
AMB	60' UP BAGGAGE EXPRESS CAR REV "HO" AMB	02	72	24
	EXPRESS REEFER KIT REVIEW "HO" AMB	10	54	08
	REA EXPRESS REEFER REVIEW "HO" AMB	07	70	18
EHB	EXPRESS REEFER GN REVIEW "HO" EH BESSEY	04	41	226
LA	1900 EXPRESS CAR MILW REV "HO" LA 1901	03	62	12
MDC	50' EXPRESS REEFER REVIEW "HO" MDC	02	71	22
	REA EXPRESS REEFER REVIEW "HO" MDC	02	67	14
MLI	50' EXPRESS REEFER REVIEW "HO" MLI	08	57	11
	52' REA EXPRESS REEVER REVIEW "O" MLI	06	59	12
TI	EXPRESS REEFER REVIEW "HO" TI 1910	07	68	12
WAL	HORSE EXPRESS CAR PRR REVIEW "HO" WAL	04	62	13

DINER PROTOTYPE DATA

	M	Y	P
PRESIDENT SERIES DINER CARS 80' PUL C&NW	04	77	64

DINER PLANS

	M	Y	P
80' DINING CAR PLANS KCS	10	44	440
CAFE CAR OF 1894 PLANS W #276	11	61	46
DAYLIGHT COFFEE SHOP CAR PLANS SP	10	48	710
DAYLIGHT DINING CAR PLANS SP	10	48	710
DAYLIGHT KITCHEN CAR PLANS SP	10	48	710
DINER HEAVY WEIGHT NYNH&H PLANS	01	38	22
DINING CAFE-PARLOR PLANS CMI #248 1907	11	74	62
DINING CAR CLASS D78C HW PLANS PRR #4490	11	74	62
DINING CAR HEAVY WEIGHT PRR #7992 PLANS	08	49	34
DINING CAR LW PLANS C&NW "400"	12	49	50
DINING CAR PLANS CMI #247	11	74	62
DINING HEAVY WEIGHT PLANS SP #10151	10	52	68
DINING PARLOR OF 1890 PLANS CMSP	06	71	44
HEAVY WEIGHT DINING CAR #1418 36 ST ATSF	02	37	62
HIAWATHA DINER DRAWING MILW	01	84	114
LIGHT WEIGHT DINING CARS ATSF #601 PLANS	07	52	62
PANAMA LIMITED DINER PLANS	05	65	35
PRESIDENTIAL DINING CARS C&NW #6932 PLNS	04	77	66
PULLMAN DINER PLANS OF 1893	04	63	39
PULLMAN PARLOR DINING LOUNGE CAR PLANS	06	66	36
SUPERLINER DINING CAR PLAN A PS	11	82	91
TROOP KITCHEN CAR FLOOR PLAN USA	01	70	87

DINER PLANS BY ROAD

RD		M	Y	P
*P	PULLMAN PARLOR DINING LOUNGE CAR PLANS	06	66	36
A	SUPERLINER DINING CAR PLAN A PS	11	82	91
ATSF	LIGHT WEIGHT DINING CARS ATSF #601 PLANS	07	52	62
	HEAVY WEIGHT DINING CAR #1418 36 ST ATSF	02	37	62
C&NW	PRESIDENTIAL DINING CARS C&NW #6932 PLNS	04	77	66
	DINING CAR LW PLANS C&NW "400"	12	49	50
CMI	DINING CAFE-PARLOR PLANS CMI #248 1907	11	74	62
	DINING CAR PLANS CMI #247	11	74	62
CMSP	DINING PARLOR OF 1890 PLANS CMSP	06	71	44
IC	PANAMA LIMITED DINER PLANS	05	65	35
KCS	80' DINING CAR PLANS KCS	10	44	440
MILW	HIAWATHA DINER DRAWING MILW	01	84	114
NYNH&H	DINER HEAVY WEIGHT NYNH&H PLANS	01	38	22
PRR	DINING CAR HEAVY WEIGHT PRR #7992 PLANS	08	49	34
	DINING CAR CLASS D78C HW PLANS PRR #4490	11	74	62
SP	DINING HEAVY WEIGHT PLANS SP #10151	10	52	68
	DAYLIGHT KITCHEN CAR PLANS SP	10	48	710
	DAYLIGHT DINING CAR PLANS SP	10	48	710
	DAYLIGHT COFFEE SHOP CAR PLANS SP	10	48	710
USA	TROOP KITCHEN CAR FLOOR PLAN USA	01	70	87
W	CAFE CAR OF 1894 PLANS W #276	11	61	46

DINER MODELS

	M	Y	P
DINER KITBASH	07	85	66
DINING CAR FROM PLASTIC SLEEPER	09	70	67
PS DINER FRIS 1948 MOD & PT	06	75	21
RECIPES FOR DINER KITBASHING 1	06	78	98
RECIPES FOR DINER KITBASHING-7 WAYS	06	78	97

DINER MODEL REVIEWS

	M	Y	P
80' STANDARD ATSF DINER REVIEW "HO" AHM	10	65	11
AM CAFE REVIEW "HO" WAL 1975	04	84	35
DINER CAR REVIEW "TT" HP	08	48	574
DINER KIT REVIEW "O" JC	03	51	53
DINING CAR CB&Q REVIEW "HO" OL 1948	09	84	37
PARLOR-BUFFET D&RGW REVIEW "ON3" CRGT	12	81	43
WOOD NP DINING CAR REVIEW "HO" LA 1902	01	67	19

DINER MODEL REVIEWS BY MFG.

MFG		M	Y	P
AHM	80' STANDARD ATSF DINER REVIEW "HO" AHM	10	65	11
CRGT	PARLOR-BUFFET D&RGW REVIEW "ON3" CRGT	12	81	43
HP	DINER CAR REVIEW "TT" HP	08	48	574
JC	DINER KIT REVIEW "O" JC	03	51	53
LA	WOOD NP DINING CAR REVIEW "HO" LA 1902	01	67	19
OL	DINING CAR CB&Q REVIEW "HO" OL 1948	09	84	37
WAL	AM CAFE REVIEW "HO" WAL 1975	04	84	35

PASSENGER EQUIPMENT

RPO PROTOTYPE DATA

	M	Y	P
CLASS M70 POSTAL CARS PRR	01	78	81

RPO PLANS

	M	Y	P
60' POSTAL CAR HEAVY WEIGHT NYC#308 PLNS	10	38	430
EXPRESS RPO 60' PLANS CP	06	59	41
LIGHT WEIGHT BAGGAGE MAIL ATSF#3407 PLAN	11	47	904
NARROW VESTIBULE RPO PLAN 1893 MILW #3	03	64	26
OLD TIME POSTAL CAR PRR #9 PLANS 1880	07	44	310
POSTAL CAR HEAVY WEIGHT N&W #96 PLANS	07	38	286
POSTAL CAR HEAVY WEIGHT NYNH&H PLAN	04	36	98
POSTAL CAR OF 1895 PLANS E #793	05	70	50
POSTAL CAR OF 1896 PLANS MILW #271	12	70	50
POSTAL CLASS M70 PLANS PRR	01	78	81
POSTAL HEAVY WEIGHT PLAN SP	02	50	46
POSTAL HEAVY WEIGHT PRR #5264 PLANS	10	51	38
WOODEN COACH OF 1870 PLANS PRR #4532	11	48	842

RPO PLANS BY ROAD

RD		M	Y	P
ATSF	LIGHT WEIGHT BAGGAGE MAIL ATSF#3407 PLAN	11	47	904
CP	EXPRESS RPO 60' PLANS CP	06	59	41
E	POSTAL CAR OF 1895 PLANS E #793	05	70	50
MILW	POSTAL CAR OF 1896 PLANS MILW #271	12	70	50
	NARROW VESTIBULE RPO PLAN 1893 MILW #3	03	64	26
N&W	POSTAL CAR HEAVY WEIGHT N&W #96 PLANS	07	38	286
NYC	60' POSTAL CAR HEAVY WEIGHT NYC#308 PLNS	10	38	430
NYNH&H	POSTAL CAR HEAVY WEIGHT NYNH&H PLAN	04	36	98
PRR	POSTAL HEAVY WEIGHT PRR #5264 PLANS	10	51	38
	POSTAL CLASS M70 PLANS PRR	01	78	81
	OLD TIME POSTAL CAR PRR #9 PLANS 1880	07	44	310
	WOODEN COACH OF 1870 PLANS PRR #4532	11	48	842
SP	POSTAL HEAVY WEIGHT PLAN SP	02	50	46

RPO MODELS

		M	Y	P
15' RAILWAY POST OFFICE KITBASH		01	79	79
FRIS RPO	MOD & PT	10	77	98
M70 MAIL CAR PRR	MOD & PT	12	78	158
RPO	MOD & PT	12	75	95

RPO MODEL REVIEWS

	M	Y	P
1900 RPO MILW REVIEW "HO" LA 1901	03	62	12
40' HARRIMAN RPO REVIEW "HO" KEN KIDDER	05	60	14
70' EXPRESS MAIL CAR MP REVIEW "HO" QC	02	71	30
GOLDEN EAGLE FAST MAIL REVIEW "HO" HIB	07	56	11
POSTAL CAR D&RG REVIEW "HON3" LA	02	67	12
RPO LISTING "N" JMC	07	78	50
RPO REVIEW "1/4" AMERICAN STANDARD CAR	07	78	41
STANDARD 74' RPO REVIEW "HO" RIV	09	66	11

RPO MODEL REVIEWS BY MFG.

MFG		M	Y	P
ASC	RPO REVIEW "1/4" AMERICAN STANDARD CAR	07	78	41
HIB	GOLDEN EAGLE FAST MAIL REVIEW "HO" HIB	07	56	11
JMC	RPO LISTING "N" JMC	07	78	50
KK	40' HARRIMAN RPO REVIEW "HO" KEN KIDDER	05	60	14
LA	1900 RPO MILW REVIEW "HO" LA 1901	03	62	12
	POSTAL CAR D&RG REVIEW "HON3" LA	02	67	12
QC	70' EXPRESS MAIL CAR MP REVIEW "HO" QC	02	71	30
RIV	STANDARD 74' RPO REVIEW "HO" RIV	09	66	11

SLEEPER PROTOTYPE DATA

	M	Y	P
PULLMAN CAR CODES	06	47	475
PULLMAN END DETAILS	11	35	299
TROOP CARS USA	12	43	550
WANDERING SLEEPERS	06	81	84

SLEEPER PLANS

	M	Y	P
ALL-ROOM SLEEPER PLANS AUTO-TRAIN #202	12	74	46
COACH 1892 PLANS MILW #413 1892 BS	02	71	60
LW SLEEPER "TWIN PEAKS" PLANS UP 1941 PS	06	75	50
PANAMA LIMITED LW SLEEPER CAR PLANS IC	05	65	34
PANAMA LIMITED SLEEPER PLAN	05	65	35
PULLMAN 12 SECTION 1 DRAWING ROOM CAR PL	11	35	294
PULLMAN 12 SECTION CAR PLANS *P	02	66	40
PULLMAN DELUXE CARS OF 1893 PLANS	04	63	41
PULLMAN LW 4 COMPART 4 BED 2 DRAW PLANS	07	38	286
PULLMAN PLANS BEDROOM SOLARIUM LOUNGE	11	35	294
PULLMAN PREWAR LIGHT WT 17 ROOMETTE PLAN	07	38	286
SLEEPER 1884 PLANS MILW NASHOTAH 1874	02	71	63
SLEEPER 1886 PLANS MILW LAKE PEPIN 1874	02	71	63
SLEEPER 8-2 RM 6 RM 6 BDRM PLAN MILW	07	72	44
SLEEPERS OF 1890 PLANS CMSP "NECEDAH"	06	71	44
STANDARD SLEEPER 72' PLANS CP	06	59	38
SUPERLINER SLEEPING CAR PLANS A PS	11	82	96
TROOP SLEEPER CAR PLANS USA #7000	12	43	550
TROOP SLEEPER FLOOR PLANS USA	01	70	86

SLEEPER PLANS BY ROAD

RD		M	Y	P
*AT	ALL-ROOM SLEEPER PLANS AUTO-TRAIN #202	12	74	46
*P	PULLMAN 12 SECTION CAR PLANS *P	02	66	40
	PULLMAN DELUXE CARS OF 1893 PLANS	04	63	41
	PULLMAN 12 SECTION 1 DRAWING ROOM CAR PL	11	35	294
	PULLMAN PLANS BEDROOM SOLARIUM LOUNGE	11	35	294
A	SUPERLINER SLEEPING CAR PLANS A PS	11	82	96
CMSP	SLEEPERS OF 1890 PLANS CMSP "NECEDAH"	06	71	44
CP	STANDARD SLEEPER 72' PLANS CP	06	59	38
IC	PANAMA LIMITED LW SLEEPER CAR PLANS IC	05	65	34
	PANAMA LIMITED SLEEPER PLAN	05	65	35
MILW	SLEEPER 1886 PLANS MILW LAKE PEPIN 1874	02	71	63
	SLEEPER 1884 PLANS MILW NASHOTAH 1874	02	71	63
	COACH 1892 PLANS MILW #413 1892 BS	02	71	60
	SLEEPER 8-2 RM 6 RM 6 BDRM PLAN MILW	07	72	44
NYC	PULLMAN LW 4 COMPART 4 BED 2 DRAW PLANS	07	38	286
	PULLMAN PREWAR LIGHT WT 17 ROOMETTE PLAN	07	38	286
UP	LW SLEEPER "TWIN PEAKS" PLANS UP 1941 PS	06	75	50
USA	TROOP SLEEPER FLOOR PLANS USA	01	70	86
	TROOP SLEEPER CAR PLANS USA #7000	12	43	550

PASSENGER EQUIPMENT

SLEEPER MODELS

		M	Y	P
SLUMBER COACH B&O	MOD & PT	11	76	123
STRECHING THE ATHEARN PULLMAN		12	60	40

SLEEPER MODEL REVIEWS

	M	Y	P
BUDD SLEEPER LISTING "HO" JMC	01	78	50
BUDD SLUMBER COACH REVIEW "N" CC	06	74	20
DUPLEX SLEEPER REVIEW "HO" RIV	06	70	19
PULLMAN CAR REVIEW "HO" V	11	41	600
PULLMAN KIT REVIEW "HO" SSM	05	49	51
PULLMAN PALACE CAR REVIEW "HO" MDC	08	67	11
SHORT PULLLMAN KIT REVIEW "HO" SMP	02	52	42
SLEEPER 10-6 REVIEW NYC "1/4" IND	09	78	34
SLEEPER C&O REVIEW "HO" L 1948 PS	12	76	32
SLEEPER PULLMAN STANDARD REVIEW "HO" EBV	11	83	52
SLEEPING CAR REVIEW "N" LIMA	01	67	16
SMOOTH SIDE STREAMLINE SLEEPER REV "HO"	12	82	61
STD PULLMAN REVIEW "HO" WAL	08	59	16
STREAMLINED PULLMAN KIT REVIEW "HO" SMP	01	50	83
STREAMLINED SLEEPER REVIEW "N" AT 1950	08	68	13
TROOP CAR REVIEW "HO" H	01	70	19
WAGNER SLEEPING CAR REVIEW "HO" CL	07	50	58

SLEEPER MODEL REVIEWS BY MFG.

MFG		M	Y	P
AT	STREAMLINED SLEEPER REVIEW "N" AT 1950	08	68	13
CC	BUDD SLUMBER COACH REVIEW "N" CC	06	74	20
CL	WAGNER SLEEPING CAR REVIEW "HO" CL	07	50	58
CY	SMOOTH SIDE STREAMLINE SLEEPER REV "HO"	12	82	61
EBV	SLEEPER PULLMAN STANDARD REVIEW "HO" EBV	11	83	52
H	TROOP CAR REVIEW "HO" H	01	70	19
IND	SLEEPER 10-6 REVIEW NYC "1/4" IND	09	78	34
JMC	BUDD SLEEPER LISTING "HO" JMC	01	78	50
L	SLEEPER C&O REVIEW "HO" L 1948 PS	12	76	32
LIMA	SLEEPING CAR REVIEW "N" LIMA	01	67	16
MDC	PULLMAN PALACE CAR REVIEW "HO" MDC	08	67	11
SMP	SHORT PULLLMAN KIT REVIEW "HO" SMP	02	52	42
	STREAMLINED PULLMAN KIT REVIEW "HO" SMP	01	50	83
SSM	PULLMAN KIT REVIEW "HO" SSM	05	49	51
V	PULLMAN CAR REVIEW "HO" V	11	41	600
WAL	STD PULLMAN REVIEW "HO" WAL	08	59	16

COACH PROTOTYPE DATA

	M	Y	P
AUTO TRAIN INTERIOR DETAIL	01	75	60
BUSINESS CAR "CHESAPEAKE" PRR #100 PLM	10	71	57
BUSINESS CARS- OFFICIAL USE ONLY	12	59	30
CLASS P58 COACH PRR #1651 1906	03	77	66
COMBINE #14 SR&RL	11	78	67
STREAMLINED COACHES OF MILW RD 1934	11	34	11
TOPLESS PASSENGER COACHES	08	75	81

COACH PLANS

	M	Y	P
35' BUSINESS CAR OF 1912 CONSTRUCT CP #5	12	56	52
60' COACH PLANS KCS	10	44	441
75' COACHES HEAVY WEIGHT NYC #409 PLANS	10	38	430
BUSINESS CAR LIGHT WEIGHT PLANS SP 1955	12	59	30
BUSINESS CAR PLANS PRR #100 "CHESAPEAKE"	10	71	56
BUSINESS CARS CANADIAN PACIFIC PLANS	04	36	98
BUSINESS HEAVY WEIGHT PLANS SP #110	12	59	32
CHAIR CAR 60' PLANS KCS	10	44	439
CHAIR CAR OF 1890 PLANS CMSP "ALEXANDRIA	06	71	44
CHAIR CAR PLANS CMI #246 1901 PULLMAN	11	74	62
CLASS P58 COACH PLANS PRR #1651 1906	03	77	66
COACH 65' WOOD SHEATH E PLN PLM CLSS A-6	06	40	346
COACH BI-LEVEL M.U. IC #1527 1971 PLAN	03	72	48
COACH BUISNESS CAR NAR GAU C&S #911 PLAN	01	49	24
COACH BUSINESS CARS MC #333 PLANS	12	67	64
COACH CLASS P-70 HVYWEIGHT PLAN PRR#1652	08	63	36
COACH CLASS PBM PLANS R #1209 OF 1925	11	84	97
COACH HARRIMAN STEEL PLANS IC #1012	03	59	45
COACH HEAVY WEIGHT NYC #830 PLANS	09	49	38
COACH LW PLANS C&NW "400"	12	49	51
COACH MU PLANS PRSL #6723	02	69	42
COACH NARROW-GAUGE PLANS D&RGW #287	12	46	846
COACH NARROW-GAUGE PLANS D&RGW #401	07	47	551
COACH OF 1860 CIVIL WAR ERA PLANS PRR	12	63	65
COACH OF 1895 PLANS N&W	07	45	289
COACH OLD TIME PLANS SP&P #1	06	67	38
COACH OLD-TIME DM&IR PLANS 1900	08	38	314
COACH OLD-TIME PLAN CS&CC #82	08	64	26
COACH OPEN PLATFORM DL&W PLANS 1870	01	39	27
COACH OPEN PLATFORM OF 1880 PLANS NYC	11	57	46
COACH OPEN PLATFORM PLANS MA&PA #20	06	68	40
COACH OPEN PLATFORM PLANS P&R #90878	07	48	482
COACH OPEN-END BOARD & BATTEN PLN EBT#10	09	61	44
COACH PLANS D&IR #3	09	67	36
COACH PLANS OF 1900 B&O #445	05	52	10
COACH PRE WAR LIGHT WEIGHT NYNH&H PLANS	01	38	22
COACH PRIVATE MR&BT PLANS 1900 ACF	04	57	44
COACH WITH STEWARDESS ROOM LW PLANS C&NW	12	49	51
COACHES LIGHT WEIGHT PLANS NYC #2562	05	46	338
COACHES LW 1934 MILW #4401 PLAN	11	34	11
DAY COACH OF 1880 PLANS	02	35	34
DAY COACH PLANS	02	39	70
DAYLIGHT DELUXE COACH PLANS SP	10	48	709
DAYLIGHT TAVERN CAR PLANS SP	10	48	709
FIRST CLASS COACH 65' PLANS CP	06	59	38
FREE LANCE COACH PLANS	01	35	5
HEAVY WEIGHT COACH PLANS ATSF #3354	05	47	402
HEAVY WEIGHT COACHES B&O CLASS A-20 PLAN	02	41	79
HEAVYWEIGHT BUSINESS CAR PLANS	02	69	66
HEAVYWEIGHT COACH DELUX ACL 76 PASS PLAN	02	41	79
HIAWATHA COACH DRAWING MILW OF 1925	01	84	114
IMLAY COACH PLANS B&O 1830	07	76	84
LUXURY PRIVATE CAR PLANS	03	60	38
NARROW VESTIBULE COACH PLANS KCP&G #101	03	58	40
OLD COACH PLANS CPA	05	53	48

PASSENGER EQUIPMENT

COACH PLANS	M	Y	P
OLD TIME BUSINESS CAR PLAN CP 1885	12	59	32
OLD TIME COACH PLANS PRR #3556	08	65	33
OLDTIME BUSINESS CAR PLANS PRR #7501	12	59	32
OPEN PLATFORM COACH OF 1865 PLANS LACK	01	39	27
OPEN PLATFORM COACH PLANS PRR #803 1880	01	53	62
PANAMA LIMITED PARLOR LW PLANS IC	05	65	35
PARLOR CAR PLANS LW C&NW "400"	12	49	50
PARLOR CLUB CAR OF 1900 MICHC PLANS	01	39	27
PASSENGER CAR DETAILED NOMENCLATURE DRAW	03	64	27
PICNIC CAR SIE #300 PLANS	02	76	78
PLATFORM COACH PLANS B&O 1835	07	76	84
PULLMAN SOLARIUM-LOUNGE PLANS 3975-S	03	43	131
STEEL SUBURBAN COACH PLAN CNJ	02	37	62
STREAMLINE BUSINESS CAR PLANS	02	69	66
SUBURBAN MU COACH & TRAILER PLNS IC#1125	04	43	182
SUBURBAN PRR #505 CLASS 54E5 PLANS	10	69	79
SUPERLINER COACH PLANS A PS	11	82	88
TRIPLE IMLAY COACH PLANS B&O 1832	07	76	84

RD	COACH PLANS BY ROAD	M	Y	P
A	SUPERLINER COACH PLANS A PS	11	82	88
ACL	HEAVYWEIGHT COACH DELUX ACL 76 PASS PLAN	02	41	79
ATSF	HEAVY WEIGHT COACH PLANS ATSF #3354	05	47	402
B&O	COACH PLANS OF 1900 B&O #445	05	52	10
	PLATFORM COACH PLANS B&O 1835	07	76	84
	TRIPLE IMLAY COACH PLANS B&O 1832	07	76	84
	IMLAY COACH PLANS B&O 1830	07	76	84
	HEAVY WEIGHT COACHES B&O CLASS A-20 PLAN	02	41	79
C&NW	COACH WITH STEWARDESS ROOM LW PLANS C&NW	12	49	51
	COACH LW PLANS C&NW "400"	12	49	51
	PARLOR CAR PLANS LW C&NW "400"	12	49	50
C&S	COACH BUISNESS CAR NAR GAU C&S #911 PLAN	01	49	24
CMI	CHAIR CAR PLANS CMI #246 1901 PULLMAN	11	74	62
CMSP	CHAIR CAR OF 1890 PLANS CMSP "ALEXANDRIA	06	71	44
CNJ	STEEL SUBURBAN COACH PLAN CNJ	02	37	62
CP	35' BUSINESS CAR OF 1912 CONSTRUCT CP #5	12	56	52
	FIRST CLASS COACH 65' PLANS CP	06	59	38
	OLD TIME BUSINESS CAR PLAN CP 1885	12	59	32
	BUSINESS CARS CANADIAN PACIFIC PLANS	04	36	98
CPA	OLD COACH PLANS CPA	05	53	48
CS&CC	COACH OLD-TIME PLAN CS&CC #82	08	64	26
D&IR	COACH PLANS D&IR #3	09	67	36
D&RGW	COACH NARROW-GAUGE PLANS D&RGW #401	07	47	551
	COACH NARROW-GAUGE PLANS D&RGW #287	12	46	846
DL&W	COACH OPEN PLATFORM DL&W PLANS 1870	01	39	27
DM&IR	COACH OLD-TIME DM&IR PLANS 1900	08	38	314
E	COACH 65' WOOD SHEATH E PLN PLM CLSS A-6	06	40	346
EBT	COACH OPEN-END BOARD & BATTEN PLN EBT#10	09	61	44
IC	PANAMA LIMITED PARLOR LW PLANS IC	05	65	35
	COACH BI-LEVEL M.U. IC #1527 1971 PLAN	03	72	48
	COACH HARRIMAN STEEL PLANS IC #1012	03	59	45
	SUBURBAN MU COACH & TRAILER PLNS IC#1125	04	43	182
KCP&G	NARROW VESTIBULE COACH PLANS KCP&G #101	03	58	40

RD	COACH PLANS BY ROAD	M	Y	P
KCS	60' COACH PLANS KCS	10	44	441
LACK	OPEN PLATFORM COACH OF 1865 PLANS LACK	01	39	27
MA&PA	COACH OPEN PLATFORM PLANS MA&PA #20	06	68	40
MC	COACH BUSINESS CARS MC #333 PLANS	12	67	64
MICHC	PARLOR CLUB CAR OF 1900 MICHC PLANS	01	39	27
MILW	HIAWATHA COACH DRAWING MILW OF 1925	01	84	114
	COACHES LW 1934 MILW #4401 PLAN	11	34	11
MR&BT	COACH PRIVATE MR&BT PLANS 1900 ACF	04	57	44
N&W	COACH OF 1895 PLANS N&W	07	45	289
NP	BUSINESS CAR LIGHT WEIGHT PLANS SP 1955	12	59	30
NYC	COACH OPEN PLATFORM OF 1880 PLANS NYC	11	57	46
	COACHES LIGHT WEIGHT PLANS NYC #2562	05	46	338
	COACH HEAVY WEIGHT NYC #830 PLANS	09	49	38
	75' COACHES HEAVY WEIGHT NYC #409 PLANS	10	38	430
NYNH&H	COACH PRE WAR LIGHT WEIGHT NYNH&H PLANS	01	38	22
P&R	COACH OPEN PLATFORM PLANS P&R #90878	07	48	482
PRR	BUSINESS CAR PLANS PRR #100 "CHESAPEAKE"	10	71	56
	CLASS P58 COACH PLANS PRR #1651 1906	03	77	66
	OLD TIME COACH PLANS PRR #3556	08	65	33
	SUBURBAN PRR #505 CLASS 54E5 PLANS	10	69	79
	OPEN PLATFORM COACH PLANS PRR #803 1880	01	53	62
	OLDTIME BUSINESS CAR PLANS PRR #7501	12	59	32
	COACH OF 1860 CIVIL WAR ERA PLANS PRR	12	63	65
	COACH CLASS P-70 HVYWEIGHT PLAN PRR#1652	08	63	36
PRSL	COACH MU PLANS PRSL #6723	02	69	42
R	COACH CLASS PBM PLANS R #1209 OF 1925	11	84	97
SIE	PICNIC CAR SIE #300 PLANS	02	76	78
SP	BUSINESS HEAVY WEIGHT PLANS SP #110	12	59	32
	DAYLIGHT DELUXE COACH PLANS SP	10	48	709
	DAYLIGHT TAVERN CAR PLANS SP	10	48	709
SP&P	COACH OLD TIME PLANS SP&P #1	06	67	38

COACH PHOTOS	M	Y	P
PRIVATE CAR "VIRGINIA" PHOTOS	06	69	46

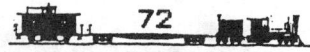

PASSENGER EQUIPMENT

COACH MODELS

Title	M	Y	P
35' BUSINESS CAR PLANS OF 1912 CP #5	12	56	52
AUTO TRAIN INTERIOR DETAILING CONSTRUCT	01	75	60
BUSINESS CAR CONSTRUCTION 1	01	69	40
BUSINESS CAR CONSTRUCTION 2	02	69	61
BUSINESS CAR CONSTRUCTION CP #32	01	57	56
BUSINESS CAR FROM PASSENGER CONVERSION	06	73	51
COACH CONSTRUCTION 1 O SCALE	09	49	14
COACH CONSTRUCTION 2 O SCALE	10	49	26
COACH KIT ASSEMBLY JC MODELS	03	49	28
COACH LW COMMUTER CONSTRUCTION RI	07	58	48
COACH TO MATCH LIONEL PULLMANS CONST	02	50	50
COMMUTER CAR BN MOD & PT	08	78	103
CP COACH MOD & PT	02	75	25
FOIL & PLASTER TO SIMULATE STAIN STEEL	06	80	80
HARRIMAN STEEL COACH CONSTRUCTION	03	59	42
KITBASH COMMUTER CARS	06	78	62
LENGHTENING MDC OVERTON PASSENGER CARS	10	80	100
MINIATURE MANSION ON RAILS 1/2" SCALE	02	77	54
MOM BUSINESS CAR SP "HO" HOFFMANN	08	52	28
MOM OPEN PLATFORM 1860 COACH "O" KRUSE	06	81	66
MOM RGS BUSINESS CAR EDNA "ON3" KRUEGER	05	80	74
MONON COACH MOD & PT	05	78	114
OLD TIME BUSINESS CAR SUPERDETAILING	12	59	60
OLDTIME LUXURY PRIVATE CAR CONSTRUCTION	03	60	34
OPEN PLATFORM COACHES MOD & PT	01	76	26
PRIVATE CAR CONST MANSION ON RAILS	05	64	39
PRIVATE CAR FOR YOUR PIKE CONSTRUCTION	02	51	50
PULLMAN SOLARIUM-LOUNGE CONSTRUCTION 1	03	43	129
PULLMAN SOLARIUM-LOUNGE CONSTRUCTION 2	04	43	184
PULLMAN SOLARIUM-LOUNGE CONSTRUCTION 3	05	43	230
PULLMAN SOLARIUM-LOUNGE CONSTRUCTION 4	06	43	276
PULLMAN SOLARIUM-LOUNGE CONSTRUCTION 5	07	43	322
READING COACHES BUILT FROM STD ATHEARNS	03	67	37

COACH MODEL REVIEWS

Title	M	Y	P
1860 COACH REVIEW "HO" M	10	58	16
1860 PASSENGER CAR REVIEW "HO" PCH 1860	09	70	14
1900 60' PARLOR CAR MILW REV "HO" LA	01	61	22
1900 MILW DAY COACH REVIEW "HO" LA	12	60	10
1906 60' COACH REVIEW "HO" KK	10	59	10
1910 PASSENGER CAR REVIEW "TT" SD	08	53	11
46' F&CC COACH REVIEW "HON3" LABELLE	07	61	10
46' V&T COACH OF 1870 REVIEW "HO" AHM	02	65	10
47' PASSENGER COACH REVIEW "HO" AHM 1875	08	74	18
50' PASSENGER COACH REVIEW "O" WAL	07	41	384
60' COACH KIT REVIEW "TT" SLM	12	50	55
60' PASSENGER CAR REVIEW "HO" WAL	12	53	13
62' COACH KIT REVIEW "O" JC	04	50	62
62' COACH REVIEW "O" JC	10	54	15
62' COACH REVIEW "O" AN	01	59	22
66' SP COACH OF 1905 REVIEW "HO" LABELLE	01	60	13
70' COACH KIT REVIEW "TT" JM	11	50	56
78' COACH NYO&W REVIEW "HO" NPP OB 1922	04	74	24
80' HEAVYWEIGHT COACH REVIEW "HO" WAL	10	77	34
83' CIRCUS COACH REVIEW "HO" WAL	08	72	21
85' USA HOSPITAL CAR REVIEW "HO" WAL ACF	02	74	29
AMCOACH REVIEW "HO" B 1975 BUDD	06	80	42
AMCOACH REVIEW "HO" WAL 1975	04	84	35
AMERICAN FLYER NYNH&H COACH REV "HO" EBV	07	82	34
ARTICULATED SP COACH REVIEW "HO" SOHO	05	77	42
BI LEVEL COACHES REVIEW "N" CC	09	82	38
BUDD COACH STREAMLINE KIT REVIEW "HO" M	09	55	16
BUDD STREAMLINE COACH REVIEW "HO" ATH	10	55	11
BUSINESS CAR 67' REVIEW "O" WAL	11	59	16
BUSINESS CAR MKT REVIEW "HO" H	01	76	38
BUSINESS CAR REVIEW "HO" L	04	76	30
BUSINESS CAR REVIEW "HO" DN	10	50	55
BUSINESS CAR SP "SUNSET" REV "HO" CY PS	07	82	36
COACH B&O TRUSS ROD REVIEW "HO" CL	12	53	22
COACH D&RG REVIEW "HON3" LA 1887 J&S	04	74	26
COACH D&RGW #319 REV "HON3" 1937 EBV	02	80	35
COACH KIT REVIEW "HO" LAC	12	49	86
COACH KIT REVIEW "HO" JGHC	12	49	85
COACH LISTING "N" RIVEROSSI	08	78	48
COACH LISTING WABASH "HO" AHM	04	78	54
COACH SR&RL REVIEW"ON2"TOY & HOBBY HOUSE	07	76	24
COACHES OF NEW HAVEN REVIEW "HO" SOHO	01	78	40
DAYLIGHT PARLOR CAR SP REVIEW "HO" SOHO	12	72	36
EXECUTIVE COACH KIT REVIEW "HO" WAL	04	58	10
GALLERY COACH REVIEW "N" RAP C&NW	03	75	24
HI-LEVEL COACH & LOUNGE REVIEW "HO" FL	12	58	17
HIAWATHA CARS MILW REVIEW "1/4" WAL	05	78	38
METROLINER A REVIEW "HO" B 1969 BUDD	07	75	24
NARROW VESTIBULE B&O COACH REV "HO" WEST	07	69	19
OLD PASSENGER CAR REVIEW "1/4" SHS	02	70	22
OLDTIME COACH KIT REVIEW "HO" BIN 1880	04	55	13
OLDTIME COACH REVIEW "G" KTTW	01	83	53
OPEN PLATFORM CAR REVIEW "HO" HIB	11	54	16
OPEN PLATFORM COACH REVIEW "HO" M	10	41	540
OPEN PLATFORM COACH REVIEW "N" RAP	05	68	18A

PASSENGER EQUIPMENT

COACH MODEL REVIEWS

	M	Y	P
PASSENGER CAR REVIEW "HO" V	07	41	383
PASSENGER CAR REVIEW "N" CC	12	68	18
PASSENGER CAR REVIEW "O" CSC	04	70	20
PASSENGER COACH KIT REVIEW "HO" LAC	10	40	580
PASSENGER COACH KIT REVIEW "HO" SMP	09	47	767
PASSENGER COACH KIT REVIEW "HO" JE	09	50	57
PASSENGER COACH KIT REVIEW "S" MIM	02	48	151
PASSENGER COACH REVIEW "HO" RCH	04	48	304
PASSENGER COACH REVIEW "HO" JC	09	48	670
PASSENGER COACH REVIEW PRR "HO" JC	03	56	9
PASSENGER KIT REVIEW "HO" BL	06	48	432
PHOTOGRAPH CAR KIT REVIEW "HO" DN	03	52	58
PUSH PULL BI-LEVEL CAR REVIEW "HO" H&R	01	68	11
SHORTY COACH REVIEW "HO" SEL	04	60	11
SHORTY METAL PASSENGER KIT REVIEW "HO" V	07	51	46
SINGLE WINDOW NYC COACH REVIEW "O" ASC	01	79	46
SP DAYLIGHT COACH REVIEW "O" BCK	08	61	12
STANDARD 74' COACH REVIEW "HO" RIV	09	66	10
STANDARD PRR COACH REVIEW "HO" ALCO	01	83	45
STEEL COACH NYC REVIEW "HO" RD	03	78	44
STEEL COACH REVIEW "O" MODEL RR COACH CO	11	37	432
STEEL OFFICE CAR ATSF REV "HO" WAL 1924	01	81	54
STREAMLINED COACH ATSF REVIEW "HO" JMC	03	69	9
STREAMLINED COACH LISTING "HO" LAMBERT	07	77	43
STREAMLINED COACH NYNH&H REVIEW "HO" EBV	07	83	28
STREAMLINED COACH REVIEW "HO" AMER	06	52	38
STREAMLINED COACH REVIEW "HO" HERK	02	63	24
STREAMLINED COACH REVIEW "HO" RIV	11	67	20
STREAMLINED NYNH&H COACH REVIEW "O" BM	04	73	28
STREAMLINER COACH REVIEW "S" AMI	01	85	52
SUPERLINER AMTRAK REVIEW "HO" CC 1979	03	84	36
TINPLATE OLDTIME COACH REVIEW "O" TH	06	51	49
UP COACH REVIEW "O" PSS	11	38	504
V&T KIMBALL COACH REVIEW "HO" LI	10	67	12

COACH MODEL REVIEWS BY ROAD

RD		M	Y	P
A	METROLINER A REVIEW "HO" B 1969 BUDD	07	75	24
	AMCOACH REVIEW "HO" WAL 1975	04	84	35
	SUPERLINER AMTRAK REVIEW "HO" CC 1979	03	84	36
	AMCOACH REVIEW "HO" B 1975 BUDD	06	80	42
ATSF	STEEL OFFICE CAR ATSF REV "HO" WAL 1924	01	81	54
	STREAMLINED COACH ATSF REVIEW "HO" JMC	03	69	9
B&O	NARROW VESTIBULE B&O COACH REV "HO" WEST	07	69	19
C&NW	GALLERY COACH REVIEW "N" RAP C&NW	03	75	24
D&RG	COACH D&RG REVIEW "HON3" LA 1887 J&S	04	74	26
D&RGW	COACH D&RGW #319 REV "HON3" 1937 EBV	02	80	35
F&CC	46' F&CC COACH REVIEW "HON3" LABELLE	07	61	10
MILW	HIAWATHA CARS MILW REVIEW "1/4" WAL	05	78	38
	1900 MILW DAY COACH REVIEW "HO" LA	12	60	10
	1900 60' PARLOR CAR MILW REV "HO" LA	01	61	22
NH	COACHES OF NEW HAVEN REVIEW "HO" SOHO	01	78	40
NYC	SINGLE WINDOW NYC COACH REVIEW "O" ASC	01	79	46
	STEEL COACH NYC REVIEW "HO" RD	03	78	44
NYNH&H	STREAMLINED NYNH&H COACH REVIEW "O" BM	04	73	28
	STREAMLINED COACH NYNH&H REVIEW "HO" EBV	07	83	28
	AMERICAN FLYER NYNH&H COACH REV "HO" EBV	07	82	34
NYO&W	78' COACH NYO&W REVIEW "HO" NPP OB 1922	04	74	24
PRR	STANDARD PRR COACH REVIEW "HO" ALCO	01	83	45
SP	DAYLIGHT PARLOR CAR SP REVIEW "HO" SOHO	12	72	36
	BUSINESS CAR SP "SUNSET" REV "HO" CY PS	07	82	36
	ARTICULATED SP COACH REVIEW "HO" SOHO	05	77	42
	66' SP COACH OF 1905 REVIEW "HO" LABELLE	01	60	13
	SP DAYLIGHT COACH REVIEW "O" BCK	08	61	12
SR&RL	COACH SR&RL REVIEW "ON2" TOY & HOBBY HOUSE	07	76	24
UP	UP COACH REVIEW "O" PSS	11	38	504
USA	85' USA HOSPITAL CAR REVIEW "HO" WAL ACF	02	74	29
V&T	46' V&T COACH OF 1870 REVIEW "HO" AHM	02	65	10
W	COACH LISTING WABASH "HO" AHM	04	78	54

PASSENGER EQUIPMENT

COACH MODEL REVIEWS BY MFG.

MFG		M	Y	P
	STEEL COACH REVIEW "O" MODEL RR COACH CO	11	37	432
	STEEL COACH NYC REVIEW "HO" RD	03	78	44
	HIAWATHA CARS MILW REVIEW "1/4" WAL	05	78	38
	ARTICULATED SP COACH REVIEW "HO" SOHO	05	77	42
AHM	47' PASSENGER COACH REVIEW "HO" AHM 1875	08	74	18
	46' V&T COACH OF 1870 REVIEW "HO" AHM	02	65	10
	COACH LISTING WABASH "HO" AHM	04	78	54
ALCO	STANDARD PRR COACH REVIEW "HO" ALCO	01	83	45
AMER	STREAMLINED COACH REVIEW "HO" AMER	06	52	38
AMI	STREAMLINER COACH REVIEW "S" AMI	01	85	52
AN	62' COACH REVIEW "O" AN	01	59	22
ASC	SINGLE WINDOW NYC COACH REVIEW "O" ASC	01	79	46
ATH	BUDD STREAMLINE COACH REVIEW "HO" ATH	10	55	11
B	METROLINER A REVIEW "HO" B 1969 BUDD	07	75	24
	AMCOACH REVIEW "HO" B 1975 BUDD	06	80	42
BCK	SP DAYLIGHT COACH REVIEW "O" BCK	08	61	12
BIN	OLDTIME COACH KIT REVIEW "HO" BIN 1880	04	55	13
BL	PASSENGER KIT REVIEW "HO" BL	06	48	432
BM	STREAMLINED NYNH&H COACH REVIEW "O" BM	04	73	28
CC	PASSENGER CAR REVIEW "N" CC	12	68	18
	BI LEVEL COACHES REVIEW "N" CC	09	82	38
	SUPERLINER AMTRAK REVIEW "HO" CC 1979	03	84	36
CL	COACH B&O TRUSS ROD REVIEW "HO" CL	12	53	22
CSC	PASSENGER CAR REVIEW "O" CSC	04	70	20
CY	BUSINESS CAR SP "SUNSET" REV "HO" CY PS	07	82	36
DN	PHOTOGRAPH CAR KIT REVIEW "HO" DN	03	52	58
	BUSINESS CAR REVIEW "HO" DN	10	50	55
EBV	AMERICAN FLYER NYNH&H COACH REV "HO" EBV	07	82	34
	STREAMLINED COACH NYNH&H REVIEW "HO" EBV	07	83	28
	COACH D&RGW #319 REV "HON3" 1937 EBV	02	80	35
FL	HI-LEVEL COACH & LOUNGE REVIEW "HO" FL	12	58	17
H	BUSINESS CAR MKT REVIEW "HO" H	01	76	38
H&R	PUSH PULL BI-LEVEL CAR REVIEW "HO" H&R	01	68	11
HERK	STREAMLINED COACH REVIEW "HO" HERK	02	63	24
HIB	OPEN PLATFORM CAR REVIEW "HO" HIB	11	54	16
JC	PASSENGER COACH REVIEW "HO" JC	09	48	670
	PASSENGER COACH REVIEW PRR "HO" JC	03	56	9
	62' COACH REVIEW "O" JC	10	54	15
	62' COACH KIT REVIEW "O" JC	04	50	62
JE	PASSENGER COACH KIT REVIEW "HO" JE	09	50	57
JGHC	COACH KIT REVIEW "HO" JGHC	12	49	85
JM	70' COACH KIT REVIEW "TT" JM	11	50	56
JMC	STREAMLINED COACH ATSF REVIEW "HO" JMC	03	69	9
KK	1906 60' COACH REVIEW "HO" KK	10	59	10
KTTW	OLDTIME COACH REVIEW "G" KTTW	01	83	53
L	BUSINESS CAR REVIEW "HO" L	04	76	30
	STREAMLINED COACH LISTING "HO" LAMBERT	07	77	43
LA	COACH D&RG REVIEW "HON3" LA 1887 J&S	04	74	26
	66' SP COACH OF 1905 REVIEW "HO" LABELLE	01	60	13
	1900 MILW DAY COACH REVIEW "HO" LA	12	60	10
	46' F&CC COACH REVIEW "HON3" LABELLE	07	61	10
	1900 60' PARLOR CAR MILW REV "HO" LA	01	61	22
LAC	PASSENGER COACH KIT REVIEW "HO" LAC	10	40	580
	COACH KIT REVIEW "HO" LAC	12	49	86
LI	V&T KIMBALL COACH REVIEW "HO" LI	10	67	12

COACH MODEL REVIEWS BY MFG.

MFG		M	Y	P
M	OPEN PLATFORM COACH REVIEW "HO" M	10	41	540
	BUDD COACH STREAMLINE KIT REVIEW "HO" M	09	55	16
	1860 COACH REVIEW "HO" M	10	58	16
MIM	PASSENGER COACH KIT REVIEW "S" MIM	02	48	151
NPP	78' COACH NYO&W REVIEW "HO" NPP OB 1922	04	74	24
PCH	1860 PASSENGER CAR REVIEW "HO" PCH 1860	09	70	14
PSS	UP COACH REVIEW "O" PSS	11	38	504
RAP	GALLERY COACH REVIEW "N" RAP C&NW	03	75	24
	OPEN PLATFORM COACH REVIEW "N" RAP	05	68	18A
RCH	PASSENGER COACH REVIEW "HO" RCH	04	48	304
RIV	COACH LISTING "N" RIVEROSSI	08	78	48
	STREAMLINED COACH REVIEW "HO" RIV	11	67	20
	STANDARD 74' COACH REVIEW "HO" RIV	09	66	10
SD	1910 PASSENGER CAR REVIEW "TT" SD	08	53	11
SEL	SHORTY COACH REVIEW "HO" SEL	04	60	11
SHS	OLD PASSENGER CAR REVIEW "1/4" SHS	02	70	22
SLM	60' COACH KIT REVIEW "TT" SLM	12	50	55
SMP	PASSENGER COACH KIT REVIEW "HO" SMP	09	47	767
SOHO	DAYLIGHT PARLOR CAR SP REVIEW "HO" SOHO	12	72	36
	COACHES OF NEW HAVEN REVIEW "HO" SOHO	01	78	40
TH	TINPLATE OLDTIME COACH REVIEW "O" TH	06	51	49
THH	COACH SR&RL REVIEW "ON2" TOY & HOBBY HOUSE	07	76	24
V	PASSENGER CAR REVIEW "HO" V	07	41	383
	SHORTY METAL PASSENGER KIT REVIEW "HO" V	07	51	46
WAL	50' PASSENGER COACH REVIEW "O" WAL	07	41	384
	85' USA HOSPITAL CAR REVIEW "HO" WAL ACF	02	74	29
	83' CIRCUS COACH REVIEW "HO" WAL	08	72	21
	BUSINESS CAR 67' REVIEW "O" WAL	11	59	16
	EXECUTIVE COACH KIT REVIEW "HO" WAL	04	58	10
	60' PASSENGER CAR REVIEW "HO" WAL	12	53	13
	80' HEAVYWEIGHT COACH REVIEW "HO" WAL	10	77	34
	AMCOACH REVIEW "HO" WAL 1975	04	84	35
	STEEL OFFICE CAR ATSF REV "HO" WAL 1924	01	81	54
WEST	NARROW VESTIBULE B&O COACH REV "HO" WEST	07	69	19

DOME CAR PROTOTYPE DATA

	M	Y	P
GREAT DOMES OF GN EMPIRE BLDR 1955	06	84	73
VISTA DOME COACHES CB&Q	08	78	69
VISTA DOME COACHES CB&Q LETTER	10	78	36

DOME CAR PLANS

	M	Y	P
DOME 85' COACH LW PLANS CB&Q SILVER DOME	07	46	446
GREAT DOME PLN GN EMPIRE BLDR 1955	06	84	75
LIGHT WT DOME LOUNGE CARS ATSF #501 PLAN	07	52	62
VISTA DOME COACH PLANS CB&Q	08	78	70

DOME CAR PLANS BY ROAD

RD		M	Y	P
ATSF	LIGHT WT DOME LOUNGE CARS ATSF #501 PLAN	07	52	62
CB&Q	VISTA DOME COACH PLANS CB&Q	08	78	70
	DOME 85' COACH LW PLANS CB&Q SILVER DOME	07	46	446
GN	GREAT DOME PLN GN EMPIRE BLDR 1955	06	84	75

PASSENGER EQUIPMENT

DOME CAR MODELS	M	Y	P
BIG DOME LOUNGE CAR CONSTRUCTION SP#2950	10	72	58
GREAT DOME CAR CONSTRUCTION GN	09	75	48
THERMOFORMING SUPERDOME WINDOWS	08	79	132

DOME CAR MODEL REVIEWS	M	Y	P
CP DOME CAR OF 1902 REVIEW "HO" WEST	07	71	26
DOME BUDD CAR LISTING "HO" SOHO	08	78	51
DOME CAR ATSF REVIEW "HO" CC	05	69	11
VISTA COME COACH REVIEW "HO" CC	02	81	56
VISTA DOME KIT REVIEW "HO" SMP	02	49	73

DOME CAR MODEL REVIEWS BY MFG.

MFG		M	Y	P
CC	DOME CAR ATSF REVIEW "HO" CC	05	69	11
	VISTA COME COACH REVIEW "HO" CC	02	81	56
SMP	VISTA DOME KIT REVIEW "HO" SMP	02	49	73
SOHO	DOME BUDD CAR LISTING "HO" SOHO	08	78	51
WEST	CP DOME CAR OF 1902 REVIEW "HO" WEST	07	71	26

OBSERVATION CAR PROTOTYPE DATA	M	Y	P
OBSERVATION CAR PLATFORM DETAIL BURL	02	62	49
STREAMLINED OBSERVATION/BUSINESS CARS	05	74	78
VANISHING OBSERVATION CAR	12	36	369

OBSERVATION CAR PLANS	M	Y	P
BUSINESS OBSERVATION DRAWING	01	69	43
CAFE/PARLOR/OBS 73' PLANS CP	06	59	38
DAYLIGHT OBSERVATION CAR PLANS SP	10	48	711
HEAVYWEIGHT CAFE-PAR-OBS CP "TRENT" PLAN	09	66	36
HIAWATHA OBSERVATION DRAWING MILW	01	84	114
HW OBSERVATION CAR PLANS UP	02	41	79
OBSERVATION LW PLANS C&NW "400"	12	49	50
OBSERVATION OLD-TIME DM&IR PLANS 1887	08	38	314
OBSERVATION-COACH 1903 PLANS D&M #100 BS	01	73	40
OBSERVATION-COACH OLD-TIME PLAN CS&CC#92	08	64	27
OBSERVATION-LOUNGE CAR PLANS PULLMAN	03	42	130
OPEN OBSERVATION D&RGW PLANS	03	48	208
OPEN OBSERVATION CAR CP #7909 PLANS	08	52	14
OPEN OBSERVATION PLANS CN #7911 1914	11	71	56
OPEN-AIR SIGHTSEEING COACH PLANS BI&B	11	62	43
PANAMA LIMITED OBSERVATION	05	65	35
PULLMAN OBSERVATION PLANS OF 1893	04	63	40

OBSERVATION CAR PLANS BY ROAD

RD		M	Y	P
	BUSINESS OBSERVATION DRAWING	01	69	43
	OBSERVATION-LOUNGE CAR PLANS PULLMAN	03	42	130
*P	PULLMAN OBSERVATION PLANS OF 1893	04	63	40
BI&B	OPEN-AIR SIGHTSEEING COACH PLANS BI&B	11	62	43
C&NW	OBSERVATION LW PLANS C&NW "400"	12	49	50
CN	OPEN OBSERVATION PLANS CN #7911 1914	11	71	56
CP	OPEN OBSERVATION CAR CP #7909 PLANS	08	52	14
	HEAVYWEIGHT CAFE-PAR-OBS CP "TRENT" PLAN	09	66	36
	CAFE/PARLOR/OBS 73' PLANS CP	06	59	38
CS&CC	OBSERVATION-COACH OLD-TIME PLAN CS&CC#92	08	64	27
D&M	OBSERVATION-COACH 1903 PLANS D&M #100 BS	01	73	40
D&RGW	OPEN OBSERVATION D&RGW PLANS	03	48	208
DM&IR	OBSERVATION OLD-TIME DM&IR PLANS 1887	08	38	314
IC	PANAMA LIMITED OBSERVATION	05	65	35
MILW	HIAWATHA OBSERVATION DRAWING MILW	01	84	114
SP	DAYLIGHT OBSERVATION CAR PLANS SP	10	48	711
UP	HW OBSERVATION CAR PLANS UP	02	41	79

OBSERVATION CAR MODELS	M	Y	P
DOME OBS CAR FROM AHM DOME COACH & OBS	07	73	62
MIDTRAIN OBSERVATION CAR KITBASH	04	79	84
MOM MOUNTAIN OBSERVATION CP CAR"HO" VIAU	12	78	101
NYC OBSERVATION MOD & PT	06	76	93
OBSERVATION CAR PLATFORM CONSTRUCTION	05	35	120
OPEN OBSERVATION CONSTRUCTION CP	11	71	56

OBSERVATION CAR MODEL REVIEWS	M	Y	P
1903 OBS-SLEEPER REVIEW CMSP "HO"LABELLE	06	61	13
1930 85' STANDARD OBS ATSF REV "HO" S	04	61	14
HARRIMANN OBS CAR REVIEW "HO" KEN KIDDER	12	64	7
OBSERVATION CAR KIT REVIEW "HO" BL	07	48	505
OBSERVATION CAR KIT REVIEW "HO" KAS	07	48	506
SL OBSERVATION REVIEW "HO" RCH	09	48	669
STREAMLINED OBSERVATION KIT REV "HO" SMP	12	48	993

OBSERVATION CAR MODEL REVIEWS BY MFG.

MFG		M	Y	P
BL	OBSERVATION CAR KIT REVIEW "HO" BL	07	48	505
KAS	OBSERVATION CAR KIT REVIEW "HO" KAS	07	48	506
KK	HARRIMANN OBS CAR REVIEW "HO" KEN KIDDER	12	64	7
LA	1903 OBS-SLEEPER REVIEW CMSP "HO"LABELLE	06	61	13
RCH~	SL OBSERVATION REVIEW "HO" RCH	09	48	669
S	1930 85' STANDARD OBS ATSF REV "HO" S	04	61	14
SMP	STREAMLINED OBSERVATION KIT REV "HO" SMP	12	48	993

PASSENGER EQUIPMENT

RAILCAR PROTOTYPE DATA

	M	Y	P
BUDD SPV-2000 UP TO DATE/SELF PROPELLED	05	81	72
COLORS FOR NS&M 700 SERIES MOTOR CAR	05	34	10
GAS ELECTRIC STREAMLINERS	10	77	125
PLACE OF GAS ELEC & M.U.S. IN OPERATIONS	02	35	31

RAILCAR PLANS

	M	Y	P
BRILL GAS-ELECTRIC DUAL 350 PLANS	03	60	44
BUDD SPV-2000 STANDARD/HIGH SPEED PLANS	05	81	73
COACH 64' MU CLASS MP-54-E PRR PLAN	10	35	266
COACH M. U. DL&W #2501 1931 PLAN	05	35	126
COMBINE GAS ELECTRIC D&RGW #592 PLAN	05	68	34
GAS ELECTRIC CAR PLANS MA&PA #62	01	66	37
GAS-ELECTRIC CAR #14 COACH MN&S PLAN	10	36	284
GAS-ELECTRIC COACH PLANS GM&N	07	35	175
GAS-ELECTRIC M-100 RPO (CIN&N) NYC PLAN	10	36	284
HALL-SCOTT MOTOR CAR PLANS NCBT #21	02	64	34
M-190 ARTICULATED RAILCAR UNIT ATSF 1930	08	54	38
MOTOR CAR & TRAILER PLANS GM&O GAS-ELECT	04	59	38
POTLATCHER RAILCAR PLANS WI&M #11	09	75	47
RDC-1 BUDD COACH PLANS	09	53	68
RDC-1 BUDD PLANS	09	50	42
RDC-2 BUDD COMBINE PLANS COACH-BAGGAGE	09	53	69
RDC-3 BUDD COMBINE PLANS COACH-BAG-MAIL	09	53	68
RDC-4 BUDD COMBINE PLANS BAGGAGE-MAIL	09	53	69
STEAM MOTOR CAR PLANS ICO	04	49	41

RAILCAR PLANS BY ROAD

RD		M	Y	P
ATSF	M-190 ARTICULATED RAILCAR UNIT ATSF 1930	08	54	38
D&RGW	COMBINE GAS ELECTRIC D&RGW #592 PLAN	05	68	34
DL&W	COACH M. U. DL&W #2501 1931 PLAN	05	35	126
GM&N	GAS-ELECTRIC COACH PLANS GM&N	07	35	175
GM&O	MOTOR CAR & TRAILER PLANS GM&O GAS-ELECT	04	59	38
ICO	STEAM MOTOR CAR PLANS ICO	04	49	41
MA&PA	GAS ELECTRIC CAR PLANS MA&PA #62	01	66	37
MN&S	GAS-ELECTRIC CAR #14 COACH MN&S PLAN	10	36	284
NCBT	HALL-SCOTT MOTOR CAR PLANS NCBT #21	02	64	34
NYC	GAS-ELECTRIC M-100 RPO (CIN&N) NYC PLAN	10	36	284
PRR	COACH 64' MU CLASS MP-54-E PRR PLAN	10	35	266
WI&M	POTLATCHER RAILCAR PLANS WI&M #11	09	75	47

RAILCAR PHOTOS

	M	Y	P
GAS ELECTRIC PHOTOS & HISTORY	02	79	148

RAILCAR MODELS

	M	Y	P
DOODLEBUG KITBASH	02	79	98
GAS ELECTRIC CAR CONSTRUCT CAR BODY	10	39	493
GAS ELECTRIC CAR CONSTRUCT MOTOR UNIT	12	39	632
GAS ELECTRIC CAR CONSTRUCT ROOF DETAIL	11	39	567
GAS ELECTRIC COMBINE CONSTRUCTION D&RGW	05	68	33
GAS-ELECTRIC CAR CONSTRUCTION	06	35	153
GAS-ELECTRICS FOR MODELING	10	36	285
HALL-SCOTT MOTOR CAR KITBASH	12	81	100
IMPROVING ATHEARNS RDC'S	11	58	56
RDC-1 BUDD CONSTRUCTION	11	52	36

RAILCAR MODEL REVIEWS

	M	Y	P
ARTICULATED GAS-ELECTRIC REVIEW "HO" WAL	04	53	60
BRILL 750 GAS ELECTRIC REVIEW "HO" S	03	61	10
GAS ELECTRIC COMBINE REVIEW "1/4" ASC	03	80	41
GAS ELECTRIC REVIEW "HO" CCF	10	80	46
GAS ELECTRIC REVIEW "HO" WALTERS	12	37	474
MCKEEN MOTOR CAR REVIEW "HO" KK 1910	11	56	22
MOTOR RAILCAR REVIEW "HO" SMP	06	49	62
RDC 1 RAIL CAR REVIEW "HO" ATH	09	53	10
RDC REVIEW "HO" ATH	08	58	9
RDC-1 BUDD RAIL CAR REVIEW "HO" ATH	06	53	56
RDC-1 BUDD REVIEW "N" CC 1950	11	81	41

RAILCAR MODEL REVIEWS BY MFG.

MFG		M	Y	P
ASC	GAS ELECTRIC COMBINE REVIEW "1/4" ASC	03	80	41
ATH	RDC REVIEW "HO" ATH	08	58	9
	RDC 1 RAIL CAR REVIEW "HO" ATH	09	53	10
	RDC-1 BUDD RAIL CAR REVIEW "HO" ATH	06	53	56
CC	RDC-1 BUDD REVIEW "N" CC 1950	11	81	41
CCF	GAS ELECTRIC REVIEW "HO" CCF	10	80	46
KK	MCKEEN MOTOR CAR REVIEW "HO" KK 1910	11	56	22
S	BRILL 750 GAS ELECTRIC REVIEW "HO" S	03	61	10
SMP	MOTOR RAILCAR REVIEW "HO" SMP	06	49	62
WAL	GAS ELECTRIC REVIEW "HO" WALTERS	12	37	474
	ARTICULATED GAS-ELECTRIC REVIEW "HO" WAL	04	53	60

PASSENGER EQUIPMENT

GENERAL PASSENGER CAR PROTOTYPE DATA

	M	Y	P
AUTOTRAIN STORY & DETAILS	12	74	48
CAR LIGHTING SYSTEMS	05	37	180
CONSIST "TWIN CITIES 400" LW C&NW	12	49	49
ELECTRIC LIGHT & HEAT TENDER CMSP #12	11	70	68
LIGHT WEIGHT "DAYLIGHT" SP	10	48	707
MILW HIAWATHA	01	84	112
MORE PASSENGER CARS OF 1890'S	06	71	43
NAME TRAINS NEEDN'T BE LONG "OLYMPIAN"	09	54	55
PASS TRAIN C&O "PERE MARQUETTE CONNECT"	11	80	68
PASSENGER CAR BLUEBOOK CAR DEFINITIONS	11	55	67
PASSENGER CAR BRAKE EQUIPMENT BLUEBOOK	07	57	65
PASSENGER CAR INTERIOR DETAILS	05	61	38
PASSENGER CAR ROOF FINISHES	02	77	121
PASSENGER CAR TRUCK BLUEBOOK	05	56	53
PASSENGER CAR UNDERBODY EQUIPMENT B PETE	09	43	408
PASSENGER CARS OF 1890 MILW ROAD	02	71	60
PASSENGER CARS OF READING	11	84	90
PASSENGER TRAIN AMTRAK "BLACKHAWK"	01	81	91
PASSENGER TRAIN AMTRAK "POTOMAC SPECIAL"	01	81	90
PASSENGER TRAIN ATSF "GRAND CANYON"	11	80	67
PASSENGER TRAIN BURL TWIN "ZEPHYRS"	11	80	69
PASSENGER TRAIN C&EI "DANVILLE FLYER"	11	80	69
PASSENGER TRAIN CARS BOOMER PETE	05	44	218
PASSENGER TRAIN CN "VIA TRAIN 179"	01	81	93
PASSENGER TRAIN CP "ATLANTIC LIMITED"	01	81	92
PASSENGER TRAIN D&H "LAURENTIAN"	11	80	68
PASSENGER TRAIN GN "DAKOTAN"	11	80	68
PASSENGER TRAIN N&W "BANNER BLUE"	11	80	69
PASSENGER TRAIN ON "TRAIN 584"	01	81	93
PASSENGER TRAIN OPERATIONS DETAILS	04	58	50
PASSENGER TRAIN PRR "CLOCKER"	11	80	67
PASSENGER TRAIN RI "PEORIA ROCKET"	01	81	92
PASSENGER TRAIN RI "QUAD CITY ROCKET"	01	81	92
PASSENGER UNDERBODY DETAILS	07	49	20
PASSENGERN TRAIN S "ASHVILLE SPECIAL"	01	81	91
PIKE SIZE PASS TRAINS YOU CAN MODEL 2	01	81	90
PIKE SIZE PASSENGER TRAINS YOU CAN MODEL	11	80	66
POSTWAR SL PASSENGER FLEET NYNH&H	01	76	56
ROOF DETAILS ON PASSENGER CARS	03	63	55
SAFETY APPLIANCES PASSENGER CARS BLUE BK	09	57	66
SP PASSENGER CAR COLOR CORRECTIONS	08	61	5
STANDARD PASSENGER CAR TRUCKS	12	34	5
STEAM GENERATOR CARS	03	82	90
STREAMLINED CAR INTERIORS BLUEBOOK	11	56	75
STREAMLINED COACHES FOR MILW IN 1934	02	34	10
STREAMLINED UP TRAIN PULLMAN BUILT 1934	02	34	6
SUPERLINER CONSISTS	11	82	96
SUPERLINERS OF AMTRAK PULLMAN STANDARD	11	82	84
TALGO TRAIN BY AMERICAN CAR & FOUNDRY	10	49	44
VENTILATOR TYPES	01	48	25

GENERAL PASSENGER CAR PLANS

	M	Y	P
"KETTLE VALLEY" CONSIST PLANS CP 1900	06	59	38
BUSINESS CAR #91 CN PLANS 1956	06	73	48
CB&Q "PIONEER ZEPHYR" CAR PLANS	10	59	52
COMMONWEALTH PASSENGER TRUCK PLANS	06	35	160
ELECTRIC LIGHT & HEAT TENDER CMSP#12 PLN	11	70	69
HIAWATHA DRAWINGS MILW	01	84	114
HOSPITAL UNIT CAR PLANS USA	08	45	322
LIGHT WEIGHT "SUPER CHIEF" CONSIST ATSF	11	38	474S
PASSENGER TRUCK PLANS	07	38	285
PASSENGER UNDERBODY DETAIL LOCATIONS	01	63	71
ROCKET 3 & 4 UNIT PLANS RI	05	80	55
SUPERLINER AMTRAK TRAIN PLANS PS	11	82	87
TALGO TRAIN PLANS AMERICAN CAR & FOUNDRY	10	49	44
VARIOUS POSTWAR LIGHTWEIGHT PLANS NYNH&H	01	76	58

GENERAL PASSENGER CAR PLANS BY ROAD

RD		M	Y	P
A	SUPERLINER AMTRAK TRAIN PLANS PS	11	82	87
ATSF	LIGHT WEIGHT "SUPER CHIEF" CONSIST ATSF	11	38	474S
CB&Q	CB&Q "PIONEER ZEPHYR" CAR PLANS	10	59	52
CMSP	ELECTRIC LIGHT & HEAT TENDER CMSP#12 PLN	11	70	69
CN	BUSINESS CAR #91 CN PLANS 1956	06	73	48
CP	"KETTLE VALLEY" CONSIST PLANS CP 1900	06	59	38
MILW	HIAWATHA DRAWINGS MILW	01	84	114
NYNH&H	VARIOUS POSTWAR LIGHTWEIGHT PLANS NYNH&H	01	76	58
RI	ROCKET 3 & 4 UNIT PLANS RI	05	80	55
USA	HOSPITAL UNIT CAR PLANS USA	08	45	322

GENERAL PASSENGER CAR PHOTOS

	M	Y	P
AMERICAN ROYAL SHOWS CAR PHOTOS	02	70	68
CITY OF PORTLAND STREAMLINER UP PHOTO	06	35	163

PASSENGER EQUIPMENT

GENERAL PASSENGER CAR MODELS

	M	Y	P
ADDING STEPS TO "N" PASSENGER CARS	03	78	131
ASSEMBING BRASS PASSENGER CARS	05	40	277
AUTO-TRAIN CARS MOD & PT	11	76	127
BUILDING 1890'S PASSENGER CARS	12	70	51
BUILDING A PASSENGER TRAIN BAGGAGE	11	38	475
BUILDING A PASSENGER TRAIN - COMBINES	01	39	28
BUILDING A PASSENGER TRAIN - DAY COACH	02	39	70
BUILDING A PASSENGER TRAIN BAG CAR FINSH	12	38	528
CAR BODIES OF LAMINATED TISSUE $1	08	70	50
CB&Q "PIONEER ZEPHYR" CAR CONSTRUCTION	10	59	50
CIRCUS TRAIN CONSTRUCTION 1	05	46	310
CIRCUS TRAIN CONSTRUCTION 2	07	46	426
CLOSE COUPLING OF PASSENGER CARS	01	40	9
CLOSE COUPLING PASS CAR SYSTEM (ROWA)	03	74	62
COACH DIAPHRAGM CONSTRUCTION	01	37	17
CP "KETTLE VALLEY" TRAIN CONSTRUCTION	06	59	26
CUSTOM CUT CLERESTORY ROOFS	04	61	44
DIAPHRAGMS ON PASSENGER CARS	07	70	74
DOODLEBUG CAR IN N SCALE CONSTRUCTION	05	76	50
FROM STEEL TO WOOD IN A FEW EASY STEPS	05	81	90
GAY 90'S WOODEN CAR SIDE CONSTRUCTION	01	41	40
HAND LETTERING YOUR PASSENGER EQUIPMENT	12	34	9
HARRIMAN PASSENGER CAR MOD & PT	08	80	112
HOSPITAL UNIT CAR MODEL	08	45	322
HOW TO MAKE MONITOR ROOFS	09	43	403
KITBASHED MODERNIZED PASSENGER CARS	02	74	40
KITBASHING STREAMLINED CAR WINDOWS	01	75	26
LIGHTWEIGHT CAR WINDOW ARRANGEMENTS	06	75	47
MODELING KCS TRAINS 9 & 10	11	80	70
MODELING VIA	05	82	62
MOM 1860 MILW PASSENGER TRAIN "HO" VIAU	06	85	94
MOM CB&Q PIONEER ZEPHYR "HO" DAVIS	11	83	86
MOM HEAVYWEIGHT PULLMAN "HO" VIAU	08	80	102
MOM PASSENGER CARS "HON3" HOMAN	07	81	55
PAINT & LETTER AMTRAK EQUIPMENT	08	74	40
PAINT & LETTERING GUIDE L&N PASS EQUIP	06	69	35
PASS TRAIN MODELING "ASHVILLE SPECIAL" S	01	81	94
PASSENGER CAR BUILDING IN HO	12	34	7
PASSENGER CAR CONSTRUCTION "O"	11	37	413
PASSENGER CAR CONSTRUCTION KINKS	04	36	99
PASSENGER CAR DIAPHRAM CONSTRUCTION	07	85	126
PASSENGER CAR END CONNECTIONS CONST	04	63	61
PASSENGER CAR ERIE MOD & PT	10	78	122
PASSENGER CAR FLOOR PLAN SOURCES	06	78	140
PASSENGER CAR FURNISHING CONSTRUCTION	08	47	640
PASSENGER CAR OF 1890'S CONST MILW	02	71	64
PASSENGER CAR ROOF CONSTRUCTION	02	35	35
PASSENGER CARS EASY CONSTRUCTION	01	43	20
PASSENGER CARS OF 1890'S CONSTRUCT CMSP	06	71	43
PASSENGER CARS OF 1900 CONSTRUCTION 1	05	52	11
PASSENGER CARS OF 1900 CONSTRUCTION 2	06	52	30
PASSENGER EXPERIMENTAL PAINT SCHEME GN	01	78	128
PASSENGER TRUCK CONSTRUCTION	12	34	4
PASSENGER TRUCK COUPLER MOUNT CONST	05	60	48
PASSENGER UNDERBODY DETAIL CONSTRUCTION1	12	62	62

GENERAL PASSENGER CAR MODELS

	M	Y	P
PIONEER ZEPHYR BURL KITBASH 1	02	82	70
PIONEER-ZEPHYR BURL KITBASH 2	03	82	74
REMOVABLE FLOORS AND ROOFS	09	71	73
SCRATCHBUILD STREAMLINE PASSENGER CARS	03	70	50
SHADOWING PASSENGER EQUIPMENT	12	74	29
SMOOTH SIDE PASSENGER CAR CN MOD & PT	10	74	18B
STEAM GENERATOR CAR KITBASH	03	82	90
STREAMLINER IN OOO SCALE (5/64)	11	39	590
WIDE DIAPHRAGM CONSTRUCTION	11	47	B96
WOOD PASSENGER CAR FINISHING MOD & PT	09	81	126
WOODEN CAR SIDES CONSTRUCTION	03	52	29
WOODEN CARS AND TRUCK CONSTRUCTION	09	42	422
WOODEN PASSENGER CAR CONSTRUCTION	02	44	60

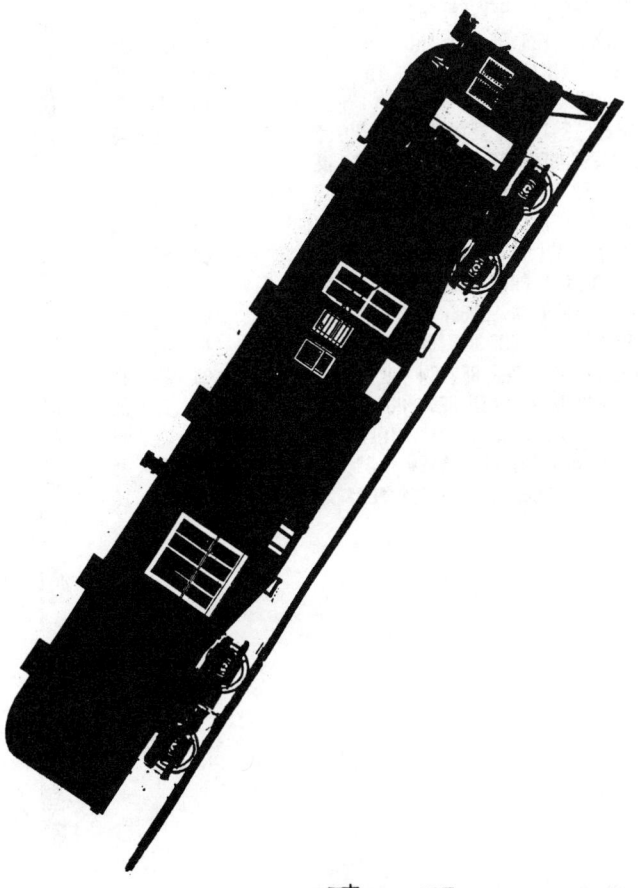

PASSENGER EQUIPMENT

GENERAL PASSENGER CAR MODEL REVIEWS

	M	Y	P
40' PASSENGER CAR OF 1890 REVIEW "HO" M	01	66	11
AMFLEET II PASS CAR REVIEW "HO" GHB	12	83	64
AMFLEET PASSENGER CAR REVIEW "HO" SOHO	07	77	37
BRITISH PASSENGER EQUIPMENT REV "OO" RP	07	60	10
BUDD METROLINER REVIEW "N" B 1966	09	70	12
CP STREAMLINED TRAIN REV "HO" PFM 1936	10	79	49
DAYLIGHT STREAMLINER SP REVIEW "HO" LE	09	79	46
DELUX PASSENGER CAR REVIEW "HO" AHM	02	66	14
HEADEND CAR LISTING D&RGW "HO" AHM	10	77	48
HEAVYWEIGHT PASSENGER CAR REVIEW "N" AHM	11	70	28
MAIL CATCHER REVIEW "1/4" CE	07	77	39
METAL PASSENGER CAR REVIEW "HO" WALTERS	09	39	482
OLDTIME PASSENGER CAR REVIEW "HO" CL	07	52	59
OPEN PLATFORM CAR REVIEWS "TT" CK	07	62	12
PASSENGER CAR KIT D&RGW REV "ON3" OWS	10	79	56
PASSENGER CAR KITS MILW REVIEW "O" LA	01	63	24
PASSENGER CAR REVIEW "HO" V	05	38	216
PASSENGER CAR REVIEW "HO" ECW	06	85	40
PASSENGER CAR REVIEW "HO" RIV	01	65	12
PASSENGER CAR REVIEW "N" AT	09	68	11
PASSENGER CAR REVIEW "N" AT	02	68	20
PASSENGER CAR REVIEW "N" CC	08	68	10
PASSENGER CAR REVIEW "N" MRC	12	69	27
PASSENGER CAR REVIEW "N" CC	11	69	29
PASSENGER CAR REVIEW "O" KAS	01	48	63
PASSENGER CAR SET ATSF LISTING "HO" AHM	11	78	62
PASSENGER CARS REVIEW "G" LGB	04	83	42
PASSENGER KIT REVIEW "HO" WAL	01	50	84
PASSENGER KIT REVIEW "HO" BL	03	50	53
PASSENGER KIT REVIEW "O" WO	02	50	75
PASSENGER TRAIN REVIEW "Z" MKL	01	74	27
PASSENGER TRAIN SETS REVIEW "O/027" WRL	04	83	48
SL PASSENGER CAR REVIEWS "HO" WE	04	66	10
STANDATD PASSENGER CAR REVIEW "HO" ATH	11	60	12
STREAMLINED CAR KIT REVIEW "OO" ZUHR	06	50	48
STREAMLINED CAR REVIEW "HO" ARR	07	52	57
STREAMLINED PASSENGER CAR REVIEW "HO RIV	02	67	14
STREAMLINED PASSENGER CAR REVIEW "HO" L	01	77	42
SUPER CHIEF CARS REVIEW "HO" OL	06	81	40
SUPERLINER A CAR REVIEW "N" CC 1979 PS	03	83	44
SV PASSENGER TRAIN REV "HON3" WEST 1918	09	71	25
TAIL SIGN LISTING "1/4" VIRDEN	01	77	49
TURBOLINER AMTRAK REVIEW "HO" JOUEF	05	77	45
WOOD PASSENGER CAR REVIEW "HO" WESTWOOD	05	67	10

GENERAL PASS CAR MODEL REVIEWS BY MFG.

MFG		M	Y	P
AHM	PASSENGER CAR SET ATSF LISTING "HO" AHM	11	78	62
	HEADEND CAR LISTING D&RGW "HO" AHM	10	77	48
	HEAVYWEIGHT PASSENGER CAR REVIEW "N" AHM	11	70	28
	DELUX PASSENGER CAR REVIEW "HO" AHM	02	66	14
ARR	STREAMLINED CAR REVIEW "HO" ARR	07	52	57
AT	PASSENGER CAR REVIEW "N" AT	09	68	11
	PASSENGER CAR REVIEW "N" AT	02	68	20
ATH	STANDATD PASSENGER CAR REVIEW "HO" ATH	11	60	12
B	BUDD METROLINER REVIEW "N" B 1966	09	70	12
BL	PASSENGER KIT REVIEW "HO" BL	03	50	53
CC	PASSENGER CAR REVIEW "N" CC	11	69	29
	PASSENGER CAR REVIEW "N" CC	08	68	10
	SUPERLINER A CAR REVIEW "N" CC 1979 PS	03	83	44
CE	MAIL CATCHER REVIEW "1/4" CE	07	77	39
CK	OPEN PLATFORM CAR REVIEWS "TT" CK	07	62	12
CL	OLDTIME PASSENGER CAR REVIEW "HO" CL	07	52	59
ECW	PASSENGER CAR REVIEW "HO" ECW	06	85	40
GHB	AMFLEET II PASS CAR REVIEW "HO" GHB	12	83	64
J	TURBOLINER AMTRAK REVIEW "HO" JOUEF	05	77	45
KAS	PASSENGER CAR REVIEW "O" KAS	01	48	63
L	STREAMLINED PASSENGER CAR REVIEW "HO" L	01	77	42
LA	PASSENGER CAR KITS MILW REVIEW "O" LA	01	63	24
LE	DAYLIGHT STREAMLINER SP REVIEW "HO" LE	09	79	46
LGB	PASSENGER CARS REVIEW "G" LGB	04	83	42
M	40' PASSENGER CAR OF 1890 REVIEW "HO" M	01	66	11
MKL	PASSENGER TRAIN REVIEW "Z" MKL	01	74	27
MRC	PASSENGER CAR REVIEW "N" MRC	12	69	27
OL	SUPER CHIEF CARS REVIEW "HO" OL	06	81	40
OWS	PASSENGER CAR KIT D&RGW REV "ON3" OWS	10	79	56
PFM	CP STREAMLINED TRAIN REV "HO" PFM 1936	10	79	49
RIV	PASSENGER CAR REVIEW "HO" RIV	01	65	12
	STREAMLINED PASSENGER CAR REVIEW "HO RIV	02	67	14
RP	BRITISH PASSENGER EQUIPMENT REV "OO" RP	07	60	10
SOHO	AMFLEET PASSENGER CAR REVIEW "HO" SOHO	07	77	37
V	PASSENGER CAR REVIEW "HO" V	05	38	216
VI	TAIL SIGN LISTING "1/4" VIRDEN	01	77	49
WAL	METAL PASSENGER CAR REVIEW "HO" WALTERS	09	39	482
	PASSENGER KIT REVIEW "HO" WAL	01	50	84
WE	SL PASSENGER CAR REVIEWS "HO" WE	04	66	10
WEST	SV PASSENGER TRAIN REV "HON3" WEST 1918	09	71	25
	WOOD PASSENGER CAR REVIEW "HO" WESTWOOD	05	67	10
WO	PASSENGER KIT REVIEW "O" WO	02	50	75
WRL	PASSENGER TRAIN SETS REVIEW "O/027" WRL	04	83	48
ZUHR	STREAMLINED CAR KIT REVIEW "OO" ZUHR	06	50	48

BILL OF LADING   FREIGHT CARS

The freight car section is broken down into eight categories: Box Cars, Flat Cars, Gondolas, Hoppers, Refrigerator Cars, Stock Cars, Tank Cars, and General Freight Cars. Cars like Auto Carriers, TOFC, Pulpwood Cars, and Disconnect Log cars have been classified as Flat Cars. Pickle Cars and Vat Cars fall under Tank Cars.

Prototype data includes articles and specifications on the real thing. In many instances there are photographs with these articles that did not get special billing in the photograph section. The plans and drawings are just that. Generally by our convention a drawing is more detailed than a plan, but this is not a hard and fast rule. The plans are listed twice: once alphabetically and once by road. The photo section shows details or unusual photos of interest to the researcher. Obviously we did not list all photos that appear in these magazines. The model section highlights exceptional models and tells how to build/kitbash/rebuild your own "gems". Finally the model review section list those items that have a chance of surviving as a recognizable entity. Included is the description, scale, and manufacturer. These are listed three ways: alphabetically, by road, and by manufacturer.

Freight car descriptors include the basic description of the car, its road, number, class, builder and date built. This data is included if available and if space permits.

MANIFEST FREIGHT CARS

	PAGE		PAGE
FREIGHT CARS	82	HOPPER MODEL REVIEWS	101
BOX CARS	84	HOPPER MODEL REVIEWS BY ROAD	101
BOX CAR PROTOTYPE DATA	84	HOPPER MODEL REVIEWS BY MFG.	102
BOX CAR PROTOTYPE DATA BY ROAD	84	REFRIGERATOR CARS	102
BOX CAR PLANS	84	REFRIGERATOR CAR PROTOTYPE DATA	102
BOX CAR PLANS BY ROAD	85	REFRIGERATOR PROTOTYPE DATA BY ROAD	102
BOX CAR PHOTOS	85	REFRIGERATOR CAR PLANS	103
BOX CAR MODELS	86	REFRIGERATOR PLANS BY ROAD	103
BOX CAR MODEL REVIEWS	87	REFRIGERATOR CAR PHOTOS	103
BOX CAR MODEL REVIEWS BY ROAD	89	REFRIGERATOR CAR MODELS	103
BOX CAR MODEL REVIEWS BY MFG.	89	REFRIGERATOR CAR MODEL REVIEWS	104
FLAT CARS	91	REFRIGERATOR MODEL REVIEWS BY ROAD	104
FLAT CAR PROTOTYPE DATA	91	REFRIGERATOR MODEL REVIEWS BY MFG.	105
FLAT CAR PROTOTYPE DATA BY ROAD	91	STOCK CARS	105
FLAT CAR PLANS	91	STOCK CAR PROTOTYPE DATA	105
FLAT CAR PLANS BY ROAD	92	STOCK CAR PLANS	105
FLAT CAR MODELS	92	STOCK CAR PLANS BY ROAD	106
FLAT CAR MODEL REVIEWS	93	STOCK CAR PHOTOS	106
FLAT CAR MODEL REVIEWS BY ROAD	93	STOCK CAR MODELS	106
FLAT CAR MODEL REVIEWS BY MFG.	94	STOCK CAR MODEL REVIEWS	106
GONDOLAS	94	STOCK CAR MODEL REVIEWS BY ROAD	106
GONDOLA PROTOTYPE DATA	94	STOCK CAR MODEL REVIEWS BY MFG.	106
GONDOLA PROTOTYPE DATA BY ROAD	94	TANK CARS	107
GONDOLA PLANS	95	TANK CAR PROTOTYPE DATA	107
GONDOLA PLANS BY ROAD	95	TANK CAR PLANS	107
GONDOLA MODELS	96	TANK CAR PLANS BY ROAD	107
GONDOLA MODEL REVIEWS	96	TANK CAR PHOTOS	107
GONDOLA MODEL REVIEWS BY ROAD	97	TANK CAR MODELS	107
GONDOLA MODEL REVIEWS BY ROAD	97	TANK CAR MODEL REVIEWS	108
GONDOLA MODEL REVIEWS BY MFG.	97	TANK CAR MODEL REVIEWS BY ROAD	108
HOPPERS	98	TANK CAR MODEL REVIEWS BY MFG.	109
HOPPER PROTOTYPE DATA	98	GENERAL FREIGHT CARS	109
HOPPER PROTOTYPE DATA BY ROAD	98	GENERAL FREIGHT PROTOTYPE DATA	109
HOPPER PLANS	98	GENERAL FREIGHT PLANS	109
HOPPER PLANS BY ROAD	99	GENERAL FREIGHT MODELS	110
HOPPER PHOTOS	99	GENERAL FREIGHT MODEL REVIEWS	110
HOPPER MODELS	100	GENERAL FREIGHT MODEL REVIEWS BY MFG.	111

NOTE: SEE PAGE 400

FREIGHT CARS

BOX CAR PROTOTYPE DATA

	M	Y	P
AUTOMOBILE TRANSPORTER BOXCAR CN	09	58	40
DF CLASS FREIGHT CARS	10	63	22
GRAIN DOORS IN STANDARD BOXCARS	03	83	139
HEATER BOXCAR CLASS XD OF PRR 1893	06	84	89
HIGHCUBE CARS THEIR LOADS	12	81	174
INSULATED BOXCARS OF B&AR	07	78	84
INSULATED BOXCARS OF SP 1960 PCF	05	85	82
JUST PLAIN OLD HAVEN BOXCAR ERROR	12	78	175
MORE ON WAGON TOP CLASS M-53 BOXCARS B&O	11	80	140
PLUG DOOR BOXCARS	03	83	133
PRIVATE OWNER BOX CARS OF 1890	11	40	619
PRR CAR W/CONSECUTIVE NUMBERING	02	81	122
SEABOARD 50T STEEL FRAME WOOD BX LETTER	04	34	7
USRA STEEL BOXCAR STANDARD NEVER BUILT	09	83	109
VENEER BOXCARS ON THE SP	04	77	76
WOOD SHEATHED BOXCARS OF CH&D 1912	05	79	86

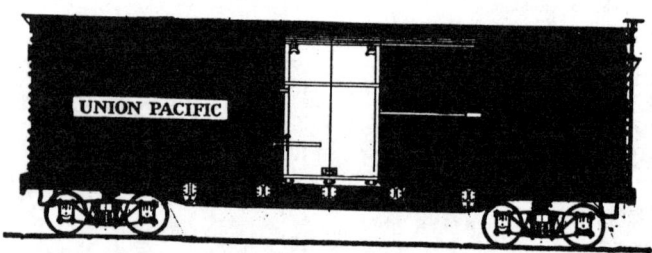

BOX CAR PROTOTYPE DATA BY ROAD

RD		M	Y	P
B&AR	INSULATED BOXCARS OF B&AR	07	78	84
B&O	MORE ON WAGON TOP CLASS M-53 BOXCARS B&O	11	80	140
CH&D	WOOD SHEATHED BOXCARS OF CH&D 1912	05	79	86
CN	AUTOMOBILE TRANSPORTER BOXCAR CN	09	58	40
PRR	PRR CAR W/CONSECUTIVE NUMBERING	02	81	122
	HEATER BOXCAR CLASS XD OF PRR 1893	06	84	89
SEA	SEABOARD 50T STEEL FRAME WOOD BX LETTER	04	34	7
SP	INSULATED BOXCARS OF SP 1960 PCF	05	85	82
	VENEER BOXCARS ON THE SP	04	77	76

BOX CAR PLANS

	M	Y	P
36' BOXCAR CH&D #48341 PLANS 1915	03	40	137
36' VENT BOX CAR PLAN ACL #28605 CL J-21	09	65	39
40 TON BOXCAR FRIS #126874 PLAN 1913	06	36	145
50 TON BOX CAR ATSF #122390 CLASS BX9	06	36	145
50 TON FURNITURE BOXCAR PLAN HPT&D #411	06	36	145
50 TON STEEL BOX B&O #272581 PLAN	07	36	178
50' ALL STEEL AUTOBOX UP #150000 CLASS XA	08	35	206
50' PLUG DR BOX CAR CL RBL-2 B #79722	12	65	48
50' PLUG/SLIDE BOX CAR PLANS CN #555559	03	68	45
70 TON BOX CAR PLANS CN #400376	04	74	55
AAR STANDARD BOXCAR PLANS P&LE #5000	10	55	38
AAR STD BOXCAR PLANS & PART DEFINITION	02	36	34
AAR STEELSHEATHED BOX CAR PLANS OF 1932	03	46	191
AAR WOOD SHEATHED BOX CAR PLANS	08	48	539
ACF BOX CAR PLANS MKT #97300 CLASS XM	12	52	76
ADAMS EXPRESS CAR #63 PLANS OF 1862	03	69	34
ALL STEEL GRAIN CAR PLANS GN #4628	07	68	26
ARA 40' CLASS X29 BOXCAR PLNS PRR #566901	04	63	63
AUTO TRANSPORTER 75' CAR PLAN CN #570424	09	58	41
AUTOMOBILE BOX CAR PLANS ATSF #10089	08	53	64
AUTOMOBILE BOX CLASS X40 PLANS PRR #36990	06	70	47
BOX CAR 50' PLANS NKP #86182 1949	05	55	34
BOX CAR CLASS XA PLANS WNY&P #6277 1875	01	62	35
BOX CAR NARROW GAUGE PLAN MILW #415	08	47	646
BOX CAR NARROW GAUGE PLANS D&RGW #3155	07	55	34
BOX CAR NARROW GAUGE PLANS D&RGW #3270	04	62	47
BOX CAR OF 1890 PLANS FE&MV #5272	02	58	43
BOX CAR OF 1890 PLANS SOO #2396	10	63	45
BOX CAR OF 1915 PLANS UP #120000	03	40	137
BOX CAR PLANS BI&B	11	62	43
BOX CAR PLANS CMI #5338	08	72	47
BOX CAR PLANS IN NARROW GAUGE B&SR #67	01	54	73
BOX CAR PLANS IN NARROW GAUGE B&SR #67 C	02	54	92
BOXCAR PLANS ET&WNC #5	07	81	62
CURVED ROOF 40 TON BOX CAR PLAN NP #39357	09	60	51
DOUBLE SHEATHED 50T BOXCAR PRR CLASS X29	01	41	41
DOUBLE SHEATHED BOX CAR PLANS EBT #170	09	61	45
EMPIRE LINE BOX CAR PLANS PRR #76182	08	57	38
FURNITURE & BUGGY CAR PLANS SLIM&S #9920	04	65	48
GRAIN CAR OF 1903 PLANS IRPC #201	11	59	34
HEATER BOXCAR CLASS XD PLANS PRR #67579	06	84	88
HOPPER BOTTOM BOX CAR PLANS B&O #190726	11	64	32
INSULATED BOX CAR PLANS FGE #82156 1954	01	66	47
INSULATED BOXCAR DRAWINGS SP #673013 PCF	05	85	82
INSULATED BOXCAR PLAN B&AR #2302	07	78	84
IRON BOX CAR OF 1862 PLANS B&O #17001	03	69	34
MERCH SERV CLASS X40B BOX PLN PRR #37007	06	70	46
MILITARY BOX CAR #194 PLANS OF 1862 USA	03	69	33
MODERN BOX CAR CLASS XML PLAN SOO #177858	09	67	48
OLD TIME BOX CAR PLANS GM&G #1006 1895	11	45	451
OUTSIDE BRACED CLASS X-23 BOXCAR CORRECT	07	71	14
OUTSIDE BRACED CLSS X-23 BOX CAR PLN PRR	04	71	36
PRIVATE OWNER BOX CARS 1890 PLANS	11	40	619
STEEL BOX CAR X-29 PLAN PRR #569056 1924	01	55	80
TRUSS ROD BOX CAR PLANS MA&PA #723	05	49	43

FREIGHT CARS

BOX CAR PLANS	M	Y	P
UNION LINE BOX CAR PLANS PRR #26598 1892	07	47	572
UNION LINE BOXCAR 1875 PLANS PRR #1586	03	46	163
USRA BOX CAR PLANS 40 TON	09	38	388
USRA STEEL BOXCAR PLANS NEVER BUILT	09	83	109
VENTILATED BOX CAR PLAN CB&Q #50000 1886	05	52	34
VENTILATED BOX CAR PLANS C&A #2873	04	62	46
VENTILATED BOX CAR PLANS C&A #2873	02	72	62
VENTILATED BOX CAR PLANS FEC #17001	12	75	59
VERT-A-PAC BOX CAR PLANS UP TTVX 810235	10	71	53
WAGON TOP BOX CAR DRAWING B&O	11	49	44
WAGON TOP BOX CLASS X318 PLN PRR #61100	06	66	32
WAGON TOP BOX PLN CLASS M53 B&O #381798	12	64	79
WAGON TOP CLASS M-53 PLANS B&O #381101	05	53	34
WIDE GAUGE BOX CAR OF 1862 PLANS G #1247	03	69	34
WOOD SHEATHED BOX CAR PLANS	12	53	94
WOOD SHEATHED BOX CAR PLANS B&O #69089	05	52	34
WOOD SHEATHED BOX CAR PLANS CNJ #10205	01	72	71
WOOD SHEATHED BOX CAR PLANS GN #9049	04	38	153
WOOD SHEATHED BOX CAR PLANS NYC&H #53896	03	54	75
WOOD SHEATHED BOX CAR PLANS SN #2340	05	58	47
WOOD SHEATHED CARS PLANS CH&D #48341	05	79	86
WOOD SHEATHED STEEL END BX PL DL&W #45000	06	63	38

RD	BOX CAR PLANS BY ROAD	M	Y	P
ACL	36' VENT BOX CAR PLAN ACL #28605 CL J-21	09	65	39
ATSF	AUTOMOBILE BOX CAR PLANS ATSF #10089	08	53	64
	50 TON BOX CAR ATSF #122390 CLASS BX9	06	36	145
B	50' PLUG DR BOX CAR CL RBL-2 B #79722	12	65	48
B&AR	INSULATED BOXCAR PLAN B&AR #2302	07	78	84
B&O	IRON BOX CAR OF 1862 PLANS B&O #17001	03	69	34
	HOPPER BOTTOM BOX CAR PLANS B&O #190726	11	64	32
	WAGON TOP BOX PLN CLASS M53 B&O #381798	12	64	79
	WAGON TOP CLASS M-53 PLANS B&O #381101	05	53	34
	WOOD SHEATHED BOX CAR PLANS B&O #69089	05	52	34
	WAGON TOP BOX CAR DRAWING B&O	11	49	44
	50 TON STEEL BOX B&O #272581 PLAN	07	36	178
B&SR	BOX CAR PLANS IN NARROW GAUGE B&SR #67	01	54	73
	BOX CAR PLANS IN NARROW GAUGE B&SR #67 C	02	54	92
BI&B	BOX CAR PLANS BI&B	11	62	43
CB&Q	VENTILATED BOX CAR PLAN CB&Q #50000 1886	05	52	34
C&A	VENTILATED BOX CAR PLANS C&A #2873	04	62	46
	VENTILATED BOX CAR PLANS C&A #2873	02	72	62
CH&D	WOOD SHEATHED CARS PLANS CH&D #48341	05	79	86
	36' BOXCAR CH&D #48341 PLANS 1915	03	40	137
CMI	BOX CAR PLANS CMI #5338	08	72	47
CN	50' PLUG/SLIDE BOX CAR PLANS CN #555559	03	68	45
	AUTO TRANSPORTER 75' CAR PLAN CN #570424	09	58	41
	70 TON BOX CAR PLANS CN #400376	04	74	55
CNJ	WOOD SHEATHED BOX CAR PLANS CNJ #10205	01	72	71
D&RGW	BOX CAR NARROW GAUGE PLANS D&RGW #3270	04	62	47
	BOX CAR NARROW GAUGE PLANS D&RGW #3155	07	55	34
DL&W	WOOD SHEATHED STEEL END BX PL DL&W #45000	06	63	38
EBT	DOUBLE SHEATHED BOX CAR PLANS EBT #170	09	61	45

RD	BOX CAR PLANS BY ROAD	M	Y	P
ET&WNC	BOXCAR PLANS ET&WNC #5	07	81	62
FE&MV	BOX CAR OF 1890 PLANS FE&MV #5272	02	58	43
FEC	VENTILATED BOX CAR PLANS FEC #17001	12	75	59
FGE	INSULATED BOX CAR PLANS FGE #82156 1954	01	66	47
FRIS	40 TON BOXCAR FRIS #126874 PLAN 1913	06	36	145
G	WIDE GAUGE BOX CAR OF 1862 PLANS G #1247	03	69	34
GM&G	OLD TIME BOX CAR PLANS GM&G #1006 1895	11	45	451
GN	ALL STEEL GRAIN CAR PLANS GN #4628	07	68	26
	WOOD SHEATHED BOX CAR PLANS GN #9049	04	38	153
HPT&D	50 TON FURNITURE BOXCAR PLAN HPT&D #411	06	36	145
IRPC	GRAIN CAR OF 1903 PLANS IRPC #201	11	59	34
MA&PA	TRUSS ROD BOX CAR PLANS MA&PA #723	05	49	43
MILW	BOX CAR NARROW GAUGE PLAN MILW #415	08	47	646
MKT	ACF BOX CAR PLANS MKT #97300 CLASS XM	12	52	76
NKP	BOX CAR 50' PLANS NKP #86182 1949	05	55	34
NP	CURVED ROOF 40 TON BOX CAR PLAN NP #39357	09	60	51
NYC&H	WOOD SHEATHED BOX CAR PLANS NYC&H #53896	03	54	75
P&LE	AAR STANDARD BOXCAR PLANS P&LE #5000	10	55	38
PRR	ARA 40' CLASS X29 BOXCAR PLNS PRR #566901	04	63	63
	EMPIRE LINE BOX CAR PLANS PRR #76182	08	57	38
	HEATER BOXCAR CLASS XD PLANS PRR #67579	06	84	88
	OUTSIDE BRACED CLSS X-23 BOX CAR PLN PRR	04	71	36
	OUTSIDE BRACED CLASS X-23 BOXCAR CORRECT	07	71	14
	AUTOMOBILE BOX CLASS X40 PLANS PRR #36990	06	70	47
	MERCH SERV CLASS X40B BOX PLN PRR #37007	06	70	46
	WAGON TOP BOX CLASS X318 PLN PRR #61100	06	66	32
	STEEL BOX CAR X-29 PLAN PRR #569056 1924	01	55	80
	DOUBLE SHEATHED 50T BOXCAR PRR CLASS X29	01	41	41
	UNION LINE BOX CAR PLANS PRR #26598 1892	07	47	572
	UNION LINE BOXCAR 1875 PLANS PRR #1586	03	46	163
SLIM&S	FURNITURE & BUGGY CAR PLANS SLIM&S #9920	04	65	48
SN	WOOD SHEATHED BOX CAR PLANS SN #2340	05	58	47
SOO	BOX CAR OF 1890 PLANS SOO #2396	10	63	45
	MODERN BOX CAR CLASS XML PLAN SOO #177858	09	67	48
SP	INSULATED BOXCAR DRAWINGS SP #673013 PCF	05	85	82
UP	BOX CAR OF 1915 PLANS UP #120000	03	40	137
	50' ALL STEEL AUTOBOX UP #150000 CLASS XA	08	35	206
USA	MILITARY BOX CAR #194 PLANS OF 1862 USA	03	69	33
USRA	USRA BOX CAR PLANS 40 TON	09	38	388
WNY&P	BOX CAR CLASS XA PLANS WNY&P #6277 1875	01	62	35

BOX CAR PHOTOS	M	Y	P
AAR STEEL BOX CAR P&LE #5000 PHOTO 1949	10	55	38
ROUND TOP BOX MILW #714305 PHOTO 1928	09	71	76
WAGON TOP BOX W/HOP DISCHARGE B&O #27998	03	65	42

FREIGHT CARS

BOX CAR MODELS		M	Y	P
40' (PS) BOXCAR MILW CONVERSION	MOD & PT	03	77	101
40' BOXCAR CENTRAL OF GEORGIA	MOD & PT	08	81	111
40' BOXCAR CGW	MOD & PT	09	80	142
40' BOXCAR EJ&E	MOD & PT	11	82	156
40' BOXCARS OF NP (4)	MOD & PT	02	85	126
40' FJ&G BOXCAR DETAILED CONSTRUCTION		08	79	90
50' BOXCAR NYC	MOD & PT	05	82	119
50' BOXCAR CI	MOD & PT	12	81	154
50' BOXCAR CN	MOD & PT	05	82	119
50' BOXCAR D&M	MOD & PT	04	78	116
50' BOXCAR DP&M	MOD & PT	04	78	117
50' BOXCAR DT&I	MOD & PT	01	82	128
50' BOXCAR MA&PA	MOD & PT	04	78	116
50' BOXCAR MT&W	MOD & PT	04	78	116
50' BOXCAR P&W	MOD & PT	04	78	116
50' BOXCAR SAL	MOD & PT	05	82	119
50' BOXCAR SP&S	MOD & PT	08	77	98
50' BOXCAR SSI RAIL	MOD & PT	04	78	115
50' BOXCAR VC	MOD & PT	04	78	116
50' BOXCAR VS	MOD & PT	04	78	116
50' CUSHION FRAME GN BOXCAR CONSTRUCTION		07	79	64
50' LUMBER CAR CN	MOD & PT	12	80	176
50'S SINGLE DOOR BOXCAR AA	MOD & PT	06	80	112
60' AUTO PARTS BOXCAR KITBASH		10	79	124
60' AUTO PARTS CAR WHEELBASE MODIFICATIO		12	85	166
60' HICUBE BOXCAR MOD & PT		06	76	94
60' HIGH CUBE WAFFLE SIDE AUTO BOX KITBA		12	79	94
A&WE FOOD CAR MOD & PT		03	76	93
AAR WOOD SHEATHED BOX CAR CONSTRUCTION		08	48	538
ABOX RAILBOX CAR	MOD & PT	09	79	58
ALL DOOR BOXCAR FJ&G	MOD & PT	08	79	108
AMERICAN LUNG ASSOC BOXCAR	MOD & PT	01	76	30
AUTOBOX KANSAS CITY SOUTHERN	MOD & PT	08	82	108
AUTOMOBILE BOX CAR CONSTRUCTION $1		05	56	26
AUTOMOBILE BOXCAR	MOD & PT	08	78	102
AUTOMOBILE CAR 40' PAINTING MILW		02	78	127
AUTOMOBILE CAR D&TSL	MOD & PT	08	78	103
AUTOMOBILE CAR EL	MOD & PT	08	78	102
AUTOMOBILE CAR IC	MOD & PT	08	78	102
AUTOMOBILE CAR MILW #13232	MOD & PT	03	77	100
AUTOMOBILE CAR PC	MOD & PT	11	78	121
BASIC BOXCAR MODELING TIPS		01	72	70
BOX CAR MODERNIZATION CONSTRUCTION		07	68	24
BOX CARS KITBASHED FOR VARIOUS LENGTHS		12	76	54
BOXCAR AD&N	MOD & PT	03	81	78
BOXCAR ASHLEY DREW & NORTHERN	MOD & PT	07	80	102
BOXCAR CENTRAL VERMONT	MOD & PT	10	80	139
BOXCAR CN	MOD & PT	02	79	131
BOXCAR DT&I	MOD & PT	05	79	107
BOXCAR G&F	MOD & PT	03	82	123
BOXCAR IT	MOD & PT	01	80	139
BOXCAR L&N	MOD & PT	02	79	132
BOXCAR M&SL	MOD & PT	06	79	109
BOXCAR MONON	MOD & PT	11	79	155
BOXCAR NORTHERN ALBERTA RAILWAY	MOD & PT	02	82	127

BOX CAR MODELS		M	Y	P
BOXCAR PAINTING W	MOD & PT	02	78	129
BOXCAR RUTLAND EPOXY RESIN	MOD & PT	09	85	100
BOXCAR ST LAWRENCE RAILROAD	MOD & PT	01	79	133
BOXCAR WESTMINSTER	MOD & PT	05	75	22
BOXCAR WP FEATHER	MOD & PT	02	81	126
BOXCARS CAMOFLAGE DT&I	MOD & PT	07	80	102
BOXCARS NYC GREEN	MOD & PT	09	80	139
BOXCARS NYS&W	MOD & PT	11	76	122
BOXCARS OF 1950'S B&M	MOD & PT	04	83	130
BOXCARS PRR STEAM ERA	MOD & PT	02	81	127
CANFOR BOXCAR	MOD & PT	10	79	130
COMBINATION DOOR BOXCAR RI	MOD & PT	04	80	122
CUSHION CAR UP AND SP	MOD & PT	11	78	120
DF BOXCAR READING	MOD & PT	06	83	123
DF BOXCAR ANN ARBOR	MOD & PT	08	82	109
DOOR AND A HALF BOX CAR CONST $1		07	56	40
FLYWHEEL BOX CAR CONSTRUCTION "O"		02	55	26
GRAIN CAR CONST ILLINOIS RIVER PACKET CO		11	59	32
GREEN BOXCAR	MOD & PT	09	78	104
HEATER BOXCAR CLASS XD OF PRR CONSTRUCT		06	84	89
HICUBE BOX FORD MOTOR CO	MOD & PT	06	80	113
HIGH-CUBE BOXCAR N&W	MOD & PT	09	78	106
INSULATED BOX CAR	MOD & PT	12	77	154
LET'S BUILD BOXCARS		03	40	131
M-26 BOXCAR B&O	MOD & PT	05	79	111
MAPLE LEAF BOXCAR CN	MOD & PT	03	80	128
MOM C&NW USRA BOXCAR "1/2"	TEABY	05	63	22
MOM RI VERT-A-PAK CAR "1/4"	HARVEY	09	74	34
MOM SP HICUBE BOXCAR "HO"	WIECZOREK	02	69	37
NARROW GAUGE BOX CAR CONSTRUCTION		07	55	20
NEW BOXCAR DETAILING		03	67	53
OUTSIDE BRACED BOX CAR CONSTRUCTION		04	71	37
OUTSIDE BRACED BOXCAR CONSTRUCTION		08	58	50
PLAIN BOX CAR	MOD & PT	08	77	98
PLAIN BOXCARS AGAIN	MOD & PT	03	79	115
PLAIN BROWN BOXCAR	MOD & PT	10	79	130
PLUG DOOR 50' BOXCAR BN	MOD & PT	07	78	113
PLUG DOOR UPDATE OF THE ATLAS BOX CAR		03	73	52
PULLMAN STANDARD PS-1 BOXCAR	MOD & PT	01	84	227
RAILBOX	MOD & PT	02	75	24
RBL BOXCAR C&NW	MOD & PT	09	82	115
ROOF HATCH BOXCAR	MOD & PT	01	79	131
SCRATCHBUILD HOUSE CARS		04	62	48
SEA SYSTEM NEW IMAGE BOXCAR	MOD & PT	01	84	226
SHEET METAL BOXCAR ARA CLASS XM 44' CNST		07	34	11
SHORTLINE LUMBER HAULERS AMC	MOD & PT	08	85	109
SHORTLINE LUMBER HAULERS MCRI	MOD & PT	08	85	110
SIMPSON LUMBER CO ALL DOOR BOXCAR	MOD&PT	03	76	92
SIXTY FOOT KITBASHED BOX CAR PRR		06	70	48
SOO LINE BOXCAR MOD & PT		04	76	88
SPENT GRAIN CAR MILW	MOD & PT	03	81	135
STEEL SHEATHED BOX CAR CONSTRUCTION		03	35	73
THREE TRUCK BOX CAR CONSTRUCTION		04	70	34
TRANSITIONAL BOXCAR CB&Q	MOD & PT	06	79	106
VENEER CAR MODELING		04	77	76

FREIGHT CARS

BOX CAR MODELS	M	Y	P
VENTELATED BOX CAR OF 1895 CONST C&A	02	72	62
WAGON TOP BOX CAR CLASS M-53 B&O #381798	12	38	533
WAGON TOP BOX CAR CONST B&O CLASS M53 $1	05	53	34
WAGON TOP BOX CAR CONSTRUCTION TINPLATE	11	49	44
WOOD PRODUCTS CAR YREKA WESTERN MOD & PT	05	81	111
WOOD SHEATHED BOX CAR CONSTRUCTION $1	06	53	49
WOOD SHEATHED BOX CAR CONSTRUCTION SN	05	58	46
WOOD SHEATHED BOXCARS GN MOD & PT	05	83	122
X-29 BOXCAR PAINTING PRR MOD & PT	02	78	125

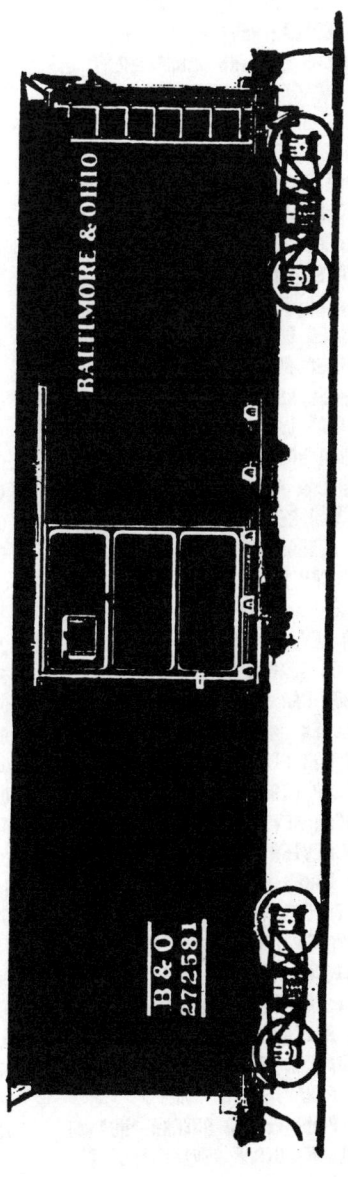

BOX CAR MODEL REVIEWS	M	Y	P
1900 BOXCAR REVIEW "HO" OC	11	62	16
1900 CAN BOX CAR REVIEW "HO" CRM	01	65	11
1900 WOOD BOXCAR REVIEW "HO" LABELLE	11	63	9
23'6" BOXCAR REVIEW "HON3" BCM	09	67	11
26' DSP&P BOXCAR REVIEW "ON3" COM 1880	01	71	32
28' OLDTIME BOX CAR REVIEW "HO" CCW	05	55	15
30' BOXCAR REBUILD D&RGW REVIEW "ON3"SRE	09	76	30
3000 SERIES D&RGW BOX CAR REV "ON3" CAM	07	61	10
34' MILW BOXCAR REVIEW "HO" LA 1890	02	71	27
34' SOO BOXCAR REVIEW "O" LA 1888	11	68	18
34' TRUSS ROD BOX CAR REVIEW "HO" CV	11	50	60
36' BOX CAR REVIEW "TT" CK	06	62	12
36' BOXCAR REVIEW "HO" MDC	05	69	8
36' BOXCAR REVIEW "HO" YE 1900	05	71	20
37' BOXCAR REVIEW "HO" BINKLEY	10	62	20
40' 40T WOOD ATSF BOXCAR REVIEW "HO" SC	07	69	16
40' AAR BOX CAR REVIEW "O" AN	09	55	16
40' AAR BOXCAR REVIEW "HO" DJB	10	85	40
40' AAR BOXCAR REVIEW "S" AMI 1937	10	83	56
40' AUTOMOBILE BOX CAR REVIEW "HO" ARD	04	58	14
40' AUTOMOBILE CAR GN REV "HO" MKM 1958	06	83	44
40' BOX CAR LISTING RI "N" KADEE	03	77	44
40' BOX CAR REVIEW "HO" KL	06	62	14
40' BOXCAR REVIEW "HO" AD	10	38	452
40' BOXCAR REVIEW "HO" KL 1947	06	69	18
40' BOXCAR REVIEW "SN3" TOM	09	67	10
40' BX-37 ATSF BOXCAR REVIEW "HO" PMI	08	75	26
40' DOUBLE DOOR BOXCAR REV "N" KD 1930	10	73	24
40' DOUBLE SHEATHED BOXCAR "HO" REV TMC	05	69	14
40' HIGH CUBE BOXCAR REVIEW "1/4" LVM	04	70	11
40' METAL END BOXCAR REVIEW "HO" ALCOE	10	68	14
40' OUTSIDE BRACED BOX CAR REV "S" KSC	12	55	22
40' PS-1 BOXCAR REVIEW "TT" GD	08	69	10
40' STEEL BOX CAR REVIEW "HO" ATHEARN	05	63	9
40' STEEL BOXCAR REVIEW "1/4" AT	05	72	24
40' STEEL BOXCAR REVIEW "1/4" AHM	01	71	34
40' STEEL BOXCAR REVIEW "N" KD 1930	07	73	24
40' STEEL BOXCAR REVIEW "O" KRIS	10	68	11
40' TRUSS ROD BOXCAR REVIEW "HO" YE	12	71	30
40' UP HIGH CUBE BOXCAR REVIEW "1/4" QC	10	71	22
40' USRA BOXCAR REVIEW "HO" CC	06	62	17
40' WOOD SHEATHED IC BOX CAR REV "HO" LA	07	65	8
40T X29 BOXCAR REVIEW "HO" TMC 1930	03	73	25
50' ALL STEEL BOXCAR REVIEW "O" NPP	06	76	35
50' AUTO BOX CAR REVIEW "HO" ATH	08	59	12
50' BOXCAR REVIEW "HO" KL	10	67	9
50' BOXCAR REVIEW "HO" KL	10	76	34
50' BOXCAR REVIEW "S" REK	07	64	6
50' CUSHION FRAME BOX CAR REV "HO" ATH	09	65	10
50' CUSHION FRAME BOXCAR REVIEW "1/4" USH	04	71	22
50' CUSHIONED BOX CAR REVIEW "HO" QC	04	66	10
50' DOUBLE PLUG DOOR BOX REVIEW "HO" DW	03	79	46
50' FLAT ROOF BOXCAR REV "N" MDC	12	79	40
50' FLAT ROOF BOXCAR REVIEW "HO" MDC	06	79	41
50' OUT BRACED AUTO BOX CAR REV "HO" MLI	04	59	14

FREIGHT CARS

BOX CAR MODEL REVIEWS	M	Y	P
50' PLUG DOOR BOXCAR REVIEW "HO" ATH	05	68	16
50' PLUG DOOR BOXCAR REVIEW "HO" KL	11	68	20
50' SINGLE DOOR BOXCAR REVIEW "HO" ATH	02	79	53
50' SINGLE DOOR BOXCAR REVIEW "N" QC	01	73	27
50' STANDARD BOXCAR 1920 REVIEW "HO" SS	05	79	45
50T X32 PRR AUTOBOX REVIEW "HO" NPP 1935	11	73	29
51' BARREL & WOODWARE CAR REV "1/4" WAL	10	72	23
51' WAFFLE SIDE BOXCAR REV "1/4" WAL PS	11	72	30
56' ALL DOOR BOXCAR S REVIEW "1/4" EPM	04	72	26
60' AIRCRAFT SKY BOXCAR REVIEW "HO" AMB	11	70	18
60' AUTO BOX REVIEW "HO" RRI	09	85	38
60' INSULATED BURL BOXCAR REVIEW HO AMB	07	71	19
70T HOGSHEAD BOX CAR REVIEW "HO" AMB	04	66	12
85' HICUBE DOUBLE DOOR BOXCAR REV "HO QC	08	69	14
86' 50T HIGH CUBE BOXCAR REV "N" RAP GSC	03	70	19
86' HIGH CUBE BOXCAR REVIEW "HO" ATH	02	70	19
86' HIGH CUBE BOXCAR REVIEW "N" MTX W&K	02	75	31
86' HY-CUBE BOXCAR REVIEW "HO" QC	11	66	19
90' SP VERT-A-PAC CAR REVIEW "HO" QC	08	71	21
92' HI CUBE BOXCAR REVIEW "HO" TI	08	68	17
AAR 40' BOX CAR KIT REVIEW "S" MIM	07	48	506
AAR 40' BOX CAR REVIEW "HO" GLO	05	48	366
AAR BOX CAR REVIEWS "HO" WAL	09	40	520
ALL METAL BOX CAR REVIEW "HO" MDC	11	50	53
ARA BOXCAR REVIEW "O" WALTEERS	11	38	504
AUTO BOX CAR REVIEW "O" HA	07	38	298
AUTO BOX CAR REVIEW "HO" COMET MODEL CO,	03	40	183
AUTO BOX KIT REVIEW "HO" ATH	03	51	52
AUTOMOBILE BOX CAR REVIEW "HO" AMB	09	57	10
AUTOMOBILE CAR REVIEW "HO" WAL	01	38	42
B&O WAGON TOP CLASS M53 REVIEW "HO" TI	12	66	22
BAY CAR KIT REVIEW "S" SSM	01	50	85
BICENTENNIAL BOXCAR LISTING "N" KADEE	02	77	46
BILLBOARD BOX CAR REVIEW "HO" LAC	09	53	14
BOX CAR 1 1/2 DOOR O BRACED LIST "N" KD	03	78	49
BOX CAR A&EC LISTING "HO" KAR-LINE	06	78	52
BOX CAR KIT REVIEW "O" ATH	11	45	504
BOX CAR KIT REVIEW "HO" LMP	01	46	66
BOX CAR KIT REVIEW "HO" MDC	04	50	60
BOX CAR KIT REVIEW "HO" M	02	55	17
BOX CAR KIT REVIEW "TT" SL	03	50	60
BOX CAR KIT REVIEW "TT" JM	01	49	101
BOX CAR KIT REVIEW GN ORANGE "HO" V	11	49	92
BOX CAR METAL KIT REVIEW "HO" MDC	08	52	46
BOX CAR MILW #507 LISTING "HO" AMB	05	78	52
BOX CAR REVIEW LMP	09	46	590
BOX CAR REVIEW "O" ATH	11	46	791
BOX CAR REVIEW "O" RAR	06	40	358
BOX CAR REVIEW C&EI "WAR BONDS" "HO" V	09	42	440
BOXCAR ATHEARN/C PAINT REVIEW "HO" BH	01	76	33
BOXCAR CA&C REVIEW "HON3" 1905 RDA	08	69	12
BOXCAR ERIE LACKAWANA REVIEW "HO" CM	11	78	61
BOXCAR REVIEW "N" CC	10	67	9
BOXCAR REVIEW "O" KRIS	03	70	22
BOXCAR REVIEW "TT" GD	09	70	20

BOX CAR MODEL REVIEWS	M	Y	P
BOXCAR SR&RL #85 REVIEW "HON30" SR	09	78	42
CENTENNIAL BOXCAR REVIEW "HO" TMC	11	74	29
COMBINATION DOOR BOXCAR "HO" DW 1965 ACF	11	81	56
COOKIE BOX CAR REVIEW D&RGW "HO" TSM	05	57	14
DOUBLE BOX CAR KIT REVIEW "HO" CRM	07	67	15
FISHBELLY BOXCAR REVIEW "N" KD 1910	07	75	26
FULL DOOR BOXCAR REVIEW "HO" AMB	04	64	10
INSULATED BOX CAR REVIEW "HO" ATT	03	68	17
INSULATED BOX CLASS RBL REVIEW "HO" DW	01	83	54
LINDSAY GHOST BOOSTER REVIEW "HO" LIN	09	50	59
METAL AUTO BOX CAR KIT REVIEW "HO" ATH	02	50	69
METAL BOX CAR REVIEW "O" MF	06	39	330
METAL BOXCAR KIT REVIEW "HO" M	10	47	860
MODERN 40' BOX CAR REVIEW "HO" KL	05	65	13
MODERN 40' BOX CAR REVIEW "HO" CC	07	65	10
MODERN 40' BOXCAR REVIEW "TT" HP	07	62	15
MODERN BOX CAR LISTING "HO" BHLW	04	77	46
MOMENTUM BOXCAR THE DRIFTER "HO" GT	06	78	54
NARROW GAUGE BOX CAR REVIEW "HO" KEM	11	49	90
NARROW GAUGE BOXCAR REVIEW "HON3" CC	05	64	6
OLD TIME BOX CAR KIT REVIEW "HO" DN	05	49	49
OUTSIDE BRACED BOX CAR KIT REVIEW "HO" U	05	49	53
OUTSIDE BRACED BOX CAR REVIEW "HO" MLI	09	56	17
OUTSIDE BRACED BOX CAR REVIEW "O" AN	07	53	56
OUTSIDE BRACED BOX CAR REVIEW "O" AN	12	53	16
OUTSIDE BRACED BOX CAR KIT REVIEW "S" NSM	11	49	96
OUTSIDE BRACED BOXCAR REVIEW "TT" ES	08	68	11
OUTSIDE BRACED WOOD BOXCAR REVIEW "N" SSP	04	68	12
PICKENS BOXCAR LISTING "HO" KAR-LINE	01	77	48
PLUG DOOR B&A BOXCAR REVIEW "HO" BHLW	04	74	20
PLUGDOOR BOXCAR REVIEW "1/4" USH	01	72	30
PS RAILBOX CAR REVIEW "HO" MDC	01	81	44
PS-1 STEEL BOXCAR REVIEW "O" AN	07	69	16
PS1 40' BOX CAR REVIEW "HO" AHM	05	62	13
PS1 40' BOXCAR REVIEW "HO" CCS 1947 PS	10	81	45
PS1 BOX CAR REVIEW "HO" KK	03	57	14
PS1 PLUG DOOR BOXCAR REV "N" B	10	69	20
PS1 STEEL BOX CAR REVIEW "HO" HD	02	65	11
RAIL BOX REVIEW "N" MDC 1974	05	80	42
RAILBOX BOX CAR LISTING "N"	08	77	40
RAILBOX BOXCAR LISTING "HO" AHM	02	77	46
RAILBOX BOXCAR REVIEW "HO" ATH	01	77	32
RAILBOX CAR REVIEW "O" QC 1975	02	84	52
RIBBED SIDE D&RGW BOXCAR REVIEW "HO" AMB	11	71	34
ROUND ROOF BOXCAR REVIEW "HO" MDC 1938	07	80	41
ROUND ROOF WAGON TOP PRR BOX REV "1" GI	11	83	48
SENTINEL BOX CAR REVIEW "O" ATH	06	48	434
STANDARD BOX CAR REVIEW "O" BR	07	38	298
STEAM SOUND BOXCAR REVIEW "HO" TMI	02	82	28
STEEL 40' BOX CAR REVIEW "HO" ATH	07	57	14
STEEL BOX CAR REVIEW "O" AN	10	53	11
STEEL UNDERFRAME X1 PRR BOXCAR "HO" WD	03	83	42
THRALL ALL DOOR BOXCAR REVIEW "HO" EBV	06	82	43
THRALL BOXCAR REVIEW "HO" LL	11	75	34
TRACK CLEANING BOXCAR REVIEW "HO" RGSR	11	83	61

FREIGHT CARS

BOX CAR MODEL REVIEWS

	M	Y	P
TRACTION BOX CAR IT REVIEW "O" AN	09	59	17
WAGON TOP BOX CAR REVIEW "OO" GMR	05	39	278
WAGON TOP CLASS M-53 B&O BOXCAR "N" QC	11	80	51
WAGON TOP PRR CLASS M53 CAR REV "HO" L	06	70	18
WOOD BOX CAR CLASS XM REVIEW "HO" U	09	52	55
WOOD BOX CAR RG REVIEW "HO" RAIL LINE	02	76	28
WOOD BOXCAR REVIEW "HO" CAM	05	77	42
WOOD SHEATHED BOXCAR REVIEW "HO" SS	12	77	48
WOODSIDE STEEL ATSF BOXCAR REV "HO" SUN	05	71	25
XFF10 RAILBOX REVIEW "N" KD 1974 FMC	08	81	39

BOX CAR MODEL REVIEWS BY ROAD

RD		M	Y	P
A&EC	BOX CAR A&EC LISTING "HO" KAR-LINE	06	78	52
ATSF	40' BX-37 ATSF BOXCAR REVIEW "HO" PMI	08	75	26
	40' 40T WOOD ATSF BOXCAR REVIEW "HO" SC	07	69	16
	WOODSIDE STEEL ATSF BOXCAR REV "HO" SUN	05	71	25
B&A	PLUG DOOR B&A BOXCAR REVIEW "HO" BHLW	04	74	20
B&O	WAGON TOP CLASS M-53 B&O BOXCAR "N" QC	11	80	51
	B&O WAGON TOP CLASS M53 REVIEW "HO" TI	12	66	22
BURL	60' INSULATED BURL BOXCAR REVIEW HO AMB	07	71	19
C&EI	BOX CAR REVIEW C&EI "WAR BONDS" "HO" V	09	42	440
CA&C	BOXCAR CA&C REVIEW "HON3" 1905 RDA	08	69	12
CAN	1900 CAN BOX CAR REVIEW "HO" CRM	01	65	11
D&RGW	30' BOXCAR REBUILD D&RGW REVIEW "ON3"SRE	09	76	30
	COOKIE BOX CAR REVIEW D&RGW "HO" TSM	05	57	14
	3000 SERIES D&RGW BOX CAR REV "ON3" CAM	07	61	10
	RIBBED SIDE D&RGW BOXCAR REVIEW "HO" AMB	11	71	34
DSP&P	26' DSP&P BOXCAR REVIEW "ON3" COM 1880	01	71	32
EL	BOXCAR ERIE LACKAWANA REVIEW "HO" CM	11	78	61
GN	40' AUTOMOBILE CAR GN REV "HO" MKM 1958	06	83	44
IC	40' WOOD SHEATHED IC BOX CAR REV "HO" LA	07	65	8
IT	TRACTION BOX CAR IT REVIEW "O" AN	09	59	17
MILW	BOX CAR MILW #507 LISTING "HO" AMB	05	78	52
	34' MILW BOXCAR REVIEW "HO" LA 1890	02	71	27
PRR	STEEL UNDERFRAME X1 PRR BOXCAR "HO" WD	03	83	42
	ROUND ROOF WAGON TOP PRR BOX REV "1" G1	11	83	48
	50T X32 PRR AUTOBOX REVIEW "HO" NPP 1935	11	73	29
	WAGON TOP PRR CLASS M53 CAR REV "HO" L	06	70	18
RBL	INSULATED BOX CLASS RBL REVIEW "HO" DW	01	83	54
RG	WOOD BOX CAR RG REVIEW "HO" RAIL LINE	02	76	28
RI	40' BOX CAR LISTING RI "N" KADEE	03	77	44
S	56' ALL DOOR BOXCAR S REVIEW "1/4" EPM	04	72	26
SOO	34' SOO BOXCAR REVIEW "O" LA 1888	11	68	18
SP	90' SP VERT-A-PAC CAR REVIEW "HO" QC	08	71	21
SR&RL	BOXCAR SR&RL #85 REVIEW "HON30" SR	09	78	42
UP	40' UP HIGH CUBE BOXCAR REVIEW "1/4" QC	10	71	22

BOX CAR MODEL REVIEWS BY MFG.

MFG	D	M	Y	P
AD	40' BOXCAR REVIEW "HO" AD	10	38	452
AHM	RAILBOX BOXCAR LISTING "HO" AHM	02	77	46
	PS1 40' BOX CAR REVIEW "HO" AHM	05	62	13
	40' STEEL BOXCAR REVIEW "1/4" AHM	01	71	34
ALCOE	40' METAL END BOXCAR REVIEW "HO" ALCOE	10	68	14
AMB	BOX CAR MILW #507 LISTING "HO" AMB	05	78	52
	70T HOGSHEAD BOX CAR REVIEW "HO" AMB	04	66	12
	FULL DOOR BOXCAR REVIEW "HO" AMB	04	64	10
	AUTOMOBILE BOX CAR REVIEW "HO" AMB	09	57	10
	60' INSULATED BURL BOXCAR REVIEW HO AMB	07	71	19
	RIBBED SIDE D&RGW BOXCAR REVIEW "HO" AMB	11	71	34
	60' AIRCRAFT SKY BOXCAR REVIEW "HO" AMB	11	70	18
AMI	40' AAR BOXCAR REVIEW "S" AMI 1937	10	83	56
AN	PS-1 STEEL BOXCAR REVIEW "O" AN	07	69	16
	OUTSIDE BRACED BOX CAR REVIEW "O" AN	07	53	56
	STEEL BOX CAR REVIEW "O" AN	10	53	11
	OUTSIDE BRACED BOX CAR REVIEW "O" AN	12	53	16
	TRACTION BOX CAR IT REVIEW "O" AN	09	59	17
	40' AAR BOX CAR REVIEW "O" AN	09	55	16
ARD	40' AUTOMOBILE BOX CAR REVIEW "HO" ARD	04	58	14
AT	40' STEEL BOXCAR REVIEW "1/4" AT	05	72	24
ATH	50' SINGLE DOOR BOXCAR REVIEW "HO" ATH	02	79	53
	RAILBOX BOXCAR REVIEW "HO" ATH	01	77	32
	50' CUSHION FRAME BOX CAR REV "HO" ATH	09	65	10
	40' STEEL BOX CAR REVIEW "HO" ATHEARN	05	63	9
	STEEL 40' BOX CAR REVIEW "HO" ATH	07	57	14
	86' HIGH CUBE BOXCAR REVIEW "HO" ATH	02	70	19
	50' PLUG DOOR BOXCAR REVIEW "HO" ATH	05	68	16
	BOX CAR REVIEW "O" ATH	11	46	791
	SENTINEL BOX CAR REVIEW "O" ATH	06	48	434
	BOX CAR KIT REVIEW "O" ATH	11	45	504
	50' AUTO BOX CAR REVIEW "HO" ATH	08	59	12
	AUTO BOX KIT REVIEW "HO" ATH	03	51	52
	METAL AUTO BOX CAR KIT REVIEW "HO" ATH	02	50	69
ATT	INSULATED BOX CAR REVIEW "HO" ATT	03	68	17
B	PS1 PLUG DOOR BOXCAR REV "N" B	10	69	20
BCM	23'6" BOXCAR REVIEW "HON3" BCM	09	67	11
BH	BOXCAR ATHEARN/C PAINT REVIEW "HO" BH	01	76	33
BHLW	MODERN BOX CAR LISTING "HO" BHLW	04	77	46
	PLUG DOOR B&A BOXCAR REVIEW "HO" BHLW	04	74	20
BIN	37' BOXCAR REVIEW "HO" BINKLEY	10	62	20
BR	STANDARD BOX CAR REVIEW "O" BR	07	38	298
CAM	WOOD BOXCAR REVIEW "HO" CAM	05	77	42
	3000 SERIES D&RGW BOX CAR REV "ON3" CAM	07	61	10
CC	RAILBOX BOX CAR LISTING "N"	08	77	40
	BOXCAR REVIEW "N" CC	10	67	9
	NARROW GAUGE BOXCAR REVIEW "HON3" CC	05	64	6
	MODERN 40' BOX CAR REVIEW "HO" CC	07	65	10
	40' USRA BOXCAR REVIEW "HO" CC	06	62	12
CCS	PS1 40' BOXCAR REVIEW "HO" CCS 1947 PS	10	81	45
CCW	28' OLDTIME BOX CAR REVIEW "HO" CCW	05	55	15
CK	36' BOX CAR REVIEW "TT" CK	06	62	12
CM	BOXCAR ERIE LACKAWANA REVIEW "HO" CM	11	78	61
CMO	AUTO BOX CAR REVIEW "HO" COMET MODEL CO.	03	40	183
COM	26' DSP&P BOXCAR REVIEW "ON3" COM 1880	01	71	32

FREIGHT CARS

BOX CAR MODEL REVIEWS BY MFG.

MFG		M	Y	P
CRM	DOUBLE BOX CAR KIT REVIEW "HO" CRM	07	67	15
	1900 CAN BOX CAR REVIEW "HO" CRM	01	65	11
CV	34' TRUSS ROD BOX CAR REVIEW "HO" CV	11	50	60
DJB	40' AAR BOXCAR REVIEW "HO" DJB	10	85	40
DN	OLD TIME BOX CAR KIT REVIEW "HO" DN	05	49	49
DW	COMBINATION DOOR BOXCAR "HO" DW 1965 ACF	11	81	56
	INSULATED BOX CLASS RBL REVIEW "HO" DW	01	83	54
	50' DOUBLE PLUG DOOR BOX REVIEW "HO" DW	03	79	46
EBV	THRALL ALL DOOR BOXCAR REVIEW "HO" EBV	06	82	43
EPM	56' ALL DOOR BOXCAR S REVIEW "1/4" EPM	04	72	26
ES	OUTSIDE BRACED BOXCAR REVIEW "TT" ES	08	68	11
G1	ROUND ROOF WAGON TOP PRR BOX REV "1" G1	11	83	48
GD	40' PS-1 BOXCAR REVIEW "TT" GD	08	69	10
	BOXCAR REVIEW "TT" GD	09	70	20
GLO	AAR 40' BOX CAR REVIEW "HO" GLO	05	48	366
GMR	WAGON TOP BOX CAR REVIEW "OO" GMR	05	39	278
GT	MOMENTUM BOXCAR THE DRIFTER "HO" GT	06	78	54
HA	AUTO BOX CAR REVIEW "O" HA	07	38	298
HD	PS1 STEEL BOX CAR REVIEW "HO" HD	02	65	11
HP	MODERN 40' BOXCAR REVIEW "TT" HP	07	62	15
JM	BOX CAR KIT REVIEW "TT" JM	01	49	101
KD	BOX CAR 1 1/2 DOOR O BRACED LIST "N" KD	03	78	49
	40' BOX CAR LISTING RI "N" KADEE	03	77	44
	BICENTENNIAL BOXCAR LISTING "N" KADEE	02	77	46
	XFF10 RAILBOX REVIEW "N" KD 1974 FMC	08	81	39
	FISHBELLY BOXCAR REVIEW "N" KD 1910	07	75	26
	40' STEEL BOXCAR REVIEW "N" KD 1930	07	73	24
	40' DOUBLE DOOR BOXCAR REV "N" KD 1930	10	73	24
KEM	NARROW GAUGE BOX CAR REVIEW "HO" KEM	11	49	90
KK	PS1 BOX CAR REVIEW "HO" KK	03	57	14
KL	50' BOXCAR REVIEW "HO" KL	10	76	34
	BOX CAR A&EC LISTING "HO" KAR-LINE	06	78	52
	PICKENS BOXCAR LISTING "HO" KAR-LINE	01	77	48
	50' BOXCAR REVIEW "HO" KL	10	67	9
	MODERN 40' BOX CAR REVIEW "HO" KL	05	65	13
	40' BOXCAR REVIEW "HO" KL	06	62	14
	50' PLUG DOOR BOXCAR REVIEW "HO" KL	11	68	20
	40' BOXCAR REVIEW "HO" KL 1947	06	69	18
KRIS	BOXCAR REVIEW "O" KRIS	03	70	22
	40' STEEL BOXCAR REVIEW "O" KRIS	10	68	11
KSC	40' OUTSIDE BRACED BOX CAR REV "S" KSC	12	55	22
L	WAGON TOP PRR CLASS M53 CAR REV "HO" L	06	70	18
LA	40' WOOD SHEATHED IC BOX CAR REV "HO" LA	07	65	8
	1900 WOOD BOXCAR REVIEW "HO" LABELLE	11	63	9
	34' MILW BOXCAR REVIEW "HO" LA 1890	02	71	27
	34' SOO BOXCAR REVIEW "O" LA 1888	11	68	18
LAC	BILLBOARD BOX CAR REVIEW "HO" LAC	09	53	14
LIN	LINDSAY GHOST BOOSTER REVIEW "HO" LIN	09	50	59
LL	THRALL BOXCAR REVIEW "HO" LL	11	75	34
LMP	BOX CAR KIT REVIEW "HO" LMP	01	46	66
	BOX CAR REVIEW LMP	09	46	590
LVM	40' HIGH CUBE BOXCAR REVIEW "1/4" LVM	04	70	11
M	METAL BOXCAR KIT REVIEW "HO" M	10	47	860
	BOX CAR KIT REVIEW "HO" M	02	55	17
MDC	PS RAILBOX CAR REVIEW "HO" MDC	01	81	44
	ROUND ROOF BOXCAR REVIEW "HO" MDC 1938	07	80	41
	RAIL BOX REVIEW "N" MDC 1974	05	80	42
	50' FLAT ROOF BOXCAR REV "N" MDC	12	79	40
	50' FLAT ROOF BOXCAR REVIEW "HO" MDC	06	79	41
	36' BOXCAR REVIEW "HO" MDC	05	69	8
	BOX CAR METAL KIT REVIEW "HO" MDC	08	52	46
	BOX CAR KIT REVIEW "HO" MDC	04	50	60
	ALL METAL BOX CAR REVIEW "HO" MDC	11	50	53
MF	METAL BOX CAR REVIEW "O" MF	06	39	330
MIM	AAR 40' BOX KIT REVIEW "S" MIM	07	48	506
MKM	40' AUTOMOBILE CAR GN REV "HO" MKM 1958	06	83	44
MLI	OUTSIDE BRACED BOX CAR REVIEW "HO" MLI	09	56	17
	50' OUT BRACED AUTO BOX CAR REV "HO" MLI	04	59	14
MTX	86' HIGH CUBE BOXCAR REVIEW "N" MTX W&K	02	75	31
NPP	50' ALL STEEL BOXCAR REVIEW "O" NPP	06	76	35
	50T X32 PRR AUTOBOX REVIEW "HO" NPP 1935	11	73	29
NSM	OUTSIDE BRACED BOXCAR KIT REVIEW "S" NSM	11	49	96
OC	1900 BOXCAR REVIEW "HO" OC	11	62	16
PMI	40' BX-37 ATSF BOXCAR REVIEW "HO" PMI	08	75	26
QC	RAILBOX CAR REVIEW "O" QC 1975	02	84	52
	WAGON TOP CLASS M-53 B&O BOXCAR "N" QC	11	80	51
	85' HICUBE DOUBLE DOOR BOXCAR REV "HO QC	08	69	14
	50' CUSHIONED BOX CAR REVIEW "HO" QC	04	66	10
	86' HY-CUBE BOXCAR REVIEW "HO" QC	11	66	19
	90' SP VERT-A-PAC CAR REVIEW "HO" QC	08	71	21
	40' UP HIGH CUBE BOXCAR REVIEW "1/4" QC	10	71	22
	50' SINGLE DOOR BOXCAR REVIEW "N" QC	01	73	27
RAP	86' 50T HIGH CUBE BOXCAR REV "N" RAP GSC	03	70	19
RAR	BOX CAR REVIEW "O" RAR	06	40	358
RDA	BOXCAR CA&C REVIEW "HON3" 1905 RDA	08	69	12
REK	50' BOXCAR REVIEW "S" REK	07	64	6
RGSR	TRACK CLEANING BOXCAR REVIEW "HO" RGSR	11	83	61
RL	WOOD BOX CAR RG REVIEW "HO" RAIL LINE	02	76	28
RRI	60' AUTO BOX REVIEW "HO" RRI	09	85	38
SC	40' 40T WOOD ATSF BOXCAR REV "HO" SC	07	69	16
SL	BOX CAR KIT REVIEW "TT" SL	03	50	60
SR	BOXCAR SR&RL #85 REVIEW "HON30" SR	09	78	42
SRE	30' BOXCAR REBUILD D&RGW REVIEW "ON3"SRE	09	76	30
SS	WOOD SHEATHED BOXCAR REVIEW "HO" SS	12	77	48
	50' STANDARD BOXCAR 1920 REVIEW "HO" SS	05	79	45
SSM	BAY CAR KIT REVIEW "S" SSM	01	50	85
SSP	OUTSIDE BRACED WOOD BOXCAR REVIEW "N"SSP	04	68	12
SUN	WOODSIDE STEEL ATSF BOXCAR REV "HO" SUN	05	71	25
TI	B&O WAGON TOP CLASS M53 REVIEW "HO" TI	12	66	22
	92' HI CUBE BOXCAR REVIEW "HO" TI	08	68	17
TMC	40' DOUBLE SHEATHED BOXCAR "HO" REV TMC	05	69	14
	40T X29 BOXCAR REVIEW "HO" TMC 1930	03	73	25
	CENTENNIAL BOXCAR REVIEW "HO" TMC	11	74	29
TMI	STEAM SOUND BOXCAR REVIEW "HO" TMI	02	82	28
TOM	40' BOXCAR REVIEW "SN3" TOM	09	67	10
TSM	COOKIE BOX CAR REVIEW D&RGW "HO" TSM	05	57	14
U	WOOD BOX CAR CLASS XM REVIEW "HO" U	09	52	55
	OUTSIDE BRACED BOX CAR KIT REVIEW "HO" U	05	49	53
USH	PLUGDOOR BOXCAR REVIEW "1/4" USH	01	72	30
	50' CUSHION FRAME BOXCAR REVIEW "1/4 USH	04	71	22

FREIGHT CARS

BOX CAR MODEL REVIEWS BY MFG.

MFG	D		M	Y	P
V	BOX CAR REVIEW C&EI "WAR BONDS" "HO"	V	09	42	440
	BOX CAR KIT REVIEW GN ORANGE "HO"	V	11	49	92
WAL	51' BARREL & WOODWARE CAR REV "1/4" WAL		10	72	23
	51' WAFFLE SIDE BOXCAR REV "1/4" WAL	PS	11	72	30
	AUTOMOBILE CAR REVIEW "HO" WAL		01	38	42
	ARA BOXCAR REVIEW "O" WALTEERS		11	38	504
	AAR BOX CAR REVIEWS "HO" WAL		09	40	520
WD	STEEL UNDERFRAME X1 PRR BOXCAR "HO" WD		03	83	42
YE	36' BOXCAR REVIEW "HO" YE 1900		05	71	20
	40' TRUSS ROD BOXCAR REVIEW "HO" YE		12	71	30

FLAT CAR PROTOTYPE DATA

D	M	Y	P
10 PAC LOADING OF TRAILERS	12	82	186
100 TON STEEL LOG CARS 1985 EVANS	07	85	78
16 AUTOBODY FLAT CAR LOAD	01	51	8
50' FLAT CARS CLASS F33 & F36 PRR	04	42	170
BI MODAL ROADRAILER	07	82	62
BULKHEAD FLAT CARS TTR CLASS BSH 71A	02	84	82
DISCONNECTED LOG CARS	01	69	92
EXOTIC FLATCAR LOADS	12	77	136
FLAT CAR LOADS (LOCOMOTIVE)	02	77	115
FLAT CAR VARIATIONS	05	47	384
FLAT CARS & TRANSFORMERS SOO LINE 1968	10	80	92
FROM BULKHEAD FLATS TO TOFC ATSF	12	84	104
FRONT RUNNER 4 WHEEL TRAILERTRAIN FLTCAR	09	85	82
MOUNTING LONG GIRDERS ON 2 CARS	11	62	88
ROADRAILERS & LOADING CARGO	07	82	111
ROADRAKER NEW DESIGN	05	83	126
SANTA FE 10-PACK ITEL	09	82	58
SP DOUBLE STACK ARTICULATED ACF 1977	10	83	92
WELL HOLE FLAT CARS OF B&M 1941	02	83	102

FLAT CAR PROTOTYPE DATA BY ROAD

RD	D	M	Y	P
ATSF	FROM BULKHEAD FLATS TO TOFC ATSF	12	84	104
	SANTA FE 10-PACK ITEL	09	82	58
B&M	WELL HOLE FLAT CARS OF B&M 1941	02	83	102
PRR	50' FLAT CARS CLASS F33 & F36 PRR	04	42	170
SOO	FLAT CARS & TRANSFORMERS SOO LINE 1968	10	80	92
SP	SP DOUBLE STACK ARTICULATED ACF 1977	10	83	92
TTR	BULKHEAD FLAT CARS TTR CLASS BSH 71A	02	84	82

FLAT CAR PLANS

D	M	Y	P
10-PACK PLANS ATSF #298956 ITEL	09	82	58
100 TON CLASS FM FLAT CAR PLAN P&LE	08	35	206
100 TON STEEL LOG CAR PLN GPSX#141 EVANS	07	85	78
42' FLAT CAR PLANS CP #34359	04	37	133
50 TON FLAT CAR C&NW #42597 PLAN 1927	07	36	178
50 TON FLAT CAR CLASS FM PLAN PRR#947580	01	62	35
50' CLASS FM SIDE GIRDER FLAT L&N PLANS	04	35	90
55' TYPE FMS FLAT CAR PLANS SOO #5776	10	80	90
BI MODAL ROADRAILER PLANS	07	82	62
BULKHEAD FLAT CAR PLAN ATSF #96178	12	84	106
BULKHEAD FLATCAR PLN TTR#82036 CL BSH71A	02	84	82
CANDA 8 TRUSS ROD FLAT CAR PLANS	08	57	40
CIRCUS 70' FLAT CAR PLANS	05	46	312
CONVERTED FLAT CAR S #117637 PLANS	04	42	168
DEPRESSED CENTER 40' FLAT CAR TPRX#1 PLN	11	52	60
DEPRESSED CTR TYPE FD FLAT SOO#54005 PLN	10	80	90
DISCONNECT LOGGING TRUCK PLANS	06	71	56
DOUBLE STACK PLANS SP #513324 ACF 1977	10	83	90
DROP CENTER FLAT CAR PLAN TPRX 1 1947	02	55	60
FLAT CAR 24' NARROW GAUGE PLAN MILW #650	09	47	718
FLAT CAR FOR HOT METAL SERVICE PLAN	05	44	216
FLAT CAR PLANS 40 TON NC&SL	10	52	74
FLAT CAR PLANS 50 TON UP CLASS F-50-9	03	38	116
FLAT CAR PLANS SIE #28	02	76	79
FLAT CAR VARIATION PLANS	05	47	384
FLAT CLASS FM W/GRINDSTONE PL PRR#473567	08	63	42
FLATCAR DRAWINGS #473567 PRR 1906	10	77	81
FOUR TRUCK FLAT CAR PLAN W #20006	06	60	42
FRONT RUNNER 4 WHEEL FLATCAR PLANS	09	85	85
GUN CARRIAGE CAR OF 1916 PLAN D&H #50001	03	63	41
HEAVY DUTY FLAT CAR PLANS IC #62499	03	73	49
HITCHHIKER FLAT CAR PLANS ACF TTX#478671	04	68	38
MILITARY FLAT CAR #295 PLANS USA 1862	03	69	33
PIGGYBACK TRAILER CAR & LOAD PLNS ET&WNC	02	44	86
TOFC FLAT CAR PLANS ATSF #293241	12	84	106
TRAILER TRAIN FINGER RACK FLAT CAR PLANS	03	76	58
TRANSFORMER CAR PLANS	01	37	25
TRANSFORMER CAR PLANS MILW #67025	02	39	82
TRANSFORMER FLAT CAR LOADS PLANS	10	80	90
USRA FLAT CAR PLANS 40 TON	03	38	116
WARTIME COMPOSITE FLAT CAR PRR #392548	06	44	247
WELL CAR PLANS B&M #5000	01	44	11
WELL HOLE FLAT CARS PLANS B&M #5006 1941	02	83	102
WELLCAR FOR KODAK COATING WHEEL PLANS	01	72	65
WOOD FLAT CAR PLANS MA&PA #120	02	68	34

FREIGHT CARS

RD	FLAT CAR PLANS BY ROAD	M	Y	P
ACF	HITCHHIKER FLAT CAR PLANS ACF TTX#478671	04	68	38
ATSF	BULKHEAD FLAT CAR PLAN ATSF #96178	12	84	106
	TOFC FLAT CAR PLANS ATSF #293241	12	84	106
	10-PACK PLANS ATSF #298956 ITEL	09	82	58
B&M	WELL CAR PLANS B&M #5000	01	44	11
	WELL HOLE FLAT CARS PLANS B&M #5006 1941	02	83	102
C&NW	50 TON FLAT CAR C&NW #42597 PLAN 1927	07	36	178
CP	42' FLAT CAR PLANS CP #34359	04	37	133
D&H	GUN CARRIAGE CAR OF 1916 PLAN D&H #50001	03	63	41
ET&WNC	PIGGYBACK TRAILER CAR & LOAD PLNS ET&WNC	02	44	86
IC	HEAVY DUTY FLAT CAR PLANS IC #62499	03	73	49
L&N	50' CLASS FM SIDE GIRDER FLAT L&N PLANS	04	35	90
MA&PA	WOOD FLAT CAR PLANS MA&PA #120	02	68	34
MILW	TRANSFORMER CAR PLANS MILW #67025	02	39	82
	FLAT CAR 24' NARROW GAUGE PLAN MILW #650	09	47	718
NC&SL	FLAT CAR PLANS 40 TON NC&SL	10	52	74
P&LE	100 TON CLASS FM FLAT CAR PLAN P&LE	08	35	206
PRR	WARTIME COMPOSITE FLAT CAR PRR #392548	06	44	247
	50 TON FLAT CAR CLASS FM PLAN PRR#947580	01	62	35
	FLATCAR DRAWINGS #473567 PRR 1906	10	77	81
	FLAT CLASS FM W/GRINDSTONE PL PRR#473567	08	63	42
S	CONVERTED FLAT CAR S #117637 PLANS	04	42	168
SIE	FLAT CAR PLANS SIE #28	02	76	79
SOO	55' TYPE FMS FLAT CAR PLANS SOO #5776	10	80	90
	DEPRESSED CTR TYPE FD FLAT SOO#54005 PLN	10	80	90
SP	DOUBLE STACK PLANS SP #513324 ACF 1977	10	83	90
TTR	BULKHEAD FLATCAR PLN TTR#82036 CL BSH71A	02	84	82
UP	FLAT CAR PLANS 50 TON UP CLASS F-50-9	03	38	116
USA	MILITARY FLAT CAR #295 PLANS USA 1862	03	69	33
USRA	USRA FLAT CAR PLANS 40 TON	03	38	116
W	FOUR TRUCK FLAT CAR PLAN W #20006	06	60	42

FLAT CAR MODELS		M	Y	P
10-PACK ATSF CONSTRUCTION	ITEL	09	82	51
50' FLAT CAR B&O	MOD & PT	08	82	113
50' FLAT CAR UP	MOD & PT	05	78	115
AUTO RACKS (BRASS)	MOD & PT	11	84	139
AUTOMOBILE TRANSPORTER 75' CONSTRUCT CN		09	58	40
BUILD A FLAT CAR		04	44	152
BUILD A LOG FLAT CAR		07	78	60
BUILDING A FLAT CAR CP #34359		04	37	133
BULKHEAD FLAT CAR KITBASH		02	84	84
CANDA PLATFORM CAR OF 1894 CONSTRUCTION		08	57	40
CONVERTED S FLAT CAR CONSTRUCTION 1928		04	42	167
CONVERTIBLE BULKHEAD FLAT CONSTRUCTION		10	76	74
CRANKSHAFT FLATCAR LOAD CONSTRUCTION		06	60	42
DISCONNECT LOGGING TRUCK CONST CORRECTIO		08	71	9
DISCONNECT LOGGING TRUCK CONSTRUCTION		06	71	56
DOUBLE STACK SP CONSTRUCTION ACF 1977		10	83	83
DROP CENTER FLAT CAR PLASTIC CONSTRUCT		02	55	62
DROP CENTER FLAT CAR WOOD CONSTRUCT	$1	02	55	58
FLAT CAR CONSTRUCTION	$1	04	53	15
FLAT CAR FROM SCRATCH CONSTRUCTION PRR		10	77	81
FLAT CAR POWDER RIVER	MOD & PT	06	79	108
FOUR TRUCK FLAT CAR CONSTRUCTION	$1	03	56	26
FOUR TRUCK FLAT CAR CONSTRUCTION WABASH		06	60	42
FREELANCE FLAT CAR CONSTRUCTION		03	58	38
FREELANCE LOG SCRATCHBUILD IN BRASS		11	81	106
FRONT RUNNER 4 WHEEL FLATCAR CONSTRUCT		09	85	86
HEAVY DUTY DEPRESSED CENTER FLAT KITBASH		04	75	38
HEAVY DUTY FLAT CAR KITBASH		03	77	48
LOADS OF LUMBER CONSTRUCTION		02	57	32
LOGGING CAR CONSTRUCTION		10	64	52
LOGGING CAR FOR QUANTITY CONSTRUCTION	$1	06	69	58
LOGGING CARS FROM BAGGAGE CARS		12	72	72
MOM OPEN TOP PULP WOOD CARS SR&RL DYXIN		12	85	101
MOM SCHNABLE FLATCAR "HO"	MANLICK	01	78	80
NOT TOO QUAINT D&RGW FLAT CAR CONSTRUCT		04	80	59
PIGGYBACK FLAT CAR CONSTRUCTION	$1	03	54	40
PIGGYBACK FLATCAR CONSTRUCTION	$1	04	68	33
PIGGYBACK VAN KITBASH CONSTRUCTION		12	75	102
PULPWOOD CAR CONSTRUCTION	$1	06	65	50
PULPWOOD CAR CONSTRUCTION SOUTHERN	$1	02	56	32
ROADRAILERS CONSTRUCT BI MODAL TRAILERS		07	82	46
ROADRAILERS CONSTRUCTION CORRECTION		08	82	131
SCRACHBUILT DEPRESSED CENTER FLAT CAR		03	78	87
SOO LINE FLATCAR & TRANSFORMER CONSTRUCT		10	80	86
SUPER SIZE 92' FLAT CAR MODEL PHOTO PRR		11	55	37
TOFC FLAT CAR CONSTRUCTION		12	84	109
TOY PARTS INTO FLAT CAR LOADS		09	79	112
TRAILER TRAIN VARIATIONS	MOD & PT	04	76	87
TRANSFORMER CAR CONRAIL	MOD & PT	12	81	156
TRANSFORMER CAR CONSTRUCTION		02	39	79

FREIGHT CARS

FLAT CAR MODEL REVIEWS	M	Y	P
16 WHEEL FLAT CAR KIT REVIEW "TT" JM	02	50	72
1890 FLAT CAR REVIEW "7/16" MEW	10	64	11
1900 FLAT CAR REVIEW "HO" HD	01	63	27
22' LOG BUGGY REVIEW "TT" CPC	08	64	10
28' LOG CAR KIT REVIEW "HON3" HD	11	65	9
30' D&RGW FLAT CAR REVIEW "HON3" ACS	12	82	48
30' D&RGW FLATCAR REVIEW "HON3" RRL 1880	08	71	27
30' FLAT CAR REVIEW "HO" MDC	07	58	9
30' FLATCAR OF 1942 REVIEW "HO" MDC 1942	06	63	9
34' MA&PA FLAT CAR REVIEW "HO" LI	12	70	38
35' TRUSS ROD FLAT CAR REVIEW "N" RLW	03	76	29
36' 30T MA&PA FLATCAR REVIEW "O" LI 1906	03	73	26
36' TRUSS ROD FLATCAR REVIEW "HO" SCSM	05	72	26
40' DISCONNECTED LOG CAR REVIEW "HO" KD	01	59	20
40' FLAT NC&SL REVIEW "HO" GC 1928 ACF	02	85	44
41 FISHBELLY FLATCAR REVIEW "O" AHM	08	71	24
41' NP LOG CAR REVIEW "HO" NWSL	11	59	21
42' FLAT CAR REVIEW "HO" MANTUA	03	56	12
42' SKELETON LOG CAR REVIEW "HO" KD	07	63	10
43' PULPWOOD CAR REVIEW "HO" KEM	07	59	14
43' PULPWOOD CAR REVIEW "O" KEM	07	59	14
50'/52' FLAT CAR REVIEW "O" FMC	10	67	14
68' FINGER RACK FLATCAR REVIEW "HO" SCC	11	71	31
70' PULPWOOD CAR REVIEW "HO" AMB	03	66	12
85' AUTO RACK REVIEW "N" RAP	06	70	24
85' CONTAINER FLAT CAR REVIEW "HO" ATH	05	71	22
85' PIGGYBACK CAR REVIEW "O" QC	12	68	13
85' PIGGYBACK FLAT CAR REVIEW "HO" SUM	10	67	11
85' TRAILER TRAIN CAR ACF REVIEW "HO" QC	01	68	14
87' FLEXIVAN CAR REVIEW "HO" QC	03	70	15
BULKHEAD FLAT CAR REVIEW "1/4" QC	01	71	26
BULKHEAD FLATCAR REVIEW "HO" SCC	06	72	23
BULKHEAD THRALL FLAT CAR REV "HO" MDC	03	82	50
CENTER BEAM LUMBER CAR REVIEW "HO" FR	09	85	33
CIRCUS FLAT CAR LISTING "1/4" C&S	10	78	54
CIRCUS FLAT CAR REVIEW "O" WAL	10	67	16
CLIMAX LOG CAR REVIEW "HO" KLW	04	77	39
DROP CENTER FLAT CAR REVIEW "HO" V	08	39	424
DUAL GAUGE IDLER CAR REVIEW "HO" BIN	04	54	12
FLAT CAR 50' LISTING "N" KADEE	03	78	49
FLAT CAR D&RGW REVIEW "ON3/HON3" PS	07	79	45
FLAT CAR KIT REVIEW "TT" HP	10	48	774
FLAT CAR KIT REVIEW "HO" LAC	02	50	71
FLAT CAR KIT REVIEW "HO" M	02	50	68
FLAT CAR KIT REVIEW "HO" U	06	50	48
FLAT CAR KIT REVIEW "HO" M	07	56	16
FLAT CAR KIT REVIEW "O" RC	07	41	383
FLAT CAR LOAD REVIEW "HO" STEWART PROD.	11	50	58
FLAT CAR REVIEW "HO" WALTERS	05	39	279
FLAT CAR REVIEW "HO" U	03	51	55
FLAT CAR REVIEW "O" NJM	05	54	11
FLAT CAR WELL HOLE REVIEW C&O "HO/4" QC	03	78	38
FLATCAR NARROW GAUGE CONV REV "HON3" WSM	05	67	10
HEAVY DUTY 47' 200T FLAT CAR REV "HO" MDC	11	55	14
IDLER FLAT CAR D&RGW REVIEW "O" TOM 1950	06	74	23

FLAT CAR MODEL REVIEWS	M	Y	P
LOG BUGGIE REVIEW "HO" MEW	03	53	64
LOG BUGGIE REVIEW "O" KEM	08	59	13
LOG BUNK REVIEW "HO" DW PCF	08	82	42
LOG CAR REVIEW "HO" HD	12	67	10
LOG CAR REVIEW "ON3" HB	11	85	54
OLD TIME FLAT CAR REVIEW "HO" ASM	11	52	70
PIGGYBACK FLAT CAR REVIEW "HO" PL	10	56	10
PIGGYBACK FLAT CAR REVIEW "HO" ULRICH	01	56	14
PULPWOOD RACK CAR REVIEW "HO" ATH	09	54	14
ROAD RAILER REVIEW "HO" DP	03	84	43
SIDE BOARD FLAT CAR REVIEW "HO" CCW	07	54	09
SWAYNE LUMBER LOG CAR REVIEW "HON3" RGM	03	79	60
TRI-LEVEL AUTO CARRIER REVIEW "1/4" QC	10	69	10
TRI-LEVEL TRAILER TRAIN CAR REV "HO" QC	10	65	11
TRILEVEL AUTORACK REVIEW "HO" CC	02	66	11
TRUCK & FREIGHT CAR COMBO REV "4MM" PPP	07	62	14
TRUSS ROD FLAT CAR REVIEW "HO" LA	08	67	12
WELL FLAT CAR PRR CLASS F33 REV "O" ALCO	12	77	46

FLAT CAR MODEL REVIEWS BY ROAD				
RD	D	M	Y	P
C&O	FLAT CAR WELL HOLE REVIEW C&O "HO/4" QC	03	78	38
D&RGW	30' D&RGW FLAT CAR REVIEW "HON3" ACS	12	82	48
	30' D&RGW FLATCAR REVIEW "HON3" RRL 1880	08	71	27
MA&PA	36' 30T MA&PA FLATCAR REVIEW "O" LI 1906	03	73	26
NC&SL	40' FLAT NC&SL REVIEW "HO" GC 1928 ACF	02	85	44
PRR	WELL FLAT CAR PRR CLASS F33 REV "O" ALCO	12	77	46

FREIGHT CARS

FLAT CAR MODEL REVIEWS BY MFG.

MFG		M	Y	P
	CLIMAX LOG CAR REVIEW "HO" KLW	04	77	39
ACS	30' D&RGW FLAT CAR REVIEW "HON3" ACS	12	82	48
AHM	41 FISHBELLY FLATCAR REVIEW "O" AHM	08	71	24
ALCO	WELL FLAT CAR PRR CLASS F33 REV "O" ALCO	12	77	46
AMB	70' PULPWOOD CAR REVIEW "HO" AMB	03	66	12
ASM	OLD TIME FLAT CAR REVIEW "HO" ASM	11	52	70
ATH	PULPWOOD RACK CAR REVIEW "HO" ATH	09	54	14
	85' CONTAINER FLAT CAR REVIEW "HO" ATH	05	71	22
BIN	DUAL GAUGE IDLER CAR REVIEW "HO" BIN	04	54	12
C&S	CIRCUS FLAT CAR LISTING "1/4" C&S	10	78	54
CC	TRILEVEL AUTORACK REVIEW "HO" CC	02	66	11
CCW	SIDE BOARD FLAT CAR REVIEW "HO" CCW	07	54	09
CPC	22' LOG BUGGY REVIEW "TT" CPC	08	64	10
DP	ROAD RAILER REVIEW "HO" DP	03	84	43
DW	LOG BUNK REVIEW "HO" DW PCF	08	82	42
FMC	50'/52' FLAT CAR REVIEW "O" FMC	10	67	14
FR	CENTER BEAM LUMBER CAR REVIEW "HO" FR	09	85	33
GC	40' FLAT NC&SL REVIEW "HO" GC 1928 ACF	02	85	44
HB	LOG CAR REVIEW "ON3" HB	11	85	54
HD	28' LOG CAR KIT REVIEW "HON3" HD	11	65	9
	LOG CAR REVIEW "HO" HD	12	67	10
	1900 FLAT CAR REVIEW "HO" HD	01	63	27
HP	FLAT CAR KIT REVIEW "TT" HP	10	48	774
JM	16 WHEEL FLAT CAR KIT REVIEW "TT" JM	02	50	72
KD	40' DISCONNECTED LOG CAR REVIEW "HO" KD	01	59	20
	FLAT CAR 50' LISTING "N" KADEE	03	78	49
	42' SKELETON LOG CAR REVIEW "HO" KD	07	63	10
KEM	LOG BUGGIE REVIEW "O" KEM	08	59	13
	43' PULPWOOD CAR REVIEW "HO" KEM	07	59	14
	43' PULPWOOD CAR REVIEW "O" KEM	07	59	14
LA	TRUSS ROD FLAT CAR REVIEW "HO" LA	08	67	12
LAC	FLAT CAR KIT REVIEW "HO" LAC	02	50	71
LI	36' 30T MA&PA FLATCAR REVIEW "O" LI 1906	03	73	26
	34' MA&PA FLAT CAR REVIEW "HO" LI	12	70	38
M	FLAT CAR KIT REVIEW "HO" M	02	50	68
	42' FLAT CAR REVIEW "HO" MANTUA	03	56	12
	FLAT CAR KIT REVIEW "HO" M	07	56	16
MDC	HEAVY DUTY 47' 200T FLAT CAR REV "HO"MDC	11	55	14
	30' FLAT CAR REVIEW "HO" MDC	07	58	9
	BULKHEAD THRALL FLAT CAR REV "HO" MDC	03	82	50
	30' FLATCAR OF 1942 REVIEW "HO" MDC 1942	06	63	9
MEW	LOG BUGGIE REVIEW "HO" MEW	03	53	64
	1890 FLAT CAR REVIEW "7/16" MEW	10	64	11
NJM	FLAT CAR REVIEW "O" NJM	05	54	11
NWSL	41' NP LOG CAR REVIEW "HO" NWSL	11	59	21
PL	PIGGYBACK FLAT CAR REVIEW "HO" PL	10	56	10
PPP	TRUCK & FREIGHT CAR COMBO REV "4MM" PPP	07	62	14
PS	FLAT CAR D&RGW REVIEW "ON3/HON3" PS	07	79	45
QC	87' FLEXIVAN CAR REVIEW "HO" QC	03	70	15
	BULKHEAD FLAT CAR REVIEW "1/4" QC	01	71	26
	FLAT CAR WELL HOLE REVIEW C&O "HO/4" QC	03	78	38
	TRI-LEVEL AUTO CARRIER REVIEW "1/4" QC	10	69	10
	85' PIGGYBACK CAR REVIEW "O" QC	12	68	13
	85' TRAILER TRAIN CAR ACF REVIEW "HO" QC	01	68	14
	TRI-LEVEL TRAILER TRAIN CAR REV "HO" QC	10	65	11

FLAT CAR MODEL REVIEWS BY MFG.

MFG		M	Y	P
RAP	85' AUTO RACK REVIEW "N" RAP	06	70	24
RC	FLAT CAR KIT REVIEW "O" RC	07	41	383
RGM	SWAYNE LUMBER LOG CAR REVIEW "HON3" RGM	03	79	60
RLW	35' TRUSS ROD FLAT CAR REVIEW "N" RLW	03	76	29
RRL	30' D&RGW FLATCAR REVIEW "HON3" RRL 1880	08	71	27
SCC	68' FINGER RACK FLATCAR REVIEW "HO" SCC	11	71	31
	BULKHEAD FLATCAR REVIEW "HO" SCC	06	72	23
SCSM	36' TRUSS ROD FLATCAR REVIEW "HO" SCSM	05	72	26
STEW	FLAT CAR LOAD REVIEW "HO" STEWART PROD.	11	50	58
SUM	85' PIGGYBACK FLAT CAR REVIEW "HO" SUM	10	67	11
TOM	IDLER FLAT CAR D&RGW REVIEW "O" TOM 1950	06	74	23
U	FLAT CAR REVIEW "HO" U	03	51	55
	FLAT CAR KIT REVIEW "HO" U	06	50	48
	PIGGYBACK FLAT CAR REVIEW "HO" ULRICH	01	56	14
V	DROP CENTER FLAT CAR REVIEW "HO" V	08	39	424
WAL	FLAT CAR REVIEW "HO" WALTERS	05	39	279
	CIRCUS FLAT CAR REVIEW "O" WAL	10	67	16
WSM	FLATCAR NARROW GAUGE CONV REV "HON3" WSM	05	67	10

GONDOLA PROTOTYPE DATA

	M	Y	P
65' BETHLEHEM MILL GONDOLAS PB&NE	06	81	88
ADDED SIDES FOR TACONITE ORE CARS	04	70	78
GONDOLA AND HOPPER CARS	02	77	62
GONDOLA LETTERING MILW	03	34	4
GONDOLA LOAD OF HOPPER CAR SIDES	12	67	66
GONDOLAS NARROW GAUGE OF D&RGW	08	78	58
HOPPER BOTTOM GONDOLA CARS	05	78	102
HOPPER BOTTOM GONDOLA OF N&W 1890	10	83	104
PROTOTYPE KITBASH BULK HEAD GONDOLA	12	78	169
STEEL COIL GONDOLAS	02	68	71
TYPES OF GONDOLA CARS	12	35	326
WHAT ROOF? SIGN ON GONDOLA	06	78	124
WHY GONDOLAS HAVE LOW SIDES	07	77	45

GONDOLA PROTOTYPE DATA BY ROAD

RD		M	Y	P
D&RGW	GONDOLAS NARROW GAUGE OF D&RGW	08	78	58
MILW	GONDOLA LETTERING MILW	03	34	4
N&W	HOPPER BOTTOM GONDOLA OF N&W 1890	10	83	104
PB&NE	65' BETHLEHEM MILL GONDOLAS PB&NE	06	81	88

FREIGHT CARS

GONDOLA PLANS	M	Y	P
42' DROP BOTTOM GONDOLA PLANS RI #187300	12	40	665
65' BETHLEHAM MILL GON PLANS PB&NE #871	06	81	89
70 TON MILL GONDOLA PLANS ATSF #170970	05	76	45
70T CLASS GS AAR STEEL GON PLNS E #44000	12	40	665
90T H.SIDE CLASS GKD GOND N&W#100054 PLN	02	45	58
BRACED DROP END GONDOLA PLANS B&O#145000	07	62	31
COMPOSITE GONDOLA PLANS IC OF 1917	01	60	75
CONTAINER CAR PLANS *SCL #50000 ACF	05	57	61
COVERED GONDOLA PLANS RI #1043	11	58	66
DOUBLE HOPPER-GONDOLA CAR PLANS B&O 1880	03	43	138
DROP BOTTOM 55T GS GONDOLA C&EI#93000 PL	02	77	62
DROP BOTTOM GONDOLA PLAN D&RGW NAR GAUGE	03	58	28
DROP SIDE GONDOLA OF 1835 PLANS B&O	07	76	85
GENERAL SERVICE DROP DOOR GONDOLA PLANS	08	70	53
GONDOLA CAR N GAUGE PLANS D&RGW #06299	02	61	39
GONDOLA CAR NARROW GAUGE PLANS D&RGW	06	43	274
GONDOLA CAR OF 1894 PLANS W #32963 SCC	01	68	39
GONDOLA CAR PLANS 50 TON SP	10	52	74
GONDOLA CAR PLANS MICHC #15317 CLASS K2	11	50	51
GONDOLA CAR PLANS PRR #315694 CLASS G22B	04	50	42
GONDOLA PLANS	03	34	6
GONDOLA PLANS	04	44	152
GONDOLA PLANS CMI #1665	08	72	47
GONDOLA PLANS ET&WNC #372	07	81	63
GONDOLA SIDE PLANS CB&Q #19540 CLASS GM	12	35	327
GONDOLA SIDE PLANS UP #11471 CLASS GMA	12	35	327
GONDOLA SIDE PLANS V #19647 CLASS G4	12	35	327
GONDOLA SIDE PLANS WM #50531 CLASS GK	12	35	327
HIGH SIDE GONDOLA PLANS V #19819 1954	12	58	58
HIGH SIDE WOOD GONDOLA PLANS BR&P #15861	04	47	296
HIGHSIDE DROP BOTTOM GOND L&N#55625 PLAN	06	45	232
HIGHSIDE DROPEND GONDOLA ATSF#166608 PLN	09	52	45
HOPPER BOTTOM GONDOLA OF 1900 PLANS	07	56	35
HOPPER BOTTOM GONDOLA PLAN	05	78	102
HOPPER BOTTOM GONDOLA PLANS WVC&P #564	10	83	104
HOPPER BOTTOM GONDOLA 1880 PLN PRR#28502	04	55	34
INTEGRAL COVER COIL CAR PLANS P&LE#42250	08	68	38
NARROW GAUGE GONDOLA PLAN D&RGW #1423	08	78	60
OLD TIME GONDOLA PLANS CL&W #6200	02	54	87
ROTARY DUMP GONDOLA PLANS CP #349410	10	71	40
SAFE LOADING MILL GONDOLA PLNS *OST#1908	01	64	52
SELF SIDE DUMPING BALLAST CAR NYC #X6665	11	36	322
TIGHT BOTTOM GOND PLNS PRR#274836 CLS GR	01	48	26
USRA 70 TON GONDOLA CAR PLANS	08	47	658
WARTIME COMPOSITE GONDOLAS PLAN S#286371	06	44	244
WOOD GONDOLA CAR PLANS MA&PA #620	01	69	45
WOODEN GONDOLA PLANS NYC&H #47463 1880	03	56	39

RD	GONDOLA PLANS BY ROAD	M	Y	P
*OST	SAFE LOADING MILL GONDOLA PLNS *OST#1908	01	64	52
*SCL	CONTAINER CAR PLANS *SCL #50000 ACF	05	57	61
ATSF	70 TON MILL GONDOLA PLANS ATSF #170970	05	76	45
	HIGHSIDE DROPEND GONDOLA ATSF#166608 PLN	09	52	45
B&O	BRACED DROP END GONDOLA PLANS B&O#145000	07	62	31
	DROP SIDE GONDOLA OF 1835 PLANS B&O	07	76	85
	DOUBLE HOPPER-GONDOLA CAR PLANS B&O 1880	03	43	138
BR&P	HIGH SIDE WOOD GONDOLA PLANS BR&P #15861	04	47	296
C&EI	DROP BOTTOM 55T GS GONDOLA C&EI#93000 PL	02	77	62
CB&Q	GONDOLA SIDE PLANS CB&Q #19540 CLASS GM	12	35	327
CL&W	OLD TIME GONDOLA PLANS CL&W #6200	02	54	87
CMI	GONDOLA PLANS CMI #1665	08	72	47
CP	ROTARY DUMP GONDOLA PLANS CP #349410	10	71	40
D&RGW	GONDOLA CAR N GAUGE PLANS D&RGW #06299	02	61	39
	NARROW GAUGE GONDOLA PLAN D&RGW #1423	08	78	60
	GONDOLA CAR NARROW GAUGE PLANS D&RGW	06	43	274
	DROP BOTTOM GONDOLA PLAN D&RGW NAR GAUGE	03	58	28
E	70T CLASS GS AAR STEEL GON PLNS E #44000	12	40	665
ET&WNC	GONDOLA PLANS ET&WNC #372	07	81	63
IC	COMPOSITE GONDOLA PLANS IC OF 1917	01	60	75
L&N	HIGHSIDE DROP BOTTOM GOND L&N#55625 PLAN	06	45	232
MA&PA	WOOD GONDOLA CAR PLANS MA&PA #620	01	69	45
MICHC	GONDOLA CAR PLANS MICHC #15317 CLASS K2	11	50	51
N&W	90T H.SIDE CLASS GKD GOND N&W#100054 PLN	02	45	58
NYC	SELF SIDE DUMPING BALLAST CAR NYC #X6665	11	36	322
NYC&H	WOODEN GONDOLA PLANS NYC&H #47463 1880	03	56	39
P&LE	INTEGRAL COVER COIL CAR PLANS P&LE#42250	08	68	38
PB&NE	65' BETHLEHAM MILL GON PLANS PB&NE #871	06	81	89
PRR	GONDOLA CAR PLANS PRR #315694 CLASS G22B	04	50	42
	HOPPER BOTTOM GONDOLA 1880 PLN PRR#28502	04	55	34
	TIGHT BOTTOM GOND PLNS PRR#274836 CLS GR	01	48	26
RI	42' DROP BOTTOM GONDOLA PLANS RI #187300	12	40	665
	COVERED GONDOLA PLANS RI #1043	11	58	66
S	WARTIME COMPOSITE GONDOLAS PLAN S#286371	06	44	244
SP	GONDOLA CAR PLANS 50 TON SP	10	52	74
UP	GONDOLA SIDE PLANS UP #11471 CLASS GMA	12	35	327
USRA	USRA 70 TON GONDOLA CAR PLANS	08	47	658
V	GONDOLA SIDE PLANS V #19647 CLASS G4	12	35	327
	HIGH SIDE GONDOLA PLANS V #19819 1954	12	58	58
W	GONDOLA CAR OF 1894 PLANS W #32963 SCC	01	68	39
WM	GONDOLA SIDE PLANS WM #50531 CLASS GK	12	35	327
WVC&P	HOPPER BOTTOM GONDOLA PLANS WVC&P #564	10	83	104

FREIGHT CARS

GONDOLA MODELS		M	Y	P
50' GONDOLA CHESSIE	MOD & PT	02	82	126
52' GONDOLA KITBASH D&H		04	83	62
52' GONDOLA PC	MOD & PT	02	77	106
65' GONDOLA KITBASH PB&NE		04	83	62
ALGOMA CENTRAL GONDOLA	MOD & PT	11	79	160
BN GONDOLA MOD & PT		01	76	30
BUILD A GONDOLA		04	44	152
COMPOSITE GONDOLA CONSTRUCTION		07	40	378
COVERED GONDOLA CONSTRUCTION ROCK ISLAND		11	58	65
DROP BOTTOM GONDOLA CONST NAR GAU D&RGW		03	58	26
DT&I GONDOLA	MOD & PT	11	77	128
GANGED GONDOLA CAR BUILDING PROCESS $1		02	67	28
GONDOLA 105 TON FROM HOPPER CAR PARTS		10	74	70
GONDOLA CAR CONSTRUCTION "S"		01	54	68
GONDOLA CAR CONSTRUCTION CL&W #6200 "O"		05	55	23
GONDOLA CAR LOADS		07	85	130
GONDOLA WABASH	MOD & PT	07	78	110
HIGH S 90T GONDOL N&W #1000544 CLASS GKD		02	45	56
HIGH SIDE DROP BOTTOM GONDOLA L&N #55625		06	45	232
HIGH SIDE GONDOLA 100T CONST V #19819		12	58	52
HIGH SIDE PULPWOOD CAR FROM TWO GONDOLAS		05	73	58
KITBASH HOPPER BOTTOM GONDOLA		05	78	100
MILL GONDOLA CONSTRUCTION $1		09	56	27
MILL GONDOLA ERIE	MOD & PT	06	85	100
MOM CP RAIL HIGHSIDE GONDOLA "HO"MANLICK		07	73	37
MOM WOOD COKE CAR "HO" ROBERTS		10	73	43
NARROW GAUGE GONDOLA CONSTRUCTION D&RGW		02	61	38
OLD TIME GONDOLA CONSTRUCTION $1		06	63	39
OLD TIME HOPPER-GONDOLA CONSTRUCTION		03	43	138
OUTSIDE BRACED GOND 1940 CROSS KIT PROJ		06	79	68
PANEL SIDE GONDOLA CONSTRUCTION $1		08	53	34
QUARRY CAR SCRATCH CONSTRUCTION $1		11	69	72
REBUILT L&N GONDOLA FOR SPECIAL SERVICE		06	83	122
SCRAP SERVICE GONDOLA	MOD & PT	01	81	128
SCRATCHBUILT HIGH SIDE GONDOLA D&RGW		08	78	66
SHEET METAL GONDOLA CONSTRUCTION		03	34	7
STEEL C&EI GONDOLA CONSTRUCTION ACF		05	59	42
STRETCHING GONDOLAS 50' + 50' = 65'		05	76	42
SULPHUR TRANSPORT GONDOLA ATSF#180157 $1		10	55	28
THRALL GONDOLA KITBASH C&GR 1980		04	83	62
TRIO OF GONDOLAS KITBASH		04	83	62
WEIGHTING GONDOLAS		06	84	133
WOOD GONDOLA CONSTRUCTION $1		02	54	74

GONDOLA MODEL REVIEWS	M	Y	P
32' D&RGW GONDOLA REVIEW "HON3" CC	07	65	10
40' 50 TON GONDOLA REVIEW "HO" RIV	05	63	7
40' 70 TON GONDOLA B&O REVIEW "O" SH	05	65	12
40' COMPOSITE GONDOLA REVIEW "HO" WAL EE	06	81	29
41' DROP BOTTOM GONDOLA REVIEW "N" DIT	12	82	65
41' GONDOLA REVIEW "1/4" AA	10	69	12
41' WOOD CHIP GONDOLA REVIEW "N" DIT	12	82	65
46' NSW GONDOLA REVIEW "HO" PMRR	08	71	25
48' 100 TON PRR GONDOLA REVIEW "S" REK	09	62	12
50 TON MILW GONDOLA REVIEW "S" WCS 1940	02	74	26
50' COVERED GONDULA REVIEW "HO" ATH	03	66	12
56' BATHTUB GONDOLA CP REV "HO" QC HSI	08	73	28
60' 70T DROP BOTTOM SP GONDOLA "HO" AMB	03	70	19
65' CLASS G26 PRR MILL GOND REV "HO" EBV	08	81	44
65' MILL GONDOLA REVIEW "S" REK	04	63	14
AUTO FRAME GONDOLA "HO" WISE-NMRA SPECIA	04	80	42
B&D CUSHION COIL CAR REVIEW "HO" AMB	10	66	18
BATHTUB GONDOLA REVIEW "HO" MDC 1976 HSI	12	81	54
CLAM SHELL GONDOLA REVIEW "HO" AHM	10	72	20
COAL GONDOLA D&RGW REVIEW "HON3" KVAL	12	65	11
COMPOSITE GONDOLA REVIEW "S" REK	01	65	13
COMPOSITE GONDOLA REVIEW "O" AN	06	54	10
DIE CAST GONDOLA REVIEW "HO" VARNEY	03	37	122
DROP BOTTOM D&RGW GONDOLA REV "HO" RRL	12	73	28
DROP BOTTOM GONDOLA D&RGW REVIEW "ON3"GL	05	77	38
DROP BOTTOM GONDOLA MILW REVIEW "HO" AMB	07	60	8
DROP BOTTOM GONDOLA REVIEW "O" MG	04	55	16
DROP END MILL GONDOLA REVIEW "N" KADEE	03	77	29
FOUR WHEEL GONDOLA 1880 REVIEW "HO" DN	10	50	57
GENERAL PURPOSE GONDOLA REVIEW "HO" U	12	70	34
GENERAL SERVICE GONDOLA REVIEW "HO" U	01	53	56
GONDOLA CAR KIT REVIEW "HO" EHB	10	48	775
GONDOLA CAR KIT REVIEW "TT" HP	10	48	774
GONDOLA CAR REVIEW "HO" DALE NEWTON	08	42	397
GONDOLA COAL LISTING "HO" WVL	11	77	54
GONDOLA D&RGW NAR GAUGE REV "HON3" BAL	03	64	12
GONDOLA HOPPER BOTTOM REVIEW "1/4" WEC	06	78	54
GONDOLA KIT REVIEW "HO" U	03	48	229
GONDOLA KIT REVIEW "OO" NASON RAILWAYS	10	41	540
GONDOLA LISTING "HO" ULRICH	08	78	50
GONDOLA REVIEW "O" LOBAUGH	12	36	376
GONDOLA REVIEW "HO" EHB	03	42	152
GONDOLA REVIEW "HO" MDC	11	51	52
GONDOLA REVIEW "HO" JE	08	53	12
GONDOLA REVIEW "HO" M	05	54	12
GONDOLA REVIEW "HO" NATIONAL CAR EAST	07	76	32
GONDOLA REVIEW "OO" NASON RAILWAYS	10	40	580
HART GONDOLA KIT REVIEW "HO" PHO	11	46	791
HIGH SIDE GONDOLA D&RGW REV "ON3" CRGT	05	80	36
HIGH SIDE GONDOLA REVIEW "ON3" VW 1874	06	71	25
LOW SIDE 50 TON GONDOLA REV "S" REX	06	55	13
MILL GONDOLA KIT REVIEW "HO" USM	08	49	49
MILL GONDOLA REVIEW "O" WALTER SYRETT	05	38	216
MINE CAR & TOOL REVIEW "HO" MEW	06	60	11
MINE CAR KIT REVIEW "HO" SSL	11	71	28

FREIGHT CARS

GONDOLA MODEL REVIEWS

	M	Y	P
OPENSIDE GONDOLA MILW REVIEW "1/48" WAL	12	72	37
RAILGON REVIEW "HO/N" MDC	04	81	54
ROTARY DUMP GONDOLA REVIEW "N" MDC	03	80	44
SPECIAL SERVICE GONDOLA REVIEW "HO" DN	07	55	9
THRALL COIL STEEL GONDOLA REVIEW "HO" OM	12	84	56
THRALL GONDOLA REVIEW "HO" MDC	04	78	41
WOOD CHIP GONDOLA REVIEW "HO" DSC	07	79	42
WOOD GONDOLA KIT REVIEW "HO" ACM	05	50	41
WOOD SIDE GONDOLA KIT REVIEW "S" MH	10	48	771
WORK GONDOLA D&RGW REVIEW "SN3" TOM	04	69	18

GONDOLA MODEL REVIEWS BY ROAD

RD		M	Y	P
B&O	B&D CUSHION COIL CAR REVIEW "HO" AMB	10	66	18
	40' 70 TON GONDOLA B&O REVIEW "O" SH	05	65	12
CP	56' BATHTUB GONDOLA CP REV "HO" QC HSI	08	73	28
D&RGW	HIGH SIDE GONDOLA D&RGW REV "ON3" CRGT	05	80	36
	DROP BOTTOM GONDOLA D&RGW REVIEW "ON3"GL	05	77	38
	DROP BOTTOM D&RGW GONDOLA REV "HO" RRL	12	73	28
	WORK GONDOLA D&RGW REVIEW "SN3" TOM	04	69	18
	GONDOLA D&RGW NAR GAUGE REV "HON3" BAL	03	64	12
	COAL GONDOLA D&RGW REVIEW "HON3" KVAL	12	65	11
	32' D&RGW GONDOLA REVIEW "HON3" CC	07	65	10
MILW	OPENSIDE GONDOLA MILW REVIEW "1/48" WAL	12	72	37
	DROP BOTTOM GONDOLA MILW REVIEW "HO" AMB	07	60	8
	50 TON MILW GONDOLA REVIEW "S" WCS 1940	02	74	26
NSW	46' NSW GONDOLA REVIEW "HO" PMRR	08	71	25
PRR	65' CLASS 626 PRR MILL GOND REV "HO" EBV	08	81	44
SP	HIGH SIDE GONDOLA REVIEW "ON3" VW 1874	06	71	25
	60' 70T DROP BOTTOM SP GONDOLA "HO" AMB	03	70	19

GONDOLA MODEL REVIEWS BY MFG.

MFG		M	Y	P
AA	41' GONDOLA REVIEW "1/4" AA	10	69	12
ACM	WOOD GONDOLA KIT REVIEW "HO" ACM	05	50	41
AHM	CLAM SHELL GONDOLA REVIEW "HO" AHM	10	72	20
AMB	60' 70T DROP BOTTOM SP GONDOLA "HO" AMB	03	70	19
	DROP BOTTOM GONDOLA MILW REVIEW "HO" AMB	07	60	8
	B&D CUSHION COIL CAR REVIEW "HO" AMB	10	66	18
AN	COMPOSITE GONDOLA REVIEW "O" AN	06	54	10
ATH	50' COVERED GONDULA REVIEW "HO" ATH	03	66	12
BAL	GONDOLA D&RGW NAR GAUGE REV "HON3" BAL	03	64	12
CC	32' D&RGW GONDOLA REVIEW "HON3" CC	07	65	10
CRGT	HIGH SIDE GONDOLA D&RGW REV "ON3" CRGT	05	80	36
DIT	41' DROP BOTTOM GONDOLA REVIEW "N" DIT	12	82	65
	41' WOOD CHIP GONDOLA REVIEW "N" DIT	12	82	65
DN	FOUR WHEEL GONDOLA 1880 REVIEW "HO" DN	10	50	57
	SPECIAL SERVICE GONDOLA REVIEW "HO" DN	07	55	9
	GONDOLA CAR REVIEW "HO" DALE NEWTON	08	42	397
DSC	WOOD CHIP GONDOLA REVIEW "HO" DSC	07	79	42
EBV	65' CLASS 626 PRR MILL GOND REV "HO" EBV	08	81	44

GONDOLA MODEL REVIEWS BY MFG.

MFG		M	Y	P
EHB	GONDOLA CAR KIT REVIEW "HO" EHB	10	48	775
	GONDOLA REVIEW "HO" EHB	03	42	152
GL	DROP BOTTOM GONDOLA D&RGW REVIEW "ON3"GL	05	77	38
HP	GONDOLA CAR KIT REVIEW "TT" HP	10	48	774
JE	GONDOLA REVIEW "HO" JE	08	53	12
KD	DROP END MILL GONDOLA REVIEW "N" KADEE	03	77	29
KVAL	COAL GONDOLA D&RGW REVIEW "HON3" KVAL	12	65	11
LOB	GONDOLA REVIEW "O" LOBAUGH	12	36	376
M	GONDOLA REVIEW "HO" M	05	54	12
MDC	BATHTUB GONDOLA REVIEW "HO" MDC 1976 HSI	12	81	54
	RAILGON REVIEW "HO/N" MDC	04	81	54
	ROTARY DUMP GONDOLA REVIEW "N" MDC	03	80	44
	THRALL GONDOLA REVIEW "HO" MDC	04	78	41
	GONDOLA REVIEW "HO" MDC	11	51	52
MEW	MINE CAR & TOOL REVIEW "HO" MEW	06	60	11
MG	DROP BOTTOM GONDOLA REVIEW "O" MG	04	55	16
MH	WOOD SIDE GONDOLA KIT REVIEW "S" MH	10	48	771
NCE	GONDOLA REVIEW "HO" NATIONAL CAR EAST	07	76	32
NR	GONDOLA KIT REVIEW "OO" NASON RAILWAYS	10	41	540
	GONDOLA REVIEW "OO" NASON RAILWAYS	10	40	580
OM	THRALL COIL STEEL GONDOLA REVIEW "HO" OM	12	84	56
PHO	HART GONDOLA KIT REVIEW "HO" PHO	11	46	791
PMRR	46' NSW GONDOLA REVIEW "HO" PMRR	08	71	25
QC	56' BATHTUB GONDOLA CP REV "HO" QC HSI	08	73	28
REK	COMPOSITE GONDOLA REVIEW "S" REK	01	65	13
	48' 100 TON PRR GONDOLA REVIEW "S" REK	09	62	12
	65' MILL GONDOLA REVIEW "S" REK	04	63	14
REX	LOW SIDE 50 TON GONDOLA REV "S" REX	06	55	13
RIV	40' 50 TON GONDOLA REVIEW "HO" RIV	05	63	7
RRL	DROP BOTTOM D&RGW GONDOLA REV "HO" RRL	12	73	28
SH	40' 70 TON GONDOLA B&O REVIEW "O" SH	05	65	12
SSL	MINE CAR KIT REVIEW "HO" SSL	11	71	28
TOM	WORK GONDOLA D&RGW REVIEW "SN3" TOM	04	69	18
U	GONDOLA LISTING "HO" ULRICH	08	78	50
	GENERAL PURPOSE GONDOLA REVIEW "HO" U	12	70	34
	GENERAL SERVICE GONDOLA REVIEW "HO" U	01	53	56
	GONDOLA KIT REVIEW "HO" U	03	48	229
USM	MILL GONDOLA KIT REVIEW "HO" USM	08	49	49
V	DIE CAST GONDOLA REVIEW "HO" VARNEY	03	37	122
VW	HIGH SIDE GONDOLA REVIEW "ON3" VW 1874	06	71	25
WAL	40' COMPOSITE GONDOLA REVIEW "HO" WAL EE	06	81	29
	OPENSIDE GONDOLA MILW REVIEW "1/48" WAL	12	72	37
WCS	50 TON MILW GONDOLA REVIEW "S" WCS 1940	02	74	26
WEC	GONDOLA HOPPER BOTTOM REVIEW "1/4" WEC	06	78	54
WSY	MILL GONDOLA REVIEW "O" WALTER SYRETT	05	38	216
WVL	GONDOLA COAL LISTING "HO" WVL	11	77	54

FREIGHT CARS

HOPPER PROTOTYPE DATA	M	Y	P
100T BIG JOHN COVERED HOPPERS OF S	05	84	82
60' WOOD CHIP CARS NP 1966 THM	05	77	60
COVERED HOPPERS 100 TON B&O #600400	04	78	99
EAST BROAD TOP COAL HOPPERS	06	80	68
H30A PRR COVERED HOPPERS 1935	10	81	66
HIAWATHA LINES COVERED HOPPER MOD & PT	06	78	101
HOPPER CARS OF 1925-1930	07	77	108
HOPPER CARS TYPES AND CLASSIFICATIONS	03	45	104
LETTER SCHEMES FOR 17 AIRSIDE CARS PHOTO	10	62	47
MINIQUAD ORE CARS ON DM&IR	02	76	57
OFFSET SIDES ON HOPPERS	06	65	59
ORTNER 5 BAY HOPPERS 1975	08	81	62
QUINTUPLE 85 TON HOPPERS PRR	07	78	84
RAPID DISCHARGE HOPPERS H230 CLASS L&N	02	83	125
REBUILT 55 TON HOPPERS MILW	11	77	67
ROLLING COALING FACILITY LS&I	08	79	86
SIDE CHUTE UP HOPPER OF 1889	03	84	75
WOOD ORE CARS 40 TON	06	78	93

HOPPER PROTOTYPE DATA BY ROAD				
RD		M	Y	P
B&O	COVERED HOPPERS 100 TON B&O #600400	04	78	99
DM&IR	MINIQUAD ORE CARS ON DM&IR	02	76	57
EBT	EAST BROAD TOP COAL HOPPERS	06	80	68
L&N	RAPID DISCHARGE HOPPERS H230 CLASS L&N	02	83	125
LS&I	ROLLING COALING FACILITY LS&I	08	79	86
MILW	REBUILT 55 TON HOPPERS MILW	11	77	67
NP	60' WOOD CHIP CARS NP 1966 THM	05	77	60
PRR	H30A PRR COVERED HOPPERS 1935	10	81	66
	QUINTUPLE 85 TON HOPPERS PRR	07	78	84
S	100T BIG JOHN COVERED HOPPERS OF S	05	84	82
UP	SIDE CHUTE UP HOPPER OF 1889	03	84	75

HOPPER PLANS	M	Y	P
100 TON QUADRUPLE HOPPER D&RGW #16872 PL	11	79	107
100T BIG JOHN COVERED HOPPERS PLN S#8696	05	84	82
100T TRIPLE HOPPER PLANS SOO #60930 MFC	12	81	115
2 BAY HOPPER PLANS CLINCHFIELD #60046 "N"	08	77	44
3 TRUCK SIDE DUMP ORE CARS PLANS LS&MC	10	67	51
30 TON HOPPER CAR PLANS EBT #805	09	61	45
30 TON TIMBER ORE CAR PLANS CP	02	66	46
4 BAY HOPPER PLAN PRR #677216 CLASS H-25	01	51	45
50 TON 2 BAY AAR STEEL HOPPER PLANS C&O	12	36	369
50 TON COVERED HOPPER PLANS E #20000 GCC	08	75	64
50 TON HOPPER CB&Q #220081 PLANS 1927	07	36	178
50 TON HOPPER CLASS HM PLANS C&O #54251	02	77	63
50 TON HOPPER COKE CAR S#110170 CLASS HC	08	35	206
60' WOOD CHIP DETAILED PLANS NP #119613	05	77	63
90T HOPPER CAR PLN ATSF #77905 CL GA123	07	67	30
AIRSLIDE COVERED HOPPER PLAN CB&Q #87370	01	61	36
ALCAN COVERED TANK HOPPER CAR PLANS 1960	05	62	57
ARTICULATED HOPPER CAR PLANS SOUTHERN	03	67	40
BALLAST HOPPER PLN 70T MILW #340970 CL KH	03	35	62
COAL HOPPER OF 1895 PLANS PY&A #1818	10	84	94
COAL HOPPER PLANS EBT #880	06	80	69
COKE CAR PLANS NYC&H #X1031	10	54	56
COMPOSITE 50T HOPPER ATSF #180572 PLANS	09	47	707
COMPOSITE HOPPER CAR PLANS ATSF #180572	08	53	65
COMPOSITE ORE CAR OF 1905 PLANS C&NW	01	75	81
CONCENTRATE CAR PLANS QM OF 1920	01	82	111
COVERED ACF HOPPER PLN CL #60046 CLSS FL3	08	52	37
COVERED CEMENT HOPPER PLANS N&W #70200	06	41	315
COVERED HOPPER 100T FMC PLAN B&O #600400	04	78	98
COVERED HOPPER CLASS H30A PLAN CR #878666	10	81	67
COVERED HOPPER OF 1899 CAR PLANS PRPM #28	03	65	42
COVERED SALT HOPPER PLANS G&Y #590001 GSC	02	68	46
COVERED SAND HOPPER PLANS NPGC #202 1925	08	64	34
GRAIN HOPPER MODIFICATION PLANS ATSF	06	47	477
GRAVEL CAR PLANS SP #310 NARROW GAUGE	08	64	34
HOPPER CAR CLASS H2A #11068 PLANS PRR	06	65	39
HOPPER CAR OF 1904 PLANS P&R #87259	09	58	65
HOPPER CAR PLANS CLASS H10 N&W #34000	06	65	39
HOPPER ORE CAR PLANS 70T 21' C&NW #121667	09	41	466
HOPPER ORE CAR PLANS CMSP #51733 1913	07	73	44
LW HOPPER CAR PLN AOC #800 4 BAY	12	37	462
MINIQUAD ORE CAR PLANS DM&IR	02	76	58
ORE CAR 95 TON PLANS QNS&L #2000 1953 PS	01	54	89
ORE CAR PLANS C&NW #121667	04	40	221
ORE CAR PLANS CP #371307	06	57	42
ORE CAR PLANS DM&IR #23002 CLASS U-15	04	40	221
ORE HOPPER CLASS U-12 DRAWING DM&N #21071	09	36	246
ORE HOPPER PLANS ET&WNC #12	07	81	62
ORTNER 5 BAY HOPPERS PLANS 1975	08	81	62
PS 125 TON HOPPER CAR MILW #100798 PLANS	02	74	59
QUAD HOPPER PLANS	11	54	35
QUINTUPLE HOPPER 85 TON PLAN PRR #180002	07	78	84
RAPID DISCHARGE HOP H230 L&N #190244 PLN	02	83	125
ROLLER BEAR HOP PLN CLASS H-11 N&W #30000	05	64	38
ROLLING COALING FACILITY LS&I PLANS	08	79	86

FREIGHT CARS

HOPPER PLANS	M	Y	P
SIDE CHUTE HOPPER CAR PLANS UP #1636	03	84	75
SIX TON COAL JIMMY PLANS	05	67	42
STEEL HOPPER CAR OF 1897 PLN PB&LE #5645	05	63	34
STERLINGWORTH STEEL HOPPER PLAN	01	78	73
TRIPLE ACF HOPPER CAR PLANS C&O #92198	12	53	76
TRIPLE HOPPER CAR PLANS P&LE #S-57490	04	53	64
USRA 55 TON HOPPER CAR PLANS	04	69	38
WARTIME COMPOSITE HOPPER B&O #30243 PLAN	06	44	244
WOOD CHIP HOPPER CAR PLANS L&N #30955	02	67	47
WOOD ORE CAR 40 TON PLAN	06	78	93
WOODEN HOPPER CAR PLANS PRR #10924	04	45	172
WOODEN HOPPER PLANS CAC #627	10	58	30
WOODSIDE COAL & ORE CAR PLANS GN #180371	12	69	70

RD	HOPPER PLANS BY ROAD	M	Y	P
AOC	LW HOPPER CAR PLN AOC #800 4 BAY	12	37	462
ATSF	COMPOSITE HOPPER CAR PLANS ATSF #180572	08	53	65
	GRAIN HOPPER MODIFICATION PLANS ATSF	06	47	477
	COMPOSITE 50T HOPPER ATSF #180572 PLANS	09	47	707
	90T HOPPER CAR PLN ATSF #77905 CL GA123	07	67	30
B&O	WARTIME COMPOSITE HOPPER B&O #30243 PLAN	06	44	244
	COVERED HOPPER 100T FMC PLAN B&O #600400	04	78	98
C&NW	HOPPER ORE CAR PLANS 70T 21' C&NW#121667	09	41	466
	ORE CAR PLANS C&NW #121667	04	40	221
	COMPOSITE ORE CAR OF 1905 PLANS C&NW	01	75	81
C&O	TRIPLE ACF HOPPER CAR PLANS C&O #92198	12	53	76
	50 TON 2 BAY AAR STEEL HOPPER PLANS C&O	12	36	369
	50 TON HOPPER CLASS HM PLANS C&O #54251	02	77	63
CAC	WOODEN HOPPER PLANS CAC #627	10	58	30
CB&Q	50 TON HOPPER CB&Q #220081 PLANS 1927	07	36	178
	AIRSLIDE COVERED HOPPER PLAN CB&Q #87370	01	61	36
CL	COVERED ACF HOPPER PLN CL #60046 CLSS FL3	08	52	37
	2 BAY HOPPER PLANS CLINCHFIELD #60046 "N"	08	77	44
CMSP	HOPPER ORE CAR PLANS CMSP #51733 1913	07	73	44
CN	ALCAN COVERED TANK HOPPER CAR PLANS 1960	05	62	57
CP	30 TON TIMBER ORE CAR PLANS CP	02	66	46
	ORE CAR PLANS CP #371307	06	57	42
CR	COVERED HOPPER CLASS H30A PLAN CR#878666	10	81	67
D&RGW	100 TON QUADRUPLE HOPPER D&RGW #16872 PL	11	79	107
DM&IR	ORE CAR PLANS DM&IR #23002 CLASS U-15	04	40	221
	MINIQUAD ORE CAR PLANS DM&IR	02	76	58
DM&N	ORE HOPPER CLASS U-12 DRAWING DM&N#21071	09	36	246
E	50 TON COVERED HOPPER PLANS E #20000 GCC	08	75	64
EBT	30 TON HOPPER CAR PLANS EBT #805	09	61	45
	COAL HOPPER PLANS EBT #880	06	80	69
ET&WNC	ORE HOPPER PLANS ET&WNC #12	07	81	62
G&Y	COVERED SALT HOPPER PLANS G&Y #590001 GSC	02	68	46
GN	WOODSIDE COAL & ORE CAR PLANS GN #180371	12	69	70
L&N	WOOD CHIP HOPPER CAR PLANS L&N #30955	02	67	47
	RAPID DISCHARGE HOP H230 L&N #190244 PLN	02	83	125
LS&I	ROLLING COALING FACILITY LS&I PLANS	08	79	86

RD	HOPPER PLANS BY ROAD	M	Y	P
LS&MC	3 TRUCK SIDE DUMP ORE CARS PLANS LS&MC	10	67	51
MILW	PS 125 TON HOPPER CAR MILW #100798 PLANS	02	74	59
	BALLAST HOPPER PLN 70T MILW#340970 CL KH	03	35	62
N&W	COVERED CEMENT HOPPER PLANS N&W #70200	06	41	315
	ROLLER BEAR HOP PLN CLASS H-11 N&W#30000	05	64	38
	HOPPER CAR PLANS CLASS H10 N&W #34000	06	65	39
NP	60' WOOD CHIP DETAILED PLANS NP #119613	05	77	63
NPGC	COVERED SAND HOPPER PLANS NPGC #202 1925	08	64	34
NYC&H	COKE CAR PLANS NYC&H #X1031	10	54	56
P&LE	TRIPLE HOPPER CAR PLANS P&LE #S-57490	04	53	64
P&R	HOPPER CAR OF 1904 PLANS P&R #87259	09	58	65
PB&LE	STEEL HOPPER CAR OF 1897 PLN PB&LE #5645	05	63	34
PRPM	COVERED HOPPER OF 1899 CAR PLANS PRPM#28	03	65	42
PRR	4 BAY HOPPER PLAN PRR #677216 CLASS H-25	01	51	45
	WOODEN HOPPER CAR PLANS PRR #10924	04	45	172
	QUINTUPLE HOPPER 85 TON PLAN PRR #180002	07	78	84
	HOPPER CAR CLASS H2A #11068 PLANS PRR	06	65	39
PY&A	COAL HOPPER OF 1895 PLANS PY&A #1818	10	84	94
QM	CONCENTRATE CAR PLANS QM OF 1920	01	82	111
QNS&L	ORE CAR 95 TON PLANS QNS&L #2000 1953 PS	01	54	89
S	50 TON HOPPER COKE CAR S#110170 CLASS HC	08	35	206
	ARTICULATED HOPPER CAR PLANS SOUTHERN	03	67	40
	100T BIG JOHN COVERED HOPPERS PLN S#8696	05	84	82
SOO	100T TRIPLE HOPPER PLANS SOO #60930 MFC	12	81	115
SP	GRAVEL CAR PLANS SP #310 NARROW GAUGE	08	64	34
UP	SIDE CHUTE HOPPER CAR PLANS UP #1636	03	84	75
USRA	USRA 55 TON HOPPER CAR PLANS	04	69	38

HOPPER PHOTOS	M	Y	P
STRAIGHT END HOPPER CMSP #25493 PHOTO	07	73	45
WAGON TOP BOX W/HOP DISCHARGE B&O #27998	03	65	42

FREIGHT CARS

HOPPER MODELS		M	Y	P
100T GRAIN HOPPER MN&S	MOD & PT	12	80	170
100T SOO TRIPLE HOPPER KITBASH 1975	MFC	12	81	114
45' COVERED HOPPER SOUTHERN	MOD & PT	02	83	127
60' WOOD CHIP CAR OF NP CONSTRUCTION 1		05	77	60
70 TON COVERED HOPPERS SCL	MOD & PT	06	82	111
ACF COVERED HOPPER N&W	MOD & PT	06	79	107
ACF HOPPER CAR AD&N	MOD & PT	03	81	78
ACF TWO BAY COVERED HOPPERS	MOD & PT	12	76	116
AIRSLIDE HOPPER SCL	MOD & PT	06	84	112
AUTOMATIC HOPPER DOOR CONSTRUCTION		08	52	41
BUILDING A 3 BAY HOPPER CAR D&H #1639		05	38	206
CARBON BLACK HOPPER CONSTRUCTION	$1	10	56	34
COKE CAR CONSTRUCTION NYC&H	$1	10	54	54
COMPOSITE HOPPER WABASH	MOD & PT	11	83	142
COMPOSITE HOPPER CONSTRUCTION	$1	12	55	64
CONCENTRATE CAR CONSTRUCTION QM 1920		01	82	110
COVERED "AIRSLIDE" HOPPER CONST CB&Q		01	61	34
COVERED GRAIN HOPPER PTLX	MOD & PT	07	78	110
COVERED HOPPER ERIE	MOD & PT	12	83	166
COVERED HOPPER B&O	MOD & PT	12	83	165
COVERED HOPPER BACON FEEDS	MOD & PT	03	77	102
COVERED HOPPER BRITISH COLUMBIA	MOD & PT	11	76	123
COVERED HOPPER C&NW	MOD & PT	12	78	154
COVERED HOPPER CAR SOUTHERN	MOD & PT	01	79	132
COVERED HOPPER CHEMPLEX PLASTIC	MOD & PT	10	80	143
COVERED HOPPER CONSTRUCTION	$1	06	55	36
COVERED HOPPER CONSTRUCTION G&Y	$1	02	68	48
COVERED HOPPER CR	MOD & PT	12	78	155
COVERED HOPPER ERIE LACKAWANNA	MOD & PT	04	79	125
COVERED HOPPER NYC	MOD & PT	12	83	166
COVERED HOPPER SOO	MOD & PT	11	75	91
COVERED HOPPER UP	MOD & PT	04	79	128
COVERED HOPPERS OF FMC CHEMICAL	MOD & PT	03	76	89
COVERED RIVETED STEEL HOPPER CONST E		08	75	58
COVERED TWIN HOPPER DT&I	MOD & PT	01	77	111
CYCLINDRICAL COVERED HOPPER CANADIAN GOV		12	82	138
DETAILING & WEATHERING LIFELIKE HOPPERS		09	76	78
DM&IR COVERED HOPPER	MOD & PT	12	74	30
ENTERPRIST BALLAST HOPPER	MOD & PT	03	77	100
FAR-MAR-CO COVERED HOPPER	MOD & PT	04	77	91
GRAIN CAR PAINTING ATSF		02	78	124
GRAIN CARS CANADIAN	MOD & PT	03	85	106
GRAIN HOPPER C&NW	MOD & PT	03	82	122
GRAIN HOPPER CONSTRUCTION ATSF		06	47	476
GRAIN HOPPER FAM	MOD & PT	11	78	119
HART SELECTIVE BALLAST CAR KITBASH		11	84	89
HOPPER CAR 2 BAY CLASS HL CONSTRUCT N&W		06	39	287
HOPPER CAR CB&Q	MOD & PT	11	79	157
HOPPER CAR CONSTRUCTION "S"		06	50	26
HOPPER CAR CONSTRUCTION IN BRASS		05	69	57
HOPPER CAR KITBASH "N"		08	77	44
HOPPER CAR SCRATCHBUILT IN BRASS		04	69	33
IMPROVING THE LOOKS OF YOUR ORE JIMMIES		07	83	88
JUMBO COVERED HOPPER AA NEW IMAGE	MOD&PT	06	80	113
MOM BN GRAIN COVERED HOPPER "HO" LOCHMAN		02	81	79

HOPPER MODELS		M	Y	P
MOM OPEN HOPPER "O"	ROMANETZ	12	72	58
MOM WELDED COVERED HOPPER "N"	MARINARO	05	73	45
OLDTIME ORE CAR CONSTRUCTION		07	78	58
ORE CAR CONSTRUCTION CP #371307		06	57	40
ORE CAR CONSTRUCTION QNS&L	$1	01	54	82
ORE CAR MINIQUAD CONVERSION CONSTRUCTION		02	76	72
ORE HOPPER D&H	MOD & PT	07	79	110
PANELED SIDE HOPPER KITBASH		12	74	76
PRIVATE NAME HOPPER	MOD & PT	07	80	103
PS COVERED HOPPER C&NW	MOD & PT	05	75	21
PS COVERED HOPPER NSO	MOD & PT	11	83	140
PUTTING MILES ON HOPPERS (DISTRESSING)		04	74	56
QUAD HOPPER CONSTRUCT LEHIGH VALLEY "S"		11	54	34
ROLLING COALING FACILITY LS&I CONSTRUCT		08	79	86
SCRATCHBUILT WARTIME HOPPER BASICS		11	78	107
SCRATCHBUILT WARTIME HOPPER FINISHING		12	78	126
SIX TON COAL JIMMY CONSTRUCTION	$1	05	67	42
STEEL HOPPER 1897 CONSTRUCTION PB&LE		05	63	27
STERLINGWORTH STEEL HOPPER CONSTRUCTION		01	78	71
TABLE SAW SURGERY ON HOPPER CAR O TO ON3		02	79	78
THREE BAY ACF DT&I HOPPER	MOD & PT	01	75	27
TIMBER ORE CAR CONSTRUCTION CP		02	66	44
TRIPLE HOPPER	MOD & PT	03	75	22
TRIPLE HOPPER KITBASHING		09	84	86
TRIPLE HOPPERS SOUTHERN	MOD & PT	08	76	95
TWIN HOPPER FRISCO	MOD & PT	02	82	126
TWIN HOPPER L&N	MOD & PT	04	79	129
TWIN HOPPER MILW #94537	MOD & PT	03	77	101
TWIN HOPPER R	MOD & PT	10	78	126
TWIN HOPPER WESTERN MARYLAND	MOD & PT	06	83	122
WOOD CHIP CAR OF NP DETAILS		06	77	74
WOOD CHIP HOPPER KITBASH AD&N		03	81	70
WOOD HOPPER CONSTRUCTION CAC #627		10	58	29
WOODCHIP CAR CONSTRUCTION	$1	07	69	53
WOODSIDE COAL & ORE CAR CONST GN #180371		12	69	69

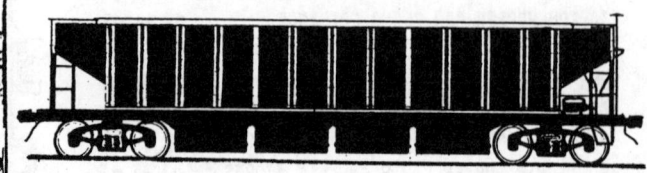

FREIGHT CARS

HOPPER MODEL REVIEWS	M	Y	P
100 TON COVERED HOPPERS REVIEW "HO" QC	09	68	16
100 TON HOPPER REVIEW "HO" MCKEAN MODELS	12	78	62
100T COVERED HOPPER B&O REV "HO" NPP FMC	09	85	46
12 YARD SIDE DUMP CAR REVIEW "HO" MEW	02	59	12
1870 NYC ORE HOPPER REVIEW "HO" HD	02	65	12
1900 ORE CAR CM&SP REVIEW "HO" GC	07	83	27
2 BAY HOPPER REVIEW "HO" U	11	55	16
25' 70 TON ORE CAR REV "1/4" AT 1950 GSC	10	72	24
26' ORE CAR REVIEW "HO" MDC	05	79	46
34' HOPPER CAR REVIEW "HO" ATH 1915	10	73	27
36' PS-3 OFFSET HOPPER REVIEW "O" QC	02	81	54
41' TRIPLE HOPPER REVIEW "HO" U 1930	08	73	25
45' COVERED HOPPER REVIEW "HO" AHM	08	75	27
45' TRIPLE HOPPER REVIEW "N" ATLAS	09	75	28
5 BAY RAPID DISCHARGE HOPPER REV "HO" MDC	08	81	40
50 TON AAR HOPPER CAR REVIEW "TT" KEM	01	55	11
50 TON COMPOSITE HOPPER REVIEW "N" KADEE	01	78	44
55 TON HOPPER REVIEW "1/4" AA	07	69	14
55 TON HOPPER REVIEW "O" MHS	05	39	279
55T TWIN HOPPER REVIEW "S" AMI	05	85	53
58' 100T AL HOPPPER S REVIEW "1/4" LVM	11	66	20
70 TON 40' COVERED HOPPER REVIEW "O" WAL	05	55	14
70 TON HOPPER REVIEW "HO" ATH	08	59	12
70 TON OFFSET HOPPER REVIEW "N" KADEE	01	78	44
70 TON PS COVERED HOPPER REVIEW "HO" MDC	08	62	10
70T COVERED HOPPER REVIEW "HO" EBV 1936	09	80	43
70T HOPPER REVIEW "N" RAP	05	67	15
70T ORE CAR REVIEW "HO" ATT 1952	04	68	16
75 TON ORE CAR REVIEW "S" DVK	07	68	13
ACF 4 BAY CENTER FLOW COVERED HOPPER AT	03	83	48
ACF CENTER FLOW HOPPER REVIEW "HO" AMB	01	65	10
ACF JUMBO COVERED HOPPER REVIEW "O" QC	09	84	40
ACL PHOSPHATE CAR REVIEW "HO" AMB	02	61	17
AIRSLIDE COVERED HOPPER REVIEW "HO" EBV	10	83	62
AIRSLIDE HOPPER REVIEW "HO" CC	02	63	27
ALUMINUM SIDE HOPPER KIT REVIEW "HO" WSP	10	48	771
CENTER FLOW COVERED HOPPER REV "HO" RAM	02	76	26
COAL HOPPER REVIEW "1/4" QC 1970 GSC	03	72	25
COMPOSITE HOPPER KIT REVIEW "S" KSC	07	56	11
COVERED HOPPER REVIEW "HO" QUALITY CRAFT	12	78	46
EMBOSSED SIDE HOPPER REVIEW "HO" V	01	40	54
HOPPER 4 BAY REVIEW "HO" LAC	08	50	44
HOPPER CAR 70 TON REVIEW "HO" WALTERS	09	78	46
HOPPER CAR CLINCHFIELD REVIEW "N" KD	01	78	51
HOPPER CAR END LISTING "HO" CARPART IND.	05	77	48
HOPPER CAR REVIEW "O" FHS	10	50	48
HOPPER CAR SET LISTING B&O "N" KADEE	08	78	51
HOPPER KIT REVIEW "HO" V	07	50	52
HOPPER KIT REVIEW "HO" M	01	49	98
HOPPER KIT REVIEW "HO" U	02	49	68
HOPPER KIT REVIEW "S" NM	07	49	49
HOPPER KIT REVIEW "TT" HP	03	49	76
HOPPER REVIEW "HON3" BIN	06	54	12
HOPPER REVIEW "O" MG	02	54	24
MINE CAR REVIEW "ON2 1/2" WMS	07	84	46

HOPPER MODEL REVIEWS	M	Y	P
MINE ORE CAR KIT REVIEW "HO" CAP	11	49	87
OFF SET HOPPER LISTING "HO" U	03	78	48
OLD TIME HOPPER REVIEW "HO" CCW	02	54	14
ORE CAR REVIEW "HO" MDC	01	61	10
ORE CAR REVIEW "N" ATLAS	02	76	26
ORE CAR REVIEW "ON2" GL	01	72	29
OUTSIDE BRACE TRIPLE HOPPER REV "HO" MDC	04	78	47
P-S 54' COVERED HOPPER REVIEW "HO" ATH	06	71	24
PANELED HOPPER REVIEW "TT" SD	12	52	58
PS HOPPER CAR VARIATIONS REV "HO" WAL	11	84	47
PS-2 CD 70 TON HOPPER REV "N" B	09	69	26
PS-2 COVERED HOPPER REVIEW "HO" RRI	01	85	53
PS-2 COVERED HOPPER REVIEW "O" QC	11	85	52
PS-3 WELDED HOPPER REVIEW "HO" TMI	09	79	52
SAND & GRAVEL HOPPER REVIEW "HO" MDC	11	54	11
SAND & GRAVEL HOPPER REVIEW "HO" MDC	09	74	20
SP NARROW GAUGE HOPPER REVIEW "HON3" EMM	08	63	6
TRIPLE HOPPER CAR REVIEW "HO" U	06	57	14
TRIPPLE HOPPER REVIEW "HO" MDC	02	57	16
TWIN BAY COVERED HOPPER "N" VL	11	85	44
WOOD HOPPER N&W REVIEW "HO" AMB	07	60	8

HOPPER MODEL REVIEWS BY ROAD				
RD		M	Y	P
B&O	100T COVERED HOPPER B&O REV "HO" NPP FMC	09	85	46
	HOPPER CAR SET LISTING B&O "N" KADEE	08	78	51
CL	HOPPER CAR CLINCHFIELD REVIEW "N" KD	01	78	51
CM&SP	1900 ORE CAR CM&SP REVIEW "HO" GC	07	83	27
GI	ORE CAR REVIEW "ON2" GL	01	72	29
N&W	WOOD HOPPER N&W REVIEW "HO" AMB	07	60	8
NYC	1870 NYC ORE HOPPER REVIEW "HO" HD	02	65	12
PS	70 TON PS COVERED HOPPER REVIEW "HO" MDC	08	62	10
S	58' 100T AL HOPPPER S REVIEW "1/4" LVM	11	66	20
SP	SP NARROW GAUGE HOPPER REVIEW "HON3" EMM	08	63	6

FREIGHT CARS

HOPPER MODEL REVIEWS BY MFG.

MFG		M	Y	P
AA	55 TON HOPPER REVIEW "1/4" AA	07	69	14
AHM	45' COVERED HOPPER REVIEW "HO" AHM	08	75	27
AMB	ACL PHOSPHATE CAR REVIEW "HO" AMB	02	61	17
	WOOD HOPPER N&W REVIEW "HO" AMB	07	60	8
	ACF CENTER FLOW HOPPER REVIEW "HO" AMB	01	65	10
AMI	55T TWIN HOPPER REVIEW "S" AMI	05	85	53
AT	45' TRIPLE HOPPER REVIEW "N" ATLAS	09	75	28
	25' 70 TON ORE CAR REV "1/4" AT 1950 GSC	10	72	24
	ACF 4 BAY CENTER FLOW COVERED HOPPER AT	03	83	48
	ORE CAR REVIEW "N" ATLAS	02	76	26
ATH	70 TON HOPPER REVIEW "HO" ATH	08	59	12
	34' HOPPER CAR REVIEW "HO" ATH 1915	10	73	27
	P-S 54' COVERED HOPPER REVIEW "HO" ATH	06	71	24
ATT	70T ORE CAR REVIEW "HO" ATT 1952	04	68	16
B	PS-2 CD 70 TON HOPPER REV "N" B	09	69	26
BIN	HOPPER REVIEW "HON3" BIN	06	54	12
CAP	MINE ORE CAR KIT REVIEW "HO" CAP	11	49	87
CC	AIRSLIDE HOPPER REVIEW "HO" CC	02	63	27
CCW	OLD TIME HOPPER REVIEW "HO" CCW	02	54	14
CPI	HOPPER CAR END LISTING "HO" CARPART IND.	05	77	48
DVK	75 TON ORE CAR REVIEW "S" DVK	07	68	13
EBV	70T COVERED HOPPER REVIEW "HO" EBV 1936	09	80	43
	AIRSLIDE COVERED HOPPER REVIEW "HO" EBV	10	83	62
EMM	SP NARROW GAUGE HOPPER REVIEW "HON3" EMM	08	63	6
FHS	HOPPER CAR REVIEW "O" FHS	10	50	48
GC	1900 ORE CAR CM&SP REVIEW "HO" GC	07	83	27
GL	ORE CAR REVIEW "ON2" GL	01	72	29
HD	1870 NYC ORE HOPPER REVIEW "HO" HD	02	65	12
HP	HOPPER KIT REVIEW "TT" HP	03	49	76
KD	HOPPER CAR CLINCHFIELD REVIEW "N" KD	01	78	51
	HOPPER CAR SET LISTING B&O "N" KADEE	08	78	51
	70 TON OFFSET HOPPER REVIEW "N" KADEE	01	78	44
	50 TON COMPOSITE HOPPER REVIEW "N" KADEE	01	78	44
KEM	50 TON AAR HOPPER CAR REVIEW "TT" KEM	01	55	11
KSC	COMPOSITE HOPPER KIT REVIEW "S" KSC	07	56	11
LAC	HOPPER 4 BAY REVIEW "HO" LAC	08	50	44
LVM	58' 100T AL HOPPPER S REVIEW "1/4" LVM	11	66	20
M	HOPPER KIT REVIEW "HO" M	01	49	98
MDC	SAND & GRAVEL HOPPER REVIEW "HO" MDC	09	74	20
	TRIPPLE HOPPER REVIEW "HO" MDC	02	57	16
	SAND & GRAVEL HOPPER REVIEW "HO" MDC	11	54	11
	OUTSIDE BRACE TRIPLE HOPPER REV "HO" MDC	04	78	47
	ORE CAR REVIEW "HO" MDC	01	61	10
	70 TON PS COVERED HOPPER REVIEW "HO" MDC	08	62	10
	5 BAY RAPID DISCHARGE HOPPER REV "HO" MDC	08	81	40
	26' ORE CAR REVIEW "HO" MDC	05	79	46
MEW	12 YARD SIDE DUMP CAR REVIEW "HO" MEW	02	59	12
MG	HOPPER REVIEW "O" MG	02	54	24
MHS	55 TON HOPPER REVIEW "O" MHS	05	39	279
MKM	100 TON HOPPER REVIEW "HO" MCKEAN MODELS	12	78	62
NM	HOPPER KIT REVIEW "S" NM	07	49	49
NPP	100T COVERED HOPPER B&O REV "HO" NPP FMC	09	85	46
QC	COVERED HOPPER REVIEW "HO" QUALITY CRAFT	12	78	46
	COAL HOPPER REVIEW "1/4" QC 1970 GSC	03	72	25
	100 TON COVERED HOPPERS REVIEW "HO" QC	09	68	16

HOPPER MODEL REVIEWS BY MFG.

MFG		M	Y	P
	PS-2 COVERED HOPPER REVIEW "O" QC	11	85	52
	36' PS-3 OFFSET HOPPER REVIEW "O" QC	02	81	54
	ACF JUMBO COVERED HOPPER REVIEW "O" QC	09	84	40
RAM	CENTER FLOW COVERED HOPPER REV "HO" RAM	02	76	26
RAP	70T HOPPER REVIEW "N" RAP	05	67	15
RRI	PS-2 COVERED HOPPER REVIEW "HO" RRI	01	85	53
SD	PANELED HOPPER REVIEW "TT" SD	12	52	58
TMI	PS-3 WELDED HOPPER REVIEW "HO" TMI	09	79	52
U	2 BAY HOPPER REVIEW "HO" U	11	55	16
	TRIPLE HOPPER CAR REVIEW "HO" U	06	57	14
	HOPPER KIT REVIEW "HO" U	02	49	68
	OFF SET HOPPER LISTING "HO" U	03	78	48
	41' TRIPLE HOPPER REVIEW "HO" U 1930	08	73	25
V	EMBOSSED SIDE HOPPER REVIEW "HO" V	01	40	54
	HOPPER KIT REVIEW "HO" V	07	50	52
VL	TWIN BAY COVERED HOPPER "N" VL	11	85	44
WAL	70 TON 40' COVERED HOPPER REVIEW "O" WAL	05	55	14
	HOPPER CAR 70 TON REVIEW "HO" WALTERS	09	78	46
	PS HOPPER CAR VARIATIONS REV "HO" WAL	11	84	47
WMS	MINE CAR REVIEW "ON2 1/2" WMS	07	84	46
WSP	ALUMINUM SIDE HOPPER KIT REVIEW "HO" WSP	10	48	771

REFRIGERATOR CAR PROTOTYPE DATA

	M	Y	P
FOUR WHEEL HORMEL REEFER CAR 1932 NA	10	70	76
PRIVATE OWNER REEFERS PHOTO ESSAY	09	40	470
REEFERS INTO BOXCARS ON MP	02	69	60
REFRIGERATOR CAR DESIGN	04	67	35

REFRIGERATOR PROTOTYPE DATA BY ROAD

RD		M	Y	P
MP	REEFERS INTO BOXCARS ON MP	02	69	60

FREIGHT CARS

REFRIGERATOR CAR PLANS

Title	M	Y	P
50' CLASS FE24 BOXCAR PLANS ATSF #10089	09	47	738
EGG REFRIGERATOR CAR PLANS NAD #6001	05	36	130
HANRAHAN AUTOMATIC REEFER PLANS CMI#1206	01	65	40
ICE SERVICE CAR PLANS LV #3206 1911	01	66	47
MECH REEFER R40-30 CLASS PLAN PFE#100028	04	67	38
MECH REEFER R70-12 CLASS PLAN PFE#301213	04	67	38
MODERN REEFER SOO CLASS RPL PLANS #10010	02	67	46
OUTSIDE BRACED CL RMJ REEFER R#19890 PLN	01	57	46
OUTSIDE BRACED REEFER PLANS PRR #5342	04	58	42
OUTSIDE BRACED REEFER PLANS R #19890	10	62	63
OVERHEAD BUNKER REEFER CAR PLN CN#212404	11	64	32
PEERBOLTE ONION SET REFRIGERATOR PLANS	08	71	35
PRIVATE OWENER WOOD REEFER PLANS	01	49	50
PRIVATE OWNER REFRIGERATOR CAR PLANS	01	49	67
REEFER & UNDERBODY & DETAILS PLANS	10	53	23
REEFER 42' PLANS	05	51	34
REEFER 50' CAR PLANS CLASS RR-30 #37343	09	47	738
REEFER CAR NARROW GAUGE PLANS D&RGW #78	04	62	46
REEFER CLASS RR40 PLANS ATSF #8225 1923	04	48	266
REFRIGERATOR CAR NARROW GAUGE PLAN D&RGW	06	43	274
REFRIGERATOR CAR PLANS 50' STEEL	12	53	94
REFRIGERATOR CAR PLANS NAD #3004 FRIGICAR	08	36	227
REFRIGERATOR CAR PLANS PFE #20001 1932	09	39	467
VENTILATED REEFER ARA *URT 35T CLASS RS	10	36	294
WOODEN REEFER CAR PLANS CN #204000 1920	07	54	34
WOODEN REEFER CAR PLANS NJ HEINZ #484	07	54	34
WOODEN REFRIGERATOR CAR PLANS CN #204000	07	59	52

REFRIGERATOR PLANS BY ROAD

RD	Title	M	Y	P
*URT	VENTILATED REEFER ARA *URT 35T CLASS RS	10	36	294
ATSF	REEFER CLASS RR40 PLANS ATSF #8225 1923	04	48	266
	50' CLASS FE24 BOXCAR PLANS ATSF #10089	09	47	738
	REEFER 50' CAR PLANS CLASS RR-30 #37343	09	47	738
CMI	HANRAHAN AUTOMATIC REEFER PLANS CMI#1206	01	65	40
CN	WOODEN REEFER CAR PLANS CN #204000 1920	07	54	34
	WOODEN REFRIGERATOR CAR PLANS CN #204000	07	59	52
	OVERHEAD BUNKER REEFER CAR PLN CN#212404	11	64	32
D&RGW	REFRIGERATOR CAR NARROW GAUGE PLAN D&RGW	06	43	274
	REEFER CAR NARROW GAUGE PLANS D&RGW #78	04	62	46
LV	ICE SERVICE CAR PLANS LV #3206 1911	01	66	47
NAD	EGG REFRIGERATOR CAR PLANS NAD #6001	05	36	130
	REFRIGERATOR CAR PLANS NAD#3004 FRIGICAR	08	36	227
PFE	REFRIGERATOR CAR PLANS PFE #20001 1932	09	39	467
	MECH REEFER R40-30 CLASS PLAN PFE#100028	04	67	38
	MECH REEFER R70-12 CLASS PLAN PFE#301213	04	67	38
PRR	OUTSIDE BRACED REEFER PLANS PRR #5342	04	58	42
R	OUTSIDE BRACED REEFER PLANS R #19890	10	62	63
	OUTSIDE BRACED CL RMJ REEFER R#19890 PLN	01	57	46
SOO	MODERN REEFER SOO CLASS RPL PLANS #10010	02	67	46

REFRIGERATOR CAR PHOTOS

Title	M	Y	P
ICE COOLED REEFER CONVERTS TO MECH PHOTO	08	67	56

REFRIGERATOR CAR MODELS

Title		M	Y	P
36' WOOD SP REEFER	MOD & PT	11	77	131
40' BOXCAR PLAIN JANE	MOD & PT	10	78	125
40' MECHANICAL REEFER	MOD & PT	03	83	114
60 TON MECHANICAL REEFER CONST *PFE		04	67	40
A.R.T. REEFER	MOD & PT	07	80	103
DOMINO PIZZA REEFER	MOD & PT	04	75	22
DRY ICE REEFER CAR SIDES SF #6004		12	40	680S
ICE REEFERS OF 60'S *PFE	MOD & PT	12	83	163
IMPROVEMENTS FOR MDC OLDTIME REEFERS		04	81	114
MECHANICAL REEFER *PFE	MOD & PT	01	77	110
MECHANICAL REEFER BAR	MOD & PT	11	76	126
MECHANICAL REEFER SWIFT	MOD & PT	12	79	160
MECHANICAL REEFERS SPFE	MOD & PT	08	80	110
MECHANICAL REEFERS UPFE	MOD & PT	08	80	110
MOM MDT #22064 REEFER "1/4"	RONK	04	43	158
OUTSIDE BRACED REEFER CONSTRUCTION PRR		04	58	40
OUTSIDE BRACED REEFER CONSTRUCTION R		10	62	60
PRIVATE OWNER REEFER SIDES IN COLOR		01	49	50S
PRIVATE OWNER REEFER SIDES IN COLOR		11	43	499
REEFER CONSTRUCTION		05	51	34
REEFER SIDES IN COLOR		10	36	280S
REEFER TIFFANY PATENT	MOD & PT	06	81	127
REEFER TROPICANA ORANGE JUICE	MOD & PT	04	79	125
REEFERS 1950'S ERA ATSF	MOD & PT	11	80	154
REEFERS OF 1880 D&RGW	MOD & PT	09	82	114
RENOVATE YOUR OLD REEFERS		01	77	94
REWORKING BRUSH PAINTED REEFER W/AIRBRUS		08	76	94
STEEL REEFER NORTHERN PACIFIC	MOD & PT	10	82	118
SWIFT REEFER CONSTRUCTION		10	53	22
WOOD REEFER CN OF 1920 CONSTRUCTION		07	59	52
WOOD SHEATHED REEFER CONSTRUCTION *GARX		04	60	32

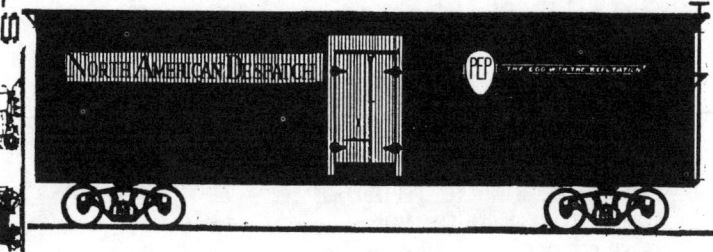

FREIGHT CARS

REFRIGERATOR CAR MODEL REVIEWS

	M	Y	P
1900 REEFER KIT REVIEW "HO" LA 1900	10	64	10
1912 REEFER REVIEW "HO" AMB	08	59	12
30' D&RGW REEFER REVIEW "HON3/ON3" TOM	12	71	42
36' DW&P REEFER REVIEW "S" CRM	05	65	10
36' PRIVATE REEFER REVIEW "S" KSC	08	58	12
36' REEFER OF 1906 REVIEW "O" TBE	02	59	13
36' REEFER REVIEW "HO" BIN	07	58	10
36' REEFER REVIEW "HO" YE 1900	05	71	20
36' WOOD REEFER REVIEW "O" AN	06	58	12
40 TON USRA REEFER REVIEW "HO" CC	08	63	13
40' REEFER KIT REVIEW "HO" CECL	09	67	14
40' WILSON REEFER REVIEW "N" CC	10	72	22
50' MECH REEFER REVIEW "HO" ATH	05	68	16
50' MECH REEFER REVIEW "HO" WAL 1960	02	73	19
50' REEFER REVIEW "N" CC	11	70	17
50' WOOD ATSF REEFER REVIEW "HO" AMB	04	73	20
60 TON MECHANICAL REEFER REV "HO" PHO	04	64	7
ARMOUR REEFER REVIEW "HO" HOWELL DAY	02	60	12
BALSA REEFER REVIEW FS	10	39	542
BILLBOARD REEFER LISTING "S" SU	12	77	62
BILLBOARD REEFER REVIEW "1/4" WALTERS	10	78	45
COMPOSITE REEFER REVIEW "O" AN	12	52	64
DOUBLE SHEATHED REEFER REVIEW "HO" TMC	01	73	35
DRY ICE REEFER REVIEW "HO" AMB	01	60	16
DRY ICE REEFER REVIEW "HO" LAC	11	48	885
EGG REEFER NAD REVIEW "HO" MBS	08	55	13
EXPRESS MILK REEFER REVIEW "HO" DN	02	52	41
HANRAHAN REEFER REVIEW "HO" LA CMI	06	65	8
HEINZ 40' REEFER LISTING "N" KADEE	03	77	44
MECHANICAL REEFER REVIEW "HO" ATH	04	77	42
METAL REEFER KIT REVIEW "HO" ATH	08	50	48
METAL REEFER REVIEW "HO" M	04	40	240
METAL REEFER REVIEW M	09	46	590
MILK REEFER KIT REVIEW "HO" LAC	06	53	59
OLYMPIA BEER REEFER REVIEW "1/4" AMB	06	75	27
PRIVATE OWNER REEFER REVIEW "HO" WAL	04	57	15
REEFER ATSF LISTING "S" SU	12	78	64
REEFER ATSF REVIEW "O" GEMO	12	42	581
REEFER BABY RUTH REVIEW "HO" COMET MODEL	03	40	183
REEFER CP CLASS RAH 1930 REVIEW "HO" AMB	08	64	6
REEFER D&RGW REVIEW "HON3" K-VAL CARS	05	64	10
REEFER KIT REVIEW "S" MIM	01	48	65
REEFER KIT REVIEW "S" SSM	07	50	55
REEFER KIT REVIEW "TT" SED	02	52	41
REEFER KIT REVIEW "O" HAWK MODEL CO.	12	39	672
REEFER KIT REVIEW "S" HM	10	46	705
REEFER KIT REVIEW "S" NIXON MODEL CO.	03	50	58
REEFER LISTING "1/4" RRR	05	78	52
REEFER MATHESON DRY ICE REVIEW "HO" LAC	06	41	331
REEFER METAL KIT REVIEW "HO" V	05	50	41
REEFER PFE SET OF 5 "N" KADEE	09	78	46
REEFER REVIEW "HO" EFMT	06	39	328
REEFER REVIEW "N" CC	10	67	9
REEFER REVIEW "O" AFM	08	53	11
REEFER REVIEW "O" JANCO MODELS	12	40	700

REFRIGERATOR CAR MODEL REVIEWS

	M	Y	P
REEFER REVIEW "TT" GD	09	70	20
REEFER/OPENING DOORS REVIEW "HO" MDC	07	56	16
REFRIGERATOR CAR ATSF REVIEW "N" QC	04	78	39
SHEET METAL REEFER REV "O" MERLE FABER	11	39	608
STEEL REEFER REVIEW "HO" ATH	05	58	9
TINPLATE REEFER KIT REVIEW "O" HT	12	50	55
TRUSS ROD REEFER KIT REVIEW "HO" CV	10	53	10
UNICEL REEFER REVIEW "HO" AMB	10	60	10
WOOD FGE REEFER REVIEW "HO" SC 1928	10	70	16
WOOD REEFER KIT REVIEW ATSF "O" AN	01	55	16

REFRIGERATOR MODEL REVIEWS BY ROAD

RD		M	Y	P
*PFE	REEFER PFE SET OF 5 "N" KADEE	09	78	46
ATSF	WOOD REEFER KIT REVIEW ATSF "O" AN	01	55	16
	50' WOOD ATSF REEFER REVIEW "HO" AMB	04	73	20
	REEFER ATSF LISTING "S" SU	12	78	64
	REFRIGERATOR CAR ATSF REVIEW "N" QC	04	78	39
CMI	HANRAHAN REEFER REVIEW "HO" LA CMI	06	65	8
CP	REEFER CP CLASS RAH 1930 REVIEW "HO" AMB	08	64	6
D&RGW	30' D&RGW REEFER REVIEW "HON3/ON3" TOM	12	71	42
	REEFER D&RGW REVIEW "HON3" K-VAL CARS	05	64	10
DW&P	36' DW&P REEFER REVIEW "S" CRM	05	65	10

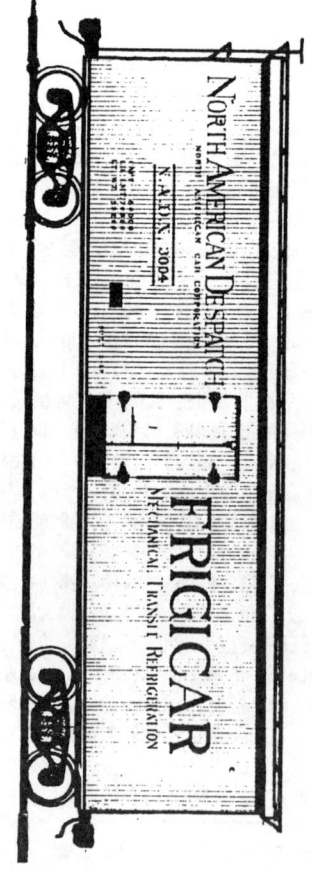

104

FREIGHT CARS

REFRIGERATOR MODEL REVIEWS BY MFG.

MFG		M	Y	P
AFM	REEFER REVIEW "O" AFM	08	53	11
AMB	1912 REEFER REVIEW "HO" AMB	08	59	12
	50' WOOD ATSF REEFER REVIEW "HO" AMB	04	73	20
	UNICEL REEFER REVIEW "HO" AMB	10	60	10
	DRY ICE REEFER REVIEW "HO" AMB	01	60	16
	REEFER CP CLASS RAH 1930 REVIEW "HO" AMB	08	64	6
	OLYMPIA BEER REEFER REVIEW "1/4" AMB	06	75	27
AN	36' WOOD REEFER REVIEW "O" AN	06	58	12
	COMPOSITE REEFER REVIEW "O" AN	12	52	64
	WOOD REEFER KIT REVIEW ATSF "O" AN	01	55	16
ATH	STEEL REEFER REVIEW "HO" ATH	05	58	9
	METAL REEFER KIT REVIEW "HO" ATH	08	50	48
	50' MECH REEFER REVIEW "HO" ATH	05	68	16
	MECHANICAL REEFER REVIEW "HO" ATH	04	77	42
BIN	36' REEFER REVIEW "HO" BIN	07	58	10
CC	40' WILSON REEFEER REVIEW "N" CC	10	72	22
	50' REEFER REVIEW "N" CC	11	70	17
	REEFER REVIEW "N" CC	10	67	9
	40 TON USRA REEFER REVIEW "HO" CC	08	63	13
CECL	40' REEFER KIT REVIEW "HO" CECL	09	67	14
CMO	REEFER BABY RUTH REVIEW "HO" COMET MODEL	03	40	183
CRM	36' DW&P REEFER REVIEW "S" CRM	05	65	10
CV	TRUSS ROD REEFER KIT REVIEW "HO" CV	10	53	10
DN	EXPRESS MILK REEFER REVIEW "HO" DN	02	52	41
EFMT	REEFER REVIEW "HO" EFMT	06	39	328
FS	BALSA REEFER REVIEW FS	10	39	542
GD	REEFER REVIEW "TT" GD	09	70	20
GEMO	REEFER ATSF REVIEW "O" GEMO	12	42	581
HA	REEFER KIT REVIEW "O" HAWK MODEL CO.	12	39	672
HD	ARMOUR REEFER REVIEW "HO" HOWELL DAY	02	60	12
HM	REEFER KIT REVIEW "S" HM	10	46	705
HT	TINPLATE REEFER KIT REVIEW "O" HT	12	50	55
JA	REEFER REVIEW "O" JANCO MODELS	12	40	700
KD	REEFER PFE SET OF 5 "N" KADEE	09	78	46
	HEINZ 40' REEFER LISTING "N" KADEE	03	77	44
KSC	36' PRIVATE REEFER REVIEW "S" KSC	08	58	12
KVAL	REEFER D&RGW REVIEW "HON3" K-VAL CARS	05	64	10
LA	1900 REEFER KIT REVIEW "HO" LA 1900	10	64	10
	HANRAHAN REEFER REVIEW "HO" LA CMI	06	65	8
LAC	MILK REEFER KIT REVIEW "HO" LAC	06	53	59
	REEFER MATHESON DRY ICE REVIEW "HO" LAC	06	41	331
	DRY ICE REEFER REVIEW "HO" LAC	11	48	885
M	METAL REEFER REVIEW "HO" M	04	40	240
	METAL REEFER REVIEW M	09	46	590
MBS	EGG REEFER NAD REVIEW "HO" MBS	08	55	13
MDC	REEFER/OPENING DOORS REVIEW "HO" MDC	07	56	16
MF	SHEET METAL REEFER REV "O" MERLE FABER	11	39	608
MIM	REEFER KIT REVIEW "S" MIM	01	48	65
NM	REEFER KIT REVIEW "S" NIXON MODEL CO.	03	50	58
PHO	60 TON MECHANICAL REEFER REV "HO" PHO	04	64	7
QC	REFRIGERATOR CAR ATSF REVIEW "N" QC	04	78	39
RRR	REEFER LISTING "1/4" RRR	05	78	52
SC	WOOD F6E REEFER REVIEW "HO" SC 1928	10	70	16
SED	REEFER KIT REVIEW "TT" SED	02	52	41
SSM	REEFER KIT REVIEW "S" SSM	07	50	55

REFRIGERATOR MODEL REVIEWS BY MFG.

MFG		M	Y	P
SU	REEFER ATSF LISTING "S" SU	12	78	64
	BILLBOARD REEFER LISTING "S" SU	12	77	62
TBE	36' REEFER OF 1906 REVIEW "O" TBE	02	59	13
TMC	DOUBLE SHEATHED REEFER REVIEW "HO" TMC	01	73	35
TOM	30' D&RGW REEFER REVIEW "HON3/ON3" TOM	12	71	42
V	REEFER METAL KIT REVIEW "HO" V	05	50	41
WAL	50' MECH REEFER REVIEW "HO" WAL 1960	02	73	19
	PRIVATE OWNER REEFER REVIEW "HO" WAL	04	57	15
	BILLBOARD REEFER REVIEW "1/4" WALTERS	10	78	45
YE	36' REEFER REVIEW "HO" YE 1900	05	71	20

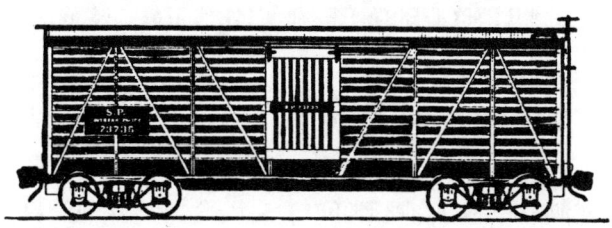

STOCK CAR PROTOTYPE DATA

	M	Y	P
BIG PIG PALACE STOCKCARS OF NP 1966 ORT	04	82	82

STOCK CAR PLANS

	M	Y	P
30 TON STEEL FRAME STOCK CAR PLANS 1912	04	41	21
40 TON AAR STOCK CAR DRAWING MP #52437	09	36	246
40 TON AAR STOCK CAR DRAWING T&P #22225	09	36	246
40T STOCK CAR PLANS SP #73735 1917	09	36	246
BIG PIG PALACE STOCKCARS PLANS NP #84300	04	82	82
CANDA CATTLE CAR OF 1893 PLANS	05	60	47
MILITARY OPEN CATTLE CAR #1134 PL 1862	03	69	33
PALACE STOCK CAR PLANS CMI #4202 1900	04	66	36
POULTRY CAR PLANS LPT #507	07	61	26
POULTRY CAR PLANS NATIONAL #6000	10	47	804
STOCK CAR 42' CLASS SK-U ATSF#60543 PLAN	03	49	48
STOCK CAR 42' PLANS	03	47	218
STOCK CAR NARROW GAUGE PLANS D&RGW	08	43	362
STOCK CAR NARROW GAUGE PLANS D&RGW #5566	11	72	54
STOCK CAR OF 1887 PLANS ML&T #3112	02	58	43
STOCK CAR OF 1903 OSL PLANS #12750	01	60	74
STOCK CAR OF 1909 PLANS PRR #647838	03	57	60
STOCK CAR PLANS 42'	08	52	45
STOCK CAR PLANS 42'	12	53	94
STOCK CAR PLANS NARROW GAUGE SP #153	01	67	51
STOCK CAR PLANS OF 1890 NYC&H #26200	02	59	46
STOCK CAR PLANS SOUTHERN #39027	04	57	47

FREIGHT CARS

RD	STOCK CAR PLANS BY ROAD	M	Y	P
ATSF	STOCK CAR 42' CLASS SK-U ATSF#60543 PLAN	03	49	48
CMI	PALACE STOCK CAR PLANS CMI #4202 1900	04	66	36
D&RGW	STOCK CAR NARROW GAUGE PLANS D&RGW	08	43	362
	STOCK CAR NARROW GAUGE PLANS D&RGW #5566	11	72	54
LPT	POULTRY CAR PLANS LPT #507	07	61	26
ML&T	STOCK CAR OF 1887 PLANS ML&T #3112	02	58	43
MP	40 TON AAR STOCK CAR DRAWING MP #52437	09	36	246
NP	BIG PIG PALACE STOCKCARS PLANS NP #84300	04	82	82
NYC&H	STOCK CAR PLANS OF 1890 NYC&H #26200	02	59	46
OSL	STOCK CAR OF 1903 OSL PLANS #12750	01	60	74
PRR	STOCK CAR OF 1909 PLANS PRR #647838	03	57	60
S	STOCK CAR PLANS SOUTHERN #39027	04	57	47
SP	40T STOCK CAR PLANS SP #73735 1917	09	36	246
	STOCK CAR PLANS NARROW GAUGE SP #153	01	67	51
T&P	40 TON AAR STOCK CAR DRAWING T&P #22225	09	36	246
USA	MILITARY OPEN CATTLE CAR #1134 PL 1862	03	69	33

STOCK CAR PHOTOS	M	Y	P
BOXCARS TO STOCK CARS CP PHOTOS	09	69	29
MODERN POULTRY CAR PHOTO	12	61	10
STOCK CAR PHOTO CP #60716	10	69	71

STOCK CAR MODELS		M	Y	P
CIRCUS STOCK CAR CONSTRUCTION	$1	07	66	33
MOM D&H STOCK CAR "HO" NELSON		02	75	51
MOM NKP 2 DECK STOCK CAR "HO"CIESWKOWSKI		06	75	61
PALACE POULTRY CAR MODEL PHOTO DYXIN		05	73	40
STEEL STOCK CAR CONSTRUCTION		02	73	46
STOCK CAR CONSTRUCTION	$1	09	53	40
STOCK CAR CONSTRUCTION NYC&HR		02	59	44
STOCK CAR CONSTRUCTION PRR #130545	$1	06	66	30
STOCK CAR CONSTRUCTION READING #19036		09	53	72
STOCK CAR CONSTRUCTION SOUTHERN		04	57	46
STOCK CAR D&RGW MOD & PT		02	80	128

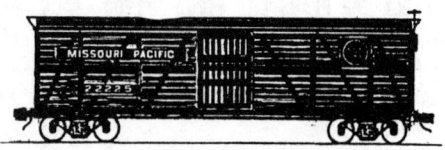

STOCK CAR MODEL REVIEWS BY ROAD			
RD	M	Y	P
ATSF DESPATCH ATSF STOCKCAR REVIEW "N" KD	10	74	23
D&RG 3' GAUGE D&RG STOCK CAR REVIEW "S" TOM	07	73	22
D&RGW STOCKCAR LISTING D&RGW "G" LBG	10	77	48
SOO 36' SOO STOCK CAR REVIEW "S" WCS 1922	07	72	22
SP 30' STOCK CAR SP REVIEW "HON3" RDA	04	65	11

STOCK CAR MODEL REVIEWS	M	Y	P
3' GAUGE D&RG STOCK CAR REVIEW "S" TOM	07	73	22
30' STOCK CAR SP REVIEW "HON3" RDA	04	65	11
36' SOO STOCK CAR REVIEW "S" WCS 1922	07	72	22
36' STOCK CAR 1914 REVIEW "HO" MLI	06	57	12
40' CLASS SM STOCK CAR REVIEW "HO" LIND	09	62	16
42' STOCK CAR REVIEW "HO" TMC	04	74	28
49' STOCK CAR REVIEW "N" MRC	12	70	38
85' STOCK CAR REVIEW "N" AT	11	70	22
ALL METAL STOCK CAR REVIEW "HO" MDC	11	50	53
CHICKEN PALACE CAR REVIEW "HO" MLI	08	54	10
CONVERTIBLE STOCK CAR KIT REV "HO" AMB	12	55	20
DESPATCH ATSF STOCKCAR REVIEW "N" KD	10	74	23
DOUBLE DECK STOCK CAR REVIEW "HO" ATT	06	68	16
LIVE POULTRY/REEFER REVIEW "HO" AMB	09	61	14
POULTRY CAR REVIEW "N" ANB	08	76	32
POULTRY CAR REVIEW "O" MLI 1920	12	76	36
STD STOCK CAR REVIEW "HO" WAL 1930	02	85	52
STOCK CAR KIT REVIEW "HO" DN	09	48	675
STOCK CAR REBUILDS REVIEW "HO" TI	10	68	20
STOCK CAR REVIEW "HO" U	03	51	55
STOCK CAR REVIEW "HO" DALE NEWTON	08	42	397
STOCK CAR REVIEW "O" NJM	03	54	13
STOCK CAR REVIEW "OO" SCALE MODELS INC	11	39	608
STOCKCAR LISTING D&RGW "G" LBG	10	77	48
TINPLATE CATTLE CAR REVIEW "O" FHS	10	52	59

STOCK CAR MODEL REVIEWS BY MFG.				
MFG		M	Y	P
AMB	CONVERTIBLE STOCK CAR KIT REV "HO" AMB	12	55	20
	LIVE POULTRY/REEFER REVIEW "HO" AMB	09	61	14
ANB	POULTRY CAR REVIEW "N" ANB	08	76	32
AT	85' STOCK CAR REVIEW "N" AT	11	70	22
ATT	DOUBLE DECK STOCK CAR REVIEW "HO" ATT	06	68	16
DN	STOCK CAR KIT REVIEW "HO" DN	09	48	675
	STOCK CAR REVIEW "HO" DALE NEWTON	08	42	397
FHS	TINPLATE CATTLE CAR REVIEW "O" FHS	10	52	59
KD	DESPATCH ATSF STOCKCAR REVIEW "N" KD	10	74	23
LBG	STOCKCAR LISTING D&RGW "G" LBG	10	77	48
LIND	40' CLASS SM STOCK CAR REVIEW "HO" LIND	09	62	16
MDC	ALL METAL STOCK CAR REVIEW "HO" MDC	11	50	53
MLI	CHICKEN PALACE CAR REVIEW "HO" MLI	08	54	10
	POULTRY CAR REVIEW "O" MLI 1920	12	76	36
	36' STOCK CAR 1914 REVIEW "HO" MLI	06	57	12
MRC	49' STOCK CAR REVIEW "N" MRC	12	70	38
NJM	STOCK CAR REVIEW "O" NJM	03	54	13
RDA	30' STOCK CAR SP REVIEW "HON3" RDA	04	65	11
SCMO	STOCK CAR REVIEW "OO" SCALE MODELS INC	11	39	608
TI	STOCK CAR REBUILDS REVIEW "HO" TI	10	68	20
TMC	42' STOCK CAR REVIEW "HO" TMC	04	74	28
TOM	3' GAUGE D&RG STOCK CAR REVIEW "S" TOM	07	73	22
U	STOCK CAR REVIEW "HO" U	03	51	55
WAL	STD STOCK CAR REVIEW "HO" WAL 1930	02	85	52
WCS	36' SOO STOCK CAR REVIEW "S" WCS 1922	07	72	22

FREIGHT CARS

TANK CAR PROTOTYPE DATA	M	Y	P
HIGH PRESSURE TANK CARS	01	82	85
MODERN CHEMICAL TANK CARS	03	79	94
TANK CAR B&SR #22 OF 1900	02	78	61
TANK CAR CLASSIFICATIONS	05	44	200
TANK CAR LOAD SIGNS	12	78	183
TANK CAR LOADING & UNLOADING	09	76	107
TANK CARS COMMON TO UNUSUAL	05	44	196
USRA TANK CARS	11	76	68

TANK CAR PLANS	M	Y	P
10,000 GAL TANK CAR PLANS	11	76	69
6000 GAL UNION TANK LINE OF 1901 PLANS	09	62	36
8000 GAL TANK CAR PLANS	11	76	69
85' TANK CAR PLANS *UTC #99399 1960	04	62	40
COAL TAR TANK CAR PLANS J&T 1926 STC	04	56	52
HEINZ 38' CLASS TW #73 BRINE TANK CAR PL	04	35	90
HIGH PRESSURE TANK CAR PLANS UTLX #89303	01	82	84
ICC-103 TANK CAR PLANS	10	37	356
INSULATED CHEM TANKER SHPX#3310 PLNS ACF	09	48	624
JUMBO 4 TRUCK TANK CAR PLANS UTLX #83699	01	82	82
LIQUID OXYGEN TANK CAR PLANS LUTLX 80011	10	63	42
MONARCH PICKLE CAR DRAWING	07	36	178
SIX DOME ACF WINE TANK CAR PLANS *SCL	10	53	74
TANK CAR 36' PLANS AAR CLASS #3000 *WTL	04	35	90
TANK CAR B&SR #22 PLANS OF 1900	02	78	61
TANK CAR NARROW GAUGE PLANS D&RGW	08	43	362
TANK CAR PLANS COMMON TO UNUSUAL	05	44	196
TANK CAR PLANS RUBBER CORP OF AMERICA	07	60	38
TANK CAR PLANS SHPX #4297 1949	02	52	38
TANK-HOPPER CAR PLANS AL CO OF CANADA	02	62	38
UNION LINE TANK CAR PLAN #7820	02	47	108

RD	TANK CAR PLANS BY ROAD	M	Y	P
*RCA	TANK CAR PLANS RUBBER CORP OF AMERICA	07	60	38
*SCL	SIX DOME ACF WINE TANK CAR PLANS *SCL	10	53	74
*UTC	85' TANK CAR PLANS *UTC #99399 1960	04	62	40
*UTL	6000 GAL UNION TANK LINE OF 1901 PLANS	09	62	36
*WTL	TANK CAR 36' PLANS AAR CLASS #3000 *WTL	04	35	90
ALCAN	TANK-HOPPER CAR PLANS AL CO OF CANADA	02	62	38
B&SR	TANK CAR B&SR #22 PLANS OF 1900	02	78	61
D&RGW	TANK CAR NARROW GAUGE PLANS D&RGW	08	43	362
J&L	COAL TAR TANK CAR PLANS J&T 1926 STC	04	56	52
LAC	LIQUID OXYGEN TANK CAR PLANS LUTLX 80011	10	63	42
SHPX	TANK CAR PLANS SHPX #4297 1949	02	52	38

TANK CAR PHOTOS	M	Y	P
DIFFERENT TWO DOME TANK PHOTO	12	63	20

TANK CAR MODELS	M	Y	P
1920 TANK CAR VARIATIONS		03	84	92
BASF WYANDOTTE CHEMICAL CARS MOD & PT	03	76	88
BEER CAN TANK CAR CONSTRUCTION	02	77	69
BOX & TANK CAR FRIS MOD & PT	11	78	122
CANADIAN GEN TRANSIT 62' TANK MOD & PT	09	77	99
CHEMICAL TANK CAR 2 DOME CONSTRUCTION	07	60	36
CHLORINE TANK CAR CONSTRUCTION	07	45	281
CHLORINE TANK CAR CONSTRUCTION $1	11	53	66
COAL TAR TANK CAR CONSTRUCTION $1	04	56	24
EARTH SCAPER DELUXE CAR LOAD CONST	05	55	41
KITBASH TANK CAR B&SR #22	02	78	62
KITBASHING AN INCLINE TANK CAR	10	75	64
LIQUID OXYGEN TANK CAR CONSRTUCTION $1	10	63	41
MODERN CHEMICAL TANK CARS CONSTRUCTION	03	79	94
MODERN TANK CARS SAFETY BARS	07	83	124
MOM CM&SP WATER CAR "HO" FORD	10	80	83
MOM LOGGING TANK CAR "ON3" DYXIN	06	76	51
PENNZOIL 3 DOME TANKER CONSTRUCTION 1915	10	85	74
PICKLE CAR CONSTRUCTION $1	11	56	46
REBUILD PLASTIC TANK CARS	09	62	34
SIMPLE DETAILS FOR MDC TANK CARS	08	83	135
SIX DOME TANK CAR CONSTRUCTION $1	10	53	44
TANK CAR MOD & PT	10	75	83
TANK CAR ALLIED CHEMICAL MOD & PT	01	84	232
TANK CAR CONSOLIDATED GAS MOD & PT	01	82	127
TANK CAR CONSTRUCTION	09	40	479
TANK CAR CONSTRUCTION USRA	09	77	56
TANK CAR PENN SALT MOD & PT	06	78	102
TANK CAR PSPX PROPANE MOD & PT	01	84	233
TANK CAR THAT NEVER WAS	02	78	65
TANK CAR WARREN PETROLEUM PROPANE MOD&PT	01	84	234
TANK-HOPPER CONSTRUCTION ALCO OF CANADA	05	62	56
TANKER CORN PRODUCTS MOD & PT	03	84	130
UPGRADE AHM VINEGAR TANK CARS	09	84	146
VINEGAR TANK CAR CONSTRUCTION	01	60	62
WOOD TANK CAR CONSTRUCTION $1	03	55	22

FREIGHT CARS

TANK CAR MODEL REVIEWS	M	Y	P
10,000 GAL TANK CAR REVIEW "S" WCS	03	74	25
2 DOME TANK CAR LISTING "ON3" ADDM	08	78	50
2 PICKLE CAR REVIEW "HO" ATH	08	59	12
20,000 GAL TANK CAR REVIEW "HO" FED	02	62	14
29' CHANGEABLE TANK "HO" REVIEW QC	08	69	9
3 DOME TANK CAR REVIEW "HO" ATH	08	50	51
36' 10,000 GAL TANK CAR REVIEW "HO" GC	02	84	41
36' 8000 GAL TANK CAR REVIEW "HO" M	01	85	66
36' TANK CAR REVIEW "HO" LA	01	69	20
36' TANK CAR REVIEW "N" RAP	05	69	16
62' TANK CAR REVIEW "HO" ATH GAT	06	68	12
76' COMPRESSED GAS TANK CAR REV O/HO QC	04	79	39
95' JUMBO GEN AMER TANKER REVIEW "N" AT	09	70	12
BASIC TANK CAR REVIEW "O" FAS	04	53	57
CHEMICAL TANK CAR REV "HO" MDC	06	60	13
CONX10 D&RGW TANK CAR REVIEW "1/4" WSM	06	75	30
ESSO TANK WAGON REVIEW "HO" US AIRFIX	01	77	43
GATX TANK TRAIN REVIEW "HO" MDC	09	83	36
LOW PRESSURE TANK CAR REVIEW "HO" TH	04	57	12
METAL TANK CAR REVIEW "HO" M	12	40	700
METAL TANK CAR REVIEW "HO" M	02	38	86
MILK TANK CAR REVIEW "HO" DALE NEWTON	04	42	202
MILK TANK CAR REVIEW "HO" NPP 1930	01	74	34
MODERN 20,000 GAL TANK CAR REV "HO" MDC	10	82	36
PICKLE CAR KIT REVIEW "O" WAL	02	48	147
PICKLE CAR REVIEW "HO" MB AUSTIN	04	40	240
PICKLE CAR REVIEW "HO" WD	10	85	45
PICKLE CAR REVIEW "HO" MB AUSTIN	08	40	460
PICKLE TANK CAR KIT "HO" UMP	02	55	18
PICKLE TANK CAR REVIEW "HO" AMB	01	58	18
SINGLE DOME TANK CAR REVIEW "S" REK	03	62	14
TANK CAR 20,000 GAL REVIEW "O" QC	01	83	52
TANK CAR BAKERS CHOCOLATE REV "HO" TH	03	58	12
TANK CAR ICC 103W REVIEW "HO" L	06	77	37
TANK CAR KIT REVIEW DT	05	38	216
TANK CAR KIT REVIEW "O" TH	04	49	75
TANK CAR LISTING "N" JMC	04	77	46
TANK CAR OF 1906 REVIEW "HO" MDC	07	69	17
TANK CAR REVIEW "HO" MC	01	38	42
TANK CAR REVIEW "HO" GLOBE	04	51	46
TANK CAR REVIEW "HO" ATH	10	50	56
TANK CAR REVIEW "ON3" BS	02	81	60
TANK CAR REVIEW "HO" M	07	59	13
TANK CAR REVIEW "HO" FUTURE DESIGNS	11	37	432
TANK CAR REVIEW "HO" M	05	56	15
TANK CAR REVIEW "HO" MODEL RAILROAD SHOP	04	38	174
TANK CAR REVIEW "O" HAWK MODEL AEROPLANE	08	37	301
TANK CAR REVIEW ACF "HO" ALCO MODELS	02	78	45
TANK NARROW GAUGE CON REVIEW "HON3" WSM	05	67	10
TEXACO TANK CAR 1930 REVIEW "N" KD	02	80	35
TINPLATE PICKLE CAR REVIEW "O" WAL	05	51	49
TRIPLE DOME TANK CAR REVIEW "HO" ATH	11	57	15
UTLX D&RGW TANK CAR REVIEW "HON3" TOM	05	76	34
UTLX TANK CAR LISTING "ON3" PFM	05	77	48
VINEGAR TANK CAR REVIEW "HO" AMB	11	58	12

TANK CAR MODEL REVIEWS	M	Y	P
WINE TANK 6 DOME CAR REVIEW "HO" TH	07	55	10
WINE TANK CAR REVIEW "1/4" LOCO WORKSHOP	11	77	43

TANK CAR MODEL REVIEWS BY ROAD				
RD		M	Y	P
ACF	TANK CAR REVIEW ACF "HO" ALCO MODELS	02	78	45
D&RGW	UTLX D&RGW TANK CAR REVIEW "HON3" TOM	05	76	34
	CONX10 D&RGW TANK CAR REVIEW "1/4" WSM	06	75	30
ICC	TANK CAR ICC 103W REVIEW "HO" L	06	77	37
J&L	20,000 GAL TANK CAR REVIEW "HO" FED	02	62	14
UTLX	UTLX TANK CAR LISTING "ON3" PFM	05	77	48

FREIGHT CARS

TANK CAR MODEL REVIEWS BY MFG.

MFG		M	Y	P
ADDM	2 DOME TANK CAR LISTING "ON3" ADDM	08	78	50
ALCO	TANK CAR REVIEW ACF "HO" ALCO MODELS	02	78	45
AMB	PICKLE TANK CAR REVIEW "HO" AMB	01	58	18
	VINEGAR TANK CAR REVIEW "HO" AMB	11	58	12
AT	95' JUMBO GEN AMER TANKER REVIEW "N" AT	09	70	12
ATH	2 PICKLE CAR REVIEW "HO" ATH	08	59	12
	3 DOME TANK CAR REVIEW "HO" ATH	08	50	51
	TANK CAR REVIEW "HO" ATH	10	50	56
	62' TANK CAR REVIEW "HO" ATH GAT	06	68	12
	TRIPLE DOME TANK CAR REVIEW "HO" ATH	11	57	15
BS	TANK CAR REVIEW "ON3" BS	02	81	60
DN	MILK TANK CAR REVIEW "HO" DALE NEWTON	04	42	202
DT	TANK CAR KIT REVIEW DT	05	38	216
FAS	BASIC TANK CAR REVIEW "O" FAS	04	53	57
FED	20,000 GAL TANK CAR REVIEW "HO" FED	02	62	14
GC	36' 10,000 GAL TANK CAR REVIEW "HO" GC	02	84	41
GLO	TANK CAR REVIEW "HO" GLOBE	04	51	46
JMC	TANK CAR LISTING "N" JMC	04	77	46
KD	TEXACO TANK CAR 1930 REVIEW "N" KD	02	80	35
L	TANK CAR ICC 103W REVIEW "HO" L	06	77	37
LA	36' TANK CAR REVIEW "HO" LA	01	69	20
LW	WINE TANK CAR REVIEW "1/4" LOCO WORKSHOP	11	77	43
M	METAL TANK CAR REVIEW "HO" M	12	40	700
	METAL TANK CAR REVIEW "HO" M	02	38	86
	TANK CAR REVIEW "HO" M	07	59	13
	TANK CAR REVIEW "HO" M	05	56	15
	36' 8000 GAL TANK CAR REVIEW "HO" M	01	85	66
MBA	PICKLE CAR REVIEW "HO" MB AUSTIN	04	40	240
	PICKLE CAR REVIEW "HO" MB AUSTIN	08	40	460
MC	TANK CAR REVIEW "HO" MC	01	38	42
MDC	GATX TANK TRAIN REVIEW "HO" MDC	09	83	36
	MODERN 20,000 GAL TANK CAR REV "HO" MDC	10	82	36
	CHEMICAL TANK CAR REV "HO" MDC	06	60	13
	TANK CAR OF 1906 REVIEW "HO" MDC	07	69	17
MRS	TANK CAR REVIEW "HO" MODEL RAILROAD SHOP	04	38	174
NPP	MILK TANK CAR REVIEW "HO" NPP 1930	01	74	34
PFM	UTLX TANK CAR LISTING "ON3" PFM	05	77	48
QC	TANK CAR 20,000 GAL REVIEW "O" QC	01	83	52
	76' COMPRESSED GAS TANK CAR REV O/HO QC	04	79	39
	29' CHANGEABLE TANK "HO" REVIEW QC	08	69	9
RAP	36' TANK CAR REVIEW "N" RAP	05	69	16
REK	SINGLE DOME TANK CAR REVIEW "S" REK	03	62	14
TH	TANK CAR KIT REVIEW "O" TH	04	49	75
	WINE TANK 6 DOME CAR REVIEW "HO" TH	07	55	10
	TANK CAR BAKERS CHOCOLATE REV "HO" TH	03	58	12
	LOW PRESSURE TANK CAR REVIEW "HO" TH	04	57	12
TOM	UTLX D&RGW TANK CAR REVIEW "HON3" TOM	05	76	34
UMP	PICKLE TANK CAR KIT "HO" UMP	02	55	18
USAI	ESSO TANK WAGON REVIEW "HO" US AIRFIX	01	77	43
WAL	PICKLE CAR KIT REVIEW "O" WAL	02	48	147
	TINPLATE PICKLE CAR REVIEW "O" WAL	05	51	49
WCS	10,000 GAL TANK CAR REVIEW "S" WCS	03	74	25
WD	PICKLE CAR REVIEW "HO" WD	10	85	45
WSM	TANK NARROW GAUGE CON REVIEW "HON3" WSM	05	67	10
	CONX10 D&RGW TANK CAR REVIEW "1/4" WSM	06	75	30

GENERAL FREIGHT PROTOTYPE DATA

	M	Y	P
4 WHEEL CARS ON US LINES 1970	08	70	70
ABREVIATIONMS IN FRT CAR REPORTING DATA	05	71	73
ARA STANDARD SAFETY APPLIANCES	02	35	49
AUTO CAR IDENTIFICATION MARKING LOCATION	12	83	171
BETTENDORF TRUCK HISTORY	06	63	61
BRAKE RIGGING FOR FREIGHT CARS OF 1880	11	68	80
CAPACITY AND LOADING LIMITS	06	37	217
COMBINATION CARS 1/2 HOPPER 1/2 BOX	06	78	125
CUSHIONED UNDERFRAMES	08	67	28
DEPRESSED CENTER FLAT CAR UNUSUAL LOADS	03	39	150
FREIGHT CAR BLUEBOOK CAR DEFINITIONS	11	55	67
FREIGHT CAR BRAKE EQUIPMENT BOOMER PETE	02	47	110
FREIGHT CAR BRAKE MECHANISMS	04	49	46
FREIGHT CAR BRAKE SYSTEMS	09	65	56
FREIGHT CAR LETTERING STANDARDS	11	34	4
FREIGHT CAR LETTERING STDS 1907 BLUEBOOK	10	57	65
FREIGHT CAR TRUCK DESIGNS	05	69	60
FREIGHT CAR TRUCK DETAILS BOOMER PETE	11	42	502
FREIGHT CAR TRUCKS BLUEBOOK	03	56	61
FREIGHT CAR UNDERBODY EQUIPMENT B. PETE	08	43	364
FREIGHT CAR UNDERBODY EQUIPMENT BLUEBOOK	06	57	59
FREIGHT TRAIN TERMINOLOGY	01	84	165
NEW FREIGHT CAR DELIVERIES BOOMER PETE	01	46	10
PAINT & LETTERING SCL FREIGHT CARS	07	68	35
PLUG DOOR OPERATION	02	68	72
POLING AND PUSH POLES	02	75	86
SAFETY APPLIANCE STANDARDS BOOMER PETE	12	45	522
SAFETY APPLIANCES ON FREIGHT CARS BLUEBK	12	56	79
STANDARD FREIGHT CAR TRUCKS	11	34	7
STENCILING "WHEN EMPTY" ON CARS	07	70	58
STRAIGHT AIR BRAKES	05	78	129
TRUCK BRAKE DETAILS	08	78	123
TRUCK MOUNTED BRAKES	11	70	87
TRUCK MOUNTED BRAKES FOR FREIGHT CARS	03	70	76
UNIT TRAINS AND THEIR MODELING	10	71	36
VERT-A-PAC CAR UP 1969 UP	10	71	51
WARTIME COMPOSITE FREIGHT CARS 1943	06	44	244
WHITE LINED CAR NUMBERS	11	66	50

GENERAL FREIGHT PLANS

	M	Y	P
ADAPTO CAR OF FUTURE PLANS ACF	01	58	31
ARCH BAR TRUCK PLAN	08	36	227
DRAWING OF SAFETY APPLIANCE LOCATIONS	12	45	523
NARROW GAUGE TRUCK PLANS	08	43	361
OLDTIME WOOD FREIGHT CAR DRAWINGS 1	08	51	19
OLDTIME WOOD FREIGHT CAR DRAWINGS 2	08	51	21
STEEL MILL SPECIAL CAR SKETCHES	11	50	16

FREIGHT CARS

GENERAL FREIGHT MODELS

	M	Y	P
ACF ADAPTO FREIGHT CAR CONSTRUCTION	01	58	28
ALUMINUM CAR SIDES	02	38	70
ARCH BAR TRUCK CONSTRUCTION	09	37	322
ARCH BAR WOOD BEAM TRUCK CONSTRUCTION	10	70	53
BUILDERS REVIEW OF ATHEARN FREIGHT CARS	03	70	22
BUILDING DETAILED FREIGHT CARS 1	01	41	5
BUILDING DETAILED FREIGHT CARS 2 (FLAT)	02	41	86
CAR LADDERS	02	38	71
CAR LOADS MOD & PT	06	76	92
CASTING YOUR OWN FREIGHT CARS	01	83	82
COMPROMISE PAINT SCHEMES MOD & PT	11	77	128
CONVERTING O GAUGE CAR KITS	08	52	58
CUSHIONED UNDERFRAME CONSTRUCTION	08	67	28
CUSTOMIZING YOUR KIT MODELS	03	56	36
DESIGNING & OBTAINING PRIVATE HERALDS	11	78	123
DEVELOPING THE FREIGHT CAR FLEET PART 1	06	77	94
DEVELOPING THE FREIGHT CAR FLEET PART 2	08	77	18
FICTITIOUS LETTERING SCHEMES MOD & PT	03	82	128
FREELANCED NARROW GAUGE FREIGHT CARS	07	81	91
FREELANCING FREIGHT CARS	11	76	54
FREIGHT CAR CONSTRUCTION	02	36	33
FREIGHT CAR HARDWARE CHOICES	04	41	209
FREIGHT CAR MODERNIZATION CONSTRUCTION	12	71	91
FREIGHT CARS IT MOD & PT	01	77	112
HOMEMADE SPRUNG TRUCKS	04	34	12
IMPROVING FREIGHT CAR REALISM	04	85	70
KADEE COUPLER BASICS	05	81	78
LITTERING FREIGHT CARS WITH A FLAIR	03	75	49
LOAD FOR DEPRESSED CENTER CAR CONSTRUCT	03	39	131
LOAD THAT REVERSES FOR OPEN CARS CONST	11	76	118
LOADS FOR FLAT CARS CONSTRUCTION	05	41	260
LOADS FOR GONDOLAS CONSTRUCTION	06	41	304
LOADS FOR OPEN CARS	07	35	170
LOADS FOR OPEN CARS CONSTRUCTION	07	36	189
LOADS OF COAL COSTRUCTION	11	49	23
LUBRICATING TRUCK JOURNALS	09	46	561
MAKING COUPLERS BY CASTING	05	45	212
MASS PRODUCING FREIGHT CARS	02	62	34
MODEL-PROTOTYPE LIST SOO FREIGHT CARS	11	82	82
MODELING NEW HIGH SPEED TRUCKS	11	34	5
MODERNIZING FREIGHT CARS CONSTRUCTION	11	73	78
MOVEABLE DRAFT GEAR FOR LONG FREIGHT CAR	11	75	56
OLD TIME WOODEN FREIGHT CAR CONSTRUCTION	08	51	18
ONE MANS MOW CAR REGISTER BARNARD	09	62	25
OUTBOARD BRAKE BEAMS CONSTRUCTION	06	61	54
OUTBOARD BRAKE BEAMS CONSTRUCTION	10	69	70
PAINT & LETTERING GUIDE L&N FREIGHT CARS	06	69	32
PLASTIC FREIGHT CAR MODIFICATIONS VARNEY	06	56	23
RAILROADS BUY ROLLING STOCK IN LARGE #S	09	77	99
REMOVABLE FLOORS AND ROOFS	09	71	73
RI NEW IMAGE CARS 1975 MOD & PT	02	76	83
SHEET METAL TRUCK CONSTRUCTION	08	35	216
SPRUNG TRUCK ADVANTAGES	01	73	94
STAFF MOUNTED BRAKE WHEELS FOR "N"	04	78	138
STEP AND GRAB IRON CONSTRUCTION	08	64	43

GENERAL FREIGHT MODELS

	M	Y	P
TRAILER HITCHES FOR FREIGHT CARS $1	10	70	72
TRUCK SPRINGING TECHNIQUES	10	47	794
UNIT TRAINS AND THEIR MODELING	10	71	36
USED CAR FLEET FOR YOUR RAILROAD	03	85	112
VENEER CAR CONVERSION TECHNIQUES	09	73	52
WEIGHTING FREIGHT CARS	02	48	102
WEIGHTING FREIGHT CARS	05	73	77
WORKING UNCOUPLING RODS	06	50	25

GENERAL FREIGHT MODEL REVIEWS

	M	Y	P
1860 FREIGHT CAR REVIEW "HO" M	06	58	14
ARCH BAR TRUCK REVIEW "ON2" SRE	07	77	31
BALSA CAR KIT REVIEW "3/16" CMS	07	37	262
COAL LOADS REVIEW ROLLER BEARING MODELS	06	77	46
EMBOSSED METAL FREIGHT CARS V	02	39	108
FINESCALE ARCH BAR TRUCK REVIEW "1/4" CE	09	77	39
FIVE FREIGHT CAR ASSORTMENT "N" KADEE	06	77	48
FIVE FREIGHT CAR SET "N" KADEE	09	77	44
FREIGHT CAR KIT REVIEW "O" POLK	11	41	599
FREIGHT CAR KIT REVIEW "HO" COMET MODELS	05	41	280
FREIGHT CAR KIT REVIEW "O" HA	04	40	240
FREIGHT CAR REVIEW "HO" PHO	07	48	508
FREIGHT CAR REVIEW "O" LIONEL	04	41	227
FREIGHT CAR REVIEW "G" KTTW	08	85	48
FREIGHT CAR REVIEW "HO" KL	11	69	30
FREIGHT CAR REVIEW "N" AT	11	67	16
FREIGHT CAR REVIEW "N" AUR	01	69	17
FREIGHT CAR REVIEW "N" CC	12	67	16
FREIGHT CAR REVIEW "N" AT	02	68	20
FREIGHT CAR REVIEW "N" LIMA	02	69	22
FREIGHT CAR REVIEW "O" MERLE FABER	09	39	482
FREIGHT CAR REVIEW "O" OHIO MODEL WORKS	03	41	176
FREIGHT CAR REVIEW "Z" MKL	03	85	35
FREIGHT CAR REVIEW "Z" KD	02	85	39
FREIGHT CAR REVIEWS "HO" VARNEY	04	42	202
FREIGHT CAR REVIEWS "O" COMM	03	42	151
FREIGHT CAR REVIEWS "N" CC	04	68	15
FREIGHT TRAIN KIT REVIEW "HO" SB	02	49	70
FREIGHT TRAIN SETS REVIEW "O/027" WRL	04	83	48
OLDTIME FREIGHT CAR REVIEW 1 "HO" AHM	11	66	22
OLDTIME FREIGHT CAR REVIEW 2 "HO" AHM	12	66	14
PLUG DOOR SET LISTING "HO" DETAILS WEST	10	77	48
ROLLERBEARING TRUCK REVIEW "HO" FMC	05	77	36
WEATHERED FREIGHT CAR REVIEW ATH HO MW	02	79	49
WELDED STEEL CARS "O" HOI	01	41	56
WHEEL SET LISTING "ON3" DURANGO PRESS	09	77	44
WOOD SIDE FREIGHT CAR REVIEW "O" ATA	03	35	82

FREIGHT CARS

GENERAL FREIGHT MODEL REVIEWS BY MFG.

```
MFG                                           M  Y  P
---    --------------------------------------- -- -- ---
AHM    OLDTIME FREIGHT CAR REVIEW 2 "HO" AHM   12 66 14
       OLDTIME FREIGHT CAR REVIEW 1 "HO" AHM   11 66 22
AT     FREIGHT CAR REVIEW "N"   AT             11 67 16
       FREIGHT CAR REVIEW "N"   AT             02 68 20
ATA    WOOD SIDE FREIGHT CAR REVIEW  "O"  ATA  03 35 82
AUR    FREIGHT CAR REVIEW "N"   AUR            01 69 17
CC     FREIGHT CAR REVIEW "N"   CC             12 67 16
       FREIGHT CAR REVIEWS "N"  CC             04 68 15
CE     FINESCALE ARCH BAR TRUCK REVIEW "1/4" CE 09 77 39
CMO    FREIGHT CAR KIT REVIEW "HO" COMET MODELS 05 41 280
CMS    BALSA CAR KIT REVIEW  "3/16"    CMS     07 37 262
COMM   FREIGHT CAR REVIEWS  "O"   COMM         03 42 151
DP     WHEEL SET LISTING "ON3" DURANGO PRESS   09 77 44
DW     PLUG DOOR SET LISTING "HO" DETAILS WEST 10 77 48
FMC    ROLLERBEARING TRUCK REVIEW  "HO"  FMC   05 77 36
HA     FREIGHT CAR KIT REVIEW "O"   HA         04 40 240
HOI    WELDED STEEL CARS    "O"   HOI          01 41 56
KD     FIVE FREIGHT CAR ASSORTMENT   "N"  KADEE 06 77 48
       FIVE FREIGHT CAR SET     "N"    KADEE   09 77 44
       FREIGHT CAR REVIEW "Z" KD               02 85 39
KL     FREIGHT CAR REVIEW "HO" KL              11 69 30
KTTW   FREIGHT CAR REVIEW "G"   KTTW           08 85 48
LIMA   FREIGHT CAR REVIEW "N" LIMA             02 69 22
LIO    FREIGHT CAR REVIEW    "O"   LIONEL      04 41 227
M      1860 FREIGHT CAR REVIEW "HO"  M         06 58 14
MF     FREIGHT CAR REVIEW "O" MERLE FABER      09 39 482
MKL    FREIGHT CAR REVIEW "Z"  MKL             03 85 35
OMW    FREIGHT CAR REVIEW "O" OHIO MODEL WORKS 03 41 176
PHO    FREIGHT CAR REVIEW       "HO"    PHO    07 48 508
POLK   FREIGHT CAR KIT REVIEW   "O"     POLK   11 41 599
R      COAL LOADS REVIEW ROLLER BEARING MODELS 06 77 46
SB     FREIGHT TRAIN KIT REVIEW    "HO"   SB   02 49 70
SRE    ARCH BAR TRUCK REVIEW "ON2" SRE         07 77 31
V      EMBOSSED METAL FREIGHT CARS  V          02 39 108
       FREIGHT CAR REVIEWS   "HO"  VARNEY      04 42 202
WRL    FREIGHT TRAIN SETS REVIEW "O/O27"  WRL  04 83 48
```

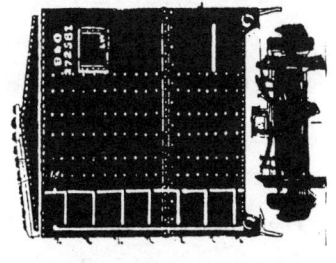

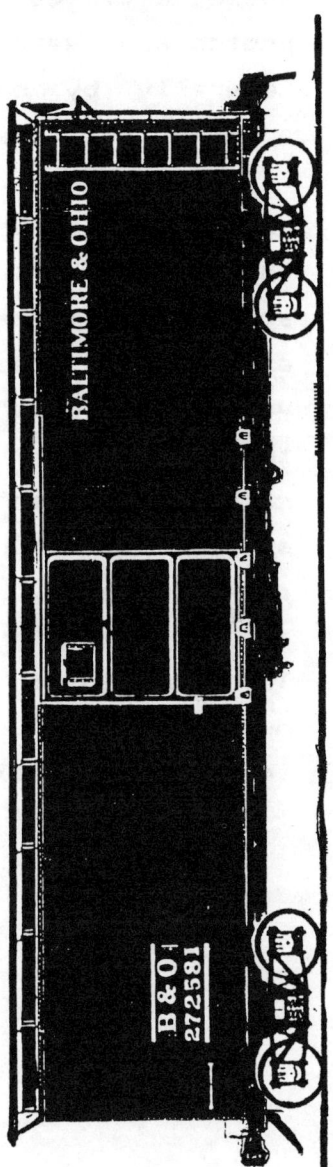

BILL OF LADING   NON-REVENUE EQUIPMENT

This section has two subsections: Cabooses and Maintanence of Way Equipment. Easch subsection is further broken down into the following subject areas:

Prototype data includes articles and specifications on the real thing. In many instances there are photographs with these articles that did not get special billing in the photograph section. The plans and drawings are just that. Generally by our convention a drawing is more detailed than a plan, but this is not a hard and fast rule. The plans are listed twice: once alphabetically and once by road. The photo section shows details or unusual photos of interest to the researcher. Obviously we did not list all photos that appear in these magazines. The model section highlights exceptional models and tells how to build/kitbash/rebuild your own "gems". Finally the model review section list those itmes that have a chance of surviving as a recognizable entity. Included is the description, scale, and manufacturer. These are listed three ways: alphabetically, by road, and by manufacturer.

The descriptor line includes a description of the car, its number, class, builder and year built. This data is included if available and if space permits.

MANIFEST NON-REVENUE CARS

	PAGE
NON-REVENUE EQUIPMENT	112
CABOOSES	114
CABOOSE PROTOTYPE DATA	114
CABOOSE PLANS	114
CABOOSE PLANS BY ROAD	115
CABOOSE PHOTOS	116
CABOOSE MODELS	117
CABOOSE MODEL REVIEWS	118
CABOOSE MODEL REVIEWS BY ROAD	119
CABOOSE MODEL REVIEWS BY MFG.	119
MOW EQUIPMENT	120
MOW PROTOTYPE DATA	120
MOW PLANS	120
MOW PLANS BY ROAD	121
MOW PHOTOS	121
MOW MODELS	121
MOW MODEL REVIEWS	122
MOW MODEL REVIEWS BY ROAD	123
MOW MODEL REVIEWS BY MFG.	123

NON-REVENUE EQUIPMENT

CABOOSE PROTOTYPE DATA	M	Y	P
BRAKE RIGGING ON 4 WHEEL CABOOSES	12	70	90
CABOOSE BRAKE GEAR	10	77	130
CABOOSE MODULAR DESIGN	06	74	35
CABOOSE PROTOTYPE INFORMATION	08	66	54
CABOOSE SAFETY APPLIANCES BLUEBOOK	09	57	65
CABOOSE TRACKS WHAT ARE THEY?	11	85	151
CABOOSES OF C&PA	10	78	93
CABOOSES OF NYO&W	11	74	24
CABOOSES, CRUMMIES AND SUCH	07	48	456
CLASSIFICATION LIGHTS ON MA&PA	09	82	138
ELIMINATION OF CABOOSES & EQUIP REPLACE	01	85	161
FAIRWELL CABOOSE	05	83	1245
PAINT & LETTERING SCL CABOOSES	07	68	36
STANDARD WAY CAR OF C&NW	07	79	93
TRANSFER CABOOSE ITS FUNCTION	08	75	85
TRANSFER CABOOSES	01	78	132
WOOD CABOOSES OF CN 1925	08	84	84
WOOD CABOOSES OF FEC 1926	08	85	60

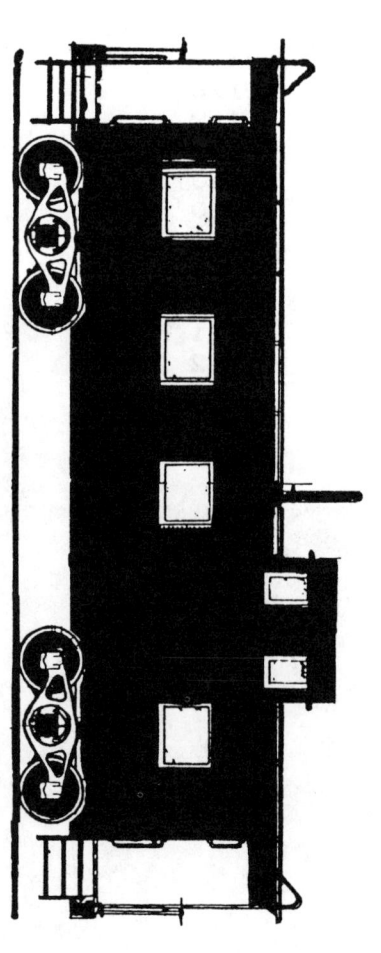

CABOOSE PLANS	M	Y	P
4 WHEEL CABOOSE PLANS D&RGW #0578 1890	02	84	70
4 WHEEL CABOOSE PLANS MA&PA #2005	01	49	29
4 WHEEL TRANSFER CABOOSE PLAN B&O #C1180	09	46	554
4 WHEEL(NO CUPOLA)CABOOSE PLAN L&NE #514	12	50	53
50 FOOT CABOOSE PLANS ACL #0802	02	70	38
BAGGAGE-PASSENGER-CABOOSE PLANS SLC	01	36	17
BAY WINDOW CABOOSE PLANS MILW #01859	12	39	638
BOBBER CABOOSE PLANS ET&WNC #205	07	81	62
BOBBER CABOOSE PLANS LV #96002	06	83	73
CABIN CAR CLASS N8 PLANS PRR #478084	04	82	80
CABOOSE #981679 CLASS N-6B PLANS PRR	12	42	564
CABOOSE 4 WHEEL PLANS CP	04	78	112
CABOOSE CA-11 PLANS UP #25800 PAC 1979	04	81	83
CABOOSE CABIN CAR CLSS N5A PL PRR#477776	11	68	51
CABOOSE CABIN CLASS N5B PLANS CORRECTION	03	69	71
CABOOSE COMBINE PLANS CB&Q #3971	12	54	33
CABOOSE NARROW GAUGE PLANS D&RGW #0505	06	70	44
CABOOSE NARROW GAUGE PLANS D&RGW #0574	01	64	30
CABOOSE OF 1915 PLANS BR&P #302	08	58	45
CABOOSE OF 1917 PLANS CGW #357	01	60	74
CABOOSE PLANS B&O #C1917	06	49	32
CABOOSE PLANS ATSF #1951	05	50	61
CABOOSE PLANS LA&T #1307	05	62	31
CABOOSE PLANS SOO #176	10	49	43
CABOOSE PLANS ATSF #1951	01	49	37
CABOOSE PLANS B&O #C1900	08	55	23
CABOOSE PLANS B&O #C1917	04	44	170
CABOOSE PLANS C&PA	10	78	93
CABOOSE PLANS CGW #355	08	76	47
CABOOSE PLANS CGW #357 1917	08	76	47
CABOOSE PLANS CLASS N-8 PRR #478084	10	61	46
CABOOSE PLANS CMI #407 SCC 1887	07	66	46
CABOOSE PLANS CNJ # 91382	08	39	390
CABOOSE PLANS CNJ # 91531 1942	03	82	84
CABOOSE PLANS CP	01	59	76
CABOOSE PLANS CV #4016	07	53	42
CABOOSE PLANS CV #4016 CLASS NE 1910	02	53	61
CABOOSE PLANS D&RGW #0574 NARROW GAUGE	02	45	74
CABOOSE PLANS DL&W #723	02	52	38
CABOOSE PLANS ERIE # 04732	11	42	500
CABOOSE PLANS FOUR VARIATIONS D&H	05	72	40
CABOOSE PLANS GN #X611 1939	09	44	406
CABOOSE PLANS KCS #582 1900	01	57	45
CABOOSE PLANS M&U	04	70	32
CABOOSE PLANS MA&PA #2002	12	64	48
CABOOSE PLANS MP	01	36	17
CABOOSE PLANS N&W #518400	08	45	315
CABOOSE PLANS N5 PRR	01	36	17
CABOOSE PLANS NP #1608	08	47	623
CABOOSE PLANS PRR #476010 CLASS ND 1905	07	52	41
CABOOSE PLANS PRR #479823 CLASS NDA 1914	07	52	41
CABOOSE PLANS READING #90258	01	54	77
CABOOSE PLANS READING #92812 OF 1931	04	39	170
CABOOSE PLANS RF&P #913	01	62	35
CABOOSE PLANS RI #18369	12	57	70

NON-REVENUE EQUIPMENT

CABOOSE PLANS	M	Y	P
CABOOSE PLANS SERIES 021 CS&CC #023 1902	09	72	36
CABOOSE PLANS SOO #176	08	54	22
CABOOSE PLANS SR&RL #551 1905 NARROW GAU	02	77	76
CABOOSE PLANS URR C-11	02	48	101
CABOOSE SIDE DOOR PLANS C&GR #508	06	72	57
CABOOSE WITH VESTIBULE END PLANS CGW #401	12	60	50
COMBINATION CABOOSE PLANS	04	52	34
COMBINATION CABOOSE PLANS CBELT #2332	05	60	54
COMBINATION CABOOSE PLANS SIERRA #9	05	68	28
DROVERS "BANANNA" CABOOSE PLANS IC #17	08	57	38
FOUR WHEEL CABOOSE #90258 PLANS R	05	37	171
FOUR WHEEL CABOOSE PLANS CB&Q #14973	11	55	42
FOUR WHEEL CABOOSE PLANS CP #3007	11	75	85
FOUR WHEEL CABOOSE PLANS D&H #10	10	65	33
FOUR WHEEL CABOOSE PLANS DL&W #506	12	44	529
FOUR WHEEL CABOOSE PLANS HU&BT #3	08	53	51
FOUR WHEEL CABOOSE PLANS MA&PA #2005 15'	05	45	200
FOUR WHEEL CABOOSE PLANS MILW #0478	03	66	51
FOUR WHEEL CABOOSE PLANS NYC #17000	05	62	31
FOUR WHEEL CABOOSE PLANS NYO&W #8105	01	74	69
FOUR WHEEL CABOOSE PLANS PRR	01	36	17
FOUR WHEEL CABOOSE PLANS PRR #980000	09	60	50
FOUR WHEEL WM #1216 PLANS	03	36	65
FREE LANCE 38' CABOOSE PLANS	12	34	10
INTERNATIONAL CABOOSE PLANS DT&I #144	06	74	39
LOGGING CABOOSE PLANS RAY #18	10	66	30
MIXED TRAIN CABOOSE PLANS MKT #350	07	63	53
OUTSIDE BRACED CABOOSE PLANS IC #8045	05	73	46
SIDE DOOR CABOOSE PLANS ATSF #849	08	52	40
SIDE DOOR CABOOSE PLANS ATSF #849	03	57	55
SIDE DOOR CABOOSE PLANS CBELT #2332	07	48	458
SIDE DOOR NARROW GAUGE CABOOSE PLAN	12	57	50
STANDARD WAY CAR PLANS C&NW #1501	07	79	93
STEEL CABOOSE PLANS MILW #01601	02	38	69
STEEL CABOOSE PLANS SEA #5602 1949	06	53	43
STEEL CABOOSE PLANS SOO #2	10	67	50
STEEL CABOOSE PLANS SOO #2 CORRECTION	01	68	70
TRANSFER CABOOSE PLANS KCT #513	07	57	52
USRA STANDARD 8 WHEEL CABOOSE PLANS 1918	01	79	97
WOOD CABOOSE PLANS CN #78021 1925	08	84	85
WOOD CABOOSE PLANS FEC #714 1926	08	85	60
WOOD SHEATH UP 3500 SERIES CABOOSE PLANS	12	41	624
WOOD SHEATHED CABOOSE DRAWING CN #78021	05	85	67
WOOD SHEATHED CABOOSE PLANS B&M #104610	04	60	38
WOOD SHEATHED CABOOSE PLANS C&O #90769	12	72	80
WOOD SHEATHED CABOOSE PLANS CN #78258	02	63	48
WOOD SHEATHED CABOOSE PLANS EBT #28	09	61	44
WOOD SHEATHED CABOOSE PLANS LV #95342	11	67	39
WOOD SHEATHED CABOOSE PLANS SOO #105	09	68	54
WOOD SHEATHED CABOOSE PLANS WABASH #465	01	64	35
WOOD SIDE DOOR CABOOSE PLANS CPA #45 1872	12	84	140
WOODEN CABOOSE PLANS NYC #19463	08	46	504
WOODEN SIDE DOOR CABOOSE PLANS FRIS #348	10	46	665
WOODEN SIDE DOOR CABOOSE PLANS IC #9405	07	71	60

RD	CABOOSE PLANS BY ROAD	M	Y	P
ACL	50 FOOT CABOOSE PLANS ACL #0802	02	70	38
ATSF	SIDE DOOR CABOOSE PLANS ATSF #849	08	52	40
	CABOOSE PLANS ATSF #1951	05	50	61
	SIDE DOOR CABOOSE PLANS ATSF #849	03	57	55
	CABOOSE PLANS ATSF #1951	01	49	37
B&M	WOOD SHEATHED CABOOSE PLANS B&M #104610	04	60	38
B&O	4 WHEEL TRANSFER CABOOSE PLAN B&O #C1180	09	46	554
	CABOOSE PLANS B&O #C1917	04	44	170
	CABOOSE PLANS B&O #C1900	08	55	23
	CABOOSE PLANS B&O #C1917	06	49	32
BR&P	CABOOSE OF 1915 PLANS BR&P #302	08	58	45
C&GR	CABOOSE SIDE DOOR PLANS C&GR #508	06	72	57
C&NW	STANDARD WAY CAR PLANS C&NW #1501	07	79	93
C&O	WOOD SHEATHED CABOOSE PLANS C&O #90769	12	72	80
C&PA	CABOOSE PLANS C&PA	10	78	93
CB&Q	FOUR WHEEL CABOOSE PLANS CB&Q #14973	11	55	42
	CABOOSE COMBINE PLANS CB&Q #3971	12	54	33
CBELT	COMBINATION CABOOSE PLANS CBELT #2332	05	60	54
	SIDE DOOR CABOOSE PLANS CBELT #2332	07	48	458
CGW	CABOOSE OF 1917 PLANS CGW #357	01	60	74
	CABOOSE WITH VESTIBULE END PLANS CGW #401	12	60	50
	CABOOSE PLANS CGW #355	08	76	47
	CABOOSE PLANS CGW #357 1917	08	76	47
CMI	CABOOSE PLANS CMI #407 SCC 1887	07	66	46
CN	WOOD SHEATHED CABOOSE DRAWING CN #78021	05	85	67
	WOOD SHEATHED CABOOSE PLANS CN #78258	02	63	48
	WOOD CABOOSE PLANS CN #78021 1925	08	84	85
CNJ	CABOOSE PLANS CNJ #91531 1942	03	82	84
	CABOOSE PLANS CNJ #91382	08	39	390
CP	FOUR WHEEL CABOOSE PLANS CP #3007	11	75	85
	CABOOSE PLANS CP	01	59	76
	CABOOSE 4 WHEEL PLANS CP	04	78	112
CPA	WOOD SIDE DOOR CABOOSE PLANS CPA #45 1872	12	84	140
CS&CC	CABOOSE PLANS SERIES 021 CS&CC #023 1902	09	72	36
CV	CABOOSE PLANS CV #4016 CLASS NE 1910	02	53	61
	CABOOSE PLANS CV #4016	07	53	42
D&H	FOUR WHEEL CABOOSE PLANS D&H #10	10	65	33
	CABOOSE PLANS FOUR VARIATIONS D&H	05	72	40
D&RGW	CABOOSE NARROW GAUGE PLANS D&RGW #0574	01	64	30
	CABOOSE PLANS D&RGW #0574 NARROW GAUGE	02	45	74
	CABOOSE NARROW GAUGE PLANS D&RGW #0505	06	70	44
	4 WHEEL CABOOSE PLANS D&RGW #0578 1890	02	84	70
DL&W	CABOOSE PLANS DL&W #723	02	52	38
	FOUR WHEEL CABOOSE PLANS DL&W #506	12	44	529
DT&I	INTERNATIONAL CABOOSE PLANS DT&I #144	06	74	39
E	CABOOSE PLANS ERIE #04732	11	42	500
EBT	WOOD SHEATHED CABOOSE PLANS EBT #28	09	61	44
ET&WNC	BOBBER CABOOSE PLANS ET&WNC #205	07	81	62
FEC	WOOD CABOOSE PLANS FEC #714 1926	08	85	60
FRIS	WOODEN SIDE DOOR CABOOSE PLANS FRIS #348	10	46	665
GN	CABOOSE PLANS GN #X611 1939	09	44	406
HU&BT	FOUR WHEEL CABOOSE PLANS HU&BT #3	08	53	51
IC	DROVERS "BANANNA" CABOOSE PLANS IC #17	08	57	38
	OUTSIDE BRACED CABOOSE PLANS IC #8045	05	73	46
	WOODEN SIDE DOOR CABOOSE PLANS IC #9405	07	71	60

Stephans_Railroad_Directory

NON-REVENUE EQUIPMENT

RD	CABOOSE PLANS BY ROAD	M	Y	P
KCS	CABOOSE PLANS KCS #582 1900	01	57	45
KCT	TRANSFER CABOOSE PLANS KCT #513	07	57	52
L&NE	4 WHEEL(NO CUPOLA)CABOOSE PLAN L&NE #514	12	50	53
LA&T	CABOOSE PLANS LA&T #1307	05	62	31
LV	BOBBER CABOOSE PLANS LV #96002	06	83	73
	WOOD SHEATHED CABOOSE PLANS LV #95342	11	67	39
M&U	CABOOSE PLANS M&U	04	70	32
MA&PA	CABOOSE PLANS MA&PA #2002	12	64	48
	FOUR WHEEL CABOOSE PLANS MA&PA #2005 15'	05	45	200
	4 WHEEL CABOOSE PLANS MA&PA #2005	01	49	29
MILW	FOUR WHEEL CABOOSE PLANS MILW #0478	03	66	51
	STEEL CABOOSE PLANS MILW #01601	02	38	69
	BAY WINDOW CABOOSE PLANS MILW #01859	12	39	638
MKT	MIXED TRAIN CABOOSE PLANS MKT #350	07	63	53
MP	CABOOSE PLANS MP	01	36	17
N&W	CABOOSE PLANS N&W #518400	08	45	315
NP	CABOOSE PLANS NP #1608	08	47	623
NYC	FOUR WHEEL CABOOSE PLANS NYC #17000	05	62	31
	WOODEN CABOOSE PLANS NYC #19463	08	46	504
NYO&W	FOUR WHEEL CABOOSE PLANS NYO&W #8105	01	74	69
PRR	CABOOSE CABIN CAR CLSS N5A PL PRR#477776	11	68	51
	CABOOSE CABIN CLASS N5B PLANS CORRECTION	03	69	71
	CABOOSE PLANS CLASS N-8 PRR #478084	10	61	46
	FOUR WHEEL CABOOSE PLANS PRR #980000	09	60	50
	CABOOSE PLANS PRR #476010 CLASS ND 1905	07	52	41
	CABOOSE PLANS PRR #479823 CLASS NDA 1914	07	52	41
	CABOOSE #981679 CLASS N-6B PLANS PRR	12	42	564
	CABIN CAR CLASS N8 PLANS PRR #478084	04	82	80
	CABOOSE PLANS N5 PRR	01	36	17
	FOUR WHEEL CABOOSE PLANS PRR	01	36	17
R	FOUR WHEEL CABOOSE #90258 PLANS R	05	37	171
	CABOOSE PLANS READING #92812 OF 1931	04	39	170
	CABOOSE PLANS READING #90258	01	54	77
RAY	LOGGING CABOOSE PLANS RAY #18	10	66	30
RF&P	CABOOSE PLANS RF&P #913	01	62	35
RI	CABOOSE PLANS RI #18369	12	57	70
SEA	STEEL CABOOSE PLANS SEA #5602 1949	06	53	43
SIE	COMBINATION CABOOSE PLANS SIERRA #9	05	68	28
SLC	BAGGAGE-PASSENGER-CABOOSE PLANS SLC	01	36	17
SOO	STEEL CABOOSE PLANS SOO #2 CORRECTION	01	68	70
	WOOD SHEATHED CABOOSE PLANS SOO #105	09	68	54
	STEEL CABOOSE PLANS SOO #2	10	67	50
	CABOOSE PLANS SOO #176	08	54	22
SR&RL	CABOOSE PLANS SR&RL #551 1905 NARROW GAU	02	77	76
UP	CABOOSE CA-11 PLANS UP #25800 PAC 1979	04	81	83
	WOOD SHEATH UP 3500 SERIES CABOOSE PLANS	12	41	624
URR	CABOOSE PLANS URR C-11	02	48	101
W	WOOD SHEATHED CABOOSE PLANS WABASH #465	01	64	35
WM	FOUR WHEEL WM #1216 PLANS	03	36	65

CABOOSE PHOTOS	M	Y	P
INTERNAT'L CABOOSE PHOTO DM&IR #C200 ICC	08	74	13
INTERNAT'L EXT VISION CABOOSE BURL#13700	06	74	36
INTERNAT'L EXT VISION CABOOSE DOD #900	06	74	35
INTERNAT'L EXT VISION CABOOSE DT&I #143	06	74	38
INTERNAT'L EXT VISION CABOOSE FRIS #1288	06	74	37
INTERNAT'L EXT VISION CABOOSE MC #644	06	74	37
INTERNAT'L EXT VISION CABOOSE MP #13578	06	74	35
INTERNAT'L EXT VISION CABOOSE N&W#518525	06	74	37
INTERNAT'L EXT VISION CABOOSE NN #6	06	74	36
INTERNAT'L EXT VISION CABOOSE NP #10401	06	74	37
INTERNAT'L EXT VISION CABOOSE SOO #58	06	74	35
INTERNAT'L EXT VISION CABOOSE SP&S #900	06	74	36
SIDE DOOR CABOOSE ATSF #915 PHOTO	12	42	566

NON-REVENUE EQUIPMENT

CABOOSE MODELS		M	Y	P
BAY WINDOW CABOOSE MODELS FOR SOUTHERN		10	84	78
BOBBER CABOOSE OF LV CONSTRUCTION		06	83	66
BRASS CABOOSE FINISHING TECHNIQUES		08	83	72
BUILDING A CABOOSE IN STYRENE		02	84	66
C&W CABOOSE	MOD & PT	02	76	84
CABIN CAR KITBASH PRR CLASS N8 & N6		04	82	79
CABOOSE AA #2841 NEW IMAGE	MOD & PT	06	80	110
CABOOSE ATSF	MOD & PT	06	78	100
CABOOSE B&O SYSTEM	MOD & PT	07	79	113
CABOOSE C&O C-20 IN 1960'S	MOD & PT	01	82	127
CABOOSE CONRAIL CLASS N8	MOD & PT	08	80	113
CABOOSE CONSTRUCTION	$1	07	53	41
CABOOSE CONSTRUCTION C&W #355 OR 357		08	76	46
CABOOSE CONSTRUCTION CNJ		08	39	387
CABOOSE CONSTRUCTION CP		01	59	74
CABOOSE CONSTRUCTION ERIE #04732		11	42	500
CABOOSE CONSTRUCTION SOO "O"	$1	08	54	20
CABOOSE DETAILING 'NEAT CABEESE'		07	73	38
CABOOSE GB&W	MOD & PT	08	75	22
CABOOSE GM&O	MOD & PT	10	75	86
CABOOSE GTW FROM ATSF	MOD & PT	03	81	134
CABOOSE KIT ASSEMBLY "O" WALTERS		09	48	597
CABOOSE LI	MOD & PT	04	77	92
CABOOSE MILW #990074	MOD & PT	03	77	99
CABOOSE N&W CLASS C-20	MOD & PT	04	83	131
CABOOSE OSCILLATION HOW TO CORRECT		08	78	121
CABOOSE PARTLY FROM SCRATCH		02	70	38
CABOOSE SANTA FE CLASS CE-8	MOD & PT	11	81	130
CABOOSE SCRATCHBUILDING		02	77	75
CABOOSE UP CA-11	MOD & PT	04	81	82
CABOOSE-COMBINE CONSTRUCTION		05	60	53
CABOOSE-COMBINE CONSTRUCTION		12	54	30
CABOOSELESS REAR PROTECTION MODELING		01	85	161
CABOOSES NEW HAVEN	MOD & PT	06	82	111
CONCOR CABOOSE COUPLER CONVERSION		06	78	134
CONVERT PASS CAR TRUCK TO BOOBER CABOOSE		04	78	112
DECREPIT CABOOSE CONSTRUCTION	$1	03	64	36
DOME FLASHER FOR CABOOSES		04	73	72
DRESSING UP THE BACHMANN CABOOSE		11	84	112
EASIEST CABOOSE DETAILING		12	73	71
FOUR WHEEL CABOOSE CONST CB&Q #14970	$1	11	55	43
FOUR WHEEL CABOOSE CONSTRUCTION		01	63	38
FOUR WHEEL CABOOSE CONSTRUCTION "TT"		01	54	76
FREE LANCE CABOOSE OF SHEET METAL		12	34	10
KITBASHED TRANSFER CABOOSE		01	78	104
MAINLINE CABOOSE FROM ATH WORK CABOOSE		07	72	42
MARKER LIGHTS DELUXE		02	76	74
MARKER LIGHTS THAT WORK CONSTRUCTION		04	67	52
MARKER LIGHTS THAT WORK CONSTRUCTION.		03	49	26
MODELING MODERN CABOOSES		06	74	42
MODERN LOGGING CABOOSE	MOD & PT	08	77	101
MODIFICATIONS OF KINSMAN CABOOSE	KSC	07	56	36
MOM CABOOSE FREELANCE "7/16"	DYXIN	02	83	91
MOM CB&Q 4 WHEEL CABOOSE "1/20"	CUPO	05	81	93
MOM COTTON BELT CABOOSE "O"	WILSON	05	83	83

CABOOSE MODELS		M	Y	P
MOM SR&RL CABOOSE #551 "1/2"°	HOUGHTON	02	84	77
N&W CABOOSE	MOD & PT	11	77	129
NARROW GAUGE CABOOSE CONSTRUCTION		12	57	50
NARROW GAUGE CABOOSE CONSTRUCTION		07	54	24
NARROW GAUGE CABOOSE CONSTRUCTION D&RGW		01	64	31
NKP CABOOSE	MOD & PT	05	85	131
OLD WOOD SHEATHED CABOOSE FROM PLAS/BODY		11	65	32
OUTSIDE BRACED BAY WINDOW CABOOSE CONST		04	71	37
PAINT & LETTERING GUIDE L&N CABOOSE		06	69	34
PARTIAL REPAINTS OF NON REV EQUIP MOD&PT		08	79	106
PRR CABOOSES OF 1950'S	MOD & PT	11	83	138
REBUILT AND SPRUNG 4 WHEEL CABOOSE CONST		05	54	34
SAFETY MESSAGES FOR CABOOSES		07	78	82
SIDE DOOR CABOOSE CONSTRUCTION ATSF #849		03	57	54
SIDE DOOR CABOOSE KITBASH M&U #00 "HO"		11	85	104
STEEL CABOOSES OF CNJ		03	82	84
SUPER DETAILED CABOOSE CONST 1 B&O C1900		08	55	22
SUPER DETAILED CABOOSE CONST 2 B&O C1900		09	55	46
THREE CABOOSE KITBASH FOR PRICE OF THREE		01	85	78
TRANSFER CABOOSE CONST FROM PICTURES		02	75	56
TRANSFER CABOOSE CONSTRUCTION B&O #C1180		09	46	554
TRANSFER CABOOSE CONSTRUCTION RI		08	59	32
TRANSFER CABOOSE CONSTRUCTION RI #19045		02	58	44
TRANSFER CABOOSE MILW FROM SCRAPS		12	82	101
WOOD CABOOSE BURL	MOD & PT	01	83	138
WOOD CABOOSE CP	MOD & PT	10	78	128
WOOD SHEATHED CABOOSE SCRATCHBUILD		05	85	66

NON-REVENUE EQUIPMENT

CABOOSE MODEL REVIEWS	M	Y	P
22' RGS CABOOSE REVIEW ON3 PFM	10	59	16
30' CABOOSE REVIEW "HON3" PT	04	69	12
30' WOOD NP CABOOSE REVIEW "S" KSC	05	55	13
34' CABOOSE KIT REVIEW "HO" CV	01	52	45
38' CABOOSE KIT REVIEW "HO" V	09	49	61
4 WHEEL BOBBER CABOOSE REV "O" AT	01	73	28
4 WHEEL CABOOSE KIT REVIEW "HO" CLIF	08	52	47
4 WHEEL CABOOSE REVIEW "HO" M	03	41	174
4 WHEEL CABOOSE REVIEW "HO" AHM	04	67	15
4 WHEEL CABOOSE REVIEW "TT" SD	02	54	22
4 WHEEL CABOOSE REVIEW C&S#1006 "HO" PFM	10	75	27
4 WHEEL CABOOSE REVIEW PRR "1/4" AMBROID	11	78	47
40' MILW CABOOSE REVIEW "HO" LA	09	66	12
8 WHEEL EBT CABOOSE REVIEW "HON3" LABELLE	09	64	11
ACF CABOOSE REVIEW ATSF "HO" ATH 1930	07	57	14
B&O CLASS I-5B BAY W CABOOSE REV "HO" TI	08	68	16
BAY WINDOW CABOOSE GN "HO" OL	11	85	58
BAY WINDOW CABOOSE P&LE REVIEW "O" ALCO	05	76	36
BAY WINDOW CABOOSE REVIEW "HO" ATH	07	68	14
BAY WINDOW CABOOSE REVIEW "HO" TI 1920	02	67	12
BICENTENNIAL CABOOSE LISTING "N" KADEE	02	77	47
BOBBER CABOOSE KIT REVIEW "HO" MEW	03	55	8
BOBBER CABOOSE LISTING DL&W "HO" EMP	10	78	54
BOBBER CABOOSE LISTING M&E "HO" EMP	10	78	54
CABIN CAR PRR CLASS N5C REVIEW "N" QC	05	80	40
CABOOSE B&M NARROW CUPOLA REV "HO" MDX	07	85	46
CABOOSE B&M WIDE CUPOLA REVIEW "HO" MDX	07	85	46
CABOOSE CLASS N6A PRR REVIEW "O" ALCO	08	76	34
CABOOSE CLASS NE5 NH REVIEW "O" ALCO	12	76	34
CABOOSE D&RGW #0584 REVIEW "ON3" CB	02	77	29
CABOOSE D&RGW REVIEW "1/4" PFM	12	78	64
CABOOSE GN BAY WINDOW REVIEW "HO" MDX	07	85	46
CABOOSE GN CLASS 200 REVIEW "HO" AMB	11	56	16
CABOOSE KIT REVIEW "HO" WAL	07	48	508
CABOOSE KIT REVIEW "HO" SS	02	49	76
CABOOSE KIT REVIEW "O" WAL	03	48	226
CABOOSE KIT REVIEW "TT" HP	03	48	224
CABOOSE KIT REVIEW "HO" MDC	01	51	63
CABOOSE KIT REVIEW "HO" SS	01	51	62
CABOOSE LISTING DL&W "S" SU	07	77	42
CABOOSE MA&PA REVIEW "HO" OVERLAND MODEL	12	78	68
CABOOSE NYO&W SERIES 800 REVIEW "HO" NPP	07	72	23
CABOOSE PRR REVIEW "O" MG	12	54	18
CABOOSE REVIEW "S" NSM	08	48	575
CABOOSE REVIEW "Z" KD	02	85	39
CABOOSE REVIEW "O" LOBAUGH	08	37	301
CABOOSE REVIEW "O" SAGINAW PATTERN & MFG	01	41	55
CABOOSE RGS REVIEW "HON3" EBV 1902 RGS	02	79	47
CABOOSE/COMBINE D&RGW REVIEW "ON3" PS	11	79	46
CENTER CUPOLA CABOOSE REVIEW "HO" V	11	50	53
COMBINATION CABOOSE KIT REVIEW "HO" ACM	08	50	47
COMPACT BODY CABOOSE UP CA-11 REV "HO" OM	03	80	38
DROVERS CABOOSE ATSF REVIEW "HO" H 1930	09	74	26
EMBOSSED SIDE CABOOSE REVIEW "HO" V	10	39	542
EXTENDED VISION CABOOSE REV "HO" ATH ICC	08	73	19

CABOOSE MODEL REVIEWS	M	Y	P
EXTENDED VISION CABOOSE REVIEW "1/4" AT	02	72	32
FOUR WHEEL CABOOSE REVIEW "HO" KD	07	62	13
INTERNATIONAL CABOOSE REVIEW "HO" OM	04	82	40
LOGGING CABOOSE REVIEW "HON3" DP	10	78	52
MKT WOOD CABOOSE REVIEW "HO" HALLMARK	11	74	34
OUTSIDE BRACED CABOOSE NC&SL REV "HO" AMB	06	58	10
OUTSIDE BRACED CABOOSE REVIEW "HO" DN	11	50	64
OUTSIDE BRACED CABOOSE REVIEW "HO" MDC	11	70	29
SHORT CABOOSE LISTING D&RGW "ON3" WSM	06	77	48
SHORT CABOOSE REVIEW D&RGW "HO" QC	07	78	48
SIDE DOOR CABOOSE KIT REVIEW "O" TC	01	50	80
SIDE DOOR CB&Q CABOOSE REVIEW "HO" TI	10	66	14
STANDARD CABOOSE C&NW REVIEW "HO" TI	07	67	14
STANDARD CABOOSE REVIEW "Z" MKL	03	85	35
STEEL CABIN CAR PRR REV "HO" ALCO 1914	06	83	38
STEEL CABOOSE C&O REVIEW "HO" NPP	12	84	48
STEEL CABOOSE R REVIEW "HO" NPP 1935	09	73	22
STEEL FRAME WOOD CABOOSE REVIEW "N" KD	11	75	28
WELDED STEEL GN CABOOSE REVIEW "HO" PFM	03	58	15
WEYERHAEUSER CABOOSE REVIEW "HO" NWSL	03	61	14
WIDE CUPOLA CABOOSE REVIEW "N" ANB	02	85	48
WOOD BAY WINDOW CABOOSE LISTING "HO" OHP	04	77	47
WOOD C&O CABOOSE REVIEW "HO" CAR SHOP	09	74	18B
WOOD CABOOSE B&O CLASS I1 REV "HO" QC	11	82	37
WOOD CABOOSE C&O REVIEW "1/4" QC	09	75	24
WOOD NYC CABOOSE REVIEW "HO" PS	11	84	60
WOOD TRUSS ROD D&H CABOOSE REV "HO" NPP	11	73	38
WOOD TRUSS ROD SOO CABOOSE REV "HO" NPP	11	72	34
WOOD UP CABOOSE REVIEW "HO" TI	11	67	16

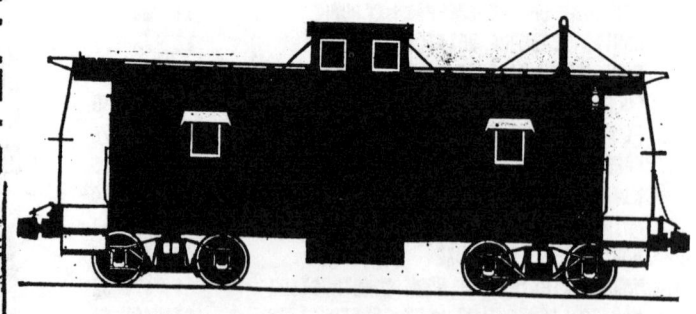

NON-REVENUE EQUIPMENT

CABOOSE MODEL REVIEWS BY ROAD

RD		M	Y	P
ATSF	ACF CABOOSE REVIEW ATSF "HO" ATH 1930	07	57	14
	DROVERS CABOOSE ATSF REVIEW "HO" H 1930	09	74	26
B&M	CABOOSE B&M WIDE CUPOLA REVIEW "HO" MDX	07	85	46
	CABOOSE B&M NARROW CUPOLA REV "HO" MDX	07	85	46
B&O	B&O CLASS I-5B BAY W CABOOSE REV "HO" TI	08	68	16
	WOOD CABOOSE B&O CLASS I1 REV "HO" QC	11	82	37
C&NW	STANDARD CABOOSE C&NW REVIEW "HO" TI	07	67	14
C&O	STEEL CABOOSE C&O REVIEW "HO" NPP	12	84	48
	WOOD CABOOSE C&O REVIEW "1/4" QC	09	75	24
	WOOD C&O CABOOSE REVIEW "HO" CAR SHOP	09	74	18B
C&S	4 WHEEL CABOOSE REVIEW C&S#1006 "HO" PFM	10	75	27
CB&Q	SIDE DOOR CB&Q CABOOSE REVIEW "HO" TI	10	66	14
D&H	WOOD TRUSS ROD D&H CABOOSE REV "HO" NPP	11	73	38
D&RGW	CABOOSE/COMBINE D&RGW REVIEW "ON3" PS	11	79	46
	CABOOSE D&RGW #0584 REVIEW "ON3" CB	02	77	29
	SHORT CABOOSE LISTING D&RGW "ON3" WSM	06	77	48
	CABOOSE D&RGW REVIEW "1/4" PFM	12	78	64
	SHORT CABOOSE REVIEW D&RGW "HO" QC	07	78	48
DL&W	CABOOSE LISTING DL&W "S" SU	07	77	42
	BOBBER CABOOSE LISTING DL&W "HO" EMP	10	78	54
EBT	8 WHEEL EBT CABOOSE REVIEW "HON3"LABELLE	09	64	11
GN	BAY WINDOW CABOOSE GN "HO" OL	11	85	58
	CABOOSE GN BAY WINDOW REVIEW "HO" MDX	07	85	46
	CABOOSE GN CLASS 200 REVIEW "HO" AMB	11	56	16
	WELDED STEEL GN CABOOSE REVIEW "HO" PFM	03	58	15
M&E	BOBBER CABOOSE LISTING M&E "HO" EMP	10	78	54
MA&PA	CABOOSE MA&PA REVIEW "HO" OVERLAND MODEL	12	78	68
MILW	40' MILW CABOOSE REVIEW "HO" LA	09	66	12
MKT	MKT WOOD CABOOSE REVIEW "HO" HALLMARK	11	74	34
NC&SL	OUTSIDE BRACED CABOOSE NC&SL REV "HO AMB	06	58	10
NH	CABOOSE CLASS NE5 NH REVIEW "O" ALCO	12	76	34
NP	30' WOOD NP CABOOSE REVIEW "S" KSC	05	55	13
NYC	WOOD NYC CABOOSE REVIEW "HO" PS	11	84	60
NYO&W	CABOOSE NYO&W SERIES 800 REVIEW "HO" NPP	07	72	23
P&LE	BAY WINDOW CABOOSE P&LE REVIEW "O" ALCO	05	76	36
PRR	CABOOSE CLASS N6A PRR REVIEW "O" ALCO	08	76	34
	STEEL CABIN CAR PRR REV "HO" ALCO 1914	06	83	38
	CABIN CAR PRR CLASS N5C REVIEW "N" QC	05	80	40
	4 WHEEL CABOOSE REVIEW PRR "1/4" AMBROID	11	78	47
R	STEEL CABOOSE R REVIEW "HO" NPP 1935	09	73	22
RGS	CABOOSE RGS REVIEW "HON3" EBV 1902 RGS	02	79	47
	22' RGS CABOOSE REVIEW ON3 PFM	10	59	16
SOO	WOOD TRUSS ROD SOO CABOOSE REV "HO" NPP	11	72	34
UP	COMPACT BODY CABOOSE UP CA-11 REV"HO" OM	03	80	38
	WOOD UP CABOOSE REVIEW "HO" TI	11	67	16

CABOOSE MODEL REVIEWS BY MFG.

MFG		M	Y	P
ACM	COMBINATION CABOOSE KIT REVIEW "HO" ACM	08	50	47
AHM	4 WHEEL CABOOSE REVIEW "HO" AHM	04	67	15
ALCO	CABOOSE CLASS N6A PRR REVIEW "O" ALCO	08	76	34
	STEEL CABIN CAR PRR REV "HO" ALCO 1914	06	83	38
	CABOOSE CLASS NE5 NH REVIEW "O" ALCO	12	76	34
	BAY WINDOW CABOOSE P&LE REVIEW "O" ALCO	05	76	36
AMB	CABOOSE GN CLASS 200 REVIEW "HO" AMB	11	56	16
	OUTSIDE BRACED CABOOSE NC&SL REV "HO AMB	06	58	10
	4 WHEEL CABOOSE REVIEW PRR "1/4" AMBROID	11	78	47
ANB	WIDE CUPOLA CABOOSE REVIEW "N" ANB	02	85	48
AT	4 WHEEL BOBBER CABOOSE REV "O" AT	01	73	28
	EXTENDED VISION CABOOSE REVIEW "1/4" AT	02	72	32
ATH	BAY WINDOW CABOOSE REVIEW "HO" ATH	07	68	14
	ACF CABOOSE REVIEW ATSF "HO" ATH 1930	07	57	14
	EXTENDED VISION CABOOSE REV "HO" ATH ICC	08	73	19
CB	CABOOSE D&RGW #0584 REVIEW "ON3" CB	02	77	29
CLIF	4 WHEEL CABOOSE KIT REVIEW "HO" CLIF	08	52	47
CS	WOOD C&O CABOOSE REVIEW "HO" CAR SHOP	09	74	18B
CV	34' CABOOSE KIT REVIEW "HO" CV	01	52	45
DN	OUTSIDE BRACED CABOOSE REVIEW "HO" DN	11	50	64
DP	LOGGING CABOOSE REVIEW "HON3" DP	10	78	52
EBV	CABOOSE RGS REVIEW "HON3" EBV 1902 RGS	02	79	47
EMP	BOBBER CABOOSE LISTING M&E "HO" EMP	10	78	54
	BOBBER CABOOSE LISTING DL&W "HO" EMP	10	78	54
H	DROVERS CABOOSE ATSF REVIEW "HO" H 1930	09	74	26
	MKT WOOD CABOOSE REVIEW "HO" HALLMARK	11	74	34
HP	CABOOSE KIT REVIEW "TT" HP	03	48	224
KD	CABOOSE REVIEW "Z" KD	02	85	39
	STEEL FRAME WOOD CABOOSE REVIEW "N" KD	11	75	28
	FOUR WHEEL CABOOSE REVIEW "HO" KD	07	62	13
	BICENTENNIAL CABOOSE LISTING "N" KADEE	02	77	47
KSC	30' WOOD NP CABOOSE REVIEW "S" KSC	05	55	13
LA	8 WHEEL EBT CABOOSE REVIEW "HON3"LABELLE	09	64	11
	40' MILW CABOOSE REVIEW "HO" LA	09	66	12
M	4 WHEEL CABOOSE REVIEW "HO" M	03	41	174
MDC	CABOOSE KIT REVIEW "HO" MDC	01	51	63
	OUTSIDE BRACED CABOOSE REVIEW "HO" MDC	11	70	29
MDX	CABOOSE B&M WIDE CUPOLA REVIEW "HO" MDX	07	85	46
	CABOOSE B&M NARROW CUPOLA REV "HO" MDX	07	85	46
	CABOOSE GN BAY WINDOW REVIEW "HO" MDX	07	85	46
MEW	BOBBER CABOOSE KIT REVIEW "HO" MEW	03	55	8
MG	CABOOSE PRR REVIEW "O" MG	12	54	18
MKL	STANDARD CABOOSE REVIEW "Z" MKL	03	85	35
NPP	STEEL CABOOSE C&O REVIEW "HO" NPP	12	84	48
	STEEL CABOOSE R REVIEW "HO" NPP 1935	09	73	22
	WOOD TRUSS ROD D&H CABOOSE REV "HO" NPP	11	73	38
	CABOOSE NYO&W SERIES 800 REVIEW "HO" NPP	07	72	23
	WOOD TRUSS ROD SOO CABOOSE REV "HO" NPP	11	72	34
NSM	CABOOSE REVIEW "S" NSM	08	48	575
NWSL	WEYERHAEUSER CABOOSE REVIEW "HO" NWSL	03	61	14
OHP	WOOD BAY WINDOW CABOOSE LISTING "HO" OHP	04	77	47
OL	BAY WINDOW CABOOSE GN "HO" OL	11	85	58
OM	COMPACT BODY CABOOSE UP CA-11 REV"HO" OM	03	80	38
	CABOOSE MA&PA REVIEW "HO" OVERLAND MODEL	12	78	68

NON-REVENUE EQUIPMENT

CABOOSE MODEL REVIEWS BY MFG.

MFG		M	Y	P
	INTERNATIONAL CABOOSE REVIEW "HO" OM	04	82	40
PFM	4 WHEEL CABOOSE REVIEW C&S#1006 "HO" PFM	10	75	27
	WELDED STEEL GN CABOOSE REVIEW "HO" PFM	03	58	15
	22' RGS CABOOSE REVIEW ON3 PFM	10	59	16
	CABOOSE D&RGW REVIEW "1/4" PFM	12	78	64
PS	WOOD NYC CABOOSE REVIEW "HO" PS	11	84	60
	CABOOSE/COMBINE D&RGW REVIEW "ON3" PS	11	79	46
PT	30' CABOOSE REVIEW "HON3" PT	04	69	12
QC	CABIN CAR PRR CLASS N5C REVIEW "N" QC	05	80	40
	WOOD CABOOSE C&O REVIEW "1/4" QC	09	75	24
	SHORT CABOOSE REVIEW D&RGW "HO" QC	07	78	48
	WOOD CABOOSE B&O CLASS I1 REV "HO" QC	11	82	37
SD	4 WHEEL CABOOSE REVIEW "TT" SD	02	54	22
SPM	CABOOSE REVIEW "O" SAGINAW PATTERN & MFG	01	41	55
SS	CABOOSE KIT REVIEW "HO" SS	01	51	62
	CABOOSE KIT REVIEW "HO" SS	02	49	76
SU	CABOOSE LISTING DL&W "S" SU	07	77	42
TC	SIDE DOOR CABOOSE KIT REVIEW "O" TC	01	50	80
TI	B&O CLASS I-5B BAY W CABOOSE REV "HO" TI	08	68	16
	BAY WINDOW CABOOSE REVIEW "HO" TI 1920	02	67	12
	STANDARD CABOOSE C&NW REVIEW "HO" TI	07	67	14
	WOOD UP CABOOSE REVIEW "HO" TI	11	67	16
	SIDE DOOR CB&Q CABOOSE REVIEW "HO" TI	10	66	14
V	CENTER CUPOLA CABOOSE REVIEW "HO" V	11	50	53
	38' CABOOSE KIT REVIEW "HO" V	09	49	61
	EMBOSSED SIDE CABOOSE REVIEW "HO" V	10	39	542
WAL	CABOOSE KIT REVIEW "O" WAL	03	48	226
	CABOOSE KIT REVIEW "HO" WAL	07	48	508
WSM	SHORT CABOOSE LISTING D&RGW "ON3" WSM	06	77	48

MOW PROTOTYPE DATA

	M	Y	P
DYNAMOMETER CARS BOOMER PETE	07	44	300
DYNAMOMETER CARS AND THEIR USES	12	73	100
FLANGER #2 FJ&G	08	79	73
FOUR WHEEL FLANGER OF CP	05	70	54
HANDCARS OF GTW 1908 SHEF	07	85	94
HOMEMADE WEED BURNERS GMI	10	59	60
OUTFIT CARS IN NARROW GAUGE	11	66	51
RAIL SERVICING CAR 1886 MICHC	01	55	75
ROTARY SNOW PLOWS	10	78	75
ROTARY SNOWPLOWS	10	78	140
RUSSELL STEEL SNOWPLOWS CR #64568	12	84	88
SCALE TEST CARS B&O X4920	01	72	84
SLEET CUTTERS	02	78	139
SYKES SEAGULL RAILBUS	04	83	115
TRACKMOBILES WHAT THEY ARE	10	80	163
WESTERN UNION WORK CARS	07	37	243
WRECK TRAINS PROTOTYPE INFORMATION	10	67	73
WRECKING CRANE CP #97	10	55	18
WRECKING TRAIN CONSIST	08	34	16

MOW PLANS

	M	Y	P
200 TON BIG HOOK PLANS	09	44	381
200 TON BUCYRUS-ERIE DERRICK PLANS	08	38	317
200 TON STEAM WRECKING CRANE UP #221	06	35	148
200T WRECKING CRANE PLANS B&O	08	50	36
23 TON TRACKMOBILE DRAWINGS	05	85	78
BOOM CAR PLANS NYC #X998	12	38	540
BUCYRUS-ERIE 250 TON STEAM CRANE PLANS	07	66	34
CAMP CAR PLANS CLASS XL PRR #492035 1910	09	66	56
CAMP CAR PLANS WESTERN UNION TELE #2308	07	37	242
CLEARANCE CAR DRAWINGS C&O #X1836	11	60	69
CONVERTIBLE BALLAST CAR PLANS CP	09	54	47
DERRICK & TOOL CAR 1888 PLANS SOO #5003	10	69	68
DERRICK CAR OF 1880 PLANS	04	55	34
DETECTOR CAR PLANS SPERRY RAIL SERVICE	01	52	42
DOUBLE ENDED SNOWPLOW PLANS HT&W	06	61	34
DYNAMOMETER CAR OF 1907 PLANS PRR	07	49	33
DYNAMOMETER CAR PLANS SP #137	07	44	303
DYNAMOMETER CAR WOOD & STEEL ATSF#29 PLN	12	70	70
FENCEMENS CAR PLANS TP&W	06	62	28
FLANGER #2 PLANS FJ&G	08	79	74
FLANGER CAR PLANS CP #400487	10	73	66
FLANGER PLANS SNOWPLOW COMPANION	02	57	53
FLANGER PLANS FJ&G #10 1890	01	55	46
FOUR WHEEL FLANGER PLANS CP #400401	05	70	55
FREELANCE BOOM CAR PLANS	06	52	48
GONDOLA MOUNTED SNOW PLOW PLANS	11	62	51
GONDOLA MOUNTED SNOWPLOW PLANS	01	57	37
HANDCAR OF 1908 PLAN GTW DRAWINGS	07	85	94
HANDCAR PLANS	06	68	44
IDLER OR BOOM CAR PLANS	08	50	38
INSPECTION CAR OF 1880 PLANS PRR #2256	07	58	57
LE TOURNEAU LETRO-PORTER DRAWINGS	08	85	96
LINK-BELT LOCOMOTIVE CRANE PLANS OF 1920	04	61	61
PAY CAR PLANS PRR #3507 1914	03	74	46
POLING CAR PLANS PRR #63 1913	07	55	34
RAIL AND TIE CAR PLANS	12	53	31
RIPTRACK CRANE PLANS	08	71	33
ROTARY SNOW PLOW PLANS UP #076 LH 1950	04	53	38
ROTARY SNOW PLOW PLANS UP #076 LH 1950 C	06	53	4
ROTARY SNOWPLOW PLANS NP #6 LESLIE BROS	03	59	40
RUSSEL STEEL SNOWPLOW PLAN CR #64568	12	84	89
SCALE TEST CAR PLANS PRR #490386	11	37	418
SP'S CAR #251 OUTHOUSE CAR PLANS 1954	05	77	81
SPEEDER & TRAILER TRUCK PLANS	01	63	57
SPEEDER RAIL TRUCK PLANS	01	63	55
STEEPLECAB SNOWPLOW PLANS AV	01	74	43
SUPPLY CAR PLANS EX-POSTAL CAR	01	53	46
SUPPLY CAR PLANS WESTERN UNION TELE#7549	02	57	63
SYKES RAILBUS PLANS NYNH&H #9013	04	83	116
SYKES RAILBUS PLANS NYO&W #801	04	83	117
TEST WEIGHT CAR PLANS PRR #490397	08	52	40
TOOL CAR OF 1875 PLANS PRR #60	10	59	40
TOOL CAR PLANS WESTERN UNION TELE #2308	07	37	243
WEDGE SNOWPLOW PLANS MP #X5808	12	72	60
WEDGE TYPE SNOW PLOW PLANS	11	43	476

NON-REVENUE EQUIPMENT

MOW PLANS	M	Y	P
WEDGE TYPE SNOWPLOW DRAWINGS	09	69	52
WORK SERVICE FLATCAR PLANS AV	05	75	57
WRECKING CRANE 30 TON PLANS ATSF #199760	01	56	33
WRECKING CRANE PLANS B&O #X45	03	40	154

RD	MOW PLANS BY ROAD	M	Y	P
#WUT	SUPPLY CAR PLANS WESTERN UNION TELE #7549	02	57	63
	TOOL CAR PLANS WESTERN UNION TELE #2308	07	37	243
	CAMP CAR PLANS WESTERN UNION TELE #2308	07	37	242
ATSF	WRECKING CRANE 30 TON PLANS ATSF #199760	01	56	33
	DYNAMOMETER CAR WOOD & STEEL ATSF#29 PLN	12	70	70
AV	WORK SERVICE FLATCAR PLANS AV	05	75	57
	STEEPLECAB SNOWPLOW PLANS AV	01	74	43
B&O	200T WRECKING CRANE PLANS B&O	08	50	36
	WRECKING CRANE PLANS B&O #X45	03	40	154
C&O	CLEARANCE CAR DRAWINGS C&O #X1836	11	60	69
CP	FLANGER CAR PLANS CP #400487	10	73	66
	FOUR WHEEL FLANGER PLANS CP #400401	05	70	55
	CONVERTIBLE BALLAST CAR PLANS CP	09	54	47
CR	RUSSEL STEEL SNOWPLOW PLAN CR #64568	12	84	89
FJ&G	FLANGER #2 PLANS FJ&G	08	79	74
	FLANGER PLANS FJ&G #10 1890	01	55	46
GTW	HANDCAR OF 1908 PLAN GTW DRAWINGS	07	85	94
HT&W	DOUBLE ENDED SNOWPLOW PLANS HT&W	06	61	34
MP	WEDGE SNOWPLOW PLANS MP #X5808	12	72	60
NP	ROTARY SNOWPLOW PLANS NP #6 LESLIE BROS	03	59	40
NYC	BOOM CAR PLANS NYC #X998	12	38	540
NYNH&H	SYKES RAILBUS PLANS NYNH&H #9013	04	83	116
NYO&W	SYKES RAILBUS PLANS NYO&W #801	04	83	117
PRR	TEST WEIGHT CAR PLANS PRR #490397	08	52	40
	PAY CAR PLANS PRR #3507 1914	03	74	46
	POLING CAR PLANS PRR #S3 1913	07	55	34
	DYNAMOMETER CAR OF 1907 PLANS PRR	07	49	33
	CAMP CAR PLANS CLASS XL PRR #492035 1910	09	66	56
	INSPECTION CAR OF 1880 PLANS PRR #2256	07	58	57
	TOOL CAR OF 1875 PLANS PRR #60	10	59	40
	SCALE TEST CAR PLANS PRR #490386	11	37	418
SOO	DERRICK & TOOL CAR 1888 PLANS SOO #5003	10	69	68
SP	DYNAMOMETER CAR PLANS SP #137	07	44	303
	SP'S CAR #251 OUTHOUSE CAR PLANS 1954	05	77	81
SRS	DETECTOR CAR PLANS SPERRY RAIL SERVICE	01	52	42
TP&W	FENCEMENS CAR PLANS TP&W	06	62	28
UP	ROTARY SNOW PLOW PLANS UP #076 LH 1950 C	06	53	4
	200 TON STEAM WRECKING CRANE UP #221	06	35	148
	ROTARY SNOW PLOW PLANS UP #076 LH 1950	04	53	38

MOW PHOTOS	M	Y	P
FLAT CAR/TENDER FOR WORK TRAIN CN PHOTO	10	55	6
FUEL TANK CAR PHOTO AT WELLS NEVADA	04	69	38
HOME GROWN MOW CARS CP	04	55	5
SAND CAR PHOTO IVORYDALE YARD B&O	11	57	8
SCALE TEST CAR PHOTO NYC #X860	02	49	54
SECTION CAR PHOTOS WI&W 1952	02	75	15
STEAM GENERATOR CAR D&H #35000 PHOTO	10	74	79
STEAM SHOVEL-CRANE UNUSUAL PHOTO	08	62	31

MOW MODELS	M	Y	P
200T WRECKING CRANE CONSTRUCTION	09	44	381
23 TON TRACKMOBILE CONSTRUCTION	05	85	78
BIG HOOK AND HOW TO BASH IT	12	75	60
BOOM CAR CONSTRUCTION NYC #X998	12	38	539
BOOM CAR FREELANCE CONSTRUCTION	06	52	48
BUILD A RAMP CAR	02	81	80
BUILD A TRACK CLEANING CAR	07	50	43
BUILD A WRECK TRAIN	03	80	80
CLEARANCE CAR CONSTRUCTION	11	60	68
COMPANY SERIVCE MOW CARS OSO MOD & PT	06	77	29
CONVERTIBLE BALAST CAR CONSTRUCTION CP	09	54	47
CRANE CONSTRUCTION POWERED BOOM	07	55	28
DIESEL ROTARY SNOWPLOW CONSTRUCTION	10	78	75
DITCHER CONSTRUCTION D&RGW	09	72	48
DYNAMOMETER CAR CONSTRUCTION BOOMER PETE	09	45	368
FLANGER CAR CONSTRUCTION CP #400487 1968	10	73	65
FLANGER CONSTRUCTION SNOWPLOW COMPANION	02	57	52
FLEA POWERED WHEEL WORKS RAIL TRUCK CONS	08	82	62
FOUR WHEEL FLANGER CONST CP #400401	05	70	55
GONDOLA MOUNTED SNOW PLOW CONSTRUCTION	11	62	50
GONDOLA MOUNTED SNOWPLOW CONST MILW	01	57	36
IMPACT DETECTOR CAR CONSTRUCTION	10	62	57
INSPECTION CAR MOD & PT	01	79	130
INSPECTION CAR BN MOD & PT	06	77	34
KITBASH A RAILBUS	06	79	70
LE TOURNEAU LETRO-PORTER CONSTRUCTION	08	85	95
LOG LOADER IN "ON3" MODEL PHOTOS	03	70	39
MODEL DYNAMOMETER CAR CONSTRUCTION	09	37	324
MODERNIZING A STEAM ROTARY SNOWPLOW	01	81	122
MOM 150T LOCO CRANE "1 1/2" RITENBURG	06	74	34
MOM 1904 DERRICK "S" AHD PHILLIPS	03	72	67
MOM 250 TON BROWN HOIST CRANE "O" SIMONS	05	52	28
MOM BIG HOOK VC #D1 "HO" WEBB	10	70	58
MOM CP 1905 FLANGER CASTO	12	74	69
MOM D&RGW DERRICK "S" MARTINSEN	07	72	32
MOM D&RGW DERRICK & IDLER "ON3" WADE	05	84	81
MOM D&RGW FLANGER KRUEGER	03	78	89
MOM D&RGW PILE DRIVER "HON3" BRACHER	11	71	49
MOM D&RGW PILE DRIVER "ON3" VASTA	05	70	33
MOM D&RGW ROTARY SNOWPLOW "HO" BRACHER	05	75	49
MOM DERRICK & TOOL CAR "1/4" SOO DYXIN	04	71	49
MOM ECC TYPE CABOOSE F&CC "ON3" KONRAD	06	79	58
MOM HANDCAR "HO" MALLORY	06	68	45
MOM JORDAN SPREADER D&RGW "ON3" NOVAK	08	70	52
MOM RGS GALLOPING GOOSE #7 "HON3"JOHNSON	01	71	43
MOM SP 1950'S CRANE "HO" HODINA	05	85	74
MOM TOOL CAR "1/4" DUPONT	12	70	76
MOM TOOL CAR "ON3" NIELSEN	01	83	115
MOM WEED SPRAYER "HO" CHAIT	08	74	50
OLDTIME WRECKING CRANE PLAN CP #97	10	55	21
OPERATING CRANE "O" ATSF	12	54	46
PANEL TRUCK CAR MILW MOD & PT	05	81	113
PASSENGER CAR TO NON REVENUE CAR	08	80	58
POWERING THE STEWART CRANE FOR SWITCHING	12	57	34
POWERING THE TRUSCALE CRANE	09	59	27

STEPHANS' RAILROAD DIRECTORY

NON-REVENUE EQUIPMENT

MOW MODELS	M	Y	P
RAIL AND TIE CAR CONSTRUCTION	12	53	30
RAIL AND TIE CAR CONSTRUCTION $1	10	68	36
RAIL CLEANING CAR CONSTRUCTION	07	41	365
RIP TRACK CRANE CONSTRUCTION $1	08	71	32
ROTARY SNOW PLOW MODIFIED CONSTRUCTION	01	73	68
SPEEDER RAIL TRUCK CONSTRUCTION	01	63	54
SPINNING POWER FOR ROTARY SNOWPLOW	01	81	124
TANK CAR COMPANY SERVICE MOD & PT	04	82	118
TOOL AND WHEEL CAR CONSTRUCTION	10	57	42
TRACK AND CLEARANCE ANALYSIS CAR CONST	08	61	42
TRACK CLEANING CAR CONSTRUCTION	11	43	500
TRACK CLEANING CAR CONSTRUCTION	09	70	62
TRANSFER CABOOSE CONSTRUCTION CN #76501	02	85	110
WEDGE TYPE SNOW PLOW CONSTRUCTION	09	69	51
WEDGE TYPE SNOWPLOW CONSTRUCTION	11	43	476
WORK CAR KITBASH A&A	05	79	83
WORK CARS FROM RETIRED EQUIPMENT	12	74	87
WORK TRAIN CABOOSE CONSTRUCTION	02	53	24
WORK TRAIN CAR CONSTRUCTION	06	53	32
WRECK TRAIN WHEEL CAR CONSTRUCTION $1	12	65	58
WRECKER CRANE KITBASHED	04	77	54
WRECKING CRANE 200T BUCYRUS-ERIE CONST	08	38	316
WRECKING CRANE 30 TON ATSF CONSTRUCTION1	01	56	32
WRECKING CRANE 30 TON ATSF CONSTRUCTION2	02	56	43
WRECKING CRANE CONSTRUCTION B&O	03	40	153
WRECKING CRANE CONSTRUCTION B&O FINISHIN	04	40	196
WRECKING CRANE CONSTRUCTION CP #97	10	55	18
WRECKING DERRICK MODEL PHOTOS	12	69	57

MOW MODEL REVIEWS	M	Y	P
120T ATSF WRECKER & BOOM CAR REV "N" DIT	11	81	50
200 TON B&O CRANE REVIEW "HO" DN	02	42	100
200T WRECKING CRANE REVIEW "HO" ATH	02	52	40
25 TON CRANE REVIEW "N" STEW AHD	08	75	30
25 TON DIESEL/ELEC CRANE REV "HO" STEW	11	57	10
25 TON OPERATING CRANE REVIEW "HO" TSM	01	59	24
35' WOOD CB&Q CABOOSE REVIEW "HO" TI	08	66	8
40' DERRICK CAR KIT REVIEW "HO" MANTUA	02	60	18
ALCO ROTARY SNOW PLOW GN REV "HO" ARISTO	02	59	16
BALAST CAR REVIEW "G" LGB	11	84	54
BLACKSMITH V&T CAR REVIEW "HO" TSM	01	61	20
BOOM CAR KIT REVIEW "HO" DALE NEWTON	12	50	58
BRILL MOTOR CAR REV "HO" NPP 1920	12	72	34
BURROW CRANE REVIEW "HO" OM BCI	08	83	35
DERRICK CAR REVIEW "HO" SRE	01	55	10
DITCHER-AMER HOIST&DERRICK REV "HO" RGM	02	78	47
DYNAMOMETER CAR ATSF REVIEW "HO" H CRLW	03	74	22
DYNAMOMETER CAR N&W #514780 REV HO NWSL	08	76	33
DYNAMOMETER CAR REVIEW "HO" DEV	04	53	59
EM80-C TRACK TESTING & CLEAN CAR "HO" B	05	81	49
FLANGER D&RGW REVIEW "HO" P 1805 D&RGW	05	74	21
FLANGER RGS REVIEW "ON3" DURANGO PRESS	11	78	46
GALLOPING GOOSE RGS REVIEW "HON3" L 1935	10	81	35
GO DEVIL REVIEW "HO" SEL	06	58	13
HANDCAR D&RGW REVIEW "O" DP	11	74	42
HANDCAR KIT REVIEW "HO" MDC	01	50	82
HANDCAR REVIEW "1/4" SELLY	04	74	29
HANDCAR REVIEW "HO" DP	01	74	37
HY-RAIL VEHICLES REVIEW "HO" B	03	85	48
JORDAN SPREADER REVIEW "HO" OM OSJ	08	82	38
JORDAN SPREADER REVIEW "HO/HON3" RGM	10	78	50
MACK BRILL RAIL BUS REVIEW "HO" HD	12	65	14
MACK NYNH&H RAILCAR REVIEW "HO" L 1920	08	83	48
MACK RAILBUS REVIEW "HO" MEW 1923	04	63	9
MAINTENANCE EQUIPMENT REVIEW "HO" BOYDE	12	66	22
MARION STEAM SHOVEL D&RGW REVIEW "HO"RGM	07	76	28
PAY CAR REVIEW "HO" BINKLEY	12	53	22
PLOW FLANGER RGS REVIEW "HON3/ON3" DP	11	77	46
POLING CAR PRR REVIEW "HO" CB	12	74	37
RAIL AND TIE CAR REVIEW "S" SM	11	73	34
RAIL AUTO REVIEW "HO" KEM	05	54	10
RAIL TRUCK REVIEW "HO" HOWELL DAY	08	64	7
RAILBUS REVIEW "HO" HD	03	67	16
RGS INSPECTION CAR REVIEW "O" SSL 1913	07	73	18
ROTARY SNOWPLOW & TENDER REV "HO" DN	07	57	9
ROTARY SNOWPLOW & TENDER REVIEW "N" DIT	11	79	45
ROTARY SNOWPLOW REVIEW "HO" NPP	05	72	22
RUSSELL SNOWPLOW REVIEW "HO" OM	07	84	36
SCALE TEST CAR REVIEW "HO" STEW	04	59	12
SIDE DUMP CAR REVIEW "HO" OM 1978	01	84	60
SNOW PLOW KIT REVIEW "HO" ST	05	50	43
SNOW PLOW WSL REVIEW "ON3" DP	04	78	50
SNOWPLOW KIT REVIEW "HO" AMB	02	50	71
SPEEDER REVIEW "HO" DP	02	77	38
SPERRY RAILCAR REVIEW "HO" H	06	70	20

NON-REVENUE EQUIPMENT

MOW MODEL REVIEWS

		M	Y	P
SUPPLY CAR REVIEW "HO" ACM		09	51	50
TOOL & WATER CAR REVIEW "O" WAL		11	55	18
TRACK CLEANING CAR "O" RIB		04	55	16
TRACK CLEANING CAR REVIEW "HO" RIB		11	56	14
TRACK CLEANING CAR REVIEW "HO" ULRICH		12	47	1042
TRACK CLEANING CAR REVIEW "HO" W&T		12	54	10
TRACK CLEANING CAR REVIEW "HO" BAU		02	54	27
TRACK MACHINE REVIEW "HO" DP		10	82	56
TRACK TEST CAR REVIEW "HO/HON3" CE		04	68	10
TRACTOR-LOCO REVIEW "1/4" SSL		03	74	24
TRANSFER CABOSE REVIEW "HO" LI		07	66	10
VELOCIPEDE REVIEW "O" MFORR		12	75	38
WATER CAR LISTING UNITAH RY "HON3" PFM		01	78	50
WEDGE SNOW PLOW REVIEW "HO" RIV		03	59	16
WESTERN UNION MATERIAL CAR REV "HO" AMB		11	59	12
WESTERN UNION MATERIAL CAR REV "HO" CLIF		09	58	11
WING SNOW PLOW KIT REVIEW B&M "S" AMB		04	55	10
WING SNOWPLOW REVIEW "HO" KEM		06	59	15
WINGED SNOWPLOW REVIEW "O" KEM		08	59	18
WORK CAR KIT REVIEW "HO" LWM		01	56	12
WORK COMBINE CABOOSE REVIEW "HO" AMB		08	67	13
WORK GOOSE RGS REVIEW "HON3" L		08	82	36
WORK TRAIN CAR REVIEW "HO" ACM		07	53	54
WORK TRAIN REVIEW "HO" TSM		03	60	12
WRECK CRANE REVIEW "HO" L		03	68	10
WRECK TRAIN CARS REVIEW "HO" L		03	68	10
WRECKER & BOOM CAR "HO" REVIEW GC		12	85	43
WRECKER CRANE & IDLER CAR "HO" B		10	80	58
WRECKER CRANE 200T REVIEW "O" MG		10	56	16
WRECKING CRANE KIT REVIEW "HO" IA		03	49	78
WRECKING CRANE OUTFIT REVIEW "N" JMC		02	79	57

MOW MODEL REVIEWS BY ROAD

RD		M	Y	P
A	EM80-C TRACK TESTING & CLEAN CAR "HO" B	05	81	49
ATSF	120T ATSF WRECKER & BOOM CAR REV "N" DIT	11	81	50
	DYNAMOMETER CAR ATSF REVIEW "HO" H CRLW	03	74	22
B&M	WING SNOW PLOW KIT REVIEW B&M "S" AMB	04	55	10
B&O	200 TON B&O CRANE REVIEW "HO" DN	02	42	100
CB&Q	35' WOOD CB&Q CABOOSE REVIEW "HO" TI	08	66	8
D&RGW	MARION STEAM SHOVEL D&RGW REVIEW "HO"RGM	07	76	28
	FLANGER D&RGW REVIEW "HO" P 1805 D&RGW	05	74	21
	HANDCAR D&RGW REVIEW "O" DP	11	74	42
GN	ALCO ROTARY SNOW PLOW GN REV "HO" ARISTO	02	59	16
N&W	DYNAMOMETER CAR N&W #514780 REV HO NWSL	08	76	33
NYNH&H	MACK NYNH&H RAILCAR REVIEW "HO" L 1920	08	83	48
PRR	POLING CAR PRR REVIEW "HO" CB	12	74	37
RGS	GALLOPING GOOSE RGS REVIEW "HON3" L 1935	10	81	35
	WORK GOOSE RGS REVIEW "HON3" L	08	82	36
	PLOW FLANGER RGS REVIEW "HON3/ON3" DP	11	77	46
	FLANGER RGS REVIEW "ON3" DURANGO PRESS	11	78	46
U	WATER CAR LISTING UNITAH RY "HON3" PFM	01	78	50
V&T	BLACKSMITH V&T CAR REVIEW "HO" TSM	01	61	20
WSL	SNOW PLOW WSL REVIEW "ON3" DP	04	78	50

MOW MODEL REVIEWS BY MFG.

MFG		M	Y	P
ACM	SUPPLY CAR REVIEW "HO" ACM	09	51	50
	WORK TRAIN CAR REVIEW "HO" ACM	07	53	54
AMB	SNOWPLOW KIT REVIEW "HO" AMB	02	50	71
	WORK COMBINE CABOOSE REVIEW "HO" AMB	08	67	13
	WING SNOW PLOW KIT REVIEW B&M "S" AMB	04	55	10
	WESTERN UNION MATERIAL CAR REV "HO" AMB	11	59	12
ARISTO	ALCO ROTARY SNOW PLOW GN REV "HO" ARISTO	02	59	16
ATH	200T WRECKING CRANE REVIEW "HO" ATH	02	52	40
B	HY-RAIL VEHICLES REVIEW "HO" B	03	85	48
	WRECKER CRANE & IDLER CAR "HO" B	10	80	58
	EM80-C TRACK TESTING & CLEAN CAR "HO" B	05	81	49
BAU	TRACK CLEANING CAR REVIEW "HO" BAU	02	54	27
BIN	PAY CAR REVIEW "HO" BINKLEY	12	53	22
BOY	MAINTENANCE EQUIPMENT REVIEW "HO" BOYDE	12	66	22
CB	POLING CAR PRR REVIEW "HO" CB	12	74	37
CE	TRACK TEST CAR REVIEW "HO/HON3" CE	04	68	10
CLIF	WESTERN UNION MATERIAL CAR REV "HO" CLIF	09	58	11
DEV	DYNAMOMETER CAR REVIEW "HO" DEV	04	53	59
DIT	ROTARY SNOWPLOW & TENDER REVIEW "N" DIT	11	79	45
	120T ATSF WRECKER & BOOM CAR REV "N" DIT	11	81	50
DN	BOOM CAR KIT REVIEW "HO" DALE NEWTON	12	50	58
	ROTARY SNOWPLOW & TENDER REV "HO" DN	07	57	9
	200 TON B&O CRANE REVIEW "HO" DN	02	42	100
DP	PLOW FLANGER RGS REVIEW "HON3/ON3" DP	11	77	46
	SPEEDER REVIEW "HO" DP	02	77	38
	HANDCAR REVIEW "HO" DP	01	74	37
	HANDCAR D&RGW REVIEW "O" DP	11	74	42
	SNOW PLOW WSL REVIEW "ON3" DP	04	78	50
	FLANGER RGS REVIEW "ON3" DURANGO PRESS	11	78	46
	TRACK MACHINE REVIEW "HO" DP	10	82	56
GC	WRECKER & BOOM CAR "HO" REVIEW GC	12	85	43
H	DYNAMOMETER CAR ATSF REVIEW "HO" H CRLW	03	74	22
	SPERRY RAILCAR REVIEW "HO" H	06	70	20
HD	RAIL TRUCK REVIEW "HO" HOWELL DAY	08	64	7
	MACK BRILL RAIL BUS REVIEW "HO" HD	12	65	14
	RAILBUS REVIEW "HO" HD	03	67	16
IA	WRECKING CRANE KIT REVIEW "HO" IA	03	49	78
JMC	WRECKING CRANE OUTFIT REVIEW "N" JMC	02	79	57
KEM	RAIL AUTO REVIEW "HO" KEM	05	54	10
	WINGED SNOWPLOW REVIEW "O" KEM	08	59	18
	WING SNOWPLOW REVIEW "HO" KEM	06	59	15
L	WRECK CRANE REVIEW "HO" L	03	68	10
	WRECK TRAIN CARS REVIEW "HO" L	03	68	10
	MACK NYNH&H RAILCAR REVIEW "HO" L 1920	08	83	48
	GALLOPING GOOSE RGS REVIEW "HON3" L 1935	10	81	35
	WORK GOOSE RGS REVIEW "HON3" L	08	82	36
LGB	BALAST CAR REVIEW "G" LGB	11	84	54
LI	TRANSFER CABOSE REVIEW "HO" LI	07	66	10
LWM	WORK CAR KIT REVIEW "HO" LWM	01	56	12
M	40' DERRICK CAR KIT REVIEW "HO" MANTUA	02	60	18
MDC	HANDCAR KIT REVIEW "HO" MDC	01	50	82
MEW	MACK RAILBUS REVIEW "HO" MEW 1923	04	63	9
MG	WRECKER CRANE 200T REVIEW "O" MG	10	56	16
NPP	ROTARY SNOWPLOW REVIEW "HO" NPP	05	72	22

NON-REVENUE EQUIPMENT

MOW MODEL REVIEWS BY MFG.

MFG		M Y P
	BRILL MOTOR CAR REV "HO" NPP 1920	12 72 34
NWSL	DYNAMOMETER CAR N&W #514780 REV HO NWSL	08 76 33
OM	BURROW CRANE REVIEW "HO" OM BCI	08 83 35
	SIDE DUMP CAR REVIEW "HO" OM 1978	01 84 60
	RUSSELL SNOWPLOW REVIEW "HO" OM	07 84 36
	JORDAN SPREADER REVIEW "HO" OM OSJ	08 82 38
P	FLANGER D&RGW REVIEW "HO" P 1805 D&RGW	05 74 21
PFM	WATER CAR LISTING UNITAH RY "HON3" PFM	01 78 50
RGM	MARION STEAM SHOVEL D&RGW REVIEW "HO" RGM	07 76 28
	JORDAN SPREADER REVIEW "HO/HON3" RGM	10 78 50
	DITCHER-AMER HOIST&DERRICK REV "HO" RGM	02 78 47
RIB	TRACK CLEANING CAR REVIEW "HO" RIB	11 56 14
	TRACK CLEANING CAR "O" RIB	04 55 16
RIV	WEDGE SNOW PLOW REVIEW "HO" RIV	03 59 16
SEL	GO DEVIL REVIEW "HO" SEL	06 58 13
SELLY	HANDCAR REVIEW "1/4" SELLY	04 74 29
SM	RAIL AND TIE CAR REVIEW "S" SM	11 73 34
SRE	DERRICK CAR REVIEW "HO" SRE	01 55 10
SSL	RGS INSPECTION CAR REVIEW "O" SSL 1913	07 73 18
	TRACTOR-LOCO REVIEW "1/4" SSL	03 74 24
ST	SNOW PLOW KIT REVIEW "HO" ST	05 50 43
STEW	25 TON DIESEL/ELEC CRANE REV "HO" STEW	11 57 10
	25 TON CRANE REVIEW "N" STEW AHD	08 75 30
	SCALE TEST CAR REVIEW "HO" STEW	04 59 12
TI	35' WOOD CB&Q CABOOSE REVIEW "HO" TI	08 66 8
TSM	BLACKSMITH V&T CAR REVIEW "HO" TSM	01 61 20
	WORK TRAIN REVIEW "HO" TSM	03 60 12
	25 TON OPERATING CRANE REVIEW "HO" TSM	01 59 24
U	TRACK CLEANING CAR REVIEW "HO" ULRICH	12 47 1042
W&T	TRACK CLEANING CAR REVIEW "HO" W&T	12 54 10
WAL	TOOL & WATER CAR REVIEW "O" WAL	11 55 18

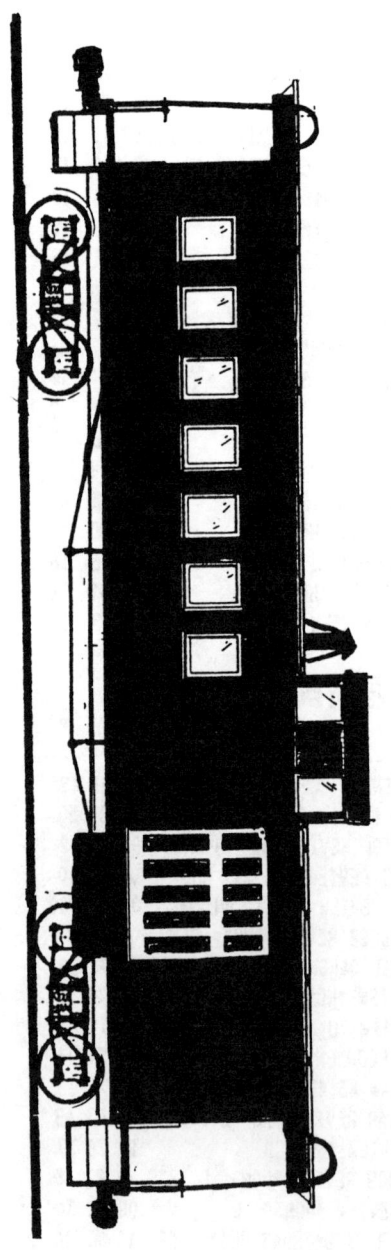

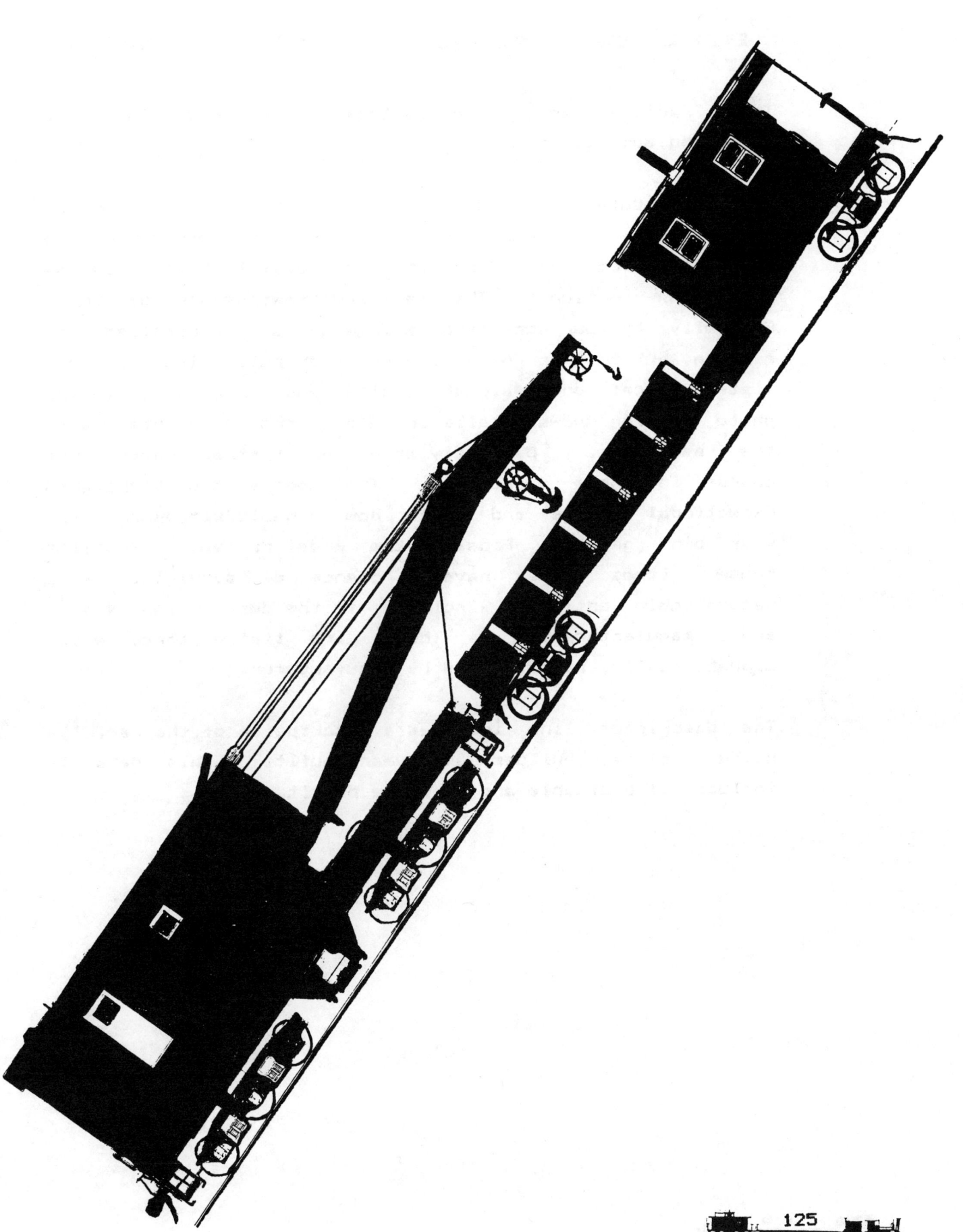

BILL OF LADING   TRACTION

The Traction Section is further broken down into the following subject areas:

Prototype data includes articles and specifications on the real thing. In many instances there are photographs with these articles that did not get special billing in the photograph section. The plans and drawings are just that. Generally by our convention a drawing is more detailed than a plan, but this is not a hard and fast rule. The plans are listed twice: once alphabetically and once by road. The photo section shows details or unusual photos of interest to the researcher. Obviously we did not list all photos that appear in these magazines. The model section highlights exceptional models and tells how to build/kitbash/rebuild your own "gems". Finally the model review section list those itmes that have a chance of surviving as a recognizable entity. Included is the description, scale, and manufacturer. These are listed three ways: alphabetically, by road, and by manufacturer.

The descriptor line includes a description of the car, its number, class, builder and year built. This data is included if available and if space permits.

MANIFEST TRACTION

	PAGE
TRACTION	126
TRACTION PROTOTYPE DATA	128
TRACTION PLANS	128
TRACTION PLANS BY ROAD	129
TRACTION MODELS	130
TRACTION MODEL REVIEWS	131
TRACTION MODEL REVIEWS BY ROAD	132
TRACTION MODEL REVIEWS BY MFG.	133

TRACTION

TRACTION PROTOTYPE DATA	M	Y	P
1000 SERIES CARS OF THE PACIFIC ELECTRIC	04	71	59
21-E TRACTION TRUCK OF 1905 BY BRILL	06	70	57
27-E TRACTION TRUCK BY BRILL	11	71	72
60' HEAVY INTERURBANS CSS&SB	03	37	95
ALL STEEL 47' INTERURBAN CARS OF PE 1913	09	39	447
ALWEG MONORAIL EQUIPMENT	12	64	44
ARTICULATED 1030 SERIES CARS MILW ELECT	05	82	77
AUTOMATIC PANTOGRAPHS	07	34	8
BRILL 27-G TRACTION TRUCKS	07	71	34
CATENARY & OVERHEAD WIRES 1	09	60	59
CATENARY & OVERHEAD WIRES 2	10	60	78
CATENARY & OVERHEAD WIRES 3	11	60	78
CATENARY & OVERHEAD WIRES 4	12	60	87
DINING TROLLIES OF CNS&M	03	75	53
ELECTROLINER TRAINS OF THE CNS&M	05	74	43
ELEVATED DETAILS	08	70	73
ELEVATED RAILROAD SUPPORTS	03	70	80
ELEVATED RAILROADS	04	76	64
ELEVATED RAPID TRANSIT LINES CITYSCAPE			106
HANGING TROLLEY WIRES PROTOTYPE IDEAS	12	48	919
INDUSTRIAL TRACTION LINE (MINE LINE)	11	64	31
INTERURBAN BOX CARS	09	46	580
INTERURBAN CARS OF BL&R 1909 CCC	01	81	97
INTERURBAN RIGHT OF WAY	07	64	28
MAXIMUM TRACTION TRUCK BY BRILL	03	70	65
MCB TRACTION TRUCK BY BRILL	05	71	61
NOITCART TRACTION	04	78	110
PACIFIC ELECTRIC TENS LETTER 1	06	71	15
PACIFIC ELECTRIC TENS LETTER 2	07	71	15
PACIFIC ELECTRIC TENS LETTER 3	11	71	24
PALACE STREETCARS OF N ORLEANS 1902	09	84	120
PORTABLE SUBSTATIONS	07	61	48
RED ARROW LIBERTY LINERS	05	74	43
RULES FOR TRACTION MODELING	08	84	96
SERIES 900 STREETCARS OF TNE MER&L	11	76	76
SMALL BAG EXPRESS SELF-PROPELLED UNIT	04	70	69
SPRINGFIELD TERMINAL RAILWAY	11	58	49
STEEL MOTOR CAR 700 SERIES #752 NS&M	04	34	7
STEEL MOTOR CAR 700 SERIES PLNS NS&M#752	04	34	6
SUBSTATIONS FOR TRACTION LINES	01	61	71
TROLLEY TO ELECTRIC PARK	02	57	58

TRACTION PLANS	M	Y	P
3 DOOR PCC CAR PLANS	08	51	31
3 OLD TIME INTERURBAN CAR PLANS	03	44	130
32' COMBINE PLANS SF&CS #10 1896 WASON	04	70	66
ARCH WINDOW COMBINE PLANS YVT #100 NILES	06	66	39
ARTICULATED 1030 SERIES CAR PLAN ME#1040	05	82	78
BIRNEY SAFETY CAR PLAN	07	39	358
BOBTAIL RPO TROLLEY CAR PLANS USR #302	09	55	40
BOX FREIGHT MOTOR UNIT PLAN CCT #7 1938	09	58	50
BOX MOTOR EXPRESS CAR DRAWINGS	03	81	88
BRILL 21-E TRACTION TRUCK PLAN	06	70	61
BRILL 27-E TRACTION TRUCK PLAN	11	71	77
BRILL 27G TRACTION TRUCK PLAN	07	71	37
BRILL 7 WINDOW TROLLEY PLN 1894 NOC&L#85	09	66	30
BRILL EUREKA MAX TRACTION TRUCK PLAN	03	70	69
BRILL MCB TRUCK DRAWING	04	71	64
CENTER DOOR COMBINE PLAN FDM&S #52	06	62	29
COMBINE COACH/BAGGAGE TROLLY PLAN CSS&SB	03	37	94
COMBINE OF 1912 PLANS SN #1005	07	60	46
COMBINE PLANS ST #16	11	58	51
COMBINE TROLLEY CAR PLAN CNS&M #253	08	70	44
COMBINE TROLLEY PLAN 1916 FDM&S #62 ACF	01	58	52
CONNECTICUT COMPAYN #1903 TROLLEY PLANS	10	40	532
DESIGNS FOR INTERURBAN LAYOUTS	03	69	38
DINING TROLLEY CAR PLAN CNS&M #409	03	75	54
DOUBLE TRUCK CAR FOR STREET RY PLAN 1925	08	36	222
DUPLEX INTERURBAN CAR PLANS ME #1180	09	68	38
ELECTROLINER TRAIN PLAN CNS&M	05	74	46
ELEVATED SUPPORTING TOWER DRAWINGS	04	76	68
EXCURSION INTERURBAN PLAN CD&M #46 1903	04	56	43
EXPRESS COACH COMBINE DRAWING PE #1360 J	04	71	62
FLOOR PLANS OF PE CLASS 1000 CARS J 1913	04	71	63
FREIGHT MOTOR PLAN CNS&M #215 1922	06	40	345
FREIGHT MOTOR PLAN I #727 1930	04	67	54
FREIGHT MOTOR PLANS C&LE #604	01	51	44
FREIGHT MOTOR UNIT OF 1930 PLANS C&LE #9	03	63	44
INTERURBAN "RED BIRD" PLAN CD&M #500	06	52	57
INTERURBAN BOX CAR PLANS	09	46	580
INTERURBAN CAR OF 1905 PLANS	02	54	52
INTERURBAN CAR OF 1907 PLAN THI&E	05	42	235
INTERURBAN CAR PLAN LSE #166	05	49	33
INTERURBAN CAR PLANS	10	41	518
INTERURBAN CAR PLANS LSE #167	04	52	14
INTERURBAN CAR PLANS BL&R #502 1909 CCC	01	81	98
INTERURBAN COACH PLANS CNS&M #420	05	50	56
INTERURBAN SLEEPING CAR PLANS	05	44	217
JEWETT WOOD SHEATHED CAR PLAN PE #1050	04	58	56
KUHLMAN CAR OF 1909 PLAN ME #1121	01	57	46
LACONIA INTERURBAN CAR PLANS PLR #10	09	57	44
LIGHTWEIGHT TROLLEY PLAN SERR #38	12	46	836
MCB BRILL TRACTION TRUCK PLANS 1905	05	71	61
MONORAIL CAR DRAWINGS	12	64	47
MONORAIL TRACK SUPPORT PLANS	12	64	46
NILES CAR OF 1907 PLAN M&N #80	03	49	40
NILES CAR OF 1908 PLAN SDS #102 NILES	07	62	30
NILES INTERURBAN COMBINE PLANS R&IR #701	05	68	31

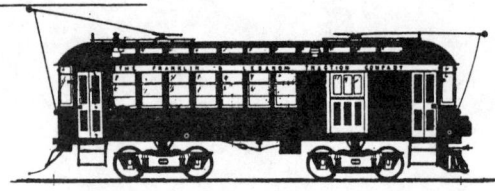

TRACTION

TRACTION PLANS	M	Y	P
OLD TIME STREETCAR PLANS PRT #537	03	50	42
OPEN TROLLEY CAR PLAN CONN #1391	05	63	48
OVERHEAD STRUCTURE PLANS FOR TROLLEYS	01	36	12
PALACE STREETCAR PLANS NOC #621 1902	09	84	120
PANTOGRAPH DRAWINGS	05	74	38
PANTOGRAPH MODEL PLANS	02	34	5
PARLOR TROLLEY CAR PLAN CD&M #500	07	57	46
PARLOR-OBSERVATION TROLLEY CAR PLANS ITR	06	64	22
PORTABLE SUBSTATION CAR PLANS NI #1	07	61	48
PULLMAN STREETCAR PLAN CRT #542 1908	12	52	70
RAIL GRINDER PLANS BIR #123	09	70	60
REFRIGERATOR TROLLEY CAR PLAN ITR #1801	10	56	47
RPO-COMBINE TROLLEY CAR PLANS I	01	46	38
SEMI CONVERTIBLE CAR PLAN EMSR #4387	12	60	74
SERIES 1000 DRAWING PE #1000 J 1913	04	71	60
SIDE DOOR INTERURBAN PLANS PSTC #73	07	59	48
SINGLE TRUCK TROLLEY PLANS	05	45	193
SNOW SWEEPER PLANS PTC #C134	10	65	38
ST LOUIS CAR COMBINE PLANS UTC	01	46	38
STEEL 47' INTERURBAN PLANS PE 1913	09	39	446
STEEL INTERURBAN PE #984 SKETCHES	08	47	654
STREET CARS OF INDIANAPOLIS PLANS	01	48	38
STREETCAR OF 900 SERIES PLAN ME #978	11	76	78
STREETCAR PLANS CSLS #542 1908 PULLMAN	02	70	60
SUBWAY TUBE CAR PLANS H&M	01	51	44
THOUGHTS ON MODULAR TRACTION DESIGN	10	85	82
TRACTION BALLAST CAR PLANS NOPS #054	03	66	37
TRACTION CAR 1100 SERIES ME #1118 PLANS	04	55	34
TRACTION CAR OF 100 SERIES PLAN IRW #128	02	71	45
TRACTION CLASS F 4 WHEEL PLAN TRCO #1668	06	72	48
TRACTION COMBINE OF 1915 PLANS OKT #1	12	66	47
TRACTION COMBINE PLANS OPS #21 NILES	02	65	31
TRACTION OBS CAR PLANS WCF&N #101	12	47	999
TRACTION SERIES 1000 CAR PLANS PE #1001	04	71	56
TRACTION STEEL OBS CAR PLANS SJ&E #200	12	66	46
TROLLEY POLE DETAIL FOR PE 1000 SERIES	04	71	64
WASON COMBINE PLANS SERY #10	03	56	34
WOOD INTERURBAN SERIES 129 PLANS CNS&M	02	41	81
WOOD SHEATHED BOX MOTOR PLAN CCT #4	01	68	42
WOOD SHEATHED COMBINE PLAN L&I	05	66	28
WOOD SHEATHED COMBINE PLANS R&IR #709	02	40	85
WOOD SHEATHED COMBINE PLANS SN #107	11	67	38
WOOD SHEATHED TRAILER OBS PLANS FDM&S#38	11	61	31
WOOD STREET CAR DRAWING 68'	09	42	423
WOODEN COMBINE OF 1902 PLANS STI #500	08	63	38
WOODEN INTERURBAN CAR PLANS SVT #115	06	52	56
WOODEN INTERURBAN CAR PLANS Y&OR #3	01	59	54

RD	TRACTION PLANS BY ROAD	M	Y	P
BIR	RAIL GRINDER PLANS BIR #123	09	70	60
BL&R	INTERURBAN CAR PLANS BL&R #502 1909 CCC	01	81	98
C&LE	FREIGHT MOTOR UNIT OF 1930 PLANS C&LE #9	03	63	44
	FREIGHT MOTOR PLANS C&LE #604	01	51	44
CCT	BOX FREIGHT MOTOR UNIT PLAN CCT #7 1938	09	58	50
	WOOD SHEATHED BOX MOTOR PLAN CCT #4	01	68	42
CD&M	EXCURSION INTERURBAN PLAN CD&M #46 1903	04	56	43
	PARLOR TROLLEY CAR PLAN CD&M #500	07	57	46
	INTERURBAN "RED BIRD" PLAN CD&M #500	06	52	57
CNS&M	COMBINE TROLLEY CAR PLAN CNS&M #253	08	70	44
	ELECTROLINER TRAIN PLAN CNS&M	05	74	46
	FREIGHT MOTOR PLAN CNS&M #215 1922	06	40	345
	WOOD INTERURBAN SERIES 129 PLANS CNS&M	02	41	81
	DINING TROLLEY CAR PLAN CNS&M #409	03	75	54
	INTERURBAN COACH PLANS CNS&M #420	05	50	56
CONN	CONNECTICUT COMPAYN #1903 TROLLEY PLANS	10	40	532
	OPEN TROLLEY CAR PLAN CONN #1391	05	63	48
CRT	PULLMAN STREETCAR PLAN CRT #542 1908	12	52	70
CSLS	STREETCAR PLANS CSLS #542 1908 PULLMAN	02	70	60
CSS&SB	COMBINE COACH/BAGGAGE TROLLY PLAN CSS&SB	03	37	94
EMSR	SEMI CONVERTIBLE CAR PLAN EMSR #4387	12	60	74
FDM&S	COMBINE TROLLEY PLAN 1916 FDM&S #62 ACF	01	58	52
	CENTER DOOR COMBINE PLAN FDM&S #52	06	62	29
	WOOD SHEATHED TRAILER OBS PLANS FDM&S#38	11	61	31
H&M	SUBWAY TUBE CAR PLANS H&M	01	51	44
I	RPO-COMBINE TROLLEY CAR PLANS I	01	46	38
	FREIGHT MOTOR PLAN I #727 1930	04	67	54
IRW	TRACTION CAR OF 100 SERIES PLAN IRW #128	02	71	45
	STREET CARS OF INDIANAPOLIS PLANS	01	48	38
ITR	PARLOR-OBSERVATION TROLLEY CAR PLANS ITR	06	64	22
	REFRIGERATOR TROLLEY CAR PLAN ITR #1801	10	56	47
L&I	WOOD SHEATHED COMBINE PLAN L&I	05	66	28
LSE	INTERURBAN CAR PLAN LSE #166	05	49	33
	INTERURBAN CAR PLANS LSE #167	04	52	14
M&N	NILES CAR OF 1907 PLAN M&N #80	03	49	40
ME	TRACTION CAR 1100 SERIES ME #1118 PLANS	04	55	34
	ARTICULATED 1030 SERIES CAR PLAN ME#1040	05	82	78
	STREETCAR OF 900 SERIES PLAN ME #978	11	76	78
	KUHLMAN CAR OF 1909 PLAN ME #1121	01	57	46
	DUPLEX INTERURBAN CAR PLANS ME #1180	09	68	38
NI	PORTABLE SUBSTATION CAR PLANS NI #1	07	61	48
NOC	PALACE STREETCAR PLANS NOC #621 1902	09	84	120
NOC&L	BRILL 7 WINDOW TROLLEY PLN 1894 NOC&L#85	09	66	30
NOPS	TRACTION BALLAST CAR PLANS NOPS #054	03	66	37
OKT	TRACTION COMBINE OF 1915 PLANS OKT #1	12	66	47
OPS	TRACTION COMBINE PLANS OPS #21 NILES	02	65	31
PCC	3 DOOR PCC CAR PLANS	08	51	31
PE	TRACTION SERIES 1000 CAR PLANS PE #1001	04	71	56
	SERIES 1000 DRAWING PE #1000 J 1913	04	71	60
	EXPRESS COACH COMBINE DRAWING PE #1360 J	04	71	62
	FLOOR PLANS OF PE CLASS 1000 CARS J 1913	04	71	63
	TROLLEY POLE DETAIL FOR PE 1000 SERIES	04	71	64
	JEWETT WOOD SHEATHED CAR PLAN PE #1050	04	58	56
	STEEL 47' INTERURBAN PLANS PE 1913	09	39	446
	STEEL INTERURBAN PE #984 SKETCHES	08	47	654

TRACTION

RD	TRACTION PLANS BY ROAD	M	Y	P
PLR	LACONIA INTERURBAN CAR PLANS PLR #10	09	57	44
PRT	OLD TIME STREETCAR PLANS PRT #537	03	50	42
PSTC	SIDE DOOR INTERURBAN PLANS PSTC #73	07	59	48
PTC	SNOW SWEEPER PLANS PTC #C134	10	65	38
R&IR	WOOD SHEATHED COMBINE PLANS R&IR #709	02	40	85
	NILES INTERURBAN COMBINE PLANS R&IR #701	05	68	31
SDS	NILES CAR OF 1908 PLAN SDS #102 NILES	07	62	30
SERR	LIGHTWEIGHT TROLLEY PLAN SERR #38	12	46	836
SERY	WASON COMBINE PLANS SERY #10	03	56	34
SF&CS	32' COMBINE PLANS SF&CS #10 1896 WASON	04	70	66
SJ&E	TRACTION STEEL OBS CAR PLANS SJ&E #200	12	66	46
SN	WOOD SHEATHED COMBINE PLANS SN #107	11	67	38
	COMBINE OF 1912 PLANS SN #1005	07	60	46
ST	COMBINE PLANS ST #16	11	58	51
STI	WOODEN COMBINE OF 1902 PLANS STI #500	08	63	38
SVT	WOODEN INTERURBAN CAR PLANS SVT #115	06	52	56
THI&E	INTERURBAN CAR OF 1907 PLAN THI&E	05	42	235
TRCO	TRACTION CLASS F 4 WHEEL PLAN TRCO #1668	06	72	48
USR	BOBTAIL RPO TROLLEY CAR PLANS USR #302	09	55	40
UTC	ST LOUIS CAR COMBINE PLANS UTC	01	46	38
WCF&N	TRACTION OBS CAR PLANS WCF&N #101	12	47	999
Y&OR	WOODEN INTERURBAN CAR PLANS Y&OR #3	01	59	54
YVT	ARCH WINDOW COMBINE PLANS YVT #100 NILES	06	66	39

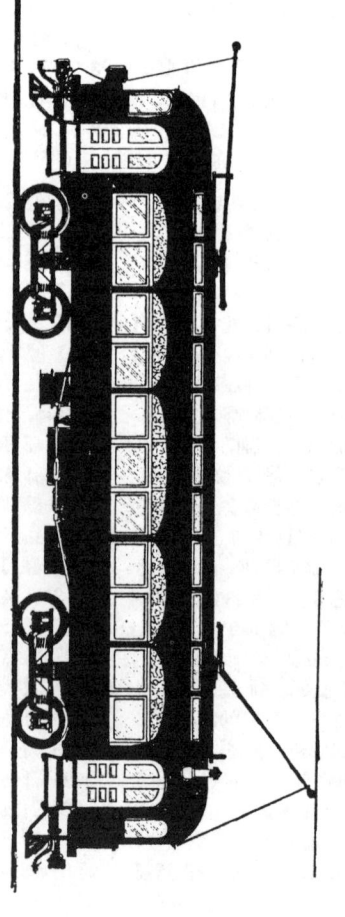

TRACTION MODELS	M	Y	P
BEAM HEADLIGHT FOR LOCO OR TROLLEY CONST	04	68	58
BOBTAIL TROLLEY CONSTRUCTION	10	48	692
BORN TO RAISE L ELEVATED CONSTRUCTION	10	84	109
BUILD A TROLLEY WORK TRAIN	05	78	96
BUILDING TROLLEY POLES	11	56	61
CATENARY & CONTROL BOOMER PETE	06	45	236
CATENARY & CONTROL CORRECTION B. PETE	07	45	275
CATENARY & OVERHEAD WIRES 3 WIRE & POLE	11	36	324
CATENARY & OVERHEAD WIRES CONTACT WIRES	03	45	126
CATENARY & OVERHEAD WIRES FOR PANTOGRAPH	10	73	56
CATENARY & OVERHEAD WIRES IDAHO MIDLAND	06	71	40
CATENARY & OVERHEAD WIRES ON BRIDGES	05	45	194
CATENARY & OVERHEAD WIRES PANTOGRAPHS	04	45	171
CATENARY & OVERHEAD WIRES TANGENT CHORD	04	40	205
CONNECTICUT COMPANY TROLLY CONSTRUCTION	10	40	531
CONSIDER ELECTRIFICATION W/OVERHEADS	09	79	61
DETAILING A MANTUA DINKY TROLLEY	07	54	28
DOUBLE TRUCK STREET CARS OF 1925	08	36	221
DOWN TO EARTH PCC CAR MODIFICATION	11	62	66
ELEVATED RAPID TRANSIT LINES CITYSCAPE	10	78	106
FISHING LURES AND TROLLEY MODELING	01	77	22
FLEXIBLE DRIVE MOTOR TRUCK CONSTRUCTION	03	46	164
FOUR HOOK TROLLEY POLE REVERSE CONSTRUCT	03	44	129
FRED TALBOT'S TROLLEYS	11	69	54
FREE LANCE TRACTION WORK CAR CONSTRUCT.	05	66	50
HOMEMADE TROLLEY POWER TRUCKS	01	54	79
HOW TO HANG TROLLEY WIRE	09	55	28
INDIANA RAILROAD HEAVY COMBINE CONST	07	43	304
INSTALLING TROLLEY WIRE	06	50	59
INSULATORS FOR CATENARY SYSTEMS	05	77	82
INTERURBAN COMBINE KITBASH "HO"	04	82	84
INTERURBAN EQUIPMENT CONSTRUCTION	10	41	517
INTERURBAN POWER TRUCK CONSTRUCTION	10	40	533
INTERURBAN TRUCK CONSTRUCTION	12	42	563
INTERURBANS IN MINIATURE	01	46	36
LAKE SHORE ELECTRIC INTERURBAN CAR CONST	04	52	14
LAKE SHORE ELECTRIC INTERURBAN CAR.CONST	05	49	33
MARKERS THAT DEMOUNT CONSTRUCTION	04	49	30
MOM 900 SERIES MILW ST. CAR "O" MATUSZAK	11	76	106
MOM INTERURBAN 1/2" DAYTON&TROY#36 DOSEY	02	70	39
MOM MILW ELECTRIC EQUIP "1/4" MATUSZAK	12	71	65
MOM TOONERVILLE TROLLEY "HO" BEGUAL	11	37	403
MOM WCF&N #381 TROLLEY "1/2"" ANDERSEN	09	85	70
OBSERVATION TROLLEY CAR WCF&N CONST	12	47	996
OVERHEAD TROLLEY	05	40	268
OVERHEAD TROLLEY FOR MODEL RAILROADS	10	34	3
OVERHEAD WIRE FOR POLE TROLLEYS	03	75	56
PACIFIC ELECTRIC INTERURBAN CAR CONST	08	47	652
PANTOGRAPH WORKING MODEL CONSTRUCTION	02	34	4
PANTOGRAPHS THAT WORK SMOOTHLY CONSTRUCT	05	74	37
PCC TRUCK KITBASH "O"	05	49	14
PE CLASSIC "HOLLYWOOD" CAR FINISHING	09	82	72
PE1940 PCC #5000 MOD & PT	05	80	108
PERFECT TROLLEY POLE CONSTRUCTION	09	82	68
PILOT MAKING FOR TRACTION CARS	11	51	47

TRACTION

TRACTION MODELS		M	Y	P
RED LINE TROLLEY	MOD & PT	11	75	90
RELIABLE OVERHEAD FOR HIDDEN TRACK		08	84	134
SCRATCHBUILD A BOX MOTOR EXPRESS CAR		03	81	88
SECOND TROLLEY POLE FOR A PCC CAR CONST		04	69	61
SECRETS OF CATENARY CONSTRUCTION		09	47	729
SINGLE TRUCK TROLLEY CAR CONSTRUCTION		05	45	192
SINGLE TRUCK TROLLEY CONSTRUCTION		02	55	70
STREETCAR UNITED RY OF ST LOUIS MOD & PT		10	81	122
SUBWAY CAR OF TOMORROW CONSTRUCTION		02	49	27
SUPPORTING STRUCTURES FOR TROLLEYS		01	36	13
TOMLINSON COUPLERS FROM MINIATURE CONNEC		08	84	80
TRACTION MODELING IN "N" SCALE		01	75	78
TRACTION TIPS BILL SCHOPP		11	52	52
TRIBOROUGH RAPID TRANSIT COMPANY		10	78	116
TROLLEY EMPIRE "O"	CLOUSER	09	56	20
TROLLEY HAS IT	BOOMER PETE	07	42	325
TROLLEY LAYOUT CONSTRUCTION		05	75	50
TROLLEY MODEL REV (14 UNITS) "O" HOFFMAN		01	50	42
TROLLEY OVERHEAD WIRE CONSTRUCTION		09	36	249
TROLLEY POLE CONSTRUCTION		03	48	194
TROLLEY SNOW SWEEPER PTC CONSTRUCTION		10	65	40
TROLLEY STANDARDS		08	41	399
TROLLEY WIRE BLUEBOOK		05	57	59
TROLLEY WIRE CATANARY CONSTTRUCTION		10	76	79
TROLLEY WIRE FOR BRANDYWINE TRANSIT		09	76	82
TROLLEY WIRE OVERHEAD TROLLEY CONSTRUCT		01	35	8
TROLLEYS THEIR CONSTRUCTION		03	42	132
UNDERFLOOR TRACTION TRUCK CONSTRUCTION		08	68	53
WHAT BROUGHT THE CATENARY DOWN		06	78	67
WOOD INTERURBAN #1009 CONSTRUCTION		10	51	31
WOOD INTERURBAN OF 1905 CONSTRUCTION		02	54	53
WORKING RADIAL COUPLER		10	83	120

TRACTION MODEL REVIEWS		M	Y	P
1907 NILES INTERURBAN REVIEW "HO" S		09	58	11
4 TRUCK 80 TON IT REVIEW "HO"SUYDAM 1924		05	60	14
B&Q CLASS 8000 REVIEW "HO" FA		10	71	23
BALTIMORE STREETCAR REV "O" LJ		07	64	11
BART TRAIN REVIEW "HO" BART MODELS 1972		08	74	16
BIRNEY SAFETY CAR REVIEW "HO" WAL		12	39	672
BIRNEY STREET CAR LISTING "HO" AHM		02	77	46
BIRNEY STREETCAR REVIEW "HON3 1/2" SOHO		05	68	13
BOSTON ELEVATED CAR REVIEW "O" BSM		01	76	34
BOSTON TROLLEY BELL REVIEW "O" FRM		01	70	22
BOSTON TYPE 4 STREETCAR REVIEW "1/4" FRM		07	71	24
BRILL MASTER UNIT STREET CAR REV HO NWSL		01	74	30
BRILL STREET CAR REVIEW "HO" MTS		01	63	27
BRILL TROLLEY CAR REVIEW PSTC "O" IND		02	60	14
BUDD MU CAR REVIEW "HO" JOUEF		11	68	12
BUTLER SHORT LINE INTER REV "17/64" JG		06	66	12
CABLE CAR KIT REVIEW "HO" DE		12	48	998
CABLE CAR KIT REVIEW "HO" DE		06	50	48
CABLE CAR REVIEW CO		02	50	69
CINCINNATI INTERURBAN REV "HO" GSB 1911		01	79	49
CITY STREETCAR REVIEW "HO" MTS		06	64	10
CSLS STREETCAR REVIEW "1/4" QC 1908 PLM		10	74	25
DIFFERENTIAL DUMP CAR REVIEW "O" FRM		02	71	26
DOUBLE TRUCK BIRNEY REVIEW "HO" KK		11	62	18
DUPLEX INTERURBAN WB&AE REVIEW "HO" GHB		05	83	45
EXPRESS MOTOR REVIEW "HO" S		09	57	12
FREIGHT MOTOR LSE REVIEW "HO/O" HORT		05	63	8
FREIGHT MOTOR PE REVIEW "HO" S 1913 PLM		12	73	30
INDIANA RAILROAD INTERURBAN REV "HO" KK		07	63	7
INTERURBAN "SN" REVIEW "HO" MEW 1912 HCC		08	67	16
INTERURBAN BOXCAR TRAILER REV "HO" SOHO		10	68	16
INTERURBAN CA&E REVIEW "HO" MTM		11	77	50
INTERURBAN CAR REVIEW "O" IND		07	48	508
INTERURBAN CNS&M REVIEW "HO" WAL		05	65	8
INTERURBAN CSS&SB REVIEW "HO" NPP		05	76	26
INTERURBAN FREIGHT CAR REVIEW "O" LC		02	38	86
INTERURBAN FREIGHT MOTOR REVIEW "HO" KK		04	66	12
INTERURBAN KIT REVIEW "HO" IND		01	50	81
INTERURBAN PRIV CAR PE REV "HO" OWS SLC		03	83	37
INTERURBAN REVIEW PAUL MOORE		02	43	101
INTERURBAN REVIEW "HO" PAM		12	52	54
INTERURBAN REVIEW "HO" S		10	56	11
IRR HIGH SPEED INTERURBAN REV "1/4" COCW		02	75	32
JEWETT COMBINE CNS&M REV "HO" S 1917		02	61	10
KEY SYSTEM INTERURBAN REVIEW "HO" KK		11	64	7
LARY TYPE B1 STREETCAR REVIEW "HO" SOHO		09	71	24
LIGHTWEIGHT INTERURBAN REVIEW "HO" PT		12	66	12
LITTLE BRILLS CSLS 5000 SERIES "HO" FTM		02	81	44
LSE INTERURBAN REVIEW "O" LA 1900		02	66	12
MANHATTAN EL CAR REVIEW "1/4" QC 1888		06	75	25
MOTOR TRUCKS REVIEW "1/4" PMT		11	77	42
MU POWER CAR REVIEW "TT" HP		08	51	52
NILES COACH OF 1906 NE REVIEW "HO" S		07	67	14
NILES INTERURBAN REVIEW "HO" S		05	57	16
NORTH SHORE COMBINE REVIEW "1/4" AN 1917		10	75	31

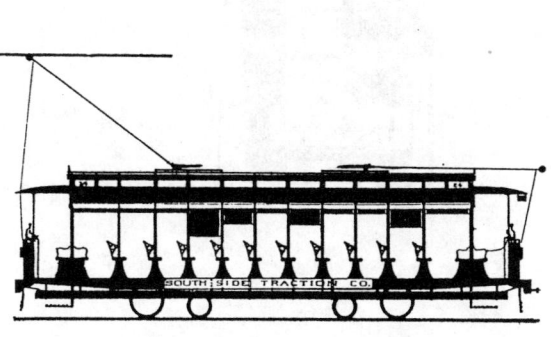

TRACTION

TRACTION MODEL REVIEWS

	M	Y	P
NORTH SHORE INTERURBAN REVIEW "HO" STS	11	48	885
NORTH SHORE JEWETT COMBINE REVIEW "HO" S	04	70	18
OHIO ELECTRIC FREIGHT MOTOR REV "HO" LA	12	61	21
OLDTIME TROLLEY REVIEW "HO" MTS 1898	01	62	14
OPEN BENCH TROLLEY REVIEW "HO" MTS	09	63	6
PARLOR CAR CNS&M REVIEW HO MTM 1922 CCC	03	79	48
PCC CAR KIT REVIEW "1/4" R&M 1936	07	71	25
PCC CAR KIT REVIEW "O" R&T	01	50	76
PE 400 CLASS INTERURBAN REV "HO" S 1911	04	63	16
PE INTERURBAN CARS REV "HO" OWS 1907	07	84	45
ROME ITALY STREET CAR REVIEW "HO" FA	07	74	24
SAN DIEGO CLASS 5 STREETCAR REV "O" PT	06	72	22
SAN DIEGO TRACTION CAR REV "HO" PT 1923	09	69	20
SINGLE TRACK BIRNEY REVIEW "1/4" PB ACC	11	74	30
STREET CAR CSLS REVIEW "1/4" ACW	11	78	54
STREET CAR KIT REVIEW "HO" PAM	09	50	56
STREET CAR REVIEW "1/4" POLK	07	78	45
STREETCAR PIT REVIEW "HO" FA	05	76	34
TINPLATE STREETCAR REVIEW "O" GM	12	50	55
TRACTION STOCK CAR REVIEW "O" MTH	01	76	40
TRACTION WYE SWITCH REVIEW RICHARD ORR	06	77	45
TRAM CAR REVIEW "HO" RIV 1900	05	64	11
TROLLEY CAR KIT "HO" BI	10	49	72
TROLLEY CAR KIT REVIEW "O" PIT	02	50	69
TROLLEY REVIEW "HO" PAM	05	54	09
TROLLEY SEAT LISTING "HO" QUALITY CAR CO	11	77	55
TROLLEY SPRINKLER CAR REVIEW "HO" MTS	02	66	15
TROLLEY SWEEPER REVIEW "HO" HUNT	11	66	18
UNDERFLOOR TRACT POWER UNIT REV "HO" TRM	04	64	9

TRACTION MODEL REVIEWS BY ROAD

RD		M	Y	P
B&Q	B&Q CLASS 8000 REVIEW "HO" FA	10	71	23
BART	BART TRAIN REVIEW "HO" BART MODELS 1972	08	74	16
BELL	BOSTON TROLLEY BELL REVIEW "O" FRM	01	70	22
C&LE	INTERURBAN FREIGHT MOTOR REVIEW "HO" KK	04	66	12
CA&E	INTERURBAN CA&E REVIEW "HO" MTM	11	77	50
CL&A	LIGHTWEIGHT INTERURBAN REVIEW "HO" PT	12	66	12
CNS&M	NORTH SHORE COMBINE REVIEW "1/4" AN 1917	10	75	31
	JEWETT COMBINE CNS&M REV "HO" S 1917	02	61	10
	PARLOR CAR CNS&M REVIEW HO MTM 1922 CCC	03	79	48
	INTERURBAN CNS&M REVIEW "HO" WAL	05	65	8
CSLS	CSLS STREETCAR REVIEW "1/4" QC 1908 PLM	10	74	25
	STREET CAR CSLS REVIEW "1/4" ACW	11	78	54
	LITTLE BRILLS CSLS 5000 SERIES "HO" FTM	02	81	44
CSS&SB	INTERURBAN CSS&SB REVIEW "HO" NPP	05	76	26
I	INDIANA RAILROAD INTERURBAN REV "HO" KK	07	63	7
IRR	IRR HIGH SPEED INTERURBAN REV "1/4" COCW	02	75	32
IT	4 TRUCK 80 TON IT REVIEW "HO" SUYDAM 1924	05	60	14
LAR	LARY TYPE B1 STREETCAR REVIEW "HO" SOHO	09	71	24
LSE	LSE INTERURBAN REVIEW "O" LA 1900	02	66	12
	FREIGHT MOTOR LSE REVIEW "HO/O" HORT	05	63	8
MAE	MANHATTAN EL CAR REVIEW "1/4" QC 1888	06	75	25
NE	NILES COACH OF 1906 NE REVIEW "HO" S	07	67	14

TRACTION MODEL REVIEWS BY ROAD

RD		M	Y	P
OER	OHIO ELECTRIC FREIGHT MOTOR REV "HO" LA	12	61	21
PE	PE 400 CLASS INTERURBAN REV "HO" S 1911	04	63	16
	FREIGHT MOTOR PE REVIEW "HO" S 1913 PLM	12	73	30
	INTERURBAN PRIV CAR PE REV "HO" OWS SLC	03	83	37
	PE INTERURBAN CARS REV "HO" OWS 1907	07	84	45
PIT	STREETCAR PIT REVIEW "HO" FA	05	76	34
PSTC	BRILL TROLLEY CAR REVIEW PSTC "O" IND	02	60	14
SDE	SAN DIEGO CLASS 5 STREETCAR REV "O" PT	06	72	22
SN	INTERURBAN "SN" REVIEW "HO" MEW 1912 HCC	08	67	16
WB&AE	DUPLEX INTERURBAN WB&AE REVIEW "HO" GHB	05	83	45

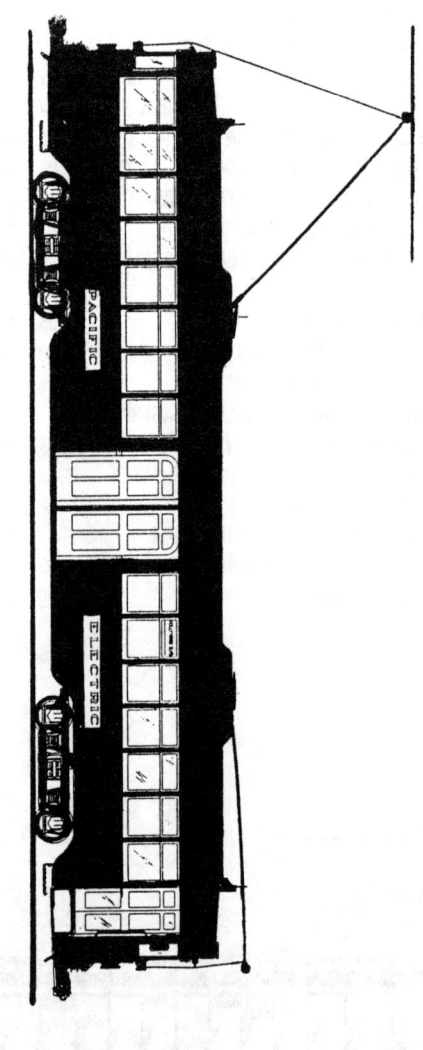

TRACTION

TRACTION MODEL REVIEWS BY MFG.

MFG		M	Y	P
ACW	STREET CAR CSLS REVIEW "1/4" ACW	11	78	54
AHM	BIRNEY STREET CAR LISTING "HO" AHM	02	77	46
AN	NORTH SHORE COMBINE REVIEW "1/4" AN 1917	10	75	31
BART	BART TRAIN REVIEW "HO" BART MODELS 1972	08	74	16
BI	TROLLEY CAR KIT "HO" BI	10	49	72
BSM	BOSTON ELEVATED CAR REVIEW "O" BSM	01	76	34
CO	CABLE CAR REVIEW CO	02	50	69
COCW	IRR HIGH SPEED INTERURBAN REV "1/4" COCW	02	75	32
DE	CABLE CAR KIT REVIEW "HO" DE	06	50	48
	CABLE CAR KIT REVIEW "HO" DE	12	48	998
FA	B&Q CLASS 8000 REVIEW "HO" FA	10	71	23
	ROME ITALY STREET CAR REVIEW "HO" FA	07	74	24
	STREETCAR PIT REVIEW "HO" FA	05	76	34
FRM	DIFFERENTIAL DUMP CAR REVIEW "O" FRM	02	71	26
	BOSTON TYPE 4 STREETCAR REVIEW "1/4" FRM	07	71	24
	BOSTON TROLLEY BELL REVIEW "O" FRM	01	70	22
FTM	LITTLE BRILLS CSLS 5000 SERIES "HO" FTM	02	81	44
GHB	DUPLEX INTERURBAN WB&AE REVIEW "HO" GHB	05	83	45
GM	TINPLATE STREETCAR REVIEW "O" GM	12	50	55
GSB	CINCINNATI INTERURBAN REV "HO" GSB 1911	01	79	49
HORT	FREIGHT MOTOR LSE REVIEW "HO/O" HORT	05	63	8
HP	MU POWER CAR REVIEW "TT" HP	08	51	52
HUNT	TROLLEY SWEEPER REVIEW "HO" HUNT	11	66	18
IND	BRILL TROLLEY CAR REVIEW PSTC "O" IND	02	60	14
	INTERURBAN KIT REVIEW "HO" IND	01	50	81
	INTERURBAN CAR REVIEW "O" IND	07	48	508
J	BUDD MU CAR REVIEW "HO" JOUEF	11	68	12
JG	BUTLER SHORT LINE INTER REV "17/64" JG	06	66	12
KK	INTERURBAN FREIGHT MOTOR REVIEW "HO" KK	04	66	12
	INDIANA RAILROAD INTERURBAN REV "HO" KK	07	63	7
	DOUBLE TRUCK BIRNEY REVIEW "HO" KK	11	62	18
	KEY SYSTEM INTERURBAN REVIEW "HO" KK	11	64	7
LA	LSE INTERURBAN REVIEW "O" LA 1900	02	66	12
	OHIO ELECTRIC FREIGHT MOTOR REV "HO" LA	12	61	21
LC	INTERURBAN FREIGHT CAR REVIEW "O" LC	02	38	86
LJ	BALTIMORE STREETCAR REV "O" LJ	07	64	11
MEW	INTERURBAN "SN" REVIEW "HO" MEW 1912 HCC	08	67	16
MTH	TRACTION STOCK CAR REVIEW "O" MTH	01	76	40
MTM	INTERURBAN CA&E REVIEW "HO" MTM	11	77	50
	PARLOR CAR CNS&M REVIEW HO MTM 1922 CCC	03	79	48
MTS	TROLLEY SPRINKLER CAR REVIEW "HO" MTS	02	66	15
	BRILL STREET CAR REVIEW "HO" MTS	01	63	27
	OPEN BENCH TROLLEY REVIEW "HO" MTS	09	63	6
	OLDTIME TROLLEY REVIEW "HO" MTS 1898	01	62	14
	CITY STREETCAR REVIEW "HO" MTS	06	64	10
NPP	INTERURBAN CSS&SB REVIEW "HO" NPP	05	76	26
NWSL	BRILL MASTER UNIT STREET CAR REV HO NWSL	01	74	30
ORR	TRACTION WYE SWITCH REVIEW RICHARD ORR	06	77	45
OWS	INTERURBAN PRIV CAR PE REV "HO" OWS SLC	03	83	37
	PE INTERURBAN CARS REV "HO" OWS 1907	07	84	45
PAM	TROLLEY REVIEW "HO" PAM	05	54	09
	INTERURBAN REVIEW "HO" PAM	12	52	54
	STREET CAR KIT REVIEW "HO" PAM	09	50	56
PB	SINGLE TRACK BIRNEY REVIEW "1/4" PB ACC	11	74	30
PIT	TROLLEY CAR KIT REVIEW "O" PIT	02	50	69
PMT	MOTOR TRUCKS REVIEW "1/4" PMT	11	77	42
POLK	STREET CAR REVIEW "1/4" POLK	07	78	45
PT	SAN DIEGO CLASS 5 STREETCAR REV "O" PT	06	72	22
	SAN DIEGO TRACTION CAR REV "HO" PT 1923	09	69	20
	LIGHTWEIGHT INTERURBAN REVIEW "HO" PT	12	66	12
QC	MANHATTAN EL CAR REVIEW "1/4" QC 1888	06	75	25
	CSLS STREETCAR REVIEW "1/4" QC 1908 PLM	10	74	25
QCC	TROLLEY SEAT LISTING "HO" QUALITY CAR CO	11	77	55
R&M	PCC CAR KIT REVIEW "1/4" R&M 1936	07	71	25
R&T	PCC CAR KIT REVIEW "O" R&T	01	50	76
RIV	TRAM CAR REVIEW "HO" RIV 1900	05	64	11
S	INTERURBAN REVIEW "HO" S	10	56	11
	EXPRESS MOTOR REVIEW "HO" S	09	57	12
	NILES INTERURBAN REVIEW "HO" S	05	57	16
	PE 400 CLASS INTERURBAN REV "HO" S 1911	04	63	16
	NORTH SHORE JEWETT COMBINE REVIEW "HO" S	04	70	18
	FREIGHT MOTOR PE REVIEW "HO" S 1913 PLM	12	73	30
	1907 NILES INTERURBAN REVIEW "HO" S	09	58	11
	JEWETT COMBINE CNS&M REV "HO" S 1917	02	61	10
	4 TRUCK 80 TON IT REVIEW "HO"SUYDAM 1924	05	60	14
	NILES COACH OF 1906 NE REVIEW "HO" S	07	67	14
SOHO	LARY TYPE B1 STREETCAR REVIEW "HO" SOHO	09	71	24
	BIRNEY STREETCAR REVIEW "HON3 1/2" SOHO	05	68	13
	INTERURBAN BOXCAR TRAILER REV "HO" SOHO	10	68	16
STS	NORTH SHORE INTERURBAN REVIEW "HO" STS	11	48	885
TRM	UNDERFLOOR TRACT POWER UNIT REV "HO" TRM	04	64	9
WAL	BIRNEY SAFETY CAR REVIEW "HO" WAL	12	39	672
	INTERURBAN CNS&M REVIEW "HO" WAL	05	65	8

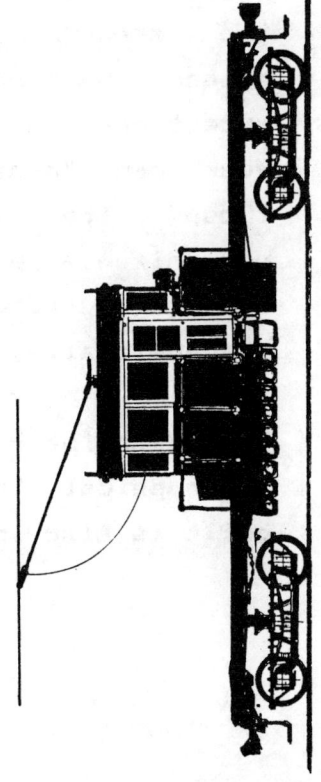

BILL OF LADING   STRUCTURES & SIGNALS

This section contains the six subsections of Bridges and Tunnels, Commercial Buildings, Depots and Stations, Railroad Structures, Signals and General Structures. Bridges and Tunnels are self-explanatory. Commercial structures include stores, factories, houses, etc. Depots and stations are just that. Railroad structures are line side buildings, roundhouses, platforms, water towers, servicing facilities and the like. Signals are signals, both electrical and mechanical, signs, telltales, etc. General structures is the catch-all.

Prototype data includes articles and specifications on the real thing. In many instances there are photographs with these articles that did not get special billing in the photograph section. The plans and drawings are just that. Generally by our convention a drawing is more detailed than a plan, but this is not a hard and fast rule. The plans are listed twice: once alphabetically and once by road. The photo section shows details or unusual photos of interest to the researcher. Obviously we did not list all photos that appear in these magazines. The model section highlights exceptional models and tells how to build/kitbash/rebuild your own "gems". Finally the model review section list those items that have a chance of surviving as a recognizable entity. Included is the description, scale, and manufacturer. These are listed three ways: alphabetically, by road, and by manufacturer.

The descriptor line includes the description. If a road or geographical location is available it is included. The year built is also included if available.

MANIFEST — STRUCTURES & SIGNALS

	PAGE
STRUCTURES & SIGNALS	134
BRIDGES & TUNNELS	136
BRIDGE & TUNNEL PROTOTYPE DATA	136
BRIDGE & TUNNEL PLANS	136
BRIDGE & TUNNEL PLANS BY ROAD	137
BRIDGE & TUNNEL PHOTOS	137
BRIDGE & TUNNEL MODELS	137
BRIDGE & TUNNEL MODEL REVIEWS	138
BRIDGE & TUNNEL MODEL REVIEWS BY MFG	139
COMMERCIAL STRUCTURES	140
COMMERCIAL BUILDING PROTOTYPE DATA	140
COMMERCIAL BUILDING PLANS	141
COMMERCIAL BUILDING PLANS BY ROAD	142
COMMERCIAL BUILDING PHOTOS	142
COMMERCIAL BUILDING MODELS	143
COMMERCIAL BUILDING MODEL REVIEWS	145
COMMERCIAL BUILDING MODEL REV BY MFG.	148
DEPOTS	150
DEPOT PROTOTYPE DATA	150
DEPOT PLANS	151
DEPOT PLANS BY ROAD	152
DEPOT MODELS	153
DEPOT MODEL REVIEWS	154
DEPOT MODEL REVIEWS BY MFG.	154
RAILROAD STRUCTURES	155
RAILROAD STRUCTURE PROTOTYPE DATA	155
RAILROAD STRUCTURE PLANS	156
RAILROAD STRUCTURE PLANS BY ROAD	158
RAILROAD STRUCTURE MODELS	159
RAILROAD STRUCTURE MODEL REVIEWS	162
RAILROAD STRUCTURE MODEL REV BY MFG.	164
RAILROAD STRUCTURE MODEL REV BY ROAD	165
SIGNALS	166
SIGNAL PROTOTYPE DATA	166
SIGNAL PLANS	166
SIGNAL PLANS BY ROAD	166
SIGNAL PHOTOS	166
SIGNAL MODELS	167
SIGNAL MODEL REVIEWS	167
SIGNAL MODEL REVIEWS BY MFG.	168
GENERAL STRUCTURES	168
GENERAL STRUCTURE PROTOTYPE DATA	168
GENERAL STRUCTURE PLANS	168
GENERAL STRUCTURE PLANS BY ROAD	168
GENERAL STRUCTURE MODELS	169
GENERAL STRUCTURE MODEL REVIEWS	170
GENERAL STRUCTURE MODEL REV BY MFG.	170

STRUCTURES & SIGNALS

BRIDGE & TUNNEL PROTOTYPE DATA

Title	M	Y	P
BASCULE BRIDGE OF C&NW	04	36	105
BASCULE DRAWBRIDGE GLOUSTER MASS B&M	11	80	82
BIG WARRIOR RIVER BRIDGE CORDOVA AL	06	78	81
BILLBOARD BRIDGES	08	80	57
BRIDGE TYPES	06	53	55
BRIDGES BOOMER PETE	12	46	828
BRIDGES WITH HANDBOOK	06	54	58
COMMON STANDARD TRESTLES	04	69	39
CONCRETE TRESTLES	11	58	40
COVERED BRIDGE WOLCOTT, VT	02	69	69
COVERED RR BRIDGES IN EXISTANCE 1984	06	84	127
CROSSING COLLIE CANYON	08	78	54
CUMBERLAND RIVER CROSSING S	02	78	76
DUBUQUE TUNNEL ON THE IC	08	57	36
GONDOLA USED AS BRIDGE	04	79	130
HIGHWAY BRIDGE PROTOTYPE	12	47	983
LATTICE TRUSS BRIDGE WESTFIELD PA	07	82	74
NORTH FOLK BRIDGE OF WP	12	78	92
ORNATE OVERPASS FOREST PARK MO WABASH	11	70	52
RATHOLE HIGHWAY BRIDGE AT LINWOOD NC S	12	81	145
SKEWED BRIDGE SPANS	03	77	114
SMALL CULVERTS	02	57	57
STEEL TRUSS BRIDGES	12	42	539
STONE ARCH BRIDGE LEWISTON, PA PRR	10	47	802
TIMBERLINED TUNNELS	09	77	62
TRESTLE INFORMATION	08	78	122
TRUSS & GIRDER BRIDGES	12	75	116
TRUSS BRIDGE BLUEBOOK	02	57	71
UNDERPASS SAN JOSE, CALIFORNIA	01	46	17
UNDERPASSES PRR RADEBAUGH PA	06	57	33
UNUSUAL CONCRETE BRIDGE	07	48	467
WITHERBY ST UNDERPASS ATSF 1924	06	80	96
WOOD HIGHWAY BRIDGE	12	43	537
WOOD KING POST TRUSS HIGHWAY BRIDGE	07	85	92
WOOD TRESTLES	09	58	59
WOOD TRESTLES 1	10	58	73
WOOD TRESTLES 2	11	58	73

BRIDGE & TUNNEL PLANS

Title	M	Y	P
B&O DOUBLE TRACK BRIDGE PLANS 1912	05	45	203
BASCULE BRIDGE PLANS B&OCT CHICAGO IL	12	73	58
BASCULE BRIDGE PLANS C&NW	04	36	104
BIG WARRIOR RIVER BRIDGE PLAN	06	78	78
BRIDGE OF A&A PLANS ARCADE, NY	09	78	84
BRIDGE OVER RHINE BENN GERMANY PLAN	10	44	436
BRIDGE OVER RIO GRANDE PLAN 1902	04	45	163
COMMON STANDARD TRESTLE PLANS	04	69	39
CONCRETE OVERPASS PLANS READING	05	42	226
COVERED BRIDGE PLANS COTTAGE GROVE, OR	04	77	52
COVERED BRIDGE PLANS SJ&LCO WOLCOTT VT	11	68	46
COVERED HGHWAY BRIDGE DRAWING CHESTER NY	04	79	72
DITCH SPANNING BRIDGE PLANS ATSF	10	61	26
DRAWBRIDGE PLANS GLOUSTER MASS B&M	11	80	83
DRAWINGS- BRIDGE HANDBOOK	06	54	58
EADS BRIDGE DBL TRACK ST LOUIS MO PLAN	12	43	549
GARABIT VIADUCT SINGLE TRACK PLAN FRANCE	08	44	347
GEORGE WASHINGTON BRIDGE, NY PLAN 1889	02	43	60
GRADE SEPARATION BRIDGE PLANS	05	38	202
GTW DOUBLE TRACK BRIDGE PLN N. FALLS, NY	09	43	402
HELLGATE, NY 4 TRACK STEEL ARCH BRIDGE	01	43	34
HIGH BRIDGE ST JOHN RIVER PLAN CANADA	08	45	329
INVERTED TRUSS BRIDGE PLANS B&M	05	42	225
KANAWHA & MICHIGAN RY BRIDGE OHIO PLAN	03	43	110
KING & QUEEN POST TRUSS BRIDGE DRAWINGS	02	51	25
KINGPOST TRUSS BRIDGE PLN FOR COUNTRY RD	04	63	42
KORNHAUS BRIDGE PLAN BERNE SWITZERLAND	11	43	497
LATTICE TRUSS BRIDGE PLANS WESTFIELD PA	07	82	74
MASONRY BRIDGE PLANS	04	48	253
MCKINLEY DOUBLE TRACK BRIDGE PLAN 1910	05	43	236
MILES GLACIER BRIDGE PLAN 1910	04	43	174
MILW SINGLE TRACK BRIGE PLAN MOBRIDGE,SD	08	43	368
MUENGSTEN VIADUCT DOUBLE TRACK GERM PLAN	01	44	32
MUNICIPAL BRIGE ST LOUIS DOUBLETRACK PLN	02	44	65
NIAGARA FALLS CLIFTON HIGHWAY BRIDGE PLA	12	44	533
NORTH FORK BRIDGE PLAN OF WP	12	78	92
NORTH SIDE POINT BRIDGE PITTSBURGH 1912	10	43	447
OLD PLATTSMOUTH TRUSS BRIDGE PLANS B&MI	04	64	26
OVERPASS AT FOREST PARK MO PLANS WABASH	11	70	53
PARABOLIC ARCH BRIDGE PLANS	04	36	90S
PLATE GIRDER BRIDGE PLANS	11	38	486
PLATE GIRDER BRIDGE PLANS.	03	43	108
PONY TRUSS BRIDGE DRAWINGS LINDSAY VA	09	51	15
PRR DOUBLE TRACK BRIDGE OVER DEL R PLAN	06	43	269
PRUSSIAN STATE RYS DOUBLETRACK BRID PLAN	06	44	254
RURAL ROAD OVERPASS PLANS	07	62	39
SCHERZER ROLLING LIFT BRIDGE PLANS	11	67	52
SHORT GIRDER BRIDGE PLANS WYOMING NY B&O	06	71	39
SHORT GIRDER OVERPASS PLANS NYC FALLS BR	10	66	54
SHORT THROUGH PLATE GIRDER BRIDGE PLANS	11	79	116
SHORT TIMBER SPAN BRIDGE PLANS	12	47	976
STEEL HIGH BRIDGE PLAN	05	42	227
STRAINING BEAM PONY TRUSS BRIDGE PLANS	10	67	47
SWING DRAW BRIDGE PLANS MILWAUKEE WIS	07	47	550
THROUGH PLATT TRUSS BRIDGE PLANS	07	53	38

STRUCTURES & SIGNALS

BRIDGE & TUNNEL PLANS

	M	Y	P
TIMBER DECK TRUSS BRIDGE PLANS	04	68	55
TIMBER TRESTLE PLANS	05	40	253
TIMBER TUNNEL PORTAL PLANS WP	05	69	42
TRESTLE BENT DRAWINGS	06	85	68
TRESTLE PLANS & DRAWINGS	02	48	96
TRUSS BRIDGE DRAWINGS	12	42	541
TRUSS BRIDGE PLANS FOUR CORNERS WY	10	75	48
UNDERPASS (MASONARY ARCH) PLANS LI	06	65	39
VIAUR VIADUCT, FRANCE 1899 PLAN	02	43	60
WITHERBY ST UNDERPASS DRAWINGS ATSF 1924	06	80	97
WOOD KING POST TRUSS HIGHWAY BRIDGE PLAN	07	85	93
WOOD TRESTLE PLANS	12	36	359
WOOD TRUSS BRIDGE PLANS	04	60	27

BRIDGE & TUNNEL PLANS BY ROAD

RD		M	Y	P
A&A	BRIDGE OF A&A PLANS ARCADE, NY	09	78	84
ATSF	DITCH SPANNING BRIDGE PLANS ATSF	10	61	26
	WITHERBY ST UNDERPASS DRAWINGS ATSF 1924	06	80	97
B&M	INVERTED TRUSS BRIDGE PLANS B&M	05	42	225
	DRAWBRIDGE PLANS GLOUSTER MASS B&M	11	80	83
B&MI	OLD PLATTSMOUTH TRUSS BRIDGE PLANS B&MI	04	64	26
B&O	B&O DOUBLE TRACK BRIDGE PLANS 1912	05	45	203
	SHORT GIRDER BRIDGE PLANS WYOMING NY B&O	06	71	39
B&OCT	BASCULE BRIDGE PLANS B&OCT CHICAGO IL	12	73	58
C&NW	BASCULE BRIDGE PLANS C&NW	04	36	104
LI	UNDERPASS (MASONARY ARCH) PLANS LI	06	65	39
MILW	MILW SINGLE TRACK BRIGE PLAN MOBRIDGE,SD	08	43	368
	SWING DRAW BRIDGE PLANS MILWAUKEE WIS	07	47	550
NYC	SHORT GIRDER OVERPASS PLANS NYC FALLS BR	10	66	54
R	CONCRETE OVERPASS PLANS READING	05	42	226
SJ&LCO	COVERED BRIDGE PLANS SJ&LCO WOLCOTT VT	11	68	46
W	OVERPASS AT FOREST PARK MO PLANS WABASH	11	70	53
WP	TIMBER TUNNEL PORTAL PLANS WP	05	69	42
	NORTH FORK BRIDGE PLAN OF WP	12	78	92

BRIDGE & TUNNEL PHOTOS

	M	Y	P
UNDERPASS N&W PHOTO	02	44	68
WOODEN TRESTLES-WORTH 1000 WORDS	08	78	100

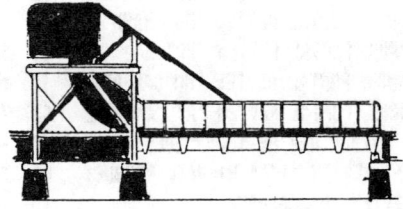

NYNH&H, NIANTIC, CT 1907

BRIDGE & TUNNEL MODELS

	M	Y	P
ARCH BRIDGE CONSTRUCTION 1	03	36	61
ARCH BRIDGE CONSTRUCTION 2	04	36	90
ARCH BRIDGE CONSTRUCTION CNCRTE ABUTMENT	06	36	155
ARCH BRIDGE CONSTRUCTION GIRDERS	07	36	191
ARCH BRIDGE CONSTRUCTION SUPPORT COLUMNS	09	36	254
BALROG GOARGE TRESTLE CONSTRUCTION	06	77	59
BASCULE BRIDGE CONSTRUCTION	09	35	240
BASCULE DRAWBRIDGE CONST GLOUSTER MASS	11	80	80
BRIDGE ABUTMENT CONSTRUCTION	12	37	460
BRIDGE CONSTRUCTION ALL KINDS IN SERIES	10	40	542
BRIDGE CONSTRUCTION TRUSS BRIDGES	12	40	672
BRIDGE CONSTRUCTION TWO GIRDER BRIDGES	11	40	603
BRIDGE ENGINEERING BOOMER PETE	03	44	120
BRIDGE KITBASH	10	73	54
BUILD SJC BRIDGES-VARIETY OF SPANS	06	84	96
COOLIE CANYON BRIDGE CONSTRUCTION	08	78	55
COVERED BRIDGE CONSTRUCTION	01	47	8
COVERED RAILROAD BRIDGE CONSTRUCT 1924	04	77	50
COVERED RAILROAD BRIDGE DIRECTORY	08	77	21
CROOKED CREEK PASS TRESTLE CONSTRUCTION	03	58	30
CROSSADA ARCH BRIDGE CONSTRUCTION	09	48	636
CUSTOM BUILT TUNNEL PORTALS	11	57	36
DECK GIRDER BRIDGE CONSTRUCTION	12	79	100
DESIGN AND CONSTRUCTION OF BRIDGES 1	02	43	68
DESIGN AND CONSTRUCTION OF BRIDGES 2	03	43	122
GIRDER BRIDGE AND APPROACHE CONSTRUCTION	05	66	24
GIRDER BRIDGE CONST MODEL IN A MINUTE 1	03	50	17
GIRDER BRIDGE CONST MODEL IN A MINUTE 2	04	50	17
GIRDER BRIDGE CONSTRUCTION	09	48	607
GIRDER DOUBLE SPAN BRIDGE CONSTRUCTION	09	42	406
GIRDER TRESTLE CONSTRUCTION	04	54	36
GIRDERS FOR BRIDGE CONSTRUCTION	03	55	60
GRADE SEPARATION BRIDGE CONSTRUCTION	05	38	203
HIGHWAY BRIDGE OF WOOD CONSTRUCTION	05	42	240
KING AND QUEEN POST TRUSS BRIDGE CONST	02	51	22
LIFT BRIDGE MODEL	05	39	259
LONG CURVED BRIDGES	02	72	81
MODERN STEEL TRUSS BRIDGE CONSTRUCTION	03	61	40
MOM CURVED CHORD PRATT TRUSS BRIDGE "HO"	10	81	65
MOM HOWE TIMBER TRUSS BRIDGE "HO"	11	79	79
MOM LIFT BRIDGE "O" SCHELBACH	09	53	22
MOM MISSOURI PACIFIC BRIDGE "S" SAPPO	09	78	58
MOM RAIL/HIGHWAY TRUSS BRIDGE "HO" SMITH	12	69	61
MOM TIMBER BRIDGES "HO" JOHNSON	09	69	39
MOM TRUSS BRIDGE MODEL "O" MOORE	10	38	413
MOM WILLIAM GORGE "HO" BIDE	05	72	35
MOM WOOD TRUSS BRIDGE "HO" SMITH	04	77	57
NEAR PERFECT HINGED BRIDGE CONSTRUCTION	11	84	100
OVERPASS GIRDER TYPE CONST NYC FALLS BRA	10	66	54
PLATE GIRDER BRIDGE CONSTRUCTION	01	35	18
PLATE GIRDER BRIDGE CONSTRUCTION.	03	43	108
PLATE GIRDER BRIDGE CONSTRUCTION..	11	38	485
PLATE GIRDER BRIDGE CONSTRUCTION...	07	51	42
PONY TRUSS BRIDGE CONSTRUCT LINDSAY VA	09	51	14
PONY TRUSS STRAINING BEAM BRIDGE CONST	10	67	45

STRUCTURES & SIGNALS

BRIDGE & TUNNEL MODELS

	M	Y	P
PRACTICAL TUNNEL MODELING	07	35	184
RAILROAD BRIDGE SELECTION	02	49	47
REMOVABLE BRIDGES FOR DOORWAYS	04	44	160
ROCK SHIELD CONSTRUCTION CAPR	02	77	92
SCHERZER COMPACT DRAWBRIDGE CONSTRUCTION	11	67	54
SKEWED DECK TRUSS BRIDGE CONSTRUCTION	02	58	54
STEEL ARCH BRIDGE CONSTRUCTION	01	51	18
STEEL TRESTLE CONST TRUSS-GIRDER-TRUSS	11	73	63
STEEL TRESTLES FROM CENTRAL VALLEY BRIDG	06	85	68
THOUGHTS ABOUT TIMBER TRESTLES CONSTRUCT	10	76	93
TIMBER DECK TRUSS BRIDGE CONSTRUCTION	04	68	52
TIMBER TRESTLE CONST-SPIDERY STRUCTURES	02	46	82
TIMBER TRESTLE CONSTRUCTION	05	40	252
TIMBER TRESTLE CONSTRUCTION	01	48	25
TIMBER TRESTLE CONSTRUCTION $1	12	63	54
TIMBER TRESTLE FOR COAL YARD CONSTRUCT	05	45	198
TIMBERED TUNNEL CONSTRUCTION	08	53	49
TRESTLE CONSTRUCTION	12	36	359
TRESTLE CONSTRUCTION BUILD ACCURATELY	02	48	96
TRUSS BRIDGE CONSTRUCTION CUT & FIT	07	53	20
TUNNEL PORTAL CONSTRUCION	02	77	67
TUNNELS TIMBERED CONSTRUCTION	09	44	394
WARREN DECK TRUSS BRIDGE CONSTRUCTION	07	40	369
WOOD TRUSS BRIDGE CONSTRUCION 36'	04	60	27

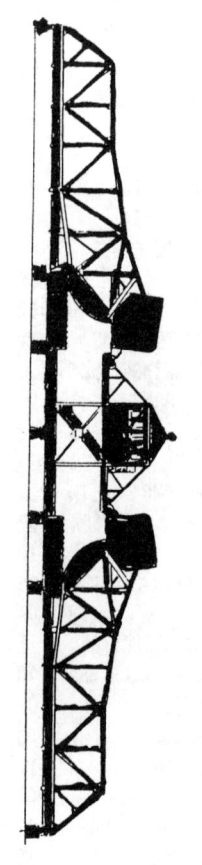

CRRNJ, NEWARK BAY, NJ 1903

BRIDGE & TUNNEL MODEL REVIEWS

	M	Y	P
65' COVERED BRIDGE REVIEW "N" MIL-SCALE	12	71	29
BASCULE BRIDGE REVIEW "HO" RMM	10	71	29
BRIDGE & CULVERT REVIEW "HO" MARION PROD	09	51	49
BRIDGE ABUTMENT/WING REVIEW "HO" AIM	08	73	26
BRIDGE KIT REVIEW "O" EH BUSSEY	06	48	446
BRIDGE KIT REVIEW "O" EH BESSEY	02	42	100
BRIDGE KIT REVIEW "O" EH BESSEY	02	41	115
BRIDGE KIT REVIEWS (3 KITS) "HO" AHM	02	72	26
BRIDGE-3 TYPE REVIEW "N" ATLAS TOOL	07	70	12
BRIDGES REVIEW "N" FALLER	05	68	17
CHALK CREEK BRIDGE REVIEW "HO" MM	01	77	39
COVERED BRIDGE REVIEW "HO" MODEL HOBBIES	09	66	9
COVERED BRIDGE REVIEW "N/HO" MIL-SCALE	11	70	14
CURVED TIMBER TRESTLE REVIEW "HO" SMO	10	53	12
CURVED TRESTLE REVIEW "HO" CAMPBELL	09	61	15
DECK GIRDER BRIDGE REVIEW "HO" CD	05	51	48
DECK GIRDER BRIDGE REVIEW "HO" LAMBERT	06	71	26
DECK PLATE GIRDER BRIDGE REVIEW "HO" C	02	63	18
DOUBLE TRACK PORTAL REVIEW "HO" ALEX	08	53	9
GENERAL PURPOSE BRIDGE REVIEW "HO" J&J	10	63	12
GIRDER BRIDGE REVIEW "HO" CD	09	50	58
GIRDER BRIDGE REVIEW "HO" MSMP	08	53	9
HIGHWAY UNDERPASS REVIEW "HO" RS	05	77	44
HOWE PONY TRUSS BRIDGE REVIEW "O" SJE	11	74	36
LIFT BRIDGE REVIEW "HO" AHM	09	73	28
MASONRY CASTING REVIEW "N" AIM PRODUCTS	06	76	26
PILE TRESTLE 54' REVIEW "HO" CAMPBELL	10	60	16
PLATE GIRDER BRIDGE PLAN	04	39	196
PLATE GIRDER BRIDGE REVIEW "HO" AHM	06	78	39
PRATT TRUSS BRIDGE REVIEW "HO" CV 1844	10	83	47
ROCK TUNNEL PORTAL REVIEW "HO" K&P	01	68	21
SHORT TRESTLE REVIEW "N" CP	10	84	60
SNOWSHEDS REVIEW "HO/N" MIL-SCALE PROD.	11	71	31
STONE ARCH BRIDGE REVIEW "HO" B&W	07	52	60
STONE CULVERT REVIEW "HO" KIMBALL-KRAFT	02	49	67
STONE PORTAL REVIEW "HO" KIMBALL-KRAFT	07	48	507
THREE SPAN PONY TRUSS BRIDGE REV "HO/S"	07	71	20
THROUGH TIMBER BRIDGE REVIEW CPC	10	62	18
THROUGH TIMBER BRIDGE REVIEW "HO" ASM	07	53	55
THROUGH TIMBER TRUSS BRIDGE REVIEW "N" C	05	72	22
TIMBER TRESTLE KITS REV "HO/HON3/N" SISP	09	72	22
TIMBER TRESTLE REVIEW "HO" AHM	06	76	26
TIMBER TRESTLE REVIEW "HO" ASM	10	53	12
TIMBER TRESTLE REVIEW "HO" CD	05	49	49
TIMBER TRESTLE REVIEW "O" LCM BLOSS	02	40	120
TIMBER TRUSS BRIDGE REVIEW "HO/HON3"HDSM	06	66	13
TIMBER TUNNEL PORTAL REVIEW "HO" HDSM	09	66	10
TIMBER TUNNEL PORTAL REVIEW "HO" SMO	01	55	14
TIMBER TUNNEL PORTAL REVIEW "HO"CAMPBELL	12	60	16
TIMBER TUNNEL PORTAL REVIEW "N" CAMPBELL	03	71	26
TRESTLE & BRIDGE REVIEW "HO" MODEL SHOP	05	40	300
TRESTLE KIT REVIEW "1/4" HI RAIL PRODUCT	02	74	25
TRESTLE REVIEW "N" CAL-SCALE	10	68	15
TRUSS BRIDGE REVIEW "HO" ASM	09	55	14
TRUSS BRIDGE REVIEW "HO" EH BESSEY	05	40	300

STRUCTURES & SIGNALS

BRIDGE & TUNNEL MODEL REVIEWS

	M	Y	P
TRUSS BRIDGE REVIEW "TT" GAMCO PRODUCTS	11	66	16
TRUSS BRIDGE SET REVIEW "N" GMX	09	85	34
TRUSS BRIDGES REVIEW "HO" VOLLMER	12	66	11
TRUSS SPAN REVIEW "HO" ATLAS TOOL	07	58	9
TUNNEL PORTAL REVIEW "HO" ARISTO-CRAFT	05	59	12
TUNNEL PORTAL REVIEW "HO" BOB'S ARTCRAFT	12	57	14
TUNNEL PORTAL REVIEW "HO" CS RAFFINGTON	09	46	591
TUNNEL PORTAL REVIEW "N" ALEX	10	69	18
TUNNEL PORTAL REVIEW "O" MODEL STRUCTURE	10	39	544
TUNNEL PORTAL/RETAIN WALLS REV "HO" H&R	08	63	12
TUNNEL PORTALS REVIEW "HO" AIM PRODUCTS	10	73	22
TUNNEL PORTALS REVIEW "HO" ALEX	05	52	53
TUNNEL PORTALS REVIEW "HO" HOBBY HAVEN	01	62	22
TUNNEL PORTALS REVIEW "HO" SCENERY PROD.	12	69	24
WARREN TRUSS BRIDGE REVIEW "HO" AHM	06	78	39
WOOD TRESTLE BENTS REVIEW "HO" HOE	09	63	14
WOOD TRUSS BRIDGE REVIEW "HO" CAMPBELL	06	69	21

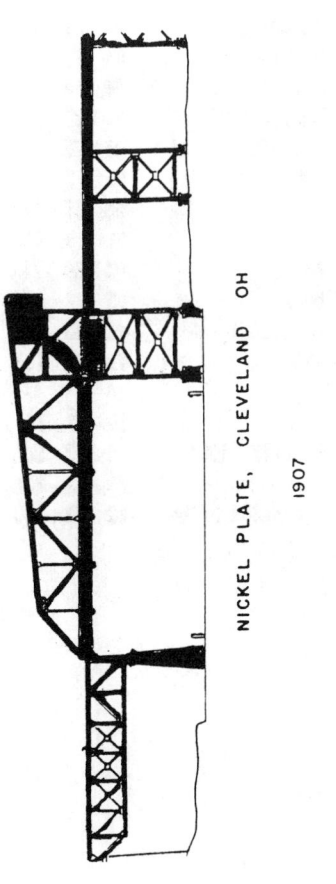

NICKEL PLATE, CLEVELAND OH 1907

BRIDGE & TUNNEL MODEL REVIEWS BY MFG

MFG		M	Y	P
AHM	BRIDGE KIT REVIEWS (3 KITS) "HO" AHM	02	72	26
	LIFT BRIDGE REVIEW "HO" AHM	09	73	28
	TIMBER TRESTLE REVIEW "HO" AHM	06	76	26
	PLATE GIRDER BRIDGE REVIEW "HO" AHM	06	78	39
	WARREN TRUSS BRIDGE REVIEW "HO" AHM	06	78	39
AIM	TUNNEL PORTALS REVIEW "HO" AIM PRODUCTS	10	73	22
	BRIDGE ABUTMENT/WING REVIEW "HO" AIM	08	73	26
	MASONRY CASTING REVIEW "N" AIM PRODUCTS	06	76	26
ALEX	DOUBLE TRACK PORTAL REVIEW "HO" ALEX	08	53	9
	TUNNEL PORTAL REVIEW "N" ALEX	10	69	18
	TUNNEL PORTALS REVIEW "HO" ALEX	05	52	53
ARISTO	TUNNEL PORTAL REVIEW "HO" ARISTO-CRAFT	05	59	12
ASM	THROUGH TIMBER BRIDGE REVIEW "HO" ASM	07	53	55
	TIMBER TRESTLE REVIEW "HO" ASM	10	53	12
	TRUSS BRIDGE REVIEW "HO" ASM	09	55	14
AT	TRUSS SPAN REVIEW "HO" ATLAS TOOL	07	58	9
	BRIDGE-3 TYPE REVIEW "N" ATLAS TOOL	07	70	12
B&W	STONE ARCH BRIDGE REVIEW "HO" B&W	07	52	60
BA	TUNNEL PORTAL REVIEW "HO" BOB'S ARTCRAFT	12	57	14
C	THROUGH TIMBER TRUSS BRIDGE REVIEW "N" C	05	72	22
	WOOD TRUSS BRIDGE REVIEW "HO" CAMPBELL	06	69	21
	CURVED TRESTLE REVIEW "HO" CAMPBELL	09	61	15
	TIMBER TUNNEL PORTAL REVIEW "HO" CAMPBELL	12	60	16
	PILE TRESTLE 54' REVIEW "HO" CAMPBELL	10	60	16
	DECK PLATE GIRDER BRIDGE REVIEW "HO" C	02	63	18
	TIMBER TUNNEL PORTAL REVIEW "N" CAMPBELL	03	71	26
CAL	TRESTLE REVIEW "N" CAL-SCALE	10	68	15
CD	TIMBER TRESTLE REVIEW "HO" CD	05	49	49
	DECK GIRDER BRIDGE REVIEW "HO" CD	05	51	48
	GIRDER BRIDGE REVIEW "HO" CD	09	50	58
CP	SHORT TRESTLE REVIEW "N" CP	10	84	60
CPC	THROUGH TIMBER BRIDGE REVIEW CPC	10	62	18
CSR	TUNNEL PORTAL REVIEW "HO" CS RAFFINGTON	09	46	591
CV	PRATT TRUSS BRIDGE REVIEW "HO" CV 1844	10	83	47
EHB	BRIDGE KIT REVIEW "O" EH BUSSEY	06	48	446
	BRIDGE KIT REVIEW "O" EH BESSEY	02	42	100
	TRUSS BRIDGE REVIEW "HO" EH BESSEY	05	40	300
	BRIDGE KIT REVIEW "O" EH BESSEY	02	41	115
FAL	BRIDGES REVIEW "N" FALLER	05	68	17
GMX	TRUSS BRIDGE SET REVIEW "N" GMX	09	85	34
GP	TRUSS BRIDGE REVIEW "TT" GAMCO PRODUCTS	11	66	16
H&R	TUNNEL PORTAL/RETAIN WALLS REV "HO" H&R	08	63	12
HDSM	TIMBER TUNNEL PORTAL REVIEW "HO" HDSM	09	66	10
	TIMBER TRUSS BRIDGE REVIEW "HO/HON3" HDSM	06	66	13
HHA	TUNNEL PORTALS REVIEW "HO" HOBBY HAVEN	01	62	22
HOE	WOOD TRESTLE BENTS REVIEW "HO" HOE	09	63	14
HR	TRESTLE KIT REVIEW "1/4" HI RAIL PRODUCT	02	74	25
J&J	GENERAL PURPOSE BRIDGE REVIEW "HO" J&J	10	63	12
K&P	ROCK TUNNEL PORTAL REVIEW "HO" K&P	01	68	21
KIK	STONE PORTAL REVIEW "HO" KIMBALL-KRAFT	07	48	507
	STONE CULVERT REVIEW "HO" KIMBALL-KRAFT	02	49	67
L	DECK GIRDER BRIDGE REVIEW "HO" LAMBERT	06	71	26
LCM	TIMBER TRESTLE REVIEW "O" LCM BLOSS	02	40	120
MAP	BRIDGE & CULVERT REVIEW "HO" MARION PROD	09	51	49

STRUCTURES & SIGNALS

BRIDGE & TUNNEL MODEL REVIEWS BY MFG

MFG		M	Y	P
MH	COVERED BRIDGE REVIEW "HO" MODEL HOBBIES	09	66	9
MM	CHALK CREEK BRIDGE REVIEW "HO" MM	01	77	39
MOD	TRESTLE & BRIDGE REVIEW "HO" MODEL SHOP	05	40	300
MS	TUNNEL PORTAL REVIEW "O" MODEL STRUCTURE	10	39	544
MSMP	GIRDER BRIDGE REVIEW "HO" MSMP	08	53	9
MSP	SNOWSHEDS REVIEW "HO/N" MIL-SCALE PROD.	11	71	31
	COVERED BRIDGE REVIEW "N/HO" MIL-SCALE	11	70	14
	65' COVERED BRIDGE REVIEW "N" MIL-SCALE	12	71	29
PMS	THREE SPAN PONY TRUSS BRIDGE REV "HO/S"	07	71	20
RMM	BASCULE BRIDGE REVIEW "HO" RMM	10	71	29
RS	HIGHWAY UNDERPASS REVIEW "HO" RS	05	77	44
SCP	TUNNEL PORTALS REVIEW "HO" SCENERY PROD.	12	69	24
SISP	TIMBER TRESTLE KITS REV "HO/HON3/N" SISP	09	72	22
SJE	HOWE PONY TRUSS BRIDGE REVIEW "O" SJE	11	74	36
SMO	TIMBER TUNNEL PORTAL REVIEW "HO" SMO	01	55	14
	CURVED TIMBER TRESTLE REVIEW "HO" SMO	10	55	12
VOL	TRUSS BRIDGES REVIEW "HO" VOLLMER	12	66	11

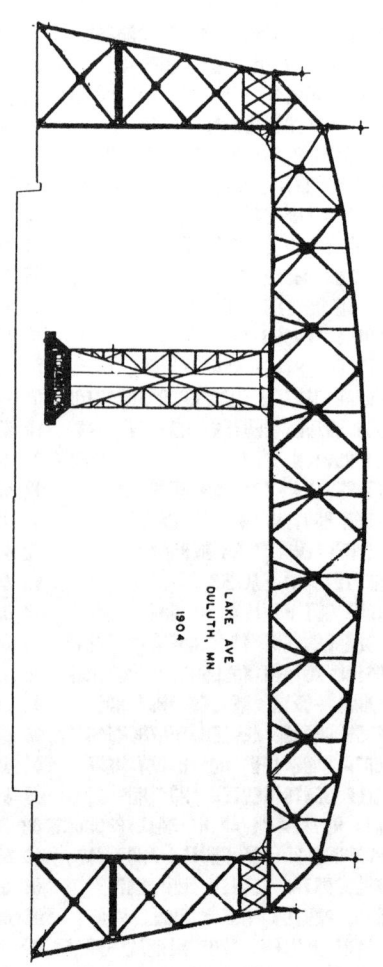

LAKE AVE DULUTH, MN 1904

COMMERCIAL BUILDING PROTOTYPE DATA

	M	Y	P
AMERICA'S LAST BEEHIVE COKE OVENS	06	81	106
ANN ARBOR CENTRAL MILLS	05	81	60
BEEHIVE COKE OVENS	06	81	100
BEEHIVE COKE OVENS ADDITION	08	81	22
BODEN BROTHERS LIVERY STABLE	12	78	100
BOOMTOWNS	05	62	22
BRICK BLOCK INDUST BLDGS BINGHAMTON NY	07	81	58
BULK PARTS- NOT REFINERIES	08	37	291
BULK TAR STORAGE FACILITIES	10	78	100
CATTLE CROSSING GUARD AT RURAL CROSSINGS	07	85	68
COAL UNLOADERS EAGLE HARBOR NY	09	77	71
CONCRETE BLOCK COAL SILO ELBA NY	03	82	94
CORNWELL COAL COMPANY COALYARD	08	71	41
CRODINES GENERAL STORE PROTOTYPE BURNS	07	78	28
DOMEX PACKAGING LTD	05	78	76
FARM MODELING	10	66	62
FARM MODELING-MORE OL' RAY	11	66	69
FIREHOUSE AT ORBISONIA PA	09	83	104
GAS STATION OF 1920 JEWEL OF RIO GRANDE	04	79	78
GRAIN LOADING INDUSTRY	10	84	152
JEFFERSON ICE DEPOT PANTIOCH ILL	10	78	60
KIMCHI GAS WORKS	04	70	59
LOGGING CAMP VANCOUVER, BC CANADA	07	66	20
LUMBER KILN & BOILER HOUSE WYMAN SAWMILL	03	78	62
LUMBER OPERATIONS AND EQUIPMENT	08	66	20
MAC DONALD COAL CO S. HANSEN, MASS	04	85	79
MACHINE SHOP RINGREE GROVE/ELGIN, ILL	03	72	62
MILL OFFICE PORTLAND OREGON	03	75	42
MORE ON STEEL MILLING	06	78	128
OIL FIELDS & EQUIPMENT	01	60	48
PERU PROPANE CORP PERU NY	03	80	74
PICKLEWORKS HOW DO THEY WORK	05	77	114
PROTOTYPE "DEPENDENCY" (OUTHOUSE)	02	63	66
STEEL MILLS ARE INTERESTING	11	77	133
STOCK PENS ON BRACH LINE	10	44	435
STRUCTURES IN THE DESERT	10	67	30
TRACKSIDE STOCK PENS SIOUX CITY, IOWA	04	83	80
WATERFRONT CAR DUMPERS	06	45	251
YOUNG & SONS COAL COMPANY WINDSOR NY D&H	12	83	100

STRUCTURES & SIGNALS

COMMERCIAL BUILDING PLANS	M	Y	P
1920'S FILLING STATION DRAWINGS	08	68	28
ANN ARBOR CENTRAL MILLS DRAWINGS	05	81	61
ARGUS TAP & DIE CO DRAWINGS	04	81	68
AWNING STORE DRAWINGS	05	53	30
BAKERY OF 1900 DRAWINGS	04	79	64
BANK BLOCK PLANS CROOKSVILLE	10	72	68
BATTERY SHOP DRAWINGS MIDDLETOWN OHIO	11	52	26
BECHAUD BREWERY BDGS PLAN FOND DU LAC WI	06	69	42
BICYCLE SHOP PLANS SAN JOSE CA 1900	09	73	40
BLOCK OF STORES DRAWING	02	77	58
BOOM TOWN BUILDING PLANS	05	62	51
BOTT'S COTTON GIN DRAWINGS	09	78	55
BOTTLED GAS PLANT DRAWINGS CLAREMONT NH	01	62	56
BRICK BLOCK INDUST BLDGS PLANS BING. NY	07	81	58
BRIDGE & STEEL WORKS PLN JOHNSON CITY TN	07	58	22
BUILDERS SUPPLY BLDG PLANS N BAY ONT CAN	02	59	33
BUILDERS SUPPLY BUILDING PLNS ELIZAB. TN	07	61	28
BULK OIL PLANT OFFICE PLANS	03	63	42
BULK OIL STORAGE TANK PLANS EAGLE WISC	06	59	48
BULK TAR STORAGE FACILITY PLANS	10	78	100
BUTTON WORKS DRAWINGS	09	79	108
BUTZ MILLING & FEED COMPANY DRAWINGS	03	78	76
BUZZARDS ROOST CO-OP DRAWINGS	03	79	92
CANAL BOAT PLANS C&O	07	76	81
CAROLINA FOUNDRY DRAWINGS	01	72	44
CATTLE CHUTE & STOCK PEN PLANS	03	41	145
CATTLE GUARD DRAWINGS	01	40	32
CENTRAL STEAM HEATING PLANT PLANS	11	78	73
CERESOTA FLOUR MILL DRAWINGS	11	76	82
CHAIR AND DESK FACTORY DRAWING	12	72	66
COAL COMPANY DRAWINGS FULTON COUNTY NY	12	79	87
COAL COMPANY OFFICE PLANS	12	35	321
COAL MINE PITHEAD STRUCTURE DRAWING	10	59	34
COAL SHED AT N ABINGTON MASS DRAWING	07	74	42
COAL YARD BUNKER PLANS CHEYENNE WY	11	64	57
COAL YARD PLANS BRIGHTWATERS, NY	10	69	50
COAL YARD PLANS ARCADIA, NY A&A	02	68	54
COAL YARD PLANS CORNWELL COAL COMPANY	08	71	41
COMPRESSED GAS FACTORY DRAWING DALLAS TX	03	71	46
CONCRETE BLOCK COAL SILO PLANS ELBA NY	03	82	96
CONCRETE BLOCK FACTORY PL LINCOLN BLOCKS	12	77	98
CONCRETE PLANT DRAWINGS	10	81	76
CONCRETE PLANT PLANS	01	58	47
COTTON GIN DRAWINGS	06	82	70
CRODINES GENERAL STORE PLANS	04	78	72
CROSBY FEED & GRAIN DRAWING	08	65	25
CRUSHED STONE MILL DRAWINGS	11	77	82
DOMEX PACKING PLANT PLANS	05	78	76
EAGLE BREWING COMPANY DRAWINGS	03	83	100
EDISON'S GREEK REVIVAL BIRTHPLACE PLANS	10	63	52
EL MOORE VILLAGE STORE PLANS	01	78	60
ELECTRIC UTILITY STRUCTURE PLANS S CA ED	07	75	50
ELECTRICAL SUBSTATION DRAWINGS	09	81	64
EVANS NAT'L BANK DRAWINGS FORESTVILLE NY	11	81	84
FACTORY BETWEEN TRACKS PLANS PIE SHAPED	07	64	40

COMMERCIAL BUILDING PLANS	M	Y	P
FACTORY DRAWINGS DILLY MFG CO	01	67	63
FEED AND SEED PLANT DRAWINGS BUNNS FEED	08	73	35
FEED STORE ELEVATION DRAWINGS	05	48	322
FEEDMILL PLANS WALES WISC	12	54	44
FERTILIZER WORKS PLANS VC FERTILIZERS	08	70	38
FIREHOUSE AT GALNA, ILL PLANS	10	60	55
FIREHOUSE DRAWINGS ORBISONIA PA	09	83	104
FLEX-ON PACKAGING CO DRAWING SENOIA GA S	04	81	64
FRAME ROW HOUSES DRAWINGS	03	77	54
FRARY & HAYDEN MARINE SUPPLY DRAWINGS	02	79	72
FRYE MACHINING COMPANY FACTORY DRAWING	04	58	33
GAS STATION OF 1920 DRAWINGS A JEWEL	04	79	80
GAS STATION, GARAGE & GROCERY PLANS	03	78	66
GAS WORKS STORAGE TANK PLANS MONTEREY CA	04	70	56
GENERAL STORE & POST OFFICE DRAWINGS	07	56	24
GENERAL STORE PLANS N ORWELL PA 1830	02	83	76
GILMORE FEED MILL DRAWINGS LAKEVILLE NY	03	81	80
GOLD MINE HOIST HOUSE & ORE BIN DRAWINGS	02	75	74
GOLD MINE PLANS HEAD FRAME BUILDING	01	75	50
GRAIN & FEED PLANS WM H ARCHER CORP	02	80	82
GRAIN ELEVATOR DRAWINGS	11	42	492
GRAIN ELEVATOR DRAWINGS OAK LAKE CANADA	08	74	54
GRAIN ELEVATOR DRAWINGS.	05	49	24
GRAIN ELEVATOR PLANS B & GREEN LEROY NY	09	72	46
GRAIN ELEVATOR PLANS MONMOUTH ILL	02	63	58
GRAIN LOADING SHED DRAWINGS	06	63	45
GRAVEL UNLOADING TRESTLE PLANS	06	76	74
GREENWICH CONN COAL COMPANY PLANS	02	58	34
GROCERY WAREHOUSE PLANS JONESBORO, TENN	07	59	42
HARDWARE STORE DRAWINGS	08	65	28
HARDWARE STORE DRAWINGS "SHANNON & CO"	06	53	17
HIGH TENSION TRANSMISSION TOWER DRAWINGS	07	75	46
IRON WORKS DRAWINGS	03	83	100
JONES CHEMICAL FACTORY DRAWINGS	03	74	44
JUNKYARD OFFICE DRAWING	10	83	106
KINGFIELD CHEMICAL CO MILL DRAWINGS	08	79	100
LIVERY STABLE PLANS BODEN BROTHERS	12	78	100
LOG LOADER PLANS MCGIFFERT LOADER	02	82	100
LOGGING CAMP STRUCTURES/CAR DRAWINGS	07	66	21
LUMBER COMPANY DRAWINGS MCGEE LUMBER	01	67	64
LUMBER KILN & BOILER HOUSE PLANS	03	78	62
LUMBER MILL DRAWINGS WYMANS MILL	09	76	48
LUMBER YARD BUILDING (CAL'S) DRAWINGS	04	73	62
MAC DONALD COAL CO DRAWING S HANSEN MASS	04	85	80
MACHINE SHOP PLANS RINGREE GROVE/ELGIN	03	72	64
MALT TOWER PLANS	07	73	56
MILL OFFICE DRAWINGS PORTLAND OREGON	03	75	44
MILLING & FEED PLANT PLANS GILBERTS, ILL	06	72	38
MILLING COMPANY DRAWINGS WILLIAMSPORT PA	07	52	11
MINE BUILDING PLANS	07	55	30
MINE HEAD BUILDING PLANS	04	66	24
MODERN GRAIN ELEVATOR DRAWING	06	57	26
MOELLER'S GENERAL STORE PLANS	05	61	30
NORDI'S GARAGE DRAWINGS TROY NY	01	85	116
OIL WELL PUMP PLANS	09	52	24

STRUCTURES & SIGNALS

COMMERCIAL BUILDING PLANS

	M	Y	P
OIL WELL RIG PLANS	09	52	21
OLD TIME GAS STATION DRAWINGS 1920	03	77	92
OPEN AIR WAREHOUSE GOVAN, SC PLANS SAL	11	62	34
OPERATING WINDMILL PLANS	09	82	67
ORE BIN PLANS URANUS MINE	05	81	84
ORE LOADING TIPPLE PLANS PARK CITY UTAH	10	60	37
PAWN SHOP DRAWING "UNCLE BEN'S"	06	53	19
PEACHEY BROS FEED MILL PLANS BURNETT WIS	05	59	26
PERKINS PRODUCE BUILDING PLANS	12	74	56
PERU PROPANE CORP BUILDING PLANS PERU NY	03	80	76
PETERS SAUSAGE FACTORY DRAWINGS	04	74	62
PICKEL FACTORY PLANS ELK MOUND WISC	02	61	30
PICKLE WORKS DRAWING PALMYRA WISC	01	55	40
PLANING MILL DRAWINGS CARRBORO NC	07	82	67
POWDER WORKS DRAWING CANNONBALL & SAFETY	04	77	68
POWER SUBSTATION DRAWINGS	04	60	47
PULP WOOD YARD OFFICE PLANS EHRHARDT SC	03	66	42
PUTTLES POT WORKS DRAWINGS (FOUNDRY)	09	75	64
QUONSET HUT FACTORY PLANS	01	62	51
RAIL TRUCK TERMINAL DRAW MINITOWWOC WISC	04	62	45
RED BARN PLANS	01	66	56
ROADSIDE FILLING STATION DRAWING	03	42	129
ROCK CRUSHER CONVEYOR & BUNKER DRAWING	12	57	62
ROCK CRUSHER DRAWINGS GATE CITY VA 1918	11	57	26
ROOFING SHOP DRAWINGS	05	53	32
ROY STREET HOUSE TEMPLATES	01	80	122
SALOON & GENERAL STORE DRAWINGS GENOA NV	11	56	30
SAND AND GRAVEL OFFICE DRAWINGS	06	76	79
SAWMILL BUILDING PLANS TACOMA WASH	08	56	37
SAWMILL PLANS	06	68	33
SECOND NATIONAL BANK DRAWINGS	05	74	35
SHACK W/OIL ROOM COAL BIN & TOILET PLANS	07	36	190
SMALL TOWN HOTEL DRAWING	08	54	16
SMALL TOWN WAREHOUSE DRAW JONESBORO TN	04	57	26
SOUVENIER FACTORY DRAWINGS	10	62	32
STAR HOTEL DRAWINGS	08	79	76
STATION DRUGSTORE DRAWINGS	05	71	38
STORE & ROOMING HOUSE DRAWINGS	01	70	66
STOREHOUSE OF CORREGATED METAL PLANS	03	70	54
STUCKUM GLUE WORKS DRAWING	10	77	78
TALL TIPPLE PLANS CANANEA MEXICO	01	77	80
TELEPHONE BOOTH PLANS P&WV FAIRHAVEN PA	02	65	47
TOBACCO WAREHOUSE DRAWING EVANSVILLE WIS	11	54	44
TRACKSIDE CATTLE PEN PLANS	09	59	58
TRACKSIDE HOUSE SHACK DRAWING	11	47	880
TRACKSIDE SHANTY DRAWINGS	09	56	25
TRACKSIDE STOCK PENS PLANS SIOUX CITY IO	04	83	82
TRIANGLE SERVICE STATION DRAWINGS	10	78	96
UNION GROVE WI TILE WORKS PLANS	12	61	44
VEGETABLE GROWERS CO-OP OFF DRAW ELBA NY	03	82	95
VERTICAL LIME KILN DRAWINGS	11	80	75
VICTORIAN HOUSE DRAWINGS	08	66	47
VILLAGE STORE BLOCK DRAWINGS	09	50	14
VILLAGE STORE DRAWING	04	55	26
VILLAGE STOREFRONT DRAWINGS	10	67	34

COMMERCIAL BUILDING PLANS

	M	Y	P
WALK UP APARTMENTS & BAR DRAW PHILA PA	05	57	26
WAREHOUSE DRAWINGS CENTRAL WAREHOUSE CO	01	67	62
WAREHOUSE FOR BUILDING MATERIALS PLANS	09	70	54
WATER TANK & SHED DRAWINGS HOLLIDAY KS	01	54	59
WATER TOWER PLANS PRAIRIE DU SAC WI	10	82	87
WAYSIDE WAREHOUSE DRAWINGS	06	74	31
WESTERN SALOON & HOTEL PLANS	03	63	47
WESTERN SAWMILL PLANS	11	61	34
WINDMILL DRAWINGS UP LARAMIE WYO	09	62	60
WOOD SHAVINGS SHED PLANS CHARLOTTE, NC	07	63	48
YOUNG & SONS COAL CO DRAWINGS WINDSOR NY	12	83	99

COMMERCIAL BUILDING PLANS BY ROAD

RD		M	Y	P
A&A	COAL YARD PLANS ARCADIA, NY A&A	02	68	54
C&NW	MILLING & FEED PLANT PLANS GILBERTS, ILL	06	72	38
C&O	CANAL BOAT PLANS C&O	07	76	81
D&H	YOUNG & SONS COAL CO DRAWINGS WINDSOR NY	12	83	99
P&WV	TELEPHONE BOOTH PLANS P&WV FAIRHAVEN PA	02	65	47
S	FLEX-ON PACKAGING CO DRAWING SENOIA GA S	04	81	64
SAL	OPEN AIR WAREHOUSE GOVAN, SC PLANS SAL	11	62	34
UP	WINDMILL DRAWINGS UP LARAMIE WYO	09	62	60

COMMERCIAL BUILDING PHOTOS

	M	Y	P
GINGERBREAD DETAIL PHOTOS	11	73	76

STRUCTURES & SIGNALS

COMMERCIAL BUILDING MODELS

	M	Y	P
1920'S FILLING STATION CONSTRUCTION	08	68	28
ALANVILLE-ELEVATED CITY	02	47	114
ALEXANDER'S SCHOOLHOUSE KIT MODIFICATION	04	56	53
APARTMENT HOUSE WITH BAR CONST PHILA PA	05	57	24
ARGUS TAP & DIE CO CONSTRUCTION	04	81	68
AUTO LIFT CONSTRUCTION	05	46	314
BAKERY OF 1900 CONSTRUCTION	04	79	62
BARREL RACK CONSTRUCTION $1	08	76	60
BATTERY SHOP CONSTRUCTION MIDDLETOWN O	11	52	26
BECHRUD BREWERY CONST FOND DU LAC WI	06	69	40
BEEHIVE COKE OVENS CONSTRUCTION	06	81	100
BETWEEN TRACKS FACTORY CONSTRUCTION	07	64	38
BLACKHOLE MINE CONSTRUCTION	12	78	72
BLACKSMITH SHOP CONSTRUCTION 1 $1	06	64	44
BLOCK OF STORES CONSTRUCTION BRANDYWINE	02	77	57
BOTT'S COTTON GIN CONSTRUCTION	09	78	54
BOTTLED GAS WORKS CONST CLAREMONT JCT NH	01	62	55
BRICK GAS STATION KITBASH	04	80	62
BRIDGE & STEEL WORKS CONST JOHNSON C. TN	07	58	20
BUILD A COAL YARD BRIGHTWATERS, NY	10	69	50
BUILDERS SUPPLY STORE CONST ELIZAB. TN	07	61	27
BUILDERS SUPPLY YARD CONST N BAY ONT CAN	02	59	32
BUILDING FLATS AS BACKGROUND STRUCTURES	06	80	88
BUILDING GLANVILLE PARK	12	77	112
BULK MATERIALS PLANT MOD & PT	03	75	20
BULK OIL DEPOT CONSTRUCTION	08	40	420
BULK OIL DEPOT CONSTRUCTION EAGLE WISC	06	59	46
BULK OIL DISTRIBUTION PLANT CONSTRUCTION	12	78	108
BULK OIL PLANT FOR EASY MODELING $1	12	69	74
BUTTON WORKS CONSTRUCTION	09	79	108
BUTZ MILLING & FEED COMPANY CONSTRUCTION	03	78	76
BUZZARDS ROOST CO-OP CONSTRUCION	03	79	90
CANADA CRUSHED & CUT STONE CONSTRUCTION	11	77	82
CAR FERRY FOR YOUR LAYOUT CONSTRUCTION	01	70	48
CATTLE GUARD CONSTRUCTION	01	40	33
CATTLE GUARD CONSTRUCTION	02	54	32
CATTLE GUARD CONSTRUCTION IN A MINUTE	12	48	914
CATTLE PEN CONSTRUCTION	09	59	57
CENTRAL STEAM HEATING PLANT CONSTRUCTION	11	78	73
CHAIR AND DESK FACTORY CONSTRUCTION $1	12	72	65
CHEMICAL FACTORY CONST JONES CHEMICAL	03	74	42
CHRISVILLE MILL FROM CON COR COURTHOUSE	06	80	54
CITY HOME CONSTRUCTION	10	46	646
CLODINES GENERAL STORE CONSTRUCTION	04	78	70
COAL BARGE CONSTRUCTION	01	61	65
COAL COMPANY CONSTRUCTION GREENWICH CONN	02	58	33
COAL COMPANY FULTON COUNTY NY	12	79	86
COAL ELEVATOR CONSTRUCTION	11	35	296
COAL MINE CONSTRUCTION BASIC LAYOUT	10	59	30
COAL MINE CONSTRUCTION PITHEAD BUILDINGS	11	59	60
COAL MINE CONSTRUCTION SHAFT/OUT BLDGS	12	59	62
COAL SHED CONSTRUCTION N ABINGTON MASS	07	74	41
COAL YARD BUNKER CONST CHEYENNE WI	11	64	56
COAL YARD CONSTRUCTION ARCADIA, NY A&A	02	68	52
COMPOUND KITBASHING A FEED MILL	01	78	112

COMMERCIAL BUILDING MODELS

	M	Y	P
COMPRESSED GAS FACTORY CONSTRUCTION	03	71	42
CONCRETE BLOCK FACTORY CONSTRUCTION	12	77	96
CONCRETE PLANT CONSTRUCTION	01	58	46
CONCRETE PLANT CONSTRUCTION	10	81	73
CONCRETE STRUCTURE CONSTRUCTION	02	78	116
CORREGATED STORE HOUSE CONSTRUCTION $1	03	70	54
COTTON GIN CONSTRUCTION	06	82	70
DODD DAM POWER COMPANY CONST HARMON, NY	11	41	548
DOLESE SAND & GRAVEL SCRATCHBUILD	08	84	63
DRIVE IN MOVIE CONSTRUCTION	03	79	118
DRUG STORE CONSTRUCTION STATION DRUGS	05	71	36
EASTWYCK & FENSTERSTOCK CONSTRUCTION CO	01	78	95
EDISON SUPPLY COMPANY KITBASH	08	83	62
EDISON'S GREEK REVIVAL HOUSE CONSTRUCTIO	10	63	50
EL MOORE VILLAGE STORE CONSTRUCTION	01	78	58
ELECTRIC UTILITY CONSTRUCTION	07	75	43
ELECTRICAL SUBSTATION CONSTRUCTION	09	81	62
ESKEW JUNKYARD CONSTRUCTION	10	83	106
FACTORY OF WOOD & BRICK CONSTRUCTION	08	70	35
FARM WAGON CONSTRUCTION	03	47	210
FEED & GRAIN BASH GAMBOL, WHAITE, & HOPE	03	85	69
FEED AND SEED PLANT CONSTRUCTION BUNNS	08	73	34
FEED MILL CONSTRUCTION 1 WALES WISC	12	54	44
FEED MILL CONSTRUCTION PEACHEY BROTHERS	05	59	26
FEED STORE CONSTRUCTION	05	48	320
FENCE OF OLD BOARDS CONSTRUCTION	02	52	49
FIELD STONE TAVERN RAYS BAR "HO" CONST	11	85	112
FIRE HOUSE AT GALENA IL CONSTRUCTION	10	60	54
FIRE HOUSE CONSTRUCTION KINGSTON NY	11	55	34
FLAT IRON COMPANY KITBASH	12	82	105
FLEX-ON PACKAGING CO CONST SENOIA GA S	04	81	63
FLOUR MILL CONSTRUCTION CERESOTA MILL	11	76	80
FOUNDRY CONSTRUCTION $1	01	72	44
FRAME ROW HOUSES CONSTRUCTION	03	77	54
FRARY & HAYDEN MARINE SUPPLY CONSTRUCTIO	02	79	72
FRISKY BRICKYARD CONSTRUCTION	01	79	158
FROM TANK CAR TO GAS STATION CONSTRUCT	03	78	104
FRONTIER TOWN STRUCTURE CONSTRUCTION	09	64	36
FRUGAL FACTORY KITBASH	08	81	67
FRYE MACHINING COMPANY FACTORY CONSTRUCT	04	58	32
GAS WORKS CONSTRUCTION MONTEREY CA $1	04	70	54
GENERAL STORE AND POST OFFICE CONSTRUCT	07	56	24
GENERAL STORE CONSTRUCTION	01	50	16
GOLD MINE CONSTRUCT GOLD IN THEM HILLS	01	75	46
GOLD MINE CONSTRUCTION ORE BIN/HOIST	02	75	72
GRAIN ELEVATOR CONST OAK RIDGE CANADA	08	74	54
GRAIN ELEVATOR CONSTRUCTION	11	42	492
GRAIN ELEVATOR CONSTRUCTION MONMOUTH IL	02	63	62
GRAIN ELEVATOR CONSTRUCTION.	05	49	24
GRAIN LOADING SHED CONSTRUCTION	06	63	44
GRANDMOTHER'S HOUSE CONSTRUCTION	10	77	88
HARDLY ABLE MFG FROM 2 SUPERIOR BAKERIES	08	85	71
HARDWARE STORE CONSTRUCTION	06	53	16
HIGHWAY CROSSING GATES (WORKING) CONST	10	62	66
HO BLAST FURNACE PHOTOS	03	59	48

STRUCTURES & SIGNALS

COMMERCIAL BUILDING MODELS

	M	Y	P
HOTEL (VILLAGE) CONSTRUCTION	08	54	16
HOTEL KITBASH DRISCOLL INN	07	75	69
HOUSE WITH GINGERBREAD DETAIL CONSTRUCT	11	73	71
INDIANA HOG FARM MODELING	02	79	106
INDUSTRIAL STORAGE TANK CONSTRUCTION	01	45	8
IRONWORKS CONSTRUCTION LEVINE BROTHERS	03	77	80
JAIL CONSTRUCTION	11	76	89
KINGFIELD CHEMICAL CO MILL CONSTRUCTION	08	79	99
KOPAY'S FURNITURE STORE SCRATCHBUILD	03	83	70
LARGE INDUSTRY FOR SMALL LAYOUT KITBASH	07	77	54
LOG LOADER KITBASH MCGIFFERT LOADER	02	82	98
LUMBER & SUPPLY YARD CONST SECOND SHED	07	60	48
LUMBER & SUPPLY YARD CONSTRUCTION SHED	06	60	46
LUMBER & SUPPLY YD CONST SELLERSVILLE PA	05	60	42
LUMBER MILL CONSTRUCTION WYMANS MILL	09	76	46
LUMBER RACK CONSTRUCTION	01	77	66
LUMBER YARD (CAL'S) CONSTRUCTION	04	73	62
MACHINE SHOP TO WOLLEN MILL KITBASH	05	77	76
MAHJEK FURNITURE CO STRUCTURE KITBASHING	10	79	101
MALT TOWER CONSTRUCTION	07	73	58
MAPLE STREET USA HOUSES KITBASHING	11	79	72
MARQUEE TRAVELING LIGHT SYSTEM	03	76	78
MEAT BUSINESS CONSTRUCTION	05	50	10
MILL FOR GRAIN FEED COAL & SALT CONST	07	52	10
MILLING & FEED PLANT CONST GILBERTS, ILL	06	72	38
MINE BUILDING CONSTRUCTION	07	55	30
MINE CONSTRUCTION	04	66	22
MODERN BLOCK OF STORES CONSTRUCTION	02	78	108
MODERN GRAIN ELEVATOR CONSTRUCTION	06	57	24
MOM AMERICAN COAL COMPANY "HO" HORNER	09	68	43
MOM BEAMER & GREEN PRODUCE "HO" MACGOWN	11	73	60
MOM CANADIAN GRAIN ELEVATOR "HO" TOKARUK	06	84	87
MOM CHURCH & CHURCH LUMBER COMPANY "HO"	07	78	91
MOM COAL MINE & DOUBLE TIPPLE "HO"	09	83	83
MOM COMBINATION GAS STAION "HO" FERGUSON	02	79	77
MOM DAVIES STEEL BLAST FURNACE 2 "HO"	10	79	68
MOM GAULEY VALLEY FEEDS "HO" RILEY	12	77	69
MOM GOLDBRICK MINE "HON3" MEEKER	06	70	68
MOM HILLSIDE BARN "O" HEWLEY	12	79	111
MOM MINING COMPLEX "HO" ROSE	08	85	70
MOM ORE TIPPLE "O" GREENBERG	03	79	98
MOM PICKS PRODUCE "N" FORD	04	76	40
MOM PISCATAQUA SAND & GRAVEL CLERKE	01	74	57
MOM RR MACHINE SHOPS "HO" BOUDREAU	12	83	116
MOM SAWMILL "KELLY'S" COWLING	06	78	83
MOM SCHLURP BREWERY "HO" FLEMING	10	75	69
MOM STOCKYARDS "HO" ANDERSON	07	82	78
MOM SWITCH SCENE "HO" BLACK	04	70	43
MOM TEN STAMP MILL "HO" WICKERSHAM	09	84	66
MOM TRAINMANS HOTEL "HO" KELLER	11	74	85
MOM VICTORIAN STORE "HO" NEWCOMB	06	77	57
MOM WILMOT TABLE CO "HO" LAWSON	04	82	71
MOM WSL CAMP CAR "ON3" FERRELL	07	79	63
MOVIE THEATER CONSTRUCTION	03	76	75
OIL FIELDS & EQUIPMENT MODELING	01	60	48

COMMERCIAL BUILDING MODELS

	M	Y	P
OIL STORAGE TANKS FOR NEXT TO NOTHING	10	83	118
OIL WELL RIG CONSTRUCTION	09	52	20
OLD FASHIONED HOUSE CONSTRUCTION.	08	66	47
OLD RED BARN CONSTRUCTION $1	01	66	54
OLD TIME GAS STATION CONSTRUCTION 1920	03	77	89
OLD TIME WESTERN SALOON CONSTRUCTION	03	63	46
OLGAS RESTAURANT PAINTING MOD & PT	02	78	122
OPEN AIR WAREHOUSE CONSTRUCTION GOVAN SC	11	62	33
OPERATING WINDMILL CONSTRUCTION	07	64	27
OPERATING WINDMILL CONSTRUCTION	09	82	66
PACKING COMPANY CONSTRUCTION	03	65	52
PAWN SHOP CONSTRUCTION	06	53	16
PENNSYLVANIA DUTCH STRUCTURE CONST	08	65	25
PERRY SHIBBEL FRUIT & PRODUCE CO-OP KITB	01	79	102
PETERS SAUSAGE COMPANY CONSTRUCTION	04	74	60
PETROLEUM BULK PLANT CONSTRUCTION	03	63	42
PICKLE FACTORY CONSTRUCTION ELK MOUND WI	02	61	29
PICKLE FACTORY CONSTRUCTION PALMYRA WISC	01	55	40
PLANING MILL CONSTRUCTION CARRBORO NC	07	82	66
PLATFORM ELEVATOR PENTHOUSE CONSTRUCTION	09	55	45
PODNER SAM'S STEAK 'N VITTLES MOD & PT	07	77	87
POTWORKS FOUNDRY CONSTRUCTION	09	75	62
POWDER WORKS CONST CANNON BALL & SAFETY	04	77	68
POWER PLANT MOD & PT	10	76	86
POWER SUBSTATION CONSTRUCTION	04	60	47
PRODUCE BUILDING CONSTRUCTION	12	74	54
PULPWOOD YARD CONSTRUCTION	03	66	40
QUONSET HUT FACTORY CONSTRUCTION	01	62	51
RAIL TRUCK TERMINAL CONST MINITOWWOC WIS	04	62	44
RAMSHACKLE SHACK CONSTRUCTION	09	43	398
RIVERFRONT FACTORY CONSTRUCTION	01	46	6
ROADSIDE DINER FROM INTERURBAN CONST	08	59	42
ROADSIDE FILLING STATION CONSTRUCTION	03	42	129
ROCK CRUSHER CONSTRUCTION GATE CITY VA	11	57	26
ROCK CRUSHER CONVEYOR & BUNKER CONSTRUCT	12	57	62
ROCK PRODUCTS BUNKER CNST LOS NIETUS CA2	11	54	55
ROCK PRODUCTS BUNKER CNST LOS NIETUS CA3	12	54	52
ROCK PRODUCTS BUNKER CONST LOS NIETOS CA	10	54	24
ROCK QUARRY FOR BUD LINE CONSTRUCTION	01	79	98
ROY STREET HOUSE CONSTRUCTION	01	80	121
SALOON & GENERAL STORE CONST GENOA NV	11	56	30
SAND & GRAVEL CO WITH UNLOAD TRESTLE CON	06	76	74
SANFORD & SON JUNKYARD CONSTRUCTION	02	83	92
SAWMILL CONSTRUCTION	06	68	28
SAWMILL CONSTRUCTION MACHINERY	07	68	50
SAWMILL CONSTRUCTION TACOMA WASH	08	56	36
SCRAPYARD SHED DRAWINGS	03	77	84
SECOND NATIONAL BANK CONSTRUCTION	05	74	34
SHAKEY CHAIR COMPANY KITBASH	10	77	52
SIGNS FOR WAREHOUSE	09	70	54
SIMPLE COAL UNLOADER CONSTRUCTION	09	77	71
SMALL TOWN WAREHOUSE CONST JONESBORO TN	04	57	26
SOUVENIR FACTORY CONSTRUCTION	10	62	32
STAR HOTEL SCRATCHBUILD	08	79	76
STAR PRINTERS KITBASH	08	80	71

STRUCTURES & SIGNALS

COMMERCIAL BUILDING MODELS

	M	Y	P
STEEL MILL MODELING	11	84	109
STORAGE SHEDS KITBASHED A PAIR	09	84	70
STORE & OFFICE CONSTRUCTION ABILENE KS	05	55	30
STORE FRONTS OF GAY NINETIES CONSTRUCT	02	49	16
STORE WITH ROOMS ABOVE CONSTRUCTION	01	70	64
STRUCTURES FROM HISTORY CONSTRUCTION	01	71	56
STUCKUM GLUE WORKS CONSTRUCTION	10	77	76
SUNNYSIDE MILL CONSTRUCTION (CAST WALLS)	02	82	78
TALL TIPPLE CONSTRUCTION AT TONOPAH	01	77	78
TELEPHONE AND UTILITY LINE CONSTRUCTION	01	68	40
TIE TREATING PLANT CONSTRUCTION	10	75	78
TILE WORKS UNION GROVE WI CONSTRUCTION	12	61	42
TOBACCO WAREHOUSE CONST EVANSVILLE WISC	11	54	44
TRACK GATES REMOTELY OPERATED CONST $1	03	67	38
TRACKSIDE HOUSE SHACK CONSTRUCTION	11	47	880
TRACKSIDE SHANTY CONSTRUCTION	09	56	25
TRANSFORMER BANK FOR INDUSTRY CONSTRUCT	01	49	14
TRIANGLE SERVICE STATION CONSTRUCTION	10	78	94
TROLLEY-STOP LUNCHONETTE CONSTRUCTION	07	77	83
URANUS #2 MINE CONSTRUCTION	05	81	83
VERTICAL LIME KILN CONSTRUCTION	11	80	74
VILLAGE STORE CONSTRUCTION	09	50	12
VILLAGE STORE CONSTRUCTION	04	55	25
VILLAGE STOREFRONT CONSTRUCTION	10	67	33
WARNING LIGHT FOR TALL BUILDINGS CONST	06	61	33
WASCO GAS STATION, GARAGE & STORE CONST	03	78	66
WATER TANK & SHED CONSTRUCT HOLLIDAY KS	01	54	58
WATER TOWER CONSTRUCT PRAIRIE DU SAC WI	10	82	86
WAYSIDE SHANTY CONSTRUCTION MP MYRICK MO	07	59	36
WAYSIDE WAREHOUSE CONSTRUCTION	06	74	30
WELTE LUMBER & MILLWORK KITBASH	05	85	68
WESTERN "BOOM TOWN" CONSTRUCTION	05	62	50
WESTERN SAWMILL CONSTRUCTION	11	61	32
WHERE'S THE FIREHOUSE CONSTRUCTION	08	46	510
WHOLESALE GROCERY WAREHOUSE CONSTRUCTION	07	59	42
WINDMILL CONSTRUCTION UP LARAMIE WYO	09	62	58
WINDOW DRESSINGS & SEASONED SIDINGS	07	78	78
WINTER ON GINGER CREEK	12	83	87
WOOD SHAVINGS SHED CONST CHARLOTTE, NC	07	63	46
WOOD WINDMILL CONSTRUCTION	05	55	40

COMMERCIAL BUILDING MODEL REVIEWS

	M	Y	P
AMERICAN STRUCTURE REVIEW "N" HELJAN	06	68	15
APARTMENT BUILDING REVIEW "HO" MMD	12	77	55
ASSAY OFFICE REVIEW "HO" SIMPSON PRODUCT	01	69	12
AYRES CHAIRS FACTORY REVIEW "HO" C	10	77	35
BACKGROUND STRUCTURE REVIEW "HO" ARISTO	05	57	12
BAKERY REVIEW "HO" REVELL	10	77	40
BANK REVIEW "HO" MMD	05	78	47
BARN & OUTBUILDINGS REVIEW "HO" REVELLE	12	59	14
BARN REVIEW "HO" SUYDAM	11	56	12
BEKINS WAREHOUSE REVIEW "HO" E SUYDAM CO	07	72	22
BLACKSMITH SHOP REVIEW "HO" DYNA MODELS	01	64	14
BLOCK OF STORES REVIEW "HO/N" MMD	05	82	44
BOARDING HOUSE REVIEW "HO" CAMPBELL	12	78	52
BOILER-PUMPHOUSE & TANK REVIEW "HO" IMW	03	59	13
BOILERHOUSE REVIEW "HO" SSL	04	69	15
BOX FACTORY REVIEW "HO" SUYDAM	08	56	14
BOX FACTORY REVIEW "N" QUALITY CRAFT	01	73	27
BREWERY LISTING "HO" MAGNUSON MODELS	11	78	63
BRICK BUILDING REVIEW "HO" VOLLMER	08	64	11
BRICK BUILDING REVIEWS "1/8" H&R	01	66	15
BROWN'S HOUSE NEVADA CITY NV REV "HO" MU	03	81	46
BUILDING FRONTS REVIEW "HO" ISLE	03	85	40
BUNGALOW REVIEW "HO" SUMMIT ENGINEERING	02	56	10
BUSINESS BLOCK REVIEW "HO" AHM	04	79	42
BUTCHER SHOP REVIEW "HO" DYNA MODELS	04	56	10
BUTLER BUILDING WAREHOUSE REVIEW "HO"PIS	02	85	37
CAFE LISTING "HO" LYTLER & LYTLER	10	78	55
CAPE COD HOUSE REVIEW "N" AHM	11	74	43
CATTLE PEN LISTING "HO" CAMPBELL	12	78	68
CATTLE PEN REVIEW "O" BOXCAR KEN	06	55	13
CEMENT PLANT REVIEW "HO" FALLER	07	77	29
CEMETERY LISTING "HO" WOODLAND SCENICS	08	78	48
CHICAGO TOWNHOUSE REVIEW "HO" SSL	10	69	19
CHURCH REVIEW "HO" AHM	09	73	27
CHURCH REVIEW "HO" CAMPBELL	02	69	16
CIMMARON SUPPLY CO WAREHOUSE REV "HO" MM	11	80	58
CITY HALL REVIEW "HO" CC	02	79	42
CITY STRUCTURES REVIEW "HO" MMD	06	77	39
COAL MINE REVIEW "HO" MINIKITS	08	67	14
COAL YARD REVIEW "HO" CC	02	79	42
COAL YARD REVIEW "HO" MODEL HOBBIES	11	51	54
COLD STORAGE BUILDING REVIEW "N" HELIAN	07	70	14
COMMERCIAL BUILDING REVIEW "N" MP	04	82	46
COMMERCIAL BUILDINGS REVIEW "N" JMC	10	73	26
COMPANY HOUSE LISTING "HO" MODEL HOBBIES	12	77	62
COMPANY HOUSES W. VA REVIEW "HO" KLW	08	80	46
CONTAINER WAREHOUSE REVIEW "HO" TIM	06	73	27
CONTEMPORARY HOUSE LISTING N MODEL POWER	02	77	46
COOPERS GARAGE REVIEW "HO" F	04	75	31
CORNER SHOP REVIEW "OO" CSML	12	84	64
CORNER STORE REVIEW "HO/N" CC	07	80	37
COUNTRY CHURCH REVIEW "HO" MODEL HOBBIES	09	56	9
COUNTRY CHURCH REVIEW "HO" SLR	09	64	8
COUNTRY GROCERY STORE REVIEW "O" CHO	03	79	46
COUNTRY STORE REVIEW "HO" CHO	10	80	45

145

STRUCTURES & SIGNALS

COMMERCIAL BUILDING MODEL REVIEWS

	M	Y	P
COUNTRY STORE REVIEW "HO" SSL 1860	02	71	20
CREOSOTING PLANT REVIEW "HO" TRI	05	63	8
CROCKER BROTHERS FEED MILLS REV "HO" F	10	80	52
DEWITTS DEPOSITORY LISTING "HO" C	05	78	53
DIE CRAFT MFG CO FACTORY REVIEW "HO" LL	03	74	28
DINGHY SHOP REVIEW "HO" CAMPBELL	12	75	34
DOCTORS OFFICE REVIEW "HO" C	01	78	42
DOLLAR BROS MOTOR EXPRESS REVIEW "O" EHD	05	79	41
DRAKE OIL WELL REVIEW "HO" STEWART PROD.	07	77	35
DRUGSTORE REVIEW "HO" SCALE STRUCTURES	01	72	20
EDISON LABORATORY REVIEW "HO" CC	02	80	50
FACTORY 1903 REVIEW "N" CONCOR	09	69	9
FACTORY CONCRETE WORKS REVIEW "N" VOL	12	70	36
FACTORY KIT REV "HO" 20TH CENTURY SALES	11	49	90
FACTORY REVIEW "HO" KIB	06	85	37
FACTORY REVIEW "HO" POLA	11	70	14
FACTORY STRUCTURE REVIEW "N" BUSCH	10	68	20
FARMHOUSE GROUP REVIEW "HO" AHM	09	72	28
FARMHOUSE REVIEW "HO" CAPBELL	09	73	20
FARMHOUSE REVIEW "N" AHM	10	74	24
FEED MILL REVIEW "HO" SUYDAM	09	56	15
FEED MILL WALES WISC REVIEW "HO" C C&NW	10	81	40
FIRE STATION OF BRICK REVIEW "HO" LL	08	76	34
FIRE STATION REVIEW "HO" HSM	03	71	30
FIREHOUSE REVIEW "HO" CON-COR	11	77	48
FIREHOUSE REVIEW "HO" AHM	03	72	24
FIREHOUSE REVIEW "HO" CAMPBELL	11	64	11
FIREHOUSE REVIEW "HO" IDEAL MODELS	08	50	47
FIREHOUSE REVIEW "HO" SUGAR PINE MODELS	02	77	40
FISHING PIER REVIEW "HO" CAMPBELL	11	77	44
FLEXI-FIT BUILDING REVIEW "HO/O" MIN	06	53	57
FLOOR & GRAIN MILL REVIEW "HO" F	11	69	19
FOUNDRY REVIEW "HO" CMI	05	78	44
FOUNDRY REVIEW "HO" BOYD MODELS	08	73	15
FRAME FALSE FRONT HDW STORE REV "HO" ESM	01	79	56
FRAME HOUSE REVIEW "N" QC	01	78	48
FRAME STORE MONTEZUMA CO REV "HO" STC	08	79	39
FREIGHT WAREHOUSE REVIEW "HO" VOLLMER	01	71	34B
FRUIT BROKERS WAREHOUSE REVIEW "HO" LAC	10	52	58
FUEL STORAGE FACILITY "Z" REVIEW WAL	12	85	45
FURNITURE FACTORY REVIEW "O" SUYDAM	12	55	18
GAS STATION BELLINGHAM WA REV "HO" CVM	07	85	44
GAS STATION ESSO REVIEW "HO" SUMMIT ENG.	08	56	13
GAS STATION REVIEW "HO" CC	02	79	42
GAS STATION REVIEW "HO" MSMW	10	84	58
GAS STATION REVIEW "N" WW	12	83	57
GAS STORAGE TANK REVIEW "HO" VOLLMER	11	63	7
GENERAL STORE 1897 REVIEW "HO" HSM	12	69	14
GENOA NEV SALOON 1851 REVIEW "HO" HSM	01	68	14
GHOST TOWN STRUCTURES REVIEW "HO" CMI	02	79	58
GRAIN ELEVATOR ELLSWORTH KS REV "HO" TIM	01	73	34
GRAIN ELEVATOR MODERN REVIEW "HO" SC	07	68	9
GRAIN ELEVATOR REVIEW "O" LIONEL	12	77	50
GRAIN ELEVATOR REVIEW "N" C	07	83	39
GRAIN ELEVATOR REVIEW "N" RAILHEAD	06	74	24

COMMERCIAL BUILDING MODEL REVIEWS

	M	Y	P
GRAIN ELEVATOR REVIEW "N" CON-COR	07	74	20
GRAIN ELEVATOR REVIEW 1927 "HO" CAMPBELL	02	74	21
GRAIN STORAGE BINS REVIEW "HO" CVM	08	84	48
GRAND CENTRAL GOLD MINE REVIEW "HO" STC	04	80	30
GRAVEL BUNKER REVIEW "N" RAILHEAD	08	76	29
GRAVITY STAMP MILL REVIEW "HO" DP	02	77	30
GRIST MILL & FEED STORRE REVIEW "HO" D	06	61	19
GRIST MILL REVIEW "HO" CAMPBELL	10	72	20
HARDWARE STORE REVIEW "HO" CMI	09	77	36
HARDWARE STORE REVIEW "HO" PNED	11	72	38
HARDWARE STORE REVIEW "HO" TIMBERLINE	09	64	9
HARDWARE STORE REVIEW"HO"LYTLER & LYTLER	05	76	29
HAUNTED HOUSE REVIEW "HO" ALEX	06	61	12
HEAVY INDUSTRY REVIEW "HO" SUYDAM	08	61	15
HOTEL REVIEW "HO" CON-COR	03	75	31
HOTEL REVIEW "N" MAGNUSON MODELS	12	78	58
HOTEL REVIEW "N" PEM	01	80	60
HOUSE AND GARAGE REVIEW "Z" BOYDE MODELS	04	75	32
HOUSE BRIDGEPORT CA REVIEW "HO" HSM 1870	04	72	23
HOUSE KIT REVIEW "HO" AHM	08	74	21
HOUSE REVIEW "HO" MODEL HOBBIES	11	52	62
HOUSE STRUCTURE REVIEW "HO" AHM	06	63	10
HOUSE VARIATIONS REVIEW "HO" AHM	03	75	24
HOUSES REVIEW "HO" LIFE LIKE	07	71	25
HOUSES UNDER CONSTRUCTION REVIEW "N" AT	12	67	14
ICE HOUSE REVIEW "HO" WS	10	81	35
ICING PLATFORM REVIEW "1/4" SUNCOAST MOD	02	68	14
INDUSTRIAL BUILDING REVIEW "N" RAILHEAD	02	74	23
JACOBS FUEL COMPANY REVIEW "HO" F	03	73	20
JUNKYARD SMILEYS TOW SERVICE REV "HO" WS	04	79	45
KALMBACH BUILDING REVIEW "HO/N" MMD	01	84	76
KOHL IRON WORKS REVIEW "HO" ESM	08	80	42
LARGE FACTORY REVIEW "N" MODEL POWER	04	77	35
LODGINGS REVIEW "HO" AYRES SCALE MODELS	04	54	16
LOGGING CAMP REVIEW "HO" SUNCOAST MODELS	08	71	25
LOGGING CAMP REVIEW "O" SUNCOAST MODELS	07	69	13
LOGGING REPAIR SHED REVIEW "HO" F	03	78	34
LOW RELIEF BUILDING REVIEW "HO" SLR	05	64	8
LOW RELIEF STRUCTURE REVIEW "HO/OO" SLR	09	63	8
LUMBER CAMPANY REVIEW "N" TPPR	07	85	48
LUMBER COMPANY REVIEW "HO" SSL	02	78	42
LUMBER COMPANY REVIEW "HO" QUALITY CRAFT	12	71	30
LUMBER YARD REVIEW "HO" MODEL HOBBIES	09	51	49
LUMBERYARD REVIEW "HO" AYRES SCALE MODEL	04	51	45
MABLES BOARDING HOUSE REVIEW "HO" D	02	81	51
MACHINERY LISTING "HO" MODEL MASTERPIECE	10	78	54
MAIN STREET USA BUILDING REV "HO" MMD	09	80	51
MARKET REVIEW "HO" SUYDAM & CO.	11	66	16
MERCURY SHOE FACTORY REVIEW "N" MMD	06	78	40
METAL FACTORY #3 REVIEW "HO" SUYDAM	01	52	46
METAL FACTORY KIT REVIEW "HO" SUYDAM	05	51	48
MINE COMPLEX REVIEW "HO" CAMPBELL	03	75	27
MINE REVIEW "N" ATLAS TOOL COMPANY	12	67	16
MINE TRAIN SET REVIEW "HO/S/O" STEW	06	71	21
MINEHAED FRAME REVIEW "HO" CAMPBELL	12	61	16

STRUCTURES & SIGNALS

COMMERCIAL BUILDING MODEL REVIEWS

	M	Y	P
MINING SUPPLY COMPANY REVIEW "HO" DP	08	78	45
MINING TOWN STORE FRONTS REV "O/HO" TY	02	79	46
MODERN FACTORY REVIEW "HO" ASM	09	55	17
MODERN FACTORY REVIEW "HO" SUYDAM	06	62	16
MODERN STORES REVIEW "HO" ASM	08	56	15
MODULAR FACTORIES REVIEW "N" HTE	12	83	50
MUNICIPAL BUILDING REVIEW "HO" MMO	01	82	39
NATIONAL BELLE MINE REVIEW "HO" TIM	04	73	24
NEWS STAND KIT REVIEW "HO" MODELTON	01	50	77
NEWSPAPER OFFICE REVIEW "HO" DP	12	78	50
NY BROWNSTONE HOUSE REVIEW "HO" SSL	06	69	20
OIL DERRICK REVIEW "HO" STAR LINE MODELS	08	48	576
OIL PUMP & SHED REVIEW "N" FAL	06	85	39
OIL PUMP JACK REVIEW "HO" RHM	08	65	9
OIL TANK & RACK REVIEW "HO" ALEX	11	55	10
OIL TANK REVIEW "N" DMK	01	83	44
OIL WELL REVIEW "HO" K&L	05	78	48
OLD TIME TOWN REIVEW "HO" ASM	12	52	54
ORE PROCESSING PLANT REVIEW "HO" SUYDAM	05	52	51
ORE TRIPLE ON EBT REVIEW "HO" W6M	09	83	40
OUTHOUSE REVIEW "HO" SELLEY	06	58	18
PERKINS PRODUCE "HO" DURANGO PRESS	06	76	31
PICKENS PLACE REVIEW "HO" CAMPBELL	11	76	39
PICKLE FACTORY REVIEW "HO" CC	11	72	23
PILLAR CRANE REVIEW "HO" ALEX	08	54	12
PIPE YARD & OFFICE REVIEW "HO" TP	07	80	44
POLE TRIMMING PLANT REVIEW "HO" TRI	07	63	11
POWER SUBSTATION REVIEW "HO" LH	12	51	57
PREFAB TRUSS CO BLDG REVIEW "HO" TRI	05	62	13
PRINTING COMAPNY REVIEW "HO" AHM	02	74	22
PROCESSING PLANT REVIEW "HO" AHM	04	73	20
PRODUCE SHED REVIEW "HO" CAMPBELL	08	73	27
PROPANE STORAGE TANK REVIEW "N" DMK	01	85	56
RED LIGHT DISTRICT HOUSE REVIEW "HO" CMI	10	75	31
REPAIR GARAGE REVIEW "HO" SUMMIT ENG.	09	56	11
RICHMOND BARREL MFG CO REVIEW "HO" C	07	80	48
ROADSIDE BUILDINGS REVIEW "HO" MH	05	65	10
RURAL BRICK HOUSE REVIEW "HO" MH	07	58	14
RURAL STRUCTURES REVIEW "N" LMS	12	84	50
SAEZ SASH & DOOR PLANING MILL REV "HO" C	12	79	33
SALIDA MACHINE SHOP REVIEW "HO" CIC	09	85	48
SALOON & GUN SHOP REVIEW "HO" MUIR	09	75	31
SALOON & STORE REVIEW "HO" CAMPBELL	07	74	18
SALOON REVIEW "HO" L&L	04	78	51
SAND TOWER REVIEW "N" KLE-WE	10	67	16
SARATOGA MINE BUILDING REVIEW "HO" L	11	84	50
SAW MILLS REVIEW "HO/O" KLW	11	78	48
SAWDUST BURNER REVIEW "HO" EHD	04	80	40
SAWMILL REVIEW "HO" SUYDAM	08	53	9
SAWMILL REVIEW "HO" FINE SCALE MINIATURE	06	76	30
SAWMILL REVIEW "HO" SUYDAM	02	56	13
SCHOOLHOUSE REVIEW "HO" ALEX	02	56	11
SCHRAMM MFG CO WOODWORKING REVIEW "HO" F	09	81	31
SEEBOLD & SONS MFG COMPANY REVIEW "HO" C	07	21	21
SERVICE STATION (ESSO) REVIEW "HO" AHM	08	71	26

COMMERCIAL BUILDING MODEL REVIEWS

	M	Y	P
SERVICE STATION 1922 REVIEW "HO" SSL	07	68	9
SERVICE STATION REVIEW "HO" AHM	12	73	29
SERVICE STATION REVIEW "N" MODEL POWER	04	77	35
SHANTY HOUSE REVIEW "HO" DYNA MODELS	02	63	26
SHERIFF'S OFFICE REVIEW "HO" CAMPBELL	08	71	24
SLAUGHTERHOUSE REVIEW "N" CON-COR	08	75	23
SMALL TOWN FACTORY REVIEW "HO" SEN	08	55	11
SOUTHERN OIL COMPANY REVIEW "HO" LL	05	79	50
STORE & APARTMENT BUILDING REV "HO" HEL	08	71	22
STORE & GARAGE REVIEW "HO" AHM	11	76	47
STORE FRONT REVIEW "1/4" VANE JONES	12	63	13
STORE KIT REVIEW "HO" MODEL HOBBIES	09	48	672
STORE REVIEW "HO" WAL	10	82	40
STORE REVIEWS "HO" AHM	06	74	18
STRUCTURE ASSORMENT REVIEW "TT" JM	08	51	55
SUBURBAN HOMES REVIEW "HO" WALTERS	06	60	12
SUPPLY BUILDING REVIEW "HO" CAMPBELL	06	70	18
SUPPLY HOUSE REVIEW "HO" SUP	05	75	28
TALK FACTORY REVIEW "HO" C	06	78	46
TILT UP NO 1 FACTORY REVIEW "HO" C	10	84	52
TOWN BUILDINGS REVIEW "HO" JMC INTERN'L	05	76	28
TOWNHOUSE KIT REVIEW "HO" IHC	12	84	45
TRACT HOUSE REVIEW "HO" SUYDAM	10	53	12
TRIANGLE BUILDING REVIEW "HO" ESM	02	80	48
TRUCK DEPOT (MODERN) REVIEW "N" MP	12	85	70
TRUCK TERMINAL #55 REVIEW "HO" F	01	71	26
TWO BROS RESTAURANT REVIEW "HO" CON-COR	10	75	28
TWO STORY SHANTY REVIEW "HO" SEELY INC	05	58	13
UNION ICE PLANT REVIEW "HO" ASM	09	51	48
USED CAR LOT REVIEW "HO" MODEL HOBBIES	12	49	82
VARIOUS BUILDING REVIEW "HO" REVELLE	01	59	14
VERTICAL OIL STORAGE TANK REV "HO" DMK	09	83	38
VICTORIAN COTTAGE REVIEW "H" CVM	09	84	52
VICTORIAN HOUSE REVIEW "1/4" 101P	02	75	28
WAREHOUSE & OFFICE "HO" CAMPBELL	06	78	53
WAREHOUSE REVIEW "1/4" QUALITY CRAFT	10	78	46
WAREHOUSE/FACTORY REVIEW "HO" QC	07	71	26
WATER STREET STORES REVIEW "HO" MMD	12	83	47
WATER TANK REVIEW "HO" WABASH VALLEY LINE	03	77	41
WATERFRONT STRUCTURES REVIEW "HO" C	06	79	45
WATERTANK & WINDMILL REVIEW "HO" TSM	02	63	29
WELLS FARGO STATION REVIEW "HO" ARGY	09	53	13
WHARF REVIEW "HO" CAMPBELL	12	70	32
WHITE CASTLE RESTAURANT REVIEW "HO" MMD	09	83	49
WILD WEST STRUCTURES REVIEW "HO" KIBRI	12	68	10
WISCHER'S WASHER BRICK FACTORY "HO" MMD	03	81	52
WOOD OIL DERRICK REVIEW "HO" CAMPBELL	06	64	11

STRUCTURES & SIGNALS

COMMERCIAL BUILDING MODEL REV BY MFG.

MFG		M	Y	P
101P	VICTORIAN HOUSE REVIEW "1/4" 101P	02	75	28
20C	FACTORY KIT REV "HO" 20TH CENTURY SALES	11	49	90
AHM	CAPE COD HOUSE REVIEW "N" AHM	11	74	43
	FARMHOUSE REVIEW "N" AHM	10	74	24
	HOUSE KIT REVIEW "HO" AHM	08	74	21
	STORE REVIEWS "HO" AHM	06	74	18
	PRINTING COMAPNY REVIEW "HO" AHM	02	74	22
	FARMHOUSE GROUP REVIEW "HO" AHM	09	72	28
	FIREHOUSE REVIEW "HO" AHM	03	72	24
	SERVICE STATION REVIEW "HO" AHM	12	73	29
	CHURCH REVIEW "HO" AHM	09	73	27
	PROCESSING PLANT REVIEW "HO" AHM	04	73	20
	HOUSE STRUCTURE REVIEW "HO" AHM	06	63	10
	HOUSE VARIATIONS REVIEW "HO" AHM	03	75	24
	STORE & GARAGE REVIEW "HO" AHM	11	76	47
	BUSINESS BLOCK REVIEW "HO" AHM	04	79	42
	SERVICE STATION (ESSO) REVIEW "HO" AHM	08	71	26
ALEX	OIL TANK & RACK REVIEW "HO" ALEX	11	55	10
	SCHOOLHOUSE REVIEW "HO" ALEX	02	56	11
	PILLAR CRANE REVIEW "HO" ALEX	08	54	12
	HAUNTED HOUSE REVIEW "HO" ALEX	06	61	12
ARGY	WELLS FARGO STATION REVIEW "HO" ARGY	09	53	13
ARISTO	BACKGROUND STRUCTURE REVIEW "HO" ARISTO	05	57	12
ASM	MODERN FACTORY REVIEW "HO" ASM	09	55	17
	MODERN STORES REVIEW "HO" ASM	08	56	15
	LODGINGS REVIEW "HO" AYRES SCALE MODELS	04	54	16
	OLD TIME TOWN REIVEW "HO" ASM	12	52	54
	UNION ICE PLANT REVIEW "HO" ASM	09	51	48
	LUMBERYARD REVIEW "HO" AYRES SCALE MODEL	04	51	45
AT	HOUSES UNDER CONSTRUCTION REVIEW "N" AT	12	67	14
	MINE REVIEW "N" ATLAS TOOL COMPANY	12	67	16
BCK	CATTLE PEN REVIEW "O" BOXCAR KEN	06	55	13
BOY	FOUNDRY REVIEW "HO" BOYD MODELS	08	73	15
	HOUSE AND GARAGE REVIEW "Z" BOYDE MODELS	04	75	32
BU	FACTORY STRUCTURE REVIEW "N" BUSCH	10	68	20
C	SALOON & STORE REVIEW "HO" CAMPBELL	07	74	18
	GRAIN ELEVATOR REVIEW 1927 "HO" CAMPBELL	02	74	21
	SEEBOLD & SONS MFG COMPANY REVIEW "HO" C	07	21	21
	GRIST MILL REVIEW "HO" CAMPBELL	10	72	20
	FARMHOUSE REVIEW "HO" CAPBELL	09	73	20
	PRODUCE SHED REVIEW "HO" CAMPBELL	08	73	27
	MINE COMPLEX REVIEW "HO" CAMPBELL	03	75	27
	DINGHY SHOP REVIEW "HO" CAMPBELL	12	75	34
	WOOD OIL DERRICK REVIEW "HO" CAMPBELL	06	64	11
	FIREHOUSE REVIEW "HO" CAMPBELL	11	64	11
	PICKENS PLACE REVIEW "HO" CAMPBELL	11	76	39
	WATERFRONT STRUCTURES REVIEW "HO" C	06	79	45
	SAEZ SASH & DOOR PLANING MILL REV "HO" C	12	79	33
	AYRES CHAIRS FACTORY REVIEW "HO" C	10	77	35
	FISHING PIER REVIEW "HO" CAMPBELL	11	77	44
	CHURCH REVIEW "HO" CAMPBELL	02	69	16
	MINEHAED FRAME REVIEW "HO" CAMPBELL	12	61	16
	WAREHOUSE & OFFICE "HO" CAMPBELL	06	78	53
	DEWITTS DEPOSITORY LISTING "HO" C	05	78	53

COMMERCIAL BUILDING MODEL REV BY MFG.

MFG		M	Y	P
	CATTLE PEN LISTING "HO" CAMPBELL	12	78	68
	TALK FACTORY REVIEW "HO" C	06	78	46
	DOCTORS OFFICE REVIEW "HO" C	01	78	42
	BOARDING HOUSE REVIEW "HO" CAMPBELL	12	78	52
	SHERIFF'S OFFICE REVIEW "HO" CAMPBELL	08	71	24
	SUPPLY BUILDING REVIEW "HO" CAMPBELL	06	70	18
	WHARF REVIEW "HO" CAMPBELL	12	70	32
	RICHMOND BARREL MFG CO REVIEW "HO" C	07	80	48
	GRAIN ELEVATOR REVIEW "N" C	07	83	39
	FEED MILL WALES WISC REVIEW "HO" C C&NW	10	81	40
	TILT UP NO 1 FACTORY REVIEW "HO" C	10	84	52
CC	GRAIN ELEVATOR REVIEW "N" CON-COR	07	74	20
	PICKLE FACTORY REVIEW "HO" CC	11	72	23
	HOTEL REVIEW "HO" CON-COR	03	75	31
	SLAUGHTERHOUSE REVIEW "N" CON-COR	08	75	23
	TWO BROS RESTAURANT REVIEW "HO" CON-COR	10	75	28
	CITY HALL REVIEW "HO" CC	02	79	42
	GAS STATION REVIEW "HO" CC	02	79	42
	COAL YARD REVIEW "HO" CC	02	79	42
	FIREHOUSE REVIEW "HO" CON-COR	11	77	48
	FACTORY 1903 REVIEW "N" CONCOR	09	69	9
	CORNER STORE REVIEW "HO/N" CC	07	80	37
	EDISON LABORATORY REVIEW "HO" CC	02	80	50
CHO	COUNTRY GROCERY STORE REVIEW "O" CHO	03	79	46
	COUNTRY STORE REVIEW "HO" CHO	10	80	45
CIC	SALIDA MACHINE SHOP REVIEW "HO" CIC	09	85	48
CMI	RED LIGHT DISTRICT HOUSE REVIEW "HO" CMI	10	75	31
	GHOST TOWN STRUCTURES REVIEW "HO" CMI	02	79	58
	HARDWARE STORE REVIEW "HO" CMI	09	77	36
	FOUNDRY REVIEW "HO" CMI	05	78	44
CSML	CORNER SHOP REVIEW "OO" CSML	12	84	64
CVM	GAS STATION BELLINGHAM WA REV "HO" CVM	07	85	44
	GRAIN STORAGE BINS REVIEW "HO" CVM	08	84	48
	VICTORIAN COTTAGE REVIEW "H" CVM	09	84	52
D	BUTCHER SHOP REVIEW "HO" DYNA MODELS	04	56	10
	SHANTY HOUSE REVIEW "HO" DYNA MODELS	02	63	26
	GRIST MILL & FEED STORRE REVIEW "HO" D	06	61	19
	BLACKSMITH SHOP REVIEW "HO" DYNA MODELS	01	64	14
	MABLES BOARDING HOUSE REVIEW "HO" D	02	81	51
DMK	PROPANE STORAGE TANK REVIEW "N" DMK	01	85	56
	OIL TANK REVIEW "N" DMK	01	83	44
	VERTICAL OIL STORAGE TANK REV "HO" DMK	09	83	38
DP	PERKINS PRODUCE "HO" DURANGO PRESS	06	76	31
	GRAVITY STAMP MILL REVIEW "HO" DP	02	77	30
	NEWSPAPER OFFICE REVIEW "HO" DP	12	78	50
	MINING SUPPLY COMPANY REVIEW "HO" DP	08	78	45
EHD	DOLLAR BROS MOTOR EXPRESS REVIEW "O" EHD	05	79	41
	SAWDUST BURNER REVIEW "HO" EHD	04	80	40
ESM	FRAME FALSE FRONT HDW STORE REV "HO" ESM	01	79	56
	KOHL IRON WORKS REVIEW "HO" ESM	08	80	42
	TRIANGLE BUILDING REVIEW "HO" ESM	02	80	48
F	JACOBS FUEL COMPANY REVIEW "HO" F	03	73	20
	COOPERS GARAGE REVIEW "HO" F	04	75	31
	SAWMILL REVIEW "HO" FINE SCALE MINIATURE	06	76	30
	FLOOR & GRAIN MILL REVIEW "HO" F	11	69	19

STRUCTURES & SIGNALS

COMMERCIAL BUILDING MODEL REV BY MFG.

MFG		M Y P
	LOGGING REPAIR SHED REVIEW "HO" F	03 78 34
	TRUCK TERMINAL #55 REVIEW "HO" F	01 71 26
	CROCKER BROTHERS FEED MILLS REV "HO" F	10 80 52
	SCHRAMM MFG CO WOODWORKING REVIEW "HO" F	09 81 31
FAL	OIL PUMP & SHED REVIEW "N" FAL	06 85 39
	CEMENT PLANT REVIEW "HO" FALLER	07 77 29
H&R	BRICK BUILDING REVIEWS "1/8" H&R	01 66 15
HEL	AMERICAN STRUCTURE REVIEW "N" HELJAN	06 68 15
	STORE & APARTMENT BUILDING REV "HO" HEL	08 71 22
HSM	HOUSE BRIDGEPORT CA REVIEW "HO" HSM 1870	04 72 23
	GENERAL STORE 1897 REVIEW "HO" HSM	12 69 14
	GENOA NEV SALOON 1851 REVIEW "HO" HSM	01 68 14
	FIRE STATION REVIEW "HO" HSM	03 71 30
HTE	MODULAR FACTORIES REVIEW "N" HTE	12 83 50
IHC	TOWNHOUSE KIT REVIEW "HO" IHC	12 84 45
IM	FIREHOUSE REVIEW "HO" IDEAL MODELS	08 50 47
IMW	BOILER-PUMPHOUSE & TANK REVIEW "HO" IMW	03 59 13
ISLE	BUILDING FRONTS REVIEW "HO" ISLE	03 85 40
JM	STRUCTURE ASSORMENT REVIEW "TT" JM	08 51 55
JMC	COMMERCIAL BUILDINGS REVIEW "N" JMC	10 73 26
	TOWN BUILDINGS REVIEW "HO" JMC INTERN'L	05 76 28
K&L	OIL WELL REVIEW "HO" K&L	05 78 48
KIB	FACTORY REVIEW "HO" KIB	06 85 37
	WILD WEST STRUCTURES REVIEW "HO" KIBRI	12 68 10
KLE	SAND TOWER REVIEW "N" KLE-WE	10 67 16
KLW	SAW MILLS REVIEW "HO/O" KLW	11 78 48
	COMPANY HOUSES W. VA REVIEW "HO" KLW	08 80 46
L	SARATOGA MINE BUILDING REVIEW "HO" L	11 84 50
L&L	HARDWARE STORE REVIEW"HO"LYTLER & LYTLER	05 76 29
	CAFE LISTING "HO" LYTLER & LYTLER	10 78 55
	SALOON REVIEW "HO" L&L	04 78 51
LAC	FRUIT BROKERS WAREHOUSE REVIEW "HO" LAC	10 52 58
LH	POWER SUBSTATION REVIEW "HO" LH	12 51 57
LIO	GRAIN ELEVATOR REVIEW "O" LIONEL	12 77 50
LJ	STORE FRONT REVIEW "1/4" VANE JONES	12 63 13
LL	DIE CRAFT MFG CO FACTORY REVIEW "HO" LL	03 74 28
	FIRE STATION OF BRICK REVIEW "HO" LL	08 76 34
	SOUTHERN OIL COMPANY REVIEW "HO" LL	05 79 50
	HOUSES REVIEW "HO" LIFE LIKE	07 71 25
LMS	RURAL STRUCTURES REVIEW "N" LMS	12 84 50
MH	USED CAR LOT REVIEW "HO" MODEL HOBBIES	12 49 82
	STORE KIT REVIEW "HO" MODEL HOBBIES	09 48 672
	COUNTRY CHURCH REVIEW "HO" MODEL HOBBIES	09 56 9
	RURAL BRICK HOUSE REVIEW "HO" MH	07 58 14
	ROADSIDE BUILDINGS REVIEW "HO" MH	05 65 10
	COMPANY HOUSE LISTING "HO" MODEL HOBBIES	12 77 62
	HOUSE REVIEW "HO" MODEL HOBBIES	11 52 62
	COAL YARD REVIEW "HO" MODEL HOBBIES	11 51 54
	LUMBER YARD REVIEW "HO" MODEL HOBBIES	09 51 49
MIN	FLEXI-FIT BUILDING REVIEW "HO/O" MIN	06 53 57
MK	COAL MINE REVIEW "HO" MINIKITS	08 67 14
MM	MACHINERY LISTING "HO" MODEL MASTERPIECE	10 78 54
	CIMMARON SUPPLY CO WAREHOUSE REV "HO" MM	11 80 58
MMD	APARTMENT BUILDING REVIEW "HO" MMD	12 77 55
	CITY STRUCTURES REVIEW "HO" MMD	06 77 39

COMMERCIAL BUILDING MODEL REV BY MFG.

MFG		M Y P
	BREWERY LISTING "HO" MAGNUSON MODELS	11 78 63
	HOTEL REVIEW "N" MAGNUSON MODELS	12 78 58
	MERCURY SHOE FACTORY REVIEW "N" MMD	06 78 40
	BANK REVIEW "HO" MMD	05 78 47
	BLOCK OF STORES REVIEW "HO/N" MMD	05 82 44
	MAIN STREET USA BUILDING REV "HO" MMD	09 80 51
	WHITE CASTLE RESTAURANT REVIEW "HO" MMD	09 83 49
	WATER STREET STORES REVIEW "HO" MMD	12 83 47
	WISCHER'S WASHER BRICK FACTORY "HO" MMD	03 81 52
	KALMBACH BUILDING REVIEW "HO/N" MMD	01 84 76
MMO	MUNICIPAL BUILDING REVIEW "HO" MMO	01 82 39
MO	NEWS STAND KIT REVIEW "HO" MODELTON	01 50 77
MP	TRUCK DEPOT (MODERN) REVIEW "N" MP	12 85 70
	LARGE FACTORY REVIEW "N" MODEL POWER	04 77 35
	SERVICE STATION REVIEW "N" MODEL POWER	04 77 35
	CONTEMPORARY HOUSE LISTING N MODEL POWER	02 77 46
	COMMERCIAL BUILDING REVIEW "N" MP	04 82 46
MSMW	GAS STATION REVIEW "HO" MSMW	10 84 58
MU	SALOON & GUN SHOP REVIEW "HO" MUIR	09 75 31
	BROWN'S HOUSE NEVADA CITY NV REV "HO" MU	03 81 46
PEM	HOTEL REVIEW "N" PEM	01 80 60
PIS	BUTLER BUILDING WAREHOUSE REVIEW "HO"PIS	02 85 37
PNED	HARDWARE STORE REVIEW "HO" PNED	11 72 38
POLA	FACTORY REVIEW "HO" POLA	11 70 14
QC	BOX FACTORY REVIEW "N" QUALITY CRAFT	01 73 27
	WAREHOUSE REVIEW "1/4" QUALITY CRAFT	10 78 46
	FRAME HOUSE REVIEW "N" QC	01 78 48
	WAREHOUSE/FACTORY REVIEW "HO" QC	07 71 26
	LUMBER COMPANY REVIEW "HO" QUALITY CRAFT	12 71 30
RE	BARN & OUTBUILDINGS REVIEW "HO" REVELLE	12 59 14
	VARIOUS BUILDING REVIEW "HO" REVELLE	01 59 14
	BAKERY REVIEW "HO" REVELL	10 77 40
RH	GRAIN ELEVATOR REVIEW "N" RAILHEAD	06 74 24
	INDUSTRIAL BUILDING REVIEW "N" RAILHEAD	02 74 23
	GRAVEL BUNKER REVIEW "N" RAILHEAD	08 76 29
RHM	OIL PUMP JACK REVIEW "HO" RHM	08 65 9
S	FURNITURE FACTORY REVIEW "O" SUYDAM	12 55 18
	BEKINS WAREHOUSE REVIEW "HO" E SUYDAM CO	07 72 22
	BARN REVIEW "HO" SUYDAM	11 56 12
	FEED MILL REVIEW "HO" SUYDAM	09 56 15
	BOX FACTORY REVIEW "HO" SUYDAM	08 56 14
	SAWMILL REVIEW "HO" SUYDAM	02 56 13
	SAWMILL REVIEW "HO" SUYDAM	08 53 9
	TRACT HOUSE REVIEW "HO" SUYDAM	10 53 12
	MODERN FACTORY REVIEW "HO" SUYDAM	06 62 16
	HEAVY INDUSTRY REVIEW "HO" SUYDAM	08 61 15
	MARKET REVIEW "HO" SUYDAM & CO.	11 66 16
	ORE PROCESSING PLANT REVIEW "HO" SUYDAM	05 52 51
	METAL FACTORY #3 REVIEW "HO" SUYDAM	01 52 46
	METAL FACTORY KIT REVIEW "HO" SUYDAM	05 51 48
SC	LOGGING CAMP REVIEW "O" SUNCOAST MODELS	07 69 13
	ICING PLATFORM REVIEW "1/4" SUNCOAST MOD	02 68 14
	GRAIN ELEVATOR MODERN REVIEW "HO" SC	07 68 9
	LOGGING CAMP REVIEW "HO" SUNCOAST MODELS	08 71 25
SEL	OUTHOUSE REVIEW "HO" SELLEY	06 58 18

STRUCTURES & SIGNALS

COMMERCIAL BUILDING MODEL REV BY MFG.

MFG		M	Y	P
	TWO STORY SHANTY REVIEW "HO" SEELY INC	05	58	13
SEN	SMALL TOWN FACTORY REVIEW "HO" SEN	08	55	11
	REPAIR GARAGE REVIEW "HO" SUMMIT ENG.	09	56	11
	GAS STATION ESSO REVIEW "HO" SUMMIT ENG.	08	56	13
	BUNGALOW REVIEW "HO" SUMMIT ENGINEERING	02	56	10
SIM	ASSAY OFFICE REVIEW "HO" SIMPSON PRODUCT	01	69	12
SL	OIL DERRICK REVIEW "HO" STAR LINE MODELS	08	48	576
SLR	LOW RELIEF STRUCTURE REVIEW "HO/OO" SLR	09	63	8
	LOW RELIEF BUILDING REVIEW "HO" SLR	05	64	8
	COUNTRY CHURCH REVIEW "HO" SLR	09	64	8
SSL	DRUGSTORE REVIEW "HO" SCALE STRUCTURES	01	72	20
	BOILERHOUSE REVIEW "HO" SSL	04	69	15
	SERVICE STATION 1922 REVIEW "HO" SSL	07	68	9
	NY BROWNSTONE HOUSE REVIEW "HO" SSL	06	69	20
	CHICAGO TOWNHOUSE REVIEW "HO" SSL	10	69	19
	LUMBER COMPANY REVIEW "HO" SSL	02	78	42
	COUNTRY STORE REVIEW "HO" SSL 1860	02	71	20
STC	FRAME STORE MONTEZUMA CO REV "HO" STC	08	79	39
	GRAND CENTRAL GOLD MINE REVIEW "HO" STC	04	80	30
STEW	DRAKE OIL WELL REVIEW "HO" STEWART PROD.	07	77	35
	MINE TRAIN SET REVIEW "HO/S/O" STEW	06	71	21
SUP	SUPPLY HOUSE REVIEW "HO" SUP	05	75	28
	FIREHOUSE REVIEW "HO" SUGAR PINE MODELS	02	77	40
TIM	CONTAINER WAREHOUSE REVIEW "HO" TIM	06	73	27
	NATIONAL BELLE MINE REVIEW "HO" TIM	04	73	24
	GRAIN ELEVATOR ELLSWORTH KS REV "HO" TIM	01	73	34
	HARDWARE STORE REVIEW "HO" TIMBERLINE	09	64	9
TP	PIPE YARD & OFFICE REVIEW "HO" TP	07	80	44
TPPR	LUMBER CAMPANY REVIEW "N" TPPR	07	85	48
TRI	CREOSOTING PLANT REVIEW "HO" TRI	05	63	8
	POLE TRIMMING PLANT REVIEW "HO" TRI	07	63	11
	PREFAB TRUSS CO BLDG REVIEW "HO" TRI	05	62	13
TSM	WATERTANK & WINDMILL REVIEW "HO" TSM	02	63	29
TY	MINING TOWN STORE FRONTS REV "O/HO" TY	02	79	46
VOL	GAS STORAGE TANK REVIEW "HO" VOLLMER	11	63	7
	BRICK BUILDING REVIEW "HO" VOLLMER	08	64	11
	FREIGHT WAREHOUSE REVIEW "HO" VOLLMER	01	71	34B
	FACTORY CONCRETE WORKS REVIEW "N" VOL	12	70	36
WAL	FUEL STORAGE FACILITY "Z" REVIEW WAL	12	85	45
	SUBURBAN HOMES REVIEW "HO" WALTERS	06	60	12
	STORE REVIEW "HO" WAL	10	82	40
WGM	ORE TRIPLE ON EBT REVIEW "HO" WGM	09	83	40
WS	JUNKYARD SMILEYS TOW SERVICE REV "HO" WS	04	79	45
	CEMETERY LISTING "HO" WOODLAND SCENICS	08	78	48
	ICE HOUSE REVIEW "HO" WS	10	81	35
WVL	WATER TANK REVIEW "HO" WABASH VALLEY LINE	03	77	41
WW	GAS STATION REVIEW "N" WW	12	83	57

DEPOT PROTOTYPE DATA

	M	Y	P
AVON STATION OF ERIE AVON, NY	12	78	94
BCR&N STANDARD STATIONS REINBECK IOWA	02	81	89
BOX CAR STATION CLARKS MILLS, PA NYC	11	34	12
BROOKFIELD WISC STATION ON MILW 1853	10	84	82
DEARBORN STATION REMEMBERED	04	79	82
DEPOT AT CANAAN CONN.	04	58	36
DEPOT AT JAMESVILLE NY DL&W	10	78	78
DEPOT AT WALLED LAKE MICH GTW	07	78	80
DOODLEBUG DEPOT OSTRANDER MINN C&NW	06	77	62
DUPLEX STAION AT LINDEN IND NKP-M	06	75	38
FREEVILLE, NY 5 SIDED DEPOT LV	02	63	38
GETTYSBURG STATION PA	02	82	84
GINGERBREAD STATION AT STRATFORD PA	12	77	92
NORTH CONWAY STATION NORTH CONWAY NH B&M	06	71	62
ROUTE 128 STATION OF THE NH	06	78	66
SAN FERNANDO STATION	12	58	64
SHEFFIELD ILL DEPOT RI 1911	11	63	44
SMALL STATIONS	01	52	12
STANDARD STATIONS OF DT&I	09	78	50
STATION AT PLAINS GEORGIA 1911 SCL	08	77	56
STATION AT STOCKYARDS WV C&O 1890	07	77	74
STATION OF SOUTHERN CENTRAL 1870	10	83	116
WALDO STATION KANSAS CITY, MO MP	02	58	50
WEST DULUTH MN STATION DW&P	07	58	31

STRUCTURES & SIGNALS

DEPOT PLANS	M	Y	P
ATSF STANDARD #4 STATION PLANS	06	83	82
AVON STATION PLANS ERIE AVON, NY	12	78	96
BCR&N STD STATIONS REINBECK IOWA DRAWING	02	81	90
BRANCH LINE DEPOT PLANS SUSSEX WIS MILW	01	49	63
CLEARWATER SMALL STATION DRAWING	09	57	40
COMBINATION DEPOT DRAWING WSL&P	02	47	122
COMBINATION FREIGHT PASSENGER DRAWING	09	52	56
COMMUTER STATION PLANS MAYFAIR IL MILW	04	76	53
COMPREHENSIVE PASSENGER STATION PLANS	09	40	495
COUNTRY FRT STN DRAW WESTERSFIELD CONN	07	54	14
DELUXE TERMINAL DRAWINGS	09	53	30
DEPOT & GENERAL OFFICE DRAWINGS	09	69	33
DEPOT AT ASHIPPUN WI PLANS C&NW	06	62	38
DEPOT AT GRAMERCY LA PLANS IC	08	62	37
DEPOT AT GREENFIELD OHIO DRAWINGS	02	70	54
DEPOT AT HOMER NY PLANS DL&W	08	65	31
DEPOT AT MENLO PARK CA PLANS SP	01	64	62
DEPOT AT PORT ALLEN LA PLANS T&P	05	63	46
DEPOT AT RICO CO OF 1891 PLANS D&RGW	10	62	38
DEPOT AT RUSHLAND PA PLANS R	12	65	57
DEPOT AT SOUTH BAY FL PLANS FEC	06	64	34
DEPOT AT TUSCALOOSA AL PLANS 1886	03	69	58
DEPOT AT WALLED LAKE MICH PLANS GTW	07	78	80
DEPOT BOARD & BATTEN GRATERFORD PA PLN R	09	63	30
DEPOT DRAWINGS LINDEN IN M-NKP	06	75	40
DEPOT DRAWINGS MOUNT HOPE NY NYC	11	75	60
DEPOT ERIE DRAWING OVERBROOK NJ	10	80	72
DEPOT GREENWOOD MASS DRAWINGS B&M	09	61	26
DEPOT OTIS STA ROCHESTER NY (NYC) PLANS	10	74	62
DEPOT PEACE DALE RI (NPIER) PLANS	09	74	42
DEPOT PLANS BENTON, WI BRANCH LINE C&NW	03	58	36
DEPOT PLANS COMBINATION FREIGHT PASS	02	36	38
DEPOT PLANS COMBINATION FREIGHT PASS.	11	49	46
DEPOT PLANS FOND DU LAC WI SOO	10	70	60
DEPOT PLANS FREIGHT/PASS ATSF PERRIS CA	11	69	50
DEPOT PLANS FRONT ROYAL VA N&W 1953	10	71	43
DEPOT PLANS HAMMONDSPORT NY B&HA	11	76	70
DEPOT PLANS LAKEWOOD RI WA	06	57	61
DEPOT PLANS LEXINGTON MASS B&M	01	57	40
DEPOT PLANS MIDLAND ONT CN	06	70	50
DEPOT PLANS ROCKINGHAM JCT NH B&M	09	57	60
DEPOT PLANS UMATILLA OR OR&NC 1882	08	61	28
DEPOT PLANS WALPOLE MA NYNH&H	09	67	40
DEPOT PLANS WEST DULUTH MN DW&P	07	58	32
DEPOT ROWLEY MASS B&M PLANS	01	74	54
DEPOT WAKEFIELD RI (NPIER) PLANS	09	74	42
DIVISION POINT DEPOT DRAW ALBUQURQUE NM	12	56	38
FIVE SIDED FREIGHT DEPOT PLN FREEVILE NY	02	63	40
FLAG DEPOT DRAWING ST. PAUL, MN MI&NW	05	47	376
FLAGSTOP STATION PLANS AIRY HALL SC SCL	01	71	64
FREIGHT DEPOT AT NORTH HILLS PA PLANS R	01	65	40
FREIGHT DEPOT DRAWING	08	45	316
FREIGHT DEPOT GLENDALE CA DRAWINGS UP	06	67	48
FREIGHT DEPOT PLANS COLDWATER NY NYC	04	68	50
FREIGHT HOUSE AT ESSINGTON PA PLANS R	05	64	30

DEPOT PLANS	M	Y	P
FREIGHT SHED & OFFICE DRAW CHAMPAIGN ILL	10	47	789
FREIGHT STATION DRAWINGS	03	73	70
FREIGHT STATION PLANS ROANOKE, VA N&W	07	71	52
GETTYSBURG STATION PA DRAWINGS	02	82	84
GINGERBREAD STATION PLANS LAURY PA LV	03	48	189
GINGERBREAD STATION STRAFFORD PA PLANS	12	77	94
INTERURBAN PASSENGER SHELTER DRAWING	12	57	73
IVY JCT STATION DRAWINGS	06	79	64
LOG CABIN DEPOT DRAWINGS COBBS JCT MO	10	80	104
MARTISCO STATION DRAWINGS NYC 1870	02	80	78
MOUNT CLARE STATION OF 1835 DRAWING B&O	07	37	241
NEWELL SC FLAGSTOP STATION DRAWINGS	04	62	39
OCTAGONAL WAY STATION RS&E PLN JORDAN NY	12	79	104
OLDTIME GENERAL PURPOSE DEPOT DRAWINGS	12	64	71
ORNATE PASS DEPOT DRAWING ALLEN LANE PA	09	54	25
PRIDES CROSSING MASS DEPOT DRAWINGS	10	58	58
ROUTE 128 STATION PLANS NH	01	78	66
RURAL FREIGHT STATION PLAN SUPLEE PA PRR	02	66	34
SHED STATION LAUREL BROOK DRAWING MA&PA	05	65	40
SHED TYPE DEPOT AT EXTON PA PLANS R	10	64	51
SMALL BRICK STATION PLANS SPREKERLS CA	11	66	54
SMALL CITY DEPOT DRAWING	03	53	62
SMALL DEPOT AT ESSINGTON PA PLANS R	05	64	30
SMALL DEPOT PLANS AT OAK GROVE MO GM&O	04	59	26
SMALL DEPOT PLANS DOSWELL VA RF&P C&O	09	69	48
SMALL DEPOT WHISTLE STOP DRAWING LV	12	46	832
SMALL STATION DRAWINGS BENTON, IND	12	43	528
SMALL STATION PLANS	10	38	410
SMALL TOWN DEPOT PLANS	01	45	4
SOUTH LYON MICH DEPOT PLANS C&O AND GTW	01	60	33
STANDARD STATION PLANS DT&I QUINCY, MI	09	78	50
STATION AT CHIPPEWA FALLS WI DRAW C&NW	03	81	84
STATION AT JAMESVILLE NY PLANS D&LW	10	78	78
STATION AT PLAINS GEORGIA PLANS SCL 1910	08	77	58
STATION AT RANDVILLE MICH PLAN	06	78	112
STATION AT STOCKYARDS WV PLANS C&O 1890	07	77	76
STATION AT WOODARD NY PLANS NYC	03	83	78
STATION DRAWING FJ&G BROADALBIN NY	08	79	70
STATION DRAWINGS BUILT AT AN ANGLE	09	80	68
STATION DRAWINGS SOUTHERN CENTRAL	10	83	116
STATION NYO&W PLANS BURNSIDE NY 1882	07	84	76
STATION PLANS	10	34	7
STATION PLANS BROOKFIELD WIS MILW 1853	10	84	86
STATION PLANS PROTECTION KS	11	79	84
STUCCO STATION PLANS IN CHICAGO ILL	07	80	87
STUCCO STATIONS PLANS CHICAGO IL CORRECT	10	80	158
SUBURBAN DEPOT PLANS CINCINNATTI, OH B&O	07	39	346
THENDRA NY STATION PLANS	03	80	86
THREE TOWER DEPOT DRAWINGS LAURENS SC	11	74	70
TOM THUMB STATION DRAWINGS MP	07	53	34
TRACTION PASSENGER TERMINAL DRAWINGS	08	76	67
TRAIN ORDER STATION DRAWINGS PRR	02	75	48
TWO LEVEL DEPOT PLANS C&O CHICAGO 63 ST.	04	57	42
TWO LEVEL STATION PLANS	05	68	44
UNION STATION ELEVATION DRAWINGS	01	48	18

STEPHANS' RAILROAD DIRECTORY

STRUCTURES & SIGNALS

	DEPOT PLANS	M	Y	P
	URBAN STATION DRAWINGS	03	51	30
	WEDGE SHAPED DEPOT PLN B&O N. ALBANY IND	11	68	62

RD	DEPOT PLANS BY ROAD	M	Y	P
ATSF	DIVISION POINT DEPOT DRAW ALBUQURQUE NM	12	56	38
	DEPOT PLANS FREIGHT/PASS ATSF PERRIS CA	11	69	50
	ATSF STANDARD #4 STATION PLANS	06	83	82
B&HA	DEPOT PLANS HAMMONDSPORT NY B&HA	11	76	70
B&M	DEPOT PLANS ROCKINGHAM JCT NH B&M	09	57	60
	DEPOT PLANS LEXINGTON MASS B&M	01	57	40
	DEPOT ROWLEY MASS B&M PLANS	01	74	54
	DEPOT GREENWOOD MASS DRAWINGS B&M	09	61	26
B&O	SUBURBAN DEPOT PLANS CINCINATTI, OH B&O	07	39	346
	MOUNT CLARE STATION OF 1835 DRAWING B&O	07	37	241
	WEDGE SHAPED DEPOT PLN B&O N. ALBANY IND	11	68	62
BCR&N	BCR&N STD STATIONS REINBECK IOWA DRAWING	02	81	90
C&NW	DEPOT PLANS BENTON, WI BRANCH LINE C&NW	03	58	36
	DEPOT AT ASHIPPUN WI PLANS C&NW	06	62	38
	STATION AT CHIPPEWA FALLS WI DRAW C&NW	03	81	84
C&O	TWO LEVEL DEPOT PLANS C&O CHICAGO 63 ST.	04	57	42
	STATION AT STOCKYARDS WV PLANS C&O 1890	07	77	76
CN	DEPOT PLANS MIDLAND ONT CN	06	70	50
D&LW	STATION AT JAMESVILLE NY PLANS D&LW	10	78	78
D&RGW	DEPOT AT RICO CO OF 1891 PLANS D&RGW	10	62	38
DL&W	DEPOT AT HOMER NY PLANS DL&W	08	65	31
DT&I	STANDARD STATION PLANS DT&I QUINCY, MI	09	78	50
DW&P	DEPOT PLANS WEST DULUTH MN DW&P	07	58	32
E	DEPOT ERIE DRAWING OVERBROOK NJ	10	80	72
	AVON STATION PLANS ERIE AVON, NY	12	78	96
FEC	DEPOT AT SOUTH BAY FL PLANS FEC	06	64	34
FJ&G	STATION DRAWING FJ&G BROADALBIN NY	08	79	70
GM&O	SMALL DEPOT PLANS AT OAK GROVE MO GM&O	04	59	26
GTW	SOUTH LYON MICH DEPOT PLANS C&O AND GTW	01	60	33
	DEPOT AT WALLED LAKE MICH PLANS GTW	07	78	80
IC	FREIGHT SHED & OFFICE DRAW CHAMPAIGN ILL	10	47	789
	DEPOT AT GRAMERCY LA PLANS IC	08	62	37
LV	GINGERBREAD STATION PLANS LAURY PA LV	03	48	189
	SMALL DEPOT WHISTLE STOP DRAWING LV	12	46	832
	FIVE SIDED FREIGHT DEPOT PLN FREEVILE NY	02	63	40
M	DEPOT DRAWINGS LINDEN IN M-NKP	06	75	40
MA&PA	SHED STATION LAUREL BROOK DRAWING MA&PA	05	65	40
MI&NW	FLAG DEPOT DRAWING ST. PAUL, MN MI&NW	05	47	376
MILW	BRANCH LINE DEPOT PLANS SUSSEX WIS MILW	01	49	63
	COMMUTER STATION PLANS MAYFAIR IL MILW	04	76	53
	STATION PLANS BROOKFIELD WIS MILW 1853	10	84	86
MP	TOM THUMB STATION DRAWINGS MP	07	53	34
N&W	DEPOT PLANS FRONT ROYAL VA N&W 1953	10	71	43
	FREIGHT STATION PLANS ROANOKE, VA N&W	07	71	52
NH	ROUTE 128 STATION PLANS NH	01	78	66
NPIER	DEPOT WAKEFIELD RI (NPIER) PLANS	09	74	42
	DEPOT PEACE DALE RI (NPIER) PLANS	09	74	42

RD	DEPOT PLANS BY ROAD	M	Y	P
NYC	DEPOT OTIS STA ROCHESTER NY (NYC) PLANS	10	74	62
	DEPOT DRAWINGS MOUNT HOPE NY NYC	11	75	60
	FREIGHT DEPOT PLANS COLDWATER NY NYC	04	68	50
	MARTISCO STATION DRAWINGS NYC 1870	02	80	78
	STATION AT WOODARD NY PLANS NYC	03	83	78
NYNH&H	DEPOT PLANS WALPOLE MA NYNH&H	09	67	40
NYO&W	STATION NYO&W PLANS BURNSIDE NY 1882	07	84	76
OR&NC	DEPOT PLANS UMATILLA OR OR&NC 1882	08	61	28
PG&CH	ORNATE PASS DEPOT DRAWING ALLEN LANE PA	09	54	25
PRR	TRAIN ORDER STATION DRAWINGS PRR	02	75	48
	RURAL FREIGHT STATION PLAN SUPLEE PA PRR	02	66	34
R	SMALL DEPOT AT ESSINGTON PA PLANS R	05	64	30
	SHED TYPE DEPOT AT EXTON PA PLANS R	10	64	51
	FREIGHT DEPOT AT NORTH HILLS PA PLANS R	01	65	40
	DEPOT AT RUSHLAND PA PLANS R	12	65	57
	DEPOT BOARD & BATTEN GRATERFORD PA PLN R	09	63	30
	FREIGHT HOUSE AT ESSINGTON PA PLANS R	05	64	30
RF&P	SMALL DEPOT PLANS DOSWELL VA RF&P C&O	09	69	48
RS&E	OCTAGONAL WAY STATION RS&E PLN JORDAN NY	12	79	104
S	NEWELL SC FLAGSTOP STATION DRAWINGS	04	62	39
SCL	FLAGSTOP STATION PLANS AIRY HALL SC SCL	01	71	64
	STATION AT PLAINS GEORGIA PLANS SCL 1910	08	77	58
SLM&S	LOG CABIN DEPOT DRAWINGS COBBS JCT MO	10	80	104
SOO	DEPOT PLANS FOND DU LAC WI SOO	10	70	60
SP	DEPOT AT MENLO PARK CA PLANS SP	01	64	62
	SMALL BRICK STATION PLANS SPREKERLS CA	11	66	54
T&P	DEPOT AT PORT ALLEN LA PLANS T&P	05	63	46
UP	FREIGHT DEPOT GLENDALE CA DRAWINGS UP	06	67	48
WA	DEPOT PLANS LAKEWOOD RI WA	06	57	61

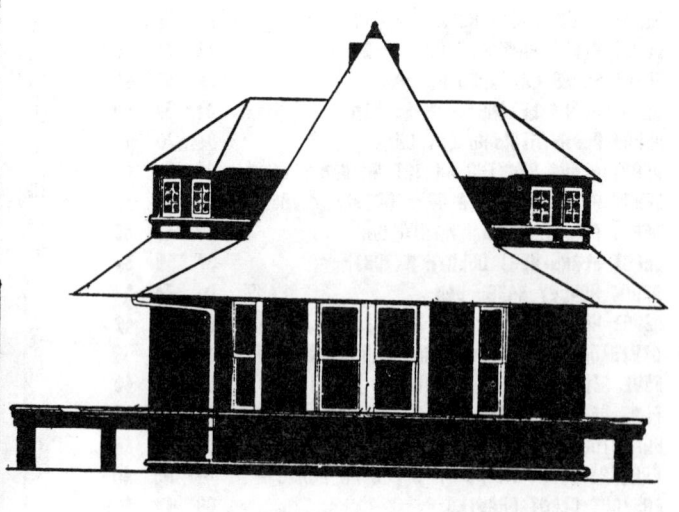

152

STRUCTURES & SIGNALS

DEPOT MODELS

Title	M	Y	P
ATSF STANDARD #4 STATION SCRATCHBUILD	06	83	80
BIG TOWN DEPOT CONSTRUCTION	01	43	4
BRANCHLINE STATION CONSTRUCTION	03	56	40
BUILD A COUNTRY STATION RUSHLAND PA R	12	65	52
CLEARWATER STATION CONSTRUCTION	09	57	40
COMMUTER STATION MAYFAIR IL (MILW) CONST	04	76	52
COMPREHENSIVE PASSENGER STATION CONSTRUC	09	40	493
COUNTRY FRT STN CONST WESTERSFIELD CONN	07	54	14
DEPOT ATTERBURY IND CONSTRUCTION PRR	04	76	41
DEPOT FLAGSTOP STN CONST NEWELL, SC S	04	62	38
DEPOT FREIGHT-PASSENGER CONSTRUCT WSL&P	02	47	122
DEPOT FRT-PASS CONSTRUCT W. HARTFORD VT	04	53	22
DEPOT FRT/PASS CONSTRUCT CRESTWOOD KY	03	55	46
DEPOT GREENWOOD MASS CONSTRUCTION B&M	09	61	26
DEPOT IN A CORNER CONSTRUCTION	02	49	36
DEPOT MOUNT HOPE NY CONSTRUCTION NYC	11	75	58
DEPOT OF 1886 CONSTRUCTION TUSCALOOSA AL	03	69	57
DEPOT OF 1900 CONSTRUCTION ALLEN LANE PA	09	54	24
DEPOT OLD TIME CONSTRUCTION $1	12	64	70
DEPOT ROWLEY MASS CONSTRUCTION B&M	01	74	50
DEPOT RURAL CONSTRUCTION GREENFIELD OHIO	02	70	52
DEPOT RURAL CONSTRUCTION PRIDES CROSS MA	10	58	58
DEPOT SOUTH LYON MICH CONST C&O-GTW	01	60	31
DEPOT SUBURBAN CONST CINCINNATI, OH B&O	07	39	345
DEPOT SUBURBAN CONSTRUCTION FINISHING	08	39	397
DEPOT SUBURBAN CONSTRUCTION.	08	46	486
DEPOT THREE TOWERED LAURENS SC CONSTRUCT	11	74	68
DEPOT TWO LEVEL CONSTRUCTION	05	68	42
DERELICT DEPOT CONSTRUCTION	11	83	112
DIVISION POINT DEPOT CONST ALBUQURQUE NM	12	56	38
DOODLEBUG DEPOT CONSTRUCTION	06	77	62
ERIE'S OVERBROOK NJ DEPOT SCRATCHBUILD	10	80	71
FLAGSTOP DEPOT CONSTRUCTION	08	59	28
FREIGHT DEPOT CONSTRUCTION	08	45	316
FREIGHT SHED & OFFICE CONST CHAMPAIGN IL	10	47	788
IVY JCT STATION CONSTRUCTION	06	79	59
LOG CABIN DEPOT CONSTRUCT COBBS JCT MO	10	80	102
MODERN RAILROAD TERMINAL CONSTRUCTION	06	41	289
MOM ATSF STATION PERRIS CA "HO" SPRAGUE	11	69	47
MOM DEPOT AT STOCKYARD WV C&O "HO"	05	78	71
MOM FREIGHT STATION "S" DYXIN	07	69	63
MOM LAKE CITY DEPOT "HO" LUNDQUIST	02	72	55
MOM MILW DEPOT "HO" MARTIN	03	84	82
MOM STATION AT OPHIR COLO "HO" GRAY	08	76	61
MOM VICTORIAN STATION "O" KUNZ	01	81	88
MOM WOLF CREEK STATION "HO" ISON	10	71	34
PLATFORMS FOR PASSENGER STATION CONST	04	73	71
RURAL FREIGHT STATION CONSTRUCTION	05	55	36
SMALL BRICK STATION CONSTRUCTION 1	11	66	52
SMALL BRICK STATION CONSTRUCTION 2	12	66	64
SMALL STATION CONSTRUCTION	10	38	409
SMALL STATION CONSTRUCTION BENTON, IND	12	43	528
SMALL TOWN DEPOT CONSTRUCTION	01	45	4
SPECKEL'S STATION ODYSSEY	11	83	120
STATION & GENERAL OFFICES CONSTRUCTION	09	69	32
STATION AT RANDVILLE, MICH CONSTRUCTION	06	78	112
STATION CONSTRUCTION BURNSIDE NY NYO&W	07	84	72
STATION FOR CLIFTON CONSTRUCTION	09	80	66
STUCCO STATIONS IN CHICAGO ILL	07	80	86
SUBURBAN STATION CONSTRUCTION	04	43	160
TERMINAL DELUXE CONSTRUCTION	09	53	30
TERMINAL FOR TRACTION LINE CONSTRUCTION	08	76	64
TERMINAL STATION CONSTRUCTION	12	50	32
TOM THUMB STATION CONSTRUCTION MP	07	53	34
TRAIN ORDER STATION CONST CANEY IND PRR	02	75	47
TWO STORY STATION CONST TUSCARORA JCT	07	55	16
UNION STATION CONSTRUCTION..	01	48	16
URBAN STATION CONSTRUCTION	03	51	28
WAYSIDE STATION CONSTRUCTION	10	34	7

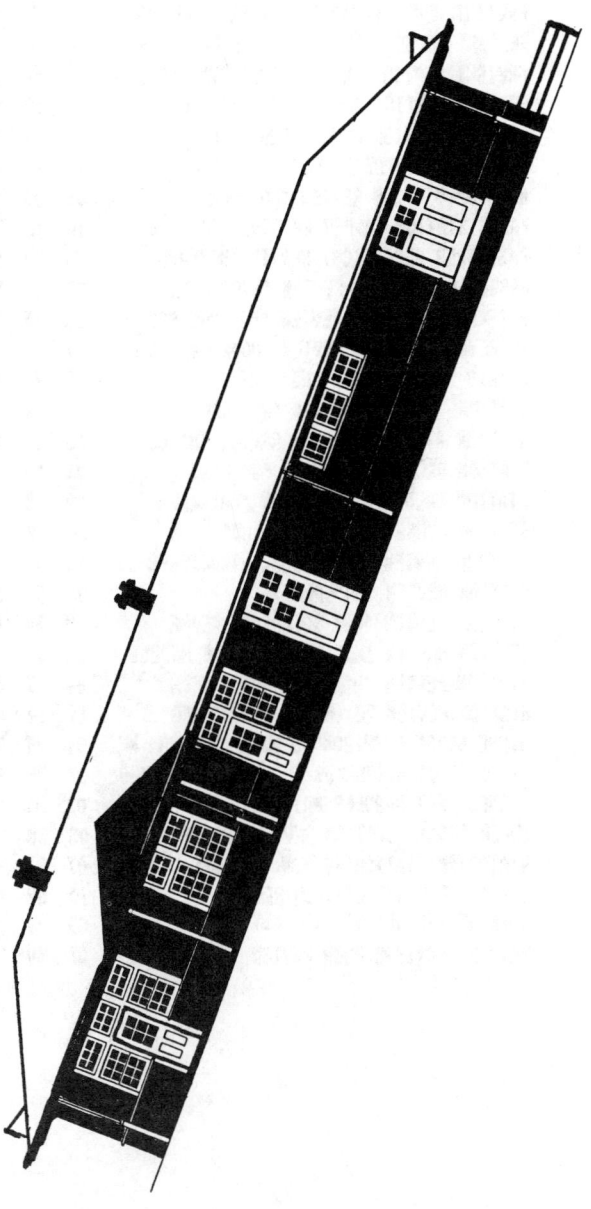

STRUCTURES & SIGNALS

DEPOT MODEL REVIEWS

	M	Y	P
BRANCHLINE FREIGHT STATION REV "HO" LADD	05	68	18B
BRICK DEPOT SMITHS CREEK MI REV "HO" CC	04	79	52
CANADIAN NATIONAL STATION REVIEW "HO"JSM	07	78	40
CLAPBOARD STATION REVIEW "O" TCM	06	50	47
COMBINATION ARLEE STATION REVIEW "N" AHM	04	74	25
COMBINATION DEPOT REVIEW "HO" AA	04	63	18
COMBINATION STATION REVIEW "HO" AHM	06	71	25
COMBINATION STATION REVIEW "HO" SLMO	03	80	46
COMBINATION STATION REVIEW "HO" SUYDAM	11	63	6
DEPOT FT WAYNE NB REVIEW "HO" AHM	01	73	29
FLAGSTOP STATION REVIEW "HO" CPC	08	62	10
FLAGSTOP STATION REVIEW "HO" F	08	72	21
FLAGSTOP STATION REVIEW "S" SU	02	73	20
FORKS CREEK STATION REVIEW "HO" SU	11	84	64
FREIGHT DEPOT 1900 REVIEW "HO" LABELLE	07	62	13
FREIGHT HOUSE 1885 REVIEW "HO" F	08	69	19
FREIGHT HOUSE BROAD TOP PA REV "HO" MH	12	54	16
FREIGHT HOUSE FACTORYVILLE PA REV"HO"SEN	10	54	15
FREIGHT STATION REVIEW "HO" DYNA MODELS	03	58	13
FREIGHT STATION REVIEW "HO" REVELLE	04	60	16
FREIGHT STATION REVIEW "HO" WMC	02	48	147
GRIZZLY FLATS DEPOT REVIEW "HO" PEM	12	76	37
MISSION STATION REVIEW "HO" ASM	05	50	43
PALMS STATION CA REVIEW 1887 "HO" DP	10	75	34
PASSENGER DEPOT 1887 REVIEW "HO" ASM	05	52	52
PASSENGER SHELTER REVIEW "O/S" MH	05	53	57
PASSENGER STATION REVIEW "HO" VOLLMER	03	73	24
PASSENGER STATION REVIEW "HO"ATLAS TOOL	09	62	14
SPARKS DEPOT REVIEW "HO" CMI	05	77	40
STATION OF 1890 REVIEW "HO" HSM	03	66	11
STATION AT FONDO LAC WI REVIEW "N" CC	05	81	46
STATION BACH MICH REVIEW "S" MIST	03	56	9
STATION CALDONIA MI REVIEW "HO" ALEX	02	55	12
STATION LYONS COLORADO "HO" MM	06	78	47
STATION REVIEW "O" MODEL STRUCTURES CO	11	42	528
STATION REVIEW "HO" ALEX	03	57	14
STATION REVIEW "HO" IDEAL AEROPLANE	09	39	484
STATION REVIEW "HO" INLAND SCALE MODELS	05	67	11
STATION REVIEW "N" MODEL POWER	04	77	35
STATION REVIEW "O" MODEL STRUCTURES	11	38	504
STONE DEPOT GUNNISON CO DSP&P REV "O" MM	09	79	39
STONE DEPOT HIGHLANDS IL REVIEW "HO" MMD	07	79	47
STONE DEPOT MARBLES MAINE REV "HO/O" TY	02	81	43
SUPER DETAIL STATION REVIEW "O" MS	05	38	216
VICTORIAN STATION REVIEW "HO" SSL	07	71	18
WAYSIDE FREIGHT STATION REVIEW "HO" C	10	69	16
WAYSIDE FREIGHT STATION REVIEW "HO" C	02	71	28
WAYSIDE WAITING ROOM REVIEW "HO" MH	06	49	56

DEPOT MODEL REVIEWS BY MFG.

MFG		M	Y	P
AA	COMBINATION DEPOT REVIEW "HO" AA	04	63	18
AHM	DEPOT FT WAYNE NB REVIEW "HO" AHM	01	73	29
	COMBINATION ARLEE STATION REVIEW "N" AHM	04	74	25
	COMBINATION STATION REVIEW "HO" AHM	06	71	25
ALEX	STATION REVIEW "HO" ALEX	03	57	14
	STATION CALDONIA MI REVIEW "HO" ALEX	02	55	12
ASM	PASSENGER DEPOT 1887 REVIEW "HO" ASM	05	52	52
	MISSION STATION REVIEW "HO" ASM	05	50	43
AT	PASSENGER STATION REVIEW "HO"ATLAS TOOL	09	62	14
C	WAYSIDE FREIGHT STATION REVIEW "HO" C	10	69	16
	WAYSIDE FREIGHT STATION REVIEW "HO" C	02	71	28
CC	BRICK DEPOT SMITHS CREEK MI REV "HO" CC	04	79	52
	STATION AT FONDO LAC WI REVIEW "N" CC	05	81	46
CMI	SPARKS DEPOT REVIEW "HO" CMI	05	77	40
CPC	FLAGSTOP STATION REVIEW "HO" CPC	08	62	10
D	FREIGHT STATION REVIEW "HO" DYNA MODELS	03	58	13
DP	PALMS STATION CA REVIEW 1887 "HO" DP	10	75	34
F	FLAGSTOP STATION REVIEW "HO" F	08	72	21
	FREIGHT HOUSE 1885 REVIEW "HO" F	08	69	19
HSM	STATION OF 1890 REVIEW "HO" HSM	03	66	11
IA	STATION REVIEW "HO" IDEAL AEROPLANE	09	39	484
ISM	STATION REVIEW "HO" INLAND SCALE MODELS	05	67	11
JSM	CANADIAN NATIONAL STATION REVIEW "HO"JSM	07	78	40
LA	FREIGHT DEPOT 1900 REVIEW "HO" LABELLE	07	62	13
LADD	BRANCHLINE FREIGHT STATION REV "HO" LADD	05	68	18B
MH	PASSENGER SHELTER REVIEW "O/S" MH	05	53	57
	FREIGHT HOUSE BROAD TOP PA REV "HO" MH	12	54	16
	WAYSIDE WAITING ROOM REVIEW "HO" MH	06	49	56
MIST	STATION BACH MICH REVIEW "S" MIST	03	56	9
MM	STONE DEPOT GUNNISON CO DSP&P REV "O" MM	09	79	39
	STATION LYONS COLORADO "HO" MM	06	78	47
MMD	STONE DEPOT HIGHLANDS IL REVIEW "HO" MMD	07	79	47
MP	STATION REVIEW "N" MODEL POWER	04	77	35
MS	STATION REVIEW "O" MODEL STRUCTURES CO	11	42	528
	SUPER DETAIL STATION REVIEW "O" MS	05	38	216
	STATION REVIEW "O" MODEL STRUCTURES	11	38	504
PEM	GRIZZLY FLATS DEPOT REVIEW "HO" PEM	12	76	37
RE	FREIGHT STATION REVIEW "HO" REVELLE	04	60	16
S	COMBINATION STATION REVIEW "HO" SUYDAM	11	63	6
SEN	FREIGHT HOUSE FACTORYVILLE PA REV"HO"SEN	10	54	15
SLMO	COMBINATION STATION REVIEW "HO" SLMO	03	80	46
SSL	VICTORIAN STATION REVIEW "HO" SSL	07	71	18
SU	FLAGSTOP STATION REVIEW "S" SU	02	73	20
	FORKS CREEK STATION REVIEW "HO" SU	11	84	64
TCM	CLAPBOARD STATION REVIEW "O" TCM	06	50	47
TY	STONE DEPOT MARBLES MAINE REV "HO/O" TY	02	81	43
VOL	PASSENGER STATION REVIEW "HO" VOLLMER	03	73	24
WMC	FREIGHT STATION REVIEW "HO" WMC	02	48	147

STRUCTURES & SIGNALS

RAILROAD STRUCTURE PROTOTYPE DATA

	M	Y	P
AMER BRIDGE STD CLASS H 66' TURNTABLE PL	07	80	78
BELLFIELD BOILERHOUSE PITTSBURGH, PA B&O	05	69	34
BETHLEHAM TWIN SPAN TURNTABLE	02	73	48
BRANCH LINE DIESEL FACILITIES RED OAK IA	01	58	58
BRICK GRADE CROSSING WATCHMAN'S TWR D&H	06	78	58
BUMPERS	12	54	42
CAR FERRY PELICAN IC	04	55	27
COAL CHUTE GATE AND APRONS	05	71	72
COALING STATION ON K&T STEARNS KY	12	59	47
COALING STATIONS	07	78	114
CRAZY PROTOTYPE WATER TANKS	06	56	53
DERAILS CAN LOCATE UNCOUPLING RAMPS	12	81	76
DIESEL & ELECTRIC SHOP PLANS AC&U	09	82	62
DIESEL FUEL TANK P&SR SAN FRANCISCO CA	03	59	37
DIESEL LOCOMOTIVE SERVICING	06	82	59
DIESEL SERVICE TERMINAL HARTFORD CT NH	10	67	52
DIFFERENT COALING STATION ORBISONIA PA	01	62	50
DUAL PURPOSE GANTRY CRANE MT UPTON PA	09	61	22
END OF LINE BUMPER CONSTRUCTION	09	34	19
ENGINE SERVICING FACILITIES	08	54	61
ENGINE TERMINAL FACILITIES	05	36	123
ENGINE TERMINAL LI OYSTER BAY	02	36	40
ENGINEHOUSE & COAL SHED HAVERHILL MASS	09	80	79
FLAGSTOP AT LURAY SC SEA	02	61	51
FLANGER SIGNS	03	85	68
FREIGHT CAR WEIGH PLATFORM	02	55	29
FREIGHT HOUSE & TEAM TRACKS	05	52	20
FREIGHT HOUSE AT LEROY NY EL	04	78	96
FREIGHT HOUSE DUBUQUE IO 1916 IC	01	82	104
FREIGHT HOUSE PLANS DUBUQUE IO 1916 IC	01	82	106
FUEL FACILITY FOR OIL STEAM LOCOS	08	67	60
GANTRY CRANES 10T ERIE 1920	10	85	76
GANTRY CRANES 20T WHITING CN TORONTO	11	83	82
HANDCAR & TOOL SHED OF MA&PA	06	78	60
ICE HOUSE CPR STANDARD #2	03	78	73
INSTRUMENT HOUSES	08	81	64
INTERLOCKING TOWER AT NORTH OLEAN NY	07	80	75
LACKAWANNA WHEEL CRANE	08	81	96
LATTICE POST WATCHMAN'S TOWER PA.	01	77	118
LINE SIDE SHED LAKE JCT, NJ LACKAWANNA	03	57	52
LOCOMOTIVE TERMINAL PLANNING	03	35	66
LOCOMOTIVE TERMINALS	10	53	52
LOCOMOTIVE TERMINALS ACTION & COLOR	05	42	236
MR VISITS A WISCONSIN CENTRAL YARD	07	52	42
OLD TIME ASH HOISTS GLAETON, PA B&SQ	05	53	64
PIGGYBACK TERMINALS	08	83	141
PROTOTYPE RIGHT OF WAY HANDBOOK	07	55	49
RAILROAD CLEANING PLANT SOUIX CITY IOWA	06	80	72
RAILROAD YARD STRUCTURES	10	77	71
RETIRED COACHES FOR MOW STRUCTURES	03	48	173
RIGHT OF WAY SIGNS	09	45	364
RIP TRACKS FOR REAL	12	45	545
ROTARY DUMP DEVICES	06	75	83
ROUNDHOUSE HOIST ANDREWS YD COLUMBIA SC	11	57	35
SAND USES & HOUSES			75

RAILROAD STRUCTURE PROTOTYPE DATA

	M	Y	P
SCOOTER SIDINGS	11	48	807
SERVICE FACILITIES FOR OIL STEAM LOCO	10	57	56
SERVICING FACILITIES FOR DIESELS	11	48	796
SIGNAL TOWER OVER HIGHWAY OVERPASS P&WR	10	62	34
STATION ORDER BOARDS	12	84	102
STEAM LOCOMOTIVE SERVICING & FACILITIES	04	82	68
SWITCH POINT HEATERS OF 1985	09	85	68
TANK CAR FACILITIES	03	77	118
TELLTALES PROPERLY PLACED ADD MUCH	04	44	155
TIE TREATMENT PLANT UP LARAMIE WYO	02	80	93
TRACK SCALE/SWITCHMAN SHNTY CR COXTON PA	07	83	60
TRACKSIDE TELEPHONE BOXES	10	68	61
TRAIN ORDER DEVICES	10	58	66
TRAIN ORDER HOLDERS	03	79	122
TRUCK UNLOADING RAMPS	10	84	141
TWO SIDED TRACK BUMPER	12	56	9
USES OF SIGNALS ON RAILROADS	01	68	75
WATER COLUMNS	07	37	258
WATER TANK AT STRAW MONTANA MILW	01	78	107
WELDING SHOP AT SODUS PT NY PRR	02	78	89
WORKINGS OF A COALING TOWER	01	82	160
YARD PEDESTRIAN ENTERANCE	07	45	287
YARD STRUCTURES DEFINITIONS/EXAMPLES	07	75	85

STRUCTURES & SIGNALS

RAILROAD STRUCTURE PLANS	M	Y	P
'YD' TOWER PLANS AT YORKDON	06	35	146
100 TON STEEL COALING STATION DRAWINGS	12	75	76
100 TON STEEL COALING STATION PLANS	09	59	48
25 TON COALING STATION PLANS MILW	05	75	65
90' TURNTABLE PLANS ABERDEEN SD	03	72	42
AMER BRIDGE STD CLASS H 66' TURNTABLE PL	07	80	78
ASH HOIST DRAWING GLAETON, PA B&SQ	05	53	64
ASHPIT DERRICK DRAWINGS	08	76	59
BAGGAGE ELEVATOR FOR TWO STORY PLAN	02	70	50
BAGGAGE ROOM BUILDING PLAN DEVON PA PRR	08	67	35
BAY WINDOW INTERLOCKING TOWER DRAWINGS	11	60	51
BETHLEHEM TWIN SPAN TURNTABLE PLANS	12	77	82
BLOCK SIGNAL CABIN DRAWINGS PRR	10	44	428
BOILER HOUSE PLNS NORTHUMBERLAND PA DL&W	04	65	48
BRANCHLINE STATION DRAWINGS	03	56	40
BRANCHLINE WATER TOWER DRAW FLEMING. NJ	05	51	44
BRANCHLINE WATERTANK PLANS BRICK BASE	10	65	52
BRANDON MANITOBA BIG COAL BUNKER PLNS CN	02	64	57
BRICK & FRAME SIGNAL TOWER DRAWINGS	01	56	44
BRICK ENGINE HOUSE DRAWINGS	03	67	57
BRICK ENGINE HOUSE PLANS ABERDEEN SD	03	72	41
BRICK ENGINEHOUSE DRAWINGS	01	55	29
BRICK INTERLOCKING TOWER PLANS RF&P	09	69	50
BRICK SAND HOUSE DRAWING	07	57	31
BRICK TRACTION SUBSTN DRAW CHESHIRE MASS	02	61	46
BRIDGE CRANE PLANS NYO&W MIDDLETOWN NY	01	77	72
BUCKET COALING STATION DRAW BRODHEAD WIS	06	55	18
BUMPER BLOCK DRAWINGS ESSINGTON PA R	05	64	31
CAR BARN FOR BWT PLANS	05	76	72
CAR RETARDER PLANS	11	61	56
CATTLE GUARD DRAWING	01	53	53
CATTLE GUARD PLANS C&NW	11	59	38
COAL BUNKER/SUPPLY SHED/FUEL TANK PLANS	08	78	72
COAL DOCK DRAWING SARGENT CO D&RGW	10	64	44
COAL LOADING DERRICK DRAWINGS	01	67	59
COAL TOWER PLANS	04	40	214
COAL TRESTLE PLANS	10	34	8
COAL UNLOADING TREST C&O PLN SHADNOAN OH	06	81	90
COAL YARD COVINGTON, OHIO PLANS PRR	03	62	44
COALING STATION 25T TW SNOW PLANS	10	80	80
COALING STATION D&RGW AT CHAMA PLANS	02	60	68
COALING STATION IN CONCRETE PLANS	02	67	33
COALING STATION PLANS	07	41	364
COALING STATION PLANS ST ALBANS VT	10	51	26
COALING STATION PLANS K&T STEARNS KY	12	59	47
COALING STN PLANS 50 TON WM BALTIMORE MD	12	62	34
COALING TOWER PLANS BLACKWATER MO. MP	01	59	52
COMBINATION ROOM FRT/PASS STN PLANS CRESTWOOD	03	55	47
CONCRETE RELAY HOUSE DRAWINGS	06	66	39
CRANE & CHAIN HOIST PLAN MILW CHILLIC,MO	05	63	45
CROSSING SIGN DRAWING	01	53	53
CROSSING WATCHMANS BOX PLANS 2 TYPES P&R	04	70	50
DIESEL & ELECTRIC SHOPS AC&Y 1947	09	82	65
DIESEL ENGINE HOUSE PLAN AVONDALE LA T&P	09	62	44
DIESEL SERVICING FACILITY PLANS	11	48	798

RAILROAD STRUCTURE PLANS	M	Y	P
DIRECT COALING STATION PLANS MP	12	57	30
DROTT TRAVELIFT CRANE PLANS	12	65	37
EIGHT SIDED GATEMANS TOWER PLANS MILW	09	60	35
ELEVATED GATE TOWER PLANS	04	35	101
ELEVATED WATCHMANS SHANTY DRW MADISON WI	05	54	16
ELEVATED WATCHMANS SHANTY PLANS ERIE PA	11	79	106
ENCLOSED UNDERSTRUCTURE WATER TOWER PLAN	11	46	729
ENCLOSED WATER TANK PLANS CP	08	60	25
ENGINE HOUSE FONDA NY DRAWINGS FJ&G	08	79	69
ENGINE HOUSE & MACHINE SHOP PLANS	12	73	51
ENGINE HOUSE 3 STALL PLANS CLAREMONT NH	01	53	13
ENGINE HOUSE DRAWING 1885 MAUCH CHUNK PA	01	47	20
ENGINE HOUSE PLANS ALAMEDA BELT LINE	04	80	82
ENGINE TERMINAL FACILITY PLANS	05	36	122
ENGINE TERMINAL FOR SHORT LINE PLANS	07	52	38
ENGINE TERMINAL LAYOUT PLANS	03	35	67
ENGINE TERMINAL PLANS DL&W	04	65	48
ENGINE TERMINAL SELKIRK NY PLANS 1 NYC	01	41	12
ENGINE TERMINAL SELKIRK NY PLANS 2 NYC	02	41	82
ENGINEHOUSE & COAL SHED DRAW HAVERHILL	09	80	80
FLAGSTOP AT LURAY SC PLANS SEA	02	61	51
FREELANCE ROUNDHOUSE DRAWINGS	02	72	67
FREIGHT HOUSE AT LEROY NY PLANS EL	04	78	96
FREIGHT HOUSE FOR WAY STATION DRAWING	08	52	49
FREIGHT HOUSE S PORTSMOUTH KY PLANS C&O	12	76	98
FREIGHT PLATFORM PLANS	02	73	45
FREIGHT SHED PLANS TORONTO ONTARIO CN	02	81	96
GANTRY CRANE 10T PLANS ERIE 1920 CIW	10	85	77
GANTRY CRANE 20T WHITING PLAN CN TORONTO	11	83	82
GANTRY CRANE PLANS	12	53	66
GATEMANS TOWER PLANS SP	08	49	25
GRADE CROSSING GATE PLANS	07	39	342
GRADE CROSSING GATE PLANS.	02	57	30
GREEN SAND BIN PLANS ST ALBANS VT CV	03	64	29
HANDCAR & TOOL SHED PLANS MA&PA	06	78	60
ICE DEPOT PLANS ANTIOCH, ILL	10	78	62
ICE HOUSE CPR STANDARD #2 PLANS	03	78	73
ICE HOUSE PLANS NORTHUBERLAWN PA DL&W	04	65	48
ICING STATION DRAWING SAVANNAH NY	10	56	42
INSPECTORS SHANTY PLANS LARAMIE WY UP	06	60	40
INTERLOCKING TOWER DETAILS-DRAWINGS	02	62	52
INTERLOCKING TOWER E STROUDSBURG PA DRAW	12	85	98
INTERLOCKING TOWER NYO&W PLANS BURNSIDE	07	84	80
INTERLOCKING TOWER PLAN E	07	38	273
INTERLOCKING TOWER PLANS	03	36	75
INTERLOCKING TOWER PLANS AT N. OLEAN NY	07	80	76
INTERLOCKING TOWER PLANS ETON JCT, MO	05	57	34
INTERLOCKING TOWER PLANS.	03	53	39
INTERLOCKING TOWER PLN ATSF ARGENTINE YD	01	57	24
JIB CRANE PLANS ST CLARE & NORTHERN	09	69	44
JUNCTION BUILDING DRAWINGS NEWFIELD NJ	06	61	44
LACKAWANNA WHEEL CRANE PLANS	08	81	96
LATTICE-POST WATCHMANS TOWER PLANS DL&W	11	63	45
LINE SHED PLANS LEAVENWORTH JCT KS	08	58	33
LINE SIDE SHED PLAN LAKE JCT, NJ LACK	03	57	52

STEPHANS' RAILROAD DIRECTORY

STRUCTURES & SIGNALS

RAILROAD STRUCTURE PLANS	M	Y	P
LOADING PLATFORM DRAWINGS PINE BUSH NY	01	76	76
LOADING RAMP PLANS JOHNSON CITY TN	10	58	36
LOADING SHED PLANS	07	69	45
MAIL CRANE PLANS OF 1869	10	59	29
MAIL HOOK AND CRANE PLANS	08	60	50
MILK STATION DRAWINGS NYO&W 1880	12	81	106
MODERN 90' TURNTABLE PLANS	08	62	46
MODERN ASH HOIST PLANS ST ALBANS VT	08	58	27
MODERN STATION AND TOWER PLANS	04	47	288
OIL SERVICE FACILITY PLANS/STEAM LOCOS	08	67	60
OIL SERVICING FACILITY DRAWINGS	01	70	46
OLGE COAL DOCK PLANS	12	45	518
ONE STALL ENGINE HOUSE PLANS	06	60	29
ONE STALL FRAME ENGINE HOUSE DRAWINGS	11	61	74
OUTBUILDING AT ESSINGTON PA PLANS R	05	64	30
PASSENGER SHELTER OF 1913 PLANS PE	06	62	67
PASSENGER SHELTER PLAN EDGEBROOK IL MILW	11	71	42
PASSENGER SHELTER PLN CB&Q W HINSDALE IN	12	68	74
PASSENGER WHISTLE STOP DRAWINGS LI	04	63	56
PRR STANDARD SCALE HOUSE PLANS WAWA PA	09	66	46
PUMP HOUSE OF 1916 PLANS S	11	60	39
RACK FOR LOCO CLEANING EQUIP PLAN EBT	08	67	27
RAILROAD CLEANING PLANT PLANS SOUIX CITY	06	80	73
RAILROAD STOREHOUSE DRAWINGS	12	70	78
RAILROAD YARD STRUCTURE PLANS	10	77	72
RAMSHACKLE YARD OFFICE DRAWINGS	11	72	57
REPAIR HOIST PLANS NP	03	68	58
RETARDER YARD TOWER PLANS ARGENTINE KS	05	58	27
RIGHT OF WAY SIGN PLANS	03	49	37
ROBERTSON CINDER CONVEYOR PLANS	03	69	50
ROUND WATER TANK PLANS NEW ENGLAND	03	52	16
ROUNDHOUSE DRAWINGS	08	81	74
ROUNDHOUSE FACILITIES PLANS MONCTON,N.B.	06	42	286
ROUNDHOUSE PLANS	06	49	30
SAND HOUSE AND TOWER PLANS CP	12	58	42
SANDHOUSE & TOWER PLANS NYC	01	80	96
SANDHOUSE AT CHAMA NM PLANS D&RGW	03	63	50
SANDHOUSE DRAWINGS	01	67	58
SANDHOUSE PLANS ARCADE, NY	09	78	86
SCALE HOUSE PLANS LEWISTOWN PA PRR	12	85	134
SECTION TOOL HOUSE DRAWINGS	06	47	466
SERVICE FACILITIES-OIL STEAM LOCOS PLANS	10	57	56
SHORTLINE RR OFFICE DRAWINGS	07	62	27
SIGNAL TOWER DATON AVE PLANS SP	09	35	233
SIGNAL TOWER DRAWING	03	47	207
SIGNAL TOWER DRAWING	03	52	27
SIGNAL TOWER PLANS EL PASO TX SP 1950	02	68	38
SIGNAL TOWER PLANS LEWISBURG PA R	02	69	70
SIGNAL TOWER PLANS NEW ORLEANS LA N&W	03	64	47
SIGNAL TOWER PLANS OF 1890 C&A 1890	04	66	48
SINGLE STALL ENGINE HOUSE PLAN CV	05	83	76
SNOW SHED PLANS	09	59	41
SNOWSHED PLANS GN	05	39	262
SQUARE WATER TOWER PLAN CP ROSSLAND B.C.	01	73	77
SQUARE WATER TOWER PLNS C&NW JEFF JCT WI	12	62	59

RAILROAD STRUCTURE PLANS	M	Y	P
STANDARD METAL STN & OUT BUILDING PLAN	03	80	78
STOCK CHUTE DOUBLE DECK PLANS	04	60	43
STONE ROUNDHOUSE DRAWINGS	12	73	52
STORAGE SHED & HANDCAR HOUSE PLANS IC	01	62	68
STORAGE SHED PLANS IC NEW ORLEANS LA	08	69	33
SWAYBACK FREIGHT STATION PLANS	01	80	118
TELEPHONE BOX PLANS	12	59	38
TELLTALE DRAWING	08	52	51
TELLTALE DRAWINGS	02	39	74
THREE STALL ROUNDHOUSE PLANS	09	56	41
TIMBER STATION & SNOW SHED PLANS RGS	01	63	48
TIMBER TRESTLE PLANS	12	63	54
TOOL & HANDCAR DRAWINGS	12	71	59
TOOL & SUPPLY FOR SIG MAINT SHED PLANS	01	36	18
TOOL AND SECTION CAR SHED PLANS	05	60	25
TOOL HOUSE DRAWING FJ&G BROADALBIN NY	08	79	72
TOWER STATION COMBINATION PLANS KANSAS	08	52	16
TRACK GANG SHELTER FROM OLD PASS CAR PLA	11	62	68
TRACK MAINTENANCE STRUCTURE DRAWINGS R	12	83	96
TRACK SCALE/SWITCHMAN SHANTY PLANS CR	07	83	60
TRACKSIDE MAIL PICKUP STAND PLANS	03	55	50
TRAIN ORDER DRAWINGS	03	79	122
TRAIN ORDER RACK PLANS G HOLLIDAY KANSAS	09	60	25
TROLLEY STOP LUNCHONETTE PLAN	07	77	84
TROLLEY TERMINAL PLANS NASHVILLE TN 1906	08	68	37
TURNTABLE BETHLEHAM TWIN SPAN PLANS	02	73	50
TURNTABLE CHESTER VT PLANS RU	08	70	56
TURNTABLE PLANS AT LAWS SP	09	65	36
WAITING SHED PLANS S	07	65	43
WAITING SHED PLANS WITH CUSPATE ROOF ME	10	65	37
WATCHMAN SHANTY DRAWING	01	46	13
WATCHMAN'S BRICK GRADE CROSSING TOWER PL	06	78	58
WATCHMANS SHANTY DRAWING	04	52	21
WATCHMANS TOWER PLANS WAUWATOSA, WI MILW	08	64	32
WATER COLUMN DRAWING B&O	04	56	36
WATER COLUMN PLANS 1	07	37	258
WATER COLUMN PLANS 2	03	40	142
WATER COLUMN PLANS 3	06	51	45
WATER CRANE OF 1891 PLANS B&O	09	61	48
WATER PLUG PLANS	02	67	45
WATER TANK & TOOL HOUSE DRAWINGS	04	59	48
WATER TANK (RECTANGULAR) DRAWINGS NP	10	73	38
WATER TANK AT STRAW MONTANA PLANS MILW	01	78	107
WATER TANK DRAWING CIRCULAR	05	52	40
WATER TANK PLANS 50,000 GALLONS	11	36	326
WATER TANK PLANS BABCOCK WIS MILW 1940	01	79	87
WATER TANK PLANS C&NW WAUKESHA, WI	08	55	34
WATER TANK PLANS ENCLOSED CP	09	72	37
WATER TANK PLANS HORIZONTAL CYLINDER	01	68	62
WATER TANK PLANS M&WR GROTON VT	11	79	108
WATER TANK PLANS PRR ORLEANS, NY	03	85	74
WATER TANK PLANS RECTANGULAR Q&TL	05	67	31
WATER TANK PLANS TAPERED DESIGN T&NO	04	63	30
WAYSIDE SHANTY MYRICK MO MP DRAWING	07	59	37
WELDING SHOP AT SODUS PT NY PLANS PRR	02	78	89

STRUCTURES & SIGNALS

RAILROAD STRUCTURE PLANS

	M	Y	P
WINDMILL PLANS GARWIN IA	02	49	42
WOOD WATER TANK PLANS ATSF 1890	02	57	46
YARD OFFICE DRAWING IC	03	57	32
YARD OFFICE DRAWINGS	01	67	61
YARD OFFICE PLANS L&N	06	63	36
YARD OFFICE PLANS NEW ORLEANS LA IC	08	66	46
YARDMASTERS OFFICE DRAWING	06	42	278

RAILROAD STRUCTURE PLANS BY ROAD

RD		M	Y	P
A&A	SANDHOUSE PLANS ARCADE, NY	09	78	86
AC&Y	DIESEL & ELECTRIC SHOPS AC&Y 1947	09	82	65
ATSF	INTERLOCKING TOWER PLN ATSF ARGENTINE YD	01	57	24
	WOOD WATER TANK PLANS ATSF 1890	02	57	46
B&O	WATER COLUMN DRAWING B&O	04	56	36
	WATER CRANE OF 1891 PLANS B&O	09	61	48
B&SQ	ASH HOIST DRAWING GLAETON, PA B&SQ	05	53	64
BWT	CAR BARN FOR BWT PLANS	05	76	72
C&NW	SQUARE WATER TOWER PLNS C&NW JEFF JCT WI	12	62	59
	CATTLE GUARD PLANS C&NW	11	59	38
	WATER TANK PLANS C&NW WAUKESHA, WI	08	55	34
C&O	FREIGHT HOUSE S PORTSMOUTH KY PLANS C&O	12	76	98
	COAL UNLOADING TREST C&O PLN SHADNOAN OH	06	81	90
CB&Q	PASSENGER SHELTER PLN CB&Q W HINSDALE IN	12	68	74
CGA	SIGNAL TOWER PLANS OF 1890 CGA 1890	04	66	48
CN	BRANDON MANITOBA BIG COAL BUNKER PLNS CN	02	64	57
	GANTRY CRANE 20T WHITING PLAN CN TORONTO	11	83	82
	FREIGHT SHED PLANS TORONTO ONTARIO CN	02	81	96
CP	ENCLOSED WATER TANK PLANS CP	08	60	25
	WATER TANK PLANS ENCLOSED CP	09	72	37
	SQUARE WATER TOWER PLAN CP ROSSLAND B.C.	01	73	77
	SAND HOUSE AND TOWER PLANS CP	12	58	42
CPR	ICE HOUSE CPR STANDARD #2 PLANS	03	78	73
CR	TRACK SCALE/SWITCHMAN SHANTY PLANS CR	07	83	60
CV	GREEN SAND BIN PLANS ST ALBANS VT CV	03	64	29
	SINGLE STALL ENGINE HOUSE PLAN CV	05	83	76
D&RGW	SANDHOUSE AT CHAMA NM PLANS D&RGW	03	63	50
	COALING STATION D&RGW AT CHAMA PLANS	02	60	68
	COAL DOCK DRAWING SARGENT CO D&RGW	10	64	44
DL&W	LATTICE-POST WATCHMANS TOWER PLANS DL&W	11	63	45
	ENGINE TERMINAL PLANS DL&W	04	65	48
	BOILER HOUSE PLNS NORTHUMBERLAND PA DL&W	04	65	48
	ICE HOUSE PLANS NORTHUBERLAWN PA DL&W	04	65	48
	INTERLOCKING TOWER E STROUDSBURG PA DRAW	12	85	98
E	GANTRY CRANE 10T PLANS ERIE 1920 CIW	10	85	77
	INTERLOCKING TOWER PLAN E	07	38	273
EBT	RACK FOR LOCO CLEANING EQUIP PLAN EBT	08	67	27
EL	FREIGHT HOUSE AT LEROY NY PLANS EL	04	78	96
FJ&G	ENGINE HOUSE FONDA NY DRAWINGS FJ&G	08	79	69
	TOOL HOUSE DRAWING FJ&G BROADALBIN NY	08	79	72
GN	SNOWSHED PLANS GN	05	39	262
IC	STORAGE SHED & HANDCAR HOUSE PLANS IC	01	62	68
	YARD OFFICE DRAWING IC	03	57	32

RAILROAD STRUCTURE PLANS BY ROAD

RD		M	Y	P
	STORAGE SHED PLANS IC NEW ORLEANS LA	08	69	33
	YARD OFFICE PLANS NEW ORLEANS LA IC	08	66	46
K&T	COALING STATION PLANS K&T STEARNS KY	12	59	47
L&N	YARD OFFICE PLANS L&N	06	63	36
LACK	LINE SIDE SHED PLAN LAKE JCT, NJ LACK	03	57	52
	LACKAWANNA WHEEL CRANE PLANS	08	81	96
LI	PASSENGER WHISTLE STOP DRAWINGS LI	04	63	56
LV	ENGINE HOUSE DRAWING 1885 MAUCH CHUNK PA	01	47	20
M&WR	WATER TANK PLANS M&WR GROTON VT	11	79	108
MA&PA	HANDCAR & TOOL SHED PLANS MA&PA	06	78	60
ME	WAITING SHED PLANS WITH CUSPATE ROOF ME	10	65	37
MILW	WATER TANK PLANS BABCOCK WIS MILW 1940	01	79	87
	CRANE & CHAIN HOIST PLAN MILW CHILLIC,MO	05	63	45
	25 TON COALING STATION PLANS MILW	05	75	65
	EIGHT SIDED GATEMANS TOWER PLANS MILW	09	60	35
	WATCHMANS TOWER PLANS WAUWATOSA, WI MILW	08	64	32
	PASSENGER SHELTER PLAN EDGEBROOK IL MILW	11	71	42
	STANDARD METAL STN & OUT BUILDING PLAN	03	80	78
	WATER TANK AT STRAW MONTANA PLANS MILW	01	78	107
	COAL BUNKER/SUPPLY SHED/FUEL TANK PLANS	08	78	72
MP	DIRECT COALING STATION PLANS MP	12	57	30
	COALING TOWER PLANS BLACKWATER MO. MP	01	59	52
	WAYSIDE SHANTY MYRICK MO MP DRAWING	07	59	37
N&W	SIGNAL TOWER PLANS NEW ORLEANS LA N&W	03	64	47
NP	WATER TANK (RECTANGULAR) DRAWINGS NP	10	73	38
	REPAIR HOIST PLANS NP	03	68	58
NYC	ICING STATION DRAWING SAVANNAH NY	10	56	42
	ENGINE TERMINAL SELKIRK NY PLANS 2 NYC	02	41	82
	ENGINE TERMINAL SELKIRK NY PLANS 1 NYC	01	41	12
	SANDHOUSE & TOWER PLANS NYC	01	80	96
NYO&W	LOADING PLATFORM DRAWINGS PINE BUSH NY	01	76	76
	BRIDGE CRANE PLANS NYO&W MIDDLETOWN NY	01	77	72
	MILK STATION DRAWINGS NYO&W 1880	12	81	106
	INTERLOCKING TOWER NYO&W PLANS BURNSIDE	07	84	80
P&R	CROSSING WATCHMANS BOX PLANS 2 TYPES P&R	04	70	50
PE	PASSENGER SHELTER OF 1913 PLANS PE	06	62	67
PRR	COAL YARD COVINGTON, OHIO PLANS PRR	03	62	44
	WATER TANK PLANS PRR ORLEANS, NY	03	85	74
	SCALE HOUSE PLANS LEWISTOWN PA PRR	12	85	134
	BLOCK SIGNAL CABIN DRAWINGS PRR	10	44	428
	BAGGAGE ROOM BUILDING PLAN DEVON PA PRR	08	67	35
	PRR STANDARD SCALE HOUSE PLANS WAWA PA	09	66	46
	WELDING SHOP AT SODUS PT NY PLANS PRR	02	78	89
Q&TL	WATER TANK PLANS RECTANGULAR Q&TL	05	67	31
R	SIGNAL TOWER PLANS LEWISBURG PA R	02	69	70
	OUTBUILDING AT ESSINGTON PA PLANS R	05	64	30
	BUMPER BLOCK DRAWINGS ESSINGTON PA R	05	64	31
	TRACK MAINTENANCE STRUCTURE DRAWINGS R	12	83	96
RF&P	BRICK INTERLOCKING TOWER PLANS RF&P	09	69	50
RGS	TIMBER STATION & SNOW SHED PLANS RGS	01	63	48
RU	TURNTABLE CHESTER VT PLANS RU	08	70	56
S	PUMP HOUSE OF 1916 PLANS S	11	60	39
	WAITING SHED PLANS S	07	65	43
SEA	FLAGSTOP AT LURAY SC PLANS SEA	02	61	51
SP	TURNTABLE PLANS AT LAWS SP	09	65	36

STRUCTURES & SIGNALS

RAILROAD STRUCTURE PLANS BY ROAD

RD		M	Y	P
	SIGNAL TOWER DATON AVE PLANS SP	09	35	233
	SIGNAL TOWER PLANS EL PASO TX SP 1950	02	68	38
	GATEMANS TOWER PLANS SP	08	49	25
T&NO	WATER TANK PLANS TAPERED DESIGN T&NO	04	63	30
T&P	DIESEL ENGINE HOUSE PLAN AVONDALE LA T&P	09	62	44
UP	INSPECTORS SHANTY PLANS LARAMIE WY UP	06	60	40
WM	COALING STN PLANS 50 TON WM BALTIMORE MD	12	62	34

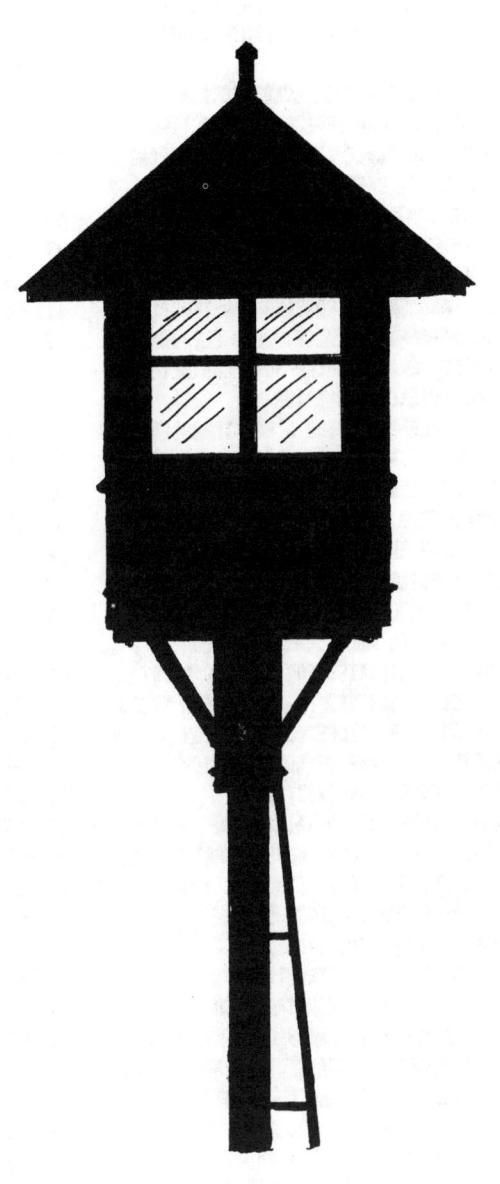

RAILROAD STRUCTURE MODELS

	M	Y	P
100 TON STEEL COALING STATION CONSTRUCT	12	75	72
25T COALING TOWER TW SNOW CONSTRUCTION	10	80	78
90' TURNTABLE CONSTRUCTION $1	03	72	43
90' TURNTABLE CONSTRUCTION ADDITION	11	72	91
ACTION GRADE CROSSING CONSTRUCTION	07	77	79
ACTION GRADE CROSSING CORRECTION 2	02	81	152
ASH HOIST CONSTRUCTION ST ALBANS VT	08	58	26
ASH PIT CONSTRUCTION JANESVILLE WIS MILW	08	57	30
ASH PIT WITH DERRICK CONSTRUCTION	08	76	58
AUTO TURNTABLE CONTROL 1	07	59	28
AUTOMATIC TURNTABLE CONST AT NEW LISBEN	10	76	48
BAGGAGE TRUCK CONSTRUCTION	07	47	540
BLOCK SIGNAL CABIN CONSTRUCTION PRR	10	44	428
BOX CAR SHED CONSTRUCTION	11	58	36
BOXCARS FOR STORAGE UNITS CONSTRUCTION	12	76	73
BRANCHLINE WATER TOWER CONST FLEMING, NJ	05	51	43
BREAKSTAND CONSTRUCTION	08	68	47
BRICK & FRAME SIGANL TOWER CONSTRUCTION1	01	56	45
BRICK & FRAME SIGNAL TOWER CONSTRUCTION2	02	56	40
BRICK ENGINE HOUSE CONSTRUCTION	01	55	28
BRICK ENGINE HOUSE CONSTRUCTION.	03	67	54
BRICK SANDHOUSE CONSTRUCTION	07	57	30
BRIDGE CRANE MODELING PROJECT NYO&W	01	77	72
BUCKET COALING STATION CONST BRODHEAD WI	06	55	18
BUILD A SWAYBACK FREIGHT STATION	01	80	118
BUILDING A TURNABLE DRIVE	05	79	100
BUMPERS AND BUMPING POST CONCTRUCTION	05	50	15
BUMPERS OF EARTH AND TIE CONSTRUCTION	03	55	36
CALL BOX CONSTRUCTION	06	44	267
CAR BARN FOR BWT CONSTRUCTION	05	76	69
CAR DUMPER THAT OPERATES CONSTRUCTION 1	12	60	64
CAR DUMPER THAT OPERATES CONSTRUCTION 2	01	61	60
CAR LOADER FOR BULK MATERIALS CONST	05	40	281
CAR SERVICE PIT CONSTRUCTION	01	50	46
CAR WASHER CONSTRUCTION	02	50	17
COAL BUNKER CONST CN BRANDON MANITOBA	02	64	56
COAL LOADER CONSTRUCTION	02	83	95
COAL TRESTLE CONSTRUCTION	10	34	7
COAL YARD COVINGTON OHIO PRR CONSTRUCTIO	03	62	40
COALING STATION CC&O	05	40	280
COALING STATION AT CHAMA CONSTRUCTION 1	02	60	68
COALING STATION AT CHAMA CONSTRUCTION 2	03	60	46
COALING STATION CONSTRUCT ST ALBANS VT 1	10	51	23
COALING STATION CONSTRUCT ST ALBANS VT 2	11	51	20
COALING STATION CONSTRUCTION 3	12	51	46
COALING STATION CONSTRUCTION 4	01	52	30
COALING STATION DIRECT DELIVERY CONST MP	12	57	30
COALING STATION RECEIVING BUNKER CONST	03	57	39
COMB TOWER-STN CONST OTTAWA JCT KS ATSF	08	52	16
CRANE WITH CHAIN HOIST CONSTRUCTION MILW	05	63	43
CRASH GATE CONSTRUCTION HAND OPERATED $1	03	76	50
DIESEL CRAWLER CRANE CONSTRUCTION	07	62	60
DIESEL ENGINE HOUSE CONSTRUCTION	02	52	10
DIESEL SERVICING CART CONSTRUCTION	05	49	27
DUAL GAUGE TURNTABLES	11	71	85

STRUCTURES & SIGNALS

RAILROAD STRUCTURE MODELS	M	Y	P
ELEVATED ENGINE TERMINAL CONSTRUCTION	05	50	34
ELEVATED WATCHMANS SHANTY CONST MADISON	05	54	16
ELEVATED WATCHMANS SHANTY CONST MADISON2	06	54	32
EMERGENCY RAIL HOLDER CONSTRUCTION	09	44	399
ENGINE HOUSE 3 STALL CONST CLAREMONT NH	01	53	12
ENGINE HOUSE 3 STALL CONSTRUCTION 2	02	53	38
ENGINE HOUSE DETAIL CONSTRUCTION $1	03	66	24
ENGINE HOUSE MODIFICATIONS MODEL HOBBIES	05	56	46
ENGINE TERMINAL LAYOUT	10	71	41
ENGINEHOUSE FREE LANCE CONSTRUCTION	03	77	51
FENCE GATES AUTOMATIC CONSTRUCTION	12	51	45
FISHBOWL ROUNDHOUSE CONSTRUCTION	03	78	84
FREELANCE FREIGHT HOUSE CONSTRUCTION	06	58	46
FREIGHT DOCK MOUNT DORA FLA CONSTRUCTION	09	80	98
FREIGHT HOUSE DETAILS CONSTRUCTION	04	56	32
FREIGHT HOUSE LCL CONSTRUCTION	10	57	35
FREIGHT PLATFORM CONSTRUCTION	02	73	43
FULLY AUTOMATIC TURNTABLE CONSTRUCTION	03	80	94
GANTRY CRANE 20T WHITING CONSTRUCTION	11	83	74
GANTRY CRANE CONSTRUCTION	12	53	65
GATEMANS SHANTY OF 1890 CONSTRUCTION	05	54	40
GATEMANS TOWER CONSTRUCTION SP	08	49	24
GRADE CROSSING CONSTRUCTION	07	39	339
GREEN SAND BIN CONSTRUCTION CV $1	03	64	28
HAND CAR SETOUT CONSTRUCTION $1	06	68	37
HANDCAR AND ITS SHED CONSTRUCTION $1	02	64	40
HILLSIDE WATER TANK KITBASH	11	84	98
ICING STATION FOR REEFERS CONSTRUCTION	10	56	42
INTERLOCKING TOWER CONSTRUCT ILLUMINATED	03	53	38
INTERLOCKING TOWER CONSTRUCTION E	07	38	272
INTERLOCKING TOWER CONSTRUCTION.	03	40	150
INTERLOCKING TOWER DETAIL CONSTRUCTION	02	62	50
INTERLOCKING TOWER WITH BAY WINDOW CONST	11	60	50
JIB CRANE CONSTRUCTION $1	09	69	44
KITBASHING A COALING STATION	07	78	64
LOADING CRANE (REMOTE CONTROL) CONST	09	56	52
LOADING CRANE CONSTRUCTION C&NW MILW, WI	08	40	433
LOADING PLATFORM CONST PINE BUSH NY	01	76	76
LOADING PLATFORM FOR WOOD BURNING LOCOS	06	73	64
LOADING RAMP CONSTRUCTION JOHNSON C. TN	10	58	36
LOADING RAMP FROM A FLAT CAR	10	84	80
LOADING SHED CONSTRUCTION	07	69	45
LOCOMOTIVE FUELING STATION CONSTRUCTION	04	40	213
MAIL PICKUP DEVICE CONSTRUCTION	10	49	15
MODEL TELLTALE CONSTRUCTION	01	76	49
MODERN SIGNAL TOWER CONSTRUCTION	09	35	232
MODERN STATION AND TOWER CONSTRUCTION	04	47	288
MODIFYING THE REVELLE ENGINEHOUSE	09	60	38
MOM COALING STATION "1/4" BRAMMER	01	72	59
MOM COALING STATION "HO" CHANDLER	01	80	82
MOM COALING STATION "N" SHAY	08	71	34
MOM COALING TOWER "HO" MEIER	05	68	41
MOM ENGINE HOUSE "HO" BOUDREAU	06	83	97
MOM ROUNDHOUSE SAN LUIS OBISPA CA PCOA	06	80	76
MOM SINGLE STALL ENGINE HOUSE "HO" COX	06	82	69

RAILROAD STRUCTURE MODELS	M	Y	P
MOM TOOL & SUPPLY SHED "1/4" PRIESTER	10	74	54
MOM TRUCK DUMP COAL LOADER "HO" CASSLER	09	79	71
MOM YARD SUPERS TOWER BARSTON CA "HO"	03	80	79
NEW TANKS FROM OLD TENDERS RUSSELL PA	09	62	46
OLD WATER TOWER CONSTRUCTION	03	54	72
OLGE COAL DOCK CONSTRUCTION	12	45	518
ONE STALL ENGINE HOUSE CONSTRUCTION	06	60	28
ONE STALL FRAME ENGINE HOUSE CONST	11	61	72
OPEN AIR ENGINE SHED CONSTRUCTION	09	47	724
PASSENGER OVERBRIDGE CONSTRUCTION	05	44	205
PASSENGER SHELTER CONST CB&Q W HINSDALE	12	68	74
PIGGYBACK TRAILER DEPOT CONSTRUCTION	08	57	46
PLANNING FOR YOUR ROUNDHOUSE	02	72	69
PLATFORM SHED CONSTRUCTION IN A MINUTE	11	48	813
RACK FOR LOCO CLEANOUT EQUIP CONST EBT$1	08	67	27
RAILROAD SIGNS	05	64	31
RAILROAD STOREHOUSE CONSTRUCTION	12	70	77
RAMSHACKLE YARD OFFICE CONSTRUCTION	11	72	57
REBUILDING TOWER 'YD' AT YORKDON PART 1	06	35	145
REBUILDING TOWER 'YD' AT YORKDON PART 2	07	35	183
REMOTE CONTROL ROUNDHOUSE DOOR CONSTRUCT	08	53	47
REPAIR HOIST CONSTRUCTION $1	03	68	57
RETARDER YARD TOWER CONST ARGENTINE KS	05	58	26
ROADS AND GRADE CROSSING CONSTRUCTION	09	80	70
ROUNDHOUSE (FREELANCE) CONSTRUCTION	02	72	65
ROUNDHOUSE ATMOSPHERE-MUST ADD DETAILS	02	45	75
ROUNDHOUSE CONSTRUCTION	08	51	14
ROUNDHOUSE DESIGNING & SCRATCHBUILDING	08	81	72
ROUNDHOUSE WITH SIX SIDES CONSTRUCTION	06	49	28
SAND HOUSE & TOWER CONSTRUCTION CP	12	58	41
SANDHOUSE AT CHAMA NM CONST D&RGW	03	63	51
SAW TOOTH ENGINE HOUSE CONSTRUCTION	08	43	344
SCRATCHBUILDING A TURNRABLE	12	77	81
SECTION TOOL HOUSE CONST ANCHORAGE KY	10	53	52
SECTION TOOL HOUSE CONSTRUCTION	06	47	466
SERVICE FACILITIES FOR DIESELS CONST	01	70	45
SERVICE FACILITIES FOR OIL STEAM LOCOS	01	70	45
SHED BUILT ON PILES CONSTRUCTION	12	62	36
SHORTLINE RR OFFICE CONSTRUCTION	07	62	26
SIGNAL TOWER CONSTRUCTION..	03	47	207
SIGNAL TOWER KIT DETAILING	03	56	24
SINGLE STALL ENGINE HOUSE SCRATCHBUILD	05	83	74
SMALL FREIGHT HOUSE CONSTRUCTION	09	51	24
SNOW SHED CONSTRUCTION 1	09	59	40
SNOW SHED CONSTRUCTION 2	10	59	70
STATION FENCE CONSTRUCTION	12	49	21
STATION PLATFORM CONSTRUCTION	12	56	60
STATION PLATFORM LAMPS CONSTRUCTION	08	50	21
STEAM FUNNEL CONSTRUCTION DENVER CO C&S	04	48	280
STRADDLE LOADER CONSTRUCTION	10	83	94
SUPPLY SHED CONSTRUCTION	09	58	26
SWITCH STAND CONSTRUCTION	03	75	50
TANK CAR WATER TANK CONSTRUCTION	02	81	72
TELEPHONE BOX AT TRACKSIDE CONSTRUCTION	06	73	69
TELEPHONE BOX FOR TRAIN CREW PRR CONST	11	53	58

STRUCTURES & SIGNALS

RAILROAD STRUCTURE MODELS	M	Y	P
TELEPHONE SHANTY CONSTRUCTION L&N	05	57	33
TELLTALE CONSTRUCTION	02	39	74
TELLTALE CONSTRUCTION IN A MINUTE	08	49	29
TERMINAL YARD FOR SHORT LINE CONST	01	67	56
THREE STALL ROUNDHOUSE CONSTRUCTION 1	09	56	40
THREE STALL ROUNDHOUSE CONSTRUCTION 2	10	56	48
TIMBER STATION & SNOWSHED CONST R&S	01	63	50
TOOL & HANDCAR SHED CONSTRUCTION	12	71	56
TRACK BUMPER CONSTRUCTION	06	53	41
TRACK GANG HEADQUARTERS CONSTRUCTION	12	83	93
TRACK GANG SHELTER FROM AN OLD CAR CONST	11	62	67
TRACKSIDE COAL BUNKER CONSTRUCTION	02	55	39
TRACTION SUBSTATION CONSTRUCTION 1	01	61	71
TRACTION SUBSTATION CONSTRUCTION 2	02	61	46
TRAIN SHED CONSTRUCT ROCHESTER NY NYC	09	53	73
TRAINSHED FOR TERMINAL CONSTRUCTION	10	53	28
TRANSFER TABLE CONST END SPACE PROBLEMS	10	55	55
TRANSFER TABLE THAT WORKS CONSTRUCTION 1	03	59	24
TRANSFER TABLE THAT WORKS CONSTRUCTION 2	04	59	40
TURNING THE TURNTABLE CONSTRUCTION	11	78	130
TURNTABLE (AUTOMATIC) CONSTRUCTION 1	06	55	22
TURNTABLE (AUTOMATIC) CONSTRUCTION 2	08	55	36
TURNTABLE (AUTOMATIC) CONSTRUCTION 1	07	44	292
TURNTABLE (AUTOMATIC) CONSTRUCTION 2	08	44	358
TURNTABLE (HAND POWERED) CONSTRUCTION	07	51	8
TURNTABLE (HAND REVOLVED) CONSTRUCTION	10	40	536
TURNTABLE CONSTRUCTION 1	09	57	46
TURNTABLE CONSTRUCTION 2	10	57	50
TURNTABLE CONSTRUCTION THE PIT AREA	08	63	39
TURNTABLE CONSTRUCTION 1	04	49	36
TURNTABLE CONSTRUCTION 2 COMPLETING IT	05	49	36
TURNTABLE CONSTRUCTION SPLIT RING CONTRL	11	57	60
TURNTABLE CONSTRUCTION THE BRIDGE	09	63	41
TURNTABLE FOR A SONG	06	43	280
TURNTABLE GEARING & PRECISION CONTROL 1	07	42	316
TURNTABLE GEARING & PRECISION CONTROL 2	08	42	360
TURNTABLE INDEXING	10	69	87
TURNTABLE MECHANISM CONSTRUCTION	04	36	94
TURNTABLE SIMPLE CONSTRUCTION	02	41	85
TURNTABLE SWITCH CONSTRUCTION	07	41	347
TURNTABLE WIRING CONRAD GEIGER	10	77	131
TURNTABLE WITH AUTO INDEXING CONSTRUCTIN	03	73	50
TURNTABLE WITH TIMBER RETAINING WALL CON	01	58	38
TWO DECK SECTION TOOL HOUSE CONST W&N	04	51	28
UMBRELLA SHEDS FOR STATIONS CONSTRUCTION	08	36	219
UNCOUPLING RAMP MANUAL CONSTRUCTION	02	52	36
WATCHMAN TOWER WAUWATOSA WI CONST MILW	08	64	32
WATCHMANS SHANTY CONSTRUCT SPEED INDIANA	09	53	50
WATCHMANS SHANTY CONSTRUCTION	01	46	13
WATER COLUMN CONSTRUCTION	06	51	44
WATER COLUMN CONSTRUCTION B&O	04	56	36
WATER COLUMN CONSTRUCTION.	03	40	143
WATER PLUG ON SHORT LINE CONSTRUCTION $1	02	67	44
WATER TANK & TOOL HOUSE CONSTRUCTION	04	59	48
WATER TANK (ENCLOSED) CONSTRUCTION	08	60	22

RAILROAD STRUCTURE MODELS	M	Y	P
WATER TANK (SQUARE) CONST CP ROSSLAND BC	01	73	73
WATER TANK AUTOMATION CONSTRUCTION	08	46	492
WATER TANK BRANCH LINE CONSTRUCTION	10	65	50
WATER TANK CONSTRUCTION NEW ENGLAND	03	52	16
WATER TANK CONSTRUCTION AN EASY WAY?	11	46	728
WATER TANK CONSTRUCTION C&NW WAUKESHA WI	08	55	26
WATER TANK WARNERVILLE CA CONSTRUCTION	02	81	119
WATER TANK WITH FUEL PLATFORM CONST V&T	04	42	160
WATER TOWER CONST JEFFERSON JCT WIS C&NW	12	62	57
WATERSPOUT PLATFORM CONSTRUCTION	09	54	37
WAYSIDE PASSENGER SHELTER CONSTRUCTION	12	51	53
WAYSIDE TELEPHONE SHACK CONSTRUCTION	09	50	51
WAYSIDE TELEPHONE SHED CONSTRUCTION	01	45	29
WOOD WATER TANK CONSTRUCTION	02	57	46
YARD INTERLOCKING TOWER CONST ATSF	01	57	24
YARD OFFICE CONSTRUCTION IC	03	57	32

STRUCTURES & SIGNALS

RAILROAD STRUCTURE MODEL REVIEWS

Title	M	Y	P
AUTOMATIC TURNTABLE REVIEW "HO" GEIGER	02	59	18
BRANCH WATER TOWER REVIEW "HO/HON3" F	11	67	18
BRICK FREIGHT HOUSE REVIEW "1/4" LJ	08	63	6
BRICK ROUNDHOUSE REVIEW "HO" VOLLMER	10	63	6
BUCKET CRANE SAND LDR REV "HO/HON3" SSMO	10	80	55
CAR REPAIR SHED REVIEW "HO" F	05	71	19
CAR REPAIR SHED REVIEW "HO" MIL-SCALE	08	69	13
CAR REPAIR SHOP REVIEW "HO" TRI	08	62	14
CAR SHOP REVIEW "HO" WGM	12	85	52
CAR WASHER REVIEW "HO" STEWART PRODUCTS	04	53	61
CINDER CONVEYER REVIEW "HO" SSL	06	73	23
COAL DOCK & SCALE HOUSE REVIEW "HO" MH	06	56	16
COAL TOWER REVIEW "HO" F	04	77	40
COALING STATION CHAMA NM REVIEW "O" SJE	06	80	46
COALING STATION REVIEW THE MODEL SHOP	06	41	331
COALING STATION REVIEW "HO" ALEX	01	54	26
COALING STATION REVIEW "HO" BOYDE CO.	04	65	14
COALING STATION REVIEW "HO" CAMPBELL	12	66	20
COALING STATION REVIEW "HO" FINE SCALE	10	70	24
COALING STATION REVIEW "HO" RCH	01	46	67
COALING STATION REVIEW "O" A MISENAR	01	40	54
COALING STATION REVIEW "O" MODEL STRUCT.	04	39	220
COALING STATION REVIEW "S" LV	04	77	42
COALING STN & ASH CONVEYOR REV "HO" ARISTO	07	57	17
COALING TOWER D&RGW CHAMA NM REV "HO" AHM	03	73	27
COMO ROUNDHOUSE REVIEW "HO" MM	03	76	27
CONTAINER CRANE REVIEW "N" VOLLMER	04	70	14
CONTAINER TRANSFER CRANE REV "HO/N" HEL	12	70	36
CORRUGATED YARD BUILDING REVIEW BOYD CO.	12	65	16
CROSSING SHANTY REVIEW "HO" Q-CAR CO.	06	77	45
CROSSING SHANTY REVIEW "HO" SSL	05	74	26
CROSSING TOWER REVIEW "N" MRW	03	83	38
DIESEL HOUSE & INTERIOR REVIEW "HO" ASM	08	50	52
DIESEL OIL TANK & PUMP HOUSE REV "HO" STEW	12	52	55
DIESEL SERVICE FACILITY REVIEW "HO" AHM	01	74	22
DIESEL SERVICING FACILITY REV "HO" STEW	02	52	45
DIESEL SHOP BUILDING REVIEW "HO" MH	09	59	14
ELECTRIC SUBSTATION REVIEW "HO" SUYDAM	11	58	14
ENCLOSED WATER TOWER REVIEW "HO" JMC	02	76	27
ENGINE HOUSE CA&C KEELER CA REV HON3 CMI	03	79	52
ENGINE HOUSE REVIEW "1/4" HEWAN	12	75	35
ENGINE HOUSE REVIEW "HO" SQ	09	82	42
ENGINE HOUSE REVIEW "HO" FINE SCALE MINI	09	69	24
ENGINE HOUSE REVIEW "HO" HELJAN	08	67	15
ENGINE HOUSE REVIEW "HO" REVELL	11	59	12
ENGINE HOUSE REVIEW "HO" TIM	05	73	27
ENGINE OIL FACILITY REVIEW "O" CSM	05	73	29
ENGINEHOUSE REVIEW "HO" MODEL HOBBIES	08	55	11
ENGINEHOUSE REVIEW "N" QUALITY CRAFT	07	77	28
FOUNDRY CB&Q AURORA IL REVIEW "N" MU	11	82	57
FREIGHT CAR REPAIR SHED REVIEW "N" MSP	01	71	28
FREIGHT HOUSE & YARD OFFICE REV 'N' QC	12	80	44
FREIGHT HOUSE REVIEW "HO" F	08	77	37
FREIGHT HOUSE REVIEW "1/4" AA	03	67	14
FREIGHT HOUSE REVIEW "HO" MODEL HOBBIES	10	77	46
FREIGHT HOUSE REVIEW "HO" SUNCOAST MODEL	04	73	26
FREIGHT STATION REVIEW "HO" AHM	06	75	26
FREIGHT STATION REVIEW "N" ATLAS TOOL CO	12	67	14
FREIGHT STORAGE SHED REVIEW "N" C	02	83	43
FREIGHTHOUSE OF 1886 PRR REVIEW "HO" ASM	01	52	44
FUEL & SAND FACILITY REVIEW "HO" AHM	06	79	38
GALLOWS TURNTABLE D&RGW REVIEW "HO" MM	11	75	29
GALLOWS TURNTABLE REVIEW "HO" MIL-SCALE	08	68	13
GALLOWS TURNTABLE REVIEW "N" MIL-SCALE	12	70	32
GANTRY CRANE REVIEW "HO" RENWAL	10	64	6
GATEMANS HOUSE REVIEW "HO" MODELTON MFG.	04	51	45
GRAVEL BUNKER REVIEW "N" KIB	12	82	57
HANDCAR HOUSE REVIEW "HO" CAMPBELL	01	75	41
HANDCAR HOUSE REVIEW "HO" J.L. MODELS	01	51	58
HANDCAR HOUSE REVIEW "HO" MODELTON MFG	03	50	58
HANDCAR SHED LISTING "HO" DURANGO PRESS	07	77	42
ICE HOUSE & YARD DETAIL REVIEW "HO" C	01	78	46
ICE STATION REVIEW "HO" FINE SCALE MINI.	03	70	16
ICING PLATFORM KIT REVIEW "HO" JL MODELS	07	51	45
ICING PLATFORM REVIEW "HO" ARVID ANDERSON	03	64	10
INTERLOCKING TOWER REVIEW "HO" AHM	12	71	32
INTERLOCKING TOWER REVIEW "HO" ALEX	04	59	12
INTERLOCKING TOWER REVIEW "HO" MH	02	53	60
INTERLOCKING TOWER REVIEW "O" MS	08	38	348
INTERLOCKING TOWER REVIEW "S" CSR	05	46	353
INTERLOCKING TOWER REVIEW "TT" CPC	06	62	11
INTERURBAN TERMINAL REVIEW "HO" SUYDAM	11	55	12
LCL FREIGHT STATION REVIEW "HO" CAMPBELL	04	64	11
LINE SIDE DETAIL REVIEW "HO" ALEX	03	76	26
LINE SIDE SHANTY REVIEW "HO" TRU SCALE	02	63	20
LOADING BAY REVIEW "HO" FRED BRONNER	10	61	12
LOADING PLATFORM FACILITY REVIEW "HO" WB	09	71	27
LOADING TANK & RACK REVIEW "HO" C	10	82	38
MAINTENANCE SHED REVIEW "HO" REVELLE	02	60	15
METAL ROUNDHOUSE REVIEW "HO" SUYDAM	11	52	65
MOM COALING STATION "HO" MECKLEM	11	68	45
MOM WOOD WATER TANK "HO" BUSCH	12	76	97
MOM YARD OFFICE "N"	08	68	31
OVERHEAD TRAVELING CRANE REVIEW "HO" VOL	02	71	24
PASSENGER & FREIGHT PLATFORM REV "HO" ASM	07	56	12
PASSENGER PLATFORM & SHED REVIEW "HO" S	05	56	16
PASSENGER PLATFORM REVIEW "N" HELJIAN	12	69	26
PASSENGER SHELTER REVIEW "O" MH	07	66	13
PILE DRIVER REVIEW "HO" HUNT	01	66	13
PILLAR CRANE REVIEW "HO" SSL	10	68	26
PLATFORM & UMBRELLA SHED REVIEW "HO" FAL	12	62	25
PLATFORM CANOPY REVIEW "HO/N" KIBRI	11	72	35
PLATFORM SHED REVIEW "HO" MIL-SCALE PROD	01	70	26
POWER HOUSE REVIEW "HO" MODEL HOBBIES	06	57	18
PRE FAB FREIGHT STATION REVIEW "HO" LM	02	74	30
PUMA HOUSE & OIL TANK REVIEW "N" STEW	05	72	21
PUMP & BOILERHOUSE REVIEW "HO" BSC	12	85	63
PUMPHOUSE REVIEW "HO" CAMPBELL	03	68	12
RAILCAR/ENGINE SHED REVIEW "HO" F	01	80	41
RAILROAD STRUCTURE REVIEW "N" HELJAN	09	68	14

STEPHANS' RAILROAD DIRECTORY

STRUCTURES & SIGNALS

RAILROAD STRUCTURE MODEL REVIEWS

	M	Y	P
RAILROAD STRUCTURES REVIEW "N" KLE-WE	11	67	24
RAILWAY TRACK SCALE REVIEW "HO" STEW	12	58	20
ROTARY CAR DUMPER REVIEW "HO" RLM	07	52	58
ROTARY DUMPER REVIEW "N" STST	12	82	45
ROUNDHOUSE COLORADO CITY REV "HO" MM	11	79	48
ROUNDHOUSE KIT REVIEW "O" SMI	04	85	44
ROUNDHOUSE REVIEW "HO" CON-COR	05	73	21
ROUNDHOUSE REVIEW "HO" FINE SCALE MINI	06	74	18
ROUNDHOUSE REVIEW "HO" MM	12	82	50
ROUNDHOUSE REVIEW "HO" SCALE STRUCTURES	09	73	19
ROUNDHOUSE REVIEW "N" HELJAN	11	68	14
ROUNDHOUSE REVIEW "O" MODEL STRUCTURES	01	40	54
SAND & PUMP HOUSE REVIEW "HO" REVELLE	09	60	11
SANDHOUSE REVIEW "HO" CAMPBELL	05	67	17
SANDHOUSE & TOWER REVIEW "HO" MH	06	59	14
SANDHOUSE CP REVIEW "HO" SSMO	04	80	37
SANDHOUSE REVIEW "N" AHM	08	70	12
SCALE STATION REVIEW "1/4" AA	03	67	14
SHANTY REVIEW "O" PNED	05	73	31
SIGNAL TOWER PRR PROTOTYPE REV "N" DIT	07	81	37
SIGNAL TOWER REVIEW "HO" FINE SCALE MINI	03	68	11
SIGNAL TOWER REVIEW "HO" VOLOMER	12	72	39
STEEL COALING TOWER REVIEW "HO" SSL	08	73	23
STOCK PENS REVIEW "HO" ACACIA SCALE MOD.	02	70	27
TAYLOR CRANE REVIEW "O" LESNEY	06	64	8
TOOL & GATEMANS SHANTY REVIEW "HO" MO	03	42	152
TOOL HOUSE REVIEW "HO/O" MODEL HOBBIES	01	51	64
TOOLHOUSE REVIEW "HO" SCALE STRUCTURES	09	70	16
TOWER & SHED REVIEW "HO/O" SUYDAM	09	54	12
TRACKSIDE STRUCTURE REVIEW "HO" MH	05	58	12
TRACKSIDE STRUCTURE REVIEW "HO" MMD	05	84	42
TRAVELING CRANE REVIEW "HO" AIRFIX	04	60	10
TURNTABLE BRIDGE REVIEW "HON2" APAG	11	78	58
TURNTABLE REVIEW "HO" AHM-AIRFIX	01	62	13
TURNTABLE REVIEW "HO" ATLAS TOOL	12	58	18
TURNTABLE REVIEW "N" RAPIDO	04	70	10
UMBRELLA SHED PLANS STOCKBRIDGE MASS	02	59	51
WATCHMAN'S SHANTY REVIEW "HO" EFMT	06	39	331
WATER & OIL COLUMN REVIEW "O" KEMTRON	10	58	18
WATER & OIL COLUMNS REVIEW "S" KEMTRON	07	58	15
WATER COLUMN REVIEW "HO" K&W SHOPS	10	39	544
WATER TANK D&RGW REVIEW "HON3" DP 1900	02	79	49
WATER TANK & COLUMN REVIEW "HO" YM	05	50	42
WATER TANK & FUEL DOCK REVIEW 2HO2 ASM	08	52	50
WATER TANK & TOOL SHED REVIEW "HO" C	04	73	21
WATER TANK 1905 DESIGN D&RG REV "O" DP	07	80	38
WATER TANK ATSF 1890 REVIEW "1/4" SC	08	68	9
WATER TANK ATSF 1900 REVIEW "S" DVK	09	69	21
WATER TANK ATSF REVIEW "HO" PMS	01	71	29
WATER TANK KIT REVIEW "HO" BELL	11	47	954
WATER TANK NP 50,000 GAL REV "N" DIT	08	80	48
WATER TANK REVIEW "O" WALTER W. SYRETT	01	38	42
WATER TANK REVIEW "1/2"" SSHK	04	85	37
WATER TANK REVIEW "HO" ALEXANDER MODELS	02	53	69
WATER TANK REVIEW "HO" ATLAS TOOL	09	62	12

RAILROAD STRUCTURE MODEL REVIEWS

	M	Y	P
WATER TANK REVIEW "HO" FRONTIER REPLICAS	05	77	40
WATER TANK REVIEW "HON3" TIMBERLINE	12	65	12
WATER TANK RGS REVIEW "O" OWS	12	79	48
WATER TANK TWIN REVIEW "HO" SSL	11	72	30
WATER TANK/TOOL SHED REVIEW "HO" F	12	74	31
WATER TOWER REVIEW "HO" STAR LINE MODELS	02	48	150
WATER TOWER REVIEW "O" MODEL STRUCTURES	09	39	482
WAYSIDE BUILDINGS REVIEW "HO" MH	07	55	12
WAYSIDE YARD OFFICE REVIEW "HO" MH	12	50	54
WOOD WATER TANK REVIEW "HO" CAMPBELL	04	65	9
WOOD WATER TANK REVIEW."HO" CAMPBELL	12	73	34
YARD BUILDING REVIEW "HO/O" EHD	06	81	32
YARD OFFICE REVIEW "1/4" AA	03	67	14
YARD OFFICE REVIEW "TT" WASC	06	66	12
YARD SHANTY REVIEW "O" MODEL STRUCTURES	10	38	452
YARD TOWER (MODERN) REVIEW "HO" KIB	12	85	68
YARD TOWER REVIEW "S" BACHMANN	01	55	17
YARDMASTERS OFFIC REVIEW "HO" MODELTON	10	50	53

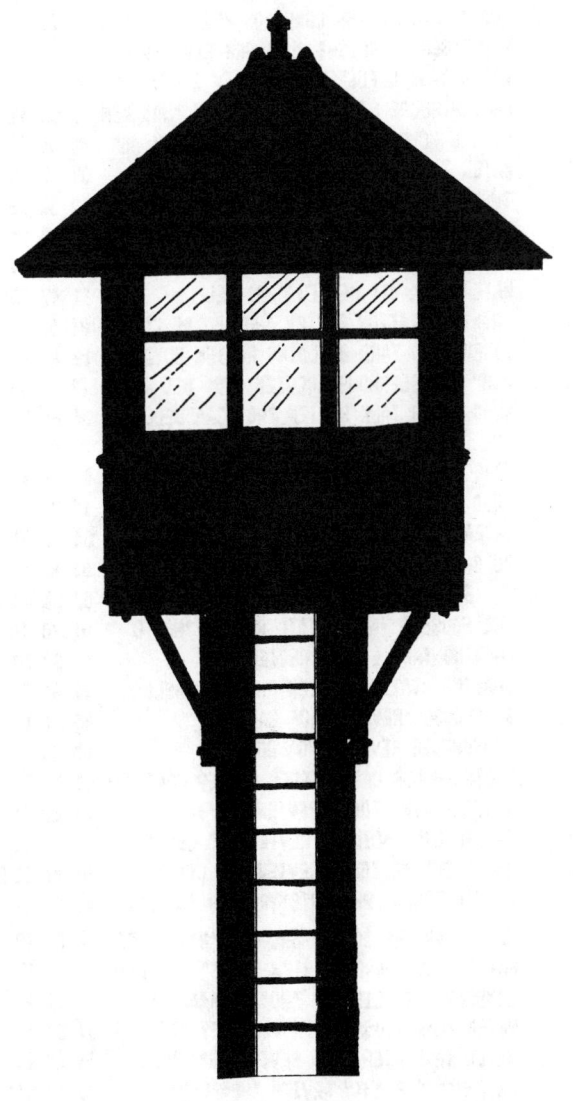

STRUCTURES & SIGNALS

RAILROAD STRUCTURE MODEL REV BY MFG.

MFG		M	Y	P
AA	ICING PLATFORM REVIEW "HO" ARVID ANDERSON	03	64	10
	FREIGHT HOUSE REVIEW "1/4" AA	03	67	14
	YARD OFFICE REVIEW "1/4" AA	03	67	14
	SCALE STATION REVIEW "1/4" AA	03	67	14
ACSM	STOCK PENS REVIEW "HO" ACACIA SCALE MOD.	02	70	27
AHM	FUEL & SAND FACILITY REVIEW "HO" AHM	06	79	38
	FREIGHT STATION REVIEW "HO" AHM	06	75	26
	COALING TOWER D&RGW CHAMA NM REV "HO" AHM	03	73	27
	SANDHOUSE REVIEW "N" AHM	08	70	12
	DIESEL SERVICE FACILITY REVIEW "HO" AHM	01	74	22
	INTERLOCKING TOWER REVIEW "HO" AHM	12	71	32
AHMA	TURNTABLE REVIEW "HO" AHM-AIRFIX	01	62	13
AIRF	TRAVELING CRANE REVIEW "HO" AIRFIX	04	60	10
ALEX	LINE SIDE DETAIL REVIEW "HO" ALEX	03	76	26
	WATER TANK REVIEW "HO" ALEXANDER MODELS	02	53	69
	COALING STATION REVIEW "HO" ALEX	01	54	26
	INTERLOCKING TOWER REVIEW "HO" ALEX	04	59	12
AMIS	COALING STATION REVIEW "O" A MISENAR	01	40	54
APAG	TURNTABLE BRIDGE REVIEW "HON2" APAG	11	78	58
ARISTO	COALING STN & ASH CONVEYOR REV "HO" ARISTO	07	57	17
ASM	PASSENGER & FREIGHT PLATFORM REV "HO" ASM	07	56	12
	WATER TANK & FUEL DOCK REVIEW 2HO2 ASM	08	52	50
	FREIGHTHOUSE OF 1886 PRR REVIEW "HO" ASM	01	52	44
	DIESEL HOUSE & INTERIOR REVIEW "HO" ASM	08	50	52
AT	WATER TANK REVIEW "HO" ATLAS TOOL	09	62	12
	TURNTABLE REVIEW "HO" ATLAS TOOL	12	58	18
	FREIGHT STATION REVIEW "N" ATLAS TOOL CO	12	67	14
B	YARD TOWER REVIEW "S" BACHMANN	01	55	17
BELL	WATER TANK KIT REVIEW "HO" BELL	11	47	954
BOY	COALING STATION REVIEW "HO" BOYDE CO.	04	65	14
	CORRUGATED YARD BUILDING REVIEW BOYD CO.	12	65	16
BSC	PUMP & BOILERHOUSE REVIEW "HO" BSC	12	85	63
C	WOOD WATER TANK REVIEW "HO" CAMPBELL	04	65	9
	LCL FREIGHT STATION REVIEW "HO" CAMPBELL	04	64	11
	HANDCAR HOUSE REVIEW "HO" CAMPBELL	01	75	41
	WOOD WATER TANK REVIEW. "HO" CAMPBELL	12	73	34
	WATER TANK & TOOL SHED REVIEW "HO" C	04	73	21
	PUMPHOUSE REVIEW "HO" CAMPBELL	03	68	12
	FREIGHT STORAGE SHED REVIEW "N" C	02	83	43
	ICE HOUSE & YARD DETAIL REVIEW "HO" C	01	78	46
	LOADING TANK & RACK REVIEW "HO" C	10	82	38
	COALING STATION REVIEW "HO" CAMPBELL	12	66	20
	SANDHOUSE REVIEW "HO" CAMPBELL	05	67	17
CC	ROUNDHOUSE REVIEW "HO" CON-COR	05	73	21
CMI	ENGINE HOUSE CA&C KEELER CA REV HON3 CMI	03	79	52
CPC	INTERLOCKING TOWER REVIEW "TT" CPC	06	62	11
CSM	ENGINE OIL FACILITY REVIEW "O" CSM	05	73	29
CSR	INTERLOCKING TOWER REVIEW "S" CSR	05	46	353
DIT	SIGNAL TOWER PRR PROTOTYPE REV "N" DIT	07	81	37
	WATER TANK NP 50,000 GAL REV "N" DIT	08	80	48
DP	WATER TANK D&RGW REVIEW "HON3" DP 1900	02	79	49
	HANDCAR SHED LISTING "HO" DURANGO PRESS	07	77	42
	WATER TANK 1905 DESIGN D&RG REV "O" DP	07	80	38
DVK	WATER TANK ATSF 1900 REVIEW "S" DVK	09	69	21
EFMT	WATCHMAN'S SHANTY REVIEW "HO" EFMT	06	39	331

RAILROAD STRUCTURE MODEL REV BY MFG.

MFG		M	Y	P
EHD	YARD BUILDING REVIEW "HO/O" EHD	06	81	32
F	ENGINE HOUSE REVIEW "HO" FINE SCALE MINI	09	69	24
	SIGNAL TOWER REVIEW "HO" FINE SCALE MINI	03	68	11
	COALING STATION REVIEW "HO" FINE SCALE	10	70	24
	COAL TOWER REVIEW "HO" F	04	77	40
	FREIGHT HOUSE REVIEW "HO" F	08	77	37
	WATER TANK/TOOL SHED REVIEW "HO" F	12	74	31
	ROUNDHOUSE REVIEW "HO" FINE SCALE MINI	06	74	18
	RAILCAR/ENGINE SHED REVIEW "HO" F	01	80	41
	CAR REPAIR SHED REVIEW "HO" F	05	71	19
	ICE STATION REVIEW "HO" FINE SCALE MINI.	03	70	16
	BRANCH WATER TOWER REVIEW "HO/HON3" F	11	67	18
FAL	PLATFORM & UMBRELLA SHED REVIEW "HO" FAL	12	62	25
FB	LOADING BAY REVIEW "HO" FRED BRONNER	10	61	12
FRR	WATER TANK REVIEW "HO" FRONTIER REPLICAS	05	77	40
GEI	AUTOMATIC TURNTABLE REVIEW "HO" GEIGER	02	59	18
HEL	PASSENGER PLATFORM REVIEW "N" HELJIAN	12	69	26
	RAILROAD STRUCTURE REVIEW "N" HELJAN	09	68	14
	ROUNDHOUSE REVIEW "N" HELJAN	11	68	14
	CONTAINER TRANSFER CRANE REV "HO/N" HEL	12	70	36
	ENGINE HOUSE REVIEW "HO" HELJAN	08	67	15
HEW	ENGINE HOUSE REVIEW "1/4" HEWAN	12	75	35
HUNT	PILE DRIVER REVIEW "HO" HUNT	01	66	13
JL	ICING PLATFORM KIT REVIEW "HO" JL MODELS	07	51	45
	HANDCAR HOUSE REVIEW "HO" J.L. MODELS	01	51	58
JMC	ENCLOSED WATER TOWER REVIEW "HO" JMC	02	76	27
K&W	WATER COLUMN REVIEW "HO" K&W SHOPS	10	39	544
KEM	WATER & OIL COLUMN REVIEW "O" KEMTRON	10	58	18
	WATER & OIL COLUMNS REVIEW "S" KEMTRON	07	58	15
KIB	YARD TOWER (MODERN) REVIEW "HO" KIB	12	85	68
	PLATFORM CANOPY REVIEW "HO/N" KIBRI	11	72	35
	GRAVEL BUNKER REVIEW "N" KIB	12	82	57
LJ	BRICK FREIGHT HOUSE REVIEW "1/4" LJ	08	63	6
LM	PRE FAB FREIGHT STATION REVIEW "HO" LM	02	74	30
LV	COALING STATION REVIEW "S" LV	04	77	42
MH	POWER HOUSE REVIEW "HO" MODEL HOBBIES	06	57	18
	COAL DOCK & SCALE HOUSE REVIEW "HO" MH	06	56	16
	FREIGHT HOUSE REVIEW "HO" MODEL HOBBIES	10	77	46
	INTERLOCKING TOWER REVIEW "HO" MH	02	53	60
	DIESEL SHOP BUILDING REVIEW "HO" MH	09	59	14
	SANDHOUSE & TOWER REVIEW "HO" MH	06	59	14
	TRACKSIDE STRUCTURE REVIEW "HO" MH	05	58	12
	WAYSIDE BUILDINGS REVIEW "HO" MH	07	55	12
	ENGINEHOUSE REVIEW "HO" MODEL HOBBIES	08	55	11
	TOOL HOUSE REVIEW "HO/O" MODEL HOBBIES	01	51	64
	WAYSIDE YARD OFFICE REVIEW "HO" MH	12	50	54
	PASSENGER SHELTER REVIEW "O" MH	07	66	13
MM	COMO ROUNDHOUSE REVIEW "HO" MM	03	76	27
	ROUNDHOUSE COLORADO CITY REV "HO" MM	11	79	48
	GALLOWS TURNTABLE D&RGW REVIEW "HO" MM	11	75	29
	ROUNDHOUSE REVIEW "HO" MM	12	82	50
MMD	TRACKSIDE STRUCTURE REVIEW "HO" MMD	05	84	42
MO	TOOL & GATEMANS SHANTY REVIEW "HO" MO	03	42	152
	GATEMANS HOUSE REVIEW "HO" MODELTON MFG.	04	51	45
	YARDMASTERS OFFIC REVIEW "HO" MODELTON	10	50	53

STRUCTURES & SIGNALS

RAILROAD STRUCTURE MODEL REV BY MFG.

MFG		M	Y	P
	HANDCAR HOUSE REVIEW "HO" MODELTON MFG	03	50	58
MOD	COALING STATION REVIEW THE MODEL SHOP	06	41	331
MRW	CROSSING TOWER REVIEW "N" MRW	03	83	38
MS	INTERLOCKING TOWER REVIEW "O" MS	08	38	348
	YARD SHANTY REVIEW "O" MODEL STRUCTURES	10	38	452
	COALING STATION REVIEW "O" MODEL STRUCT.	04	39	220
	WATER TOWER REVIEW "O" MODEL STRUCTURES	09	39	482
	ROUNDHOUSE REVIEW "O" MODEL STRUCTURES	01	40	54
MSP	CAR REPAIR SHED REVIEW "HO" MIL-SCALE	08	69	13
	GALLOWS TURNTABLE REVIEW "HO" MIL-SCALE	08	68	13
	GALLOWS TURNTABLE REVIEW "N" MIL-SCALE	12	70	32
	FREIGHT CAR REPAIR SHED REVIEW "N" MSP	01	71	28
	PLATFORM SHED REVIEW "HO" MIL-SCALE PROD	01	70	26
MU	FOUNDRY CB&Q AURORA IL REVIEW "N" MU	11	82	57
OWS	WATER TANK RGS REVIEW "O" OWS	12	79	48
PMS	WATER TANK ATSF REVIEW "HO" PMS	01	71	29
PNED	SHANTY REVIEW "O" PNED	05	73	31
QC	ENGINEHOUSE REVIEW "N" QUALITY CRAFT	07	77	28
	FREIGHT HOUSE & YARD OFFICE REV "N" QC	12	80	44
QCC	CROSSING SHANTY REVIEW "HO" Q-CAR CO.	06	77	45
RAP	TURNTABLE REVIEW "N" RAPIDO	04	70	10
RCH	COALING STATION REVIEW "HO" RCH	01	46	67
RE	SAND & PUMP HOUSE REVIEW "HO" REVELLE	09	60	11
	MAINTENANCE SHED REVIEW "HO" REVELLE	02	60	15
	ENGINE HOUSE REVIEW "HO" REVELL	11	59	12
REN	GANTRY CRANE REVIEW "HO" RENWAL	10	64	6
RLM	ROTARY CAR DUMPER REVIEW "HO" RLM	07	52	58
S	PASSENGER PLATFORM & SHED REVIEW "HO" S	05	56	16
	TOWER & SHED REVIEW "HO/O" SUYDAM	09	54	12
	ELECTRIC SUBSTATION REVIEW "HO" SUYDAM	11	58	14
	INTERURBAN TERMINAL REVIEW "HO" SUYDAM	11	55	12
	METAL ROUNDHOUSE REVIEW "HO" SUYDAM	11	52	65
SC	FREIGHT HOUSE REVIEW "HO" SUNCOAST MODEL	04	73	26
	WATER TANK ATSF 1890 REVIEW "1/4" SC	08	68	9
SJE	COALING STATION CHAMA NM REVIEW "O" SJE	06	80	46
SL	WATER TOWER REVIEW "HO" STAR LINE MODELS	02	48	150
SMI	ROUNDHOUSE KIT REVIEW "O" SMI	04	85	44
SQ	ENGINE HOUSE REVIEW "HO" SQ	09	82	42
SSHK	WATER TANK REVIEW "1/2" SSHK	04	85	37
SSL	ROUNDHOUSE REVIEW "HO" SCALE STRUCTURES	09	73	19
	STEEL COALING TOWER REVIEW "HO" SSL	08	73	23
	CINDER CONVEYER REVIEW "HO" SSL	06	73	23
	PILLAR CRANE REVIEW "HO" SSL	10	68	26
	TOOLHOUSE REVIEW "HO" SCALE STRUCTURES	09	70	16
	CROSSING SHANTY REVIEW "HO" SSL	05	74	26
	WATER TANK TWIN REVIEW "HO" SSL	11	72	30
SSMO	SANDHOUSE CP REVIEW "HO" SSMO	04	80	37
	BUCKET CRANE SAND LDR REV "HO/HON3" SSMO	10	80	55
STEW	PUMA HOUSE & OIL TANK REVIEW "N" STEW	05	72	21

RAILROAD STRUCTURE MODEL REV BY MFG.

MFG		M	Y	P
	CAR WASHER REVIEW "HO" STEWART PRODUCTS	04	53	61
	RAILWAY TRACK SCALE REVIEW "HO" STEW	12	58	20
	DIESEL OIL TANK & PUMP HOUSE REV"HO"STEW	12	52	55
	DIESEL SERVICING FACILITY REV "HO" STEW	02	52	45
STST	ROTARY DUMPER REVIEW "N" STST	12	82	45
TIM	WATER TANK REVIEW "HON3" TIMBERLINE	12	65	12
	ENGINE HOUSE REVIEW "HO" TIM	05	73	27
TRI	CAR REPAIR SHOP REVIEW "HO" TRI	08	62	14
TSM	LINE SIDE SHANTY REVIEW "HO" TRU SCALE	02	63	20
VOL	BRICK ROUNDHOUSE REVIEW "HO" VOLLMER	10	63	6
	SIGNAL TOWER REVIEW "HO" VOLOMER	12	72	39
	CONTAINER CRANE REVIEW "N" VOLLMER	04	70	14
	OVERHEAD TRAVELING CRANE REVIEW "HO" VOL	02	71	24
WASM	YARD OFFICE REVIEW "TT" WASC	06	66	12
WB	LOADING PLATFORM FACILITY REVIEW "HO" WB	09	71	27
WGM	CAR SHOP REVIEW "HO" WGM	12	85	52
WSY	WATER TANK REVIEW "O" WALTER W. SYRETT	01	38	42
YM	WATER TANK & COLUMN REVIEW "HO" YM	05	50	42

RAILROAD STRUCTURE MODEL REV BY ROAD

RD		M	Y	P
CA&C	ENGINE HOUSE CA&C KEELER CA REV HON3 CMI	03	79	52
CB&Q	FOUNDRY CB&Q AURORA IL REVIEW "N" MU	11	82	57
CMI	ROUNDHOUSE COLORADO CITY REV "HO" MM	11	79	48
CP	SANDHOUSE CP REVIEW "HO" SSMO	04	80	37
D&RG	WATER TANK 1905 DESIGN D&RG REV "O" DP	07	80	38
D&RGW	WATER TANK D&RGW REVIEW "HON3" DP 1900	02	79	49
	GALLOWS TURNTABLE D&RGW REVIEW "HO" MM	11	75	29
	COALING TOWER D&RGW CHAMA NM REV"HO" AHM	03	73	27
PRR	SIGNAL TOWER PRR PROTOTYPE REV "N" DIT	07	81	37
	FREIGHTHOUSE OF 1886 PRR REVIEW "HO" ASM	01	52	44
RGS	WATER TANK RGS REVIEW "O" OWS	12	79	48

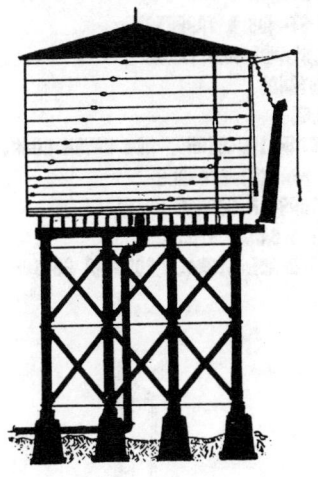

STRUCTURES & SIGNALS

SIGNAL PROTOTYPE DATA

Title	M	Y	P
BALL AND BANJO SIGNALS	09	47	721
BANJO SIGNALS INTO 1930'S C&NW	08	80	136
BLOCK & INTERLOCKING SIGNAL DIFFERENCES	05	53	61
DETAILING A SIGNAL SYSTEM CONSTRUCTION	01	67	44
DWARF SIGNALS WHERE TO USE THEM	04	53	71
FLANGER SIGNS	05	44	207
FLANGER SIGNS AND TELLTALES	06	51	57
FLANGER WARNING SIGNS	05	70	59
FOLLOWING SIGNAL PROTOTYPES	09	37	307
INSTRUMENT CASES & WHERE TO FIND THEM	06	81	74
LANTERN SIGNALS	08	57	66
LIGHTED RAILROAD SIGNALS	05	52	37
LOWER QUADRANT SEMAPHORES	12	58	63
MECHANICAL INTERLOCKING & SIGNALING 1	01	61	46
MOTOR SECTION CAR SIGNAL	10	70	69
RAILROAD CROSSING SIGNS	11	43	506
RED LIGHTS & GREEN SIGNALS BOOMER PETE	05	47	368
SEARCHLIGHT SIGNALS	01	83	111
SEMAPHORE MOUNTING ON ATSF	04	47	299
SEMAPHORE SIGNAL BLADE SHAPES	06	63	61
SIGNAL ASPECTS & INDICATIONS	10	70	54
SIGNAL ASPECTS & THEIR INDICATIONS	05	62	47
SIGNAL ASPECTS CHART	11	48	825
SIGNAL BRIDGE C&NW	01	46	17
SIGNAL EQUIPMENT & LINESIDE SIGNALS	01	36	5
SIGNAL IN MIDDLE OF TRACK?	10	78	149
SIGNAL LOCATIONS BLUEBOOK	03	57	67
SIGNAL RULES & TYPES	09	76	54
SIGNAL SIZE TEMPLATES	01	36	68
SIGNALING PRACTICE	09	34	5
SIGNALING THROUGH HISTORY 1830-1924	12	64	87
SIGNALS--WHAT? WHY? WHERE? BOOMER PETE	04	43	168
SMASHBOARD SIGNALS PLYMOUTH WISC C&NW	08	83	68
STANDARD SIGNAL ASPECTS & CHART	07	35	186
SWINGING GATE CROSSINGS HIGHLAND PARK CA	08	82	100
SWITCH INDICATORS	12	36	353
SWITCH STAND APPURTENANCES	04	81	72
SWITCH STANDS	05	48	329
SWITCH STANDS & TARGETS	06	65	58
SWITCH STANDS AND TARGETS	02	81	81
SWITCHSTANDS	03	38	98
TELLTALES	11	56	58
TRAIN STARTING SIGNAL NEW HAVEN CONN.	10	65	57
USE OF BRACKET SIGNALS	09	36	261
VARIATIONS IN SIGNAL PRACTICE	01	71	79
WHAT IS A BANJO SIGNAL	12	79	181
WIG WAG GRADE SIGNAL CROSSING SWITCH	04	49	57

SIGNAL PLANS

Title	M	Y	P
BALL AND BANJO SIGNAL DRAWINGS	09	47	720
CANTILEVER SIGNAL BRIDGE PLANS	08	70	60
CANTILEVER SIGNAL BRIDGE PLN IHB CHICAGO	08	63	35
CROSSING GATE PLANS FOR TRAINS PLANS	06	48	395
CROSSING GATE PLANS WESTERN RY SIGNAL CO	10	62	68
CROSSING SIGN DRAWING	06	52	29
CROSSING SIGNAL DRAWING	09	52	76
DWARF COLOR LIGHT SIGNAL DRAWING	03	52	55
DWARF SIGNAL PLANS	05	41	264
FREE LANCE SIGNAL BRIDGE DRAWINGS	12	79	69
GRADE CROSSING BLINKER SIGNAL PLANS	04	49	56
GRADE CROSSING FLASHING SIGNAL PLANS	01	52	54
INSTRUMENT CASES PLANS	06	81	74
OLD DILLY OF A SIGNAL PLANS	10	63	58
POSITION SIGNAL DRAW B&O CLARKSBURG W.VA	06	40	321
RELAY BOX & CABLE POST DRAWING	06	52	42
RIGHT OF WAY SIGN PLANS B&O	06	40	323
SEARCHLIGHT SIGNAL PLANS	10	34	14
SEARCHLIGHT SIGNAL PLANS	07	41	368
SEARCHLIGHT SIGNALS PLANS	01	83	111
SEMAPHORE AT FREEVILLE, NY PLANS LV	02	63	40
SEMAPHORE LOWER QUADRANT PLANS	12	58	63
SIGNAL BRIDGE PLANS B&M STANDARD	01	54	102
SIGNAL DRAWING SUPPLEMENT	01	36	65
SIGNAL HEAD DRAWINGS	01	71	80
SIGNAL MAST PLANS	03	52	30
SIGNAL PLANS POSITION LIGHTS PRR	07	40	376
SIGNAL PLANS TRI COLOR SIGNAL TYPE G	09	40	502
SIGNAL PLANS TYPE D COLOR LIGHT SIGNAL	11	40	608
SIGNAL TOWER IN MINIMUM SPACE PLANS	01	69	72
SIGNAL TYPE DRAWINGS	05	47	368
SMASHBOARD PLANS	07	60	27
STANDARD SIGNAL BRIDGE PLANS PRR	09	38	364
SWINGING GATE CROSSINGS PLNS HIGHLAND CA	08	82	101
SWITCH STAND APPURTENANCES DRAWINGS	04	81	72
TRACKSIDE SIGN PLANS	09	35	235
WAYSIDE SIGNAL SIGNS	01	52	35

SIGNAL PLANS BY ROAD

RD	Title	M	Y	P
B&M	SIGNAL BRIDGE PLANS B&M STANDARD	01	54	102
B&O	POSITION SIGNAL DRAW B&O CLARKSBURG W.VA	06	40	321
	RIGHT OF WAY SIGN PLANS B&O	06	40	323
IHB	CANTILEVER SIGNAL BRIDGE PLN IHB CHICAGO	08	63	35
LV	SEMAPHORE AT FREEVILLE, NY PLANS LV	02	63	40
PRR	STANDARD SIGNAL BRIDGE PLANS PRR	09	38	364
	SIGNAL PLANS POSITION LIGHTS PRR	07	40	376

SIGNAL PHOTOS

Title	M	Y	P
HOESCHEN GRADE CROSSING SIGNAL PHOTO	08	71	70

STRUCTURES & SIGNALS

SIGNAL MODELS	M	Y	P
A DILLY OF A SIGNAL NH	10	63	55
ADDING THREE COLOR SIGNALS	04	72	37
BLOCK SIGNALING	02	37	55
CANTILEVER SIGNAL BRIDGE CONSTRUCTION	08	70	57
COLOR LIGHT SIGNAL CONSTRUCTION	03	52	30
CROSSING BLINKING/DINGING SIGNAL CONST	09	58	35
CUSTOM SIGNAL BRIDGES FROM KITS	03	55	27
DETAILING A SIGNAL SYSTEM CONSTRUCTION	01	67	44
DWARF SIGNALS BY THE DOZEN	10	54	44
FIBER OPTIC STREET LAMPS	05	76	96
FREE LANCE SIGNAL BRIDGE SCRATCHBUILD	12	79	68
GRADE CROSSINGS FLASHER IN "N" CONSTRUCT	03	79	108
GROUND THROW/HIGH LEVEL SWITCH STAND	06	82	100
HALL DISK SIGNAL CONSTRUCTION	05	55	42
HIGHWAY CROSSING FLASHER CONSTRUCTION	03	36	72
HIGHWAY CROSSING FLASHER CONSTRUCTION.	07	56	45
HOME AND DISTANT SIGNALS CONST	06	36	147
HOW TO DESIGN INTERLOCKING SIGNAL FRAMES	02	61	57
HOW TO USE SIGNALS BOOMER PETE	03	46	170
HOW TO USE SIGNALS ALL KINDS	11	50	44
INDIRECTLY LIGHTED SEARCHLIGHT SIGNAL	10	34	14
INEXPENSIVE SIGNALS	01	42	15
INTERLOCKING SIGNAL CONSTRUCTION	03	60	32
MANUAL SIGNALING HAS ADVANTAGES	10	38	407
MECHANICAL INTERLOCKING SIGNAL CONST	12	40	668
MODULAR SIGNALS EASES MAINTENANCE	11	83	110
OLD STYLE DOUBLE BALL SIGNAL MARYLAND	03	42	114
OLD TIME BALL SIGNAL CONSTRUCTION $1	05	65	44
OPERATING BLOCK SIGNAL CONSTRUCTION	05	50	24
OPERATING MAIL CRANE CONSTRUCTION	06	79	104
OPERATING WIG WAG SIGNAL CONSTRUCTION	01	81	89
PLEXIGLASS SIGNAL LIGHTING	09	52	67
SCALE SEMAPHORE SIGNALS	08	73	75
SEARCHLIGHT SIGNAL & PRISM MAST CONST	03	52	31
SEARCHLIGHT SIGNAL MECHANISM	02	73	60
SEARCHLIGHT SIGNALS WITH FIBER OPTICS	01	76	82
SEMAPHORES FROM LOST WAX PARTS	04	61	50
SIGNAL BRIDGE CONSTRUCTION	01	54	102
SIGNAL BRIDGE CONSTRUCTION STANDARD PRR	09	38	364
SIGNAL BRIDGE DOUBLE TRACK CONSTRUCTION	08	54	26
SIGNAL BRIDGES CANTILEVERED CONSTRUCTION	08	63	34
SIGNAL RELAY BOX CONSTRUCTION	10	56	39
SIGNAL RELAY CONSTRUCTION	03	36	70
SIGNAL RELAY SHED CONSTRUCTION	10	47	806
SIGNAL TOWER IN MINIMUM SPACE CONST	01	69	71
SIGNALING FOR TWO RAIL	06	37	218
SIGNALING FOR TWO RAIL SYSTEM	10	35	259
SIGNALS	03	78	116
SIGNALS FOR THE LAYOUT	04	43	168
SLO-ACTION SEMAPHORE MECHANISM CONST	09	61	46
SOLENOID OPERATED SEMAPHORE & SA SIGNALS	09	34	7
SUPER SEMAPHORE CONSTRUCTION	03	54	32
SWITCH STANDS DUMMY	09	55	55
SWITCH STANDS IN N SCALE THAT WORK $1	06	76	82
SWITCH STANDS O GAUGE	09	35	228

SIGNAL MODELS	M	Y	P
THREE COLOR SIGNALS COLOR ORDER	07	78	131
THREE COLOR SIGNALS ON THE TSL	06	72	60
THREE POSITION SEMAPHORE SIGNAL	03	39	117
TO SCALE SIGNALS	04	41	201
TOWER COLOR SIGNALS	04	51	51
TRACKSIDE SIGN CONSTRUCTION	09	35	234
TRAIN ORDER SEMAPHORE CONSTRUCT C&NW $1	01	69	67
TRAIN ORDER SIGNAL CONSTRUCTION	10	58	66
USING IC'S FOR SIGNALING	04	78	84
WOOD & METAL SIGNAL CONSTRUCTION	03	52	33
WORKING DWARF AND DISTANT SEMAPHORES	06	61	46
WORKING HIGHWAY CROSSINGS	11	62	55
WORKING SEMAPHORE CONSTRUCTION	09	41	454
WORKING SEMAPHORE CONSTRUCTION CORRECT	10	41	496
WORKING SEMAPHORE CONSTRUCTION.	06	55	25

SIGNAL MODEL REVIEWS	M	Y	P
BANJO SIGNAL REVIEW "HO" HI BALLER CORP	05	56	12
COLOR LIGHT SIGNALS REVIEW "O" MRS	07	37	262
COLOR LIGHT TYPE G SIGNAL REVIEW "HO" OD	08	59	14
COLOR SIGNALS REVIEW "HO" CHM	01	54	32
CROSSING GATE REVIEW "O" WALTERS	10	40	580
CROSSING GATE REVIEW "HO" KKR	01	54	34
CROSSING GATES "O" WALTERS	07	40	410
CROSSING GATES REVIEW "HO" DON FOWLER	03	55	10
CROSSING SIGNAL REVIEW "O" WALTERS	10	54	16
CROSSING WARNING REVIEW "HO/O" GMR	12	41	660
CROSSING WIG WAG REVIEW "HO" DON FOWLER	06	56	13
DUMMY SIGNAL REVIEW "HO" WALTERS	06	49	58
DUMMY SIGNALS LISTING "HO" MODEL POWER	06	77	49
DWARF SIGNAL 2 & 3 COLOR REVIEW "HO" HI	07	48	509
DWARF SIGNALS REVIEW "O" PIONEER CO.	02	42	101
DWARF SWITCH SIGNAL REVIEW "O" DIM	01	52	45
HIGH LEVEL SWITCH STAND REVIEW "HO" MEW	09	49	62
HIGHWAY CROSSING GUARD REVIEW "O" KK	08	59	13
OPERATING SEMAPHORE REVIEW "HO" N&G	04	84	420
OPERATING SEMAPHORE REVIEW "HO" PFM	02	83	42
OPERATING SEMAPHORE REVIEW "HO" KKR	01	53	54
POSITION LIGHT SIGNAL REVIEW "HO" CAPL	02	47	171
POSITION LIGHT SIGNAL REVIEW "HO" KEM	11	57	14
SEARCH LIGHT SIGNAL REVIEW "HO" OLYMPIA	03	59	13
SEMAPHORE REVIEW "O" WALTERS	07	40	410
SEMAPHORE SIGNAL REVIEW "O" WALTERS	07	38	298
SIGNAL BRIDGE REVIEW "O" BACHMANN	01	55	17
SIGNAL BRIDGE REVIEW "O" EH BESSEY	04	47	344
SIGNAL BRIDGE REVIEW "O" K&W MFG CO.	02	41	115
SIGNAL KIT LISTING "HO" N&G	05	77	49
SIGNAL REVIEW "HO" ECA	01	49	93
SIGNAL REVIEW "HO" KURTZ-KRAFT MODELS	11	50	54
SIGNAL REVIEW "HO" WALTERS	01	56	10
SIGNAL REVUEW "HO" KEMTRON	02	57	19
SIGNALS REVIEW "O" WALTERS	12	56	22
SMALL SWITCH STAND REVIEW "O" POLKS	08	41	437
SWITCH STAND REVIEW "O" MDC	03	48	228
SWITCH STAND REVIEW MODEL ENGINEER WORKS	02	46	141
SWITCHSTAND REVIEW "O" MULTIPLEX MFG CO	05	38	216
TWO INDICATOR SIGNAL REVIEW "HO" WALTERS	10	50	52

STRUCTURES & SIGNALS

SIGNAL MODEL REVIEWS BY MFG

MFG		M	Y	P
B	SIGNAL BRIDGE REVIEW "O" BACHMANN	01	55	17
CAPL	POSITION LIGHT SIGNAL REVIEW "HO" CAPL	02	47	171
CHM	COLOR SIGNALS REVIEW "HO" CHM	01	54	32
DF	CROSSING WIG WAG REVIEW "HO" DON FOWLER	06	56	13
	CROSSING GATES REVIEW "HO" DON FOWLER	03	55	10
DIM	DWARF SWITCH SIGNAL REVIEW "O" DIM	01	52	45
ECA	SIGNAL REVIEW "HO" ECA	01	49	93
EHB	SIGNAL BRIDGE REVIEW "O" EH BESSEY	04	47	344
GMR	CROSSING WARNING REVIEW "HO/O" GMR	12	41	660
HI	DWARF SIGNAL 2 & 3 COLOR REVIEW "HO" HI	07	48	509
HIB	BANJO SIGNAL REVIEW "HO" HI BALLER CORP	05	56	12
K&W	SIGNAL BRIDGE REVIEW "O" K&W MFG CO.	02	41	115
KEM	POSITION LIGHT SIGNAL REVIEW "HO" KEM	11	57	14
	SIGNAL REVUEN "HO" KEMTRON	02	57	19
KK	HIGHWAY CROSSING GUARD REVIEW "O" KK	08	59	13
KKR	OPERATING SEMAPHORE REVIEW "HO" KKR	01	53	54
	CROSSING GATE REVIEW "HO" KKR	01	54	34
	SIGNAL REVIEW "HO" KURTZ-KRAFT MODELS	11	50	54
MDC	SWITCH STAND REVIEW "O" MDC	03	48	228
MEW	SWITCH STAND REVIEW MODEL ENGINEER WORKS	02	46	141
	HIGH LEVEL SWITCH STAND REVIEW "HO" MEW	09	49	62
MP	DUMMY SIGNALS LISTING "HO" MODEL POWER	06	77	49
MULT	SWITCHSTAND REVIEW "O" MULTIPLEX MFG CO	05	38	216
N&G	SIGNAL KIT LISTING "HO" N&G	05	77	49
	OPERATING SEMAPHORE REVIEW "HO" N&G	04	84	42D
OD	COLOR LIGHT TYPE G SIGNAL REVIEW "HO" OD	08	59	14
	SEARCH LIGHT SIGNAL REVIEW "HO" OLYMPIA	03	59	13
PC	DWARF SIGNALS REVIEW "O" PIONEER CO.	02	42	101
PFM	OPERATING SEMAPHORE REVIEW "HO" PFM	02	83	42
POLK	SMALL SWITCH STAND REVIEW "O" POLKS	08	41	437
WAL	SEMAPHORE REVIEW "O" WALTERS	07	40	410
	CROSSING GATES "O" WALTERS	07	40	410
	CROSSING GATE REVIEW "O" WALTERS	10	40	580
	SEMAPHORE SIGNAL REVIEW "O" WALTERS	07	38	298
	SIGNALS REVIEW "O" WALTERS	12	56	22
	SIGNAL REVIEW "HO" WALTERS	01	56	10
	CROSSING SIGNAL REVIEW "O" WALTERS	10	54	16
	DUMMY SIGNAL REVIEW "HO" WALTERS	06	49	58
	TWO INDICATOR SIGNAL REVIEW "HO" WALTERS	10	50	52

GENERAL STRUCTURE PROTOTYPE DATA

	M	Y	P
BUMPING POSTS AND CAR STOPS	04	83	100
CAR FERRY ON GREAT LAKES	04	78	78
CAR FERRY THAT'S UNUSUAL	06	70	73
DETAILS FOR FLAT ROOFS	05	77	110
FACTORY OFFICE AND SUPPLY BUILDING	06	78	82
GEOLOGY-BASIS FOR SCENERY	12	77	140
HOT BOX DETECTION	05	80	62
INDUSTRIES FOR YOUR PIKE	01	54	90
MILEPOSTS AND SCALE MILES	02	82	96
ORDER BOARDS	08	84	136
PORTABLE AUTO UNLOADER OF NYC	01	78	57
PROTOTYPE RIGHT OF WAY HANDBOOK	07	55	49
RAILROAD LINE TELEPHONE POLES HOW TO USE	10	81	92
SCRAP RAIL USES ON A LAYOUT & ROAD	10	71	65
STOCK GUARDS-RIGHT OF WAY DETAILS	09	79	107
TELEPHONE POLES NOT ALWAYS ROUND	07	77	109
TRAIN DEFECT DETECTION INSTALLATIONS	03	84	94

GENERAL STRUCTURE PLANS

	M	Y	P
BUMPING POSTS AND CAR STOPS DRAWINGS	04	83	101
CROSS TIE STACKING PLAN	01	52	17
FLAT FRONT BLDG DRAWINGS CHICAGO HOUSES	11	69	40
GREAT LAKE CAR FERRY PLAN	04	78	78
PORTABLE AUTO UNLOADER PLAN	01	78	57
SINGS-FENCES-RELAY BOXES DRAWINGS	08	79	65
STOCK GUARD PLANS	09	79	107
TRAIN DEFECT DETECTION INSTALLATION DRAW	03	84	95

GENERAL STRUCTURE PLANS BY ROAD

RD		M	Y	P
FJ&G	SINGS-FENCES-RELAY BOXES DRAWINGS	08	79	65

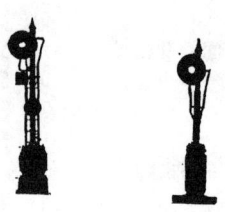
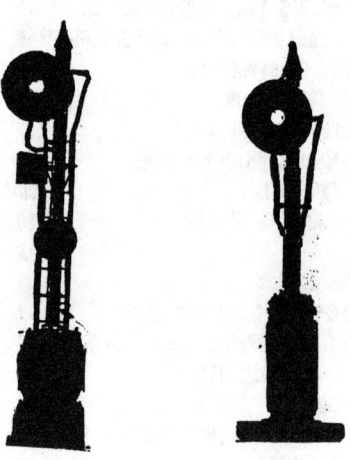

STRUCTURES & SIGNALS

GENERAL STRUCTURE MODELS

Title	M	Y	P
100 STRUCTURES FROM PLASTIC KITS	09	65	22
48 STAR FLAGS	07	83	90
50 STAR FLAGS	07	84	98
ACRYLIC PLASTIC FOR STRUCTURES	07	75	70
AGING OF BOARDS AND SHINGLES	04	71	46
ANIMATED CARNIVAL ATTRACTIONS	02	69	49
ART OF USING MIRRORS	12	81	109
ASPARAGUS FERN INTO CORN FIELD	04	81	98
BACKLIGHTED TRANSPARENCIES (INT DETAIL)	07	73	40
BENDING ANGLE STOCK	08	70	57
BILLBOARDS FOR TODAY	11	77	106
BILLBOARDS USED IN '20'S & '30'S	09	75	57
BILLBORAD CONSTRUCTION	05	79	104
BRANCHLINE INDUSTRIES	11	69	70
BROADWAY POSTERS	01	83	120
BUCKETS FOR COALING STATIONS	08	77	110
BUILD J&SW STRUCUTRES/PAINT/WEATHERING	11	82	98
BUILD SJC STRUCTURES-SMALL COLORFUL BLDS	05	84	56
BUILD THE W&SF STRUCTURES OF PAULS VALLY	06	83	74
BUILDING A CONCRETE HIGHWAY FROM STYRENE	12	77	130
BUILDING SIGNS FOR BINGHAMTON BRICK BLOC	07	81	98
BUILDING WITH WOOD	06	62	35
BUILDING YOUR FIRST WOOD STRUCTURE KIT	08	82	84
BUILDINGS: LOCATION & CONSTRUCTION	12	48	944
CAMPBELL MODEL DISPLAYS	09	74	35
CARDBOARD BUILDING CONSTRUCTION	11	44	478
CARNIVAL RIDE IDEAS	07	67	56
CASTING PARTS IN POLYSTER RESIN	11	81	116
CHAIN LINK FENCE MODELING	09	80	72
CIRCA THIRTY DIORAMA	09	75	52
CIRCUS POSTERS FOR YOUR LAYOUT	10	76	78
CLAY FOR MODELING STRUCTURES	09	73	61
COKE BILLBOARDS FROM THE PAST	12	75	78
COMPRESSING STRUCTURE TECHNIQUES	02	69	75
CONCRETE HIGHWAYS	08	78	122
CONCRETE WALL SECTIONS CONSTRUCTION	09	77	48
CORREGATED IRON STRUCTURES CONSTRUCTION	09	47	704
CORRUGATED SIDING CONSTRUCTION	02	77	123
CREATING SHINGLES AND A MOOD	11	83	87
CYCLONE FENCES	09	77	112
DESIGN AND CONSTRUCTION OF BUILDINGS 1	02	43	68
DESIGN AND CONSTRUCTION OF BUILDINGS 2	03	43	122
DETAILED DOORWAY CONSTRUCTION	12	65	64
DIRT HIGHWAY CROSSING CONSTRUCTION	12	83	126
DRIVE THAT PILE!	08	78	78
EMPTY LOT MOD & PT	08	77	100
EVERGREENS EVERYWHERE WITH BUMPY CHENILL	10	78	68
FALSE FRONT BUILDINGS HIDE FIREPLACE	03	82	100
FATHER NATURES TREES	03	82	107
FEED MILL SIGNS	03	81	118
FELT GRASS AND WEEDS	01	82	118
FINISHING TOUCHES ON STRUCTURES	02	59	48
FIRE ESCAPE CONSTRUCTION	05	71	40
FLAT BACKGROUND TREES	05	83	88
FLORAL SHOP TREES (PINE TREES)	08	83	70

GENERAL STRUCTURE MODELS

Title	M	Y	P
FROM TRASH TO DETAIL TREASURES	08	80	60
FURNISH YOUR HOMES WITH TRASH	07	80	82
GROWING A FOREST OVERNIGHT-WIRE TREES	05	82	100
GUIDELINES FOR MODELING TOWNS & CITIES	08	77	70
HIGHWAY CROSSING ON CURVED TRACK	10	77	132
HOW TO MAKE NEAT SIGNS	08	73	43
HOW TO MODEL BUILDINGS - ARCHITECTS VIEW	07	47	564
IMPROVING AND DETAILING STRUCTURES	01	74	63
INTERIOR LIGHTING TIPS	11	83	124
INVESTMENT CAST WINDOW LINTELS	05	71	37
JUTE TREES (EVERGREENS) CONSTRUCTION	10	83	124
KIBASHING STRUCTURES	08	80	70
LADDERS OF IRON CONSTRUCTION	12	51	39
LAMPS FOR STATIONS	10	39	504
LICHEN AND HOW TO USE IT	11	81	112
LIGHT TOWER KITBASH	04	81	88
MAKE RR TRAVEL POSTERS FOR YOUR LAYOUT	04	78	86
MAKING A STREET LAMP	02	83	120
MAKING FENCES	09	82	112
MAKING PALLETS	10	83	122
MALT TOWER SIGNS	07	73	56
MANY STRUCTURES FROM ONE KIT	12	63	40
MARVELEOUS MOSS	06	73	67
MATERIALS & TECHNIQUES OF STRUCTURES	09	51	8
MICROGLAZING WINDOWS-SOME NOTES	01	71	81
MODEL HOT BOX DETECTORS	05	80	62
MODELING A DERAIL ON D&RGW	07	79	99
MODELING A SCRAP STEEL CAR LOAD	06	77	58
MODELING LE WOT BOG	06	79	90
MODELING WATER EPOXY BASICS	03	82	98
MODELING WITH PHOTOS	01	85	119
MODELING WITH SPRUES $1	07	69	64
MODERN BILLBOARD SIGNS	02	75	46
MODIFIED KIT BUILDINGS ON W&V JCT RR	04	79	74
MODIFYING KIT STRUCTURES	05	75	38
MODULAR ASSEMBLY OF BUILDINGS	02	74	60
MUSEUM DIORAMA BUILDING SMETHPORT PA	09	81	103
NEW ENGLAND STONE WALL CONSTRUCTION	12	81	95
NORTH SHORE POSTERS OF 1920	07	80	95
ODDS & ENDS- STRUCTURE DETAILING	06	45	242
OPERATING CLAMSHELL BUCKET	05	73	80
OPERATING TRAFFIC CIRCLE $1	02	68	65
PAINTING SCALE FIGURES	09	81	69
PALLETS FOR SHIPMENT CONSTRUCTION	01	74	80
PEEL & STICK WALLS	11	79	152
PIGEON CREED STRUCTURES	12	67	54
PLANT YOUR STRUCTURES IN THE GROUND	06	80	99
PLASTIC BEARS	03	82	109
PLASTIC STRUCTURAL SHAPES IN ABS	05	69	54
RAILROAD ICE FOR REEFERS	11	75	113
RAILWAY SIGNS-SIGNALS & OTHER DETAILS	12	80	123
REAL GLASS FOR WINDOWS	10	78	138
REALISTIC MODEL WINDOW GLASS	01	78	106
REALISTIC STRUCTURE DETAIL	09	39	456
RECRUITING POSTERS FOR YOUR LAYOUT	07	76	58

STRUCTURES & SIGNALS

GENERAL STRUCTURE MODELS

	M	Y	P
REDUCED DEPTH STRUCTURES FOR ATMOSPHERE	11	69	40
REDUCTION COPYING SIGNS	02	79	137
REMODELING MODELS	06	78	90
REPAIR MODEL STRUCTURES	06	78	90
RIGHT OF WAY GUARDS, RAILRACKS, GUY WIRE	08	35	211
ROOF SHINGLE CONSTRUCTION	01	49	49
SAFETY CAGE LADDER CONSTRUCTION	01	80	130
SCALE ADVERTISEMENT SIGNS CONSTRUCTION	02	77	87
SCALE BEES	02	74	45
SCALE SIGN CONSTRUCTION WITH A CAMERA	06	77	119
SCALE STRUCTURES SOME GOOD/SOME NOT GOOD	07	73	78
SCRAP RAIL USES ON A LAYOUT & ROAD	10	71	65
SCRATCHBUILDING YOUR 1ST WOOD STRUCTURE	07	83	91
SHAPING CORBELS	05	71	42
SHINGLES GALORE CONSTRSUCTION	01	64	51
SHIP MODEL ADDENDUM	02	78	142
SHIP MODELS	11	77	143
SHIP MODELS FOR RAILROADS	02	78	26
SHRINK MODELING USING SHRINKY DINKS	11	81	98
SIGNS FOR KITTY HAWK CENTRAL	01	82	117
SIGNS FOR MODELS CO-OPS	09	73	58
SIGNS FOR STRUCTURES & STREETCARS	06	72	43
SIGNS FOR TRACKSIDE	11	76	110
SIGNS OF THE TIMES FROM OLD MAGAZINE ADS	02	82	104
SIX BUILDINGS FROM THREE KITS	02	84	86
SOLUTION TO SHORT SIDING REMOTE UNLOAD F	12	81	107
STACK BY STACK LUMBER CONSTRUCTION	10	82	98
STAINED GLASS WINDOWS	07	78	78
STEP AND STAIR CONSTRUCTION	04	45	162
STEP BY STEP BACKDROP PAINTING	02	82	93
STORE SIGNS AND BILLBOARDS	01	73	66
STREET LIGHT CONSTRUCTION $1	01	73	67
STRIPWOOD STRUCTURES CONSTRUCTION	10	52	36
STRUCTURE ARRANGEMENT & DETAIL IN TOWNS	05	73	48
STRUCTURE SELECTION THOUGHTS	06	73	63
STRUCTURES AND TREES ON THE NY&Q	03	69	54
STRUCTURES FOR GOLD HILL CENTRAL CONST	04	84	96
STRUCTURES FROM THE GROUND UP CONST	07	67	48
STRUCTURES GENERAL CONSTRUCTION	11	48	815
TANK PARTS FROM AUTO FREEZEOUT PLUGS	01	78	144
TOY PARTS INTO FLAT CAR LOADS	09	79	112
TREES BY THE BUSHEL 2	08	77	188
TREES BY THE BUSHEL- AND BELIEVABLE!	06	77	87
UNIO PACIFIC BILLBOARDS	01	79	106
USE MIRRORS TO EXPAND SCENES	07	81	76
USING SMALL SHEETS OF PLASTIC BRICK	10	70	81
WHISTLE STOP TOWN MODEL	06	43	256
WINDOW DETAILING	04	64	51
WINDOW PANE CONSTRUCTION	11	63	57
WOOD HIGHWAY CROSSING CONSTRUCTION	12	84	86
WOOD SPLINT BIULDING CONSTRUCTION	04	56	44

GENERAL STRUCTURE MODEL REVIEWS

	M	Y	P
BLACKSMITH SHOP MACHINERY REVIEW "HO" RGM	06	78	43
CONTAINER CRANE REVIEW "HO" ROWA	11	71	28
PRINTED SIGNS LISTING TINY SIGNS	12	77	62
STRUCUTRES REVIEW "N" BACHMANN	05	69	17

GENERAL STRUCTURE MODEL REV BY MFG.

MFG		M	Y	P
B	STRUCUTRES REVIEW "N" BACHMANN	05	69	17
RGM	BLACKSMITH SHOP MACHINERY REVIEW "HO"RGM	06	78	43
ROWA	CONTAINER CRANE REVIEW "HO" ROWA	11	71	28

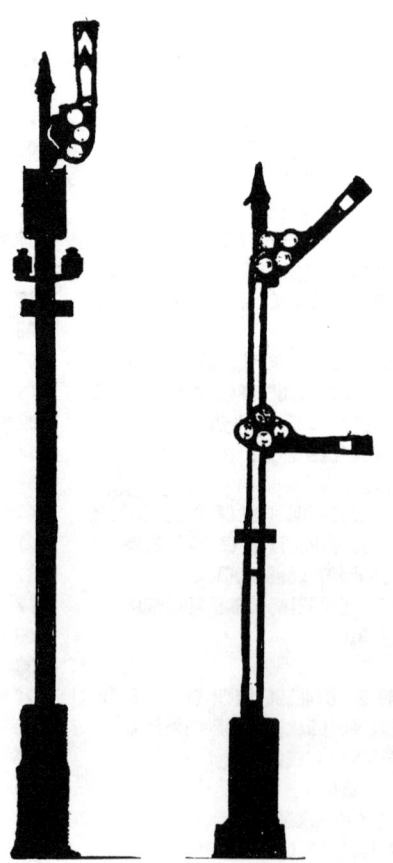

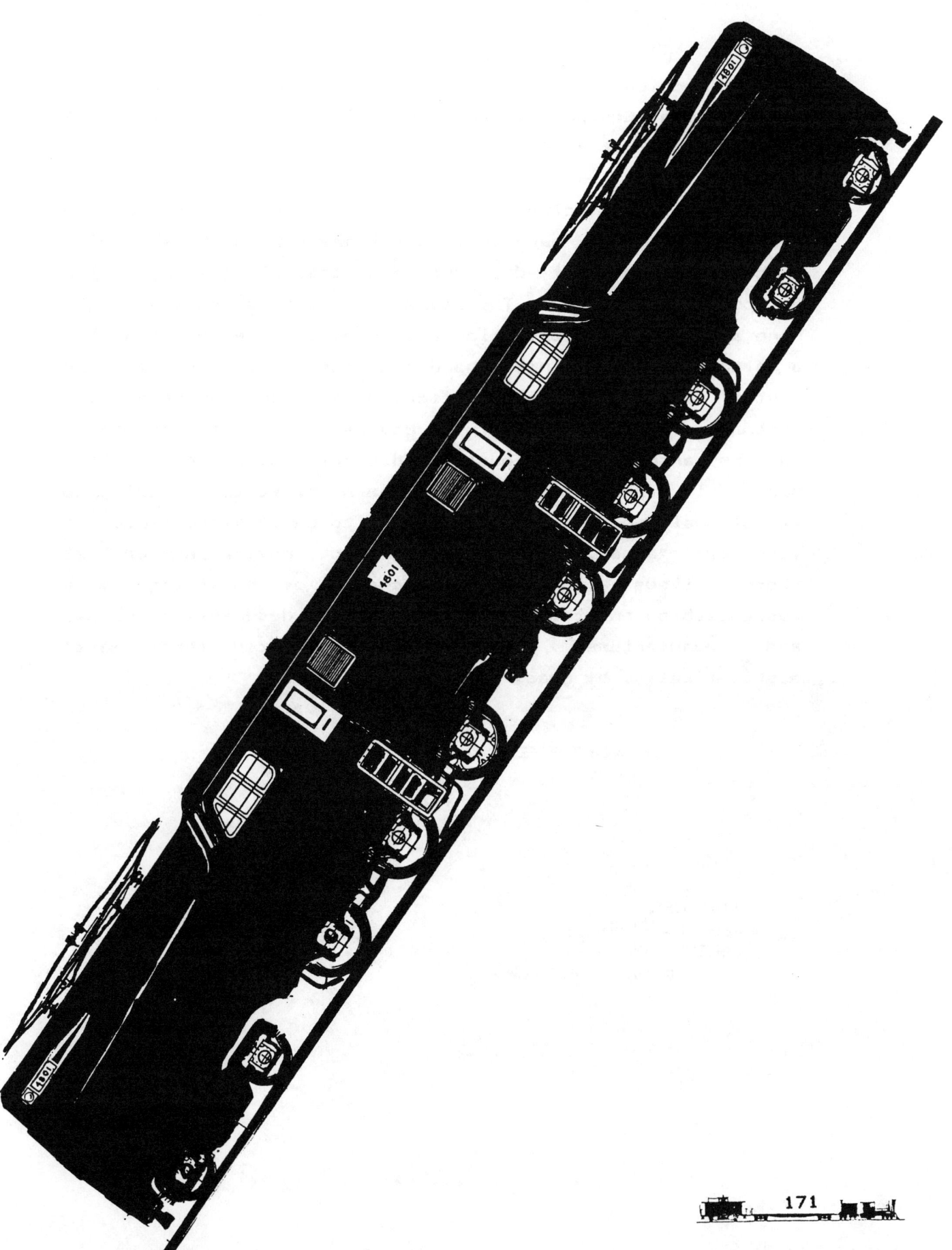

BILL OF LADING   VEHICLES

This section contains information on Road Vehicles, Construction Equipment, and the like. It lists the five areas of interest as follows:

Prototype data includes articles and specifications on the real thing. In many instances there are photographs with these articles that did not get special billing in the photograph section. The plans and drawings are just that. Generally by our convention a drawing is more detailed than a plan, but this is not a hard and fast rule. The plans are listed twice: once alphabetically and once by road. The photo section shows details or unusual photos of interest to the researcher. Obviously we did not list all photos that appear in these magazines. The model section highlights exceptional models and tells how to build/kitbash/rebuild your own "gems". Finally the model review section list those items that have a chance of surviving as a recognizable entity. Included is the description, scale, and manufacturer. These are listed three ways: alphabetically, by road, and by manufacturer.

MANIFEST   VEHICLES

	PAGE
VEHICLES	172
VEHICLE PLANS	173
VEHICLE MODELS	173
VEHICLE MODEL REVIEWS	173

VEHICLES

VEHICLE PLANS	M	Y	P
BAGGAGE & EXPRESS WAGON PLANS	01	57	34
BAGGAGE WAGON PLANS	08	55	42
BULLDOG MACK TRUCK DRAWINGS	01	61	67
CONTAINER TRAILER PLANS	10	83	96
LOGGING WAGON PLANS	12	60	60

VEHICLE MODELS	M	Y	P
BAGGAGE & EXPRESS WAGON CONSTRUCTION	01	57	34
BIG TRUCK KITBASH	02	78	84
BULLDOG MACK TRUCK CONSTRUCTION	01	61	66
CONSTRUCTION EQUIPMENT 1	01	78	95
DRAY LINE TRUCK CONSTRUCTION	04	60	52
EASTERN TRUCK TRACTORS MOD & PT	09	77	101
FIRE TRUCK (MODEL T) CONSTRUCTION	10	60	59
FORK LIFT THAT MOVES CONSTRUCTION	09	68	28
LOGGING WAGON CONSTRUCTION	12	60	60
MOM MACK BULLDOG RAILTRUCK "1/24" AVIS	09	82	50
PIGGYBACK TRAILER MOD & PT	07	76	105
PLASTIC VEHICLE KITBASH	05	62	54
ROAD TRUCKS FOR YOUR LAYOUT	05	43	218
STEAM SHOVEL CONSTRUCTION	02	85	70
STRUCTURAL STEEL CARRYING FLATBED KITBAS	03	77	88
TRACATORS FOR YOUR TERMINALS	07	82	88
TRACTOR TRAILER CROSSKIT IDEAS	01	62	67
TRUCK & RECREATION VEHICLE CONSTRUCTION	03	81	98
WHITE FREIGHTLINER MOD & PT	06	76	92

VEHICLE MODEL REVIEWS	M	Y	P
1932 FORD ROADSTER REVIEW "HO" WW	05	78	41
ARMY VEHICLE REVIEW "HO" AHM	07	63	8
ATLAS MOTORING CARS REVIEW "HO" ATLAS	12	62	16
BAGGAGE WAGON REVIEW "N" AL	12	85	50
BROUGHAM COACH REVIEW "HO" JORDAN PROD.	11	63	15
CAR & TRUCK REVIEW "HO" LESNEY	06	64	8
CAR & TRUCK REVIEW "N" BOYDE	07	71	21
CHEVY 1957 BEL AIR REVIEW "HO/N" AL	10	84	55
CIRCUS EQUIPMENT REVIEW "HO" SISC	08	63	9
CONSTRUCTION EQUIPMENT REVIEW "1/50" GES	02	74	33
CONSTRUCTION EQUIPMENT REVIEW "HO" AHM	03	65	12
CONTAINER TRUCK REVIEW "HO" HE	06	85	45
DELIVERY WAGON REVIEW "HO" JORDAN PROD	03	63	11
DELIVERY WAGON REVIEW "HO" JORDAN PROD.	08	63	12
DITCHDIGGER REVIEW "1/100" DMT	09	84	50
EUCLID SCRAPER REVIEW "HO" STEWART PROD.	10	59	12
EXPRESS BAGGAGE TRUCK REV "O" FRED STOES	06	48	438
FIRE ENGINE 1880 REVIEW "HO" RHM	09	63	14
FIRE TRUCK 1915 REVIEW "HO" JORDAN PROD.	01	62	24
FLAT BED TRUCK REVIEW "OO" COC	10	85	54
FORD 1934 PICKUP LISTING "HO" WHEELWORKS	05	77	48
FORD 1935 SEDAN LISTING "HO" MSMW	05	77	48
FORD AUTO TRANSPORT REVIEW "HO" REVELLE	09	62	15
FORD MODEL A REVIEW "HO" JORDON PRODUCTS	07	70	12
FORD MODEL T LISTING "N" GREENHALGH	01	77	48

VEHICLE MODEL REVIEWS	M	Y	P
FORD ROADSTER 1925 REVIEW "HO" JORDAN	03	67	14
GLOBAL VAN LINES TRUCK REVIEW"HO"REVELLE	02	60	13
GMC BUS REVIEW PIRATE MODELS	12	77	45
HIGHWAY TRACTOR REVIEW "HO" ATHEARN	05	76	30
HIGHWAY TRUCK REVIEW "HO" PR	12	85	45
HIGHWAY TRUCKS S ERTL	09	78	46
KLEIBER STAKE TRUCK REVIEW "HO" SSL	12	76	45
KLEIBER TRUCK OF 1920 LISTING "HO" SSL	04	77	46
LINE SIDE VEHICLES REVIEW "HO" FB	04	59	13
MACK DUMP TRUCK REVIEW "HO" JORDAN PROD.	11	62	14
MACK HIGHWAY TRUCK REVIEW "HO" CC	03	78	42
MACK TRUCK REVIEW "HO" JORDAN PRODUCTS	08	62	13
MAIL TRUCK REVIEW "HO" JORDAN PRODUCTS	06	69	17
MODEL T FORD REVIEW "HO" JORDAN PROD.	07	59	12
MODEL T FORD REVIEW "HO" JORDAN PRODUCTS	11	55	22
P&H MINING SHOVEL REVIEW "HO" CPR	06	84	36
PACKARD VICTORIA 1930 REVIEW "1/4" REN	10	75	26
PIGGYBACK TRAILER REVIEW "HO" QC	04	68	17
RD-8 CATERPILLAR TRACTOR REVIEW "HO" HHS	03	76	35
ROAD ROLLER REVIEW "HO" SSD	11	85	49
ROAD TRUCK REVIEW "HO" VARNEY	06	58	13
SCALE CAR & TRUCK REVIEW "Z" NOCH	11	84	58
SCALE VEHICLES REVIEW "HO" VIKING	02	67	10
SCALE VEHICLES REVIEW "S" MINIATURE TOYS	04	74	27
SPEEDER FAIRMONT MOD M-19 REV "O/ON3"PEM	02	78	48
TANK TRUCK REVIEW "HO" ULRICH	02	58	10
TRACTOR-SEMITRAILER REVIEW "N" BOYDE	06	70	22
TROLLEY BUS REVIEW "N" EHEIM	08	66	9
TRUCK & CAR REVIEW "HO" LESNEY	11	63	18
TRUCK REVIEW "HO" FRED BRONNER	10	61	42
TRUCK TRAILER REVIEW "N" CONCOR	02	70	27
TRUCKS REVIEW "N" BOYDE MODELS	02	70	16
TRUCKS TO SCALE REVIEW "N" BOYDE	06	69	17
UPS HIGHWAY TRAILER REVIEW "HO" TK	12	84	46
US AUTO REVIEW "N" BOYDE	10	68	22
US AUTOS REVIEW "HO" JORDAN PRODUCTS	02	56	15
VEHICLES REVIEW "HO" WIKING	12	60	21

BILL OF LADING — PROTOTYPE EXAMPLES

This section concerns itself with things the real railroads do that modelers can follow. It includes items that do not seem like what a prototype would do . It also includes roads that you can model (UCMI). As well, the descriptor line defines the contents.

MANIFEST — PROTOTYPE EXAMPLES

	PAGE
PROTOTYPE MODELING IDEAS	174
RAILROADS YOU CAN MODEL	175
PROTOTYPE TRACKWORK	175
PROTOTYPE EXAMPLES	176

PROTOTYPE MODELING IDEAS

RAILROADS YOU CAN MODEL		M	Y	P
ADIRONDACK RAILWAY OF NEW YORK	UCMI	03	80	84
ALAMEDA BELT LINE OAKLAND CA	UCMI	04	80	80
AROOSTOCK VALLEY RAILROAD	UCMI	07	66	28
ASHLEY, DREW & NORTHERN	UCMI	02	81	108
BIGHORN LUMBER COMPANY	UCMI	04	81	76
BUFFALO CREEK & GAULEY	UCMI	11	59	42
C&NW PRAIRIE BRANCH	UCMI	02	79	94
CHATTAHOOCHEE VALLEY	UCMI	12	73	72
CHICAGO & NORTH WESTERN BELT	UCMI	06	37	204
CLOQUET TERMINAL (D&NE)	UCMI	08	63	52
CNJ SEASHORE LINE	UCMI	09	85	58
COAL UNLOADING DOCKS PRR CLEVE OHIO	UCMI	09	47	719
COLORADO OF THE EAST	UCMI	06	63	33
DSP&P BRANCH OF BN	UCMI	12	80	104
DURANGO YARD D&RG	UCMI	07	81	82
EBT HAND CAR LINE	UCMI	12	71	70
FJ&G	UCMI	08	79	58
FORT DODGE DEMOINES & SOUTHERN RY	UCMI	11	68	36
FOX LAKE JCT MILW	UCMI	02	76	48
GALVESTON WARVES	UCMI	05	83	58
GENESEE & WYOMING RAILROAD	UCMI	12	76	58
GRAHAM COUNTY RAILROAD	UCMI	04	62	24
GREYCOURT INTERCHANGE ON ERIE	UCMI	08	80	92
IRON RIDGE & MAYVILLE RAILWAY	UCMI	06	54	48
KAW VALLEY TRACTION	UCMI	02	72	38
L&N EVANSVILLE DIVISION	UCMI	05	85	88
LACKAWANNA RAILROAD PROTOTYPE	UCMI	05	38	183
LEHIGH VALLEY YOU CAN MODEL IT	UCMI	12	66	52
LITTLEST YARD YOU CAN BUILD	UCMI	05	68	52
LONG ISLAND MONTAUK YARD	UCMI	03	66	52
M&K JCT W. VA. HELPER TERMINAL	UCMI	03	62	30
MANN'S CREEK RAILROAD	UCMI	07	72	30
MARTHA'S VINEYARD RAILROAD	UCMI	06	80	82
MARYLAND & PENNSYLVANIA	UCMI	05	65	38
MILW KINGSBURY BRANCH	UCMI	04	75	52
MILW MAYFAIR JCAT CHICAGO ILL	UCMI	03	76	60
MINERAL RAILWAY TO TIDEWATER	UCMI	08	62	28
MODELING THE AUTO-TRAIN	UCMI	12	74	48
MODERN SOO LINE GENERAL INFORMATION	UCMI	10	82	63
MODERN SOO LINE POWER/ROLLING STOCK	UCMI	11	82	78
MORE TRACK IN THE STREETS	UCMI	02	69	38
MOUNTAIN RAILROADS & MODELING THEM	UCMI	10	74	34
N&W	UCMI	08	37	276
NARRAGANSETT PIER	UCMI	09	74	37
NEWTON BRANCH OF R TERMINAL	UCMI	11	62	39
NORFOLK SOUTHERN AT SOUTH DURHAM	UCMI	06	74	54
NP - P&L BRANCH OPERATIION	UCMI	01	74	64
P&WR	UCMI	08	72	48
PLYMOUTH MOUNTAIN JUNCTION	UCMI	02	73	38
PROTOTYPE SIDING YOU CAN MODEL	UCMI	07	79	70
PRR GALLITZIN PA	UCMI	04	40	219
QUINCY RAILROAD	UCMI	04	63	32
ROWLAND SPRINGS RAILROAD	UCMI	06	74	44
SAN FRANCISCO BELT LINE NICKLE	UCMI	04	80	64
SHORT LINE TO THE SEA	UCMI	08	64	46

RAILROADS YOU CAN MODEL		M	Y	P
SOO LINE EASTERN DIVISION	UCMI	10	82	66
SOUTHERN'S MURPHY BRANCH	UCMI	10	84	68
SOUTHWEST FOREST INDUSTRIES	UCMI	03	84	70
ST GOTTHARD LINE	UCMI	07	39	355
STEAM IN 1975 AT BN TIE PLANT	UCMI	10	75	78
STEWARTSTOWN RAILROAD	UCMI	10	66	50
STONEWELL YARD MILWAUKEE WI MILW	UCMI	01	72	50
STREET TRACKAGE OF C&S AND ATSF	UCMI	04	68	43
THE ABERDEEN & ROCKFISH	UCMI	11	65	33
THE AE&FRE YOU CAN BUILD IT	UCMI	09	67	24
TOPEKA KANSAS AREA	UCMI	01	38	9
TRACTION TERMINAL AT 69TH ST. P&WR	UCMI	02	67	30
TWEETSE:NARROW GAUGE ON BLUE RIDGE	UCMI	07	81	66
UNION TRANSPORTATION COMPANY	UCMI	04	64	28
UP OREGON DIVISION	UCMI	09	73	54
VERMONT GRANITE ROADS	UCMI	10	75	52
WABASH COLUMBIA CENTRALIA BRANCH	UCMI	01	66	38
WALPOLE & THE KISSING BRIDE	UCMI	09	67	38
WASHINGTON IDAHO & MONTANA (WI&M)	UCMI	09	75	40
WESTERN PACIFIC WYE	UCMI	03	36	68
WHITE PASS & YUKON	UCMI	03	53	44
WHITE SULPHER SPRINGS STATION	UCMI	11	63	36
WINCHESTER & WESTERN	UCMI	10	74	44
YANCEY RAILROAD	UCMI	08	74	33

PROTOTYPE TRACKWORK	M	Y	P
ABANDONED TRACKAGE BOOMER PETE	07	49	16
BUMPERS	12	54	42
DUAL GAUGE TRACKWORK	07	52	55
FREIGHT YARD DESIGN	01	50	31
HUMP YARD THAT IS FULLY AUTOMATIC	11	61	57
IRON RIDGE & MAYVILLE RAILWAY	06	54	48
PROTOTYPE TRAIN YARDS HANDBOOK	06	55	47
RAIL SIZE	09	67	59
STUB SWITCHES	01	66	75
TRACKWORK IN STREETS 1	01	63	59
TRACKWORK IN STREETS 2	02	63	67
TRACKWORK IN STREETS 3	03	63	61
TRANSITION FISH PLATES-WORTH 1000 WORDS	11	78	161

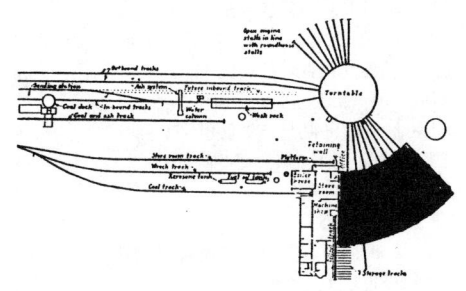

PROTOTYPE MODELING IDEAS

PROTOTYPE EXAMPLES	M	Y	P
6TH STREET UNDERPASS WILMINGTON DEL	06	58	42
A JOG IN THE TRACK	08	73	57
ACL COLOR CHART	10	47	812
AIN'T PROTOTYPE CUT & TUNNEL NYC BEACON	03	80	155
AN OLD TIME STATION DETAIL	12	61	79
B&A COLOR CHART	07	47	554
B&M COLOR CHART	12	46	835
B&O COLOR CHART	08	46	497
BALLASTING VARIOUS TYPES OF TRACK	04	72	74
BARSTOW YARD AT ATSF	07	77	90
BLUERIDGE SUMMIT, MD DEPOT 1899 WM	11	62	60
BOXCARS AS BILLBOARDS	03	81	106
BUMPING POSTS AND CAR STOPS	04	83	100
BUSINESS CARS- OFFICIAL USE ONLY	12	59	30
C&NW COLOR CHART	01	45	10
C&O COLOR CHART	10	44	446
CABOOSE SERVICE FACILITIES W	08	78	76
CABOOSE SERVICE FACILITIES OF ATSF	08	78	74
CABOOSE SERVICE FACILITIES OF C&NW	08	78	72
CABOOSE SERVICE FACILITIES OF MILW	08	78	73
CANADIAN PACIFIC COLOR CHART	06	46	384
CAR SHOPS AT UNION BRIDGE MA WM	04	65	42
CATSASUQUA CROSSING LV AND R	05	58	42
CB&Q COLOR CHART	12	44	537
CENTRAL OF GEORGIA COLOR CHART	06	47	479
CHAMA N. MEXICO MIDPOINT ON NARROW GAUGE	02	60	36
CHICAGO & EAST ILLINOIS COLOR CHART	07	45	278
CIVIL WAR RAILROADING	04	64	41
CN COLOR CHART	07	48	473
CNJ COLOR CHART	08	47	639
COALING STATION ON K&T STEARNS KY	12	59	47
COALING TOWER AT BLACKWATER, MO. MP	01	59	52
COLOR CHART ATSF	04	44	161
COLOR CHART L&N	04	45	160
COMPLETE FREIGHT YARD FUNCTIONING	10	47	805
COTTON BELT COLOR CHART	09	47	730
COUNTRY JUNCTION NEWFIELD, NJ R	06	61	43
COUNTRY JUNCTION NEWFIELD, NJ PRR	06	61	43
CROSS TIE END OF LINE BUMPER	06	63	48
CROSSING GATES AT DOVER N.H. B&M	02	65	32
DELTA MO & OFFICIAL CAR OF MA&PA	03	65	45
DENVER & RIO GRAND WESTERN COLOR CHART	09	44	391
DEPOT AT LEAVENWORTH JCT KANSAS CGW	08	58	32
DETAIL AT SAIS SWITCH NM ATSF	10	63	54
DIESEL FUEL TANK P&SR SAN FRANCISCO CA	03	59	37
DIESEL LOCOMOTIVE SERVICING	06	82	59
DRYING OUT UNDERGROUND RAILWAYS	07	79	131
DULUTH & NORTHEASTERNS CLOQUET SHOPS	08	63	52
EIGHT SIDED GATEMANS TOWER MILW	09	60	34
ELEVATED RAILROADS	04	76	64
ERIE COLOR CHART	07	44	297
ESPEE REBUILT STATION HUMPHRES CA	06	59	42
FALL RIVER LINE NH	04	64	50
FLOP OVER TURNOUT THROWS	09	48	629
FREEVILLE, NY 5 SIDED DEPOT LV	02	63	38
GORDON, PA JUNCTION R	09	58	32
GRADE CROSSINGS	02	48	100
GRADE CROSSINGS AT TURNOUTS	07	59	58
GREAT NORTHERN COLOR CHART	05	45	213
GUARD RAIL USES	11	73	93
HELPER ENGINE BASE SARGENT CO D&RGW	10	64	44
HELPER SERVICE CONCEPT	04	49	42
HELPER TERMINAL M&K JCT W. VA.	03	62	30
HOMEMADE WEED BURNERS GMI	10	59	60
HUMP YARD THAT IS FULLY AUTOMATIC	11	61	57
ILLINOIS CENTRAL COLOR CHART	10	45	399
IMPROVISED PIGGYBACK RAMPS	06	63	50
INDUSTRIAL SPUR INTO A WAREHOUSE	02	67	53
INTERCHANGE AT LOMBARD MONTANA MP&MLW	08	60	32
INTERCHANGE TRACKS	03	64	63
JERSEY SHORT LINE TRACKAGE	04	64	28
KANSAS CITY SOUTRN COLOR CHART	12	45	532
KNUCKLE-LINK-PIN COUPLER COMBINATION	08	48	549
LEHIGH VALLEY COLOR CHART	09	45	366
LINE CROSSING WAUKESHA WISC SOO/C&NW	SOO	57	30
LOCOMOTIVE CHANGE POINTS	01	50	47
LOCOMOTIVE CLASSIFICATION LIGHTS	01	71	77
LUMBER RAILROAD OPERATIONS	08	66	20
MAINE CENTRAL COLOR CHART	05	47	377
MILWAUKEE COLOR CHART	01	46	12
MINIATURE AIR HOSES	08	37	290
MISSOURI PACIFIC COLOR CHART	08	45	330
MISSOURI PACIFIC COLOR CHART CORRECTION	11	45	480
MITCHEL YARD MILWAUKEE WI C&NW	05	73	60
MIX & MATCH MOTIVE POWER	03	63	43
MKT COLOR CHART	06	48	395
MONON COLOR CHART	08	48	531
MONTREAL TERMINAL THROAT	07	57	60
MOUNTING LONG GIRDERS ON 2 CARS	11	62	88
MOVEABLE FROG TURNOUT ON CN	11	71	18
NASHVILLE CHAT & ST LOUIS COLOR CHART	01	47	29
NICKEL PLATE COLOR CHART	04	47	308
NORFOLK & WESTERN COLOR CHART	02	47	112
NORTHERN PACIFIC COLOR CHART	11	44	486
NOTES ON DIESELS FOR MODEL RAILROADS	03	72	34
NY NH & HARTFORD COLOR CHART	09	46	582
NYC COLOR CHART	11	46	754
OLD BOXCARS NEED NEVER DIE!	10	63	36
OLD CUMBERLAND RIVER CROSSING S	02	78	76
OLD TIMERS SELECTION OF PHOTOS	01	60	76
OLD TRACK AT TUNNEL HILL, GA	04	62	34
ORE TRIPLE AT PARK CITY, UTAH UP	10	60	36
PASSENGER TRAIN UNUSUAL OPERATIONS	12	64	67
PERE MARQUETTE COLOR CHART	07	46	438
PIGGY BACK RAMPS	08	59	47
PLYMOUTH, WIS JUNCTION SMASHBOARD	07	60	26
PROTOTYPE EQUIPMENT OF 1880'S	07	50	16
PRR COLOR CHART	05	44	206
PRR COLOR CHARTS	03	46	188
RACK RAILROADS	08	76	70

PROTOTYPE MODELING IDEAS

PROTOTYPE EXAMPLES	M	Y	P
RAIL & FLANGE GREASERS	02	83	156
RAILROAD CLEANING PLANT SOUIX CITY IOWA	06	80	72
READING COLOR CHART	02	45	59
REASON FOR TUNNEL/NON TUNNEL RO WAY	05	81	128
RESOLVING PULLMAN SPACE PRACTICES	08	36	228
RETURN LOOPS AND WYES	02	76	41
REVERSE CURVE ON BRIDGES	05	79	107
RF&P COLOR CHART	11	45	478
RIDE THE GM&O DOODLEBUG	04	59	24
RIGHT OF WAY AND SCENERY MILW	08	37	280
ROCK ISLAND COLOR CHART	03	48	178
SEABOARD COLOR CHART	06	45	241
SHAMOKIN, PA ON PRR	08	61	24
SHORT LINE ENGINE TERMINAL B&S	10	58	55
SHORT LINE TERMINAL BEVIER & SOUTHERN	08	65	24
SIDETRACK DETAILS	11	68	71
SIGNALING THROUGH HISTORY 1830-1924	12	64	87
SMASHBOARD SIGNALS PLYMOUTH WISC C&NW	08	83	68
SNOW SHEDS ERECTION AT CRITICAL POINTS	09	59	40
SOO COLOR CHART	03	47	205
SOUTHERN COLOR CHART	05	46	324
SOUTHERN PACIFIC COLOR CHART	06	44	259
SPUR THROUGH A PLATFORM PRR AT NABETH PA	03	60	59
ST LOUIS SAN FRAN COLOR CHART	10	46	644
STATION AT SAYNER WI MILW	12	63	37
STATION AT WESTMINISTER MD WM	01	64	71
STATION IN THE STREET ST PETE FLA ACL	05	59	52
STUB TERMINAL GTW AT PORTLAND ME	01	66	48
STUDY IN CLUTTER	04	60	46
SWITCH POINT HEATERS OF 1985	09	85	68
SWITCH TO NOWHERE? LASALLE CO UP	04	78	109
TANK CAR LOADING & UNLOADING	09	76	107
TEHACHAPI LOOP	04	80	132
TERMINAL AT QUINCY CA QUINCY RAILROAD	04	63	32
TERMINAL AT TIBURON, CA NWP	05	60	50
TRACK PLAN INSPITE OF THE DEVIL	03	64	48
TRACK PROFILES	12	82	124
TRACKS IN CENTER OF THE ROAD	03	50	44
TRAIN ORDER SIGNALS	04	64	34
TURNOUT TIES AND PROTOTYPE PRACTICE	07	66	54
TWO FOOT CARS OF BI&B	11	62	42
UNION PACIFIC COLOR CHART	08	44	346
UNIT TRAINS	09	76	104
UNUSUAL TURNOUT IN CITY STREET	05	62	46
VIRGINIAN COLOR CHART	04	46	254
WABASH COLOR CHART	02	46	117
WABASH COLOR CHARTS	02	48	121
WALLACE JUNCTION, IND MONON	12	60	48
WATER TANK CONVERTED TO GRAIN BIN BURL	11	59	71
WAYSIDE STATION STOCKBRIDGE, MASS NH	02	59	50
WEEDS ON THE PROTOTYPE	10	48	706
WESTERN PACIFIC COLOR CHART	03	45	110
WHAT AMTRAK MEANS TO MODEL RAILROADING	01	72	34
WHERE TO PLACE THE THIRD RAIL	07	64	55
WHITE SULPHER SPRINGS VA STATION	11	63	36
WINDSOR LOCKS CONN SWITCHING CORNER NH	11	60	44
WIRE TRAINS ON ELECTRIC LINES	06	85	118
WRECK TRAINS BOOMER PETE	08	50	35
WYE AND ITS USE	08	83	135
YARD DESIGN AND TRACKAGE PRINCIPALS	06	75	80
ZOO JUNCTION PHILADELPHIA PA	12	58	66

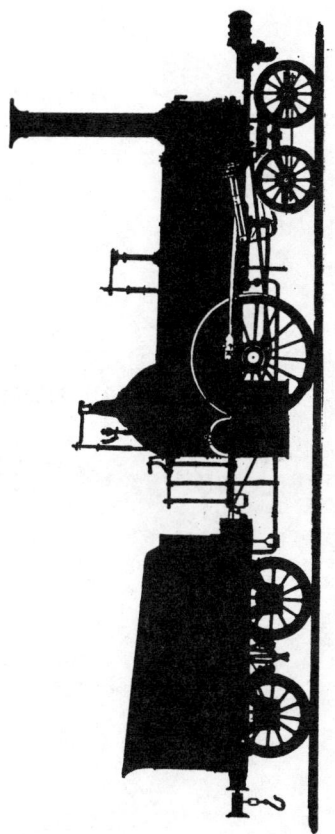

BILL OF LADING   RAILROAD HISTORIES

Railroad Histories are articles on specific railroads. In some instances they are they result of reseaching the olden days of the road. In some instances they are current happenings, at the time of publication, which are now history. The descriptor line contains the road abbreviation plus an idea of the subject matter contained in the article.

MANIFEST   ROAD HISTORIES

RAILROAD HISTORIES

RAILROAD HISTORIES

RAILROAD HISTORIES	M	Y	P
HISTORY OF A&A PASS AS IMPORTANT AS FRT	09	78	78
HISTORY OF A&R INDUSTRIES-DIESEL & STEAM	11	65	33
HISTORY OF AB 2 MI ISLAND HOPPER	04	80	80
HISTORY OF AD&N WOOD PRODUCTS INDUSTRY	02	81	108
HISTORY OF AE&FRE ONE MAN RAILROAD	09	67	24
HISTORY OF ATSF CAJON PASS	10	56	22
HISTORY OF ATSF TEHACHAPI LOOP	04	80	132
HISTORY OF AUTO-TRAIN	12	74	48
HISTORY OF AV THE POTATO PIKE	07	66	28
HISTORY OF B&CH	10	75	52
HISTORY OF B&M	10	75	52
HISTORY OF B&M NORTH CONWAY NH	06	71	62
HISTORY OF B&O AMER. 1ST COMMON CARRIER	07	76	74
HISTORY OF B&O M&K JCT W. VA.	03	62	30
HISTORY OF BC&G NV SHORT LINE	11	59	42
HISTORY OF BHL LOGGING IN VANCOUVER 1920	04	81	76
HISTORY OF BN TIE TREATING	10	75	78
HISTORY OF BSRR TRAP ROCK LINE	08	64	46
HISTORY OF C&LE ALL STEEL FRT MOTORS	03	63	44
HISTORY OF C&NW PRAIRIE BRANCH	02	79	94
HISTORY OF C&O WHITE SULPHER SPRINGS	11	63	36
HISTORY OF C&O SOUTH PORTSMOUTH	04	78	100
HISTORY OF CAC MINES TO SHIPS	08	62	28
HISTORY OF CASEY JONES THE ENGINEER	11	47	922
HISTORY OF CHV ALABAMA SHORT LINE	12	73	72
HISTORY OF CL	11	78	85
HISTORY OF CN	10	75	52
HISTORY OF CNJ SEASHORE LINE	09	85	58
HISTORY OF CP	10	75	52
HISTORY OF CP KETTLE VALLEY LINE	05	68	52
HISTORY OF D&GR DURANGO YARD	07	81	82
HISTORY OF D&NE CLOQUET SHOPS	08	63	52
HISTORY OF DSP&P RAILROAD IN THE CLOUDS	12	80	104
HISTORY OF E GREYCOURT INTERCHANGE	08	80	92
HISTORY OF EBT 24" GAUGE HAND CARS	12	71	70
HISTORY OF EN SHORT HISTORY	05	62	24
HISTORY OF ET&WNC BLUE RIDGE NARROW GAUG	07	81	66
HISTORY OF FDM&S	11	68	36
HISTORY OF FJ&G DELAWARE OTSEGO SYSTEM	08	79	58
HISTORY OF G&Y PA OIL ROAD	12	76	58
HISTORY OF GB&W 256 LOCAL OWNED MILES	02	78	66
HISTORY OF GB&W KEWAUNEE DIV UCMI	04	78	58
HISTORY OF GCO SHAY OPERATED SHORT LINE	04	62	24
HISTORY OF GH&H WHARVE RAILROAD	05	83	58
HISTORY OF GT	10	75	52
HISTORY OF GWH WHARVE RAILROAD	05	83	58
HISTORY OF H&SO THE JELLO ROUTE	04	79	119
HISTORY OF JCE IN TRANSITION	06	77	80
HISTORY OF KCKW LASTED LONGER THAN MOST	02	72	38
HISTORY OF L&N EVANSVILLE DIVISION	05	85	88
HISTORY OF LI MONTAUK TERMINAL	03	66	52
HISTORY OF LV HISTORIC SITE	12	66	52
HISTORY OF LVT LIBERTY BELL LINE	06	61	38
HISTORY OF M&WR	10	75	52
HISTORY OF MA&PA AUTOMOATIC BACKGROUND	05	65	38
HISTORY OF MC	10	75	52
HISTORY OF MCR NARROW GAUGE-COAL ROAD	07	72	30
HISTORY OF MILW FOX LANE JCT	02	76	48
HISTORY OF MILW KINGSBURY BRANCH	04	75	52
HISTORY OF MILW MAYFAIR JCT	03	76	60
HISTORY OF MILW STOWELL YARD	01	72	50
HISTORY OF MV 19TH CENTURY TOURIST ROAD	06	80	82
HISTORY OF NH	10	75	52
HISTORY OF NH SYKES RAILBUS 1925	04	83	115
HISTORY OF NP PALOUSE & LEWISTON BRANCH	01	74	64
HISTORY OF NPIER NJ TO NH	09	74	37
HISTORY OF NS SOUTH DURHAM, NC	06	74	54
HISTORY OF P&WR A LITTLE OF EVERYTHING	08	72	48
HISTORY OF P&WR 69TH ST TERMINAL	02	67	30
HISTORY OF PRR SHAMOKIN PA	08	61	24
HISTORY OF PRR ZOO JUNCTION PA	12	58	66
HISTORY OF Q BACK COUNTRY LINE	04	63	32
HISTORY OF QC	10	75	52
HISTORY OF R NEWTON BRANCH	11	62	39
HISTORY OF RS 2'/INTERURBAN/STANDARD	06	74	44
HISTORY OF S MURPHY BRANCH	10	84	68
HISTORY OF SCPA 24" SHAYS	05	71	56
HISTORY OF SF&CS 8 MILE RURAL ELCTRIC	04	70	67
HISTORY OF SFB	04	80	65
HISTORY OF SFI ARIZONA LOGGER	03	84	70
HISTORY OF SJ&LC	10	75	52
HISTORY OF SN LINE OF DIVERSITY	07	70	46
HISTORY OF SN STEEPLE CAB LOCOS	09	77	64
HISTORY OF SOO LINE GENERAL INFO MODERN	10	82	63
HISTORY OF SOO LINE POWER/ROLLING STOCK	11	82	78
HISTORY OF ST DIESEL SHORT LINE	11	58	49
HISTORY OF STEW 1855-1966	10	66	50
HISTORY OF SVS LATER LOCOMOTIVES	03	81	138
HISTORY OF TM&BC 1860-1940	11	82	108
HISTORY OF UTC JERSEY SHORT LINE	04	64	28
HISTORY OF VERMONT GRANITE ROADS	10	75	52
HISTORY OF VIA CANADAS GOV'T TRAINS	05	82	62
HISTORY OF W COLUMBIA-CENTRALIA BRANCH	01	66	38
HISTORY OF WI&M AND POTLASH LUMBER	09	75	40
HISTORY OF WI&W 18 MILES IN VIRGINIA	10	74	44
HISTORY OF WJ&S JERSEY ELECTRIC LINE	02	69	41
HISTORY OF WP&Y PROUD RAILROAD	03	53	44
HISTORY OF Y 10.6 MILES IN N CAROLINA	08	74	33
HISTORY OF YVA BRIEF HISTORY	08	84	73

BILL OF LADING — MODEL LAYOUTS

This section covers layouts and the basic building of them. The sub-categories include Model Trackwork (including switch machines), Prototype Trackwork, Layout Design, Layout Operation, Layout Plans, Layout Building, Scenery, and Layout Visits. All are self-explanatory. The layout visit section contains many interesting model ideas. In many instances layout plans are included that are not in the plans section. Often the "trick" techniques of the layouts specialty are described - sometimes in detail - sometimes not. The model photography is generally good. The layout visits descriptor contains the name of the layout and when available the scale and the owners last name. (At times its the author of the article.) Layout building concerns itself with all aspects of layout construction. The operation section will give you ideas on what to do with or how to run your pike when it is finished.

MANIFEST — MODEL LAYOUTS

	PAGE
MODEL LAYOUTS	180
LAYOUT DESIGN	181
LAYOUT PLANS	182
LAYOUT BUILDING	183
MODEL TRACKWORK	185
SCENERY	188
LAYOUT OPERATION	190
LAYOUT VISITS	192

MODEL LAYOUTS

LAYOUT DESIGN	M	Y	P
4 X 8 TRACK PLANNING BASICS	06	81	70
ACCOMODATING A 16' DOOR	06	62	56
ADD A TERMINAL MODULE	10	72	66
ARTIFICIAL HAZARDS ON LAYOUTS	11	47	898
AT&S OPERATIONS LAYOUT HOSS	11	72	62
BASEMENT LAYOUT OBSTACLE COURSE RRING	12	56	66
BASHING A 4 X 8 LAYOUT	09	84	112
BELT LINE LAYOUT	01	55	56
BIG FOUR PLANNING RULES	06	39	295
BUILD YOUR PIKE ON PAPER FIRST	02	43	64
CENTRAL MICHIGAN LAYOUT ODEGARD	11	72	68
CLEARANCE ON CURVES	08	34	14
CLEARANCES FOR CURVED TRACK ON BRIDGES	03	77	116
COMMUTER TRACK PLANS	09	72	38
CONSIDER THIS IN YOUR TRACK PLANNING	12	62	85
CORNERS OF YOUR LAYOUT	07	35	176
CROSSOVERS AND LADDER TRACK	02	37	71
CUBICLE RAILROADS	05	75	40
CURVE LAYOUT-MIGHTY BANTAM	11	53	60
CURVE REALISM PLANNING	02	66	37
CURVES AND OPERATION	05	37	163
CURVES LAYED OUT WITH TEMPLATES	05	43	226
DEAMON S CURVES - BEWARE!	08	53	48
DESIGNING PORTABLE LAYOUTS	07	67	32
DESIGNING THE NEW CARRABASSET & DEAD RIV	11	81	86
DESIGNS FOR INTERURBAN LAYOUTS	03	69	38
DIESEL SERVICING FACILITIES	10	65	45
DM&S RR LAYOUT-PLANS "HO" WESTCOTT	02	35	40
DOODLING BY SQUARES LAYOUT DESIGN	11	80	102
DOUBLE DECK LAYOUT WITHOUT SPIRAL	02	84	140
EASMENT TEMPLATES	10	69	60
EASY TO LAY OUT TURNOUTS	10	43	436
ELLIPTICAL TRANSITION CURVE MAKER	09	62	57
EVOLUTIONARY TRACK PLANNING	03	70	36
EXPANDABLE TRACK PLANS	12	68	60
FACTS ABOUT TRACK SECTIONAL & FLEXIBLE	07	80	66
FIE ON OVAL OPERATIONS	10	63	34
FOLD AWAY LAYOUT TABLE	11	74	92
FREIGHT YARD DESIGN AND TRACKAGE	05	35	123
FUNDIMENTAL LAYOUT DESIGN CONCEPTS	12	72	90
HELPER GRADE LAYOUT SILAS	11	72	64
IDEAS FOR SPACE UTILIZATION	11	47	916
INDUSTRIES FOR YOUR PIKE	01	54	90
INTERCHANGE TABLE WITHOUT TURNOUTS	08	79	84
INTERCHANGES ADDING THEM TO YOUR LAYOUT	02	82	76
JUNCTIONS AND CROSSINGS	06	35	149
JUNCTIONS AND CROSSINGS GEMS OF PLANNING	08	47	624
JUNCTIONS AND CROSSINGS OF THE PROTOTYPE	12	47	984
LAYOUT DESIGN BASICS	11	36	317
LAYOUT DRAWING STANDARD SYMBOLS	10	36	293
LAYOUT PLANS BY FORMULA	06	68	46
LAYOUT SURGERY	05	76	41
LIMITING NOISE IN TRACKAGE	02	54	42
LOCOMOTIVE MINIMUM RADIUS TABLE	02	52	59
LOCOMOTIVE TERMINALS	01	38	24
LOCOMOTIVE TERMINALS ACTION & COLOR	05	42	236
LOCOMOTIVE TERMINALS & ENGINE FACILITIES	08	62	24
LOCOMOTIVE TERMINALS DESIGN	10	53	54
LOCOMOTIVE TERMINALS-4 VERSIONS	11	46	726
MAIN LINE TRACK DESIGN	09	64	22
MODEL RAILROAD STANDARDS	07	35	189
MODERATION IN PLANNING	04	76	60
MODULAR RAILROADING "ON3"	01	81	70
MODULAR SECTION LAYOUTS	01	72	66
MOSTEST TRACK IN LEASTEST SPACE	01	65	36
MY POSTWAR PLANS & IDEAS BOOMER PETE	04	45	166
MY POSTWAR PLANS: LUMBER, RAIL & PLASTER	05	45	196
NO STOOP RAILROADS ARMSTRONG	01	56	51
NONBRANCHING BRANCH LINE LAYOUT	04	57	52
OVALS & WELTERWEIGHT LAYOUTS	02	81	104
PARABOLIC CURVES FOR MODEL RAILROAD USE	11	35	288
PASSENGER STATION TRACKAGE	04	35	95
PLAN LAYOUT TO FURNISH FREIGHT TRAFFIC	10	35	255
PLANNING A NEW LAYOUT	06	72	28
PLANNING FOR REALISM IN LAYOUTS	10	34	10
PLANNING ROUNDHOUSE TRACKAGE	02	72	69
PRAIRE PROBLEMS ARMSTRONG	07	53	46
REALISTIC OPERATION BOOMER PETE	03	39	127
REALISTIC PERFORMANCE ON MODEL PIKES	05	63	38
RIBBONS OF STEEL GOOD TRACKWORK B. PETE	07	46	418
RIGHT OF WAY DIMENSIONS (VARIOUS GAUGES)	07	35	189
ROUNDHOUSE LAYOUT	04	67	64
SCALE RULE & RADIUS FINDER	06	43	267
SCALES AND GAUGES SMALL	05	35	125
SCALING TRACK PLANS TO VARIOUS GAUGES	11	68	52
SECOND CHANCE TRACK PLANNING	01	64	66
SHORT LINE MIXED TRAINS	02	55	52
SIDE TRACK PLANNING	07	51	18
SMALL RADIUS LAYOUTS	04	50	33
SMALL STATION LAYOUTS	11	38	470
SNAP TRACK TIMESAVER	10	76	67
SNEAK OFF TRACKS	04	46	240
SPIRAL TRACKAGE	09	48	691
SPIRAL TRANSITION CURVES WITH EASEMENTS	10	69	58
SPIRAL TRANSITIONS IN EXISTING TRACK	11	69	83
STACKED MAIN LINES FOR ADDED MILEAGE	11	66	36
STARTER RAILROAD THAT GROWS	12	73	54
STRUCTURE ARRANGEMENT & DETAIL IN TOWNS	05	73	48
SUPERELEVATED SIDINGS ON CURVES	06	78	137
SUPERELEVATED TRACK	05	78	132
SWING AWAY TRACK SECTION ROOM ACCESS	07	73	76
SWITCHBACKS	12	50	29
SWITCHING IN HO BY REMOTE CONTROL	04	39	181
TERMINAL LAYOUTS	04	50	30
TERMINAL TURNOUTS BOOMER PETE	05	46	318
TEST TRACK LAYOUT-A LITTLE OF EVERYTHING	03	74	55
THINK BIG IN SMALL PLACES	05	76	66
THOUGHTS ON MODULAR TRACTION DESIGN	10	85	82
THREE IN ONE BENCHWORK	10	72	63
TIMESAVER IN A LOOP	02	79	124

MODEL LAYOUTS

LAYOUT DESIGN

	M	Y	P
TIMESAVER LAYOUT ALLEN	11	72	66
TOTAL LAYOUT DESIGN BASICS	06	82	90
TRACK LAYOUT PLANNING HINTS	05	34	8
TRACK PLAN DESIGNED FOR GROWTH	12	76	105
TRACK PLAN DRAWING MADE EASY	07	82	64
TRACK PLAN HUNTING FOR A PROTOTYPE	09	70	30
TRACK PLANNING	10	41	495
TRACK PLANNING 1 USEFUL TRICKS	10	52	48
TRACK PLANNING 2 USEFUL TRICKS	11	52	40
TRACK PLANNING 3 USEFUL TRICKS	04	53	34
TRACK PLANNING FOR OPERATION	01	54	62
TRACK PLANNING FOR SMALL SPACES	12	74	83
TRACK PLANNING GORRE & DAPHETID	03	63	28
TRACK PLANNING VARIATIONS ON AN OVAL	09	52	38
TRACK PLANS FOR RAILROADS THAT GROW	01	50	23
TRACK TEMPLATES	04	78	136
TRANSFER TERMINAL FOR DUAL GAUGE	05	71	34
TRANSITION CURVES IN YARDS	06	78	136
TUNNELS ADD ILLUSION OF LENGTH	12	45	525
TUXEDO JUNCTION LAYOUT DESIGN	12	52	18
TUXEDO JUNCTION TRACK DESIGN	04	54	44
TWO IN ONE RAILROAD	06	53	44
UNCOUPLING RAMP LOCATION	07	51	22
UNCOUPLING RAMP LOCATIONS	08	69	75
USE OF INDUSTRIES IN LAYOUT PLANNING	10	63	38
WALK IN LAYOUT IN PHASES	06	71	54
WARF TRACKAGE	06	65	20
WHERE TO LOCATE INDUSTRIES	06	50	10
WUT PORTABLE SYSTEM CLUB	11	72	60
WYE AND ITS USE	08	83	135
YARD DESIGN & TRACKAGE AN EVOLVING YARD	11	71	62
YARD DESIGN (KICKBACK HUMP YARD)	09	74	52
YARD DESIGN AND TRACKAGE BOOMER PETE	10	38	433
YARD DESIGN AND TRACKAGE (COMPACT YARDS)	02	44	56
YARD DESIGN AND TRACKAGE PRINCIPLES	06	75	80
YARD DESIGN HANDBOOK	08	55	47

LAYOUT PLANS

	M	Y	P
ARCADE & ATTICA PLAN	09	78	82
ARCADIA TERMINAL STREET & DOCK RR PLAN	12	77	79
BAY CITY SOUTHERN PLAN	10	78	72
BLACK RIVER LINES PLAN	09	78	62
BRANDYWINE SHORTLINE PLANS	12	77	87
CHATTANOOGA AREA MODEL RR CLUB PLANS HO	10	77	92
CLIMAX FALLS II PLAN	08	78	87
CLINCHFIELD PROJECT PLAN	11	78	91
CLINCHFIELD RAILROAD PLANS MULTI-GAUGE	12	78	87
COLRAIN VALLEY RAILROAD PLANS	11	77	60
CUMBERLAND & OHIO PLANS	01	78	56
D&S RAILROAD PLANS	02	78	91
ERIE MAHINING DIVISION PLANS	11	78	103
GBW KEWAUNEE DIVISION PLANS	04	78	63
GM&G RAILROAD PLANS	12	78	82
GREAT SOUTHERN LINES PLAN	05	78	59
LAKES & NORTHWESTERN RAILROAD PLANS	01	77	56
MAD RIVER NAVIGATION RAILWAY PLANS	07	77	48
MARQUETTE UNION TERMINAL PLAN	06	78	74
MIDLAND VALLEY RAILROAD PLANS	06	77	54
MOHAWK & HUDSON RAILROAD PLAN	03	78	53
MUSKINGOM VALLEY TRACTION LINES PART 1	06	77	106
NORTHERN ALLEN PARK LINES PLAN	07	78	88
OAKVILLE CENTRAL PLAN	12	78	106
OCEAN VIEW UNIFIED RAILROAD PLAN	09	78	73
OHIO RIVER & MUSKINGUM RR PART 1 PLANS	06	77	106
OHIO SOUTHERN RAILROAD PLAN	07	78	73
OMAHA & NORTH WESTERN LINE PLANS "HO"	07	77	62
PATERSON & EASTERN RAILROAD	01	77	55
PATERSON TERMINAL TRANSFER RAILWAY PLAN	01	77	55
PATERSON, TWIN RIVERS & EASTERN RR PLANS	01	77	56
PENN-READING SEASHORE PLAN	08	78	84
PRR SCIOTA VALLEY SUBDIVISION	06	77	106
QUONSET & EAST DOUGLAS RAILWAY PLAN	05	78	91
RACQUETTE RIVER RAILROAD PLANS	10	77	97
ROAD TO ENCHANTMENT PLAN	01	91	84
ROCK POINT & COAST RAILROAD PLAN	10	78	67
ROYAL GEORGE WESTERN	01	77	70
SANDRIC & LAKE SUPERIOR RAILROAD PLANS	08	77	76
SANTA FE IN "HO" PLAN	12	78	159
SECAUCUS & BLACKWATER PLAN	04	78	107
SIERRA GRANDE & WESTERN PLAN	02	78	100
THIRD STREET INDUSTRIAL DISTRICT TRACKPL	11	85	116
THREE TRACK PLANS FOR THE JM&J LINES	12	79	122
TRIBOROUGH RAPID TRANSIT COMPANY PLANS	10	78	116
TWO PLANS FOR L SHAPE SPACE	02	78	88
UNION SOUTHWESTERN RAILWAY	01	77	56
WALK IN TRACK PLAN IDEA 6 X 13	02	77	64
WHITEHALL & VALLEY JUCTION PLAN	07	78	56

MODEL LAYOUTS

LAYOUT BUILDING	M	Y	P
25 YEARS OF TRACK PLANS ARMSTRONG	01	59	58
50,000 SPIKES BENCHWORK ALLEN	02	42	68
50,000 SPIKES BRIDGES ALLEN	05	42	224
50,000 SPIKES LANDSCAPING ALLEN	07	42	328
50,000 SPIKES PAST HISTORY GEORGE ALLEN	09	41	445
50,000 SPIKES PRELIMINARY PLAN ALLEN	12	41	619
50,000 SPIKES RIVER/SWAMP/MILL/WATERFALL	04	42	176
50,000 SPIKES ROADBED & NOISE ALLEN	03	42	122
50,000 SPIKES ROUND UP BAGGAGE CAR ALLEN	11	41	553
50,000 SPIKES UP GOES THE CEILING ALLEN	10	41	504
50,000 SPIKES YARDMASTERS OFFICE ALLEN	06	42	278
AMERICAN MODELS IN SWEDEN LANAL	02	42	62
APARTMENT PIKE WESTCOTT	09	51	40
BASIC BENCHWORK CONSTRUCTION	05	68	65
BEDROOM RAILROAD CONSTRUCTION	11	56	54
BENCH AND ROADBED CONSTRUCTION METHODS	06	70	30
BENCHWORK CONSTRUCTION	12	41	608
BENCHWORK CONSTRUCTION 1	11	47	884
BENCHWORK CONSTRUCTION 2	12	47	972
BENCHWORK CONSTRUCTION SIMPLE & STURDY	03	54	28
BENCHWORK CONSTRUCTION USE CIRCULAR SAW	05	67	43
BENCHWORK LUMBER SIZES	11	52	76
BENCHWORK MODULES MOVE THEM WHOLE!	06	74	60
BI LEVEL BENCHWORK TECHNIQUES	02	83	83
BOOKSHELF LAYOUT CONSTRUCTION PART 1	01	77	53
BOOKSHELF LAYOUT CONSTRUCTION PART 2	02	77	95
BREAKAWAY BENCHWORK FRAMEWORK	07	50	29
BREAKAWAY BENCHWORK ROADBED	08	50	16
BUILD A CHANGEABLE SCENERY PIKE	06	62	30
BUILD CLINCH BUILDING SCENERY	05	79	58
BUILD CLINCH FULL OPERATIONS	07	79	72
BUILD CLINCH RAILROAD - THE BEGINNING	11	78	85
BUILD CLINCH RAILROAD BENCHWORK	12	78	86
BUILD CLINCH STRUCTURES & DETAILS	06	79	80
BUILD CLINCH WIRING TWO TRAIN OPERATION	03	79	99
BUILD CLINCHFIELD TRACKLAYING	01	79	74
BUILD E&O BENCHWORK	12	66	38
BUILD E&O ENLARGING IT "N"	05	67	26
BUILD E&O EQUIPMENT AND OPERATION	04	67	48
BUILD E&O R IS FOR ROADBED	01	67	37
BUILD E&O WIRING	03	67	32
BUILD E&O ZIP TEXTURE SCENERY	02	67	48
BUILD GOLD HILL CENTRAL IN 6 HOURS	03	84	84
BUILD GREAT SOUTH PASS BENCHWORK	05	56	36
BUILD GREAT SOUTH PASS CONTROL PANEL	09	56	61
BUILD GREAT SOUTH PASS ENGINEERS CAB	10	56	63
BUILD GREAT SOUTH PASS PLANNING	04	56	40
BUILD GREAT SOUTH PASS SCENERY	12	58	78
BUILD GREAT SOUTH PASS SWITCH MACHINES	08	56	52
BUILD GREAT SOUTH PASS TRACK LAYING	06	56	45
BUILD GREAT SOUTH PASS TRNTBL	11	57	60
BUILD GREAT SOUTH PASS TRNTBL HANDCRANK	10	57	50
BUILD GREAT SOUTH PASS TURNTABLE 1	09	57	46
BUILD GRR EASY STORE "N" GREEN RIVER RR	12	80	74
BUILD GRR LAY TRACK/WIRE/SCENERY	01	81	114
BUILD GRR WIRING/STRUCTURES/LANDSCAPE	03	81	73
BUILD GV&W ONE SCENE AT A TIME	09	84	67
BUILD IT IN HO OR N BENCHWORK TO TRACK	12	68	52
BUILD IT IN HO OR N FINAL TOUCHES	05	69	36
BUILD IT IN HO OR N FINISHING TOUCHES	03	69	54
BUILD IT IN HO OR N TRACK AND STRUCTURES	02	69	54
BUILD IT IN HO OR N WHO SAID FLAT WORLD	04	69	52
BUILD IT IN HO OR N WIRING	01	69	59
BUILD J&SW "HO" FIRST LOOK	02	82	62
BUILD J&SW ADD BACK ALLEY & WARF	02	83	62
BUILD J&SW ADDING COLOR	10	82	100
BUILD J&SW BACKDROPS & WIDE OPEN SPACES	01	83	78
BUILD J&SW BENCHWORK AND ROADBED	04	82	90
BUILD J&SW LOCOMOTIVE & CAR WEATHERING	12	82	74
BUILD J&SW STRUCTURES/PAINT/WEATHERING	11	82	98
BUILD J&SW TERRAIN HARDSHELL & ROCKS	08	82	67
BUILD J&SW TRACK & CONTROL	06	82	62
BUILD J&SW TRACK & CONTROL CORRECTION	10	82	147
BUILD KHC "HO" BENCHWORK/TRACKWORK	12	81	78
BUILD KHC STRUCTURES/SCENERY/DETAILS	01	82	70
BUILD KR&D ADD COLOR AND FOLIAGE	07	72	36
BUILD KR&D BENCHWORK KINNICKINNIC RY	01	72	60
BUILD KR&D HARBOR/CAR FERRY/LOAD APRON	08	72	32
BUILD KR&D HARD SHELL TERRAIN	05	72	36
BUILD KR&D OPERATIONS	02	73	56
BUILD KR&D TRACK/TURNOUTS/SWITCHSTANDS	02	72	51
BUILD KR&D WIRING	03	72	52
BUILD MA&PA INDUSTRY & HISTORY	01	65	28
BUILD MA&PA BELOW TRACK SCENERY	08	65	47
BUILD MA&PA CAB CONTROL	06	65	40
BUILD MA&PA GRADES	09	65	48
BUILD MA&PA HERITAGE	05	65	38
BUILD MA&PA HILLS WITH HARD SHELL	03	65	38
BUILD MA&PA OPERATIONS	11	65	54
BUILD MA&PA STARTING BENCHWORK	12	64	26
BUILD MA&PA WALK AROUND CONTROL	04	65	38
BUILD MA&PA YARD	02	65	48
BUILD PIKE TO SUIT YOURSELF ARMSTRONG	11	54	66
BUILD PINE TREE CENTRAL SCENERY	02	53	58
BUILD PUGET JUNCTION	05	66	37
BUILD SJC BRIDGES-VARIETY OF SPANS	06	84	96
BUILD SJC L GIRDER BENCHWORK & ROADBED	12	83	118
BUILD SJC LOCOMOTIVES AND CARS	07	84	84
BUILD SJC OPERATION	08	84	98
BUILD SJC SAN JUAN CENTRAL "HO" 1ST LOOK	11	83	88
BUILD SJC SCENERY--ACRES OF ROCK W/FOAM	04	84	56
BUILD SJC STRUCTURES-SMALL COLORFUL BLDS	05	84	56
BUILD SJC TRACK LAYING--NO DERAILMENTS	02	84	90
BUILD SJC WIRING--DYNATROL SYSTEM	03	84	66
BUILD SPRR FRAMEWORK	12	65	40
BUILD SPRR MINING TOWN	04	66	22
BUILD SPRR OPERATIONS	06	66	42
BUILD SPRR POWERING	02	66	56
BUILD SPRR SCENERY	03	66	29
BUILD SPRR THROW THE TRACK ON	01	66	30

MODEL LAYOUTS

LAYOUT BUILDING	M	Y	P
BUILD THE LQ&N $300 RAILROAD	12	84	123
BUILD THE MM&N COMPACT STARTER LAYOUT	12	84	98
BUILD THE W&SF STRUCTURES OF PAULS VALLY	06	83	74
BUILD TIDEWATER CENTRAL BENCHWORKRK	12	56	28
BUILD TIDEWATER CENTRAL PLASTER/DRY COLO	01	57	62
BUILD UC1 UNION CENTRAL HISTORY	09	71	51
BUILD W&SF BACKDROPS LAYERED LANDSCAPES	11	82	120
BUILD W&SF BASIC SCENERY & TERRAIN	02	83	107
BUILD W&SF BENCHWORK FOUNDATION OF A MRR	03	82	68
BUILD W&SF LAYING FLEXTRACK	05	82	88
BUILD W&SF PLANNING "HO"	01	82	86
BUILD W&SF WASHITA CANYON CONSTRUCTION	08	84	58
BUILD W&SF WIRING WITH COMMAND CONTROL	09	82	90
BUILDING A LAYOUT SO IT CAN BE MOVED	11	62	44
BUILDING GOPHER GULCH & PINE RIDGE	02	79	102
BUILDING THE B&R "HO"	01	52	22
BUILDING THE BRANDYWINE SHORT LINE	12	77	86
BUILDING THE PORTAGE HILL EXPANSION	12	62	52
BUILDING THE PORTAGE HILL FINAL EXPANSIO	07	63	32
BWT CONSTRUCTION BENCHWORK/PLOTTING PLAN	05	75	50
BWT CONSTRUCTION CAR BARNS	05	76	69
BWT CONSTRUCTION FINAL OVERHEAD WIRES	10	76	79
BWT CONSTRUCTION MORE TRACK LAYING	09	75	72
BWT CONSTRUCTION OVERHEAD WIRES	09	76	82
BWT CONSTRUCTION PASSENGER TERMINAL	08	76	64
BWT CONSTRUCTION PROTOTYPE CONTROLLERS	03	76	68
BWT CONSTRUCTION STREETS AND SIDEWALKS	11	75	80
BWT CONSTRUCTION TRACKWORK AND OVERHEAD	07	75	60
BWT CONSTRUCTION WIRING THE CITY DIVISIO	01	76	85
CABLE SUSPENDED LAYOUT	05	51	24
CENTRALIZED TRAFFIC CONTROL CENTER	01	84	186
CIRCULAR COFFEE TABLE LAYOUT	06	66	40
COFFEE TABLE "N" SCALE EMPIRE DAVIS	10	79	94
COFFEE TABLE RAILROAD	02	56	26
CS CONSTRUCTION BUILD CANADIAN SOUTHERN	01	71	45
CS CONSTRUCTION CONTROL AND SCENERY	03	71	61
DISPLAY MODULES TAKE OUT LAYOUTS	06	73	56
DROP LEAF MODULE FOR BOOKSHELF LAYOUT	02	80	112
EVERGREEN CENTRAL CONSTRUCTION	11	53	28
EVERGREEN CENTRAL CONSTRUCTION SCENERY	12	53	50
FLIP OVER RAILROAD	07	55	18
FOLD AWAY LAYOUT	01	73	70
FOLDING ROLLAWAY LAYOUT	12	78	104
GARAGE LAYOUT THAT IS SUSPENDED	09	47	726
GSV MOVES-BEGIN ANEW DO IT RIGHT	06	72	28
HIDEAWAY CABINET RAILROAD	09	48	592
HIDEAWAY WALL LAYOUT	12	77	102
HIDEAWAY WALL LAYOUT CONSTRUCTION	12	77	102
HIGH ALTITUDE RAILROADING-7' ABOVE FLOOR	01	49	44
HINGED YARDS ARE EASIER FOR WIRING	09	83	76
HOW I BUILT MY LAYOUT PAGE	10	42	460
HOW TO BUILD GOOD BENCHWORK	09	52	12
JEFFERSON MEMPHIS & NORTHERN "HO"	10	79	92
JEROM & SOUTHWESTERN JR "N" CONSTRUCT	01	85	91
JIGSAW RAILROAD	10	51	28
JOPLIN & SOUTHERN CONST BENCH/TRACK/WIRE	12	85	136
L GIRDER BENCHWORK	01	81	82
L GIRDER CLEATS	02	77	123
L GIRDER FRAMEWORK	09	63	44
LASTCHANCE & FAIRPLAY WESTCOTT	09	56	54
LAYING OUT CURVES WITH A TRIPOD	02	68	51
LAYOUT FOR 4-12-2S ARMSTRONG	04	65	34
LAYOUT FOR CHRISTMAS MORNING CONSTRUCTIO	12	80	110
LAYOUT IN A FORTNIGHT	12	51	12
LAYOUTS IN SUBASSEMBLIES PTS TRAF INTERE	01	68	49
LIFT AWAY RAILROAD CONSTRUCTION	02	49	28
LIGHTING A BOOKSHELF RAILROAD	04	80	106
LIVING ROOM LAYOUT IN A CABINET	01	70	52
LONDON'S BENCHWORK & TRACKWORK	05	73	36
M&I CONST BUILD MARQUETTE & INDEPENDENCE	12	75	62
M&I CONSTRUCTION CONTROL PANEL & WIRING	02	76	60
M&I CONSTRUCTION STRUCTURES AND SCENERY	04	76	44
MAKING ROOM FOR MAKING TRACKS SEMI ATTIC	08	84	76
MODIFIED GIRDER CONSTRUCTION	01	78	141
MODULE IN A BOX CONSTRUCTION	10	82	94
NEW MODEL RAILROAD BOOMER PETE	02	42	56
NOEL CENTRAL SCENERY	01	56	58
PETITE BELT LINE-BACK TO BASICS	12	76	101
PIECES OF SUNSET MODULAR CONSTRUCTION	11	73	68
PINE PLANK SHELF LAYOUT	04	66	32
PINE TREE CENTRAL FINISHING	05	53	46
PINE TREE CENTRAL GETTING STARTED	12	52	12
PING-PONG & WALLPAPER PASTE TABLE LAYOUT	05	54	26
PIPE BENCHWORK	02	48	116
PORTABLE SECTION LAYOUT	06	67	25
PORTAGE HILL & COMIONIPAW SCENERY	05	62	26
QUIET OPERATION	09	51	54
RAILROAD COFFEE TABLE "N" BEGIN CONST	12	70	61
RAILROAD COFFEE TABLE LAYING TRACK	01	71	66
RAILROAD COFFEE TABLE SCENERY/STRUCTURES	04	71	30
RAILROAD COFFEE TABLE UP AND OVER	02	71	53
RAILROAD COFFEE TABLE WIRING "N"	03	71	51
RAISE AWAY LAYOUT CONSTRUCTION	10	68	68
REBUILDING GLENCOE SKOKIE VALLEY "HO"	01	49	8
REHABILITATING THE MIDLAND ELECTRIC	10	81	84
ROADBED CONSTRUCTION & TRACKLAYING	06	67	51
ROCHESTER REGIONAL CONSTRUCTION 1	02	74	55
ROCHESTER REGIONAL CONSTRUCTION 2	03	74	56
ROLLAWAY PIKE CONSTRUCTION	09	50	30
RUMPUS ROOM RAILROADING	01	53	42
SEABOARD CENTRAL "HO" OVERVIEW CONSTRUCT	12	85	86
SEASIDE LAYOUT WESTCOTT	02	42	66
SHOWCASE RAILROAD CONSTRUCTION	03	41	134
STARTING A LAYOUT BOOMER PETE	02	38	49
STEAMING UP (LIVE STEAM) GEISSEL	08	64	28
STEEL MILL RAILROAD RAU	11	50	12
STORAGE CABINET LAYOUT	08	61	50
SUITCASE RAILROAD	12	53	46
SUITCASE RAILROAD CONSTRUCTION	06	56	24
SUNSET VALLEY CONSTRUCTION & CONTROL	05	79	87

STEPHANS_RAILROAD_DIRECTORY

MODEL LAYOUTS

LAYOUT BUILDING	M	Y	P
SUNSET VALLEY EPILOGUE & QUESTIONS	05	80	100
SUNSET VALLEY MOTIVE POWER/ROLLING STOCK	09	79	87
SUNSET VALLEY MOUNTAINS AND BUILDINGS	07	79	78
SUNSET VALLEY OPERATIONS	11	79	118
SUPPORTING YOUR MODEL RAILROAD	08	35	204
SUSPENDED LAYOUT IN GARAGE	05	57	46
SWITCHING LAYOUTS PART 2	09	77	28
TIMESAVER CONSTRUCTION "HON3"	06	81	96
TRACK & ROADBED ON GLENCOE SKOKIE	04	49	14
TRACK BASE CONSTRUCTION (ROADBED)	05	48	332
TRACK PLANNING GUIDE	03	57	61
TUPPER LAKE & FAUST JCT "HO" SUITCASE	12	53	46
TUXEDO JUCTION RESEARCHING W/ OPEN MIND	11	52	12
TUXEDO JUNCTION "HO" ALLEN	10	52	12
TUXEDO JUNCTION AIR OPERATED SWITCHES	06	54	26
TUXEDO JUNCTION BUILDING STORES	06	53	16
TUXEDO JUNCTION CASTING PARTS	08	54	33
TUXEDO JUNCTION CONVERT PLANS	07	53	30
TUXEDO JUNCTION CREATIVE MODELING	01	53	19
TUXEDO JUNCTION DWARF SIGNAALS	10	54	44
TUXEDO JUNCTION ELECTRO/PNEUMATIC	11	54	60
TUXEDO JUNCTION GANTRY CRANE	12	53	65
TUXEDO JUNCTION LAYOUT DESIGN	12	52	18
TUXEDO JUNCTION LIMITING NOISE IN TRACKS	02	54	42
TUXEDO JUNCTION PLAN REVISION	02	53	16
TUXEDO JUNCTION PROTOTYPE JUNKET	05	53	30
TUXEDO JUNCTION SIGNAL CIRCUITS	12	54	66
TUXEDO JUNCTION SOUP LADLE FOUNDRY	07	54	30
TUXEDO JUNCTION TERMINAL DELUXE	09	53	30
TUXEDO JUNCTION TERMINAL FINISHING	10	53	28
TUXEDO JUNCTION TRACK DESIGN	04	54	44
TUXEDO JUNCTION TRACK LAYING	03	54	60
TUXEDO JUNCTION TRACK LAYING.	05	54	40
TUXEDO JUNCTION UNUSUAL TOOLS	08	53	24
TUXEDO JUNCTION VARIABLE TRANSFORMERS	02	55	48
TUXEDO JUNCTION WORKING DRAWING BOARD	03	53	18
TUXEDO JUNCTION YOUR PLAN: ONLY STARTER	11	53	52
TWO LEVEL COMPACT LAYOUT CONSTRUCTION	01	70	60
UNIFORM ROADBED SECTIONS BY THE MILE	06	75	64
WE BUILT IT IN 6 DAYS SHOW LAYOUT	10	76	94
XMAS JULY AND ALWAYS ARMSTRONG	10	54	49
YULETIDE CENTRAL	11	54	28
YULETIDE CENTRAL SCENERY	12	54	84

MODEL TRACKWORK	M	Y	P
AUTOMATIC HO GAUGE UNCOUPLING	01	35	16
AUTOMATIC SIDING STOP	12	38	546
BALLAST BOARDS -- SINK TRACKS IN YARDS	12	69	46
BALLASTING TRACK	03	77	97
BASIC TRACK ELEMENTS BLUEBOOK	10	56	65
BEGINNING BENCHWORK	12	71	66
BELL CRANKS FOR TURNOUTS HOW TO USE 'EM	06	50	28
BLEND YOUR BALLAST FOR REALISM	07	66	41
BONDED BALLAST FOR NATURAL APPEARANCES	07	66	42
BRASS AND NICKEL SILVER TRACK TOGETHER	10	78	160
BUILD A TWO RAIL MODEL RAILROAD	11	34	10
BUILD J&SW TRACK & CONTROL	06	82	62
BUILD J&SW TRACK & CONTROL CORRECTION	10	82	147
BUILD SJC TRACK LAYING--NO DERAILMENTS	02	84	90
BUILD W&SF LAYING FLEXTRACK	05	82	88
BUILD YOUR OWN SWITCH MACHINES	08	78	92
BUILDING TURNOUTS AT THE WORK BENCH	06	83	92
CALSA TIE LAYING METHOD USING FIXTURES	11	77	115
CANTED RAILS	07	85	131
CAST PLASTER ROADBEDS	09	62	40
CHOKE CONTROLS FOR TURNOUTS	09	47	706
CLEAN TRACK, CLEAN WHEELS	11	85	96
CODE 40 & 55 RAIL FOR "N" SCALE	02	78	147
CODE 40 N GAUGE TURNOUTS BUILT IN PLACE	03	79	126
COLORING TRACK FOR MAXIMUM EFFECT	02	83	104
COLORING YOUR RAILS BY CHEMICAL ACTION	03	45	117
CONCEALED MOUNTING OF SWITCH MACHINES	04	64	59
CONNECTING CONCEALED SWITCH MACHINES	11	44	480
CONSTRUCTION METHOD FOR OO OR HO TRACK	08	34	14
CONVERTED SWITCH MACHINE	06	47	479
CONVERTING COMMERCIAL TURNOUTS	11	55	64
CORRECTING TIGHT GAUGE ON CURVES	04	78	137
COUNTERWEIGHT TURNOUT CONTROL	08	68	56
CRIMP LINK SWITCH MACHINE INSTALLATION	12	74	61
CROSSINGS	01	37	15
CURVED TRACKWORK	10	56	54
CURVES EASEMENTS & FLEXIBLE TRACK	04	80	142
CURVES SHORT RADIUS	01	37	26
DERAILMENTS AND WHY BOOMER PETE	04	38	157
DETAILED CROSSING CONSTRUCTION	02	51	46
DIODE MATRIX SYSTEMS FOR TURNOUT CONTROL	05	82	68
DOUBLE CROSSOVER CONSTRUCTION	09	39	441
DOUBLE CROSSOVER WIRING	01	83	166
DOUBLE SLIP SWITCH MACHINE LINKAGE	03	82	107
DOUBLE SLIP SWITCH OPERATION	06	78	136
DRAWBRIDGE BUMP ELININATION	05	70	63
DUAL GAUGE TRACKAGE	01	54	71
DUAL GAUGE TURNOUT CONSTRUCTION	04	64	46
EASEMENT CALCULATIONS SIMPLIFIED	05	57	40
EASEMENTS AND BALLASTING	03	54	60
EASING THE TOPS & BOTTOMS OF GRADES	11	74	79
EFFICIENT TURNOUT CONTROL	01	47	18
ELECTROMECHANICAL RAMP FOR KADEE COUPLER	09	76	80
END TWIN COIL SWITCH MACHINE FRUSTRATION	04	83	86
ERECTING TROLLEY WIRE	02	39	57

MODEL LAYOUTS

MODEL TRACKWORK

Title	M	Y	P
EXCAVATING A LAYOUT IN SAND	01	55	62
FACTS ABOUT TRACK SECTIONAL & FLEXIBLE	07	80	66
FUNDAMENTALS OF TRACKWORK	08	48	553
GAUNTLET TRACK & HOW TO WIRE IT	04	75	86
GAUNTLET TRACKS	04	48	255
GEMS OF TRACK PLANNING-STATION/JUNCTION	04	48	246
GRADE CALCULATION	09	36	255
GRADE CALCULATION (% OF GRADE CHART)	06	39	296
GRADES BASIC PRINCIPALS	03	68	30
GRADES ON THE MA&PA	09	65	48
GROUND THROW/HIGH LEVEL SWITCH STAND	06	82	100
HAND LAYING N GUAGE CODE 40 TRACK	02	76	42
HAND LAYING TRACK SYSTEM	06	75	62
HAND MAKING TURNOUTS	05	45	204
HANDLAYING HIGH SPEED TURNOUTS	09	81	80
HELIX TRACK OPERATION & RELIABILITY	07	85	128
HIDDEN MAGNE-ELECTRIC UNCOUPLING RAMPS	12	83	104
HIDING ATLAS SWITCH MACHINES	08	77	82
HIDING ATLAS SWITCH MACHINES.	10	85	138
HINGED POINT TURNOUTS	08	84	75
HINGED YARDS ARE EASIER FOR WIRING	09	83	76
HO TURNOUT ADJUSTMENT	08	50	39
HOMASOTE	07	67	61
HOMOSOTE ROADBED	01	55	34
HOT PROBE TURNOUT CONTROL	06	83	141
HOW TO BUILD TURNOUTS	05	55	38
HOW TO FIGURE GRADES	10	57	60
HOW TO HAND LAY TRACK E JERSY GAN DANCER	08	85	66
HOW TO INSULATE & WIRE DOUBLE CROSSOVERS	09	43	412
HOW TO LAY TRACK	06	52	18
IMPROVED RIGHT OF WAY WITH DETAILS	11	38	479
IMPROVING ATLAS N SCALE TURNOUTS	02	85	102
INEXPENSIVE TURNOUT CONTROL	02	71	85
INSULATED RAIL JOINT CONSTRUCTION	12	36	368
INTERCHANGE TABLE WITHOUT TURNOUTS	08	79	84
INTERURBAN CONSTRUCTION PE	12	52	29
JIGS FOR SPEEDY TIE LAYING	07	66	38
JOINING TRACK ON CURVES	03	78	125
LAP TURNOUTS SPACE SAVING DESIGN	03	57	35
LAYING FLEXIBLE TRACK BASICS	02	81	102
LAYING OUT TURNOUTS	11	34	8
LAYING SMALL GAUGE TRACK	07	36	190
LAYING SMOOTH TRACK BOOMER PETE	11	37	411
LAYING STRAIGHT TRACK	04	78	135
LOCATION TURNOUTS ON CURVES	03	64	55
MAINTENANCE FREE TURNOUTS	05	78	62
MAKING A SWITCH MACHINE	09	38	375
MAKING TURNOUTS THAT WORK	12	35	317
MANUAL MECHANICAL TURNOUT CONTROL	12	76	56
MANUAL TURNOUT CONTROL MECHANISM	02	85	131
MANUAL TURNOUT THROW THAT IS PRACTICAL	06	69	48
MARK 7 TURNOUT CONTROL	12	77	123
MARK 7 TURNOUT CONTROL CONSTRUCTION	12	77	123
MAXIMUM LAYOUT GRADES	12	78	185
MECHANICAL TURNOUT CONTROL REVISITED	04	79	92
MECHANICAL TURNOUT CONTROLS	03	77	17
MIDLIN CORK BASE HO TRACK	03	51	15
MIDLIN TRACK HOW TO LAY IT	08	47	644
MODELING A DERAIL ON D&RGW	07	79	99
NEW METHOD OF LAYING SCALE TRACK	10	34	9
NOISE ABSORBING BALLAST-SEARCH F/SILENCE	07	49	10
PANEL LIGHT INDICATIONS OF DOUBLE SLIP S	10	77	131
PARABOLIC CURVES	03	34	8
PASSING TRACK WIRING IMPROVED	09	68	40
PC TIES FOR SPIKELESS TRACKLAYING	03	66	55
PNEUMATIC OPERATED SWITCH MACHINES	06	54	26
POWER FOR DISTANT SWITCH MACHINES	05	80	98
PRACTICAL SWITCH MACHINE	08	56	42
QUICK GETAWAY CLAMP CONSTRUCTION	01	83	172
R IS FOR ROADBED IN "N" SCALE	01	67	37
RACK RAILROAD TURNOUTS	08	76	76
RAIL SIZE CHART	04	81	135
RAILS IN ALL SCALES	11	62	83
RAILS LAID IN STREETS	01	73	92
RECYCLE RAIL BOOMER PETE	10	42	458
RELIABLE OVERHEAD FOR HIDDEN TRACK	08	84	134
RERAILERS	08	37	283
RETRACTABLE UNCOUPLING RAMP	02	71	58
ROADBED AND TRACKLAYING ON MA&PA	12	64	33
ROADBED BASICS	09	81	96
ROTARY SWITCHERS FOR TURNOUT CONTROL	04	79	109
SCALE SIZE RAIL AND WHERE TO USE IT	04	69	51
SCALE TURNOUT CONSTRUCTION 1	10	55	42
SCALE TURNOUT CONSTRUCTION 2	11	55	58
SCENERY MATERIAL APPLICATOR	01	83	165
SEARCH FOR PERFECT SWITCH MACHINE	11	77	64
SECTIONAL TRACK	02	69	53
SELF GUARDING FROGS BOOMER PETE	11	38	492
SIDINGS AND PASSING TRACKS	08	35	205
SIMPLE SWITCH MACHINE LINKAGE	04	78	91
SIMPLE TURNOUT CONSTRUCTION PB MRR CLUB	05	85	126
SIMPLE TURNOUT CONTROL	03	78	125
SIMPLE TURNOUT CONTROL MECHANISM	06	75	57
SIMPLE TURNOUT CONTROL.	03	81	140
SIMULATING PROTOTYPE TRACKWAY	07	73	30
SMALL GAUGE TRACK CONSTRUCTION	02	35	36
SMOOTH SWITCH TRACKWORK	05	62	62
SPACE SAVING TURNOUTS	10	44	442
SPRING SWITCH FOR TURNOUTS	05	77	114
SPRING SWITCH WYE	02	55	38
SQUIGGLE TRACK	05	54	40
STANDARD AREA DOUBLE SLIP SWITCH PLAN	01	35	12
STANDARD THIRD RAIL PRACTICE	02	35	33
STEAM ROAD TURNOUT FOR CITY PAVEMENTS	03	64	35
STREET TRACKAGE	01	55	58
STREET TRACKAGE OF C&S AND ATSF	04	68	43
STRIP TRACK CONSTRUCTION INEXPENSIVE	03	34	1
SUPERELEVATION	05	78	132
SUPERELEVATIONS AND SPIRALS	08	44	336
SWITCH AND SIGNAL RODDING	04	40	191

MODEL LAYOUTS

MODEL TRACKWORK	M	Y	P
SWITCH CONTROL CONSTRUCTION	08	34	12
SWITCH FROG DRAWINGS	08	66	41
SWITCH LAYOUT TEMPLATES #6 FOR O/OO/HO	05	36	118
SWITCH MACHINE LINKAGE	04	55	39
SWITCH MACHINE MAINTENANCE	05	65	59
SWITCH MACHINES THAT ARE HIDDEN	10	76	56
SWITCH MOTORS FOR TURNOUTS	01	76	71
SWITCH POINT CONTROLS-PRACTICAL & SIMPLE	09	43	391
SWITCH STAND CONSTRUCTION	03	75	50
SWITCH STAND HAND OPERATED CONSTRUCTION	12	61	69
SWITCH STANDS IN N SCALE THAT WORK $1	06	76	82
TAILOR MADE TRACK	04	54	66
TEAM TRACKS AND THEIR USES	05	75	81
THERMAL SWITCH MACHINE	07	65	30
THIRD RAIL BOOMER PETE	07	38	279
TIE LAYING MADE EASY	01	51	52
TIES & ROADBED FROM ONE PIECE OF WOOD	08	36	217
TIES AND BALLAST	02	42	65
TIGHTENING TURNOUT RIVETS	06	78	135
TIPS ON INSTALLING GROUND THROWS	11	62	74
TRACK BALLASTING MADE EASY	01	78	108
TRACK COMPONENTS	02	63	77
TRACK CONSTRUCTION GRADES & CURVES	06	44	266
TRACK CONTACTS ABC OF MODEL RAILROADS	05	73	52
TRACK CROSSING CONSTRUCTION	09	56	46
TRACK CROSSINGS ADD INTEREST	01	47	24
TRACK EASMENTS NOMOGRAPH	11	49	98
TRACK LAYING JIG	10	43	434
TRACK LAYING ON PILLAR TO POST RAILROAD	06	48	408
TRACK LAYING WITH PAINT	03	82	105
TRACK LAYING WITH SMALL RAIL	02	65	65
TRACK MEASUREMENTS BLUEBOOK	09	56	59
TRACK PLANNING KIT REVIEW VALCAM ASSOC	04	77	34
TRACK PLANNING TEMPLATE REVIEW AM	05	78	40
TRACK PROFILES	12	82	124
TRACK SUPERELEVATION	01	65	71
TRACK SWITCH DETAIL	01	39	7
TRACK SYMPOSIUM	06	48	388
TRACK TERMINOLOGY	05	45	213
TRACK TROUBLES FIXING THEM	10	45	406
TRACKWORK BOOMER PETE	03	40	146
TRACKWORK 3A	10	50	19
TRACKWORK 3B FROM THE GROUND UP	11	50	26
TRACKWORK A NEW FIELD FOR REALISM	10	36	279
TRACKWORK IS A MODEL TOO	01	55	48
TRACKWORK THAT WORKS	02	43	56
TRIBOROUGH RAPID TRANSIT 1 BROWSKY	10	78	116
TRIPLE GAUGE TRACKWORK CHALLENGE	02	80	96
TROLLEY SPRUNG TURNOUT CONSTRUCTION	07	55	26
TROLLEY TRACK FROM TIN CANS	03	43	113
TROLLEY TRACKWORK TIPS	07	46	439
TURNOUT CHOICE OF SIZES	11	76	53
TURNOUT CONNECTOR FOR POSITIVE ACTION	09	46	561
TURNOUT CONSTRUCTION BETTER WAYS	09	51	27
TURNOUT CONSTRUCTION FOR ANY SITUATION	04	63	43

MODEL TRACKWORK	M	Y	P
TURNOUT CONTROL WITH MOTORS/ELECTRONICS	09	85	92
TURNOUT DETAILING	10	37	363
TURNOUT FABRICATION DATA	03	77	70
TURNOUT FROGS USING A PATTERN	08	66	40
TURNOUT INSTALLATION IN HO	07	50	44
TURNOUT SPLIT SWITCH PREVENTION	06	36	150
TURNOUT TEMPLATES	03	57	19
TURNOUT TROUBLES	09	45	353
TURNOUTS ABC'S OF RAILROADING	09	68	57
TURNOUTS AND CROSSINGS	09	48	630
TURNOUTS ARE EASY TO BUILD BOOMER PETE	08	40	429
TURNOUTS BASIC UNDERSTAND/TROUBLESHOOT	10	80	107
TURNOUTS BY THE DOZEN BUILT UP FGOM JIGS	07	72	46
TURNOUTS CONSTRUCTION ON PILLAR TO POST	07	48	476
TURNOUTS DIMENSIONS FOR SWITCHES CHART	07	72	48
TURNOUTS DOUBLE SLIP TYPE CONSTRUCTION 1	09	53	62
TURNOUTS DOUBLE SLIP TYPE CONSTRUCTION 2	10	53	64
TURNOUTS FOR BEGINNERS	05	41	243
TURNOUTS FOR DUAL GAUGE	08	46	499
TURNOUTS JIG MADE EPOXY MOUNTED	03	73	36
TURNOUTS OF CODE 70 NIAG RAIL CONSTRUCT	04	61	32
TURNOUTS SMALL	04	46	243
TURNOUTS SPRING SWITCH TYPE	11	48	820
TURNOUTS SPRING SWITCH TYPE.	05	46	337
TURNOUTS STUB SWITCH TYPE	10	65	24
TURNOUTS STUB TYPE FROM RTR TURNOUTS	09	61	32
TURNTABLE DRIVE MECHANISM	06	70	74
TURNTABLE INDEXING	10	69	87
ULTRARELIABLE HAND LAID TURNOUTS	03	77	68
UNCOUPLING RAMP THAT IS MOVEABLE	08	73	58
UNIFORM ROADBED SECTIONS BY THE MILE	06	75	64
WHAT RAIL IS BEST?	02	48	114
WIRING A DOUBLE CROSSOVER	09	70	75
WIRING A DOUBLE SLIP SWITCH	01	69	92
WIRING A DOUBLE TRACK CROSSING	04	78	139
WIRING CROSSINGS	02	74	84
WIRING HAND LAID CROSSINGS	07	82	131
WIRING SHINOHARA 3 WAY TURNOUTS	04	78	136
WIRING SWITCH MACHINES	08	78	121
ZERO DERAILMENTS ABC'S OF MODEL RRING	12	76	88

MODEL LAYOUTS

SCENERY

Title	M	Y	P
A USE FOR HALF A CAR	01	37	10
AIDS FOR S SCALE MEN	11	61	55
ALCOHOL DYES FOR WOOD	07	71	69
ANOTHER LOOK AT LICHEN	11	74	87
APTAKISIC LIFT OUT TOWN	09	72	41
ART OF USING MIRRORS	12	81	109
ATTENTION TO DETAILS	12	46	838
BACKDROP COLLAGE	10	75	66
BACKDROP PAINTING	04	77	116
BACKDROPS	11	40	591
BACKDROPS CREATE YOUR OWN	07	85	71
BAG & BAGGAGE CONSTRUCTION	04	47	276
BALSAWOOD CLIFFS TO HIDE SWITCH MACHINES	06	63	49
BARREL MAKING IN A MINUTE	06	50	15
BELOW TRACK SCENERY ON TABLE TOP LAYOUT	08	65	47
BILLBOARD CONSTRUCTION	03	47	208
BILLBOARD CONSTRUCTION.	10	55	31
BILLBOARD FENCE $1	11	64	33
BILLBOARD SIGN CUTOUTS	02	80	110
BILLBOARDS FROM MATCHBOOK COVERS	09	74	52
BLACK LIGHTS FOR LAYOUTS	07	51	26
BLENDING AND ISOLATION OF SCENERY	11	49	18
BLENDING FOREGROUND AND BACKGROUND	10	60	29
BLUEPRINT FOR RAILROAD SCENIC DESIGN	08	49	10
BUILD J&SW ADDING COLOR	10	82	100
BUILD J&SW BACKDROPS & WIDE OPEN SPACES	01	83	78
BUILD J&SW TERRAIN HARDSHELL & ROCKS	08	82	67
BUILD SJC SCENERY--ACRES OF ROCK W/FOAM	04	84	56
BUILD W&SF BASIC SCENERY & TERRAIN	02	83	107
BUILD W&SF WASHITA CANYON CONSTRUCTION	08	84	58
BUILDING ANIMALS FROM CARDSTOCK & FILLER	03	68	70
BUILDING SCENIC FORMS	09	82	70
BUSHES FOR YOUR LAYOUT	07	84	62
CAMPFIRE THAT BURNS MODELING	03	85	88
CEDAR SHINGLES FOR ROOFS	11	69	68
CEILING TILE ROCKS	04	81	66
CELOTEX INSULATING CEMENT SCENERY	09	60	52
CHANGE SCENERY-REPLACE ROCK WITH TRESTLE	03	80	100
CLIFFSIDE RAILROAD SCENE CONSTRUCTION	06	61	28
COLORING YOUR LANDSCAPE	02	51	36
COMMON SIGNS FOR YOUR RIGHT OF WAY	02	75	44
CONCEALING COLUMNS	04	50	44
CONCEALING COLUMNS	07	69	28
CONCEALING COLUMNS AS INDUSTRIES	01	49	40
CONCEALING CORNERS	01	43	16
CONCEALING CORNERS.	07	58	51
CONTINOUS GRAVEL PIT LOADING OPERATION	01	64	41
CORRUGATED SIDING BY THE TON	11	85	80
COUNTRY ROAD CONSTRUCTION	03	48	168
COURTHOUSE LANDSCAPING	04	49	13
CREATING LIFE LIKE TREES	02	50	22
CULVERT CONSTRUCTION	09	53	20
CULVERTS IN A MINUTE	11	50	24
CULVERTS OF ROCK CONSTRUCTION	08	54	48
CUSTOM BUILT TUNNEL PORTALS	11	57	36

SCENERY

Title	M	Y	P
CUTS AND FILLS BOOMER PETE	01	41	34
CUTS, ROCK CUTS, AND FILLS	02	54	34
DIORAMA SCENERY TECHNIQUES	12	40	657
DIORAMAS SMALL DISPLAY OR WHOLE LAYOUT	08	38	333
DRAINAGE SYSTEMS & SPANNING THEM SP	10	61	26
DRESSING STORE WINDOWS	02	50	44
DROP-IN SCENERY EASIER AND MAYBE BETTER	04	70	48
EASILY MADE STREET LIGHTS	12	62	73
FARM MODELING	10	66	62
FARM MODELING-MORE OL' RAY	11	66	69
FELT GRASS AND WEEDS	01	82	118
FENCES ADD INTEREST	02	47	118
FENCES FOR THE RIGHT OF WAY	10	43	449
FIGURES DRESS THEM FOR VARIOUS PERIODS	10	59	28
FIGURES-PLAY LIFE INTO YOUR LAYOUT	09	46	558
FULLY AUTOMATIC TURNTABLE CONSTRUCTION	03	80	94
FURNACE FILTER CONIFER FORESTS	04	80	96
GATES AT CROSSINGS IN AN EVENING	03	45	110
GOOD LOOKING HIGHWAYS	11	43	496
GRADE CROSSING SURFACES IN A MINUTE	02	49	24
GRADE CROSSINGS	02	48	100
HARD SHELL SCENERY	03	65	22
HARD SHELL TERRAIN	05	72	36
HIGHWAY CROSSING MODELING	01	53	48
HILLS REALISTIC	04	41	185
HINTS ON PLANNING SCENERY	08	43	355
HOW ABOUT A LAKE	12	48	912
HOW TO MAKE NEAT SIGNS	08	73	43
HOW TO MAKE TREES	04	47	276
HOW TO PROCESS LICHEN FOR COLOR	01	60	38
HOW TO RAISE A FOREST	04	43	166
INSTANT SCENERY FROM A CAN	01	80	102
IVY FOR BUILDING SIDES	01	76	74
KITTY LITTER SCENERY	03	76	48
LAKES OF REAL WATER	03	49	35
LAMINATED STYROFOAM SCENERY	09	59	34
LANDSCAPING FOR BEGINNERS	01	49	25
LARGE PINE TREE SOURCES	01	85	114
LET'S MAKE A POND	01	68	43
LIFT OUT SCENERY	03	53	33
LIFT OUT SCENERY FOR ACCESS	04	57	58
LITTER AROUND BUILDINGS ADDS REALISM	10	70	36
LOGGING INCLINE CONSTRCUTION	04	65	22
MAKE BETTER TREES FROM BOUGHT ONES	01	73	64
MAKE YOUR OWN CHIMNEYS SMOKE	10	49	24
MAKE YOUR OWN SALE FIGURES	02	65	26
MAKING MINIATURE FIGURES JOHN ALLEN	09	49	18
MAKING SMALL GAUGE PEOPLE FROM STRING	07	36	200
MAKING TREES	11	48	826
MARVELEOUS MOSS	06	73	67
MIN MIRROR SCENERY CONSTRUCTION	12	85	100
MINIATURE FIGURE CONSTRUCTION	08	55	25
MINIMIZING MONOTONY WITH SCENERY	06	64	30
MODEL CULVERTS OF MANY STYLES CONSTRUCT	04	39	193
MODEL MANURE HOW TO MAKE IT	10	80	158

MODEL LAYOUTS

SCENERY

Title	M	Y	P
MODEL SCENERY PLANNING	10	41	509
MODEL THE GROUND-AVOID GULF COURSE LOOK	06	80	70
MODELING AN INDUSTRY THAT ISN'T THERE	07	80	107
MODELING FURLOWS SLOUGH(BEGINNING WATER)	03	81	94
MODELING GREAT AMERICAN DESERTS	12	83	111
MODELING MOUNTAINS	12	78	182
MODELING NIAGARA EXCARPMENT ROCK FORMATI	12	80	118
MODELING TEXTURES WITH SANDPAPER	06	61	50
MODELING TREES OF ALL KINDS	07	72	72
MODELING WATER EPOXY BASICS	03	82	98
MODELING WATER ON J&SW	02	83	69
MODELING WATER W/ACRYLIC GLOSS MEDIUM	01	84	152
MODELING WITH FIBER OPTICS	04	73	52
MOLDING HUMAN FIGURES	02	47	100
MOUNT ALEXANDER CONSTRUCTION JOHN ALLEN	12	49	22
MOUNTAINS SIMPLE & INEXPENSIVE	05	42	241
MOUNTAINS SIMPLE CONSTRUCTION	05	34	11
MOVABLE MOUNTAINSIDE FOR TUNNEL ACCESS	09	65	27
MOVING CARS ON MODEL RAILROADS	07	71	73
MOVING MOUNTAINS ROCK FORMING	09	80	64
NEW USES FOR OLD RAILS	05	59	46
NEW WAY OF OBTAINING SCENIC EFFECTS	02	35	47
ORNAMENTAL STATION LIGHTS CONSTRUCTION	09	53	70
PALM TREE CONSTRUCTION $1	12	68	46
PALM TREES REVISITED $1	08	75	44
PAPER TOWEL SCENERY PAPER-MACHE	07	52	35
PEOPLE FOR THE PH&C	11	63	40
PERSPECTIVE AND COLOR IN MODELS	10	47	790
PERSPECTIVE CORNERED FOR DISTANT ILLUSIO	12	44	544
PINE BARK SCENERY	10	76	54
PINE FOREST QUICK & INEXPENSIVE	08	85	80
PINE TREE MODELING	05	58	32
PLANNING FOR SCENERY	06	38	237
PLANNING YOUR RAILSCAPE	09	48	619
PLASTER AND DRY COLOR	01	57	62
PLASTER GAUZE SCENERY	11	80	114
PLASTIC LAKES & STREAMS	11	51	8
PLOWED FIELDS AND SUCH	12	45	530
POWER OPERATED SUN AUTOMATIC DAYLIGHT	12	48	938
PRISMOIDAL FORMS SIMPLIFY SCENERY	07	74	73
PUT YOUR FIGURES TO WORK	07	57	50
RAILRACK CONSTRUCTION	09	49	13
RAILROAD SIGNS	11	56	19
REALISM IN THE LITTLE THINGS OF SCENERY	10	60	40
REALISTIC SCENERY	08	42	362
REDUCED DEPTH MODELING	02	70	76
RETAINING WALLS IN A MINUTE	06	49	11
RIGHT OF WAY DETAILING	04	74	36
RIGHT OF WAY SIGNS	10	48	720
RIVER BANKS	12	43	548
RIVERS MODELING A LARGE RIVER	10	53	33
RIVERS SMALL STREAMS	09	53	18
RIVERS-REALISTIC	04	41	185
ROADS & HIGHWAYS MODELING	11	53	46
ROADS & HIGHWAYS ON YOUR LAYOUT	12	75	84

SCENERY

Title	M	Y	P
ROADS AND GRADE CROSSING CONSTRUCTION	09	80	70
ROCK CASTING TECHNIQUES FROM MUSEUM	01	61	57
ROCK CASTING WITH RUBBER MOLDS	05	67	32
ROCK COLORING	10	68	72
ROCK MOLDS FROM PLASTIC WORMS	07	83	84
ROCK OUTCROPPINGS	03	45	112
ROCK WALL CASTING IN HOME MADE PANS	03	76	65
ROCK-FILL CRIB WALL CONSTRUCTION	02	85	98
ROCKS AND HOW TO FOIL THEM	08	67	24
ROCKS HOW TO DETAIL THEM	12	59	35
ROOT TREES FOR SCENIC VARIETY	08	84	94
ROWBOATS SCRATCHBUILD THEM	03	85	104
RUBBER ROCKS-WIRE WEEDS & OTHER TIPS	12	85	156
RUFF HILL ON MA&PA THE HARD SHELL WAY	03	65	38
RUSHING WATER CONSTRUCTION-TURBULENCE	12	85	112
SAGUARO CACTUS CONSTRUCTION	02	57	29
SAND TABLE LAYOUTS	12	36	367
SANDSTONE CLIFF SCENERY	05	43	229
SCALE TREES	08	52	57
SCENERY	04	38	137
SCENERY	10	55	59
SCENERY AND FOLIAGE TEXTURING	09	74	56
SCENERY AT PIT RIVER SP BRIDGE	04	62	20
SCENERY DETAILS ALONG THE NYC	08	39	393
SCENERY FUNDAMENTALS	12	50	12
SCENERY IMPROVEMENTS ON PILLAR TO POST	06	48	408
SCENERY ON CANANDAIGUA & SOUTHERN	03	71	61
SCENERY ON RIGHT OF WAY B&O	06	40	318
SCENERY PERSPECTIVE OL' RAY	04	67	62
SCENERY PROFILES HELP LAYOUT	10	81	68
SCENERY TECHNIQUES ON THE NY&Q	05	69	36
SCENERY WITHOUT TALENT	02	64	44
SCENIC BACKGROUNDS 20 MILES IN 1/8 INCH	03	48	176
SCENIC ILLUSIONS(DOUBLE LAYOUT FOR $1)	08	67	38
SCENIC KINKS-IMPROVING APPEARANCES	10	38	420
SCRAP RAIL USES ON A LAYOUT & ROAD	10	71	65
SIDEWALKS-PATHWAYS TO DETAIL	05	85	104
SIGNAL DETAILS FOR THE RIGHT OF WAY	06	75	66
SIGNS AND POSTER CONSTRUCTION	06	37	206
SIGNS FOR FLANGER	11	39	586
SIGNS FOR ROADSIDES	12	53	34
SIGNS FOR THE LAYOUT HIGHWAY-BILLBOARD	12	72	62
SIGNS FOR TRACKSIDE	11	76	110
SIGNS FROM CATALOGS & OTHER SOURCES	12	72	63
SIGNS OF THE TIMES BILLBOARDS	06	50	30
SIMULATING CHAIN LINK FENCE FOR "N"	04	78	139
SIMULATING MORTAR JOINTS	12	78	183
SKY BACKDROP CONSTRUCTION	12	56	62
SMALL CULVERT CONSTRUCTION IN A MINUTE	08	48	541
SMOKEY BEAR POSTERS	10	85	88
SNOW AT CONDOR PASS CONSTRUCTION	12	84	136
SNOW FENCES	11	39	586
SNOW ON WINTER PARK MODEL RAILROAD	01	80	116
SNOWSHED CONSTRUCTION	05	39	262
STAGE SET SCENERY	12	38	519

MODEL LAYOUTS

SCENERY

	M	Y	P
STANDARD CONCRETE CULVERTS	11	63	55
STATION ACCESS-SEMAPHORE/EXPRESS WAGONS	11	38	464
STATUES AND MONUMENTS FOR PARKS	11	75	82
STEP BY STEP BACKDROP PAINTING	02	82	93
STREET SCENERY	08	41	408
STRUCTURES WITH A PURPOSE	12	55	54
STYROFOAM MOUNTAINS	03	84	88
STYROFOAM SCENERY LIGHTS-STRONG-EASY	01	65	56
SUDDEN SCENERY	03	66	29
SUDDEN SCENERY 5' X 8' IN TWO NIGHTS	08	71	49
SUMMIT SCENERY ON NEB&W	03	84	100
TALL PRAIRIE GRASS MODELING	03	85	62
TECHNIQUE FOR DISGUISE TWO TIER TRACK	12	71	49
TELEGRAPH POLES DON'T FORGET 'EM	08	53	44
TELEPHONE POLL CONSTRUCTION IN A MINUTE	09	48	603
THREE DIMENSIONAL POND CONSTRUCTION	04	58	26
TIMBER-R-R-R LOGS & STUMPS	05	64	26
TIPS ON MAKING REALISTIC BACKDROPS	08	52	36
TOWN OR CITY BACKDROPS	10	42	448
TRADEMARKED CRATES ON CARS & PLATFORMS	12	54	69
TREATMENT OF SCENERY COLOR/ILLUMINATION	02	49	31
TREE BUILDING WITH PICTURE WIRE $1	01	74	44
TREE STUMPS OF RUBBER	04	70	33
TREE TRUNKS AND STUMP CONSTRUCTION	09	57	26
TREES AND SHRUBS	12	56	44
TREES AND TERRAIN	04	55	23
TREES FOR YOUR LAYOUT	11	44	484
TREES FROM RUBBERIZED WOOL IN A MINUTE $1	05	68	51
TREES MAKING THEM MORE REALISTIC	02	65	58
TREES OF LICORICE ROOTS	08	69	34
TREES SORGHUM TYPE	08	72	61
TREES YOU NEED THOUSANDS	08	73	33
TREES-REALISTIC	04	41	185
TUNNEL LININGS OF FOIL MOLDED ROCK	11	69	45
TUNNEL PORTALS	06	46	380
TUNNEL PORTALS 1	04	54	27
TUNNEL PORTALS 2	05	54	24
TUNNEL PORTALS CONSTRUCTION	05	39	243
TUNNELS PREFABRICATED	10	48	746
TURNING PLASTER INTO SCENERY	01	51	12
TURNPIKE TO NOWHERE	12	63	48
URBAN SCENERY OF SEVERNA INDUSTRIAL PARK	12	75	54
VEGETATION IN MINIATURE	03	51	16
WATER AND HOW TO MODEL IT	10	85	78
WATERFALLS AND HOW TO BUILD THEM $1	12	75	81
WATERFALLS FOR A DOLLAR $1	07	73	43
WATERFALLS MADE AS EASY AS ABC	02	43	62
WATERFRONT SCENERY	10	54	36
WATERWAYS, WATER SURFACES AND WAVES	12	76	86
WEEDS GROWN ON WLC	09	64	28
WHEAT FIELDS-BELLY ACRES	02	45	60
WHITE WATER SIMULATION	08	80	55
WINTER ON GINGER CREEK	12	83	87
WRECK SCENE FOR YOUR PIKE	04	50	36
ZAP TEXTURING FOR FOLIAGE	09	80	90

SCENERY

	M	Y	P
ZAP TEXTURING FOR FOLIAGE ADDENDUM	03	81	28
ZIP TEXTURING LOOKS FINE!	04	65	25
ZIP TEXTURING TECHNIQUES	02	67	48

LAYOUT OPERATION

	M	Y	P
ALL IN THE CARDS OPERATION	01	65	52
AUTOMATIC RAILROAD	02	48	95
AXMINSTER & POTOMAC OPERATION	02	52	26
BRIDGE TRAFFIC CAN BE FUN	05	77	84
BUILD E&O EQUIPMENT AND OPERATION	04	67	48
BUILD SJC OPERATION	08	84	98
BUILD SPRR OPERATIONS	06	66	42
CAR CARDS AND WAYBILLS	08	60	26
CAR DISTRIBUTION REALISTIC TRAFFIC GENER	02	60	33
CARD ORDER OPERATION SYSTEM	12	52	48
CARD ORDER SYSTEM OF OPERATION	09	58	22
CARD ORDERS SIMPLIFIED	02	77	86
CARD SYSTEM OF OPERATION THE LAST WORD	12	61	52
CARD SYSTEM OF OPERATION VICTORIA NORTHE	05	58	50
CARGO OPERATIONS	03	74	66
CENTRALIZED TRAFFIC CONTROL CENTER	01	84	186
CLOCKS AND TIMING IN OPERATION	03	66	26
CLOCKS AND TIMING WHY USE SCALE TIME?	06	66	22
CLUB OPERATION & OPERATION BOOMER PETE	01	40	6
COAL DOCK OPERATIONS N. OHIO BELT LINE	10	79	75
COLOR CODED ROUTING ON THE PUTENTAKE	10	48	702
COLOR CODED TACK CAR FORWARDING REFINEMN	07	72	41
COLOR CODED TACKS OPERATION	07	65	20
CONCEPT MAKES THE RAILROAD GO	02	60	30
CONSIDER WAY FREIGHT OPERATION	11	68	60
CRYSTAL RIVER SOUTHERN OPERATION	08	68	36
DIGIT SYSTEM OF OPERATION	05	64	32
DIGITAL FAST TIME CLOCK THOMSEN	11	74	82
DIRECTING FREIGHT TRAFFIC	08	38	342
DISPATCHING & SCHEDULING ROLLING STOCK	07	62	48
DISPATCHING ROLLING STOCK SUNSET VALLEY	11	75	72
DIVISION POINTS ON SHORT LINES OPERATION	01	57	52
DIVISION POINTS OPERATION	11	52	32
DIVISION POINTS SWITCHING OPERATIONS	02	63	49
DOCK RAILWAY OPERATION	02	73	56
DOVER FOXCRAFT & CARLISLE OPEARTION	03	65	46
DROP THAT SLEEPER CAR	04	48	250
FAST FREIGHT OPERATIONS	12	49	16
FAST TIME CLOCKS	11	55	53
FLYING SWITCH OPERATIONS	01	74	42
GIVE THE YARDMASTER A BREAK	09	78	126
GSV PLANNED FOR OPERATION	08	72	41
HOW "PASS THE BUCK" SYSTEM WORKS	01	40	21
HOW TO DESIGN A TIMETABLE	07	58	28
HUMP YARD OPERATION	02	50	14
ITS MORE THAN HORSEPOWER	11	78	135
JERSEY EASTERN SWITCHING OPERATIONS	11	84	104
KEEPING TRACK	02	78	118

MODEL LAYOUTS

LAYOUT OPERATION	M	Y	P
LIMITED OPERATION	03	78	108
LOADED & EMPTY FREIGHT CAR MOVEMENTS	08	63	27
LUMBER ROAD OPERATION	08	66	20
MAIN LINE TRAIN MOVEMENTS	10	61	54
MODEL RAILROAD OPERATING BOOMER PETE	09	38	361
MORE OPERATIONS ON SUNSET VALLEY	01	73	56
MOVING ORE ON SIERRA PINTADA	06	66	42
MY LAYOUT SAGLE	02	41	96
NO PRIORITIES NEEDED BOOMER PETE	12	41	626
ON CAR WAYBILLS FOR OPERATION	11	75	86
OPERATING A SMALL LAYOUT	07	78	54
OPERATING ALTURAS & LONE PINE	02	83	72
OPERATING LINGO	01	64	70
OPERATING NIGHT ON A CLUB ROAD	09	36	258
OPERATING NIGHT ON MR&T	03	85	76
OPERATING ON ALTURAS AND LONE PIKE	09	66	22
OPERATING THE ALLEGHENY & LAKE ERIE	09	52	16
OPERATING THE CERRO AZUL	11	51	40
OPERATING THE GULF MIDLAND	07	51	24
OPERATING THE LINNVILLE & WESTERN SMALL	04	51	42
OPERATING THE MODEL RAILROAD	01	39	3
OPERATING THE SILVER FALLS & KLAMATH	08	51	38
OPERATING YOUR MODEL RAILROAD	11	75	45
OPERATION CAN BE REALISTIC TOO	03	35	59
OPERATION IN "OO"	08	61	44
OPERATION KEY TO AUTHENIC RAILROADING	10	57	24
OPERATION OF CANANDAIGUA & SOUTHERN	03	71	61
OPERATION OF ROYAL GEORGE	05	73	63
OPERATION ON ALAGASH & PENOBSCOT	03	51	34
OPERATION ON COLRAIN VALLEY	11	77	58
OPERATION ON S&LS AFTER 20 YEARS	08	80	62
OPERATION ON TEXAS & RIO GRANDE WESTERN1	12	58	32
OPERATION ON TEXAS & RIO GRANDE WESTERN2	01	59	86
OPERATION ON THE DELAWARE	12	62	38
OPERATION ON WINCHESTER VALLEY	01	51	38
OPERATION PROS & CONS	01	80	136
OPERATION UNLIMITED	12	60	55
OPERATIONS AT FILLMORE ENGINE FACILITY	11	77	90
OPERATIONS ON CLINCHFIELD	07	79	72
OPERATIONS ON MA&PA	11	65	54
OPERATIONS ON SUNSET VALLEY	06	70	36
OPERATIONS ON THE GUM STUMP AND SNOWSHOE	04	66	32
OPERATIONS UUNLIMITED	06	62	44
PASSENGER TERMINAL OPERATION	11	74	66
PASSENGER TRAIN OPERATION	06	51	8
POINT TO POINT OPERATION	10	52	26
ROUTE SWITCHING OPERATIONS	03	50	24
RUNNING THE CLUB PIKE BOOMER PETE	02	40	87
RUNNING THE MIDLAND BOOMER PETE	05	40	264
SANTE FE CENTRAL OPERATIONS	03	68	35
SCALE SPEED COMPUTATION & NOMOGRAPH	11	49	52
SCALE SPEED OPERATION	08	53	45
SCALE SPEED TABLE	06	44	257
SCALE TIME	07	35	173
SCHEDULING FROM SCRATCH	12	64	54
SHIFT TIME OPERATION	04	83	88
SHORT LINE MIXED TRAIN OPERATIONS	02	55	52
SHORT LINE RAILROADING	05	51	8
SMALL TIMETABLE OPERATION	05	55	43
STANDARD TIME FAST CLOCK CONSTRUCTION	02	60	38
SUNSET VALLEY OPERATIONS	11	79	118
SWITCHING AROUND A DERAILMENT AT LEADHIL	01	80	134
SWITCHING BLACKHOLE MINE	12	78	72
SWITCHING PROBLEM	10	78	92
SWITCHING SECRETS FOR SIMPLIFICATION	06	63	54
SWITCHING WYE PROBLEM	03	80	116
TAB ON CAR OPERATION	12	81	84
TAB SYSTEM OF FREIGHT CAR FORWARDING	02	75	67
TELEPHONES FOR YOUR RAILROAD	07	59	26
TIMECARDS FOR YOUT LAYOUT	02	48	123
TIMETABLE OPERATION	03	35	63
TIMETABLE OPERATION CLUB PIKE	02	40	87
TIMING CLOCKS	10	64	34
TRAFFIC GENERATION OPERATION	11	77	108
TRAIN MAKEUP AND SWITCHING BOOMER PETE	10	40	562
TRAIN ORDER DISPATCHING	04	61	36
TRAIN ORDERS & TIMETABLES	08	35	208
TRAIN SPEED	08	52	63
WASTE TIME & MONEY RAILROAD	08	35	215
WATERFRONT INDUSTRIAL LAYOUT OPERATION	06	57	34
WAY FREIGHT OPERATION	02	50	28
WAY FREIGHT SWITCHING OPERATION B. PETE	12	48	929
WAY FREIGHT SWITCHING OPERATION W. AGONY	07	60	22
WAY TRAFFIC ON YAMPA VALLEY RAILROAD	10	77	114
WELL PLANNED LAYOUTS	07	48	486
WESTCHESTER CLUB PHILLIPS	09	39	433
WHEEL REPORTS FOR EASY OPERATION	05	84	102
YARD HOPPING ON GLENCOE SKOKIE	07	59	22
YARD OPERATION AT WESTPORT	09	83	116
YARD SWITCHING PROTOTYPE STYLE	07	61	38

MODEL LAYOUTS

LAYOUT VISITS		M	Y	P
150 X 40 "HO" RAILROAD		07	72	56
1908 AKSARBEN NO 2 GAUGE DISPLAY		09	74	64
2" FINE SCALE DIORAMA	BROWN	08	69	48
2000 FEET OF TRACK "O"	TOLSTEAD	01	38	15
3RD TRY RAILROAD "HO"	L'HEUREUX	12	66	58
45 YEARS ON TOLUCA LINES "O"	TAYLOE	03	73	39
50' ANNIVERSARY MR GOODWILL TOUR		01	84	100
A "FINISHED" LAYOUT "HO"	THOMAS	12	74	64
A DAY AT SHOES MEADOWS "HON3"	OLSON	05	76	54
A TASTE OF 1/48	LARSON	12	73	62
ABERFOYLE JUNCTION "O"	DUBREY	03	79	66
ABERJONA VALLEY "O"	BLACKBURN	11	77	99
ABERJONA VALLEY RAILROAD "O"	BLACKBURN	10	43	438
ABERJONA VALLEY RAILROAD "O"	BLACKBURN	12	50	20
ACORN & GREAT OAK RAILROAD		05	53	49
ACROSS THE CONTINENT IN 1885	WELCH	06	60	22
AE&N RAILROAD "O"	TOLSTEAD	08	55	16
AE&N VISIT "17/64"	TOLSTEAD	01	43	28
AHWAHNEE WESTERN "3 1/4"	HORNER	02	34	9
AHWAHNEE WESTERN LIVE STEAM ABANDONED		10	35	264
AL SCHUTZ'S LAYOUT "O" B. PETE	SCHUTZ	01	45	18
ALBERTA PACIFIC "N"	PAULL	03	76	52
ALHAMBRA & LILLIPUTIA "HO"	WALD	05	73	56
ALLEGHENY & OHIO "HO"	HEDIGER	07	75	67
ALLEGHENY ROUTE "O"	RAY	06	37	201
ALLEGHENY VALLEY "HO" PITTSBURGH RR CLUB		03	50	12
ALONG THE WOOD ACRES ROUTE	HOUGHTON	12	40	662
ALPENA & HARWOOD WESTERN RAILROAD	MORSE	01	53	45
ALTURAS & LONE PINE	TOWERS	12	62	74
ALTURAS & LONE PINE "HO"	TOWERS	01	83	67
AMERICAN CENTRAL "1/4"	STOVICEK	02	72	42
ANOTHER WORLDS FAIR LAYOUT "O"		04	39	187
APARTMENT DWELLERS RAILROAD	GRUTSCH	04	74	66
APARTMENT NARROW GAUGE LINE "HO"	JOHNSON	06	77	84
APPACAHIAN SOUTHERN "HO"	ARMSTRONG	06	82	93
ARCADE & ATTICA		09	79	79
ARCADIA TERMINAL STREET & DOCK HO	LAIER	12	77	76
ARIZONA-NEVADA & WEST PACAIFIC	RICHARDSO	01	59	33
ASHDOWN FOREST RY BRITISH "O"	RICHARDS	06	58	22
ATLANTIC & WESTERN "HO/HON3"	SHOUP	06	85	56
ATSF ARGENTINE DIV "HO"	HITCHCOCK	12	83	72
ATSF HO DIVISION "HO"	BARWIN	05	56	20
ATSF SILSBEE DISTRICT "N"	WELBORN	06	84	102
ATTIC & PACIFIC "O"	ASHLEY	12	46	834
ATTIC TRACK PLN FOR HE WHO WANTS EVERTHI		05	61	49
AUSTRALIIAN O SCALE PIKE	WATSON	09	47	722
B&M BRANCH LINE	CHESEBROUGH	11	61	45
B&O VISIT "O"	SAGLE	10	45	400
BACK YARD RAILROAD	STOMP	05	53	40
BALTIMORE & OHIO VALLEY RR "O"	ALEXANDER	03	39	123
BALWYN PACIFIC "O"	LOWRY	12	45	540
BATHROOM CENTRAL	HUDSON	09	78	99
BAY CITY SOUTHERN	HOINSKA	10	78	70
BAY FIELD & IRON RIVER RAILWAY		07	59	50
BAY LINE SIMPLE EFFECTIVE LAYOUT "O"		07	35	173
BAY POINT & CLAYTON VALLEY "HO"	HARTLEY	08	73	48
BAY SHORE ELECTRIC "O"	CUTHBERT	09	48	600
BAY SHORE ELECTRIC "O"	CUTHBERT	06	59	22
BAY SHORE ELECTRIC RAILROAD "O"	CUTHBERT	01	45	6
BAY STATE WESTERN RAILROAD "O"	CLUB	01	40	18
BC&E "TT"	SCHWARTZ	11	51	17
BELLEFONTE & SNOWSHOE	YUNGKOTRTH	09	63	51
BELLEVUE & CASCADE "HON3"	LEE	05	83	72
BELMONT SHORE LINES BELMONT SHORE CLUB		03	78	58
BEMIS STREET RAILWAY "HO"	CLARK	11	70	70
BENTON GALENA & SLAG HILL	RESCHENBERG	07	57	36
BERKELEY & LINCOLN RAILROAD "O"	WILHELM	07	37	237
BERN & WAGONLIT RAILROAD "Z"	MCKEE	12	82	82
BERRYVILLE & SUMMIT POINT RY	ODEGARD	10	57	49
BIG ROUNDHOUSE-BIG YARD "HO"	LANDESCO	02	57	50
BIGGEST RR IN FLORIDA NAT'L ENQUIRER		04	79	66
BIRTH OF HO	WESTCOTT	12	42	552
BLACK RIVER LINES	KANNA	09	78	60
BLIND MANS MODEL RAILROAD	FRANK	02	61	54
BLOCKING TRAINS ON YOUR LAYOUT		01	53	27
BLUE STAR PACIFIC "HO"	SUGIYAMA	11	74	88
BRADLEY, EPWORTH & SOUTHERN	MILLER	04	79	94
BRITIANS BEST 7MM		01	61	28
BRITISH LAYOUT "HO"	AHEARN	01	41	9
BRITISH MODEL RAILWAY SCENE	FREEZER	10	81	102
BROOKFIELD & WESTERN "HO" BOOMER PETE		04	40	202
BROOKLYN EAST RIVER TERMINAL "HO"	CREA	04	83	98
BTR RR UNCONVENTIONAL RR "HO"	CURRON	09	80	104
BUCKINGHAM BRANCH LINE "OO"	DENNY	04	66	38
BUCKLEY & ONARCA RAILROAD	BARON	12	66	48
BUD LINES "N"	PETTY	04	77	58
BUFFALO CENTRAL	RYAN	06	48	392
BUHL PLANETARIUM LAYOUT & VILLAGE BRIGHT		07	79	100
BUILDING A HO MODEL RAILROAD	TONNER	05	45	202
BUILT UP TRACK SECTION LAYOUT	PAGE	07	47	556
BULLFROG LOGGING COMPANY "HON3"	JOHNSTON	04	67	28
BURLINGTON NORTHERN		04	78	108
C&NW GALENA DIVISION "HO"	CERNY	03	83	98
C&O 21 YEARS OLD	GWINN	05	34	2
CA&D "HO"	FRYE	04	58	22
CABRIALES IN VENEZUELA PART 1 "O"	MILLER	04	36	92
CABRIALES IN VENEZUELA PART 2 "O"	MILLER	05	36	120
CACTUS GULCH "HO"	JOHNSON	12	52	24
CAJON PASS "HO"	ARMSTRONG	10	56	22
CALAPOOYA PACIFIC "HO/HON3"	GATES	05	81	54
CALIFORNIA CENTRAL RAILROAD "OO"	LYON	02	38	73
CAMBRIA & BLACK MOUNTAIN "O"	CHARLES	11	64	27
CANADIAN CENTRAL "O"	CROOKFORD	09	37	330
CANADIAN GREAT WESTERN "O"	CLUB	03	43	116
CANADIAN GREAT WESTERN "O" TORONTO CLUB		07	53	10
CANADIAN PACIFIC "HO"	GARDNER	01	80	110
CANADIAN PIKE "HO"	HESELTON	10	41	501
CARLSBAD, EAST PORTAL & ZENITH "N"		04	82	98
CAROLINA MIDLAND RY "HO"	ROBL	02	79	68
CARRABASSET & DEAD RIVER "HON2 1/2"		11	79	86

STEPHANS' RAILROAD DIRECTORY

MODEL LAYOUTS

LAYOUT VISITS

Layout	Name	M	Y	P
CARRABASSET & DEAD RIVER "HON2 1/2".		02	80	62
CARRIZO & NORTH GRAND "HO"	TOCQUIGNY	11	53	42
CARSON VALLEY & LOCK AVE RAILROAD	PARKS	09	78	120
CASCADE VALLEY "O"	MILLER	09	82	80
CAT MOUNTAIN & SANTA FE	SPERANDEO	03	80	62
CAT MOUNTAIN & SF REBUILT "HO"	BARROW	05	84	66
CECILE MINING COMPANY "ON3"	HAMILTON	10	79	66
CEMENT PLANT RAILROAD "HO"	MARATIN	06	52	14
CENTERVILLE CUTOFF TINPLATE "O"		05	50	35
CENTINELA VALLEY RAILROAD "O"	B. PETE	04	42	184
CENTRAL & ONTARIO "O"	BRUNGER	09	85	96
CENTRAL APPALACHIAN RAILWAY	LARSON	03	57	48
CENTRAL ATTICA "O"	GOEHST	11	38	467
CENTRAL ILLINOIS RAILROAD "O"	ANDERSON	07	42	338
CENTRAL INDIANA "HO"	BLACK	06	72	30
CENTRAL JERSEY "O"	EVANS	09	52	46
CENTRAL NEW ENGLAND RAILROAD "O"	BARR	07	35	174
CENTRAL TRACTON LINES "O"	SMALL	12	65	60
CENTRALIA & CHESTER	RESCHENBERG	07	58	37
CHANNEL RAILROAD LINE "O"	CLUB	11	41	578
CHATTANOOGA MODEL RAILROAD CLUB HO		10	77	91
CHELSEA & ACTION AIR LINE	WESTCOTT	11	68	56
CHESAPEAKE & ALLEGHENY "HO"	DOLKOS	06	73	34
CHESTER VALLEY OUTSTANDING LAYOUT	GEISSL	11	69	75
CHESTER VALLEY RAILROAD "O"	GEISSEL	08	39	383
CHICAGO SALT LAKE & PACIFIC "O"	MASON	05	37	175
CHILDRENS MUSEUM LIONEL LAYOUT "O"		03	81	103
CHINOOK UNION LINES "HO"	EVANS	04	42	164
CHITLIN VALLEY "HO"	MITCHELL	03	51	24
CIMARRON VALLEY "HO"	FRICK	10	63	60
CINCINNATI & WESTERN "O"	THORNBURGH	05	41	246
CIRCA THIRTY DIORAMA		09	75	52
CIRCUS TRAIN ON SUNSET VALLEY	CHUBB	01	72	57
CLIFTON & NORTHWESTERN		10	68	42
CLIFTON & SOUTHWESTERN	ODEGARD	10	68	43
CLIMAX FALLS II	O'CONNELL	08	78	86
CLINCHFIELD RAILROAD PROJECT HISTORY		11	78	154
CLOUSERS TERRIFIC TROLLEYS "O"	CLOUSER	03	62	36
CN CLOVERLEAF DIVISION "HO"	REGULA	04	63	106
COAST LINE ELECTRIC INTERURBAN "O"	CLUB	05	39	242
COBWEBS, DUST & ASHES "HO"	FRYE	03	77	57
COLORADO & CALIFORNIA SOUTHERN "HON3"		10	60	26
COLORADO & SOUTHWESTERN "HO"	DANNEMAN	12	80	95
COLORADO MIDLAND "HO"	PRICE	08	80	94
COLORADO MIDLAND "O"	BOOMER PETE	10	43	444
COLORADO WESTERN & GULF DUAL GUAGE	SMALL	09	59	53
COLRAIN VALLEY RAILROAD "HO"	SEFFIEBEN	11	77	58
COLUMBIA GLADE CREEK & WESTERN		04	58	48
COMPLETE TINPLATE LAYOUT "O"	REICHERT	10	36	298
CONNECTICUT MIDLAN "O"	HOUSE	01	46	18
CONNOTTON VALLEY & STRAITSVILLE "HON3"		07	81	50
CONOCIQUINET RAILWAYS "O"	GURLEY	05	64	51
CONTINELA VALLEY "O"	BOOMER PETE	08	47	620
CONVOLUTIONS & WESTERN "HO"	ARMSTRONG	07	52	26
CP IN MINIATURE "HO"	HOUGH	12	68	40

LAYOUT VISITS

Layout	Name	M	Y	P
CRAIGARD MODEL RAILROAD "O"	LANAL	08	34	2
CRANDIC "N"	LAWA	07	85	56
CRIPPLE CREEK & WESTERN "HO"	RANDALL	04	62	35
CROOKED MOUNTAIN LINES "O"	HEGGE	04	57	22
CROOKED MOUNTAIN LINES CLOSE UP "O"	HEGGE	12	76	94
CULVER MILITARY LAYOUT	SCHOOL	08	71	37
CUMBERLAND & OHIO	FRANCVIGLIA	01	78	54
CUMBERLAND & SUSQUEHANNA RR	MELLANDER	05	70	30
CUMBERLAND VALLEY SYSTEM "N"	REID	08	81	54
D&RG SAN JUAN EXTENSION "HON3"	DANNEMAN	05	85	58
D&RGW E. HARTFORD DIVISION	KALBFLEISCH	07	69	32
D&RGW PANORAMIC DIV "HO"	HOLTZ	04	82	62
D&RGW SECTIONAL LAYOUT	BENDER	04	78	92
D&S RAILROAD	MUELLER	02	78	90
DAYTON & WESTERN "1/4"	GORATH	08	73	60
DAYTON DULUTH & WESTERN "HO"	FINK	02	77	50
DAYTON FRANKLIN & HAMILTON "HO"	HETZEL	12	80	87
DELAWARE & LEHIGH "HO"	LUTZ	07	83	82
DELAWARE & WESTERN "S"	TITMAN	09	59	24
DELAWARE & WESTERN RAILROAD "O"	SMITH	11	40	598
DELTA LINES "O"	ELLISON	08	41	392
DELTA LINES "O"	ELLISON	11	55	26
DENVER & WESTERN "ON2 1/2"	NORTH	06	79	73
DENVER & WESTERN "S"	HEIMBURGER	06	81	80
DENVER MODEL RAILROAD CLUB "HO"		01	81	76
DENVER TERMINAL D&RGW	HOLTZ	08	85	62
DESERT LINES "O"	ANDES	11	66	44
DESTINATIONS UNLIMITED LAYOUT	WELCH	05	68	32
DETROIT UNDER WIRE "HO"	HEDIGER	09	75	58
DETROIT UNION RAILROAD "O"	CLUB	03	37	102
DETROIT UNION RAILROAD "O"	GOTTLIEB	04	43	175
DETROIT UNION RR "O" DETROIT MRR CLUB		05	36	119
DETROIT, LINVILLE & ASTERN "O"	GOTTLIEB	07	36	173
DEVILS GULCH "OO"	HECKMANN	01	68	36
DEW VALLEY RAILROAD "HO"	GREER	11	71	45
DIABLO VALLEY LINE "HO/O"	TOWERS	02	62	30
DIABLO VALLEY LINES "HO"	CLUB	03	84	58
DIAMOND VALLEY LINE "HO"	GILL	07	83	66
DIMINUTIVE & OBSTINATE RR "OO"	STOCK	04	34	1
DIRGE MOUNTAIN & ICHABOD RIVER "HO"	KRUSE	10	81	70
DISPLAY MODEL RAILROAD "O"	MEREDITH	06	34	5
DISPLAY RAILROAD "HO"	HOBBY SHOP	02	40	73
DOGHOUSE DIVISION OF SP	TOWERS	09	61	50
DOUBLE CROSSING RAILROAD	WEGNER	07	74	45
DOUGLASS PRIZE WINNING LAYOUTS		09	43	392
DOVER HILL WESTERN "HO"	VONDRAK	05	80	80
DOVER HILL WESTERN "HO"	VONDRAK	08	75	40
DOWNTOWN CHICAGO "HO"	PALMITER	08	81	82
DP&AP RAILROAD "TT"	HARDING	11	66	32
DRAGO & EAST RIDGE RAILWAY		01	61	51
DUAL GAUGE LAYOUT	WASH DC	02	48	104
DUNWOOD WESTERN LINES "O"	CLUB	07	34	5
DUQUESNE	DOLKOS	03	83	58
DURHAM & SOUTHERN "HO"	PAINE	04	69	28
DWARF LINES "E"	RITTER	07	35	180

MODEL LAYOUTS

LAYOUT VISITS

Title	Author	M	Y	P
E.L. MOORES LEGACY		02	80	102
EAST BAY GIANT CLUB "HO/O"	TOWERS	06	62	46
EAST HAVEN RAILROAD & WHARF	SAUNDERS	11	62	73
EAST SIDE "HO"	MOORE	08	58	20
EAST SKINNY "HO"	ROMANO	06	75	42
EAST TEXAS & BAYEUX JUNCTION "ON2"		12	82	94
EAST VALLEY LINES	TOWER	04	78	102
EASTERN LINES	WESTCHESTER CLUB	10	37	373
EASTERN LINES "O"	WESTCHESTER CLUB	01	47	17
EASTERN NEW JERSEY RAILROAD "HO"	CLUB	09	46	557
EASTERN RR ASSOCIATION "N"	GRAFF	12	62	110
EBT "HON3"	TAYLOR	10	83	108
EBT TRACK PLANS	LUTZ	12	71	53
EC&O VISIT "O"	STARK	09	43	400
ELIZABETH TERMINAL RR "O"	ROSENFIELD	10	45	407
EMPIRE IN HO BOOMER PETE	YATES	12	39	648
ENJ RAILROAD "HO"	BREIKORN	04	45	158
ENPORT, ROGUE RIVER & THATAWAY "N"		12	84	94
EPITHET CREEK RAILROAD & ITS TRACK PLAN		06	72	54
ERIE & EASTERN RAILROAD "O"	PHILLIPS	02	38	63
ERIE MAHINING DIVISION	SLAWSEER	11	78	100
ESPEE "O"	PHILLIPS	08	57	24
EXPANDABLE RAILROAD "HO"	BURTON	10	55	36
FALL RIVER LOGGING COMPANY "HO"	MILLER	10	64	46
FAROVIA RAPID TRANSIT		11	35	285
FAWRCARNEDD RR "OON3"	BRACKENBOROUGH	02	67	35
FEATHER RIVER ROUTE	ARMSTRONG	02	54	58
FERROEQUINOLOGY AT ICU COLLEGE LAYOUT		02	79	118
FH&Q RAILROAD "O"	QUARMBY	03	35	58
FITCHBURG & SOUTHBRIDGE "HO"	TYLICK	09	85	72
FIVE LAYOUTS OF DETROIT MODEL CLUB		09	74	44
FLORENCE & EDDIESVILLE "O"	HOHFIELD	01	50	20
FLYING HORSESHOE	ARMSTRONG	12	53	42
FOUR BY EIGHT LAYOUTS	ARMSTRONG	02	53	52
FOX RIVER GROVE RAILROAD "HO"	STASTNY	02	75	62
FRANKLIN EASTERN RAILROAD "O"	FISK	03	53	12
FREIGHT SERVICE LAYOUT "HO"	SANDERS	06	36	144
FROGVILLE, PUNKIN, CTR & WESTERN "O"		10	46	606
GAME ROOM RAILROAD	BORTHWICK	02	58	60
GENERIC RAILROAD "O"	MANWARREN	05	84	92
GENOA & EASTERN RIVER COUNTRY	ODEGARD	06	65	29
GERRITON & WESTERN	ROBINSON	01	80	78
GLIMPSES OF P&L "HO"	HITCHINS	12	49	64
GM&G	DAVIS	12	78	80
GM&O WESTERN DISTRICT		04	59	53
GN WISKEY RIVER DIV "HO"	O'ROURKE	12	82	84
GOLD COAST RAILROAD "HO"	RUSSELL	11	80	100
GOLDEN GATE FAIR LAYOUT "O" BOOMER PETE		05	39	231
GOLDEN VALLEY 1 "O" BOOMER PETE	SMITH	11	44	492
GOLDEN VALLEY 2 "O" BOOMER PETE	SMITH	12	44	538
GOLETA VALLEY LIVE STEAM	LEBECK	09	76	70
GOPHER GULCA & PINE RIDGE	CANNER	11	63	42
GORRE & DAPHETID "HO"	ALLEN	03	51	11
GORRE & DAPHETID "HO"	ALLEN	01	48	20
GORRE & DAPHETID "HO" RR DREAM J. ALLEN		12	81	66

LAYOUT VISITS

Title	Author	M	Y	P
GORRE & DAPHETID (NEW) "HO"	ALLEN	03	56	20
GORRE & DAPHETID BRIDGES	ALLEN	02	59	28
GORRE & DAPHETID PASSENGERS "HO"	ALLEN	01	69	46
GORRE & DAPHETID THE BEGINNING "HO"	ALLEN	09	61	33
GORRE & DEPHETIDS LATEST "HO"	ALLEN	06	57	36
GRAHAMSVILLE & PEEKAMOOSE "O"	WAKEFIELD	11	59	24
GRAND ISLAND CENTRAL TINPLATE "O"	WOOD	04	50	72
GRANGER DENROCK & SOUTHERN "HO"	BRAET	12	81	89
GRASSFLAT, POSSOMTROT & BUG TUSSEL "HO"		06	84	62
GREAT BYRON & WESTERN "HO"	WITTMUS	12	83	84
GREAT LAKES TRACTION "HO/O"	RECEIVES	09	62	49
GREAT NORTH ROAD "ON3 1/2"	JAQUIS	05	62	32
GREAT NORTHERN "HO"	NIXEN	06	76	52
GREAT NORTHERN PACIFIC "S"	BENNETT	02	85	62
GREAT SOUTHERN "O"	JOINER	06	80	60
GREAT SOUTHERN "O"	COLE	07	46	422
GREAT SOUTHERN RR MODEL CLUB ATLANTA		05	78	56
GREAT SOUTHERN REVISITED "O"	JOINER	06	83	58
GREAT WESTERN MODEL RAILROAD "1/4"	BELING	06	34	2
GREEN MOUNTAIN CENTRAL RAILROAD	SNYDER	05	59	50
GREENWICH VALLEY "HO"	HUBBELL	12	41	614
GREENWICH VALLEY SYSTEM "HO"	HUBBELL	06	40	311
GREY BURROW LINES	BAUSTERT	08	62	48
GRIZZLY FLATS RAILROAD 1 TO 1	KIMBALL	04	77	77
GROVE STREET & PACIFIC RR "HO"	SMITH	05	38	191
GTW DETROIT DIVISION "HO"	HEDIGER	03	74	36
GULCH ROUTE "O"	KALMBACH	01	36	7
H&H RAILROAD "O"	BROOK	12	35	325
HAMILTON & WESTERN RR "O"	CONROY	07	41	352
HAMILTON BAY CITY "HO"	LEE	10	68	45
HAMILTON CLUB "O"	TOVEE	05	47	388
HAPPY VALLEY RAILROAD "O"	RUSSELA	05	37	165
HARBOR VIEW TRACTION "HO"	BERTZ	07	58	38
HARDSCRABLLE "HON3"	ARMSTRONG	01	62	41
HARPERS FERRY VIGNETTE		08	52	30
HEAVENLY TRAINS DAILY "HO"	DAILY	12	65	38
HI RAIL PIKE "O"	SWAN	03	50	71
HIDEAWAY RAILROAD "HO"		11	48	850
HIGHLAND & WESTERN RAILROAD "HO"	WASHBURN	01	38	9
HISTORY OF GR LAKES TRACTION FACT/FICTN		09	62	49
HISTORY OF QUONSET & EAST DOUGLAS		05	78	89
HO RAILROAD THAT GREW MORE	SUKALAC	12	65	50
HOBBY LOBBY LAYOUT "HO"	WINDOLPH	08	82	90
HOLLOW TREE RAILROAD "HO"	THRASHER	11	43	480
HORSESHOE CURVE	ARMSTRONG	07	54	35
HORSESHOE CURVE "HO"	KENDALL	10	75	49
HOUSTON, EAT & WEST TEXAS "HO"		12	79	80
HUDSON VALLEY RAILROAD CLUB	EIGHMEY	08	38	340
HUFF 'N' PUFF RAILROAD "HO"	BLISS	10	51	16
HUNGRY HORSE TIMBER COMPANY	WESTCOTT	03	58	46
HUNTINGTON & HOUSATONIC "HO"	EVANS	07	71	32
I BUILD A RAILROAD "HO"	WAGNER	09	41	450
I BUILD MY PIKE FOR STRUCTURES "HO"		12	62	45
IDAHO MIDLAND "HO"	HICKLEY	05	69	28
IDAHO NORTHERN PART 1 "HO"	ZINN	01	77	92

MODEL LAYOUTS

LAYOUT VISITS

Title	Author	M	Y	P
ILLINOIS & WESTERN "O"	STERANT	12	43	533
INDIAN CREEK VALLEY RAILWAY "HO"	CLARK	12	85	76
INDUSTRIAL RAILROAD	BOGART	02	49	30
INDUSTRIAL NARROW GAUGE "HON2.5"	HAGER	07	65	44
INTERLAKE VULCANIAN "HO"	MARTIN	11	81	66
INTERLAKE VULCANIAN RAILWAY "HO"	MARTIN	10	72	44
INTERSTATE & WESTERN	ODEGARD	08	67	48
INTERSTATE LINES "O"	DENNETT	04	38	149
INTERURBAN IN NATURAL HABITAT		08	59	24
INTRODUCING THE ALLAGASH CARTEL	HANSON	01	78	62
IRONHEAD TIMBER COMPANY "HO"	CLARKE	10	85	60
ISLAND CENTRAL LINES "HO"	ALBERTSON	06	81	60
IT "JUST GROWED" "HO"	TRAUB	08	41	402
ITS BUILT WITH KITS	BARNETT	07	63	42
JAMESTOWN BOBSVILLE & TOMSBURG "O"		09	37	309
JASPER & KEYSTONE	KIBBEE	06	82	54
JERSEY CENTRAL "O"	CAROLINE	03	38	103
JERSEY COAST & WESTERN "O"	KING	06	49	9
JOAN WENTZ'S LAYOUT "O"		01	45	11
JUNCTION LAYOUT		01	36	14
JUNCTION LAYOUT	LARSON	04	55	50
JUSTIFYING TWO COMPANIES	FREEZER	05	64	44
KANSAS CITY SOUTHERN	HUNT	03	78	70
KANSAS MISSOURI & ARKANSAS "O"	WATT	12	36	366
KENILWORTH & WESTERN "O"	ALGER	01	50	60
KENT & SURREY RAILWAY	JAGGER	04	35	97
KIEWA VALLEY RAILROAD	BARNETT	12	57	44
KING KOLE MINING COMPANY "S"	TITMAN	02	71	50
KNEE HIGH CHESSIE "O"	BOLLINGER	08	53	16
LA GRANDE "HO"	SCOTT	04	85	104
LAKE EDITH RAILWAY LIVE STEAM IN CANADA		02	39	64
LAKE EDITH RAILWAY OUTDOOR "O"	ROWAN	10	41	516
LAKE ERIE & SOUTHERN	DOSEY	11	49	37
LAKE ERIE & SOUTHERN 1/2"	DOSEY	02	68	35
LAKE FOREST & SCGATIVILLE	LINDENSTRUTH	11	73	50
LAKE GEORGE & BOULDER OUTDOOR GM	SMALL	04	72	58
LAKE PORT & TERMINAL "HO"	GOSHERT	04	68	26
LAKE SHORE ELECTRIC "HO"	DARST	01	70	57
LAKE SHORE LINE "HO"	WESTCOTT	05	35	121
LAKE SHORE SOUTHERN "N"	STEINBERG	01	81	102
LAKE SUPERIOR & WESTERN "O"	ANDERSON	06	68	50
LAKE TAHOE RY & TRANSPORTATION "ON3"		09	81	54
LANCASTER SOUTH & EASTERN "HO"	WATKINS	07	70	30
LAVEGAS MINERAL & MINING COMPANY "ON3"		10	79	97
LAYOUT IN A CLOSET "N"	BAKER	07	84	81
LAYOUT ON THE BIAS		09	53	46
LC&J RAILROAD	COOK	09	71	32
LILLIPUT RAILROAD OBITUARY "HO"	TURNER	12	35	313
LINDEN VALLEY RAILWAY "HO"	MONEY	05	83	98
LISBEN, NECEDAH & L SUPERIOR	RESCHENBERG	06	58	44
LITTLE C&O "O"	LOCKMAN	01	51	48
LITTLE CANADIAN PACIFIC "O"	HEARN	08	52	10
LITTLE ISLAND RAILROAD "OO"	SMALL	06	35	142
LITTLE L&N "O"	TANKSLEY	02	48	92
LITTLE L&N "O"	TANKSLEY	06	53	10
LITTLE LITTLE NORTH SHORE "HO"	WAGNER	09	42	412
LITTLE NYC "O"	GOLDING	08	37	273
LITTLE SOUTHERN RAILWAY "O"	HAVERLY	10	35	268
LITTLE SP "HO"	WAHLER	04	51	22
LITTLE TH&B "O"	CLUB	10	39	500
LITTLE V&T "HO"	ANDERSON	12	51	18
LITTLEST B&O "HO"	SAGLE	06	56	36
LITTLETON & BOX SPRINGS	MEYER	09	68	31
LIVE STEAMERS		11	38	496
LORING ELLIOTTS' LAYOUT "O"		07	34	2
LOS OSOS VALLEY "O"	THORP	09	80	74
LOST RIVER DISTRICT "N"	ANTHONY	02	85	106
LOTS OF LOCOMOTIVES "O"	CARTER	04	53	12
LUCAS COUNTY TRACTION CO "HO"	RAMSEY	04	85	64
LUCAS LINE "HO"	LUCAS	05	42	220
LUCKEY SHORT LINE	RESCHENBERG	06	63	34
LUNAR RAILROAD		04	78	87
M&H LINES "HO"	CONRAD	02	42	74
MAD RIVER NAVIGATION COMPANY	SPENCER	05	73	54
MAD RIVER NAVIGATION RAILWAY	SPENCER	07	77	46
MADDER VALLEY RAILWAY	AHERN	01	46	30
MAINE CENTRAL INNSMOUTH BRANCH	LEWTAS	06	83	104
MAJOR CONSTRUCTION PROJECT RR	MARTIN	06	51	22
MANESTA LINE "HO"	WEIDHAAS	07	70	54
MANHATTAN BEACH RAILWAY "O"	ALLEN	07	38	269
MANSFIELD JUNCTION "HO"	BOUDREAU	10	84	95
MARAIS RAILWAY & NAVIGATION "HO"	MARTIN	11	60	30
MARKLIN MODELING	BARSCH	12	82	98
MARQUETTE UNION TERMINAL R.R.	ROBINSON	06	78	71
MARQUETTE UNION TERMINAL RR	ROBINSON	04	52	32
MARTHA'S VINEYARD "HON3"		06	80	86
MARYSVILLE & WELLINGTON NORTHRN	HOLLIDGE	03	61	49
MASHAPAUG & WISCASSET "HO/HON3"	CLERKE	03	82	58
MASHAPAUG & WISCASSETT "HO"	CLERKE	07	69	30
MASSACHUSETTS MODEL RAILROAD SOC	B. PETE	07	40	393
MATAPEDIA CENTRAL "S"	FIRIOTTE	07	48	465
MAYLAND & SUSQUEHANNA "HO"	ROBERTSON	02	84	58
MAYWOOD CENTRAL "HO"	DECHO	01	62	36
MCBURNEY'S POINT "HO"	MAGUIRE	11	52	22
ME, HIM, HER PIKE	DICKINSON	01	63	40
MEADMORE MODEL RW AUSTRALIA "O"	1932	04	34	4
MERLINS MAGIC	SWINERS	06	65	22
MERRIMAL SOUTHEASTERN "HO"	ODEGARD	01	80	94
MESCAL LINES "HON3"	OLSON	01	84	125
METROPOL & WESTERN	BORTHWICK	10	59	62
MIAMI ROAD "O"	FESSLER	12	69	42
MICHAEL KUEHNS RAILROAD		02	78	120
MID WESTERN CENTRAL	BEDROWSKY	11	68	58
MIDDELTOWN & MYSTIC MINES "HO"	SMALLSHAW	07	69	34
MIDDLETOWN & MYSTIC MINES "HO"	SMALLSHAW	05	82	58
MIDGET PACIFIC "HO"	KNOX	04	38	152
MIDLAND CENTRAL "HO"	LEUPOLD	12	76	50
MIDLAND ELECTRIC "HO"	GOEHMANN	07	80	58
MIDLAND VALLEY RAILROAD "HO"	MORRISON	06	77	52
MIDWEST PACIFIC "O"	STEWART	05	43	221

MODEL LAYOUTS

LAYOUT VISITS		M	Y	P
MILLCREEK ROAD "O/ON3"	SCHWARM	06	71	30
MILLERS LINES "HO"	MILLER	11	81	94
MILW ELECTRIC LINES TROLLEY WING DING "O"		05	33	12
MILW ELECTRIC TROLLEY WING DING "O"		05	53	12
MILW UNION TERMINAL OBITUARY	B. PETE	06	47	468
MILWAUKEE & SHEBOYGAN "O"	WILBERT	02	84	100
MILWAUKEE & SHEBOYGAN "O"	WILBERT	11	67	34
MILWAUKEE & WESTERN	BARNETT	11	70	76
MILWAUKEE ROAD "O"	GILCHER	02	36	47
MILWAUKEE ROAD "O"	CLUB	03	37	109
MILWAUKEE UNION TERMINAL "O"	CLUB	06	34	6
MILWAUKEE UNION TERMINAL RR "O"	CLUB	06	35	157
MINERAL POINT & NORTHERN RY "HO"	LARSON	05	81	66
MINITOUR PIKE "S" AUTOMATIC/SCENIC	MERTZ	08	63	44
MINNEAPOLIS MODEL RAILROAD "O"	CLUB	04	37	129
MISSISSIPPI RAILROAD "HO"	FLOURNUT	01	43	12
MODEL A CITY "HO"	SUMNER	01	85	86
MODEL MEET AT TAKARAZUKA JAPAN		12	67	48
MODEL RAILROAD OF GEORGE STOCK		01	37	1
MODEL RAILROAD CLUB-PROGRESS REPORT		10	83	70
MODEL RAILROADING AT THE OHIO STATE FAIR		08	83	82
MODEL RAILROADING ON THE MANOR	MONTAGU	03	79	110
MODEL RAILROADING UNDER THE CHANDELIER		06	78	107
MODEL RR CLUB OF MILWAUKEE-50 YEARS		10	84	100
MODEL RR IN A CORNER "HO"	LEHMAN	03	85	90
MODIFYING EXISTING TRACK PLANS		10	50	24
MODULAR RAILROADING "ON3"	HAMILTON	01	81	70
MODULE IN A BOX "N"	SPANO	10	82	94
MOHAWK & HUDSON RAILROAD	PASTON	03	78	52
MOHAWK VALLEY "OO"	ANDERSON	02	36	36
MOJAVE WESTERN "HO"	MILLER	04	84	66
MON-YOUGH VALLEY	THORNILEY	02	66	48
MONASHEE WESTERN "HO"	HOLLAND	04	80	100
MONTANA & PUGET SOUND	ARMSTRONG	12	59	52
MONTAUK VALLEY "HO" 25 YRS AND COUNTING		12	79	106
MOONSHINE STILLRIVER & BOOTLEG VALLEY RR		04	63	54
MOTH LAKE & MOUNT ARAB "HO"	BLUMENSCAME	06	79	66
MOTIVE POWER OF THE D&O "HO"	STOCK	06	35	151
MOUNT ROYAL BELT LINE "O"	CLUB	04	39	180
MOUNTAIN ROUTE "O"	HOHL	07	34	7
MT RUSHMORE IN "HO"	FURNISH	03	75	63
MUDDY & OIL CREEK RAILROAD "HO"	COLLOM	03	36	74
MUSS, CUSS & FUSS "HO"	VONDRAK	08	85	130
MY MODEL RAILROAD "OO"	KIRCH	02	44	66
MY RAILROAD JUST GROWED "HON3"	LIVINGSTON	09	62	28
N SCALE MODULAR TWIN CITIES	SCHAFER	10	77	55
N SCALE RAILROAD	LEACH	03	78	96
N SCALE SAVED SPACE FOR ME	EDELMAN	12	67	36
N&O OLD KING COLE "OO" BOOMER PETE	COLE	08	48	524
NACIONALED DE MINATURA "HO"	DE LA TORRE	03	45	114
NARROW GAUGE OPHIR "TN3 1/4"	MOORE	10	62	40
NATIONAL ENQUIRER OUTDOOR LAYOUT		03	78	99
NAZARETH TRANSIT COMPANY "O"	ZELLER	08	35	200
NEEHI VALLEY (COFFEE TABLE "N")	BRODIE	05	75	58
NEVADA & WESTERN "HO"	ROSS	10	61	29
NEVADA SHORTLINE "O"	ROBBIS	10	70	44
NEW CASTLE & FRENCHTOWN RR "HO"	CROSBY	12	48	920
NEW DETROIT UNION RAILROAD SOC MODEL ENG		06	36	152
NEW ENGLAND, BERKSHIRE & WESTERN "HO"		09	83	58
NEW HAVEN CLUB "O"	WESTCOTT	09	53	24
NEW HAVEN OVERHEAD "HO"	SCHLEGEL	03	37	101
NEW HAVEN RAILROAD "HO"	ALDRICH	09	80	58
NEW JERSEY NORTHERN "HO"	DALBERG	02	73	52
NEW LISDON "N" MODULE	ODEGARD	10	76	46
NEW YORK & NEW ENGLAND "O"	CLUB	04	37	139
NEW YORK CENTRAL LINES "O"	BLACKBURN	10	37	353
NEW YORK WORLDS FAIR RAILROAD "O"		03	39	136
NEWBURG ON FRISCO "HO"	JESTER	06	84	64
NOEL CENTRAL "HO"	MR STAFF	12	55	32
NOITCART TRACTION	BRUNSKY	04	78	110
NONCONFORMIST RAILROAD "HO"	BRAY	04	41	205
NOOK & CRANNY RAILROAD	ARMSTRONG	03	55	40
NORFOLK & OHIO "OO"	APPEL	11	58	28
NORTH JERSEY RAP TRANSIT OUTDOOR	QUINBY	11	39	553
NORTH MERRICK & INDIAN "HO"	BENZING	10	52	30
NORTH MOUNTAIN RAILROAD "O"	FRIEND	11	37	422
NORTH PENNSYLVANIA RR CO LTD "HO"		02	82	108
NORTHERN ALLEN PARK LINES	GUNTHER	07	78	86
NORTHERN OF NEW JERSEY	BORTHWICK	03	59	59
NORTHERN RAILWAY "HO"	LATHAM	11	48	803
NORTHERN RR OF NEW JERSEY "O"	CAROLINE	08	42	378
NORTHERN SIERRA & FALL CREEK "HO"	PATRONE	09	84	62
NORTHFIELD CENTRAL "O"	MEREDITH	06	36	149
NORTHWEST & PACIFIC "HO"	WESTCOTT	12	36	364
NORTHWESTERN PACIFIC "N"	FUZAK	05	84	63
NORTON BROS CONNECTING RR "N"	ANTHONY	09	81	94
NTRAK TODAY "N"	FITZGERALD	11	85	70
NWRR	TOMBS	08	65	44
NYC "1/4"	LAFAYE	01	72	54
NYO&W "O"	MIDDLETOWN NY CLUB	08	41	412
O GAUGE IN TWIN CITIES	WESTCOTT	08	51	8
OAHU RAILWAY & LAND CO "HON3"	WHITTED	03	65	32
OAKVILLE CENTRAL RAILROAD	MITCHELL	12	78	106
OCEAN VIEW UNIFIED RAILROAD	GOOGAN	09	78	72
OFFICE WALL TRANSFER LAYOUT		11	76	102
OHIO & MICHIGAN ELECTRIC LINES	EDSON	02	43	80
OHIO CENTRAL SYSTEM	WESTCOTT	07	56	38
OHIO ELECTRIC "HO"	DURFLINGER	11	62	36
OHIO MICHIGAN & SOUTH SHORE "HO"	HEDIGER	03	75	46
OHIO SOUTHERN	HEDIGER	07	78	70
OLD COLONY LINES	ARMSTRONG	02	60	55
OLD COLONY RAILROAD "O"	LEONARD	12	36	360
OLD WORLD LAYOUT "HO"	BROOKS	07	71	64
OMAHA & NORTHWESTERN PLAN FOR ALL REASON		07	77	62
ONE MAN CLASS 1 TRACK PLAN	SEELEY	04	70	30
ONEONTA SNY "HO"	SHELDON	07	68	28
ONTARIO & EASTERN "HO"	BASCOM	03	82	67
ONTARIO CENTRAL "HO"	BAILEY	10	80	110
OO GAUGE ROAD	ANDERSON	05	35	114
ORANGE VALLEY LINES "HO"	PERRY	11	42	496

STEPHANS' RAILROAD DIRECTORY

MODEL LAYOUTS

LAYOUT VISITS

Layout	Scale	Author	M	Y	P
OREGON PACIFIC RAILWAY	"O"	ZEHRUNG	08	34	6
OSHKOSH MODEL RAILROADERS	"O"	CLUB	03	40	138
OSSAGE RAILROAD	"HO"	MARTIN	10	50	12
OTTUMWA CENTRAL	"N"	ODEGARD	05	74	50
OUTDOOR HO PIKE			09	66	48
OUTDOOR INTERSTATE CENTRAL 1/20		BLOSSER	01	51	24
OUTDOOR LINE (110V) "2 1/8"		BRINK	01	34	10
OUTDOOR RAILROAD	"1/2"	HOWARD	03	41	139
OUTDOOR RAILROAD	"O"	NERVO	01	34	3
OZARK "HO" RR MADE OF MEMORIES		HUSMAN	01	82	100
OZARK VALLEY LINES	"O"	PIRTLE	06	82	86
OZARK WILDERNESS LINES	"HO"	HART	01	81	108
PACIFIC BEACH AND WESTERN	"HO"	SLOCUM	10	66	40
PACIFIC ELECTRIC	"O"	EVERETT	08	83	54
PACIFIC SOUTHERN	"HO"	KELLY	11	83	68
PAGET SOUND SHORE LINE	"HO"		05	59	23
PALISADES MINING COMPANY	"HO"	EGGERT	07	80	70
PANHANDLE & SANTA FE	"HO"	LOTT	02	81	74
PANHANDLE RAILWAY		TIPTON	06	78	107
PANHANDLE TRACTION	"HO"	HOHMAN	10	64	42
PAPER VALLEY RAILROAD	"O"	HEDIGER	04	79	115
PASKENTA RAILWAY & NAV	"HON3"	SMITH	07	84	54
PASSAIC & DEL VALLEY LARGE SCALE LAYOUT			07	39	362
PD&Q HOW IT GREW		SMALL	08	52	35
PE SYSTEM	"1/4"	EVERETT	03	73	53
PEEWEE VALLEY	"HO"	PITCHER	06	45	235
PENINSULA MRR ASSOCIATION			08	85	54
PENN ROAD	"HO"	SCHMIDT	09	38	371
PENN, SANTA FE & PACIFIC	"O"	BEEMAN	10	76	62
PENN-ERIE	"OO"	WINTHER	07	34	16
PENN-READING SEASHORE LINES	"N"	FOLS	08	78	82
PENNEANTE LINES	"HO"	STOUT	01	41	16
PENNSY SOUTHERN	"O"	WAGNER	04	47	278
PENNSYLVANIA & WESTBROOK	"HO"	BAILEY	11	82	110
PENNSYLVANIA MODEL RAILROAD	"O"	ALBRECHT	01	34	8
PENNSYLVANIA RR	"HO"	SALZGABER	03	81	62
PEORIA & WESTERN	"O"	MEANS	02	38	53
PEORIA & WESTERN	"O"	MEANS	07	36	179
PEORIA & WESTERN	"O"	MEANS	09	35	244
PF&W TRACTION	"HO"	MEHLENBECK	02	44	84
PIEDMONT & SHORE	"OOO"	YOUNG	02	64	50
PIEDMONT & WESTERN	"HO"	JONES	02	80	98
PIEDMONT TRACTION SYSTEM	"O"	DALE	01	35	11
PIGEON CREEK		BARON	12	67	53
PIKE KIDS CAN GROW WITH		PARKS	09	78	121
PIKE THAT "JACK" BUILT	"HO"	PARRAY	06	52	10
PIKES YOU CAN LIVE WITH		ARMSTRONG	05	56	40
PIKESVILLE RAILROAD	"HO"	BROADRICK	11	50	20
PINE CONE VALLEY	"ON2"	BOUTELL	04	52	26
PINE TREE CENTRAL ADD ON	"HO"	AIREY	12	73	49
PINE VALLEY RAILROAD	"HO"	DELAUNIERE	05	74	40
PINT SIZE & PORTABLE	"HO"	MILLER	02	46	86
PLATONICA RIVER SOUTHERN			02	52	32
PLEASANT HILL & SUNNYDALE		MITCHELL	05	76	66
PLM DANS LA MASSIF (3 LEVELS)	"HO"		05	83	90
PM&LS RAILROAD HO SCALE		TOMPKINS	08	46	494
POCAHONTAS JUNCTION	"O"	ARMSTRONG	01	58	60
POOR MANS THROAT		ARMSTRONG	07	55	36
PORT ABLE RAILROAD		SMALL	06	51	26
PORT CARIDOU RR & WESTERN NAVIGATION CO			09	77	52
PORTABLE EXHIBITION LAYOUT			02	36	44
POTOMAC & WESTERN	"HO"	MCBRIDE	08	47	626
PRACTICAL APARTMENT PIKE	"HO"	MILLER	04	49	20
PRIZE WINNING LAYOUTS			12	35	328
PROVING GROUND RAILROAD		MR STAFF	03	52	10
PRR IN MINIATURE		BISHOP	09	34	13
PRR VISIT	"O"	BLOOMBERG	06	43	261
PRR VISIT	"O"	ALBRECHT	02	37	45
PUBLIC BELT OF NEW ORLEANS		WELCH	02	61	44
PUGET SOUND SHORE LINE	"HO"	CHAUDIERE	02	60	26
PULLMAN & GHOST RIDGE	"HO"	BRANDT	06	85	96
PURR (MA&PA)		SIMA	06	69	65
QUARTZ HILL TRAMWAY	"HON2 1/2"	DEVERE	04	83	66
QUIST STRUCTURES ON P&P	"HO"	BELL	11	61	38
RACQUETTE RIVER RAILROAD		BLUMENSCHINE	10	77	97
RAILROAD EMPIRE	"HO"	VERMILYEA	11	41	570
RAILROAD IN A CABOOSE	"HO"	SCHREIER	04	60	24
RAILROAD IN AUSTRALIA	"OO"	SHENNEN	08	42	382
RAILROAD THAT GOES PLACES		ARMSTRONG	09	54	40
RAILROAD TO ENCHANTMENT			01	78	90
RAILROADING IN THE OIL FIELDS		WEBB	01	60	48
RAILROADING OUTDOORS	"O"	LANE	04	51	8
RAILROADS FOR EVERY HOME		WESTCOTT	12	55	70
RAILWAYS OF AMERICA	"O"	LOWRY	08	74	30
RAINY RIVER TRANSIT	"HO"	WILLIAMS	09	45	360
RALEIGH, GULF & SOUTHWESTERN		ODEGARD	02	59	54
RAYTOWN & ADAVILLE TROLLEY LINE	"O"	REGER	10	43	455
RECTORY RAILROAD	"HO"	ALBAUGH	03	46	184
REDESIGN A LAYOUT TINPLATE SCALE		KAHLER	09	35	242
RESTLESS RAILROAD	"ON3"	ALEXANDER	06	63	24
RIDE OF YOUR LIFE		DETLEFSEN	12	61	30
RIO GRANDE & SAN JUAN	"SN3 1/2"	PRUITT	10	71	46
RIO GRANDE EAST HARTFORD DIV	"HO"		05	82	55
RIO GRANDE SHORT LINE	"HO"	WOODHEAD	07	42	340
RIO GRANDE SOUTHERN		NYCE	07	82	92
RIO GRANDE SOUTHERN	"HON3"	SYLVESTER	04	80	54
RIO GRANDE SOUTHERN	"HON3"	HITZEMAN	02	79	80
RIVERSIDE JUNCTION	"HO"	SCHUBERT	06	85	92
ROCK CANYON & WESTERN RR	"HO"	GRAVES	09	48	604
ROCK MILL LINE	"1/4"	STANDERY	10	72	70
ROCK POINT & COAST		LUTZ	10	78	64
ROCKEY RIVER TRACTION		WAGNER	06	47	473
ROCKLAND RAILROAD		RAMSDELL	11	47	910
ROCKLAND RAILROAD	"O"	ROBB	02	51	27
ROLLAWAY "N" GAUGE LAYOUT			12	77	86
ROLLING HILLS RAILROAD	"O"	CHERRNAY	01	82	62
ROSSADORA WESTERN	"HO"	ROSS	02	74	46
ROYAL GEORGE WESTERN	"N"	WIDMAR	01	77	68
RUBE GOLDBERG LAYOUT	"O"	BOOMER PETE	02	44	80
S&C VISIT	"O"	ABRAHAM	01	42	4

MODEL LAYOUTS

LAYOUT VISITS

Title	Author	M	Y	P
SAFARZE LOOVILLE & NAWINS "HO" BOWEN		09	36	256
SAGATUKETT RIVER RAILROAD SILAS		03	72	60
SALT CREEK RAILROAD "HO" WESTCOTT		03	61	24
SAN DIABLO GADGET EMPIRE "O" BONDURANT		02	52	14
SAN DIEGO CLUB "HO/O" TOWERS		10	63	27
SAN DIEGO MODEL RR MUSEUM		02	85	78
SAN FRANCISCO BELT LINE NICKLE		04	80	65
SAN JACINTO DISTRICT "HO" SPERANDEO		02	80	107
SAN JOSE SOCIETY MODEL RAILROADERS "N"		01	85	73
SAN JUAN & NORTHERN "ON3" BERMAN		10	80	66
SAN MARINO & SANTA FE "Q" CRONKHITE		11	38	461
SAND HILL & WESTERN RAILROAD "HO" MOORE		11	69	61
SAND TABLE LAYOUT		12	36	367
SANDRIC & LAKE SUPERIOR "HO" LUNDBURG		08	77	74
SANDY FLAT & CENTRAL "HO" FRISCHMAN		11	76	96
SANTA ANA VALLEY LINES "HO" CLUB		07	45	276
SANTA FE "HO" NIELSON		12	78	159
SANTA FE "O" BOOMER PETE WANAMAKER		08	45	319
SANTA FE MODEL SYSTEM "1/4" CRONDKITE		03	41	125
SANTA FE PACIFIC OUTDOOR "O" SPIRI		10	36	292
SANTALAND & SOUTHERN "HO" SHEDD		11	64	36
SARANAC & WOLF POND "HO" BLUMENCHINE		01	75	52
SBSS&C "HO" WESTCOTT		08	44	348
SCENICED & UNDECIDED "N" SPANO		05	80	75
SECAUCUS & BLACKWATER RAILROAD		04	78	107
SENECA VALLEY LINES "HO"		11	79	100
SENECA VALLEY RAILROAD BORTHWICK		08	62	53
SETON VALLEY LINES "O" PIERCE		12	42	544
SHASTA SOUTHERN "1/4" GILL		04	73	48
SHEEPSHANKS & SHORT SIDINGS ARMSTRONG		05	58	38
SHELF LAYOUTS ODEGARD		07	60	44
SHELF RAILROADS		03	52	48
SHOWCASE RAILROAD "HO" BOOMER PETE		11	40	610
SIERRA & WHITE RIVER "HO" MARTIN		02	83	78
SIERRA CENTRAL RAILROAD "HO" FAUL		12	70	57
SIERRA GRANDE & WESTERN OLAFSON		02	78	98
SIERRA PACIFIC PASADENA CLUB		03	78	90
SIERRA PACIFIC "HO" TOWERS		09	60	22
SIERRA PASS REVISITED "1/4" ARMSTRONG		05	72	42
SIERRA SANTA FE PARROTT		07	74	48
SIERRA SILVERTON RAILROAD "HO" PETHOUD		07	83	98
SIMPATICO "HO" KUYKENDALL		07	74	30
SLEEPY VALLEY & WESTERN "HO" HORNER		07	69	33
SLEEPY VALLEY & WESTERN "HO" HORNER		03	82	63
SMALL LAYOUT FOR OPERATION WELCH		11	64	74
SMALL POINT TO POINT LAYOUT "HO" LAING		10	35	261
SMALL PORTABLE LAYOUT "O" DOOLEY		01	47	30
SMALL YARDS WITH A FUTURE		09	58	49
SOMERS JUNCTION RAILROAD BARON		01	68	52
SOMERSET & MOUNT VERNON "HO" CONSTABLE		08	79	82
SOMETIMES YOU NEED A SHOEHORN CUSHMAN		07	63	27
SOO LINES MODEL PORTABLE RR HEDIGER		05	80	95
SOUTH BAY CENTRAL "O" VONDRAK		05	80	68
SOUTH MIDLAND RAILWAY "O" TURNER		03	35	67
SOUTH RIDGE LINES "HO" FREYTAG		11	80	95

LAYOUT VISITS

Title	M	Y	P
SOUTH SHASTA LINE "O" HAUMANN	05	84	112
SOUTH TROY ENGLISH & WICKLIFFE "HO"	11	75	50
SOUTHERN CONSOLIDATED "HO" OAKES	10	81	58
SOUTHERN MODEL RAILWAY "O" WAYMEYER	09	34	2
SOUTHERN PACIFIC LIMITED BLAIR	12	39	628
SOUTHERN RAILROAD "N" 3' WIDE CHASE	12	72	52
SOUTHERN RAILROADS ARMSTRONG	03	56	52
SOUTHERN WESTCHESTER RAILROAD "O" READER	08	36	224
SOUTHWESTERN & PACIFIC "N" DAVIS	12	80	138
SP BRANCH "O" NUREMBERG	10	47	798
SPARE TIME LINES "HO" GROTH	10	73	51
SPRING GLEN INTERCONNECTING LINES "O"	02	35	30
SQUARE PIKE ALEXANDER	03	54	51
SS&GW RAILROAD-BAJA ARRIBA 1884 BOOM	10	79	89
ST CLAIR NORTHERN SCHULTZ	09	73	37
ST CLAIR NORTHERN REVISITED SCHULTZ	08	76	54
ST DENIS "S" PETERSON	05	50	28
ST JOSEPH & SOUTHERN RESCHENBERG	08	57	50
ST LOUIS UNION STATION BORTHWICK	10	60	60
ST PAUL LAYOUT "O" VALENTINE	12	44	530
STARTING 2ND 50 YEARS WITH A "Z" LAYOUT	01	84	148
STERLING VALLEY RAILROAD "OO" SMITH	02	35	38
STERLING VALLEY RAILROAD "HO" SMITH	01	42	22
STILLWATER VALLEY ROOT "HO" LYLE	06	74	58
STONY CREEK & WESTERN "HO" FREITAG	07	82	56
SUGAR RIVER & RIDGEFIELD MILLER	06	67	31
SUNSET VALLEY EVOLUTION CHUBB	03	79	79
SUNSET VALLEY FAN TRIP CHUBB	01	74	47
SUNSET VALLEY STORY CHUBB	01	79	66
SUSQUEHANNA & WESTERN "O" TAFEL	05	37	174
SWEETWATER RR "HO" FAMILY RM LAYOUT WYATT	09	81	86
SWISS MODELING IN ISRAEL	07	61	32
SWITCHING LAYOUTS PART 1 MILLER	06	77	107
T&E RAILROAD RICHARDSON	06	51	18
TABLE TOP TROLLEY "HO" SENNHAUSER	04	54	38
TAILORED FOR WAY FREIGHTS	01	51	32
TANNE HILL RAILROAD "HO" TANNEHILL	12	49	38
TAPPAN ZEE "HO" SCHLEGEL	06	42	270
TCHOPITOULAS RAILWAY & NAVIGATION "HO"	04	81	90
TERMINAL & TIDEWATER SWITCHING PIKE SMAL	09	47	725
TERMINAL CENTRAL "HO" ECK	10	73	44
TERMINAL LAYOUTS	08	49	38
TERMINAL SOLUTION "HO" SCHOOF	07	85	132
TERMITE TIMBER COMPANY "HO" ULLIAN	01	75	54
TERMITE TIMBER COMPANY "ON3" WESTCOTT	10	54	38
TEXAS & SANTA FE "O" CRONKHITE	10	36	282
TEXAS CRAWFORD & PRAIRIE "HO" HS OF ME	09	79	66
TEXAS SUBDIVISON "N"	12	79	114
TEXAS, SALTAIR & WESTERN "HO" RADEBAUGH	01	60	28
TH&B VERSIONS 1,2&3 "HO" HENDREN	10	69	41
THE BEGINNING BURGER	09	35	230
THE BIGGEST MULTI LEVEL LAYOUT ARMSTRONG	04	54	59
THE SHELF LINE "HO" COCHRAN	06	69	50
THE WAY TO MY HOBBY "S" BISMARCK	09	65	28
THREE LAYOUTS IN ONE RESCHENBERG	08	58	46

MODEL LAYOUTS

LAYOUT VISITS

Title	Author	M	Y	P
TIMBER RIVER RAILROAD "HO"	TEW	01	85	96
TIMESAVER LAYOUT "HO"	VONDRAK	11	77	96
TINPLATE LAYOUT "O"	BROWN	12	49	61
TIOGA PASS "HO"	FINDLEY	08	82	50
TOCOPILLA LIGHT OUTDOOR #1	LEVER	06	75	59
TOLUCA "O"	TOWERS	08	65	36
TOMAHAWK TRAIL RAILROAD "TT"	CHURCH	09	62	30
TOOLOMNE FORKS LUMBER "1/4 FS"	BROWN	08	75	50
TOURING THE NORTHWEST LAYOUTS W/WESTCOTT		08	50	10
TOWERMANS DREAM	HAMMOND	08	59	38
TRACK PLAN FOR APARTMENTS	SEELEY	10	67	38
TRACTION WITH IDEAS		02	61	26
TRAIL OF TWO RAILROADS	WELCH	11	71	40
TRAIN GALLERY "HO"	MAJOR	04	85	84
TRAVELING LAYOUT SHOW "HO"	WILSON	11	83	98
TRAVELING ROAD "O"	HEIBERG	02	50	38
TRL CO 1/4	ALEXANDER	10	46	636
TROLL & ELFIN "HO"	KNOTTS	04	82	102
TRUCKEE & WESTERN "TT"	MORAN	07	67	25
TRUE APARTMENT RAILROAD "HO"	BLANC	07	35	181
TRUNDLE LAYOUT "HO"	KUYKENDALL	11	73	59
TUPPER LAKE & FAUST JUCTION	BLUMENCHINE	03	75	72
TURTLE CREEK & WESTERN "HO"	MC CLANAHAN	10	48	698
TUSCARRORAH & EDINGTON RAILROAD		12	51	30
TUXEDO JUNCTION A WHOLE BARN!		04	53	18
TWO POINT TO POINT ROADS	WELSH	04	60	40
TWO RAILROADS ON WATERMAN AVENUE		11	74	48
TWO ROOM RAILROAD	HINRICHS	04	44	163
TYLER MT & BEAVER CREEK "HO"	SUMNER	11	82	108
UNION CONNECTING GOLDEN SPIKE"O"	B. PETE	02	39	61
UNION CONNECTING RAILROAD	SMALL	02	38	59
UNION CONNECTING RAILROAD "O"	CLUB	01	35	13
UNION HOBOKEN & OVERLAND "HO"		05	83	66
UNION PACIFIC JR "O"	BULL	07	41	341
UNITED SYSTEMS "O"	GOODWIN	02	41	69
UNLIKELY & IMPROBABLE RY "HO"	HENDERSON	06	79	98
UTAH COLORADO WESTERN "HO"	NICHOLAS	11	85	82
UTAH MIDLAND "HO"	LINDOA	05	79	68
UTAH PACIFIC "HO"	OLIVER	08	68	34
UTAH PACIFIC "HO"	OLIVER	10	58	24
UTAH PACIFIC "HO"	OLIVER	07	62	44
UTE CITY BRANCH "ON3"	LEE	06	84	58
UTE SHORT LINE "HO"	COCHRAN	11	49	24
V&T "N"	RIDDLEBAUGH	04	84	92
VACATION OUTDOOR RAILROAD "O"	KAY	07	52	31
VALLEY MODEL RAILROAD CLUB	GATHMAN	08	66	36
VARIETY IN 5 X 10 LAYOUT		08	53	40
VERDUGO VALLEY "HO"	GLENDALE	12	60	28
VERY SHORT SHORT-LINE	DURFEE	04	83	76
VICTORIA NORTHERN "HO"	DOHN	08	62	40
VICTORIAN RAILWAY "HON2 1/2"	MAIN	02	70	42
VIRGINIAN & OHIO "HO"	MCCLELLAND	11	82	68
VLA-CI RR SPACE AGE COMPLEX	RIEHEL	04	83	77
VOS MOUNTAIN RAILROAD "HO"	KAYLE	06	83	90
W&W LINES "HO"	HYAM	08	42	368
WAIST LINE "HO"	FULLER	10	59	24
WARRIOR RIVER INTERURBAN "O"	BOGART	10	38	414
WARTIME HO LAYOUT	BOOMER PETE	02	45	64
WASSENAAR RAILWAY COMPANY "S"	DRIELSMA	10	70	36
WATERFRONT AT WISCASSET	CLARKE	02	78	58
WATERFRONT RAILROADS	BORTHWICK	09	60	28
WATHUNG & RAITAN "HO"	ISLEY	01	76	50
WATKINS WALFORD & WESTERN RR "N"	LARSON	11	74	94
WAWBEEK & SUNMOUNT "HO"		11	79	98
WAY OUT WEST "HO"	NELSON	11	41	563
WEBER VALLEY RAILROAD "HO"	SPANGLER	12	84	76
WEBSTER GROVES "O"	MUELLER	09	72	42
WELLINGTON LINES "O"	MARR	02	51	44
WEST BAY LINES O-S-HO	TOWERS	01	64	38
WEST MIDLAND LINES "OO"	BEAL	08	38	323
WESTCHESTER ELECTRIC	ISSACS	06	69	36
WESTCHESTER RAILROAD "HO"	ISSACS	05	60	22
WESTERN & ATLANTIC "O"	WESTCHESTER CLUB	08	36	209
WESTERN FUN IN 81 PREVIEWS		06	81	54
WESTERN LOGGING COMPANY "HO"	SPEARS	12	63	45
WESTERN MODEL RAILROADS		10	48	727
WESTERN NEW ENGLAND RAILROAD "HO"	WEBB	10	58	48
WESTERN PACIFIC "N"	ANDERSON	07	84	63
WESTERN PACIFIC RAILWAY "O"	JOHNSON	09	37	319
WESTERN RAILROAD "O"	LYTLE	05	39	240
WESTERN VALLEY "HO"	PORTER	09	55	38
WESTFIELD VISIT "O"	WOODRUFF	12	44	550
WESTWARD HO "HO"	COPE	01	53	32
WHARF & INDUSTRY TRACK PLAN	WHITMORE	02	68	45
WHEELING CLUB LAYOUT "O"		05	39	257
WHITE PLAINS MODEL RR CLUB "HO"		11	84	74
WHITE RIVER & NACHES "N"	NAFF	02	81	98
WHOPPER-POO LARGE LAYOUT OF MONTH		12	41	630
WIERD AND WONDERFUL	SCHAMPEL	01	66	44
WIND RIVER & NORTHERN	KAEGI	01	73	49
WISCASSET & OSWEGO RY "HON3"	RESCHENBERG	01	58	40
WOODLAND VALLEY & WESTERN "HO"	POWERS	04	75	58
WORLD IN MY LAP "Z"	SMITH	10	75	42
WORLD'S SMALLEST RAILROAD "1/16"	WALTER	01	38	5
YAMPA VALLEY "HO"	ROTHE	08	84	70
YARD & OUORNER SHELF LAYOUT	KLATT	02	67	52
YORK LUMBER CO. "HO"	BOWDEN	11	57	32
YOUNGSTOWN UNION TERMINAL RAILROAD "O"		07	37	256
ZACK & SOUTHERN "O"	DAVIDSON	10	66	33
ZOO JUNCTION	BORTHWICK	12	58	66

BILL OF LADING   ELECTRONICS/COMPUTERS

This section concerns itself with the electrical aspects of model railroading. It covers everything from storage battery running of trains to integrated circuits to computers. The descriptor line is self-explanatory.

MANIFEST   ELECTRONICS/COMPUTERS

	PAGE
ELECTRICAL & ELECTRONICS	200
COMPUTERS	201
GENERAL ELECTRONICS	201

ELECTRICAL & ELECTRONICS

COMPUTERS	M	Y	P
C/MRI CAB CONTROL SOFTWARE	12	85	114
C/MRI COMPUTER CAB CONTROL HARDWARE	10	85	66
C/MRI COMPUTER LAYOUT WIR/CAB CONTROL IO	11	85	98
C/MRI COMPUTER MRR INTERFACE CPN/LAYOUT	02	85	92
C/MRI CONNECTING RAILROAD TO IO CARDS	07	85	87
C/MRI CONNECTING UBEC TO COMPUTER	04	85	90
C/MRI IO CIRCUITS	05	85	92
C/MRI OPTIMIZED DETECTOR NOT COMPUTERIZE	08	85	87
C/MRI TESTING WITH SOFTWARE	06	85	80
C/MRI UNIVERSAL BUS EXTENDER CARD	03	85	92
CAR SELECTION PROGRAM TSR80	04	84	50
COMPUTER INDEX PROGRAM FOR MODEL RRS	01	84	34
COMPUTER SIMULATIONS ENGINES	04	85	142
COMPUTER SIMULATIONS RAIL DISPATCHER	04	85	143
COMPUTERIZED HUMP YARD	01	79	92
COMPUTERIZED TRAFFIC GENERATOR	02	84	72
COMPUTERIZING THE GREAT SOUTHERN	04	83	91
COMPUTERS IN MODEL RAILROADING PART 1	09	77	83
MODEL RAILROADING IN BINARY GAUGE	12	84	91
RAILOGIC: TWO HOBBIES DO TEAMWORK	09	76	45

GENERAL ELECTRONICS	M	Y	P
36 VOLT TRACK CIRCUIT	02	49	52
AC SOLENOID SIGNAL RELAY	06	34	13
AC/DC MAIL TRANSFORMERS	05	85	101
ACTION GRADE CROSSING CONSTRUCTION	07	77	79
ACTION GRADE CROSSING CORRECTION	02	78	146
ACTION GRADE CROSSING CORRECTION 2	02	81	152
ADD PULSE FEATURE TO ADD-ON THROTTLE	03	82	88
ADDING THREE COLOR SIGNALS	04	72	37
AIRPORT RUNWAY SEQUENCE FLASHER CKT	05	82	82
ALTERNATING CURRENT POWER SUPPLIES	10	38	418
ALTERNATING CURRENT POWER SUPPLY	06	34	8
ANYONE CAN WIRE THIS TRANSISTOR THROTTLE	08	63	48
APPROACH INDICATOR LAMPS	05	72	60
ARC WELDER FLASH CIRCUIT	07	81	74
ASTRAC	04	78	138
ASTRAC AND WALKAROUND CONTROL	04	66	46
ASTRAC SYSTEM ON THE RIGHT TRACK?	12	63	33
AUDIBLE SHORT CIRCUIT ALARM EVANS	05	84	104
AUTO GENERATOR CUTOUT FOR SIGNALS	12	36	365
AUTO TRAIN CONTROL W/TRI COLOR SIGNALS	10	75	76
AUTO TRAIN CONTROL: A NEW GAME TODAY	06	76	47
AUTO TURNTABLE CONTROL 1	07	59	28
AUTO TURNTABLE CONTROL 2	08	59	56
AUTOMATIC ACCELERATION	12	40	682
AUTOMATIC CONTROL ABC OR PCC	06	76	105
AUTOMATIC CONTROL CIRCUIT	11	43	504
AUTOMATIC INTERLOCKING	09	37	312
AUTOMATIC INTERLOCKING.	06	46	376
AUTOMATIC REVERSE	12	38	523
AUTOMATIC STOPPING CIRCUIT	05	45	204
AUTOMATIC SWITCHING CIRCUIT GIERHART	11	85	114
AUTOMATIC TRAIN CONTROL	01	82	68
AUTOMATIC TRAIN CONTROL SIMPLIFIED	03	48	171
AUTOMATIC TRAIN CONTROL.	07	64	42
AUTOMATIC TRAIN CONTROL..	05	65	45
BATTERY OPERATED DOME FLASHER CKT REVISE	05	82	83
BEAM HEADLIGHT FOR LOCO OR TROLLEY CONST	04	68	58
BETTER CONTROL	05	49	17
BETTER CONTROL CAB CONTROL	09	49	24
BETTER CONTROL ROUTE BOARDS	11	49	48
BETTER CONTROL ROUTE CAB CONTROL	10	49	30
BETTER CONTROL TWO OR MORE TRAINS	08	49	20
BETTER CONTROL WIRING YOUR RAILROAD	06	49	24
BETTER SPEED CONTROL 5 TYPES	04	56	54
BIPOLAR TRANSISTOR BRIDGE MANN	08	85	82
BIT FOR MODEL IRON HORSE RHE	12	40	681
BLACK LIGHT MAGIC	10	71	35
BLOCK CONTROL	02	47	116
BLOCK OCCUPANCY DETECTOR FOR CC CKT MANN	02	84	97
BLOCK SIGNALING WITHOUT RELAYS	12	34	11
BLOCK SIGNALING YOUR RAILROAD BOOMER PET	12	38	513
BLOCKING & CONTROLLING A ENGINE TERMINAL	07	54	45
BUILD A BETTER THROTTLE CASE	12	61	63
BUILD A BLINKER FLASHING LIGHTS	02	78	102
BUILD A CORDLESS WALK AROUND THROTTLE	05	78	80

ELECTRICAL & ELECTRONICS

	M	Y	P
BUILD A DIGITAL FAST CLOCK	09	83	66
BUILD A DIGITAL FAST CLOCK CORRECTION	11	83	168
BUILD A DIGITAL FAST CLOCK.	11	78	76
BUILD A TETHERED TRANSISTOR THROTTLE	10	78	88
BUILD LIGHTED PUSHBUTTON SWITCHES	03	82	110
BULBS FOR MODEL RAILROAD USE	05	51	53
CAB CONTROL & SIGNALING	09	36	247
CAB CONTROL ON THE MA&PA	06	65	40
CAB CONTROL WIRING	06	68	53
CAB CONTROL-ROBOT RELAYS	02	41	90
CAMPBELL SIGNAL MONITOR	02	68	66
CAPACITORS GENERAL INFORMATION	03	65	59
CAPY DETECTION CIRCUITS	04	73	45
CAR LIGHTING CIRCUIT SIMPLIFIED	04	55	44
CATENARY & OVERHEAD WIRES	08	35	214
CENTRALIZED TRAFFIC CONTROL CENTER	01	84	186
CHASE LIGHT CIRCUITS	03	81	108
CHEAP & DIRTY CORDLESS THROTTLE WOODBURY	02	85	117
CHOOSING AND USING DIODE RECTIFIERS	11	72	72
CHOOSING CORRECT WIRE SIZE	07	49	37
CIRCUIT BREAKER PROTECTION	08	54	40
CIRCUIT BREAKERS	11	44	488
CIRCUIT BREAKERS.	08	46	505
CIRCUITS FOR TRANSISTOR THROTTLES 2	02	62	56
CIRCUITS FOR TRANSISTOR THROTTLES 3	03	62	76
CODED CONTROL OF SIGNALS	09	71	63
CODING YOUR CIRCUITS	08	52	59
COMMAND CONTROL COMPARISON (7 SYSTEMS)	04	80	90
COMMAND CONTROL DOGBONE WIRING KELLER	05	85	101
COMMAND CONTROL QUESTIONS	05	83	80
COMMAND CONTROL WIRING ON W&SF	09	82	90
COMMAND CONTROL: AN UPDATE	03	84	57
COMMERCIAL COMMAND CONTROL SYSTEMS	11	79	80
COMMON RAIL EXPLANATION	04	52	39
COMMON RAIL WIRING ON A SINGLE POWER PAC	12	78	182
CONNECTING TRANSFORMERS IN PARALLEL	07	35	187
CONSTANT CURRENT POWER SOURCE & DIRT BUT	03	57	34
CONSTANT INTENSITY FOR LIONEL PASS CARS	11	83	119
CONSTANT LIGHTING FOR LOCOMOTIVES	09	74	74
CONSTANTNT DIRECTION LIGHTS FOR ZERO-1	02	85	120
CONTACT DETECTION SYSTEM FOR SIGNALS	03	64	30
CONTACTOR SIGNALING	08	37	284
CONTACTOR SIGNALS FOR TRACTION LINES	07	66	50
CONTACTS GALORE FOR SWITCHES & CROSSINGS	03	70	49
CONTROL BOARDS BOOMER PETE	05	41	253
CONTROL CIRCUITS BOOMER PETE	06	39	320
CONTROL OF ELECTRIC TRAINS	05	40	271
CONTROL PANEL CASE CONSTRUCTION	02	55	44
CONTROL PANEL LIGHTS	01	57	33
CONTROL PANEL PLANNING	06	50	32
CONTROL PANEL WIRING	02	45	68
CONTROL PANEL WITH ETCHED DIAGRAMS	06	76	84
CONTROLLING FACTORS ELECTRICAL CONTROLS	08	77	84
CONTROLLING HIDDEN STORAGE TRACKS	05	64	46
CORRECTING ENGINES DIRECTION OF TRAVEL	06	78	140

	M	Y	P
CROSSING FLASHER & BELL RINGER CIRCUIT	03	83	105
CTC CONTROL	07	37	237
CTC FOR THE CAT MOUNTAIN LINE	05	84	74
CTC-16 RECEIVERS IN POWERED DIESEL UNIT	09	81	72
CTC-16 AUDIBLE SHORT CIRCUIT ALARM	05	83	81
CTC-16 BUILD YOUR OWN FOR $200	12	79	64
CTC-16 COMES TO SUNSET VALLEY	01	83	103
CTC-16 COMES TO SUNSET VALLEY CORRECTION	05	83	81
CTC-16 COMMAND STATION	01	80	86
CTC-16 COMMAND SYSTEM IMPROVEMENT	05	83	80
CTC-16 EPILOGUE MORE QUESTIONS	12	80	132
CTC-16 EPILOGUE MORE QUESTIONS CORRECTIO	02	81	162
CTC-16 HAND HELD THROTTLE	03	80	89
CTC-16 LETTERS	06	80	18
CTC-16 MULTIPLE POWER STATION USE	08	82	130
CTC-16 POWER STATION CONSTRUCTION	02	80	89
CTC-16 RECEIVERS	04	80	71
CTC-16 TROUBLESHOOTING HINTS REID	11	83	118
CTC-16 TURNTABLE WIRING	05	83	81
CTC-16E COMMAND/POWER STATION CONSTRUCT	05	84	84
CTC-16E LAYOUT WIRING/AUX POWER STATIONS	07	84	66
CTC-16E NEXT GENERATION COMMAND CONTROL	04	84	85
CTC-16E THROTTLES-DEDICATED OR T/BUS	06	84	68
CTC-16E TWO RECEIVER CONFIGURATIONS	08	84	86
CTC/DIGITAL RECEIVER FOR "N" MANN	11	84	128
CUSTOM BUILDING A MOTOR	10	67	55
CUSTOM BUILDING A MOTOR ADDENDUM	02	68	71
DELAWARE TOWER CAB CONTROL	03	58	50
DETROIT WIRING SYSTEM	02	78	146
DIESEL CONTROLLER CONSTRUCTION	03	57	22
DIESEL ENGINE SOUND GENERATOR WITH IC'S	03	82	87
DIESEL ENGINE SOUND SIMULATOR CKT SMITH	02	84	96
DIESEL HORN CIRCUIT HAMMOND	11	83	116
DIESEL HORN CIRCUIT REED SWITCH ACTIVATO	04	69	56
DIESEL HORN CKT 1 WEBB	02	85	119
DIESEL HORN CKT 2 MANN	05	85	101
DIESEL HORN MFG BY MOUNTAIN AUTOMATION	12	78	65
DIESEL HORN SIMULATION MONSTER-HORN	12	66	50
DIESEL SOUND GENERATOR CIRCUIT 2	01	83	116
DIESEL SOUND SYSTEM CIRCUITS	07	81	74
DIESEL SOUND SYSTEM CIRCUITS CORRECT 1	11	81	105
DIESEL SOUND SYSTEM CIRCUITS CORRECT 2	05	82	84
DIESEL SOUND SYSTEM CIRCUITS CORRECT 3	09	82	87
DIESEL WARNING FLASHER CKT WEBB	02	85	119
DIFFERENCE BETWEEN CAN & MICRO MOTORS	05	79	138
DIGITAL DISPLAYS FOR YOUR RAILROAD	11	76	74
DIGITAL FAST CLOCK CIRCUITS	01	82	69
DIGITAL FAST TIME CLOCK THOMSEN	11	74	82
DIGITAL FAST TIME CLOCK CIRCUIT	05	82	84
DIGITRACK 1600 COMMAND CONTROL SYSTEM	08	72	37
DIODE LIGHTING FOR LOCOS & CARS	05	74	61
DIODE MATRIX SYSTEMS FOR TURNOUT CONTROL	05	82	68
DIODE ROUTING SIMPLIFIED	09	65	16
DIRECT CURRENT POWER SUPPLIES	06	39	311
DIRECT CURRENT POWER SUPPLY	08	34	5

ELECTRICAL & ELECTRONICS

Title	M	Y	P
DIRECTIONAL CONSTANT LIGHTING FOR CC	11	83	117
DIRT CUTTING HOT SPOT FOR TX THROTTLE	11	61	54
DOME FLASHER CKT BATTERY OPERATED	11	83	118
DOUBLE CROSSOVER WIRING	01	83	166
DOUBLE HEADING WITH COMMAND CONTROL	08	85	82
DOUBLE POLE SWITCHES/ROTARY SWITCH MACH	09	52	62
DRUM TYPE CONTROLLER CONSTRUCTION	02	45	78
DRY CELL DIESEL HORN	04	64	38
DUAL POLARIZED FEEDER WIRING	08	73	64
DYNATROL SYSTEMS--WIRING ON SJC	03	84	66
EFFECTIVE LAYOUT LIGHTING PART 1	01	77	84
EFFECTIVE LAYOUT LIGHTING PART 2	06	77	26
ELECTRICAL DEMONS & HOW TO SLAY THEM 1	10	51	40
ELECTRICAL DEMONS & HOW TO SLAY THEM 2	11	51	32
ELECTRICAL DEMONS & HOW TO SLAY THEM 3	12	51	32
ELECTRICAL DEMONS & HOW TO SLAY THEM 4	01	52	56
ELECTRICAL DEMONS & HOW TO SLAY THEM 5	02	52	53
ELECTRICAL DEVICES CAPACITORS	12	57	74
ELECTRICAL DEVICES CIRCUIT BREAKERS	04	58	58
ELECTRICAL DEVICES ELECTRICAL SWITCHES	07	57	58
ELECTRICAL DEVICES FUSES	05	58	52
ELECTRICAL DEVICES LAMPS	03	58	55
ELECTRICAL DEVICES LOCOMOTIVE MOTORS	05	57	66
ELECTRICAL DEVICES METERS	02	58	64
ELECTRICAL DEVICES OSCILLATORS	06	58	52
ELECTRICAL DEVICES RECTIFIERS	06	57	65
ELECTRICAL DEVICES RESISTORS	08	57	60
ELECTRICAL DEVICES RHEOSTATS	11	57	73
ELECTRICAL DEVICES TERMINAL STRIPS	01	58	68
ELECTRICAL DEVICES TRANSFORMERS	04	57	69
ELECTRICAL FACTS FOR BEGINNERS-METERS	02	50	64
ELECTRICAL MEASUREMENT	02	38	65
ELECTRICAL PRIMER BOOMER PETE	01	43	23
ELECTRICAL SPLICE TECHNIQUES	08	36	227
ELECTRICAL WINDSHIELD WIPER MOTORS	01	42	7
ELECTRICITY BLUEBOOK	08	56	45
ELECTRICITY FOR BEGINNERS CAPACITORS	08	49	31
ELECTRICITY FOR BEGINNERS CIRCUIT BREAKE	01	50	72
ELECTRICITY FOR BEGINNERS GENERAL	05	49	40
ELECTRICITY FOR BEGINNERS POWER DISTRIB	10	49	38
ELECTRICITY FOR BEGINNERS POWER PACKS	08	49	31
ELECTRICITY FOR BEGINNERS POWER SUPPLIES	06	49	33
ELECTRICITY FOR BEGINNERS RECTIFIERS	07	49	30
ELECTRICITY FOR BEGINNERS REVERSE METHOD	11	49	64
ELECTRICITY FOR BEGINNERS RHEOSTATS	12	49	67
ELECTRICITY FOR BEGINNERS STORAGE BATTER	09	49	35
ELECTRO-PNEUMATIC CONTROL	11	54	60
ELECTRONIC SIMULATED HOT BOX DETECTORS	05	80	64
ELECTRONICALLY CONTROLLED ELECTRIC LOCO	08	83	98
ELECTRONICS TECHNOLOGY APPLIED TO RR	12	76	108
ELIMINATING JERKY STARTS	02	56	59
END TWIN COIL SWITCH MACHINE FRUSTRATION	04	83	86
ENGINEER CONTROL 1	03	47	192
ENGINEER CONTROL 2	04	47	282
ENGINEER CONTROL 2 CORRECTION	05	47	416
ENGINEERING REPORT ON SSF GENERATORS	12	71	62
EXPANDING YOUR POWER SUPPLY	09	54	34
FAST CIRCUIT BREAKER	08	67	46
FIVE LIGHT FLASHER FOR SIGNS	10	64	50
FIVE VOLT IC POWER SUPPLY HANSEN	12	76	108
FLASHER CIRCUIT FOR GRADE CROSSING COR	04	77	106
FLASHER CIRCUIT FOR GRADE CROSSINGS	07	66	17
FLASHER CIRCUIT FOR GRADE CROSSINGS.	12	76	111
FLASHING LIGHT CIRCUIT TROUBLE SHOOTING	02	69	78
FLASHING LIGHTS FOR RAILROADS	04	68	64
FOOLPROOF CONTROL PLUGS	03	80	130
FOUR ASPECT SIGNALING CIRCUIT	01	37	9
FREQUENCY CONTROL SYSTEM BY ALPHATRONICS	07	78	132
FUEL & WATER SIMULATOR FOBES	05	85	100
FUNDIMENTALS OF CONTROL	01	37	20
GAPS AND FEEDERS IN WIRING	07	72	52
GETTING STARTED WITH GOOD WIRING	11	71	66
GRADUAL MOTOR STARTING	06	65	54
GREAT SEABOARD GOES TWO RAIL	05	37	169
HANDHELD ADD ON THROTTLE	12	78	184
HEADLIGHT BRIGHTNESS BOOSTER THORNE	09	70	63
HEADLIGHT REVERSAL IMPROVED	10	67	66
HEAVY DUTY TRANSFORMER CONSTRUCTION 1	02	51	30
HEAVY DUTY TRANSFORMER CONSTRUCTION 2	03	51	46
HIGH FREQUENCY LIGHTING	07	62	64
HIGH VOLTAGE SIGNALING TRACK CIRCUIT 60V	05	42	222
HIGHWAY & MARS LIGHT FLASHERS RODGERS	11	63	66
HIGHWAY CROSIING CONTROL CIRCUIT	07	44	315
HIGHWAY CROSSING WARNING ACTUATION	11	62	55
HIGHWAY FLASHER PRODUCES COLD LIGHT	02	71	42
HIGHWAY SIGNAL OPERATION FROM THE TRACK	09	69	62
HIGHWAY SIGNAL OPERATION FROM TRACK CORR	11	69	83
HOOKUP WIRE CHART	11	53	80
HOT PROBE TURNOUT CONTROL	06	83	141
HOW TO SIMULATE A ROTATING BEACON	07	78	92
HOW TO WIRE YOUR TRACK	08	48	534
HUMP YARD THAT IS FULLY AUTOMATIC	11	61	57
HYBRID MOTOR TRUCK	05	46	322
IC LOCO/CABOOSE WARNING FLASHER CONST	03	77	50
IDIOT-PROOF TRANSISTOR THROTTLE	01	81	100
ILLUMINATED TRACK DIAGRAM	04	34	5
ILLUMINATED TRACK DIAGRAMS	07	74	62
ILLUMINATED TRACK DIAGRAMS ULTRAVIOLET	05	75	66
IMPROVED PULSE WITH ORDINARY POWER PACKS	07	67	35
IMPROVED VOLTAGE REG (CORRECTION)	11	84	130
IMPROVED VOLTAGE REG THROTTLE W/MOMENTUM	08	84	102
INDEPENDENT OPER OF 4 UNITS IN 1 BLOCK	07	66	26
INEXPENSIVE DIESEL HORN FLEET	02	84	98
INSTALLING WORKING HEADLIGHTS	07	73	66
INSULATING GAPS 1	12	51	23
INSULATING GAPS 2	01	52	36
INTEGRATED CIRCUIT PRIMER	10	76	50
INTEGRATED CIRCUIT TRACK DETECTOR	03	81	108
INTEGRATED PHOTODETECTOR	09	81	92
INTERFACING OPTIMIZED DETECTOR IC SIGNAL	11	83	119

ELECTRICAL & ELECTRONICS

Title	M	Y	P
KEEP HEADLIGHTS BURNING SILICON DIODES	12	62	68
LAMP BULBS METER YOUR CONTROL	01	62	66
LAMPS AS CURRENT LIMITERS - DIODES	06	67	60
LAMPS FOR MODEL RAILROADS TABLE	01	46	15
LED USE INFORMATION	05	82	85
LIGHT ACTUATED ACTION CROSSING CIRCUIT 2	01	83	116
LIGHT BEAMS DETECT TRAINS MILLER	09	73	59
LIGHTING THE LAYOUT ONE BULB NOT ENOUGH	11	74	90
LIGHTING YOUR VILLAGE	07	47	555
LIGHTS AND MARKERS FOR CARS	03	73	38
LIGHTS FOR SIGNALS	05	40	276
LIGHTS THAT STAY LIT IN PASSENGER CARS	04	50	18
LOCO CONTROL PROBLEM W/SELECT POWER PACK	05	82	138
LOCOMOTIVE CONTROLLER	04	43	163
LOGIC THEORY FOR BEGINNERS	11	83	116
LOOP WYE & RETURN CUT OFF WIRING	01	69	82
MAGNETIC MAGIC WITH REED CONTACTS	01	63	16
MAKE YOUR OWN MINIATURE CONNECTORS	07	78	81
MAKE YOUR OWN POWER PACK	10	66	36
MARKER LIGHT CKT PIKE	11	83	116
MARKER LIGHTS DELUXE	02	76	74
MARQUEE TRAVELING LIGHT SYSTEM	03	76	78
MARS LIGHTS (AUTOMATIC)	11	76	115
MASTER ZONE LAYOUT CONTROL	02	74	66
MASTER ZONE LAYOUT CONTROL CORRECTION	04	74	86
MASTER ZONE LAYOUT CONTROL INDICATORS	10	74	66
MASTER ZONE LAYOUT CONTROL WALK AROUND	04	74	68
MASTER ZONE LAYOUT CONTROL MASTER PANEL	05	74	62
MATRIX CONTROL OF SWITCH MACHINES	11	68	44
MINIATURE LAMP BULBS	01	74	78
MODIFIED CTC SIGNAL DECODER PATTERSON	08	85	83
MOMENTUM THROTTLE CIRCUITS YURKON	02	85	116
MOTOR BRUSH PHYSICS	12	66	76
MOTOR CHARACTERISTICS	07	36	176
MOTOR CHART	12	47	1008
MOTOR MAGNETS AND HOW TO CHARGE THEM	09	72	59
MOTOR MAINTENANCE	02	44	76
MOTOR-GENERATOR FOR DC POWER	10	39	508
MOTORMANS CONTROLLER	09	54	52
MULTI-UNIT REVERSING FOR CTC SYSTEMS	11	84	129
MULTICONTACT REMOTE CONTROL SWITCH LEVER	08	48	544
MULTIPURPOSE LED FLASHER (CORRECTION)	11	84	130
MULTIPURPOSE LED FLASHER CIRCUIT	08	84	103
NEW CONTROL BOARD	01	37	22
OHMITE CALCULATORS PARRALLEL RESIST OHMS	07	45	285
ON BOARD EXHAUST SOUND CIRCUIT	05	82	82
ON BOARD STEAM SOUND CIRCUIT	01	83	116
ON BOARD STEAM SOUND CIRCUIT IMPROVEMENT	05	83	82
ON BOARD STEAM SOUND FOR N SCALE	05	83	82
ONE AND TWO BATTERY WIRING	08	42	370
ONE BUTTON LADDER CONTROL	08	75	72
ONE COIL SWITCH MACHINE	06	64	47
ONE CONTACT SIGNALING CIRCUIT	08	62	52
OP AMP DETECTION CIRCUIT PAUL	08	73	65
OPTIMIZED DETECTOR AN UPDATE CKT	03	83	102
OPTIMIZED DETECTOR CIRCUIT	03	82	86
OPTIMIZED DETECTOR CIRCUIT Q&A	09	82	87
OTTLEROTTLE CIRCUIT TESTER	01	68	66
PACEMAKER THROTTLE	12	77	107
PACEMAKER THROTTLE CORRECTION	02	78	146
PC BOARD LIGHT CIRCUITS	02	85	114
PC BOARDS MAKE WIRING EASIER	08	63	46
PERFECT SWITCH MACHINE	11	77	64
PHOTOELECTRIC DETECTOR CIRCUIT	09	81	92
PLUG IN STRUCTURE WIRING	10	68	58
POLARIZED RELAY FOR REVERSING LOCOMOTIVE	10	45	396
POLARIZED RELAYS	05	64	50
POLARIZED REVEARSING RELAY	12	37	444
POSSIBILITY OF RADIO CONTROL ON MODEL RR	12	52	39
POWER FEEDERS	03	44	116
POWER FOR DISTANT SWITCH MACHINES	05	80	98
POWER FOR YOUR TURNTABLE	05	48	350
POWER PACK SELECTION	06	48	404
POWER PACK SELECTION.	10	52	40
POWER PLANT-POWER SUPPLY WITH METERS 1	12	44	534
POWER PLANT-POWER SUPPLY WITH METERS 2	01	45	22
PRACTICAL CONTROL PANEL WIRING	07	65	37
PRACTICAL LAYOUT LIGHTING	07	74	51
PRACTICAL SWITCH CONTROL BOOMER PETE	10	44	444
PREFAB ASSEMBLIES FOR SIGNALING	09	55	41
PRINTED CIRCUIT THROTTLE (TAT III LAYOUT	09	64	55
PROTECTION FOR TRANSISTORS FROM RELAYS	01	64	83
PROTOTYPE ACTION THROTTLE: PART 1	01	79	112
PS1 DYNATROL RRL RECEIVER FOR ATLAS RS-3	09	85	116
PULSE ADD-ON THROTTLE CIRCUIT CORRECTION	01	83	116
PULSE POWER LATEST DEVELOPMENTS	08	54	52
PULSE POWER WHAT IS IT?	02	54	80
PULSE POWER TOWARD PERFECT MOTOR RESPONC	01	65	60
PULSE TONE WALKAROUND CONTROL SYS CORREC	07	81	74
PULSE TONE WALKAROUND CONTROL SYSTEM	02	81	84
PULSE-POWER MEASUREMENT	06	85	106
PURE PULSE TRANSISTOR THROTTLE	01	65	63
PURE PULSE TRANSISTOR THROTTLE CORRECTIN	04	65	57
PUSH BUTTONS BY THE DOZEN CONSTRUCTION	07	60	41
QUADRANT THROTTLE CONSTRUCTION	05	52	31
RADIO CONTROL-NO SECTIONAL TRACK NEEDED	04	41	194
REALISTIC CONTROL FOR GRADE CROSS FLASH	02	77	68
RECESSED CONTROL PANEL CONSTRUCTION	10	56	32
RECTIFIERS	06	45	240
RECTIFIERS FOR POWER & REVERSAL	05	38	181
REDUCING MOTOR STATIC	04	67	59
REFRIGERATOR CAR SOUND SIMULATOR CKT	11	83	118
RELAY INTERLOCKING CTC SYSTEM B. PETE	09	44	393
RELAY TERM GLOSSARY	11	45	464
RELAYLESS SIGNALING WITH TWIN-T	10	64	56
RELAYS	03	52	24
RELAYS AND HOW THEY CONTROL	09	44	396
RELAYS BUILDING YOUR OWN	12	44	525
RELAYS FOR SIGNALING BOOMER PETE	11	45	463
RELAYS- ROBOTS THAT HELP RUN MODEL RYS	10	45	404

ELECTRICAL & ELECTRONICS

Title	M	Y	P
RELAYS.	07	56	39
RELIABLE TINPLATE WIRING	07	50	40
RESISTOR QUESTIONS ANSWERED	08	65	55
REVERSE SWITCHES.	03	40	145
REVERSING HEADLIGHT FOR LIONEL AC	08	85	82
REVERSING REMOTE CONTROL	02	35	44
REVERSING VOLT METER	11	41	567
REVISED SIGNAL CIRCUITS	12	55	77
REWINDING HO MOTORS CORRECTION	11	46	725
REWINDING HO MOTORS TO 12V STANDARD	10	46	634
RHEOSTAT ADJUSTMENT BY REMOTE CONTROL	09	55	50
RHEOSTAT HOMEMADE FOR HO	10	51	34
RHEOSTATS	10	44	432
RHEOSTATS IN TANDEM	09	54	45
RHEOSTATS WITH CHART	05	48	354
ROUTE CAB CONTROL ADDED CONTACTS	05	57	52
ROUTE CAB CONTROL BLOCKS & SIGNALS	09	57	52
ROUTE CAB CONTROL BRANCH LINES ETC	07	57	54
ROUTE CAB CONTROL ROUTE CAB CIRCUITRY	08	57	52
ROUTE CAB CONTROL TRAIN OPER AT ITS BEST	04	57	60
ROUTE CAB CONTROL TURNOUT CONTROL	06	57	54
ROUTE CAB CONTROL YARDMASTER	08	57	56
ROUTE INDICATOR FOR THE CONTROL PANL CKT	03	83	103
ROUTE INTERLOCKING 1	09	46	574
ROUTE INTERLOCKING 2	10	46	654
ROUTE INTERLOCKING 3	11	46	739
ROUTE SELECTION WITH FEWER DIODES	11	71	68
ROUTING THROUGH TURNOUTS WITH DIODES	04	65	50
SCALE TIME CLOCK CONSTRUCTION	08	44	340
SCHMIDT TRIGGER FOR PULSE CONTROL CKT	04	66	58
SCR THROTTLE SYSTEM CONSTRUCTION	06	77	70
SCR THROTTLE WITH MOMENTUM EFFECTS	03	68	54
SCR TIME DELAY CIRCUIT	08	67	62
SEARCHLIGHT SIGNAL CKT MITCHELL	02	84	97
SENSITIVE BLOCK IN USE DETECTOR	03	69	65
SEPARATED RETURN LOOP CONTROL	03	74	41
SEQUENCE LIGHTING DRUM CONTROLLER	12	52	44
SEVEN CIRCUITS FOR TX THROTTLES	01	62	58
SEVEN CIRCUITS FOR TX THROTTLES COR1	03	62	10
SEVEN CIRCUITS FOR TX THROTTLES COR2	03	62	76
SHORT CIRCUITS FOOLPROOFING	08	47	639
SIGNAL CIRCUIT DESIGN	08	48	565
SIGNAL CIRCUITS	12	54	66
SIGNAL CIRCUITS FOR BEGINNERS	02	53	48
SIGNAL DETECTION WITH AN SCR	03	68	60
SIGNAL RELAY CONSTRUCTION	04	44	172
SIGNALING CIRCUITS	03	81	108
SIGNALING CIRCUITS CORRECTION 3-81 P108	07	81	74
SIGNALING PRIMER BOOMER PETE	03	42	115
SILENT SOLENOIDS FOR SIGNALS	03	43	112
SILICON CONTROLLED RECTIFIERS POWER PACK	03	67	42
SIMPLE BUT SURE BLOCK SIGNALS	10	65	57
SIMPLE DETECTION CIRCUIT ROSENBAUM	02	85	121
SIMPLE ELECTRICAL TOOLS & TESTS	08	45	326
SIMPLE INTERLOCKING FUNDAMENTALS	06	44	262
SIMPLE POLARITY INDICATOR CONSTRUCT #1	11	70	56
SIMPLE SIGNALING	03	38	93
SIMPLE SIGNALS FOR TRACTION LINES	03	66	45
SIMPLE SOUND MAKER FOR MODEL RAILROADS	04	67	56
SIMPLE TURNOUT CONTROL MECHANISM	06	75	57
SIMPLEST OF TRANSISTOR THROTTLES	08	76	44
SIMPLIFIED PRACTICAL CONTROL BOOMER PETE	09	39	448
SIMPLIFIED SWITCH MACHINE CONTROL	11	58	60
SINGLE TRACK PROTECTION CONTROLLER	11	81	104
SINGLE TRACK PROTECTION CONTROLLER REVIS	03	82	87
SLAVE DRIVER MU BOOSTER FOR CC-16 MANN	11	83	117
SLO-MO-SHON CONSTRUCTION SWITCH MACHINE	01	77	64
SNAP ACTION POWER FOR SWITCH MACHINES 1	08	64	52
SNAP ACTION POWER FOR SWITCH MACHINES 2	12	64	81
SNEAKY FAULTS OF TRANSISTOR THROTTLES	10	61	48
SOLID STATE TURNOUT CONTROL MINDY	05	84	104
SOLID STATE TURNTABLE CONTROL	07	82	79
SOUND EFFECTS USING ELECTRIC GADGETS	04	41	192
SOUND EFFECTS CHIPS	11	80	113
SOUND EFFECTS CHIPS CORRECTION	03	81	109
SPEED CONTROL FOR SWITCHING & TURNTABLES	09	66	41
SPEED DETECTOR CIRCUITS	02	82	88
SPEED DETECTOR CIRCUITS CORRECTION 2-85	07	82	126
SPEED SIGNALING	12	54	88
SSF GENERATOR FOR TRAIN LIGHT CONTROL	12	71	60
STANDARD RELAY CIRCUITS-7 OF THEM	11	45	463
STANDARD THREE INDICATOR SIGNAL CIRCUIT	10	39	510
STARTING CIRCUITS FOR YOUR CONTROL	01	35	6
STEAM WHISTLE CIRCUIT	05	83	82
STEAM WHISTLE CKT HAMMOND	11	84	128
STORAGE BATTERIES	07	44	298
STROBE LIGHT CKT PIKE	11	83	116
STUD CONTACT POEWER DISTRIBUTION	05	64	59
SWITCH MACHINE A HOMEMADE MAGNETIC	07	34	9
SWITCH MACHINE CONTACT USES	03	63	69
SWITCH MACHINE CONTACT USES MORE	04	63	69
SWITCH MACHINE CONTACT USES STILL MORE	05	63	58
SWITCH MACHINE CONTROL AT LOW COST	04	52	30
SWITCH MACHINE POWER SUPPLY FYFFE	01	69	84
SWITCH MACHINES	03	50	45
SWITCH MACHINES FROM DOOR BELLS	06	41	307
SWITCH MOTOR CONSTRUCTION	05	37	181
SWITCH MOTORS FOR TURNOUTS	01	76	71
TAT IV CLARIFICATION	07	69	23
TAT IV IMPROVED TRANSISTOR THROTTLE	03	69	12
TELEPHONE SYSTEM USED ON CM&SF	08	82	64
TELEPHONE SYSTEM USED ON CM&SF CORRECTIO	10	82	147
TENDER PICKUPS	04	47	290
TERMINAL BOARD USE FOR EASE OF WIRING	09	79	25
THERMAL SWITCH MACHINE	07	65	30
THIRD RAIL SHOE CONSTRUCTION	09	37	311
THREE COLOR SIGNAL CONTROL 1	06	76	68
THREE COLOR SIGNAL CONTROL 2	08	76	80
THREE COLOR SIGNALS ON THE TSL	06	72	60
THREE COLOR SIGNALS WITH ONE LAMP	12	74	78

ELECTRICAL & ELECTRONICS

	M	Y	P
THREE CONTROLS FROM TWO WIRES	11	67	61
THREE INDICATOR SIGNAL LETTERS	11	39	588
THROTTLE BOOSTER CIRCUITS	03	73	62
THROTTLE BOOSTER CIRUITS CORRECTION	05	73	77
THROTTLE CASES MAKE IT LOOK GOOD	05	70	51
THROTTLE METER CONSTRUCTION	12	80	128
TIMER MOTOR SOURCES	02	77	125
TINPLATE CONTROL OF TWO OR MORE TRAINS	04	50	74
TINPLATE CONVERSION MOTOR TRUCK	09	46	564
TOGGLE SWITCH CAB CONTROL/MULTIPLE PACKS	03	73	33
TOTAL STEAM SOUND CIRCUITS	05	81	88
TRACK & CONTROL ON J&SW	06	82	62
TRACK & CONTROL ON J&SW CORRECTION	10	82	147
TRACK CIRCUITS OPEN AND CLOSED	04	36	89
TRACK CONNECTORS FOR TWO RAIL	11	35	292
TRACK DETECTION CIRCUITS OF NMRA	03	49	12
TRACK DIAGRAM & INTERLOCKING CABINET	03	61	54
TRACK INDICATING CONTROL BOARD	03	56	46
TRACKSIDE CONTACT SIGNALING	05	53	44
TRAFFIC SIGNAL SEQUENCE CKT	05	82	82
TRAIN ANNUNCIATOR APPLICATION FOR TWIN-T	04	60	51
TRAIN CONTROL FOR CROSSINGS	07	45	282
TRAIN CONTROL HOMEMADE UNIT	04	45	156
TRAIN CONTROL METHODS 1	01	72	73
TRAIN CONTROL METHODS 2	02	72	71
TRAIN DETECTION USING COMPARATORS	09	81	92
TRAIN DETECTOR CKT PIKE	11	83	116
TRAIN OPERATION VERSUS POWER PACKS	01	71	60
TRAIN SITUATION INDICATOR	12	73	82
TRAIN SITUATION INDICATOR UPDATE1	09	81	92
TRAIN SITUATION INDICATORS	11	80	110
TRAIN SPEEDOMETER	05	54	36
TRANSFORMER PHASING	12	70	88
TRANSFORMER PROTECTION	05	44	213
TRANSFORMERS	12	46	822
TRANSFORMERS AND POWER SUPPLIES	03	80	150
TRANSISTOR HEAT SINKS	01	75	70
TRANSISTOR THROTTLE BASIC & ADD ON CONST	06	75	52
TRANSISTOR THROTTLE TROUBLE SHOOTING	11	64	48
TRANSISTOR THROTTLES IMPROVING CONTROL	11	60	56
TRANSISTORS FOR MODEL CIRCUITRY	05	63	50
TRANSISTORS FOR MODEL RAIL USE LISTINGS	01	75	71
TRANSISTORS FOR MODEL RAILROAD USE	10	69	82
TRANSISTORS FOR MODEL RAILROADERS	09	61	61
TRAVELING ENGINEERS MOVE WITH TRAIN	02	52	50
TRICOLOR LED SIGNAL CIRCUIT	11	81	103
TRICOLOR LED SIGNAL IMPROVEMENTS	09	82	87
TROLLEY CONTROL	12	54	60
TROUBLE SHOOTING TRANSISTORS	05	60	57
TTL TRAIN DETECTION CIRCUITS	01	77	98
TTL TRAIN DETECTION CIRCUITS CORRECTION	07	77	108
TURBINE SOUND CIRCUIT	09	82	86
TURBINE SOUND CIRCUIT CORRECTION	10	82	147
TURNOUT CONTROL WITH MOTORS/ELECTRONICS	09	85	92
TURNOUT INDICATOR LAMPS THAT REMEMBER	10	73	61
TURNOUT INDICATOR WITH NO CONTACTS	05	68	54
TURNOUT POSITION INDICATOR CIRCUIT	09	81	92
TURNOUT POSITION INDICATOR CIRCUIT UP 1	05	82	84
TURNOUT POSITION INDICATOR CIRCUIT UP 2	03	83	105
TURNTABLE ALIGNMENT WITH PHOTOCELLS	11	66	58
TURNTABLE WIRING	11	66	71
TV REMOTE SPEED & DIRECTION CONTROL	03	82	88
TWIN COIL MACHINE POWER REQUIREMENTS	12	81	178A
TWIN T DETECTION CKT BUGS	08	80	135
TWIN T REVISITED UPDATE ON DETECTION CKT	08	80	80
TWIN T VS 2-D SIGNAL DETECTOR CIRCUITS	11	64	70
TWIN-T CIRCUITS 1	06	58	36
TWIN-T CIRCUITS 2	07	58	42
TWIN-T CIRCUITS 3	08	58	41
TWIN-T CIRCUITS REVISITED	10	72	80
TWIN-T SIGNAL SYSTEM ON SUNSET VALLEY	10	70	38
TWIN-T SILENT SIGNALS	08	60	51
TWO CAB WIRING BASICS	01	85	107
TWO COLOR SIGNAL LIGHTING	09	71	64
TWO RAIL CROSSING CIRCUIT	09	36	266
TWO RAIL SIGNAL CIRCUIT	07	38	282
TWO RAIL SIGNALING CIRCUIT	10	44	443
TWO RAIL SIGNALING KITS BY KRAMBLE	12	35	330
TWO RAIL SIGNALING-NO RELAYS	02	40	65
TWO RAIL SIMPLIFIED	07	37	246
TWO RAIL TRACK CIRCUIT SYMPOSIUM	07	47	536
TWO RAIL TRACK MADE EASY BOOMER PETE	09	40	484
TWO RAIL TRACK WIRING	12	49	30
TWO RAIL TRAIN CONTROL	10	41	497
TWO RAIL WIRING BASICS	03	81	110
TWO WAY AUTOMATIC TRAIN CONTROL	08	44	339
TX THROTTLE MODERNIZATION OF POWER PACK	01	70	76
UNCOUPLING RAMP ELECTROMAGNETIC CONSTRUC	01	61	54
UNUSUAL ELECTRICAL DEVICES	02	45	71
USE DIODES TO IMPROVE NORMAL WIRING	11	72	71
USE SNAP SWITCHES FOR POWER ROUTINGS/PAN	08	85	108
USEABLE MOTORS FROM AUTOS	08	43	354
USING 50 CYCLE AC EQUIPMENT	05	78	131
USING IC'S FOR SIGNALING	04	78	84
USING TTR'S FOR POWER SUPPLY/CONST LIGHT	08	79	79
VARIABLE TRANSFORMERS	02	55	48
VARIABLE TRANSFORMERS QUESTIONS/ANSWERS	04	55	56
VARIACS	01	41	8
VOLTAGE CONTROLLED STEAM SOUND CIRCUIT	09	82	86
VOLTAGE CONTROLLED STEAM SOUND CIRCUIT C	11	82	171
VOLTAGE REGULATOR FOR PULS THROTTLE CKT	11	83	116
VOLTMETER SPEEDOMETER	06	52	28
WALK AROUND CONTROL SYSTEM ON OHIO SOUTH	05	79	71
WALKAROUND CAB CONTROL PROBLEMS SOLVED	11	65	47
WALKAROUND CONRTOL BLOCK CONNECTING	03	69	52
WALKAROUND CONTROL 1	09	72	50
WALKAROUND CONTROL 2	07	78	127
WALKAROUND CONTROL 1	04	65	38
WALKAROUND CONTROL 2 FOR TWO TRAINS	07	65	40
WALKAROUND LOCOMOTIVE CONTROL	10	65	34

ELECTRICAL & ELECTRONICS

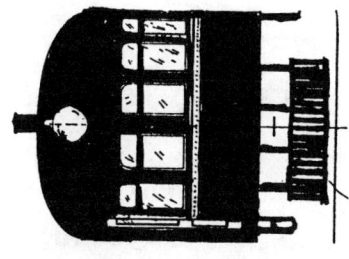

	M	Y	P
WALKAROUND LOCOMOTIVE CONTROL.	06	66	38
WALKAROUND THROTTLE PULSE/MEMORY UPGRADE	01	82	68
WALKAROUND TRANSISITOR THROTTLE DESIGN	01	75	74
WARTIME MOTORS FROM SCRAP	12	42	536
WHICH TRAIN CONTROL IS BEST FOR YOU?	03	48	204
WHISTLE BELL STEAM AND EXHAUST SOUNDS	05	66	44
WHISTLE BELL STEAM AND EXHAUST SOUNDS C	07	66	15
WHISTLE HANDLE FOR FYFFE ST SOUND GENERA	06	79	110
WINDING YOUR OWN TRANSFORMERS	06	62	59
WIRE FOR TRACK AND ACCESSORIES	01	64	78
WIRELESS THROTTLE CONST NO MOD TO CTC-16	03	83	86
WIRELESS THROTTLE CONTROLLER/POWER PACK	04	83	68
WIRING A DOUBLE CROSSOVER	09	70	75
WIRING A DOUBLE SLIP SWITCH	01	69	92
WIRING A LAYOUT	07	78	127
WIRING A LAYOUT FIRST STEP FORWARD	03	78	127
WIRING CROSSINGS	02	74	84
WIRING CROSSINGS AND TURNOUTS	03	49	18
WIRING FOR MODEL RAILROADS	10	36	290
WIRING HAND LAID CROSSINGS	07	82	131
WIRING SPLIT RINGS FOR TURNTABLES	12	77	84
WIRING SWITCH MACHINES	03	63	70
WIRING THE NY&Q	01	69	59
WIRING THE PORTAGE HILL	08	62	34
WIRING THE PORTAGE HILL CONTROL PANELS	10	62	52
WIRING THE PORTAGE HILL REVERSING SECT	09	62	37
WIRING TIPS FOR BEGINNERS	01	74	70
WIRING TURNING TRACKS BLUEBOOK	04	57	68
WIRING YOUR 1ST LAYOUT OBVIOUS NOT BEST	04	75	40
WIRING YOUR LAYOUT 2 RAIL	08	42	371
WIRING YOUR LAYOUT 3 RAIL OR TROLLEY	09	42	417
WIRING YOUR LAYOUT CONTROL BOARD	11	42	505
WIRING YOUR LAYOUT CONTROL BOARD COREECT	04	43	181
WIRING YOUR LAYOUT CONTROL BORAD CONST	12	42	560
WIRING YOUR LAYOUT CONTROL PANEL	10	42	467
WIRING YOUR LAYOUT CONTROL TYPES	07	42	318
WIRINGS BASIC RULES	02	56	36
WORKING MARS LIGHTS HULEN	03	75	74
WORKING SIGNALS FOR LAYOUTS	12	50	42
WOUND FIELD MOTORS	03	52	52
X SECTION SIMPLIFIED CAB CONTROL	09	58	52
ZERO 1 FOR N SCALE	07	83	62

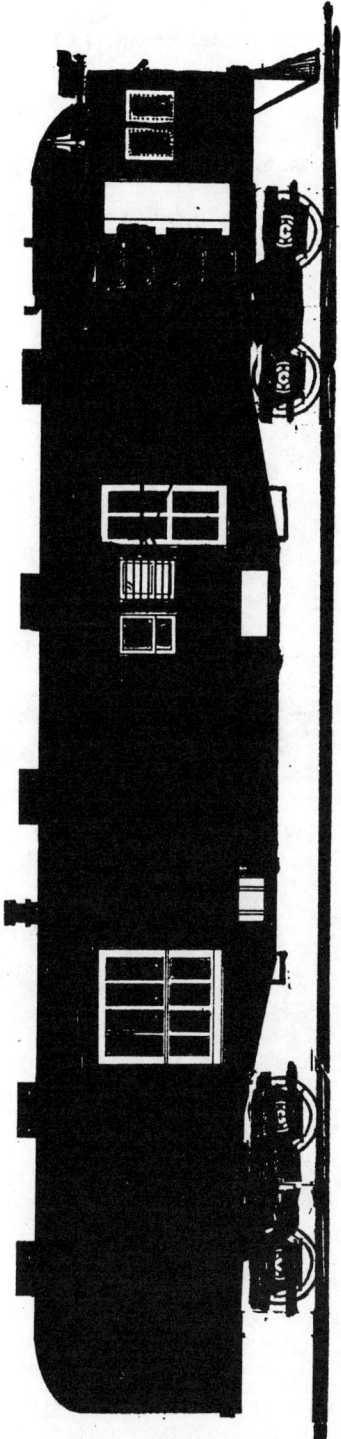

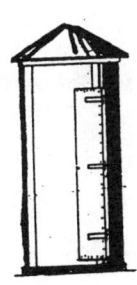

BILL OF LADING   TOOLS & MATERIALS

In this section raw materials, their properties and uses, are listed. Also the tools of the trade are identified. These include the basic tools like screwdrivers and hammers to the exotic model lathes. The descriptor line is self-explanatory.

MANIFEST   TOOLS & MATERIALS

	PAGE
TOOLS & MATERIALS	208
TOOLS	209
MATERIALS	210

TOOLS & MATERIALS

TOOLS	M	Y	P
ADJUSTABLE DRIVE QUARTERING JIG	01	71	44
AIR COMPRESSOR CONSTRUCTION	02	49	25
AIR PAINTING EQUIPMENT	06	67	40
AIRBRUSHES MAKE YOUR OWN	07	71	62
ALL SCALE DRILL & WIRE CHART	04	61	39
BELT DRIVE FOR SENSITIVE DRILL	01	70	80
BENCH AND STORAGE CHEST CONSTRUCTION	10	74	56
BENDING ANGLE STOCK	08	70	57
BETTER MODELS WITH A SURFACE PLATE	07	74	34
BUILD A PIN JIG	11	68	78
BUILD A PORTABLE OVEN	06	80	98
BUILD A VAPOR DEGREASER	04	79	90
BUILD A WOODEN CALIPER	05	80	96
CALCULATORS AS TOOLS FOR MODELING	01	75	84
CARRYING CASE CONST TRANSPORT/STORAGE	06	59	36
CARRYING CASE FOR MODELS CONSTRUCTION	11	49	32
CART FERRY STORAGE & CONSTRUCTION	09	74	66
CASTING WITH VACUUM DE-AIRING	09	75	68
COMBINATION SQUARES THEIR USE & CARE	06	50	37
CONVERSION TABLES FOR SCALE MODELS	04	74	49
COUPLER AND DIAPHRAGM CHECK GAUGE	07	56	37
CUSTOM CLAMPS	12	78	185
CUTTING BOARD DELUX CONSTRUCTION	07	77	51
DECAL APPLICATION JIG	03	81	96
DECIMAL EQUIVALENTS FOR DRILLS	03	57	20
DELUXE CUTTING AND DRAFTING BOARD	07	77	51
DELUXE HOBBYBENCH	10	80	121
DELUXE SPRAY BOOTH CONSTRUCTION	08	83	103
DENTAL TOOLS FOR MODELING	04	75	62
DENTISTS SPOON AS A TOOL	10	74	55
DIE CASTINGS WITH YOUR OWN DIES	01	44	16
DIES THEIR USE & CARE	10	50	69
DRILL PRESS CONSTRUCTION SENSITIVE	08	69	58
DRILL PRESSES & DRILLING SPEEDS TABLE	09	73	74
DRILL SCREW AND TAP SIZES	11	56	69
DRILL SCREW AND TAP SIZES.	01	42	29
DRILLS (TWIST DRILLS) USE & CARE	04	53	53
DRILLS AND DRILLING	07	68	47
DRILLS THEIR USE AND CARE	02	50	48
DRIVER QUARTERING JIG	10	61	47
ECONOMY SURFACE PLATES	09	76	72
FILE SELECTION AND USE	10	79	160
FILES THEIR USE AND CARE	11	49	74
FILES AND RASPS	03	43	127
GANTRY LADDER FOR LAYOUT BUILDING	11	68	66
GLUE GUNS AND HOT GLUE	11	75	92
GRADIENT GAUGE CONSTRUCTION	01	43	10
HACKSAW BLADES	05	43	217
HAMMERS HOW THEY WORK	09	72	75
HAND TAPS AND THEIR USES	01	74	89
HELPING THIRD HAND	12	74	88
HOMEMADE MINIATURE CLAMP	03	84	142
HOMEMADE SOLDERING TORCH	09	68	30
LATHE MACHINING IN MINIATURE	09	75	66
LATHE OPERATION THE ABC'S	09	78	132
LATHES REVIEW FOR MODEL BUILDERS	03	70	44
LAYOUT TOOLS FOR SCRATCHBUILDING	02	69	46
LIQUID LEVEL FOR LAYOUTS	12	50	61
LOCOMOTIVE TEST RACKS	08	71	66
MASTER RIVETER WITH MINI RIVETER	10	79	76
MICRO FILES FOR DETAIL WORK	06	69	47
MINIATURE OILSTONE BENCH GRINDER	06	78	94
MOBILE HOBBY BENCH CONSTRUCTION	09	81	106
MODEL BEGINNERS TOOL BOX	04	82	72
MODELMAKING WORKBENCH CONSTRUCTION	04	72	53
MODLERS HAND SAWS-ALL TYPES	04	74	80
MOTOR TOOLS 1	06	56	41
MOTOR TOOLS 2 BLUEBOOK	07	56	53
NEEDLE POINT APPLICATOR REVIEW A-WEST	08	77	30
OVEN FOR SETTING EPOXY JOINTS & CASTINGS	04	74	46
PAINT JAR RACK CONSTRUCTION	05	84	99
PARTS CATCHER APRON	04	84	138
PLIERS AND THEIR USES	04	46	260
PORTABLE WORKSHOP CARRYING CASE CONST	03	75	69
POWER SAW FOR SMALL PARTS	03	75	78
PUNCHES & THEIR USES	01	69	93
QUARTERING JIG REVIEW NWSL	03	77	38
QUARTERING JIG FOR DRIVERS	05	67	30
QUICK GETAWAY CLAMP CONSTRUCTION	01	83	172
RENEWABLE AIR SUPPLY FOR AIRBRUSH PAINT	12	79	112
RIVET FORMING MACHINE	06	51	25
RIVET PUNCH BUILD YOUR OWN	03	60	28
ROLLTOP WORKBENCH	03	77	98
SANDBAGS, FROGS & JAWS (CLAMPS)	05	81	101
SANDBLAST SYSTEM BUILD YOUR OWN	09	77	68
SCENERY MATERIAL APPLICATOR	01	83	165
SCREWDRIVERS AND HOW TO USE THEM	11	72	84
SCREWDRIVERS THEIR CARE & USES	01	51	65
SCRIBING JIG FOR WOOD/STYRENE/METAL	02	77	94
SHAPING TOOLS FOR STYROFOAM	06	67	28
SHEET METAL AND WIRE GAUGES	02	43	83
SIMPLE POLARITY INDICATOR CONSTRUCT $1	11	70	56
SIMPLE PUNCHES FOR MODLERS	06	77	64
SKY HOOK CONSTRUCTION-REACH THE BACK!	10	49	34
SMALL CLAMPS BIG HELPS	04	48	256
SMALL TOOL CLINIC	10	47	824
SOFT SOLDERING TOOLS	06	36	151
SOLDERING HEAT CONTROL	11	46	745
SOLDERING TOOLS	05	34	13
SOLDERING TOOLS 1	04	39	200
SOLDERING TOOLS 2	05	39	260
SOLDERING TOOLS AND METHODS	05	49	30
SPIKE DRIVER	04	77	86
STRIPWOOD CUTTING TOOL	08	70	76
SURFACE GAUGE VERSATILE TOOLS $1	11	71	69
SURFACE GAUGE FOR A DOLLAR $1	08	72	60
TAPS AND DIES	04	43	179
TAPS AND HOW TO USE THEM	12	67	73
TAPS THEIR USE AND CARE	12	48	934
TEST STAND FOR LOCOMOTIVE MOTORS	06	79	93

TOOLS & MATERIALS

TOOLS	M	Y	P
THREE-D PANTOGRAPH FOR DRAWING	09	65	42
THREE-D PANTOGRAPH FOR DRAWING CONTINUED	11	65	60
THUMB TACH FOR MODEL RAILROAD USE	09	76	66
TIE CUTTING JIG	06	65	30
TOOL DEMAGNETIZER	06	44	254
TOOLS THE UNUSUAL ONES	08	53	24
TOOLS BLUEBOOK	01	56	63
TOOLS FOR GENERAL SERVICING EQUIPMENT	06	69	63
TOOLS FOR GENERAL SIMPLE METAL WORKING	10	69	80
TOOLS FOR WORKING BRASS	07	71	44
TOOLS IN GENERAL ASSEMBLING PLASTIC KITS	07	69	66
TOOLS IN GENERAL ASSEMBLING WOOD KITS	08	69	69
TOOLS IN GENERAL MAKE MODELING EASIER	11	40	594
TOOLS OF THE HOBBIEST TRADE	12	77	168
TOOLS OF THE MODEL RAILROADER	12	77	168
TRAUBS RIVET MACHINE	01	78	72
TRAY FOR ASSEMBLING MODELS	03	62	52
TWO IN ONE CABINET	04	48	285
ULTRAMINI SURFACE GAUGE CONSTRUCTION	02	81	130
UNDER LAYOUT SCOOTER CONSTRUCTION	01	55	45
UNDER TABLE CREEPER CONSTRUCTION	06	47	478
UNIMAT MODIFICATIONS	10	76	57
USEFUL MODELING TOOLS	05	47	380
USING A MICROMETER	08	78	124
USING METAL WORKING TOOLS	11	82	126
WHEEL COLLET FOR YOUR WORKSHOP	07	72	55
WHEEL PULLER	09	76	77
WILD WILLIES LIGHTED KD UNCOUPLING TOOL	08	81	81
WOOD SCREW REFERENCE	09	53	43
WORK STATION & SHOP	07	75	76
WORKBENCH CAR CLAMP	01	55	66
WORKSHOP DATA AND DETAIL DIMENSIONS	08	74	47
WORKSHOP IN A BOX CONSTRUCTION	02	56	38

MATERIALS	M	Y	P
ACC BONDING OF MODEL PARTS	11	72	74
ACRYLIC PLASTICS FOR STRUCTURES	07	75	70
ADHESIVES BASICS FOR CHOOSING RIGHT ONE	02	83	114
BLACKENING SOLUTION REVIEW A-WEST	05	77	39
BRASS WIRE IN MILLMETER SIZES	03	78	127
CARPET TAPE SIDING ATTACHMENT	10	84	148
GALVANIZED SHEET IRON	07	37	255
HO SCALE LUMBER SOURCES	06	78	140
HOMASOTE	07	67	61
LICHEN AND HOW TO USE IT	11	81	112
LOW MELTING POINT ALLOYS	06	78	137
LUBRICANTS OF TEFLON	03	75	35
MAKING ITEMS FROM BALL POINT PENS	11	78	146
METALS FOR MOLDING CHARACTERISTICS	01	77	129
NICKEL SILVER ADVANTAGES	04	39	208
PERFECT FILLER PUTTY FOR PLASTICS	06	83	141
PLASTER MIXES	04	65	26
PLASTIC STRUCTURAL SHAPES IN ABS	05	69	54
REAL LEXAN	08	78	101
SCENERY PLASTER TYPES	04	65	29
SELECTING ADHESIVES	12	78	178
SELF HARDENING SEALANTS FOR AXELS	05	71	64
SILICONE RUBBER ADHESIVE	02	64	70
SMALL DIAMETER WIRE	01	77	131
SMALL SCREWS-NUTS-WASHERS	02	78	148
SMALL SPRING AVAILABILITY	12	78	187
STRATHMORE BOARD USE	06	74	81
STUCK ON ADHESIVES	03	80	132
STYRENE BUILDING MATERIALS REVIEW	09	77	34
TESTIMONIAL TO STYRENE	05	70	66
TRACK CLEANER LISTING AHM	07	77	43
X-30 ADHESIVE REVIEW PACER INDUSTRIES	03	77	29

STEPHANS' RAILROAD DIRECTORY

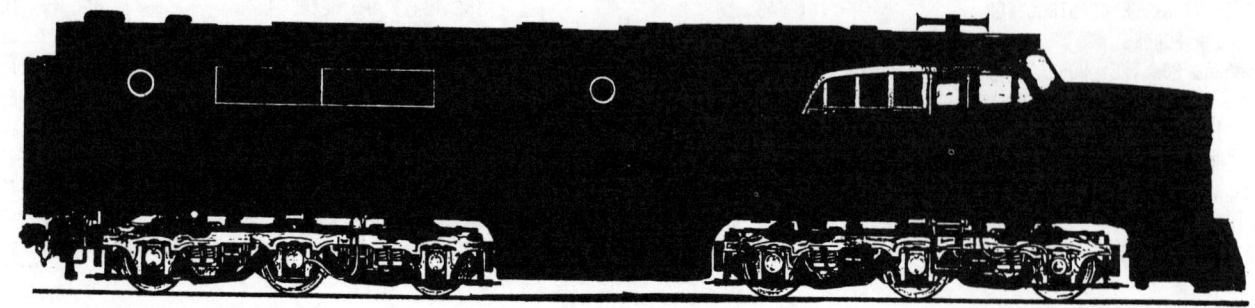

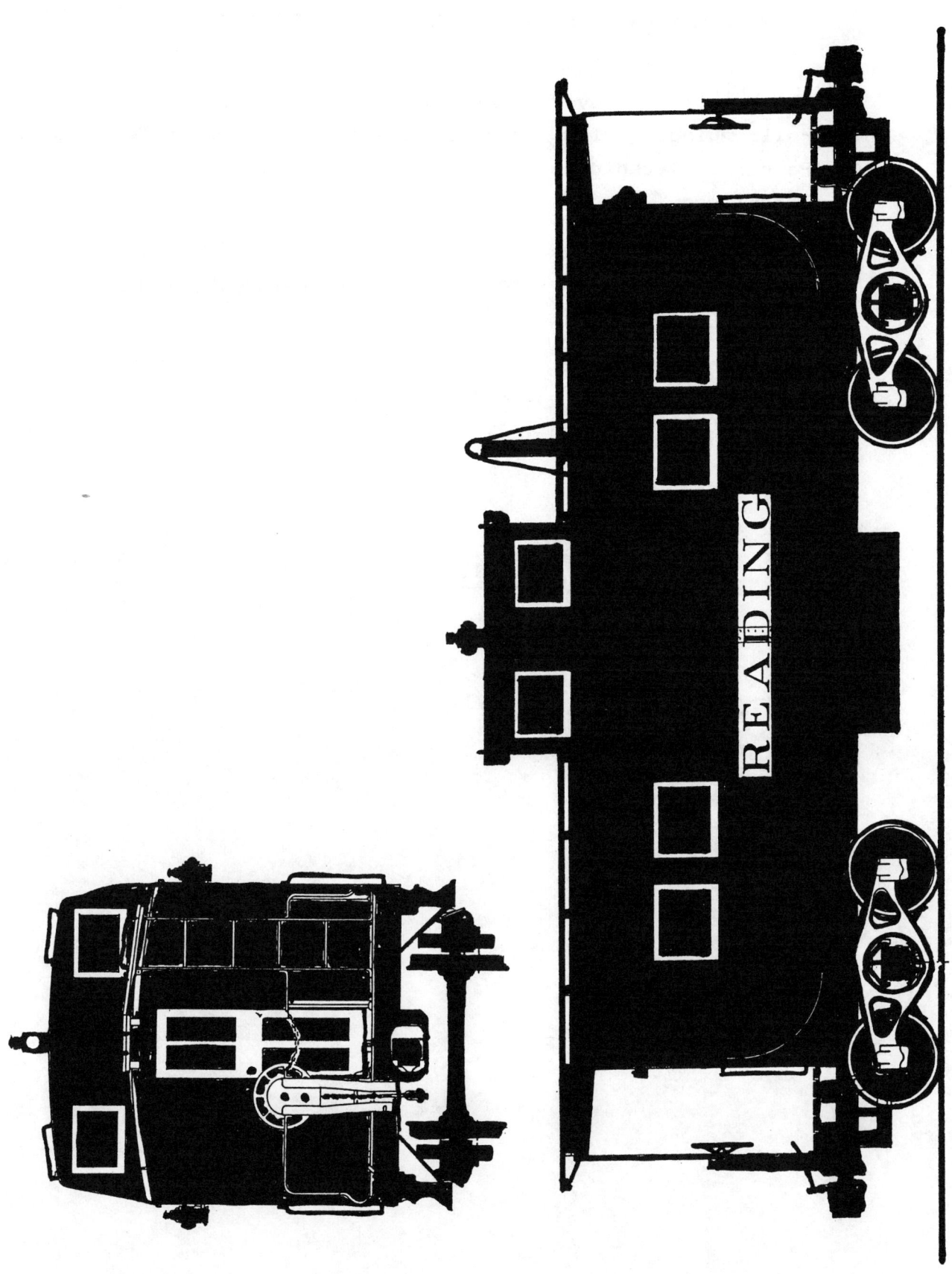

BILL OF LADING TECHNIQUES

This section covers the many "how to" do things in model railroading. Its four sections are Modeling Techniques, Painting Techniques, Weathering Techniques, and Photography Techniques.

MANIFEST TECHNIQUES

	PAGE
TECHNIQUES	212
MODELING TECHNIQUES	213
PAINTING TECHNIQUES	215
WEATHERING TECHNIQUES	216
PHOTOGRAPHY	216

TECHNIQUES

MODELING TECHNIQUES	M	Y	P
"FIVE FOOT RULER" MODEL PHOTO MEASURES	02	73	54
ABC'S OF DRILLING	11	77	70
ACC ADHESIVE USE & TIPS	01	76	49
ACC BONDING OF MODEL PARTS	11	72	74
ACCURATE DRILLING	09	54	68
ACCURATE MEASUREMENTS	07	70	60
ADDING RIVETS TO LOCOMOTIVES	07	36	184
ADJUSTING MOTOR BRUSH TENSION	01	66	35
AIRBRUSH PAINTING BASICS	12	83	80
ANCHORS FOR CONCRETE AND MASONRY	12	76	134
ART OF SOLDERING 2	08	51	26
ART OF SOLDERING 3	09	51	32
ASSEMBLING CASTINGS	05	38	186
BACKDROPS CREATE YOUR OWN	07	85	71
BACKLIGHTED TRANSPARENCIES (INT DETAILS)	07	73	40
BAKING PLASTIC MODELS	08	81	121
BENDING ANGLE STOCK	08	70	57
BENDING METAL ANGLES	04	40	213
BENDING T-STRAPPING	09	42	410
BETTER MODELS WITH A SURFACE PLATE	07	74	34
BLD A FRT CAR WITH CAMERA & STEEL TAPE 1	03	50	18
BLD A FRT CAR WITH CAMERA & STEEL TAPE 2	04	50	34
BLEND YOUR BALLAST FOR REALISM	07	66	41
BOILER WEIGHT INSTALLATION	10	77	134
BRASS CABOOSE FINISHING TECHNIQUES	08	83	72
BRUSH PAINTED BOXCARS	05	81	112
BUILD A VAPOR DEGREASER	04	79	90
BUILD J&SW BACKDROPS & WIDE OPEN SPACES	01	83	78
BUILDING PLASTIC STRUCTURE KITS DETAILS	06	85	62
BUILDING WITH SHEET STYRENE NEW MATERIAL	11	59	48
BUILDING WITH SHEET STYRENE VERSATILITY	12	59	74
CALCULATORS AS TOOLS FOR MODELING	01	75	84
CAMERA AS A MODELING TOOL	11	66	63
CAR CONSTRUCTION METHODS	05	38	179
CARBON ROD SOLDERING	11	54	38
CARS FROM COLORED PAPER	12	44	552
CASTING IN RUBBER MOLDS	07	56	46
CASTING OF SMALL PARTS AT HOME	04	35	93
CASTING PARTS IN POLYSTYRENE RESIN	11	81	116
CASTING WITH CERRO	08	59	50
CASTING WITH CERRO BEND	07	54	30
CASTING WITH VACUUM DE-AIRING	09	75	68
CASTING YOUR OWN FREIGHT CARS	01	83	82
CASTINGS MAKE YOUR OWN	10	53	60
CASTINGS FOR SCRATCHBUILDING INTRO	01	73	79
CHEMICALLY COLOR BRASS TO LOOKLIKE STEEL	08	36	234
CHOKE CABLE CONTROLS	09	72	79
CLEANING DIRTY TRUCKS	12	37	451
CLEANING DIRTY WHEELS $1	12	75	80
CLEANING FLASH ESSENTIAL IN GOOD MODELIN	12	50	37
CLEARANCES FOR TRACK AND STRUCTURES	02	40	86
COLD CASTING SMALL DETAIL PARTS	03	61	28
COMPOUND CURVES CONSTRUCTION	04	82	148
CONDITION YOUR PIKE AFTER SUMMER LAYOFF	10	53	71
CONTACT CEMENTS-HOW TO USE	03	71	78

MODELING TECHNIQUES	M	Y	P
CUTTING COMMERCIAL WOOD	03	55	34
CUTTING PLASTIC CASTINGS	08	78	122
CUTTING SHEET BRASS	04	77	110
CUTTING THREADS USING TAPS AND DIES	01	78	84
CUTTING WINDOWS IN METAL CAR SIDES	02	70	80
DECAL APPLICATION JIG	03	81	96
DECAL LIGHT BOX FOR TRIMMING	03	68	56
DECAL MAKING	06	49	14
DECAL MAKING	05	55	50
DECAL MODIFICATION FOR PRIVATE ROADS	05	81	111
DEHUMIDIFERS IN BASEMENTS	06	78	135
DERAILMENTS BANISHED-COMPLETELY!	07	63	39
DIE CASTINGS HOME MADE	05	41	237
DIE CASTINGS WITH CARDBOARD DIES	08	54	33
DIES THAT ARE LAMINATED CONSTRUCTION	10	36	287
DIRTY WHEELS AND TRACK	03	84	144
DON'T BUILD CARS THIS WAY-PITFALLS	04	48	244
DOUBLE SLIP SWITCH MACHINE LINKAGE	03	82	107
DOWN SCALING A BUILDING	07	63	31
DRAWBAR PULL DETERMINATION	07	48	473
DRILLING AND TAPPING HOLES IN METAL	01	67	71
DRILLING HOLES IN RODS (ENDS)	11	74	108
DRILLING HOLES IN RODS (SIDE)	11	74	104
DRILLS AND DRILLING	07	68	47
DRIVE WHEEL MACHINING	07	37	254
DRY BRUSH WEATHERING TECHNIQUES	06	84	112
DUST ELIMINATION FROM LAYOUT ROOMS	09	67	53
DUST ELIMINATION FROM PIKES	01	63	68
DUST-STROYER FOR REMOVING DUST	06	85	104
ELIMINATE FLYWHEEL VIBRATIONS	06	78	114
ELIMINATING JERKY STARTS	02	56	59
EQUIPMENT DRAWINGS FROM PHOTOS	08	77	106
EYEPINS HAVE MANY USES	09	77	114
FATHER NATURES TREES	03	82	107
FINE SPRAY FROM AIRBRUSHES	02	73	88
FIRE ESCAPE CONSTRUCTION	05	71	40
FLAT BACKGROUND TREES	05	83	88
FLUID DISPENCER FOR WHEEL CLEANING $1	03	70	70
FLYWHEEL MECHANICS FOR N GAUGE	12	69	62
FREEING UP YOUR LOCOMOTIVE	07	39	360
GEARS AND GEARING	02	66	65
GOOD LOCO PERFORMANCE THROUGH ADJUSTMENT	09	44	405
GROOMING THE IRON HORSE FOR OPERATION	01	68	64
HAND LETTERING TECHNIQUES	03	71	77
HARD SILVER SOLDERING	08	76	99
HAVING YOUR CONTROL PANEL IN A STRUCTURE	06	78	110
HAZARDS: MECHANICAL & ELECTRICAL IN MRR	04	76	92
HINGED YARDS ARE EASIER FOR WIRING	09	83	76
HOW TO HAND LAY TRACK E JERSY GAN DANCER	08	85	66
HYDRAULIC ACTUATORS FOR TURNOUTS ETC	08	70	61
I DIDN'T LIKE SOLDER	05	39	259
IMPROVED TURBINE LOCOMOTIVE PERFORMANCE	03	70	64
IMPROVING YOUR BASEMENT FOR PIKE LIFE	02	49	11
IN DEFENSE OF THE SABLE (BRUSH PAINTING)	05	81	94
INSULATING CAR WHEELS FOR TWO RAIL USE	01	36	14

TECHNIQUES

MODELING TECHNIQUES	M	Y	P
INTERIOR LIGHTING TIPS	11	83	124
INVESTMENT CAST WINDOW LINTELS	05	71	37
KADEE CONVERSIONS IN "N" FROM RAPIDO	08	78	121
KADEE COUPLER BASICS	05	81	78
KADEE COUPLER MOUNTING ATH DIESEL SWITCH	05	85	120
KADEE COUPLER MOUNTING TECHNIQUES	04	85	129
KEEPING BRASS BRIGHT	02	76	96
KEEPING PAINT FROM DRYING IN BOTTLE	07	84	111
KEEPING YOUR PIKE IN TOP SHAPE	02	52	28
LATHE FROM ELECTRIC DRILL	02	67	56
LATHE MACHINING IN MINIATURE	09	75	66
LATHE OPERATION DRILLING	11	78	164
LATHE OPERATION THE ABC'S	09	78	132
LATHE OPERATION TOOLS AND TECHNIQUES	10	78	156
LAYOUT MAINTENANCE	02	78	118
LAYOUT MAINTENANCE HANDBOOK	05	54	61
LETTERING REMOVAL	07	84	111
LOCATING ELECTRICAL TROUBLES	05	44	201
LOCATING HOLES ACCURATELY	08	74	60
LOCO CONTROL PROBLEM W/SELECT POWER PACK	05	82	138
LOCOMOTIVE PERFORMANCE	09	70	39
LOCOMOTIVE TEST RACKS	08	71	66
LUBRICANTS OF TEFLON	03	75	35
LUBRICATION FOR LOCOMOTIVES SYMPOSIUM	12	47	974
LUBRICATION OF IMPORTED LOCOMOTIVES	12	63	52
LUBRICATION OF MODELS	04	39	202
LUBRICATION OF NEW LOCOMOTIVES	10	63	69
LUBRICATION TESTS	05	68	19
MAINTAINING & TROUBLESHOOTING LOCOS	06	80	90
MAINTAINING LOCOMOTIVES CLEAN/LUB/REPAIR	02	85	75
MAINTENANCE SHORT CUTS	10	50	36
MAKING PARTS OUT OF PAPER	09	44	404
MAKING PARTS WITH BRASS	07	71	44
MAKING SMALL CASTINGS WITH SOAP MOLDS	06	35	159
MAKING YOUR OWN DRY TRANSFERS	02	80	70
MANUAL TURNOUT CONTROL MECHANISM	02	85	131
MASTER RIVETER WITH MINI RIVETER	10	79	76
MEASURING STRUCTURES	10	79	106
MEASURING WITHOUT A TAPE USE A CAMERA	06	77	118
MERCURY POOL CONTACTS	07	48	490
METAL MILLING FOR MODELERS	03	69	46
METRIC CONVERSION FACTORS	02	77	14
MICROFLAME TORCH USE	08	69	39
MODEL WITH BURNING TOOLS	07	62	42
MODEL WORK BENCH CONSTRUCTION 2ND TRY	07	84	90
MODELING WATER W/ACRYLIC GLOSS MEDIUM	01	84	152
MODELING WITH HARDWOOD VENEER	05	80	93
MODELS BY THE MILLIONS RTV MOLDS	09	61	53
MODULAR SIGNALS EASES MAINTENANCE	11	83	110
MOMENTUM IN BRASS STEAM LOCOS	12	69	64
MOTOR MAINTENANCE	04	56	47
MOUNTING KADEES ON LONG CARS	02	83	154
NOMOGRAPH SCALING OF PLANS	04	40	222
NUT BOLT WASHER CASTINGS ATTACHMENT	05	77	115
OIL FOR YOUR CARS	02	40	108
OPERATING CLASS LIGHTS WITH FIBER OPTICS	07	70	68
OVERHAUL OF BRASS FROM STORAGE	03	85	134
PAINTING CORRUGATED ROOFS	04	83	148
PEEL & STICK WALLS	11	79	152
PHOTOENGRAVED DETAIL	10	53	69
PHOTOETCHING FLAT PARTS	09	70	48
PHOTOSTATIC REDUCTION AND ENLARGEMENT	06	78	138
PNEUMATIC SWITCH & SIGNAL OPERATION 1	05	42	212
PNEUMATIC SWITCH & SIGNAL OPERATION 2	06	42	290
PREPARING A BRASS DIESEL FOR PAINTING	04	84	104
PREPARING PLASTIC FOR METAL PLATING	08	77	110
PUT ON A HAPPY FACE FIGURE DETAILING	05	84	111
RAIL CLEANER CONSTRUCTION	05	75	56
RAIL CLEANING DEVICE	05	70	48
RAISED LETTER SIGNS & BUILD PLATES	04	71	50
RAPID AGING WITH PHOTO LAMPS	01	78	136
REDUCING OVERSIZE FLANGES	07	68	64
REDUCING OVERSIZE FLANGES	03	75	52
REDUCTION COPYING SIGNS	02	79	137
REMOTORING FOR BETTER PERFORMANCE	12	85	94
REMOVING WHITE DEPOSITS FROM ZINC ALLOYS	04	73	83
RENEWABLE AIR SUPPLY FOR AIRBRUSH PAINT	12	79	112
RESISTANCE SOLDERING	11	78	80
RIVET DETAILS	06	68	55
RIVET MAKING TO SCALE	10	41	510
ROCK MOLDS FROM PLASTIC WORKS	07	83	84
ROLLING STOCK CONSTRUCTION HINTS	04	34	13
RUBBER STAMP LETTERING	01	51	56
RUNNING ON DIRTY TRACK	09	82	97
SALVAGING SHEET METAL FROM OIL CANS	09	51	38
SANDBAGS, FROGS & JAWS (CLAMPS)	05	81	101
SANDING FLAT SURFACES FLAT	03	81	149
SCALE ELEVATIONS WITH A CAMERA	06	77	120
SCALE, SCALE RULES, AND SCALE PLANS	03	62	69
SCALING PHOTOS FOR MODEL DATA	09	63	64
SELECTIVE COMPRESSION	11	77	82
SHADOW DETAILS FOR BACKGROUND MODELS	07	84	94
SHAPING CORBELS	05	71	42
SHEET METAL CUTTING	04	55	32
SHRINK MODELING USING SHRINKY DINKS	11	81	98
SIDE ROD BIND CORRECTIONS SIX CAUSES	02	71	67
SILENT SPRAY SYSTEM	09	69	71
SILK SCREEN FOR ROAD NAMES	08	67	44
SILVER SOLDERING	09	66	31
SIMPLE METAL TURNING WITHOUT A LATHE	11	42	510
SIMPLE TURNOUT CONTROL PB MRR CLUB	05	85	126
SMALL MACHINE SCREWS REFERENCE CHART	12	53	78
SOLDERING COPPER STRUCTURAL SHAPES	05	81	133
SOLDERING DETAIL ONTO BRASS	08	69	36
SOLDERING FUXES	03	66	60
SOLDERING MADE EASY	08	43	349
SOLDERING RAIL JOINTS	02	78	148
SOLDERING TOOLS AND METHODS	05	55	48
SOLDERING WIRE HANDRAILS ON PLASTIC LOCO	02	77	119
SOLDERING WITH A BLOWPIPE	02	43	84

TECHNIQUES

MODELING TECHNIQUES	M	Y	P
SOLDERING WITH AN IRON	11	68	67
SOLDERING ZAMAK	12	56	50
SPIKING RAIL	11	63	76
SPLICING WIRES	08	48	536
SPRAY WEATHERING WITHOUT AN AIRBRUSH	10	84	98
SPRINGING DRIVER TECHNIQUES	09	70	72
STAINING WOOD FOR MODEL STRUCTURES	05	62	42
STRATHMORE BOARD USE	06	74	81
STRATHMORE ILLUSTRATION BOARD USE	02	59	62
STRIPWOOD CAR FLOORS	12	55	61
STRIPWOOD CUTTING TOOL	08	70	76
TAPERED BOILER SECTIONS	06	69	72
TENDER TO LOCO DRIVES	10	69	88
TEST STAND FOR LOCOMOTIVE MOTORS	06	79	93
THERMOFORMING SUPERDOME WINDOWS	08	79	132
TIE RACK BECOMES THIRD HAND	09	77	116
TINPLATING FOR SOLDERING	07	73	75
TOO SMALL TO HANDLE?	09	41	460
TORQUE ARM DRIVE FOR STEAM LOCOMOTIVES	11	80	116
TRACK LAYING WITH PAINT	03	82	105
TRACK MAINTENANCE BOOMER PETE	09	41	459
TROUBLE SHOOTING WORM GEARS	06	62	63
TRUCK LUBRICATION	06	79	139
TUNING AND BREAKING IN RTR LOCOMOTIVES	12	69	80
TURQUE ARMS FOR KTM GEAR BOXES	09	83	80
UNCOUPLING DEVICE CONSTRUCTION	05	50	62
UNDERPAINTING FOR DETAILS	11	80	119
USE MIRRORS TO EXPAND SCENES	07	81	76
USING A MICROMETER	08	78	124
USING DISCARDED MATERIALS	08	36	226
USING METAL WORKING TOOLS	11	82	126
USING SMALL SHEETS OF PLASTIC BRICK	10	70	81
WASH AND DRYBRUSH WEATHERING	05	84	98
WATER AND HOW TO MODEL IT	10	85	78
WEIGHING CARS	09	77	112
WHEEL SET GAUGE CHECKER	06	85	114
WHERE TO OIL YOUR ENGINES	07	68	56
WILD WILLIES LIGHTED KD UNCOUPLING TOOL	08	81	81
WINDING SPRINGS FOR MRR USE	06	65	57
WORK WITH METAL	01	77	126
WORKING WITH COMMON PLASTICS	04	61	63
WORM & PINION GEARS	10	43	432
YOU TOO CAN SOLDER	05	46	326
ZAP TEXTURING FOR FOLIAGE	09	80	90
ZAP TEXTURING FOR FOLIAGE ADDENDUM	03	81	28

BOSTON, REVERE BEACH & LYNN 1903

PAINTING TECHNIQUES	M	Y	P
AIR PAINTING EQUIPMENT	06	67	42
AIRBRUSH PAINTING BASICS	12	83	80
AIRBRUSH PAINTING TECHNIQUES	07	74	38
AIRBRUSHES MAKE YOUR OWN	07	71	62
BACKDROP PAINTING	04	77	116
BACKDROPS CREATE YOUR OWN	07	85	71
BAKING PLASTIC MODELS	08	81	121
BRUSH PAINTED BOX CARS	05	81	112
BRUSH PAINTING	02	76	85
BUILD J&SW BACKDROPS & WIDE OPEN SPACES	01	83	78
BUILD W&SF BACKDROPS LAYERED LANDSCAPES	11	82	120
CAR & LOCOMOTIVE COLORING AND PAINTING	07	36	171
CAR LETTERING BY HAND	10	34	4
CLOUD PAINTING	03	84	102
COLOR MIXTURE INDEX	04	71	29
COLORING THE RIGHT WAY STATIONS/BRIDGES	03	36	68
CONRAIL INSIGNIA & LETTERING	11	76	86
CUSTOM DECALS MAKE YOUR OWN	12	73	53
DECAL APPLICATION	11	45	452
DECAL APPLICATION	02	54	63
DECAL MAKING	06	49	14
DECAL MODIFICATION FOR PRIVATE ROADS	05	81	111
DECAL SCRATCH LETTERING	03	61	50
DELUXE SPRAY BOOTH CONSTRUCTION	08	83	103
DRY TRANSFER LETTERING	09	67	49
EXPERIMENTAL PAINT SCHEMES	01	78	126
FINE SPRAY FROM AIRBRUSHES	02	73	88
HAND LETTER AND STRIPE MODELS	08	56	20
IN DEFENSE OF THE SABLE (BRUSH PAINTING)	05	81	94
INDEX OF 295 PAINT SHOP PROJECTS	09	79	60
LET'S PAINT A BACKDROP	11	77	74
LETTERING CARS & SIGNS	12	63	62
LETTERING REMOVAL	07	84	111
LETTERING STORE WINDOWS	09	58	56
LOCOMOTIVE HIGHLITING TECHNIQUES	06	65	32
MODELING WATER W/ACRYLIC GLOSS MEDIUM	01	84	152
N SCALE LETTERING	04	78	134
PAINT & LETTER L&N LOCOS & CARS	06	69	30
PAINT & LETTER SCL LOCOS & CARS	07	68	34
PAINT & WEATHERING FINISHING TOUCHES	11	83	107
PAINT JAR BECOMES A SPRAY GUN	11	64	47
PAINT JAR RACK CONSTRUCTION	05	84	99
PAINT SPRAY OUTFIT REVIEW WR BROWN CORP	10	77	42
PAINT STORAGE	11	74	27
PAINTING & FINISHING BLUEBOOK	02	56	55
PAINTING & LETTERING	10	37	358
PAINTING & LETTERING	11	46	732
PAINTING & SHADING STRUCTURES	04	52	10
PAINTING BACKGROUNDS BLDGS IN PERSPECTIV	02	44	72
PAINTING BACKGROUNDS SCENIC ART	01	44	8
PAINTING COLORED BACKDROPS	01	64	42
PAINTING CORRUGATED ROOFS	04	83	148
PAINTING IMPORTED LOCOMOTIVES	12	63	52
PAINTING LOCOMOTIVES	01	66	58
PAINTING SCALE FIGURES	09	81	69

TECHNIQUES

PAINTING TECHNIQUES

Title	M	Y	P
PAINTING SCENERY	04	48	260
PAINTING STEAM LOCOMOTIVES (PS-4)	08	64	35
PAINTING STONES	12	44	547
PAINTING STRAIGHT STRIPES	06	78	106
PAINTING WITH A THROAT ATOMIZER	05	49	15
PAINTING WITH SPRAY CANS	12	77	148
PAINTING WITH STOVE POLISH	04	54	64
PAINTS & PAINTING	07	51	29
PREPARING A BRASS DIESEL FOR PAINTING	04	84	104
PRIMER ON METAL MODELS	03	66	64
PROFESSIONAL PAINTING	03	59	28
PUT ON A HAPPY FACE FIGURE DETAILING	05	84	111
RENEWABLE AIR SUPPLY FOR AIRBRUSH PAINT	12	79	112
SHADOW DETAILS FOR BACKGROUND MODELS	07	84	94
SHADOWING PASSENGER EQUIPMENT	12	74	29
SILENT SPRAY SYSTEM	09	69	71
SILK SCREEN FOR ROAD NAMES	08	67	44
SILK SCREEN PRINTING	03	53	28
SIMPLE AIR SUPPLY FOR SPRAY PAINTING	04	77	93
SPRAY PAINTING MODELS EQUIPMENT	01	40	34
SPRAY PAINTING MODELS-STEPS FOR REEFER	02	40	74
SPRAY WEATHERING WITHOUT AN AIRBRUSH	10	84	98
STEP BY STEP BACKDROP PAINTING	02	82	93
STRIPING WITH CELLOPHANE	08	53	36
TIPS ON PAINTING	08	68	58
UNDERPAINTING FOR DETAILS	11	80	119
USING TRANSFERS FOR LETTERING	08	68	26
WASHING MODELS BEFORE PAINTING	11	77	132

WEATHERING TECHNIQUES

Title	M	Y	P
AGING & WEATHERING CARS	12	55	44
AGING & WEATHERING CARS & LOCOS	01	56	36
AGING & WEATHERING WITH CASEIN	02	66	26
AGING WITH CHALKS	12	72	46
ART OF WEATHERING AND AGING	04	77	60
COLORING TRACK FOR MAXIMUM EFFECT	02	83	104
DRY BRUSH WEATHERING TECHNIQUES	06	84	112
HEAVY WEATHERING MOD & PT	09	80	138
PAINT & WEATHERING FINISHING TOUCHES	11	83	107
QUICK WEATHERING WITH CHALKS	02	84	64
SPRAY WEATHERING WITHOUT AN AIRBRUSH	10	84	98
THIS BUSINESS OF WEATHERING	09	64	50
WASH AND DRYBRUSH WEATHERING	05	84	98
WEATHERING	04	77	91
WEATHERING A COMBINE BRINGS IT TO LIFE	12	79	79
WEATHERING CARS AND LOCOMOTIVES	07	84	86
WEATHERING EQUIPMENT	12	39	617
WEATHERING FREIGHT CARS	01	55	42
WEATHERING HOPPER CARS	09	76	78
WEATHERING ROLLING STOCK ON J&SW	12	82	74
WEATHERING WITH A BRUSH	10	75	61
WEATHERING WITH CASEIN COLORS	11	60	34
WEATHERING WOODEN CARS	10	72	56

PHOTOGRAPHY

Title	M	Y	P
"5' RULER" MODEL PHOTOGRAPHY MEASURES	02	73	54
BETTER MODEL PHOTOS	02	39	76
CAMERA AS A MODELING TOOL	11	66	63
CLOUDS IN MODEL PHOTOGRAPHY	08	69	32
COLOR PHOTOGRAPHY IN MODEL RAILROADS	12	77	116
CONTRAST AND SHADOW DETAILS IN PHOTOS	11	70	85
FAULTS SEEN IN MODEL PHOTOS	02	71	35
GRANDEST LAYOUT OF ALL PHOTO TRICKS	10	62	65
INSTANT DIORAMAS FOR PHOTOGRAPHS	05	75	55
MODEL COLOR PHOTOGRAPHY	06	66	59
MODEL PHOTOGRAPHY ALMOST MUCH FUN AS MRR	01	80	83
MODEL PHOTOGRAPHY MADE EASY	03	72	68
MODEL PHOTOGRAPHYS NEW DIMENSIONS	08	60	36
MODEL PHOTOS WITH A BOX CAMERA	05	68	30
MODEL RAILROAD PHOTOGRAPHS	06	35	160
MODEL RAILROAD PHOTOGRAPHY	09	84	93
PERSPECTIVE IN PHOTOGRAPHING MODELS	02	49	45
PHOTO CONTEST WINNERS 1985	03	85	82
PHOTO MODELS THROUGH "SMOKED" GLASS	01	85	76
PHOTOGENIC MODELING	01	64	54
PHOTOGRAPHING A MODEL SCENE	03	66	34
PHOTOGRAPHING SMALL MODELS	01	35	4
PHOTOGRAPHING THE CLINCHFIELD	11	78	154
PHOTOGRAPHY FOR MODEL RAILROADERS	08	63	22
POSING BENCH FOR MODEL RR EQUIPMENT	09	77	51
PROJECTED PHOTOGRAPHIC BACKGROUNDS	12	69	76
REALISM IN MODEL PHOTOGRAPHY	01	49	36
REALISTIC MODEL PHOTOGRAPHS	07	46	432
RIDE YOUR OWN MODEL CABOOSE	11	66	61
SPECIAL CAMERA FOR MODEL RR PHOTOS	08	73	50
SUNLIGHT IN MODEL PHOTOS	05	70	32
USING CAMERA FOR SCALE SIGNS & ELEVATION	06	77	118

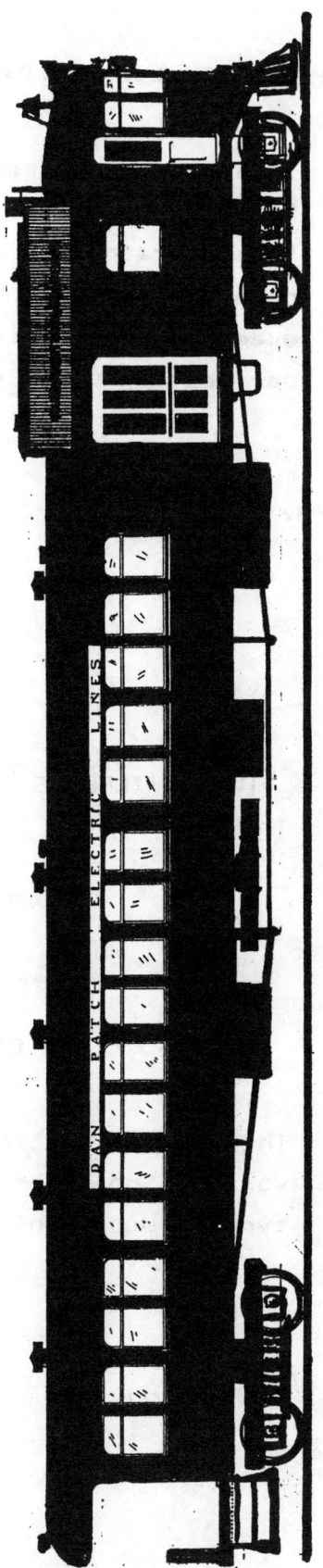

217

BILL OF LADING — TOY & TINPLATE TRAINS

This section relates specifically to Toy and Tinplate Trains. All of the entries are specifically related to these trains. Articles that concern themselves with more general topics will be found under these headings. As an example: Building of tinplate box cars would be in the box car section under models.

MANIFEST — TOY & TINPLATE TRAINS

	PAGE
TOY & TINPLATE TRAINS	218

BILL OF LADING — ROSTERS

The Roster listings show locomotives or rolling stock of the various roads or builders. The descriptor line includes the type of equipment and dates covered when available.

	PAGE
RAIL ROSTERS	218

TOYS & TINPLATE

TOY & TINPLATE TRAINS	M	Y	P
CONFESSIONS OF A TINPLATER	09	36	244
DECADE WHEN DREAMS CAME TRUE 1900-1910	08	77	51
DEJAMMING LIONELS MILK CAR	02	50	53
DEPARTMENT-STORE LAYOUTS AND DISPLAYS	07	76	51
FUN AND FASCINATION OF TRAINS	01	78	122
FUN AT CHRISTMAS LIO LAYOUT AT S&L OFFIC	12	83	128
HISTORY OF TINPLATE RAILROADS	09	35	236
KENDALE LINES TINPLATE BURDNO	07	49	22
LIONEL'S SANTA FE F3 "O"	12	81	118
LONG LIVE THE KING RENAISSANCE OF "O"	06	84	82
MAGICAL CATALOGS OF CHRISTMASSES PAST	12	78	110
MAGNE-TRACTION BY LIONEL	09	50	44
MAKE YOUR OWN TINPLATE SEITCHES	08	50	54
MODEL RAILROADING 1898	09	40	500
MODEL RAILROADING WITH TINPLATE O SCALE	09	34	10
OLDEST MODEL RAILROAD 1905	09	37	310
REGEARING TINPLATE LOCOMOTIVES	09	36	251
REMOTE CONTROL TRACK USES TINPLATE	09	50	45
ROMANCE IN TINPLATE COLLECTING	11	36	332
SARASOTA LIONEL TRAIN MUSEUM	12	82	120
STREAMLINED STEAM TOYS & THEIR PROTOTYPE	12	79	118
TINPLATE CONVERSION	06	37	220
TINPLATE REALISM	06	49	21
TINPLATE TRACK TIPS	06	50	40
TINPLATE TRAINS IN AMERICA (HIST SURVEY)	07	76	46
TINPLATE TROUBLE SHOOTING	12	48	936
TINPLATE WAS MADE TO OPERATE	12	78	113
TOY TRAIN CATALOGS	12	78	110
TRACK LAYOUTS FOR LIONEL	11	52	72

ROSTERS

RAIL ROSTERS	M	Y	P
PANAMA LIMITED CONSIST IC	05	65	34
ROSTER OF 4-8-4'S LOCOMOTIVES ON NP	03	77	61
ROSTER OF FREIGHT CARS CL	07	79	61
ROSTER OF LOCOS B&O 1840	07	76	80
ROSTER OF LOCOS CL ALL TIME	07	79	60
ROSTER OF LOCOS GB&W	02	78	70
ROSTER OF LOCOS N&W 4-6-2'S E CLASS	08	77	63
ROSTER OF LOCOS N&W 4-8-2 MOUNTAINS	12	77	70
ROSTER OF LOCOS SD40-2 1972	07	76	64
ROSTER OF LOCOS SOO 1977-82	11	82	80
ROSTER OF MP15 LOCOS	10	78	85
ROSTER OF ROLLING STOCK AD&N	02	81	112
ROSTER OF SOO CABOOSES 1966-81	11	82	80
ROSTER OF USRA 0-6-0 SWITCHERS	09	39	461
ROSTER OF USRA 2-8-2 LIGHT MIKADOS	06	41	309

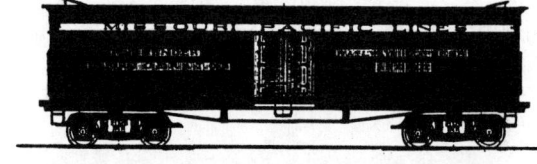
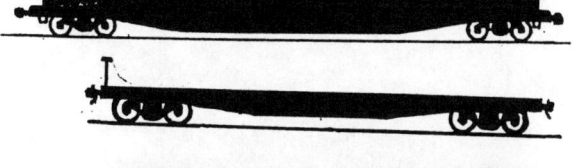

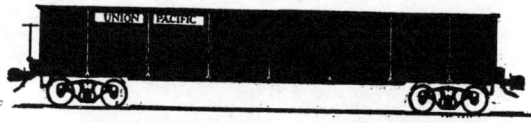
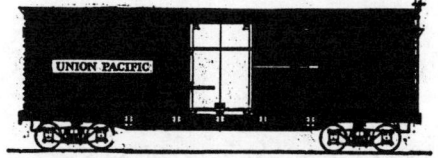

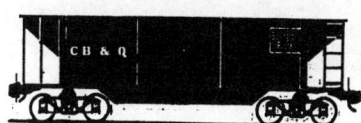

BILL OF LADING — LITERATURE REVIEWS

Literature review has three sub categories. Prototype books are about real railroads. Modeling books are about models and model aspects of railroading. Videos list video tapes as they are released. The descriptor lists the full title of the entry. If space permits the author (or publisher) is listed at the end of the line.

MANIFEST — LITERATURE REVIEWS

	PAGE
RAIL LITERATURE REVIEWS	220
PROTOTYPE BOOKS	221
MODELING BOOKS	227
VIDEOS	229

LITERATURE REVIEWS

PROTOTYPE BOOKS

Title	Author	M	Y	P
100 YEARS OF CAPITAL TRACTION	KING	03	74	17
100 YEARS OF RAILROAD CARS	LUCAS	03	59	17
100 YEARS OF STEAM LOCOMOTIVES	LUCAS	02	58	22
1941 LOCOMOTIVE CYCLOPEDIA	KALMBACH	09	72	7
2' CYCLOPEDIA VOLUME 1 KINGFIELD MAINE		08	77	23
4-10-2: THREE BARRELS OF STEAM	BOYNTON	01	74	19
400 STORY (C&NW)	SCRIBBINS	10	82	126
50 BEST LOCOMOTIVES OF THE B&O	BARR	11	77	150
50 BEST OF B&O 2		02	78	38
50 BEST OF B&O 3		02	78	38
50 BEST OF B&O 4	THOMPSON	12	78	40
50 BEST OF B&O 5	LORENZ	02	80	125
50 BEST OF NYC 1	HARWOOD	12	78	40
50 BEST OF PRR		02	78	38
50 BEST OF W&M 1	ROUSE	12	78	40
57 MAINTENANCE PLANS OF PRR	BOYNTON	01	78	35
ABE'S GRAPHIC CHARTS OF PA LOCOS(REPRINT		12	76	124
ALCO ROTARY SNOW PLOW 1909 REPRINT		03	74	18
ALCO USRA LOCOMOTIVES 1919 REPRINT		03	74	18
ALL ABOARD AMERICA		07	77	101
ALLEGHENY: LIMA'S FINEST (2-6-6-6)		01	85	135
ALONG THE IRON TRAIL	RICHARDSON	11	38	502
AMERICA'S COLORFUL RAILROADS	BALL	02	79	21
AMERICA'S NEW RAILROADS	CARPER	03	81	144
AMERICAN LOCOS AN ENGINEERING HISTORY		09	68	18A
AMERICAN NARROW GAUGE	KRAUSE	01	79	39
AMERICAN RAILROAD PASSENGER CAR	WHITE	09	85	111
AMERICAN RAILROAD PASSENGER CARS	WHITE	10	78	153
AMERICAN SHORT LINE RAILWAY GUIDE	LEWIS	06	79	132
AMERICAS RAILROADS:2ND GENERATION	BALL	01	81	168
AMERICAS SHORT LINE RAILWAY GUIDE	LEWIS	08	76	24
AMTRAK AT MILEPOST 10	ZIMMERMAN	02	82	44
AMTRAK CAR & LOCOMOTIVE SPOTTER 4TH EDIT		12	80	68
APEX OF THE ATLANTICS	WESTING	11	63	23
ARCADE & ATTICA RAILROAD	LEWIS	03	73	16
ARTICULATED LOCOMOTIVES	WIENER	04	71	6
ARTICULATED LOCOMOTIVES OF WP	NOBEL	05	63	14
ATCHINSON TOPEKA & SANTA FE RAILWAY VOL1		05	85	116
ATSF CAR & LOCO PLANS FOR MODEL RR		01	78	34
B&O POWER 1829-1969	SAGLE	03	65	14
BADGER TRACTION CENT ELECTRIC RAILFANS		12	69	13
BALDWIN LOCO WORKS GEN CATALOG 1915 REFR		03	74	18
BALDWIN LOGGING LOCOMOTIVES 1913 REPRINT		03	74	18
BALDWIN NARROW GAUGE LOCOS 1872-1876 REP		03	74	18
BALDWIN VULCAN COMPOUNDS 1900 REPRINT		03	74	18
BEAUTY OF RAILWAYS PITTMAN PUBLICATIONS		05	61	10
BIG BLOW UP SUPER TURBINES	COCKLE	09	78	26
BLUE RIDGE TROLLEY H&F	HARWOOD	12	75	42
BRADFORD & FOSTER BROOK (B&FB)	KILMER	02	75	22
BRADFORD, BORDELL & KINZUA	BARBER	02	72	11
BRIDGE & TRESTLE HANDBOOK MRR	MALLERY	10	58	21
BRIDGES & STRUCTURES OF AMERICAN RAIL RD		05	77	34
BRITISH RAILWAY LOCOMOTIVES 1803-1853		12	63	16
BRITISH STEAM RAILWAYS	NOCK	08	65	17
BUDD RDC IN CANANDA	CORLEY	06	68	17
BURLINGTON IN TRANSITION	CORBIN	02	68	22
BURLINGTON NORTHERN 1971 MOTIVE POWER AN		03	72	6
BURLINGTON NORTHERN 1973 ANNUAL	WAGNER	08	74	14
BURLINGTON NORTHERN 1977-80 ANNUAL		05	82	129
BURLINGTON NORTHERN PASSNGR CARS	RUDISEL	01	75	20
BUSTED AND STILL RUNNING (B&SR)	MEAD	03	69	8
BUSTED AND STILL RUNNING B&SR	MEAD	09	71	7
BUTTE ANACONDA BAP		03	71	10
C&O FREIGHT CARS PRIOR TO 1945	FREYTAG	01	75	23
C&O POWER	SHUSTER	02	66	18
C&S - NARROW GAUGE	FERRELL	08	82	120
CAB FORWARD REVISED SP	CHURCH	10	83	136
CABLE CAR IN AMERICA	HILTON	03	72	5
CABOOSE CARS OF THE SANTA FE RAILWAY		09	78	26
CABOOSES OF NH AND NYC RAILROADS		08	82	117
CALIFORNIA CENTRAL COAST RAILWAYS		04	81	130A
CALL THE BIG HOOK	DOUGHERTY	05	85	116
CANADIAN NATIONAL RAILWAYS STORY	DORIN	05	76	24
CANADIAN NATIONAL STEAM POWER	CLEGG	11	74	25
CANADIAN PACIFIC DIESEL LOCOMTIVES	DEAN	06	82	49
CANADIAN PACIFIC IN THE ROCKIES	BAIN	03	80	138
CANADIAN PACIFIC RAILWAY	DORIN	07	75	17
CANADIAN RAILWAY SCENES 1	WOLF	07	84	108
CANADIAN STEAM	MORGAN	05	62	16
CAR & LOCO CYCLOPEDIA OF AMER PRACT 1984		05	85	118
CAR & LOCOMOTIVE CYCLOPEDIA 1980		12	80	68
CAR BUILDERS CYCLOPEDIA 1937		12	37	468
CAR NAMES, NUMBERS, & CONSISTS	WAYMER	11	72	15
CARS OF PACIFIC ELECTRIC VOL I	SWEET	05	65	19
CARS OF PACIFIC ELECTRIC VOL II	SWEET	11	65	16
CARS OF SACRAMENTO NORTHERN		03	73	16
CASS COLLECTION	KILLORAN	08	82	120
CAVALCADE OF THE RAILS	MORSE	09	40	524
CENTENNIALS IN ACTION UP	COCKLE	02	81	117
CENTRAL AMERICAN HOLIDAY	BEST	07	61	16
CENTRAL PACIFIC & SOUTHERN PACIFIC RR		07	63	13
CENTRAL RR OF NJ STEAM LOCO PLANBOOK		05	84	118
CENTRAL VERMONT RAILWAY VOL II	JONES	07	82	107
CENTRAL VERMONT RAILWAY: YANKEE TRAD V 5		01	83	161
CENTURY OF DELUXE RAILWAY CARS IN CANADA		12	83	145
CENTURY OF READING CO MOTIVE POWER		08	41	438
CENTURY OF SP STEAM LOCOMOTIVES	DUNSCOMB	12	63	16
CHALLENGER LOCOMOTIVES UP	KRATVILLE	11	81	150
CHANGE AT PARK STREET UNDER BOSTON SUBWY		03	73	16
CHARACTERISTICS CHARTS CNE 1923		11	78	144
CHARACTERISTICS CHARTS NYNH&H 1959		11	78	144
CHESAPEAKE & OHIO DIESEL REVIEW		06	82	49
CHESAPEAKE & OHIO RAILWAY	DORIN	05	82	125
CHICAGO & ILLINOIS MIDLAND	WALLIN	04	80	108
CHICAGO & NORTHWESTERN POWER	DORIN	03	73	18
CHICAGO'S PASSENGER TRAINS	OLMSTED	12	84	188
CHICAGO'S RAPID TRANSIT		07	74	8
CHICAGO'S RAPID TRANSIT VOL II 1977		07	77	101
CHICAGO'S SURFACE LINES	LIND	11	77	147
CINCINATTI CARS NO. 3 CABLE CARS	WAGNER	02	70	10

LITERATURE REVIEWS

PROTOTYPE BOOKS

Title	Author	M	Y	P
CINCINATTI STREETCARS #4	WAGNER	02	71	5
CINCINATTI STREETCARS #5	WAGNER	03	72	7
CINCINATTI'S STREETCAR VOL 7	WAGNER	05	77	25
CINCINNATI & LAKE ERIE RR (C&LE)	KEENAN	10	75	20
CINCINNATI STREET CARS 6 1912-22	WRIGHT	03	74	18
CINDERS AND SMOKE	OSTERWALD	09	66	15
CITY & INTERURBAN CARS 1913 BRILL REPRIN		12	66	24
CITY MAKERS	NADEAU	04	66	13
CIVIL WAR RAILROADS	ABDILL	02	62	22
CIVIL WAR RAILROADS AND MODELS	ALEXANDER	10	78	152
CLASSIC AMERICAN RAILROAD STATIONS		04	81	132
CLIMAX AN UNUSUAL STEAM LOCOMOTIVE	TABER	07	61	16
CLIMAX CATALOG REPRINT		12	68	22
COACH CABBAGE AND CABOOSE ATSF	MCCALL	06	80	126
COAL BOATS TO TIDEWATER	WAKEFIELD	04	66	13
COLLECTORS BOOK OF THE LOCO	ALEXANDER	04	67	8
COLOR PICTORIAL OF NORTHEASTERN RAILFAN		02	82	54
COLOR TREASURY OF MODEL TRAINS		04	74	18
COLORADO MIDLAND	CAFKY	07	65	12
COLORADO MIDLAND GUIDE & DATA BOOK		04	81	133
COLORADO RAIL ANNUAL 15		05	82	128
COLORADO ROAD	WAGNER	05	72	5
COMMUTER RAILROADS	DORIN	04	71	12
COMPENDIUM OF SIGNALS (POOR)	KARL	09	72	10
CORSICANA & THE ENNIS SUB (SP)	OLMSTED	11	84	132
COUNTRY RR STATIONS IN AMERICA	GRANT	02	79	24
CP IN SOUTHERN ONTARIO VOL 1		05	83	115
CP IN THE ROCKIES VOL 1-8		05	83	115
CROOKEDEST RAILROAD IN THE WORLD	WURM	10	83	136
CURVED SIDE CARS	WAGNER	03	66	17
CZ:STORY OF THE CALIFORNIA ZEPHYR		09	76	27
D DAY ON WESTERN PACIFIC	STAFF	01	83	161
D&RGW NARROW GAUGE PLANS	HEIMBURGER	04	77	21
DAWN OF THE DIESEL AGE	KIRKLAND	01	84	50
DAYLIGHT 4449'S FAMILY ALBUM SP	JOHNSEN	10	84	118
DAYTON COVINGTON & PIQUA TRACTION CO		10	74	28
DECADE OF THE TRAINS 1940'S	BALL	11	80	152
DECADE OF TRAINS THE 1940'S	BALL	11	78	142
DECLINE OF STEAM	GIFFORD	06	65	16
DESCRIPTIVE LIST OF CARS OF PULLMAN CO.		09	70	6
DESSINS FERROVIAIRES SCRAPBOOKS 17 TO 19		08	67	8
DESSINS FERROVIARIES SCRAPBOOKS 27		04	68	7
DESSINS FERROVIARIES SCRAPBOOKS 28 TO 32		05	69	6
DESSINS FERROVIARIES SCRAPBOOKS 33 TO 37		03	70	10
DESSINS FERROVIARIES SCRAPBOOKS 38 TO 42		03	71	10
DESSINS FERROVIARIES SCRAPBOOKS 43 TO 47		05	71	6
DESSINS FERROVIARIES SCRAPBOOKS 48 TO 52		09	72	10
DESTINATION LOOP	CUDAHY	05	83	115
DIESEL & ELECT LOCO LETTERING DIAGRAM NH		02	73	18
DIESEL LOCOMOTIVE ROSTERS	MACDONALD	06	82	48
DIESEL LOCOMOTIVES OF NYC SYSTEM	EDSON	01	79	39
DIESEL LOCOS OF THE NEW HAVEN	CAVANAUGH	06	81	124
DIESEL SPOTTERS GUIDE	PINKEPANK	06	67	15
DIESELS FROM EDDYSTONE:STORY OF BALDWIN		10	84	116
DIESELS OF THE ESPEE VOL 1 ALCO PA'S		11	76	32

PROTOTYPE BOOKS

Title	Author	M	Y	P
DIESELS OF THE SUNRISE TRAIL (LI)	SCALA	05	85	117
DINKIES, DAMS, AND SAWDUST	KLINE	11	77	148
DL&W RAILROAD IN THE 20TH CENTURY	TABER	04	81	132
DOING THE WHITE PASS (WP&Y)	CLIFFORD	12	83	145
DOMELINERS	DORIN	10	73	20
DOODLEBUGS	MCCALL	06	78	24
DOWN AMONG THE SUGAR CANE	BUTLER	03	81	144
DUNELAND ELECTRIC (CSS&SB)	KAPLAN	07	85	103
EARLY AMERICAN STEAM LOCOMOTIVES	KINERT	01	63	30
EARLY RAILWAYS	SNELL	08	65	16
EAST BROAD TOP	RAINEY	06	82	48
EAST BROAD TOP TO THE MINES & BACK		03	81	143
ED NOWAKS NYC	NOWAK	10	84	116
EDMONTONS ELECTRIC TRANSIT	HATCHER	12	83	144
ELECTRIC CARS OF JAPAN	KIDDER	01	66	17
ELECTRIC RAILWAY 1889 REPRINT	WHIPPLE	11	80	152
ELECTRIC RAILWAY PIONEER (NWP)	DEMORO	07	83	113
ELECTRIC RAILWAY TRUCKS	HARPER	06	68	17
ELECTRIC RAILWAYS OF INDIANA #104		07	61	17
ELECTRIC RAILWAYS OF IOWA CENT ELEC RFAN		08	57	18
ELECTRIC RAILWAYS OF NORTHEASTERN OHIO		02	66	18
ELECTRIC TRACTION ON PRR 1895-1968		12	80	69
ELECTRIC WAY ACROSS THE MOUNTAINS	MILW	02	81	117
ELECTRIFICATION BY GE		03	77	108
ENCYCLOPEDIA OF N AMERICAN RAILROADING		12	81	170
ERA OF STREETCARS IN WINNIPEG 1881-1955		01	72	12
ERIE LACKAWANA STORY	CARLETON	06	76	42
ERIE LACKAWANNA FREIGHT EQUIP DIAGRAM BK		12	80	68
EVENING BEFORE THE DIESEL	FOSS	04	81	133
EVERYWHERE WEST:THE BURLINGTON RTE	DORIN	03	77	106
EXAMPLES OF GRADES & LOCO PERFORMANCE		01	85	135
EXTRA SOUTH	REID	08	64	12
F UNITS	MULHEARN	07	83	112
FAMOUS AMERICAN TRAINS		01	35	23
FARES PLEASE! THOSE PORTLAND TROLLEY YRS		03	81	143
FLYING SCOTSMAN	PEGLER	12	70	14
FOGG & STEAM	CLODFELTER	04	79	20
FORT WAYNE AND WABASH VALLEY TROLLEYS		02	84	109
FREIGHT CARS ROLLING	SAGLE	05	61	10
FREIGHT TERMINALS & TRAINS	DROEGE	12	37	468
FRENCH STEAM LOCOMOTIVES 1840-1950		12	75	42
FRISCO DIESEL POWER	MARRE	03	85	123
FRISCO POWER	COLLIAS	11	84	132
FRISCO SOUTHWEST	MCCALL	10	82	126
FROM ABBEY TO ZURRA VIA BAGDAD CP	WILSON	08	81	100
FROM HORSECARS TO STREAMLINERS	LIND	12	78	38
FROM INVERNESS TO CREWE	EVANS	09	66	15
G-FILES WESTSIDE MODEL INDEX		09	78	30
GEORGIA RAILROAD ALBUM	BECKUM	11	85	147
GHOST LUMBER TOWNS OF CENTRAL PA.	KLINE	01	71	7
GHOST TOWN ALBUM	FLORIN	02	63	16
GHOST TOWN TRAILS	FLORIN	11	64	13
GIANT'S LADDER	BONER	03	63	16
GILPIN GOLD TRAM	FERRELL	11	71	6
GOLDEN STATE RAILS	FOX	06	81	124

LITERATURE REVIEWS

PROTOTYPE BOOKS		M	Y	P
GRAND TRUNK WESTERN	DORIN	02	78	36
GRASS BETWEEN THE RAILS (MILW)		10	73	20
GREAT AMERICAN SCENIC RAILROADS	BERGER	11	85	146
GREAT NORTHERN RAILWAY	PFM	08	79	32
GREAT THIRD RAIL	CAMPBELL	04	62	17
GROWING UP WITH TRAINS:N CALIF ALBUM		05	84	117
GROWING UP WITH TRAINS:S CALIF ALBUM		05	84	117
HANDBOOK OF AMERICAN RAILROADS	LEWIS	06	52	42
HANDBOOK OF AMERICAN RAILROADS.	LEWIS	04	57	18
HANDSOMEST TRAINS IN WORLD (LV)	KARMER	11	80	148
HAWAIIAN RAILROADS	HUNGERFORD	07	64	12
HEISLER LOCOMOTIVE	KLINE	08	82	117
HIGH IRON	BEEBE	11	38	502
HIGHBALL A PAGENT OF TRAINS REPRNT	BEEBE	12	61	88
HIGHLINERS	BEEBE	04	40	234
HISTORIC ALPINE TUNNEL DSP&P	HELMERS	04	79	22
HISTORIC LOCOMOTIVE DRAWINGS 4MM	ROCHE	04	64	13
HISTORIC LOCOMOTIVE POCKETBOOK	CASSERLY	07	61	16
HISTORICAL LOCOMOTIVES	STROMBECK-BECKER	10	36	308
HISTORY OF BRIDGE ENGINEERING REPRINT		01	69	6
HORSECARS, CABLE CARS & OMNIBUSES	WHITE	12	75	40
I LIKE TRAINS	KALMBACH	03	81	142
I REMEMBER PENNSY (PRR)	WOOD	10	74	28
ILLUSTRATED CN & CP RAIL MOT POWER 80-81		06	81	126
ILLUSTRATED TREASURY OF ALCO	KERR	04	81	132
INDUSTRIAL ARCHEOLOGY	SANDE	07	77	105
INSIDE MUNI(MUNICIPAL RR OF SAN FRAN)		01	83	161
INTERURBAN ERA	MIDDLETON	11	61	19
INTERURBAN TO MILWAUKEE	BENEDICT	06	63	17
IOWA TROLLEYS		06	75	18
IRON HORSE AT WAR	VALLE	11	78	142
IRON HORSE AT WAR 1	VALLE	05	78	34
IRON HORSES OF THE SANTA FE TRAIL	WORLEY	09	65	19
JANE'S WORLD RAILWAYS 1983-84		01	84	50
JOHN BULL	WHITE	02	82	46
JOHN STEPHENSON CO ELECT RY CATALOG 1905		01	73	11
KATY DIAGRAM BOOKS	VINCENT	05	71	6
KATY STANDARD PLANS (MKT)	SAPP	05	82	128
KETTLE VALLEY AND ITS RAILWAYS	RIEGGER	12	82	40
KEY ROUTE, PART ONE (CER)	DEMORO	09	85	112
KEY SYSTEM ALBUM	WALKER	11	79	23
KING OF RAILWAY LOCOMOTIVES REPRINT	BRIT	10	71	5
KINSEY, PHOTOGRAPHER:LOCOMOTIVE PORTRAIT		03	85	123
LA RAILWAY THROUGH THE YEARS	EASLON	01	75	23
LAKE SUPERIOR IRON ORE RAILROADS	DORIN	11	69	7
LAST OF 3 FOOT LOGGERS	KRIEG	07	63	13
LAST OF STEAM	COLLIAS	12	60	22
LAST OF THE GREAT STATIONS	BRADLEY	12	79	152
LEHIGH VALLEY RAILROAD	ARCHER	09	78	30
LETTERING GUIDE OF EARLY COLO NAR GAUGE		04	71	12
LIFE & TIMES OF THE PACIFIC ELECTRIC		01	84	49
LIMA LOCOMOTIVES 1911 CATALOG REPRINT		05	63	13
LINCOLN LAND TRACTION	JOHNSON	04	66	13
LINES WEST (GREAT NORTHERN)	WOOD	01	68	25
LITTLE JEWEL (SOO)	ABBEY	07	85	104

PROTOTYPE BOOKS		M	Y	P
LOCO, TROLLEY & RAIL CAR BUILDERS	ARNOLD	07	65	12
LOCOMOTIVE	LOEWY	08	37	300
LOCOMOTIVE 346 D&RG 2-8-0	RAMSEY	12	81	170
LOCOMOTIVE CATECHISM 1908 REPRINT		02	79	31
LOCOMOTIVE CYCLOPEDIA 1930		12	37	468
LOCOMOTIVE DIRECTORY 1906 REPRO	GREGG	09	72	6
LOCOMOTIVE QUARTERLY VOLUME 1 #1		01	77	101
LOCOMOTIVES & LOCOMOTIVE BUILDING	FORNEY	09	63	16
LOCOMOTIVES IN MY LIFE	WOOD	01	77	105
LOCOMOTIVES OF DM&IR	KING	10	84	118
LOCOMOTIVES OF MY LIFE	WOOD	12	75	42
LOCOMOTIVES OF SOUTH AFRICAN RAILWAYS		01	71	7
LOCOMOTIVES OF THE EMPIRE BUILDER	MARTIN	09	72	10
LOCOMOTIVES OF THE READING	WARNER	08	63	15
LOCOMOTIVES THAT BALDWIN BUILT	WESTING	02	67	17
LOGGING RAILROAD ERA OF LUMBERING PA 8		11	73	22
LOGGING RAILROADS OF RUSK CO WISC	BROWN	05	83	115
LOGGING RAILROADS OF THE WEST	ADAMS	12	61	88
LOGGING RAILROADS OF THE WHITE MOUNTAINS		06	81	126
LOS ANGELES PACIFIC ALBUM	SWETT	02	67	16
MA&PA	HILTON	06	81	126
MAIN LINE MEXICO (NDM)	EDMUNDSON	11	65	16
MAINE CENTRAL RR MOUNTAIN DIVISION	BUX	11	85	147
MAINE CENTRAL RR PHOTO ALBUM	ROBERTSON	02	81	117
MAINTENANCE OF WAY & STRUCTURES	WILLARD	12	37	468
MANSIONS ON RAILS	BEEBE	12	59	24
MARKET STREET RAILWAY REVISITED	SWETT	03	73	16
MARSHALL PASS (RIO GRANDE)	BORNEMANN	04	81	133
MARSHALLS BOOK OF RAILWAYS	WALLER	12	61	90
MATCAHES, FLUMES & RAILS	STEPHENS	08	78	28
MECHANICAL DEPARTMENT FACILITIES NH		11	78	144
MEET THE MAINE CENTRAL		05	82	128
MEMORIES OF BOSTON & MAINE	MAYWOOD	11	85	146
MEN & IRON	HUNGERFORD	07	38	306
METROPOLITAN CORRIDOR	STILGOE	12	83	145
MEXICAN NARROW GAUGE	BEST	03	69	8
MIBA REPORTS 1,2,3,4		01	78	26
MILWAUKE		12	72	
MILWAUKEE ROAD BI POLAR ELECTRICS	HOLLEY	08	82	117
MILWAUKEE ROAD EAST	DORIN	10	78	152
MILWAUKEE ROAD ELECTRIFICATION	BRAIN	12	61	90
MILWAUKEE ROAD WEST	WOOD	12	72	15
MINERAL BELT VOL 1 & 2	DIGERNESS	02	79	20
MINNESOTA LOGGING RAILROADS	KING	04	82	138
MINUTEMAN STEAM: B&M STEAM LOCOS 1911-58		05	83	113
MISSABE ROAD DM&IR	KING	02	74	20
MISSOURI PACIFIC ANNUAL 1975-6	EAGAN	05	77	31
MISSOURI PACIFIC P-73 CLASS 4-6-2	PFM	04	79	22
MIXED TRAIN DAILY REPRINT	BEEBE	02	62	20
MODEL RAILROADER CYCLOPEDIA VOL 2		10	80	28
MODERN RAILWAY	PARMELE	10	40	584
MOFFAT ROAD	BOLLINGER	03	63	16
MOHAWK THAT REFUSED TO ABDICATE/OTHERS		04	76	18
MONTANAS TROLLEYS VOL II		03	71	10
MOPAC POWER	COLLIAS	10	80	27

STEPHANS' RAILROAD DIRECTORY

LITERATURE REVIEWS

PROTOTYPE BOOKS

Title	Author	M	Y	P
MORE RAILROADS YOU CAN MODEL	SCHAFER	07	78	28
MORE WELCH HIGHLAND RAILWAY	LEE	08	67	8
MOTIVE POWER OF UNION PACIFIC	KRATVILLE	03	59	20
MOUNTAIN TO MILL C&WY	MCKENZIE	05	83	113
MOVIE RAILROADS	JENSEN	02	82	52
MR CYCLOPEDIA VOL 1 STEAM LOCOMOTIVES		08	60	16
MR LINCOLNS MILITARY RAILROADS	MEREDITH	07	79	36
N&W HANDBOOK	WALLACE	02	81	116
N&W: GIANT OF STEAM	JEFFRIES	11	80	149
NARROW GAUGE NOSTALGIA REISSUE	TURNER	02	72	11
NARROW GAUGE PICTORIALS	RUBB	05	83	114
NARROW GAUGE PORTRAIT S. PACIFIC COAST		07	76	16
NARROW GAUGE RAILWAYS OF CANADA	LAVALLEE	12	76	122
NARROW GAUGE SILVERTON TRAIN (D&RGW)		04	73	19
NARROW GAUGE TO COMBRES (C&T)	OSTERWALD	02	73	18
NARROW GAUGE: STORY OF BRB&L	STANLEY	02	81	117
NEBRASKA CB&Q DEPOTS	RAPP	12	70	12
NEVADA COUNTY NARROW GAUGE	BEST	09	65	19
NEVER ON WEDNESDAY:1ST DECADE RG ZEPHYRS		04	81	130A
NEW ENGLAND ALCOS IN TWILIGHT	HARTLEY	03	85	123
NEW ENGLAND SHORT LINES 1970-80	NELLIGAN	05	83	114
NEW ENGLANDS DIESELS	ALBERT	08	78	25
NEW HAVEN RR FREIGHT & WORK CAR PLANBOOK		07	77	98
NEWPORT BY TROLLEY	O'HANLEY	08	77	22
NO ROYAL ROAD	CUSTER	11	37	428
NORFOLK & WESTERN	STRIPLIN	05	82	129
NORTH AMERICAN STEAM LOCOS:THE NORTHERNS		03	76	22
NORTH SHORE	MIDDLETON	04	65	15
NORTH SHORE LINE MEMORIES CNS&M	CAMPBELL	12	80	69
NORTH WESTERN PACIFIC PICTORIAL	FOX	10	83	136
NORTHERN ALBERTA RAILWAYS		05	83	115
NORTHERN INDIANA RAILWAYS	BRADLEY	11	53	88
NORTHERN PACIFIC	WOOD	04	69	7
NORTHWEST RAIL PICTORIAL	WING	10	84	116
NOTABLE LOCOMOTIVES OF 1906	REPRINT	02	79	32
NWI'S GUIDE TO RR PHOTOGRAPHY	SCHMIDT	03	77	106
NYC LATER POWER: 1910-68	STAUFER	06	82	49
NYC SYSTEM, GONE BUT NOT FORGOTTON		10	84	116
NYO&W SCRANTON DIVISION	BOX	11	85	147
ONE MAN'S RAILWAY	SNELL	05	84	118
ONTARIO & QUEBEC RAILWAY	WILSON	05	85	116
OTTO PERRY: MASTER RAILROAD PHOTOGRAPHER		12	82	40
OUR GM SCRAPBOOK	KALMBACH	04	72	8
OVERLAND LIMITED	BEEBE	03	64	14
OVERLAND TO THE ROCKIES	FOX	03	85	122
PACIFIC SLOPE RAILROADS	ABDILL	12	59	25
PACIFIC STREAM	EVANS	09	61	18
PASS TRAIN CARS SANTA FE 1870-1971 VOL 1		03	74	17
PASSENGER TERMINALS & TRAINS	DROEGE	12	37	468
PASSENGER TRAIN EQUIP SANTA FE VOL II		09	76	26
PAY LOCOMOTIVE		11	78	144
PC SYSTEM BI ANNUAL	REID	02	75	22
PCC FROM COAST TO COAST	SCHNEIDER	01	84	49
PCC: THE CAR THAT FOUGHT BACK	CARLSON	04	81	130A
PENN STATION ITS TUNNELS & SIDE RODDERS		02	79	21

PROTOTYPE BOOKS

Title	Author	M	Y	P
PENNSY CAR PLANS	WAYNER	12	70	11
PENNSY POWER	STAUFER	01	63	30
PEOPLE'S RAILWAY (MSP)	PERLES	09	81	138
PEORIA WAY (TP&W)	MCMILLAN	09	85	111
PERE MARQUETTE POWER	DIXON	07	85	103
PFE ICE REFRIGERATOR CARS 1906-32		01	79	40
PICTORAL HISTORY OF JNR OKAJOKI TO HIKAK		09	66	14
PIEDMONT AND NORTHERN	FETTERS	03	76	23
PINO GRANDE, MICH LOG RR-CALIF LUMBER CO		03	67	20
PINO GRANDE: LOGGING RR OF MICH-CAL LUMB		01	85	135
PITCH PINE AND PROP TIMBER	KLINES	01	72	12
PITTSBURGH AND LAKE ERIE RAILROAD	MCLEAN	03	81	144
POCKET ENCYCLOPEDIA BRITISH STEAM LOCOS		12	73	24
PORT OF NEW YORK	CONDIT	05	82	128
PORTAITS OF THE IRON HORSE	HENRY	12	36	468
PORTRAIT OF AN ENGINE SP #4294	BOTHMAN	11	69	7
PORTRAITS OF THE IRON HORSE	HENRY	11	37	428
PRIVATE PASSENGER CAR ANNUAL VOL1	BRIGGS	11	80	149
PROTOTYPE RAILROAD COLOR GUIDE	GERITY	10	82	122
PRR STANDARD MAINTENANCE OF WAY PLANS		09	67	15
PUTNAM DIVISION:NYC BYGONE RT WESTCHESTE		12	81	168
Q DEFINITIVE HISTORY OF B&O Q CLASS MIKA		01	79	39
QUARTER CENTURY OF ATSF PASS CONSISTS		11	85	146
RAIL CANADA VOLUME 1		10	76	91
RAIL CANADA VOLUME 2	LEWIS	05	79	39
RAIL CANADA VOLUME 3	LEWIS	08	79	37
RAIL CANADA VOLUME 4	LEWIS	10	83	134
RAIL FACTS AND FEATS	MARSHALL	08	74	14
RAIL VENTURES	SWANSON	07	83	113
RAIL-SCAN	KNEITEL	05	83	115
RAILROAD CAR JOURNAL V1 BOXCARS		01	72	13
RAILROAD IN THE CLOUDS:AL AGE OF STEAM		06	78	28
RAILROAD OF NEVADA & E CALIF VII	MYRICK	03	64	12
RAILROAD PROTOTYPE LETTERING DIAGRAMS V3		08	63	15
RAILROAD SLANGUAGE	ANS PUBLISHER	07	52	61
RAILROAD STATION	MEEKS	04	57	18
RAILROAD STATION PLAN BOOK	EDMONSON	07	77	98
RAILROAD THAT RAN BY THE TIDE (IL)		12	72	15
RAILROAD, WHAT IS IT?, WHAT IT DOES		02	79	29
RAILROADERS	LEUTHNER	02	84	109
RAILROADING THROUGH CAJON PASS	WALKER	01	79	36
RAILROADS AN AMERICAN JOURNEY	BALL	11	76	32
RAILROADS IN THE LEHIGH VALLEY	KULP	10	63	18
RAILROADS IN THE WOODS	LABBE	12	61	88
RAILROADS OF ARIZONA VOL 1	MYRICK	08	76	22
RAILROADS OF ARIZONA VOL II	MYRICK	06	81	126
RAILROADS OF ARIZONA VOL III	MYRICK	10	84	118
RAILROADS OF HAWAII	BEST	03	79	35
RAILROADS OF KANSAS CITY	LYNCH	12	84	188
RAILROADS OF NEVADA & E CALIF V1	MYRICK	02	63	16
RAILROADS OF THE BLACK HILLS	FIEDLER	01	65	13
RAILROADS OF THE YOSEMITE VALLY	JOHNSTON	02	64	25
RAILROADS THROUGH THE COEUR D'ALENES		10	83	134
RAILROADS YOU CAN MODEL	KALMBACH	07	76	16
RAILS	BALL	05	82	129

LITERATURE REVIEWS

PROTOTYPE BOOKS

Title	Author	M	Y	P
RAILS 'NEATH THE PALMS	MANN	05	85	117
RAILS ACROSS THE MIDLANDS	COOK	04	65	15
RAILS ACROSS THE TUNDRA (AL)	COHEN	01	85	136
RAILS AOUND THE LOOP (GB&L)	MORGAN	06	77	35
RAILS AROUND GOTHAM		05	82	128
RAILS IN THE SHADOW OF MT SHASTA	SIGNOR	05	84	118
RAILS NORTH	CLIFFORD	06	82	49
RAILS TO CARRY COPPER (MA)	CHAPPELL	04	75	18A
RAILS TO THE BIG VEIN	MELLANDER	09	81	138
RAILS TO THE MINARETS (SPLC)	JOHNSTON	10	80	30
RAILS TO THE MINES:TAIWANS FORGOTTON RYS		02	79	32
RAILS TO THE PINES CR&M.	BROWN	06	81	126
RAILS TO THE RISING SUN	SMALL	02	66	18
RAILS TO THE ROCKIES	LEPAK	06	77	35
RAILS TO THE SETTING SUN	SMALL	04	72	8
RAILS UNDER THE MIGHTY HUDSON	CUDAHY	01	77	102
RAILS UP THE RARITAN (RR)	DIEBERT	12	83	144
RAILS WEST	ABDILL	11	61	19
RAILS, SAGEBRUSH AND PINE	FARRELL	02	68	24
RAILWAY ENG & MAINT CYCLOPEDIA 1929		12	37	468
RAILWAY HOLIDAY IN SPAIN	ROWE	12	67	9
RAILWAY MILEPOSTS: BC VOL 1 CPR MAINLINE		02	82	54
RAILWAY MILEPOSTS:BRITISH COLUMBIA VOL 2		05	85	118
RAILWAY SIGNALING	KING	12	37	468
RAILWAY STATIONS OF WESTERN CANADA		03	81	143
RAINBOW ROUTE	MEARS	01	76	23
READING POWER PICTORIAL	BERTROM	07	74	10
READINGS VICTORIAN STATIONS 1890		05	77	34
RED ARROW	DEGREW	03	73	15
RED ARROW, FIRST 100 YEARS	DEGRAW	09	85	111
RED CAR DAYS, MEMORIES OF THE PE	LONG	02	84	109
RED RIVER PAUL BUNYANS OWN LUMBER CO &RR		02	81	117
RED TRAINS IN EAST BAY (SP)	FORD	05	79	37
RED TRAINS REMEMBERED (SP)	FORD	11	80	152
REDWOODS, IRON HORSES & THE PACIFIC CW		12	71	12
REFLECTIONS: NICKEL PLATE YRS 1881-1981		04	81	130A
REMEMBER WHEN TROLLEY WIRES SPAN COUNTRY		02	81	117
REQUIEM FOR NARROW GAUGE (D&RGW)	GRENARD	07	85	104
RHODE ISLAND TRANSIT ALBUM		12	79	155
RIDE THE BIG RED CARS	CRUMP	05	63	14
RIDE THE SANDY RIVER SR&RL	CORNWALL	12	73	22
RIO GRANDE CAR PLANS	WAYNER	11	69	7
RIO GRANDE DIESELS VOL 1	STRAPAC	12	83	143
RIO GRANDE DIESELS VOL 2	STRAPAC	12	84	18B
RIO GRANDE NARROW GAUGE	NORWOOD	07	83	112
RIO GRANDE SKI TRAIN	PATTERSON	09	85	110
RIO GRANDE STEAM LOCOMOTIVES: STD GAUGE		04	82	138
RIO GRANDE WEST	HILL	12	82	40
RIVERSIDE & ARLINGTON ELECTRIC RY	SWETT	04	63	19
ROARING U50'S, UP TWIN DIESELS	KEEKLEY	06	79	130
ROCK ISLAND DIESEL LOCOMOTIVES	MARRE	08	82	120
ROCK ISLAND RECOLLECTIONS	OLMSTED	10	82	126
ROLLING STOCK OF JAPAN	YAMAZAKI	05	67	17
ROUND THE WORLD IN NARROW GAUGE	ALLEN	01	73	10
ROUTE OF THE ELECTROLINERS	BENEDICT	05	64	12

PROTOTYPE BOOKS

Title	Author	M	Y	P
ROUTE OF THE MINUTE MAN B&M	NELLIGAN	02	81	117
ROYAL BLUE HERITAGE	WOOD	02	79	30
RR THAT LIGHTED S. CALIFORNIA	JOHNSTON	07	65	12
RUNNING A MOUNTAIN RAILROAD (C&TS)		12	81	173
RUTLAND ROAD	SHAUGHNESSY	04	65	15
RUTLAND ROAD 2ED EDITION	SHAUGHNESSY	05	82	128
SACRAMENTO NORTHERN	SWETT	07	63	13
SACRAMENTO NORTHERN ALBUM #34 REPRINT		12	73	22
SAGA OF THE SOO, WEST FROM SHOREHAM		01	77	101
SAIL & RAIL	WAKEFIELD	06	82	49
SAN ANTONIO AND ARKANSAS PASS RAILWAY		10	83	134
SAN DIEGO & ARIZONA	HANFT	05	85	117
SANTA FE DEPOTS-THE WESTERN LINES POUNDS		01	85	136
SANTA FE SYSTEM STANDARDS		12	78	38
SANTA FE SYSTEM STANDARDS VOL 3		02	79	31
SANTA FE'S DIESEL FLEET		08	76	24
SANTA FE'S EARLY DIESEL DAZE 1935-53		03	81	143
SANTA FE'S HI LEVEL CARS	KOGAN	08	76	20
SANTA FE'S RATON PASS	HARPER	01	84	51
SEARCH FOR STEAM	COLLIAS	12	72	15
SEATTLE CAR & FOUNDRY CO CATALOG 1913		07	75	18
SESQUEHANNA NYS&W	KRAUSE	11	80	150
SEVEN SHORT LINES, THEIR LIVES & TIMES		04	62	17
SHAY	APPEL	10	83	136
SHAY MODELERS HANDBOOK: LIMA CLASS "C"		05	85	115
SHIPS & NARROW GAUGE RAILS	BEST	09	64	12
SHORT LINE ODYSSEY	YOUNG	02	82	54
SHORT LINE TO PARADISE (YV)	JOHNSTON	04	63	19
SHORTLINE RAILROADS OF ARKANSAS	HULL	10	69	7
SILVER SAN JUAN (RGS)	FERRELL	02	74	20
SILVER SHORT LINE (V&T)	WURM	10	83	136
SLIM RAILS THROUGH THE SAND	TURNER	01	64	18
SNOWPLOW	BEST	03	67	20
SOUTH PACIFIC COAST	MACGREGOR	03	69	8
SOUTHERN CALIFORNIA & THE PACIFIC ELECTR		02	81	117
SOUTHERN PACIFIC MOTIVE POWER ANNUAL '71		03	73	19
SOUTHERN PACIFIC NARROW GAUGE	FERRELL	12	82	40
SP DAYLIGHT TRAIN 98-99	WRIGHT	11	78	145
SP LOCOMOTIVE DIRECTORY 84		11	84	134
SP MOTIVE POWER ANNUAL 1973	STRAPAC	01	75	22
SP MOTIVE POWER ANNUAL 1974-76		01	78	24
SP STEAM LOCOMOTIVES	DUKE	05	63	14
SP&S THE NORTHWESTS OWN RAILWAY	WOOD	11	74	26
SPEEDWAY TO SUNSHINE (FEC)	BRAMSON	09	85	110
SPIRIT OF THE SOUTH SHORE (CSS&SB)	RAIA	09	85	111
ST LOUIS CAR COMPANY ALBUM	YOUNG	01	85	135
STAIRWAY TO THE STARS	ABBOTT	09	78	29
STATEN ISLAND RAPID TRANSIT		04	66	14
STEAM IN CANADA	LEWIS	09	85	112
STEAM IN NIAGARA	PANKO	04	84	110
STEAM IN THE ROCKIES A D&RG ROSTER	HAUCK	05	64	12
STEAM LOCO DIAGRAMS OF THE C&O	STAUFER	07	65	13
STEAM LOCOMOTIVE IN AMERICA	BRUCE	09	53	80
STEAM LOCOMOTIVES	KALMBACH	12	53	99
STEAM LOCOMOTIVES & HISTORY (G) & (WPR)		01	77	102

LITERATURE REVIEWS

PROTOTYPE BOOKS

Title	Author	M	Y	P
STEAM LOCOMOTIVES IN JAPAN	YAMAZAKI	11	63	23
STEAM LOCOMOTIVES OF BURLINGTON	CORBIN	08	60	16
STEAM LOCOMOTIVES OF EAST EUROPE	DURRANT	02	67	16
STEAM LOCOS OF MEIJI ERA		05	69	7
STEAM LOCOS OF THE FRISCO LINE	STAGNER	03	77	108
STEAM POWER NYC VOL 1 MODERN POWER		11	61	22
STEAM RAILROADS OF CENTRAL NEW YORK		10	73	21
STEAM TRAINS TO BRUCE (CP)	BEAUMONT	11	78	145
STEAMERS OF THE D&H RAILROAD	REZNAK	07	72	77
STEAMS FINEST HOUR	MORGAN	12	59	25
STEEL RAILS	STEVERS	12	37	468
STEEL RAILS TO THE SUNSET	ZIEL	01	66	16
STEEL TRAILS--EPIC OF RAILROADS	STEVERS	06	34	14
STEMWINDERS IN LAUREL HIGHLANDS	KLINE	11	77	148
STOCK CARS OF THE SANTA FE RAILWAY	BERRY	02	82	52
STORY OF HIAWATHA (MILW)		07	85	104
STORY OF TUNNELS	BLACK	07	38	306
STREAMLINE ERA	REED	10	76	92
STREAMLINED STEAM		01	73	10
STREAMLINER CARS: VOL 1 PULLMAN-STANDARD		12	81	173
STREATOR CONNECTION (CONRAIL)		05	82	125
STREET RAILWAY ERA IN SEATTLE	BLANCHARD	03	69	8
STREETCARS OF NEW ORLEANS VII	HENNICK	10	65	17
STRUCTURES OF THE EARLY WEST		11	76	33
SUDBURY STREETCARS (SCCE)	KNOWLES	12	83	145
SUGAR TRAINS PICTORIAL	CONDE	05	76	25
SUGAR TRAMP CGW	MORGAN	12	76	121
SUPER CHIEF: TRAIN OF THE STARS ATSF		03	81	143
SURFACE CARS OF PHILADELPHIA	COX	03	66	17
SWITZERLAND TRIAL OF AMERICA	CROSSEN	08	79	37
TEHACHAPI (SP)	SIGNOR	01	84	50
TEXAS & PACIFIC	WATSON	06	79	133
TEXAS STATE RAILROAD BRANCH LINE	GRAPHIC	03	80	139
THE DIESEL YEARS	OLMSTED	03	76	23
THE LAST WHISTLE (OS)	WAGNER	07	75	17
THE MA&PA HIST OF MARYLAND & PENN	HILTON	10	63	18
THE MOUNTAINS (4-8-2)	PFM	03	79	36
THE NOT&L STORY	BLOWER	02	67	16
THEY BUILT THE WEST	QUIETT	02	35	53
THIS WAS RAILROADING	ABDILL	11	58	22
THOSE AMAZING CLASS D LOCOS	ALBRECHT	02	82	54
THOSE DAYLIGHT 4-8-4'S	CHURCH	08	67	8
THREE FEET ON THE PANHANDLE (W&WA)		12	83	144
THROUGHBREDS NYC HUDSONS	STAUFER	08	76	22
THUNDER IN THE MOUNTAINS	JOHNSTON	09	68	188
TICKET TO TOLTEC D&RGW	OSTERWALD	01	77	101
TIMBER	ANDREWS	01	69	8
TIME OF THE TROLLEY	MIDDLETON	03	68	9
TRACKS, TIRES & WIRES	MCCALEB	06	82	49
TRACTION CLASSICS THE INTERURBANS		02	84	109
TRACTION FANS DIRECTORY FOR 1962	JONES	06	62	18
TRACTION PHOTO ALBUM 1	JONES	01	63	30
TRAFFORD TROLLEYS (WP&P)	ALBERT	03	81	143
TRAGIC TRAIN "CITY OF SAN FRANCISCO"		11	77	148
TRAIL OF IRON (CP)	MCKEE	11	84	134

PROTOTYPE BOOKS

Title	Author	M	Y	P
TRAIN FREQS		01	83	161
TRAIN SHED 7 STRUCTURES	GREGG	07	73	8
TRAIN SHED 8 PASSENGER CARS	GREGG	07	73	8
TRAIN SHED CYCLOPEDIA 79	GREGG	02	80	122
TRAIN TRIPS: EXPLORING AMERICA BY RAIL		08	81	100
TRAIN WATCHERS GUIDE TO N AMERICAN RRS		07	84	108
TRAINS	HENRY	06	34	14
TRAINS 2ND EDITION	HENRY	08	39	422
TRAINS OF DISCOVERY: WESTERN RR & NATL PK		03	85	123
TRAINS OF THE NORTHEAST CORRIDOR		08	82	120
TRAINS ON AVENUE DE RUMINE	COLUZZI	05	84	116
TRAINS WE RODE VOLUME 2	BEEBE	02	67	17
TRAINS, TRACKS & TRAVEL	VAN METRE	12	37	468
TRAINS, TRACKS, & TRAVEL 5TH ED	VANMETRE	08	39	422
TRAINS.	HENRY	12	37	468
TRAINSHED CYCLOPEDIA 80	GREGG	02	80	122
TROLLEY TALK VOLUME 1 WAGNER CAR CO PUB		08	77	23
TROLLEY TALK VOLUME 3	WAGNER	04	70	6
TROLLEY TALK VOLUME 3 REPRINT		12	79	155
TROLLEY TITANS	CARSON	02	82	54
TROLLEY TO THE PAST	YOUNG	01	84	50
TROLLEYS OF BERKS COUNTY PA	FOESIG	04	71	10
TROLLEYS TO THE SURF-STORY OF LA&P	MYERS	10	77	112
TUMULT ON THE MOUNTAINS	CLARKSON	01	65	13
TWEETSIE COUNTRY (ET&WNC)	FERRELL	05	77	24
TWILIGHT OF STEAM LOCOMOTIVES	ZIEL	02	64	25
TWIXT RAIL AND SEA REPRINT BRITISH		10	71	8
UINATAH RAILWAY	BENDER	04	71	10
UNDER SIDEWALKS OF NEW YORK	CUDAHY	04	80	110
UNION PACIFIC 1977-1980	COCKLE	09	81	136
UNION PACIFIC 8444	KINDIG	01	79	39
UNION PACIFIC CABOOSES		03	79	44
UNION PACIFIC FREIGHT CARS OF THE '50'S		03	80	139
UNION PACIFIC RR PAINTING GUIDE 1903-30		02	82	52
UNION PACIFIC STREAMLINERS	RANKS	11	75	102
UP MOTIVE POWER REVIEW 1968-77		07	79	36
USRA 2-8-8-2 SERIES 2ND EDITION	DRESSLER	09	85	112
V&O STORY	MCCLELLAND	03	85	122
V&T LOCOMOTIVES	KOEGIN	02	81	117
VALLEY RAILWAYS	SIEBERT	07	83	113
VANCOUVER ISLAND RAILROADS	GOLDEN WEST	01	77	103
VANISHING MARKERS	FISHER	10	77	113
VIRGINIA & TRUCKEE	BEEBE	10	63	18
VIRGINIAN RAILWAY	REID	01	62	25
VIRGINIAN RAILWAY (PAPERBACK)	REID	03	81	142
WABASH	HEIMBURGER	11	84	132
WATER LEVEL ROUTE (NYC)	KNOLL	07	85	104
WAYCARS OF THE CB&Q	HOLBROOK	01	79	40
WELLSVILLE, ADDISON & GALETON RAILROAD		03	73	16
WELSH HIGHLAND RAILWAY	LEE	08	67	8
WENDOVER, ACME & VIRGINA POINT	REEVES	12	81	173
WEST MIDLAND (BRITISH)	BEAL	01	53	83
WESTERN GHOST TOWNS	FLORIN	11	64	13
WESTERN MARYLAND STEAM ALBUM	PRICE	11	85	146
WESTERN PAC STEAM LOCOS, PASS TRAINS, CARS		09	81	136

LITERATURE REVIEWS

PROTOTYPE BOOKS

Title	Author	M	Y	P
WESTERN PACIFIC PICTORIAL	RYCZKOWSKI	02	81	117
WESTERN PACIFIC'S DIESEL YEARS	STRAPAC	03	81	144
WESTERN STEAM SPECTACULAR	STRAPAC	05	82	125
WHEN STEAM WAS KING	STEWART	04	71	10
WHITE FRONT CARS OF SAN FRANCISCO		04	72	9
WHITE FRONT CARS OF SAN FRANCISCO	SWETT	09	79	37
WHO MADE ALL OUR STREETCARS GO?	FARRELL	04	75	18A
WILDCATTING ON THE MOUNTAINS	KLINE	01	71	7
WILLAMETTE LOCOMOTIVE	HAUFF	11	84	134
YELLOW CARS OF LOS ANGELES	WALKER	01	78	32
YONDER COMES THE TRAIN	PHILLIPS	06	66	15
ZEPHYRS & COMMUTERS (CB&Q/BN)	OLMSTED	09	85	112
ZEPHYRSM CHIEFS, & OTHER ORPHANS	FRAILEY	01	78	34

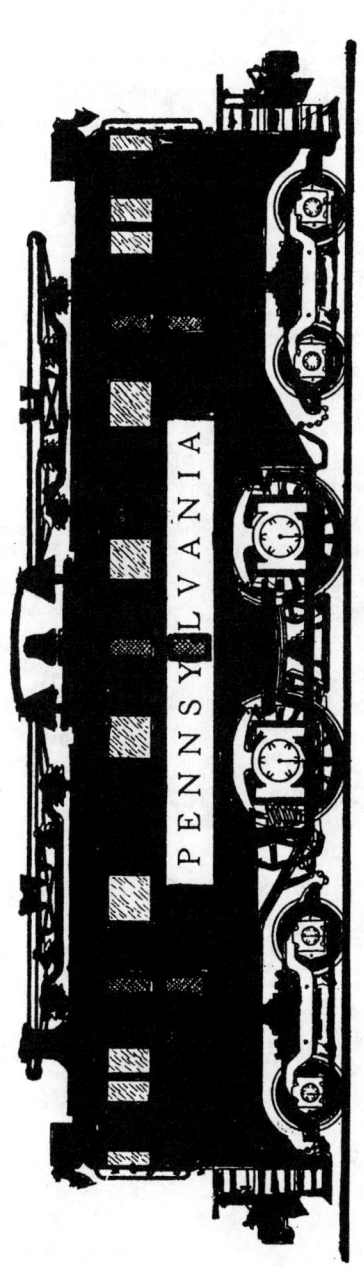

MODELING BOOKS

Title	Author	M	Y	P
101 MODEL RAILROAD LAYOUTS	GARRISON	02	84	106
101 TRACK PLANS	WESTCOTT	12	56	25
18 TAYLOR MADE MRR TRACK PLANS	ARMSTRONG	04	84	108
34 NEW ELECTRONIC PROJECTS FOR MRR		10	82	122
35 MODEL BUILDING PROJECTS	OLEVSKY	09	78	27
764 HELPFUL HINTS FOR MRR	WARREN	10	65	16
A.C. GILBERT'S HERITAGE	HEIMBURGER	10	83	134
ABC MINIATURE RAILWAYS	WILSON	12	61	90
ABC NARROW GAUGE RAILWAYS	DAVIES	12	61	90
ADVANCED MODEL RAILROADING	HERTZ	05	55	09
AIRBRUSH TECHNIQUES	KOHL	06	65	17
ALL ABOARD: JOSHUA LIONEL COWEN/TRAIN CO		04	82	134
ALL ABOUT N GAUGE MODEL RRING	GARRISON	07	83	112
ALL TIME INDEX	WAYNER	04	71	10
ANIMATED SCALE MODELS HANDBOOK	FRANK	07	82	102
ANTIQUE TOY TRAINS	GODEL	03	77	107
ARCHITECTURAL AND INTERIOR MODELS		11	70	12
ART OF BRASS IN MODEL RAILROADING VOL 1		05	83	112
BEST OF MRING MAGAZINES TRACK PLANS		02	84	106
BLUEPRINTS FOR ATLAS SNAP TRACK	ATLAS	08	68	4
BOOK OF RULES FOR MODEL RRERS	SAGLE	05	44	232
BRIDGE & TRESTLE HANDBOOK REVISED		02	73	18
BRIDGE AND TRESTLE HANDBOOK REVISED		05	77	31
BRIDGES & BUILDINGS FOR MODEL RAILROADS		02	66	18
BRIDGES AND TRESTLES MODEL STRUCTURES CO		01	49	57
BROWN BOOK (BRASS PRICE LISTING)	BROWN	01	81	165
BROWN BOOK 2ND ED	BROWN	10	83	134
BUILD YOUR OWN MODEL CARS/LOCOS	KALMBACH	02	55	22
BUILDING & LAYING "O" TRACKWORK	CARTER	08	52	51
BUILDING & OPERATING MODEL RAILROADS		11	79	23
BUILDING PLASTIC RR MODELS	SCHLEICHER	02	80	120
CERRO BOND CASTING	COFFEY	10	73	20
CLASSIC ARTICLES FROM MR	KALMBACH	08	81	98
CLOCKWORK, STEAM, & ELECTRIC	REDER	04	73	19
CLOSE-UP PHOTOGRAPHY	WHITE	07	85	103
COLLECTING MODEL TRAINS	HERTZ	04	57	18
COLLECTORS & BLDRS GUIDE TO STEAM LOCOS		12	81	166
COLLECTORS GUIDE & HISTORY LIONEL TRAINS		12	75	40
COLLECTORS GUIDE TO N SCALE	MUMMERT	02	81	116
COLLECTORS GUIDE TO N SCALE	WINGARD	03	85	122
COLLECTORS GUIDE TO POSTWAR LIONEL	TUOHY	12	75	41
COMPLETE BOOK OF MODEL RAILROADING	HERTZ	02	52	47
COMPLETE BOOK OF MODEL RAILROADING	SUTTN	02	65	20
COMPLETE BOOK OF PLASTIC MODEL KITS		06	62	18
COMPOSITE PRODUCT REVIEW INDEX	SWIFT	10	83	132
CRAFT OF MODEL RAILWAYS	BEAL	11	37	428
CREATIVE LAYOUT DESIGN	ARMSTRONG	05	79	35
CTC-16E MODEL RR COMMAND SYSTEM		01	85	134
DIRECTORY OF MODEL RAILROAD SCALE DRAWIN		10	83	134
EASY TO BUILD MODEL RAILROAD FREIGHT CAR		03	72	6
EASY TO BUILD MODEL RR STRUCTURES	ANDERS	11	58	22
ELECTRICAL HANDBOOK FOR MRR	MALLERY	02	56	20
ENJOYING LIONEL FUNDIMENSIONS TRAINS		08	82	116
FRANK ELLISON ON MODEL RAILROADS		01	55	24
FREIGHT CAR LETTERING PLAN BOOK	MEYER	04	66	14

LITERATURE REVIEWS

MODELING BOOKS

Title	M	Y	P
GREENBERG OP/REP MANUAL LIONEL-FUN D TRA	11	79	24
GREENBERG'S AF S GAUGE OPER & REP MANUAL	01	85	134
GREENBERG'S GUIDE TO IVES TRAINS 1901-32	12	84	17
GREENBERG'S OPERATING/REAPIR MANUAL L-F	08	82	116
GREENBERG'S PRICE GUIDE LIONEL 1945-82	08	82	116
GREENBERG'S PRICE GUIDE N GAUGE TRAINS	04	82	135
GREENBERG'S PRICE GUIDE TO LIONEL TRAINS	11	77	150
GREENBERGS OP INSTRUMENTS W/LAYOUTS LIO	10	78	152
GREENBERGS PRICE GUIDE TO LIONEL TRAINS	07	78	35
GREENBERGS REPAIR/OP MANUAL LIONEL TRAIN	07	78	34
HANDBOOK FOR MODEL RAILROADERS 2ND WAL	08	39	422
HO NARROW GAUGE YOU CAN BUILD FURLOW	12	84	17
HO RAILROAD THAT GROWS WESTCOTT	05	58	16
HO SCALE MODEL DIESELS SODERQUIST	01	84	49
HOW TO BUILD MODEL RAILROAD BENCHWORK	05	80	133
HOW TO BUILD MODEL RAILROADS & EQUIPMENT	02	57	21
HOW TO BUILD REALISTIC MODEL RR SCENERY	05	82	124
HOW TO BUILD YOUR OWN SWITCH MACHINES	12	80	68
HOW TO IMPROVE YOUR MODEL RAILROAD YATES	12	53	100
HOW TO OPERATE LIONEL & AF TRAINS/ACCESS	12	80	66
HOW TO OPERATE YOUR MODEL RAILROAD CHUBB	12	77	164
HOW TO PHOTOGRAPH SCALE MODELS PAINE	01	85	134
HOW TO RUN A RAILROAD	01	78	26
HOW TO WIRE YOUR MODEL RAILROAD WESTCOTT	09	50	61
HOW TO WIRE YOUR MODEL RR (ENLARGED)	07	54	13
IAN ALLEN BOOK OF MRR BRYANT	04	61	11
INDOOR MODEL RAILWAYS "HO/OO" TWINING	03	38	128
INTERNATIONAL MODEL RAILWAYS GUIDE	01	81	166
INTERNATIONAL MODEL RAILWAYS GUIDE STEIN	10	78	154
KING SIZE PLAN BOOK FOR HO RAILROADS UCM	08	66	13
LBSC'S SHOP, SHED & ROAD	10	70	8
LENAHANS LOCOMOTIVE LEXICON	08	75	18
LIONEL COLL GUIDE & HIST VOL 5 ARCHIVES	02	82	43
LIONEL COLL GUIDE & HIST VOL 6 ADS & ART	02	82	43
LIONEL COLLECTORS GUIDE/HISTORY VOL 3	02	79	30
LIONEL TRAINS-STD OF THE WORLD 1900-1943	08	77	22
LOCOMOTIVE PLAN PACKAGE MODEL CRAFTSMAN	05	45	217
MAKE YOUR OWN MODEL RAILROAD TRACK GEE	09	61	18
MAKING & OPERATING MODEL RAILROADS YATES	10	38	452
MINIATURE STEAM LOCOMOTIVES WOODSTOCK	05	65	19
MODEL CARS & LOCOMOTIVES "O" TAYLOR	06	40	358
MODEL RAILROAD BUYER'S GUIDE BOYNTON	05	77	34
MODEL RAILROAD CONVERSION MANUAL HERTZ	08	40	464
MODEL RAILROAD PHOTOGRAPHY GARRISON	08	81	100
MODEL RAILROAD RIGHT OF WAY WILSON	03	35	81
MODEL RAILROAD SCRATCH BLDG WESOLOWSKI	09	81	133
MODEL RAILROAD TRACK PLAN BOOK ARMSTRONG	12	80	66
MODEL RAILROADING PAUST	08	81	100
MODEL RAILROADING LIONEL CORP	01	51	83
MODEL RAILROADING TREND BOOKS	02	57	21
MODEL RAILROADING A FAMILY GUIDE	09	79	38
MODEL RAILROADING HANDBOOK FAWCET	02	52	46
MODEL RAILROADING HANDBOOK SCHLEICHER	12	75	40
MODEL RAILROADING HANDBOOK V2 SCHLEICHER	02	79	21
MODEL RAILROADING HANDBOOK VOL 11	09	79	30
MODEL RAILROADING HANDBOOK VOL III	07	82	102
MODEL RAILROADING IN SMALL SPACES	12	82	38
MODEL RAILROADING WITH JOHN ALLEN	11	81	148
MODEL RAILROADS ALEXANDER	01	41	54
MODEL RAILROADS IN THE HOME MAY	12	39	670
MODEL RAILWAY ELECTRIFICATION CARTER	07	38	306
MODEL RAILWAY ENCYCLOPEDIA (BRITISH)	12	50	80
MODEL RAILWAY ENGINES MINN	02	70	7
MODEL RAILWAYS BEFORE THE CAMERA SCHMIDT	01	74	19
MODEL RAILWAYS HANDBOOK 6TH EDITION	03	63	16
MODEL RR LAYOUT & TRACK DESIGN BODEL	10	61	18
MODEL SOLDIER GUIDE RISLEY	02	66	18
MODEL TRACTION HANDBOOK FOR MODEL RR ERS	09	75	21
MODELING NARROW GAUGE RAILROADS PRICE	09	85	110
MODULAR MODELING MANUAL INGRAHAM	10	83	132
MODULAR RAILROADING TARJANY	11	80	146
N SCALE MODEL RAILROADING MANUAL	05	85	115
N SCALE PRIMER LARSON	07	74	8
NN3 MANUAL SLOAN	06	81	124
NTRAK 10TH ANNIVERSARY SCRAPBOOK	12	83	143
NTRAK MODULE "HOW TO" BOOK FITZGERALD	12	84	17
ON THE RIGHT TRACK HISTORY LIONEL TRAINS	04	77	21
PADDINGTON TO SEAGOOD:THE STORY OF A MRR	04	47	349
PAINTING & DECALING MRR EQUIPMENT	07	65	13
PATTERN MAKING & MACHINING FOR MOD RRERS	06	82	48
PFM 25 YEARS OF FINE MODELS KUHL	06	79	133
PHOTO-PLAN-PAK PE-1 OLSEN	12	62	27
PHOTO-PLAN-PAK SN-6 BREWSTER	02	62	22
POPULAR MODEL RAILROADS YOU CAN BUILD	04	78	129
POPULAR PICTURE & PLAN BOOK RR CARS/LOCO	11	51	58
PRACTICAL ELECTRONIC PROJECTS FOR MRR	03	75	17
PRACTICAL GUIDE TO MODEL RAILROADING	09	52	75
PROTOTYPE RAILROAD MODELING 1	12	81	166
RAILWAY MODELING IN MINIATURE BEAL	02	36	52
RIDING THE TINPLATE RAILS HERTZ	05	45	217
SCALE MODEL RAILROADING WHITE	12	64	12
SCALE MODEL WEATHERING NASH	02	80	122
SCENERY & DIORAMAS SCHLEICHER	10	83	132
SCENERY FOR MODEL RAILROADS MCCLANAHAN	08	67	8
SCENERY FOR MODERN RAILROADS MCCLANAHAN	10	58	20
SCENERY IDEAS SELLIOS	09	81	133
SCR HOBBY MANUAL REICH	02	64	26
SCRATCHBUILDING & KITBASHING MRR STATION	06	78	22
SIGNALING WALTERS	09	40	524
SIMPLIFIED TRACKWORK FOR MRR BUILDERS	01	35	23
SMALL RAILROADS YOU CAN BUILD HAYDEN	12	78	36
SMALL RAILROADS YOU CAN BUILD KALMBACH	02	55	22
SN3 MODELING HEIMBURGER	12	82	38
SO YOU WANT TO BUILD A LIVE STEAM LOCO	05	75	19
STYRENE FABRICATION & PLAN PKG ARMITAGE	01	64	18
SWITCH THAT CAR-DON'T JUST MOVE IT	09	78	30
TACKLE MODEL RAILWAYS THIS WAY CARTER	09	61	18
TAT IV CONSTRUCTION 2ND EDITION BLUNT	11	70	8
TAT IV CONSTRUCTION MANUAL BLUNT	11	69	8
TIMBER TRESTLES SAUNDERS	11	48	859

LITERATURE REVIEWS

MODELING BOOKS

Title	Author	M	Y	P
TOY COLLECTOR	HERTZ	01	72	13
TOY, TINPLATE & SCALE MODEL RR	WALTHERS	10	51	42
TRACK PLANNING IDEAS FROM MR	KALMBACH	04	81	128
TRACK PLANS	RAPIDO	11	70	8
TRACKWORK HANDBOOK 2ND EDITION	MALLERY	07	77	104
TRACKWORK HANDBOOK FOR MODEL RAILROADERS		03	70	7
TRACTION GUIDEBOOK FOR MODEL RAILROADS		10	74	29
TRACTION HANDBOOK VOLUME 1	FOULDS	07	73	9
TRANSISTOR REFERENCE BOOK	KILPATRICK	10	63	18
TROLLEY TALK (NEWSLETTER)	WAGNER	02	79	29
WEATHERING LOCOMOTIVES WITH AN AIRBRUSH		06	65	17
WHY NOT BUILD A MODEL RAILROAD	BATHGATE	08	45	346
WORLD LOCOMOTIVE MODELS	DOW	01	74	18
WORLD OF MODEL TRAINS	WILLIAMS	02	72	11
YOUR INTRODUCTION TO S GAUGE	HEIMBURGER	10	82	122

VIDEOS

Title		M	Y	P
611 STORY (N&W 4-8-4)	VIDEO	09	84	140
AUTUMN LEAVES-ATLANTA 83 (N&W 4-8-4)	VID	09	84	140
BERKSHIRE THROUGH THE BLUEGRASS	VIDEO	06	83	134
BIGGEST LITTE RY IN THE WORLD (BRIT)	VID	01	84	196
BIRMINGHAM SPECIAL SP	VIDEO	01	84	198
BLACK RIVER FREIGHT (BR&W)	VIDEO	02	84	116
BRITISH CAVALCADE 1 & 2	VIDEO	01	85	34D
CALIFORNIA DIESELS	VIDEO	01	85	34B
CANAL ROUTE	VIDEO	02	84	115
CASS	VIDEO	11	83	157
CHALLENGER 82	VIDEO	04	83	118
CHICAGO TRAIN WATCHER	VIDEO	06	83	136
CLASS J HIGHBALL (N&W 4-8-4)	VIDEO	01	84	200
CUMBRES & TOLTEC RAILROAD	VIDEO	03	84	111
CUMBRES & TOLTEC SCENIC RAILROAD	VIDEO	01	84	200
DATELINE D&H: BINGHAMTON NY	VIDEO	04	83	120
DAYLIGHT 4449 '84	VIDEO	12	84	170
DAYLIGHT DELIGHT (SP 4-8-4)	VIDEO	02	85	28
DAYLIGHT ON TEHACHAPI	VIDEO	06	85	30
DIESELS OF THE UNION PACIFIC	VIDEO	06	85	28
DIESELS ON THE UNION PACIFIC SEQUEL	VID	06	85	28
DIESELS WEST	VIDEO	11	82	35
EAST BROAD TOP	VIDEO	06	84	120
EMPIRE ON PARADE (GN)	VIDEO	02	85	30B
EXCURSION TO THE THIRTIES	VIDEO	01	83	131
EXTRA 767 WEST (NKP BERKSHIRE)	VIDEO	11	83	156
FAST FREIGHT (B&O)	VIDEO	02	84	113
FESTINIOG RAILWAY	VIDEO	08	83	117
FIRST GEN DIESELS:A SEARCH FOR SURVIVORS		10	85	120
FLIGHT OF THE CENTURY (NYC)	VIDEO	02	85	30
FORTIES MEMORY	VIDEO	12	84	171
GETTING AROUND (DST)	VIDEO	09	84	141
GLORY MACHINES	VIDEO	06	85	26
GOOSE TRAIN (OP&E)	VIDEO	11	83	157
GREAT AGE OF STEAM	VIDEO	03	84	111
JERSEY DIESELS:THE DIESELS OF NJ TRANSIT		06	85	30

VIDEOS

Title		M	Y	P
LEGEND OF RIO GRANDE ZEPHYR	VIDEO	06	84	120
LITTLE ENGINES THAT COULD	VIDEO	03	85	110
LONESOME VALLEY SPECIAL (S&A 4-6-2)	VIDEO	11	83	156
NO TRAINS TO SAVOY	VIDEO	02	84	115
OTTO PERRY PARTS 1,2 & 3	VIDEO	01	83	130
OVER, UNDER, AROUND, AND THROUGH (CL)		01	85	34B
PHOENIX ENGINE 4-8-4 (B&O)	VIDEO	06	83	136
QUEEN OF THE FLEET (N&W 4-8-4)	VIDEO	03	84	112
RAILROAD AT WORK (MILW)	VIDEO	03	84	112
READING 2124 (4-8-4)	VIDEO	08	83	119
RETURN OF THE DAYLIGHT (1981)	VIDEO	12	84	170
RIDE THE LAST OF THE BIG RED CARS PE	VID	09	84	141
RIO GRANDE NARROW GAUGE IN THE 50'S	VID	08	83	116
RIO GRANDE WORK TRAIN 81	VIDEO	01	83	130
RISE & FALL OF THE STEAM LOCO (BRIT)	VID	01	84	196
ROTARY ON CUMBRES (C&TS)	VIDEO	11	83	157
ROTARY WORKOUT (C&TS)	VIDEO	04	85	117
RUSTIC NEW ENGLAND STEAM	VIDEO	06	83	135
SACRAMENTO BOUND	VIDEO	11	82	34
SILVERTON IN WINTER (D&SI)	VIDEO	08	83	117
SIX ONE ONE (N&W 611)	VIDEO	03	85	111
SLIM RAILS THRU THE SAN JUANS C&TS	VIDEO	09	84	140
SOUTHERN RAILWAY STEAM ACTION 1983	VIDEO	06	84	121
SOUTHERN STYLE (S #4501)	VIDEO	10	85	122
STEAM DOUBLE HEADER TO CUMBRES	VIDEO	04	85	116
STEAM OVER SHERMAN (UP)	VIDEO	02	85	27
SUSQUEHANNA TODAY (S&W)	VIDEO	12	84	171
THUNDERING RAILS	VIDEO	02	84	113
TRAINWATCHER FIVE	VIDEO	06	84	121
TROLLEY CAVALCADE	VIDEO	06	83	135
UNION PACIFIC CENTENNIALS	VIDEO	10	85	120
UP DOUBLEHEADER	VIDEO	11	82	34
UP STEAM EXPRESS:3985 CHALLENGER	VIDEO	04	83	118
VALLEY LINE	VIDEO	11	82	35
WHEELING IN THE RAT HOLE	VIDEO	04	83	118
WHEELS OF STEEL	VIDEO	01	84	198
WORLDS FAIR DAYLIGHT (4449)	VIDEO	03	85	110

BILL OF LADING   GENERAL RAILROADING

This section is the catch-all for all those miscellaneous items that do not clearly fall into a specific category. We initially attempted to divide this into model related and prototype related but finally gave up as many were both. This section really has to be "read" to get the full benefit from it. Many items appear here as well as under a specific heading.

MANIFEST   GENERAL RAILROADING

GENERAL RAILROADING

	M	Y	P
10 ACRES OF 3" LIVE STEAM	07	69	36
10 PRINCIPALS FOR PLANNING FAMILY MOD RR	12	82	126
150 X 40 "HO" RAILROAD	07	72	56
1908 ARSARBEN NO 2 GAUGE DISPLAY	09	74	64
20 QUESTIONS ABOUT MODEL RAILROADING	12	69	52
33,000 MILES ON LITTLE B&O	11	48	851
50 YEARS OF MODEL RR BLACKBURN REMEMBERS	11	77	99
A JOG IN THE TRACK	08	73	57
ABOUT TO FLOURISH? LIVE STEAM UPDATE	06	81	92
ACCOUNTING FOR CASH FARES	05	37	180
ADD A BRANCH LINE	05	71	29
ADD A WHARF TO INCREASE TRAFFIC	06	65	20
ADD MODEL CAR FITTINGS FOR REALISM	04	63	60
ADDED DETAILS MAKE LAYOUTS REALISTIC 1	09	62	70
ADDED DETAILS MAKE LAYOUTS REALISTIC 2	10	62	76
ADHESIVES BASICS FOR CHOOSING RIGHT ONE	02	83	114
ADVENTURE IN LIVE STEAM 3/4 SCALE MODEL	08	77	46
ADVENTURES IN OO GAUGE	08	37	278
ADVENTURES IN OO GAUGE A NEW WORLD	11	36	327
ADVENTURES IN OO GAUGE TWO RAIL POWER	12	36	362
AIR BRAKE VALVE ACTION	08	68	40
AIRBRUSH PAINTING BASICS	12	83	80
AMAZING 4-8-4 SIMULATES SOUNDS & MOTIONS	07	85	84
AMERICA'S LAST BEEHIVE COKE OVENS	06	81	106
AN UPDATE ON "S" SCALE	06	81	82
ANCHORS FOR CONCRETE AND MASONRY	12	76	134
ANOTHER SCALE FOR O GAUGE?	07	34	3
APTAKISIC LIFT OUT TOWN	09	72	41
ARA TYPE HO GAUGE COUPLER	02	35	46
ARE SCALES NEW TO YOU?	12	72	14
ART OF MODEL RAILROADING 1	08	64	20
ART OF MODEL RAILROADING 2 MAIN LINE	09	64	22
ART OF MODEL RAILROADING 3 TIMING	10	64	34
ART OF MODEL RAILROADING 4 SPACE/TIME	11	64	24
ART OF MODEL RAILROADING 5 OPERATION	12	64	54
ART OF MODEL RAILROADING 1 ELLISON	03	44	108
ART OF MODEL RAILROADING 2 ELLISON	04	44	156
ART OF MODEL RAILROADING 3 ELLISON	05	44	208
ART OF MODEL RAILROADING 4 ELLISON	06	44	255
ART OF MODEL RAILROADING 5 ELLISON	07	44	304
ART OF MODEL RAILROADING 6 ELLISON	08	44	343
ART OF SCRATCHBUILDING	05	60	26
ARTISTRY IN 1" SCALE	02	58	28
ARTISTRY IN BRASS-BOB IUEG	09	48	601
ASSEMBLING KADEE "N" COUPLERS	05	73	75
ATHEARN: INNOVATOR OF MRR INDUSTRY	11	81	72
AUSTRAILIAS BEYER-GARRATT ON NSWG	05	66	32
AUTOMATIC AIR BRAKES	07	36	175
AUTOMATIC BRAKE SYSTEM FOR "HO" CARS	08	81	106
AUTOMATIC CAR IDENTIFICATION SYS LABELS	12	69	86
AUTOMATIC CAR IDENTIFICATION SYSTEM	07	69	72
AUTOMATIC MODEL COUPLER HISTORY	06	72	70B
AUTOMATIC UNCOUPLING	04	41	191
AVERAGE MODELER--ABOVE AVERAGE MODELS	12	73	84
AXLE LOAD VS RAIL WEIGHT	10	64	62

	M	Y	P
B&S- LEGALIZED LUNACY	09	43	388
BACKDROPS CREATE YOUR OWN	07	85	71
BACKLIGHTED TRANSPARENCIES (INT DETAIL)	07	73	40
BALLON POWERED RAILROAD	11	49	47
BARNUM HAD IT-SHOWMANSHIP! BOOMER PETE	06	41	295
BEGINNERS HANGUPS PROB KEEP INTEREST UP	01	70	82
BENCHWORK BLUEBOOK SHEET 1	09	55	43
BETTER LAYOUT LIGHTING	05	63	40
BI LEVEL BENCHWORK TECHNIQUES	02	83	83
BICENTENNIAL COLORS- PATRIOTIC LOCOS	07	76	45
BICYCLE RAILWAY LOCO 1889	01	51	10
BILEVEL COMMUTER CARS BEHIND STEAM	01	78	121
BILL CLOUSER ON FINE SCALE	03	71	55
BLACK LIGHT MAGIC	10	71	35
BLUEBOOK 01 BENCHWORK	09	55	43
BLUEBOOK 02 SCENERY	10	55	58
BLUEBOOK 03 PASSENGER & FREIGHT CARS	11	55	67
BLUEBOOK 04 TYPES OF LOCOMOTIVES	12	55	73
BLUEBOOK 05 TOOLS	01	56	63
BLUEBOOK 06 PAINTING & FINISHING	02	56	55
BLUEBOOK 07 FREIGHT TRUCKS	03	56	61
BLUEBOOK 08 VALVE GEAR	04	56	57
BLUEBOOK 09 PASSENGER TRUCKS	05	56	53
BLUEBOOK 10 MOTOR TOOLS	06	56	41
BLUEBOOK 11 MOTOR TOOLS	07	56	53
BLUEBOOK 12 ELECTRICITY	08	56	45
BLUEBOOK 13 TRACK MEASUREMENT	09	56	59
BLUEBOOK 14 BASIC TRACK ELEMENTS	10	56	65
BLUEBOOK 14 STREAMLINED CAR INTERIORS	11	56	75
BLUEBOOK 15 FREIGHT CAR SAFETY APPLIANCE	12	56	79
BLUEBOOK 17 LOCOMOTIVE & TENDER DETAILS	01	57	67
BLUEBOOK 18 TRUSS BRIDGES	02	57	71
BLUEBOOK 19 SIGNAL LOCATIONS	03	57	67
BLUEBOOK 20 WIRING TURNING TRACKS	04	57	68
BLUEBOOK 21 TROLLEY DETAILS	05	57	59
BLUEBOOK 22 FREIGHT CAR UNDERBODY DETAIL	06	57	59
BLUEBOOK 23 PASSENGER CAR BRAKE EQUIP	07	57	65
BLUEBOOK 24 TRAIN WHISTLE & LANTERN SIG	08	57	66
BLUEBOOK 25 SAFETY APPLIANCE-PASS/CABOOS	09	57	65
BLUEBOOK 26 FREIGHT CAR LETTERING STDS	10	57	65
BLUEBOOK 27 ID-EMD DIESEL YARD SWITCHERS	11	57	71
BLUEBOOK 28 GP-9 DIESEL COLOR CHART B&M	12	57	80
BLUEBOOK 28 GP9 DIESEL COLOR CHART GTW	12	57	81
BLUEBOOK 29 E8 UNIT COLOR CHARTS IC	01	58	74
BLUEBOOK 29 F7 DIESEL COLOR CHART S	01	58	73
BLUEBOOK 30 GP-9 DIESEL COLOR CHART NP	02	58	70
BLUEBOOK 30 GP7 DIESEL COLOR CHART W	02	58	69
BLUEBOOK 31 GP9 DIESEL COLOR CHART C&NW	03	58	65
BLUEBOOK 32 F7 DIESEL COLOR CHART CB&Q	04	58	66
BLUEBOOK 32 GP-9 DIESEL COLOR CHART R	04	58	65
BLUEBOOK 33 F7 DIESEL COLOR CHART NYC	05	58	58
BLUEBOOK 33 GP-9 DIESEL COLOR CHART GN	05	58	57
BLUEBOOK 34 F UNIT DIESEL CLR CHART B&LE	06	58	58
BLUEBOOK 34 F UNIT DIESEL COLOR CHART MP	06	58	57
BLUEBOOK 35 F UNIT DIESEL CLR CHART ACL	07	58	56

GENERAL RAILROADING

	M	Y	P
BLUEBOOK 35 GP-9 DIESEL COLOR CHART C&O	07	58	55
BLUEBOOK 36 F UNIT DIESEL CLR CHART FRIS	08	58	56
BLUEBOOK 36 F UNIT DIESEL CLR CHARTS PRR	08	58	55
BLUEBOOK 37 F UNT DIESEL CLR CHART D&RGW	09	58	64
BLUEBOOK 37 GP DIESEL COLOR CHARTS L&N	09	58	63
BLUEBOOK 38 WOOD TRESTLES	09	58	59
BLUEBOOK 39 WOOD TRESTLES	10	58	73
BLUEBOOK 40 F UNIT DIESEL COLOR CHART UP	10	58	75
BLUEBOOK 40 GP DIESEL COLOR CHART D&LW	10	58	76
BLUEBOOK 41 WOOD TRESTLES	11	58	73
BLUEBOOK 42 F UNIT DIESEL CLR CHARTS KCS	11	58	78
BLUEBOOK 42 GP DIESEL COLOR CHARTS WP	11	58	77
BLUEBOOK 43 EMD ROAD SWITCHERS	12	58	87
BLUEBOOK 44 STEAM LOCO DETAIL SAFETY APP	01	59	95
BLUEBOOK 45 E UNIT DIESEL CLR CHART C&EI	01	59	98
BLUEBOOK 45 F UNIT DIESEL COLOR CHART NP	01	59	97
BLUEBOOK 46 STEAM LOCOMOTIVE DETAILS	02	59	71
BLUEBOOK 47 GP DIESEL COLOR CHART FEC	02	59	73
BLUEBOOK 47 GP DIESEL COLOR CHARTS B&O	02	59	74
BLUEBOOK 48 STEAM LOCOMOTIVE DETAILS	03	59	67
BLUEBOOK 49 F UNIT DIESEL CLR CHART SOO	03	59	70
BLUEBOOK 49 GP DIESEL COLOR CHARTS NKP	03	59	69
BLUEBOOK 50 STEAM LOCOMOTIVE DETAILS	04	59	63
BLUEBOOK 51 F UNIT DIESEL COLOR CHART CN	04	59	66
BLUEBOOK 51 GP DIESEL COLOR CHARTS FRIS	04	59	65
BLUEBOOK 52 STEAM LOCOMOTIVE DETAILS	05	59	63
BLUEBOOK 53 F UNIT DIESEL CLR CHART B&O	05	59	66
BLUEBOOK 53 GP DIESEL COLOR CHARTS MKT	05	59	65
BLUEBOOK 54 STEAM LOCOMOTIVE DETAILS	06	59	63
BLUEBOOK 55 E UNIT DIESEL CLR CHART PRR	06	59	65
BLUEBOOK 55 E UNIT DIESEL CLR CHARTS C&O	06	59	66
BLUEBOOK 56 STEAM LOCOMOTIVE DETAILS	07	59	63
BLUEBOOK 57 F UNIT DIESEL COLOR CHART SP	07	59	66
BLUEBOOK 57 GP DIESEL COLOR CHARTS ACL	07	59	65
BLUEBOOK 58 STEAM LOCOMOTIVE DETAILS	08	59	63
BLUEBOOK 59 GP DIESEL COLOR CHART IC	08	59	66
BLUEBOOK 59 GP DIESEL COLOR CHART MP	08	59	65
BLUEBOOK 60 ALCO ROAD SWITCHERS	09	59	63
BLUEBOOK 61 E UNIT DIESEL CLR CHART CB&Q	11	59	78
BLUEBOOK 61 F UNIT DIESEL CLR CHART B&M	10	59	78
BLUEBOOK 61 F UNIT DIESEL COLOR CHART GN	11	59	77
BLUEBOOK 61 GP DIESEL COLOR CHARTS PRR	10	59	77
BLUEBOOK 63 E UNIT DIESEL COLOR CHART SP	12	59	90
BLUEBOOK 63 F UNIT DIESEL CLR CHARTS C&O	12	59	89
BLUEBOOK 64 GP DIESEL COLOR CHART S	01	60	82
BLUEBOOK 64 GP DIESEL COLOR CHART SOO	01	60	A1
BLUEBOOK 65 F UNIT DIESEL CLR CHART FEC	03	60	66
BLUEBOOK 65 F UNIT DIESEL CLR CHART MKT	03	60	65
BLUEBOOK 66 E UNIT DIESEL COLOR CHART S	04	60	66
BLUEBOOK 66 GP DIESEL COLOR CHART UP	04	60	65
BLUEBOOK 67 F UNIT DIESEL COLOR CHART SP	05	60	61
BLUEBOOK 67 GP DIESEL COLOR CHART L&N	05	60	62
BLUEBOOK 68 F UNIT DIESEL COLOR CHART W	06	60	57
BLUEBOOK 68 F UNIT DIESEL COLOR CHART HM	06	60	58
BLUEBOOK 69 E UNITS OF EMD	07	60	57
BLUEBOOK 70 E UNIT DIESEL CLR CHART C&NW	08	60	58
BLUEBOOK 70 F UNIT DIESEL COLOR CHART R	08	60	57
BLUEBOOK 71 TRACTION OVERHEAD SYSTEMS	09	60	59
BLUEBOOK 72 TRACTION OVERHEAD SYSTEMS	10	60	71
BLUEBOOK 73 TRACION OVERHEAD SYSTEMS	11	60	79
BLUEBOOK 74 TRACTION OVERHEAD SYSTEMS	12	60	87
BLUEBOOK 75 DIESEL COLOR CHART E	01	61	78
BLUEBOOK 75 DIESEL COLOR CHART SP	01	61	77
BLUEBOOK 76 DIESEL COLOR CHART ATSF	03	61	62
BLUEBOOK 76 DIESEL COLOR CHART FEC	03	61	61
BLUEBOOK 77 WORKING W/COMMON PROBLEMS	04	61	63
BLUEBOOK 78 E UNIT COLOR CHART ALCO LV	05	61	63
BLUEBOOK 78 E UNIT DIESEL CLR CHART FRIS	05	61	64
BLUEBOOK 79 ALCO DEISEL COLOR CHART LI	06	61	64
BLUEBOOK 79 EMD DIESEL COLOR CHART C&IM	06	61	63
BLUEBOOK 80 F UNIT DIESEL CLR CHART ACL	07	61	57
BLUEBOOK 80 F UNIT DIESEL CLR CHART CGA	07	61	58
BLUEBOOK 81 ALCO DIESEL COLOR CHART MILW	08	61	57
BLUEBOOK 81 FL-9 DIESEL COLOR CHART NH	08	61	58
BLUEBOOK 82 TRANSISTORS FOR MODEL RR	09	61	61
BLUEBOOK 83 ALCO DIESEL COLOR CHART GN	10	61	73
BLUEBOOK 83 EMD DIESEL COLOR CHART CB&Q	10	61	74
BLUEBOOK 84 WHEEL CONTOUR RP-25	01	62	69
BLUEBOOK 85 DIESEL AIR & ELECTRICAL CONN	04	62	61
BLUEBOOK 86 SIGNAL ASPECTS/INDICATIONS	05	62	47
BLUEBOOK 87 WINDING YOUR OWN TRANSFORMER	06	62	59
BLUEBOOK 88 F UNIT DIESEL CLR CHART MILW	08	62	57
BLUEBOOK 88 F UNITS DIESEL CLR CHART T&P	08	62	58
BLUEBOOK 89 F UNITS DIESEL CLR CHART WP	09	62	56
BLUEBOOK 89 SW UNITS DIESEL CLR CHART RI	09	62	55
BLUEBOOK 90 TRACKWORK IN STREETS	01	63	59
BLUEBOOK 91 TRACKWORK IN STREETS	02	63	67
BLUEBOOK 92 TRACKWORK IN STREETS	03	63	61
BLUEBOOK 93 PASSENGER CAR END CONNECTION	04	63	61
BLUEBOOK 94 DIESEL COLOR CHART NSO	07	63	52
BLUEBOOK 94 DIESEL COLOR CHART C&W	07	63	51
BLUEBOOK 94 DIESEL COLOR CHART L&HR	07	63	51
BLUEBOOK 95 COMMON STAND CONCRETE CULVER	11	63	55
BLUEPRINT FOR A RAILROAD	07	47	542
BOB WHELOVE: SCRATCHBUILDER	05	77	52
BOILER FRAME AND CYLINDER FASTEN METHODS	01	72	81
BOOMER PETE KIBITZES	05	42	230
BOOMER PETE LOOKS AROUND	03	43	136
BOOMER PETE RIDES THE CAB	01	38	18
BOOMER PETE TAKES A TRIP ON C&NW	06	42	264
BOOMING IN HO BOOMER PETE	06	38	228
BRASS LOCOMOTIVES BASICS	08	85	76
BREAKING UP FREIGHT TRAINS	05	55	46
BRUCE GREENBERGS TRAVELING TRAIN SHOW	04	82	106
BUDD RDC IN A STANDARD TRAIN	01	78	120
BUILD A LITTLE AT A TIME	01	62	28
BUILD A MODEL RAILROAD LOCATING THE LINE	02	34	10
BUILD A MODEL RAILROAD TRACK PLANNING	03	34	12
BUILD A MODEL RAILROAD XMAS PRESENT	01	34	4
BUILD A RAILROAD ROOM	03	49	16

GENERAL RAILROADING

	M	Y	P
BUILD YOUR FIRST CAR	06	47	462
BUILDING A PLASTIC SHOWCASE	01	48	44
BUILDING A TURNTABLE DRIVE	05	79	100
BUILDING LOCOMOTIVES FROM KITS & PARTS	12	72	50
BUILDING PLASTIC STRUCTURE KITS DETAILS	06	85	62
BUREAU OF MODEL STANDARDS BY MR	10	35	269
BUSINESS CRS- OFFICIAL USE ONLY	12	59	30
BUYING A TRAIN SET WHAT'S AVAILABLE	12	80	142
BUYING THAT FIRST DEPOT PROTECTION KS	11	79	82
CAB RIDE OVER CAJON PASS	07	83	108
CABLE RAILWAYS	02	73	35
CALCULATORS AS TOOLS FOR MODELING	01	75	84
CANTED RAILS	07	85	131
CAR RETARDERS & THEIR USE	07	84	136
CARPETING THE LAYOUT ROOM	09	83	120
CART FERRY STORAGE & CONSTRUCTION	09	74	66
CASE FOR MOUSEPOWER	02	50	26
CATTLE CROSSING GUARD AT RURAL CROSSINGS	07	85	68
CHANGE OF PACE-HARRY ALBRECHT B. PETE	08	44	352
CHARLIE MEAD CUSTOM LOCO REBUILDER INTER	05	67	39
CHOO-CHOO BARN HOBBY TO BUSINESS	07	79	94
CHOOSING A TRAIN SET "HO"	12	85	124
CHRONOLOGY OF THE VARNEY LINE	01	85	123
CIRCA THRITY DIORAMA	09	75	52
CIRCUS MODELING	10	76	70
CIVIL WAR RAILROADS	03	61	32
CLARIFYING THE COMMON GAUGES & SCALES	07	34	3
CLEAN TRACK, CLEAN WHEELS	11	85	96
CLEARANCE CHARTS FOR VARIOUS GAUGES	11	56	69
CLEARANCES FUN MOVING OVERSIZE LOADS	02	64	36
CLINCHFIELD TAKES TO THE ROADS	07	79	104
COCOONING FOR LOCOMOTIVE STORAGE	10	81	90
COLETA VALLEY WESTERN LIVE STEAM	09	69	54
COLLECTING MAGAZINES OLD ONES CAN HELP	07	78	101
COLORFUL CONTROL PANELS	05	82	94
COMMAND CONTROL: AN UPDATE	03	84	57
CONRAIL ROLLING STOCK	11	76	86
CONSIDER NARROW GAUGE	08	78	89
CONTINUOUS CAB SIGNALS	03	37	93
CONVERSATION WITH LINN WESTCOTT	10	77	61
CONVERSION CHART FOR PLAN PHOTOSTATS	08	47	647
CONVERTING MEASUREMENTS	11	45	456
CONVERTING SCALE DRAWINGS	01	56	21
COUPLER INFORMATION	04	65	57
COUPLER TRICKS WITH KADEE'S	02	58	58
COUPLERS ADVANTAGES OF MAGNETICS	03	64	40
COUPLERS AUTOMATICS FROM DUMMIES	01	47	32
COUPLERS BASICS & NOMENCLATURE	12	67	38
COUPLERS FOR NARROW & DUAL GAUGE	06	65	30
COUPLERS FOX TYPE	04	73	46
COUPLERS MAGNETIC FOR O SCALE 1	05	72	62
COUPLERS MAGNETIC FOR O SCALE 2	06	72	58
COUPLERS MAGNETIC FOR O SCALE 3	08	72	58
COUPLERS MAKING THEM AUTOMATIC	10	46	643
COUPLERS NARROW GAUGE WORKING	11	69	64
COUPLERS NMRA TRICKS	05	58	44
COUPLERS OLD KADEE'S TO MAGNETIC	12	63	68
COUPLERS WORKING FROM DUMMIES	04	67	53
COWLES LOCOMOTIVE 1886-FLAT DRIVE WHEELS	08	51	56
CREATING A BALANCED FREIGHT CAR FLEET	10	81	80
CRIMP LINK SWITCH MACHINE INSTALLATION	12	74	61
CRITERIA FOR EXCELLENCE IN MODEL RAILS	01	56	23
CROSSWORD- RAILROAD ABBREVIATION	11	81	140
CROSSWORD-SCHOOL MODEL RAILROAD CLUB	06	82	102
CURVES ON THE MODEL RAILROAD	12	34	3
DAYS THAT WERE BOOMER PETE	12	42	550
DELUXE HOBBYBENCH	10	80	121
DEPARTMENT-STORE LAYOUTS AND DISPLAYS	07	76	51
DERAILMENTS	01	75	45
DESK DRAWER MODEL RAILROADING	06	73	19
DIESELS I LIKE 'EM	11	63	48
DIFFERENCE BETWEEN CAN & MICRO MOTORS	05	79	138
DIODE MATRIX SYSTEMS FOR TURNOUT CONTROL	05	82	68
DIRTY WHEELS AND TRACK	03	84	144
DISPLAY CASES OF PLEXIGLAS	12	76	92
DISPLAYING TRAIN NUMBERS	06	35	160
DISPLAYS FOR TREASURED MODELS	06	67	40
DISTRIBUTION OF FREIGHT CAR TYPES 1931	04	35	88
DON'T BUILD THEM LIKE THEY USED TO-NOSTA	12	85	141
DON'T WASTE AISLE SPACE	08	74	62
DOWN & UP GRADE TRACKS AT TUNNEL PORTAL	01	78	119
DOWN TO EARTH-PARTLY EXCAVATED BASEMENT	03	44	128
DR JECKYLL'S LOCOMOTIVE BOOMER PETE	07	45	272
DRAFT GEAR O GAUGE	10	36	297
DREAM COME TRUE-SAN DIEGO MODEL RR MUSEU	12	82	132
DUST ELIMINATOR FROM LAYOUT ROOMS	09	67	53
DUST-STROYER FOR REMOVING DUST	06	85	104
E.L. MOORES LEGACY	02	80	102
ECHO MOUNTAIN INCLINE RAILROAD	02	73	36
ECHOS ADD TO SOUND EFFECTS	12	73	42
ELECTROMECHANICAL RAMP FOR KADEE COUPLER	09	76	80
ELIMINATION OF CABOOSES & EQUIP REPLACE	01	85	161
EMD HISTORY IN MODELS	10	72	51
EMPLOYEES TIMETABLES OPERATING INFORM	11	75	68
END TWIN COIL SWITCH MACHINE FRUSTRATION	04	83	86
ENGINEERING REPORT ON SSF GENERATORS	12	71	62
EQUIPMENT AVAILABLE FOR "OO"	12	41	657
ESTHETICS AND MODEL RAILROADING	12	83	136
EUROPES AUTOMATIC COUPLER	04	73	46
EXCAVATING A BASEMENT FOR RAILROADING	02	48	84
EXPERIENCE A GOOD TEACHER	01	37	12
FA'S SHARKS & KADEE COUPLERS	02	79	126
FACTS ABOUT TRACK SECTIONAL & FLEXIBLE	07	80	66
FAIRHILL CENTRAL ROOM 402 LEARNING PRGRM	11	79	134
FAIRWELL CABOOSE	05	83	124
FAST FREIGHT LINES	12	53	37
FERROEQUINOLOGY AT ICU-1981	06	82	96
FIGURING ELEVATION ON PROTOTYPE CURVES	07	36	175
FINDING DRAW BAR PULL	02	34	9
FINE SCALE WHEEL STANDARDS	08	75	54

GENERAL RAILROADING

Title	M	Y	P
HOSE CONNECTIONS MADE EASILY	09	37	313
HOUSE OF HOBBIES 15" GAUGE BOOMER PETE	08	39	413
HOW "T" RAIL WAS BORN	09	48	626
HOW A DIESEL WORKS	09	84	84
HOW A STEAM LOCOMOTIVE WORKS	10	82	80
HOW A STEAM LOCOMOTIVE WORKS CORRECTION	11	82	170
HOW I BUILD MY LOCOMOTIVES & CARS	10	62	46
HOW I LIVE WITH A MODEL RAILROADER	04	69	45
HOW LONG SHOULD A TRAIN BE?	10	72	37
HOW MANY CARS?	03	39	146
HOW MANY PASSENGER CARS IN A TRAIN?	10	36	296
HOW TO MOVE A MODEL RAILROADER-BY WIFE	10	69	25
HOW TO USE A SCALE RULE	08	72	74
HUMDINGERS-SUPERDETAILS OF FOWLER	11	41	558
I'LL TAKE S GAUGE	03	54	48
I'VE A MODEL HUSBAND-A WIFE'S VIEW	03	34	9
IDEA BEHIND MODEL RAILROAD BOOMER PETE	02	43	74
IDEAL BASEMENT	08	78	117
IF I COULD DO IT AGAIN - MY MISTAKES	04	66	49
IF I HAD A MILLION-WHAT A RAILROAD	05	51	14
IMPROVED DISPLAY SHELVES	01	69	79
IMPROVING ATLAS N SCALE TURNOUTS	02	85	102
IMPROVING HOOK HORN MAGNETIC UNCOUPLERS	12	63	71
INDEX OF 295 PAINT SHOP PROJECTS	09	79	60
INEXPENSIVE TURNOUT CONTROL	02	71	85
INFORMATION RETREIVAL FOR MRR'ERS	07	78	117
INSIDE FACES OF MRR CLUBS	09	62	63
INSTALLING NMRA COUPLERS	05	55	51
INTERCHANGE TABLE WITHOUT TURNOUTS	08	79	84
INTERIOR LIGHTING TIPS	11	83	124
INTERLOCKING FOR MODEL RAILROADS	11	35	290
INTRODUCING BOOMER PETE	10	37	378
IT'S A COVERUP-RR CONTROLS IN STATION	06	78	110
JAPANEESE MODEL RAILROADING	10	64	22
JEWELRY ON WHEELS 1/2 SIZE TT	09	48	626
JOHN ALLEN TRIBUTE (10 PAGES)	04	73	35
JOHN CASSADY & 1 1/2" SCALE OUTDOOR RR	08	82	94
JOHN PAGE-BILL SCHOOP'S TROLLEYS	09	85	128
JOHN PAGE-DON'T TOUCH THE TRACK 115V	12	85	122
JOHN PAGE-ELLISONS WAY TO BETTER OPERATI	08	85	102
JOHN PAGE-JIM DECHERT'S "FATSO"	09	85	128
JOHN PAGE-JOHN ALLEN'S GORRE & DAPHETID	07	85	106
JOHN PAGE-LOCO TRACTIVE EFFORT CONTEST	11	85	133
JOHN PAGE-MEL THORNBURGH'S WORKSHOP	10	85	100
KADEE COUPLER BASICS	05	81	78
KADEE COUPLER MOUNTING ATH DIESEL SWITCH	05	85	120
KADEE COUPLER MOUNTING TECHNIQUES	04	85	129
KEEP THEM RUNNING TIPS	07	36	176
KEEPING TRACK OF TONNAGE	04	37	146
L GIRDER BENCHWORK	01	81	82
LAYING FLEXIBLE TRACK BASICS	02	81	102
LAYOUT SOUND EFFECTS:THE 4TH DIMENSION	10	84	88
LAZIEST MODEL RAILROAD THAT EVER LIVED	07	78	104
LEVEL TRACK ISN'T LEVEL	03	37	93
LEWIS' LIVE STEAM HERITAGE	06	72	34
FINER THAN FINE SCALE "1/4AAR"	08	69	48
FINGER LAKES NY LIVE STEAM	08	83	74
FIRST AID HINTS FOR THE MODEL RAILROAD	03	35	61
FLANGER SIGNS	03	85	68
FLANGER SIGNS AND TELLTALES	06	51	57
FLYING SWITCH OPERATIONS	01	74	42
FOLD OUT PLATE OF CAR DETAILS	10	35	258S
FOR BEGINNERS ONLY BOOMER PETE	04	39	171
FOR BEGINNERS ONLY PART 2 BOOMER PETE	11	39	576
FOREGIN CARS ON THE HOME ROAD	01	44	14
FORTY FIVE YEARS AFTER THE BUG BIT	12	83	90
FRANK ELLISONS LEGACY	07	76	87
FREE LANCE LAYOUTS PROS & CONS	08	70	30
FREELANCING-OFT MALIGNED DIVISION	10	40	529
FREIGHT CAR TRUCK DETAILS BOOMER PETE	11	42	502
FREIGHT CARS NOW BOOMER PETE	06	43	270
FULGUREX MODELS OF SWITZERLAND	11	76	58
FULL HEIGHT LADDERS ON HICUBE CARS	01	78	119
FULLY AUTOMATIC TURNTABLE CONSTRUCTION	03	80	94
FUN AT CHRISTMAS L10 LAYOUT AT S&L OFFIC	12	83	128
G SCALE: STANDARD & NARROW GAUGE	02	84	57
GARDEN RAILROAD IN SPAIN	07	85	82
GAS ELECTRIC PHOTOS & HISTORY	02	79	148
GEORGE PETERS: LOCOMOTIVE BUILDER	08	80	74
GETTING STARTED IN MODEL RAILROADING	12	74	79
GETTING STARTED IN MODEL RAILROADING.	12	78	140
GETTING THE MOST FROM YOUR RAILROAD	06	56	33
GHOSTS OF ALLENTOWN TERMINAL	08	81	93
GLOSSARY TO MODEL RAILROAD TERMS	12	85	178
GRADES BASIC PRINCIPALS	03	68	30
HAND OPERATED NMRA UNCOUPLING	12	55	51
HAND SIGNALS FOR RAILROADS ARE UNIVERSAL	09	64	46
HAND TRAIN & WHISTLE SIGNALS	12	48	928
HANDBOOK BRIDGES	06	54	58
HANDBOOK COUPLERS	07	54	57
HANDBOOK ENGINE SERVICING FACILITIES	08	54	61
HANDBOOK LAYOUT MAINTENANCE	05	54	61
HANDMADE BRASS FROM JAPAN	03	73	64
HAZARDS: MECHANICAL & ELECTRICAL IN MRR	04	76	92
HELIX TRACK OPERATION & RELIABILITY	07	85	128
HERALDS OF THE FULL SCALE ROADS	04	35	98
HERE AND THERE BOOMER PETE	04	41	198
HERE'S "OO" AGAIN	11	84	125
HERE'S OO GAUGE	02	34	1
HIDDEN MAGNE-ELECTRIC UNCOUPLING RAMPS	12	83	104
HIDING ATLAS SWITCH MACHINES	10	85	138
HIGH SPEED MILWAUKEE ATLANTICS	05	35	137
HISTORY OF MODEL RAILROADING	02	37	49
HO GAUGE STANDARDS NMRA	04	36	110
HO KITS:BETTER OR WORSE	08	53	15
HOBBY SHOP OF JIM HARPER	01	81	86
HOBBYISTS DREAM-BARGAINS!	09	76	91
HOBO SIGNS	12	65	76
HOPKINSVILLE & SOUTHERN THE JELLO ROUTE	04	79	119
HORSESHOE CURVE OF PRR	08	78	101

STEPHANS' RAILROAD DIRECTORY

GENERAL RAILROADING

	M	Y	P
LGB CHRISTMAS LAYOUT IN A MALL	12	84	132
LIONEL OFFERS DC NOW	12	80	114
LIST OF HISTORICAL GROUPS 1977	02	78	138
LITTLE ATSF PAPER WEIGHT TO LOCO	01	48	42
LITTLE THINGS MAKE A LAYOUT	07	43	300
LIVE STEAM IN FLORIDA	04	79	98
LIVE STEAM IN MISSOURI	09	80	106
LIVE STEAM IN THE GARDEN STATE	09	68	32
LIVE STEAM MEET AT LOS ANGELES CALIF	03	60	22
LIVE STEAM ON THE WEST COAST	11	65	30
LOCO ADJUSTMENTS AND SUCH	04	48	283
LOCOMOTIVE BUILT TO 1/305 SCALE	10	70	68
LOCOMOTIVE PERFORMANCE ANALYSIS	08	74	27
LOCOMOTIVE SELECTION BOOMER PETE	08	38	326
LOCOMOTIVES & CARS OF JW BARNARD	06	64	24
LONG LIVE THE KING RENAISSANCE OF "O"	06	84	82
LOWERING FUEL CONSUMPTION BOOMER PETE	12	37	451
MAGIC OF GARDEN RAILWAYS	10	85	94
MAGNETIC COUPLERS FOR "O" SCALE	01	65	50
MAGNETIC SCALE COUPLERS	08	52	45
MAINTAINING & TROUBLESHOOTING LOCOS	06	80	90
MAINTAINING LOCOMOTIVES CLEAN/LUB/REPAIR	02	85	75
MAINTENANCE OF SCALE	10	44	451
MAKING A TRAIN SET A REAL MODEL RAILROAD	02	56	62
MAKING DETAIL PARTS FOR MODELS	12	73	84
MAKING ROOM FOR MAKING TRACKS SEMI ATTIC	08	84	76
MANUAL SWITCH MACHINE WITH WEIGHTS	08	44	339
MANUAL TURNOUT CONTROL MECHANISM	02	85	131
MARKLIN: A BRIEF HISTORY	02	80	100
MARVELOUS MOSS	06	73	67
MATCHING DIESEL SPEEDS	07	84	133
MEASURING SCALE SPEED	11	64	26
MEASURING STRUCTURES	10	79	106
MECHANICAL INTERLOCKING & SIGNALING 1	01	61	46
MECHANICAL INTERLOCKING & SIGNALING 2	02	61	57
MECHANICAL INTERLOCKING & SIGNALING 3	03	61	54
MECHANICAL INTERLOCKING & SIGNALING 4	04	61	50
MECHANICAL INTERLOCKING & SIGNALING 5	06	61	46
MECHANICAL TURNOUT CONTROL REVISITED	04	79	92
MEET GORDON VARNEY	07	46	444
MEMEORIES OF CHRISTMAS PILGRAMAGES	12	79	129
METAMORPHOSIS OF A MODEL RAILROADER	04	49	34
MICHIGAN TRACTION OUTDOOR SYSTEM	04	74	58
MINIATURE DISPLAY CASES	06	85	90
MODEL & MANUFACTURER AVAIL POST VJ DAY	09	45	375
MODEL RAILROAD "CORPORATE" IMAGES	08	80	98
MODEL RAILROAD CHARACHTERS I HAVE KNOWN	05	69	51
MODEL RAILROAD CLUB ORGANIZATION B. PETE	06	40	339
MODEL RAILROAD ERA	12	37	453
MODEL RAILROAD IN 6 OLD REEFERS	05	44	214
MODEL RAILROAD MOVIE	01	39	14
MODEL RAILROAD PERIODICALS OF THE WORLD	06	66	54
MODEL RAILROAD PRODUCTS FROM EUROPE	09	82	74
MODEL RAILROAD WIFE DISTAFF SIDE VIEW	05	68	29
MODEL RAILROADER STORY	02	37	41
MODEL RAILROADER THREE YEAR INDEX 1934-6	02	37	64
MODEL RAILROADERS ON THE LOOSE IN ENGLAN	02	71	69
MODEL RAILROADING AS & WHERE YOU LIKE IT	04	85	75
MODEL RAILROADING BY MAIL ORDER	09	80	84
MODEL RR AS 5TH GRADE CLASS PROJECT	12	75	86
MODEL STANDARDS FOR O GAUGE	01	34	2
MODEL WORK BENCH CONSTRUCTION 2ND TRY	07	84	90
MODELING A DERAIL ON D&RGW	07	79	99
MODELING AND MARRIAGE	12	71	82
MODELING IN THE SOVIET UNION	06	78	119
MODELING NARROW GAUGE	06	64	56
MODELING NARROW GAUGE SPECIFICATIONS	03	68	49
MODELING NARROW GAUGE.	05	71	54
MODELING SOME AD&N EQUIPMENT	03	81	78
MODELING TRAINS IN 7/16 SCALE	04	66	34
MODELING WHAT YOU DON'T MODEL	04	78	124
MODELING WITH FIBER OPTICS	04	73	52
MODELING WITH SPRUES $1	07	69	64
MODELMAKING WORKBENCH CONSTRUCTION	04	72	53
MODULAR RAILROADING "ON3"	01	81	70
MODULAR SIGNALS EASES MAINTENANCE	11	83	110
MOST REALISTIC LAYOUT	09	72	40
MOTOR OVERHEATING	01	63	79
MOUNTING KADEES ON LONG CARS	02	83	154
MOVEABLE FROG TURNOUT ON CN	11	71	18
MOVING A LAYOUT	06	82	127
MOVING THE MOUNTAINS A CLUB IS EVICTED	04	82	108
MR 50 FORUM 1 MODEL RAILROADER FUTURE	01	84	166
MR 50 FORUM 2 LAYOUTS OF THE FUTURE	01	84	172
MR 50 FORUM 3 MODEL RRING GOES HIGH TECH	01	84	174
MR CAPSULE HISTORY	01	84	218
MR EDITORS	01	84	184
MR INTERVIEWS LARRY KEELER PIONEER SPIRT	01	79	92
MR MILEPOST 50	01	84	181
MR VISIT WITH ED RAVENSCROFT SKOKE LINE	10	81	95
MR VISITS A CUSTOM BUILDER JERRY WHITE	09	54	20
MR VISITS HORNBY HOBBIES (ZERO 1)	10	80	114
MR VISITS KADEE	10	83	98
MR VISITS MANTUA METAL PRODUCTS	11	84	118
MR VISITS NORTHEASTERN SCALE MODELS	11	83	84
MR VISITS UNCLE ERIC (ERIC LANAL)	01	79	134
MR'S 50TH ANNIVERSARY CONFERENCE	10	83	148
MRR REHABILITATION SAVED MY LIFE	03	84	96
MULTIPLE UNIT CONTROL	05	36	132
MUSEUM BEHIND THE SCENE	11	56	26
MUSEUM BEHIND THE SCENE TREES & SHRUBS	12	56	44
MY ADVENTURES IN MODEL LAND 1	03	43	114
MY ADVENTURES IN MODEL LAND 2	04	43	164
MY ADVENTURES IN MODEL LAND 3	05	43	224
MY ADVENTURES IN MODEL LAND 4	06	43	268
MY ADVENTURES IN MODEL LAND 5	07	43	308
MY ADVENTURES IN MODEL LAND 6	08	43	358
MY FAVORITE MODEL RAILROADER--MY DAD	05	75	69
N GAUGE ELECTROMAGNETIC UNCOUPLER	02	79	92
N SCALE CONVERSION TABLE	10	70	83

GENERAL RAILROADING

Title	M	Y	P
N SCALE QUESTIONS AND ANSWERS	10	74	82
N SCALE STANDARDS	09	71	48
N&W JAWN HENRY STEAM TURBINE 1950	10	75	98
N&W MODELER GOES WESTERN	09	75	78
NAMING YOUR MODEL RAILROAD	04	75	68
NARROW GAUGE BASICS BROAD OVERVIEW	07	81	56
NARROW GAUGE IN THE REDWOODS DICKINSON	09	67	15
NARROW GAUGE MYSTIQUE	07	81	49
NATURE OF HO GAUGE	12	34	2
NEW AUTOMATIC COUPLERS	10	42	454
NMRA ADOPTS STANDARDS REALISTIC STREETS	09	36	243
NMRA JUDGING CRITERIA	02	70	78
NMRA STANDARDS GAUGE	06	60	27
NMRA WHEEL STANDARDS	03	36	60
NTRAK STORY GROUP ACTIVITY AT ITS BEST	12	76	80
NY SOUTHERN TIER SHORT LINE ASSOCIATION	02	60	42
OBITUARY AL KALMBACH	01	82	60
OBITUARY LINN H WESTCOTT	11	80	65
OL' REPROBATE - WASTED SPACE	02	78	138
OLD TIME MODELING IDEAS	04	55	53
ON NARROW GAUGE BOOMER PETE	01	42	18
ONE ANSWER TO LAYOUT DUST	09	73	42
ONLY WHEN VISITORS COME-TRAIN MISBEHAVES	03	75	66
OO OR HO GAUGE--WHICH??	01	35	7
OOO GAUGE SMALLEST OF SMALL	02	64	48
OPERATING CLASS LIGHTS WITH FIBER OPTICS	07	70	68
OPERATING YOUR MODEL RAILROAD	11	75	45
ORGANIZED CLUBS - WHY NOT??	04	66	44
ORGANIZED CLUBS YOU CAN HAVE THEM!	11	65	44
OUTDOOR HO GAUGE--WHY NOT?	09	64	42
OUTDOOR HO PIKES	09	66	48
OUTDOOR RAILROAD COMING TRUE	04	63	58
OVERPASS DISGUISING TUNNEL KELSO WA	07	78	109
PARTS CATCHER APRON	04	84	138
PARTS DIAGRAM OF A STEAM LOCOMOTIVE	05	70	72
PASSENGER STEAM-OL' RAY SAYS	01	70	36
PAUL BUNYANS RAILROAD BOOMER PETE	03	45	120
PE CARS OF BILL HOFFMAN	09	64	20
PEN AND INK DRAWINGS	07	53	30
PENNSYLVANIA LIVE STEAMERS	09	71	55
PERFECT FILLER PUTTY FOR PLASTICS	06	83	141
PERSPECTIVE DIORAMA 1916 DALLAS TEXAS	08	83	78
PETE RIDES THE BRANCH LINE BOOMER PETE	10	39	520
PIKE & WORKSHOP IN A TRAILER	04	63	37
PIONEERING IN #1 GAUGE	06	38	235
PLANNING FOR YOUR ROUNDHOUSE	02	72	69
PLASTIC KITS BUILT SEVERAL WAYS??	11	67	32
PLASTIC WHEELS-WHAT'S WRONG WITH THEM?	11	47	890
PLIGHT OF A SALESMAN-TRAVEL & SCRATCHBLD	03	66	50
PNEUMATIC SWITCH & SIGNAL OPERATION	06	47	452
POLING AND PUSH POLES	02	75	86
PRACTICAL THROTTLE HANDLE FOR TAT IV	07	71	58
PRESENTING THE ACE 3000	06	82	77
PREVENTING THEFT	04	83	139
PROPOSED HON2 STANDARDS	11	69	82
PROTOTYPE ATMOSPHERE IN MODELING	11	61	42
PROTOTYPE CAR BLDG CONTEST 1925 D&H	08	77	79
PROTOTYPE DIESEL CAB PROJ PART 2(11/76)	10	80	98
PROTOTYPE HAND LETTERING	06	78	124
PROTOTYPE RIGHT OF WAY HANDBOOK	07	55	49
PROTOTYPE TRAIN YARDS HANDBOOK	06	55	47
PUBLIC OPEN HOUSE TOO MUCH OF GOOD THING	10	76	103
QUESTIONS FOR CHRISTMAS LAYOUTS	12	80	80
RACK RAILROAD MODELING	08	76	70
RACK RAILROADS	08	76	70
RADIUM TRAIN-REAL HOTSHOT	06	49	16
RAIL & FLANGE GREASERS	02	83	156
RAIL ALTERNATIVE TO PANAMA CANAL	09	49	64
RAIL CLEANER CONSTRUCTION	05	75	56
RAIL CLEANING DEVICE	05	70	48
RAIL SIZE	09	67	59
RAILRAOD ODDITIES AERIAL RAILROAD 1872	09	50	72
RAILROAD LINGO 1 GLOSSARY	09	53	21
RAILROAD LINGO 1-37	01	37	34
RAILROAD LINGO 10-35	10	35	277
RAILROAD LINGO 10-36	10	36	310
RAILROAD LINGO 11-35	11	35	302
RAILROAD LINGO 11-36	11	36	344
RAILROAD LINGO 12-36	12	36	378
RAILROAD LINGO 2 GLOSSARY	10	53	63
RAILROAD LINGO 2-35	02	35	54
RAILROAD LINGO 3 GLOSSARY	11	53	91
RAILROAD LINGO 3-36	03	36	82
RAILROAD LINGO 4 GLOSSARY	12	53	26
RAILROAD LINGO 4-35	04	35	110
RAILROAD LINGO 5-35	05	35	137
RAILROAD LINGO 6-35	06	35	167
RAILROAD LINGO 7-35	07	35	194
RAILROAD LINGO 8-35	08	35	222
RAILROAD LINGO 9-36	09	36	271
RAILROAD ODDITIES 1893 STREAMLINER	05	50	64
RAILROAD ODDITIES STEAM ELEVATED 1886	11	50	82
RAILROAD ODDITIES COUPLERS OF EARLY TYPE	01	52	75
RAILROAD ODDITIES GOAT POWERED RAILROAD	05	50	64
RAILROAD ODDITIES JULL CENTRIFUGAL SNOW	12	51	22
RAILROAD ODDITIES ONE RAIL STM TRAM 1868	12	50	76
RAILROAD ODDITIES RIVER XING ON ICE 1880	06	51	4
RAILROAD WITH EYE FOR THE PUBLIC	08	61	30
RAILROADING AS AN ART FORM	07	76	89
RAILROADING IN A RAESTRICTED AREA	07	40	398
RAILROADS AND THE ENVIRONMENT	08	76	25
RAILROADS OF TOMORROW	07	76	68
RAILWAYS OF AMERICA-LARGEST TRAIN DISPLA	08	74	30
REALISTIC SOUND IN O SCALE 1	07	69	58
REALISTIC SOUND IN O SCALE 2	08	69	61
REASON FOR TUNNEL/NON TUNNEL RIGHT OF WY	05	81	128
REASSEMBLING DISMANTLED LAYOUTS	09	68	56
REFLECTIONS ON THE HOBBY-GOOD OL' DAYS	07	84	92

GENERAL RAILROADING

	M	Y	P
RELATIONS BETWEEN SCALE & APPARENT SPEED	04	35	87
RELIABLE OVERHEAD FOR HIDDEN TRACK	08	84	134
REMEMBERING JOHN ALLEN	12	81	73
REMOVABLE FLOORS AND ROOFS	09	71	73
REMOVING WHITE DEPOSITS FROM ZINC ALLOYS	04	73	83
REVERSE CURVE ON BRIDGES	05	79	107
RIDE THE GM&O DOODLEBUG	04	59	24
RIGHTS OF TRAINS	01	37	11
ROADS AND GRADE CROSSING CONSTRUCTION	09	80	70
ROCKETS ON THE RAILS TGV & BULLETS/ETC	07	84	120
ROLLING STOCK SELECTION	10	48	721
ROTARY SWITCHERS FOR TURNOUT CONTROL	04	79	109
ROUNDHOUSE LAYOUT	04	67	64
RULES FOR TRACTION MODELING	08	84	96
RUNNING ON DIRTY TRACK	09	82	97
S SCALE TODAY	05	76	76
SAFETY IN MODELING	03	72	33
SANDBAGS, FROGS & JAWS (CLAMPS)	05	81	101
SCALE & GAUGE BASICS	12	82	80
SCALE & GAUGE TABULATION	03	35	78
SCALE BEES	02	74	45
SCALE CONVERSION TECHNIQUES	07	53	30
SCALE MODELS FROM DRAWINGS	01	36	15
SCALE RATIO AND GAUGE ABC OF MODEL RRING	12	68	77
SCALE RELATIONSHIPS	02	67	65
SCALE RULES 1	11	68	50
SCALE RULES 2	12	68	73
SCALE RULES IN VARIOUS PROPORTIONS	02	68	34
SCALE TO PROTOTYPE RELATIONSHIP	04	55	7
SCALE, SCALE RULES, AND SCALE PLANS	03	62	69
SCALES AND GAUGES INTRODUCTION Z TO GM	12	85	92
SCALING PHOTOS FOR MODEL DATA	09	63	64
SCHOOL FOR MODEL RAILROADERS	03	80	106
SCRATCHBUILDING YOUR 1ST WOOD STRUCTURE	07	83	91
SEE THE WORKS OF LOCOS BY X-RAY	11	39	594
SEE THEM MODELS ROLL BOOMER PETE	12	43	554
SELECTIVE COMPRESSION SPACE SAVING	07	71	31
SELF HARDENING SEALANTS FOR AXELS	05	71	64
SEVEN AGES OF RAILROAD MODELING	08	75	36
SIDE ROD BIND CORRECTIONS SIX CAUSES	02	71	67
SIMPLE TURNOUT CONTROL	03	81	140
SIMPLE TURNOUT CONTROL PB MRR CLUB	05	85	126
SIX AGES OF RAILROAD MODELING	01	49	17
SLOT CARS & TRAINS AT ODDS--NO!	02	79	102
SMALL SCALE AIR RAIL "1/384" BAYHA	08	82	76
SMALL WORLD- WHITCOMB IN GUATEMALA	10	78	148
SMOOTH RUNNING HO ROAD BOOMER PETE	07	39	351
SMOOTH RUUNING CLUB BOOMER PETE	03	38	108
SOCIETY FOR MODEL ENGINEERS	03	80	109
SOLAR POWERED TRAIN	09	78	115
SOME "HO" EXPERIENCES	11	37	419
SOUND IDEA-8 TRACK RECORDER USE	04	79	102
SOUND PRACTICES IN MODEL RAILROADING	12	64	59
SP #4449 GS-4 CROSS COUNTRY RUN 1941	06	84	123
SP DOUBLE STACK ARTICULATED ACF 1977	10	83	92
SPACE SAVING GRACE OF HO GAUGE	06	34	9
SPELING ERRORS ON ROLLING STOCK	06	78	118
SPRING FEVER ALA RAILROAD BOOMER PETE	04	46	255
SPRUNG TRUCK ADVANTAGES	01	73	94
STANDARD CAR DESIGN	10	35	2585
STARTING A MRR CLUB	09	62	64
STARTING TRAINS FROM TERMINALS	04	37	146
STEAM IN YOUR BACKYARD?	10	85	90
STEAM LOCO INFORMATION FOR THE NOVICE	12	79	174
STEAM LOCOMOTIVE THROTTLE CONSTRUCTION	06	57	46
STEAM LOCOMOTIVES WHAT, WHY, WHEN	10	82	70
STEAM LOCOMOTIVES WHAT, WHY, WHEN ADDEND	12	82	23
STEAM LOCOMOTIVES WHAT, WHY, WHEN CORRCT	11	82	170
STEAM TROLLEY CAR 1884 BALDWIN	01	51	10
STEAMING ALONG BOOMER PETE	01	39	18
STEEL & WOOD BRIDGE SIDE BY SIDE VERMONT	07	78	108
STORAGE TRACKS-UNPLUGGING THE YARD	03	71	33
STRETCHING A TOO SHORT MAINLINE	05	61	33
STUB SWITCH VS SPLIT SWITCH	12	62	88
STYROFOAM AND CARRYING EQUIPMENT	11	64	41
SUBURBAN TRAIN OPERATION	01	76	47
SUGGESTED O GAUGE STANDARDS	06	34	3
SUPER SCRATCH BLDR LIVE ST R. MCALLISTER	06	76	88
SWING AWAY TRACK SECTION ROOM ACCESS	07	73	76
SWITCHING PROTOTYPE STYLE	12	79	126
SWTICH STANDS AND TARGETS	02	81	81
SYMPTOMS OF MODEL RAILROADS MALADY	06	51	7
TABLE OF GAUGES	12	73	41
TACKLING EQUIPMENT STORGAE PROBLEM	02	79	145
TACTICS & STRATEGY FOR MARRIED MRRERS	12	74	90
TANK CAR LOADING & UNLOADING	09	76	107
TEAM DRILL AND INTERCHANGE TRACKS	04	73	86
TEAM TRACKS AND THEIR USES	05	75	81
TELEGRAPH COMMUNICATION ON RAILROADS	02	37	70
TELEGRAPH SOUND EFFECTS MACHINE CONST	08	53	37
TEMPORARY STANDARDS FOR "O" GAUGE	01	36	24
TERMINALS-STUB END SWITCHING	03	42	108
TEST TRACK LAYOUT-A LITTLE OF EVERYTHING	03	74	55
THE CASE FOR COLLECTING MODELS	01	71	11
THE REAL THING (STARUCCA VIADUCT/ETC)	07	43	312
THIS IS HH GAUGE	04	46	262
THORNBURGH'S 61 LOCOMOTIVES	10	39	506
THREE KINDS OF SCALE SPEED	05	36	115
TIPS FOR TRAIN SET BUYERS	12	77	66
TOMLINSON COUPLERS FROM MINIATURE CONNEC	08	84	80
TONNAGE RATINGS FOR MODEL STEAM LOCOS	03	60	40
TONNAGE RATINGS TRACTIVE EFFORT OR SPEED	11	78	135
TORQUE ARM DRIVE FOR STEAM LOCOMOTIVES	11	80	116
TOWARDS RELIABLE OPERATION	09	79	72
TOY TRAIN MUSEUM TCA LANCASTER PA	12	85	108
TRACK & SIGNAL QUESTIONS & ANSWERS	01	45	128
TRACK AND CLEARANCE GAUGE IN N	10	77	131
TRACK COMPONENTS	02	63	77
TRACK PROFILES	12	82	124
TRACTION CAN'T BE BEAT	04	69	59

GENERAL RAILROADING

Title	M	Y	P
TRADE TOPICS TESTING	03	52	15
TRAIN MARKERS	05	35	117
TRAIN MARKERS FLAGS & LIGHTS	05	36	132
TRAIN MARKERS FOR REALISM	01	34	11
TRAIN MEETING ITSELF?	07	78	106
TRAIN OPERATION VERSUS POWER PACKS	01	71	60
TRAIN ORDERS TAKEN ON THE RUN	08	37	285
TRAIN SETS 1954	11	53	31
TRAIN SETS FOR 1956	12	55	26
TRAIN YOU CAN MODEL ET&WNC	07	81	65
TRAINLAND USA IOWA LIONEL "O"	11	85	118
TRANSISTOR THROTTLES WORTH THE COST?	06	63	46
TROLLEY LINE ADDITION TO A LAYOUT	03	70	33
TRUCK MOUNT YOUR COUPLERS	09	56	29
TRUCK MOUNTING "N" SCALE KADEES	01	80	132
TURN LEVER FOR SWITCH CONTROL	02	74	44
TURNOUT CHOICE OF SIZES	11	76	53
TURNOUT CONTROL WITH MOTORS/ELECTRONICS	09	85	92
TURNOUT ON A BRIDGE BELLOWS FALLS VT	07	78	107
TURNOUTS BASIC UNDERSTAND/TROUBLESHOOT	10	80	107
TURNTABLE DRIVE MECHANISM	06	70	74
TWENTY YEARS OF MODEL RAILROADING	01	54	40
TWO CAB WIRING BASICS	01	85	107
UNCLE ERIC REWIRED	01	79	144
UNCOUPLING RAMP CONSTRUCTION NMRA	05	57	36
UNCOUPLING RAMP REMOTE CONTROL CONST	01	58	37
UNCOUPLING RAMP RETRACTABLE CONSTRUCTION	07	56	55
UNCOUPLING RAMP.RETRACTABLE CONSTRUCTION	05	61	32
UNDECORATED RAILROAD LEASING CO. SPOUF	04	77	81
UNIT TRAINS	09	76	104
UNIT TRAINS AND THEIR MODELING	10	71	36
UNMATCHED PASSENGER TRAINS EXIST?	10	78	136
UNUSUAL 1/4" SCALE EQUIVALENT CHART	05	37	163S
UNUSUAL SCENIC RAILWAYS	04	76	49
VARNEY MODEL COMPANY GORDON REMEMBERED	01	85	120
VARNEY MODEL COMPANY (LETTER)	03	85	18
VARNEY MODEL COMPANY LETTER 2	04	85	15
VENERABLE J HAROLD GEISSEL	07	76	54
VIDEO & YOUR HOME LAYOUT	09	84	110
VIRTUES OF FINE SCALE	01	61	30
VISIT WITH ED RADEBAUGH 1922 TO TOADY	09	79	100
WALKAROUND OPERATION	05	72	31
WALTERS: FIRST 50 YEARS	05	82	70
WATER AND HOW TO MODEL IT	10	85	78
WATER UNDER THE BRIDGE MR 10 YRS B. PETE	01	44	22
WAY BACK WHEN IN MODEL RAILROADING	01	49	22
WE'RE GOING INTO CANTON ON TIME C JONES	12	81	96
WHAT AMTRAK MEANS TO MODEL RAILROADING	01	72	34
WHAT ARE LOST WAX CASTINGS	11	53	89
WHAT DIESELS REPLACED WHAT STEAM ENGINES	03	72	39
WHAT IS A TRAIN MAKEUP?	10	65	61
WHAT YOU CAN DO IN SN2	07	64	37
WHAT'S COOKIN' (AFTER THE WAR) B. PETE	04	44	166
WHEEL CONTOUR RP-25	01	62	69
WHEEL GAUGING AND SPACING	11	67	44
WHEEL GAUGING AND SPACING.	08	68	62
WHEEL RETARDERS	03	78	130
WHEEL SET GAUGE CHECKER	06	85	114
WHEELS FINE FLANGING THE EASY WAY	08	75	68
WHEELS WHY NOT SMALLER FLANGES	07	60	32
WHISTLE SIGNALS	08	57	66
WHITE LINED CAR NUMBERS	11	66	50
WHY JOIN A CLUB? PROS!	08	64	44
WILD WILLIES LIGHTED KD UNCOUPLING TOOL	08	81	81
WONDERFUL WORLD OF LIVE STEAM	05	65	22
WOOD CARS...LITTLE ENGINE	02	57	42
WOOD CARVED LOCOS OF ERNEST WARTHER	04	70	60
WOOD WIZARD FRANK KAPPLER VISIT A MFGR	12	79	133
WOODEN DISPLAY MODELS STROMBECKER	09	51	51
WORK STATION & SHOP	07	75	76
WORKING COUPLERS	08	43	348
WORKING RADIAL COUPLER	10	83	120
WORLD'S LARGEST LOCOMOTIVE ROSTER LOWRY	09	55	22
YARD DESIGN AND TRACKAGE PRINCIPLES	06	75	80
YARD DESIGN HANDBOOK	08	55	47
YARD LIMITS DEFINED	11	36	333
Z SCALE ABC'S	04	85	58
Z SCALE MODEL RAILROADING	10	75	42
ZINC ALLOY CASTING DETERIORATION	07	71	72

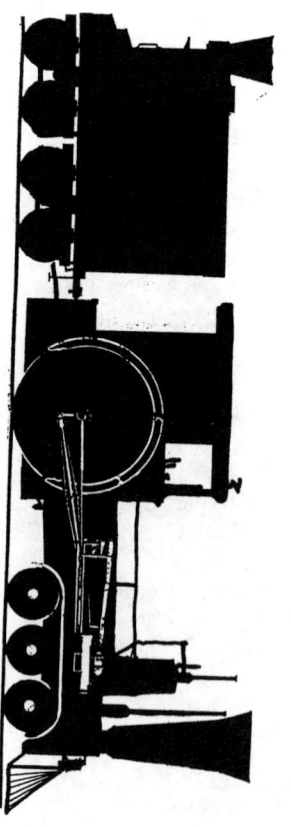

239

Trains

BILL OF LADING   THE SOURCE (HISTORY)

Trains made its debut in November of 1940. It has been published monthly since. This magazine is predominantly on prototype roads. It was known for a brief time as Trains and Travel but then reverted to its original name which it bears today. It, too, has absorbed other smaller magazines in order to improve its content. The publisher does have some back issues available. The current subscription rate is $25.00 a year. For back issues and subscription write:

>Trains
>1027 N. Seventh Street
>Milwaukee, Wi 53233

BILL OF LADING   LOCOMOTIVES

The locomotive section is broken down into five categories. Steam Locomotives, Tenders, Diesel Locomotives, Electric Locomotives and the catch-all of General Locomotives. Each of these categories is then broken into the three sub categories. Prototype Data, Plans and Drawings, and Photos.

The prototype data section contains articles on the specific prototype, tables that list prototype specifications and other listings of information of interest. The descriptor line contains the definition of the locomotive, the class, road and road number when available, the builder, and on occasion the year built. All of this information is taken from the article as written. We have made no attempt to research further when the information is not provided. The plans and drawings section lists just that. Again the type of locomotive is followed by class, road, road number, builder, and date. Over the years plans and drawings have improved in quality and detail tremendously. We have tried to specify a plan as a less detailed layout than a drawing. While this is a general practice it is not a rule. Photos come next. We have not tried to list all photos but rather only photos that show detail that would be of interest to the researcher. The same elements are included in the descriptor. Look at the "Prototype Data" section too as many times photographs accompany those entries but those photos did not get billing in the photo section. The three above are presented twice. Once in their alphabetical listing and for those associated with a specific road by road. This should help you LOP&G fans.

Hopefully this overall format will become as easy for you to use as it has for us. If you can suggest improvements please drop us a line.

MANIFEST LOCOMOTIVES

	PAGE
LOCOMOTIVES	242
STEAM LOCOMOTIVES	244
STEAM LOCOMOTIVE PROTOTYPE DATA	244
STEAM LOCO PROTOTYPE DATA BY ROAD	250
STEAM LOCOMOTIVE PLANS	255
STEAM LOCOMOTIVE PLANS BY ROAD	255
STEAM LOCOMOTIVE PHOTOS	256
STEAM LOCOMOTIVE PHOTOS BY ROAD	261
TENDERS	266
TENDER PROTOTYPE DATA	266
TENDER PROTOTYPE DATA BY ROAD	266
TENDER PLANS	266
TENDER PHOTOS	266
TENDER PHOTOS BY ROAD	266
DIESEL LOCOMOTIVES	266
DIESEL LOCOMOTIVE PROTOTYPE DATA	266
DIESEL LOCO PROTOTYPE DATA BY ROAD	268
DIESEL LOCOMOTIVE PHOTOS	269
DIESEL LOCOMOTIVE PHOTOS BY ROAD	274
DIESEL LOCOMOTIVE PLANS	278
DIESEL LOCOMOTIVE PLANS BY ROAD	278
ELECTRIC LOCOMOTIVES	278
ELECTRIC LOCOMOTIVE PROTOTYPE DATA	278
ELEC LOCO PROTOTYPE DATA BY ROAD	279
ELECTRIC LOCOMOTIVE PLANS	279
ELECTRIC LOCOMOTIVE PHOTOS	280
ELECTRIC LOCOMOTIVE PHOTOS BY ROAD	280
GENERAL LOCOMOTIVES	281
GENERAL LOCOMOTIVE PROTOTYPE DATA	281
GENERAL LOCO PROTOTYPE DATA BY ROAD	281

NOTE: SEE PAGE 400

LOCOMOTIVES

STEAM LOCOMOTIVE PROTOTYPE DATA

	M	Y	P
0-10-0 LOCOMOTIVE FOR 6% GRADES	10	44	39
0-10-0 23 5/8 GAUGE BALDWIN	08	83	51
0-10-0T SCTC #598	09	64	44
0-10-0T SCTC #598 SPECS	10	64	45
0-10-2 IC 3600 CLASS #3601 B 1922	03	53	53
0-10-2 SWITCHER URR #303 BALDWIN 1936	07	53	54
0-12-2 SYNCHROMESH LOCO OF ARGENTINA	06	57	27
0-2-2-0 #10 MT WASHINGTON COG RAILWAY	05	73	41
0-4-0 A-DUMMY SWITCHER ACL #1434 B 1905	06	50	45
0-4-0 FIRELESS COOKER SOP 1910	01	52	19
0-4-0 FIRELESS LOCOMOTIVE	03	49	56
0-4-0 INSPECTION LOCO R "BLACK DIAMOND"	09	49	51
0-4-0 LOCO CATAWISSA LSCH #1832	10	46	66
0-4-0 LOCOMOTIVE NYC ELEVATED 1879	05	43	28
0-4-0 NW #3 VULCAN	01	53	58
0-4-2 CH&B #2 PORTER	08	46	41
0-4-4 FORNEY LOCOMOTIVE NYC ELEVATED	05	43	28
0-4-4 SUBURBAN ENGINE NY&H #26	03	43	30
0-4-4-0 IN/OUTSIDE FRAMED LOCOS MEXICO	06	63	23
0-4-4T SR&RL #6	08	83	22
0-4-6 FAIRLIE HERO #187 TW&W	03	43	44
0-4-6 FORNEY C. H. WARREN (B&P) 1886	03	43	44
0-6-0 CAMELBACK SWITCHER CNJ #37	06	53	58
0-6-0 CLASS E10 ACL #1124 B 1912	06	50	45
0-6-0 CLASS E13 ACL #1150 B 1920	06	50	45
0-6-0 CLASS L-10 SIX COUPLED NP #1168	07	49	50
0-6-0 CONVERTED TO SADDLETANK LOCO MP	07	49	54
0-6-0 IC SWITCHER #333 COOKE 1918	03	53	52
0-6-0 LOCOMOTIVE OF 1863 DT&I	01	42	37
0-6-0 NOCATEE CRATE CO #8 B 1914	03	51	14
0-6-0 USRA SHIFTER CLASS B-28 PRR #7641	10	49	16
0-6-0'S CHANGING OF GUARD TAYLOR YD SP	06	78	37
0-6-0T CLASS L-4 SHOP SWITCHER NP #10 B	07	49	50
0-6-0T DISGUISED AS A STREETCAR B&O #316	03	44	38
0-6-0T IC SHOP SWITCHER #3287 B 1898	03	53	52
0-8-0 CAMELBACK SWITCHER CNJ #294 1918	06	53	58
0-8-0 CLASS E14 ACL #1227 BALDWIN 1923	06	50	45
0-8-0 CLASS G1 8 COUPLED NP #1172 BLW'19	07	49	50
0-8-0 CLASS G2 8 COUPLED NP #1181 ALCO	07	49	50
0-8-0 CLASS SA V #2 ALCO 1909	12	53	52
0-8-0 CLASS SB V #253	12	53	52
0-8-0 CLASS U4A IHB	02	42	43
0-8-0 IC 3500 CLASS SWITCHER #3532 1921	03	53	52
0-8-0 SWITCHER C&BL #47 LIMA 1941	01	44	46
0-8-0 SWITCHER G #801	02	77	52
0-8-0 U4A CLASS IHB #102	01	68	18
0-8-0T FROM 2-8-0 NW #809 1898	01	53	57
0-8-2 IC 3650 CLASS SWITCHER#3699 B 1911	03	53	53
0-8-8-0 CLASS CC2 COMPOUND PRR 1919 B	10	49	17
2-10-0 BIRTH OF BALDWIN LOCO PHOTO ESSAY	05	74	32
2-10-0 CLASS I1S PRR #4300 1923 B	11	83	58
2-10-0 CLASS M NP #2 BALDWIN 1886	07	49	51
2-10-0 CLASS O ACL #8005 B 1920	06	50	46
2-10-0 COLOSSUS OF THE DECAPODS	11	83	54
2-10-0 DECAPOD ON SHAMOKIN BRANCH PRR	11	57	24

STEAM LOCOMOTIVE PROTOTYPE DATA

	M	Y	P
2-10-0 DECAPOD TYPE LOCOMOTIVES	02	52	18
2-10-0 IC 3610 SERIES MIKADO #3610	03	53	55
2-10-10-2 COMPOUND ATSF #3000 TS 1911	09	51	45
2-10-10-2 MALLET ATSF #3000 1911	02	45	31
2-10-10-2 ODD MALLET ATSF #3001	11	57	21
2-10-10-2 V #800 ALCO 1918	12	53	56
2-10-2 CLASS 61 T&P #505 B 1918	02	78	28
2-10-2 CLASS I 2 WM 1112	11	83	54
2-10-2 CLASS K1SA R #3011 1922 B	11	83	58
2-10-2 CLASS N1 PRR 50 LOCO TRAIN PHOTOS	08	49	64
2-10-2 CLASS Q1 ACL #2001 B 1925	06	50	46
2-10-2 CLASS S1 B&O #6200 1927 B	11	83	58
2-10-2 COMPOUND ATSF #911	09	51	47
2-10-2 IC 2700 SERIES #2700 IC SHOPS	03	53	56
2-10-2 IC 2800 SERIES #2801	03	53	56
2-10-2 SANTA FE #524 "SNUFF DIPPER" T&P	10	72	44
2-10-2 SANTA FE SOLD TO OTHER ROADS W	11	49	50
2-10-2+2-6-2 TRACTOR S #5046	11	57	22
2-10-4 CLASS J1 PRR	10	49	18
2-10-4 CLASS J12 TEXAS TYPE PRR	06	43	30
2-10-4 CLASS T CGW #884 LIMA 1930	02	78	28
2-10-4 CLASS T1 C&O #3000 LIMA 1930	10	62	20
2-10-4 CLASS T1 C&O #3004	10	49	18
2-10-4 CLASS T1 T&P #610 LIMA 1925	02	78	28
2-10-4 LOCOMOTIVES OF T&P	02	78	22
2-10-4 SPECIFICATIONS BY ROAD	08	75	26
2-10-4 TEXAS CLASS I T&P #660	02	53	26
2-10-4 TEXAS TYPE CLASS H1G B&LE #647 B	12	44	19
2-10-4 TEXAS TYPE LOCOMOTIVES ATSF	08	75	ALL
2-10-4 THE ULTIMATE DEVELOPMENT	08	75	18
2-4-2 COLUMBIA TYPE ACL #93 B 1895	06	50	42
2-4-2 K88 ROGERS LOCO IN NEW ZEALAND	09	83	23
2-4-4 INSPECTION LOCO AD&SL #99	08	44	36
2-4-4 JOHN BULL	12	81	19
2-4-4T SUBURBAN LOCOMOTIVE IC #1402	10	43	44
2-4-6 INSPECTION LOCO SL&AD SLW 1892	09	49	50
2-6-0 BROOKS-SCANLON #7 PORTER	03	51	13
2-6-0 DOWLING & CAMP #12 B 1906	03	51	15
2-6-0 IC MOGUL #3709 1901	03	53	53
2-6-0 MANATEE CRATE CO #401	03	51	12
2-6-0 MAT #100 MOGUL	03	67	47
2-6-0 MOGUL REFUSED TO CAPITULATE	05	84	29
2-6-0 MOGULS OF MARIETTA	03	68	26
2-6-2 3 CYLINDER SCOTTISH LOCOMOTIVE	07	63	46
2-6-2 BROOKS-SCANLON #3	03	51	15
2-6-2 CLASS T NP #2360 BROOKS 1906	07	49	51
2-6-2 PEAVY-WILSON LUMBER CO #6 B 1914	03	51	14
2-6-6 C&NP #24 1893 BROOKS LOCO WORKS	08	46	41
2-6-6 MASON BOGIE DSP&P #55	04	43	24
2-6-6-2 BEYER GARRATT	07	82	45
2-6-6-2 COMPOUND GOES SIMPLE PRR #7518	10	49	10
2-6-6-2 HOW TO SCRAP PHOTO ESSAY	12	73	38
2-6-6-2 IC HUMP POWER #6003 RLW 1919	03	53	56
2-6-6-2 MALLET COMPOUND ATSF #1157 1910	02	45	32
2-6-6-2 MALLET COMPOUND ATSF #1158 1910	02	45	32

LOCOMOTIVES

STEAM LOCOMOTIVE PROTOTYPE DATA

	M	Y	P
2-6-6-2 MALLET FLEXIBLE BOILER ATSF#3321	02	45	33
2-6-6-2 MALLET FLEXIBLE BOILER ATSF#3322	02	45	33
2-6-6-2 ODD MALLET ATSF #1157	11	57	21
2-6-6-2 ODD MALLET GW #652	11	57	21
2-6-6-4 ARTICULATED CLASS A N&W #1212	06	45	30
2-6-6-4 CLASS A N&W 1238 ONE OF A KIND	03	50	35
2-6-6-4 CLASS A N&W #1212 1936 N&W SHOP	04	47	15
2-6-6-4 LOCOMOTIVES-TWIN STACKS	08	79	44
2-6-6-6 ALLEGHENY CLASS H-8 C&O #1603 L	05	48	39
2-6-6-6 ALLEGHENY CLASS H-8 C&O LIMA	07	56	50
2-6-6-6 CLASS A6 V #900 LIMA 1945	12	53	55
2-6-8-0 ODD MALLET CLASS 0 B&O #2421	11	57	20
2-6-8-0 ODD MALLET E #2900	11	57	20
2-8-0 CAMELBACK CNJ #678 ALCO	06	53	59
2-8-0 CLASS H10 PRR STANDARDS	10	73	24
2-8-0 CLASS H8SB PRR STANDARDS	10	73	24
2-8-0 CLASS H9 PRR STANDARDS	10	73	24
2-8-0 CLASS N2 CP #3718 1946 CP SHOP	05	47	60
2-8-0 CLASS Y NP #36 SLW 1898	07	49	51
2-8-0 CLASS Y-2 NP #1275 1901	07	49	52
2-8-0 CLASS Y-3 NP #1212 SLW 1901	07	49	52
2-8-0 COMPOUND SOO #429	09	51	48
2-8-0 COMPOUND W&LE #251 B 1903	09	51	46
2-8-0 CONSOLIDATION "NARROW GAUGE BOOMER"	01	50	42
2-8-0 CONSOLIDATION "UNCLE DICK" NM&SP B	10	46	60
2-8-0 CONSOLIDATION CLASS Z REBUILT C&NW	12	43	35
2-8-0 CONSOLIDATION DEVELOPMENT D&H 1	04	67	38
2-8-0 CONSOLIDATION DEVELOPMENT D&H 2	05	67	20
2-8-0 CONSOLIDATION DEVELOPMENT D&H 3	06	67	39
2-8-0 CONSOLIDATION USWD #3029	07	45	40
2-8-0 D&H #853 ERECTION PHOTO ESSAY	12	74	49
2-8-0 IC 700 SERIES CONSOLIDATION #700	03	53	53
2-8-0 IC 900 SERIES CONSOLIDATION #906 B	03	53	53
2-8-0 NW #7	01	53	58
2-8-0 S #385 IN NEW JERSEY	05	66	48
2-8-0 SIDE RODS BUT NO CYCLINDERS	07	67	26
2-8-0 USA SWITCHER #6998 (ALASKA ROAD)	01	44	46
2-8-2 ATSF #4007 COFFIN FEEDWATER HEATER	08	63	49
2-8-2 BIG DUTCH MIKADOS READING	06	85	32
2-8-2 CANADIAN BUILT LOCO FOR INDIA	04	44	15
2-8-2 CLASS AM-2 AB&CO #332 ALCO 1914	06	50	47
2-8-2 CLASS AM-2 ACL #7332 ALCO 1914	06	50	47
2-8-2 CLASS H-6E NKP #633 LIMA 1923	10	62	20
2-8-2 CLASS J4A MIKADO L&N #1903 B 1929	02	47	61
2-8-2 CLASS L1 PRR 1914 PRR SHOPS	06	85	34
2-8-2 CLASS L2 USRA PRR #9630	10	49	17
2-8-2 CLASS M ACL #813 B 1911	06	50	45
2-8-2 CLASS M1A READING 1912 READING SHP	06	85	34
2-8-2 CLASS M1SA READING 1913 BALDWIN	06	85	34
2-8-2 CLASS M1SA READING REBUILT 1917 B	06	85	34
2-8-2 CLASS M1SB READING 1916 BALDWIN	06	85	34
2-8-2 CLASS M2 ACL #836 B 1918	06	50	46
2-8-2 CLASS MB V #453 B 1910	12	53	53
2-8-2 CLASS MC V #462 B 1912	12	53	53
2-8-2 CLASS MCA V #484	12	53	54

STEAM LOCOMOTIVE PROTOTYPE DATA

	M	Y	P
2-8-2 CLASS MD V #410 REBUILT #700 B	09	52	22
2-8-2 CLASS N2 C&EI	01	42	51
2-8-2 CLASS O-8 GN SPECIFICATIONS	01	69	41
2-8-2 CLASS P1N CP #5200 CP SHOPS	05	47	60
2-8-2 CLASS Q3 B&O 1918 BALDWIN	06	85	34
2-8-2 CLASS R FRENCH SUPPLY COUNCIL LIMA	11	46	61
2-8-2 CLASS W NP #1529 ALCO 1904	07	49	52
2-8-2 CLASS W2 NP #1917 BROOKS 1904	07	49	52
2-8-2 CLASS W5 NP #1844 1923 SLW	07	49	52
2-8-2 FOR SALE - NO SALE USA	09	82	37
2-8-2 IC 1200 SERIES MIKADO #1207	03	53	54
2-8-2 IC 1500 SERIES MIKADO #1561	03	53	54
2-8-2 IC 1700 SERIES MIKADO #1711	03	53	55
2-8-2 IC 2100 SERIES MIKADO #2115	03	53	55
2-8-2 IC 3766 SERIES MIKADO #3792	03	53	55
2-8-2 IMPRESSIONS OF CP #5137 PHOTO ESSA	09	61	40
2-8-2 LIGHT MIKADO FIRST USRA LOCOMOTIVE	12	60	47
2-8-2 MIKADO CLASS H-10 NYC WHY LANDMARK	06	75	50
2-8-2 MIKADO CLASS O-8 GN #3397	01	69	38
2-8-2 MIKADO CLASS P-2H CP#5417 CLC 1943	01	44	44
2-8-2 MIKADO CLASS S NKP	10	62	18
2-8-2 MIKADO TYPE LOCOS NEW-FOR SALE	05	61	52
2-8-2 MIKADO USWD #1624	07	45	40
2-8-2 NARROW GAUGE MIKADO D&RGW	09	61	20
2-8-2 SUPERCHARGED MIKADO IC #3791	08	46	40
2-8-2+2-8-0 TRACTOR S #4576	11	57	22
2-8-4 BANTAM WEIGHT BERKSHIRE NSO #600	09	84	52
2-8-4 BERKSHIRE #759 REFERBISHING NKP	03	69	29
2-8-4 BERKSHIRE CLASS M-1 L&N #1967 B	05	53	22
2-8-4 BERKSHIRE CLASS M-1 L&N BIG EMMA	12	72	22
2-8-4 BERKSHIRE CLASS N-1 PM #1222 LIMA	08	43	25
2-8-4 BERKSHIRE CLASS S-1 NKP #730 LIMA	08	43	25
2-8-4 BERKSHIRE CLASS S-3 NKP #776 LIMA	09	49	39
2-8-4 BERKSHIRE CLASSES S-3 & S-4 ERIE	02	48	8
2-8-4 BERKSHIRE RF&P #574 LIMA 1943	06	43	24
2-8-4 BORN AGAIN BERKSHIRE LIMA	05	80	22
2-8-4 CANADA'S ONLY 2-8-4'S TH&B	06	85	41
2-8-4 CLASS A1 IC #8049 LIMA	01	52	16
2-8-4 CLASS A1 LIMA #1 DEMONSTRATOR	02	78	28
2-8-4 CLASS AS TH&B #202 1928 MLW	06	85	40
2-8-4 CLASS BA V #505 LIMA	11	46	61
2-8-4 CLASS BA V #505 LIMA 1946	12	53	54
2-8-4 CLASS J4 C&NW #2806 1927 ALCO	06	85	42
2-8-4 CLASS K4 C&U #2744 LIMA	11	46	61
2-8-4 CLASS S NKP #703 ALCO 1934	10	62	20
2-8-4 CLASS S-4 E #3389 LIMA 1929	10	62	20
2-8-4 DEMONSTRATOR 1 LIMA LOCO WORKS	01	52	17
2-8-4 LIMA CLASS MIKADO #8015 1926	03	53	55
2-8-8 MIKADO CLASS 282-S-227 PGE #160	02	46	47
2-8-8-0 CLASS HC1 SIMPLE PRR #3700 1919	10	49	17
2-8-8-2 ARTICULATED CLASS Y-6 N&W #2197	09	53	32
2-8-8-2 ARTICULATED CLASS Y-6A N&W #2156	08	43	24
2-8-8-2 CLASS AF V #610	12	53	56
2-8-8-2 CLASS AF V #610 REBUILT #700 B	09	52	22
2-8-8-2 CLASS HH1 PRR (FORMER N&W)	10	49	18

LOCOMOTIVES

STEAM LOCOMOTIVE PROTOTYPE DATA

	M	Y	P
2-8-8-2 CLASS LS1 S #4009 1918 BALDWIN	08	85	50
2-8-8-2 CLASS US V #711 ALCO 1919	12	53	54
2-8-8-2 CLASS USE V #741	12	53	54
2-8-8-2 CLASS XX BR&P #801 WRECK	02	52	56
2-8-8-2 CLASS Y6A N&W #2156 N&W SHOPS	04	47	15
2-8-8-2 CLASS Z-3 NP #4025 ALCO 1913	07	49	53
2-8-8-2 CLASS Z-4 NP #4503 RLW 1923	07	49	53
2-8-8-2 FROM LARGEST TO SOME OF LARGEST	04	82	42
2-8-8-2 MALLET ATSF #1700	02	45	30
2-8-8-2 N&W Y6 CLOSE UP PHOTO ESSAY	11	60	60
2-8-8-4 CLASS EM-1 YELLOWSTONE B&O #7600	10	44	20
2-8-8-4 CLASS Z-5 NP #5005 BALDWIN 1930	07	49	53
2-8-8-4 NP CLASS Z4 AND SISTERS STATISTS	03	82	27
2-8-8-4 ONCE WORLDS LARGEST LOCO NP#500	03	82	22
2-8-8-8-2 TRIPLEX CLASS P1 E#5014 B 1914	11	44	14
2-8-8-8-4 CLASS XA TRIPLEX V#700 B 1916	09	52	22
4-10-0 "EL GOBERNADOR" SP 1883'S BIGGEST	08	42	18
4-10-2 BALDWIN ENGINE #60000 1926	04	54	50
4-10-2 COMPOUND BALDWIN LOCO WORKS#60000	09	51	44
4-12-2 CLASS 9000 UP 1926 BLW	07	84	19
4-12-2 UNION PACIFIC #9085 1926	01	45	38
4-2-0 H&NY LOCO 1864 ROGERS	12	46	61
4-2-0 INSPECTION LOCO LV #1 1884	09	49	50
4-2-2 BALDWIN EXPERIMENTAL OF 1880 P&R	11	49	54
4-2-2 BRITISH GN #1 PHOTO	06	82	19
4-2-2 CS FONTAINE LOCOMOTIVE	12	47	61
4-2-2 INSPECTION LOCO E&WV #40	01	49	64
4-2-2 LJIP #1 YANKEE COME HOME	09	84	21
4-2-4 CP HUNTINGTON SP #1	03	51	48
4-4 BALDWIN FREIGHT LOCO 1850 W&W	10	41	2
4-4-0 AMERICAN AT HENRY FORD MUSEUM	10	74	22
4-4-0 AMERICAN CLASS D-16 PRR	08	54	22
4-4-0 AMERICAN LOCOMOTIVES OF ROGERS	07	51	48
4-4-0 AMERICAN PP&B #2 1889 ROGERS	09	43	38
4-4-0 AMERICAN THE LAST LOCO NP #684	08	53	14
4-4-0 CLASS D-21 AMERICAN L&N #143 B	02	47	61
4-4-0 CLASS D16-D16SB DIFFERENCES PRR	08	54	26
4-4-0 CLASS EA V #295 B 1906	12	53	52
4-4-0 DOWLING & CAMP #103 B 1913	03	51	15
4-4-0 INSPECTION LOCO B&A #31 1869	09	49	50
4-4-0 INSPECTION LOCO CB&Q #475	09	49	51
4-4-0 MASON (LAST ENGINE)	02	45	34
4-4-0 MODIFIED TO 2-6-0 CRB&L #9	09	50	44
4-4-0 NYC #999	07	41	35
4-4-0 NYC LOCOMOTIVE #999	04	66	18
4-4-0 PACIFIC RR #6 OF 1852	09	51	7
4-4-0 TAUNTON LOCOMOTIVES OF 1880	12	44	18
4-4-0 V&T GOES TO HOLLYWOOD	01	41	24
4-4-0 VARIETES B&P	07	43	29
4-4-0 YUCATAN RAILWAYS #81	06	46	32
4-4-0'S WEREN'T ALL AT THE FAIR	09	77	42
4-4-2 ATLANTIC CLASS A STREAMLINED MILW	05	52	36
4-4-2 CAMELBACK ATLANTIC CNJ #803 R 1912	06	53	56
4-4-2 CLASS A16 C&O	11	41	31
4-4-2 CLASS E1 MOTHER HUBBARD PRR #700	10	49	15

STEAM LOCOMOTIVE PROTOTYPE DATA

	M	Y	P
4-4-2 CLASS E28 BALDWIN COMPUND PRR#7451	10	49	15
4-4-2 CLASS E6 PRR STANDARDS	10	73	24
4-4-2 CLASS I ACL #89 B 1895	06	50	42
4-4-2 CLASS J N&W #611 FINEST STEAM LOCO	01	83	44
4-4-2 CLASS J N&W #611 GREEN FLAGS 1950	01	83	42
4-4-2 COLE COMPUND PRR #7452 ALCO 1905	10	49	15
4-4-2 COMPOUND NYC&H #3000 SLW	09	51	48
4-4-2 FRENCH COMPOUND PRR #2512 1904	10	49	15
4-4-2 HIAWATHA MILW	04	41	46
4-4-2 HIAWATHA UNDER STREAMLINER MILW	12	84	30
4-4-2 IC BRANCH LINE ATLANTIC #2009 R	03	53	56
4-4-2 INSPECTION LOCO READING #100	08	44	36
4-4-4 JUBILEE CLASS F-2A CP #3002 MLW	04	53	36
4-4-4 JUBILEE UNDER THE STREAMLINER CP	12	84	29
4-4-4 LOCOMOTIVE "LADY BALTIMORE" B&O	09	42	12
4-4-4 PRR CLASS T1 UNDER THE STREAMLINER	12	84	34
4-4-4 WITNESSING OF A CRIME	04	83	22
4-4-4-4 CLASS T1 PRR#6110 ST LAST CHANCE	03	77	20
4-4-4-4 DUPLEX CLASS N-1 B&O	09	64	24
4-4-4-4 DUPLEX CLASS T-1 PRR	07	43	32
4-4-4-4 DUPLEX CLASS T-1 PRR 1842	07	51	28
4-4-6-2 ATASF #1301 LARGEST PASS LOCO	08	63	48
4-4-6-2 MALLET COMPOUND ATSF #1398 1909	02	45	30
4-6-0 AMERICAN TYPE 10 WHEELER LV #149	08	54	50
4-6-0 BALDWIN DEMONSTRATOR OF 1891	06	57	36
4-6-0 BE&CH #31 ENGINED WALKED IN SLEEP	07	49	40
4-6-0 C&NW #836 SIMPLE TO COMP TO SIMPLE	04	62	49
4-6-0 CAMELBACK CNJ # 180 BLW	06	53	56
4-6-0 CAMELBACK CNJ #423 B 1893	06	53	56
4-6-0 CAMELBACK CNJ #754 BALDWIN	03	56	26
4-6-0 CAMELBACK CNJ #788 1918	06	53	56
4-6-0 CLASS AW-4 AB&CO #124 1907	06	50	47
4-6-0 CLASS AW-4 ACL #7124 B 1907	06	50	47
4-6-0 CLASS G5 LI STANDARDS 1923 PRR	10	73	26
4-6-0 CLASS G5 PRR STANDARDS	10	73	24
4-6-0 CLASS G5'S OF LI	05	79	35
4-6-0 CLASS K14 ACL #254 B 1910	06	50	43
4-6-0 CLASS K6 ACL #359 B 1904	06	50	43
4-6-0 CLASS L6SA R STANDARDS 1905 B	10	73	26
4-6-0 CLASS L8 & T40 CNJ STANDARD 1918 B	10	73	26
4-6-0 CLASS S-4 NP #1379 BALDWIN 1902	07	49	48
4-6-0 CLASS T40 SP STANDARDS 1917 SP	10	73	26
4-6-0 COMPOUND PLANT SYSTEM #119 B	09	51	46
4-6-0 LOP&G #101	03	51	14
4-6-0 MANATEE CRATE CO #1252	03	51	15
4-6-0 NP STEAMS LAST DAYS PHOTO ESSAY	02	61	24
4-6-0 OF IC	02	41	46
4-6-0 REBUILD ACL #386 B 1920	06	50	43
4-6-0 TALES OF A TEN WHEELER NP #1356	08	56	14
4-6-0 TEN WHEELER #1 CL TOMS ENGINE	03	73	18
4-6-0 TEN WHEELER #20 F&CC SLW 1899	10	54	53
4-6-0 TEN WHEELER ACL #210	11	43	24
4-6-0 TEN WHEELER CLASS G5S PRR	10	73	20
4-6-0 TEN WHEELER CNJ #774	10	71	18
4-6-0 TEN WHEELERS OF 1890	08	43	46

LOCOMOTIVES

STEAM LOCOMOTIVE PROTOTYPE DATA

	M	Y	P
4-6-0 V&T #26 SUICIDE	02	60	26
4-6-2 B&O PRESIDENT SERIES	03	41	13
4-6-2 CLASS AJ-2 AB&CO #175 LIMA 1914	06	50	47
4-6-2 CLASS AJ-2 ACL #7175 LIMA 1914	06	50	47
4-6-2 CLASS E4 N&W #598 ROLLING MUDFENCE	02	85	29
4-6-2 CLASS I5 & CONTEMPORARY SPECIFICAT	09	81	24
4-6-2 CLASS I5 NYNH&H LOCOMOTIVES	09	81	20
4-6-2 CLASS K-5 PACIFIC L&N 275 ALCO	02	47	61
4-6-2 CLASS K4 PRR	12	40	11
4-6-2 CLASS K5 PACIFICS PRR #5698 1927	10	49	16
4-6-2 CLASS P ACL #263 B	06	50	43
4-6-2 CLASS P-4 ACL #457 B 1917	06	50	44
4-6-2 CLASS P-5A ACL #1530 ALCO 1918	06	50	44
4-6-2 CLASS P-5B ACL #1732 B 1922	06	50	44
4-6-2 CLASS PA V #212 1928	12	53	52
4-6-2 CLASS PS4 S	06	41	35
4-6-2 CLASS Q NP #2080 BALDWIN 1903	07	49	48
4-6-2 CLASS Q2 NP # 2176 ALCO 1906	07	49	48
4-6-2 CLASS Q4 NP #2222 1910	07	49	48
4-6-2 CLASS Q5 NP #2241 1920	07	49	48
4-6-2 CLASS Q6 NP #2256 1923	07	49	49
4-6-2 CLASS S3A1 FW&D #553	08	69	18
4-6-2 ENGINE # 50000 OF AMERICAN LOCO CO	11	52	48
4-6-2 FIREFLY FRIS	09	41	19
4-6-2 FIRST PACIFIC 1889 CM&STP SHOPS	05	43	44
4-6-2 IC 2031 SERIES #2037 ALCO 1905	03	53	51
4-6-2 IC 1000 SERIES #1002	03	53	51
4-6-2 IC 1135 SERIES #1171	03	53	51
4-6-2 LITRI #10 SMALLEST PACIFIC BUILT	04	83	35
4-6-2 M&O #268 TO GM&O #576 AFTER MERGER	10	43	48
4-6-2 NH STREAMLINER CLASS I5	12	84	31
4-6-2 PACIFIC "CINCINNATIAN" B&O #5301 B	10	53	30
4-6-2 PACIFIC "MADAM QUEEN" MP #6000	02	50	12
4-6-2 PACIFIC "MARIE" NC&SL #535	01	67	20
4-6-2 PACIFIC #295 L&N 1940	03	59	20
4-6-2 PACIFIC CLASS C-3G CP #2400 CLC	01	44	44
4-6-2 PACIFIC CLASS G-5 CP #1200 1944	07	44	40
4-6-2 PACIFIC CLASS K-4 PRR #5495	04	46	38
4-6-2 PACIFIC CLASS K-4S PRR 1928 PRR	08	56	44
4-6-2 PACIFIC CLASS K-5 PRR	09	57	52
4-6-2 PACIFIC CLASS P-13 SP #633 B 1928	04	43	5
4-6-2 PACIFIC CLASS P-7 PRESIDENTS B&O	06	51	45
4-6-2 PACIFIC CLASS PS-4 S	10	50	20
4-6-2 PACIFIC K-4 PRR #1737 1927 PRR	04	52	28
4-6-2 PACIFIC K4 "BROADWAY LIMITED" PRR	10	68	41
4-6-2 PACIFIC TYPE E	11	40	7
4-6-2 PACIFICS CP #1262	02	54	51
4-6-2 PS2 CLASS PACIFICS S	12	78	28
4-6-2 REBORN LOCOMOTIVE MP #6001	10	78	26
4-6-4 C&NW CLASS E4 UNDER STREAMLINER	12	84	32
4-6-4 CLASS 3460 ATSF #3462 1937 BALDWIN	06	85	22
4-6-4 CLASS 3460 STREAMLINED ATSF #3460	06	85	22
4-6-4 CLASS E4 C&NW 1938 ALCO	06	85	22
4-6-4 CLASS F-7 CMSP&P 1938 ALCO	06	85	22
4-6-4 CLASS F6 CMSP&P(MILW) #6402 B 1934	12	63	20

STEAM LOCOMOTIVE PROTOTYPE DATA

	M	Y	P
4-6-4 CLASS H1 "ROYAL HUDSON" CP #2857	08	69	20
4-6-4 CLASS J HUDSON NYC	11	57	44
4-6-4 CLASS J-1A HUDSON NYC #5200 ALCO	02	56	45
4-6-4 CLASS K-3Q MODIFIED PACIFIC NYC	02	56	45
4-6-4 CLASS L-2 HUGE HUDSONS C&O #305	05	61	46
4-6-4 CP H1 SPECIFICATIONS	08	69	26
4-6-4 HIAWATHA UNDER STREAMLINER MILW	12	84	33
4-6-4 HUDSON "LORD BALTIMORE" B&O	09	42	12
4-6-4 HUDSON CLASS J-1 NYC 1931	10	68	41
4-6-4 HUDSON CLASS J-3 NYC #5273 ALCO	03	52	30
4-6-4 HUDSON CLASS L-2 C&O #305 B 1941	09	43	35
4-6-4 HUDSON CONVERTED FROM 2-8-2 W #700	02	45	35
4-6-4 IC HUDSON REBUILD #2499 IC SHOPS	03	53	56
4-6-4 LORD BALTIMORE DIES B&O 1935	09	49	62
4-6-4 MODERN FRENCH LOCOMOTIVES	03	47	22
4-6-4 NYC #5344 MOST FAMOUS HUDSON ALCO	01	50	47
4-6-4 OF FRANCE 1910	02	56	46
4-6-4 SL HUDSON "BLUEBIRD" ATSF #3460 B	01	53	52
4-6-4 SL HUDSON CLASS E-4 C&NW #4002	11	53	54
4-6-6-4 3000 SERIES UP #3951 PHOTO	07	43	27
4-6-6-4 ARTICULATED CL #655 ALCO 1943	07	43	40
4-6-6-4 CHALLENGER CLASS 307 MB UP #3977	08	44	29
4-6-6-4 CHALLENGER CLASS L97 D&RGW #3800	08	44	29
4-6-6-4 CHALLENGERS LAST CHANCE NP #5140	05	78	25
4-6-6-4 CLASS Z-8 NP #5139 ALCO	07	49	53
4-6-6-4 LOCOS OF D&H	08	41	19
4-6-6-4 UP #3967 ALCO 1942	11	43	25
4-6-6-4 UP 3985 RESTORATION	11	82	32
4-8-0 CAMELBACK MASTODON CNJ #477	06	53	59
4-8-0 CYRANO DE NW #495	01	53	59
4-8-0 MONON #225 1898 BROOKS LOCO WORKS	02	84	30
4-8-0 SWITCHER NW #1100 B 1910	01	53	57
4-8-0'S TO MALLETS TO JAWN HENRY N&W	10	84	36
4-8-2 CLASS AM-1 AB&CO #372 ALCO 1924	06	50	47
4-8-2 CLASS AM-1 ACL #7372 ALCO 1924	06	50	47
4-8-2 CLASS J-1 ACL #1401 BLW	06	50	44
4-8-2 CLASS J1C NC&SL #567 B 1925	12	63	24
4-8-2 CLASS J2 NC&SL #579 ALCO 1930	12	63	24
4-8-2 CLASS J3 NC&SL #587 ALCO 1942	12	63	24
4-8-2 CLASS J3 TP&W #80 ALCO 1937	12	63	24
4-8-2 CLASS M1 FREIGHT LOCOMOTIVES PRR	11	47	62
4-8-2 CLASS M1 PRR #6783 PHOTO ESSAY	05	58	31
4-8-2 CLASS QR-1 NDEM B 1946	12	63	24
4-8-2 CLASS R10 B&M #4117 BEAUTIFUL BALD	10	68	18
4-8-2 IC #2500	10	41	13
4-8-2 IC 2500 SERIES #2511 IC SHOPS 1937	03	53	52
4-8-2 IC 2600 SERIES #2600 IC SHOPS 1942	03	53	52
4-8-2 IC MOUNTAIN #2431 ALCO 1923	03	53	50
4-8-2 MOUNTAIN C&O #316 ALCO 1911	02	56	45
4-8-2 MOUNTAIN CLASS L-4B NYC #3135 LIMA	09	44	17
4-8-2 MOUNTAIN CLASS M SEA #240 ALCO	12	52	52
4-8-2 MOUNTAIN CLASS M-1 & M-2 T&P #908	09	46	27
4-8-2 MOUNTAIN CLASS MT-1 SP #4300 ALCO	05	44	26
4-8-2 MOUNTAIN CLASS R-1D B&M #4113 1941	02	48	46
4-8-2 MOUNTAIN CLASS U-1F CN #6060 1945	10	45	38

LOCOMOTIVES

STEAM LOCOMOTIVE PROTOTYPE DATA

	M	Y	P
4-8-2 MOUNTAIN PRR CLASS M-1 1926	03	43	4
4-8-2 MOUNTAIN TYPE 2600 CLASS IC #2600	05	43	29
4-8-2 MOUNTAIN TYPE L&HR#10 BALDWIN 1944	12	44	19
4-8-2 WHAT HAPPENED TO C&O #317	07	83	42
4-8-2'S SELECTED US ROAD SPECS	10	79	24
4-8-2-2-8-4 GARRATT #4015	01	77	20
4-8-4 CLASS J3 NC&SL #587	06	44	16
4-8-4 CLASS T2B LV #5220	06	44	16
4-8-4 "SUPER" NORTHERNS NYC 5500 CLOSE	02	75	47
4-8-4 ATSF #3764 CAPROTTI VALVE GEAR B	08	63	47
4-8-4 CLASS 1901 MP #1922 1930 LIMA	05	84	24
4-8-4 CLASS 2101 MP #2101 1940 MP SHOPS	05	84	24
4-8-4 CLASS 2201 MP #2208 1943 BALDWIN	05	84	24
4-8-4 CLASS A NP #2600 SLW 1926	07	49	49
4-8-4 CLASS A-1 NP #2626 ALCO 1930	07	49	49
4-8-4 CLASS A-3 NP #2666 BALDWIN 1934	07	49	49
4-8-4 CLASS A-4 NP #2676 BALDWIN 1941	07	49	49
4-8-4 CLASS HS-1A COMPOUND NYC #800	02	55	48
4-8-4 CLASS J N&W #600 1941 N&W SHOPS	04	47	14
4-8-4 CLASS K3 ON W&LE	03	79	44
4-8-4 CLASS M68 D&RGW #1804 1938 BALDWIN	05	84	24
4-8-4 CLASS O20 SOO #5000 1938 LIMA	08	67	18
4-8-4 CLASS O5 BURL PHOTO ESSAY	05	57	31
4-8-4 CLASS R-1 ACL #1800 B 1938	06	50	44
4-8-4 CLASS S DEVELOPER PAUL KIEFER NYC	03	84	46
4-8-4 CLASS S-1 GN SPECIFICATIONS	01	69	41
4-8-4 CLASS S1A NYC #6009	11	50	15
4-8-4 CLASS S2 MILW	12	41	39
4-8-4 CLASS U2H CN #6249	06	44	16
4-8-4 DAYLIGHT LIKE NO OTHER SP	10	84	24
4-8-4 DIARY OF A LOCOMOTIVE ATSF #3761 B	03	48	16
4-8-4 LOCOMOTIVES ON ROCK ISLAND	03	81	22
4-8-4 LOCOS OF UP	01	41	28
4-8-4 MONTANA TYPE CLASS S1 & S2 GN#2577	07	67	18
4-8-4 MOUNTAIN "FOUR ACES" TIMKEN NP	11	58	16
4-8-4 NIAGARA NYC #6000 ALCO 1945	05	45	36
4-8-4 NORTHERN CGA #455 LIMA 1944	01	45	39
4-8-4 NORTHERN CLASS 481 WP #485 LIMA	03	44	37
4-8-4 NORTHERN CLASS A-1 A-2 A-4 A-5 NP	04	48	28
4-8-4 NORTHERN CLASS A-4 NP #2670 B	06	43	25
4-8-4 NORTHERN CLASS G8-6 SP #4462 LIMA	03	44	37
4-8-4 NORTHERN CLASS GS-4 SP #4454 LIMA	10	43	46
4-8-4 NORTHERN CLASS H C&NW	07	42	5
4-8-4 NORTHERN CLASS H C&NW 3000 SERIES	10	70	20
4-8-4 NORTHERN CLASS J N&W #600 1941	06	45	30
4-8-4 NORTHERN CLASS J STEAM POWER N&W	12	64	44
4-8-4 NORTHERN CLASS J-3 C&O #600 LIMA	09	43	34
4-8-4 NORTHERN CLASS J-3 NC&SL	12	63	22
4-8-4 NORTHERN CLASS J-3A C&O #605	09	43	34
4-8-4 NORTHERN CLASS K-62 D&H #308 ALCO	10	43	46
4-8-4 NORTHERN CLASS L-1 CBELT #815	04	43	4
4-8-4 NORTHERN CLASS M-68 D&RGW #1804 B	12	43	29
4-8-4 NORTHERN CLASS N-73 MP#2208 B 1943	12	43	29
4-8-4 NORTHERN CLASS R67B RI #5000 SLW	06	52	28
4-8-4 NORTHERN CLASS S-2 MILW #206	11	44	40

STEAM LOCOMOTIVE PROTOTYPE DATA

	M	Y	P
4-8-4 NORTHERN CLASS S-2 MILW #238	01	48	18
4-8-4 NORTHERN CLASS S-3 MILW #262 1944	11	44	40
4-8-4 NORTHERN CLASS T-1 R	12	60	17
4-8-4 NORTHERN CLS GS-4 DAYLIGHT SP#4454	10	52	20
4-8-4 NORTHERN CP LONELY CANADIAN 4-8-4S	01	76	20
4-8-4 NORTHERN SERIES 2900 ATSF #2903 B	06	44	17
4-8-4 NORTHERN SERIES 3776 ATSF #3780 B	06	44	17
4-8-4 NORTHERN STREAMLINED	03	73	35
4-8-4 NORTHERN TYPE R1 #5100 ALCO 1944	01	45	39
4-8-4 PHOTO IDENTIFICATION QUIZ RUN GEAR	08	64	27
4-8-4 PROPOSED CONSTANT TORQUE LOCO B&O	08	49	28
4-8-4'S OF MP SEDALIA SHOPS	05	84	20
4-8-4-4-8-4 BEYER-GARRATT #6003	07	54	18
4-8-6 GIGER LOCOMOTIVE (PROPOSED)	03	50	16
4-8-8-4 BIG BOY UP	11	58	40
4-8-8-4 BIG BOY UP 4000 SERIES 1941	07	43	24
4-8-8-4 BIG BOY UP #4022 ALCO 1941	08	52	58
4-8-8-4 LOOK AT BIG BOY PHOTO ESSAY UP	05	56	31
6-4-4-6 CLASS S1 BIG ENGINE PRR #6100	10	49	16
6-4-4-6 PRR CLASS S1 UNDER THE STREAMLIN	12	84	35
6-8-6 CLASS S2 TURBINE PRR #6200 1944	10	49	19
6-8-6 STEAM TURBINE CLASS S-2 PRR #6200	01	45	15
AB&C LOCOMOTIVES TO ACL	11	76	31
ACE 3000 WHAT IS IT?	12	80	12
ACL STEAM POWER	06	50	42
AIR BRAKES IMPORTANCE OF BEING ABLE STOP	10	75	44
AMERICAN LOCOMOTIVE COMPANY HISTORY	11	52	48
ARTICULATED RUNNING GEAR IDENT PHOT QUIZ	12	64	39
ARTICULATION THE ABC'S	08	61	42
AUXILIARY SAND BOXES D&RGW	06	41	46
B&O "WARBABY" REBUILDING	05	43	40
B&O ARTICULATEDS FROM SAL ROSTER	08	79	49
BACKHEAD LAYOUTS	06	48	15
BAKER VALVE GEAR	05	84	35
BALDWIN DISK DRIVER DETAILS	04	47	35
BALDWIN VALUCLAIN NOMAD OF THE '90'S	06	57	36
BAY STATE LOCOMOTIVES	11	42	28
BELL RINGERS AND HOW THEY WORK	04	46	56
BEST TEN WHEELER IN THE WHOLE WIDE WORLD	06	77	28
BEYER-GARRATT CONTORTION FIRST LOCOS	06	55	16
BIG ENGINE THAT DIDN'T UP #8444	02	76	44
BIG PERFORMANCE STEAM LOCOMOTIVES	06	68	38
BIG STEAM COMPARISON TABLE	11	58	50
BIG STEAM POWER SCOREBOARD	06	68	44
BRAND NEW WOODBURNERS 2-6-0 & 0-4-4T	08	62	47
BRITISH LOCO PORTFOLIO	10	41	14
BUILDERS PLATES BADGES OF DISTINCTION	06	62	24
BUILT AT BREWSTER W&LE SHOPS	11	84	52
BURDEN BEARING STEAM LOCOMOTIVE	08	70	42
CAB FORWARD LOCOMOTIVES UNLIMITED NON SP	02	69	24
CABS CASEY CALLED IT A CABIN	12	56	46
CAMELBACK CLASSICS PHOTO ESSAY	01	62	44
CAMELBACK LOCOMOTIVES LETTERS	04	41	47
CAMELBACK LOCOMOTIVES 1	02	41	16
CASE FOR AMERICAN STEAM LOCOMOTIVES	08	67	22

LOCOMOTIVES

STEAM LOCOMOTIVE PROTOTYPE DATA

	M	Y	P
CASE FOR THE FRENCH STEAM LOCOMOTIVE	12	66	23
CASS SHAY WORLD'S LARGEST (LETTER)	10	67	50
CGW INTERESTING & ODD STEAM POWER	09	65	20
CNJ CAMELBACK LOCOMOTIVES	06	53	57
COMPOUND LOCOMOTIVES	09	51	44
CONTEMPORARIES OF NKP S CLASS 2-8-4	10	62	27
CONTROLS IN CAB OF STEAM LOCOMOTOVES	11	44	24
COUNTERBALANCING CONNECTING RODS	05	45	22
CP TRIPLE HEADER PHOTO ESSAY	08	60	46
D&H STEAM LOCOMOTIVE DEVELOPMENT LOREE	07	52	20
DID WE SCRAP THEM TOO SOON? STEAM LOCOS	06	74	36
DISTINGUISHING FEATURES OF STEAM ON S	10	71	36
DL&W STEAM LOCOMOTIVE DEVELOPMENT	09	65	28
DRIVING WHEEL PHOTO QUIZ	01	80	20
DUAL HEADLIGHTS FOR PRR	07	48	5
DUPLEX DRIVE LOCOS STEAMS LAST STAND	11	59	16
DUPLEX DRIVE LOCOS STEAMS LAST STAND ADD	03	60	54
EASTERN KENTUCKY STEAM POWER L&N	03	50	10
ELESCO FEEDWATER LOCO CLAN	09	78	21
ENGINES BY HERBERT WALLIS GTW	02	43	10
EVOLUTION OF STREAMLINE ENCLOSURE	07	52	15
EVOLUTIONARY STAGES OF LACKAWANNA LOCOS	07	42	51
EXPERIMENTAL D&H #1403 ALCO 1933	01	45	33
FACTORS IN LOCOMOTIVE DESIGN	12	41	42
FAMOUS ALCO LOCOMOTIVES	10	48	26
FEEDWATER HEATERS	06	42	5
FIRELESS LOCOMOTIVES	07	45	34
FIRST LOCOMOTIVE IN MAINE "PIONEER"	06	43	37
FLYING SCOTSMAN PHOTO ESSAY	01	70	16
FORNEY "ARIEL" LOCO EARLY CAB FORWARD	03	48	20
FORNEY AND FAIRLIE LOOK ALIKES	03	43	44
GARRATT LOCOMOTIVES OF GREAT BRITAIN	06	44	32
GARRATTS IN CRISIS	04	66	25
GARRATTS IN SOUTH AFRICA	04	61	36
GATHERING OF IRON HORSES SACRAMENTO CAL	08	81	16
GEARED POWER OF PICKERING LUMBER	01	55	28
GIESL OBLONG INJECTOR EXTEND STEAMS LIFE	01	68	27
GLOVER MACHINE WORKS LOCO PRODUCTION	03	68	26
GREAT DYNAMOMETER TEST LOCO S #610	02	78	33
GREAT NORTHERN ARTICULATED LOCOMOTIVES	12	43	28
HEISLER OF 1940 (FIRELESS)	02	83	39
HELPER ENGINES	04	43	28
HIAWATHA MILW	02	41	47
HIGH SPEED WATER SCOOPS	04	45	6
HISTORY OF ALCO JOHN PLAYER-MAN IN POWER	04	44	6
HOW TO START A SHAY PHOTO ESSAY	08	67	44
I1 THAT LOST HER CYLINDER HEAD	06	81	36
ILLINOIS CENTRAL STEAM POWER RENAISSANCE	03	53	50
IMAGINARY STEAM POWER ON S	06	50	52
INSPECTION LOCOMOTIVES	08	44	36
INSPECTION LOCOMOTIVES	09	49	50
JAWN HENRY 1954-1957	03	58	6
JAWN HENRY CRUSHES A CABOOSE	05	58	60
JOINTED BOILER MALLET LOCOMOTIVES ATSF	02	45	29
KITSON MEYER LOCOMOTIVES	08	61	40

STEAM LOCOMOTIVE PROTOTYPE DATA

	M	Y	P
LAST LOCO MALLET?	06	81	33
LIMA LOCOMOTIVE WORKS -LOCOS NEVER BUILT	03	52	18
LIMA LOCOMOTIVE WORKS SUPER POWER	01	52	13
LIMA MASTERS OF LOCOMOTIVES DESIGN	06	48	12
LOCOMOTIVE "GENERAL" RESTORATION OF	07	62	18
LOCOMOTIVE "MALLET-GARRATT" PROPOSED	02	73	36
LOCOMOTIVE BUILDERS PLATES	02	48	50
LOCOMOTIVE ESTHETICS AND ARCHITECTURE	04	56	26
LOCOMOTIVE FACES-SMOKEBOXES	08	56	21
LOCOMOTIVE INJECTORS AND HOW THEY WORK	01	48	42
LOCOMOTIVE MONARCH! KING GEORGE V	04	73	36
LOCOMOTIVE UTILIZATION	11	46	17
LOCOMOTIVES IN WWI & WWII USWD	12	64	20
LOCOMOTIVES OF CAPITAL LIMITED 1933-36	03	50	38
LOCOMOTIVES OF MP	05	42	4
LOCOMOTIVES OF NDEM PHOTO ESSAY	04	62	26
LOCOMOTIVES OF WISCONSIN CENTRAL	04	43	44
LOCOMOTIVES ON DISPLAY (LIST)	05	56	53
LOCOMOTIVES YOU DIDN'T EXPECT TO MEET	01	59	20
LOCOS WE SAW BUT NEVER SAW-UNDER STREAML	12	84	28
LONG-LEGGED STEAM LOCOMOTIVES	07	80	22
M-10002 UP NORTHROP COAL TURBINE	10	57	25
MALLET MAKESHIFT LOCOMOTIVES	11	57	19
MILWAUKEE ROAD POWER PHOTO ROSTER	12	45	30
MODERNIZATION OF OLD STEAM LOCOMOTIVES	01	49	48
N&W MODERN STEAM POWER	04	47	14
N&W NOMAD MOUNTAIN TO WHEELING	03	79	44
N&W STEAM LOCOMOTIVE DEVELOPMENT	11	54	19
N&W UNUSUAL LOCOMOTIVES	01	53	57
N&W'S NOMAD MOUNTAINS	02	79	48
NAME THE NAMED STEAM LOCOS PHOTO QUIZ	03	74	44
NAT'L PARK SERV REPLICAS JUPITER/UP #119	10	79	67
NORTHERN PACIFIC STEAM POWER	07	49	47
NYNH&H WARTIME REBUILDING	02	43	12
OR&NC ENGINES OF 1889	06	43	40
PARADE OF THE IRON HORSE	11	43	18
PILOTS AND COWCATCHERS--SYMBOLISM OF ART	01	56	39
POLE ROAD LOCOMOTIVES OF EARLY DAYS	02	48	27
PROPOSED BUT NEVER BUILT LOCOMOTIVES	09	75	30
PRR UNUSUAL LOCOMOTIVES	10	49	14
PRR UNUSUAL LOCOMOTIVES OF PRR	10	62	36
READER STEAM POWER GI IN CIVVIES	08	66	27
READERS DECISION FOR STEAM	12	64	40
REBIRTH OF WORLDS MOST BEAUTIFUL 4-8-4	07	75	16
RETURN OF THE CHALLENGER	03	54	6
ROSTER OF LOCOS NKP CLASS S STATISTICS	10	62	24
SALUTE TO THE GENERAL	03	57	15
SCRAPPED-END OF LINE FOR WEARY STEAM	02	51	47
SCRAPPING AND DISMANTLING STEAM LOCOS	06	42	32
SECONDHAND LOCOMOTIVE PHOTO QUIZ	03	75	29
SECONDHAND SHORTLINE STEAM PHOTO QUIZ	12	63	40
SHAY COLUMBIA LIMA 1893	09	41	14
SHAY INSULAR LUMBER COMPANY #8 LIMA	01	52	14
SHAY LAST BUILT BY LIMA NMLC #7	07	77	22
SHAY LOCOMOTIVE FOLLY WORTH A FORTUNE	08	67	33

LOCOMOTIVES

STEAM LOCOMOTIVE PROTOTYPE DATA

	M	Y	P
SHAY LOCOMOTIVE VALVE ACTUATION	03	66	59
SHAY LOCOMOTIVES	07	41	28
SHAY OF LIMA STONE COMPANY #10	12	54	52
SMOKE BOX FRONT/LOCO NATIONALITY PH QUIZ	09	65	25
SMOKE DEFLECTORS HOW TO GET RID OF SMOKE	03	50	32
SONG OF THE SHAY	08	51	22
SOUTHERN VALVE GEAR	05	84	35
SOVIET SEARCH FOR SUPER POWER	01	61	26
SP ARTICULATED LOCOMOTIVES	04	41	41
SP CAB IN FRONT LOCOMOTIVES	08	68	20
SP CAB-IN-FRONT	05	41	41
SP CLASS AC CAB IN FRONT LOCOMOTIVE	11	62	28
SPARK DEFECTORS	02	46	48
SPECIFICATIONS OF L&N CLASS M1 LOCOS	12	72	36
STANDARDIZATION OF STEAM LOCOMOTIVES	12	47	43
STEAM CENTIPEDE STILLBORN	02	73	36
STEAM ENGINE SERVICING ON D&TSL	10	47	21
STEAM LOCOMOTIVE - TO BE REPLACED?	03	41	5
STEAM LOCOMOTIVE MACHINERY DETAILS	09	85	36
STEAM QUIZ BY WILLIAM YOUNG	01	66	49
STEAM SAFARI D-I-E-S-E-L?	06	54	19
STEAM SAFARI EUREKA FOUND'EM	05	54	54
STEAM SAFARI IN CANADA	04	54	24
STEAM TURBINE LOCOMOTIVES C&O 1947 B	08	47	7
STEAM-ELECTRIC TUG OF WAR	07	70	18
STEPHENSON VALVE GEAR	05	84	35
STREAMLINE A STEAM LOCO HOW TO DO IT	03	73	35
STREAMLINED MAKESHIFTS	03	50	46
STYLE OF STEAM IN ITS BIRTHPLACE BRITIAN	11	68	29
SUPER ARTICULATED LOCOMOTIVES (PROPOSED)	08	51	46
SUPERIORITIES OF AMERICAN LOCOMOTIVES	08	67	23
SWITCH ENGINES	02	42	4
TALL STACKED OLD TIMERS	06	45	36
THREE CYLINDER LOCOMOTIVES	03	66	59
TREVITHICK LOCOMOTIVES OF EARLY 1800'S	07	63	40
TURBINES PROPOSED BY C&O	05	45	5
TWENTIES REVISITED PHOTO ESSAY	05	70	29
UGLY STEAM LOCOS-ROLLING MUD FENCE	02	85	29
UNUSUAL STEAM LOCOMOTIVES ATSF	08	63	47
VALVE GEAR 5 TYPES	05	84	34
VALVE GEAR STEPHENSON	05	84	35
VALVE GEAR WALSCHAERT	05	84	35
VALVE GEAR WALSCHAERT HOW IT WORKS	11	47	26
VALVE GEAR YOUNG	05	84	35
VALVE GEAR YOUNG ROTARY VALVES	07	47	64
VIRGINIAN STEAM POWER	12	53	50
WALSCHAERT VALVE GEAR	05	84	35
WAR BABIES RAILROADS REBUILD LOCOS	05	43	41
WAR ENGINES - PERSIA - BRITISH ISLES	07	43	48
WASHING LOCOMOTIVES	01	42	26
WASHOUT IN THE ROUNDHOUSE	01	57	39
WATER HOLES FOR IRON HORSES	06	44	18
WHEELS-HIGH WHEELS-LOW EFFICIENCY	02	57	16
WHY NP CLASS Z5 WAS BUILT	11	41	46
WOOD BURNING LOCOMOTIVES	11	46	52
WOOD BURNING LOCOS ON FLORIDA LUMBER RDS	03	51	12
YOUNG VALVE GEAR	05	84	35

STEAM LOCO PROTOTYPE DATA BY ROAD

RD		M	Y	P
AB&CO	2-8-2 CLASS AM-2 AB&CO #332 ALCO 1914	06	50	47
	4-8-2 CLASS AM-1 AB&CO #372 ALCO 1924	06	50	47
	4-6-2 CLASS AJ-2 AB&CO #175 LIMA 1914	06	50	47
	4-6-0 CLASS AW-4 AB&CO #124 1907	06	50	47
ACL	0-8-0 CLASS E14 ACL #1227 BALDWIN 1923	06	50	45
	4-6-0 TEN WHEELER ACL #210	11	43	24
	2-10-0 CLASS O ACL #8005 B 1920	06	50	46
	2-8-2 CLASS M2 ACL #836 B 1918	06	50	46
	2-8-2 CLASS M ACL #813 B 1911	06	50	45
	0-6-0 CLASS E13 ACL #1150 B 1920	06	50	45
	0-6-0 CLASS E10 ACL #1124 B 1912	06	50	45
	0-4-0 A-DUMMY SWITCHER ACL #1434 B 1905	06	50	45
	4-8-4 CLASS R-1 ACL #1800 B 1938	06	50	44
	4-8-2 CLASS J-1 ACL #1401 BLW	06	50	44
	4-6-2 CLASS P-5B ACL #1732 B 1922	06	50	44
	4-6-2 CLASS P-5A ACL #1530 ALCO 1918	06	50	44
	4-6-2 CLASS P-4 ACL #457 B 1917	06	50	44
	4-6-2 CLASS P ACL #263 B	06	50	43
	4-6-0 CLASS K14 ACL #254 B 1910	06	50	43
	4-6-0 REBUILD ACL #386 B 1920	06	50	43

LOCOMOTIVES

STEAM LOCO PROTOTYPE DATA BY ROAD

RD		M	Y	P
	4-6-0 CLASS K6 ACL #359 B 1904	06	50	43
	4-4-2 CLASS I ACL #89 B 1895	06	50	42
	2-4-2 COLUMBIA TYPE ACL #93 B 1895	06	50	42
	ACL STEAM POWER	06	50	42
	2-8-2 CLASS AM-2 ACL #7332 ALCO 1914	06	50	47
	4-8-2 CLASS AM-1 ACL #7372 ALCO 1924	06	50	47
	4-6-2 CLASS AJ-2 ACL #7175 LIMA 1914	06	50	47
	4-6-0 CLASS AW-4 ACL #7124 B 1907	06	50	47
	2-10-2 CLASS Q1 ACL #2001 B 1925	06	50	46
	AB&C LOCOMOTIVES TO ACL	11	76	31
AD&SL	2-4-4 INSPECTION LOCO AD&SL #99	08	44	36
AL	2-8-0 USA SWITCHER #6998 (ALASKA ROAD)	01	44	46
ATSF	4-8-4 NORTHERN SERIES 2900 ATSF #2903 B	06	44	17
	4-8-4 NORTHERN SERIES 3776 ATSF #3780 B	06	44	17
	4-8-4 DIARY OF A LOCOMOTIVE ATSF #3761 B	03	48	16
	2-6-6-2 MALLET FLEXIBLE BOILER ATSF#3322	02	45	33
	2-6-6-2 MALLET FLEXIBLE BOILER ATSF#3321	02	45	33
	2-6-6-2 MALLET COMPOUND ATSF #1158 1910	02	45	32
	2-6-6-2 MALLET COMPOUND ATSF #1157 1910	02	45	32
	2-10-10-2 MALLET ATSF #3000 1911	02	45	31
	4-4-6-2 MALLET COMPOUND ATSF #1398 1909	02	45	30
	2-8-8-2 MALLET ATSF #1700	02	45	30
	JOINTED BOILER MALLET LOCOMOTIVES ATSF	02	45	29
	2-10-2 COMPOUND ATSF #911	09	51	47
	2-10-10-2 COMPOUND ATSF #3000 TS 1911	09	51	45
	4-6-4 SL HUDSON "BLUEBIRD" ATSF #3460 B	01	53	52
	2-6-6-2 ODD MALLET ATSF #1157	11	57	21
	2-10-10-2 ODD MALLET ATSF #3001	11	57	21
	4-8-4 ATSF #3764 CAPROTTI VALVE GEAR B	08	63	47
	4-4-6-2 ATASF #1301 LARGEST PASS LOCO	08	63	48
	2-8-2 ATSF #4007 COFFIN FEEDWATER HEATER	08	63	49
	UNUSUAL STEAM LOCOMOTIVES ATSF	08	63	47
	2-10-4 TEXAS TYPE LOCOMOTIVES ATSF	08	75	ALL
	4-6-4 CLASS 3460 STREAMLINED ATSF #3460	06	85	22
	4-6-4 CLASS 3460 ATSF #3462 1937 BALDWIN	06	85	22
B&O	4-6-2 PACIFIC "CINCINNATIAN" B&O #5301 B	10	53	30
B&A	4-4-0 INSPECTION LOCO B&A #31 1869	09	49	30
B&LE	2-10-4 TEXAS TYPE CLASS H16 B&LE #647 B	12	44	19
B&M	4-8-2 MOUNTAIN CLASS R-1D B&M #4113 1941	02	48	46
	4-8-2 CLASS R10 B&M #4117 BEAUTIFUL BALD	10	68	18
B&O	2-8-8-4 CLASS EM-1 YELLOWSTONE B&O #7600	10	44	20
	0-6-0T DISGUISED AS A STREETCAR B&O #316	03	44	38
	B&O "WARBABY" REBUILDING	05	43	40
	4-6-2 B&O PRESIDENT SERIES	03	41	13
	4-6-4 HUDSON "LORD BALTIMORE" B&O	09	42	12
	4-4-4 LOCOMOTIVE "LADY BALTIMORE" B&O	09	42	12
	4-6-2 PACIFIC CLASS P-7 PRESIDENTS B&O	06	51	45
	4-8-4 PROPOSED CONSTANT TORQUE LOCO B&O	08	49	28
	4-6-4 LORD BALTIMORE DIES B&O 1935	09	49	62
	2-6-8-0 ODD MALLET CLASS O B&O #2421	11	57	20
	4-4-4-4 DUPLEX CLASS N-1 B&O	09	64	24
	2-8-2 CLASS Q3 B&O 1918 BALDWIN	06	85	34
	2-10-2 CLASS S1 B&O #6200 1927 B	11	83	58
B&P	0-4-6 FORNEY C. H. WARREN (B&P) 1886	03	43	44
BE&CH	4-6-0 BE&CH #31 ENGINED WALKED IN SLEEP	07	49	40
BR&P	2-8-8-2 CLASS XX BR&P #801 WRECK	02	52	56
C&O	4-8-2 WHAT HAPPENED TO C&O #317	07	83	42
C&A	2-6-0 MOGUL REFUSED TO CAPITULATE	05	84	29
C&BL	0-8-0 SWITCHER C&BL #47 LIMA 1941	01	44	46
C&EI	2-8-2 CLASS N2 C&EI	01	42	51
C&NP	2-6-6 C&NP #24 1893 BROOKS LOCO WORKS	08	46	41
C&NW	2-8-0 CONSOLIDATION CLASS Z REBUILT C&NW	12	43	35
	4-8-4 NORTHERN CLASS H C&NW	07	42	5
	4-6-4 SL HUDSON CLASS E-4 C&NW #4002	11	53	54
	4-6-0 C&NW #836 SIMPLE TO COMP TO SIMPLE	04	62	49
	4-8-4 NORTHERN CLASS H C&NW 3000 SERIES	10	70	20
	2-8-4 CLASS J4 C&NW #2806 1927 ALCO	06	85	42
	4-6-4 CLASS E4 C&NW 1938 ALCO	06	85	22
	4-6-4 C&NW CLASS E4 UNDER STREAMLINER	12	84	32
C&O	4-6-4 HUDSON CLASS L-2 C&O #305 B 1941	09	43	35
	4-8-4 NORTHERN CLASS J-3 C&O #600 LIMA	09	43	34
	4-4-2 CLASS A16 C&O	11	41	31
	STEAM TURBINE LOCOMOTIVES C&O 1947 B	08	47	7
	2-6-6-6 ALLEGHENY CLASS H-8 C&O #1603 L	05	48	39
	4-8-4 NORTHERN CLASS J-3A C&O #605	09	43	34
	2-10-4 CLASS T1 C&O #3004	10	49	18
	4-8-2 MOUNTAIN C&O #316 ALCO 1911	02	56	45
	2-10-4 CLASS T1 C&O #3000 LIMA 1930	10	62	20
	2-6-6-6 ALLEGHENY CLASS H-8 C&O LIMA	07	56	50
	4-6-4 CLASS L-2 HUGE HUDSONS C&O #305	05	61	46
C&U	2-8-4 CLASS K4 C&U #2744 LIMA	11	46	61
CB&Q	4-4-0 INSPECTION LOCO CB&Q #475	09	49	51
CBELT	4-8-4 NORTHERN CLASS L-1 CBELT #815	04	43	4
CGA	4-8-4 NORTHERN CGA #455 LIMA 1944	01	45	39
CGW	CGW INTERESTING & ODD STEAM POWER	09	65	20
	2-10-4 CLASS T CGW #884 LIMA 1930	02	78	28
CH&B	0-4-2 CH&B #2 PORTER	08	46	41
CL	4-6-6-4 ARTICULATED CL #655 ALCO 1943	07	43	40
	4-6-0 TEN WHEELER #1 CL TOMS ENGINE	03	73	18
CM&STP	4-6-2 FIRST PACIFIC 1889 CM&STP SHOPS	05	43	44
CMSP&P	4-6-4 CLASS F-7 CMSP&P 1938 ALCO	06	85	22
CN	4-8-4 CLASS U2H CN #6249	06	44	16
	4-8-2 MOUNTAIN CLASS U-1F CN #6060 1945	10	45	38
	4-8-4 NORTHERN STREAMLINED	03	73	35
CNJ	CNJ CAMELBACK LOCOMOTIVES	06	53	57
	4-8-0 CAMELBACK MASTODON CNJ #477	06	53	59
	2-8-0 CAMELBACK CNJ #678 ALCO	06	53	59
	0-8-0 CAMELBACK SWITCHER CNJ #294 1918	06	53	58
	0-6-0 CAMELBACK SWITCHER CNJ #37	06	53	58
	4-6-0 CAMELBACK CNJ #788 1918	06	53	56
	4-6-0 CAMELBACK CNJ # 180 BLW	06	53	56
	4-4-2 CAMELBACK ATLANTIC CNJ #803 R 1912	06	53	56
	4-6-0 CAMELBACK CNJ #423 B 1893	06	53	56
	4-6-0 CAMELBACK CNJ #754 BALDWIN	03	56	26
	4-6-0 CLASS L8 & T40 CNJ STANDARD 1918 B	10	73	26
	4-6-0 TEN WHEELER CNJ #774	10	71	18
CP	4-6-2 PACIFIC CLASS G-5 CP #1200 1944	07	44	40
	4-6-2 PACIFIC CLASS C-3G CP #2400 CLC	01	44	40
	2-8-2 MIKADO CLASS P-2H CP#5417 CLC 1943	01	44	44
	2-8-2 CLASS P1N CP #5200 CP SHOPS	05	47	60

LOCOMOTIVES

STEAM LOCO PROTOTYPE DATA BY ROAD

RD		M	Y	P
	2-8-0 CLASS N2 CP #3718 1946 CP SHOP	05	47	60
	4-4-4 JUBILEE CLASS F-2A CP #3002 MLW	04	53	36
	4-6-2 PACIFICS CP #1262	02	54	51
	4-6-4 CP H1 SPECIFICATIONS	08	69	26
	CP TRIPLE HEADER PHOTO ESSAY	08	60	46
	2-8-2 IMPRESSIONS OF CP #5137 PHOTO ESSA	09	61	40
	4-6-4 CLASS H1 "ROYAL HUDSON" CP #2857	08	69	20
	4-8-4 NORTHERN CP LONELY CANADIAN 4-8-4S	01	76	20
	4-4-4 JUBILEE UNDER THE STREAMLINER CP	12	84	29
CRB&L	4-4-0 MODIFIED TO 2-6-0 CRB&L #9	09	50	44
CS	4-2-2 CS FONTAINE LOCOMOTIVE	12	47	61
D&H	4-8-4 NORTHERN CLASS K-62 D&H #308 ALCO	10	43	46
	4-6-6-4 LOCOS OF D&H	08	41	19
	EXPERIMENTAL D&H #1403 ALCO 1933	01	45	33
	D&H STEAM LOCOMOTIVE DEVELOPMENT LOREE	07	52	20
	2-8-0 CONSOLIDATION DEVELOPMENT D&H 1	04	67	38
	2-8-0 CONSOLIDATION DEVELOPMENT D&H 2	05	67	20
	2-8-0 CONSOLIDATION DEVELOPMENT D&H 3	06	67	39
	2-8-0 D&H #853 ERECTION PHOTO ESSAY	12	74	49
D&RGW	4-6-6-4 CHALLENGER CLASS L97 D&RGW #3800	08	44	29
	4-8-4 NORTHERN CLASS M-68 D&RGW #1804 B	12	43	29
	AUXILIARY SAND BOXES D&RGW	06	41	46
	2-8-2 NARROW GAUGE MIKADO D&RGW	09	61	20
	4-8-4 CLASS M68 D&RGW #1804 1938 BALDWIN	05	84	24
D&TSL	STEAM ENGINE SERVICING ON D&TSL	10	47	21
DL&W	DL&W STEAM LOCOMOTIVE DEVELOPMENT	09	65	28
DO&C	2-6-0 DOWLING & CAMP #12 B 1906	03	51	15
	4-4-0 DOWLING & CAMP #103 B 1913	03	51	15
DSP&P	2-6-6 MASON BOGIE DSP&P #55	04	43	24
DT&I	0-6-0 LOCOMOTIVE OF 1863 DT&I	01	42	37
E	2-8-8-8-2 TRIPLEX CLASS P1 E#5014 B 1914	11	44	14
	4-6-2 PACIFIC TYPE E	11	40	7
	2-8-4 BERKSHIRE CLASSES S-3 & S-4 ERIE	02	48	8
	2-6-8-0 ODD MALLET E #2900	11	57	20
	2-8-4 CLASS S-4 E #3389 LIMA 1929	10	62	20
E&WV	4-2-2 INSPECTION LOCO E&WV #40	01	49	64
F&CC	4-6-0 TEN WHEELER #20 F&CC SLW 1899	10	54	53
FRIS	4-6-2 FIREFLY FRIS	09	41	19
FW&D	4-6-2 CLASS S3A1 FW&D #553	08	69	18
G	0-8-0 SWITCHER G #801	02	77	52
GM&O	4-6-2 M&O #268 TO GM&O #576 AFTER MERGER	10	43	48
GN	GREAT NORTHERN ARTICULATED LOCOMOTIVES	12	43	28
	4-8-4 CLASS S-1 GN SPECIFICATIONS	01	69	41
	2-8-2 CLASS O-8 GN SPECIFICATIONS	01	69	41
	4-8-4 MONTANA TYPE CLASS S1 & S2 GN#2577	07	67	18
	2-8-2 MIKADO CLASS O-8 GN #3397	01	69	38
GTW	ENGINES BY HERBERT WALLIS GTW	02	43	10
GW	2-6-6-2 ODD MALLET GW #652	11	57	21
H&NY	4-2-0 H&NY LOCO 1864 ROGERS	12	46	61
IC	2-4-4T SUBURBAN LOCOMOTIVE IC #1402	10	43	44
	4-8-2 MOUNTAIN TYPE 2600 CLASS IC #2600	05	43	29
	4-6-0 OF IC	02	41	46
	4-8-2 IC #2500	10	41	13
	2-8-2 SUPERCHARGED MIKADO IC #3791	08	46	40
	0-10-2 IC 3600 CLASS #3601 B 1922	03	53	53

STEAM LOCO PROTOTYPE DATA BY ROAD

RD		M	Y	P
	0-8-2 IC 3650 CLASS SWITCHER#3699 B 1911	03	53	53
	0-8-0 IC 3500 CLASS SWITCHER #3532 1921	03	53	52
	0-6-0 IC SWITCHER #333 COOKE 1918	03	53	52
	0-6-0T IC SHOP SWITCHER #3287 B 1898	03	53	52
	4-8-2 IC 2600 SERIES #2600 IC SHOPS 1942	03	53	52
	4-8-2 IC 2500 SERIES #2511 IC SHOPS 1937	03	53	52
	4-6-2 IC 2031 SERIES #2037 ALCO 1905	03	53	51
	4-6-2 IC 1135 SERIES #1171	03	53	51
	4-6-2 IC 1000 SERIES #1002	03	53	51
	4-8-2 IC MOUNTAIN #2431 ALCO 1923	03	53	50
	ILLINOIS CENTRAL STEAM POWER RENAISSANCE	03	53	50
	2-8-4 CLASS A1 IC #8049 LIMA	01	52	16
	2-6-6-2 IC HUMP POWER #6003 RLW 1919	03	53	56
	4-6-4 IC HUDSON REBUILD #2499 IC SHOPS	03	53	56
	4-4-2 IC BRANCH LINE ATLANTIC #2009 R	03	53	56
	2-10-2 IC 2800 SERIES #2801	03	53	56
	2-10-2 IC 2700 SERIES #2700 IC SHOPS	03	53	56
	2-10-0 IC 3610 SERIES MIKADO #3610	03	53	55
	2-8-4 LIMA CLASS MIKADO #8015 1926	03	53	55
	2-8-2 IC 3766 SERIES MIKADO #3792	03	53	55
	2-8-2 IC 2100 SERIES MIKADO #2115	03	53	55
	2-8-2 IC 1700 SERIES MIKADO #1711	03	53	55
	2-8-2 IC 1500 SERIES MIKADO #1561	03	53	54
	2-8-2 IC 1200 SERIES MIKADO #1207	03	53	54
	2-8-0 IC 900 SERIES CONSOLIDATION #906 B	03	53	53
	2-8-0 IC 700 SERIES CONSOLIDATION #700	03	53	53
	2-6-0 IC MOGUL #3709 1901	03	53	53
IHB	0-8-0 CLASS U4A IHB	02	42	43
	0-8-0 U4A CLASS IHB #102	01	68	18
L&HR	4-8-2 MOUNTAIN TYPE L&HR#10 BALDWIN 1944	12	44	19
L&N	2-8-2 CLASS J4A MIKADO L&N #1903 B 1929	02	47	61
	4-6-2 CLASS K-5 PACIFIC L&N 275 ALCO	02	47	61
	4-4-0 CLASS D-21 AMERICAN L&N #143 B	02	47	61
	EASTERN KENTUCKY STEAM POWER L&N	03	50	10
	2-8-4 BERKSHIRE CLASS M-1 L&N #1967 B	05	53	22
	4-6-2 PACIFIC #295 L&N 1940	03	59	20
	2-8-4 BERKSHIRE CLASS M-1 L&N BIG EMMA	12	72	22
	SPECIFICATIONS OF L&N CLASS M1 LOCOS	12	72	36
LACK	EVOLUTIONARY STAGES OF LACKAWANNA LOCOS	07	42	51
LI	4-6-0 CLASS 65 LI STANDARDS 1923 PRR	10	73	26
LIRR	4-6-0 CLASS 65'S OF LI	05	79	35
LJIP	4-2-2 LJIP #1 YANKEE COME HOME	09	84	21
LOP&G	4-6-0 LOP&G #101	03	51	14
LR	4-6-2 LITRI #10 SMALLEST PACIFIC BUILT	04	83	35
LSC	SHAY OF LIMA STONE COMPANY #10	12	54	52
LSCH	0-4-0 LOCO CATAWISSA LSCH #1832	10	46	66
LV	4-8-4 CLASS T2B LV #5220	06	44	16
	4-2-0 INSPECTION LOCO LV #1 1884	09	49	50
	4-6-0 AMERICAN TYPE 10 WHEELER LV #149	08	54	50
M	4-8-0 MONON #225 1898 BROOKS LOCO WORKS	02	84	30
MAT	2-6-0 MAT #100 MOGUL	03	67	47
MILW	4-8-4 NORTHERN CLASS S-3 MILW #262 1944	11	44	40
	4-8-4 NORTHERN CLASS S-2 MILW #206	11	44	40
	4-8-4 CLASS S2 MILW	12	41	39
	4-4-2 HIAWATHA MILW	04	41	46

LOCOMOTIVES

STEAM LOCO PROTOTYPE DATA BY ROAD

RD		M Y P
	HIAWATHA MILW	02 41 47
	4-8-4 NORTHERN CLASS S-2 MILW #238	01 48 18
	4-4-2 ATLANTIC CLASS A STREAMLINED MILW	05 52 36
	4-6-4 CLASS F6 CMSP&P(MILW) #6402 B 1934	12 63 20
	4-6-4 HIAWATHA UNDER STREAMLINER MILW	12 84 33
	4-4-2 HIAWATHA UNDER STREAMLINER MILW	12 84 30
MP	4-8-4 NORTHERN CLASS N-73 MP#2208 B 1943	12 43 29
	LOCOMOTIVES OF MP	05 42 4
	4-6-2 PACIFIC "MADAM QUEEN" MP #6000	02 50 12
	0-6-0 CONVERTED TO SADDLETANK LOCO MP	07 49 54
	4-8-4 CLASS 2201 MP #2208 1943 BALDWIN	05 84 24
	4-8-4 CLASS 2101 MP #2101 1940 MP SHOPS	05 84 24
	4-8-4 CLASS 1901 MP #1922 1930 LIMA	05 84 24
	4-8-4'S OF MP SEDALIA SHOPS	05 84 20
	4-6-2 REBORN LOCOMOTIVE MP #6001	10 78 26
MWCOG	0-2-2-0 #10 MT WASHINGTON COG RAILWAY	05 73 41
N&W	2-8-8-2 ARTICULATED CLASS Y-6A N&W #2156	08 43 24
	2-6-6-4 CLASS A N&W #1212 1936 N&W SHOP	04 47 15
	2-8-8-2 CLASS Y6A N&W #2156 N&W SHOPS	04 47 15
	4-8-4 CLASS J N&W #600 1941 N&W SHOPS	04 47 14
	N&W MODERN STEAM POWER	04 47 14
	2-6-6-4 ARTICULATED CLASS A N&W #1212	06 45 30
	4-8-4 NORTHERN CLASS J N&W #600 1941	06 45 30
	2-6-6-4 CLASS A N&W 1238 ONE OF A KIND	03 50 35
	2-8-8-2 ARTICULATED CLASS Y-6 N&W #2197	09 53 32
	N&W UNUSUAL LOCOMOTIVES	01 53 57
	N&W STEAM LOCOMOTIVE DEVELOPMENT	11 54 19
	4-8-4 NORTHERN CLASS J STEAM POWER N&W	12 64 44
	N&W NOMAD MOUNTAIN TO WHEELING	03 79 44
	N&W'S NOMAD MOUNTAINS	02 79 48
	UGLY STEAM LOCOS-ROLLING MUD FENCE	02 85 29
	4-6-2 CLASS E4 N&W #598 ROLLING MUDFENCE	02 85 29
	4-4-2 CLASS J N&W #611 FINEST STEAM LOCO	01 83 44
	4-4-2 CLASS J N&W #611 GREEN FLAGS 1950	01 83 42
	4-8-0'S TO MALLETS TO JAWN HENRY N&W	10 84 36
NC&SL	4-8-4 CLASS J3 NC&SL #587	06 44 16
	4-8-2 CLASS J3 NC&SL #587 ALCO 1942	12 63 24
	4-8-2 CLASS J2 NC&SL #579 ALCO 1930	12 63 24
	4-8-2 CLASS J1C NC&SL #567 B 1925	12 63 24
	4-8-4 NORTHERN CLASS J-3 NC&SL	12 63 22
	4-6-2 PACIFIC "MARIE" NC&SL #535	01 67 20
NDEM	LOCOMOTIVES OF NDEM PHOTO ESSAY	04 62 26
	4-8-2 CLASS QR-1 NDEM B 1946	12 63 24
NH	4-6-2 NH STREAMLINER CLASS I5	12 84 31
NKP	2-8-4 BERKSHIRE CLASS S-1 NKP #730 LIMA	08 43 25
	2-8-4 BERKSHIRE CLASS S-3 NKP #776 LIMA	09 49 39
	CONTEMPORARIES OF NKP S CLASS 2-8-4	10 62 27
	ROSTER OF LOCOS NKP CLASS S STATISTICS	10 62 24
	2-8-4 CLASS S NKP #703 ALCO 1934	10 62 20
	2-8-2 CLASS H-6E NKP #633 LIMA 1923	10 62 20
	2-8-2 MIKADO CLASS S NKP	10 62 18
	2-8-4 BERKSHIRE #759 REFERBISHING NKP	03 69 29
NM&SP	2-8-0 CONSOLIDATION "UNCLE DICK" NM&SP B	10 46 60
NMLC	SHAY LAST BUILT BY LIMA NMLC #7	07 77 22
NP	4-8-4 NORTHERN CLASS A-4 NP #2670 B	06 43 25

STEAM LOCO PROTOTYPE DATA BY ROAD

RD		M Y P
	WHY NP CLASS Z5 WAS BUILT	11 41 46
	4-8-4 NORTHERN CLASS A-1 A-2 A-4 A-5 NP	04 48 28
	2-8-0 CLASS Y-2 NP #1275 1901	07 49 52
	2-8-0 CLASS Y-3 NP #1212 SLW 1901	07 49 52
	2-8-0 CLASS Y NP #36 SLW 1898	07 49 51
	2-10-0 CLASS M NP #2 BALDWIN 1886	07 49 51
	2-6-2 CLASS T NP #2360 BROOKS 1906	07 49 51
	0-8-0 CLASS G2 8 COUPLED NP #1181 ALCO	07 49 50
	0-8-0 CLASS G1 8 COUPLED NP #1172 BLW'19	07 49 50
	0-6-0 CLASS L-10 SIX COUPLED NP #1168	07 49 50
	0-6-0T CLASS L-4 SHOP SWITCHER NP #10 B	07 49 50
	4-8-4 CLASS A-4 NP #2676 BALDWIN 1941	07 49 49
	4-8-4 CLASS A-3 NP #2666 BALDWIN 1934	07 49 49
	4-8-4 CLASS A-1 NP #2626 ALCO 1930	07 49 49
	4-8-4 CLASS A NP #2600 SLW 1926	07 49 49
	4-6-2 CLASS Q6 NP #2256 1923	07 49 49
	4-6-2 CLASS Q5 NP #2241 1920	07 49 48
	4-6-2 CLASS Q4 NP #2222 1910	07 49 48
	4-6-2 CLASS Q2 NP # 2176 ALCO 1906	07 49 48
	4-6-2 CLASS Q NP #2080 BALDWIN 1903	07 49 48
	4-6-0 CLASS S-4 NP #1379 BALDWIN 1902	07 49 48
	NORTHERN PACIFIC STEAM POWER	07 49 47
	4-6-6-4 CLASS Z-8 NP #5139 ALCO	07 49 53
	2-8-8-4 CLASS Z-5 NP #5005 BALDWIN 1930	07 49 53
	2-8-8-2 CLASS Z-4 NP #4503 RLW 1923	07 49 53
	2-8-8-2 CLASS Z-3 NP #4025 ALCO 1913	07 49 53
	2-8-2 CLASS W2 NP #1917 BROOKS 1904	07 49 52
	2-8-2 CLASS W NP #1529 ALCO 1904	07 49 52
	4-4-0 AMERICAN THE LAST LOCO NP #684	08 53 14
	2-8-2 CLASS W5 NP #1844 1923 SLW	07 49 52
	4-8-4 MOUNTAIN "FOUR ACES" TIMKEN NP	11 58 16
	4-6-0 TALES OF A TEN WHEELER NP #1356	08 56 14
	4-6-0 NP STEAMS LAST DAYS PHOTO ESSAY	02 61 24
	4-6-6-4 CHALLENGERS LAST CHANCE NP #5140	05 78 25
	2-8-8-4 NP CLASS Z4 AND SISTERS STATISTS	03 82 27
	2-8-8-4 ONCE WORLDS LARGEST LOCO NP#500	03 82 22
NSO	2-8-4 BANTAM WEIGHT BERKSHIRE NSO #600	09 84 52
NW	4-8-0 CYRANO DE NW #495	01 53 59
	0-4-0 NW #3 VULCAN	01 53 58
	2-8-0 NW #7	01 53 58
	4-8-0 SWITCHER NW #1100 B 1910	01 53 57
	0-8-0T FROM 2-8-0 NW #809 1898	01 53 57
NY&H	0-4-4 SUBURBAN ENGINE NY&H #26	03 43 30
NYC	4-8-2 MOUNTAIN CLASS L-4B NYC #3135 LIMA	09 44 17
	4-8-4 CLASS S1A NYC #6009	11 50 15
	4-4-0 NYC #999	07 41 35
	4-8-4 NIAGARA NYC #6000 ALCO 1945	05 45 36
	4-6-4 NYC #5344 MOST FAMOUS HUDSON ALCO	01 50 47
	4-6-4 CLASS J-1A HUDSON NYC #5200 ALCO	02 56 45
	4-6-4 CLASS K-3Q MODIFIED PACIFIC NYC	02 56 45
	4-6-4 CLASS J HUDSON NYC	11 57 44
	4-6-4 HUDSON CLASS J-3 NYC #5273 ALCO	03 52 30
	4-8-4 CLASS HS-1A COMPOUND NYC #800	02 55 48
	4-4-0 NYC LOCOMOTIVE #999	04 66 18
	4-6-4 HUDSON CLASS J-1 NYC 1931	10 68 41

LOCOMOTIVES

STEAM LOCO PROTOTYPE DATA BY ROAD

RD		M	Y	P
	4-8-4 "SUPER" NORTHERNS NYC 5500 CLOSE	02	75	47
	2-8-2 MIKADO CLASS H-10 NYC WHY LANDMARK	06	75	50
	4-8-4 CLASS S DEVELOPER PAUL KIEFER NYC	03	84	46
NYC&H	4-4-2 COMPOUND NYC&H #3000 SLW	09	51	48
NYCE	0-4-0 LOCOMOTIVE NYC ELEVATED 1879	05	43	28
	0-4-4 FORNEY LOCOMOTIVE NYC ELEVATED	05	43	28
NYNH&H	NYNH&H WARTIME REBUILDING	02	43	12
	4-6-2 CLASS I5 NYNH&H LOCOMOTIVES	09	81	20
OR&NC	OR&NC ENGINES OF 1889	06	43	40
P&R	4-2-2 BALDWIN EXPERIMENTAL OF 1880 P&R	11	49	54
PGE	2-8-8 MIKADO CLASS 282-S-227 PGE #160	02	46	47
PLU	GEARED POWER OF PICKERING LUMBER	01	55	28
PM	2-8-4 BERKSHIRE CLASS N-1 PM #1222 LIMA	08	43	25
PP&B	4-4-0 AMERICAN PP&B #2 1889 ROGERS	09	43	38
PRR	6-8-6 STEAM TURBINE CLASS S-2 PRR #6200	01	45	15
	2-10-4 CLASS J12 TEXAS TYPE PRR	06	43	30
	4-4-4-4 DUPLEX CLASS T-1 PRR	07	43	32
	4-8-2 MOUNTAIN PRR CLASS M-1 1926	03	43	4
	4-6-2 CLASS K4 PRR	12	40	11
	4-8-2 CLASS M1 FREIGHT LOCOMOTIVES PRR	11	47	62
	DUAL HEADLIGHTS FOR PRR	07	48	5
	4-6-2 PACIFIC CLASS K-4 PRR #5495	04	46	38
	4-4-4-4 DUPLEX CLASS T-1 PRR 1842	07	51	28
	PRR UNUSUAL LOCOMOTIVES	10	49	14
	6-8-6 CLASS S2 TURBINE PRR #6200 1944	10	49	19
	2-10-4 CLASS J1 PRR	10	49	18
	2-8-8-2 CLASS HH1 PRR (FORMER N&W)	10	49	18
	2-8-8-0 CLASS HC1 SIMPLE PRR #3700 1919	10	49	17
	0-8-8-0 CLASS CC2 COMPOUND PRR 1919 B	10	49	17
	2-8-2 CLASS L2 USRA PRR #9630	10	49	17
	6-4-4-6 CLASS S1 BIG ENGINE PRR #6100	10	49	16
	0-6-0 USRA SHIFTER CLASS B-28 PRR #7641	10	49	16
	4-6-2 CLASS K5 PACIFICS PRR #5698 1927	10	49	16
	4-4-2 COLE COMPUND PRR #7452 ALCO 1905	10	49	15
	4-4-2 CLASS E28 BALDWIN COMPUND PRR#7451	10	49	15
	4-4-2 FRENCH COMPOUND PRR #2512 1904	10	49	15
	4-4-2 CLASS E1 MOTHER HUBBARD PRR #700	10	49	15
	2-6-6-2 COMPOUND GOES SIMPLE PRR #7518	10	49	10
	2-10-2 CLASS N1 PRR 50 LOCO TRAIN PHOTOS	08	49	64
	4-4-0 AMERICAN CLASS D-16 PRR	08	54	22
	4-4-0 CLASS D16-D16SB DIFFERENCES PRR	08	54	26
	4-6-2 PACIFIC CLASS K-5 PRR	09	57	52
	2-10-0 DECAPOD ON SHAMOKIN BRANCH PRR	11	57	24
	4-6-2 PACIFIC K-4 PRR #1737 1927 PRR	04	52	28
	4-6-2 PACIFIC CLASS K-4S PRR 1928 PRR	08	56	44
	PRR UNUSUAL LOCOMOTIVES OF PRR	10	62	36
	4-6-0 TEN WHEELER CLASS G5S PRR	10	73	24
	2-8-0 CLASS H10 PRR STANDARDS	10	73	24
	2-8-0 CLASS H9 PRR STANDARDS	10	73	24
	2-8-0 CLASS H8SB PRR STANDARDS	10	73	24
	4-6-0 CLASS G5 PRR STANDARDS	10	73	24
	4-4-2 CLASS E6 PRR STANDARDS	10	73	24
	4-6-2 PACIFIC K4 "BROADWAY LIMITED" PRR	10	68	41
	2-8-2 CLASS L1 PRR 1914 PRR SHOPS	06	85	34
	4-4-4-4 CLASS T1 PRR#6110 ST LAST CHANCE	03	77	20

STEAM LOCO PROTOTYPE DATA BY ROAD

RD		M	Y	P
	2-10-0 CLASS I1S PRR #4300 1923 B	11	83	58
	4-4-4 WITNESSING OF A CRIME	04	83	22
	6-4-4-6 PRR CLASS S1 UNDER THE STREAMLIN	12	84	35
	4-4-4 PRR CLASS T1 UNDER THE STREAMLINER	12	84	34
R	4-4-2 INSPECTION LOCO READING #100	08	44	36
	0-4-0 INSPECTION LOCO R "BLACK DIAMOND"	09	49	51
	4-8-4 NORTHERN CLASS T-1 R	12	60	17
	4-6-0 CLASS L6SA R STANDARDS 1905 B	10	73	26
	2-8-2 CLASS M1SA READING REBUILT 1917 B	06	85	34
	2-8-2 CLASS M1SB READING 1916 BALDWIN	06	85	34
	2-8-2 BIG DUTCH MIKADOS READING	06	85	32
	2-8-2 CLASS M1A READING 1912 READING SHP	06	85	34
	2-8-2 CLASS M1SA READING 1913 BALDWIN	06	85	34
	2-10-2 CLASS K1SA R #3011 1922 B	11	83	58
RF&P	2-8-4 BERKSHIRE RF&P #574 LIMA 1943	06	43	24
RI	4-8-4 NORTHERN TYPE RI #5100 ALCO 1944	01	45	39
	4-8-4 NORTHERN CLASS R67B RI #5000 SLW	06	52	28
	4-8-4 LOCOMOTIVES ON ROCK ISLAND	03	81	22
RRR	READERS DECISION FOR STEAM	12	64	40
	READER STEAM POWER GI IN CIVVIES	08	66	27
S	4-6-2 CLASS PS4 S	06	41	35
	4-6-2 PACIFIC CLASS PS-4 S	10	50	20
	IMAGINARY STEAM POWER ON S	06	50	52
	2-8-2+2-8-0 TRACTOR S #4576	11	57	22
	2-10-2+2-6-2 TRACTOR S #5046	11	57	22
	2-8-0 S #385 IN NEW JERSEY	05	66	48
	GREAT DYNAMOMETER TEST LOCO S #610	02	78	33
	DISTINGUISHING FEATURES OF STEAM ON S	10	71	36
	2-8-8-2 CLASS LS1 S #4009 1918 BALDWIN	08	85	50
	4-6-2 PS2 CLASS PACIFICS S	12	78	28
SAL	B&O ARTICULATEDS FROM SAL ROSTER	08	79	49
SCTC	0-10-0T SCTC #598 SPECS	10	64	45
	0-10-0T SCTC #598	09	64	44
SEA	4-8-2 MOUNTAIN CLASS M SEA #240 ALCO	12	52	52
SL&AD	2-4-6 INSPECTION LOCO SL&AD SLW 1892	09	49	50
SOO	2-8-0 COMPOUND SOO #429	09	51	48
	4-8-4 CLASS O20 SOO #5000 1938 LIMA	08	67	18
SOP	0-4-0 FIRELESS COOKER SOP 1910	01	52	19
SP	4-8-4 NORTHERN CLASS GS-6 SP #4462 LIMA	03	44	37
	4-8-2 MOUNTAIN CLASS MT-1 SP #4300 ALCO	05	44	26
	4-6-2 PACIFIC CLASS P-13 SP #633 B 1928	04	43	5
	4-8-4 NORTHERN CLASS GS-4 SP #4454 LIMA	10	43	46
	SP CAB-IN-FRONT	05	41	41
	SP ARTICULATED LOCOMOTIVES	04	41	41
	4-10-0 "EL GOBERNADOR" SP 1883'S BIGGEST	08	42	18
	4-2-4 CP HUNTINGTON SP #1	03	51	48
	4-8-4 NORTHERN CLS GS-4 DAYLIGHT SP#4454	10	52	20
	SP CLASS AC CAB IN FRONT LOCOMOTIVE	11	62	28
	4-6-0 CLASS T40 SP STANDARDS 1917 SP	10	73	26
	SP CAB IN FRONT LOCOMOTIVES	08	68	20
	0-6-0'S CHANGING OF GUARD TAYLOR YD SP	06	78	37
	4-8-4 DAYLIGHT LIKE NO OTHER SP	10	84	24
SR&RL	0-4-4T SR&RL #6	08	83	22
T&P	4-8-2 MOUNTAIN CLASS M-1 & M-2 T&P #908	09	46	27
	2-10-4 TEXAS CLASS I T&P #660	02	53	26

LOCOMOTIVES

STEAM LOCO PROTOTYPE DATA BY ROAD

RD		M	Y	P
	2-10-2 CLASS 61 T&P #505 B 1918	02	78	28
	2-10-4 CLASS T1 T&P #610 LIMA 1925	02	78	28
	2-10-4 LOCOMOTIVES OF T&P	02	78	22
	2-10-2 SANTA FE #524 "SNUFF DIPPER" T&P	10	72	44
TH&B	2-8-4 CLASS A5 TH&B #202 1928 MLW	06	85	40
	2-8-4 CANADA'S ONLY 2-8-4'S TH&B	06	85	41
TP&W	4-8-2 CLASS J3 TP&W #80 ALCO 1937	12	63	24
TW&W	0-4-6 FAIRLIE HERO #187 TW&W	03	43	44
UP	4-6-6-4 CHALLENGER CLASS 307 MB UP #3977	08	44	29
	4-8-8-4 BIG BOY UP 4000 SERIES 1941	07	43	24
	4-6-6-4 UP #3967 ALCO 1942	11	43	25
	4-8-4 LOCOS OF UP	01	41	28
	4-6-6-4 3000 SERIES UP #3951 PHOTO	07	43	27
	4-12-2 UNION PACIFIC #9085 1926	01	45	38
	M-10002 UP NORTHROP COAL TURBINE	10	57	25
	4-8-8-4 BIG BOY UP	11	58	40
	4-8-8-4 BIG BOY UP #4022 ALCO 1941	08	52	58
	4-8-8-4 LOOK AT BIG BOY PHOTO ESSAY UP	05	56	31
	BIG ENGINE THAT DIDN'T UP #8444	02	76	44
	4-6-6-4 UP 3985 RESTORATION	11	82	32
	4-12-2 CLASS 9000 UP 1926 BLW	07	84	19
URR	0-10-2 SWITCHER URR #303 BALDWIN 1936	07	53	54
USA	2-8-2 FOR SALE - NO SALE USA	09	82	37
USRA	2-8-2 LIGHT MIKADO FIRST USRA LOCOMOTIVE	12	60	47
USWD	2-8-2 MIKADO USWD #1624	07	45	40
	2-8-0 CONSOLIDATION USWD #3029	07	45	40
	LOCOMOTIVES IN WWI & WWII USWD	12	64	20
V	2-8-4 CLASS BA V #505 LIMA	11	46	61
	VIRGINIAN STEAM POWER	12	53	50
	2-8-2 CLASS MD V #410 REBUILT #700 B	09	52	22
	2-8-8-2 CLASS AF V #610 REBUILT #700 B	09	52	22
	2-10-10-2 V #800 ALCO 1918	12	53	56
	2-8-8-2 CLASS AF V #610	12	53	56
	2-8-8-2 CLASS USE V #741	12	53	54
	2-8-8-2 CLASS US V #711 ALCO 1919	12	53	54
	2-8-4 CLASS BA V #505 LIMA 1946	12	53	54
	2-8-2 CLASS MCA V #484	12	53	54
	2-8-2 CLASS MC V #462 B 1912	12	53	53
	2-8-2 CLASS MB V #453 B 1910	12	53	53
	0-8-0 CLASS SB V #253	12	53	52
	0-8-0 CLASS SA V #2 ALCO 1909	12	53	52
	4-6-2 CLASS PA V #212 1928	12	53	52
	4-4-0 CLASS EA V #295 B 1906	12	53	52
	2-6-6-6 CLASS AG V #900 LIMA 1945	12	53	55
	2-8-8-8-4 CLASS XA TRIPLEX V#700 B 1916	09	52	22
V&T	4-4-0 V&T GOES TO HOLLYWOOD	01	41	24
	4-6-0 V&T #26 SUICIDE	02	60	26
W	4-6-4 HUDSON CONVERTED FROM 2-8-2 W #700	02	45	35
	2-10-2 SANTA FE SOLD TO OTHER ROADS W	11	49	50
W&LE	2-8-0 COMPOUND W&LE #251 B 1903	09	51	46
	4-8-4 CLASS K3 ON W&LE	03	79	44
	BUILT AT BREWSTER W&LE SHOPS	11	84	52
W&W	4-4 BALDWIN FREIGHT LOCO 1850 W&W	10	41	2
WC	LOCOMOTIVES OF WISCONSIN CENTRAL	04	43	44
WM	2-10-2 CLASS I 2 WM 1112	11	83	54

STEAM LOCO PROTOTYPE DATA BY ROAD

RD		M	Y	P
WP	4-8-4 NORTHERN CLASS 481 WP #485 LIMA	03	44	37
YU	4-4-0 YUCATAN RAILWAYS #81	06	46	32

STEAM LOCOMOTIVE PLANS

	M	Y	P
4-10-0 "EL GOBERNADOR" PLANS CP 1883	08	42	18
4-2-2 DRAWINGS LJIP #1	09	84	26
4-4-4-4-2 PROPOSED COMPOUND DRAWING	06	74	45
4-4-4-4-4 & PEDESTAL TENDER PROPOSED DRA	06	74	45
4-4-4-4-4 PROPOSED COMPOUND DRAWING	06	74	49
4-4-6 PROPOSED LIMA DRAWING	06	74	38
4-6-4-4-4 PROPOSED COMPOUND DRAWING	06	74	49
4-6-6-4 CLASS M-2 W&M #1203 PLANS	12	47	30
4-8-4 SUPER NORTHERN COMPOSITE DRAWING	02	75	52
SHAY DRAWING	07	41	32
SHAY PART IDENTIFCATION DRAWING	08	67	43
WALSCHAERT VALVE GEAR DRAWINGS	11	47	26

STEAM LOCOMOTIVE PLANS BY ROAD

RD		M	Y	P
CP	4-10-0 "EL GOBERNADOR" PLANS CP 1883	08	42	18
LJIP	4-2-2 DRAWINGS LJIP #1	09	84	26
W&M	4-6-6-4 CLASS M-2 W&M #1203 PLANS	12	47	30

LOCOMOTIVES

STEAM LOCOMOTIVE PHOTOS	M	Y	P
0-12-0T OF 1863 PHOTO P&R	07	80	23
0-4-0 "DUMMY" ACL #1434 PHOTO B 1905	12	77	52
0-4-0 CAMELBACK READING #1187 PHOTO	05	59	59
0-4-0 LACKAWANNA #7 PHOTO	02	42	7
0-4-0T PHOTO ROCK #3	08	42	44
0-4-2 BROCKINGS & PEACH ORCHARD #1 PHOTO	04	81	41
0-4-2T BALDWIN PLANTATION #1112 PHOTO	05	83	29
0-4-4-6 CLASS S1 PRR #6100 PHOTO	10	62	37
0-4-4T SOUTHERN #1509 "MAUD" PHOTO	08	42	35
0-6-0 CLASS 1-5A MILW #1455 PHOTO 1903	12	45	31
0-6-0 CLASS B6A WASHT #22 PHOTO	10	62	38
0-6-0 CLASS T2 NH #2423 PHOTO	03	45	40
0-6-0 CN #7518 PHOTO CLC	02	42	6
0-6-0 FRISCO #746 PHOTO	04	47	37
0-6-0 PACIFIC ELECTRIC #1507 PHOTO	06	42	2
0-6-0 PM&Y #9159 CLC PHOTO	02	42	7
0-6-0 SPOKANE PORTLAND & SEATTLE #1 PHOTO	02	42	4
0-6-0 SWITCHER MP #9301	11	77	57
0-6-0 USRA B&O #353 PHOTO BALDWIN 1918	02	42	6
0-6-0T LEHIGH VALLEY #3359 PHOTO BALDWIN	09	42	25
0-6-0T MAUDE CG #8 PHOTO B 1886	06	54	10
0-6-4T H&TL #8 "ST LOUIS" PHOTO MMW 1887	08	72	34
0-6-4T H&TL #9 "SCHOOLCRAFT" PHOTO MMW	08	72	34
0-6-6T GTW #30 PHOTO	02	43	10
0-8-0 2-8-0 REBUILD PHOTO D&H #159 1925	05	67	22
0-8-0 CLASS AS11 S #1894 PHOTO	10	71	32
0-8-0 CLASS B4 PHOTO D&H #83	04	67	41
0-8-0 CLASS S1A N&W #201 PHOTO	11	54	25
0-8-0 CLASS SW8 MP #9773 PHOTO LIMA 1928	05	42	7
0-8-0 CLASS Y3 NH #3420 PHOTO 1920	03	45	40
0-8-0 CLASS Y4 NH # 8604 PHOTO 1924	03	45	40
0-8-0 CN #8353 PHOTO	02	42	7
0-8-0 CNJ #305 PHOTO	08	69	43
0-8-0 CNJ #323 PHOTO BALDWIN 1930	02	42	6
0-8-0 ET&WNC #7 PHOTO ALCO 1906	12	42	19
0-8-0 HEAVY SWITCHER LACK #214 PHOTO	02	42	6
0-8-0 LEHIGH & NEW ENGLAND #132 PHOTO	02	42	7
0-8-8-0 CLASS H D&H #1610 PHOTO D&H SHOP	07	52	21
0-8-8-0 CLASS H HELPER D&H #1611 PHOTO	01	64	36
0-8-8-0 ERIE #2601 UGLY PHOTO	02	85	35
0-8-8-0 MALLET D&H #1600 PHOTO ALCO 1910	07	52	21
2-10-0 CLASS FS1 L&NE #402 PHOTO	11	83	57
2-10-2 3900 SERIES ATSF #3920 PHOTO	08	75	24
2-10-2 B&M #3004 FRONT VIEW PHOTO	06	46	27
2-10-2 C&S #900 PHOTO BALDWIN 1915	11	83	44
2-10-2 CLASS F81 D&RGW #1254 PHOTO ALCO	03	46	42
2-10-2 CLASS L1 NH #3221 PHOTO 1918	03	45	37
2-10-2 CLASS Q1 ACL #2006 PHOTO	12	77	50
2-10-2 CLASS X NYO&W #351 PHOTO ALCO	08	42	28
2-10-2 S #5023 PHOTO	10	73	36
2-10-2 T&P #524 PHOTO	10	72	47
2-10-2 USRA ACL #2007 PHOTO B 1925	08	64	43
2-10-4 ATSF #3829 PHOTO B 1919	08	75	25
2-10-4 BURL #6325 PHOTO	06	68	42
2-10-4 CLASS 2104-S-566 C&O #3004 PHOTO	03	41	10

STEAM LOCOMOTIVE PHOTOS	M	Y	P
2-10-4 CLASS 5000 ATSF #5004 PHOTO 1936	08	75	32
2-10-4 CLASS T1 T&P #600 PHOTO LIMA	02	78	24
2-10-4 CLASS T1A T&P #610 PHOTO LIMA	02	78	24
2-10-4 CLASS T1B T&P #637 PHOTO LIMA	02	78	24
2-10-4 CLASS T1C T&P #640 PHOTO LIMA	02	78	24
2-10-4 CLASS T1D T&P #660 PHOTO LIMA	02	78	24
2-2-0 LILLIPUT LV #24 PHOTO 1862	12	52	55
2-4-0 M&E #7 (SCRAP) PHOTO ALCO 1905	07	52	8
2-4-2 BEAUFORT & MOREHEAD #4 PHOTO	12	52	56
2-4-2T PHOTO SP #1010	12	42	2
2-4-4-2 TAUPO TOCARA #7 N ZEALAND PHOTO	07	63	11
2-6-0 "SIDNEY DILLON" NC #2 PHOTO	01	42	39
2-6-0 ATSF #477 PHOTO	06	69	45
2-6-0 CAMELBACK NYO&W #272 PHOTO	06	42	44
2-6-0 CASSVILLE & EXETER #345 PHOTO	06	42	51
2-6-0 CLASS K1 NH #420 PHOTO 1900	03	45	40
2-6-0 CLASS M4 SP #1681 PHOTO CLW 1900	06	72	36
2-6-0 CR&SJ #2 PHOTO BALDWIN 1902	09	43	12
2-6-0 DETROIT & MACKINAC #116 PHOTO	03	44	35
2-6-0 HIMMLEBERG-HARRISON LUMB CO # 8 PH	04	81	37
2-6-0 MISSISSIPPI RY #10 PHOTO B 1917	05	47	43
2-6-0 OUACHITA & NORTHWESTERN # 2 PHOTO	04	81	38
2-6-0 RF&P #18 PHOTO RLW 1889	04	51	28
2-6-2 ATSF #1207 PHOTO BALDWIN 1903	06	72	34
2-6-2 B&HS #250 PHOTO 1926 B	04	81	38
2-6-2 CLASS K1 MILW #941 PHOTO ALCO	12	45	31
2-6-2 CLIFFSIDE RR # 108 PHOTO	04	81	37
2-6-2 RGE #101 PHOTO SLW 1900	06	72	35
2-6-2 SUPER SMOKEBOX NP #2406 PHOTO 1916	02	69	47
2-6-2+2-6-2 GARRETT PHOTO	06	42	4
2-6-2T TECOPA RR #1 PHOTO BALDWIN 1910	06	72	35
2-6-6-0 DNW&P #200 PHOTO	11	83	44
2-6-6-2 ATSF #1157 UGLY PHOTO	02	85	35
2-6-6-2 ATSF #3321 PHOTO B 1911	08	75	24
2-6-6-2 C&O #1605 PHOTO	06	68	42
2-6-6-2 CLASS H1 CGW #608 PHOTO	09	65	22
2-6-6-2 CLASS L62 D&RGW #1052 PHOTO	03	46	41
2-6-6-2 CLASS MM2 SP #4207 PHOTO 1911 B	08	68	28
2-6-6-2 CLASS N3S MILW #9314 PHOTO	12	45	37
2-6-6-2 PHOTO GN #1800	11	61	29
2-6-6-2 PHOTO SUMPTER VALLEY #250	11	42	49
2-6-6-2 WESTERN PACIFIC #208 PHOTO ALCO	03	42	41
2-6-6-4 BACKHEAD DETAIL PHOTO	08	79	46
2-6-6-4 CLASS A N&W #1200 PHOTO	10	84	41
2-6-6-4 CLASS A N&W #1238 PHOTO	11	54	25
2-6-6-4 CLASS R1 SAL #2501 PHOTO B 1935	08	79	47
2-6-6-4 CLASS R1 SAL #2508 PHOTO B	08	79	45
2-6-6-4 N&W #1212 PHOTO N&W SHOPS 1936	08	79	47
2-6-6-4 P&WV #1101 PHOTO B 1935	08	79	47
2-6-6-4 SAL CLASS R1/R2 DIFFERENCES PHOT	08	79	48
2-6-6-6 ALLEGHENY C&O #1605 PHOTO LIMA	06	74	38
2-6-6-6 C&O 1600 SERIES PHOTOS	03	42	51
2-6-6-6 CLASS H8 C&O #1605 PHOTO L 1941	06	52	26
2-8-0 ARCHABALD 500 LB BOILER D&H #1402	06	67	40
2-8-0 BACKHEAD D&H "HORATIO ALLEN" PHOTO	06	67	42

LOCOMOTIVES

STEAM LOCOMOTIVE PHOTOS	M	Y	P
2-8-0 CA&S #320 PHOTO 1904 BLW	04	81	39
2-8-0 CAMELBACK CLASS P NYO&W #217 PHOTO	08	42	28
2-8-0 CAMELBACK L&NE #152 PHOTO	06	42	42
2-8-0 CAMELBACK REBUILDS PHOTO D&H #942	04	67	42
2-8-0 CK&S #201 PHOTO SLW 1905	04	81	38
2-8-0 CLASS C48 D&RGW #1176 PHOTO 1906	03	46	42
2-8-0 CLASS C7 MILW #1350 PHOTO ALCO	12	45	32
2-8-0 CLASS E1A CAMELBACK PHOTO D&H #244	04	67	38
2-8-0 CLASS E2 CAMELBACK PHOTO D&H #357	04	67	40
2-8-0 CLASS E2A CAMELBACK PHOTO D&H #339	04	67	41
2-8-0 CLASS E3A CAMELBACK PHOTO D&H #221	04	67	45
2-8-0 CLASS E3A CAMELBACK PHOTO D&H #26	04	67	42
2-8-0 CLASS E3A CAMELBACK PHOTO D&H #793	07	52	21
2-8-0 CLASS E3A CAMELBACK PHOTO D&H #806	04	67	43
2-8-0 CLASS E3A CAMELBACK PHOTO D&H #819	04	67	44
2-8-0 CLASS E3A CAMELBACK PHOTO D&H #891	04	67	46
2-8-0 CLASS E4 CAMELBACK PHOTO D&H #349	04	67	41
2-8-0 CLASS E5 CAMELBACK PHOTO D&H #1011	05	67	20
2-8-0 CLASS E5 PHOTO D&H #1054 1908	05	67	20
2-8-0 CLASS E5 PHOTO D&H #1060 1912	05	67	20
2-8-0 CLASS E5 W/DABEG HEATER D&H #1076	05	67	22
2-8-0 CLASS E5A 300 LB BOILER D&H #1114	06	67	43
2-8-0 CLASS E5A FOUR ACES PHOTO D&H#1111	06	67	43
2-8-0 CLASS E6 PHOTO D&H #1200 1916	05	67	23
2-8-0 CLASS E6A PHOTO D&H #1218 1918	05	67	23
2-8-0 CLASS E6A WELDED BOILER D&H #1219	05	67	24
2-8-0 CLASS E71 D&H "HORATIO ALLEN" 1927	07	52	22
2-8-0 CLASS E71 D&H "JAMES ARCHBALD"ALCO	07	52	23
2-8-0 CLASS E71 D&H "JOHN JERVIS" 1927	07	52	22
2-8-0 CLASS F5 NH #153 PHOTO 1912	03	45	37
2-8-0 CLASS G6H B&A #1045 PHOTO SLW	04	42	42
2-8-0 CLASS H5-39 M&SL #455 PHOTO ALCO	12	42	44
2-8-0 CLASS H9 WM #810 PHOTO	11	83	56
2-8-0 CLASS MS1 S #4767 PHOTO	02	43	20
2-8-0 COMPOUND PHOTO D&H #1400 S 1924	06	67	40
2-8-0 CONSOLIDATION CG #509 PHOTO B 1906	06	54	10
2-8-0 CONSOLIDATION OR&NC #83 PHOTO	06	43	40
2-8-0 CONSOLIDATION PHOTO C&I #14	03	71	41
2-8-0 D&H #1400 UGLY PHOTO	02	85	34
2-8-0 H&TL "KITCHIGAMI" CAMELBACK PHOTO	08	72	33
2-8-0 H&TL #13 "VOYAGEUR" PHOTO B 1900	08	72	34
2-8-0 J. JERVIS 400 LB BOILER D&H #1401	06	67	40
2-8-0 L LOREE 500 LB BOILER D&H #1403 PH	06	67	41
2-8-0 MOTHER HUBBARD D&H #793 ALCO 1903	07	52	21
2-8-0 MP #100 PHOTO (INJECTOR PIPING)	01	48	43
2-8-0 PERSHING LOCO PHOTO USA #5724	12	64	30
2-8-0 S #390 ON ARMSTRON TURNTABLE PHOTO	03	73	33
2-8-0 SD&AE #50 PHOTO	06	72	36
2-8-0 TUNNEL EXTENDED STACK GN#1106 PHOT	11	61	29
2-8-0 UPSIDE DOWN VULCAN IOWAC #81	10	55	44
2-8-0 USRA READER RR #1702 PHOTO	01	66	28
2-8-0 WESTERN PACIFIC #1 PHOTO BALDWIN	03	42	41
2-8-0 WESTERN PACIFIC #124 PHOTO BALDWIN	03	42	41
2-8-0 WITH TENDER BOOSTER PHOTO C&I #19	03	71	41
2-8-2 + 2-8-2 GARRATT PHOTO	03	66	50

STEAM LOCOMOTIVE PHOTOS	M	Y	P
2-8-2 1200 SERIES PHOTO MP #1201	11	77	50
2-8-2 AL #701 PHOTO 1927	04	53	45
2-8-2 B&O #4132 PHOTO	08	42	51
2-8-2 BURL CLASS O3 #5325 PHOTO	06	52	4
2-8-2 CLASS H10 NYC #8000 PHOTO LIMA	06	75	52
2-8-2 CLASS H10 PRR #952 PHOTO	06	75	52
2-8-2 CLASS H5G B&A #1218 PHOTO	04	42	42
2-8-2 CLASS J1 NH #3000 PHOTO 1916	03	45	35
2-8-2 CLASS J2A L&N #1480 PHOTO 1914	12	72	34
2-8-2 CLASS J4 L&N #1863	12	72	34
2-8-2 CLASS J4A L&N #1892 PHOTO	06	75	52
2-8-2 CLASS J4A L&N #1892 PHOTO	12	72	34
2-8-2 CLASS J5 L&N #1999 PHOTO 1924	12	72	34
2-8-2 CLASS K27 D&RGW #459 PHOTO 1903	03	46	43
2-8-2 CLASS K37 D&RGW #490 PHOTO 1928	03	46	43
2-8-2 CLASS K3A C&O #2318 PHOTO	06	75	52
2-8-2 CLASS K59 D&RGW #1212 PHOTO B 1913	03	46	39
2-8-2 CLASS L1 PRR #1556 PHOTO	10	62	39
2-8-2 CLASS L1 PRR #2861 EMERSON FIREBOX	10	62	39
2-8-2 CLASS L1AS MILW #8518 PHOTO 1909	12	45	32
2-8-2 CLASS L2 MILW #474 PHOTO BALDWIN	12	45	32
2-8-2 CLASS L3 MILW #360 PHOTO	12	45	33
2-8-2 CLASS M2AS CNJ #875 PHOTO	06	42	9
2-8-2 CLASS M50 M&SL #631 PHOTO	12	42	37
2-8-2 CLASS W3 NP #1728 PHOTO ALCO 1913	02	46	26
2-8-2 CLASS W3 NP #1814 PHOTO	03	82	24
2-8-2 COLUMBUS & GREENVILLE #503 PHOTO	04	81	41
2-8-2 D&SL #407 PHOTO	11	83	45
2-8-2 DM&IR TOP PHOTO	03	58	31
2-8-2 DT&I #800 LIMA 1940 PHOTO	06	42	5
2-8-2 KENTUCKY & TENESEE #7 PHOTO	04	81	39
2-8-2 MIKADO PHOTO C&I #20 PHOTO	03	71	41
2-8-2 MIKADO PHOTO C&I #4 PHOTO	03	71	41
2-8-2 MIKADO PHOTO C&I #5 PHOTO	03	71	41
2-8-2 S #4501 COLOR PHOTO	10	73	30
2-8-2 S #4888 PHOTO	10	71	32
2-8-2 SEA #357 UGLY PHOTO	02	85	34
2-8-2 SUMPTER & CHOCTAW #105 PHOTO	03	44	36
2-8-2 TATUM LUMBER CO #6 PHOTO	04	81	40
2-8-2 USRA MIKADO PHOTO B&O #4500	12	60	49
2-8-2 V #457 UGLY PHOTO	02	85	34
2-8-2 WESTERN PACIFIC #301 PHOTO ALCO	03	42	41
2-8-2T K&M #559 PHOTO	09	47	54
2-8-4 600 SERIES NSO #600 PHOTO B 1940	11	61	32
2-8-4 B&M #4015 COFFIN HEATER PHOTO	02	42	32
2-8-4 CLASS A B&A #1426 PHOTO LIMA 1926	04	42	42
2-8-4 CLASS BK MP #1922 PHOTO	05	42	6
2-8-4 CLASS BK MP #2101 PHOTO	05	42	6
2-8-4 CLASS JA NEW ZEALAND #1210 PHOTO	05	70	24
2-8-4 CLASS K4 C&O #2744 PHOTO	06	52	26
2-8-4 CLASS M1 L&N #1954 PHOTO B 1942	12	72	35
2-8-4 CLASS M1 L&N #1967 PHOTO B 1944	12	72	35
2-8-4 CLASS M1 L&N #1970 PHOTO LIMA 1949	12	72	35
2-8-4 CLASS S2 NKP #759 PHOTO	01	69	36
2-8-4 E #3360 PHOTO	06	68	42

LOCOMOTIVES

STEAM LOCOMOTIVE PHOTOS	M	Y	P
2-8-4 ERIE #3360 BALDWIN 1928 PHOTO	06	42	5
2-8-4 NORFOLK SOUTHERN #600 PHOTO 1940	08	42	34
2-8-4 OR&LC #80 PHOTO	07	44	39
2-8-8-0 CLASS M25 DM&N #210 PHOTO	11	80	33
2-8-8-0 DM&N #2008 PHOTO	11	80	33
2-8-8-2 CC&O #731 PHOTO	10	83	28
2-8-8-2 CLASS AC1 SP #4004 PHOTO	11	62	29
2-8-8-2 CLASS AC2 SP #4028 PHOTO	11	62	29
2-8-8-2 CLASS AC2 SP #4028 PHOTO 1911 B	08	68	27
2-8-8-2 CLASS AC3 SP #4041 PHOTO 1927 B	08	68	29
2-8-8-2 CLASS AC9 SP #3800 PHOTO 1939 L	08	68	30
2-8-8-2 CLASS HH1 PRR #373 PHOTO	10	62	38
2-8-8-2 CLASS L107 D&RGW #3500 PHOTO	03	46	41
2-8-8-2 CLASS L131 D&RGW #3618 PHOTO	03	82	25
2-8-8-2 CLASS L131 D&RGW #3618 PHOTO 1927	03	46	40
2-8-8-2 CLASS L131 D&RGW #3608 PHOTO BLW	04	63	22
2-8-8-2 CLASS L2 WM #924 PHOTO	11	83	56
2-8-8-2 CLASS L95 D&RGW #1075 PHOTOO	03	46	41
2-8-8-2 CLASS M DM&N #206 PHOTO	11	80	33
2-8-8-2 CLASS M1 DM&N #208 PHOTO	11	80	33
2-8-8-2 CLASS M137 WP #259 PHOTO 1938	11	80	36
2-8-8-2 CLASS MC2 SP #4004 PHOTO 1909 B	08	68	27
2-8-8-2 CLASS MC4 SP #4022 PHOTO 1911 B	08	68	27
2-8-8-2 CLASS MCC SP #4043 PHOTO 1913 B	08	68	28
2-8-8-2 CLASS ML MP #4000 PHOTO BALDWIN	05	42	4
2-8-8-2 CLASS Y2 N&W #1700 PHOTO 1918	10	84	42
2-8-8-2 CLASS Y3A N&W #2063 PHOTO ALCO	10	84	42
2-8-8-2 CLASS Y4 N&W #2087 PHOTO ALCO	10	84	42
2-8-8-2 CLASS Y6 N&W #2197 PHOTO	06	68	42
2-8-8-2 CLASS Y6A N&W #2156 PHOTO 1942	10	84	42
2-8-8-2 CLASS Y6B N&W #2197 PHOTO	11	54	25
2-8-8-2 CLASS Y6B N&W #2197 PHOTOGRAPH	10	84	42
2-8-8-2 CLASS Z4 NP #4503 PHOTO	03	82	24
2-8-8-2 CLASS Z5 NP #5002 PHOTO	04	82	44
2-8-8-2 D&RGW #3600 FRONT CLOSE UP PHOTO	05	53	31
2-8-8-2 MALLET N&W #2197 PHOTO	06	74	41
2-8-8-2 NP #4023 PHOTO	02	41	11
2-8-8-4 CLASS M3 DM&IR #223 PHOTO 1941	11	80	36
2-8-8-4 CLASS M4 BACKHEAD PHOTO	11	80	37
2-8-8-4 CLASS M4 DM&IR #231 PHOTO	11	80	36
2-8-8-8-2 TRIPLEX PHOTO E #5016 B 1914	12	52	38
4-10-2 3 CYLINDER SP #5024 PHOTO 1925	06	74	41
4-12-2 OF 1926 PHOTO UP #9000	07	80	25
4-12-2 UP #9000 PHOTO	07	84	21
4-12-2 UP #9000 PHOTO ALCO 1926	06	72	37
4-4-0 "EDWARD KIDDER" W&WR PHOTO	08	42	35
4-4-0 ALBANY & NORTHERN #10 PHOTO 1890	03	44	34
4-4-0 B&P #2 "WM R ROBESON" PHOTO	07	43	28
4-4-0 B&P #62 "STOUGHTON" PHOTO	07	43	28
4-4-0 BALDWIN G&J #3 1902	10	55	64
4-4-0 C&NW #17 PHOTO SLW 1895	07	43	14
4-4-0 C&NW CLASS C5 #685 PHOTO SLW 1888	07	43	29
4-4-0 C&PA #6 PHOTO	07	44	30
4-4-0 CAMELBACK LACKAWANNA #952 PHOTO	07	42	51
4-4-0 CG #349 PHOTO B 1891	06	54	10

STEAM LOCOMOTIVE PHOTOS	M	Y	P
4-4-0 CLASS H8 MILW #34 PHOTO 1904 ROG	12	45	33
4-4-0 CLASS J N&W #19 PHOTO	12	64	46
4-4-0 CNJ #379 PHOTO	03	47	53
4-4-0 CSP&KC #68 PHOTO	09	65	22
4-4-0 GS&G #10 PHOTO	03	44	34
4-4-0 GTW #416 PHOTO	02	43	11
4-4-0 KANSAS PACIFIC "SEMINOLE" PHOTO	05	42	26
4-4-0 LACKAWANA & BLOOMSBURG #2 PHOTO	12	40	2
4-4-0 LNA&C #5 PHOTO	03	44	33
4-4-0 LNA&C #9 PHOTO	03	44	33
4-4-0 LS&MC #136 "SAXON" PHOTO	03	42	21
4-4-0 MA&PA #6 PHOTO RLW 1901	07	52	8
4-4-0 NYNH&H #891 FAMOUS LOCOMOTIVE	12	42	46
4-4-0 SOUTHERN #3841 PHOTO	04	44	37
4-4-0 SOUTHERN #3859 PHOTO 1880	01	45	22
4-4-0 STREAMLINED LACKAWANNA #988	07	42	51
4-4-0 UP #768 CENTER/REAR CAB PHOTO	01	59	23
4-4-0 WISCONSIN CENTRAL #57 PHOTO SLW	04	43	44
4-4-0 WISCONSIN CENTRAL #16 SLW 1882	04	43	44
4-4-0 WM CROOKS SP&P	11	57	15
4-4-2 ANN ARBOR #1614 PHOTO	09	51	28
4-4-2 ATLANTIC CLASS E4 E#536	11	40	6
4-4-2 ATLANTIC CLASS E5 E#537	11	40	6
4-4-2 B&S #274 (RENUMBERED B&O #1484)PHO	02	47	49
4-4-2 CLASS A MILW #3 HIAWATHA PHOTO	12	45	34
4-4-2 CLASS B MILW #3135 PHOTO 1886 B	12	45	33
4-4-2 CLASS B7 MILW #3135 BALDWIN	12	45	33
4-4-2 CLASS E2 ATLANTIC C&EI #222 PHOTO	04	81	35
4-4-2 CLASS H1 NH #1101 PHOTO 1907	03	45	37
4-4-2 CLASS J N&W #606 PHOTO	12	64	46
4-4-2 CLASS J N&W #611 PHOTO ESSAY	01	83	40
4-4-2 INTER #9 W/SOUTHERN VLAVE GEAR PHO	02	54	58
4-4-2 MOTHER HUBBARRB R #343 PHOTO	02	41	16
4-4-2 ROGERS IC #1014 PHOTO ROGERS 1916	09	52	36
4-4-2 S #1914 PHOTO RLW 1906	07	54	20
4-4-2 SINGLE DOME PFW&C #27 PHOTO	04	57	49
4-4-4 READING #110 UGLY PHOTO	02	85	35
4-4-4-4 CLASS N1 DUPLEX B&O #5600 PHOTO	06	78	39
4-4-4-4 CLASS T1 PRR #6110 PHOTO BALDWIN	01	43	29
4-4-6-4 CLASS Q2 PRR PHOTO	10	44	5
4-4-6-4 Q2 PRR #6131 PHOTO	11	59	23
4-4-0 WISCONSIN CENTRAL #90 SLW 1886	04	43	44
4-6-0 ATLANTA & WEST POINT #228 PHOTO	08	42	34
4-6-0 ATSF #466 PHOTO BALDWIN 1894	06	72	34
4-6-0 B&O SOUTH-WESTERN #131 PHOTO BLW	08	43	47
4-6-0 BCR&N #105 PHOTO BLW 1892	08	43	46
4-6-0 BCR&N #71 PHOTO BLW 1896	08	43	46
4-6-0 BLACK MOUNTAIN #1 PHOTO	04	81	34
4-6-0 CAMELBACK CLASS U1 NYO&W #246 PHOT	08	42	28
4-6-0 CLASS G0 CBELT #665 SCULLIN DRIVES	07	51	38
4-6-0 CLASS G4 NH #815 PHOTO 1904	03	45	37
4-6-0 CLASS G5 PRR #5741 PHOTO 1923 PRR	10	73	28
4-6-0 CLASS G6PS MILW #1108 PHOTO	12	45	34
4-6-0 CLASS G8A MILW #2639 PHOTO	12	45	34
4-6-0 CLASS S10 NP #328 PHOTO ROG 1905	11	81	42

LOCOMOTIVES

STEAM LOCOMOTIVE PHOTOS	M	Y	P
4-6-0 CM&SP #820 PHOTO BALDWIN 1892	08	43	46
4-6-0 COLLINS & GLENVILLE #105 PHOTO	03	44	36
4-6-0 COLUMBUS & GREENVILLE # 216 PHOTO	04	81	35
4-6-0 DO&S #2 PHOTO 1907 RL	08	47	61
4-6-0 ET&WNC #10 PHOTO BALDWIN 1910	12	42	19
4-6-0 IC #382 AFTER WRECK PHOTO	04	57	58
4-6-0 LOP&G #100 PHOTO 1936	01	75	60
4-6-0 LOP&G #102 PHOTO 1910	03	44	32
4-6-0 MKT #269 PHOTO	01	43	13
4-6-0 MOTHER HUBBARD CNJ #409 PHOTO	03	47	53
4-6-0 MP #338 PHOTO (REAR)	06	76	39
4-6-0 NP #1354 PHOTO	02	41	11
4-6-0 RUTLAND #45 PHOTO	02	46	29
4-6-0 RUTLAND #57 PHOTO	02	46	29
4-6-0 SUSQUEHANNA #215 PHOTO	08	42	5
4-6-0 TEN WHEELER OR&NC #45 PHOTO	06	43	40
4-6-0 TEN WHEELER PHOTO MP #2325	11	77	52
4-6-0 TEXAS-MEXICAN RY #16 PHOTO	04	51	32
4-6-0 WESTERN PACIFIC #77 PHOTO ALCO	03	42	41
4-6-0 WISCONSIN CENTRAL #211 PHOTO BLW	04	43	44
4-6-2 "LEGIONNAIRE" PHOTO CGW #932	09	65	22
4-6-2 AB&C #71 PHOTO SLW 1911	04	81	36
4-6-2 AL #902 PHOTO BALDWIN 1945	04	63	45
4-6-2 BALDWIN T&P #700 PHOTO	07	72	36
4-6-2 C&EI #1008 PHOTO	02	41	38
4-6-2 C&EI #1008 STREAMLINED PHOTO	02	41	39
4-6-2 CLASS E N&W #597 UGLY PHOTO	02	85	35
4-6-2 CLASS F19 C&O #475 PACIFIC PHOTO	01	41	22
4-6-2 CLASS F19 C&O #490 PHOTO	06	83	23
4-6-2 CLASS F3S MILW #164 PHOTO	12	45	35
4-6-2 CLASS F4MS MILW #6207 PHOTO	12	45	35
4-6-2 CLASS F5B MILW #6361 PHOTO	12	45	35
4-6-2 CLASS G3C CP #2317 PHOTO	02	79	2
4-6-2 CLASS G3S CNJ #831 PHOTO	03	41	10
4-6-2 CLASS GS2 SP #4328 PHOTO	01	42	6
4-6-2 CLASS I1 NH #1026 PHOTO 1926	03	45	36
4-6-2 CLASS I2 NH #1318 PHOTO 1913	03	45	36
4-6-2 CLASS I4 NH #1362 PHOTO 1916	03	45	35
4-6-2 CLASS K1 WM #154 PHOTO	05	41	29
4-6-2 CLASS K2 E #2900 LIMA 1913 PHOTO	11	40	8
4-6-2 CLASS K2A E #2905 ALCO 1917 PHOTO	11	40	9
4-6-2 CLASS K2A ERIE #2912 PHOTO	11	40	9
4-6-2 CLASS K2A L&N #158 PHOTO	02	43	21
4-6-2 CLASS K3 NYC #4806 PHOTO	04	78	36
4-6-2 CLASS K4 E #2711 ALCO 1913 PHOTO	11	40	10
4-6-2 CLASS K4A ERIE #2752 PHOTO	11	40	10
4-6-2 CLASS K4B ERIE #2744 PHOTO	11	40	10
4-6-2 CLASS K5 E #2509 ALCO 1910 PHOTO	11	40	8
4-6-2 CLASS K5 PRR #5698 WALSCHAERTS VLV	08	79	30
4-6-2 CLASS K5 PRR #5699 CAPROTTI VALVE	08	79	30
4-6-2 CLASS K5A E #2940 B 1923 PHOTO	11	40	11
4-6-2 CLASS K5B ERIE #2960	11	40	11
4-6-2 CLASS P MP #1727 PHOTO	05	42	5
4-6-2 CLASS P1 D&H #653 1931 D&H SHOPS	07	52	24
4-6-2 CLASS P16B GM&O #5296 PHOTO	12	50	38

STEAM LOCOMOTIVE PHOTOS	M	Y	P
4-6-2 CLASS P44 D&RGW #1003 PHOTO B 1913	03	46	39
4-6-2 CLASS P5B ACL #1652 PHOTOS	06	76	29
4-6-2 CLASS P7D B&O #5303 PHOTO	11	81	548
4-6-2 CLASS PS4 CRESCENT LIMITED S #1396	07	64	28
4-6-2 CLASS PS4 S #1408 PHOTO 1928 B	10	71	32
4-6-2 CLASS SP3 PM #721 PHOTO	08	45	20
4-6-2 CLASS USRA ERIE #2919 PHOTO	11	40	11
4-6-2 CM&STP #796 PHOTO	05	43	44
4-6-2 CM&STP #830 PHOTO	05	43	44
4-6-2 CNJ #830 PHOTO	08	69	42
4-6-2 CNJ #831 PHOTO	08	69	42
4-6-2 ERIE #953 PHOTO	08	42	5
4-6-2 K4 LOEWY PACIFIC PRR #1120 PHOTO	08	56	53
4-6-2 K4 PACIFIC PRR #1737 PHOTO 1914	08	56	52
4-6-2 K4 PACIFIC PRR #5471 PHOTO 1956	08	56	53
4-6-2 K4 PACIFIC PRR #5495 PHOTO 1928	08	56	52
4-6-2 K4 W/12 WHEEL TENDER PRR #5432 PHO	10	62	40
4-6-2 K4 W/BOOSTER PRR #3676 PHOTO	10	62	40
4-6-2 K4 W/ELEPHANT EARS PRR #5038 PHOTO	10	62	41
4-6-2 K4 W/FRONT-END THROTTLE PRR #3847	10	62	41
4-6-2 K5 PRR #5698 PHOTO	09	57	54
4-6-2 L&N #218 PHOTO	08	42	32
4-6-2 LIGHT PACIFIC RF&P #258 PHOTO	11	46	40
4-6-2 M&SL #503 PHOTO BROOKS 1921	12	42	43
4-6-2 MISSOURI PACIFIC #6001 PHOTO	06	74	41
4-6-2 NP #2218 PHOTO	02	41	11
4-6-2 PACIFIC E #2512 1905	11	40	6
4-6-2 PACIFIC ACL #1533 PHOTO	12	77	50
4-6-2 PACIFIC MOBILE & OHIO #268 PHOTO	04	81	36
4-6-2 PRR #5699 CAPROTTI VALVE GEAR PHOT	09	57	55
4-6-2 PRR K4 WITH DISK DRIVERS PHOTO	06	47	8
4-6-2 S #1332 PHOTO 1914	07	54	21
4-6-2 S #1406 PHOTO	10	71	32
4-6-2 SUSQUEHANNA #953 PHOTO	08	42	4
4-6-2 UP #2889 PHOTO 1914 LIMA	05	76	52
4-6-2 W/FRANKLIN POPPET VALVES PRR #5399	10	62	41
4-6-4 B&A #619 FRONT VIEW PHOTO	06	46	26
4-6-4 C&O #490 STREAMLINED PHOTO	09	71	17
4-6-4 CENTURY HUDSON J3 NYC #5450 PHOTO	11	57	53
4-6-4 CLASS 3460 ATSF #3462 PHOTO 1937 B	03	41	10
4-6-4 CLASS F6 MILW #6414 PHOTO	12	45	36
4-6-4 CLASS F7 MILW HIAWATHA PHOTO ALCO	12	45	36
4-6-4 CLASS I5 WH #1400 PHOTO 1942	03	45	35
4-6-4 CLASS J2B B&A #605 PHOTO ALCO 1930	04	42	42
4-6-4 CLASS S4 CB&O #3000 PHOTO	03	41	10
4-6-4 EMPIRE HUDSON J3 NYC #5429 PHOTO	11	57	53
4-6-4 LACKAWANNA #1155 PHOTO	03	77	37
4-6-4 NYC #4689 PHOTO	12	44	37
4-6-4 NYC #5285 PHOTO	12	44	37
4-6-4 PIONEER HUDSON J1 NYC #5200 PHOTO	11	57	52
4-6-4 SHROUDED HUDSON NYC PHOTO	12	44	36
4-6-4 SUPER HUDSON J3 NYC #5405 PHOTO	11	57	52
4-6-4-4 Q1 (SHOPPED) PRR #6130 PHOTO	11	59	23
4-6-4-4 STREAMLINED Q1 FRT PRR#6130 PHOT	11	59	23
4-6-6-2 CLASS MM2 MODIFIED SP#4210 PHOTO	08	68	28

LOCOMOTIVES

STEAM LOCOMOTIVE PHOTOS	M	Y	P
4-6-6-2 CLASS MM2 SP #4210 UGLY PHOTO	02	85	34
4-6-6-4 CLASS J D&H PHOTO ALCO	07	52	24
4-6-6-4 CLASS L105 D&RGW #3704 PHOTO	03	46	40
4-6-6-4 CLASS L105 D&RGW #3708 PHOTO B	06	52	34
4-6-6-4 CLASS L97 D&RGW #3800 PHOTO 1943	03	46	40
4-6-6-4 CLASS M2 WM #1203 PHOTO	05	41	29
4-6-6-4 CLASS M2 WM #1203 PHOTO	11	83	56
4-6-6-4 CLASS Z6 SP&S #900 PHOTO	02	50	33
4-6-6-4 CLASS Z7 NP #5123 PHOTO ALCO	02	46	26
4-6-6-4 CLASS Z8 NP #5138 DETAIL PHOTO	04	65	40
4-6-6-4 SP&S #900 FRONT END PHOTO	02	53	36
4-6-6-4 WESTERN PACIFIC #402 PHOTO B	03	42	41
4-8-0 CAMELBACK PHOTO C&EI #171 1899 PCLW	02	55	53
4-8-0 CLASS TW3 SP #2933 PHOTO SLW 1892	06	72	37
4-8-0 D&H "L. LOREE" #1403 1933	07	52	23
4-8-0 N&W #1100 SWITHCER EXPERIMENT	10	84	44
4-8-2 CLASS A3 SP&S #700 PHOTO	02	50	33
4-8-2 CLASS M1 PRR #4700 PHOTO 1923	08	79	24
4-8-2 CLASS M1 PRR #6800 PHOTO B 1926	08	79	25
4-8-2 CLASS M1A PRR #6707 PHOTO BALDWIN	08	79	31
4-8-2 CLASS M67 D&RGW #1501 PHOTO ALCO	03	46	37
4-8-2 CLASS M75 D&RGW #1600 PHOTO B 1926	03	46	38
4-8-2 CLASS MT MP #5321 PHOTO	05	42	7
4-8-2 CLASS O3 BURL #5301 PHOTO 1915	12	40	28
4-8-2 CLASS O5 BURL #5604 PHOTO 1930	12	40	29
4-8-2 CLASS R1 NH #3326 PHOTO 1919	03	45	36
4-8-2 CLASS R2 NH #3500 PHOTO	06	42	9
4-8-2 CLASS R2 NH #3507 PHOTO 1924	03	45	36
4-8-2 CLASS R3 NH #3551 PHOTO 1926	03	45	35
4-8-2 CLASS R3A NYNH&H #3553 PHOTO	03	41	2
4-8-2 CLASS T3 B&O UGLY PHOTO	02	85	33
4-8-2 CLASS Y NYO&W #405 PHOTO SLW 1923	08	42	29
4-8-2 CLASS Y NYO&W #407 PHOTO	06	42	44
4-8-2 CLASS Y2 NYO&W #455 PHOTO ALCO	08	42	26
4-8-2 CN #6060 COLOR PHOTO	12	73	32
4-8-2 ERECTION PHOTO S CLASS 7S-1	03	77	41
4-8-2 GULF MOBILE & NORTHERN # 400 PHOTO	04	81	37
4-8-2 IC #2600 PHOTO ESSAY 1942	07	66	30
4-8-2 MOUNTAIN RF&P #504 PHOTO ALCO 1925	11	46	40
4-8-2 NYC #3000 FACE PHOTO	12	40	43
4-8-2 RF&P UGLY PHOTO	02	85	33
4-8-2 SOUTHERN #1471 PHOTO	04	44	37
4-8-2 T&P #904 PHOTO	05	48	32
4-8-2 USRA MOUNTAIN C&O #133 PHOTO ALCO	09	66	18
4-8-2 WESTERN PACIFIC #175 PHOTO ALCO	03	42	41
4-8-4 BIG APPLE CG #451 PHOTO LIMA 1943	06	54	10
4-8-4 C&O #600 UGLY PHOTO	02	85	31
4-8-4 CB&Q #5625 PHOTO 1938 CB&Q SHOPS	05	43	2
4-8-4 CLASS A NP #2609 UGLY PHOTO	02	85	34
4-8-4 CLASS GS2 SP #4411 PHOTO	01	42	6
4-8-4 CLASS H C&NW #3006 PHOTO 1929 B	10	70	24
4-8-4 CLASS J N&W #600 PHOTO	11	54	25
4-8-4 CLASS J N&W #600 PHOTOGRAPH	12	64	46
4-8-4 CLASS J N&W #600 PHOTOGRAPHS	06	74	41
4-8-4 CLASS J1 N&W #600 (WARTIME) PHOTO	11	54	25

STEAM LOCOMOTIVE PHOTOS	M	Y	P
4-8-4 CLASS J3A C&O #610 PHOTO LIMA 1934	06	52	26
4-8-4 CLASS K D&H PHOTO	07	52	24
4-8-4 CLASS L2A NYC #2995	12	44	37
4-8-4 CLASS M64 D&RGW #1700 PHOTO B 1929	03	46	37
4-8-4 CLASS M68 D&RGW #1801 PHOTO B 1938	03	46	37
4-8-4 CLASS R67B RI #5027 PHOTO	03	81	22
4-8-4 CLASS S2 MILW #238 PHOTO B 1929	12	45	36
4-8-4 CLASS S3 MILW #287 PHOTO ALCO 1929	12	45	37
4-8-4 D&RGW #1702 PHOTO	07	72	24
4-8-4 FAST FREIGHT PHOTOS FRIS #4503	11	42	46
4-8-4 J CLASS N&W #602 TOP SIDE DETAIL	08	53	47
4-8-4 LACKAWANNA #1635 PHOTO	11	43	6
4-8-4 MOUNTAIN CLASS N N&W #200 PHOTO	02	79	50
4-8-4 PHOTO CP #3101	01	66	12
4-8-4 RF&P #553 PHOTO 1937 B	05	68	34
4-8-4 UP #8444 PHOTO	09	73	28
4-8-4 UP #8444 TOP VIEW PHOTO	04	80	33
4-8-8-2 CLASS AC11 SP #4272 PHOTO 1942 B	08	68	30
4-8-8-2 CLASS AC12 SP #4294 PHOTO 1943 B	08	68	30
4-8-8-2 CLASS AC4 SP #4102 1928 B PHOTO	08	668	29
4-8-8-2 CLASS AC4 SP #4102 PHOTO	08	68	29
4-8-8-2 CLASS AC5 SP #4114 PHOTO	11	62	29
4-8-8-2 CLASS AC5 SP #4114 PHOTO 1919 B	08	68	29
4-8-8-2 CLASS AC7 SP #4159 PHOTO 1937 B	08	68	30
4-8-8-2 CLASS AC8 SP #4185 PHOTO	11	62	29
4-8-8-2 SP #4102 FRONT PHOTO	08	68	1
4-8-8-4 4000 SERIES UP #4000 PHOTO	07	43	26
4-8-8-4 BUILDERS PHOTO UP #4002	12	41	46
6-8-6 PRR #6800 STEAM TURBINE PHOTO	06	47	15
BACKHEAD PHOTO 2-8-2 WAR DEPT PHOTO	12	64	28
BACKHEAD PHOTO N&W MOUNTAIN	02	79	49
BILL WITBECKS SOUTH PHOTOS LITTLE LOCOS	04	75	22
BONEYARD OS TEAM LOCOS PHOTO NC&SL	06	73	32
CLIMAX MIDDLEFORK RR #3 PHOTO	12	48	56
FIRELESS LOCOMOTIVE PHOTOS	09	65	10
HEISLER MEADOW RIVER LUMBER #6 PHOTO	04	81	40
HEISLER MIDDLEFORK RR #7 PHOTO	12	48	56
JAWN HENRY N&W #2300 PHOTO	11	54	29
LAIRD CROSSHEAD DETAIL PHOTO	12	64	27
SHAY #4 ED HINES WESTERN LUMBER PHOTO	06	42	4
SHAY 2 TRUCK ARGENTINE CENTRAL #4 PHOTO	11	83	45
SHAY 2 TRUCK SUPERHEATED LIMA #1 PHOTO	08	67	38
SHAY 3 TRUCK FEEDWATER HEAT ABIT#70 PHOT	08	67	40
SHAY 3 TRUCK LARGEST WM #6 LIMA PHOTO	08	67	40
SHAY 3 TRUCK PACIFIC COAST SLCO PHOTO	08	67	40
SHAY 3 TRUCK SUPERHEATED BRADEN CO #19 L	08	67	38
SHAY 4 TRUCK S #4001 PHOTO LIMA	08	67	38
SHAY C&O #12 & #2 PHOTO LIMA 1906	10	65	53
SHAY LIMA'S LAST WM #6 PHOTO	12	53	9
SHAY MUTT & JEFF PHOTO LIMA 1920	07	61	45
STEAM LOCOMOTIVE CAB DETAIL PHOTO	05	53	12
STREAMLINED STEAM LOCOMOTIVE PHOTOS	08	67	29
TE1 CLASS #2300 N&W STEAM TURBINE/ELECT	10	84	45

LOCOMOTIVES

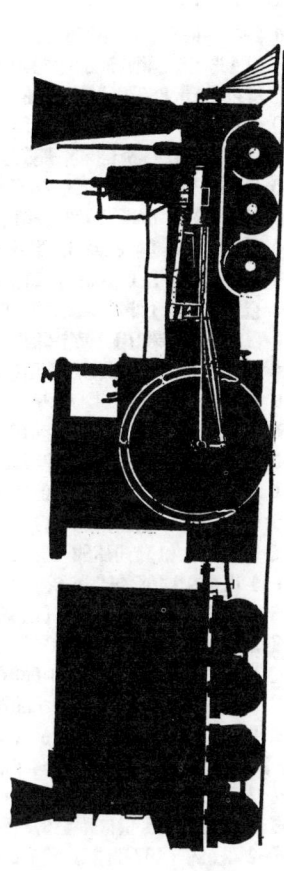

STEAM LOCOMOTIVE PHOTOS BY ROAD

RD		M	Y	P
	4-6-0 ATSF #466 PHOTO BALDWIN 1894	06	72	34
B&A	4-6-4 CLASS J2B B&A #605 PHOTO ALCO 1930	04	42	42
	2-8-4 CLASS A B&A #1426 PHOTO LIMA 1926	04	42	42
	2-8-2 CLASS H5G B&A #1218 PHOTO	04	42	42
	2-8-0 CLASS 66H B&A #1045 PHOTO SLW	04	42	42
	4-6-4 B&A #619 FRONT VIEW PHOTO	06	46	26
B&M	2-8-4 B&M #4015 COFFIN HEATER PHOTO	02	42	32
	2-10-2 B&M #3004 FRONT VIEW PHOTO	06	46	27
B&O	0-6-0 USRA B&O #353 PHOTO BALDWIN 1918	02	42	6
	2-8-2 B&O #4132 PHOTO	08	42	51
	4-6-2 CLASS P7D B&O #5303 PHOTO	11	81	548
	4-8-2 CLASS T3 B&O UGLY PHOTO	02	85	33
	2-8-2 USRA MIKADO PHOTO B&O #4500	12	60	49
	4-4-4-4 CLASS N1 DUPLEX B&O #5600 PHOTO	06	78	39
B&P	4-4-0 B&P #62 "STOUGHTON" PHOTO	07	43	28
	4-4-0 B&P #2 "WM R ROBESON" PHOTO	07	43	28
B&PO	0-4-2 BROCKINGS & PEACH ORCHARD #1 PHOTO	04	81	41
B&S	4-4-2 B&S #274 (RENUMBERED B&O #1484) PHO	02	47	49
BCR&N	4-6-0 BCR&N #71 PHOTO BLW 1896	08	43	46
	4-6-0 BCR&N #105 PHOTO BLW 1892	08	43	46
BMT	4-6-0 BLACK MOUNTAIN #1 PHOTO	04	81	34
BURL	4-8-2 CLASS O5 BURL #5604 PHOTO 1930	12	40	29
	4-8-2 CLASS O3 BURL #5301 PHOTO 1915	12	40	28
	2-8-2 BURL CLASS O3 #5325 PHOTO	06	52	4
	2-10-4 BURL #6325 PHOTO	06	68	42
C&E	2-6-0 CASSVILLE & EXETER #345 PHOTO	06	42	51
C&EI	4-6-2 C&EI #1008 STREAMLINED PHOTO	02	41	39
	4-6-2 C&EI #1008 PHOTO	02	41	38
	4-8-0 CAMELBACK PHOTO C&EI #171 1899 PCLW	02	55	53
	4-4-2 CLASS E2 ATLANTIC C&EI #222 PHOTO	04	81	35
C&GR	2-8-2 COLUMBUS & GREENVILLE #503 PHOTO	04	81	41
	4-6-0 COLUMBUS & GREENVILLE #216 PHOTO	04	81	35
C&I	2-8-2 MIKADO PHOTO C&I #4 PHOTO	03	71	41
	2-8-2 MIKADO PHOTO C&I #5 PHOTO	03	71	41
	2-8-0 CONSOLIDATION PHOTO C&I #14	03	71	41
	2-8-0 WITH TENDER BOOSTER PHOTO C&I #19	03	71	41
	2-8-2 MIKADO PHOTO C&I #20 PHOTO	03	71	41
C&NW	4-4-0 C&NW CLASS C5 #685 PHOTO SLW 1888	07	43	29
	4-4-0 C&NW #17 PHOTO SLW 1895	07	43	14
	4-8-4 CLASS H C&NW #3006 PHOTO 1929 B	10	70	24
C&O	2-10-4 CLASS 2104-S-566 C&O #3004 PHOTO	03	41	10
	4-6-2 CLASS F19 C&O #475 PACIFIC PHOTO	01	41	22
	2-6-6-6 C&O 1600 SERIES PHOTOS	03	42	51
	2-8-2 CLASS K3A C&O #2318 PHOTO	06	75	52
	2-6-6-6 ALLEGHENY C&O #1605 PHOTO LIMA	06	74	38
	4-6-2 CLASS F19 C&O #490 PHOTO	06	83	23
	SHAY C&O #12 & #2 PHOTO LIMA 1906	10	65	53
	4-8-4 C&O #600 UGLY PHOTO	02	85	31
	2-6-6-6 CLASS H8 C&O #1605 PHOTO L 1941	06	52	26
	4-8-4 CLASS J3A C&O #610 PHOTO LIMA 1934	06	52	26
	2-8-4 CLASS K4 C&O #2744 PHOTO	06	52	26
	4-8-2 USRA MOUNTAIN C&O #133 PHOTO ALCO	09	66	18
	2-6-6-2 C&O #1605 PHOTO	06	68	42
	4-6-4 C&O #490 STREAMLINED PHOTO	09	71	17
C&PA	4-4-0 C&PA #6 PHOTO	07	44	30

STEAM LOCOMOTIVE PHOTOS BY ROAD

RD		M	Y	P
A&N	4-4-0 ALBANY & NORTHERN #10 PHOTO 1890	03	44	34
AB&C	4-6-2 AB&C #71 PHOTO SLW 1911	04	81	36
ABIT	SHAY 3 TRUCK FEEDWATER HEAT ABIT#70 PHOT	08	67	40
ACL	4-6-2 CLASS P5B ACL #1652 PHOTOS	06	76	29
	2-10-2 USRA ACL #2007 PHOTO B 1925	08	64	43
	0-4-0 "DUMMY" ACL #1434 PHOTO B 1905	12	77	52
	2-10-2 CLASS Q1 ACL #2006 PHOTO	12	77	50
	4-6-2 PACIFIC ACL #1533 PHOTO	12	77	50
AL	2-8-2 AL #701 PHOTO 1927	04	53	45
	4-6-2 AL #902 PHOTO BALDWIN 1945	04	63	45
ARC	SHAY 2 TRUCK ARGENTINE CENTRAL #4 PHOTO	11	83	45
ATSF	4-6-4 CLASS 3460 ATSF #3462 PHOTO 1937 B	03	41	10
	2-6-6-2 ATSF #3321 PHOTO B 1911	08	75	24
	2-10-2 3900 SERIES ATSF #3920 PHOTO	08	75	24
	2-10-4 ATSF #3829 PHOTO B 1919	08	75	25
	2-10-4 CLASS 5000 ATSF #5004 PHOTO 1936	08	75	32
	2-6-6-2 ATSF #1157 UGLY PHOTO	02	85	35
	2-6-0 ATSF #477 PHOTO	06	69	45
	2-6-2 ATSF #1207 PHOTO BALDWIN 1903	06	72	34

LOCOMOTIVES

STEAM LOCOMOTIVE PHOTOS BY ROAD

RD		M	Y	P
C&S	2-10-2 C&S #900 PHOTO BALDWIN 1915	11	83	44
C&GL	4-6-0 COLLINS & GLENVILLE #105 PHOTO	03	44	36
CA&S	2-8-0 CA&S #320 PHOTO 1904 BLW	04	81	39
CB&Q	4-6-4 CLASS S4 CB&Q #3000 PHOTO	03	41	10
CB&Q	4-8-4 CB&Q #5625 PHOTO 1938 CB&Q SHOPS	05	43	2
CBELT	4-6-0 CLASS 60 CBELT #665 SCULLIN DRIVES	07	51	38
CC&O	2-8-8-2 CC&O #731 PHOTO	10	83	28
CG	4-8-4 BIG APPLE CG #451 PHOTO LIMA 1943	06	54	10
	2-8-0 CONSOLIDATION CG #509 PHOTO B 1906	06	54	10
	4-4-0 CG #349 PHOTO B 1891	06	54	10
	0-6-0T MAUDE CG #8 PHOTO B 1886	06	54	10
CGW	2-6-6-2 CLASS H1 CGW #608 PHOTO	09	65	22
	4-6-2 "LEGIONNAIRE" PHOTO CGW #932	09	65	22
CLIF	2-6-2 CLIFFSIDE RR # 108 PHOTO	04	81	37
CM&SP	4-6-0 CM&SP #820 PHOTO BALDWIN 1892	08	43	46
CM&STP	4-6-2 CM&STP #830 PHOTO	05	43	44
	4-6-2 CM&STP #796 PHOTO	05	43	44
CN	0-8-0 CN #8353 PHOTO	02	42	7
	0-6-0 CN #7518 PHOTO CLC	02	42	6
	4-8-2 CN #6060 COLOR PHOTO	12	73	32
CNJ	4-6-2 CLASS G3S CNJ #831 PHOTO	03	41	10
	0-8-0 CNJ #323 PHOTO BALDWIN 1930	02	42	6
	2-8-2 CLASS M2AS CNJ #875 PHOTO	06	42	9
	0-8-0 CNJ #305 PHOTO	08	69	43
	4-6-2 CNJ #831 PHOTO	08	69	42
	4-6-2 CNJ #830 PHOTO	08	69	42
	4-6-0 MOTHER HUBBARD CNJ #409 PHOTO	03	47	53
	4-4-0 CNJ #379 PHOTO	03	47	53
CP	4-8-4 PHOTO CP #3101	01	66	12
	4-6-2 CLASS G3C CP #2317 PHOTO	02	79	2
CR&SJ	2-6-0 CR&SJ #2 PHOTO BALDWIN 1902	09	43	12
CSP&KC	4-4-0 CSP&KC #68 PHOTO	09	65	22
D&H	0-8-8-0 CLASS H HELPER D&H #1611 PHOTO	01	64	36
	2-8-0 D&H #1400 UGLY PHOTO	02	85	34
	4-8-0 D&H "L. LOREE" #1403 1933	07	52	23
	2-8-0 CLASS E71 D&H "JAMES ARCHBALD"ALCO	07	52	23
	2-8-0 CLASS E71 D&H "JOHN JERVIS" 1927	07	52	22
	2-8-0 CLASS E71 D&H "HORATIO ALLEN" 1927	07	52	22
	0-8-8-0 CLASS H D&H #1610 PHOTO D&H SHOP	07	52	21
	0-8-8-0 MALLET D&H #1600 PHOTO ALCO 1910	07	52	21
	2-8-0 CLASS E3A CAMELBACK PHOTO D&H #793	07	52	21
	2-8-0 MOTHER HUBBARD D&H #793 ALCO 1903	07	52	21
	4-6-6-4 CLASS J D&H PHOTO ALCO	07	52	24
	4-8-4 CLASS K D&H PHOTO	07	52	24
	4-6-2 CLASS P1 D&H #653 1931 D&H SHOPS	07	52	24
	2-8-0 CLASS E5A 300 LB BOILER D&H #1114	06	67	43
	2-8-0 CLASS E5A FOUR ACES PHOTO D&H#1111	06	67	43
	2-8-0 L LOREE 500 LB BOILER D&H #1403 PH	06	67	41
	2-8-0 ARCHABALD 500 LB BOILER D&H #1402	06	67	40
	2-8-0 J. JERVIS 400 LB BOILER D&H #1401	06	67	40
	2-8-0 COMPOUND PHOTO D&H #1400 S 1924	06	67	40
	2-8-0 CLASS E6A WELDED BOILER D&H #1219	05	67	24
	2-8-0 CLASS E6A PHOTO D&H #1218 1918	05	67	23
	2-8-0 CLASS E6 PHOTO D&H #1200 1916	05	67	23
	2-8-0 CLASS E5 W/DABEG HEATER D&H #1076	05	67	22
	0-8-0 2-8-0 REBUILD PHOTO D&H #159 1925	05	67	22
	2-8-0 CLASS E5 CAMELBACK PHOTO D&H #1011	05	67	20
	2-8-0 CLASS E5 PHOTO D&H #1060 1912	05	67	20
	2-8-0 CLASS E5 PHOTO D&H #1054 1908	05	67	20
	2-8-0 CLASS E3A CAMELBACK PHOTO D&H #891	04	67	46
	2-8-0 CLASS E3A CAMELBACK PHOTO D&H #221	04	67	45
	2-8-0 CLASS E3A CAMELBACK PHOTO D&H #819	04	67	44
	2-8-0 CLASS E3A CAMELBACK PHOTO D&H #806	04	67	43
	2-8-0 CAMELBACK REBUILDS PHOTO D&H #942	04	67	42
	2-8-0 CLASS E3A CAMELBACK PHOTO D&H #26	04	67	42
	0-8-0 CLASS B4 PHOTO D&H #83	04	67	41
	2-8-0 CLASS E4 CAMELBACK PHOTO D&H #349	04	67	41
	2-8-0 CLASS E2A CAMELBACK PHOTO D&H #339	04	67	41
	2-8-0 CLASS E2 CAMELBACK PHOTO D&H #357	04	67	40
	2-8-0 CLASS E1A CAMELBACK PHOTO D&H #244	04	67	38
	2-8-0 BACKHEAD D&H "HORATIO ALLEN" PHOTO	06	67	42
D&M	2-6-0 DETROIT & MACKINAC #116 PHOTO	03	44	35
D&RGW	2-8-8-2 CLASS L131 D&RGW #3618 PHOTO	03	82	25
	4-6-6-4 CLASS L105 D&RGW #3708 PHOTO B	06	52	34
	2-8-8-2 D&RGW #3600 FRONT CLOSE UP PHOTO	05	53	31
	2-8-8-2 CLASS L131 D&RGW #3608 PHOTO BLW	04	63	22
	2-8-2 CLASS K37 D&RGW #490 PHOTO 1928	03	46	43
	2-8-2 CLASS K27 D&RGW #459 PHOTO 1903	03	46	43
	2-8-0 CLASS C48 D&RGW #1176 PHOTO 1906	03	46	42
	2-10-2 CLASS F81 D&RGW #1254 PHOTO ALCO	03	46	42
	2-6-6-2 CLASS L62 D&RGW #1052 PHOTO	03	46	41
	2-8-8-2 CLASS L95 D&RGW #1075 PHOTOO	03	46	41
	2-8-8-2 CLASS L107 D&RGW #3500 PHOTO	03	46	41
	2-8-8-2 CLASS L131 D&RGW#3618 PHOTO 1927	03	46	40
	4-6-6-4 CLASS L105 D&RGW #3704 PHOTO	03	46	40
	4-6-6-4 CLASS L97 D&RGW #3800 PHOTO 1943	03	46	40
	4-6-2 CLASS P44 D&RGW #1003 PHOTO B 1913	03	46	39
	2-8-2 CLASS K59 D&RGW #1212 PHOTO B 1913	03	46	39
	4-8-2 CLASS M75 D&RGW #1600 PHOTO B 1926	03	46	38
	4-8-2 CLASS M67 D&RGW #1501 PHOTO ALCO	03	46	37
	4-8-4 CLASS M64 D&RGW #1700 PHOTO B 1929	03	46	37
	4-8-4 CLASS M68 D&RGW #1801 PHOTO B 1938	03	46	37
	4-8-4 D&RGW #1702 PHOTO	07	72	24
D&SL	2-8-2 D&SL #407 PHOTO	11	83	45
DM&IR	2-8-2 DM&IR TOP PHOTO	03	58	31
	2-8-8-4 CLASS M3 DM&IR #223 PHOTO 1941	11	80	36
	2-8-8-4 CLASS M4 DM&IR #231 PHOTO	11	80	36
DM&N	2-8-8-2 CLASS M DM&N #206 PHOTO	11	80	33
	2-8-8-2 CLASS M1 DM&N #208 PHOTO	11	80	33
	2-8-8-0 DM&N #2008 PHOTO	11	80	33
	2-8-8-0 CLASS M25 DM&N #210 PHOTO	11	80	33
DNW&P	2-6-6-0 DNW&P #200 PHOTO	11	83	44
DO&S	4-6-0 DO&S #2 PHOTO 1907 RL	08	47	61
DT&I	2-8-2 DT&I #800 LIMA 1940 PHOTO	06	42	5
E	4-6-2 CLASS K5B ERIE #2960	11	40	11
	4-6-2 CLASS K5A E #2940 B 1923 PHOTO	11	40	11
	4-6-2 CLASS USRA ERIE #2919 PHOTO	11	40	11
	4-6-2 CLASS K4B ERIE #2744 PHOTO	11	40	10
	4-6-2 CLASS K4A ERIE #2752 PHOTO	11	40	10
	4-6-2 CLASS K4 E #2711 ALCO 1913 PHOTO	11	40	10

LOCOMOTIVES

STEAM LOCOMOTIVE PHOTOS BY ROAD

RD		M	Y	P
	4-6-2 CLASS K2A ERIE #2912 PHOTO	11	40	9
	4-6-2 CLASS K2A E #2905 ALCO 1917 PHOTO	11	40	9
	4-6-2 CLASS K2 E #2900 LIMA 1913 PHOTO	11	40	8
	4-6-2 CLASS K5 E #2509 ALCO 1910 PHOTO	11	40	8
	4-6-2 PACIFIC E #2512 1905	11	40	6
	4-4-2 ATLANTIC CLASS E4 E#536	11	40	6
	4-4-2 ATLANTIC CLASS E5 E#537	11	40	6
	4-6-2 ERIE #953 PHOTO	08	42	5
	2-8-4 ERIE #3360 BALDWIN 1928 PHOTO	06	42	5
	0-8-8-0 ERIE #2601 UGLY PHOTO	02	85	35
	2-8-8-8-2 TRIPLEX PHOTO E #5016 B 1914	12	52	38
	2-8-4 E #3360 PHOTO	06	68	42
ET&WNC	0-8-0 ET&WNC #7 PHOTO ALCO 1906	12	42	19
	4-6-0 ET&WNC #10 PHOTO BALDWIN 1910	12	42	19
FRIS	4-8-4 FAST FREIGHT PHOTOS FRIS #4503	11	42	46
	0-6-0 FRISCO #746 PHOTO	04	47	37
G&J	4-4-0 BALDWIN G&J #3 1902	10	55	64
GM&N	4-8-2 GULF MOBILE & NORTHERN # 400 PHOTO	04	81	37
GM&O	4-6-2 CLASS P16B GM&O #5296 PHOTO	12	50	38
GN	2-8-0 TUNNEL EXTENDED STACK GN#1106 PHOT	11	61	29
	2-6-6-2 PHOTO GN #1800	11	61	29
GS&G	4-4-0 GS&G #10 PHOTO	03	44	34
GTW	4-4-0 GTW #416 PHOTO	02	43	11
	0-6-6T GTW #30 PHOTO	02	43	10
H&TL	2-8-0 H&TL "KITCHIGAMI" CAMELBACK PHOTO	08	72	33
	0-6-4T H&TL #9 "SCHOOLCRAFT" PHOTO MMW	08	72	34
	0-6-4T H&TL #8 "ST LOUIS" PHOTO MMW 1887	08	72	34
	2-8-0 H&TL #13 "VOYAGEUR" PHOTO B 1900	08	72	34
HHL	2-6-0 HIMMLEBERG-HARRISON LUMB CO # 8 PH	04	81	37
IC	4-6-0 IC #382 AFTER WRECK PHOTO	04	57	58
	4-8-2 IC #2600 PHOTO ESSAY 1942	07	66	30
	4-4-2 ROGERS IC #1014 PHOTO ROGERS 1916	09	52	36
INTER	4-4-2 INTER #9 W/SOUTHERN VLAVE GEAR PHO	02	54	58
IOWAC	2-8-0 UPSIDE DOWN VULCAN IOWAC #81	10	55	44
K&M	2-8-2T K&M #559 PHOTO	09	47	54
K&T	2-8-2 KENTUCKY & TENESEE #7 PHOTO	04	81	39
L&B	4-4-0 LACKAWANA & BLOOMSBURG #2 PHOTO	12	40	2
L&N	4-6-2 L&N #218 PHOTO	08	42	32
	4-6-2 CLASS K2A L&N #158 PHOTO	02	43	21
	2-8-2 CLASS J4A L&N #1892 PHOTO	06	75	52
	2-8-2 CLASS J5 L&N #1999 PHOTO 1924	12	72	34
	2-8-2 CLASS J4 L&N #1863	12	72	34
	2-8-2 CLASS J4A L&N #1892 PHOTO	12	72	34
	2-8-4 CLASS M1 L&N #1954 PHOTO B 1942	12	72	35
	2-8-4 CLASS M1 L&N #1967 PHOTO B 1944	12	72	35
	2-8-4 CLASS M1 L&N #1970 PHOTO LIMA 1949	12	72	35
	2-8-2 CLASS J2A L&N #1480 1914	12	72	34
L&NE	0-8-0 LEHIGH & NEW ENGLAND #132 PHOTO	02	42	7
	2-8-0 CAMELBACK L&NE #152 PHOTO	06	42	42
	2-10-0 CLASS FS1 L&NE #402 PHOTO	11	83	57
LACK	0-4-0 LACKAWANNA #7 PHOTO	02	42	7
	0-8-0 HEAVY SWITCHER LACK #214 PHOTO	02	42	6
	4-4-0 STREAMLINED LACKAWANNA #988	07	42	51
	4-4-0 CAMELBACK LACKAWANNA #952 PHOTO	07	42	51
	4-8-4 LACKAWANNA #1635 PHOTO	11	43	6

STEAM LOCOMOTIVE PHOTOS BY ROAD

RD		M	Y	P
	4-6-4 LACKAWANNA #1155 PHOTO	03	77	37
LNA&C	4-4-0 LNA&C #9 PHOTO	03	44	33
	4-4-0 LNA&C #5 PHOTO	03	44	33
LOP&G	4-6-0 LOP&G #102 PHOTO 1910	03	44	32
	4-6-0 LOP&G #100 PHOTO 1936	01	75	60
LS&MC	4-4-0 LS&MC #136 "SAXON" PHOTO	03	42	21
LV	0-6-0T LEHIGH VALLEY #3359 PHOTO BALDWIN	09	42	25
	2-2-0 LILLIPUT LV #24 PHOTO 1862	12	52	55
M&E	2-4-0 M&E #7 (SCRAP) PHOTO ALCO 1905	07	52	8
M&SL	2-8-0 CLASS H5-39 M&SL #455 PHOTO ALCO	12	42	44
	4-6-2 M&SL #503 PHOTO BROOKS 1921	12	42	43
	2-8-2 CLASS M50 M&SL #631 PHOTO	12	42	37
MA&PA	4-4-0 MA&PA #6 PHOTO RLW 1901	07	52	8
MILW	4-4-2 CLASS B7 MILW #3135 BALDWIN	12	45	33
	2-6-2 CLASS K1 MILW #941 PHOTO ALCO	12	45	31
	0-6-0 CLASS 1-5A MILW #1455 PHOTO 1903	12	45	31
	2-6-6-2 CLASS N3S MILW #9314 PHOTO	12	45	37
	4-8-4 CLASS S3 MILW #287 PHOTO ALCO 1929	12	45	37
	4-8-4 CLASS S2 MILW #238 PHOTO B 1929	12	45	36
	4-6-2 CLASS F7 MILW HIAWATHA PHOTO ALCO	12	45	36
	4-6-2 CLASS F6 MILW #6414 PHOTO	12	45	36
	4-6-2 CLASS F3S MILW #164 PHOTO	12	45	35
	4-6-2 CLASS F4MS MILW #6207 PHOTO	12	45	35
	4-6-2 CLASS F5B MILW #6361 PHOTO	12	45	35
	4-6-0 CLASS G8A MILW #2639 PHOTO	12	45	34
	4-6-0 CLASS G6PS MILW #1108 PHOTO	12	45	34
	4-4-2 CLASS A MILW #3 HIAWATHA PHOTO	12	45	34
	4-4-0 CLASS H8 MILW #34 PHOTO 1904 ROG	12	45	33
	2-8-2 CLASS L3 MILW #360 PHOTO	12	45	33
	2-8-2 CLASS L1AS MILW #8518 PHOTO 1909	12	45	32
	2-8-2 CLASS L2 MILW #474 PHOTO BALDWIN	12	45	32
	2-8-0 CLASS C7 MILW #1350 PHOTO ALCO	12	45	32
	4-4-2 CLASS B MILW #3135 PHOTO 1886 B	12	45	33
MKT	4-6-0 MKT #269 PHOTO	01	43	13
MP	2-8-4 CLASS BK MP #1922 PHOTO	05	42	6
	4-6-2 CLASS P MP #1727 PHOTO	05	42	5
	2-8-8-2 CLASS ML MP #4000 PHOTO BALDWIN	05	42	4
	4-8-2 CLASS MT MP #5321 PHOTO	05	42	7
	0-8-0 CLASS SW8 MP #9773 PHOTO LIMA 1928	05	42	7
	2-8-4 CLASS BK MP #2101 PHOTO	05	42	6
	4-6-2 MISSOURI PACIFIC #6001 PHOTO	06	74	41
	4-6-0 MP #338 PHOTO (REAR)	06	76	39
	2-8-2 1200 SERIES PHOTO MP #1201	11	77	50
	4-6-0 TEN WHEELER PHOTO MP #2325	11	77	52
	0-6-0 SWITCHER MP #9301	11	77	57
	2-8-0 MP #100 PHOTO (INJECTOR PIPING)	01	48	43
MRL	HEISLER MEADOW RIVER LUMBER #6 PHOTO	04	81	40
N&W	2-8-8-2 MALLET N&W #2197 PHOTO	06	74	41
	4-8-4 CLASS J N&W #600 PHOTOGRAPHS	06	74	41
	4-4-2 CLASS J N&W #611 PHOTO ESSAY	01	83	40
	4-4-0 CLASS J N&W #19 PHOTO	12	64	46
	4-4-2 CLASS J N&W #606 PHOTO	12	64	46
	4-8-4 CLASS J N&W #600 PHOTOGRAPH	12	64	46
	4-6-2 CLASS E N&W #597 UGLY PHOTO	02	85	35
	TE1 CLASS #2300 N&W STEAM TURBINE/ELECT	10	84	45

LOCOMOTIVES

STEAM LOCOMOTIVE PHOTOS BY ROAD

RD		M	Y	P
	4-8-0 N&W #1100 SWITHCER EXPERIMENT	10	84	44
	2-8-8-2 CLASS Y6B N&W #2197 PHOTOGRAPH	10	84	42
	2-8-8-2 CLASS Y6A N&W #2156 PHOTO 1942	10	84	42
	2-8-8-2 CLASS Y4 N&W #2087 PHOTO ALCO	10	84	42
	2-8-8-2 CLASS Y3A N&W #2063 PHOTO ALCO	10	84	42
	2-8-8-2 CLASS Y2 N&W #1700 PHOTO 1918	10	84	42
	2-6-6-4 CLASS A N&W #1200 PHOTO	10	84	41
	4-8-4 J CLASS N&W #602 TOP SIDE DETAIL	08	53	47
	2-6-6-4 CLASS A N&W #1238 PHOTO	11	54	25
	2-8-8-2 CLASS Y6B N&W #2197 PHOTO	11	54	25
	0-8-0 CLASS S1A N&W #201 PHOTO	11	54	25
	4-8-4 CLASS J N&W #600 PHOTO	11	54	25
	4-8-4 CLASS J1 N&W #600 (WARTIME) PHOTO	11	54	25
	JAWN HENRY N&W #2300 PHOTO	11	54	29
	2-8-8-2 CLASS Y6 N&W #2197 PHOTO	06	68	42
	BACKHEAD PHOTO N&W MOUNTAIN	02	79	49
	4-8-4 MOUNTAIN CLASS N N&W #200 PHOTO	02	79	50
	2-6-6-4 N&W #1212 PHOTO N&W SHOPS 1936	08	79	47
NC	2-6-0 "SIDNEY DILLON" NC #2 PHOTO	01	42	39
NC&SL	BONEYARD OS TEAM LOCOS PHOTO NC&SL	06	73	32
NH	4-8-2 CLASS R2 NH #3500 PHOTO	06	42	9
	0-8-0 CLASS Y4 NH # 8604 PHOTO 1924	03	45	40
	0-8-0 CLASS Y3 NH #3420 PHOTO 1920	03	45	40
	0-6-0 CLASS T2 NH #2423 PHOTO	03	45	40
	2-6-0 CLASS K1 NH #420 PHOTO 1900	03	45	40
	2-10-2 CLASS L1 NH #3221 PHOTO 1918	03	45	37
	4-4-2 CLASS H1 NH #1101 PHOTO 1907	03	45	37
	4-6-0 CLASS 64 NH #815 PHOTO 1904	03	45	37
	2-8-0 CLASS F5 NH #153 PHOTO 1912	03	45	37
	4-8-2 CLASS R2 NH #3507 PHOTO 1924	03	45	36
	4-8-2 CLASS R1 NH #3326 PHOTO 1919	03	45	36
	4-6-2 CLASS I2 NH #1318 PHOTO 1913	03	45	36
	4-6-2 CLASS I1 NH #1026 PHOTO 1926	03	45	36
	4-8-2 CLASS R3 NH #3551 PHOTO 1926	03	45	35
	2-8-2 CLASS J1 NH #3000 PHOTO 1916	03	45	35
	4-6-2 CLASS I4 NH #1362 PHOTO 1916	03	45	35
NKP	2-8-4 CLASS S2 NKP #759 PHOTO	01	69	36
NP	2-8-8-2 NP #4023 PHOTO	02	41	11
	4-6-2 NP #2218 PHOTO	02	41	11
	4-6-0 NP #1354 PHOTO	02	41	11
	2-8-8-2 CLASS Z5 NP #5002 PHOTO	04	82	44
	2-8-8-2 CLASS Z4 NP #4503 PHOTO	03	82	24
	2-8-2 CLASS W3 NP #1814 PHOTO	03	82	24
	4-6-0 CLASS S10 NP #328 PHOTO ROG 1905	11	81	42
	4-8-4 CLASS A NP #2609 UGLY PHOTO	02	85	34
	4-6-6-4 CLASS Z8 NP #5138 DETAIL PHOTO	04	65	40
	2-6-2 SUPER SMOKEBOX NP #2406 PHOTO 1916	02	69	47
	4-6-6-4 CLASS Z7 NP #5123 PHOTO ALCO	02	46	26
	2-8-2 CLASS W3 NP #1728 PHOTO ALCO 1913	02	46	26
NSO	2-8-4 NORFOLK SOUTHERN #600 PHOTO 1940	08	42	34
	2-8-4 600 SERIES NSO #600 PHOTO B 1940	11	61	32
NYC	4-8-2 NYC #3000 FACE PHOTO	12	40	43
	4-6-4 PIONEER HUDSON J1 NYC #5200 PHOTO	11	57	52
	4-6-4 SUPER HUDSON J3 NYC #5405 PHOTO	11	57	52
	4-6-4 EMPIRE HUDSON J3 NYC #5429 PHOTO	11	57	53

STEAM LOCOMOTIVE PHOTOS BY ROAD

RD		M	Y	P
	4-6-4 CENTURY HUDSON J3 NYC #5450 PHOTO	11	57	53
	4-6-4 SHROUDED HUDSON NYC PHOTO	12	44	36
	4-8-4 CLASS L2A NYC #2995	12	44	37
	4-6-4 NYC #4689 PHOTO	12	44	37
	4-6-4 NYC #5285 PHOTO	12	44	37
	2-8-2 CLASS H10 NYC #8000 PHOTO LIMA	06	75	52
	4-6-2 CLASS K3 NYC #4806 PHOTO	04	78	36
NYNH&H	4-8-2 CLASS R3A NYNH&H #3553 PHOTO	03	41	2
	4-4-0 NYNH&H #891 FAMOUS LOCOMOTIVE	12	42	46
NYO&W	4-8-2 CLASS Y NYO&W #405 PHOTO SLW 1923	08	42	29
	4-6-0 CAMELBACK CLASS U1 NYO&W #246 PHOT	08	42	28
	2-8-0 CAMELBACK CLASS P NYO&W #217 PHOTO	08	42	28
	2-10-2 CLASS X NYO&W #351 PHOTO ALCO	08	42	28
	4-8-2 CLASS Y2 NYO&W #455 PHOTO ALCO	08	42	26
	4-8-2 CLASS Y NYO&W #407 PHOTO	06	42	44
	2-6-0 CAMELBACK NYO&W #272 PHOTO	06	42	44
OR&LC	2-8-4 OR&LC #80 PHOTO	07	44	39
OR&NC	2-8-0 CONSOLIDATION OR&NC #83 PHOTO	06	43	40
	4-6-0 TEN WHEELER OR&NC #45 PHOTO	06	43	40
P&R	0-12-0T OF 1863 PHOTO P&R	07	80	23
P&WV	2-6-6-4 P&WV #1101 PHOTO B 1935	08	79	47
PFW&C	4-4-2 SINGLE DOME PFW&C #27 PHOTO	04	57	49
PM	4-6-2 CLASS SP3 PM #721 PHOTO	08	45	20
PM&O	4-6-2 PACIFIC MOBILE & OHIO #268 PHOTO	04	81	36
PM&Y	0-6-0 PM&Y #9159 CLC PHOTO	02	42	7
PRR	4-4-4-4 CLASS T1 PRR #6110 PHOTO BALDWIN	01	43	29
	4-6-2 K4 PACIFIC PRR #1737 PHOTO 1914	08	56	52
	4-6-2 K4 PACIFIC PRR #5495 PHOTO 1928	08	56	52
	4-6-2 K4 LOEWY PACIFIC PRR #1120 PHOTO	08	56	53
	4-6-2 K4 PACIFIC PRR #5471 PHOTO 1956	08	56	53
	4-6-2 K5 PRR #5698 PHOTO	09	57	54
	4-6-2 PRR #5699 CAPROTTI VALVE GEAR PHOT	09	57	55
	4-6-4-4 STREAMLINED Q1 FRT PRR#6130 PHOT	11	59	23
	4-6-4-4 Q1 (SHOPPED) PRR #6130 PHOTO	11	59	23
	4-4-6-4 Q2 PRR #6131 PHOTO	11	59	23
	4-4-6-4 CLASS Q2 PRR PHOTO	10	44	5
	2-8-2 CLASS H10 PRR #952 PHOTO	06	75	52
	2-8-8-2 CLASS HH1 PRR #373 PHOTO	10	62	38
	2-8-2 CLASS L1 PRR #1556 PHOTO	10	62	39
	2-8-2 CLASS L1 PRR #2861 EMERSON FIREBOX	10	62	39
	0-4-4-6 CLASS S1 PRR #6100 PHOTO	10	62	37
	4-8-2 CLASS M1 PRR #4700 PHOTO 1923	08	79	24
	4-8-2 CLASS M1 PRR #6800 PHOTO B 1926	08	79	25
	4-6-2 CLASS K5 PRR #5699 CAPROTTI VALVE	08	79	30
	4-6-2 CLASS K5 PRR #5698 WALSCHAERTS VLV	08	79	30
	4-8-2 CLASS M1A PRR #6707 PHOTO BALDWIN	08	79	31
	4-6-2 W/FRANKLIN POPPET VALVES PRR #5399	10	62	41
	4-6-2 K4 W/ELEPHANT EARS PRR #5038 PHOTO	10	62	41
	4-6-2 K4 W/FRONT-END THROTTLE PRR #3847	10	62	41
	4-6-2 K4 W/BOOSTER PRR #3676 PHOTO	10	62	40
	4-6-2 K4 W/12 WHEEL TENDER PRR #5432 PHO	10	62	40
	6-8-6 PRR #6800 STEAM TURBINE PHOTO	06	47	15
	4-6-2 PRR K4 WITH DISK DRIVERS PHOTO	06	47	8
	4-6-0 CLASS 65 PRR #5741 PHOTO 1923 PRR	10	73	28
Q&NW	2-6-0 QUACHITA & NORTHWESTERN # 2 PHOTO	04	81	38

LOCOMOTIVES

STEAM LOCOMOTIVE PHOTOS BY ROAD

RD	Description	M	Y	P
R	4-4-2 MOTHER HUBBARRB R #343 PHOTO	02	41	16
	0-4-0 CAMELBACK READING #1187 PHOTO	05	59	59
	4-4-4 READING #110 UGLY PHOTO	02	85	35
RF&P	2-6-0 RF&P #18 PHOTO RLW 1889	04	51	28
	4-8-2 RF&P UGLY PHOTO	02	85	33
	4-8-4 RF&P #553 PHOTO 1937 B	05	68	34
	4-8-2 MOUNTAIN RF&P #504 PHOTO ALCO 1925	11	46	40
	4-6-2 LIGHT PACIFIC RF&P #258 PHOTO	11	46	40
RGE	2-6-2 RGE #101 PHOTO SLW 1900	06	72	35
RI	0-4-0T PHOTO ROCK #3	08	42	44
	4-8-4 CLASS R67B RI #5027 PHOTO	03	81	22
S	2-8-0 CLASS MS1 S #4767 PHOTO	02	43	20
	0-4-4T SOUTHERN #1509 "MAUD" PHOTO	08	42	35
	4-4-0 SOUTHERN #3841 PHOTO	04	44	37
	4-8-2 SOUTHERN #1471 PHOTO	04	44	37
	4-6-2 CLASS PS4 CRESCENT LIMITED S #1396	07	64	28
	4-4-2 S #1914 PHOTO RLW 1906	07	54	20
	4-6-2 S #1332 PHOTO 1914	07	54	21
	4-8-2 ERECTION PHOTO S CLASS 7S-1	03	77	41
	SHAY 4 TRUCK S #4001 PHOTO LIMA	08	67	38
	4-4-0 SOUTHERN #3859 PHOTO 1880	01	45	22
	4-6-2 S #1406 PHOTO	10	71	32
	2-8-2 S #4888 PHOTO	10	71	32
	0-8-0 CLASS AS11 S #1894 PHOTO	10	71	32
	4-6-2 CLASS PS4 S #1408 PHOTO 1928 B	10	71	32
	2-8-0 S #390 ON ARMSTRON TURNTABLE PHOTO	03	73	33
	2-8-2 S #4501 COLOR PHOTO	10	73	30
	2-10-2 S #5023 PHOTO	10	73	36
S&C	2-8-2 SUMPTER & CHOCTAW #105 PHOTO	03	44	36
SAL	2-6-6-4 SAL CLASS R1/R2 DIFFERENCES PHOT	08	79	48
	2-6-6-4 CLASS R1 SAL #2501 PHOTO B 1935	08	79	47
	2-6-6-4 CLASS R1 SAL #2508 PHOTO B	08	79	45
SD&AE	2-8-0 SD&AE #50 PHOTO	06	72	36
SEA	2-8-2 SEA #357 UGLY PHOTO	02	85	34
SLCO	SHAY 3 TRUCK PACIFIC COAST SLCO PHOTO	08	67	40
SP	2-4-2T PHOTO SP #1010	12	42	2
	4-6-2 CLASS GS2 SP #4328 PHOTO	01	42	6
	4-8-4 CLASS GS2 SP #4411 PHOTO	01	42	6
	4-10-2 3 CYLINDER SP #5024 PHOTO 1925	06	74	41
	4-6-6-2 CLASS MM2 SP #4210 UGLY PHOTO	02	85	34
	4-8-8-2 CLASS AC8 SP #4185 PHOTO	11	62	29
	4-8-8-2 CLASS AC5 SP #4114 PHOTO	11	62	29
	2-8-8-2 CLASS AC2 SP #4028 PHOTO	11	62	29
	2-8-8-2 CLASS AC1 SP #4004 PHOTO	11	62	29
	2-6-6-2 CLASS MM2 SP #4207 PHOTO 1911 B	08	68	28
	2-8-8-2 CLASS AC2 SP #4028 PHOTO 1911 B	08	68	27
	2-8-8-2 CLASS MC4 SP #4022 PHOTO 1911 B	08	68	27
	2-8-8-2 CLASS MC2 SP #4004 PHOTO 1909 B	08	68	27
	4-8-8-2 CLASS AC12 SP #4294 PHOTO 1943 B	08	68	30
	4-8-8-2 CLASS AC11 SP #4272 PHOTO 1942 B	08	68	30
	2-8-8-2 CLASS AC9 SP #3800 PHOTO 1939 L	08	68	30
	4-8-8-2 CLASS AC7 SP #4159 PHOTO 1937 B	08	68	30
	4-8-8-2 CLASS AC5 SP #4114 PHOTO 1919 B	08	68	29
	4-8-8-2 CLASS AC4 SP #4102 1928 B PHOTO	08	668	29
	2-8-8-2 CLASS AC3 SP #4041 PHOTO 1927 B	08	68	29
	2-8-8-2 CLASS MCC SP #4043 PHOTO 1913 B	08	68	28
	4-6-6-2 CLASS MM2 MODIFIED SP #4210 PHOTO	08	68	28
	4-8-8-2 CLASS AC4 SP #4102 PHOTO	08	68	29
	4-8-8-2 SP #4102 FRONT PHOTO	08	68	1
	2-6-0 CLASS M4 SP #1681 PHOTO CLW 1900	06	72	36
	4-8-0 CLASS TW3 SP #2933 PHOTO SLW 1892	06	72	37
SP&P	4-4-0 WM CROOKS SP&P	11	57	15
SP&S	4-6-6-4 CLASS Z6 SP&S #900 PHOTO	02	50	33
	4-8-2 CLASS A3 SP&S #700 PHOTO	02	50	33
	4-6-6-4 SP&S #900 FRONT END PHOTO	02	53	36
SV	2-6-6-2 PHOTO SUMPTER VALLEY #250	11	42	49
T&P	2-10-4 CLASS T1 T&P #600 PHOTO LIMA	02	78	24
	2-10-4 CLASS T1A T&P #610 PHOTO LIMA	02	78	24
	2-10-4 CLASS T1B T&P #637 PHOTO LIMA	02	78	24
	2-10-4 CLASS T1C T&P #640 PHOTO LIMA	02	78	24
	2-10-4 CLASS T1D T&P #660 PHOTO LIMA	02	78	24
	2-10-2 T&P #524 PHOTO	10	72	47
	4-8-2 T&P #904 PHOTO	05	48	32
	4-6-2 BALDWIN T&P #700 PHOTO	07	72	36
TL	2-8-2 TATUM LUMBER CO #6 PHOTO	04	81	40
UP	4-8-8-4 BUILDERS PHOTO UP #4002	12	41	46
	4-8-8-4 4000 SERIES UP #4000 PHOTO	07	43	26
	4-4-0 UP #768 CENTER/REAR CAB PHOTO	01	59	23
	4-6-2 UP #2889 PHOTO 1914 LIMA	05	76	52
	4-12-2 UP #9000 PHOTO	07	84	21
	4-8-4 UP #8444 TOP VIEW PHOTO	04	80	33
	4-12-2 OF 1926 PHOTO UP #9000	07	80	25
	4-12-2 UP #9000 PHOTO ALCO 1926	06	72	37
	4-8-4 UP #8444 PHOTO	09	73	28
USA	2-8-0 PERSHING LOCO PHOTO USA #5724	12	64	30
USWD	BACKHEAD PHOTO 2-8-2 WAR DEPT PHOTO	12	64	28
V	2-8-2 V #457 UGLY PHOTO	02	85	34
WASHT	0-6-0 CLASS B6A WASHT #22 PHOTO	10	62	38
WC	4-6-0 WISCONSIN CENTRAL #211 PHOTO BLW	04	43	44
	4-4-0 WISCONSIN CENTRAL #57 PHOTO SLW	04	43	44
	4-4-0 WISCONSIN CENTRAL #90 SLW 1886	04	43	44
	4-4-0 WISONSIN CENTRAL #16 SLW 1882	04	43	44
WH	4-6-4 CLASS I5 WH #1400 PHOTO 1942	03	45	35
WM	4-6-2 CLASS K1 WM #154 PHOTO	05	41	29
	4-6-6-4 CLASS M2 WM #1203 PHOTO	05	41	29
	2-8-8-2 CLASS L2 WM #924 PHOTO	11	83	56
	4-6-6-4 CLASS M2 WM #1203 PHOTO	11	83	56
	2-8-0 CLASS H9 WM #810 PHOTO	11	83	56
	SHAY LIMA'S LAST WM #6 PHOTO	12	53	9
	SHAY 3 TRUCK LARGEST WM #6 LIMA PHOTO	08	67	40
WP	2-6-6-2 WESTERN PACIFIC #208 PHOTO ALCO	03	42	41
	4-6-6-4 WESTERN PACIFIC #402 PHOTO B	03	42	41
	4-8-2 WESTERN PACIFIC #175 PHOTO ALCO	03	42	41
	2-8-0 WESTERN PACIFIC #124 PHOTO BALDWIN	03	42	41
	2-8-0 WESTERN PACIFIC #1 PHOTO BALDWIN	03	42	41
	4-6-0 WESTERN PACIFIC #77 PHOTO ALCO	03	42	41
	2-8-2 WESTERN PACIFIC #301 PHOTO ALCO	03	42	41
	2-8-8-2 CLASS M137 WP #259 PHOTO 1938	11	80	36

LOCOMOTIVES

TENDER PROTOTYPE DATA

	M	Y	P
"CANTEEN" TENDERS FOR 2-6-6-4 N&W	12	55	22
DOGHOUSES FOR BRAKEMEN	11	59	35
REMEMBER "US" ON TENDERS?	04	83	3
ROCK ISLAND DESTINCTIVE TENDERS	07	69	45
TAKING WATER ON THE FLY	04	49	39
TENDERS FOR PRR 4-8-2 MOUNTAINS SPECS	10	79	29
TENDERS WITHOUT 'EM LITTLE ENG COULDN'T	12	55	21

TENDER PROTOTYPE DATA BY ROAD

RD		M	Y	P
N&W	"CANTEEN" TENDERS FOR 2-6-6-4 N&W	12	55	22
PRR	TENDERS FOR PRR 4-8-2 MOUNTAINS SPECS	10	79	29
RI	ROCK ISLAND DESTINCTIVE TENDERS	07	69	45

TENDER PLANS

	M	Y	P
TENDER PAIR PROPOSED DRAWING	06	74	45
PEDESTAL TENDER DRAWING	06	74	45

TENDER PHOTOS

	M	Y	P
4-6-0 TENDER MP #338 PHOTO (REAR)	06	76	39
4-8-2 TENDER PRR #3000 REAR VIEW	12	40	44
BOOSTER TENDER UNION RAILROAD	12	55	23
CENTIPEDE TENDER PHOTO NYC	12	55	22
DISSIMILAR TRUCK TENDER PHOTO C&O	12	55	23
NYC TENDER #2961 DETAIL PHOTO	04	44	22

TENDER PHOTOS BY ROAD

RD		M	Y	P
C&O	DISSIMILAR TRUCK TENDER PHOTO C&O	12	55	23
MP	4-6-0 TENDER MP #338 PHOTO (REAR)	06	76	39
NYC	NYC TENDER #2961 DETAIL PHOTO	04	44	22
	CENTIPEDE TENDER PHOTO NYC	12	55	22
PRR	4-8-2 TENDER PRR #3000 REAR VIEW	12	40	44

DIESEL LOCOMOTIVE PROTOTYPE DATA

	M	Y	P
1000 HP MLW A1A-A1A COMPOUND TO B-B	07	73	39
1000 HP SWITCHER LIMA HAMILTON'S FIRST	09	49	8
1500 HP ALCO/GE ROAD SWITCHER NP #158	07	49	51
1978 MOTIVE POWER SURVEY 30TH ANNUAL	11	78	30
1979 MOTIVE POWER 31ST SCRAMBLE TO UNTAN	11	79	23
1980 MOTIVE POWER 32ND SHORTAGE TO SURPL	10	80	48
1981 MOTIVE POWER SURVEY 33RD DIV/0 MILE	11	81	50
1982 MOTIVE POWER SURVEY #34 AMER LOCOS	10	82	40
1984 MOTIVE POWER SURVEY 36TH	11	84	46
1985 MOTIVE POWER SURVEY 37TH	10	85	24
2-8-8-2 FROM LARGEST TO SOME OF LARGEST	04	82	42
415 DEMONSTRATOR D.C. (GENERATOR)	11	66	18
44 TON UNITS GE	05	75	42
44 TON UNITS PRR	05	75	40
6000 HP EXPERIMENTAL BALDWIN	01	63	38
660 HP ALCO/GE SWITCHER NP #125 1940	07	49	51
ALCO CENTURIES LONG HAULS	01	77	46
ALCO CENTURIES TRANSFER OPERATIONS	01	77	47
ALCO CHALLENGES THE BIG E (EMD)	06	71	31
ALCO IN A WAR BONNET ATSF	03	71	19
ALCO LOCOMOTIVE SHOWROOM 1967-68	12	67	31
ALCO LOCOMOTIVES 1957 FOB SCHENECTADY NY	05	57	20
ALCO LOCOMOTIVES IN MAINE	08	81	30
ALCO MONSTERS OF MINGO JUNCTION	01	77	42
ALCO'S 75000TH LOCOMOTIVE	11	46	42
ALCOS LOYALL, KY FANS	06	77	48
ALCOS OF C&NW	10	85	50
ALCOS OPERATING PHOTO FEATURE	11	64	10
ALCOS OVER LINEVILLE	09	83	36
ALCOS WHERE YOU'D LEAST XPECT ALCOS	08	81	40
ALL DIESEL ISSUE--THE FIRST	05	62	ALL
AMERICAN LOCOMOTIVE COMPANY HISTORY	07	54	23
AMERICAN LOCOMOTIVE COMPANY IN DIESELS	12	65	40
AMTRAK DIESEL FLEET	08	72	13
AMTRAK UNIT DISTRIBUTION	12	75	22
AMTRAKS DIESEL UNITS & TURBOTRAINS	03	73	16
AS-6-16 BALDWIN MILW #2104	06	66	18
ATOMIC LOCOMOTIVES	05	56	29
BAGGAGE CAR LOCOMOTIVES RI EMD 1929	12	65	34
BALDWIN LOCOMOTIVE WORKS	05	62	42
BALDWIN LOCOMOTIVE WORKS HISTORY	12	67	22
BB VS CC DEBATE FOR DIESEL LOCOMOTIVES	10	63	6
BICENTENIAL LOCOMOTIVES BYE-BYE	03	77	50
BIG BLOW FROM MOSCOW	07	60	27
BL-2 UNITS EMD BORDEN TANK + P5A = BL2	10	75	29
BURLINGTON ZEPHYRS	09	52	32
C LINE TESTING FM	06	50	16
C LINE UNITS FM 1948	12	48	40
C LINER UNITS CP ELUSIVE C-LINERS	07	72	40
C UNITS ALCO'S ANSWER	09	65	7
C&O DIESELIZATION PROGRAM	06	52	22
C-C UNITS OF ACL	08	64	40
C420 REBUILD ALCO W/STRANGE NOSE GB&W	01	85	47
C430 R #5212 AC/DC TRANSMISSION ALCO	11	66	18
C628 & C855 ALCO CENTURY UNITS	11	63	22

LOCOMOTIVES

DIESEL LOCOMOTIVE PROTOTYPE DATA

	M	Y	P
CABLE AND HOSE CONNECTIONS FOR DIESELS	12	61	52
CENTER CAB 2500 HP ROAD DIESEL PRR #8948	01	52	8
CENTIPEDE CONNECTION 1 EARLY HISTORY	05	82	38
CENTIPEDE CONNECTION 2 MEXICAN EXPERIENC	05	82	46
CENTIPEDE CONNECTION 3 PRR PERSONALITY	05	82	48
CENTURY SP #9019 HYDAULIC DRIVE ALCO	11	66	18
CFA16-4 SPECIFICATIONS FAIRBANKS MORSE	07	75	27
COMPLES DIESEL LOCOMOTIVE	03	48	38
CONCEIVED OF CANNIBALISM LOCOS CN 1959	04	77	40
COVERED WAGONS THE CIRCLE GROWS SMALLER	07	78	26
COW & CALF TRANSFER UNITS EMD	01	65	24
COW & CALF UNITS IC	03	53	54
CUSTOM BUILT GE UNITS WP&Y 1954	02	56	36
DD35 UNITS EMD	11	63	21
DECIPHERING DIESELDOM-NUMBER CODES	01	62	32
DEMONSTRATION FREIGHT UNITS 1939 EMD	02	60	18
DES 1000 HP ACL #611 ALCO/GE 1940	06	50	46
DESIGN FACTORS FOR DIESELS	06	62	26
DIESEL BUILDER PHOTO QUIZ	04	60	42
DIESEL CAB INTERIORS AND CONTROLS	08	83	20
DIESEL CATALOG 1974	01	74	36
DIESEL FROM D TO L CYCLES & CYLINDERS	05	79	44
DIESEL FROM D TO L DESIGN	04	79	22
DIESEL FROM D TO L STOPPING & STARTING	06	79	46
DIESEL FUEL TECHNICAL ANALYSIS	05	73	36
DIESEL HYDRAULIC UNITS OF KARUS-MAFFEI.	10	61	43
DIESEL HYDRAULIC UNITS OF KARUSS-MAFFEI	09	60	11
DIESEL HYDRAULICS FROM ROCKIES TO BERKSH	06	76	40
DIESEL HYDRAULICS ON RG ROCKIES WEEKEND	02	62	34
DIESEL HYDRAULICS ON RIO GRANDE 2	11	62	36
DIESEL IN THE ROCKIES	09	42	26
DIESEL LASHUPS ON ACL	12	69	44
DIESEL LOCOMOTIVE CAB INTERIORS	09	78	27
DIESEL LOCOMOTIVE DEVELOPMENT EMD	09	49	14
DIESEL OPERATION ON THE D&M	09	69	40
DIESEL RUNNING GEAR PHOTO QUIZ	08	65	47
DIESEL SPOTTER CHART (SILHOUETTES)	11	48	44
DIESEL SPOTTER CHART CORRECTION	01	49	60
DIESEL STREAMLINERS	12	68	31
DIESEL THAT COULDN'T REPLACE STEAMER PRR	05	75	40
DIESEL THAT WAS DRAFTED ALCO USA	03	80	24
DIESEL THAT WON'T DIE CN #7700 30 YR OLD	02	60	41
DIESELIZATION WITH A DIFFERENCE BRITISH	09	60	19
DIESELS IN WAUSAU WI	04	79	44
DIESELS INVADE BIRTHPLACE OF STEAM	04	56	40
DIESELS OF MEXICO YOU DIDN'T EXPECT	07	64	41
DIESELS OF MIXED PARENTAGE	01	65	8
DIESELS PULL MONON TRAINS	07	47	43
DL-109 UNITS ALCO RUNNING BIG REBEL GM&O	01	76	28
DL-600 3/4 HOOD ALCO ATSF #800 1959	07	59	12
DL109 HOW TO BUILD ONE ALCO	03	77	26
DUNGAREES FOR THE DIESEL	05	53	50
E UNIT REBUILD EXAMPLES ATSF	08	53	9
E UNITS EARLY EMD HOW THEY BUILT THEM	12	68	24
E UNITS EARLY EMD:EARLY NOSES YESTERYEAR	12	71	38

DIESEL LOCOMOTIVE PROTOTYPE DATA

	M	Y	P
E UNITS EMD ESTHETIC E'S BUMPED STEAM	05	64	20
E'S AND EVERYTHING ELSE	07	78	30
E-7 EMD ACL #532 1939	06	50	46
E7 INDESTRUCTIBLE LOCOMOTIVES	01	79	44
E7 REPUTATION FOR RELIABILITY	01	79	48
E7 THE ESSENCE OF THE E7	01	79	30
E8 EMD IC UNITS #4018 1936	03	53	54
E8'S THREE LOVELY LADIES	06	68	23
E9'S AS FUEL TENDERS A	05	78	13
EARLY DAYS OF DIESELDOM	05	62	24
ELECTO-MOTIVE DIVISION OF GE	09	72	ALL
ELECTRO-MOTIVE DIVISION OF GE	11	48	46
EMD 567 IS DEAD LONG LIVE 645	11	66	20
EMD AN INSTANT HISTORY	09	72	56
EMD BIGGER & BETTER SUPER DIESELS	07	63	6
EMD DASH 2 MODELS LITTLE CHANGE LAGRANGE	04	72	16
EMD EARLY STREAMLINED UNITS BURL #9900	01	64	22
EMD EXPORT UNITS	08	66	18
EMD LA GRANGE PLANT DAYBREAK AT LAGRANGE	08	76	29
EMD LOCOMOTIVES 1957 FOB LA GRANGE NY	05	57	18
EMD NEVER ENDING PURSUIT 1967	12	67	36
EMD NEW CATALOG OF ROAD POWER	11	66	22
EMD WHEN DIESEL MARKET IS SATURATED	10	52	23
EMD'S 10,000 UNIT DELIVERED	08	51	6
ERIE BUILT UNITS WHEN GE HELPED FM	12	71	29
EXECUTIVE E CONRAIL	01	84	24
F UNITS CALIFORNIAS FINAL FOUR	11	78	38
F UNITS F MEANS FREIGHT	05	65	40
F'S 2, GOATS 0	01	84	54
F3 EMD 4500 HP NP #6504 1947	07	49	50
F3 UNITS EMD	12	46	52
F40 A DEFENSE OF	12	85	82
F7A SPECIFICATIONS EMD	07	75	27
FA UNITS ALCO DIESELS DIDN'T QUITE DO IT	07	75	22
FA UNITS HISTORY ALCO BID TO BE BEST	06	75	22
FA2 SPECIFICATIONS ALCO	07	75	27
FAIRBANKS-MORSE CLIMAXES A TREND	01	53	9
FAIRBANKS-MORSE DIESELS	06	44	5
FAIRBANKS-MORSE LOCOS 1957 FOB BELOIT WI	05	57	22
FAIRBANKS-MORSE ON STAGE	09	70	23
FIRST GENERATION DIESELS EAST	12	69	20
FL9-27 YEARS LATER	09	83	30
FM 2000 HP DIESEL DISPLAY ON C&NW	06	49	26
FM 2000 HP SWITCHERS	12	47	41
FM DIESEL UNIT HISTORY BORN AT BELOIT	11	64	36
FM FLEET FINALE	09	85	18B
FT & F-2 EMD ACL #332	06	50	47
FT EMD 5400 HP NP #6001 1944	07	49	53
FT UNITS EMD FAIRWELL TO THE FT	03	62	42
FT'S ERIE EARLY ENCOUNTERS	06	84	29
GAS TURBINE LOCOMOTIVE OF UP "BIG BLOW"	07	53	19
GAS TURBINES FOR UP	02	53	6
GAS-TURBINE LOCOMOTIVES/ALLIS CHAMBERS	06	44	5
GE A BELIEF IN SIMPLICITY 1967	12	67	40
GE EARLY UNITS WHERE WOULD WE BE W/OUT?	11	66	41

LOCOMOTIVES

DIESEL LOCOMOTIVE PROTOTYPE DATA

Title	M	Y	P
GE V8 LOCO OF 1913 DAN PATCH #100	06	59	21
GEEP! EVERYMAN'S LOCOMOTIVE EMD	12	65	20
GENERAL ELECTRIC LOCOS 1957 FOB ERIE PA	05	57	24
GM SCRAPBOOK MARKET ORIENTED CATALOG	01	71	40
GP NEW SERIES EMD BIGGEST NEWS SINCE 39	07	65	3
GP18 & 20 LOW NOSES & SUPERCHARGERS EMD	12	65	24
GP28,30,35 & 40 MORE AND MORE HORSES	12	65	26
GP30'S WHY THEIR AGELESS	04	80	31
GP35 UNITS EMD SUPER GEEP	11	63	21
GP38-2 NAMED UNITS FOR BICENTENNIAL IC	03	75	12
GP7 & 9 FLOWERS OF FUCTIONALISM EMD	12	65	22
GP7 EMD IC UNITS #6900	03	53	54
GP9 CN #4571 DON'T SAY "JUST A GEEP"!	01	82	52
H10-44 AND H12-44 FM ON MILW 1945	01	80	26
HEADLIGHT HIGHLIGHTS ON DIESELS	04	66	59
HEATER CAR HC53 S	07	63	45
HH660 ALCO L&N #10 PHOTO	03	78	50
HOW THE DIESEL WORKS WITH CUTAWAY DWGS	10	52	28
INGERSOL RAND: CATALYST OF DIESELIZATION	12	70	24
LA GRANGE INFLUENCE	09	72	30
LA GRANGE LOCOMOTIVE LANDMARKS	09	72	38
LASH'EM UP HOW TO MATE MAKES & MODELS	12	68	45
LATE NEWS ON GAS TURBINES	12	53	7
LEHIGH VALLEY DIESEL COLOR SCHEMES	01	74	29
LIMA ALA ARMCO STEEL	01	73	40
LIMA HAMILTON DIESELS RED DIAMOND DIESEL	11	63	26
LINGERING LEGACY OF THE F	06	83	32
LOCOMOTIVE SHOWROOM 1957	05	57	16
M-1000 UP STREAMLINER	11	63	44
MOBILE SERVICE STAT. FOR DIESEL SWITCHER	04	41	34
MOTIVE POWER FREEZE-THAWING MILW	11	78	30
MRS1 ALCO WI&W #2098 ALCO 1979	09	79	19
OPPOSED PISTON DIESEL UNITS FM	05	47	25
PA ALCO UNITS SALUTE TO DIFFERENT DIESEL	11	66	26
PA'S NOT PUT OUT TO PASTURE PHOTO ESSAY	07	68	20
PITTSBURGH THE PARTY'S OVER	05	83	10
POSTWAR PARADE GAS TURBINES	11	45	32
PRECISION NATIONAL CORP (LOCO DEALERS)	06	72	26
PROMISED LAND ALCOS S2 TO M420	06	83	38
PRR DIESEL FLEET AMERICA'S LARGEST	04	64	38
READING DIESELIZATION	05	62	16
REBUILDING DIESEL UNITS TP&W	01	55	58
REMANUFACTURING EMD UNITS F3 TO GP20	03	61	25
REMOTE CONTROLLED DIESELS-WHY & WHEREFOR	02	83	34
REVOLUTION OF FRONT DIESEL CARS	07	81	48
RF16 BALDWIN SHARKS	08	78	16
RF16 SPECIFICATIONS BALDWIN LIMA HAMILTO	07	75	27
ROAD ENGINE NUMBERS MILW	10	46	31
ROCK ISLAND DIESEL DIVERSITY	12	65	28
RS3-THE LAST LARGE FLEET A	02	80	22
RSD1 ARMY LOCOMOTIVE DISPOSITIONS	04	80	48
RSD1 REPATRIATED FROM USA	04	80	44
RUSSIAN BUILT ALCOS SPECIFICATIONS	03	80	29
SD SIX MOTOR UNITS EMD	02	66	20
SD18,24,35,SDP35 AND MORE TO COME	02	66	24
SD7 & 9 GEEPS BIG SISTERS EMD	02	66	22
SDP45 7 AXLE DIESEL BN #6599	12	84	20
SERVICING FACILITIES FOR DIESELS	11	40	15
SHARK NOSE STEAM LOCOS T1 520 IN AUSTRAL	10	80	26
SHORTAGE OF DIESEL UNITS ON CLINCHFIELD	02	67	24
SHRAKS SURVIVE ONCE AGAIN	08	78	16
SLAVE UNITS L&N-MIDTRAIN	11	64	4
SLUGS ON THE ROAD	07	84	42
SOUTHERN RAILWAY DIESELIZATION	12	49	14
SWITCHER B&O #195 6 CYL/GOING STRONG	11	56	26
SWITCHERS EMD DIESELS WITHIN YARD LIMITS	11	64	20
TECHNOLOGY OF DIESEL LOCO OPERATION	12	70	18
TEN DISTINCTIVE DIESELS	12	71	20
THREE THAT SURVIVED PRE GM EMD LOCOS	09	72	42
TRAINMASTER PLUGGED-IN STILL TOILS	08	73	46
TRAINMASTER RETIREMENT N&W #173	02	77	42
TRAINMASTER TRIBUTE FM	08	73	28
TURBINES ARE A-COMIN'	06	52	8
U25B BIOG. THE OTHER DIESEL THAT DID IT	08	82	42
U25B BIOGRAPHY ON THE ROPES	09	82	40
U25B U25C UNITS GE	11	63	24
U25B UNITS GE A LOCOMOTIVE IS BORN	09	62	18
U25B UNITS GE WHAT'S NEW!	08	60	40
U50 UNITS GE	11	63	25
UB25B & U28C GE REACTION TO COMPETITION	11	65	14
VERMONT DIESELS OF CP	05	50	16
VEST POCKET GAS SWITCHER LIMA	01	52	19
WESTINGHOUSE ELEC & MFG DIESEL HISTORY	12	69	28
WHATS DOING IN DIESELDOM 1964 CATALOG	11	63	20
WHEEL ARRANGEMENTS OF DIESEL LOCOMOTIVES	11	64	35
WHEN THEY CAPITALIZED DIESEL DELUXE	12	68	31

DIESEL LOCO PROTOTYPE DATA BY ROAD

RD	Title	M	Y	P
A	RS3-THE LAST LARGE FLEET A	02	80	22
	E9'S AS FUEL TENDERS A	05	78	13
	AMTRAK UNIT DISTRIBUTION	12	75	22
	AMTRAKS DIESEL UNITS & TURBOTRAINS	03	73	16
	AMTRAK DIESEL FLEET	08	72	13
ACL	DIESEL LASHUPS ON ACL	12	69	44
	C-C UNITS OF ACL	08	64	40
	FT & F-2 EMD ACL #332	06	50	47
	DES 1000 HP ACL #611 ALCO/GE 1940	06	50	46
	E-7 EMD ACL #532 1939	06	50	46
ATSF	ALCO IN A WAR BONNET ATSF	03	71	19
	E UNIT REBUILD EXAMPLES ATSF	08	53	9
	DL-600 3/4 HOOD ALCO ATSF #800 1959	07	59	12
B&O	SWITCHER B&O #195 6 CYL/GOING STRONG	11	36	26
BN	SDP45 7 AXLE DIESEL BN #6599	12	84	20
BURL	EMD EARLY STREAMLINED UNITS BURL #9900	01	64	22
	BURLINGTON ZEPHYRS	09	52	32
C&NW	ALCOS OF C&NW	10	85	50
	FM 2000 HP DIESEL DISPLAY ON C&NW	06	49	26

LOCOMOTIVES

DIESEL LOCO PROTOTYPE DATA BY ROAD

RD		M	Y	P
C&O	C&O DIESELIZATION PROGRAM	06	52	22
CL	SHORTAGE OF DIESEL UNITS ON CLINCHFIELD	02	67	24
CN	GP9 CN #4571 DON'T SAY "JUST A GEEP"!	01	82	52
	CONCEIVED OF CANNIBALISM LOCOS CN 1959	04	77	40
	DIESEL THAT WON'T DIE CN #7700 30 YR OLD	02	60	41
CP	C LINER UNITS CP ELUSIVE C-LINERS	07	72	40
	VERMONT DIESELS OF CP	05	50	16
CR	EXECUTIVE E CONRAIL	01	84	24
D&M	DIESEL OPERATION ON THE D&M	09	69	40
DPE	GE V8 LOCO OF 1913 DAN PATCH #100	06	59	21
E	FT'S ERIE EARLY ENCOUNTERS	06	84	29
GB&W	C420 REBUILD ALCO W/STRANGE NOSE GB&W	01	85	47
GM&O	DL-109 UNITS ALCO RUNNING BIG REBEL GM&O	01	76	28
IC	GP38-2 NAMED UNITS FOR BICENTENNIAL IC	03	75	12
	GP7 EMD IC UNITS #6900	03	53	54
	COW & CALF UNITS IC	03	53	54
	E8 EMD IC UNITS #4018 1936	03	53	54
L&N	HH660 ALCO L&N #10 PHOTO	03	78	50
	SLAVE UNITS L&N-MIDTRAIN	11	64	4
	MOBILE SERVICE STAT. FOR DIESEL SWITCHER	04	41	34
LV	LEHIGH VALLEY DIESEL COLOR SCHEMES	01	74	29
M	DIESELS PULL MONON TRAINS	07	47	43
MILW	H10-44 AND H12-44 FM ON MILW 1945	01	80	26
	MOTIVE POWER FREEZE-THAWING MILW	11	78	30
	AS-6-16 BALDWIN MILW #2104	06	66	18
	ROAD ENGINE NUMBERS MILW	10	46	31
N&W	TRAINMASTER RETIREMENT N&W #173	02	77	42
NDEM	DIESELS OF MEXICO YOU DIDN'T EXPECT	07	64	41
NP	FT EMD 5400 HP NP #6001 1944	07	49	53
	1500 HP ALCO/GE ROAD SWITCHER NP #158	07	49	51
	660 HP ALCO/GE SWITCHER NP #125 1940	07	49	51
	F3 EMD 4500 HP NP #6504 1947	07	49	50
NYC	DIESEL HYDRAULICS FROM ROCKIES TO BERKSH	06	76	40
PA	PA'S NOT PUT OUT TO PASTURE PHOTO ESSAY	07	68	20
PRR	DIESEL THAT COULDN'T REPLACE STEAMER PRR	05	75	40
	44 TON UNITS PRR	05	75	40
	PRR DIESEL FLEET AMERICA'S LARGEST	04	64	38
	CENTER CAB 2500 HP ROAD DIESEL PRR #8948	01	52	8
R	C430 R #5212 AC/DC TRANSMISSION ALCO	11	66	18
	READING DIESELIZATION	05	62	16
RG	DIESEL HYDRAULICS ON RIO GRANDE 2	11	62	36
	DIESEL HYDRAULICS ON RG ROCKIES WEEKEND	02	62	34
RI	ROCK ISLAND DIESEL DIVERSITY	12	65	28
	BAGGAGE CAR LOCOMOTIVES RI EMD 1929	12	65	34
S	HEATER CAR HC53 S	07	63	45
	SOUTHERN RAILWAY DIESELIZATION	12	49	14
SP	CENTURY SP #9019 HYDAULIC DRIVE ALCO	11	66	18
TP&W	REBUILDING DIESEL UNITS TP&W	01	55	58
UP	M-1000 UP STREAMLINER	11	63	44
	GAS TURBINES FOR UP	02	53	6
	GAS TURBINE LOCOMOTIVE OF UP "BIG BLOW"	07	53	19
USA	DIESEL THAT WAS DRAFTED ALCO USA	03	80	24
WI&W	MRS1 ALCO WI&W #2098 ALCO 1979	09	79	19
WP&Y	CUSTOM BUILT GE UNITS WP&Y 1954	02	56	36

DIESEL LOCOMOTIVE PHOTOS

	M	Y	P
1000 HP ALCO SWITCHER MILW #1672 PHOTO	12	45	38
1000 HP BALDWIN #58501 1925 PHOTO	05	62	44
1000 HP BALDWIN #61000 1929 PHOTO	05	62	44
1000 HP BALDWIN STOCK SWITCHER PHOTO	05	62	46
1000 HP BALDWIN SWITCHER MILW #1680 PHOTO	12	45	38
1000 HP BALDWIN SWITCHER PRR #9276 PHOTO	05	62	46
1000 HP DE 66 ALCO SWIT D&RGW #105 PHOTO	03	46	44
1000 HP EMD SWITCHER MILW #1650 PHOTO	12	45	39
1000 HP EMD SWITCHER W/STEAM GEN PHOTO	03	62	9
1000 HP FM SWITCHER MILW #1502 PHOTO	12	45	38
1000 HP SWITCHER NH #0600 PHOTO 1944	03	45	38
1200 HP SWITCHER W/HOOD TANKS CBL PHOTO	05	58	9
125T GE PHOTO FACE KE #402	07	69	30
136 TON SWITCHER C&NW #1199 PHOTO	02	79	11
144T CENTER CAB GE BN #1101 PHOTO	04	83	19
1500 HP ALCO NYC #1091 PHOTO	12	69	25
1500 HP SMALL NOSE BALDWIN MP #203 PHOTO	05	62	49
171 TON INGERSOL RAND IC #9200 PHOTO	12	70	38
2000 HP DUAL PURPOSE NH #0714 PHOTO	03	45	38
2ST PLYMOUTH US ARMY BICENTENNIAL COLORS	02	76	16
300 HP BOXCAB BALDWIN LI PHOTO 1927	05	62	44
300 HP INTERURBANISH BALDWIN #2 PHOTO	05	62	44
3000 HP 2-D + D-2 B CAB SEA #4500 PHOTO	05	62	49
380 HP DE 26 GE SWITCHER D&RGW #38 PHOTO	03	46	44
380 HP SWITCHER NH #0806 PHOTO 1936	03	45	39
4-8-8-4 6000 HP B PROTOTYPE #600 PHOTO	05	62	48
4-8-8-4 CENTIPEDE PRR #5823 PHOTO	05	62	49
4000 HP EMD PASSENGER MILW #13 PHOTO	12	45	30
44 TON GE HT&W #16 PHOTO	01	71	33
44T SLG&W BICENTENNIAL COLORS PHOTO	07	76	16
44T SWITCHER MP PHOTO	02	42	7
5400 HP EMD FREIGHT MILW #40 PHOTO	12	45	30
5400 HP WESTERN PACIFIC #503 PHOTO	03	42	41
550 SWITCHER RI #529 PHOTO EMD	11	64	21
600 HP ALCO SWITCHER NH #0900 PHOTO 1937	03	45	39
600 HP BALDWIN PROTOTYPE SWITCHER PHOTO	05	62	46
600 HP BALDWIN STOCK SWITCHER PHOTO	05	62	46
600 HP SWITHCER LACKAWANNA #426 PHOTO	11	64	21
660 HP DE 60 BALDWIN SWIT D&RGW #67 PHOTO	03	46	43
660 HP INGERSOL RAND SWIT NH #0901 PHOTO	03	45	39
660 HP SWITCHER NH #0939 PHOTO 1936	03	45	39
70T GE OL&B #102 PHOTO	11	78	23
70T LA&SO #76 BICENTENNAIL COLORS PHOTO	07	76	16
85T GE PHOTO FACE KE #753	07	69	30
85T GE PHOTO FACE KE #766	07	69	30
90 TON GE LUS #41 BICENTENNIAL COLORS PH	11	75	25
900 HP ALCO ACIP BICENTENNIAL COLORS PHO	10	75	16
900 HP EARLY BALDWIN PHOTO PBR #32 1937	05	62	44
900 HP EMC SWITCHER #518 PHOTO EMD	11	64	21
A1A-A1A B PASS DEMONSTRATOR #2000 PHOTO	05	62	48
A1A-A1A BALDWIN LOCO/BAG CNW#5000A PHOTO	05	62	49
A1A-A1A DOUBLE ENDED B CNJ # 200 PHOTO	05	62	48
A1A-A1A ERIE BUILT FM ATSF #90 PHOTO	11	64	42
AB MODEL 1000 RI #750 PHOTO GE 1940	05	64	25
ALCO GE SWITCHER NYC #85 PHOTO	02	42	5

STEPHANS' RAILROAD DIRECTORY

LOCOMOTIVES

DIESEL LOCOMOTIVE PHOTOS

Title	M	Y	P
ALCO HOOD UNITS SEA #1680 PHOTO	11	61	35
ALCO MC #961 PAINT SCHEME PHOTO	11	67	8
ARMCO LIMA SWITCHER PHOTOS E170 SERIES	01	73	42
AS616 BALDWIN HOOD PHOTOS C&O #2209	03	71	13
AS616 BALDWIN PHOTO FACE UP #262	07	69	30
AS616 BALDWIN TRO #52 PHOTO	09	79	34
AS616 RAY #76 BICENTENNIAL COLORS PHOTO	05	76	17
B&M FM SPEED MERCHANT PAINT SCHEME PHOTO	01	58	9
B&M-MAINE CENTRAL FLYING YANKEE PHOTO	01	64	24
B-B GM&O #1900 INGALLS SHIPBUILDING PHOT	01	67	9
B36-8 AT GE #606 PROTOTYPE PHOTO	04	83	4
B6-4 & 5 INGERSOL RAND NW #1200 PHOTO	12	70	35
BABY FACE BALDWIN PHOTO MP #205	11	77	56
BALDWIN DIESEL HYDRAULIC PI #3001	12	69	48
BALDWIN ROAD SWITCHER S&A #109 PHOTO	11	61	34
BL1 C&O #83 PHOTO	12	65	20
BL1 DEMONSTRATOR #499 1949 PHOTO	12	65	20
BL2 B&M #557 & 54 TWO PAINT SCHEMES PHO	03	81	34
BL2 DETAIL FRONT PHOTO B&AR #56	07	65	31
BL2 MONON #36 PHOTO	12	65	21
BOXCAB #1000 CNJ PHOTO	08	78	49
BOXCAB DIESEL 4-8-4 NYC #1550 PHOTO	04	54	12
BOXCAB IRD #91 BICENTENNIAL COLORS PHOTO	06	76	15
BOXCAB PHOTO UNC #3	02	71	51
BQ23-7 GE SCL #5132 PHOTO	02	79	11
BRANCH LINE DIESELS FROM MILW SHOPS#5900	09	48	4
BULLDOG NOSE SUPER CHIEF POWER ATSF PHOT	05	62	41
BURL #9900 PHOTO	01	64	22
BURL SILVER CHARGER PHOTO	01	64	26
BURL SILVER KING & QUEEN SHOVEL NOSE PHO	01	64	25
C-C CENTER CAB 2000 HP DSS&A #300 PHOTO	05	62	47
C36-7 EXPORT MODEL PHOTO	11	84	12
C415 ALCO 44T WTC #684 PHOTO	06	74	27
C415 ALCO RI #415 PHOTO 1966	01	67	10
C415 CENTURY PHOTO RI #420 ALCO	12	67	34
C420 ALCO V&MA #202	11	78	23
C420 CENTURY PHOTO SEA #125 ALCO	12	67	32
C424 CENTURY PHOTO W #B905	12	67	32
C424 GB&W #312 PHOTO	06	82	19
C425 CENTURY PHOTO SP&S #315	12	67	33
C425 CNW #4256 PHOTO	03	84	44
C425 LV #2451 PHOTO	05	76	9
C430 ALCO NYC #2058 PHOTO 1967	11	68	11
C430 CENTURY PHOTO R #5212 ALCO	12	67	33
C430 MORRISTOWN & ERIE #17 PHOTO	10	84	13
C6-1 INGERSOL RAND DL&W #451 PHOTO	12	70	40
C628 ALCO PHOTO FACE SP #7105	07	69	31
C628 CENTURY ALCO 2750 HP ACL#3001 PHOTO	08	64	41
C628 CENTURY ALCO D&H #604 PHOTO 1964	11	64	50
C628 CENTURY PHOTO SP #4850 ALCO	12	67	35
C630 CENTURY PHOTO ACL #2011 ALCO	12	67	35
C636 ALCO PHOTO IC #1101 1968	09	68	31
C643 CENTURY HYDRAULIC PHOTO SP #9019	12	67	35
C855 CENTURY PHOTO UP #61 ALCO	12	67	35
CAB UNIT 1500 HP BALDWIN SEA #2700 PHOTO	05	62	48
CABLESS BN #4500 PHOTO	07	82	19
CF16-4 CF20-4 FM C-LINER NYC #5006 PHOTO	11	64	42
CITY OF SAN FRANCISCO #M-10004 PHOTO	01	64	25
CP16-5 CP20-5 CP24-5 FM C-LINER PHOTO	11	64	42
CV DIESELS COATS OF MANY COLORS PHOTO	11	79	34
DD-35 EMD PHOTO FACE UP #94B	07	69	31
DD35A UP #74 2 GP35'S UNDER ONE ROOF	11	66	25
DDA40X UP #6922 PHOTO	09	78	39
DDA40X UP #900 PHOTOS	01	71	46
DE 225 EMD UNITS D&RGW #540 PHOTO EMD	03	46	39
DES3 BOXCAB NYC #543 PHOTO	12	69	26
DIESEL FACE PHOTOS 1975-79	10	80	42
DIESEL HYDRAULICS OF B NYC #20 PHOTO	05	62	49
DIESEL LOCOMOTIVE FACES PHOTO ESSAY	07	69	30
DL109 GM&O #270 PHOTO	06	71	32
DL109 MILW #14A HIAWATHA PHOTO	06	71	32
DL109 NH #0700 PHOTO	06	71	32
DL109-110 PAIR PHOTO S #6400-6425	06	71	35
DOUBLE CAB BALDWIN 2000 HP CNJ #2905 PHO	12	69	24
DR4-415 BALDWIN CNJ #73 PHOTO	12	69	26
DRS-6-6-15 BALDWIN NW #1500 PHOTO	05	62	47
DS4-4-100 SCL #93 PHOTO	12	69	49
DS44-10 USSC #29 BICENTENNIAL COLORS PHO	06	76	18
DT-6-6-24 CENTER CAB PRR #8954 PHOTO	05	62	47
E3 NW #400 TIMKEN TRUCKS PHOTO GE 1939	05	64	25
E3 PURPLE ACL CHAMPION #P1000 PHOTO	09	78	34
E3 UP #LA5 & 6 CITY OF LOS ANGELES PHOT	05	64	24
E5 BURL SILVER METEOR & COMET PHOTO	05	64	24
E7 EMD PRR #5901 PHOTO	12	69	21
E7 FRISCO TEXAS SPECIAL #2000 PHOTO	01	79	35
E7 W #1000 PHOTO GE 1946	05	64	26
E8 BURL #9946 PHOTO GE	05	64	26
E8 PRR #5765-5766 W/RADIO PHOTO GE	05	64	27
E8 RI #652 BICENTENNIAL COLORS COLOR PHO	10	76	19
E8 SOUTHERN #6910 PHOTO	06	74	29
E9 IC PANAMA LTD #4034 PHOTO GE	05	64	27
E9 SP #6051 WITH DYNAMIC BRAKES PHOTO GE	05	64	27
ERIE BUILT FM NYC #4402 PHOTO	12	69	27
F2 A&EC #400 PHOTO EMD 1940	05	65	44
F2 BURL #158 & 153 PHOTO EMD 1946	05	65	44
F3 EMD PHOTO FACE WP #805-D	07	69	30
F3 ICG #1610 PHOTO	01	79	2
F3-F3B PRR #9543 PHOTO EMD 1948	05	65	45
F3-F3B TP&W #100 & 101 PHOTO EMD	05	65	44
F3A ACL #307 PHOTO	12	69	46
F3B GE ACL #130-C PHOTO	12	69	46
F40PH A #100 PHOTO	12	75	18
F40PH EMD MBTA #1000 PHOTO EMD	01	79	2
F40PH-2 CNJ #413 PHOTO	05	82	19
F40PH-2M PHOTO SPEND RAIL SERVICE	04	83	19
F45 ATSF #1900 PHOTO	01	71	42
F45 GN #434 PHOTO	01	71	43
F7 A-B-A RI #1118 PHOTO EMD 1949	05	65	45
F7 CHINEFIELD COAL CO #014 PHOTO	10	78	75
F7 EMD PHOTO FACE D&RGW #5641	07	69	30

LOCOMOTIVES

DIESEL LOCOMOTIVE PHOTOS	M	Y	P
F7B GE #9676-B PHOTO	12	69	47
F9 ATSF #289C PHOTO EMD 1956	05	65	47
F9 LOEWRY STYLED NP PHOTO EMD 1954	05	65	47
F9 MILW CLASS 17.5 E-F-4 PHOTO EMD 1954	05	65	46
F90PH CTA #102 PHOTO	12	77	74
FA2 ALCO WM #302 PHOTO	12	69	20
FIRST ATSF DIESEL FREIGHT UNT PHOTO 1871	06	41	2
FL9 NH #2001 & 2000 PHOTO EMD	05	65	47
FM DIESEL STATIONARY POWER PLANTS	02	71	15
FP 45 PHOTO ATSF #100 EMD	12	67	38
FP45 ATSF #100 PHOTO	01	71	42
FP7 AL #1776 BICENTENNIAL COLORS PHOTO	04	76	7
FP7 GOLD MOVIE LOCO "TIME EXPRESS" PHOTO	06	79	3
FP7 SEABOARD SYSTEM #118 PHOTO	09	83	21
FP7-F7B 500 PHOTO EMD 1949	05	65	45
FPA2 ALCO APSM #901 PHOTO	09	78	2
FS DIESEL PHOTO MP #508	11	77	54
FT A&B EMD R #259 PHOTO	12	69	24
FT ATSF #158 DETAIL PHOTO	11	65	28
FT DEMONSTRATOR EMD #103 PHOTO 1939	05	65	42
FT EMD UNITS ATSF #100 PHOTO	09	72	41
FT GN #5900 PHOTO EMD 1945	05	65	43
FT KTY #56A PHOTO	12	69	47
FT LACKAWANNA #601 PHOTO 1945	05	65	43
FT-FTSB RI #73 PHOTO EMD 1945	05	65	43
GP-38 PHOTO MC #251 EMD	12	67	36
GP-40 PHOTO IC #3058 EMD	12	67	37
GP10 GULD & MISSISSIPPI #8009 PHOTO	10	85	14
GP15-1 EMD FRIS #105 PHOTO	12	77	20
GP15-1 NORTHWESTERN #4402 PHOTO BABY GEP	09	76	6
GP15T APALACHICOLA NORTHERN #721 PHOTO	09	83	20
GP15T TURBOCHARGED B C&O #1510 PHOTO	01	83	17
GP18 C&NW #1776 BICENTENNIAL COLORS PHOT	11	75	25
GP18 MP #1976 BICENTENNIAL COLORS PHOTO	06	76	19
GP18 PHOTO LOW NOSE B&M #1770	12	65	24
GP18 SEABOARD #400 PHOTO EMD 1960	12	65	24
GP20 PHOTO CBELT #816 EMD 1961	12	65	25
GP20 PHOTO DEMONSTRATORS #5628 EMD 1962	12	65	24
GP20 PHOTO STEAM HEADLIGHT WP #2001 EMD	12	65	25
GP20 PHOTO W/OUT DYNAMIC BRAKES NYC#6110	12	65	25
GP28 PHOTO NO TURBOCHARGE/DYNMIC IC#9430	12	65	27
GP30 EMD PHOTO FACE D&RGW #3006	07	69	30
GP30 PHOTO COW & CALF UP #729	12	65	26
GP30 PHOTO NO MU CONTROLS PHELPS DODGE27	12	65	26
GP30 PHOTO ON ALCO TRUCKS GM&O #506	12	65	27
GP30 READING #5514 EMD PHOTO	12	65	26
GP35 EMD PHOTO FACE D&RGW #3029	07	69	30
GP35 PHOTO HIGH SHORT HOOD N&W #231	12	65	27
GP35 SOO #1776 BICENTENNIAL COLORS PHOTO	11	75	25
GP35 WTC #308 PHOTO	03	75	17
GP38 B&AR #81 PHOTO EMD	11	66	22
GP38 ICG #1776 BICENTENNIAL COLORS PHOTO	05	75	14
GP38 NL&G #46 PHOTO	09	83	21
GP38 P&W #2011 PHOTO	05	85	14
GP38-2 ICG #9568 PHOTO	10	79	19

DIESEL LOCOMOTIVE PHOTOS	M	Y	P
GP38-2 B&M #200 BICENTENNIAL COLORS PHOT	06	75	17
GP38-2 D&S #2000 BICENTENNIAL COLORS PHO	05	76	17
GP38-2 GM&O #746 COLOR PHOTO	06	74	30
GP38-2 GM&O #753 PHOTO	01	74	40
GP38-2 GT&I #1776 BICENTENNIAL COLORS PH	11	75	25
GP38-2 SOUTH SHORE LAKE #2001 PHOTO	04	81	11
GP38-2W CP #5560 PHOTO	01	74	41
GP38AC GTW #1776 BICENTENNIAL COLORS PHO	04	76	16
GP38AC ICG #1776 BICENTENNIAL COLORS PHO	11	75	42
GP39 C&O #3906 PHOTO	01	71	41
GP39-2 KENNECOTT COPPER #785 PHOTO EMD	04	77	9
GP40 CR #3091 IN ROYAL BLUE PHOTO	08	76	67
GP40 KATY #200 BICENTENNIAL COLORS PHOTO	06	76	17
GP40 NYC #3019 PHOTO EMD 1905	11	66	23
GP40 TP&W #1000 NEW COLORS PHOT EMD	04	75	14
GP40-2 B&M #314 PHOTO	03	78	15
GP40-2 B&O #4108 PHOTO	01	74	43
GP40-2 EMD ALASKA #3015 PHOTO	03	79	2
GP40P-2 SP #3197 PHOTO	03	75	17
GP40TC GO #500 PHOTO	06	78	2
GP40X 3500 HP UP #9000 PHOTO EMD	05	78	15
GP50 FRISCO #3100 PHOTO	03	81	18
GP7 ALGOMA CENTRAL #168 PHOTO	03	79	2
GP7 B&A #1776 BICENTENNIAL COLORS PHOTO	03	75	14
GP7 B&M #1557 WITH STRIPES PHOTO	05	75	14
GP7 C&WY #200 BICENTENNIAL COLORS PHOTO	07	75	3
GP7 CF&W #531 PHOTO	10	84	13
GP7 COLUMBUS & GREENVILLE #608 PHOTO	12	78	23
GP7 CONRAIL #5902 PHOTO	12	78	23
GP7 D&TSL #76 BICENTENNIAL COLORS PHOTO	07	76	17
GP7 LOW NOSE AL #1837 PHOTO	02	67	10
GP7 MC #572 PHOTO	04	79	67
GP7 MP #1776 BICENTENNIAL COLORS PHOTO	06	76	19
GP7 PHOTO ATSF #2651 EMD	12	65	22
GP7 PHOTO DEMONSTRATOR #922 EMD	12	65	22
GP7 PHOTO LACK #952 EMD 1951	12	65	23
GP7 PHOTO USA #1826 EMD	12	65	22
GP7 RI #4508 IN INGRAHAM COLORS PHOTO	06	75	7
GP9 CN #1776 BICENTENNIAL COLORS PHOTO	04	76	16
GP9 EMD PHOTO FACE UP #274	07	69	30
GP9 EMD UNITS IC #9242 PHOTO	09	72	41
GP9 PHOTO COW & CALF UP #140 EMD 1954	12	65	23
GP9 PHOTO LATE MODEL GN #727 EMD 1958	12	65	23
GP9 PHOTO PHELPS DODGE #38 EMD	12	65	23
GP9 SP #3001 MULTI HEAD LIGHT PHOTO	11	68	10
GP9E SP #3187 COMMUTER PHOTO	09	82	18C
GTEL GE PHOTO FACE UP #25	07	69	31
H-10-44 FM PHOTO FACE D&RGW #123	07	69	31
H10-44 APA #200 BICENTENNIAL COLORS PHOT	07	76	17
H10-44 FM #1802 PHOTO 1944	11	64	40
H12-44 FM SP #1577 PHOTO 1956	11	64	40
H12-44TS FM SP #542 PHOTO 1956	11	64	40
H15-44 FM PHOTO 1947	11	64	41
H15-44 FM CNJ #1511 PHOTO	02	79	42
H16-44 FM NH #1610 PHOTO 1954	11	64	41

LOCOMOTIVES

DIESEL LOCOMOTIVE PHOTOS	M	Y	P
H16-66 FM C&NW #1672 PHOTO 1951	11	64	43
H20-44 FM AC&Y #505 1947	11	64	41
H20-44 FM SWPC #410 PHOTO	09	79	34
H20-44 UP #410 PHOTO	05	85	14
H24-55 FM TRAINMASTER PRR #8706 1926 PHO	11	64	43
H3-1 INGERSOL RAND BUSH #5 PHOTO	12	70	40
H6-1 INGERSOL RAND NH #0907 PHOTO	12	70	41
HR616 CN #2100 PHOTO BOMBARDIER	06	82	16
IC GREEN DIAMOND PHOTO	01	64	25
INGERSOL RAND EARLY DIESEL PHOTOS	12	70	28
KANSAS STAR #4037 MOVIE LOCO PHOTO	12	77	74
KM PHOTO ALBUM	03	64	11
LIMA PHOTO CATALOG OF DIESEL LOCOS	11	63	30
LITTLE JOE EMDIZED CAB PHOTO MILW	03	67	10
LRC MLW PHOTO	01	74	37
LRC PROTOTYPE PHOTO OF MLW	03	73	14
M-10000 PHOTO UP	09	42	5
M420 P&W #2001 PHOTO 1974 MLW	05	74	16
M420TR MLW ALCAN #26 PHOTO	01	74	39
M420W CN #2500 PHOTO	01	74	41
M640 CP #4744 PHOTO	01	74	45
M640 MLW CP #4744 PHOTO	05	71	12
MID TRAIN CONTROL CAR PHOTO S #5960	04	66	10
MODEL 40 EMD #1134 PHOTO	11	64	22
MP15 S #2349 PHOTO	12	77	20
MP15 BRC #534 BICENTENNIAL COLORS PHOTO	11	75	42
MP15 URR #17 BICENTENNIAL COLORS PHOTO	06	76	18
MRS-1 MILITARY ROAD SWITCHER-1 EMD PHOTO	08	52	16
MRS1 ALASKA #1718 PHOTO EMD	09	83	21
NC1 SWITCHER BIS #71 & #72 PHOTO	11	64	23
NC2 SWITCHER MP #4100 PHOTO EMD	11	64	23
NW SWITCHER KCT #60 PHOTO	11	64	23
NW1 SWITCHER RI #703 PHOTO EMD	11	64	22
NW1A SWITCHER SOO #2100 PHOTO EMD	11	64	22
NW2 IHB #1976 BICENTENNIAL COLORS PHOTO	06	76	18
NW2 SWITCHER ATSF #2367 PHOTO 1943	11	64	22
NW3 SWITCHER GN #5400 PHOTO EMD 1939	11	64	26
NW4 SWITCHER MP #4102 PHOTO	11	64	27
NW5 BN #992 PHOTO	02	82	35
NW5 SWITCHER GN #187 PHOTO	11	64	26
PA ALCO PHOTO FACE SP #6043	07	69	30
PA POSTLUDE PHOTO ESSAY	11	67	29
PA1 ALCO DEMONSTRATOR PHOTO	12	69	23
PA1 ALCO LV #606 PHOTO	12	69	25
RF16 BALDWIN SHARK D&H #1216 COLOR PHOTO	01	75	2
RP-E4D NORFOLK SOUTHERN #9719 PHOTO	06	85	15
RS-1 CHOP NOSE A&STAB #910 PHOTO	12	69	45
RS11 DW&P #3605 BICENTENNIAL COLORS PHOT	05	76	17
RS11 GIL #7414 PHOTO	10	84	12
RS12 MICHIGAN NORTHERN #212 PHOTO	12	78	2
RS1325 SWITCHER C&IM #31 PHOTO	11	64	26
RS3 ALCO BN #4082 PHOTO	09	78	2
RS3 D&H #1976 BICENTENNIAL COLORS PHOTO	05	76	17
RS3 ERIE WESTERN PHOTOS #1602	10	78	75
RS36 ALCO D&H #5015 PHOTO	11	72	17

DIESEL LOCOMOTIVE PHOTOS	M	Y	P
RSD NKP #329 PHOTO	11	83	23
RSD12 ALCOS LS&I #1853 PHOTO	01	79	67
RSD15 LS&I #2402 PHOTO	11	84	14
RSD15 LS&I #2402 PHOTO	05	84	17
RSD15 SLUG ATSF PHOTO	01	71	13
RSD5 ALCO PHOTO FACE UTAH #300	07	69	31
S-4 SLUG PHOTO NW #BU9	02	66	8
S12 NOD #1 BICENTENNIAL COLORS PHOTO	02	76	16
S12 SIERRA RR #44 PHOTO	03	81	19
S2 ACL #45 PHOTO	12	69	48
S2 SBUF #76 BICENTENNIAL COLORS PHOTO	02	76	17
S2 WABASH #318 PHOTO	12	69	49
S4 BAY COLONY #1061 PHOTO	09	83	21
S4 MCO #136 BICENTENNIAL COLORS PHOT	06	76	18
SC EMD SWITCHER EMPIRE COKE #570 PHOTO	09	72	27
SC SWITCHER ATSF #2301 PHOTO EMD	11	64	21
SD-40 EMD PHOTO FACE SP #8413	07	69	31
SD-45 EL #803 PHOTO	05	69	22
SD-7 EMD #990 DEMONSTRATOR PHOTO	05	52	8
SD18 PHOTO C&IM #60 EMD 1961	02	66	24
SD24 C&NW #6626 PHOTO	01	83	18C
SD24 PHOTO BURL #505 EMD	02	66	24
SD24 PHOTO DEMONSTRATOR #5579 EMD 1958	02	66	24
SD24 PHOTO NO CAB BOOSTER UP	02	66	24
SD35 PHOTO ACL #1000 EMD 1964	02	66	24
SD35 PHOTO B&O #7403 EMD	02	66	20
SD38 PHOTO B&LE #861 EMD	12	67	38
SD38-2 BESSEMER #873 PHOTO	01	74	42
SD38-2 EJ&E #668 BICENTENNIAL COLORS PHO	07	76	17
SD38-2 NA #401 PHOTO	04	76	14
SD38-2 YD #1776 BICENTENNIAL COLORS PHOT	07	76	16
SD39 TURBOCHARGED SP #5301 PHOTO	01	71	41
SD40 KCS #616 BICENTENNIAL COLORS PHOTO	06	76	17
SD40 PHOTO MP #709 EMD	12	67	39
SD40 PRR #6100 PHOTO EMD 1966	08	66	48
SD40 SP #7342 PHOTO	03	81	19
SD40 SP #8430 W/OBSERV PLATFORMS EMD PHO	11	66	23
SD40-2 BICENTENNIAL COLORS MILW #156 PHO	02	75	3
SD40-2 BN #1976 BICENTENNIAL COLORS PHOT	07	75	14
SD40-2 CP RAIL #5777 PHOTO	09	76	49
SD40-2 MILW #156 BICENTENNIAL COLORS PHO	11	75	42
SD40-2 RED N&W #6175 PHOTO	10	78	76
SD40-2 UP #3222 PHOTO	01	74	42
SD40A IC #6070 PHOTO	01	71	44
SD40T-2 TUNNEL MOTOR PHOTO D&RGW #5342	01	75	17
SD45 ATSF #1819 PHOTO EMD	11	66	22
SD45 EMD AD DETAILED PHOTOS	04	66	31
SD45 N&W #1776 BICENTENNIAL COLORS PHOTO	11	75	42
SD45 PHOTO ATSF #1827 EMD	12	67	39
SD45 TUNNEL MOTOR SP #9169 PHOTO EMD	05	72	16
SD45 UP #60 PHOTO	11	80	15
SD45-2 ATSF #5688 PHOTO	01	74	44
SD45-2 ATSF #5700 BICENTENNIAL COLORS PH	05	75	14
SD45-2 ATSF #5701 BICENTENNIAL COLORS PH	11	75	42
SD45-2 EL #3679 PHOTO	01	74	44

LOCOMOTIVES

DIESEL LOCOMOTIVE PHOTOS	M	Y	P
SD45T-2 CBELT #9389 BICENTENNIAL COLORS	07	75	14
SD45T-2 SP #9168 PHOTO	01	74	45
SD45T-2SSW SP #9389 BICENTENNIAL COLORS	11	75	42
SD50 SEABOARD SYSTEM #8509 PHOTO	05	83	18A
SD60 DEMONSTRATOR PHOTO EMD	10	84	17
SD7 PHOTO CGA #201 EMD 1953	02	66	22
SD7 PHOTO MILW #2202 EMD 1952	02	66	22
SD7 W/DYNAMIC BRAKES PHOTO PRR #8589 EMD	02	66	22
SD9 PHOTO A&STAB #505 EMD	02	66	23
SD9 PHOTO SOO #2381 EMD 1954	02	66	23
SD9 W/STEAM GENERATOR NWH #1723 EMD	02	66	23
SDL39 MILW #582 PHOTO	01	71	41
SDP-45 BUILDER AD SP #3200 PHOTO	10	67	6
SDP35 IN FAMILY LINES COLORS #1 PHOTO	11	77	75
SDP35 PHOTO SEA #1100 EMD	02	66	24
SDP40 BN #1976 BICENTENNIAL COLORS PHOTO	11	75	42
SDP40 GN #322 W/STEAM GENERATOR EMD PHOT	11	66	23
SDP40F AMTRAK #539 PHOTO	01	74	37
SDP45 PHOTO SP #3200 EMD	12	67	39
SEA #2027 SILVER METEOR PHOTO	01	64	26
SG-1 SLUG PHOTO MILW	04	71	12
SHARKNOSE BALDWIN B&O #866 PHOTO	05	62	48
SHARKNOSE BALDWIN PRR #9721	12	69	22
SHOP LOCO 6 NP "RANCHERO" PHOTO	03	58	51
SILVER CHARGER PHOTO BURL #9908	05	62	29
SILVER KING/QUEEN STREAMLINER PHOTO BURL	12	68	34
SLUG C&NW #BU32 PHOTO	11	71	28
SPD45 EL #3638 BICENTENNIAL COLORS PHOTO	04	76	16
SPIRIT OF 76 SCL TRAIN PHOTOS	02	73	13
STEAM TURBINE UP #61 PHOTO	09	56	30
SW SWITCHER EMD #7800 PHOTO	11	64	23
SW-1000 PHOTO D&RGW #141 EMD	12	67	37
SW-1500 PHOTO RI #930 EMD	12	67	37
SW1 CRT #1 PHOTO	11	83	23
SW1 ITC #603 BICENTENNIAL COLORS PHOTO	07	76	52
SW1 NH #8518 PHOTO	12	78	2
SW1 SWITCHER FWB #1 PHOTO 1939	11	64	22
SW1000 BURL #9316 EMD	11	66	24
SW1001 BIS #19 PHOTO	01	74	38
SW1001 DED #217 PHOTO	01	71	44
SW1200 C&I #36 BICENTENNIAL COLORS PHOTO	07	76	17
SW1200 SWITCHER CBL #1202 1954	11	64	27
SW1200 SWITCHER N&PBL #106 PHOTO EMD	11	64	24
SW1200 SWITCHER NH #646 FLEX TRUCKS PHOT	11	64	27
SW1500 A&BB #1501 PHOTO	05	834	18A
SW1500 BN #313 PHOTO	01	74	38
SW1500 IU #23 BICENTENNIAL COLORS PHOTO	07	76	16
SW1500 K&IT #67 PHOTO	11	66	24
SW600 SWITCHER CL #100 PHOTO EMD	11	64	24
SW7 PHOTO C&I #45	03	71	42
SW7 SWITCHER IC #9319 PHOTO EMD 1950	11	64	25
SW8 SD&AE #1126 PHOTO	02	80	17
SW8 SWITCHER EMD #800 PHOTO 1950	11	64	25
SW8 SWITCHER LV #268 DYNAMIC BRAKES PHOT	11	64	27
SW9 EMD PHOTO FACE CARB #282	07	69	31

DIESEL LOCOMOTIVE PHOTOS	M	Y	P
SW9 EMD PHOTO FACE UP #1846	07	69	31
SW9 HB&T #31 BICENTENNIAL COLORS PHOTO	05	76	16
SW9 PI&SH #1775 BICENTENNIAL COLORS PHOT	10	75	17
SW9 S #1733 PHOTO	11	77	75
SW9 SWITCHER NYC #8923 PHOTO EMD 1951	11	64	25
SW900 BUICK #1776 BICENTENNIAL COLORS PH	11	75	25
SW900 MPCE #1 BICENTENNIAL COLORS PHOTO	10	75	17
SW900 RST #141 BICENTENNIAL COLORS PHOTO	05	76	16
SW900 VS #955 PHOTO	12	69	48
TA EMD UNIT RI #60 PHOTO	09	72	41
TA RI #601 PHOTO GE 1937	05	64	23
TE70-4S SP #7030 PHOTOS	05	78	2
TE70-4S SP #7032 TEST RUN PHOTO 1978	04	79	68
TR2 CGW #59 COW & CALF PHOTO EMD	01	65	26
TR2 SP #4601 & 4701 COW & CALF PHOTO EMD	01	65	28
TR2 UP #1875 A&B COW & CALF PHOTO EMD	01	65	28
TRAINMASTER COW-BALDWIN B-65 CALF EL PHO	02	66	11
TRAINMASTER FM R #863 PHOTO	12	69	21
TRAINMASTER TO SLUG N&W #9910 PHOTO	09	76	49
U18B BABY BOAT SCL #323 PHOTO	08	73	15
U18B NAMED LOCOS MC #400 PHOTO	10	75	19
U18B SCL #250 PHOTO 1973 GE	04	74	15
U18B SCL #303 PHOTO 1973	01	74	40
U23-C PC #6712 PHOTO	01	74	42
U23B GE D&H #304 PHOTO 1908	12	68	8
U23B MISSOURI PACIFIC #2266 PHOTO	03	75	17
U23B PHOTO MONON #601 PHOTO 1910 GE	08	70	21
U23B S #3907 PHOTO 1973	01	74	40
U25B SP #6800 BICENTENNIAL COLORS PHOTO	06	76	19
U25C GE 2500 HP ACL #3001 PHOTO	08	64	41
U28B TRANSKENTUCKY TRANSPORT #248 PHOTO	05	82	19
U30-B FRISCO #846 PHOTO	01	74	43
U30-C MP #963 PHOTO	01	74	42
U30B PHOTO IC #5002	06	67	9
U30B PHOTO NYC #2836	12	67	42
U30C LOW HOOD N&W #8002 PHOTO	07	74	3
U30C PHOTO D&H #701	06	67	8
U30C PHOTO PRR #6539	12	67	42
U30C SOO #805 SIMPLIFIED PAINT PHOTO	01	75	17
U30C XTRA RELIABILITY LOCO L&N #1499 PHO	12	72	20
U30CG ATSF #400 PHOTO STYLED	03	68	11
U30CG PHOTO ATSF #400 SEMI-STREAMLINED	12	67	43
U33B PHOTO GE DEMONSTRATOR #302	12	67	41
U33B SCL #1734 PHOTO	01	74	43
U33C BN #5741 PHOTO	01	74	44
U33C SJ GROVES & SONS #508 PHOTO	02	70	13
U34CH E #3351 PHOTO	01	74	37
U36B AUTO TRAIN #4000 PHOTO	01	74	43
U36B SCL #1776 BICENTENNIAL COLORS PHOTO	11	75	42
U36C NDM #8909 PHOTO	01	74	45
U50 GE UP #43 PHOTO	12	68	52
UB30B GE ACL #978 PHOTO	12	69	45
UNUSUAL ALCO HOOD UNIT RS&S #11 PHOTO	04	66	39
UP #M-10001 PHOTO	01	64	25
WHITCOMB CHICAGO GRAVEL CO #506 PHOTO	10	74	37
XPLORER VS F UNIT NYC PHOTO	08	56	8

LOCOMOTIVES

DIESEL LOCOMOTIVE PHOTOS BY ROAD

RD		M	Y	P
A	SDP40F AMTRAK #539 PHOTO	01	74	37
	F40PH A #100 PHOTO	12	75	18
A&EC	F2 A&EC #400 PHOTO EMD 1940	05	65	44
A&STAB	RS-1 CHOP NOSE A&STAB #910 PHOTO	12	69	45
	SD9 PHOTO A&STAB #505 EMD	02	66	23
A&BB	SW1500 A&BB #1501 PHOTO	05	834	18A
AC&Y	H20-44 FM AC&Y #505 1947	11	64	41
ACIP	900 HP ALCO ACIP BICENTENNIAL COLORS PHO	10	75	16
ACL	E3 PURPLE ACL CHAMPION #P1000 PHOTO	09	78	34
	S2 ACL #45 PHOTO	12	69	48
	UB30B GE ACL #978 PHOTO	12	69	45
	F3B GE ACL #130-C PHOTO	12	69	46
	F3A ACL #307 PHOTO	12	69	46
	C630 CENTURY PHOTO ACL #2011 ALCO	12	67	35
	SD35 PHOTO ACL #1000 EMD 1964	02	66	24
	U25C GE 2500 HP ACL #3001 PHOTO	08	64	41
	C628 CENTURY ALCO 2750 HP ACL#3001 PHOTO	08	64	41
AL	MRS1 ALASKA #1718 PHOTO EMD	09	83	21
	GP40-2 EMD ALASKA #3015 PHOTO	03	79	2
	FP7 AL #1776 BICENTENNIAL COLORS PHOTO	04	76	7
	GP7 LOW NOSE AL #1837 PHOTO	02	67	10
ALCA	M420TR MLW ALCAN #26 PHOTO	01	74	39
ALGC	GP7 ALGOMA CENTRAL #168 PHOTO	03	79	2
APA	H10-44 APA #200 BICENTENNIAL COLORS PHOT	07	76	17
APSM	FPA2 ALCO APSM #901 PHOTO	09	78	2
AS	ARMCO LIMA SWITCHER PHOTOS E170 SERIES	01	73	42
ATR	U36B AUTO TRAIN #4000 PHOTO	01	74	43
ATSF	SD45-2 ATSF #5700 BICENTENNIAL COLORS PH	05	75	14
	SD45-2 ATSF #5701 BICENTENNIAL COLORS PH	11	75	42
	SD45-2 ATSF #5688 PHOTO	01	74	44
	FP45 ATSF #100 PHOTO	01	71	42
	F45 ATSF #1900 PHOTO	01	71	42
	RSD15 SLUG ATSF PHOTO	01	71	13
	FT EMD UNITS ATSF #100 PHOTO	09	72	41
	U30CG ATSF #400 PHOTO STYLED	03	68	11
	U30CG PHOTO ATSF #400 SEMI-STREAMLINED	12	67	43
	SD45 PHOTO ATSF #1827 EMD	12	67	39
	FP 45 PHOTO ATSF #100 EMD	12	67	38
	F9 ATSF #289C PHOTO EMD 1956	05	65	47
	SD45 ATSF #1819 PHOTO EMD	11	66	22
	GP7 PHOTO ATSF #2651 EMD	12	65	22
	A1A-A1A ERIE BUILT FM ATSF #90 PHOTO	11	64	42
	FT ATSF #158 DETAIL PHOTO	11	65	28
	NW2 SWITCHER ATSF #2367 PHOTO 1943	11	64	22
	SC SWITCHER ATSF #2301 PHOTO EMD	11	64	21
	BULLDOG NOSE SUPER CHIEF POWER ATSF PHOT	05	62	41

DIESEL LOCOMOTIVE PHOTOS BY ROAD

RD		M	Y	P
	FIRST ATSF DIESEL FREIGHT UNT PHOTO 1871	06	41	2
B&A	GP7 B&A #1776 BICENTENNIAL COLORS PHOTO	03	75	14
B&AR	GP38 B&AR #81 PHOTO EMD	11	66	22
	BL2 DETAIL FRONT PHOTO B&AR #56	07	65	31
B&LE	SD38 PHOTO B&LE #861 EMD	12	67	38
B&M	BL2 B&M #557 & 54 TWO PAINT SCHEMES PHO	03	81	34
	GP40-2 B&M #314 PHOTO	03	78	15
	GP7 B&M #1557 WITH STRIPES PHOTO	05	75	14
	GP38-2 B&M #200 BICENTENNIAL COLORS PHOT	06	75	17
	GP18 PHOTO LOW NOSE B&M #1770	12	65	24
	B&M-MAINE CENTRAL FLYING YANKEE PHOTO	01	64	24
	B&M FM SPEED MERCHANT PAINT SCHEME PHOTO	01	58	9
B&O	GP40-2 B&O #4108 PHOTO	01	74	43
	SD35 PHOTO B&O #7403 EMD	02	66	20
	SHARKNOSE BALDWIN B&O #866 PHOTO	05	62	48
BESS	SD38-2 BESSEMER #873 PHOTO	01	74	42
BIS	SW1001 BIS #19 PHOTO	01	74	38
	NC1 SWITCHER BIS #71 & #72 PHOTO	11	64	23
BN	NW5 BN #992 PHOTO	02	82	35
	144T CENTER CAB GE BN #1101 PHOTO	04	83	19
	CABLESS BN #4500 PHOTO	07	82	19
	RS3 ALCO BN #4082 PHOTO	09	78	2
	SW1500 BN #313 PHOTO	01	74	38
	SDP40 BN #1976 BICENTENNIAL COLORS PHOTO	11	75	42
	SD40-2 BN #1976 BICENTENNIAL COLORS PHOT	07	75	14
	U33C BN #5741 PHOTO	01	74	44
BRC	MP15 BRC #534 BICENTENNIAL COLORS PHOTO	11	75	42
BUI	SW900 BUICK #1776 BICENTENNIAL COLORS PH	11	75	25
BURL	SILVER KING/QUEEN STREAMLINER PHOTO BURL	12	68	34
	F2 BURL #158 & 153 PHOTO EMD 1946	05	65	44
	SW1000 BURL #9316 EMD	11	66	24
	SD24 PHOTO BURL #505 EMD	02	66	24
	E5 BURL SILVER METEOR & COMET PHOTO	05	64	24
	E8 BURL #9946 PHOTO GE	05	64	26
	BURL SILVER CHARGER PHOTO	01	64	26
	BURL SILVER KING & QUEEN SHOVEL NOSE PHO	01	64	25
	BURL #9900 PHOTO	01	64	22
	SILVER CHARGER PHOTO BURL #9908	05	62	29
BUSH	H3-1 INGERSOL RAND BUSH #5 PHOTO	12	70	40
C&GR	GP7 COLUMBUS & GREENVILLE #608 PHOTO	12	78	23
C&I	SW1200 C&I #36 BICENTENNIAL COLORS PHOTO	07	76	17
	SW7 PHOTO C&I #45	03	71	42
C&IM	SD18 PHOTO C&IM #60 EMD 1961	02	66	24
	RS1325 SWITCHER C&IM #31 PHOTO	11	64	26
C&NW	SD24 C&NW #6626 PHOTO	01	83	18C
	136 TON SWITCHER C&NW #1199 PHOTO	02	79	11
	GP18 C&NW #1776 BICENTENNIAL COLORS PHOT	11	75	25
	SLUG C&NW #BU32 PHOTO	11	71	28
	H16-66 FM C&NW #1672 PHOTO 1951	11	64	43
C&O	GP15T TURBOCHARGED 8 C&O #1510 PHOTO	01	83	17
	AS616 BALDWIN HOOD PHOTOS C&O #2209	03	71	13
	GP39 C&O #3906 PHOTO	01	71	41
	BL1 C&O #83 PHOTO	12	65	20
C&WY	GP7 C&WY #200 BICENTENNIAL COLORS PHOTO	07	75	3
CARB	SW9 EMD PHOTO FACE CARB #282	07	69	31

LOCOMOTIVES

DIESEL LOCOMOTIVE PHOTOS BY ROAD

RD		M	Y	P
CBELT	SD45T-2 CBELT #9389 BICENTENNIAL COLORS	07	75	14
	GP20 PHOTO CBELT #816 EMD 1961	12	65	25
CBL	SW1200 SWITCHER CBL #1202 1954	11	64	27
	1200 HP SWITCHER W/HOOD TANKS CBL PHOTO	05	58	9
CF&W	GP7 CF&W #531 PHOTO	10	84	13
CGA	SD7 PHOTO CGA #201 EMD 1953	02	66	22
CL	SW600 SWITCHER CL #100 PHOTO EMD	11	64	24
CN	HR616 CN #2100 PHOTO BOMBARDIER	06	82	16
	GP9 CN #1776 BICENTENNIAL COLORS PHOTO	04	76	17
	M420W CN #2500 PHOTO	01	74	41
CNJ	F40PH-2 CNJ #413 PHOTO	05	82	19
	H15-44 FM CNJ #1511 PHOTO	02	79	42
	BOXCAB #1000 CNJ PHOTO	08	78	49
	DOUBLE CAB BALDWIN 2000 HP CNJ #2905 PHO	12	69	24
	DR4-415 BALDWIN CNJ #73 PHOTO	12	69	26
	A1A-A1A DOUBLE ENDED B CNJ # 200 PHOTO	05	62	48
CNW	C425 CNW #4256 PHOTO	03	84	44
	GP15-1 NORTHWESTERN #4402 PHOTO BABY GEP	09	76	6
	A1A-A1A BALDWIN LOCO/BAG CNW#5000A PHOTO	05	62	49
CP	SD40-2 CP RAIL #5777 PHOTO	09	76	49
	M640 CP #4744 PHOTO	01	74	45
	GP38-2W CP #5360 PHOTO	01	74	41
	M640 MLW CP #4744 PHOTO	05	71	12
CR	GP7 CONRAIL #5902 PHOTO	12	78	23
	GP40 CR #3091 IN ROYAL BLUE PHOTO	08	76	67
CRT	SW1 CRT #1 PHOTO	11	83	23
CTA	F90PH CTA #102 PHOTO	12	77	74
CV	CV DIESELS COATS OF MANY COLORS PHOTO	11	79	34
D&H	RS3 D&H #1976 BICENTENNIAL COLORS PHOTO	05	76	17
	RF16 BALDWIN SHARK D&H #1216 COLOR PHOTO	01	75	2
	RS36 ALCO D&H #5015 PHOTO	11	72	17
	U30C PHOTO D&H #701	06	67	8
	U23B GE D&H #304 PHOTO 1908	12	68	8
	C628 CENTURY ALCO D&H #604 PHOTO 1964	11	64	50
D&RGW	SD40T-2 TUNNEL MOTOR PHOTO D&RGW #5342	01	75	17
	F7 EMD PHOTO FACE D&RGW #5641	07	69	30
	GP30 EMD PHOTO FACE D&RGW #3006	07	69	30
	GP35 EMD PHOTO FACE D&RGW #3029	07	69	30
	H-10-44 FM PHOTO FACE D&RGW #123	07	69	31
	SW-1000 PHOTO D&RGW #141 EMD	12	67	37
	380 HP DE 26 GE SWITCHER D&RGW #38 PHOTO	03	46	44
	1000 HP DE 66 ALCO SWIT D&RGW #105 PHOTO	03	46	44
	660 HP DE 60 BALDWIN SWIT D&RGW#67 PHOTO	03	46	43
	DE 225 EMD UNITS D&RGW #540 PHOTO EMD	03	46	39
D&S	GP38-2 D&S #2000 BICENTENNIAL COLORS PHO	05	76	17
D&TSL	GP7 D&TSL #76 BICENTENNIAL COLORS PHOTO	07	76	17
DED	SW1001 DED #217 PHOTO	01	71	44
DL&W	C6-1 INGERSOL RAND DL&W #451 PHOTO	12	70	40
DSS&A	C-C CENTER CAB 2000 HP DSS&A #300 PHOTO	05	62	47
DW&P	RS11 DW&P #3605 BICENTENNIAL COLORS PHOT	05	76	17
E	U34CH E #3351 PHOTO	01	74	37
EJ&E	SD38-2 EJ&E #668 BICENTENNIAL COLORS PHO	07	76	17
EL	SPD45 EL #3638 BICENTENNIAL COLORS PHOTO	04	76	16
	SD45-2 EL #3679 PHOTO	01	74	44
	TRAINMASTER COW-BALDWIN B-65 CALF EL PHO	02	66	11

DIESEL LOCOMOTIVE PHOTOS BY ROAD

RD		M	Y	P
FAM	SDP35 IN FAMILY LINES COLORS #1 PHOTO	11	77	75
FRIS	GP50 FRISCO #3100 PHOTO	03	81	18
	GP15-1 EMD FRIS #105 PHOTO	12	77	20
	U30-B FRISCO #846 PHOTO	01	74	43
FWB	SW1 SWITCHER FWB #1 PHOTO 1939	11	64	22
GB&W	C424 GB&W #312 PHOTO	06	82	19
GIL	RS11 GIL #7414 PHOTO	10	84	12
GM&O	GP38-2 GM&O #746 COLOR PHOTO	06	74	30
	GP38-2 GM&O #753 PHOTO	01	74	40
	DL109 GM&O #270 PHOTO	06	71	32
	B-B GM&O #1900 INGALLS SHIPBUILDING PHOT	01	67	9
	GP30 PHOTO ON ALCO TRUCKS GM&O #506	12	65	27
GN	F45 GN #434 PHOTO	01	71	43
	FT GN #5900 PHOTO EMD 1945	05	65	43
	SDP40 GN #322 W/STEAM GENERATOR EMD PHOT	11	66	23
	GP9 PHOTO LATE MODEL GN #727 EMD 1958	12	65	23
	NW5 SWITCHER GN #187 PHOTO	11	64	26
	NW3 SWITCHER GN #5400 PHOTO EMD 1939	11	64	26
GO	GP40TC GO #500 PHOTO	06	78	2
GT&I	GP38-2 GT&I #1776 BICENTENNIAL COLORS PH	11	75	25
GTW	GP38AC GTW #1776 BICENTENNIAL COLORS PHO	04	76	16
HB&T	SW9 HB&T #31 BICENTENNIAL COLORS PHOTO	05	76	16
HT&W	44 TON GE HT&W #16 PHOTO	01	71	33
IC	SD40A IC #6070 PHOTO	01	71	44
	GP9 EMD UNITS IC #9242 PHOTO	09	72	41
	171 TON INGERSOL RAND IC #9200 PHOTO	12	70	38
	U30B PHOTO IC #5002	06	67	9
	C636 ALCO PHOTO IC #1101 1968	09	68	31
	GP-40 PHOTO IC #3058 EMD	12	67	37
	GP28 PHOTO NO TURBOCHARGE/DYNMIC IC#9430	12	65	27
	E9 IC PANAMA LTD #4034 PHOTO GE	05	64	27
	IC GREEN DIAMOND PHOTO	01	64	25
	SW7 SWITCHER IC #9319 PHOTO EMD 1950	11	64	25
ICG	GP38-2 ICG #9568 PHOTO	10	79	19
	F3 ICG #1610 PHOTO	01	79	2
	GP38 ICG #1776 BICENTENNIAL COLORS PHOTO	05	75	14
	GP38AC ICG #1776 BICENTENNIAL COLORS PHO	11	75	42
IHB	NW2 IHB #1976 BICENTENNIAL COLORS PHOTO	06	76	18
IRD	BOXCAB IRD #91 BICENTENNIAL COLORS PHOTO	06	76	15
ITC	SW1 ITC #603 BICENTENNIAL COLORS PHOTO	07	76	52
IU	SW1500 IU #23 BICENTENNIAL COLORS PHOTO	07	76	16
K&IT	SW1500 K&IT #67 PHOTO	11	66	24
KATY	GP40 KATY #200 BICENTENNIAL COLORS PHOTO	06	76	17
KC	GP39-2 KENNECOTT COPPER #785 PHOTO EMD	04	77	9
KCS	SD40 KCS #616 BICENTENNIAL COLORS PHOTO	06	76	17
KCT	NW SWITCHER KCT #60 PHOTO	11	64	23
KE	85T GE PHOTO FACE KE #753	07	69	30
	85T GE PHOTO FACE KE #766	07	69	30
	125T GE PHOTO FACE KE #402	07	69	30
KTY	FT KTY #56A PHOTO	12	69	47
L&N	U30C XTRA RELIABILITY LOCO L&N #1499 PHO	12	72	20
LA&SO	70T LA&SO #76 BICENTENNAIL COLORS PHOTO	07	76	16
LACK	FT LACKAWANNA #601 PHOTO 1945	05	65	43
	GP7 PHOTO LACK #952 EMD 1951	12	65	23
	600 HP SWITCHER LACKAWANNA #426 PHOTO	11	64	21

LOCOMOTIVES

DIESEL LOCOMOTIVE PHOTOS BY ROAD

RD		M	Y	P
LI	300 HP BOXCAB BALDWIN LI PHOTO 1927	05	62	44
LS&I	RSD15 LS&I #2402 PHOTO	11	84	14
	RSD15 LS&I #2402 PHOTO	05	84	17
	RSD12 ALCOS LS&I #1853 PHOTO	01	79	67
LUS	90 TON GE LUS #41 BICENTENNIAL COLORS PH	11	75	25
LV	C425 LV #2451 PHOTO	05	76	9
	PA1 ALCO LV #606 PHOTO	12	69	25
	SW8 SWITCHER LV #268 DYNAMIC BRAKES PHOT	11	64	27
M	U23B PHOTO MONON #601 PHOTO 1910 GE	08	70	21
M&E	C430 MORRISTOWN & ERIE #17 PHOTO	10	84	13
MBTA	F40PH EMD MBTA #1000 PHOTO EMD	01	79	2
MC	GP7 MC #572 PHOTO	04	79	67
	U18B NAMED LOCOS MC #400 PHOTO	10	75	19
	ALCO MC #961 PAINT SCHEME PHOTO	11	67	8
	GP-38 PHOTO MC #251 EMD	12	67	36
MCO	S4 MCO #136 BICENTENNIAL COLORS PHOT	06	76	18
MILW	SD40-2 BICENTENNIAL COLORS MILW #156 PHO	02	75	3
	SD40-2 MILW #156 BICENTENNIAL COLORS PHO	11	75	42
	DL109 MILW #14A HIAWATHA PHOTO	06	71	32
	S6-1 SLUG PHOTO MILW	04	71	12
	SDL39 MILW #582 PHOTO	01	71	41
	LITTLE JOE EMDIZED CAB PHOTO MILW	03	67	10
	SD7 PHOTO MILW #2202 EMD 1952	02	66	22
	F9 MILW CLASS 17.5 E-F-4 PHOTO EMD 1954	05	65	46
	1000 HP EMD SWITCHER MILW #1650 PHOTO	12	45	39
	1000 HP BALDWIN SWITCHER MILW #1680 PHOTO	12	45	38
	1000 HP ALCO SWITCHER MILW #1672 PHOTO	12	45	38
	1000 HP FM SWITCHER MILW #1502 PHOTO	12	45	38
	5400 HP EMD FREIGHT MILW #40 PHOTO	12	45	30
	4000 HP EMD PASSENGER MILW #13 PHOTO	12	45	30
MN	RS12 MICHIGAN NORTHERN #212 PHOTO	12	78	2
MP	BABY FACE BALDWIN PHOTO MP #205	11	77	56
	FS DIESEL PHOTO MP #508	11	77	54
	U23B MISSOURI PACIFIC #2266 PHOTO	03	75	17
	GP18 MP #1976 BICENTENNIAL COLORS PHOTO	06	76	19
	GP7 MP #1776 BICENTENNIAL COLORS PHOTO	06	76	19
	U30-C MP #963 PHOTO	01	74	42
	SD40 PHOTO MP #709 EMD	12	67	39
	NW4 SWITCHER MP #4102 PHOTO	11	64	27
	NC2 SWITCHER MP #4100 PHOTO EMD	11	64	23
	1500 HP SMALL NOSE BALDWIN MP #203 PHOTO	05	62	49
	44T SWITCHER MP PHOTO	02	42	7
MPCE	SW900 MPCE #1 BICENTENNIAL COLORS PHOTO	10	75	17
N&PBL	SW1200 SWITCHER N&PBL #106 PHOTO EMD	11	64	24
N&W	SD40-2 RED N&W #6175 PHOTO	10	78	76
	SD45 N&W #1776 BICENTENNIAL COLORS PHOTO	11	75	42
	TRAINMASTER TO SLUG N&W #9910 PHOTO	09	76	49
	U30C LOW HOOD N&W #8002 PHOTO	07	74	3
	GP35 PHOTO HIGH SHORT HOOD N&W #231	12	65	27
NA	SD38-2 NA #401 PHOTO	04	76	14
NDM	U36C NDM #8909 PHOTO	01	74	45
NH	SW1 NH #8518 PHOTO	12	78	2
	DL109 NH #0700 PHOTO	06	71	32
	H6-1 INGERSOL RAND NH #0907 PHOTO	12	70	41
	FL9 NH #2001 & 2000 PHOTO EMD	05	65	47

DIESEL LOCOMOTIVE PHOTOS BY ROAD

RD		M	Y	P
	H16-44 FM NH #1610 PHOTO 1954	11	64	41
	SW1200 SWITCHER NH #646 FLEX TRUCKS PHOT	11	64	27
	380 HP SWITCHER NH #0806 PHOTO 1936	03	45	39
	660 HP SWITCHER NH #0939 PHOTO 1936	03	45	39
	660 HP INGERSOL RAND SWIT NH #0901 PHOTO	03	45	39
	600 HP ALCO SWITCHER NH #0900 PHOTO 1937	03	45	39
	2000 HP DUAL PURPOSE NH #0714 PHOTO	03	45	38
	1000 HP SWITCHER NH #0600 PHOTO 1944	03	45	38
NKP	RSD NKP #329 PHOTO	11	83	23
NL&G	GP38 NL&G #46 PHOTO	09	83	21
NOD	S12 NOD #1 BICENTENNIAL COLORS PHOTO	02	76	16
NP	F9 LOEWRY STYLED NP PHOTO EMD 1954	05	65	47
	SHOP LOCO 6 NP "RANCHERO" PHOTO	03	58	51
NSO	RP-E4D NORFOLK SOUTHERN #9719 PHOTO	06	85	15
NW	B6-4 & 5 INGERSOL RAND NW #1200 PHOTO	12	70	35
	S-4 SLUG PHOTO NW #BU9	02	66	8
	E3 NW #400 TIMKEN TRUCKS PHOTO GE 1939	05	64	25
	DRS-6-6-15 BALDWIN NW #1500 PHOTO	05	62	47
NWH	SD9 W/STEAM GENERATOR NWH #1723 EMD	02	66	23
NYC	C430 ALCO NYC #2058 PHOTO 1967	11	68	11
	1500 HP ALCO NYC #1091 PHOTO	12	69	25
	DES3 BOXCAB NYC #543 PHOTO	12	69	26
	ERIE BUILT FM NYC #4402 PHOTO	12	69	27
	U30B PHOTO NYC #2836	12	67	42
	GP40 NYC #3019 PHOTO EMD 1905	11	66	23
	GP20 PHOTO W/OUT DYNAMIC BRAKES NYC#6110	12	65	25
	CF16-4 CF20-4 FM C-LINER NYC #5006 PHOTO	11	64	42
	SW9 SWITCHER NYC #8923 PHOTO EMD 1951	11	64	25
	DIESEL HYDRAULICS OF B NYC #20 PHOTO	05	62	49
	BOXCAB DIESEL 4-8-4 NYC #1550 PHOTO	04	54	12
	XPLORER VS F UNIT NYC PHOTO	08	56	8
	ALCO GE SWITCHER NYC #85 PHOTO	02	42	5
OL&B	70T GE OL&B #102 PHOTO	11	78	23
P&W	GP38 P&W #2011 PHOTO	05	85	14
	M420 P&W #2001 PHOTO 1974 MLW	05	74	16
PBR	900 HP EARLY BALDWIN PHOTO PBR #32 1937	05	62	44
PC	U23-C PC #6712 PHOTO	01	74	42
PI	BALDWIN DIESEL HYDRAULIC PI #3001	12	69	48
PI&SH	SW9 PI&SH #1775 BICENTENNIAL COLORS PHOT	10	75	17
PRR	E7 EMD PRR #5901 PHOTO	12	69	21
	SHARKNOSE BALDWIN PRR #9721	12	69	22
	SD7 W/DYNAMIC BRAKES PHOTO PRR #8589 EMD	02	66	22
	U30C PHOTO PRR #6539	12	67	42
	F3-F3B PRR #9543 PHOTO EMD 1948	05	65	45
	SD40 PRR #6100 PHOTO EMD 1966	08	66	48
	H24-55 FM TRAINMASTER PRR #8706 1926 PHO	11	64	43
	E8 PRR #5765-5766 W/RADIO PHOTO GE	05	64	27
	4-8-8-4 CENTIPEDE PRR #5823 PHOTO	05	62	49
	DT-6-6-24 CENTER CAB PRR #8954 PHOTO	05	62	47
	1000 HP BALDWIN SWITCHER PRR #9276 PHOTO	05	62	46
R	C430 CENTURY PHOTO R #5212 ALCO	12	67	33
	TRAINMASTER FM R #863 PHOTO	12	69	21
	FT A&B EMD R #259 PHOTO	12	69	24
	GP30 READING #5514 EMD PHOTO	12	65	26
RAY	AS616 RAY #76 BICENTENNIAL COLORS PHOTO	05	76	17

STEPHANS' RAILROAD DIRECTORY

LOCOMOTIVES

DIESEL LOCOMOTIVE PHOTOS BY ROAD

RD		M	Y	P
RI	E8 RI #652 BICENTENNIAL COLORS COLOR PHO	10	76	19
	GP7 RI #4508 IN INGRAHAM COLORS PHOTO	06	75	7
	TA EMD UNIT RI #60 PHOTO	09	72	41
	C415 CENTURY PHOTO RI #420 ALCO	12	67	34
	C415 ALCO RI #415 PHOTO 1966	01	67	10
	SW-1500 PHOTO RI #930 EMD	12	67	37
	F7 A-B-A RI #1118 PHOTO EMD 1949	05	65	45
	FT-FTSB RI #73 PHOTO EMD 1945	05	65	43
	TA RI #601 PHOTO GE 1937	05	64	23
	AB MODEL 1000 RI #750 PHOTO GE 1940	05	64	25
	NW1 SWITCHER RI #703 PHOTO EMD	11	64	22
	550 SWITCHER RI #529 PHOTO EMD	11	64	21
RS&S	UNUSUAL ALCO HOOD UNIT RS&S #11 PHOTO	04	66	39
RST	SW900 RST #141 BICENTENNIAL COLORS PHOTO	05	76	16
S	MP15 S #2349 PHOTO	12	77	20
	SW9 S #1733 PHOTO	11	77	75
	E8 SOUTHERN #6910 PHOTO	06	74	29
	U23B S #3907 PHOTO 1973	01	74	40
	DL109-110 PAIR PHOTO S #6400-6425	06	71	35
	MID TRAIN CONTROL CAR PHOTO S #5960	04	66	10
S&A	BALDWIN ROAD SWITCHER S&A #109 PHOTO	11	61	34
SBUF	S2 SBUF #76 BICENTENNIAL COLORS PHOTO	02	76	17
SCL	BQ23-7 GE SCL #5132 PHOTO	02	79	11
	U36B SCL #1776 BICENTENNIAL COLORS PHOTO	11	75	42
	U18B BABY BOAT SCL #323 PHOTO	08	73	15
	SPIRIT OF 76 SCL TRAIN PHOTOS	02	73	13
	U18B SCL #250 PHOTO 1973 GE	04	74	15
	U33B SCL #1734 PHOTO	01	74	43
	U18B SCL #303 PHOTO 1973	01	74	40
	DS4-4-100 SCL #93 PHOTO	12	69	49
SD&AE	SW8 SD&AE #1126 PHOTO	02	80	17
SEA	C420 CENTURY PHOTO SEA #125 ALCO	12	67	32
	SDP35 PHOTO SEA #1100 EMD	02	66	24
	SEA #2027 SILVER METEOR PHOTO	01	64	26
	ALCO HOOD UNITS SEA #1680 PHOTO	11	61	35
	3000 HP 2-D + D-2 B CAB SEA #4500 PHOTO	05	62	49
	CAB UNIT 1500 HP BALDWIN SEA #2700 PHOTO	05	62	48
SL&W	44T SL&W BICENTENNIAL COLORS PHOTO	07	76	16
SOO	U30C SOO #805 SIMPLIFIED PAINT PHOTO	01	75	17
	GP35 SOO #1776 BICENTENNIAL COLORS PHOTO	11	75	25
	SD9 PHOTO SOO #2381 EMD 1954	02	66	23
	FP7-F7B SOO PHOTO EMD 1949	05	65	45
	NW1A SWITCHER SOO #2100 PHOTO EMD	11	64	22
SP	SD40 SP #7342 PHOTO	03	81	19
	GP9E SP #3187 COMMUTER PHOTO	09	82	18C
	TE70-4S SP #7030 PHOTOS	05	78	2
	TE70-4S SP #7032 TEST RUN PHOTO 1978	04	79	68
	GP40P-2 SP #3197 PHOTO	03	75	17
	U25B SP #6800 BICENTENNIAL COLORS PHOTO	06	76	19
	SD45T-2SSW SP #9389 BICENTENNIAL COLORS	11	75	42
	SD45 TUNNEL MOTOR SP #9169 PHOTO EMD	05	72	16
	SD45T-2 SP #9168 PHOTO	01	74	45
	SD39 TURBOCHARGED SP #5301 PHOTO	01	71	41
	SD-40 EMD PHOTO FACE SP #8413	07	69	31
	PA ALCO PHOTO FACE SP #6043	07	69	30

DIESEL LOCOMOTIVE PHOTOS BY ROAD

RD		M	Y	P
	C628 ALCO PHOTO FACE SP #7105	07	69	31
	SDP-45 BUILDER AD SP #3200 PHOTO	10	67	6
	SDP45 PHOTO SP #3200 EMD	12	67	39
	C643 CENTURY HYDRAULIC PHOTO SP #9019	12	67	35
	C628 CENTURY PHOTO SP #4850 ALCO	12	67	35
	SD40 SP #8430 W/OBSERV PLATFORMS EMD PHO	11	66	23
	H12-44TS FM SP #542 PHOTO 1956	11	64	40
	H12-44 FM SP #1577 PHOTO 1956	11	64	40
	E9 SP #6051 WITH DYNAMIC BRAKES PHOTO GE	05	64	27
	TR2 SP #4601 & 4701 COW & CALF PHOTO EMD	01	65	28
SP&S	C425 CENTURY PHOTO SP&S #315	12	67	33
SWPC	H20-44 FM SWPC #410 PHOTO	09	79	34
TP&W	GP40 TP&W #1000 NEW COLORS PHOT EMD	04	75	14
	F3-F3B TP&W #100 & 101 PHOTO EMD	05	65	44
TRO	AS616 BALDWIN TRO #52 PHOTO	09	79	34
UNC	BOXCAB PHOTO UNC #3	02	71	51
UP	H20-44 UP #410 PHOTO	05	85	14
	DDA40X UP #6922 PHOTO	09	78	39
	GP40X 3500 HP UP #9000 PHOTO EMD	05	78	15
	SD45 UP #60 PHOTO	11	80	15
	SD40-2 UP #3222 PHOTO	01	74	42
	DDA40X UP #900 PHOTOS	01	71	46
	GTEL GE PHOTO FACE UP #25	07	69	31
	DD-35 EMD PHOTO FACE UP #94B	07	69	31
	AS616 BALDWIN PHOTO FACE UP #262	07	69	30
	GP9 EMD PHOTO FACE UP #274	07	69	30
	SW9 EMD PHOTO FACE UP #1846	07	69	31
	C855 CENTURY PHOTO UP #61 ALCO	12	67	35
	U50 GE UP #43 PHOTO	12	68	52
	DD35A UP #74 2 GP35'S UNDER ONE ROOF	11	66	25
	SD24 PHOTO NO CAB BOOSTER UP	02	66	24
	GP9 PHOTO COW & CALF UP #140 EMD 1954	12	65	23
	GP30 PHOTO COW & CALF UP #729	12	65	26
	E3 UP #LA5 & 6 CITY OF LOS ANGELES PHOT	05	64	24
	UP #M-10001 PHOTO	01	64	25
	TR2 UP #1875 A6B COW & CALF PHOTO EMD	01	65	28
	STEAM TURBINE UP #61 PHOTO	09	56	30
	M-10000 PHOTO UP	09	42	5
URR	MP15 URR #17 BICENTENNIAL COLORS PHOTO	06	76	18
USA	2ST PLYMOUTH US ARMY BICENTENNIAL COLORS	02	76	16
	GP7 PHOTO USA #1826 EMD	12	65	22
USSC	DS44-10 USSC #29 BICENTENNIAL COLORS PHO	06	76	18
UTAH	RSD5 ALCO PHOTO FACE UTAH #300	07	69	31
V&MA	C420 ALCO V&MA #202	11	78	23
VGW	TR2 CGW #59 COW & CALF PHOTO EMD	01	65	26
VS	SW900 VS #955 PHOTO	12	69	48
W	S2 WABASH #318 PHOTO	12	69	49
	C424 CENTURY PHOTO W #B905	12	67	32
	E7 W #1000 PHOTO GE 1946	05	64	26
WM	FA2 ALCO WM #302 PHOTO	12	69	20
WP	F3 EMD PHOTO FACE WP #805-D	07	69	30
	GP20 PHOTO STEAM HEADLIGHT WP #2001 EMD	12	65	25
	5400 HP WESTERN PACIFIC #503 PHOTO	03	42	41
WTC	GP35 WTC #308 PHOTO	03	75	17
	C415 ALCO 44T WTC #684 PHOTO	06	74	27
YD	SD38-2 YD #1776 BICENTENNIAL COLORS PHOT	07	76	16

LOCOMOTIVES

DIESEL LOCOMOTIVE PLANS

	M	Y	P
2000 HP FM ROAD DIESEL DRAWINGS KCS#60A	05	47	24
AMT-125 AMFLEET 1000 DRAWING A	02	76	9
C636 DRAWING CENTURY ALCO	12	67	34
DD-40A DRAWINGS EMD 1966	07	65	9
GP-38 DRAWINGS EMD 1966	07	65	8
GP-40 DRAWINGS EMD 1966	07	65	8
GP38-2 DRAWING EMD	09	76	46
GP39-2 EMD BUILDER DRAWING	01	74	41
MP-15 DRAWING EMD	09	76	46
SD-38 DRAWINGS EMD 1966	07	65	9
SD-40 DRAWINGS EMD 1966	07	65	8
SD-45 DRAWINGS EMD 1966	07	65	8
SD35 EMD 2500 HP ACL #1000 DRAWING	08	64	41
SD40-2 DRAWING EMD	09	76	47
SD40-2 DRAWING EMD	09	76	47
SDP-40 DRAWINGS EMD 1966	07	65	8
SW1000 DRAWINGS EMD 1966	07	65	9
SW1500 DRAWINGS EMD 1966	07	65	9
TRAINMASTER SEE THROUGH DRAWING	08	73	30
U18BT GE BUILDER DRAWING	01	74	38
U23B DRAWING GE	09	76	46
U25C DRAWING GE 1965	11	65	14
U30C DRAWING GE	09	76	47
U36B GE DRAWINGS	04	79	24
UB25-B DRAWING GE 1965	11	65	14

DIESEL LOCOMOTIVE PLANS BY ROAD

RD		M	Y	P
A	AMT-125 AMFLEET 1000 DRAWING A	02	76	9
ACL	SD35 EMD 2500 HP ACL #1000 DRAWING	08	64	41
KCS	2000 HP FM ROAD DIESEL DRAWINGS KCS#60A	05	47	24

DIESEL LOCOMOTIVES

	M	Y	P
PROMISED LAND ALCO FANS PARADISE	05	83	42

ELECTRIC LOCOMOTIVE PROTOTYPE DATA

	M	Y	P
0361 SERIES ELECTRICS NYNH&H	03	71	47
1-D-1 NYC CLASS T1 #3104 1904 ALCO	07	70	24
16 WHEEL ELECT PIEDMONT & NORTHERN #5611	04	45	32
2-8-2 BOXCAB ELECTRIC PRR #5940 LIMA	01	52	19
4-8-4 CLASS R-1 PRR #4999 1934	10	49	19
AC-DC RECTIFIER UNITS NYNH&H	03	57	18
ALCO GE GAS TURBINE ELECTRIC #101	01	49	5
AMTRAK LOCOMOTIVE DISTRIBUTION	12	75	22
B-D + D-B CLASS W1 GN #5019 1934	07	70	34
BOXCAB CLASS EP1 NYNH&H #01 1905 BW	07	70	26
BUTTE ANACONDA & PACIFIC ELECTRIFICATION	07	63	16
C-C CLASS E-50 MEL #200 GE 1968	07	70	37
CLASSIC ELECTRIC LOCOMOTIVES	07	70	20
COAL TURBINE ELECTRIC UP #80 & 80B	03	63	14
COAL TURBINE ELECTRIC UP #80 ALCO 1962	01	63	13
DD1 ELECTRIC UNITS PRR	10	56	28
DETROIT TOLEDO & IRONTON ELECTRICS	09	76	22
E2B & E3B ELECTRIC UNITS PRR	02	54	15
E3 BIPOLAR ELECTRICS MILW 1920 GE	08	49	12
E44 ELECTRIC UNITS PRR ENTER NEW DESIGN	02	61	22
EL2B GE V #125 1948	12	53	55
EL3A V #101 1925	12	53	55
ELECTRIC MOTORS BY TRUCKS PHOTO QUIZ	02	68	45
ELECTRIFICATION ITS ADVANTAGES	04	62	18
ELECTRIFICATION ITS DISADVANTAGES	12	62	40
ELECTRIFICATION ITS PROSPECTS IN 1970	07	70	39
ELECTRO LINER LEGEND NEVER DONE BETTER	11	82	48
ELECTROLINER LEGEND CNS&M OPTIMIST	10	82	34
FF1 ELECTRIC EXPERIMENT PRR #3931 1917	10	49	19
FF2 ELECTRICS PRR	06	58	45
GAS ELECTRIC CARS OF EMD	11	63	38
GAS ELECTRIC CARS TAKE SEATS OUT = LOCO	12	73	40
GAS ELECTRIC LOCOS EPILOGUE	12	73	45
GAS ELECTRIC UNITS, CONTROL OF LTD POWER	01	74	26
GAS TURBINE "BLUE GOOSE" BY WEST-BALDWIN	01	53	25
GAS TURBINE 101 BY ALCO-GE	07	49	14
GAS TURBINE LOCOMOTIVES OF UP 8500 HP	03	56	18
GEARLESS BIPOLAR CLASS EP-2 MILW #10251	07	70	31
GG1 CURTAIN CALL PRR	06	67	18
GG1 ELECTRICS PRR	03	64	20
GG1 GOES IN GRACE	02	84	2A
GG1 ONE LAST TIME, ONE LAST G NYC	08	84	29
GG1 PRR #4824 1934	07	70	32
GG1 REPAIRED AT STRASBURG PA PC	01	75	12
GREAT NORTHERN ELECTRIC LOCOMOTIVES	05	43	4
GREAT NORTHERN ELECTRIC LOCOMOTIVES	12	61	23
HEILMANN EXPERIMENTAL LOCOMOTIVE OF 1890	01	58	40
INTERURBAN FREIGHT UNITS ON OE 1941	10	68	48
LACKAWANNA & WYOMING VALLEY BOXCAB LOCOS	02	66	26
MEET BLACK MARIA OF 1894	10	59	24
MODERN POWER IT F#70	04	41	35
MONTREAL SUBURBAN ELECTRIFICATION CN	03	75	20
MYSTIQUE OF ELECTRIFICATION	07	70	44
NEW LIFE FOR JUICE JACKS MILW	03	52	56
P5 ELECTRICS PRR BEFORE GG1	09	75	44

LOCOMOTIVES

ELECTRIC LOCOMOTIVE PROTOTYPE DATA

	M	Y	P
PRR HISTORY OF ELECTRIFICATION	04	46	40
REELECTRIFICATION OF THE NYNH&H	08	64	20
SIDE ROD BOXCAB CLASS LC-1 N&W #2501 BW	07	70	29
SOUTH AMERICAN ELECTRIC LOCOMOTIVES	04	44	14
STEAM TURBINE ELECTRICS C&O #500	11	50	33
STEAM-ELECTRIC TUG OF WAR	07	70	18
STEEPLE CAB GE B&O #1 1895	07	70	22
TURBINE ELCTRIC 500 SERIES C&O 1947	10	59	42
UPDATING PENNSY ELECTRICS	09	67	6
WHAT'S NEW UNDER PENNSY PANTOGRAPHS	06	58	45

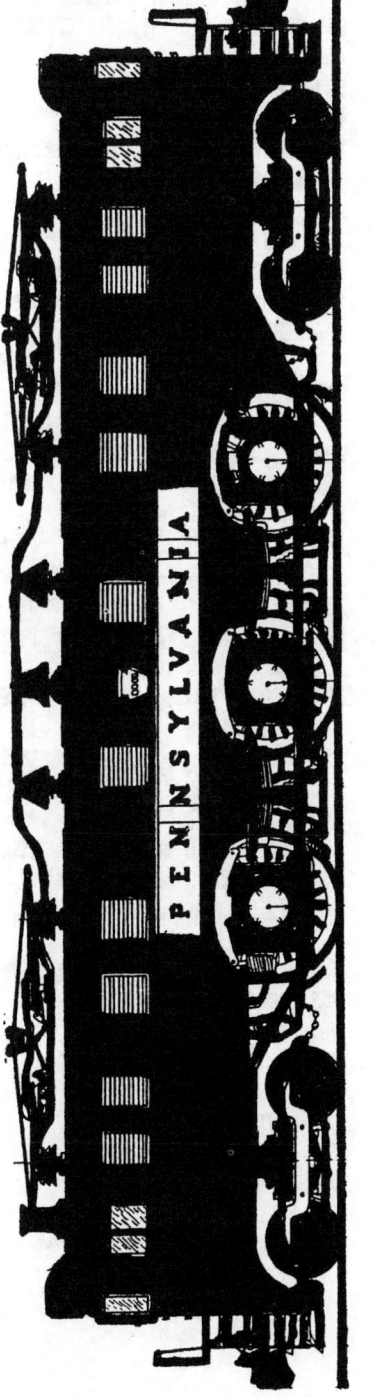

ELEC LOCO PROTOTYPE DATA BY ROAD

RD		M	Y	P
A	AMTRAK LOCOMOTIVE DISTRIBUTION	12	75	22
BA&P	BUTTE ANACONDA & PACIFIC ELECTRIFICATION	07	63	16
C&O	TURBINE ELCTRIC 500 SERIES C&O 1947	10	59	42
	STEAM TURBINE ELECTRICS C&O #500	11	50	33
CN	MONTREAL SUBURBAN ELECTRIFICATION CN	03	75	20
CNS&M	ELECTROLINER LEGEND CNS&M OPTIMIST	10	82	34
DT&I	DETROIT TOLEDO & IRONTON ELECTRICS	09	76	22
GE	STEEPLE CAB GE B&O #1 1895	07	70	22
GN	GREAT NORTHERN ELECTRIC LOCOMOTIVES	05	43	4
	GREAT NORTHERN ELECTRIC LOCOMOTIVES	12	61	23
	B-D + D-B CLASS W1 GN #5019 1934	07	70	34
IT	MODERN POWER IT F#70	04	41	35
L&WV	LACKAWANNA & WYOMING VALLEY BOXCAB LOCOS	02	66	26
MEL	C-C CLASS E-50 MEL #200 GE 1968	07	70	37
MILW	E3 BIPOLAR ELECTRICS MILW 1920 GE	08	49	12
	NEW LIFE FOR JUICE JACKS MILW	03	52	56
	GEARLESS BIPOLAR CLASS EP-2 MILW #10251	07	70	31
N&W	SIDE ROD BOXCAB CLASS LC-1 N&W #2501 BW	07	70	29
NYC	GG1 ONE LAST TIME, ONE LAST G NYC	08	84	29
	1-D-1 NYC CLASS T1 #3104 1904 ALCO	07	70	24
NYNH&H	AC-DC RECTIFIER UNITS NYNH&H	03	57	18
	REELECTRIFICATION OF THE NYNH&H	08	64	20
	0361 SERIES ELECTRICS NYNH&H	03	71	47
	BOXCAB CLASS EP1 NYNH&H #01 1905 BW	07	70	26
OE	INTERURBAN FREIGHT UNITS ON OE 1941	10	68	48
P&N	16 WHEEL ELECT PIEDMONT & NORTHERN #5611	04	45	32
PC	GG1 REPAIRED AT STRASBURG PA PC	01	75	12
PRR	DD1 ELECTRIC UNITS PRR	10	56	28
	P5 ELECTRICS PRR BEFORE GG1	09	75	44
	FF2 ELECTRICS PRR	06	58	45
	WHAT'S NEW UNDER PENNSY PANTOGRAPHS	06	58	45
	4-8-4 CLASS R-1 PRR #4999 1934	10	49	19
	FF1 ELECTRIC EXPERIMENT PRR #3931 1917	10	49	19
	GG1 ELECTRICS PRR	03	64	20
	2-8-2 BOXCAB ELECTRIC PRR #5940 LIMA	01	52	19
	E2B & E3B ELECTRIC UNITS PRR	02	54	15
	E44 ELECTRIC UNITS PRR ENTER NEW DESIGN	02	61	22
	UPDATING PENNSY ELECTRICS	09	67	6
	GG1 CURTAIN CALL PRR	06	67	18
	PRR HISTORY OF ELECTRIFICATION	04	46	40
	GG1 PRR #4824 1934	07	70	32
UP	GAS TURBINE LOCOMOTIVES OF UP 8500 HP	03	56	18
	COAL TURBINE ELECTRIC UP #80 & 80B	03	63	14
	COAL TURBINE ELECTRIC UP #80 ALCO 1962	01	63	13
V	EL2B GE V #125 1948	12	53	55
	EL3A V #101 1925	12	53	55

ELECTRIC LOCOMOTIVE PLANS

	M	Y	P
E252B GE 2500 HP DRAWING	05	76	15
ELECTROLINER ZEPHYR DRAWINGS CNS&M	10	82	36

LOCOMOTIVES

ELECTRIC LOCOMOTIVE PHOTOS

	M	Y	P
139T GE ELECTRIC NYC #1174 PHOTO	03	43	14
2-2+2+2+2-2 CM&SP #10203 PHOTO	11	54	14
2-C + C-2 GE PHOTO NH #0361 1938	03	71	48
260T 1-C+C-1 GN #5011 PHOTO GE	12	61	30
30T STEEPLE CAB H&N #1 BICENT COLORS PHO	05	76	16
70 TON ELECTRIC YARD GOAT PHOTO MILW#E80	02	66	8
ASEA 6000 HP B-B DEMONSTRATOR A #X995	01	77	67
BOXCAB BA&P #44 PHOTO	01	74	12
BOXCAB ELECTRIC BA&P #50 PHOTO	02	79	34
BOXCAB ELECTRIC P&N #5610 PHOTO	04	42	25
CITY OF DECATUR ELECTROLINER IC#300 PHOT	01	49	35
COMPACT SHIFTER PRR #3921 PHOTO	07	61	38
DDPE #100 PHOTO	05	78	2
E57B BOXCAB GE 1916 MILW PHOTO	01	76	16
E60 DW #WFU2 PHOTO	11	83	22
E60C GE PROTOTYPE PHOTO 1972	01	73	7
E60CP FIRST OF GG1 SUCCESSOR A #951 PHOT	03	75	2
E70 LITTLE JOE MILW 1947 GE PHOTO	01	76	16
E8 BOOSTER C&NW #504 PHOTO	06	73	13
EF1 LOCO NYNH&H #083 PHOTO 1912	03	45	33
EF2 LOCO NYNH&H #0112 PHOTO	03	45	34
EF3 LOCO MILW #E28 PHOTO	12	45	37
EF3 LOCO NYNH&H #0153 PHOTO 1942	03	45	34
ELECTRIC PHOTO B&O #1 OF 1894	04	43	17
ELECTRIC PHOTO B&O #18 OF 1927	04	43	17
ELECTRIC PHOTO B&O #5 OF 1903	04	43	17
EP1 LOCO NYNH&H #012 PHOTO 1906	03	45	32
EP2 GE LOCO MILW #E4 PHOTO	12	45	39
EP2 LOCO NYNH&H #0319 PHOTO 1919	03	45	33
EP3 LOCO NYNH&H #0351 PHOTO 1931	03	45	34
EP3 WESTINGHOUSE MILW #10300 PHOTO	12	45	38
EP4 LOCO NYNH&H #0361 PHOTO 1938	03	45	34
EY LOCO NYNH&H #0200 PHOTO 1911	03	45	32
FF2 PRR #5 PHOTO (EX GN) 30 YEARS NEW	06	58	49
GAS ELECTRIC ARMORED USA #10001 PHOTO	12	73	48
GAS ELECTRIC CBA PHOTO	12	73	47
GAS ELECTRIC DPE #101 PHOTO	12	73	47
GAS ELECTRIC EEC #11 PHOTO	12	73	49
GAS ELECTRIC GE CAR TAT #1 PHOTO	11	73	47
GAS ELECTRIC JS #4 PHOTO	12	73	49
GAS ELECTRIC TRANSFER LOCO EEC #1006 PHO	12	73	46
GG1 1/2 UNIT REBUILD PHOTO PC	04	71	14
GG1 CR #4800 BICENTENNIAL COLORS PHOTO	06	76	8
GG1 FACE PHOTO PRR #4800	02	83	02
GG1 PHOTO PRR #4935	08	77	2
GG1 PRR #4877 & 4936 PHOTOS	09	81	2
GG1 PRR #4935 PHOTO	02	79	2
GM10B DEMONSTRATOR PHOTO 1976	10	76	11
GM6C PROTOTYPE SKETCHES	04	75	13
HOOSIC TUNNEL MOTORS B&M #5005 PHOTO	02	42	36
IC # 10001 PHOTO	07	41	21
P5B PRR #4702 PHOTO	09	75	48
ROAD ELECTRIC NYC #1144 PHOTO 1906	02	42	6
STEEPLE CAB ST #15 PHOTO	08	46	49
SWITCHER PE #1603 PHOTO	06	42	22

ELECTRIC LOCOMOTIVE PHOTOS BY ROAD

RD		M	Y	P
A	E60CP FIRST OF GG1 SUCCESSOR A #951 PHOT	03	75	2
	ASEA 6000 HP B-B DEMONSTRATOR A #X995	01	77	67
B&M	HOOSIC TUNNEL MOTORS B&M #5005 PHOTO	02	42	36
B&O	ELECTRIC PHOTO B&O #18 OF 1927	04	43	17
	ELECTRIC PHOTO B&O #5 OF 1903	04	43	17
	ELECTRIC PHOTO B&O #1 OF 1894	04	43	17
BA&P	BOXCAB BA&P #44 PHOTO	01	74	12
	BOXCAB ELECTRIC BA&P #50 PHOTO	02	79	34
C&NW	E8 BOOSTER C&NW #504 PHOTO	06	73	13
CBA	GAS ELECTRIC CBA PHOTO	12	73	47
CM&SP	2-2+2+2+2-2 CM&SP #10203 PHOTO	11	54	14
CR	GG1 CR #4800 BICENTENNIAL COLORS PHOTO	06	76	8
DPE	DDPE #100 PHOTO	05	78	2
	GAS ELECTRIC DPE #101 PHOTO	12	73	47
DW	E60 DW #WFU2 PHOTO	11	83	22
EEC	GAS ELECTRIC TRANSFER LOCO EEC #1006 PHO	12	73	46
	GAS ELECTRIC EEC #11 PHOTO	12	73	49
GN	260T 1-C+C-1 GN #5011 PHOTO GE	12	61	30
H&N	30T STEEPLE CAB H&N #1 BICENT COLORS PHO	05	76	16
IC	IC # 10001 PHOTO	07	41	21
	CITY OF DECATUR ELECTROLINER IC#300 PHOT	01	49	35
JS	GAS ELECTRIC JS #4 PHOTO	12	73	49
MILW	E70 LITTLE JOE MILW 1947 GE PHOTO	01	76	16
	E57B BOXCAB GE 1916 MILW PHOTO	01	76	16
	70 TON ELECTRIC YARD GOAT PHOTO MILW#E80	02	66	8
	EP2 GE LOCO MILW #E4 PHOTO	12	45	39
	EP3 WESTINGHOUSE MILW #10300 PHOTO	12	45	38
	EF3 LOCO MILW #E28 PHOTO	12	45	37
NH	2-C + C-2 GE PHOTO NH #0361 1938	03	71	48
NYC	ROAD ELECTRIC NYC #1144 PHOTO 1906	02	42	6
	139T GE ELECTRIC NYC #1174 PHOTO	03	43	14
NYNH&H	EF3 LOCO NYNH&H #0153 PHOTO 1942	03	45	34
	EF2 LOCO NYNH&H #0112 PHOTO	03	45	34
	EP4 LOCO NYNH&H #0361 PHOTO 1938	03	45	34
	EP3 LOCO NYNH&H #0351 PHOTO 1931	03	45	34
	EP2 LOCO NYNH&H #0319 PHOTO 1919	03	45	33
	EF1 LOCO NYNH&H #083 PHOTO 1912	03	45	33
	EY LOCO NYNH&H #0200 PHOTO 1911	03	45	32
	EP1 LOCO NYNH&H #012 PHOTO 1906	03	45	32
P&N	BOXCAB ELECTRIC P&N #5610 PHOTO	04	42	25
PC	GG1 1/2 UNIT REBUILD PHOTO PC	04	71	14
PE	SWITCHER PE #1603 PHOTO	06	42	22
PRR	FF2 PRR #5 PHOTO (EX GN) 30 YEARS NEW	06	58	49
	P5B PRR #4702 PHOTO	09	75	48
	GG1 FACE PHOTO PRR #4800	02	83	02
	GG1 PRR #4877 & 4936 PHOTOS	09	81	2
	COMPACT SHIFTER PRR #3921 PHOTO	07	61	38
	GG1 PHOTO PRR #4935	08	77	2
	GG1 PRR #4935 PHOTO	02	79	2
ST	STEEPLE CAB ST #15 PHOTO	08	46	49
TAT	GAS ELECTRIC GE CAR TAT #1 PHOTO	11	73	47
USA	GAS ELECTRIC ARMORED USA #10001 PHOTO	12	73	48

LOCOMOTIVES

GENERAL LOCOMOTIVE PROTOTYPE DATA

	M	Y	P
1948 MOTIVE POWER 1ST SHIFT FROM STEAM	04	49	26
1949 MOTIVE POWER SURVEY 2ND ANNUAL	04	50	16
1950 MOTIVE POWER SURVEY 3RD ANNUAL	04	51	20
1951 MOTIVE POWER SURVEY 4TH ANNUAL	04	52	52
1952 MOTIVE POWER SURVEY 5TH ANNUAL	05	53	50
1953 MOTIVE POWER SURVEY 6TH ANNUAL	05	54	48
1954 MOTIVE POWER SURVEY 7TH ANNUAL	05	55	45
1955 MOTIVE POWER SURVEY 8TH ANNUAL	05	56	25
1956 MOTIVE POWER SURVEY 9TH 90% DIESEL	05	57	53
1957 MOTIVE POWER 10TH ANNUAL RECESSION	05	58	52
1958 MOTIVE POWER SURVEY 11TH ANNUAL	05	59	22
1959 MOTIVE POWER 12TH ANNUAL WHY IMPORT	05	60	43
1960 MOTIVE POWER 13TH ANNUAL LOCO LAG	06	61	34
1961 MOTIVE POWER SURVEY 14TH ANNUAL	06	62	26
1962 MOTIVE POWER SURVEY 15TH DIESEL DIF	06	63	18
1963 MOTIVE POWER 16TH 4 MOTORS ENOUGH?	08	64	40
1964 MOTIVE POWER 17TH ANNUAL 2500HP	08	65	23
1965 MOTIVE POWER 18TH HOW HIGH THE HP?	09	66	20
1966 MOTIVE POWER 19TH HOW TO MERGE IT	10	67	20
1967 MOTIVE POWER 20TH IRON HORSE OPERA	11	68	20
1968 MOTIVE POWER 21ST HP ALONE NOT LOCO	07	69	20
1969 MOTIVE POWER 22ND YR OF INTERMEDIAT	08	70	20
1970 MOTIVE POWER 23RD LOCOS BACKGROUND	11	71	24
1971 MOTIVE POWER 24TH ONLY EMD/GE LEFT	08	72	40
1972 MOTIVE POWER 25TH BEG-BORROW OR BUY	09	73	20
1973 MOTIVE POWER 26TH OLD/NEW/BORROW/BLU	10	74	46
1974 MOTIVE POWER 27TH POINTLESS ARROW	12	75	22
1975 MOTIVE POWER 28TH REBUILD OR REPLAC	09	76	41
2-8-8-2 VS. 2-8+8-2 AND ALL THAT	05	82	3
ATOMIC LOCOMOTIVES	07	55	21
COAL TURBINE LOCOMOTIVE OF UP #80	01	63	13
FACTORS IN MOTIVE POWER DESIGN	09	48	28
FLYING SCOTSMAN	10	45	18
HITLER'S SUPER LOCOMOTIVES	08	84	38
HOOD UNITS IN STEAM	11	57	29
LIMA'S LAST LOCOMOTIVE	11	51	6
LOCO FACE QUIZ	08	57	56
LOCO FACE QUIZ METAMORPHOSES	11	57	23
LOCOMOTIVE BUILDING PROGRAM 1943	09	43	38
LOCOMOTIVE NAMES THE UNUSUAL ONES	01	57	25
LOCOMOTIVE PHOTO QUIZ	10	45	34
LOCOMOTIVE ROAD & TYPE PHOTO QUIZ	09	61	39
LOCOMOTIVES NEW LOOK	06	48	48
LOCOMOTIVES NUMBERED 9000 ON CN	02	53	22
LOCOMOTIVES OF LACKAWANA	12	78	48
LOCOMOTIVES OF THE FUTURE	01	43	28
LOCOMOTIVES OF THE SANTA FE (ATSF)	05	49	51
MOTIVE POWER THAT WON THE WEST	05	69	54
NEW HAVEN POWER PHOTO REVIEW	03	45	32
POSTSCRIPT AT POTOMIC YARD ALEXANDRIA VA	10	78	22
SAND FOR RAILS	08	46	18
STEAM TURBINE DRIVING GEAR PRR 1945	06	45	26
STEAM TURBINE LOCOMOTIVES COALS NEW HOPE	06	47	14
STEAM-DIESEL-ELECT-TURBINE-ATOMIC LOCOS	03	53	12
WHAT'LL YOU HAVE-STEAM OR DIESEL?	09	55	8

GENERAL LOCOMOTIVE PROTOTYPE DATA BY ROAD

RD		M	Y	P
ATSF	LOCOMOTIVES OF THE SANTA FE (ATSF)	05	49	51
CN	LOCOMOTIVES NUMBERED 9000 ON CN	02	53	22
EL	LOCOMOTIVES OF LACKAWANA	12	78	48
NH	NEW HAVEN POWER PHOTO REVIEW	03	45	32
PRR	STEAM TURBINE DRIVING GEAR PRR 1945	06	45	26
UP	COAL TURBINE LOCOMOTIVE OF UP #80	01	63	13

STEPHANS' RAILROAD_DIRECTORY

BILL OF LADING   PASSENGER EQUIPMENT

The passenger equipment section is broken down into eleven categories: Baggage Cars, RPO's, Express Cars, Combines, Coaches, Diners, Sleepers, Dome Cars, Observation Cars, Self Motorized Cars, and General Passenger Equipment. These eleven have the following three subject areas:

Prototype data includes articles and specifications on the real thing. In many instances there are photographs with these articles that did not get special billing in the photograph section. The plans and drawings are just that. Generally by our convention a drawing is more detailed than a plan, but this is not a hard and fast rule. The plans are listed twice: once alphabetically and once by road. The photo section shows details or unusual photos of interest to the researcher. Obviously we did not list all photos that appear in these magazines.

The passenger descriptor line includes the description of the car, its road, number, class, builder, and date built. As much of this information that is available or that will fit is included.

MANIFEST   PASSENGER CARS

	PAGE
PASSENGER EQUIPMENT	282
BAGGAGE CARS	284
BAGGAGE CAR PROTOTYPE DATA	284
EXPRESS CARS	284
EXPRESS CAR PROTOTYPE DATA	284
DINERS	284
DINER PROTOTYPE DATA	284
DINER PHOTOS	284
DINER PHOTOS BY ROAD	284
DINER RECIPES	284
RPO CARS	284
RPO PROTOTYPE DATA	284
RPO PHOTOS	284
SLEEPERS	285
SLEEPER PROTOTYPE DATA	285
SLEEPER PROTOTYPE DATA BY ROAD	285
SLEEPER PHOTOS	285
SLEEPER PHOTOS BY ROAD	285
COACHES	284
COACH PROTOTYPE DATA	284
COACH PROTOTYPE DATA BY ROAD	284
COACH PLANS	284
COACH PHOTOS	284
COACH PHOTOS BY ROAD	284
DOME CARS	285
DOME CAR PROTOTYPE DATA	285
DOME CAR PROTOTYPE DATA BY ROAD	285
DOME CAR PHOTOS	285
DOME CAR PHOTOS BY ROAD	285
OBSERVATION CARS	285
OBSERVATION CAR PROTOTYPE DATA	285
OBSERVATION CAR PHOTOS	285
OBSERVATION CAR PHOTOS BY ROAD	286
RAILCARS	286
RAILCAR PROTOTYPE DATA	286
RAILCAR PROTOTYPE DATA BY ROAD	286
RAILCAR PLANS	286
RAILCAR PHOTOS	286
RAILCAR PHOTOS BY ROAD	287
GENERAL PASSENGER CARS	287
GENERAL PASSENGER CAR PROTOTYPE DATA	287
GENERAL PASS CAR PROTOTYPE DATA BY ROAD	289
GENERAL PASSENGER CAR PLANS	287
GENERAL PASSENGER CAR PHOTOS	287
GENERAL PASSENGER CAR PHOTOS BY ROAD	287

NOTE: SEE PAGE 400

PASSENGER EQUIPMENT

BAGGAGE CAR PROTOTYPE DATA

	M	Y	P
BAGGAGE CAR LOCOMOTIVE RI EMD 1929	12	65	34

EXPRESS CAR PROTOTYPE DATA

	M	Y	P
RUSH-PERISHABLE EXPRESS REEFERS	03	42	12

RPO PROTOTYPE DATA

	M	Y	P
MAIL PICKUP ON B&M	03	49	50

RPO PHOTOS

	M	Y	P
OPEN PLATFORM RPO CMSP #225 PHOTO	02	71	34

DINER PROTOTYPE DATA

	M	Y	P
DINING CAR SERVICE AND OPERATION.	01	41	5
DINING CAR SERVICE AND OPERATIONS	09	51	36
TABLE FOR ONE NYC	01	52	46

DINER RECIPES

	M	Y	P
LOBSTER ALA NEWBURG NYC	01	52	47
MOUNTAIN TROUT AU BLEU RECIPE ATSF	06	52	57

DINER PHOTOS

	M	Y	P
BUFFET PHOTO NYC #440 PULL 1910	01	60	20
CAFE-CHAIR CAR PHOTO GCE #1008 PULL 1905	01	60	21
DINER CLASS 900 PHOTO C&NW "LELAND" 1896	01	60	20
DINER PHOTO C&O #961 PULL 1917	01	60	20
DINER PHOTO MILW "WAUWATOSA" BS 1909	01	60	21
METROLINER SNACKBAR COACH A #867 PHOTO	02	74	13

DINER PHOTOS BY ROAD

RD		M	Y	P
A	METROLINER SNACKBAR COACH A #867 PHOTO	02	74	13
C&NW	DINER CLASS 900 PHOTO C&NW "LELAND" 1896	01	60	20
C&O	DINER PHOTO C&O #961 PULL 1917	01	60	20
GCE	CAFE-CHAIR CAR PHOTO GCE #1008 PULL 1905	01	60	21
MILW	DINER PHOTO MILW "WAUWATOSA" BS 1909	01	60	21
NYC	BUFFET PHOTO NYC #440 PULL 1910	01	60	20

COACH PROTOTYPE DATA

	M	Y	P
BED FOR THE COACH PASSENGER	08	53	6
BILEVEL COACHES ON NW	01	58	12
BUSINESS CAR DESIGNED FOR LIVING	11	49	40
DAY COACHES	08	51	38
PARLOR CAR SERVICE ON THE LI	05	68	24
PRIVATE CAR "VIRGINA CITY"	04	56	23
PRIVATE CARS SCRUMPTIOS STEAMCARS	11	60	52
PRIVATE CARS- PINS CUSHIONS	04	78	20
SUPERLINER HIGH POINTS	06	79	16
UNUSUAL MYSTERY COACH B&M	09	49	54

COACH PROTOTYPE DATA BY ROAD

RD		M	Y	P
B&M	UNUSUAL MYSTERY COACH B&M	09	49	54
LI	PARLOR CAR SERVICE ON THE LI	05	68	24
NW	BILEVEL COACHES ON NW	01	58	12

COACH PHOTOS

	M	Y	P
72 PASSENGER COACH PHOTO KCS #274 1965	01	66	8
BILEVEL COMMUTER CAR CTA #7754 PHOTO	10	79	19
BILEVEL COMMUTER CAR PHOTO BN #744	08	74	15
BUFFET-LOUNGE COACH IC #3857	01	60	19
BUSINESS CAR 1A NORFOLK SOUTHERN PHOTO	05	84	12
CHAIR CAR PHOTO PRR #800 PULL 1905	01	60	18
GALLERY COMMUTER COACH C&NW #1 PHOTO	06	55	9
HARRIMAN COACH IC #880 AC&F 1913	01	60	19
HAWKER SIDDELEY BILEVEL CARS GO PHOTO	06	78	2
HIGH LEVEL CHAIR CAR ATSF PHOTO	11	54	9
PASSENGER COACH PHOTOS C&GR #B23 & #B27	01	61	52
PRIVATE CAR PHOTO OSL #1903 PULL	01	60	26
STD P70 COACH PHOTO PRR #8055 AC&F 1914	01	60	18

COACH PHOTOS BY ROAD

RD		M	Y	P
ATSF	HIGH LEVEL CHAIR CAR ATSF PHOTO	11	54	9
BN	BILEVEL COMMUTER CAR PHOTO BN #744	08	74	15
C&GR	PASSENGER COACH PHOTOS C&GR #B23 & #B27	01	61	52
C&NW	GALLERY COMMUTER COACH C&NW #1 PHOTO	06	55	9
CTA	BILEVEL COMMUTER CAR CTA #7754 PHOTO	10	79	19
GO	HAWKER SIDDELEY BILEVEL CARS GO PHOTO	06	78	2
IC	HARRIMAN COACH IC #880 AC&F 1913	01	60	19
	BUFFET-LOUNGE COACH IC #3857	01	60	19
KCS	72 PASSENGER COACH PHOTO KCS #274 1965	01	66	8
NSO	BUSINESS CAR 1A NORFOLK SOUTHERN PHOTO	05	84	12
OSL	PRIVATE CAR PHOTO OSL #1903 PULL	01	60	26
PRR	STD P70 COACH PHOTO PRR #8055 AC&F 1914	01	60	18
	CHAIR CAR PHOTO PRR #800 PULL 1905	01	60	18

COACH PLANS

	M	Y	P
SUPERLINER DRAWINGS	06	79	17

PASSENGER EQUIPMENT

SLEEPER PROTOTYPE DATA

	M	Y	P
AMTRAK SLUMBER-COACHES	11	78	48
BEEBE PONDERS THE PULLMANS	10	61	36
BUDGET SLEEPING CARS	03	63	36
BUNKING DOWN IN AMTRAK AMCOACH	08	78	12
COAST TO COAST SLEEPER OF 1885 FI	01	47	63
GAP BETWEEN RECLINER SEAT & UPPER BERTH	11	78	55
GEORGE PULLMAN & SLEEPING CARS	08	41	17
HOTEL PULLMAN	02	42	44
I'VE BEEN RIDING THE PULLMANS	05	44	6
MODERN SCHLAFWAGEN	12	40	39
MR PULLMAN REVISITED	01	65	20
NIGHT PASSAGE ON B&O	06	58	43
PULLMAN CAR NAMES	06	41	40
SLUMBERCOACHES WHAT PRICE SLEEP	01	57	40
TROOP SLEEPER	11	43	36

SLEEPER PROTOTYPE DATA BY ROAD

RD		M	Y	P
A	BUNKING DOWN IN AMTRAK AMCOACH	08	78	12
B&O	NIGHT PASSAGE ON B&O	06	58	43
FI	COAST TO COAST SLEEPER OF 1885 FI	01	47	63

SLEEPER PHOTOS

	M	Y	P
ALL ROOM SLEEPER PHOTO "MARYLAND" UPCC	01	60	25
PULLMAN BRAQUE MONDE WAGNER PALACE CAR	11	69	26
PULLMAN CULVER WHITE GM&O PHOTO	11	69	30
PULLMAN FIRST ALL ALUM GM PULLMAN PHOTO	11	69	30
PULLMAN FIRST ALL STEEL JAMESTOWN PHOTO	11	69	31
PULLMAN MANILY NYC #628 WAGNER PALACE CR	11	69	26
PULLMAN PALACE CAR PHOTOS	11	69	28
PULLMAN PIONEER PHOTO 1891	11	69	25
PULLMAN SLEEPING CAR #9 PHOTO	11	69	25
PULLMAN STEVENSON SP&S PHOTO 1908	11	69	27
SILVER PALACE SLEEPING CAR CP PHOTO	11	69	27
SLEEPER 12-1 PHOTO PUERTO PULL 1917	01	60	24
SLEEPER PHOTO B&O GREEN BANK PULL 1938	01	60	24
SLEEPER PHOTO CGA OOSTANULA PULL	01	60	24
SLEEPING CAR 7 ROOMETTE PHOTO NH #2056	01	60	25
SLUMBER COACH BULR NORTHERN ZEPHYR PHOTO	02	57	8

SLEEPER PHOTOS BY ROAD

RD		M	Y	P
B&O	SLEEPER PHOTO B&O GREEN BANK PULL 1938	01	60	24
BURL	SLUMBER COACH BULR NORTHERN ZEPHYR PHOTO	02	57	8
CGA	SLEEPER PHOTO CGA OOSTANULA PULL	01	60	24
CP	SILVER PALACE SLEEPING CAR CP PHOTO	11	69	27
GM&O	PULLMAN CULVER WHITE GM&O PHOTO	11	69	30
NH	SLEEPING CAR 7 ROOMETTE PHOTO NH #2056	01	60	25
NYC	PULLMAN MANILY NYC #628 WAGNER PALACE CR	11	69	26
SP&S	PULLMAN STEVENSON SP&S PHOTO 1908	11	69	27

DOME CAR PROTOTYPE DATA

	M	Y	P
DOME CAR BY BUDD CONSTRUCTION	02	48	48
POSTWAR PARADE VISTA DOME/ASTRO LINERS	09	45	9
SUPER DOME POSTCRIPT	06	80	28
VISTA DOMES OF 1906 ON CP	07	49	58
WHO HAD FIRST DOME CP 1902	02	54	10

DOME CAR PROTOTYPE DATA BY ROAD

RD	D	M	Y	P
CP	WHO HAD FIRST DOME CP 1902	02	54	10
	VISTA DOMES OF 1906 ON CP	07	49	58

DOME CAR PHOTOS

	M	Y	P
DOME COACH PHOTO GN #1320	08	55	9
DOME-LOUNGE CAR AMTRAK SP #3603 PHOTO	06	73	30
DOMES GO NORTH CN PHOTO	08	64	13
FULL DOME SP #3600 PHOTO	11	54	8
MODEL DOME CAR PHOTO SP #3601 1955	07	55	10
VISTA DOME NP #552 PHOTO	11	54	9

DOME CAR PHOTOS BY ROAD

RD		M	Y	P
SP	DOME-LOUNGE CAR AMTRAK SP #3603 PHOTO	06	73	30
CN	DOMES GO NORTH CN PHOTO	08	64	13
GN	DOME COACH PHOTO GN #1320	08	55	9
NP	VISTA DOME NP #552 PHOTO	11	54	9
SP	FULL DOME SP #3600 PHOTO	11	54	8
	MODEL DOME CAR PHOTO SP #3601 1955	07	55	10

OBSERVATION CAR PROTOTYPE DATA

	M	Y	P
DRUMHEADS OF NASHVILLE	05	72	35
HIAWATHA OBSERVATION CAR EMD DETAIL	07	52	17
OBSERVATION CARS FLYING CINDERS & DUST	08	47	55
SKY TOP OBSERVATION HIAWATHA MILW	03	49	8

OBSERVATION CAR PHOTOS

	M	Y	P
HIAWATHA OBSERVATION PHOTO MILW	06	59	32
OBS PHOTO CMI TRYPHENA PULL	01	60	23
OBS PHOTO ROCK #1664 PULL 1909	01	60	23
OBSERVATION D&RG CAL ZEPHYR PHOTO	01	69	33
OBSERVATION PHOTO UP COLORADO CLUB	01	60	22
PARLOR OBS CAR PHOTO IT #514 DCC 1911	01	60	26
PARLOR OBS PHOTO ATSF #1204 PULL 1910	01	60	22
ROUND END OBS PRAIRIE HOME KCS PHOTO	07	61	53
SKYTOP LOUNGE OBSERVATION PHOTO CN	07	71	34
SKYTOP OBSERVATION DELL RAPIDS MILW PHOT	05	76	19
STRATES SHOWS OBSERVATION PHOTO	04	63	10

PASSENGER EQUIPMENT

OBSERVATION CAR PHOTOS BY ROAD

RD		M	Y	P
	STRATES SHOWS OBSERVATION PHOTO	04	63	10
ATSF	PARLOR OBS PHOTO ATSF #1204 PULL 1910	01	60	22
CMI	OBS PHOTO CMI TRYPHENA PULL	01	60	23
CN	SKYTOP LOUNGE OBSERVATION PHOTO CN	07	71	34
D&RG	OBSERVATION D&RG CAL ZEPHYR PHOTO	01	69	33
IT	PARLOR OBS CAR PHOTO IT #514 DCC 1911	01	60	26
KCS	ROUND END OBS PRAIRIE HOME KCS PHOTO	07	61	53
MILW	HIAWATHA OBSERVATION PHOTO MILW	06	59	32
	SKYTOP OBSERVATION DELL RAPIDS MILW PHOT	05	76	19
ROCK	OBS PHOTO ROCK #1664 PULL 1909	01	60	23
UP	OBSERVATION PHOTO UP COLORADO CLUB	01	60	22

RAILCAR PROTOTYPE DATA

	M	Y	P
ANCIENT ANCESTOR TO RDC C&NW 2680	08	59	51
BUDD INTRODUCES RDC-1	11	49	4
DOODLEBUGS THAT ENDURED BUILT IN AUSTRAL	04	78	44
DOODLEBUGS THAT ENDURED SOUND DIFFERENT	05	78	28
GAS ELECRIC CGW #M300	11	63	38
GAS ELECTRIC CARS DIRGE FOR DOODLEBUGS	05	61	26
GAS ELECTRIC CARS OF EMD	11	63	38
GAS ELECTRIC CARS THE BEGINNING	11	73	36
GAS ELECTRIC OF MR STRANG	05	79	22
GAS ELECTRIC UNITS, CONTROL OF LTD POWER	01	74	26
GREAT RDC RACE ON B&O	10	55	16
JET POWERED RDC CAR OF NYC 183.85 MPH	10	66	16
LAND O'CORN BUS ON STEEL WHEELS IC	05	71	26
LITTLE MACK ON THE ROAD TO PARADISE	10	77	53
MCKEEN CARS KNIFE NOSES & PORTHOLES	07	60	30
NO RPO THIS CHRISTMAS	12	77	16
PROPOSED BUT NEVER BUILT RAILCARS	09	75	32
RAILCARS OF EARLY 1930'S BY BUDD	04	73	24
RDC CARS BY BUDD RDC-1,2,3	05	50	11
RDC CARS BY BUDD, ALL ABOUT THEM	03	53	17
RDC CARS OF THE B&O	08	55	28
RDC CARS OF THE B&O RDC BREAKS THROUGH	01	57	42
RDC ON RI	12	65	37
RDC PHOTO QUIZ	06	71	37
RDC ROLL CALL	05	55	37
RDC SERVICE ON THE PACIFIC GREAT EASTERN	02	58	24
RDC UPDATE FOR RED LION	12	77	15
RPO WASHINGTON - NEW YORK SERVICE	03	72	6
WHAT BECAME OF ALL THOSE RDC'S?	12	68	38

RAILCAR PLANS

	M	Y	P
RAIL CAR TYPE RE44B16M8 DRAWING	12	73	42

RAILCAR PROTOTYPE DATA BY ROAD

RD		M	Y	P
B&O	RDC CARS OF THE B&O RDC BREAKS THROUGH	01	57	42
	GREAT RDC RACE ON B&O	10	55	16
	RDC CARS OF THE B&O	08	55	28
C&NW	ANCIENT ANCESTOR TO RDC C&NW 2680	08	59	51
CGW	GAS ELECRIC CGW #M300	11	63	38
IC	LAND O'CORN BUS ON STEEL WHEELS IC	05	71	26
NYC	JET POWERED RDC CAR OF NYC 183.85 MPH	10	66	16
PGE	RDC SERVICE ON THE PACIFIC GREAT EASTERN	02	58	24
RI	RDC ON RI	12	65	37

RAILCAR PHOTOS

	M	Y	P
BUDD RPO UP #5909 PHOTO	02	71	34
BUDD STAINLESS MU ELECTRIC COMMUTER CAR	12	63	12
FREIGHT GAS ELECTRIC PE #1502 PHOTO	07	74	55
GAS ELECTRIC BR&P #1002 PHOTO	11	73	42
GAS ELECTRIC CMSP #5 PHOTO 1913 GE	11	73	44
GAS ELECTRIC DPE #100 PHOTO 1913 GE	12	73	44
GAS ELECTRIC GE DEMONSTRATOR #3 PHOTO	11	73	38
GAS ELECTRIC GE DEMONSTRATOR #7 PHOTO	11	73	38
GAS ELECTRIC MIDGET P&LE #500 PHOTO	11	73	47
GAS ELECTRIC MIV #1 PHOTO GE	11	73	44
GAS ELECTRIC S #1 PHOTO 1911 GE	11	73	44
JITNEY #15 CBELT	09	71	18
M-160 BRILL RAILER ATSF #25 PHOTO 1931	05	69	22A
MCKEEN RAILCAR RI #9023 PHOTO	11	79	36
METROLINER PHOTOS PC #880 BUDD	03	69	8
RDC CAB END DETAIL PHOTO A #28	08	79	13
RDC DOODLEBUG BURL #9838 PHOTO	07	72	32
RDC DOODLEBUG MILW #5927 PHOTO	07	72	32
SHORTENED GAS ELECTRIC PHOTO PE #1649	02	61	8
SKUNK CW #M-300 PHOTO 1963	01	64	9
SPV-2000 BUDD RAIL CAR PHOTO	03	78	67
TURBINE RAIL CAR BY BUDD PHOTO GT-1	12	66	10
UNUSUAL MOTOR CAR PHOTOS P&N	08	41	48

PASSENGER EQUIPMENT

RAILCAR PHOTOS BY ROAD

RD		M	Y	P
A	RDC CAB END DETAIL PHOTO A #28	08	79	13
ATSF	M-160 BRILL RAILER ATSF #25 PHOTO 1931	05	69	22A
BR&P	GAS ELECTRIC BR&P #1002 PHOTO	11	73	42
BURL	RDC DOODLEBUG BURL #9838 PHOTO	07	72	32
CBELT	JITNEY #15 CBELT	09	71	18
CMSP	GAS ELECTRIC CMSP #5 PHOTO 1913 GE	11	73	44
CW	SKUNK CW #M-300 PHOTO 1963	01	64	9
DPE	GAS ELECTRIC DPE #100 PHOTO 1913 GE	12	73	44
F&NW	UNUSUAL MOTOR CAR PHOTOS P&N	08	41	48
MILW	RDC DOODLEBUG MILW #5927 PHOTO	07	72	32
MIV	GAS ELECTRIC MIV #1 PHOTO GE	11	73	44
P&LE	GAS ELECTRIC MIDGET P&LE #500 PHOTO	11	73	47
PC	METROLINER PHOTOS PC #880 BUDD	03	69	8
PE	SHORTENED GAS ELECTRIC PHOTO PE #1649	02	61	8
	FREIGHT GAS ELECTRIC PE #1502 PHOTO	07	74	55
RI	MCKEEN RAILCAR RI #9023 PHOTO	11	79	36
S	GAS ELECTRIC S #1 PHOTO 1911 GE	11	73	44
UP	BUDD RPO UP #5909 PHOTO	02	71	34

GENERAL PASSENGER CAR PLANS

	M	Y	P
FLOOR PLANS VARIATIONS PIONEER III CARS	11	56	46
PASSENGER FLOOR PLANS DENVER ZEPHYR BURL	11	63	46

GENERAL PASSENGER CAR PHOTOS

	M	Y	P
CHESSIE SPECIAL #2101 COLOR PHOTO	07	77	2
COLONIAL HERFORD FARM COACH PHOTO	04	69	11
ESCORT CAR US ARMY #617	06	63	8
PIONEER ZEPHYR PHOTO BURL	06	60	8
SILVER KING/QUEEN STREAMLINER PHOTO BURL	12	68	34
SPIRIT OF 76 SCL TRAIN PHOTOS	02	73	13
TURBO TRAIN PHOTO CN	07	70	14
UNITED AIRCRAFT TURBO LINER PHOTO	01	66	10

GENERAL PASSENGER CAR PHOTOS BY ROAD

RD		M	Y	P
BURL	PIONEER ZEPHYR PHOTO BURL	06	60	8
	SILVER KING/QUEEN STREAMLINER PHOTO BURL	12	68	34
CHESS	CHESSIE SPECIAL #2101 COLOR PHOTO	07	77	2
CN	TURBO TRAIN PHOTO CN	07	70	14
SCL	SPIRIT OF 76 SCL TRAIN PHOTOS	02	73	13

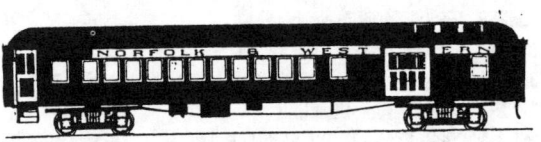

GENERAL PASSENGER CAR PROTOTYPE DATA

	M	Y	P
20TH CENTURY LIMITED TALES OF CENTURY	05	54	16
A TRAIN OF FOOLS	09	75	26
AEROTRAIN COAST TO COAST	01	57	36
AEROTRAIN HERE COMES TOMARROW	09	55	46
AEROTRAIN-ONE FOR THE BUDGET	05	56	16
ALF LANDON TRAIN STOMPING	11	84	44
AMERICAS UNREMARKED INN KEEPERS-THE RR	10	65	26
AMTRAK 1190 CARS	12	71	16
AMTRAK 6 WIGGINS	12	84	50
AMTRAK CAR INSPECTION STANDARDS	01	75	22
AMTRAK CONSISTS OF TRAINS MAY 1, 1975	01	76	48
AMTRAK ERA SERVICE ON THE SOUTHERN	10	74	26
AMTRAK FRENCH TURBO TRAIN CHICAGO IL PHO	10	73	13
AMTRAK LEGISLATION PERTAINING TO OPERATN	05	75	52
AMTRAK PASSENGER FLEET PHOTO ESSAY	07	72	16
AMTRAK QUESTIONS & ANSWERS	08	71	10
AMTRAK SAMPLER, NOTES ON 17,451 MILES	11	72	20
AMTRAK STATE SUBSIDIES	07	74	35
AMTRAKS LEGAL ASPECTS	08	72	37
AMTRAKS TURBOTRAINS BIG NEWS SINCE 747?	01	74	20
ASTRO-DOME TRAIN SEATTLE TO PORTLAND UP	04	51	41
AUTOTRAIN PIGGYBACK AUTOS & PEOPLE	02	62	38
AUTOTRAIN SELLS SOMETHING PEOPLE WANT	01	73	22
AUTOTRAIN THIS HIGHWAY ISN'T ON AUTO MAP	12	74	22
BILEVEL CARS IC LOWDOWN ON HIGHLINERS	02	72	42
BLUE COMET WONDER TRAIN OF 1929 CNJ B	06	56	14
BLUE TRAIN OF SOUTH AFRICA	03	70	18
BRIGHTON BELLE TRAIN WAS A WAY OF LIFE	07	72	38
BRITISH RAIL HISTORY PHOTOS	12	72	18
BROADWAY LIMITED CHRISTMAS EVE	12	48	27
BROADWAY LIMITED PENNYS FINEST 1898-1962	02	62	16
BROADWAY LIMITED SECOND ENGINE 28 PRR	03	75	42
BUDD STREAMLINER KEEPS THE FAITH	05	56	20
BULLET TRAIN FROM JAPAN REVISITED	10	73	38
CALIF ZEPHYR HER SPIRIT WILL NEVER DIE	01	73	18
CALIFORNIA ZEPHYR DESIRES TO BE ELSEWHER	02	52	15
CALIFORNIA ZEPHYR SCHEDULED FOR SCENERY	06	50	36
CALIFORNIA ZEPHYR SEARCH VANISHING MAGIC	04	75	42
CALIFORNIA ZEPHYR WP PHOTO ESSAY	09	70	29
CANADIAN OF THE CANADIAN PACIFIC	08	55	18
CAPITOL LIMITED	03	50	36
CENTURY OF PROGRESS 9000 +50 CB&Q	04	84	3
CHESHIRE STREAMLINER B&M	03	55	7
CHESSIE SPECIAL #2101 CONSIST	07	77	3
CHESSIE TRAIN THAT WAS BUT NEVER WAS	07	68	38
CHICAGO-TWIN CITIES LIMITED CB&Q	08	70	36
CHIEF OF THE ATSF	11	48	38
CINCINNATIAN THE DAY IT STOPPED	01	73	27
CITY OF DENVER C&NW UP	07	46	30
CITY OF MIAMI MOST TALKED OF TRAIN IN US	01	75	33
CITY STREAMLINERS OF THE UNION PACIFIC	09	42	4
CLASSIC PASSENGER CARS	01	60	16
COACH TRAVEL ON THE ERIE	05	72	20
COAST TO COAST ON AN IRON OCEAN	08	71	36
COMMUTER OPERATIONS ON ERIE LACKAWANA	04	71	38

PASSENGER EQUIPMENT

GENERAL PASSENGER CAR PROTOTYPE DATA

Title	M	Y	P
COMMUTER OPERATIONS ON THE GO GOT	10	68	20
COMMUTER OPEREATIONS ON THE READING	10	63	21
COMMUTER SERVICE ECONOMICS	04	52	24
COMMUTER SERVICE IN DETROIT AREA OF GTW	12	55	18
COMMUTER TRAIN SPRING FEVER	12	58	40
COMMUTER TRAINS IN CHICAGO IC	12	56	16
COMMUTER TRAINS IN CHICAGO IC	10	43	3
COMMUTER TRAINS OF CHICAGO	08	48	46
COMMUTERS 34,000 DAILY ON THE NYC	07	65	21
COMMUTERS FROM PHILADELPHIA TO NEW YORK	04	49	44
COMMUTERS IF NYC SAYS YES	08	65	48
CONGRESSIONAL NY TO WASHINGTON PRR	06	52	50
CONSOLIDATION OF NAME TRAINS	02	64	44
CRESCENT LIMITED 1891-1964 S	07	64	20
CRESCENT LIMITED TO WASHINGTON DC S	09	46	10
DAYLIGHT LIKE NO OTHER SP	10	84	24
DENVER ZEPHYR OVERNIGHT-EVERY NIGHT	11	63	45
DETOUR ROUTES FOR "JAMES W RILEY" AMTRAK	11	74	16
DINING CAR SERVICE & OPER HOW TO RUN IT	03	76	50
DINING CAR SERVICE ON THE ROCK	02	53	18
DISCONTINUANCE OF SERVICE UNDER SEC 13A	01	76	12
DIXIE FLAGLER C&EI	02	41	38
DIXIE FLYER NC&SL RIDE THRU HISTORYLAND	02	51	42
EARLY DAYS OF DIESELDOM	05	62	24
EARLY PASSENGER SERVICE ON CGA	12	47	20
EL CAPITAN NIGHT RIDE	03	51	36
ELECTROLINERS EASTBOUND	02	64	4
EMPIRE BUILDER CLEAN WINDOW TRAIN	05	58	22
EMPIRE SERVICE TRAINS OF PENN CENTRAL	11	68	40
EMPIRE STATE EXPRESS NYC	11	41	21
EUROPEAN PASSENGER CAR TRENDS	09	64	6
FAVORITE PASSENGER CAR TYPES	05	58	16
FLYING SCOTSMAN	10	45	18
FRONTENAC LETS GO TO QUEBEC CP	12	45	10
GEORGIAN ACF FIRST POSTWAR COACHES L&N	01	47	48
GETTING THERE WAS HALF THE FUN	09	75	23
GOLDEN ARROW LONDON TO PARIS	03	54	24
GOLDEN GATE SPECIAL FINEST TRAIN WORLD	04	63	25
HIAWATHA STORY	12	50	26
HIGH LEVEL PASSENGER CARS OF ATSF	10	56	21
HITLER'S SUPER PASSENGER CARS	08	84	38
HOOSIER 5 O'CLOCK MONON	09	45	40
HOW SUPER ARE SUPERLINERS?	05	79	14
HUMMING BIRD ACF 1ST POSTWAR COACHES L&N	01	47	48
HUSHED CORRIDORS & CRASHING VESTIBULES	12	84	52
HUSTLER STREAMLINER SP	01	50	36
IF I RAN PASSENGER TRAINS	02	58	19
INTERLINE TICKETS AND HOW THEY WORK	03	48	14
INVETERATE TRAIN RIDERS NOTES	07	66	20
IS THE PASSENGER TRAIN OBSOLETE?	07	56	31
JAMES E STRATES SHOWS TRAIN	04	85	42
JEFFERSONIAN	07	41	42
KIDDIE SPECIAL TRAINS OF THE L&N	08	61	45
LARK THE NIGHT FLIGHT	04	49	40
LOS ANGELES-SAN FRANCISCO SERVICE ON SP	08	50	36

GENERAL PASSENGER CAR PROTOTYPE DATA

Title	M	Y	P
MAIL TRAIN OF 1899 ON THE GN	03	50	40
MAP OF AMTRAK ROUTES 1975	01	76	52
MERCHANTS LIMITED TO BOSTON ON NH	02	49	28
METROLINERS THIS THE WAY TO WASHINGTON?	08	70	25
METROLINERS WHATS RIGHT/WRONG WITH THEM	07	69	27
MEXICAN TRAINS - AMERICAN PASSENGER CARS	06	73	20
MIXED TRAIN OPERATION ON THE GEORGIA	09	67	20
MODE OF TRAVEL-THE SILVER COMET	07	83	24
MONTREALER A BOOTLEGGER	05	72	44
MOUNTAINEER OF C&NW-SOO-CP	10	48	36
NAMEKAGEN NOBODY KNEW THIS MOTOR TRAIN	08	84	22
NEW ENGLAND STATES BOSTON-CHICAGO NYC	09	51	20
NEW YORK-BOSTON WHITE TRAIN EVEN COAL	03	61	37
NIGHT FERRY LONDON TO PARIS	03	54	24
NO PASSENGER TRAINS BY 1970?	12	58	42
NORTH COAST LIMITED	12	52	48
NORTH COAST LIMITED OF NP	08	63	28
NORTHEAST CORRIDOR PROJECT	11	67	18
NOTABLE TRAINS OF CHICAGO GREAT WESTERN	01	68	34
NP LIKES PASSENGERS	12	59	32
OLYMPIAN HIAWATHA MILW	06	49	40
ON THE VERGE OF VIA	08	78	28
OPERATION STREAMLINER CITY OF LA UP	07	51	20
ORIENT EXPRESS OMNIPRESENT	02	69	40
PAINTING PASSENGER EQUIPMENT	04	49	48
PAN-AMERICAN NEW ORLEANS VIA L&N	01	47	52
PANAMA EXPRESS PULLMAN & VERY DELUXE	03	63	16
PAOLI LOCAL OF THE PRR	02	47	14
PASSENGER CARS BUILT BY ACF	04	51	12
PASSENGER CARS OF AMER CAR AND FOUNDRY	04	51	12
PASSENGER RESERVATION SYSTEM OF THE PRR	09	50	14
PASSENGER SERVICE ON THE CB&Q	03	49	26
PASSENGER SERVICE ON THE GTW	12	49	46
PASSENGER SERVICE ON THE KCS	11	67	40
PASSENGER SERVICE ON THE NYNH&H	02	50	21
PASSENGER SERVICE ON THE VIRGINIAN	08	56	18
PASSENGER SERVICE ON WESTERN MARYLAND	07	53	14
PASSENGER TRAIN ECONOMICS-IN THE RED?	10	51	18
PASSENGER TRAIN HISTORY	06	41	10
PASSENGER TRAINS OF 1957	06	58	16
PASSENGER WINDOW WASHERS-A LOST ART?	06	75	20
PASSENGERS-KEEP'EM HAPPY	08	57	44
PENINSULA 400 STREAMLINER	07	48	38
PENNSYLVANIA SPECIAL BROADWAY LTD PRR	03	52	52
PEORIA ROCKET TALES	12	81	45
PERFECT PASSENGER TRAIN	05	66	52
PIONEER III CONCEPT BY BUDD	11	56	42
PIONEER III CONCEPT BY BUDD	09	58	10
PIONEER LIMITED ROLLS-ROYCE OF RR MILW	07	61	20
PIONEER ZEPHYR BURL	09	52	24
POSTWAR STREAMLINERS ON THE GN	11	51	36
POWHATAN ARROW NEW FINE FEATHERS N&W	02	50	14
PRR FIRST POST WAR COACHES	02	47	6
PULLMAN COMPANY EASTERN SERVICE IN 1927	10	67	24
PULLMAN COMPANY HISTORY POSTSCRIPT	11	69	20

PASSENGER EQUIPMENT

GENERAL PASSENGER CAR PROTOTYPE DATA	M	Y	P
PULLMAN PALACE CARS	03	59	49
PULLMANS-ALL RED PRR-ALL PRR RED NO!	09	67	38
PUSH-PULL TRAINS OF THE C&NW FOR PROFIT	08	60	42
RAILWAY POST OFFICE SERVICE HISTORY	02	71	26
RAPIDO CN MOST TALKED ABOUT TRAIN	03	67	20
RDC SERVICE IN NEW ENGLAND ON NYC	03	51	23
READINGS NEW BLUE PASSENGER FLEET	04	65	17
RIO GRANDE ZEPHYR	05	80	26
ROCKEY MOUNTAIN ROCKET	04	53	63
ROYAL BLUE LINES TRAINS OF B&O	08	72	20
SAN FRANCISCO OVERLAND SP	01	52	36
SCENIC RAILWAYS SELL SOMETHING PEOP WANT	01	73	22
SECOND GENERATION STREAMLINERS	09	65	8
SERVICING THE SP DAYLIGHT	02	49	12
SIMPLON-ORIENT EXPRESS	02	69	40
SOLID CLANK OF 6 WHEEL TRUCKS	05	73	20
SOUTHLAND 4 ROADS--SEVEN STATES	10	47	27
STEAM GENERATORS FOR HEATING & COOLING	08	51	14
STREAMLINER SERVICE ON ACL	03	58	18
STREAMLINER SHOWING	05	56	14
STREAMLINERS TRAVEL WEST 1964	10	64	20
STREAMLINERS OF THE UNITED STATES	07	48	45
SUNBEAM STREAMLINER SP	01	50	36
SUNSET LIMITED SP	02	48	38
SUNSET LIMITED 20 MINUTES AT EL PASO SP	05	52	66
SUNSHINE SPECIAL PASSENGER CARS MP	02	67	41
SUPER CHIEF DESIGNED FOR DIESELS ATSF	05	62	30
SUPER CHIEF DINING CAR SERVICE ATSF	11	70	28
SUPER CHIEF ON THE ATSF SUPER TRAIN	06	70	20
SUPER CONTINENTAL OF CANADIAN NATIONAL	08	55	18
SUPERLINER DESIGN	08	82	26
TALGO MOST DERAIL PROOF TRAIN ON RAILS?	09	54	6
TALGO THE PIONEER STREAMLINER ACF	05	56	16
TALGO TRAIN X AC&F	06	49	5
TEXAS ZEPHYR DENVER-DALLAS BURL	10	49	40
THE 400 ON STILTS NW BILEVEL CARS	01	59	16
TOMORROW'S DAYLINER CONCEPTS	04	59	37
TRAIN TIME PASSENGER LUXURY TRAVEL	61		12
TRAIN X EXPERIMENTAL RUNS	07	52	6
TUBULAR TRAIN OF THE PRR	10	56	21
TUNNEL CARS FOR HOLIDAY ON ICE WAGONS	06	65	9
TURBO TRAIN ON TOUR PHOTO ESSAY AMTRAK	11	71	20
TURBO TRAIN TRIP TRAIN 153	10	76	42
TURBO TRAINS BY DOT-UNITED AIRCRAFT	06	71	29
TURBO TRAINS HARDWARE EQUAL TO HARD SELL	04	69	20
TURBO TRAINS OF THE CANADIAN NATIONAL	04	71	19
TWENTIETH CENTURY LIMITED CHRONICLE	08	62	16
TWIN ZEPHYRS RIDING THE WEST WIND BURL	04	45	10
VANDALISM ON METROLINER ROUTE	02	71	20
WAR TIME UTILIZATION OF PASSENGER CARS	12	43	32
WASHINGTONIAN B&O DAY TRAIN	10	51	36
WASHINGTONIAN A BOOTLEGGER	05	72	44
WHO SHOT THE PASSENGER TRAIN?	04	59	14
X TRAIN STREAMLINER PULLMAN STANDARD	05	56	18
XPLORER TRAIN OF NYC 1956	07	56	6
ZEPHYRETTE	07	52	26

RD	GENERAL PASSENGER CAR PROTOTYPE DATA BY ROAD	M	Y	P
A	AMTRAK SAMPLER, NOTES ON 17,451 MILES	11	72	20
	AMTRAK PASSENGER FLEET PHOTO ESSAY	07	72	16
	AMTRAK FRENCH TURBO TRAIN CHICAGO IL PHO	10	73	13
	AMTRAK QUESTIONS & ANSWERS	08	71	10
	AMTRAK 1190 CARS	12	71	16
	TURBO TRAIN ON TOUR PHOTO ESSAY AMTRAK	11	71	20
	AMTRAKS LEGAL ASPECTS	08	72	37
	AMTRAK 6 WIGGINS	12	84	50
	MAP OF AMTRAK ROUTES 1975	01	76	52
	AMTRAK CONSISTS OF TRAINS MAY 1, 1975	01	76	48
	AMTRAK LEGISLATION PERTAINING TO OPERATN	05	75	52
	AMTRAK CAR INSPECTION STANDARDS	01	75	22
	DETOUR ROUTES FOR "JAMES W RILEY" AMTRAK	11	74	16
	AMTRAK STATE SUBSIDIES	07	74	35
	AMTRAKS TURBOTRAINS BIG NEWS SINCE 747?	01	74	20
ACL	STREAMLINER SERVICE ON ACL	03	58	18
ATSF	SUPER CHIEF DESIGNED FOR DIESELS ATSF	05	62	30
	SUPER CHIEF ON THE ATSF SUPER TRAIN	06	70	20
	SUPER CHIEF DINING CAR SERVICE ATSF	11	70	28
	CHIEF OF THE ATSF	11	48	38
	HIGH LEVEL PASSENGER CARS OF ATSF	10	56	21
B&M	CHESHIRE STREAMLINER B&M	03	55	7
B&O	ROYAL BLUE LINES TRAINS OF B&O	08	72	20
	CINCINNATIAN THE DAY IT STOPPED	01	73	27
	WASHINGTONIAN B&O DAY TRAIN	10	51	36
BURL	CALIFORNIA ZEPHYR DESIRES TO BE ELSEWHER	02	52	15
	PIONEER ZEPHYR BURL	09	52	24
	TWIN ZEPHYRS RIDING THE WEST WIND BURL	04	45	10
	TEXAS ZEPHYR DENVER-DALLAS BURL	10	49	40
C&EI	DIXIE FLAGLER C&EI	02	41	38
C&NW	PUSH-PULL TRAINS OF THE C&NW FOR PROFIT	08	60	42
	CITY OF DENVER C&NW UP	07	46	30
	MOUNTAINEER OF C&NW-SOO-CP	10	48	36
	NAMEKAGEN NOBODY KNEW THIS MOTOR TRAIN	08	84	22
CB&Q	CHICAGO-TWIN CITIES LIMITED CB&Q	08	70	36
	PASSENGER SERVICE ON THE CB&Q	03	49	26
	CENTURY OF PROGRESS 9000 +50 CB&Q	04	84	3
CGA	EARLY PASSENGER SERVICE ON CGA	12	47	20
CGW	NOTABLE TRAINS OF CHICAGO GREAT WESTERN	01	68	34
CHESS	CHESSIE SPECIAL #2101 CONSIST	07	77	3
CN	TURBO TRAINS OF THE CANADIAN NATIONAL	04	71	19
	RAPIDO CN MOST TALKED ABOUT TRAIN	03	67	20
	SUPER CONTINENTAL OF CANADIAN NATIONAL	08	55	18
CNJ	BLUE COMET WONDER TRAIN OF 1929 CNJ B	06	56	14
CP	FRONTENAC LETS GO TO QUEBEC CP	12	45	10
	CANADIAN OF THE CANADIAN PACIFIC	08	55	18
E	COACH TRAVEL ON THE ERIE	05	72	20
EL	COMMUTER OPERATIONS ON ERIE LACKAWANA	04	71	38
G	MIXED TRAIN OPERATION ON THE GEORGIA	09	67	20
GM	AEROTRAIN-ONE FOR THE BUDGET	05	56	16
GN	POSTWAR STREAMLINERS ON THE GN	11	51	36
	MAIL TRAIN OF 1899 ON THE GN	03	50	40
GOT	COMMUTER OPERATIONS ON THE GO GOT	10	68	20
GTW	PASSENGER SERVICE ON THE GTW	12	49	46
	COMMUTER SERVICE IN DETROIT AREA OF GTW	12	55	18

PASSENGER EQUIPMENT

GENERAL PASSENGER CAR PROTOTYPE DATA BY ROAD

RD		M	Y	P
IC	PANAMA EXPRESS PULLMAN & VERY DELUXE	03	63	16
	BILEVEL CARS IC LOWDOWN ON HIGHLINERS	02	72	42
	COMMUTER TRAINS IN CHICAGO IC	10	43	3
	COMMUTER TRAINS IN CHICAGO IC	12	56	16
KCS	PASSENGER SERVICE ON THE KCS	11	67	40
L&N	KIDDIE SPECIAL TRAINS OF THE L&N	08	61	45
	GEORGIAN ACF FIRST POSTWAR COACHES L&N	01	47	48
	HUMMING BIRD ACF 1ST POSTWAR COACHES L&N	01	47	48
	PAN-AMERICAN NEW ORLEANS VIA L&N	01	47	52
MILW	PIONEER LIMITED ROLLS-ROYCE OF RR MILW	07	61	20
	OLYMPIAN HIAWATHA MILW	06	49	40
	HIAWATHA STORY	12	50	26
MP	SUNSHINE SPECIAL PASSENGER CARS MP	02	67	41
N&W	POWHATAN ARROW NEW FINE FEATHERS N&W	02	50	14
NC&SL	DIXIE FLYER NC&SL RIDE THRU HISTORYLAND	02	51	42
NH	MERCHANTS LIMITED TO BOSTON ON NH	02	49	28
NP	NORTH COAST LIMITED	12	52	48
	NORTH COAST LIMITED OF NP	08	63	28
	NP LIKES PASSENGERS	12	59	32
NW	THE 400 ON STILTS NW BILEVEL CARS	01	59	16
NYC	TWENTIETH CENTURY LIMITED CHRONICLE	08	62	16
	20TH CENTURY LIMITED TALES OF CENTURY	05	54	16
	COMMUTERS 34,000 DAILY ON THE NYC	07	65	21
	COMMUTERS IF NYC SAYS YES	08	65	48
	EMPIRE STATE EXPRESS NYC	11	41	21
	RDC SERVICE IN NEW ENGLAND ON NYC	03	51	23
	NEW ENGLAND STATES BOSTON-CHICAGO NYC	09	51	20
	XPLORER TRAIN OF NYC 1956	07	56	6
NYNH&H	PASSENGER SERVICE ON THE NYNH&H	02	50	21
PC	EMPIRE SERVICE TRAINS OF PENN CENTRAL	11	68	40
PRR	CONGRESSIONAL NY TO WASHINGTON PRR	06	52	50
	PENNSYLVANIA SPECIAL BROADWAY LTD PRR	03	52	52
	BROADWAY LIMITED PENNYS FINEST 1898-1962	02	62	16
	PAOLI LOCAL OF THE PRR	02	47	14
	PRR FIRST POST WAR COACHES	02	47	6
	PULLMANS-ALL RED PRR-ALL PRR RED NO!	09	67	38
	PASSENGER RESERVATION SYSTEM OF THE PRR	09	50	14
	TUBULAR TRAIN OF THE PRR	10	56	21
	BROADWAY LIMITED SECOND ENGINE 28 PRR	03	75	42
R	COMMUTER OPEREATIONS ON THE READING	10	63	21
	READINGS NEW BLUE PASSENGER FLEET	04	65	17
RI	DINING CAR SERVICE ON THE ROCK	02	53	18
S	CRESCENT LIMITED TO WASHINGTON DC S	09	46	10
	CRESCENT LIMITED 1891-1964 S	07	64	20
	AMTRAK ERA SERVICE ON THE SOUTHERN	10	74	26
SP	SAN FRANCISCO OVERLAND SP	01	52	36
	SUNSET LIMITED 20 MINUTES AT EL PASO SP	05	52	66
	SUNSET LIMITED SP	02	48	38
	SERVICING THE SP DAYLIGHT	02	49	12
	DAYLIGHT LIKE NO OTHER SP	10	84	24
	LOS ANGELES-SAN FRANCISCO SERVICE ON SP	08	50	36
	HUSTLER STREAMLINER SP	01	50	36
	SUNBEAM STREAMLINER SP	01	50	36

GENERAL PASSENGER CAR PROTOTYPE DATA BY ROAD

RD		M	Y	P
UP	CITY STREAMLINERS OF THE UNION PACIFIC	09	42	4
	ASTRO-DOME TRAIN SEATTLE TO PORTLAND UP	04	51	41
	OPERATION STREAMLINER CITY OF LA UP	07	51	20
V	PASSENGER SERVICE ON THE VIRGINIAN	08	56	18
VIA	ON THE VERGE OF VIA	08	78	28
WM	PASSENGER SERVICE ON WESTERN MARYLAND	07	53	14
WP	CALIFORNIA ZEPHYR WP PHOTO ESSAY	09	70	29

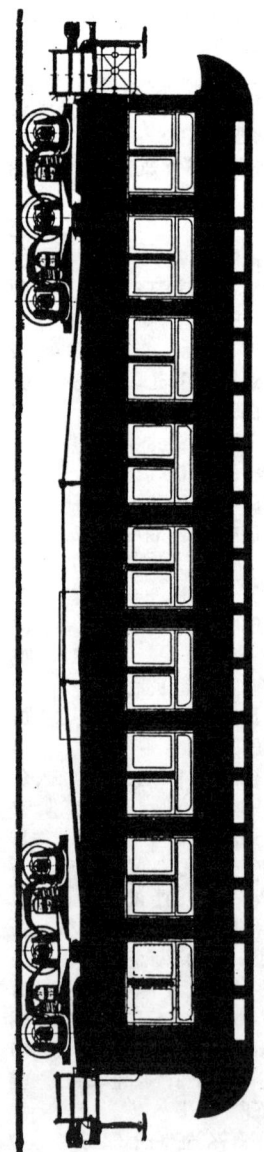

291

BILL OF LADING   FREIGHT CARS

The freight car section is broken down into eight categories: Box Cars, Flat Cars, Gondolas, Hoppers, Refrigerator Cars, Stock Cars, Tank Cars, and General Freight Cars. Cars like Auto Carriers, TOFC, Pulpwood Cars, and Disconnect Log cars have been classified as Flat Cars. Pickle Cars and Vat Cars fall under Tank Cars.

Prototype data includes articles and specifications on the real thing. In many instances there are photographs with these articles that did not get special billing in the photograph section. The plans and drawings are just that. Generally by our convention a drawing is more detailed than a plan, but this is not a hard and fast rule. The plans are listed twice: once alphabetically and once by road. The photo section shows details or unusual photos of interest to the researcher. Obviously we did not list all photos that appear in these magazines.

Freight car descriptors include the basic description of the car, its road, number, class, builder and date built. This data is included if available and if space permits.

MANIFEST FREIGHT CARS

	PAGE
FREIGHT CARS	292
BOX CARS	294
BOX CAR PROTOTYPE DATA	294
BOX CAR PROTOTYPE DATA BY ROAD	294
BOX CAR PHOTOS	294
BOX CAR PHOTOS BY ROAD	294
FLAT CARS	294
FLAT CAR PROTOTYPE DATA	294
FLAT CAR PLANS	295
FLAT CAR PHOTOS	295
FLAT CAR PHOTOS BY ROAD	295
GONDOLAS	295
GONDOLA PROTOTYPE DATA	295
GONDOLA PROTOTYPE DATA BY ROAD	295
HOPPERS	295
HOPPER PROTOTYPE DATA	295
HOPPER PROTOTYPE DATA BY ROAD	295
HOPPER PHOTOS	295
HOPPER PHOTOS BY ROAD	296
REFRIGERATOR CARS	296
REFRIGERATOR CAR PROTOTYPE DATA	296
REFRIGERATOR CAR PHOTOS	296
STOCK CARS	296
STOCK CAR PHOTOS	296
TANK CARS	296
TANK CAR PROTOTYPE DATA	296
TANK CAR PROTOTYPE DATA BY ROAD	296
TANK CAR PHOTOS	296
GENERAL FREIGHT CARS	297
GENERAL FREIGHT PROTOTYPE DATA	297
GENERAL FRT PROTOTYPE DATA BY ROAD	297

NOTE: SEE PAGE 400

FREIGHT CARS

BOX CAR PROTOTYPE DATA

	M	Y	P
93' #85000 BOXCARS VS 40' #89133 WABASH	05	64	3
HOW TO BUILD A PULLMAN STD BOXCAR	09	53	65
NEW 50 TON PACKAGE BOXCAR PS1	08	52	63
NEW GAEX-DF BOXCAR GEN AMER-EVANS 1952	08	52	63
OUTSIZE BOX CAR OF THE SOUTHERN #9799	03	62	48
SMART MONEY RIDES ON BOXCARS MA&PA	09	78	22
UNLOADING GRAIN BOX CARS ROTARY DUMP	10	58	48

BOX CAR PROTOTYPE DATA BY ROAD

RD		M	Y	P
MA&@A	SMART MONEY RIDES ON BOXCARS MA&PA	09	78	22
S	OUTSIZE BOX CAR OF THE SOUTHERN #9799	03	62	48
W	93' #85000 BOXCARS VS 40' #89133 WABASH	05	64	3

BOX CAR PHOTOS

	M	Y	P
40' BOXCAR NEW COLORS B&M #74063 PHOTO	09	56	8
40' BOXCAR PHOTO B&AR #9025	08	61	11
40' BOXCAR PHOTO GN #18626 1956	09	56	8
50' BOXCAR ADN #8105 PHOTO	09	78	26
50' BOXCAR CR #1094 PHOTO	09	78	26
50' BOXCAR E&LS #9032 PHOTO	09	78	24
50' BOXCAR H&S #2032 PHOTO	09	78	26
50' BOXCAR MD&W #10175 PHOTO	09	78	24
50' BOXCAR MT&W #4046 PHOTO	09	78	24
50' BOXCAR PI #1844 PHOTO	09	78	26
50' BOXCAR RR #465 PHOTO	09	78	24
50' BOXCAR VN #7721 PHOTO	09	78	24
50' INSUL BOX CFP#464 BICENT COLOR PHOTO	04	76	16
70T INSULATED BOX W/NEW SAFETY UP#491048	10	66	11
78' AUTO PARTS CONTAINER ATSF #90060 PHO	04	63	11
COKE CARRYING CARS N&W #72082 PHOTO 1964	02	65	11
DD 15500 SERIES BOXCAR DSS&A PHOTO	12	57	8
DD BOXCAR PHOTO GN #3500	09	56	8
FURNITURE CAR CGW #50534 PHOTO	01	68	36
PALLETIZED LOAD BOXCAR PHOTO SP #219900	05	65	13
PLUG DOOR BOXCAR CP #81039 PHOTO	01	68	9
SKY BOXCAR FOR STABILIZERS SP 1965	01	66	11
THRALL ALL DOOR BOXCAR PHOTO	11	68	10
TWO AXLE GENERAL MILLS#6000 BOXCAR PHOTO	03	70	15
WAGON TOP BOXCAR B&O #381587 PHOTO	12	73	3

BOX CAR PHOTOS BY ROAD

RD		M	Y	P
ADN	50' BOXCAR ADN #8105 PHOTO	09	78	26
ATSF	78' AUTO PARTS CONTAINER ATSF #90060 PHO	04	63	11
B&AR	40' BOXCAR PHOTO B&AR #9025	08	61	11
B&M	40' BOXCAR NEW COLORS B&M #74063 PHOTO	09	56	8
B&O	WAGON TOP BOXCAR B&O #381587 PHOTO	12	73	3
CFP	50' INSUL BOX CFP#464 BICENT COLOR PHOTO	04	76	16
CGW	FURNITURE CAR CGW #50534 PHOTO	01	68	36
CP	PLUG DOOR BOXCAR CP #81039 PHOTO	01	68	9
CR	50' BOXCAR CR #1094 PHOTO	09	78	26
DSS&A	DD 15500 SERIES BOXCAR DSS&A PHOTO	12	57	8
E&LS	50' BOXCAR E&LS #9032 PHOTO	09	78	24
GN	40' BOXCAR PHOTO GN #18626 1956	09	56	8
	DD BOXCAR PHOTO GN #3500	09	56	8
H&S	50' BOXCAR H&S #2032 PHOTO	09	78	26
MD&W	50' BOXCAR MD&W #10175 PHOTO	09	78	24
MT&W	50' BOXCAR MT&W #4046 PHOTO	09	78	24
N&W	COKE CARRYING CARS N&W #72082 PHOTO 1964	02	65	11
PI	50' BOXCAR PI #1844 PHOTO	09	78	26
RR	50' BOXCAR RR #465 PHOTO	09	78	24
SP	PALLETIZED LOAD BOXCAR PHOTO SP #219900	05	65	13
	SKY BOXCAR FOR STABILIZERS SP 1965	01	66	11
UP	70T INSULATED BOX W/NEW SAFETY UP#491048	10	66	11
VN	50' BOXCAR VN #7721 PHOTO	09	78	24

FLAT CAR PROTOTYPE DATA

	M	Y	P
FREIGHTLINERS THEIR DEFENSE	01	75	54
HEAVY GENERATOR FLAT CAR LOAD	01	52	10
LONG FLAT CAR LOADS	10	51	8
ONE MILLION LB GENERATOR FLAT CAR LOAD	02	75	17
PERLMANS PIGGYBACK	10	57	6
PIGGYBACK & THE PORTAGER DREAM 1	04	77	44
PIGGYBACK & THE PORTAGER DREAM 2	05	77	44
PIGGYBACK AUTOMOBILE TRAFFIC	12	62	18
PIGGYBACK CONCEPT	08	52	24
PIGGYBACK CONCEPT PERFOMANCE	07	60	46
PIGGYBACK CONCEPT THE PARAPHERNALIA	06	60	37
PIGGYBACK CONCEPT-WHTA PRICE?	05	60	30
PIGGYBACK FLAT X-15972	12	53	6
PIGGYBACK-MOST REALISTIC APPROACH	05	55	7
PIGGYBACK: BOOM OR BUST	03	54	21
ROADRAILER III	10	77	7
ROADRUNNER ALA 1937--A FAILURE	08	52	26
SCHNABEL HEAVY DUTY FLAT CAR BY WESTINGH	07	73	20
TOFC INNOVATIONS	09	61	11
VERSA-DECK 89' FLAT CAR ACF	04	68	9
WORLD'S LARGEST FLAT CAR PRR #470245	02	53	9

FREIGHT CARS

FLAT CAR PHOTOS

	M	Y	P
108' BOILER DRUM FLATCAR LOAD PHOTO	03	70	15
138T TELESCOPE FLAT CAR LOAD PHOTO P-S	02	64	13
172000 LB 129' FLAT CAR LOAD PHOTO	04	66	13
350T 24 WHEEL FLAT CAR GE #40005 PHOTO	04	64	10
70' BULKHD FLT W/CAST IRON PIPE L&N22300	01	66	9
AIRJET TANK LOADS S #4999 PHOTO	05	63	9
AUTO CARRIERS (ENCLOSED) SP #907671 PHOT	04	74	15
AUTORACK W/VANDAL SCREENS SP #510516 PHO	08	66	10
CATTLEBACK OPERATIONS TOFC PHOTO	02	68	9
CONVERTIBLE FLAT CAR PHOTO SP #514000	01	62	9
ENCLOSED BI LEVEL AUTO CARRIER ATSF PHOT	10	76	17
HOODED FLATCAR PHOTO GTW #675049	01	66	11
ICBM CARRING FLAT CAR PHOTOS	05	60	8
ISOCRACKING REACTOR VESSEL CAR LOAD L&N	10	63	60
PLATED COIL CAR PHOTO #50900 THRALL	02	4	12
PORT-A-BULK STORAGE TANK FLATCAR LOAD PH	03	70	15
POWER PLANT GENERATOR FLATCAR PHOTOS	03	70	14
TRANSFORMER FLAT CAR LOAD PHOTO	07	59	32
TRANSFORMER LOAD PHOTO NYC #499088	03	53	6
TRIPLE DECK AUTO CARRIER PHOTOS	04	60	8
TRUCK ON TRAILER OF FLATCAR PHOTO	02	67	27
WAGONS AS PIGGYBACK LAOD PHOTO SP	07	68	8
WELL FALT CAR PHOTO PRR (500,000 LBS)	02	53	59
WIND TUNNEL DOOR LOAD NYC #499071 PHOTO	05	63	9

FLAT CAR PHOTOS BY ROAD

RD		M	Y	P
ATSF	ENCLOSED BI LEVEL AUTO CARRIER ATSF PHOT	10	76	17
GE	350T 24 WHEEL FLAT CAR GE #40005 PHOTO	04	64	10
L&N	70' BULKHD FLT W/CAST IRON PIPE L&N22300	01	66	9
	ISOCRACKING REACTOR VESSEL CAR LOAD L&N	10	63	60
NYC	TRANSFORMER LOAD PHOTO NYC #499088	03	53	6
	WIND TUNNEL DOOR LOAD NYC #499071 PHOTO	05	63	9
S	PLATED COIL CAR PHOTO #50900 THRALL	02	4	12
	AIRJET TANK LOADS S #4999 PHOTO	05	63	9
SP	CONVERTIBLE FLAT CAR PHOTO SP #514000	01	62	9
	AUTO CARRIERS (ENCLOSED) SP #907671 PHOT	04	74	15
	AUTORACK W/VANDAL SCREENS SP #510516 PHO	08	66	10
	WAGONS AS PIGGYBACK LAOD PHOTO SP	07	68	8
TOFC	CATTLEBACK OPERATIONS TOFC PHOTO	02	68	9

FLAT CAR PLANS

	M	Y	P
PORTAGER TOFC FOUR WHEEL DRAWINGS	04	77	48

GONDOLA PROTOTYPE DATA

	M	Y	P
49' COIL STEEL CAR PHOTOS PRR #387009	05	66	11
85' ALUMINUM COVERED GONDOLA ROCK #2099	03	61	9
88T ORE CAR GONDOLA DEMONSTRATOR BLH PHO	05	60	8
ALUMINUM ORE GONDOLA PHOTO	04	66	11
FAST DUMP GONDOLA ESPEE PHOTO	12	61	8
FLIP TOP COAL GONDOLA PHOTO BSPX #217	10	75	19
STEEL COIL GONDOLA PHOTO PRR #387000	03	65	12
WELDED ALUMINUM GONDOLA KAISER#163 PHOTO	02	57	9

GONDOLA PROTOTYPE DATA BY ROAD

RD		M	Y	P
PRR	49' COIL STEEL CAR PHOTOS PRR #387009	05	66	11
	STEEL COIL GONDOLA PHOTO PRR #387000	03	65	12
ROCK	85' ALUMINUM COVERED GONDOLA ROCK #2099	03	61	9
SP	FAST DUMP GONDOLA ESPEE PHOTO		12 61	8

HOPPER PROTOTYPE DATA

	M	Y	P
ARTICULATED HOPPER OF THE SOUTHERN	10	65	4
GRAVEL CAR COMPARISONS & CRITIQUES	01	75	38
HOPPER CARS	07	46	40
HOPPER CARS OF C&O SPECIFICATIONS	04	56	21
NEW COVERED 2 BAY HOPPER ACF 1952	08	52	63
PS-2 COVERED HOPPER INTRODUCTION	06	53	10
ROTO DUMP HOPPERS OF RMC	01	69	24

HOPPER PROTOTYPE DATA BY ROAD

RD		M	Y	P
C&O	HOPPER CARS OF C&O SPECIFICATIONS	04	56	21
RMC	ROTO DUMP HOPPERS OF RMC	01	69	24
S	ARTICULATED HOPPER OF THE SOUTHERN	10	65	4

HOPPER PHOTOS

	M	Y	P
100T SIDE GATE 100 XHC HOPPER PHOTO L&N	03	67	8
135T COVERED HOPPER ACL #50000 PHOTO	02	64	12
2800 CUBIC FT TANK HOPPERS SAL #7145 PHO	01	65	13
70T ORE JENNY FOAM INSULATION PRR #13978	01	65	12
90T 25' TACONITE HOPPER PHOTO LS&I #8563	05	65	13
95T 6 BAY HOPPER PHOTO N&W #76950	02	64	15
98 1/2T 29' SPEC CAR SP #345198 PHOTO	04	60	9
ALCAN TANK-HOPPER ESPEE PHOTO	12	61	8
ALUMINUM FMC HOPPER PHOTO	09	66	10
BIG JOHN 100T COVERED HOPPER S#8033 PHOT	06	62	10
CENTERFLOW REFRIG HOPPER NP #419903 PHOT	05	69	22C
DIA-FLO COVERED HOPPER GACX #50396 PHOTO	02	64	12
FIBERGLASS HOPPER COVERS ICG#361935 PHOT	01	74	13
HOPPER CLASS H39A PHOTO PRR #275089 1961	09	62	40
ICE BREAKER HOPPER PHOTO B&O #828123	04	65	13
ORE CAR #1502 25T D&IR PHOTO 1889	12	75	48
ORE CAR #7013 35T D&IR PHOTO	12	75	48
ORE JENNY CLASS G-39 PRR #14000 PHOTO	09	62	40
STRANGE ORE CARS? WABASH MINES#241-A-B-C	05	65	13
TRIPLE HOPPER PHOTO RTMX #8000	11	72	17

FREIGHT CARS

RD	HOPPER PHOTOS BY ROAD	M	Y	P
	ALUMINUM FMC HOPPER PHOTO	09	66	10
	TRIPLE HOPPER PHOTO RTMX #8000	11	72	17
ACL	135T COVERED HOPPER ACL #50000 PHOTO	02	64	12
B&O	ICE BREAKER HOPPER PHOTO B&O #828123	04	65	13
D&IR	ORE CAR #7013 35T D&IR PHOTO	12	75	48
	ORE CAR #1502 25T D&IR PHOTO 1889	12	75	48
GACX	DIA-FLO COVERED HOPPER GACX #50396 PHOTO	02	64	12
ICG	FIBERGLASS HOPPER COVERS ICG #361935 PHOT	01	74	13
L&N	100T SIDE GATE 100 XHC HOPPER PHOTO L&N	03	67	8
LS&I	90T 25' TACONITE HOPPER PHOTO LS&I #8563	05	65	13
N&W	95T 6 BAY HOPPER PHOTO N&W #76950	02	64	15
NP	CENTERFLOW REFRIG HOPPER NP #419903 PHOT	05	69	22C
PRR	70T ORE JENNY FOAM INSULATION PRR #13978	01	65	12
	HOPPER CLASS H39A PHOTO PRR #275089 1961	09	62	40
	ORE JENNY CLASS G-39 PRR #14000 PHOTO	09	62	40
S	BIG JOHN 100T COVERED HOPPER S #8033 PHOT	06	62	10
SAL	2800 CUBIC FT TANK HOPPERS SAL #7145 PHO	01	65	13
SP	98 1/2T 29' SPEC CAR SP #345198 PHOTO	04	60	9
	ALCAN TANK-HOPPER ESPEE PHOTO	12	61	8
W	STRANGE ORE CARS? WABASH MINES #241-A-B-C	05	65	13

REFRIGERATOR CAR PROTOTYPE DATA	M	Y	P
NEW UNICEL REEFER PRESSED STEEL CAR CO	08	52	62
REFRIGERATOR CAR ICING IN 45 SECONDS	12	55	24
REFRIGERATOR CARS FRESH FRUIT EVERYDAY	12	42	26
REFRIGERATOR CARS PERISHABLE--RUSH!!!	02	49	26

REFRIGERATOR CAR PHOTOS	M	Y	P
VENTILATOR REEFER #WFE #49846 PHOTO	01	41	35

STOCK CAR PHOTOS	M	Y	P
PIG PALACE STOCK CAR NP #84200 PHOTO 1964	02	65	11
PIG PALACE STOCK CAR PHOTO NP #84000	05	58	8
STOCK CAR LOADING PHOTO	10	74	42

TANK CAR PROTOTYPE DATA	M	Y	P
HOT DOG TANK CARS UNION TANK #42998	12	57	55
TANK CARS ARE INDISPENSABLE	10	48	42
TANK TRAIN CARS & OPERATIONS	02	74	3
TANK TRAIN TETE-A-TETE	10	78	16

TANK CAR PHOTOS	M	Y	P
15,000 GAL LIQUID GAS TANK CAR PHOTOS	01	62	9
22,900 GAL WHALE BELLY TANK MCPX #23000	01	66	9
30,800 GAL RAILKING TANK CAR PHOTO	08	62	9
32,800 GAL LP GAS TANK PHILGAS #30030 PH	02	64	11
32,800 GAL LPG GAT TANK CAR #33102 PHOTO	03	65	11
38,000 GAL RAIL WHALE PRR #50001 PHOTO	04	66	11
38,500 GAL TANK CAR UTLX #89701 PHOTO	12	63	12
50,000 GAL LAND TANKER UTLX #83699 PHOTO	09	63	12
50,000 GAL TANK CAR UNION TANK #83699 PHO	05	65	13
60,000 GAL TANKER GATX #96500 PHOTO	12	65	12
84' 159T CO2 TANK CAR PHOTO GATX	09	69	11
LARAGEST TANK CAR PHOTOS	04	60	9
PICKLE CAR PARAMOUNT FOODS PHOTO 1932	01	64	8
RAIL-KING TANK ACF PHOTO SHPX #30000	08	62	9
VAT TYPE OIL TANK CAR PHOTO	03	68	43
VINEGAR CAR STD BRANDS SBIX #1634 PHOTO	01	64	8

TANK CAR PROTOTYPE DATA BY ROAD				
RD		M	Y	P
GATX	60,000 GAL TANKER GATX #96500 PHOTO	12	65	12
PRR	38,000 GAL RAIL WHALE PRR #50001 PHOTO	04	66	11
SBIX	VINEGAR CAR STD BRANDS SBIX #1634 PHOTO	01	64	8
UTLX	50,000 GAL LAND TANKER UTLX #83699 PHOTO	09	63	12

FREIGHT CARS

GENERAL FREIGHT PROTOTYPE DATA

Title	M	Y	P
A HISTORY OF CONTAINERIZATION	06	60	37
AAR CAR SERVICE DIV SEND US EMPTIES-NOW!	09	53	35
CAR LEASING GATX NATX SHPX UTLX & ALL	10	66	38
CAR LOCATING COMPUTER ON BURL	08	68	6
COAL TRAFFIC GOING GOING GONE?	10	67	37
COAL TRAFFIC ON THE C&O	04	56	16
COAL TRAFFIC ON THE N&W	11	47	13
CONSTRUCTION AGGREGATE GRAVEL TRAINS	01	75	36
CONTAINER TRAFFIC LAND BRIDGE IN MEXICO	05	75	36
CONTAINER TRAFFIC TRAINS FOR TOMORROW	04	76	40
CONTAINER TRAINS TO HALIFAX ON THE CN	03	71	24
CONTAINERS NEXT GENERATION TECHNOLOGY	08	76	41
CONVEYOR CARS NW #12	01	53	59
FAST FREIGHT SERVICE ON THE CBELT	11	49	44
FAST FREIGHT SERVICE ON THE M&SL	08	49	40
FAST FREIGHT SERVICE ON THE UP	04	47	42
FREIGHT ON THE SEABOARD AIR LINE	05	63	20
FREIGHT SCHEDULES ON THE D&RGW	09	68	20
FREIGHT SERVICE ON THE GTW	01	47	14
FREIGHT TRAFFIC ON THE MP	01	57	44
GARBAGE TRAIN PROPOSALS TALE OF 3 TRAINS	02	75	44
GRADIENT FACTOR IN FRT TRAIN OPERATION	08	70	44
HITLER'S SUPER FREIGHT CARS	08	84	38
HOTBOX DETECTORS "ON TRAIN"	01	74	3
INEFFICIENT OPERATIONS A HISTORY LESSON	03	68	38
INEFFICIENT OPERATIONS NO FRT CAR SHORT	05	68	44
INEFFICIENT OPERATIONS SOL TO PROBLEM	04	68	36
INEFFICIENT OPERATIONS WHY FRT CARS SIT?	02	68	40
INT FF SERVICE BOSTON-CHICAGO B&M-CV-CN-	08	50	18
INTEGRAL TRAIN CONCEPT	01	68	20
INTEGRAL TRAIN CONCEPT HOTSHOT TO LANDSH	01	72	20
IOWA DIVISION MEAT TRAIN ON THE IC	10	58	40
IRON ORE TRAFFIC PRR #2 HAULER	09	62	34
KATY KOMET TRAIN OF THE MKT	09	53	28
MINIQUAD ORE CARS ON THE DM&IR 4 CARS= 1	02	76	12
NORTHEAST CORRIDOR POSSIBILITIES	08	74	20
PACIFIC ELECTRIC FREIGHT SERVICE	06	48	18
PACIFIC ELECTRIC SERVICE	05	46	40
PERISHABLE FREIGHT OPERATIONS ON THE WP	08	52	54
PIGGYBACK TRAFFIC ON THE SP	09	56	16
POCATELLO-PORTLAND FAST FREIGHT RUN UP	05	50	20
POTATO TRAFFIC ON ATSF	09	53	60
PULPWOOD TRAINS CAN BE PROFITABLE	03	75	26
PUSH BUTTONS AT PIG'S EYE YARD MILW	10	59	18
SACRAMENTO DIV OPERATIONS OF THE SP	08	58	40
SHORTHAUL 97 FREIGHT TRAIN OF THE SEA	02	74	36
SPEEDWEST FREIGHT SERVICE ON C&O	08	52	28
TARIFFS AND PRICING FOR THE FUTURE	02	63	38
THREE PIECE FREIGHT TRUCK ROCK&ROLL/BRAK	08	83	46
THREE PIECE FREIGHT TRUCKS AT BARGAN PCS	07	83	50
TRAIN LENGTH ARE THEY TOO LONG?	12	58	46
TRAIN SLACK END RESULT WHATS WRONG W/RR	02	76	22
TRAINMAKER CONCEPT YARD OF FUTURE	12	57	50
WHAT'S NEW IN FREIGHT EQUIPMENT	08	52	62

GENERAL FRT PROTOTYPE DATA BY ROAD

RD	Title	M	Y	P
ATSF	POTATO TRAFFIC ON ATSF	09	53	60
B&M	INT FF SERVICE BOSTON-CHICAGO B&M-CV-CN-	08	50	18
BURL	CAR LOCATING COMPUTER ON BURL	08	68	6
C&O	COAL TRAFFIC ON THE C&O	04	56	16
	SPEEDWEST FREIGHT SERVICE ON C&O	08	52	28
CBELT	FAST FREIGHT SERVICE ON THE CBELT	11	49	44
CN	CONTAINER TRAINS TO HALIFAX ON THE CN	03	71	24
D&RGW	FREIGHT SCHEDULES ON THE D&RGW	09	68	20
DM&IR	MINIQUAD ORE CARS ON THE DM&IR 4 CARS= 1	02	76	12
GTW	FREIGHT SERVICE ON THE GTW	01	47	14
IC	IOWA DIVISION MEAT TRAIN ON THE IC	10	58	40
M&SL	FAST FREIGHT SERVICE ON THE M&SL	08	49	40
MILW	PUSH BUTTONS AT PIG'S EYE YARD MILW	10	59	18
MKT	KATY KOMET TRAIN OF THE MKT	09	53	28
MP	FREIGHT TRAFFIC ON THE MP	01	57	44
N&W	COAL TRAFFIC ON THE N&W	11	47	13
NW	CONVEYOR CARS NW #12	01	53	59
PE	PACIFIC ELECTRIC SERVICE	05	46	40
	PACIFIC ELECTRIC FREIGHT SERVICE	06	48	18
PRR	IRON ORE TRAFFIC PRR #2 HAULER	09	62	34
SEA	SHORTHAUL 97 FREIGHT TRAIN OF THE SEA	02	74	36
	FREIGHT ON THE SEABOARD AIR LINE	05	63	20
SP	PIGGYBACK TRAFFIC ON THE SP	09	56	16
	SACRAMENTO DIV OPERATIONS OF THE SP	08	58	40
UP	POCATELLO-PORTLAND FAST FREIGHT RUN UP	05	50	20
	FAST FREIGHT SERVICE ON THE UP	04	47	42
WP	PERISHABLE FREIGHT OPERATIONS ON THE WP	08	52	54

BILL OF LADING   NON-REVENUE EQUIPMENT

This section has two subsections: Cabooses and Maintanence of Way Equipment. Easch subsection is further broken down into the following subject areas:

Prototype data includes articles and specifications on the real thing. In many instances there are photographs with these articles that did not get special billing in the photograph section. The plans and drawings are just that. Generally by our convention a drawing is more detailed than a plan, but this is not a hard and fast rule. The plans are listed twice: once alphabetically and once by road. The photo section shows details or unusual photos of interest to the researcher. Obviously we did not list all photos that appear in these magazines.

The descriptor line includes a description of the car, its number, class, builder and year built. This data is included if available and if space permits.

MANIFEST   NON-REVENUE CARS

	PAGE
NON-REVENUE EQUIPMENT	298
CABOOSES	300
CABOOSE PROTOTYPE DATA	300
CABOOSE PROTOTYPE DATA BY ROAD	300
CABOOSE PHOTOS	300
CABOOSE PHOTOS BY ROAD	300
MOW EQUIPMENT	300
MOW PROTOTYPE DATA	300
MOW PROTOTYPE DATA BY ROAD	300
MOW PHOTOS	301
MOW PHOTOS BY ROAD	301

NON-REVENUE EQUIPMENT

CABOOSE PROTOTYPE DATA

	M	Y	P
30' CRESCENT CUPOLA CABOOSE GN #X310	05	56	8
BRIGHT GREEN CABOOSE TP&W #N	08	49	50
CABOOSE ANATOMY	04	44	13
CABOOSE WORLD OF WAYNE LEEMAN	04	79	32
CABOOSES TRAVELING OFFICES	04	44	8
EXTENDED VISION CABOOSE FRIS #204	06	59	11
FAREWELL CABOOSE	09	85	34
WANING WAYCAR	01	83	4

CABOOSE PROTOTYPE DATA BY ROAD

RD		M	Y	P
FRIS	EXTENDED VISION CABOOSE FRIS #204	06	59	11
GN	30' CRESCENT CUPOLA CABOOSE GN #X310	05	56	8
TP&W	BRIGHT GREEN CABOOSE TP&W #N	08	49	50

CABOOSE PHOTOS

	M	Y	P
AUTO TRAIN CABOOSE #92 FROM FEC PHOTO	12	76	19
BAY-COM-CUPOLA CABOOSE MP #997-R PHOTO	03	65	33
CABOOSE WITH BOXCAR SIDES CN #79399 PHOT	10	70	17
DOME CABOOSE CP #437448 PHOTO	08	54	53
INTERNATIONAL CABOOSE PHOTO LI #54	06	59	8
SIDE DOOR CABOOSE CBELT #2305 PHOTO	05	84	12
SIDE DOOR CABOOSE PHOTO B&AR #C42	04	65	13
STD CABOOSE LV #1776 BICENT COLORS PHOTO	04	76	17
STD CABOOSE PHOTO B&O #C300	04	53	14
STD CABOOSE PHOTO R #92900 1965 COLORS	01	66	10
STEEL STANDARD CABOOSE PHOTO BURL #13548	03	55	8

CABOOSE PHOTOS BY ROAD

RD		M	Y	P
B&AR	SIDE DOOR CABOOSE PHOTO B&AR #C42	04	65	13
B&O	STD CABOOSE PHOTO B&O #C300	04	53	14
BURL	STEEL STANDARD CABOOSE PHOTO BURL #13548	03	55	8
CBELT	SIDE DOOR CABOOSE CBELT #2305 PHOTO	05	84	12
CN	CABOOSE WITH BOXCAR SIDES CN #79399 PHOT	10	70	17
CP	DOME CABOOSE CP #437448 PHOTO	08	54	53
LI	INTERNATIONAL CABOOSE PHOTO LI #54	06	59	8
LV	STD CABOOSE LV #1776 BICENT COLORS PHOTO	04	76	17
MP	BAY-COM-CUPOLA CABOOSE MP #997-R PHOTO	03	65	33
R	STD CABOOSE PHOTO R #92900 1965 COLORS	01	66	10

MOW PROTOTYPE DATA

	M	Y	P
BURDEN BEARING STEAM LOCOMOTIVE	08	70	42
DUAL PURPOSE INSPECTION CARS	02	47	69
FIRE FIGHTING TRAIN BIG ONE AT SHED 27	11	51	20
JORDAN SPREADERS MULTIDEXTEROUS MACHINES	06	69	38
MAINTENANCE OF WAY MACHINERY	04	72	24
OHIO LOCOMOTIVE CRANE OVERTURE	07	82	36
PAY CAR IT WAS MORE THAN JUST PAY	12	74	44
PILE DRIVERS OF NYC	11	52	54
PROLIFIC PILE DRIVER SCL #6	06	69	18A
RAIL DEFECT DETECTOR CAR "TAKE HER OUT"	02	51	16
RAIL DETECTOR CAR MADE BY SP #0-1000	04	46	58
RAILCAR CRB&L #1	09	50	44
ROTARY PLOWS FIGHTING SNOW FOR PROFIT	03	76	22
SELF PROPELLED PIGGYBACK SHOVEL CP	02	61	39
SHAY ENGINE ROTARY SNOWPLOW SOO #X10 L	11	63	35
SNOWPLOWS-BEYOND THE 100" ISOLINE CP&CN	02	80	46
SPERRY RAIL DEFECT DETECTOR CAR	10	41	28
SPERRY RAIL SERVICE CAR #130	01	63	44
TRACK DESTROYERS (MILITARY)	02	45	36
WHAT IS A LIDGERWOOD? CM&SP #X302	01	45	40
WHAT SPERRY CARS LOOK FOR	02	83	23
WHEEL CHECKERS CATCH BROKEN FLANGES	06	57	43
WRECK TRAINS THE BIG HOOK	04	50	41
WRECKMASTERS MOON PRR	10	82	22

MOW PROTOTYPE DATA BY ROAD

RD		M	Y	P
CBR&L	RAILCAR CRB&L #1	09	50	44
CM&SP	WHAT IS A LIDGERWOOD? CM&SP #X302	01	45	40
CP	SNOWPLOWS-BEYOND THE 100" ISOLINE CP&CN	02	80	46
	SELF PROPELLED PIGGYBACK SHOVEL CP	02	61	39
NYC	PILE DRIVERS OF NYC	11	52	54
PRR	WRECKMASTERS MOON PRR	10	82	22
SCL	PROLIFIC PILE DRIVER SCL #6	06	69	18A
SOO	SHAY ENGINE ROTARY SNOWPLOW SOO #X10 L	11	63	35
SP	FIRE FIGHTING TRAIN BIG ONE AT SHED 27	11	51	20
	RAIL DETECTOR CAR MADE BY SP #0-1000	04	46	58

NON-REVENUE EQUIPMENT

MOW PHOTOS	M	Y	P
BALLAST CLEANING MACHINE PRR PHOTO	11	44	43
BIG HOOK DERAILMENT PHOTO EL	06	77	33
BUICK SPECIAL RAILCAR PHOTO BURL	12	55	53
CABOSE REBUILD B&M #C90 PHOTO	07	63	9
CLEARANCE CAR PHOTO NYC	10	42	41
CLEARANCE TRUCK PHOTO CR	02	81	15
DYNAMOMETER CAR IC #30 PHOTO	02	70	14
EC-1 TRACK GEOMETRY CAR UP PHOTO PLA	08	75	16
FLANGER PHOTO SP #7319	12	57	34
GAS ELECTRIC LINE CAR NYW&B #X1 PHOTO GE	11	73	47
MCKEON MOTOR CAR PHOTO UP #M-18	05	80	40
MOBILE HOME ON FLATCAR PHOTOS NP #201638	02	70	15
MOTOR CAR #4900 SCL PHOTO	06	70	17
PACKARD INSPECTION CAR PHOTO PI&SH 1931	02	55	21
PEAKING POWER UNIT PHOTO FM	08	62	9
PILE DRIVER #6 SCL #765450 PHOTO	06	69	1
PILE DRIVER PHOTO COLUMBIAN NAT'L RY	06	62	12
PONTIAC INSPECTION CAR PHOTO WSL	07	71	32
PORT-A-BULK STORAGE TANK FLATCAR LOAD PH	03	70	15
RAIL TRUCK SWITCHER PHOTO VALLEY RAIL RD	04	52	58
RAILCAR #2 WM AT EDGEMONT MD PHOTO	10	76	34
RAILMOBILE PHOTOS E&LS	07	84	37
ROTARY SNOWPLOW LIMA SHAY RI #95377 PHOT	11	67	9
SCALE TEST CAR OF 1891 PC #8000 PHOTO	06	74	35
SIDEWAYS FLAT CAR TRANSFER TABLE PHOTO	10	68	9
SNOW MELTER ON B&M PHOTO	11	45	43
SNOWPLOW FROM TENDER CNW #X262667 PHOTO	05	67	47
SPERRY RAIL CAR PHOTO SRS #131	01	64	30
SPERRY RAIL SERVICE CAR PHOTOS	01	83	33
THROUGH CABIN CAR PRR #478179 PHOTO	03	63	9
TRANSFER CABOOSE ON SWITCHER UNDERFRAME	03	66	55
TWO "BIG HOOKS" IN OPERATION S #903018	03	77	17
WHALE BOTTOM BOOM CAR PHOTO ATSF #181493	02	66	10
WRECK CRANE CNJ #6 PHOTO	11	67	8
WRECK CRANE PHOTO RRR #X01	04	68	12

RD	MOW PHOTOS BY ROAD	M	Y	P
ATSF	WHALE BOTTOM BOOM CAR PHOTO ATSF #181493	02	66	10
B&M	SNOW MELTER ON B&M PHOTO	11	45	43
	CABOSE REBUILD B&M #C90 PHOTO	07	63	9
BURL	BUICK SPECIAL RAILCAR PHOTO BURL	12	55	53
CNJ	WRECK CRANE CNJ #6 PHOTO	11	67	8
CNW	SNOWPLOW FROM TENDER CNW #X262667 PHOTO	05	67	47
CR	CLEARANCE TRUCK PHOTO CR	02	81	15
E&LS	RAILMOBILE PHOTOS E&LS	07	84	37
EL	BIG HOOK DERAILMENT PHOTO EL	06	77	33
IC	DYNAMOMETER CAR IC #30 PHOTO	02	70	14
NP	MOBILE HOME ON FLATCAR PHOTOS NP #201638	02	70	15
NYC	CLEARANCE CAR PHOTO NYC	10	42	41
NYW&B	GAS ELECTRIC LINE CAR NYW&B #X1 PHOTO GE	11	73	47
PC	SCALE TEST CAR OF 1891 PC #8000 PHOTO	06	74	35
PI&SH	PACKARD INSPECTION CAR PHOTO PI&SH 1931	02	55	21
PRR	BALLAST CLEANING MACHINE PRR PHOTO	11	44	43
	THROUGH CABIN CAR PRR #478179 PHOTO	03	63	9
RI	ROTARY SNOWPLOW LIMA SHAY RI #95377 PHOT	11	67	9
RRR	WRECK CRANE PHOTO RRR #X01	04	68	12
S	TWO "BIG HOOKS" IN OPERATION S #903018	03	77	17
SCL	MOTOR CAR #4900 SCL PHOTO	06	70	17
	PILE DRIVER #6 SCL #765450 PHOTO	06	69	1
SP	FLANGER PHOTO SP #7319	12	57	34
SRS	SPERRY RAIL CAR PHOTO SRS #131	01	64	30
UP	MCKEON MOTOR CAR PHOTO UP #M-18	05	80	40
VAL	RAIL TRUCK SWITCHER PHOTO VALLEY RAIL RD	04	52	58
WM	RAILCAR #2 WM AT EDGEMONT MD PHOTO	10	76	34
WSL	PONTIAC INSPECTION CAR PHOTO WSL	07	71	32

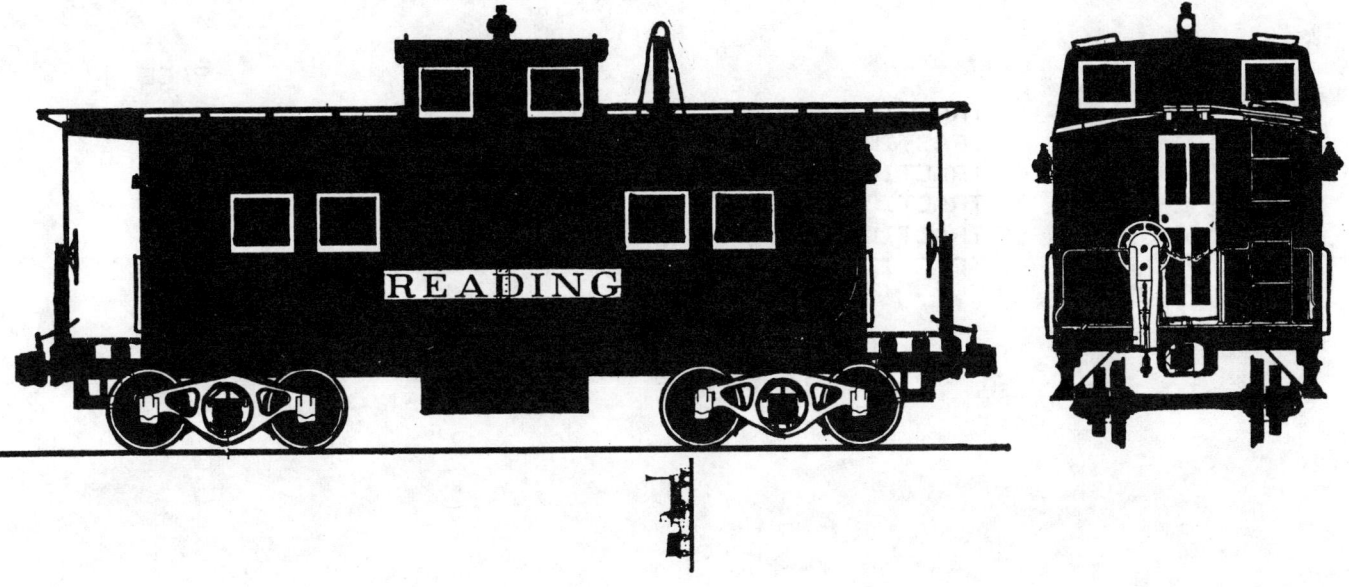

BILL OF LADING — TRACTION

The Traction Section is further broken down into the following subject areas:

Prototype data includes articles and specifications on the real thing. In many instances there are photographs with these articles that did not get special billing in the photograph section. The plans and drawings are just that. Generally by our convention a drawing is more detailed than a plan, but this is not a hard and fast rule. The plans are listed twice: once alphabetically and once by road. The photo section shows details or unusual photos of interest to the researcher. Obviously we did not list all photos that appear in these magazines.

The descriptor line includes a description of the car, its number, class, builder and year built. This data is included if available and if space permits.

MANIFEST — TRACTION

	PAGE
TRACTION	302
TRACTION PROTOTYPE DATA	303
TRACTION PROTOTYPE DATA BY ROAD	303
TRACTION PHOTOS	303
TRACTION PHOTOS BY ROAD	303
TRACTION IN GENERAL	303

TRACTION

TRACTION PROTOTYPE DATA

Title	M	Y	P
BRIGHTLINER SUBWAY CARS BY BUDD	03	65	16
BRILL HEAVYWEIGHT CARS ON THE MRR	11	68	44
BUDD RAPID TRANSIT CARS	10	60	8
BULLET CARS BY BRILL	07	66	26
CHICAGO SUBWAY 39 YEARS OF PLANNING	05	43	37
COMBINES AND COACHES OF THE CSS&SB	08	72	26
COMBINES OF THE I&C TRACTION CO	02	64	50
COMBINES OF THI&E WILEY HIGH SCHOOL #122	08	64	38
CURVED SIDE LIGHTWEIGHT CARS OF CIN CAR	07	65	28
ELECTRIFICATION ITS PROSPECTS IN 1970	07	70	39
ELECTROLINER TRAINS OF THE CNS&M	03	65	34
EXIT THE TROLLEY	11	54	53
HOLLAND INTURURBAN SLEEPING CAR-CLASSIC	04	64	24
INSULL'S INTERURBANS	04	56	31
INTERURBANS IN THE COUNTRY	06	49	36
IOWA LAND OF STEAM ROAD TROLLEYS	01	56	27
JEWETT CARS OF 1912 ON THE LVT	09	69	37
JEWETT CENTER DOOR CARS ON SLE 1910	02	73	38
KEY SYSTEMS FORMER NEW YORK CITY EL CARS	02	43	35
KUHLMAN CARS ON THE CSCO	05	66	42
LIBERTY LINERS NORTH SHORE RED ARROW	04	64	7
LINE CAR IT #1700	09	55	41
MULTIPLE UNIT ELECTRICS	06	43	14
MYSTIQUE OF ELECTRIFICATION	07	70	44
NEW CARS FOR SOUTH SHORE...FINALLY!	01	82	48
OHIO TROLLEY LINES TWILIGHT OF TROLLEY	06	51	40
PARLOR CAR CONNR #500 1904 BRILL	01	69	26
PARLOR OBSERVATION CAR OF WCF&N	09	58	47
PARLOR OBSERVATION CAR OF WCF&N 1915 M&C	02	68	46
PRIVATE CAR EL VIENTO JEWEL BOX ON WHEEL	11	69	38
RED DEVIL CARS OF THE C&LE	10	63	44
RISE AND FALL OF THE INTERURBAN	10	49	48
RUN AN INTERURBAN EXCURSION W/OUT JUICE	07	59	40
SEASHORE ELECTRIC RAILWAY & MUSEUM.	09	56	51
SOUTHEASTERN PA TRANSPORT AUTHOR #9102	06	78	2
SPEED ON TRACTION LINES	04	67	24
SUBWAYS OF NEW YORK CITY	10	42	4
TROLLEYS NORTH OF LAKE ERIE ONTARIO CAN	10	57	31
UTAH INTERBANS	09	42	10
WASH BALTIMORE & ANNAPOLIS ELECTRIC RR	01	66	46

TRACTION PROTOTYPE DATA BY ROAD

RD	Title	M	Y	P
C&LE	RED DEVIL CARS OF THE C&LE	10	63	44
CNS&M	ELECTROLINER TRAINS OF THE CNS&M	03	65	34
	LIBERTY LINERS NORTH SHORE RED ARROW	04	64	7
CONNR	PARLOR CAR CONNR #500 1904 BRILL	01	69	26
CSCO	KUHLMAN CARS ON THE CSCO	05	66	42
CSS&SB	NEW CARS FOR SOUTH SHORE...FINALLY!	01	82	48
	COMBINES AND COACHES OF THE CSS&SB	08	72	26
CSUB	CHICAGO SUBWAY 39 YEARS OF PLANNING	05	43	37
I&C	COMBINES OF THE I&C TRACTION CO	02	64	50
IT	LINE CAR IT #1700	09	55	41
LVT	JEWETT CARS OF 1912 ON THE LVT	09	69	37
MRR	BRILL HEAVYWEIGHT CARS ON THE MRR	11	68	44
SLE	JEWETT CENTER DOOR CARS ON SLE 1910	02	73	38
THI&E	COMBINES OF THI&E WILEY HIGH SCHOOL #122	08	64	38
WB&AE	WASH BALTIMORE & ANNAPOLIS ELECTRIC RR	01	66	46
WCF&N	PARLOR OBSERVATION CAR OF WCF&N	09	58	47
	PARLOR OBSERVATION CAR OF WCF&N 1915 M&C	02	68	46

TRACTION PHOTOS

Title	M	Y	P
COACH-LOUNGE C&LE #110 PHOTO CCC 1930	10	63	44
INTERURBAN #1 NIR PHOTO	12	53	44
LINE CAR #1100 PHOTO CSS&SB	10	47	40
OHIO ELECTRIC #164 COMBINE PHOTO	11	49	36
WORK MOTOR INDIANA RAILROAD #787 PHOTO	04	42	23

TRACTION PHOTOS BY ROAD

RD	Title	M	Y	P
C&LE	COACH-LOUNGE C&LE #110 PHOTO CCC 1930	10	63	44
CSS&SB	LINE CAR #1100 PHOTO CSS&SB	10	47	40
NIR	INTERURBAN #1 NIR PHOTO	12	53	44

TRACTION IN GENERAL

Title	M	Y	P
ELECTRIC RAILROADING PHOTO ESSAY	10	46	20
SAN FRANCISCO CABLE CARS SOLE SURVIVORS	11	47	8
ZEPHYRETTE	07	52	26

BILL OF LADING   STRUCTURES & SIGNALS

This section contains the six subsections of Bridges and Tunnels, Commercial Buildings, Depots and Stations, Railroad Structures, Signals and General Structures. Bridges and Tunnels are self-explanatory. Commercial structures include stores, factories, houses, etc. Depots and stations are just that. Railroad structures are line side buildings, roundhouses, platforms, water towers, servicing facilities and the like. Signals are signals, both electrical and mechanical, signs, telltales, etc. General structures is the catch-all.

Prototype data includes articles and specifications on the real thing. In many instances there are photographs with these articles that did not get special billing in the photograph section. The plans and drawings are just that. Generally by our convention a drawing is more detailed than a plan, but this is not a hard and fast rule. The plans are listed twice: once alphabetically and once by road. The photo section shows details or unusual photos of interest to the researcher. Obviously we did not list all photos that appear in these magazines.

The descriptor line includes the description. If a road or geographical location is available it is included. The year built is also included if available.

MANIFEST STRUCTURES & SIGNALS

	PAGE
STRUCTURES & SIGNALS	304
BRIDGES & TUNNELS	306
BRIDGE & TUNNEL PROTOTYPE DATA	306
BRIDGE & TUNNEL PROTOTYPE DATA BY ROAD	306
BRIDGE & TUNNEL PLANS	306
BRIDGE & TUNNEL PHOTOS	306
BRIDGE & TUNNEL PHOTOS BY ROAD	306
COMMERCIAL STRUCTURES	306
COMMERCIAL BUILDING PHOTOS	306
DEPOTS	307
DEPOT PROTOTYPE DATA	307
DEPOT PROTOTYPE DATA BY ROAD	307
DEPOT PLANS	307
DEPOT PHOTOS	307
DEPOT PHOTOS BY ROAD	307
RAILROAD STRUCTURES	307
RAILROAD STRUCTURE PROTOTYPE DATA	307
RAILROAD STRUCTURE PROTOTYPE DATA BY RD	308
RAILROAD STRUCTURE PHOTOS	308
RAILROAD STRUCTURE PHOTOS BY ROAD	308
SIGNALS	308
SIGNAL PROTOTYPE DATA	308
SIGNAL PROTOTYPE DATA BY ROAD	308
SIGNAL PHOTOS	308
SIGNAL PHOTOS BY ROAD	308

STRUCTURES & SIGNALS

BRIDGE & TUNNEL PROTOTYPE DATA

	M	Y	P
AL SMITH HUDSON RIVER BRIDGE NYC 1924	09	53	58
ARCH & SUSPENSION BRIDGE - NIAGARA FALLS	12	57	44
BOX GERDER BRIDGE ON BN	03	84	31
BRIDGE THAT BALKED QUEBEC BRIDGE	03	85	27
BUILD A BRIDGE AROUND EXISTING TRACK	11	45	42
CANADIAN NATIONAL RAILWAYS BRIDGES	01	41	15
CANYON DIABLO BRIDGE ATSF	07	52	18
CASCADE TUNNEL CONQUERED BY GN	11	61	23
CASCADE TUNNEL GN	06	41	4
CASCADE TUNNEL THE REASON GN ELECTRIFIED	12	61	23
CASCADE TUNNEL THROUGH THE CASCADES	09	52	20
CIMARRON BRIDGE RI ENGINEERING FEAT	02	53	48
CONCRETE VIADUCT ACL JAMES RIVER VA	10	55	55
COVERED BRIDGES CROSSINGS UNDER COVER	06	55	44
DALE CREEK'S TRESTLES UP	12	51	30
DETROIT RIVER TUNNEL DETROIT MI	10	64	40
ENGLEWOOD TUNNEL	11	42	18
ENLARGEMENT OF "RAT HOLE" DIV TUN CNO&TP	03	62	4
GREAT SALT LAKE TRESTLE	03	84	8
HELL GATE BRIDGE CASSATT'S DREAM	10	54	27
HIGH VIEW TUNNEL VIEWS O&W 1954	02	76	50
HOOSAC TUNNEL 1875 B&M	02	42	28
HOOSAC TUNNEL FITCHBURG DIV B&M	12	47	52
HOOSAC TUNNEL NOTABLE ENGINEERING FEAT	06	52	20
HOOSAC TUNNEL THE GREAT BORE	06	60	18
KEDDIE WYE BRIDGE NOTABLE ENGINEER FEAT	03	53	48
KINZUA VIADUCT ERIE NOTE ENGINEER FEAT	07	53	25
MISSISSIPPI RIVER BRIDGE STONE ARCH TYPE	12	53	48
MISSISSIPPI RIVER PONTOON BRIDGE FLOATS	01	52	43
MOFFAT TUNNEL UNDER CONTINENTAL DIVIDE	10	53	60
NATURAL TUNNEL IN VIRGINIA S	01	44	34
NEW & OLD TUNNELS	09	42	42
POUGHKEEPSIE BRIDGE NOTE ENGINEER FEAT	05	53	26
REOPENING OF TUNNEL 1943 D&SL	02	44	10
SALT LAKE FILL SP	01	57	9
SPIRAL TUNNELS IN THE ROCKIES CP	04	52	22
ST CLAIR TUNNEL GTW	09	64	36
STARRUCCA VIADUCT LAINESBORO PA	05	72	20
THOMAS VIADUCT LATAROBELS FOLLY B&O	12	52	20
TUNNEL CONSTRUCTION 1	09	64	36
TUNNEL CONSTRUCTION 2	10	64	40
TUNNEL DOORS ON EBT	01	52	50
TUNNELS IN NEW ENGLAND	01	57	16
TUNNELS ON RAILROADS 300 US MILES	05	46	10
VERTICAL LIFT BRIDGE AT BUZZARDS BAY NH	10	55	56

BRIDGE & TUNNEL PLANS

	M	Y	P
HARLEM RIVER BRIDGE DRAWINGS WS&Y	12	47	12

BRIDGE & TUNNEL PROTOTYPE DATA BY ROAD

RD		M	Y	P
ACL	CONCRETE VIADUCT ACL JAMES RIVER VA	10	55	55
ATSF	CANYON DIABLO BRIDGE ATSF	07	52	18
B&M	HOOSAC TUNNEL 1875 B&M	02	42	28
	HOOSAC TUNNEL FITCHBURG DIV B&M	12	47	52
B&O	THOMAS VIADUCT LATAROBELS FOLLY B&O	12	52	20
BN	BOX GERDER BRIDGE ON BN	03	84	31
CN	CANADIAN NATIONAL RAILWAYS BRIDGES	01	41	15
CNO&TP	ENLARGEMENT OF "RAT HOLE" DIV TUN CNO&TP	03	62	4
CP	SPIRAL TUNNELS IN THE ROCKIES CP	04	52	22
D&SL	REOPENING OF TUNNEL 1943 D&SL	02	44	10
E	KINZUA VIADUCT ERIE NOTE ENGINEER FEAT	07	53	25
EBT	TUNNEL DOORS ON EBT	01	52	50
GN	CASCADE TUNNEL GN	06	41	4
	CASCADE TUNNEL THE REASON GN ELECTRIFIED	12	61	23
	CASCADE TUNNEL CONQUERED BY GN	11	61	23
	CASCADE TUNNEL THROUGH THE CASCADES	09	52	20
	MISSISSIPPI RIVER BRIDGE STONE ARCH TYPE	12	53	48
GTW	ST CLAIR TUNNEL GTW	09	64	36
NH	VERTICAL LIFT BRIDGE AT BUZZARDS BAY NH	10	55	56
NYC	HELL GATE BRIDGE CASSATT'S DREAM	10	54	27
	AL SMITH HUDSON RIVER BRIDGE NYC 1924	09	53	58
O&W	HIGH VIEW TUNNEL VIEWS O&W 1954	02	76	50
RI	CIMARRON BRIDGE RI ENGINEERING FEAT	02	53	48
S	NATURAL TUNNEL IN VIRGINIA S	01	44	34
SP	SALT LAKE FILL SP	01	57	9
UP	DALE CREEK'S TRESTLES UP	12	51	30

BRIDGE & TUNNEL PHOTOS

	M	Y	P
BRIDGE PHOTO ESSAY	03	66	31
CULVERT BRIDGE PHOTO ON B&M	10	65	10
DUAL PURPOSE BRIDGE 1867 PHOTO WDSVLL NH	06	59	35
LIFT SPAN BRIDGE GALENA RIVER IL PHOTO	05	73	16
PRE STRESSED CONCRETE SLAB TRESTLE ACL	03	60	9
STARRUCCA VIADUCT PHOTO	01	57	54
STARRUCCA VIADUCT & C424 PHOTO	09	63	32
STARRUCCA VIADUCT PHOTO	02	46	17
STARRUCCA VIADUCT PHOTOGRAPH	11	62	48
TIFFANY BRIDGE WIS C&NW PHOTO	06	77	35
TUNKHANNOCK PA VIADUCT PHOTO	08	52	48

BRIDGE & TUNNEL PHOTOS BY ROAD

RD		M	Y	P
ACL	PRE STRESSED CONCRETE SLAB TRESTLE ACL	03	60	9
B&M	CULVERT BRIDGE PHOTO ON B&M	10	65	10
C&NW	TIFFANY BRIDGE WIS C&NW PHOTO	06	77	35

COMMERCIAL BUILDING PHOTOS

	M	Y	P
COAL MINE BARRETT W VA EAST ASSN COAL PH	05	68	10
FILLING STATION ON FLANGED WHEELS PHOTO	03	66	55
MOTEL FROM EX-BOXCARS PHOTO	08	65	61

STRUCTURES & SIGNALS

DEPOT PROTOTYPE DATA

	M	Y	P
ARCADIA FLA DEPOT SAL	04	83	50
ATLANTA TERMINAL	08	59	19
BIG CITY PASSENGER STATION STATUS LIST	05	73	14
BROAD ST STATION PHILADELPHIA PA PRR	12	83	40
CENTRAL UNION TERMINAL TOLEDO OHIO	10	53	20
CHICAGO'S STATIONS GATES TO EVERYWHERE	08	48	22
CHICHAGO STATIONS NEW SHED IC	06	45	38
DEPOT AT ESSEX JCT VERMONT 1881-1958	08	58	50
DEPOT PORTLAND UNION STATION B&M	08	84	20
DEPOT STRATFORD TX SP	04	84	32
DETROIT THE STATION LOOKS LIKE A HOTEL	08	78	41
DETROITS LAST DEPOT	09	78	44
GRAND CENTRAL STATION CHICAGO IL FAREWEL	09	69	20
GRAND CENTRAL TERMINAL NEW YORK CITY NY	03	43	8
GRAND CENTRAL TERMINAL NEW YORK NY	05	75	22
JACKSONVILLE TERMINAL JACKSONVILLE FL	06	78	22
JACKSONVILLE TERMINAL JACKSONVILLE FLA	05	49	12
MONTREAL TERMINAL MONTREAL CANADA CN	11	43	30
MONTREAL W. STATION/THREE ROUT TERMINAL	10	45	28
NEW STATION CONCEPTS	04	59	45
NORTH STATION BOSTON MA	09	48	14
PENNSYLVANIA STATION NY, NY PRR	04	46	35
PHILADELPHIA PA 6-11-23 FIRE BROAD ST ST	11	43	26
RAILROAD NAMES ON STATION PHOTO	07	79	38
RAILROAD TERMINALS 1	09	85	20
RAILROAD TERMINALS 2	10	85	40
SMALL TOWN DEPOTS-OUT OF WAY PLACES	05	78	20
ST ALBANS DEPOT ST ALBANS VT CV	06	58	56
STATION LOCATION QUIZ	10	57	52
UNION DEPOT DULUTH MN ONE THAT ENDURED	11	73	20
UNION PASSENGER TERMINAL NEW ORLEANS LA	09	54	14
UNION STATION JOLIET IL	03	52	14
UNION STATION AUGUSTA GA TORN DOWN NOW	02	73	42
UNION STATION CHICAGO IL PHOTO ESSAY	08	65	28
UNION STATION DENVER CO 1881-1970	06	70	40
UNION STATION HISTORY ST LOUIS MO	03	78	20
UNION STATION KANSAS CITY MO	04	65	42
UNION STATION LOS ANGELES CA	05	44	4
UNION STATION LOUISVILLE KY L&N	05	72	26
UNION STATION NASHVILLE TN L&N	05	72	26
UNION STATION ST. LOUIS MO	08	43	48
UNION STATION WASHINGTON DC	12	40	13
UNION STATION WASHINGTON DC $72000/DAY	01	43	38
UNION STATION YARDS WASHINGTON DC	10	52	51
UNION TERMINAL CINCINNATI OH	03	41	15
UNION TERMINAL CINCINNATI OH A MEMOIR	02	72	18
UNION TERMINAL CINCINNATI OHIO	05	53	14
UNION STATION CHICAGO, ILL	03	44	4

DEPOT PLANS

	M	Y	P
UNION DEPOT DULUTH MN DRAWING	11	73	21
UNION STATION AUGUSTA GA ELEVATION DRAW	02	73	44

DEPOT PROTOTYPE DATA BY ROAD

RD		M	Y	P
B&M	DEPOT PORTLAND UNION STATION B&M	08	84	20
CN	MONTREAL TERMINAL MONTREAL CANADA CN	11	43	30
CV	ST ALBANS DEPOT ST ALBANS VT CV	06	58	56
IC	CHICHAGO STATIONS NEW SHED IC	06	45	38
L&N	UNION STATION LOUISVILLE KY L&N	05	72	26
	UNION STATION NASHVILLE TN L&N	05	72	26
PRR	BROAD ST STATION PHILADELPHIA PA PRR	12	83	40
SAL	ARCADIA FLA DEPOT SAL	04	83	50
SP	DEPOT STRATFORD TX SP	04	84	32

DEPOT PHOTOS

	M	Y	P
DEPOT CANAAN CONN PHOTO	09	78	50
MP DIVISION OFFICE & DEPOT WICHITA KS	12	65	13
OLD STATIONS NY & PA PHOTOS	11	45	40
STONE RECESSED DEPOT WIND EL TENAFLY NJ	07	67	29

DEPOT PHOTOS BY ROAD

RD		M	Y	P
EL	STONE RECESSED DEPOT WIND EL TENAFLY NJ	07	67	29
MP	MP DIVISION OFFICE & DEPOT WICHITA KS	12	65	13

RAILROAD STRUCTURE PROTOTYPE DATA

	M	Y	P
BIG BIG DOME REPAIR SHOP UNION TANK	01	59	6
CEDAR GROVE TOWER 1937 SHREVEPORT LA	09	62	32
DIESEL CAB AS A GUARDHOSE BOISE ID	06	80	50A
ENGLEWOOD YARD HOUSTON TX SP	04	56	57
ERECTING CRANE IN OPER (4-8-2 LIFTING)	02	75	38
EXCHANGING TURNTABLES 60' FOR 80' B&O	01	45	21
LOCOMOTIVE SQUAREHOUSE HAVRE MONT GN	10	46	48
PROVISO YARD CHICAGO ILL C&NW	10	44	6
RAILROAD HEADQUARTERS PHOTO QUIZ	04	73	46
RUSSELL CAR SHOPS OF THE C&O	03	56	50
SAND FOR RAILS	08	46	18
SELKIRK YARD ALBANY NY NYC	07	48	18
SOMETHING ABOUT A DEPOT	11	62	39
STREAMLINER CAR WASH	06	51	48
TRACK PANS WATER ON THE FLY MC	12	51	42
WATER HOLES FOR IRON HORSES	06	44	18

STRUCTURES & SIGNALS

RAILROAD STRUCTURE PROTOTYPE DATA BY RD

RD		M	Y	P
B&O	EXCHANGING TURNTABLES 60' FOR 80' B&O	01	45	21
C&NW	PROVISO YARD CHICAGO ILL C&NW	10	44	6
C&O	RUSSELL CAR SHOPS OF THE C&O	03	56	50
CN	ERECTING CRANE IN OPER (4-8-2 LIFTING)	02	75	38
GN	LOCOMOTIVE SQUAREHOUSE HAVRE MONT GN	10	46	48
MC	TRACK PANS WATER ON THE FLY MC	12	51	42
NYC	SELKIRK YARD ALBANY NY NYC	07	48	18
SP	ENGLEWOOD YARD HOUSTON TX SP	04	56	57

RAILROAD STRUCTURE PHOTOS

	M	Y	P
ARMSTRONG TURNTABLE & S #390 2-8-0 PHOTO	03	73	33
COAL CHUTE PHOTO BUREAU ILL ROCK ISLAND	04	47	32
CONCRETE COALING TOWER GORDON AK MP PHOT	11	77	51
DOUBLE TURNTABLE COLOGNE GERMANY PHOTO	01	46	52
FRT DOCKS AT WEEHAWKEN MANHATTAN NY PHOT	02	46	21
INTERLOCKING TOWER GIBSON CITY IL PHOTO	01	70	38
MODERNISTIC COAL CHUTE CLIFTON FORGE C&O	06	52	27
RAILROAD OFFICE DOORS & TOWERS PHOTOS	03	81	38
RUTLAND VT YARDS 1874 & 1957 PHOTOS	09	57	38
YARD OFFICE FROM OBSERVATION CAR ENDS PH	08	66	47

RAILROAD STRUCTURE PHOTOS BY ROAD

RD		M	Y	P
C&O	MODERNISTIC COAL CHUTE CLIFTON FORGE C&O	06	52	27
E	FRT DOCKS AT WEEHAWKEN MANHATTAN NY PHOT	02	46	21
MP	CONCRETE COALING TOWER GORDON AK MP PHOT	11	77	51
RI	COAL CHUTE PHOTO BUREAU ILL ROCK ISLAND	04	47	32

SIGNAL PROTOTYPE DATA

	M	Y	P
BALL SIGNAL-LAST IN US MC WINFIELD NH	01	80	42
BRITISH SIGNALS & WHY THEY LOOK THAT WAY	08	55	44
CAB & POSITION LIGHT SIGNALS ON PRR	04	46	48
CAB SIGNALS	04	44	21
CROSSING SIGNS	06	51	54
CTC CENTRALIZED TRAFFIC CONTROL BEGIN	09	47	14
ELECTRO PNEUMATIC SEMAPHORES	02	48	43
HIGH WIND INDICATOR	06	79	31
ICC SIGNALING REQUIREMENTS	11	50	44
INTERLOCKING SIGNAL TOWERS	10	44	10
INTERLOCKING TOWERS	04	42	28
RAILROAD CROSSING MARKER D&H	06	52	59
RAILROAD CROSSING-DOUBLE CROSSING	11	51	50
RAILROAD GRADE CROSSING SIGNS	04	50	34
RAILROAD SIGNAL 2 TRAINS 1 TRACK	06	57	44
RAILROAD SIGNALS WHERE TRACKS CROSS	07	57	44
SEMAPHORS 44 ON BRIDGE FOR 3 TRACKS	04	45	36
SIGNALING ORDERED ON HIGH SPEED LINES	08	47	4
TRACK CIRCUITS & HOW THEY WORK	08	42	31
WHAT THE SIGNALS SAY	09	43	13
WHISTLE SIGNAL MEANINGS	03	45	6

SIGNAL PROTOTYPE DATA BY ROAD

RD		M	Y	P
D&H	RAILROAD CROSSING MARKER D&H	06	52	59
MC	BALL SIGNAL-LAST IN US MC WINFIELD NH	01	80	42
PRR	CAB & POSITION LIGHT SIGNALS ON PRR	04	46	48

SIGNAL PHOTOS

	M	Y	P
BNAJO SIGNAL PHOTO RUTHERFORD PA R	03	42	52
CLIPPED SIGNAL PHOTO MONTREAL CANADA	02	71	47
HIGH BALL SIGNAL WILMINGTON DEL PHOTO	10	54	60
SIGNAL BRIDGE PHOTO E. JERSEY CITY TERM.	12	40	19
SIGNAL IN MIDDLE OF TRACK D&H FT ANN NY	08	57	96

SIGNAL PHOTOS BY ROAD

RD		M	Y	P
D&H	SIGNAL IN MIDDLE OF TRACK D&H FT ANN NY	08	57	96
R	BNAJO SIGNAL PHOTO RUTHERFORD PA R	03	42	52

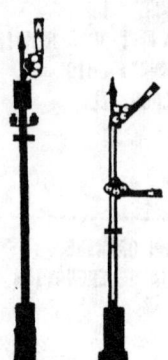

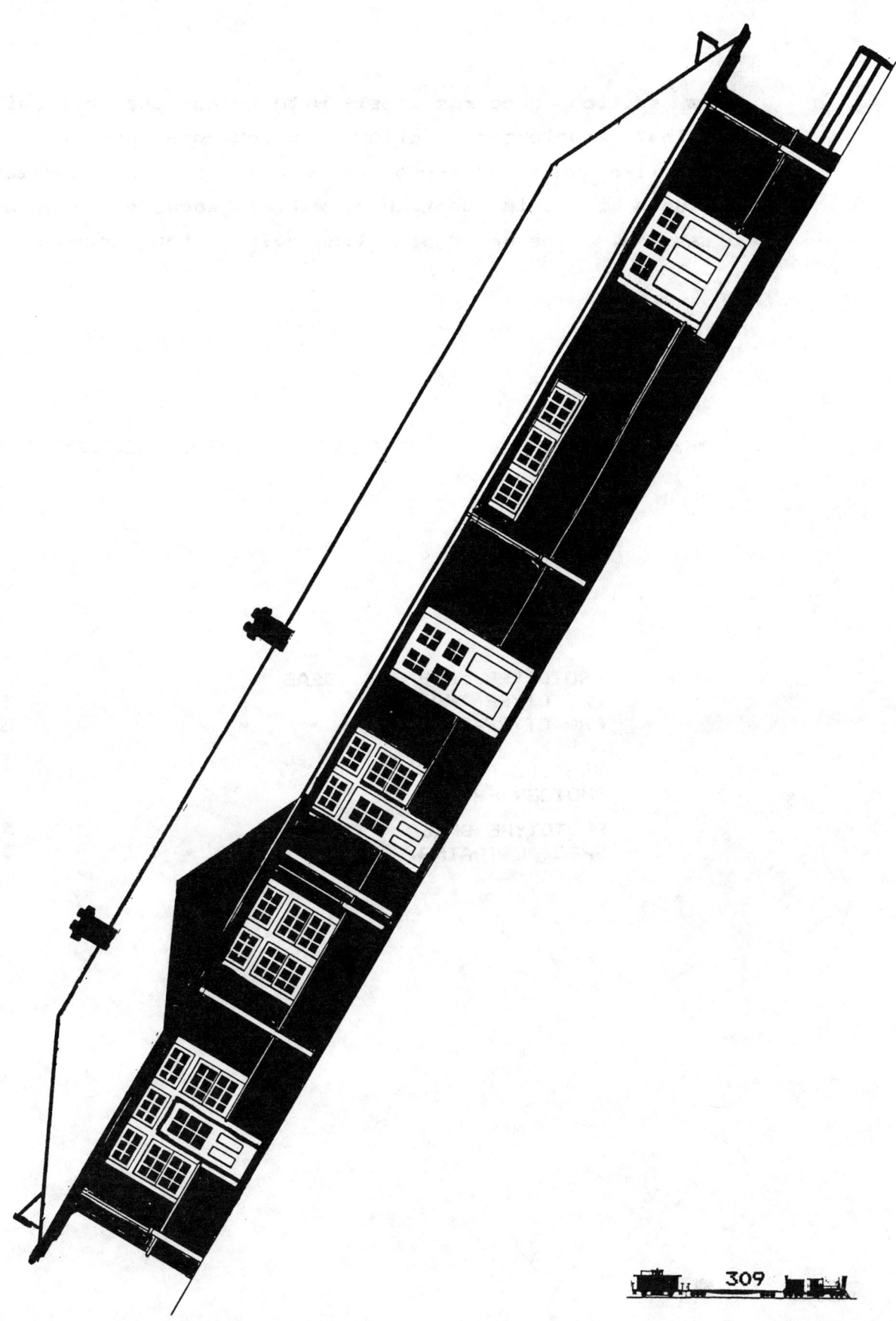

BILL OF LADING   PROTOTYPE EXAMPLES

This section concerns itself with things the real railroads do that modelers can follow. It includes items that do not seem like what a prototype would do. Photo essays are included in this section as well as speed surveys and rail disasters. The descriptor line defines the contents.

MANIFEST   PROTOTYPE EXAMPLES

	PAGE
PROTOTYPE MODELING IDEAS	310
PROTOTYPE TRACKWORK	311
PROTOTYPE EXAMPLES	311
WRECKS	311
VEHICLE PHOTOS	311
PHOTOGRAPHY	311
PROTOTYPE SPEED	312
SPECIAL TRAINS	312

PROTOTYPE MODELING IDEAS

PROTOTYPE EXAMPLES

	M	Y	P
BUSIEST RAILROAD PRR	10	41	26
CLEARING YARD OF BELT RAILWAY OF CHICAGO	09	66	44
ELECTRIFICATION OF THE MILWAUKEE	07	41	5
ENGLEWOOD YARD HOUSTON TX SP	04	56	57
HORSESHOE CURVE PRR	03	41	28
LOCUST POINT B&O SHIPPING OUTLET	09	41	26
POTOMAC YARD ALEXANDRIA VA	11	40	23
SPIRAL TUNNELS ON CP	12	40	7
WP WYE KEDDIE CALIFORNIA PHOTO	12	40	22

PROTOTYPE TRACKWORK

	M	Y	P
AUTOMATED TRAIN YARD	03	61	22
BATTLE CREEK YARD BATTLE CREEK MI GTW	01	63	18
CAR RETARDERS IN TRAIN YARDS	03	43	25
CATENARY MAINTENANCE NH	11	52	50
ENOLA YARD ENOLA PA PRR 12000 CARS A DAY	09	53	22
FITZPATRICK YARD RUSSELL KY C&O	03	61	18
NUMBER TEN SWITCH	04	48	30
PROVISO YARD CHICAGO IL C&NW	10	44	6
PUZZLE SWITCH ON C&WI	12	45	41
RIGHT OF WAY TERMS & DEFINITIONS	04	72	26
SOUTHERN RAILWAY YARD PROGRAM	06	53	50
WELDED RAIL ONE INSTEAD OF MANY	03	42	22
WELDED RAIL AND ITS PAYOFFS	02	50	36
WELDED RAIL NO CLICKETY-CLACK	09	49	52
WEST OAKLAND YARD WEST OAKLAND CA SP	04	47	58

VEHICLE PHOTOS

	M	Y	P
HOPPER CAR AS TRUCK BED PHOTO	03	70	29

PHOTOGRAPHY

	M	Y	P
CATCHING A TRAIN BY PLANE	01	50	16
FAVORITE RAIL PHOTO OF PRESTON GEORGE	06	80	31
FAVORITE RR PHOTOS OF WARREN MCGEE	01	80	31
HIGH SPEED TRAIN PHOTOGRAPHS	09	48	60
HOW TO TAKE STANDARD LOCOMOTIVE PICTURES	02	48	52
IMAGINATIVE PHOTOGRAPHY ON ESPEE	02	50	47
LOW ANGLE RAILROAD PHOTOS	06	48	62
MOUNTAIN RAILROAD PHOTOGRAPHY	07	48	58
PHOTOS OF L.C. MCCLURE	11	83	39
PLAN FOREGROUNDS IN RAILROAD PHOTOS	03	48	54
PRIZE WINNING LOCOMOTIVE PHOTOS	08	42	4
RAILROAD PHOTOGRAPHS OF AE BROWN	02	84	32
RAILROAD PHOTOGRAPHS OF JOE SADLER	08	78	18
RAILROAD PHOTOGRAPHS PAUL STRINGHAM	11	77	35
RAILROAD PHOTOGRAPHY	11	40	4
RAILROAD PHOTOGRAPHY	12	41	20
RAILROAD PHOTOGRAPHY CHARLES SMALL	04	48	62
RAILROAD PHOTOGRAPHY COLD WEATHER	11	47	56
RAILROAD PHOTOGRAPHY PHOTO ESSAY	12	45	20
RAILROAD PHOTOGRAPHY IN EASTERN EUROPE	08	77	22
RAILROAD PHOTOGRAPHY OF VICTOR HAND	10	78	35
RAILROAD PHOTOS NAUTAKA HRONA	11	82	28
RAILROAD PHOTOS OF JOHN W. MAYWELL	04	82	31
RAILROAD PHOTOS OF LINN WESTCOTT	03	85	34
RAILROAD PHOTOS OF OTTO PERRY	06	82	31
RAILROAD PHOTOS- BOB HALE	07	77	34
SCHUYLKILL PHOTOGRAPHS A GOOD DAY 1948	07	78	44
SUPER POWER PORTRAITIST: JARDINE OF LIMA	02	77	22
TRACKS WITHOUT TRAINS	06	78	52

WRECKS

	M	Y	P
IMPERIAL VALLEY FLOOD 1906	07	50	44
JOHNSTOWN PA FLOOD 5-31-1889 BLACK WALL	03	53	27
MONTANA WRECK NP 9-20-1954	09	56	21
MONTGOMERY AL WRECK 9-27-64 BURLINGTON	10	65	23
NEWARK BAY BRIDGE NJ WRECK 9-27-59 CNJ	02	60	36
RERAIL A 2-8+8-2 1946 D&RWG	05	82	20
VAUGHN MS CASEY JONES WRECK 4-30-00 IC	05	65	20
WASHINGTON DC RUNAWAY U STA 2-10-53 PRR	08	53	18

Bascule Bridge,
Straus heel trunnion type.
Chicago River

PROTOTYPE MODELING IDEAS

PROTOTYPE SPEED	M	Y	P
1954 SPEED SURVEY	05	55	16
1955 SPEED SURVEY	05	56	40
1956 SPEED SURVEY 20 YEARS OF SPEED	05	57	40
1957 SPEED SURVEY BEGINNING OF THE END?	05	58	40
1958 SPEED SURVEY WERE STILL THE FASTEST	05	59	40
1959 SPEED SURVEY THE FRENCH DID IT	05	60	18
1960 SPEED SURVEY LOOK AT CENTRAL 60	06	61	20
1961 SPEED SURVEY NYC STILL ON TOP	06	62	40
1962 SPEED SURVEY CENTRAL KEEPS THE CAKE	06	40	62
1963 SPEED SURVEY FEWER PASS FASTER FRT	06	64	36
1964 SPEED SURVEY JAPAN TAKES BLUE RIBBO	06	65	20
1965 SPEED SURVEY JAPAN GOES TO 106.2MPH	06	66	40
1966 SPEED SURVEY PASS SLOWING DOWN	05	67	32
1967 SPEED SURVEY SETTING STAGE FOR SPED	06	68	24
1968 SPEED SURVEY EUROPE MATCHS OUR BEST	06	69	18
1968 SPEED SURVEY OVERTAKEN OVERSEAS	07	69	38
1969 SPEED SURVEY TOMARROWS TRAIN/OLD TR	09	70	36
1970 SPEED SURVEY ON EVE OF RAILPAX	06	71	40
1971 SPEED SURVEY AMTRAK ABANDONED RACES	06	72	38
1972 SPEED SURVEY FEW POSITIVE ACHIEVEME	07	73	40
CHICAGO TO MILWAUKEE SPEED RUN MILW	05	68	20
CITY OF MILWAUKEE 400 SCHEDULE C&NW	03	56	24
CITY OF NEW ORLEANS SPEED E9 OF IC	03	66	52
EMPIRE STATE EXPRESS SPEED RUN 1939	05	65	24
FM & VHF RADIO COMMUNICATION	01	73	37
JERSEY CITY TO PITTSBURGH FAST FREIGHTS	06	66	25
NYC PASSENGERS HOW FAST IN 1957?	02	57	19
OPERATING TIMETABLE PREPARATION	08	45	34
PORT AUTHORITY TRANS-HUDSON SPEED TEST	10	65	20
ROYAL HUDSON SPEED 98 MPH CP	12	64	37
SPEED ON TRACTION LINES	04	67	24
TIMETABLE REFERENCE MARKS	03	64	51
TIMING TRAIN SPEED CHART	09	42	21
TRAIN SCHEDULE FACTORS	03	46	22
TWIN ZEPHYR SPEED CB&Q AMERICA'S FASTEST	11	64	28

SPECIAL TRAINS	M	Y	P
ARMY NAVY GAME SPECIAL TRAINS	01	53	16
ASIA EXPRESS	04	42	4
AUTOTRAIN EXCURSION CHICAGO TO LA	06	56	42
BOAT TRAIN ON D&RGW	11	46	30
BROWN BROTHERS HARRIMAN AND CO SPECIAL	09	69	47
CHICAGO TO MILWAUKEE HIAWATHA RUN MILW	07	53	27
CIRCUS MOVES BY RAIL	08	45	28
CIRCUS TRAIN SCHLITZ SPECIAL	07	66	46
CIRCUS TRAINS SPECIAL CARS GALORE	07	46	42
CRESCENT LIMITED TO WASHINGTON DC S	09	46	10
DAYLIGHT OF THE SOUTHERN PACIFIC	01	42	4
DEATH VALLEY SCOTTY SPECIAL	02	53	14
EMPIRE BUILDER AT MARIAS PASS	05	44	10
ERIE LIMITED	12	42	7
FUNERAL CAR OF ABRAHAM LINCOLN	06	41	24
FUNERAL TRAIN OF DWIGHT D EISENHOWER	06	69	14
FUNERAL TRAIN OF ROBERT F KENNEDY	08	68	10
FUNERAL TRAIN OF WARREN G. HARDING	09	82	20
FUNERAL TRAIN OF WINSTON CHURCHILL	05	65	8
GM EXECUTIVE TRAIN TO WHITE SULPHUR SPGS	04	73	20
HARRISBURG PA CHAMBER OF COMMERCE SPECAL	04	53	33
JERRETT AND PALMER SPECIAL 1876	12	42	10
KENTUCKY DERBY SPECIAL TRAINS AND CARS	05	66	20
LINDBERG NEWSREEL TRAIN.	10	52	18
NERVE GAS TRANSPORT TRAINS	11	70	12
NEW YORK-BOSTON WHITE "GHOST" TRAIN	01	43	34
NEWSPAPER SPECIAL OF 1912	10	43	17
OVERNIGHTER FREIGHT SERVICE ON THE PM	08	41	37
PENNSYLVANIA SPECIAL 127 MPH	04	43	25
PRESIDENTIAL TRAIN TRAVEL NIXON METROLIN	04	70	10
PRESIDENTIAL TRAIN TRAVEL TRUMAN CAMPAGN	03	49	16
PRIVATE CAR "CORNHUSKERS CLUB"	03	66	24
PRIVATE CAR "VIRGINIA CITY"	04	56	23
PRIVATE CAR OF COLE BROTHERS CIRCUS	11	49	40
PRIVATE CARS LUXURIOUS RIDING	01	51	12
RACE HORSE TRANSPORTATION	08	46	42
SAGA OF THE 400 C&NW	11	41	4
SHRINE SPECIAL 1952 CONVENTION TRAINS	10	53	54
SPECIAL TRAIN "COMBAT CANCER" 1968 S	05	70	27
STRICKEN PRESIDENT GARFIELD TO SEASHORE	09	52	58
SUNBEAM - DALLAS TO HOUSTON SP	12	44	38
TWENTIETH CENTURY LIMITED 40 YRS OLD NYC	07	42	26
TWENTIETH CENTURY LIMITED CONSIST	07	42	27

BILL OF LADING   RAILROAD HISTORIES

Railroad Histories are articles on specific railroads. In some instances they are they result of reseaching the olden days of the road. In some instances they are current happenings, at the time of publication, which are now history. The descriptor line contains the road abbreviation plus an idea of the subject matter contained in the article.

MANIFEST   ROAD HISTORIES

RAILROAD HISTORIES

RAILROAD HISTORIES

Title	M	Y	P
EXTRA 1555 WEST UP	05	50	20
HIST OF ATSF RAILCAR DAILY EXCEPT SUNDAY	08	45	27
HISTORY OF A REISTRIP REMEMBERS	01	81	44
HISTORY OF A CHICAGO MY KND OF TOWN?	11	84	41
HISTORY OF A AMTRAK EAST	07	74	28
HISTORY OF A AMTRAK SOUTH	07	74	32
HISTORY OF A OPERATING MANS RAILROAD	05	83	12
HISTORY OF A TRAIN TIME AT HAMMOND	09	85	46
HISTORY OF A&D SOUTHERN WAIF	12	50	40
HISTORY OF A&EC STATE OWNED RR N. CARO	02	43	40
HISTORY OF A&N SHORTLINE DOWN SOUTH	04	69	24
HISTORY OF A&WP WEST POINT ROUTE	06	43	9
HISTORY OF AB CALIFORNIA ISLAND CITY	08	41	42
HISTORY OF AB&C DIXIE FLAGLER	05	77	20
HISTORY OF AB&C THE 6:57	08	42	10
HISTORY OF ACL ALONG THE 5543 MILE LINE	08	49	14
HISTORY OF ACL MONTGOMERY DIVISION	12	77	48
HISTORY OF ACL STEAM IN VA PHOTO ESSAY	10	55	51
HISTORY OF ACL STREAMLINERS	03	58	18
HISTORY OF ACL WAYFARERS OF WAYCROSS	12	69	44
HISTORY OF AF LOS ANGELES CABLE CAR	11	42	44
HISTORY OF AL INTEGRATION IN THE NORTH	07	71	36
HISTORY OF AL UNCLE SAM'S RAILROAD	09	49	22
HISTORY OF AL COLD WAR RAILROADING	05	63	40
HISTORY OF AL THE BEAR & THE BIG HOOK	04	67	23
HISTORY OF AL THE RR THAT HAD IT TO GOOD	09	55	23
HISTORY OF AL UNCLE SAMS EXPERIMENT	04	63	42
HISTORY OF AL&C TOURISTS & TONNAGE	09	84	42
HISTORY OF ARIZONA COPPER HAULERS	07	56	26
HISTORY OF ARL BALLOON STACKS/LINK PINS	06	56	47
HISTORY OF AS LIMAS LOCOMOTIVES	01	73	40
HISTORY OF ATSF RATON PASS	08	46	30
HISTORY OF ATSF A DAY ON THE SANTA FE	12	49	40
HISTORY OF ATSF CHICAGO TO CAILFORNIA	07	44	20
HISTORY OF ATSF MAGDALENA BRANCH	09	59	23
HISTORY OF ATSF MAINLINE IN WARTIME	07	45	9
HISTORY OF ATSF MOJAVE CROSSING	08	77	31
HISTORY OF ATSF SUPER RAILROAD	01	54	15
HISTORY OF ATSF TEHACHAPI	01	77	24
HISTORY OF ATSF TO LA ON CHIEF	11	48	38
HISTORY OF ATSF -LOS ANGELES DIV	06	47	19
HISTORY OF ATSF BLUE GOOSE & KIN	06	85	20
HISTORY OF ATSF CAJON PASS	10	41	38
HISTORY OF ATSF CAJON PASS REVISITED	09	74	20
HISTORY OF ATSF CLAIRVOYANCE IN CAJON	05	76	22
HISTORY OF ATSF MIDDLE DIVISION	04	84	20
HISTORY OF ATSF RE-ARRANGING CAJON	10	72	8
HISTORY OF ATSF SUPER CHIEF/EL CAPTAIN	12	82	40
HISTORY OF B&A NYC'S NEW ENGLAND PORTAL	07	49	28
HISTORY OF B&A OVER THE BERKSHIRES	04	42	32
HISTORY OF B&AN END OF A TRADITION	12	51	44
HISTORY OF B&AR POTATOES FEED THIS RR	06	49	12
HISTORY OF B&CH GRANITE FROM VERMONT	09	41	15
HISTORY OF B&E BRANCH LINE	05	47	14
HISTORY OF B&H RAILFANS UTOPIA	04	41	36
HISTORY OF B&H RENT IT FOR $35.00	02	59	40
HISTORY OF B&LE 9035 HOPPERS & A HOTSHOT	09	57	16
HISTORY OF B&M HOOSIC TUNNEL	06	60	18
HISTORY OF B&M ED FRENCH	02	44	40
HISTORY OF B&M HOOSAC TUNNEL	02	42	26
HISTORY OF B&M MAKE IT ON YOUR OWN	08	80	44
HISTORY OF B&M RIVER LINE	01	82	35
HISTORY OF B&M COMING OUT OF CORP. CHAOS	09	80	44
HISTORY OF B&M DIESELS & COVERED BRIDGES	01	49	16
HISTORY OF B&M JOY & PAIN ON B&M	12	70	46
HISTORY OF B&M NEW HAMPSHIRE PHOTO ESSAY	07	55	53
HISTORY OF B&M NORTHWEST KINGDOM	02	82	22
HISTORY OF B&ML CIVIC FUNCTION S. LINE	04	44	4
HISTORY OF B&O DAN WILLARD	06	44	22
HISTORY OF B&O 100TH ANNIVERSASRY 1927	09	77	20
HISTORY OF B&O BALTIMORE DIVISION	09	44	26
HISTORY OF B&O CUMBERLAND DIVISION	11	45	8
HISTORY OF B&O DANIEL WILLARD	10	43	18
HISTORY OF B&O GREAT RDC RACE	10	55	16
HISTORY OF B&O RDC CARS	08	55	28
HISTORY OF B&O ROYAL BLUE LINE RECALL	08	72	20
HISTORY OF B&O CT&V SUBDIVISION	04	83	42
HISTORY OF B&O IRON HORSE DAYS	11	64	8
HISTORY OF B&O LAKE BRANCH PHOTO ESSAY	01	56	47
HISTORY OF B&O OLD CHICAGO DIVISION	03	73	27
HISTORY OF B&O OVER ALLEGHENIES DAYLIGHT	10	51	36
HISTORY OF B&O ROYAL BLUE LINE 1890-1958	08	58	10
HISTORY OF B&O-BALT BELT LINE	04	43	9
HISTORY OF B&O-CUMBERLAND DIV	08	60	28
HISTORY OF B&O-HELPER TURN OUT OF M&K	09	60	39
HISTORY OF B&P VARIETIES IN OLD POWER	07	43	29
HISTORY OF B&S MOGUL & MIKES	10	61	38
HISTORY OF B&SQ SUNSET OF AN EMPIRE	02	47	38
HISTORY OF B&SQ SOLE LEATHER LINE	02	72	36
HISTORY OF B&WO BACK BAY RAILROAD	10	77	28
HISTORY OF BA&H STEAM & CHAMPAGNE	12	46	35
HISTORY OF BA&P	09	44	6
HISTORY OF BA&P ELECTRIFICATION MADEGOOD	07	63	16
HISTORY OF BC&G LAST TRAIN FROM WIDEN	05	64	46
HISTORY OF BD PRR BRANCH LINE	03	42	26
HISTORY OF BEEC	03	70	8
HISTORY OF BEM SIDEWINDERS & SING ENG	01	62	25
HISTORY OF BI&B BORN & BURIED IN 6 MONTH	09	59	34
HISTORY OF BM&E FINEST DIRT TRACK RR	05	74	25
HISTORY OF BM&LP AMERICAS FINEST RAIL RD	10	74	17
HISTORY OF BMT SOUTH TOE RAMBLER	08	74	36
HISTORY OF BN WISHRAM WAHINGTON	08	81	20
HISTORY OF BN FAREWELL CB&Q/GN/NP/SP&S	06	70	25
HISTORY OF BN MERGER APPROVAL	05	70	3
HISTORY OF BN WINDOW TO THE FUTURE	11	83	47
HISTORY OF BR TRAFFIC LINK	07	41	36
HISTORY OF BR&P BILL NOONAN	01	44	48
HISTORY OF BRB&L 3 FOOT GAUGE	01	46	30
HISTORY OF BRC A RAILWAYS RAILROAD	09	66	36
HISTORY OF BRC HOW THE BELT CAME TO BE	10	66	42

STEPHANS' RAILROAD DIRECTORY

RAILROAD HISTORIES

	M	Y	P
HISTORY OF BRI A NEW START	09	66	14
HISTORY OF BUC SHORT ON LINE LONG ONTIME	12	50	45
HISTORY OF BURL GREYHOUNDS	06	59	43
HISTORY OF BURL PIONEER ZEPHYR	09	52	24
HISTORY OF BURL WIND RIVER CANYON	07	45	26
HISTORY OF BURL 4-8-4 PHOTO ESSAY	05	57	31
HISTORY OF BUT (EL & NORFOLK & WESTERN)	02	76	29
HISTORY OF C&C 64 ANGELS FOR A SHORTLINE	06	55	23
HISTORY OF C&EI CENTURY OLD	08	49	16
HISTORY OF C&EI CANT KEEP A GOOD RR DOWN	10	54	18
HISTORY OF C&GR DELTA ROUTE	10	82	27
HISTORY OF C&GR PREDECEASORS	10	82	31
HISTORY OF C&GR THE DELTA ROUTE	09	58	40
HISTORY OF C&HC MASON BOGIES & 3% GRADES	08	72	29
HISTORY OF C&I THIS IS A SHORTLINE?	03	71	38
HISTORY OF C&IM OASIS IN DIESELDOM	08	55	22
HISTORY OF C&LC HOW TO OWN/OPER SHORTLIN	02	68	20
HISTORY OF C&MI REVISITED	03	60	20
HISTORY OF C&NW MEMORIAL DAY	05	47	35
HISTORY OF C&NW GENEVA DIVISON	08	44	30
HISTORY OF C&NW MOUNTAINEER	10	48	36
HISTORY OF C&NW PENINSULA 400 STREAMLIN	07	48	38
HISTORY OF C&NW THE BIG SHOW	10	49	11
HISTORY OF C&NW THE OLD C&NW	07	43	9
HISTORY OF C&NW BRASS POUNDERS	06	82	22
HISTORY OF C&NW EMPLOYEES OWNED ALCOS	10	85	50
HISTORY OF C&NW FLIGHT OF THE FALCON	02	79	22
HISTORY OF C&NW GALENA DIVISION	04	52	14
HISTORY OF C&NW LAKE STREET TOWER	02	41	4
HISTORY OF C&NW LANCASTER DIVISION	06	71	24
HISTORY OF C&NW NO HERO FOR NORTHWESTERN	01	71	27
HISTORY OF C&NW SPINE LINE STRATEGY	09	84	9
HISTORY OF C&NW THE NAMEKAGON	08	84	22
HISTORY OF C&NW WHAT ARE THEY DOING?	07	58	16
HISTORY OF C&O SOFT COAL	04	45	22
HISTORY OF C&O COAL, COAL & MORE COAL	11	49	22
HISTORY OF C&O KEN BROWNE	04	54	19
HISTORY OF C&O TIDE 470 COAL TRAFFIC	04	56	16
HISTORY OF C&O A SONG OF SEPTEMBER	09	55	14
HISTORY OF C&O SAND PATCH PA	01	80	44
HISTORY OF C&O SPEEDWEST SERVICE	08	52	28
HISTORY OF C&OG ROUSE POINT	02	41	37
HISTORY OF C&PA PENNSYLVANIA PYGMY	07	44	28
HISTORY OF C&TS NATIONS NEWEST NARROW GA	04	71	22
HISTORY OF C&W ROBERT E LEE'S RAILROAD	06	49	47
HISTORY OF C&WC CAROLINA RAILROADING	10	49	46
HISTORY OF CA&C NOW SP	03	47	14
HISTORY OF CA&C TRACK OF CA&C	01	78	52
HISTORY OF CA&E	04	56	31
HISTORY OF CA&E ROARING ELGIN	01	52	22
HISTORY OF CAD 10.3 MILES & 9 LIVES	11	81	57
HISTORY OF CANADIAN RAILROADS	11	85	27
HISTORY OF CAPR WHAT A PLACE TO BUILD RR	10	52	14
HISTORY OF CASS 12 MPH TO ELKINS	03	66	28
HISTORY OF CASS SAVED:SWITCHBACKS/SHAYS	01	64	38

	M	Y	P
HISTORY OF CB&Q BUDA S CURVE	10	46	44
HISTORY OF CB&Q GALESBURG DIVISION	02	47	52
HISTORY OF CB&Q WAY OF THE ZEPHYRS	04	53	56
HISTORY OF CB&Q FINEST TRAINS ON EARTH	08	70	36
HISTORY OF CB&Q INSIDE BURLINGTON	12	55	43
HISTORY OF CB&Q SOMONAUK IL 1947	04	77	52
HISTORY OF CB&Q WARTIME FRT OPERATIONS	03	43	20
HISTORY OF CB&Q WHAT MAKES IT TICK	11	55	16
HISTORY OF CB&Q WYOMING LINE RELOCATION	11	50	20
HISTORY OF CBELT FAST FREIGHT	11	49	44
HISTORY OF CBELT GOES LIKE A BLUE STREAK	11	62	18
HISTORY OF CBELT STEAM PHOTO ESSSAY	03	56	55
HISTORY OF CC&C SHORTLINE SCRAPBOOK	06	54	54
HISTORY OF CC&CH	04	47	24
HISTORY OF CC&M PROPOSED	03	45	26
HISTORY OF CC&O MAINLINE SWITCHBACK	08	85	24
HISTORY OF CCW ABSORBED BY IOWA	07	65	16
HISTORY OF CGW GREAT TRAINS OF GW	01	68	34
HISTORY OF CHESS CINCINATTI OHIO	04	77	16
HISTORY OF CHESS STEAM SPECIAL	03	79	29
HISTORY OF CHESS B&O & THE DOMINO THEORY	06	85	3
HISTORY OF CHESS CHAPTERS OF CHESSIE	02	76	3
HISTORY OF CI OLD ALCOS NEVER DIE	07	82	26
HISTORY OF CL A CASE FOR CLINCHFIELD	10	83	24
HISTORY OF CL ORIGINAL SURVEY	04	47	24
HISTORY OF CL PHOTO ESSAY	06	54	41
HISTORY OF CL HERE COMES CLINCHFIELD	08	61	30
HISTORY OF CLIF NOT ANOTHER LIKE IT	11	55	28
HISTORY OF CMI MARTYR TO COMMERCE	05	43	9
HISTORY OF CMI 4' 8 1/2" NARROW GAUGE	08	57	17
HISTORY OF CMI RAILROAD BECAME A LEGEND	09	57	42
HISTORY OF CN WINNIPEG	10	60	24
HISTORY OF CN ARE YOU LISTENING MR GORO	02	54	48
HISTORY OF CN DONALD GORDON	03	56	42
HISTORY OF CN INTERURBAN TO ST ANNE	09	52	54
HISTORY OF CN LOCOMOTIVES NUMBERED 9000	02	53	22
HISTORY OF CN LOS ANGELES DIV	04	47	42
HISTORY OF CN MINITOBA-WINNIPEG FUNNEL	11	85	42
HISTORY OF CN N. AMERICAS LONGEST ROAD	10	49	20
HISTORY OF CN AB SABOURIN'S LAST TRIP	11	85	58
HISTORY OF CN BAY-VIEW ONTARIO	07	80	29
HISTORY OF CN CASE OF CONTRASTS	04	71	18
HISTORY OF CN MANITOBA PURE RAILROAD	11	85	42
HISTORY OF CN NEWFOUNDLAND NARROW GAUGE	07	71	36
HISTORY OF CN OVERHAUL AN IMAGE	06	61	38
HISTORY OF CN- DETROIT-SARNIA FERRIES	03	65	24
HISTORY OF CN-LAKE SUPERIOR LINE	06	41	36
HISTORY OF CN-LYNN LAKE EXTENSION	04	55	16
HISTORY OF CN-PRINCE EDWARD ISLAND	09	63	25
HISTORY OF CNJ JERSEY'S OWN	12	46	42
HISTORY OF CNJ COSTLIEST RR 1/2 ABANDON	11	48	52
HISTORY OF CNJ MUCH TAXED SYSTEM	03	48	6
HISTORY OF CNJ #2000	03	84	20
HISTORY OF CNJ ABRIDGED/ORPHANED/UNNEEDE	03	84	20
HISTORY OF CNJ HAD A GREAT FALL	03	72	20

RAILROAD HISTORIES

	M	Y	P
HISTORY OF CNJ TALE OF TWO RAILROADS	02	65	20
HISTORY OF CNO&TP RAT HOLE DIVISION	01	61	18
HISTORY OF CNO&TP RAT HOLE DIV NO MORE	01	64	17
HISTORY OF CNS&M INSULL	04	56	31
HISTORY OF CNS&M FREIGHT & PASSENGERS	10	44	30
HISTORY OF CNS&M INTERURBAN AT SUNSET	01	63	30
HISTORY OF CNYE DREAM ROAD OF 1906	10	46	15
HISTORY OF CO&E MARIOTT IL	09	80	36
HISTORY OF CP KETTLE VALLEY LINE	05	68	37
HISTORY OF CP CROWS NEST PASS	04	42	14
HISTORY OF CP 2-10-4 SELKIRK #5927	09	50	16
HISTORY OF CP COMES THE REVOLUTION	08	55	18
HISTORY OF CP CROWS NEST PASS	07	84	27
HISTORY OF CP IMPOSSIBLE RAILROAD	08	53	24
HISTORY OF CP KETTLE VALLEY LINE	10	51	14
HISTORY OF CP MOUNTAINEER	10	48	36
HISTORY OF CP RIVER LINE	01	82	35
HISTORY OF CP RY THAT MADE CANADA WHOLE	08	80	22
HISTORY OF CP IRIS G TRAIN BARGE	03	77	43
HISTORY OF CP LYNDONVILLE SUBDIVISION	12	48	12
HISTORY OF CP NORTHEAST KINGDOM	02	82	22
HISTORY OF CP ROGERS PASS	11	85	32
HISTORY OF CP THOSE ELUSIVE C-LINERS	07	72	40
HISTORY OF CP WINTER IN ONTARIO	12	80	41
HISTORY OF CP WINTER ON GLORY ROAD	11	55	27
HISTORY OF CP&LT SONG OF THE SHAY	08	51	22
HISTORY OF CPA SPIKE OF GOLD	05	42	8
HISTORY OF CPA JOINING THE NATION	05	69	ALL
HISTORY OF CPA TRACK LAYING EXTRAVAGANZA	01	43	6
HISTORY OF CR BREAK IT UP	06	77	40
HISTORY OF CR STANLEY CRANE	07	81	14
HISTORY OF CR WANT TO BUY CONRAIL?	09	83	12
HISTORY OF CR COMPARE CR TO CONRAL	10	77	42
HISTORY OF CR FROM INSIDE OUT	01	81	33
HISTORY OF CR FROM INSIDE OUT PART 2	02	81	44
HISTORY OF CR MASSILLON OHIO 1979	09	80	28
HISTORY OF CR MOUNTAIN ROAD REVISITED	01	85	24
HISTORY OF CR&IC UNCOMMON INTERURBAN	04	51	36
HISTORY OF CR&SJ MARBLE ROAD	09	43	8
HISTORY OF CRB&L LUMBER TO COAL	09	50	42
HISTORY OF CS	03	85	22
HISTORY OF CS&CC FORGOTTON RAILROAD	07	42	14
HISTORY OF CS&CC MOTIVE POWER CORRECTION	09	42	48
HISTORY OF CSS&SB INSULL	04	56	31
HISTORY OF CSS&SB SOUTH SHORE LINE	11	42	16
HISTORY OF CSS&SB AND THEN THERE WAS ONE	02	65	44
HISTORY OF CSS&SB RR WITH ORANGE TRAINS	05	53	20
HISTORY OF CSS&SB S SHORE CLIMBS OFF ST.	02	57	10
HISTORY OF CUR NOT JUST ANOTHER BRANCH	02	54	54
HISTORY OF CV CN VERMONT STEPCHILD	05	49	36
HISTORY OF CV RIVER LINE	01	82	35
HISTORY OF CV NORTHEAST KINGDOM	02	82	22
HISTORY OF CW WESTWARD BY RAILCAR	09	47	40
HISTORY OF D&H COAL LINE	01	45	24
HISTORY OF D&H PHOTO ESSAY	10	54	41

	M	Y	P
HISTORY OF D&H ROAD OF NEW IDEAS	08	43	4
HISTORY OF D&H 150 YEARS & STILL SOLVENT	05	73	26
HISTORY OF D&H BETTER LATE THAN NEVER	01	59	40
HISTORY OF D&H BIG LITTLE D&H	12	76	12
HISTORY OF D&M FAREWELL TO MAROON/GRAY	08	81	25
HISTORY OF D&M 7 DIESELS/262 RTE MILES	09	69	40
HISTORY OF D&M THEY SHED NO TEARS	07	51	40
HISTORY OF D&NE YOUR TRAIN IS COMING	03	55	52
HISTORY OF D&RGW MONARCH BRANCH	11	49	18
HISTORY OF D&RGW "SFT" CONCEPT	07	72	20
HISTORY OF D&RGW FAST FREIGHT	09	68	20
HISTORY OF D&RGW HELPER DISTRICT	04	63	21
HISTORY OF D&RGW MAIN LINE AT CUMBRES	09	44	18
HISTORY OF D&RGW MONARCH BRANCH	07	65	42
HISTORY OF D&RGW PALMERS LITTLE ROAD	06	45	8
HISTORY OF D&RGW SALT LAKE DIVISION	04	58	18
HISTORY OF D&RGW SILVERTON BRANCH	08	42	12
HISTORY OF D&RGW THROUGH THE ROCKIES	09	49	40
HISTORY OF D&RGW TINTIC LOOP	12	41	40
HISTORY OF D&RGW INTO FREEZING DARKNESS	04	56	48
HISTORY OF D&RGW MONARCH BRANCH	03	77	30
HISTORY OF D&RGW RIO GRANDE REVISITED	04	65	20
HISTORY OF D&RGW SANTA FE BRANCH	09	41	5
HISTORY OF D&RGW SNOW REMOVAL	10	69	20
HISTORY OF D&RGW UTAH DIVISION	07	85	24
HISTORY OF D&RGW WET MOUNTAIN VALLEY	08	66	38
HISTORY OF D&RGW WHEN THISTLE VANISHED	07	83	14
HISTORY OF DA LAND OF EVANGELINE	06	51	24
HISTORY OF DC&S LAST TIME I SAW #134	03	64	48
HISTORY OF DL&W D&H/B&H/SUSIE Q	08	85	40
HISTORY OF DL&W ROUTE OF PHOEBE SNOW	06	50	18
HISTORY OF DL&W LACKAWANNA CUTOFF	10	45	8
HISTORY OF DL&W SUNBURY BRANCH	12	40	18
HISTORY OF DL&W WHERE IS ROLLING STOCK?	08	85	44
HISTORY OF DL&W A BRIEF HISTORY	11	43	5
HISTORY OF DL&W LIFE AFTER LACKAWANNA	07	85	36
HISTORY OF DL&W STEAM OUT OF SCRANTON	09	65	28
HISTORY OF DM&CI IOWA INTERURBAN	06	41	42
HISTORY OF DM&IR ORE EXTRA	11	59	26
HISTORY OF DM&IR SHORT CARS HEAVY TRAIN	11	41	6
HISTORY OF DM&N HALF CENTRY OF ARTICULAT	11	80	30
HISTORY OF DP PROPOSED	03	45	28
HISTORY OF DSP&P OLD SOUTH PARK	11	43	8
HISTORY OF DUD&T	11	73	20
HISTORY OF DW&P CN IN MINNESOTA	03	74	20
HISTORY OF DW&P HILL LINE	03	85	16
HISTORY OF E ELEAZAR LORD	05	44	40
HISTORY OF E FRED UNDERWOOD	03	44	40
HISTORY OF E 999 MILES	03	46	10
HISTORY OF E GULF SUMMIT 1946	12	66	42
HISTORY OF E ROUTE OF THE FLYING SAUCER	05	51	24
HISTORY OF E EARLY FT'S	06	84	29
HISTORY OF E&B BION ARNOLD	08	78	34
HISTORY OF E&LS	07	84	31
HISTORY OF E&M 1 0-4-0T 2 1/2 MILES TRAK	05	65	29

RAILROAD HISTORIES

	M	Y	P
HISTORY OF EBT COAL HAULER	08	41	4
HISTORY OF EBT PHOTO ESSAY	11	53	31
HISTORY OF EBT TWIN STACKS ROCKHILL FUR	01	82	22
HISTORY OF EBT THE GREAT REVIVAL	12	60	26
HISTORY OF EJ&S CROSSING OVER JORDAN	01	62	22
HISTORY OF EL LOCOMOTIVE CYCLOPEDIA	12	78	48
HISTORY OF EL PROJECTED MERGER	07	60	18
HISTORY OF EMC THE OTHER ERIE	09	73	41
HISTORY OF EMD AN INSTANT HISTORY	09	72	56
HISTORY OF EP&S STRANGE STORY	02	66	44
HISTORY OF ER ELLIS ATWOOD	05	48	49
HISTORY OF ES MONORAIL TO NOWHERE	10	51	24
HISTORY OF ET&WNC TENN NARROW GAUGE	12	42	18
HISTORY OF ET&WNC TALE OF TWO 2-8-0'S	07	60	28
HISTORY OF ET&WNC TWEETSIES LAST TRIP	01	51	24
HISTORY OF F&CC ORE & SCENIC EMPIRE	12	41	4
HISTORY OF FEC CASE OF THE CAR COUNTERS	04	78	29
HISTORY OF FEC FLANGER'S KEY WEST LINE	01	53	48
HISTORY OF FEC KEY WEST LINE	11	47	44
HISTORY OF FEC LAKE HARBOR BRANCH	05	47	48
HISTORY OF FEC METAMORPHIS ROAD	06	70	3
HISTORY OF FEC RICH ROAD-POOR ROAD	04	41	18
HISTORY OF FEC FLANGER SYSTEM RECALL	10	70	44
HISTORY OF FEC WHERE DID IT GO?	02	75	22
HISTORY OF FJ&G AMBIDEXTROUS SHORT LINE	03	59	40
HISTORY OF FR&P POTOMAC YARD VIRGINIA	11	40	23
HISTORY OF FRIS DIXON HILL IMPROVEMENT	04	45	16
HISTORY OF FRIS SOUTHEASTERN JUNCTION	12	43	37
HISTORY OF FRIS TULSA-OKLAHOMA CITY RTE	01	48	7
HISTORY OF FRIS SPRINGFIELD YARD	01	81	22
HISTORY OF G PHOTO ESSAY	11	54	41
HISTORY OF G MIXED TRAIN OPERATIONS	09	67	20
HISTORY OF G&GE SAVED BY THE SHOVEL	02	56	38
HISTORY OF G-P DEMI EMPIRE	05	68	19
HISTORY OF GAS&C	04	69	24
HISTORY OF GB&W	09	42	27
HISTORY OF GCO CINDERS	08	66	13
HISTORY OF GCO SIDEWINDERS & SING ENG	01	62	25
HISTORY OF GIL 4000 MILE CR ALTERNATIVE	04	84	10
HISTORY OF GIL HIGH GREEN FOR GILFORD	09	83	15
HISTORY OF GM&N GULF MOBILE & NORTHERN	01	41	12
HISTORY OF GM&O EXPANSION	02	48	10
HISTORY OF GM&O MERGER CHILD	01	41	12
HISTORY OF GMI RARE & WONDERFUL	09	57	26
HISTORY OF GMT RAILS TO SUNRISE	04	66	44
HISTORY OF GN BIEBER LINE	01	45	6
HISTORY OF GN BIEBER LINE	07	49	42
HISTORY OF GN CASCADE DIVISION	11	61	23
HISTORY OF GN CASCADE TUNNEL	06	41	4
HISTORY OF GN CASCADE TUNNEL LINE RELO	12	49	24
HISTORY OF GN JAMES J HILL	12	54	22
HISTORY OF GN MARIAS PASS	05	44	10
HISTORY OF GN CASCADE TUNNEL	09	52	20
HISTORY OF GN TAKES MONEY TO MAKE MONEY	11	51	36
HISTORY OF GN THE EMPIRE BUILDER	05	58	22
HISTORY OF GN BATTLING BLIZZARDS	02	73	20
HISTORY OF GN BRASS POUNDERS	06	82	22
HISTORY OF GNO	04	69	24
HISTORY OF GR&I WRECK AT PIERSON MI	01	74	32
HISTORY OF GRA AMERICAS VERY FIRST RR	04	75	28
HISTORY OF GTW PHOTO ESSAY	03	61	42
HISTORY OF GTW BATTLE CREEK YARDS	01	63	18
HISTORY OF GTW DURAND MI-GTW HOT SPOT	12	45	44
HISTORY OF GTW ROUTE OF FREIGHT 400S	01	47	14
HISTORY OF GTW THEY KEEP THEIR WORD	12	55	18
HISTORY OF H&BTM BRIDGE LINE	03	47	46
HISTORY OF H&H FROM NOWHERE TO NO PLACE	02	51	13
HISTORY OF H&TL MASON BOGIES & 3% GRADES	08	72	29
HISTORY OF HIL MICHIGAN GOT INTO RAILBUS	10	76	46
HISTORY OF HT&W 11 MILES, 6 EMPLOY,2 LOC	09	62	25
HISTORY OF HY&T ILLINOIS SHORT LINE	01	47	46
HISTORY OF I DEATH FOR THE INDIANA	04	42	18
HISTORY OF IC EDGEWOOD CUTOFF	11	42	18
HISTORY OF IC FERRYBOAT "PELICAN"	06	51	14
HISTORY OF IC MADISON BRANCH	02	71	37
HISTORY OF IC EDGEWOOD CUTOFF	08	52	52
HISTORY OF IC IOWA DIVISION MEAT TRAINS	10	58	40
HISTORY OF IC LOCOMOTIVE PORTFOLIO	05	41	36
HISTORY OF IC MAIN LINE OF MID AMERICA	10	48	16
HISTORY OF IC PANAMA LIMITED	03	63	18
HISTORY OF IC WOODVILLE BRANCH	06	79	40
HISTORY OF ICG FULTON TRIANGLE	02	83	27
HISTORY OF IM NOT OFFICIALLY LISTED	06	50	48
HISTORY OF INTER WHISTLE IN THE VALLEY	08	53	26
HISTORY OF IOWA ABSORBS CCW	07	65	16
HISTORY OF IT CLASS 1 FREIGHT LINE	09	41	36
HISTORY OF IT PRAIRIE STATE RAILROAD	09	50	36
HISTORY OF IT TRACTION IN TWILIGHT	09	55	31
HISTORY OF IT FROM TRACTION TO TENANT	05	81	22
HISTORY OF IT PERILS OF PRR SECONDARY	06	81	40
HISTORY OF JT THRESHOLD TO FLORDIA	05	49	12
HISTORY OF K&T IN THE HILLS OF KENTUCKY	07	49	12
HISTORY OF K&T RR CHANGED MOTIVE POWER	07	74	20
HISTORY OF KCE RANDOLPH TO TOGUS	09	51	25
HISTORY OF KCKV NOT A RADIO STATION	04	61	22
HISTORY OF KCS PUT IT BACK TOGETHER	09	79	22
HISTORY OF KCS ROUTE OF SOUTHERN BELLE	07	49	18
HISTORY OF KCS THE RR THAT UNRAVELED	08	79	22
HISTORY OF KCS WE WILL NOT QUIT PASSENGE	11	67	40
HISTORY OF L&A STEAM PHOTO ESSAY	03	55	41
HISTORY OF L&N 100,000 KIDS FRIENDS	08	61	45
HISTORY OF L&N HURRICANE EMMA 1947	11	47	24
HISTORY OF L&N A SPOT IN MY HEART	05	76	42
HISTORY OF L&N BIG EMMA 2-8-4'S	12	72	22
HISTORY OF L&N CC&O CONNECTION	08	85	24
HISTORY OF L&N SHORT LINE DIVISION	02	68	27
HISTORY OF L&N THIS IS THE L&N	03	55	17
HISTORY OF L&NW	05	85	24
HISTORY OF LCL ALLIGATORS & CYPRESS	11	51	14
HISTORY OF LE MR SPENCE & HIS STEAM LOC	03	63	45

RAILROAD HISTORIES

	M	Y	P
HISTORY OF LE&P NEVER BUILT	05	48	54
HISTORY OF LEI 2ND ED RR IN US 1809	02	43	30
HISTORY OF LESM LITTLE COTTONWOOD CANYON	11	51	26
HISTORY OF LI 1 IN 5 PASSENGERS RIDE IT	03	49	40
HISTORY OF LI SHE MAKES A COMEBACK	12	57	14
HISTORY OF LI WHICH PLAN D'YA READ?	12	52	26
HISTORY OF LI BACK FROM LOONEYVILLE?	01	71	20
HISTORY OF LI DECIDING THE FUTURE 5:15	02	71	40
HISTORY OF LI&M ST LOUIS MO SHORTLINE	04	52	20
HISTORY OF LITRI SMALLEST PACIFIC BUILT	04	83	35
HISTORY OF LK&W KANSAS SHORTLINE	05	48	16
HISTORY OF LNP&W MERGES WITH UP	02	52	10
HISTORY OF LO&S BIG PLANS NARROW GAUGE	10	43	37
HISTORY OF LS&I ORE HAULER	12	54	54
HISTORY OF LS&MC PART OF NYC	03	42	18
HISTORY OF LV WYOMING DIVISION	01	47	26
HISTORY OF LV ASA PACKERS RAILROAD	12	50	18
HISTORY OF LV ROUTE OF BLACK DIAMOND	04	49	36
HISTORY OF LV STEAM PHOTO ESSAY	12	55	55
HISTORY OF LV TALE OF TWO RAILROADS	02	65	20
HISTORY OF LVT ARCH WIND/WALKOVER SEATS	09	69	37
HISTORY OF LVT LIBERTY BELL ROUTE	01	51	44
HISTORY OF M	07	47	ALL
HISTORY OF M 549 MILE X ROUTE	07	42	46
HISTORY OF M TODAYS MONON	03	51	16
HISTORY OF M DIESELS PULL MONON TRAINS	07	47	43
HISTORY OF M GROWTH OF A RAILROAD	07	47	55
HISTORY OF M PHOTO ESSAY	07	54	41
HISTORY OF M PHOTO STORY	07	47	33
HISTORY OF M ROAD UPGRADING GUINEA PIG	07	47	15
HISTORY OF M THE SYSTEM & ITS TRAFFIC	07	47	20
HISTORY OF M THIS RAILROAD IS A FACTORY	07	47	49
HISTORY OF M ALWAYS UNCOMMON	02	84	20
HISTORY OF M MONON MEMOIR	02	84	22
HISTORY OF M&BIG D-DAY ON THE BIGBEE	07	59	37
HISTORY OF M&D	10	78	48
HISTORY OF M&E MATTER OF PAPER PROFITS	11	50	50
HISTORY OF M&ET TRACTION DIESEL STYLE	03	69	43
HISTORY OF M&HM FROM NOWHERE TO SOMEWHER	06	65	13
HISTORY OF M&O MOBILE & OHIO	01	41	12
HISTORY OF M&PP 12,109 FT ABOVE SEA LEVE	02	49	50
HISTORY OF M&SL FAST FREIGHTS	08	49	40
HISTORY OF M&SL NEW BEGINNING	12	42	32
HISTORY OF M&SL IN THE NEWS AGAIN	03	59	16
HISTORY OF M&SL RETURNED FROM THE DEAD	02	49	36
HISTORY OF M&WR VERMONT SHORT LINE	11	41	38
HISTORY OF M-CL LUMBER RAILROAD	03	43	32
HISTORY OF MA SUDDENLY FAMOUS	01	61	37
HISTORY OF MA COPPER HAULERS	07	56	26
HISTORY OF MA&PA NARROW TO STD GAUGE	12	41	6
HISTORY OF MBL HIGH TRESTLES-OCEAN MISTS	08	71	25
HISTORY OF MC MOUNTAIN SUBDIVISION	01	50	10
HISTORY OF MC&SA STEAMING IN THE RAIN	08	60	26
HISTORY OF MCR WHERE TIME STOOD STILL	07	55	43
HISTORY OF MCRI LOGGING LINE 1959	02	59	18
HISTORY OF MCRI STEAM BELOW SHASTA	10	71	42
HISTORY OF ME JUMBLED OWNERS	08	47	44
HISTORY OF MEL OHIO ROBOT RAILROAD	03	79	22
HISTORY OF MEXICAN RAILROADS 1	01	83	23
HISTORY OF MEXICAN RAILROADS 2	02	83	44
HISTORY OF MF	03	70	8
HISTORY OF MI THE MISSISSIPPIAN	02	58	15
HISTORY OF MIDC DIDNT HEAR OF? NO MORE!	06	72	20
HISTORY OF MILW NEW LISBON WI	07	41	43
HISTORY OF MILW THE HIAWATHA STORY	12	50	26
HISTORY OF MILW ELECTRIC OVER ROCKIES	07	41	7
HISTORY OF MILW FAMOUS #15	07	53	27
HISTORY OF MILW FROM 10 TO 2900 MILES	02	82	49
HISTORY OF MILW JUICE JACKS	03	52	56
HISTORY OF MILW MILWAUKEE CITY	04	48	19
HISTORY OF MILW RYEGRASS & EVERGREEN	06	79	18
HISTORY OF MILW TOMARROWS RAILRD TODAY	02	44	24
HISTORY OF MILW 4-6-4 90MPH CHIC TO MILW	06	50	14
HISTORY OF MILW CHARGING BUFFALO ROUTE	09	84	32
HISTORY OF MILW CHESTNUT STREET LINE	08	52	21
HISTORY OF MILW FAIRBANKS-MORSE LOCOS	01	80	26
HISTORY OF MILW LIONEL IN 1:1 SCALE	12	77	26
HISTORY OF MILW SNOW REMOVAL	12	44	20
HISTORY OF MILW STILL SPRINT-ING ALONG	09	83	17
HISTORY OF MILW TACOMA HILL & SLUGS	03	78	35
HISTORY OF MILW WITHDRAWL FROM THE WEST	09	80	32
HISTORY OF MILW-BELLEVUE & CASCADE BRANC	04	54	58
HISTORY OF MISSC STEAM PHOTO ESSAY	08	55	49
HISTORY OF MIT TWILIGHT	11	48	12
HISTORY OF MJ&MW THE CROOKEDEST RAILROAD	06	53	45
HISTORY OF MKT THE KATY	01	43	12
HISTORY OF MKT CAN MR B SAVE MISS KATY?	08	66	24
HISTORY OF MKT KATY IS NOT A MUSEUM	09	82	22
HISTORY OF MKT KATY SERVES THE SOUTHWEST	04	49	16
HISTORY OF MKT WHAT'S THE CURE?	08	60	18
HISTORY OF MLC SAVED:SWITCHBACKS/SHAYS	01	64	38
HISTORY OF MN MICHIGAN GOT INTO RAILBUS	10	76	46
HISTORY OF MN&S PASSENGER TO FREIGHT	06	59	16
HISTORY OF MO OLD 2 X 6	05	53	28
HISTORY OF MONTREALS RAILROADS	08	44	10
HISTORY OF MP KINGSVILLE DIVISION	06	49	16
HISTORY OF MP PORT ISABEL BRANCH	08	41	32
HISTORY OF MP ASSISTANT TRAINMASTER	11	77	48
HISTORY OF MP KIRKWOOD HILL	07	43	18
HISTORY OF MP MILESTONE 51	01	54	50
HISTORY OF MP CURTAIN CALL IN COAL FIELD	10	55	25
HISTORY OF MRS TRACKS TO VICTORY	09	45	26
HISTORY OF MT&MW BILL THOMAS	02	56	41
HISTORY OF MWCOG MT WASHINGTON COGG RY	06	46	28
HISTORY OF MWCOG NEW STEAM ON MOUNTAINS	05	73	41
HISTORY OF MWCOG OLDEST/HIGHEST IN EAST	06	41	28
HISTORY OF MWCOG CELEBRATION TRAIN	07	59	46
HISTORY OF MWCOG STEEP BUT SLOW	07	56	38
HISTORY OF N&CA NOW SP	03	47	14
HISTORY OF N&N MICHIGAN LOSES A RAILROAD	06	49	50

RAILROAD HISTORIES

	M	Y	P
HISTORY OF N&PBL FERTILIZER ROUTE	05	50	46
HISTORY OF N&W SOFT COAL	04	45	22
HISTORY OF N&W ABINGDON MIXED TRAIN	10	52	52
HISTORY OF N&W ABINGTON BRANCH	07	57	31
HISTORY OF N&W COAL TRAFFIC	11	47	13
HISTORY OF N&W 4-4-2 CLASS J #611	01	83	44
HISTORY OF N&W AFTER DARK PHOTO ESSAY	11	57	30
HISTORY OF N&W MORNING AFTER STEAM	09	59	27
HISTORY OF N&W N&W SHOPS	10	84	36
HISTORY OF N&W TRAINMASTER RETIREMENT	02	77	42
HISTORY OF N&W V STU SAUNDERS	02	63	26
HISTORY OF N&WO	08	42	48
HISTORY OF NC LOCO SIDNAY DILLON	01	42	38
HISTORY OF NC&SL DIXIE FLYER	02	51	43
HISTORY OF NC&SL DIXIE SUCCESS STORY	01	48	44
HISTORY OF NC&SL DIXIE LINE PHOTO ESSAY	02	56	47
HISTORY OF NC&SL GLIDERS/Y JACKETS/STRIP	12	63	22
HISTORY OF NC&SL SIX TRAINS AT WINSTEAD	09	85	42
HISTORY OF NCB PHELPS-DODGE COPPER CORP	07	66	36
HISTORY OF NF NEWFOUNDLAND NARROW GAUGE	11	44	30
HISTORY OF NH CEDAR HILL YARD	10	48	12
HISTORY OF NH OLD COLONY LINES	04	48	6
HISTORY OF NH PAT MCGINNIS	09	54	46
HISTORY OF NH RE-ELECTRIFIED	08	64	20
HISTORY OF NH CURIOUS CONNOISSEURS	05	83	22
HISTORY OF NH PASSENGERS & TRAILER TRUCK	02	50	21
HISTORY OF NH WHAT HAPPENED TO NEW HAVEN	09	82	16
HISTORY OF NKP BELLVIEW OHIO	11	49	13
HISTORY OF NKP FIRST 56 ENGINE #758	10	62	33
HISTORY OF NKP NICKEL-PLATED RAILROAD	05	48	20
HISTORY OF NKP BERKSHIRES ON THE MOVE	09	55	18
HISTORY OF NN SCHIZOPHRENIC ROAD	07	61	33
HISTORY OF NN ALCOS IN ACTION	09	78	40
HISTORY OF NN HARD TIMES IN ELY NV	01	78	30
HISTORY OF NP BITTER ROOT BRANCH	01	47	40
HISTORY OF NP WALLACE BRANCH	02	41	7
HISTORY OF NP MAIN STREET OF NORTHWEST	02	46	10
HISTORY OF NP NORTH COAST LIMITED	12	52	48
HISTORY OF NP LOOKOUT PASS WALLACE BRANC	09	55	55
HISTORY OF NP NORTH COAST LIMITED	08	63	28
HISTORY OF NPIER LONGEST SHORTLINE IN RI	05	63	47
HISTORY OF NS&W SMOKE OVER STERLING	06	68	18
HISTORY OF NSO PASSENGER 1924-FRT 1947	01	51	18
HISTORY OF NSO TOBACCO BELT ROAD	04	42	30
HISTORY OF NW BILEVEL CARS	01	59	16
HISTORY OF NWP REDWOOD EMPIRE ROUTE	06	46	6
HISTORY OF NY&LB STEAM RULES!	01	55	41
HISTORY OF NYC AL PERLMAN	06	57	16
HISTORY OF NYC 20TH CENTURY LIMITED	08	62	16
HISTORY OF NYC ALBANY BYPASS	09	53	58
HISTORY OF NYC BEELINER TO HITOP	01	54	53
HISTORY OF NYC BUF-NIAGARA FALLS LINE	12	44	29
HISTORY OF NYC HUDSON RIVER ROUNDHOUSE	06	44	12
HISTORY OF NYC LAKE PLACID BRANCH	09	50	22
HISTORY OF NYC NEW ENGLAND STATES	09	51	20
HISTORY OF NYC OTTAWA TO HUNGERFORD CTY	05	52	30
HISTORY OF NYC ROBERT YOUNG 1	12	47	64
HISTORY OF NYC ROBERT YOUNG 2	01	48	60
HISTORY OF NYC SELKIRK YARD	07	48	18
HISTORY OF NYC WEST SIDE FREIGHT LINE	06	44	6
HISTORY OF NYC AND HOW IT GREW	09	47	47
HISTORY OF NYC NORWALK BRANCH 1948	10	80	55
HISTORY OF NYC PAUL KIEFER'S 4-8-4	03	84	46
HISTORY OF NYC PRINCELY NEW YORK CENTRAL	11	48	16
HISTORY OF NYC SPUYTEN DUYVIL 3RD TRICK	03	47	38
HISTORY OF NYC&N BOSTON VIA MANHATTAN EL	12	47	13
HISTORY OF NYNH&H 4-6-2 CLASS I5 LOCOS	09	81	20
HISTORY OF NYNH&H LOSS-5500/DAY	07	41	15
HISTORY OF NYNH&H MARINE OPERATIONS	08	43	32
HISTORY OF NYNH&H NEW CANAAN BRANCH	09	45	18
HISTORY OF NYNH&H PENN CENTRAL MERGER	01	70	20
HISTORY OF NYNH&H WHAT NEXT?	01	62	20
HISTORY OF NYNH&H WHAT WENT WRONG	10	61	18
HISTORY OF NYO&W COAL ROAD TO BRIDGE RT	08	49	36
HISTORY OF NYO&W LAMENT FOR OLD WEMAN	02	81	31
HISTORY OF NYO&W NEW TRAFFIC	08	42	20
HISTORY OF NYO&W OBIT OF AN OLD LADY	07	57	23
HISTORY OF NYP&C PROJECTED	06	43	26
HISTORY OF NYS&W SUSQUEHANNA	07	46	10
HISTORY OF NYS&W DELAWARE WATER GAP	09	48	26
HISTORY OF NYW&B GRASS GROWS ON WESTCHES	10	51	42
HISTORY OF OA&E INTERURBAN A-FLOAT	03	80	42
HISTORY OF ON DIESELS TO DESOLATION	01	60	28
HISTORY OF ON SILVER BONANZA	08	49	24
HISTORY OF OR&LC	03	47	26
HISTORY OF OR&LC NARROW GAUGE ON OAHU	07	44	36
HISTORY OF OR&NC ENGINES OF 1889	06	43	41
HISTORY OF OR&W LAST OHIO NARROW GAUGE	04	50	24
HISTORY OF ORO DAM BUILDING RAILROAD	01	66	20
HISTORY OF P&C HENS ARE STILL LAYING	02	45	23
HISTORY OF P&EA ROAD OF EFFICIENCY PLUS	02	53	24
HISTORY OF P&EL WORLDS STEEPEST ADHESION	06	69	42
HISTORY OF P&LE LITTLE GIANT, FREE AGAIN	07	81	36
HISTORY OF P&N CATENARY OVER CAROLINAS	06	54	48
HISTORY OF P&N INTERURBAN IN LONG PANTS	07	54	48
HISTORY OF P&N THE FINAL REPORT	01	70	10
HISTORY OF P&PU THE PEORIA GATEWAY	07	44	8
HISTORY OF P&W UNMERGER DAY IN NEW ENGLA	04	73	16
HISTORY OF P&WV MIDDLE OF ALPHABET RTE	11	56	14
HISTORY OF PAN COAST TO COAST	01	50	44
HISTORY OF PC KANKAKEE BELT ROUTE	02	69	20
HISTORY OF PC MANAGEMENT PROBLEMS	05	71	20
HISTORY OF PC PRE-MERGER FORECASTS	01	58	24
HISTORY OF PC IRONIES-WHEN DENATIONALIZD	11	72	25
HISTORY OF PE FREIGHT RUNS	05	46	40
HISTORY OF PE BUSTLINE FREIGHT	06	48	18
HISTORY OF PE ORANGE EMPIRE	06	42	10
HISTORY OF PEC BUENA VISTA STORY	08	82	22
HISTORY OF PGE TO ALASKA SOMEDAY	11	50	22
HISTORY OF PGE 347 BRITSH COLUMBIA MILES	12	44	6

RAILROAD HISTORIES

	M	Y	P
HISTORY OF PGE OUT OF NOWHERE TO SOMEWHE	06	60	29
HISTORY OF PGE STEPS INTO FUTURE	07	60	40
HISTORY OF PI&SH THE SHAWMUT LINE	02	55	16
HISTORY OF PLU ITS POWER	01	55	28
HISTORY OF PM LUMBER ROAD TO INTERLINE	08	45	8
HISTORY OF PM OVERNIGHTER SERVICE	08		36
HISTORY OF PM&Y THE MUD HOP	09	81	36
HISTORY OF PRES 2.5 MIL A VERY SHORTLINE	03	58	28
HISTORY OF PRR HORSESHOE CURVE	03	41	28
HISTORY OF PRR 100 YEARS OF OPERATION	04	46	ALL
HISTORY OF PRR ALTOONA SHOPS	01	46	20
HISTORY OF PRR BALTIMORE-HARRISBURG LIN	08	44	38
HISTORY OF PRR CHES BAY FERRIES & FLOAT	08	50	14
HISTORY OF PRR CONEMAUGH DAM RELOCATION	05	47	32
HISTORY OF PRR CONEMAUGH DIV DE-DIESEL	09	55	42
HISTORY OF PRR EPOCH OF ELECTRIFICATION	04	46	40
HISTORY OF PRR ERA OF IMPROVEMENT	04	46	26
HISTORY OF PRR HORSESHOE CURVE	05	52	28
HISTORY OF PRR IS IT COMING BACK?	12	54	16
HISTORY OF PRR MADISON HILL GRADE	07	62	34
HISTORY OF PRR NEW YORK DIVISION	01	42	8
HISTORY OF PRR ONCE UPON THE PENNSY	02	53	52
HISTORY OF PRR PITTSBURGH-ALTOONA LINE	04	57	17
HISTORY OF PRR RRING W/OUT PRECEDENT	02	51	36
HISTORY OF PRR 1 THROUGH 9999	06	70	38
HISTORY OF PRR 2-10-0 SHAMOKIN BRANCH	11	57	24
HISTORY OF PRR ATTERBURYS ENG 72"DRIVERS	11	79	44
HISTORY OF PRR ATTERBURYS ENGINES	10	79	23
HISTORY OF PRR BEGINNINGS	04	46	14
HISTORY OF PRR BROAD ST STATION	12	83	40
HISTORY OF PRR DECLINE & FALL OF STEAM	10	49	4
HISTORY OF PRR ELECTRIFICATION MITE BEEN	03	78	30
HISTORY OF PRR JAMES MILLER SYMES	07	55	15
HISTORY OF PRR KISKMINEATAS JUNCTION	05	47	27
HISTORY OF PRR NATIONS #2 ORE HAULER	09	62	34
HISTORY OF PRSL 3 MO. FEAST 9 MO FAMINE	06	48	22
HISTORY OF PRSL RIVAL SYSTEMS/NOW FRIEND	08	41	21
HISTORY OF PSL WHO PAINTS HOPPERS YELLOW	02	60	29
HISTORY OF PT DOWN-EAST	11	46	48
HISTORY OF Q CALIF MOUNTAIN MIDGET	03	54	16
HISTORY OF QA&P QUANAH MEANS QUICK	02	61	35
HISTORY OF QM DEAD BUT NOT BURIED	01	60	40
HISTORY OF QNS&L TOMORROW'S RAILROAD	11	60	35
HISTORY OF R POTTSVILLE	07	46	38
HISTORY OF R LOCOMOTIVE GROWTH	09	41	20
HISTORY OF R TAKE A RIDE ON READING	08	47	14
HISTORY OF R FIRES & PASSENGERS	10	63	21
HISTORY OF R READING'S RAMBLE	04	61	18
HISTORY OF RAILROADS OF MARYLAND	05	44	28
HISTORY OF RAILROADS OF MASSACHUSETTS	03	44	14
HISTORY OF RAL BOULEVARD FOR BULLETS	06	58	50
HISTORY OF RAY LOGGERS & LOKEYS	04	60	44
HISTORY OF RCBH&W S. DAKOTA SHORTLINES	12	47	45
HISTORY OF RF&P CAPITAL CITIES ROUTE	11	41	33
HISTORY OF RF&P GATEWAY BLUE TO GRAY	11	77	26
HISTORY OF RF&P RICHMOND-WASHINGTON	11	46	33
HISTORY OF RGS CALLS IT QUITS	06	52	14
HISTORY OF RGS SAN JUAN SCENIC LINE	02	42	8
HISTORY OF RGS WHEN ALL LED TO ORLANDO	10	69	38
HISTORY OF RI DENISE OF CHI/RI/PACIFIC	09	80	22
HISTORY OF RI DIESEL DIVERSITY	12	65	28
HISTORY OF RI DINING SERVICE	02	53	18
HISTORY OF RI DIRECTED SERVICE ORDERS	09	81	48
HISTORY OF RI DISPATCH IN THE 70'S	07	80	44
HISTORY OF RI IN RETROSPECT	06	80	3
HISTORY OF RI PEORIA ROCKET	12	81	45
HISTORY OF RI REBIRTH OF A RAILROAD	12	47	22
HISTORY OF RI ROCK REBORN	03	83	48
HISTORY OF RI ROCKEY MT ROCKY	04	53	63
HISTORY OF RI THE VIOLET HOUR	03	83	22
HISTORY OF RI WHAT HAPPENED TO RI	03	83	31
HISTORY OF RI COULD THE ROCK HAVE MADEIT	03	83	47
HISTORY OF RI LGST # OF 4-8-4 OF ANY RD	03	81	22
HISTORY OF RI ROCK BECAME A SAD ROAD	07	75	19
HISTORY OF RMC THE PURE RAILROAD	01	69	20
HISTORY OF ROC 40 YEARS OF RUST	05	42	47
HISTORY OF ROY PROPOSED LINE	03	45	29
HISTORY OF RPL&N 6 MAN RAILROAD	06	43	35
HISTORY OF RR MONEY MAKING FEDERAL LINE	01	44	38
HISTORY OF RRR DECISION FOR STEAM	12	64	40
HISTORY OF RRR TRAIN TIME IN ARKANSAS	03	63	40
HISTORY OF RU GREEN MOUNTAIN ROUTE	03	46	28
HISTORY OF RU HOW RARE THE RUTLAND	04	50	12
HISTORY OF RU WHENCE THE RUTLAND?	05	64	38
HISTORY OF RV NEW JERSEY STREAK OF RUST	10	50	36
HISTORY OF S POMONA YARD	03	80	49
HISTORY OF S SOUTHLAND CARRIER	04	44	24
HISTORY OF S BLUE RIDGE MOUNTAINS	08	45	22
HISTORY OF S ENGINEERS I HAVE KNOWN	07	54	16
HISTORY OF S LINES TO ASHEVILLE	09	48	48
HISTORY OF S PS2 PACIFICS	12	78	28
HISTORY OF S RAT HOLE DIVISION	07	51	14
HISTORY OF S ABOUT THE MAIN LINE	10	71	31
HISTORY OF S CAROLINA DIVISION	11	84	26
HISTORY OF S CRESCENT LIMITED	07	64	20
HISTORY OF S RABBIT CHASES BEAGLE UP RAT	04	76	22
HISTORY OF S SALUDA HILL PHOTO ESSAY	04	55	49
HISTORY OF S THE RR THAT STAYED OUT OF A	10	784	26
HISTORY OF S&A	10	46	58
HISTORY OF S&NC LIFE AFTER MILW?	10	81	26
HISTORY OF S&NY COAL & LUMBER	01	43	14
HISTORY OF SOO CP SUBSIDARY	02	45	14
HISTORY OF SAL THROUGH HEART OF SOUTH	02	49	16
HISTORY OF SCL ACL + SEA = SCL	10	64	24
HISTORY OF SCL ACL + SAL = SCL	10	67	20
HISTORY OF SCL LINEVILLE SUBDIVISION	11	76	22
HISTORY OF SCL CLEARWATER FOR TRAINWATCH	04	75	33
HISTORY OF SCL RALEIGH DIVISION	06	80	22
HISTORY OF SD&AE CARRISO GORGE	09	48	18
HISTORY OF SD&AE CARRISO GORGE	07	43	4

321

RAILROAD HISTORIES

	M	Y	P
HISTORY OF SD&AE NO MANANA MUCHACHU	06	51	38
HISTORY OF SEA CORBIN DIVISION	08	85	24
HISTORY OF SEA COWAN TENN	04	84	42
HISTORY OF SEA SMELL OF COAL SMOKE	02	74	36
HISTORY OF SEA TALE OF 2 FREIGHT TRAINS	05	63	20
HISTORY OF SEA WET ROCK-DRY ROCK	10	84	46
HISTORY OF SFB FETCH & CARRY LINE	02	50	18
HISTORY OF SH RESIDENTS RUN THEIR OWN	10	46	51
HISTORY OF SHRT CLEVELAND RIDES RAPIDS	04	55	42
HISTORY OF SIE GREAT REVIVAL OF STEAM	06	73	38
HISTORY OF SIE SHOOTING STARS	07	51	18
HISTORY OF SIRT LITTLE KNOWN RR OF B&O	02	51	20
HISTORY OF SJ&LC 96 MILE VERMONT LINE	05	47	50
HISTORY OF SJ&LC COLLEGE TAKES TO RAILS	03	49	12
HISTORY OF SJ&LCO VT METAMORPHOSIS	12	52	22
HISTORY OF SLKC PROPOSED LINE	03	45	30
HISTORY OF SMA COPPER HAULERS	07	56	26
HISTORY OF SMT	12	49	28
HISTORY OF SN EAST BAY PHOTO ESSAY	07	55	31
HISTORY OF SN LONGEST ELEC MAIN LINE	03	41	36
HISTORY OF SOO MOUNTAINEER	10	48	36
HISTORY OF SOO FIRST YEAR REPORT	08	62	36
HISTORY OF SOO SHE'S NOT SLEEPING	12	58	14
HISTORY OF SOO STEAM PHOTO ESSAY	06	55	51
HISTORY OF SP $7.50 TO LA	08	50	36
HISTORY OF SP 20 MINUTES AT EL PASO	05	52	66
HISTORY OF SP CARQUINEZ FERRIES	08	46	36
HISTORY OF SP CASCADE LINE	01	44	19
HISTORY OF SP CLOUDCROFT BRANCH	02	48	44
HISTORY OF SP DONNER PASS PHOTO ESSAY	12	81	30
HISTORY OF SP KEELER BRANCH	03	47	14
HISTORY OF SP KEELER BRANCH PHOTO ESSAY	02	55	35
HISTORY OF SP LARGEST US ROAD	03	45	8
HISTORY OF SP PIGGYBACK CHAMP	09	56	16
HISTORY OF SP SANTA CRUZ BRANCH	07	48	47
HISTORY OF SP SANTA MARGARITA HILL PHOT	06	54	31
HISTORY OF SP SHASTA DIVISION	12	51	36
HISTORY OF SP SHASTA ROUTE	01	46	16
HISTORY OF SP STRANDED IN DONNER PASS	01	53	50
HISTORY OF SP SUNSET LUMBER	02	48	38
HISTORY OF SP TEHACHAPI	01	77	24
HISTORY OF SP TEHACHAPI EARTHQUAKE	11	52	14
HISTORY OF SP TEHACHAPI LOOP	12	46	14
HISTORY OF SP WEST OAKLAND YARD	04	47	58
HISTORY OF SP YUMA DIVISION	02	57	38
HISTORY OF SP BROKEN JAWBONE TUNNEL 29	08	83	34
HISTORY OF SP CASCADE SUMMIT	07	82	32
HISTORY OF SP CHARLES EDISON TYNER 1	09	83	48
HISTORY OF SP CHARLES EDISON TYNER 2	10	83	46
HISTORY OF SP COAST DAYLIGHT PHOTO ESSAY	05	55	51
HISTORY OF SP PANAMA PACIFIC	09	77	48
HISTORY OF SP SAN FRAN OVERLAND TRADITIO	01	52	36
HISTORY OF SP SCHELLVILLE TURN	02	84	12
HISTORY OF SP THE HILL	02	85	22
HISTORY OF SP THE HILL SACRAMENTO DIV	08	58	40
HISTORY OF SP WEATHJER WHY THE MAP BLED	07	83	14
HISTORY OF SP&S UP THE COLUMBIA	08	44	24
HISTORY OF SP&S NORTHWESTS OWN RAILROAD	04	60	26
HISTORY OF SP&S FASTEST RR IN PACIFIC NW	03	60	34
HISTORY OF SPA	12	46	54
HISTORY OF SPC PICNIC LINE	07	48	47
HISTORY OF SPI 1906	07	49	36
HISTORY OF SPI UP TO CANADA?	06	56	18
HISTORY OF SR&RL 67 YEARS IN MAINE	08	46	10
HISTORY OF SR&RL WONDERFUL LITTLE RR	10	65	36
HISTORY OF SSE PROJECTED	03	45	27
HISTORY OF SSL SHORTLINE CALLED SKANEATE	05	71	41
HISTORY OF SSP GENEROUS TO UNFORTUNATE	07	55	48
HISTORY OF ST LAST VERMONT ELECTRIC	08	46	48
HISTORY OF STRR ROAD TO PARADISE	04	61	25
HISTORY OF SV SUMPTER'S LAST STAND	02	47	20
HISTORY OF SW (NOW CLINCHFIELD)	04	47	24
HISTORY OF SYC WANDERING RAILS	08	47	29
HISTORY OF T TENNESSEE IS TOUGH	09	68	24
HISTORY OF T&P STRAIGHT THROUGH TEXAS	03	50	18
HISTORY OF T&P QUEEN OF RED RIVER VALLEY	05	77	40
HISTORY OF TC&GB COPPER HAULERS	07	56	26
HISTORY OF TE DALLAS TEXAS	07	44	16
HISTORY OF TE GONE BUT NOT FORGOTTON	10	66	41
HISTORY OF TENNC 248 MILES	01	46	8
HISTORY OF TRO CHEMICAL HAULER	10	57	54
HISTORY OF TSM HOW YOU FIXED FOR SHAYS	04	60	38
HISTORY OF UCKC RR IN A COPPER MINE	03	74	36
HISTORY OF UP CITY OF LOS ANGELES	07	51	20
HISTORY OF UP AMES MONUMENT	10	48	52
HISTORY OF UP CITY OF LOS ANGELES	08	77	51
HISTORY OF UP IDAHO NORTHERN BRANCH	12	47	15
HISTORY OF UP IN OREGON	12	50	46
HISTORY OF UP JOINING THE NATION	05	69	ALL
HISTORY OF UP N PLATTE YARD	09	50	10
HISTORY OF UP SHERMAN HILL	06	52	16
HISTORY OF UP SHERMAN HILL RELOCATION	11	53	21
HISTORY OF UP SPIKE OF GOLD	05	42	8
HISTORY OF UP ASTRA DOMES IN NORTHWEST	04	51	41
HISTORY OF UP BLUE MOUNTAINS PHOTO ESSAY	12	54	41
HISTORY OF UP DOWN HUMBOLTS GOLDEN ROAD	01	78	38
HISTORY OF UP HARD ROAD TO VEGAS	01	78	22
HISTORY OF UP LOS ANGELES DIVISION	04	58	46
HISTORY OF UP SNOW REMOV YELLOWSTONE LIN	05	52	20
HISTORY OF UP WATER STATION 25	01	78	27
HISTORY OF USA CLAIBORNE-POLK RR	10	68	36
HISTORY OF USA FORT LEONARD WOOD	10	41	18
HISTORY OF USA TRANSPORT CORP SCHOOL	04	55	40
HISTORY OF USN NAVAL AIR STATION RR	03	53	24
HISTORY OF USSC SOUTH PASS RR	09	67	26
HISTORY OF UTAH REVISITIED	08	81	34
HISTORY OF UTAH BLACK DIAMONDS/WH DIESEL	01	56	40
HISTORY OF UV GRASS ROOTS RAILROAD	05	44	16
HISTORY OF V SOFT COAL	04	45	22
HISTORY OF V COAL CARRIER	01	50	20

RAILROAD HISTORIES

	M	Y	P
HISTORY OF V NORFOLK & WESTERN MERGER	02	63	26
HISTORY OF V BLACK UPHOLSTERY & COMM EXH	08	56	18
HISTORY OF V&MA JACK OF ALL RAILROADS	10	78	48
HISTORY OF V&T BONANZA RAILROAD	01	48	20
HISTORY OF V&T LAST TRAIN FROM CARSON C	08	50	44
HISTORY OF V&T QUEEN OF SHORT LINES	01	78	50
HISTORY OF VAC ABINDON BRANCH	06	84	21
HISTORY OF VALLEY RAILROAD (MUSEUM)	02	80	35
HISTORY OF VBR EX ARMY 0-6-0 LOCOS	10	62	42
HISTORY OF VC DONT LOOK GIFT HORSE MOUTH	11	67	16
HISTORY OF VER	05	64	38
HISTORY OF VER FROM RUTLAND ASHES	06	66	6
HISTORY OF VR	07	85	16
HISTORY OF W AT CHICAGO	02	41	41
HISTORY OF W ENGINEERING	07	50	22
HISTORY OF W LOCOMOTIVES	07	50	24
HISTORY OF W OPERATIONS	07	50	18
HISTORY OF W TRAFFIC	07	50	14
HISTORY OF W WE ARE NOT ASHAMED OF SERV	07	50	12
HISTORY OF W&LE NO PASSENGER ROAD	06	42	37
HISTORY OF W&LE INSTANT NEWS COVERAGE	07	77	52
HISTORY OF W&OD 93 YR OLD ROAD	04	48	42
HISTORY OF W&OD GEORGE BAGGETT	10	54	48
HISTORY OF WA OSCAR GREENE	06	67	46
HISTORY OF WA&G PREDESSORS	02	72	36
HISTORY OF WA&G WHERE 1ST GENERATION=2ND	03	72	38
HISTORY OF WAS ROLLING DOWN TO JUNCTION	05	76	27
HISTORY OF WB&AE MILE A MINUTE ARTICULAT	01	66	46
HISTORY OF WCF&N ELECT LINE MANY TALENTS	01	49	12
HISTORY OF WEST VIRGINA SHORTLINES	03	70	8
HISTORY OF WF&S BRACKET THE BRAZOS	11	45	22
HISTORY OF WFE 1828-1978	06	79	40
HISTORY OF WIN ABOUT TO BOW OUT	07	52	52
HISTORY OF WM A MIXING OF COLORS	06	80	44
HISTORY OF WM FAST FREIGHT LINE	05	41	20
HISTORY OF WM FAST FREIGHT LINE	03	54	48
HISTORY OF WM PHOTO ESSAY	03	54	31
HISTORY OF WM TRAINS THAT COST TOO MUCH	07	53	14
HISTORY OF WM GOING OUT QUIETLY	05	80	44
HISTORY OF WMW&N BRACKET THE BRAZOS	11	45	22
HISTORY OF WP BIEBER LINE	01	45	6
HISTORY OF WP BIEBER LINE	07	49	42
HISTORY OF WP FEATHER RIVER ROUTE	03	42	28
HISTORY OF WP WATERS OF THE WEST	07	53	50
HISTORY OF WP WOBBLY COMES OF AGE	08	53	49
HISTORY OF WP ZEPHYRETTE	07	52	26
HISTORY OF WP DOWN HUMBOLTS GOLDEN ROAD	01	78	38
HISTORY OF WP GARBAGE EXPRESS	05	85	52
HISTORY OF WP HIGH TRAILS FROM UTAH	01	78	34
HISTORY OF WP&Y 3' GAUGE	09	42	35
HISTORY OF WP&Y GATEWAY TO THE YUKON	01	51	36
HISTORY OF WP&Y INTEGRATION IN THE NORTH	07	71	36
HISTORY OF WP&Y MODERN NARROW GAUGE	03	63	30
HISTORY OF WP&Y SCENIC RTE OF THE WORLD	02	63	18
HISTORY OF WPA WANDERING WEST PENN	02	50	43

	M	Y	P
HISTORY OF WPBT INTERCHANGE WITH CUBA	08	54	46
HISTORY OF WPR WEST POINT ROUTE	06	43	9
HISTORY OF WRA WEST POINT ROUTE	06	43	9
HISTORY OF WRB ONE MAN RAILROAD IN RI	07	41	22
HISTORY OF WS SHIPPER OWNS HIS OWN TRAIN	09	71	38
HISTORY OF WSL HISTORY BORN AGAIN	10	58	17
HISTORY OF WSSB SOUTHBOUND BEHIND STEAM	03	57	25
HISTORY OF WVN	03	70	8
HISTORY OF WVPP SAVED:SWITCHBACKS/SHAYS	01	64	38
HISTORY OF Y NEE BLACK MOUNTAIN	08	74	38
HISTORY OF YD THAT SOUNDS LIKE A RR	05	70	42
HISTORY OF YV 78 MILES OF TRACK	04	43	21
HISTORY OF YVT TRACKMOBILE REPLCE TRACTI	02	84	44
HISTORY OF YVT UNION PACIFICS INTERURBAN	10	75	22
HSITORY OF IC IM COMMUTERS	12	56	16

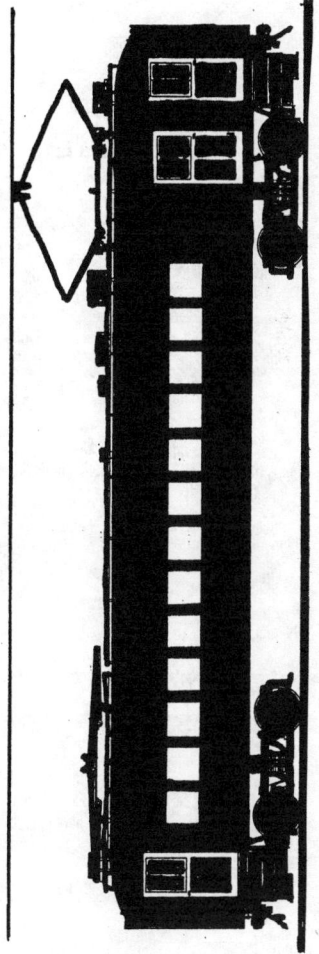

BILL OF LADING ROSTERS

The Roster listings show locomotives or rolling stock of the various roads or builders. The descriptor line includes the type of equipment and dates covered when available.

MANIFEST   ROSTERS

RAIL ROSTERS

PAGE
324

ROSTERS

	M	Y	P
ROSTER OF ROAD POWER MILW PHOTO ROSTER	12	45	30
ROSTER OF 2-8-0 WAR DEPT LOCOMOTIVES	12	64	33
ROSTER OF 4-8-2 M1 LOCOS ON PRR	11	79	47
ROSTER OF 4-8-4 LOCOS IN US	02	75	51
ROSTER OF ALCO LOCOMOTIVES (USA)	03	80	29
ROSTER OF ALCO LOCOS ALCO CATALOG	07	54	28
ROSTER OF ALCO LOCOS AT LOYALL, KY	06	77	51
ROSTER OF ALCO LOCOS MAINE CENTRAL	08	81	32
ROSTER OF ALCO LOCOS PORTLAND TERMINAL	08	81	32
ROSTER OF ALCO PA LOCOMOTIVES	11	66	38
ROSTER OF ALCO UNITS IN 1920'S	12	65	43
ROSTER OF AMERICAN LOCOS IN CHINA	11	72	40
ROSTER OF ARTICULATED LOCOMOTIVES	11	80	34
ROSTER OF BALDWIN DIESEL LOCO TYPES PHOT	05	62	44
ROSTER OF BALDWIN LOCOS IN JAPAN	10	63	42
ROSTER OF BOXCARS	09	78	25
ROSTER OF BRITISH DIESEL LOCOS PHOTOS	09	60	22
ROSTER OF BUDD RDC CARS	03	53	22
ROSTER OF BUDD-MICHELINS	04	73	27
ROSTER OF BUSINESS CARS CR	01	84	27
ROSTER OF CAB FORWARD LOCOMOTIVES	08	68	26
ROSTER OF CAB FOWARD LOCOS PHOTOS	04	41	42
ROSTER OF CAMELBACK LOCOS CNJ PHOTO	06	53	56
ROSTER OF CARS ON SHRT CLEVELAND OHIO	04	55	48
ROSTER OF CENTURY LOCOS CONRAIL	01	77	45
ROSTER OF COMMUTER LOCOS IC	12	56	22
ROSTER OF DIESEL LOCOS FEC	04	78	30
ROSTER OF DIESEL LOCOS B&LE	09	57	23
ROSTER OF DIESEL LOCOS C&I	03	71	42
ROSTER OF DIESEL LOCOS D&M	09	69	41
ROSTER OF DIESEL LOCOS P&WV	11	56	18
ROSTER OF DIESEL LOCOS R PHOTO ESSAY	05	62	19
ROSTER OF DIESEL LOCOS RF&P	11	77	31
ROSTER OF DIESEL LOCOS RI PAST/PRESENT	12	65	35
ROSTER OF DIESEL-ELECTRIC LOCOS LI	12	57	27
ROSTER OF DIESELS & RAILCARS VIETNAM	04	69	39
ROSTER OF EBT	11	53	39
ROSTER OF ELECTRIC LOCOS CN	03	75	25
ROSTER OF ELECTRIC LOCOS DRT	10	64	46
ROSTER OF ELECTRIC LOCOS ON NH	08	64	26
ROSTER OF ELECTRIC LOCOS READING RR	10	63	26
ROSTER OF ELECTRIC P5A LOCOMOTIVES	09	75	50
ROSTER OF ELECTRIC SERVICE CARS LI	12	57	27
ROSTER OF EMD DEMONSTRATOR LOCOS	09	72	58
ROSTER OF EQUIPMENT-SEASHORE ELECT MUSUM	09	56	54
ROSTER OF FM LOCOS 1944-64 PHOTOS	11	64	40
ROSTER OF FM TRAINMASTER LOCOMOTIVES	08	73	40
ROSTER OF GARRATT LOCOMOTIVES	06	44	39
ROSTER OF GE GAS ELECTRIC CARS	11	73	42
ROSTER OF GE GAS ELECTRIC CARS-LATE	12	73	44
ROSTER OF GEARED LOCOS PLU PHOTO ROSTER	01	55	28
ROSTER OF GG1 LOCOMOTIVES	03	64	30
ROSTER OF GREEK LOCOS	06	64	22
ROSTER OF H1 ROYAL HUDSONS CP	08	69	24
ROSTER OF LIMA DIESEL LOCOS	11	63	28
ROSTER OF LOCO CURIOSITIES IN CINCINATTI		12	67	48
ROSTER OF LOCOS 2-10-4 PHOTO ROSTER		08	75	26
ROSTER OF LOCOS A	1	08	72	13
ROSTER OF LOCOS A	2	07	73	14
ROSTER OF LOCOS A	3	10	77	45
ROSTER OF LOCOS A	4	01	84	14
ROSTER OF LOCOS A 1975		12	75	28
ROSTER OF LOCOS A RS3		02	80	25
ROSTER OF LOCOS A&EC 1942		02	43	46
ROSTER OF LOCOS A&WP		06	43	13
ROSTER OF LOCOS AA		10	77	45
ROSTER OF LOCOS ACL PHOTO ROSTER		06	50	42
ROSTER OF LOCOS AL		05	63	44
ROSTER OF LOCOS AL 1954		09	55	29
ROSTER OF LOCOS AL RSD1		04	80	45
ROSTER OF LOCOS ALGC		09	84	45
ROSTER OF LOCOS AS		01	73	43
ROSTER OF LOCOS ATSF 1953		01	54	29
ROSTER OF LOCOS ATSF 2-10-4		08	75	31
ROSTER OF LOCOS AUTO TRAIN		12	74	26
ROSTER OF LOCOS B&O CUMBERLAND DIVISION		11	45	21
ROSTER OF LOCOS B&AR 1949		06	49	15
ROSTER OF LOCOS B&CH		09	41	18
ROSTER OF LOCOS B&M		09	80	50A
ROSTER OF LOCOS B&O TRANSPORT MUSEUM		06	54	26
ROSTER OF LOCOS BA&P		07	63	27
ROSTER OF LOCOS BEM		01	62	28
ROSTER OF LOCOS BERKSHIRE 2-8-4 TYPE		06	43	24
ROSTER OF LOCOS BMT		08	74	38
ROSTER OF LOCOS BRB&L 1945		01	46	40
ROSTER OF LOCOS BRC		09	66	46
ROSTER OF LOCOS BRC		10	66	46
ROSTER OF LOCOS BURL		12	55	50
ROSTER OF LOCOS BURL PHOTO		12	40	32
ROSTER OF LOCOS C&A 2-6-0'S 1900		05	84	30
ROSTER OF LOCOS C&C		06	55	24
ROSTER OF LOCOS C&EI 1954		10	54	23
ROSTER OF LOCOS C&EI 1949		08	49	20
ROSTER OF LOCOS C&GR		10	82	28
ROSTER OF LOCOS C&HC		08	72	32
ROSTER OF LOCOS C&I STEAM		03	71	40
ROSTER OF LOCOS C&I STEAM PHOTOS		03	71	41
ROSTER OF LOCOS C&IM		08	55	26
ROSTER OF LOCOS C&LC		02	68	23
ROSTER OF LOCOS C&MI SECOND HAND POWER		08	55	27
ROSTER OF LOCOS C&O 1949		11	49	29
ROSTER OF LOCOS CAD		11	81	58
ROSTER OF LOCOS CANADIAN ALCOS		05	83	44
ROSTER OF LOCOS CBELT		11	62	21
ROSTER OF LOCOS CI		07	82	27
ROSTER OF LOCOS CMI		09	57	48
ROSTER OF LOCOS CN MLW/BOMBARDIER		07	83	46
ROSTER OF LOCOS COVERED WAGONS		07	78	29
ROSTER OF LOCOS CP ALCO'S		07	83	48
ROSTER OF LOCOS CR		10	77	46

ROSTERS

	M	Y	P
ROSTER OF LOCOS CR&SJ	09	43	12
ROSTER OF LOCOS D&H	10	77	45
ROSTER OF LOCOS D&M	08	81	27
ROSTER OF LOCOS D&NE	03	55	54
ROSTER OF LOCOS D&RGW (PHOTO) 1945	03	46	36
ROSTER OF LOCOS DL&W 1950	06	50	26
ROSTER OF LOCOS DM&IR	02	55	46
ROSTER OF LOCOS DRL&W	03	74	24
ROSTER OF LOCOS DUD&T	11	73	24
ROSTER OF LOCOS DV&RL	03	74	24
ROSTER OF LOCOS DW&P	03	74	24
ROSTER OF LOCOS E 160 PACIFICS	11	40	12
ROSTER OF LOCOS E 1950	05	51	30
ROSTER OF LOCOS E&LS DIESEL	07	84	38
ROSTER OF LOCOS E&LS STEAM	07	84	32
ROSTER OF LOCOS EARLY U25B'S 1962 GE	08	82	44
ROSTER OF LOCOS EMC	09	73	44
ROSTER OF LOCOS EMD EARLY E UNITS	12	71	43
ROSTER OF LOCOS ETHEOPIAN RAILROADS	11	69	37
ROSTER OF LOCOS FA ALCO UNITS	06	75	26
ROSTER OF LOCOS FL9 UNITS	09	83	32
ROSTER OF LOCOS FRIS SPRINGFIELD YARD	01	81	30
ROSTER OF LOCOS GCO	01	62	28
ROSTER OF LOCOS GMI	09	57	28
ROSTER OF LOCOS GN O-8 CLASS	01	69	42
ROSTER OF LOCOS HERSHEY CUBA	01	59	35
ROSTER OF LOCOS IC PHOTO	03	53	50
ROSTER OF LOCOS IN ANGOLA	04	72	44
ROSTER OF LOCOS IN BRAZIL	11	81	38
ROSTER OF LOCOS IN BRAZIL	01	70	28
ROSTER OF LOCOS IN CENTRAL PERU	01	55	54
ROSTER OF LOCOS IN GUATAMALA IRCA	09	54	45
ROSTER OF LOCOS IN JAVA	10	71	28
ROSTER OF LOCOS IN MEXICANO ALL TIME	05	61	23
ROSTER OF LOCOS IN SUMATRA	07	73	28
ROSTER OF LOCOS IN TAIWAN	02	78	47
ROSTER OF LOCOS IN THAILAND	07	67	42
ROSTER OF LOCOS INGERSOL RAND	12	70	32
ROSTER OF LOCOS INTER	08	53	31
ROSTER OF LOCOS IT	06	81	56
ROSTER OF LOCOS JAPAN RAILROADS	10	59	33
ROSTER OF LOCOS JNR	04	62	45
ROSTER OF LOCOS JT	05	49	15
ROSTER OF LOCOS K&T	07	74	24
ROSTER OF LOCOS KCS	09	79	31
ROSTER OF LOCOS KCS 1949	07	49	20
ROSTER OF LOCOS L&A	07	49	20
ROSTER OF LOCOS L&N	03	55	27
ROSTER OF LOCOS L&N ALL	11	79	26
ROSTER OF LOCOS L&N 1979	11	79	24
ROSTER OF LOCOS L&NW DIESEL	05	85	29
ROSTER OF LOCOS L&NW STEAM	05	85	28
ROSTER OF LOCOS LE PHOTO ROSTER	03	63	46
ROSTER OF LOCOS LI	03	49	47
ROSTER OF LOCOS LS&I	12	54	56
ROSTER OF LOCOS LS&I	12	54	56
ROSTER OF LOCOS M (STEAM)	07	47	47
ROSTER OF LOCOS M&D	10	78	55
ROSTER OF LOCOS M&ET	03	69	46
ROSTER OF LOCOS M&SL 1942	12	42	45
ROSTER OF LOCOS M&WR 1942	11	41	43
ROSTER OF LOCOS MA&PA 1940	12	41	13
ROSTER OF LOCOS MIDC	06	72	24
ROSTER OF LOCOS MILW (PHOTOS)	12	45	30
ROSTER OF LOCOS MILW 13TH LARGEST	11	78	32
ROSTER OF LOCOS MILW TACOMA HILL	03	78	38
ROSTER OF LOCOS MILW FM'S	01	80	28
ROSTER OF LOCOS MKT	09	82	25
ROSTER OF LOCOS MN&S	06	59	20
ROSTER OF LOCOS N&W	10	84	38
ROSTER OF LOCOS N&W NEW!	09	59	32
ROSTER OF LOCOS N&W 1954	11	54	24
ROSTER OF LOCOS N&W 4-8-4'S	03	79	46
ROSTER OF LOCOS NH 1949	02	50	26
ROSTER OF LOCOS NKP	05	48	29
ROSTER OF LOCOS NP PHOTO ROSTER	07	49	47
ROSTER OF LOCOS NP 1946	02	46	26
ROSTER OF LOCOS NS&W	06	68	21
ROSTER OF LOCOS NYO&W	08	42	29
ROSTER OF LOCOS NYO&W	07	57	27
ROSTER OF LOCOS P&LE	07	81	41
ROSTER OF LOCOS P&WV STEAM	11	56	19
ROSTER OF LOCOS PM 1945	08	45	21
ROSTER OF LOCOS PRR 1963	04	64	44
ROSTER OF LOCOS PRR CLASS A5 0-4-0	05	75	44
ROSTER OF LOCOS PRR CLASS G5 4-6-0	10	73	22
ROSTER OF LOCOS PRR CLASS GS4 44T DIESEL	05	75	44
ROSTER OF LOCOS Q ALL TIME	03	54	19
ROSTER OF LOCOS QM	01	60	41
ROSTER OF LOCOS RAY	04	60	47
ROSTER OF LOCOS RGS 1941	02	42	19
ROSTER OF LOCOS RMC	01	69	24
ROSTER OF LOCOS RR	01	44	41
ROSTER OF LOCOS RV 1945	03	46	34
ROSTER OF LOCOS S	12	49	18
ROSTER OF LOCOS S	10	74	28
ROSTER OF LOCOS SCTC	10	64	45
ROSTER OF LOCOS SEABOARD SYSTEM	11	83	52
ROSTER OF LOCOS SOO	12	58	23
ROSTER OF LOCOS SP 1956	05	56	26
ROSTER OF LOCOS SR&RL AFTER RENUMBERING	10	65	45
ROSTER OF LOCOS SSL	05	71	44
ROSTER OF LOCOS SSP	07	55	50
ROSTER OF LOCOS T	09	68	27
ROSTER OF LOCOS T&P 1949	03	50	25
ROSTER OF LOCOS TENNC 1945	01	46	10
ROSTER OF LOCOS U25B LATE 1962 GE	09	82	42
ROSTER OF LOCOS UCKC	03	74	38
ROSTER OF LOCOS US ARMY WAR YEARS	12	64	22
ROSTER OF LOCOS V 1948	01	50	25

STEPHANS' RAILROAD DIRECTORY

ROSTERS

	M	Y	P
ROSTER OF LOCOS V PHOTO ROSTER	12	53	52
ROSTER OF LOCOS V&MA	10	78	55
ROSTER OF LOCOS V&RL	03	74	24
ROSTER OF LOCOS V&T ALL TIME	01	48	28
ROSTER OF LOCOS VBR	10	62	45
ROSTER OF LOCOS VIA	11	84	23
ROSTER OF LOCOS VIA MLW BOMBARDIER	07	83	46
ROSTER OF LOCOS VIETNAM	03	69	25
ROSTER OF LOCOS W 1950	07	50	26
ROSTER OF LOCOS W PHOTO	02	41	44
ROSTER OF LOCOS WA&G FORDS TO FS	03	72	41
ROSTER OF LOCOS WESTERN ROUTES	11	84	48
ROSTER OF LOCOS WESTINGHOUSE	12	69	40
ROSTER OF LOCOS WM	05	41	28
ROSTER OF LOCOS WM	06	80	49
ROSTER OF LOCOS WM	03	54	55
ROSTER OF LOCOS WP	03	42	40
ROSTER OF LOCOS WP&Y	01	51	42
ROSTER OF LOCOS WP&Y 1942	09	42	37
ROSTER OF LOCOS WRA	06	43	13
ROSTER OF LOCOS WSL	10	58	22
ROSTER OF LOCOS WSSB	03	57	28
ROSTER OF LOCOS Y	08	74	38
ROSTER OF LOCOS YD	05	70	44
ROSTER OF LOCOS YVT	02	84	46
ROSTER OF MIKADO LOCOS D&RGW	09	61	23
ROSTER OF MOTIVE POWER EQUIPMENT IT 1950	09	50	40
ROSTER OF NH LOCOMOTOVIES (PHOTO)	03	45	32
ROSTER OF PASSENGER CARS A	12	71	16
ROSTER OF PASSENGER CARS A	01	84	14
ROSTER OF PASSENGER CARS ALGC	09	84	45
ROSTER OF PASSENGER CARS KCS	11	67	43
ROSTER OF PASSENGER CARS RAL	06	58	55
ROSTER OF PASSENGER CARS S	10	74	28
ROSTER OF PASSENGER CARS VIA	11	84	23
ROSTER OF PASSENGER EQUIP ACL 1957	03	58	23
ROSTER OF PASSENGER EQUIPMENT LI	12	57	27
ROSTER OF PASSENGER LOCOS KCS	11	67	47
ROSTER OF PRESERVED AMER LOCOS PRE 1870	09	84	22
ROSTER OF RAILCARS INGERSOL RAND	12	70	32
ROSTER OF RAILROAD COVERED BRIDGES 1955	06	55	48
ROSTER OF RDC CARS	03	57	6
ROSTER OF RDC CARS BY ROAD	05	55	38
ROSTER OF RDC'S BY RAILROAD	12	68	39
ROSTER OF ROLLING STOCK A	07	73	14
ROSTER OF ROLLING STOCK ATR	12	74	28
ROSTER OF ROLLING STOCK C&LC	02	68	23
ROSTER OF ROLLING STOCK MIDC	06	72	24
ROSTER OF SELF PROPELLED CARS C&I	03	71	45
ROSTER OF SHAY LOCOS OF TAIWAN	02	78	51
ROSTER OF SLUGS BUILT 1970-84	07	84	46
ROSTER OF T1 4-8-4 LOCOMOTIVES	12	60	20
ROSTER OF TRAIN CHESSIE	07	68	47
ROSTER OF TUNNEL LOCOMOTIVES B&O	04	43	16
ROSTER OF US LOCOMOTIVES IN FRANCE	10	70	40
ROSTER OF VARNISH ON CLINCHFIELD 1973	03	73	23

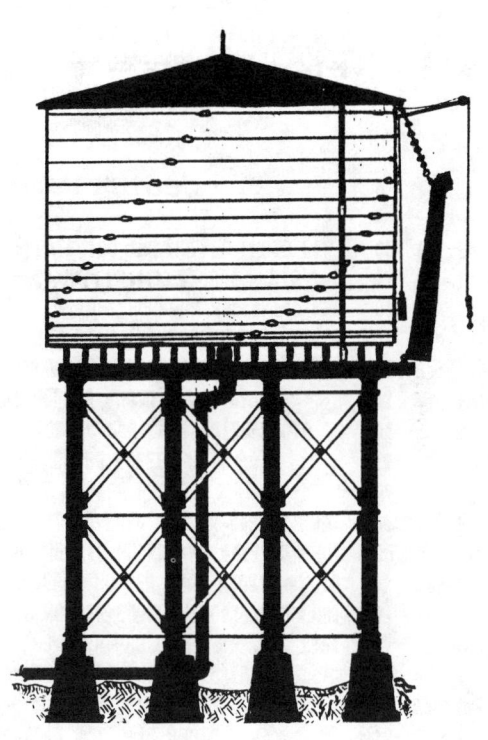

BILL OF LADING   LITERATURE REVIEWS

Literature reviews are Prototype books and are about real railroads. The descriptor lists the full title of the entry. If space permits the author (or publisher) is listed at the end of the line.

MANIFEST   LITERATURE REVIEWS

	PAGE
RAIL LITERATURE REVIEWS	328
PROTOTYPE BOOKS	329

LITERATURE REVIEWS

Title	Author	M	Y	P
100 GREATEST ADVERTISEMENTS	WATKINS	07	60	64
100 YEARS OF STEAM LOCOMOTIVES	LUCAS	04	58	63
1851 AM RAILWAY GUIDE/POCKET COMPANION		02	46	9
1966 CAR & LOCO CYCLOPEDIA OF AMER PRACT		04	67	53
20TH CENTURY	BEEBE	12	62	50
4000 MILES ON THE FOOTPLATE	NOCK	10	53	73
50 BEST OF B&O	BARR	12	77	61
5:10 TO SUBURBIA	OLMSTED	09	76	58
700	COLQUOHOUN	12	68	59
90 YEARS OF BUFFALO RAILWAYS	GORDON	11	70	56
ABANDONED RAILROADS OF BEDFORD	SULZER	01	61	57
ACE CORSON-RAILROADER 1878-1960	RAMSEY	03	65	54
ACL RAILROAD STEAM LOCOS, SHIPS, HISTORY		07	68	53
ACQUAINTANCE WITH ALCO	OLMSTEAD	05	69	66
AE STILWELL PROMOTER WITH A HUNCH	BRYANT	01	74	51
AGE OF STEAM	BEEBE	12	57	64
ALASKA RAILROAD	FITCH	10	68	52
ALASKA RAILROAD (2 VOLS)	PRINCE	06	67	52
ALBUM OF WESTERN LOCOMOTIVES	DUNSCOMB	08	50	54
ALGOMA CENTRAL RAILROAD	NOCK	08	76	56
ALL ABOARD WITH EM FRIMBO	HISS	02	76	60
ALL ABOARD! HISTORY OF RR IN MICHIGAN		12	71	53
ALONG THE IRON TRACK	RICHARDSON	07	67	53
AMBASSADOR ON RAILS	FANT	10	48	5
AMERICAN HERITAGE DECEMBER 1957		04	58	64
AMERICAN HERITAGE HISTORY OF RR IN AMER		04	76	57
AMERICAN LOCOMOTIVE ENGINEERING		05	68	53
AMERICAN LOCOMOTIVES	WHITE	03	70	54
AMERICAN LOCOMOTIVES	ALEXANDER	03	51	56
AMERICAN LOCOMOTIVES 1871-1881	HARDY	11	50	62
AMERICAN RAILROAD JOURNAL 1966		08	66	52
AMERICAN RAILROAD POLITICS 1914-70	KERR	01	70	55
AMERICAN SHORT LINE RR GUIDE	LEWIS	02	77	57
AMERICAN STEAM LOCOS 1 EVOLUTION	SWENGEL	09	68	54
ANOTHER DAY, ANOTHER DOLLAR	WINTERICH	11	47	59
APEX OF THE ATLANTICS	WESTING	06	64	51
ARID DOMAIN (SP)	GREEVER	08	55	63
ARKANSAS VALLEY INTERURBAN		12	56	62
ARTICULATED LOCOMOTIVES OF THE WP		07	59	56
AUSTRIA FOR RAILFANS	MARSH	01	69	55
B&O IN THE CIVIL WAR	BAIN	09	66	52
B&O POWER	SAGLE	06	65	52
BACKWOODS RAILROADS OF THE WEST		08	64	52
BASALT: COLORADO MIDLAND TOWN	DANIELSON	02	67	56
BEAUTY OF RAILWAYS	ELLIS	12	61	55
BERKSHIRE ERA	REHOR	09	68	54
BESSEMER & LAKE ERIE RR 1869-1969	BEAVER	11	70	57
BIG BOY	KRATVILLE	10	65	56
BIG DAN: STORY OF A COLORFUL RAILROADER		11	46	60
BIG IVY (FICTION)	MCCAGUE	12	55	63
BONANZA RAILROADS	KNEISS	01	42	49
BONANZA RAILROADS.	KNEISS	02	48	54
BOOKS THE TEN BEST RAILROAD BOOKS		12	56	53
BRITIANS RAILWAY LIVERIES	CARTER	09	53	74
BRITIANS RAILWAYS AT WAR 1939-45	NOCK	03	76	57
BRITISH EXPRESS LOCOMOTIVE DEVELOPMENT		10	53	72
BRITISH PACIFIC LOCOMOTIVES	ALLEN	12	63	49
BRITISH RAILWAYS IN ACTION	NOCK	08	57	61
BRITISH RAILWAYS TODAY & TOMARROW	ALLEN	07	59	56
BRITISH STEAM HORSES	DOW	10	50	55
BROTHERHOOD/SLEEPING CAR PORTERS	BRAZEAL	02	47	65
BURLINGTON IN TRANSITION	CORBIN	08	68	54
BURLINGTON NORTHERN ANNUAL 74-5	WAGNER	06	76	57
BURLINGTON ROUTE	OVERTON	04	71	50
BURLINGTON WEST	OVERTON	01	42	8
BUSTED AND STILL RUNNING (B&SR)	MEAD	05	69	66
C&NW STEAM POWER	KNUDSEN	03	66	62
C&O POWER	SHUSTER	06	66	58
CAB FORWARD	CHURCH	03	70	54
CABLE CAR CARNIVAL	BEEBE	08	51	58
CABLE CAR DAYS IN SAN FRANCISCO	KAHN	04	42	49
CABLE CAR DAYS IN SAN FRANCISCO.	KAHN	12	44	44
CABLE CARS OF SAN FRANCISCO	PALMER	07	59	56
CALIFORNIA WESTERN RAILROAD	BORDEN	12	57	65
CANADIAN NATIONAL RAILWAYS 1 & 2	STEVENS	10	62	51
CANADIAN PACIFIC	MCDOUGALL	12	69	54
CAR NAMES & CONSIST	WAYNER	12	63	52
CASE PROBLEMS IN TRANSPORTATION MGMT		12	57	64
CASEY JONES' LOCKER	SHAW	07	60	62
CATENARY THROUGH THE COUNTIES	CLEGG	05	68	52
CAVALCADE OF NEW ZEALAND LOCOS	PALMER	09	57	64
CENTRAL AMERICAN HOLIDAY	BEST	04	61	53
CENTRAL MASS	FISHER	03	77	58
CENTURY OF CHICAGO STREETCARS	JOHNSON	12	64	54
CENTURY OF LOCOMOTIVES		09	57	64
CENTURY OF SP STEAM LOCOMOTIVES	DUNSCOMB	12	63	48
CENTURY PLUS OF LOCOMOTIVES		11	68	54
CHAPELON:GENIUS OF FRENCH STEAM	ROGERS	04	76	58
CHESSIE'S ROAD	TURNER	12	56	59
CHICAGO ELEVATED RR CONSOLID OF OPERATIO		02	68	55
CINCINATTI LOCOMOTIVE BUILDERS 1845-68		04	67	53
CIVIL WAR RAILROADS	ABDILL	07	62	53
CLEAR THE TRACK	WOLFE	09	52	63
CLEAR THE TRACKS (DL&W)	BROMLEY	12	43	47
CLIMAX	TABER	06	61	59
CLIMAX PATENT GEARED LOCOMOTIVES		12	63	54
CLOUD CLIMBING RAILROAD	NEAL	04	69	51
CN RAILWAY'S STORY	DORIN	08	76	56
COLLIS POTTER HUNTINGTON	EVANS	01	67	53
COLORADO MIDLAND	CAFKY	10	65	56
COLORADO ROAD	WAGNER	12	73	51
COMMUTER RAILROADS	DORIN	07	71	54
COMPETITION AND RR PRICE DISCRIMINATION		06	71	55
CONCISE CYCLOPEDIA OF WORLD RY LOCOS		05	60	59
COST DATA FOR MGMT OF RR PASS SERVICES		09	57	64
COVERED BRIDGES OF MID ATLANTIC STATES		01	60	53
COVERED BRIDGES OF THE NORTHEAST	ALLEN	04	58	64
CP & SP RAILROADS	BEEBE	12	63	50
CP RAILWAY:MOTIVE POW/ROLL STK/HISTORY		08	76	56
CROOKEDEST RAILROAD IN THE WORLD	WURM	10	54	63

STEPHANS' RAILROAD DIRECTORY

LITERATURE REVIEWS

Title	Author	M	Y	P
CROSSTIES THROUGH CAROLINA	GILBERT	12	69	53
CRYSTAL RIVER PICTORIAL	MCCOY	12	73	51
CUMBRES & TOLTEC SCENIC RAILROAD	ROSS	12	73	51
CURVED SIDE CARS	WAGNER	11	65	54
DECLINE OF STEAM	GIFFORD	10	65	56
DELAWARE & HUDSON	SHAUGHENESSY	04	71	50
DENVER & RIO GRANDE W NARROW GAUGE PLANS		02	77	58
DENVER, SOUTH PARK, & PACIFIC	POOR	03	50	56
DESTINATION TOPOLOBAMPO (KCM&O)	KERR	05	69	66
DEVELOPMENT OF LOCO ENGINE	SINCLAIR	04	72	55
DIE DAY IN LA		03	65	54
DIESEL SPOTTERS GUIDE	PINKEPANK	08	67	52
DIESEL YEARS	OLMSTED	05	76	62
DIESEL-ELECTRIC LOCOMOTIVE	FOELL	11	46	60
DIESEL-ELECTRIC LOCOMOTIVE HANDBOOK		07	51	56
DIESEL-ELECTRIC LOCOMOTIVES		02	68	55
DIESELS OF ESPEE VOL I:ALCO PA'S	CORTANI	05	76	59
DIESELS WEST	MORGAN	06	64	51
DILEMMA OF FREIGHT TRANSPORTATION	REGULA	06	71	55
DILWORTH STORY (EMD)	RECK	05	55	64
DOWN AT THE DEPOT	ALEXANDER	03	71	51
DOWN, BRAKES	SHAW	09	62	51
EARL CLARKS 67 DIRECTORY WORLD ELEC LINE		02	68	54
EARLY AMERICAN STEAM LOCOMOTIVES	KINERT	10	64	54
EASTERN STEAM PICTORIAL	PENNYPACKER	07	67	52
EDAVILLE RAILROAD	MOODY	08	48	60
ELECTRIC INTERURBAN RAILWAYS IN AMERICA		01	61	55
ELECTRIC LOCOMOTIVE ROSTERS	WAYNER	11	65	54
ELECTRIC RAILROADS OF INDIANA	MARLETTE	12	60	56
ELECTRIC RAILWAY PICTORIAL		02	46	9
ELECTRIC RAILWAYS OF INDIANA #104		04	61	53
ELECTRIC RAILWAYS OF INDIANA PART 1		09	58	56
ELECTRIC RAILWAYS OF INDIANA-2		08	59	55
ELECTRIC RAILWAYS OF IOWA		02	58	55
ELECTRIC RAILWAYS OF MICHIGAN		01	61	57
ELECTRIC RAILWAYS OF NOTHEASTERN OHIO		11	66	53
ELECTRIC RAILWAYS OF WISCONSIN		10	54	63
EMPIRE THAT MISSOURI PACIFIC SERVES		02	58	55
END OF THE LINE	MORGAN	01	56	55
ENTERPRISE DENIED: ORIGINS/DELINE US RRS		12	72	58
ERIE POWER	WESTING	04	72	55
EXTRA SOUTH	REID	01	65	54
FACINATING RAILROAD BUSINESS	HENRY	02	48	54
FAIRWELL TO STEAM	PLOWDEN	12	67	52
FALL OF A RAILROAD EMPIRE (NH)	STAPLES	10	48	56
FAMOUS LOCOMOTIVES OF THE WORLD	ELLIS	02	58	55
FAR WHEELS	SMALL	07	60	62
FAREWELL TO CUMBRES	CHAPPELL	12	68	60
FASCINATION OF RAILWAYS	LLOYD	12	51	53
FASTEST HOUND DOG IN ST OF MAINE	GOULD	02	56	57
FIDDLE HILL	MCCAGUE	06	61	60
FIDDLEWOWN & COPPEROPOLIS (BRITISH RD)		06	60	61
FIGHT FOR CONTROL (NYC)	KARR	02	58	55
FINAL YEARS (NYO&W)	KRAUSE	12	77	62
FIRST QUARTER CEN OF STEAM LOCOS N AMERI		02	57	55
FIRST TRANSCONTINENTAL RAILROAD	GALLOWAY	05	50	57
FOCUS: RAILROAD IN TRANSITION	CARPER	05	69	66
FRANK JONES: KING OF ALEMAKERS	BRIGHTON	03	77	58
FREIGHT CARS ROLLING	SAGLE	07	61	54
FRENCH MINOR RAILWAYS	DAVIES	04	68	54
FRIENDLY SOO	SUPREY	05	54	64
FRISCO FOLKS	BAIN	12	63	53
FROM CAB TO CABOOSE	NOBLE	07	64	51
FROM MINE TO MARKET (N&W)	LAMBIE	02	55	55
FROM THE HILLS TO THE HUDSON (P&HR)	LUCIS	07	45	43
FURTHER SELECTION OF LOCOS I HAVE KNOWN		02	66	58
GALVESTON-HOUSTON ELECTRIC RAILWAY	WOODS	01	61	57
GARRATT LOCOMOTIVE	DURRANT	07	71	54
GATEWAY TO THE NORTHWEST	DONOVAN	06	5	62
GEORGIA RAILROAD & WEST POINT RTE	PRINCE	12	62	53
GEORGIAN LOCOMOTIVE	BRYANT	12	62	54
GIANTS LADDER	BONER	04	63	55
GILPIN GOLD TRAM	FERRELL	12	73	51
GILPIN TRAM	HOLLENBECK	07	59	56
GOLD RUSH NARROW GAUGE	MARTIN	03	71	55
GOLDEN RAILS	KRATVILLE	09	66	53
GOLDEN SPIKE A CENTENNIAL REMEMBERANCE		08	69	53
GOV'T PROMO OF AMER CANALS/RR 1800-90		09	64	53
GRAND CENTRAL	MARSHALL	02	47	64
GRANGER COUNTRY	LEWIS	09	49	60
GREAT CENTRAL (3 VOLS)	DOW	06	72	49
GREAT CENTRAL ALBUM	DOW	06	72	49
GREAT CENTRAL STEAM	TUPLIN	06	72	49
GREAT IRON TRAIL	HOWARD	10	64	53
GREAT LAKES CAR FERRIES	HILTON	04	63	54
GREAT LOCOMOTIVE CHASE	ROBERTS	02	58	55
GREAT POEMS FROM RAILROAD MAGAZINE		08	68	54
GREAT RAILROAD PAINTINGS	GOLDSBOROUGH	02	77	58
GREAT RAILROAD PHOTOGRAPHS (USA)	BEEBE	12	64	51
GREAT RAILROAD STORIES OF THE WORLD		06	55	62
GREAT RAILWAY BAZAAR:BY TRAIN THRU ASIA		09	76	56
GREAT THRID RAIL		08	62	52
GREAT TRAINS OF ALL TIME	HUBBARD	12	63	52
GULF MOBILE & OHIO	LEMLY	07	54	60
GULF TO ROCKIES	OVERTON	08	54	56
HANDBOOK OF AMERICAN RAILROADS	LEWIS	05	52	76
HAWAIIAN RAILROADS	HUNGERFORD	02	65	58
HEADLIGHTS AND MARKERS	DONOVAN	08	46	47
HEADLIGHTS AND MARKERS.	DONOVAN	05	69	66
HEAR THE TRAIN BLOW	BEEBE	12	52	60
HENRY MEIGGS, YANKEE PIZARRO	STEWART	02	47	65
HERE COMES THE SCHOOL TRAIN	BUNCE	01	54	64
HIAWATHA STORY	SCRIBBINS	03	71	51
HIGH GREEN AND BARK PEELERS	NEAL	12	50	64
HIGH ROAD TO PROMONTORY	KRAUS	08	69	52
HISTORIC ALPINE TUNNEL	HELMERS	09	64	53
HISTORIC CARS OF SEASHORE TROLLEY MUSEUM		09	67	53
HISTORIC LOCO DRAWINGS IN 4MM SCALE		07	65	52
HISTORIC RAILWAY DISASTERS 2ND EDIT	NOCK	01	70	54
HISTORY OF CN RAILWAY	STEVENS	08	76	56

STEPHANS' RAILROAD DIRECTORY

LITERATURE REVIEWS

Title	Author	M	Y	P
HISTORY OF RUSSIAN RAILWAYS	WESTWOOD	03	65	54
HISTORY OF WISCONSIN CENTRAL	MARTIN	04	41	49
HOOT, TOOT & WHISTLE HT&W	CARMAN	08	64	53
ILLINOIS TRACTION SYSTEM		06	55	62
ILLUSTRATED CATALOG OF LOCOMOTIVES		12	60	54
IMPACT OF RAILWAYS ON VICTORIAN CITIES		08	71	50
INLAND EMPIRE: D.C. CORBIN & SPOKANE		03	67	52
INTEGRAL TRAIN SYSTEMS	KNEILING	02	70	53
INTERCITY ELEC RAILWAY INDUSTRY OF CANAD		09	66	50
INTERURBAN ERA	MIDDLETOWN	11	61	52
INTERURBAN INTERLUDE	QUINBY	12	69	54
INTERURBAN TO MILWAUKEE		12	63	52
INTERURBANS OF THE EMPIRE STATE		11	49	65
INTERURBANS OF UTAH	SWETT	01	55	64
IRON HORSE RAMBLES & READING T-1'S YOUNG		12	63	52
IRON HORSES	ALEXANDER	01	42	8
IRON HORSES OF THE SANTA FE TRAIL	WORLEY	11	65	51
IRON HORSES TO PROMONTORY	BEST	08	69	52
IRON ROAD TO EMPIRE (ROCK ISLAND)	HAYES	12	55	63
JANES WORLD RAILWAYS 9TH ED	SAMPSON	02	67	55
JAY GOULD	GRODINSKY	09	58	54
JOSIAH WHITE/PRINCE OF PIONEERS -	MORTON	04	47	68
KANSAS WEST	ANDERSON	12	64	51
KATY NORTHWEST (MKT)	HOFSOMMER	01	77	59
KATY RAILROAD: LAST FRONTIER	MASTERSON	09	53	78
L&N RAILROAD 1850-1959	HERR	02	60	55
L&N STEAM LOCOMOTIVES	PRINCE	01	60	52
LACKAWANNA STORY (1ST 100 YRS)	DL&W	06	51	58
LAKE SHORE ELECTRIC TCLSE	CHRISTIANSEN	03	65	55
LAST DAYS OF STEAM	COLLIAS	04	61	53
LAST OF 3' LOGGERS	KRIEG	08	63	53
LAST SPIKE IS DRIVEN		08	69	52
LAST STEAM LOCOS OF W. EUROPE	WALLIS	08	63	53
LETS OPERATE A RAILROAD	ROXBURY	09	57	65
LIFE & DECLINE OF AMERICAN RR	STOVER	08	71	50
LIFE ON THE HEAD END	ADAMS	10	58	57
LINES WEST	WOOD	06	69	51
LITTLE ENGINES AND BIG MEN	LATHROP	08	55	62
LITTLE RAILWAYS OF THE WORLD	SHAW	01	59	54
LOCO PRACTICE & PERFORMANCE IN 20TH CENT		10	49	64
LOCOMOTIVE 4501	MORGAN	02	70	52
LOCOMOTIVE ADVERTISING IN AMER 1850-1900		09	61	54
LOCOMOTIVE CYCLOPEDIA		08	48	60
LOCOMOTIVE CYCLOPEDIA 15TH ED	COMBES	12	57	64
LOCOMOTIVE CYCLOPEDIA OF AMER PRACT 50-2		09	51	55
LOCOMOTIVE ENGINEER 1863-1963	RICHARDSON	10	64	54
LOCOMOTIVE ENGINEERS ALBUM	ABDILL	07	66	52
LOCOMOTIVE, TROLLEY & RAIL CAR BUILDERS		10	65	57
LOCOMOTIVES AND CARS SINCE 1900	LUCAS	07	59	56
LOCOMOTIVES I HAVE KNOWN	MASKELYNE	01	61	56
LOCOMOTIVES OF DICKSON MFG CO	BEST	09	69	50
LOCOMOTIVES OF JERSEY CENTRAL	CARTER	04	58	64
LOCOMOTIVES OF MANY LANDS	ALLEN	01	55	65
LOCOMOTIVES OF OUR LIVES	PENNOYER	10	54	63
LOCOMOTIVES OF PRR 1834-1924	WARNER	10	59	56
LOCOMOTIVES OF READING 1836-1923	WARNER	12	63	53
LOCOMOTIVES OF THE LNWR (BRITISH)		04	49	60
LOCOMOTIVES OF THE SP COMPANY	BEST	11	41	49
LOCOMOTIVES OF THE WP	DUNSCOMB	12	54	64
LOCOMOTIVES ON PARADE	HUNGERFORD	03	41	48
LOCOMOTIVES THAT BALDWIN BUILT	WESTING	05	68	53
LOCOS & TRAINS OF L&AKS RAILWAYS	BROWN	10	53	72
LOGGING ALONG THE DENVER & RIO GRANDE		12	73	51
LOGGING RAILROADS OF THE WEST	ADAMS	12	61	53
LONDONS HISTORIC RAILWAY STATIONS		06	74	51
LONDONS TERMINI	JACKSON	08	71	50
LONG LOOK AT STEAM	OLMSTED	10	65	56
LOUISIANA ITS STREET & INTERURBAN RWYS 1		12	63	53
LOUISVILLE & NASHVILLE RAILROAD	HERR	07	64	52
LOUISVILLE & NASHVILLE RR 1850-1942	HERR	06	43	36
LUCIUS BEEBE READER	CLEGG	07	68	53
MA & PA	HILTON	12	63	51
MAGIC OF RAILWAYS	HARTMANN	07	60	61
MAIL BY RAIL	LONG	07	52	64
MAIN LINE (SP)	KING	01	49	62
MAIN LINE MEXICO	EDMONSON	07	64	51
MAIN LINE OF MID AMERICA IC	CORLISS	09	51	55
MAINE SCENIC ROUTE	CRITTENDEN	04	68	54
MAINE TWO FOOTERS	MOODY	01	60	52
MAKIN' TRACKS	MAYER	02	76	59
MAKING OF A RAILWAY	ROLT	06	72	49
MANCHESTER & ONEIDA RAILWAY	DONOVAN	12	57	65
MANSIONS ON RAILS	BEEBE	10	59	55
MAPS OF SOUTHERN PACIFIC	DUNSCOMB	07	49	64
MARKER	WENDELING	01	49	62
MEN OF FIRE	HUNGERFORD	03	47	61
METROPOLITIAN RAILWAY	BAKER	11	51	52
MEXICAN NARROW GAUGE	BEST	10	69	52
MIDLAND COMPOUNDS	NOCK	07	65	53
MIDLAND RAILWAY (ENGLAND)	ELLIS	10	54	64
MILE HIGH TROLLEYS	JONES	07	69	52
MILEPOSTS ON THE PRAIRIE	DONOVAN	04	51	54
MILWAUKEE ROAD	DERLETH	06	48	58
MILWAUKEE ROAD ELECTRIFICATION	BRAIN	09	61	55
MINISINK VALLEY EXPRESS PJM&NY	BEST	12	56	62
MISSABEE IRON RANGER MAGAZINE 4-61		09	61	54
MIXED TRAIN DAILY	BEEBE	11	47	59
MIXED TRAIN DAILY 4TH EDITION	BEEBE	06	62	59
MODERN AUSTRALIAN & NEW ZEALAND TRAINS		09	66	53
MODERN HEISLER (CATALOG REPRINT)		02	68	54
MODERN RAILWAYS	ALLEN	12	60	54
MODERN WONDERBOOK OF TRAINS/RR	CARLISLE	02	47	65
MODERN WORLD BOOK OF RAILWAYS	TOWNEND	02	50	56
MOFFAT ROAD D&SL	BOLLINGER	12	62	52
MOGULS AND IRON MEN	MCCAGUE	11	65	53
MONORAILS	BOTZOW	07	60	64
MORE CLASSIC TRAINS	DUBIN	07	76	60
MOTIVE POWER OF THE UP	KRATVILLE	04	59	55
MR PULLMANS ELEGANT PALACE CAR	BEEBE	12	62	49
MY AMERICAN PILGRIMAGE	CHRISTOWE	09	47	70

LITERATURE REVIEWS

Title	Author	M	Y	P
MY BEST RAILROAD PHOTOGRAPHS	KINDIG	08	49	62
MY IRON JOURNEY:A LIFE WITH STEAM/STEEL		04	69	51
NAMIB NARROW GAUGE	MOIR	04	68	54
NARROW GAUGE ALBUM	WHITEHOUSE	12	57	65
NARROW GAUGE COUNTRY	LIND	07	64	52
NARROW GAUGE IN ROCKIES	BEEBE	12	58	56
NARROW GAUGE NOSTALGIA	TURNER	02	67	56
NARROW GAUGE RAILWAYS OF EUROPE	ALLEN	12	60	55
NARROW GAUGE RALWAYS IN AMERICA	FLEMING	02	50	56
NARROW GAUGE TO CENTRAL & SILVER PLUME		12	73	51
NARROW GAUGE TO CUMBRES	OSTERWALD	12	73	51
NARROW GAUGE TO SILVERTON		08	55	64
NARROW GAUGE TO THE REDWOODS	DICKINSON	04	68	54
NASHVILLE, CHAT & ST LOUIS HIST/ST LOCOS		07	68	53
NATCHEZ ROUTE (MISSC)	PRICE	12	77	63
NEVADA COUNTY NARROW GAUGE	BEST	10	65	57
NEW JERSEY CENTRAL ALBUM	CARTER	03	65	54
NEW JERSEY SHORT LINE RAILROADS	JOHNSTON	08	59	55
NEW TECHNOLOGIES IN RR RATE MAKING		06	71	55
NEW YORK STATE RAILWAYS	KING	09	52	64
NICKEL PLATE ROAD	HAMPTON	03	48	52
NICKEL PLATE STORY	REHOR	08	66	54
NIGHT BOAT	HILTON	02	69	54
NIGHT TRAIN	DUKE	12	62	54
NORTH ARKANSAS LINE-M&NA	FAIR	11	73	51
NORTH SHORE CNS&M	MIDDLETON	12	64	54
NORTHERN PACIFIC RAILROAD	STINDT	02	66	58
NORTHERN PACIFIC: MAIN ST OF NORTHWEST		11	69	52
NORTHERN RAILS	SMITH	02	68	54
NORTHERN RR OF THE CIVIL WAR	WEBER	02	53	62
NORTHERNS	FARRELL	04	76	57
NORTHWESTERN PACIFIC RAILROAD	BORDEN	07	49	65
NORTHWESTERN PENNSYLVANIA RAILROAD		02	77	58
NOT&L STORY (NORTHERN OHIO TRACTION/LIGH		12	67	51
NWI'S GUIDE TO RAILROAD PHOTOGRAPHY		07	76	57
NYC EARLY POWER VOL II 1831-1916	STAUFER	08	68	54
O&W	HELMER	06	60	60
OFFICIAL GUIDE 1868 REPRINT		05	69	66
OIL LAMPS AND IRON PONIES	SHAW	12	49	58
ON PARADE	HUNGERFORD	12	57	65
ON RAILWAYS AT HOME AND ABROAD	WALLIS	12	51	53
ON THE MAIN LINE	ALEXANDER	03	72	55
OPERATIONS SANTA FE	ARMITAGE	08	48	60
ORIENT EXPRESS	BARSLEY	07	69	51
OVERLAND LIMITED	BEEBE	07	64	51
PA BOOK	YOUNG	05	76	59
PACIFIC COAST SHAY	RANGER	10	65	56
PACIFIC SLOPE RAILROADS	ADBILL	01	60	53
PASSENGER TRAIN ANNUAL #2	KEEFE	12	77	61
PENISNULA SERVICE	STINDT	12	57	65
PENN CNETRAL SYSTEM BI ANNUAL	REID	06	76	57
PENNSY POWER	STAUFER	08	63	54
PENNSY POWER II	STAUFER	05	69	66
PENNSYLVANIA RR:PICTORIAL HSTY	ALEXANDER			54
PGE-RAILWAY TO THE NORTH	RAMSEY	03	65	54
PHANTOM BRAKEMAN (FICTION)	HUBBARD	07	60	64
PICTORAL ENCYCLOPEDIA OF RAILWAYS	ELLIS	10	68	52
PICTORIAL SUPPLEMENT TO DSP&P	KINDIG	07	60	60
PICTURE HISTORY OF B&O MOTIVE PWR	SAGLE	05	53	64
PICTURE HISTORY OF RAILWAYS	ELLIS	12	56	59
PICTURE HISTORY OF US TRANSPORTATION		04	59	56
PIONEER RAILROAD (C&NW)	DOUGLAS	03	49	60
POCKET GUIDE TO AMERICAN LOCOS	LUCAS	07	54	60
POGO'S TRAIN RIDE	NORLING	02	45	37
POPULAR PICTURE & PLAN BK OF RR CARS/LOC		03	52	62
PORTRAIT OF THE RAILS:FROM STEAM TO DIES		11	73	55
POUNDING WHEELS (FICTION)	HALE	08	47	60
PRACTICAL EVALUATION OF RR MOTIVE POWER		09	48	62
PROVACTIVE PEN OF LUCIUS BEEBE ESQ		07	68	53
PRR A PICTORIAL HISTORY	ALEXANDER	02	72	54
PUGET SOUND ELECTRIC RAILWAY	SWETT	09	61	54
PULLMAN PANORAMA VOL 1	WAYNER	05	69	66
PULLMAN: EXPER IN INDUS ORDER/COMMUN PLN		12	71	54
QUEST FOR CRISIS	SITES	12	63	48
QUICK REVIEW OF EAST BROAD TOP	MANNIX	09	61	54
RAILROAD	MC PHERSON	02	77	58
RAILROAD ALBUM	O'CONNELL	05	54	64
RAILROAD AND SPACE PROGRAM	MAZLISH	09	66	51
RAILROAD AVENUE (REPRINT)	HUBBARD	10	65	57
RAILROAD CABOOSE	KNAPKE	01	69	55
RAILROAD CONDUCTOR	WINKLER	02	49	59
RAILROAD ENGINEERING VOL 1	HAY	08	54	56
RAILROAD EQUIPMENT FINANCING	STREET	01	60	52
RAILROAD FOR TOMORROW	HUNGERFORD	04	46	50
RAILROAD INDUSTRY	YOUNG	01	42	8
RAILROAD MEN	KALISHER	07	62	53
RAILROAD PASS SERVICE COSTS & FIN RESULT		02	57	55
RAILROAD PASSENGER CAR	MENCKEN	04	58	63
RAILROAD POLICE	DEWHURST	12	57	65
RAILROAD POST OFFICE HISTORY	MCKEE	10	73	50
RAILROAD SCENE	MIDDLETON	08	71	49
RAILROAD STATIONS	MEEKS	08	57	61
RAILROAD THAT DIED AT SEA (FEC)	PARKS	05	69	66
RAILROAD THAT LIGHTED S. CALIF	JOHNSTON	11	65	54
RAILROADING AROUND THE WORLD	FARRINGTON	12	55	62
RAILROADING FROM THE HEAD END	FARRINGTON	05	43	48
RAILROADING FROM THE REAR END	FARRINGTON	02	47	65
RAILROADING IN 18 COUNTRIES	GRAY	02	56	56
RAILROADING THE MODERN WAY	FARRINGTON	10	51	55
RAILROADING WEST:A CONTEMPORARY GLIMPSE		10	76	58
RAILROADS & STEAMERS OF LKE TAHOE	MCKEON	07	49	65
RAILROADS AT WAR	KIP	12	44	44
RAILROADS COME TO IOWA	PETERSON	01	61	57
RAILROADS DOWN THE VALLEYS	MILLS	05	51	60
RAILROADS IN THE DAYS OF STEAM		01	61	57
RAILROADS IN THE WOODS	LABBE	12	61	53
RAILROADS OF AMERICA	DONOVAN	11	49	65
RAILROADS OF AMERICA	ARMITAGE	10	53	72
RAILROADS OF CHICAGO	KALMBACH	10	50	54
RAILROADS OF NEVADA & E CALIF 1	MYRICK	08	63	53

LITERATURE REVIEWS

Title	Author	M	Y	P
RAILROADS OF NEVADA & E CALIF 2	MYRICK	08	64	49
RAILROADS OF NEW YORK	O'CONNOR	02	50	56
RAILROADS OF THE BALCK HILLS	FIELDER	03	67	52
RAILROADS OF THE CONFEDERACY	BLACK	02	53	62
RAILROADS OF THE HOUR	FARRINGTON	01	59	55
RAILROADS OF TODAY 1949	FARRINGTON	09	49	60
RAILROADS OF YOSEMITE VALLEY	JOHNSTON	09	64	52
RAILROADS TODAY & YESTERDAY	BUEHR	04	58	64
RAILROADS: AN AMERICAN JOURNEY	BALL	03	76	58
RAILS ACROSS THE MIDLANDS	COOK	12	64	54
RAILS AROUND GOLD HILL	CAFKY	01	56	54
RAILS FROM THE WEST	HINCKLEY	08	69	52
RAILS OF THE SILVER GATE	DODGE	09	61	54
RAILS SUGARBRUSH AND PINE	FERRELL	04	68	54
RAILS THAT CLIMB	BOLLINGER	01	51	56
RAILS THROUGH DIXIE	KRAUSE	09	66	51
RAILS TO POSSUM TROT	STOWE	02	68	54
RAILS TO THE HIGH COUNTRY	LIND	06	62	59
RAILS TO THE NORTH STAR	PROSSER	06	67	51
RAILS WEST	ADBILL	04	61	52
RAILWAY CAR BUILDERS OF US & CANADA		04	58	64
RAILWAY ENGINEERS	NOCK	12	56	59
RAILWAY GAME	LUKASIEWICZ	02	77	58
RAILWAY MAGAZINE MISCELLANY	MAXWELL	09	58	54
RAILWAY MEMORIES (BRITISH)	BUCKNALL	04	49	60
RAILWAY REMINISCENCES OF 3 CONTINENTS		03	70	54
RAILWAY SIGNALING	TAYLOR	02	50	57
RAILWAYS IN NEW ZEALAND	PALMER	12	60	56
RAILWAYS OF BRITIAN	NOCK	09	48	62
RAND MCNALLY HANDY RR ATLAS OF THE US		10	65	57
RAPIDLY ROUND THE BEND	ELLIS	01	60	54
READING STEAM PICTORIAL	PENNYPACKER	07	64	52
READINGS VICTORIAN STATIONS	LEWIS	12	77	61
REBEL OF ROCKIES, THE D&RGW RR	ATHEARN	12	64	53
RED ARROW	DEGRAW	03	74	50
RED FOR DANGER	ROLT	04	57	62
REDWOOD RAILWAYS	KNEISS	04	57	62
REGULATION OF TRANSPORT INNOVAT COAL TRA		06	67	51
REVOLUTION IN TRANSPORTATION	RUPPENTHAL	08	64	53
RIDE THE BIG RED CARS PE	CRUMP	02	67	55
RIDING THE RAILS	MATHERS	02	77	58
RIGHT OF WAY:GUIDE TO ABANDONED RR IN US		10	73	49
RIGHTS OF TRAINS	JUSSERAND	09	58	56
RIO GRANDE	BEEBE	12	62	49
RIO GRANDE PICTORIAL	MCCOY	12	73	51
ROAD FROM UPPER DARBY	COX	02	68	54
ROAD OF THE CENTURY (NYC)	HARLOW	08	47	60
ROAD TO PARADISE	MOEDINGER	08	62	52
ROADWAY AND TRACK	RENCH	04	47	68
ROCKFORD & INTERURBAN RAILWAY		12	57	65
ROLL OF TRANSPORTATION IN DEV OF VERMONT		07	47	68
ROMANCE & HISTORY OF THE RAILROADS	RICE	04	42	49
ROUND THE WORLD ON THE NARROW GAUGE		04	68	54
ROUNDHOUSE PARADISE & MR PICKERING		09	66	50
ROUTE OF ELECTROLINERS CNS&M		07	64	52
ROUTE OF THE ORANGE LIMITED R&E	GORDON	06	55	62
RPO HANDBOOK VOLUME 1		09	61	54
RR OF AMERICA:MOTIVE POWER OF D&H		10	41	49
RUDOLF DIESEL	NITSKE	10	65	55
RUINS IN THE SKY	FAWCETT	08	59	54
RULER OF READING FRANKLIN GOWEN 1836-89		01	48	55
RUSSIAN LOCOMOTIVE TYPES	WESTWOOD	09	61	55
RUSSIAN RAILWAYS	GARBUTT	08	49	62
RUSSIAN STEAM LOCOMOTIVES	PRICE	07	61	54
RUTLAND ROAD	SHAUGHNESSY	02	66	58
SACRAMENTO NORTHERN	SWETT	12	63	53
SANTA FE'S DIESEL FLEET	MCMILLAN	06	76	57
SANTA FE-STEEL RAILS THRU CALIF	DUKE	09	64	54
SANTE FE/RR THAT BUILT AN EMPIRE/MARSHAL		02	46	52
SAPBUSH RUN	O'DONNELL	07	49	66
SCENES FROM THE SHORE LINES	OLMSTED	03	65	54
SCENIC LINE OF THE WORLD	CHAPPELL	12	73	51
SEVEN SHORT LINES	YOUNG	08	62	53
SHAY LOCOMOTIVE	KOCH	04	72	55
SHIPS AND NARROW GAUGE RAILS	BEST	01	65	54
SHORT LINE ANNUAL 1960-61	YOUNG	08	62	53
SHORT LINE JUNCTIONS	WAGNER	12	56	59
SHORTLINE RAILROADS OF ARKANSAS	HULL	12	69	53
SILVERTON TRAIN	HUNT	01	56	54
SINGING RAILS	PEASE	12	48	64
SLIM PRINCESS	HUNGERFORD	12	56	62
SMALLER ELECTRIC RAILWAYS OF ILLINOIS		12	56	62
SMOKE ABOVE THE PLAINS UP	EHERNBERGER	06	66	58
SMOKE ACROSS THE PRAIRIE	EHERNBERGER	07	65	53
SMOKE DOWN THE CANYONS	GSCHWIND			51
SMOKE OVER DIXIE UP	EHERNBERGER	06	66	58
SNOWPLOW	BEST	07	67	53
SOME CLASSIC LOCOMOTIVES	ELLIS	07	50	56
SOME CLASSIC TRAINS	DUBIN	12	64	52
SOO LINE	MORRISSETTE	11	65	54
SOUTH PACIFIC COAST	MAC GREGOR	11	69	52
SOUTH WESTERN RAILWAY	ELLIS	01	59	55
SOUTHERN PACIFIC	WILSON	04	52	64
SOUTHERN PACIFIC MOTIVE POWER ANNUAL		06	76	57
SOUTHERN STEAM POWER	RANKS	02	67	54
SOUTHERN STEAM SPECIALS	ZIEL	02	77	58
SP MOTIVE POWER ANNUAL 66-67	STRAPAC	02	68	54
SPLENDOUR OF STEAM	ELLIS	11	65	52
ST JOSEPH VALLEY RAILWAY	GALLOWAY	12	56	62
ST LOUIS-SAN FRAN TRANS CONTINENTAL RR		01	74	51
ST PANCRAS STATION	SIMMONS	09	69	50
STARLIGHT ON THE RAILS & OTHER SONGS		03	76	59
STEAM & TROLLEY DAYS ON FJ&G	NESTLE	01	59	56
STEAM FAN TRIP ACROSS THE MIDWEST		03	65	55
STEAM IN THE SIXTIES	ZIEL	10	68	53
STEAM LOCOMOTIVES & BOATS S RY SYSTEM		07	65	53
STEAM LOCOMOTIVES CGW 2-8-0 TYPE	BROWN	12	77	63
STEAM LOCOMOTIVES CYCLOPEDIA VOL 1		12	60	55
STEAM LOCOMOTIVES IN AMERICA	BRUCE	04	53	80
STEAM LOCOMOTIVES IN JAPAN	USUI	11	62	54

LITERATURE REVIEWS

Title	Author	M	Y	P
STEAM LOCOMOTIVES OF EASTERN EUROPE		03	67	54
STEAM LOCOS OF BURLINGTON RTE	CORBIN	06	60	61
STEAM ON Q (CB&Q)	EDMONSON	09	61	55
STEAM POWER OF NYC STEAM 1915-55	STAUFEL	12	61	55
STEAM STEEL & LIMITEDS	KRATVILLE	12	62	51
STEAM TRAINS OF THE SOO	SUPREY	08	64	50
STEAM WIDE & NARROW	WOJTAS	01	60	54
STEAMCARS TO COMSTOCK	BEEBE	09	57	64
STEAMS FINEST HOUR	MORGAN	02	60	56
STEEL RAILS TO VICTORY	ZIEL	07	71	54
STEEL TRAILS & IRON HORSES	BUCHNAN	08	55	63
STEELS RAILS TO SUNRISE LI	ZIEL	03	66	61
STEELWAYS OF NEW ENGLAND	HARLOW	08	46	46
STORY OF AMERICAN RAILROADS	HOLBROOK	01	48	55
STORY OF EDDYSTONE 1928 REPRINT	BALDWIN	02	76	61
STORY OF ENG CASEY JONES' LAST TRIP	WEBB	11	52	64
STORY OF SETTLE-CARLISLE LINE (BRITISH)		04	49	58
STORY OF STEAMTOWN & EDAVILLE	ZIEL	11	65	54
STREAMLINE DECADE	BUSH	04	76	59
STREAMLINE ERA	REED	04	76	59
STREET CARS & INTERURBANS OF YESTERDAY		07	60	62
STREET RAILWAYS OF TORONTO	PURSLEY	01	59	56
SUPER POWER STEAM LOCOMOTIVES	COOK	09	67	52
SUSQUEHANNA TROLLEYS	GORDON	09	52	64
SWITZERLAND FOR RAILFANS	PRIGMORE	01	69	55
SWITZERLAND TRAIL OF AMERICA	CROSSEN	12	62	53
SWITZERLANDS AMAZING RAILWAYS	ALLEN	01	55	64
TANDEM COMPOUND LOCOMOTIVES	KALLA-BISHOP	08	50	52
THEN CAME THE RAILROADS	CLARK	02	60	56
THEY FOOLED THE REDWOODS	JOHNSTON	10	68	53
THIS WAS RAILROADING (SP)	ABDILL	12	58	56
THOSE DAYLIGHT 4-8-4'S	CHURCH	09	67	53
THREE BARRELS OF STEAM	BOYNTON	02	76	60
THUNDER LAKE NARROW GAUGE	HUSTON	09	61	54
TICKET TO TOLTEC	OSTERWALD	02	77	58
TIME OF THE TROLLEY	MIDDLETON	06	68	53
TM:MILW ELECTRIC RY & LIGHT CO	CANFIELD	03	74	50
TO THE GREAT OCEAN	TUPPER	04	69	51
TORONTO TROLLEY CAR STORY	SWETT	12	63	53
TRACKS OF THE BLACK BEAR (ALGC)	WILSON	08	76	56
TRACKS TROUBLE & TRIUMPH	BROEHL	02	55	55
TRAIL OF THE ZEPHYRS (BURL)	OLMSTEAD	08	71	49
TRAIN FERRIES OF WESTERN EUROPE	WALLIS	06	69	52
TRAIN TO YESTERDAY		08	55	64
TRAIN WRECK	GRISWOLD	09	70	52
TRAIN WRECKS	REED	05	69	66
TRAINS ALBUMS OF PHOTOGRAPHS #1,2,3,4		03	43	47
TRAINS IN TRANSITION	BEEBE	01	42	8
TRAINS ROLLING	MCBRIDE	10	53	72
TRAINS WE RODE VOL 1	BEEBE	01	67	56
TRAINS WE RODE VOL II	BEEBE	07	68	53
TRAINS, TRACK & TRAVEL	VAN METRE	09	44	40
TRAINS, TRACKS AND TRAVEL	VAN METRE	09	50	56
TRANSPORTATION CENTURY	FOX	12	68	58
TREASURY OF RAILROAD FOLK LORE	BOTKIN	12	53	64
TROLLEY CAR TREASURY	ROWSOME	12	56	59
TRUE ADVENTURES OF RAILROADERS	MORGAN	07	54	61
TURBINES WESTWARD	LEE	12	76	58
TWEETSIE ET&WNC	SCHEER	02	59	56
TWENTY FOUR INCHES APART	MOIR	03	65	54
TWILIGHT OF STEAM LOCOMOTIVES	ZIEL	12	63	49
TWO MILLION MILES OF TRAIN TRAVEL	ALLEN	07	66	54
UNION PACIFIC STREAMLINERS	RANKS	12	76	57
UNITAH RAILWAY	BENDER	08	71	49
UNIVERSAL RAILWAYS	WILSON	02	59	56
UNUSUAL LOCOMOTIVES	CARTER	12	60	55
US STEAM LOCO DIRECTORY	KOENIGSBERG	11	68	54
VAN HORNE'S ROAD (CP)	LAVALLEE	08	76	56
VANISHING MARKERS	FISHER	03	77	58
VICTORY RODE THE RAILS	TURNER	02	54	64
VIRGINIA & TRUCKEE	BEEBE	06	49	60
VIRGINIAN RAILWAY	REID	11	61	53
WAITING FOR THE 5:05	GROW	12	77	63
WALKING BEAMS & PADDLE WHEELS	HARLAN	05	52	80
WAR ON THE LINE (ENGLANDS SOUTHERN RY)		08	47	60
WASHINGTON & OLD DOMINION RR	WILLIAMS	03	74	50
WESTERN TRAINS	STEINHEIMER	06	66	59
WESTWARD TO PROMONTORY	COMBS	08	69	52
WHAT MAKES THE LOCOMOTIVE GO	SAGLE	05	50	56
WHEELS	OWEN	04	69	51
WHEELS ACROSS AMERICA	HORNUNG	02	60	56
WHEN BEAUTY RODE THE RAILS	BEEBE	12	62	50
WHEN MCQUEEN WAS KING	LYONS	12	56	59
WHERE STEAM STILL SERVES		09	61	54
WHERE TO WATCH TRAINS	LADD	12	77	60
WHO'S WHO IN RAILROADING	MOORE	01	67	56
WHO'S WHO IN RAILROADING 14TH ED	MOORE	07	60	64
WILD TRAIN (W&A)	O'NEILL	09	57	64
WITH A CINDER IN MY EYE	DOWNING	01	52	56
WORK OF GIANTS	GRISWOLD	10	64	53
WORLD RAILWAYS	SAMPSON	03	52	62
WORLD RAILWAYS 1958-59	SAMPSON	04	59	56
YONDER COMES THE TRAIN	PHILLIPS	09	66	53

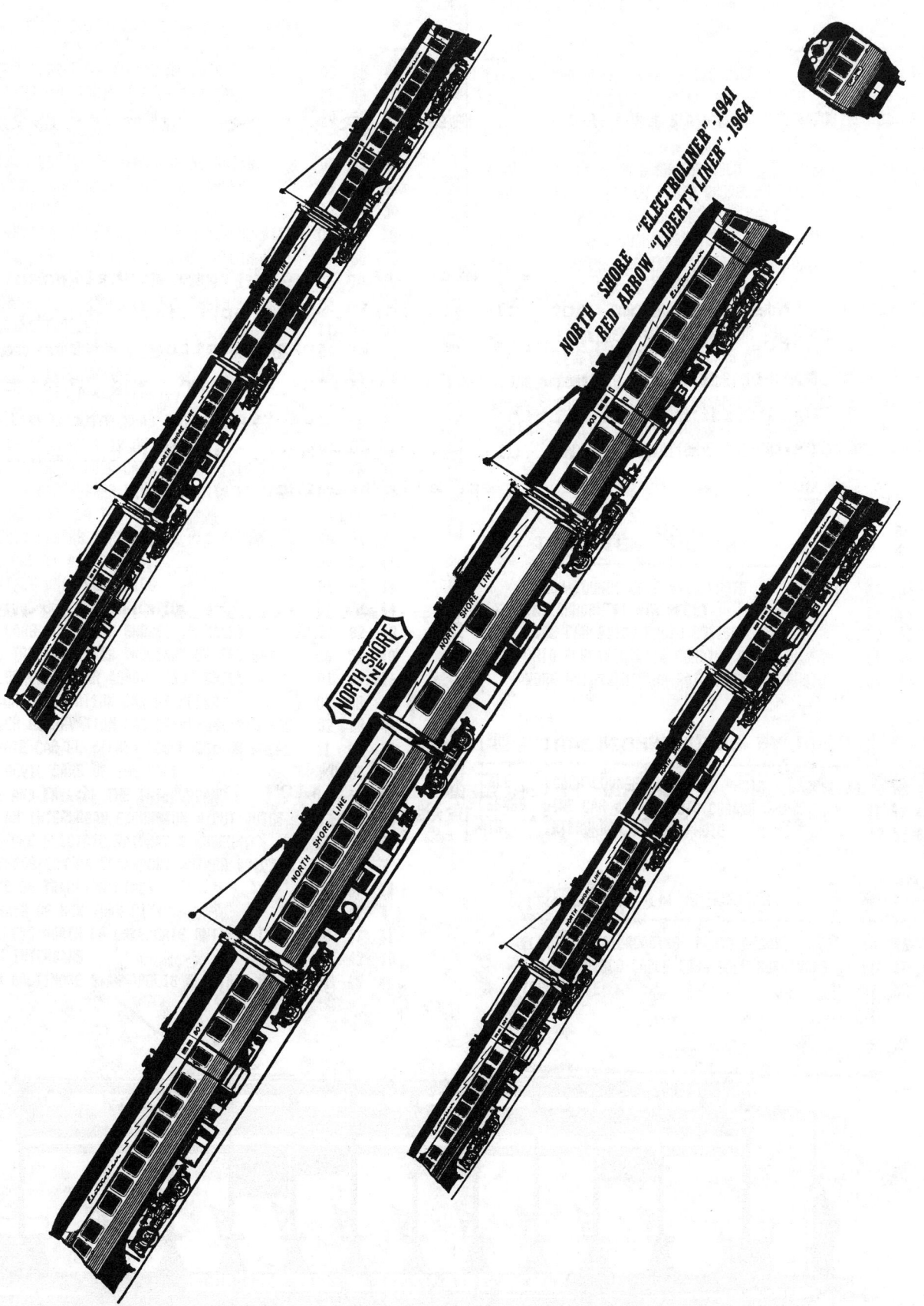

BILL OF LADING — GENERAL RAILROADING

This section is the catch-all for all those miscellaneous items that do not clearly fall into a specific category. Three sub categories make up this section. General Railroading, General Railroading Fiction and General Railroading Non-Fiction. This section really has to be "read" to get the full benefit from it. Many items appear here as well as under a specific heading.

MANIFEST — GENERAL RAILROADING

	PAGE
GENERAL RAILROADING	336
GENERAL RAILROADING FICTION	338
GENERAL RAILROADING NON-FICTION	337
GENERAL RAILROADING	338

GENERAL RAILROADING

GENERAL RAILROADING NON-FICTION

Title	M	Y	P
"OH HELL" ALBERTSON - ENGINEER	11	42	4
11 HOURS WITH A 111 YEAR OLD LOCOMOTIVE	10	67	44
2-8-4 NKP #759 CLOSE UP	05	71	36
4-4-0 + E-44 LIGHTNING STRIKES TWICE	03	78	52
4-4-2 CLASS J N&W #611 FINEST STEAM LOCO	01	83	44
4-8-4 REBORN	04	77	20
9900 TONS OF TRAIN GM&O	03	78	44
A MAN AND HIS TOWER	03	84	40
A TRAIN OF FOOLS	09	75	26
ACL TRAIN RECOVERING TIME-I REMEMBER	02	77	46
AMTRAK-8 TRAINS-14 DAS-4400 MILES	11	78	51
ANNISTON ALA STEAM LOCOMOTIVE MEET 1969	02	70	20
AS CENTURYS DIDN'T PASS IN THE NIGHT	11	74	53
BEAR AND THE SEMAPHORE	04	43	39
BELLEFONTAINE OH LOCO EXPLOSION 4-25-42	07	74	36
BENS REVENGE--STEEL ERECTION ON UP	08	77	55
BLACK CAT WRECK	11	55	54
BLUE COMET SPECIAL-YESTERDAY BECAME TODA	08	76	23
BOILERWASH EXTRA	04	79	50
BRAODWAY LIMITED SECOND ENGINE 28 PRR	03	75	42
BREAK UP CONRAIL JERVIS LANGDON	06	77	40
BREAKING IN A STREAMLINER "HIAWATHA"	03	72	18
CAB RIDE TO BURBANK TOWER SP	05	45	32
CHARGING WRAITHLIKE FROM SNOW A	12	82	54
CHIEF DISPATCHER ON THE WABASH	09	58	16
CHILDS GARDEN OF RAILROADING ESSAY	01	67	24
CLEAN FLUES-WASH BOILERS--HARD WORK!	03	72	44
CONDUCTOR MOEDINGER RIDES AGAIN	06	76	22
CONFESSIONS OF A EMD WATCHER	09	72	46
CONFESSIONS OF A TRAIN WATCHER D. MORGAN	05	57	26
DAY IN THE LIFE OF AN ENGINEER	10	48	44
DEATH VALLEY SCOTTY SPECIAL	02	53	14
DIARY OF A RAILROADER RIGHT SIDE OF CAB	07	58	42
DIARY OF A RAILROADER STEAMS DEMISE	11	58	21
DIARY OF A RAILROADER WALT THRALL	01	58	44
DIARY OF A RAILROADER XTRA ON MT ROAD	04	58	46
DIARY OF ANNE DOVEL SHE LOVES LOCOS	07	60	22
DIESEL GENERATIONS-FIREMAN NOTES	02	80	28
DIPLOMAT MY DAD FIRED IT	11	74	37
EDUCATION OF DIESEL RAILROAD MAN	05	85	54
EX-FLYBOY RAILROADING IN BLUE MOUNTAINS	09	73	35
EXPOSITION FLYER SWIFTEST TRAIN IN WORLD	03	67	38
EXTRA BOARD DIARY RR FACTS THROTTLE JOCK	11	74	43
FIRE THEY STOPPED THE TRAINS FOR	10	57	42
FIREMAN DREW A MIKADO-I WAS LUCKY	02	62	42
FIREMAN-FIRELIGHT ON THE SKY	01	62	36
FIREMANS MANUAL CONTINGENCIES NOT COVERD	04	76	48
FLORIDIAN GET BORED-THINK GREYHOUND	04	80	26
FOUR FOR EASTBOUND	10	77	31
FOUR LOCHINVARS FLASH THRU THE NIGHT	12	73	28
FROM THROTTLE TO TYPEWRITER	09	55	48
GETTING THERE WAS HALF THE FUN	09	75	23
GG1 ELECTRICS RIDE IN THE CAB PRR	10	47	16
GG1 MY OWN (ALMOST)	12	81	50
GO WEST, MIDDLE AGED MAN, GO WEST	07	67	20
HISTORY OF RAY 3 NOTCHES TO WILLITS	04	72	48
HOBO'S LAMENT LOOKING FOR A RIDE	04	78	52
HOW TO BE AN ASSISTANT TRAINMASTER	11	77	48
HUGH MCCARTHY-BORN TO RAILROAD	10	55	41
I PULLED EMERGENCY BREAK ON 99	01	83	20
I REMEMBER BUCYRUS TO BELGIUM 1944	11	68	46
IC #5 4-6-2 #1199	11	71	22
INVETERATE TRAIN RIDERS NOTES	07	66	20
ISN'T THAT A FLYING COW?	02	54	22
JARRETT AND PALMER SPECIAL WHIRLED ACROS	04	55	27
JOURNEY INTO THE UNKNOWN	04	69	35
LADY AND THE PENNSY	12	82	48
LAST RIDE TO LEADVILLE C&S 1936	12	82	26
LOST GENERATION	10	49	45
MAKE MINE AN UPPER	06	48	16
MAN IN A HURRY ENGINEER N&W J CLASS LOCO	12	64	44
MAN WHO KNOWS HOW TO RUN FAN TRIPS	07	81	20
MASTER MECHANIC STEAM ENGINES	09	76	27
MAYFAIR TOWER IS LAST OUTPOST	12	52	17
MINNESOTA RRS--JIM HILL COUNTRY	08	43	35
MONMOUTH ME WRECK 12-7-06 MC MAN ERROR	03	55	48
MONTANA WRECK NP 9-20-54	09	56	21
MORSE MEMORIES	10	77	22
MOTORMEN	12	80	52
MY FIRST TRIP WEST 1949	01	82	44
MY RIDE ON THE ROCK	03	83	37
NIGHT 4922 BLEW UP NYC K-5B PACIFIC	07	74	36
NIGHT RIDE (RANDOM THOUGHTS)	02	44	30
OH TO BE A STEWARD	06	52	56
ONCE AGAIN WITH CONDUCTOR MOEDINGER	12	76	22
ONE DAY IN MAY ON CNJ	08	69	42
OUR TRAIN WAS SNOWBOUND	03	52	13
OUTSIDERS (NEW ZEALAND) VIEW OF AMTRAK	03	76	43
OVERLAND DIARY 1869	05	69	51
PANAMA EXPRESS MY FINEST TRAIN TRIP	04	50	36
PAY CAR IT WAS MORE THAN JUST PAY	12	74	44
PIERSON MI WRECK 8-15-00 GR&I	01	74	32
PRR NEW YORK DIVISION FIREMEN	03	77	22
PRR K4 VS J-1 FROM THE CAB 1931	10	68	41
PRR K4'S AT 94.7 MPH	05	73	46
PULLMAN CONDUCTOR BILL MUEDINGER	05	72	38
PULLMAN CONDUCTOR DIARY 1 MILLION MILES+	02	70	41
PULLMAN CONDUCTOR DIARY TROOP TRAVEL/JET	03	70	40
PULLMAN CONDUCTOR LIFE NOT ALL BAD	10	72	38
RAILROAD PRESIDENTS	11	60	24
RAILROAD REFLECTIONS IN & OUT OF UNIFORM	09	68	47
RAILROADS OF MY FATHERS YOUTH	05	82	24
REAR END BRAKEMAN D&RGW	12	40	5
RECOLLECTING OF AN OMAHA BRASS POUNDER	06	82	22
RIDE A CAB SP 4460 SERIES	11	44	6
RIDE WITH KINGS 4-6-0 RIDE	06	69	44
ROAD FORMAN HIS DAY	07	72	26
ROUNDHOUSE FOREMAN MY FIRST NIGHT	02	70	25
SEATTLE NIGHTS	12	85	37
SERVICEMANS RAILROAD NOTES AND PHOTOS	11	45	28

GENERAL RAILROADING

GENERAL RAILROADING NON-FICTION

Title	M	Y	P
SIERRA NEVADA STRANDED CITY SAN FRAN SP	01	53	50
SO THIS IS STEAM	06	62	18
STEAM AN AUSTRALIAN ENGINEERS ESTIMATE	05	66	18
STUDENT DAZE ON THE WESTERN	10	85	32
SURPRISE RAILROAD TESTS	03	80	45
TANK-TOWN TUTOR STATION MASTER	06	52	55
THAT DEPOT AND ME	01	65	38
THIRTY YEARS OF TRAIN WATCHING THOUGHTS	11	70	20
THIS CAN'T BE MILLBORN NJ	09	78	28
THREE POWER LOCOMOTIVES OF DL&W	07	71	44
THREE TALES OF TRAIN TRAVEL	04	69	31
THRILLS OF THE CAB NYC 1949	05	84	42
TIME FOR REMEMBERING 100T CONTOLLED FURY	02	68	48
TO HELL (MUCKRAKING) IN A DAYCOACH	06	68	48
TORONTO TO MONTREAL ON 15 TRAINS	12	79	44
TRACKSIDE: ONE MANS GENESIS	06	78	44
TRAINMASTER REFLECTIONS CLYDE CARLEY	02	58	40
TRAVEL VIGNETTES	05	51	17
TRAVELING SALESMAN DIARY	11	41	28
TRAVELING SALESMEN ON GEORGIA ROAD	05	42	42
TRAVELING SHOWS - BY RAIL	08	44	6
TREVITHICK LOCOMOTIVES OF EARLY 1800'S	07	63	40
TURBO TRAIN TRIP TRAIN 153	10	76	42
TWELVE HOURS WITH NYC #6009	11	50	15
UP ENGINEER JIM MACMAHON	10	50	41
UP FAN TRIP LOCOMOTIVE #8444	01	70	41
USA RAILPASS I WAS RELUCTANT TO LEAVE #7	12	76	40
USA RAILPASS LESS THAN 2 CENTS PER MILE	11	76	40
VALEDICTORY FOR CN 4-8-4 #6218	04	72	19
VERDI VILLIANS TRAIN ROBBERY	04	58	54
WELLS FARGO ROBBERY VERDI NEVADA 11/1870	04	58	54
WHILE THE KEY WAS DISAPPEARING-TELEGRAPH	06	75	44
WORKING BN'S CHICAGO FUNNEL	10	81	40
WRECKMASTERS MOON PRR	10	82	22
YES, I DID WANT TO RUN A RAILROAD	07	78	22

GENERAL RAILROADING FICTION

Title	M	Y	P
MEMOIRS OF ENGINE 38 (FANTASY)	07	46	24
RAILROAD PLANS FOR TOMORROW	09	44	8
RAILROADS OF MY STATE COUNT SHOTTSKI	07	43	6

GENERAL RAILROADING

Title	M	Y	P
0-4-4-0 IN/OUTSIDE FRAMED LOCOS MEXICO	06	63	23
112 MPH BEHIND A BRITISH 4-6-2	10	60	20
1940 REVISITED PHOTO ESSAY	11	60	29
1953 SPEED SURVEY	05	54	22
1954 SPEED SURVEY	05	55	16
1956 SPEED SURVEY 20 YEARS OF SPEED	05	57	40
1959 SPEED SURVEY THE FRENCH DID IT	05	60	18
1960 SPEED SURVEY LOOK AT CENTRAL GO	06	61	20
1961 SPEED SURVEY NYC STILL ON TOP	06	62	40
1962 SPEED SURVEY MORE AT 65 OR BETTER	06	63	38
1963 SPEED SURVEY FEWER PASS FASTER FRT	06	64	36
1966 SPEED SURVEY PASS SLOWING DOWN	05	67	32
1970 SPEED SURVEY ON EVE OF RAILPAX	06	71	40
1972 SPEED SURVEY FEW POSITIVE ACHIEVEME	07	73	40
1972.MOTIVE POWER 25TH BEG BORROW OR BUY	09	73	20
1977 MOTIVE POWER SURVEY #29	10	77	42
1978 MOTIVE POWER SURVEY 30TH ANNUAL	11	78	30
1979 MOTIVE POWER SURVEY 31ST UNTANGLE	11	79	23
1981 MOTIVE POWER SURVEY 33RD DIV/0 MILE	11	81	50
1982 MOTIVE POWER SURVEY #34 AMER LOCOS	10	82	40
1983 MOTIVE POWER SURVEY 35TH	11	83	47
1985 MOTIVE POWER SURVEY 37TH	10	85	24
2-10-4 TO REVELSTOKE CP #5927	09	50	16
2-8-2 FOR SALE - NO SALE USA	09	82	37
2-8-8-2 VS. 2-8+8-2 AND ALL THAT	05	82	3
20TH CENTURY LTD TALES OF CENTURY NYC	05	54	16
25 YEARS OF TRAINS MAGAZINE	11	65	20
4-4-0'S WEREN'T ALL AT THE FAIR	09	77	42
50 YEARS OF FAN TRIPS MASS BAY RAILFANS	02	85	44
6000 MILE RAILFAN TOUR OF 1938	08	80	28
8 HOURS AT BEREA OHIO TOWER	10	57	16
86 MPH BEHIND 4-4-4-4 B&O	09	64	24
999 MILES ON THE ERIE	03	46	10
A HISTORY OF CONTAINERIZATION	06	60	37
A VERY SPECIAL SPECIAL NRHS TRIP 7-19-59	12	60	33
AB BRAKE VALVE OPERATION	05	50	44
ABANDONED RAILROADS A TREND?	02	67	8
ABC'S OF THE RDC	05	55	39
ABE LINCOLN & AMERICAN RAILROADS	06	41	21
ACL & ROLLER BEARINGS	02	82	48
AEROTRAIN HERE COMES TOMORROW	09	55	46
AEROTRAIN ON ATSF	06	56	42
AFRICAN RAILROADS (CONGO-OCEAN)	01	44	10
AIR BRAKES BRAKE LOAD TO TARE RATIO	12	75	48
AIR BRAKES IMPORTANCE OF BEING ABLE STOP	10	75	44
AIR BRAKES POST ZEPHYR BRAKING	01	76	40
AIR VERSUS TRAIN TRAVEL	10	50	16
AIRLINES WILL NOT RUIN RR PASSENGER BUS.	06	46	33
ALBUM OF MEMORIES--ROBERT HANFT	11	74	22
ALCO IN WAR BONNET ATSF	03	71	19
ALCO? BALDWIN? LIMA? YES!	10	85	22
ALCOS BID TO BE THE BEST	06	75	22
ALF LANDON TRAIN STOMPING	11	84	44
ALL ABOARD MIXED EMOTIONS ABOUT BOARDING	02	67	28
ALL AMERICAN RAILROAD THIS IS WAY TO RUN	12	85	28

STEPHANS' RAILROAD DIRECTORY

GENERAL RAILROADING

Title	M	Y	P
ALTOONA AT NIGHT PHOTO ESSAY	04	48	10
AMERICA RAILROAD - LAND OF WONDERS	06	83	20
AMERICAN RAILFAN IN HINDUSTAN	02	84	48
AMERICAN RAILROADING 1940-49	11	50	6
AMERICAN RAILWAY PROGRESS EXPOSITION	01	64	44
AMERICAN SHORT LINE RAILROAD ASSOCIATION	09	46	28
AMERICAN STEAM IN FRANCE	10	70	36
AMERICAS FIRST TRANSCONTINENTAL PAN	01	54	56
AMERICAS UNREMARKED INN KEEPERS-THE RRS	10	65	26
AMTRACK CRITIQUE:DELIVER ME BY NIGHT OWL	03	81	31
AMTRAK 1190 CARS	12	71	16
AMTRAK 6623 MILES 142 HRS 10 MINUTES	12	73	22
AMTRAK APPROACHES A 3 WAY STUB SWITCH	04	72	14
AMTRAK CRITIQUE:NO WAY TO TREAT A BOMB	03	81	32
AMTRAK EAST	07	74	28
AMTRAK FIRST CLASS	08	83	16
AMTRAK FROM ZEPHYR TO VIA	03	82	40
AMTRAK QUESTIONS & ANSWERS	08	71	10
AMTRAK SAMPLER, NOTES ON 17,451 MILES	11	72	20
AMTRAK SOUTH	07	74	32
AMTRAK TIMETABLE OF 11-14-71	01	72	12
AMTRAK: HOW MUCH MONEY IS ENOUGH?	12	74	12
AMTRAKING WEST IN SEARCH OF FLYING SCOTS	01	72	36
AMTRAKS LOCOMOTIVE & ROLLING STOCK ACQUI	07	73	14
ANYTHING CAN HAPPEN ON A FAN TRIP	03	48	40
APPLE TRAFFIC ON THE GN	01	41	35
ARE THESE PEOPLE RAIL EMBALMERS/ENTHUSIA	09	69	44
ARIZONA COPPER HAULERS	07	56	26
ARMY NAVY GAME SPECIAL TRAINS	01	53	16
ARTIST AND THE RAILROAD PHOTO ESSAY	05	59	27
ARTISTS EXCURSION NOTES 1859	12	40	24
ASIAN RAIL TRENDS IN CAPSULE	02	65	4
ASSISTANT DIVISION ENGINEER PC	04	72	20
ATSF-SP MERGER IN AGAIN	12	83	8
AUTOMATIC TRAIN YARDS	03	61	22
AUTOTRAIN PIGGYBACK AUTOS & PEOPLE	02	62	38
AUTOTRAIN SELLS SOMETHING PEOPLE WANT	01	73	22
AXIS RAIL TRANSPORTATION	02	44	4
B&O COMES BACK	02	64	23
B&O TRANSPORTATION MUSEUM	06	54	24
BACKWARDS OIL TRAIN ON B&O	04	83	42
BALDWIN-LIMA HAMILTON MERGER	10	50	6
BANKRUPCY & REORGANIZATION OF RR ANAL	02	73	26
BATTLE CREEK YARD BATTLE CREEK MI GTW	01	63	18
BATTLING BLIZZARDS ON THE GN	02	73	20
BAYVIEW TOWER HAMILTON ONTARIO	05	48	12
BEAR & THE BIG HOOK WILDLIFE VS ALASKA R	04	67	23
BED FOR THE COACH PASSENGER	08	53	6
BEFORE AND AFTER AMTRAK PHOTO ESSAY	07	71	12
BELLEFONTAIE PROFILE OF A RR TOWN PHOTOS	07	63	29
BELOW THE MASON & DIXON LINE	08	42	32
BEST TRAIN WATCHING SEAT B&M READING MAS	01	85	44
BETHLEHEM PAS 6 RAILROADS	09	43	27
BICYCLING BY RAIL	08	49	52
BIG BLUE TRAIN (SOUTH AFRICA)	03	70	18
BIG ENGINE THAT DIDN'T UP #8444	02	76	44
BIG FIVE RAILROADS 1985	09	85	9
BILL WITBECKS SOUTH PHOTOS LITTLE LOCOS	04	75	22
BIRTHPLACE OF STEAM BRITIAN	06	59	24
BIRTHPLACE OF STEAM CHANNEL CROSSING	08	59	24
BIRTHPLACE OF STEAM HITLERS 2-10-0'S	09	59	18
BIRTHPLACE OF STEAM LONDON AT 96 MPH	07	59	24
BIRTHPLACE OF STEAM MUSSOLINIS STATION	09	59	18
BLACK RR EMPLOYEES: OPPORTUNITY & DISCRI	08	73	20
BLAIRSVILLE & INDIANA TOURIST RAILROAD	01	77	52
BN LAND GRANT THAT BLEW UP MT ST HELEN'S	08	80	17
BOAT TRAIN SOUTH AFRICAN STEAM STYLE	06	81	28
BOMBARDIER INC--RAIL NEWS	05	82	15
BOOKS THE TEN BEST RAILROAD BOOKS	12	56	53
BOOMER - INTINERARY RAILROADERS	10	42	43
BOSS OF FREIGHT CAR FLEET ARTHUR GASS	02	52	20
BRITISH INTER-CITY #125 SPEED RECORD	10	79	45
BRITISH RAIL HISTORY PHOTOS	12	72	18
BRITISH RAILWAYS IN WARTIME	05	46	32
BRITISH SCHOOL BOYS VIEW OF NYNH&H	06	42	46
BRITISH SIGNALS & WHY THEY LOOK THAT WAY	08	55	44
BRITISH SPEED TRIALS 100 MPH+	11	49	16
BROWN BROTHERS HARRIMAN AND CO SPECIAL	09	69	47
BUDD RAPID TRANSIT CARS	10	60	8
BUFFALO NY TRAIN WATCHING	02	76	29
BULLET TRAIN FROM JAPAN REVISITED	10	73	38
BULLETINS FROM OLD ROUNDHOUSE WALLS	06	71	38
BURLINGTON ZEPHYRS	09	52	32
BUSINESS CAR TRIP ON CB&Q	03	48	21
BUSY SWITCH REPLACEMENT NYC	06	45	6
BUTTE ANACONDA & PACIFIC ELECTRIFICATION	07	63	16
BY RAIL TO GUATEMALA	04	43	30
C&O PUTS COAL ON ROLLER BEARINGS	02	47	6
CABLE HELPERS FOR LOCOMOTIVES	06	56	51
CALIF ZEPHYR HER SPIRIT WILL NEVER DIE	01	73	18
CALIFORNIA IN WINTER PHOTO ESSAY	02	74	18
CALIFORNIA PASSENGER RECONFIGURATION	04	83	16
CALLING ALL CANDIDATES POLITICAL TRAINS	03	60	24
CAN EUROPES RAIL MAGIC BE IMPORTED?	07	74	48
CAN RAIL LABOR BE RESPONSIBLE?	11	83	5
CANADA 67-TRAINS VS CARS & JETS	08	66	16
CANADIAN BROAD GAUGE	05	41	35
CANADIAN NATIONAL NEW LINE	02	44	38
CANDIDATES TRAVEL BY RAIL FORD-BUCKLEY	01	77	14
CAR FERRIES AN ENDANGERED SPECIES	01	75	42
CAR LEASING GATX NATX SHPX UTLX AND ALL	10	66	38
CAR RETARDERS IN TRAIN YARDS	03	43	25
CARNIVAL TRAINS	10	54	56
CAROLINA INCIDENT 4%+ GRADES	12	42	16
CASE FOR AMERICAN STEAM LOCOMOTIVES	08	67	22
CASE FOR STEAM TOURIST RAILROADS	04	68	40
CASE FOR THE FRENCH STEAM LOCOMOTIVE	12	66	23
CASE FOR THE PASSENGER VEEP	12	53	15
CASE OF RAILWAY MANIA IN US	05	77	22
CASE OF THE CALIFORNIA K4	12	83	58

GENERAL RAILROADING

	M	Y	P
CASEY JONES A BRAVE ENGINEER	12	54	51
CASEY JONES DIED 50 YEARS AGO	04	50	48
CASEY JONES MONUMENT	10	47	56
CATENARY MAINTENANCE NH	11	52	50
CEDAR HILL YARD NEW HAVEN CONN NH	10	48	12
CENSUS OF AMERICAN LOCOMOTIVES	11	82	40
CENTRAL STATES DISPATCH SERVICE	03	52	26
CENTRAL VERMONT ROCKET	02	83	14
CHANGE AT THE JUNCTION OTTAWA JCT KS	07	67	44
CHESSIE CAT	03	41	22
CHICAGO KALEIDOSCOPE PHOTO ESSAY	08	76	48
CHICAGO RAILROAD CAPITAL OF THE WORLD	08	48	14
CHICAGO THE NATIONS XROADS 21ST ST TOWER	12	50	12
CHICAGO'S STATIONS GATES TO EVERYWHERE	08	48	22
CIMARRON BRIDGE RI ENGINEERING FEAT	02	53	48
CINCINNATI CURIOSITIES IN ROLLING STOCK	12	67	44
CINCINNATIAN THE DAY IT STOPPED	01	73	27
CIRCUS MOVES BY RAIL	08	45	28
CIRCUS SHOW TRAIN ROYAL AMEARICAN SHOWS	04	65	34
CIRCUS TRAINS SPECIAL CARS GALORE	07	46	42
CITY OF MILWAUKEE 400 SCHEDULE C&NW	03	56	24
CITY OF NEW ORLEANS SPEED E9 OF IC	03	66	52
CITY OF THE IRON HORSE BIRMINGHAM AL	05	45	6
CIVIL WAR RAILROADS	01	56	22
CLASSIFICATION SIGNALS DISCONTINUED	10	47	59
CLEAN UP THE YARD S YARD PROGRAM	06	53	50
CLOCK RUNNING DOWN FOR RAIL COMPUTERS?	10	83	30
COAL TRAFFIC GOING GOING GONE?	10	67	37
COAST TO COAST ON AN IRON OCEAN	08	71	36
COAST TO COAST ON PANAMA RAILROAD	01	50	44
COASTING DOWN THE ANDES	12	40	35
COLORADO RAILROADS	04	41	5
COLORADO'S UNMARKED TESTIMONIAL TO RRING	09	81	44
COMES THE STREAMLINED DAWN	05	46	5
COMMON CARRIER TEST TRACKS	01	72	26
COMMUTER SERVICE ECONOMICS	04	52	24
COMPUTERS & RAILROADS HOW THEY RELATE?	09	67	42
COMPUTERS ON THE SOUTHERN	03	69	16
CONGRESS ON CONRAIL	11	81	23
CONNECTICUT TRAIN WATCHING	03	73	42
CONQUEST OF THE ROCKIES	10	47	42
CONRAIL DID BETTER THAN HITLER HUNTERS	02	80	6
CONRAIL THE OTHER BIG FIASCO	02	80	5
CONTROLS IN CAB OF STEAM LOCOMOTIVES	11	44	24
COOKES & CONSOLIDATIONS AMONG CUBAN CANE	05	83	26
CORRIDOR YOU SELDOM SEE A INSIDE OUT	03	85	41
COUPLERS BRAGGING OR BASHFULNESS	01	70	48
CRANE ON CONRAIL	07	81	14
CRIPPLE CREEK COLORADO SHORT LINE	02	41	34
CROSSWORD PUZZLE 100 PER-CENT BONA FIDE	04	84	49
CROSSWORD PUZZLE ACROSTIC	09	82	38
CROSSWORD PUZZLE DEVILISHLY DIFFICULT	12	75	47
CROSSWORD PUZZLE DIVISION POINTS	11	81	33
CROSSWORD PUZZLE ESPEE EXOTICA	04	85	49
CROSSWORD PUZZLE OTTOMWA STA & OTHERS	12	77	31

	M	Y	P
CROSSWORD PUZZLE PENNZY PUNDIT	06	79	39
CROSSWORD PUZZLE RAILROAD-IT'S EASY	12	74	43
CROSSWORD PUZZLE TOUGH TRAIN	01	73	39
CROSSWORD PUZZLE TOUGHER TRAIN	11	73	35
CROSSWORD PUZZLE TOUGHER YET TRAIN	04	74	35
CROSSWORD PUZZLE VANISHED VARNISH	11	80	49
CULPRIT WAS A WATER SCOOP = WRECK	07	79	50
CUMBERLAND MO. NARROWS	11	44	36
DARJEELING HIMALAYAN TRAINS	01	46	42
DAVIN MOFFATS DREAM COMES TRUE	01	42	28
DAY AT CANTON S.D. PHOTO STORY	05	45	14
DAY AT GENEVA ILL	08	44	30
DECLINE & DECAY OF RAILWAY EXPRESS	07	79	22
DEEP IN DIXIE	02	52	48
DELIVERING EMD'S LOCOMOTIVES	11	80	50
DENVER AT DAWN--CHICAGO AT DUSK	09	52	27
DENVER RAILFAN	03	41	24
DEPARTED RIVER QUEENS	01	84	47
DEREGULATION REALLY REREGULATION	01	80	22
DIESEL DIETS WHAT YOU SHOULD KNOW	05	73	36
DIESEL FORM D TO L MAGNETS & MAINTENANCE	07	79	44
DIESEL IN THE ROCKIES	09	42	26
DIESELIZATION ON MULLET ROAD A&EC	01	47	64
DIESELS ON THE PENNSYLVANIA	03	47	4
DIFFERENCE OF DECADES PHOTO ESSAY	08	82	31
DIM CARS ON PRR	07	82	30
DISPATCHER RAILROADS TRAFFIC COP	02	48	18
DISPATCHERS-SUMMIT SECOND TRICK	09	51	14
DIVERSIFICATION OF RAILROADS	02	64	28
DO SOME SHORT LINES MAKE TOO MUCH MONEY?	02	53	50
DOES BRITAIN NEED A NATIONAL RAILWAY?	08	83	28
DON'T SELL RAILROADS SHORT- IMPROVEMENTS	04	45	34
DON'T SELL THE SHORTLINES SHORT	01	49	26
DORNER STAYS OPEN	03	84	24
DOUBLE TRACK TRAINS TRACK GA 18' 8 1/2"	03	76	28
DOWN IN MAINE - TWO FOOTERS	02	43	28
DREAMS OF RAILROADS DASHED BY ICC	03	45	26
DRINKING ON THE RAILS: THE SOLUTION	07	83	6
DRIVING WHEEL PHOTO QUIZ	01	80	20
DRUNK DRIVING RAILROAD STYLE	06	83	6
DUTCH RAILROADS DURING THE WAR	12	46	27
EARLY DAYS OF DIESELDOM	05	62	24
EARLY DAYS ON THE SOO	02	50	51
EAST TO WEST AND BACK S 4501-AMTRAK-CZ	05	73	22
EASTBAY RAILROADING (CALIFORNIA)	08	41	44
ECONOMIC ANALYSIS OF THE RAILROADS	03	70	23
ED BEWLEYS PHOTOGRAPHS	03	42	8
EDISON: A RAILROAD MAN	03	47	44
EDWIN HAWLEY RAILROAD CONGLOMERATE	09	52	52
EISENHOWERS INAUGURATION	04	53	16
ELECTRICS IN THE CASCADES MILW PHOTO ESS	07	73	29
ELIZABETH NJ SEE THE TRAINS OF NY CITY	05	49	46
EMD AN INSTANT HISTORY	09	72	56
EMD PHOTO QUIZ	09	72	44
EMPIRE BUILDER AT MARIAS PASS	05	44	10

STEPHANS_RAILROAD_DIRECTORY

GENERAL RAILROADING

	M	Y	P
EMPIRE STATE EXPRESS SPEED RUN 1939	05	65	24
ENGINE CHANGE IN CITIES POLICY	05	83	20
ENGINEER EVANGELIST DAVID J FANT	12	85	46
ENGINEER-RIGHT HAND MAN IN THE CAB	05	48	40
ENGLEWOOD UNION STATION CHICAGO ILL	02	46	31
ENOLA YARD ENOLA PA PRR 12000 CARS A DAY	09	53	22
EQUIPMENT IDENTIFICATION BY TRUCKS QUIZ	04	64	49
EQUIPMENT THRUSTS WHAT ARE THEY	08	49	45
ERIE RAILROADS WITH RADIOS	10	50	42
ESCAPE BY TRAIN	10	53	62
EUROPEAN PASSENGER CAR TRENDS	09	64	6
EVOLUTION OF THE RAILROAD 1800	03	51	41
EXCESSIVE SPEED + CURVE = WRECK NYC J3	04	85	50
EXPO 74 RAILROAD EXHIBITS SPOKANE WA	08	74	17
EXTRA 454 SOUTH S	09	64	47
FA PHOTO ESSAY	07	75	22
FAIRTRAN- 2 F UNITS RESURRECTED	03	84	36
FALLEN FLAGS AKRON CANTON & YOUNGSTOWN	05	74	45
FALLEN FLAGS ALTON RAILROAD	04	74	28
FALLEN FLAGS ANN ARBOR	01	84	38
FALLEN FLAGS ATLANTA BIRMINGHAM & COAST	06	74	24
FALLEN FLAGS ATLANTIC COAST LINE	04	74	25
FALLEN FLAGS B&O	04	74	27
FALLEN FLAGS BURLINGTON RTE (CB&Q)	04	74	23
FALLEN FLAGS C&O	04	74	24
FALLEN FLAGS CENTRAL NEW JERSEY	01	84	36
FALLEN FLAGS CENTRAL OF GEORGIA	04	74	22
FALLEN FLAGS CHARLESTON & W CAROLINA	06	74	22
FALLEN FLAGS CHICAGO & EATERN ILLINOIS	05	74	41
FALLEN FLAGS CHICAGO GREAT WESTERN	06	74	21
FALLEN FLAGS CI&L (MONON)	04	74	26
FALLEN FLAGS CLINCHFIELD	01	84	43
FALLEN FLAGS COLUMBUS & GREENVILLE	06	74	25
FALLEN FLAGS DENVER & SALT LAKE	04	74	26
FALLEN FLAGS DETROIT TOLEDO & IRONTON	01	84	38
FALLEN FLAGS DETROIT TOLEDO SHORE LINE	01	84	38
FALLEN FLAGS DSS&A	04	74	28
FALLEN FLAGS ERIE	06	74	23
FALLEN FLAGS ERIE	01	84	35
FALLEN FLAGS FRISCO	01	84	45
FALLEN FLAGS GEORGIA & FLORIDA	05	74	43
FALLEN FLAGS GEORGIA & WEST POINT	01	84	41
FALLEN FLAGS GREAT NORTHERN	05	74	42
FALLEN FLAGS GULF MOBILE & OHIO	06	74	23
FALLEN FLAGS ILLINOIS CENTRAL	05	74	46
FALLEN FLAGS ILLINOIS TERMINAL	01	84	39
FALLEN FLAGS KANSAS OKLAHOMA & GULF	05	74	41
FALLEN FLAGS LACKAWANNA	04	74	25
FALLEN FLAGS LEHIGH & HUDSON RIVER	01	84	35
FALLEN FLAGS LEHIGH & NEW ENGLAND	04	74	26
FALLEN FLAGS LEHIGH VALLEY	01	84	35
FALLEN FLAGS LITCHFIELD & MADISON	05	74	43
FALLEN FLAGS LONG ISLAND	06	74	25
FALLEN FLAGS LOUISVILLE & NASHVILLE	01	84	42
FALLEN FLAGS MINN NORTHFIELD & SOUTHERN	01	84	40
FALLEN FLAGS MINNEAPOLIS & ST PAUL	04	74	20
FALLEN FLAGS MISSISSIPPI CENTRAL	06	74	26
FALLEN FLAGS NC&SL	04	74	28
FALLEN FLAGS NEW YORK ONTARIO & WESTERN	06	74	26
FALLEN FLAGS NICKEL PLATE (NYC&SL)	04	74	27
FALLEN FLAGS NORFOLK SOUTHERN	05	74	44
FALLEN FLAGS NORTHERN ALBERTA RAILWAY	01	84	39
FALLEN FLAGS NORTHERN PACIFIC	04	74	24
FALLEN FLAGS NYC	05	74	42
FALLEN FLAGS NYNH&H	06	74	24
FALLEN FLAGS PENN CENTRAL	01	84	36
FALLEN FLAGS PENN-READING SEASHORE LINE	01	84	38
FALLEN FLAGS PERE MARQUETTE	06	74	21
FALLEN FLAGS PITTSBURG & WEST VIRGINIA	05	74	41
FALLEN FLAGS PRR	04	74	23
FALLEN FLAGS QUANAH ACME & PACIFIC	01	84	44
FALLEN FLAGS READING	01	84	37
FALLEN FLAGS ROCK ISLAND	01	84	45
FALLEN FLAGS RUTLAND RAILROAD	06	74	22
FALLEN FLAGS SAVANNAH & ATLANTA	06	74	20
FALLEN FLAGS SEABOARD AIR LINE	05	74	44
FALLEN FLAGS SEABOARD COAST LINE	01	84	42
FALLEN FLAGS SPOKANE INTERNATIONAL	06	74	19
FALLEN FLAGS SPOKANE PORTLAND & SEATTLE	05	74	46
FALLEN FLAGS ST LOUIS SOUTHWESTERN CBELT	05	74	45
FALLEN FLAGS TENNESSEE CENTRAL	06	74	20
FALLEN FLAGS TEXAS & PACIFIC	06	74	19
FALLEN FLAGS TEXAS PACIFIC & WESTERN	01	84	40
FALLEN FLAGS VIRGINIAN	04	74	22
FALLEN FLAGS WABASH	04	74	20
FALLEN FLAGS WESTERN MARYLAND	05	74	46
FALLEN FLAGS WESTERN PACIFIC	01	84	45
FALLEN FLAGS WHEELING & LAKE ERIE	06	74	19
FALLS CREEK PA AREA OF RAILROAD THRILLS	01	48	39
FAREWELL TO GEORGIA MIXED TRAINS	08	83	14
FAVORITE LOCO PHOTOS OF JOHN B ALLEN	04	81	34
FEATHERBED, AGAIN OR YET	01	84	5
FIRELESS STRIPED ELEPHANT WITH 6 LEGS	02	83	39
FIREMEN-FEED AN ELEPHANT AT 60 MPH	11	59	37
FIRST ENCOUNTER WITH CONRAIL ENOLA YARD	03	79	49
FIRST FA'S THEN SURPRISE HOPEWELL JCT NY	07	79	19
FIRST RAILFAN TRIP IN USA 8-24-34	09	62	29
FITTING FINISH AT PULLMAN	08	81	2
FITZPATRICK YARD RUSSELL KY C&O	03	61	18
FLOATING BRIDGE "PELICAN" IC	06	51	14
FLOOD NEAR PERORIA ILL, ROCK ISLAND	08	43	42
FLYING ABDICATION	11	72	14
FM & VHF RADIO COMMUNICATION	01	73	37
FM DIESEL STATIONARY POWER PLANTS	02	71	15
FREIGHT CAR OWNERSHIP & PURCHASE	12	44	27
FREIGHT ON THE SEABOARD AIR LINE	05	63	20
FREIGHTLINERS THEIR DEFENSE	01	75	54
FUEL SUPPLY INDICATES RR ELECTRIFICATION	04	48	4
FUNERAL TRAIN OF DWIGHT D EISENHOWER	06	69	14
FUNERAL TRAIN OF ROBERT F KENNEDY	08	68	10

GENERAL RAILROADING

	M	Y	P
FUNERAL TRAIN OF WILLIAM G HARDING	07	62	32
FUNERAL TRAIN OF WINSTON CHURCHILL	05	65	8
GANDY DANCING IN KAMKI TACHO JAPAN	08	79	21
GAS ELECTRIC OF MR STRANG	05	79	22
GATHERING OF IRON HORSES SACRAMENTO CAL	08	81	16
GG1 AT CHERRY HILL PA PC	01	75	12
GLAMOR GIRL UP CHALLENGER SERVICE	08	41	28
GM GOES TO GREENBRIER A REPEATS PULLMAN	04	73	20
GM&O PHOTO STUDY	09	82	31
GO ONE WAY RETURN ANOTHER RAIL TRIPS	04	53	59
GOLDEN AGE OF RAILROAD CONSTRUCTION	02	49	40
GOLDEN AGE OF WESTERN RAILROADING PHOTOS	12	53	16
GRADE CROSIING COLLISION PHOTO ESSAY	02	75	14
GREAT CRASH AT CRUSH PLANNED WRECK	09	77	30
GREAT DYNAMOMETER TEST LOCO S #610	02	78	33
GREAT UNEXPECTED 24 HOUR FAN TRIP	09	82	50
GREAT WORK OF THE OVERLAND ROUTE	05	69	42
GRIF TELLERS TRAINS	12	79	26
GROSS TON/MILES PER TRAIN/HOUR ANALYSIS	04	70	37
GROUCHO, HARDO & RIO CHICO RR (MOVIE)	05	41	45
HAPPY BIRTHDAY EMMA 2-6-0 WARD KIMBALL	02	82	42
HARRIMAN LEGACY	04	79	3
HARRISBURG PA RAIL CENTER	12	49	11
HE BUILT HIS OWN RAILROAD	07	52	57
HE SOLD STREAMLINING OTTO KUHLER	07	52	12
HE STYLES STREAMLINERS RAY LOWERY	12	48	16
HENRY FORD & HIS ELECTRIC LOCOMOTIVE	09	76	22
HIGH SPEED WATER SCOOPS	04	45	6
HIGH VIEW TUNNEL VIEWS D&W 1954	02	76	50
HILL TOPPER REQUIEM FOR A LIGHTWEIGHT A	04	80	20
HITLERS SUPER RAILWAY	08	84	38
HORSE & FLAT CAR? RUN YOUR OWN RAILROAD	06	84	46
HORSESHOE CURVE	05	52	28
HOW BIG WAS BIG IN RAILROAD WORLD	02	79	44
HOW MANY CLASS 1 RAILROADS IN 1982?	02	82	3
HOW SUPER ARE SUPERLINERS?	05	79	14
HOW TO ARGUE FOR THE RAILS	10	60	22
HOW TO MAKE PASSENGER SERVICE WELL	04	59	14
HOW TO OPERATE A FAN TRIP	05	55	27
HOW TO REPLACE A RAILWAY CARTOON FEATURE	05	65	26
HOW TO RETIRE A STEAM LOCOMOTIVE	01	53	19
HOW TO RUN A RR IN THE NORTHEAST	08	74	20
HOW TO SPONSOR A STREAMLINER	11	79	30
HOW TO START A SHAY PHOTO ESSAY	08	67	44
HOW TO TOTE 600 TONS SCHNABEL FLAT CAR	07	73	20
HOW TO USE OPTIONAL ROUTES	04	47	19
HUB OF WASHINGTON TERMINAL IVY CITY ENG	04	50	44
I DON'T LIKE SHORT LINES -HOWEVER----	02	59	48
I LIKE TRAINS	01	41	29
I LIKE TRAINS (STILL!) AL KALMBACH	11	60	56
I STILL LIKE TRAINS AL KALMBACH	08	54	14
I'VE BEEN RIDING THE PULLMANS	05	44	6
ICC AUTHORIZATION OF NEW RR CONSTRUCTION	05	45	24
ICC EVALUATION BY RALPH NADER	11	70	44
ICC ITS COST TO YOU AND ME	10	72	24

	M	Y	P
ICED AND AIRLESS AT CASCADE SUMMIT	07	82	32
ICG-ESPEE JUST A BIG LIONEL TRAIN SET	12	84	36
IF I RAN PASSENGER TRAINS	02	58	19
ILLINOIS EXCURSION PHOTO STORY	11	44	26
IMPACT OF RAILROADS ON US HISTORY	07	76	ALL
IMPERIAL VALLEY FLOOD OF 1906	07	50	44
IMPORTANT BUSINESS BY RAIL	04	53	24
IN THE ARMY NOW - LOCOMOTIVES DRAFTED	09	43	36
INEFFICIENT OPERATIONS A HISTORSY LESSON	03	68	38
INEFFICIENT OPERATIONS NO FRT CAR SHORT	05	68	44
INEFFICIENT OPERATIONS SOL TO PROBLEM	04	68	36
INEFFICIENT OPERATIONS WHY FRT CARS SIT?	02	68	40
INSPECTION & REPAIR OF MOTIVE PWR & CARS	05	42	34
INSPECTION STOPS	01	51	16
INSTANT WHEEL REPAIR-MARION OHIO E	01	44	31
INT FF SERVICE BOSTON-CHICAGO B&M-CV-CN-	08	50	18
INTEGRAL TRAIN CONCEPT	01	68	20
INTERLINE TICKETS AND HOW THEY WORK	03	48	14
INTERSTATE COMMERCE COMMISS IT MUST GO!	01	67	36
INTERSTATE RAILROAD SYSTEM STRACNET	04	82	14
INVASION RAILROADS	10	44	24
IRON ORE TRAFFIC PRR #2 HAULER	09	62	34
IS IT A CRIME TO BE A RAILROAD?	08	61	20
IS THERE A "BEST" RAILROAD?	09	64	20
IS THIS LINCOLN CHANGING TRAINS?	11	53	50
IT'S DYING WHERE IT ALL BEGAN BRITISH ST	01	66	24
ITS THE PITS -TURNTABLE MISHAPS PHOTOS	04	81	20
JAWN HENRY CRUSHES A CABOOSE	05	58	60
JERSEY CITY TO PITTSBURGH FAST FREIGHTS	06	66	25
JERSEY MEADOWS RAILROAD WORKSHOP EAST	06	51	19
JFK WHAT HE MEANT TO RAILROADING	02	64	49
JITNEY #15 CBELT	09	71	18
JOHN L. LEWIS & THE DIESEL LOCOMOTIVE	12	46	4
JOHNSTOWN PA FLOOD 5-31-1889 "BLACK WALL	03	53	27
JSS STEAM ON THE ZAMBESI	05	66	44
JSS JET SERCH FOR STEAM ENGLAND	01	66	24
JSS NEW SOUTH WALES GARRATT LOCOS	03	66	46
JSS REPUBLIC OF SOUTH AFRICA	02	66	50
JSS RHODESIA RAILWAYS GARRATTS IN CRISIS	04	66	25
JSS STEAM AT NAIROBI AFRICA	06	66	20
JSS STEAM IN FRANCE 141-R MEANS USA	07	66	42
JSS STEAM IN SPAIN UNCOMMON GARRATTS	08	66	32
JSS STEAM ON ISLE OF MANX	09	66	24
JUPITER & 119 ON SINGLE TRACK	05	69	49
KANSAS CITY MO FLOODS 1951	12	51	14
KAUAI ISLAND SUGAR RAILROAD HAWAII	07	44	34
KEDDIE WYE BRIDGE NOTABLE ENGINEER FEAT	03	53	48
KEEP RAILROADS-SELL TRACK TO UNCLE SAM	03	67	35
KEEP THEM ROLLING PHOTO ESSAY	11	46	20
KEEPING THE RAIL LINE OPEN	02	41	21
KEEPING UP WITH VIA	02	80	13
KEN BROWNE INTERVIEW	04	54	19
KENTUCKY DERBY SPECIAL TRAINS AND CARS	05	66	20
KENTUCKY RAILWAY MUSEUM PLEASURES/PITFAL	09	68	40
KNEILING VS USRA	09	75	52

GENERAL RAILROADING

Title	M	Y	P
KUHLER - HE SOLD STREAMLINING	07	52	12
LA DIESELS WHERE THE DOGERS WENT	07	59	16
LA OVER MOUNTAINS TO CITY OF ANGELS	08	59	42
LAKE MICHIGAN CAR FERRIES	09	42	14
LAKE MICHIGAN CAR FERRIES FLOATING RR	08	49	46
LAND BARGE #244 ALCO POWERED	08	81	42
LAPLAND EXPRESS ELECTRIC RAILWAY	11	42	32
LAST LOCO MALLET?	06	81	33
LAST STEAM-A BRIEF ODYSSEY	02	80	20
LETTER TO MODEL RAILROADER	09	82	28
LIKE RAILROADS! BUT INVEST IN THEM?	06	73	27
LIMA ALA ARMCO STEEL	01	73	40
LIMA'S LAST LOCOMOTIVE	11	51	6
LIMA: AN INFORMAL LOOK	06	81	20
LINCOLN AND THE RAILROADS	02	46	40
LINDBERG NEWSREEL TRAIN	10	52	18
LINE SHRINKAGE = SURVIVAL?	01	69	44
LIST OF RR TOOLS 1892 RULE 417 WC	05	44	42
LITTLE ENGINE THAT COULD 2-6-0T JUNG LOC	04	74	32
LIVINGSTON MONTANA RAILROAD TOWN PHOTOS	09	54	27
LNP&W MERGES WITH UP	02	52	10
LOCOMOTIVE FIREMEN	12	45	16
LOCOMOTIVE MESSENGERS DEL. OF NEW LOCOS	01	44	28
LOCOMOTIVE MONARCH! KING GEORGE V	04	73	36
LOCOMOTIVE WEST TEST	04	58	53
LOCOMOTIVES NEW LOOK	06	48	48
LOOK AT THE OFFICIAL GUIDE RECENTLY?	09	63	18
LOVE THOSE DIESELS	04	77	26
LOWREY: HE STYLES STREAMLINERS	12	48	16
LRC EQUIPMENT ON AMTRACK	01	81	18
MAIL PICKUP ON B&M	03	49	50
MAIL-KEY RAILROADERS	04	41	28
MAINE TWO FOOTERS 5 ROADS	07	42	40
MAINLINE HOT SPOT HARRISBURG PA	02	45	16
MAINLINE TO VICTORY	03	42	4
MAJOR TRACKAGE RIGHT LIST	01	79	24
MAKING MONEY IN THE RAILROAD BUSINESS	12	53	27
MAKING OF AN UNDER 30 TRAINWATCHER	11	78	26
MAP OF AMTRAK ROUTES 1975	01	76	52
MAP OF EXPANDED CHESSIE 1976	02	76	2
MARKER LIGHTS SERVE DEFINITE PURPOSE	12	47	52
MARRIED TO A TRAIN	03	50	43
MAXIMIZING TONNAGE ON LINE	01	58	18
MEMO TO MGM MOVIES	12	56	44
MEMORIAL DAY ON C&NW	05	47	35
MERGER MADDENERS QUIZ	02	63	35
MERGERS--WHERE ARE WE	03	64	7
MEXICAN RAILFAN TRIP	04	61	20
MID POWER TRAINS	07	84	18A
MIDCONTINENT MAKES A TRAIN MOVE	03	70	48
MIDNIGHT LOCAL NYC	11	51	24
MILE 435.9 A STATION TOO LATE, TOO FAR	09	85	20
MILE 435.9 TRAINS DEPART AFTER 50+ YEARS	10	85	40
MILEPOST SPEED CHART	01	48	48
MILES OF MEMORIES	12	51	22
MILITARY RAIL SERVICE IN ITALY	02	45	8
MILWAUKEE CITY OF STREAMLINERS	04	48	19
MISS 2,000,000 MILES RR STEWARDESS-NURSE	01	55	25
MIXED TRAIN FAREWELL	04	83	30
MIXED TRAINS ARE UNRELIABLE	11	47	40
MONTREAL W. STATION/THREE ROUT TERMINAL	10	45	28
MONTREALS RAILROADS	08	44	10
MOPAC REPLACES A SWITCH	12	47	51
MORE MILES ON MORE RAILROADS ON BUDGET	04	53	26
MOST CHERISHED STEAM PHOTOS G. BEST	06	72	31
MOTION PICTURE "GREAT LOCOMOTIVE CHASE"	05	56	21
MOTION PICTURE "RAILROADS"	01	49	40
MOTION PICTURE TRAINS LIGHTS CAM ACTION	04	62	34
MOTIVE POWER THAT WON THE WEST	05	69	54
MOVE A CN STEEL WATER TOWER 1934	02	78	52
MOVING TONNAGE BY RAIL	10	80	34
MR PULLMAN REVISITED	01	65	20
MT WASHINGTON COG RAILWAY	07	59	46
N&W SPRING CLEANING	05	41	42
NAKITA KHRUSHCHEV RIDES THE RAILS	12	59	17
NAME THAT TRAIN PHOTO QUIZ	08	59	22
NAMES OF RAILROAD TOWNS	05	52	60
NAMES OF RAILROADS	02	43	6
NARROW GAUGE SUMMER	08	50	12
NARROW GAUGE VACATION D&RGW	05	51	46
NATIONALIZATION NO, STATELIZATION YES	04	85	44
NATIONALIZATION OF BRITISH RAILWAYS	12	47	6
NATIONALIZATION OF RAILROADS IN USA	05	70	5
NATIONALIZED RAILROADS COMPAIRED TO US	08	71	20
NATIONS CROSSROADS-18-TRUNKS AT ST LOUIS	07	42	30

GENERAL RAILROADING

Title	M	Y	P
NERVE GAS TRANSPOT TRAINS	11	70	12
NEW DIESELS - OLD PULLMANS PRIMERA NORTH	02	83	44
NEW DIESELS - OLD PULLMANS SEGUNDA SOUTH	01	83	22
NEW ENGLAND RAILFAN ON B&M	01	41	19
NEW TRAINS MORE SPLASH THAN SPEED	05	56	40
NEW YORK CITY RAILROADING PHOTO ESSAY	06	63	27
NEW YORK-BOSTON WHITE TRAIN EVEN COAL	03	61	37
NEWFOUNDLAND'S NARROW GAUGE	11	44	30
NIGHT DRAGONS AND GEEPS	07	83	26
NORTH PLATTE YARD NORTH PLATTE NE UP	09	50	10
NORTHWEST PASSAGE 1947 VERSION MILW	04	47	6
NP LIKES PASSENGERS	12	59	32
NRHS 50TH ANNIVERSARY FAN TRIP	12	85	22
NUMBER TEN SWITCH	04	48	30
NY TO CHICAGO THE LONG WAY ON 9 ROADS	02	52	36
NYC COMPANY PHOTOGRAPHER PHOTO ESSAY	04	74	36
NYC PASSENGERS HOW FAST?	02	57	19
NYC PRESIDENT A.E. PERLMAN	08	74	42
OBITUARY AL KALMBACH	01	82	3
OBITUARY ALFRED E. PERLMAN NYC	07	83	5
OBITUARY EDWARD HUNGERFORD	09	48	4
OBITUARY F NELSON BLOUNT	01	68	12
OBITUARY FREEMAN HUBBARD	11	81	4
OBITUARY JOHN W. BARIGER	03	77	6
OBITUARY LINN WESTCOTT	11	80	4
OBITUARY LUCIUS BEEBE	04	66	4
OBITUARY ROBERT R YOUNG NYC	04	58	6
OFF THE BEATEN PATH ON HELPERS	05	51	31
OFFICIAL GUIDE TO THE RAILWAYS	04	51	18
OHIO'S ROBOT RAILROAD (MEL)	03	79	22
OLD IRISH MONORAIL SYSTEM 1855-1924	11	44	42
OLD RAILROAD FOLDERS TIMETABLE & MAPS	07	45	20
ON THE READING PHOTO STORY	07	46	38
ON THE VERGE OF VIA	08	78	28
ON WATCHING TRAINS E. DEERFIELD MASS	05	79	28
ONTARIO NORTHERN IMAGE CHANGE	06	66	11
ONTARIO VIA WEEKEND	11	83	30
OPERATING TIMETABLE PREPARATION	08	45	34
OPERATION STREAMLINER CITY OF LA UP	07	51	20
OTIS & COMPANY OFFERS TO BUY PULLMAN CO.	10	45	4
OTTO KUHLER-AN ORIGINAL	10	75	33
OUT WITH THE TRACK GANG	12	77	34
OVER THE ROCKY MOUNTAINS PHOTO FEATURE	02	44	18
OVER THE YEARS ON THE OVERLAND ROUTE	05	69	34
PARADE OF THE IRON HORSE	11	43	18
PASSENGER AGENTS	02	41	12
PASSENGER CARS BUILT BY ACF	04	51	12
PASSENGER CONDUCTORS	12	43	40
PASSENGER SERVICE IT CAN BE PROFITABLE	09	49	26
PASSENGERS-KEEP'EM HAPPY	08	57	44
PASSING THROUGH EUROPE BACK IN BRITAN	05	81	44
PASSING THROUGH EUROPE, FRANCE AND SPAIN	02	81	22
PAUL KIEFER CLASS S 4-8-4'S FATHER NYC	03	84	46
PC GEOGRAPHICAL TRAFFIC MAP	10	73	16
PC TRUSTEES MAP LESS 5000 MILES	04	73	6
PC TRUSTEES SYSTEM MAP	08	72	16
PENNSYLVANIA SPECIAL BROADWAY LTD PRR	03	52	52
PEORIA GATEWAY RAILROADS	07	44	8
PEORIA IL BIGGEST LITTLE RAILROAD CENTER	04	49	12
PETER HELCK RAILROAD ARTIST	10	41	22
PHILADELPHIA PA 6-11-23 FIRE BROAD ST ST	11	43	26
PHLLYS PERSONALITY TRAINS	01	48	14
PHOTO WORKS OF L.C. MCCLURE	11	83E	39
PHOTOS OF L.C. MCCLURE	11	83	39
PIGGYBACK & THE PORTAGER DREAM 1	04	77	44
PIGGYBACK & THE PORTAGER DREAM 2	05	77	44
PIGGYBACK AUTOMOBILE TRAFFIC	12	62	18
PIGGYBACK-MOST REALISTIC APPROACH	05	55	7
PLACE TO WATCH TRAINS-DENVER UNION STN	04	58	28
POOL TRAINS CN&CP	07	43	30
PORT AUTHORITY TRANS-HUDSON SPEED TEST	10	65	20
POSTWAR PARADE GAS TURBINES	11	45	32
POSTWAR PARADE VISTA DOME/ASTRO LINERS	09	45	9
POWER POOLS DIESELS ON DECLINE?	10	85	24
PRELUDE TO PROMONTORY	05	69	31
PRESIDENTAIL ADDRESS PLANES GA DEPOT	01	77	12
PRESIDENTAIL TRAIN TRAVEL NIXON METROLIN	04	70	10
PROMISE OF PROMINTORY	05	69	57
PROMISE OF THE '90'S BALD ERECTING SHOP	02	55	14
PROMISED LAND ALCO GLAMOUR GIRLS	07	83	44
PROPOSED ICG MAP	03	72	13
PROVISO YARD CHICAGO ILL C&NW	10	44	6
PSSING THROUGH EUROPE RHINE NYC&HR 4-4-2	04	81	44
PSSNG THROUGH EUR.:WIDE,STD,NARROW,NRWER	03	81	44
PUSH BUTTONS AT PIG'S EYE YARD MILW	10	59	18
PUZZLE SWITCH ON C&WI	12	45	41
RACE FOR ACE- 614T	04	85	10
RADIO & RAILROADING	07	44	18
RAIL ABANDONMENTS 1917-1940	02	41	50
RAIL EMBARGOES-STOP TRAINS BEFORE DERAIL	10	80	32
RAIL FLOOD PHOTO ESSAY	10	72	16
RAIL INTERESTS IN NEW ORLEANS LA	01	47	58
RAIL PHOTOS NEAR CHICAGO	12	40	27
RAIL TRAFFIC IN POSTWAR GERMANY	12	48	22
RAIL TRIP ON CP 1	08	42	36
RAIL VS TRUCKING COSTS	12	75	45
RAIL-SHAPED LIKE A CAPTIAL I	02	83	20
RAILFAN BRIT RAIL PASS 2523 MILE TRIP	07	75	46
RAILFAN INGENUITY	11	40	19
RAILFAN, INC.	06	59	47
RAILFANS ON PARADE-VANISHED FOR THE DUR.	09	42	21
RAILFANS--WHAT MAKES THEM TICK	03	62	21
RAILROAD ADVENTURE IN MEXICO	03	44	26
RAILROAD ADVERTISING	06	56	22
RAILROAD ART BY READERS	06	62	31
RAILROAD BUILDER HENRY FARNAM RI	12	48	42
RAILROAD BUILDER HENRY FARNUM UPDATE RI	04	49	56
RAILROAD BUILDERS ISAMBARD K. BRUNEL	09	48	40
RAILROAD COMMUTERS-HOW MANY? WHERE?	06	77	42
RAILROAD CONSOLIDATIONS	11	47	6

STEPHANS' RAILROAD DIRECTORY

GENERAL RAILROADING

	M	Y	P
RAILROAD DAY IN 1894	09	49	36
RAILROAD ECONOMIC PROBLEMS IN 1971	06	71	19
RAILROAD FAIR IN CHICAGO	09	49	11
RAILROAD FREIGHT: WHAT IT IS/IT MIGHT BE	08	52	8
RAILROAD GONE FROM OUR TOWN	05	41	18
RAILROAD HEADQUARTERS PHOTO QUIZ	04	73	46
RAILROAD IMAGE AS GOOD AS YOU THINK	12	59	22
RAILROAD ISSUED PAPER MONEY	07	43	43
RAILROAD LEGAL DEPARTMENTS	05	43	31
RAILROAD LICENSE PLATES	07	82	56
RAILROAD MANAGEMENT TRAINING PROGRAMS	04	70	40
RAILROAD MAP OF THE UNITED STATIES	05	51	34
RAILROAD MEN PHOTO ESSAY	11	72	29
RAILROAD MERGERS & CONSOLIDATIONS 1	04	74	20
RAILROAD MERGERS & CONSOLIDATIONS 2	05	74	40
RAILROAD MERGERS & CONSOLIDATIONS 3	06	74	18
RAILROAD NOW A TURNPIKE	12	46	54
RAILROAD OF SCOTLAND ENVIRONS OF INVERNS	06	83	27
RAILROAD PAINTINGS-AGAIN	06	61	49
RAILROAD PHOTOGRAPHS OF AE BROWN	02	84	32
RAILROAD PHOTOS OF LINN WESTCOTT	03	85	34
RAILROAD POINT OF LAW HITTING COWS	11	44	23
RAILROAD POINT OF LAW - CEMETARIES	09	44	42
RAILROAD POLICE BADGES	06	82	53
RAILROAD PRESIDENTS PHOTO QUIZ	10	73	46
RAILROAD PSYCHASTHENIA	12	48	52
RAILROAD QUESTION OF SURVIVAL	10	57	49
RAILROAD RADIO--LISTENING IN	11	81	30
RAILROAD RESERVATIONS	10	45	16
RAILROAD RIVER QUIZ	08	58	48
RAILROAD ROUTS ACROSS THE ROCKIES (9)	10	47	44
RAILROAD SHOWROOM ATLANTIC CITY NJ	11	53	24
RAILROAD SOUNDS ARE MUSIC	02	42	26
RAILROAD TERMS	10	80	36
RAILROAD TICKET MAN	06	45	31
RAILROAD TO A VOLCANO - URUAPAN MEXICO	06	44	26
RAILROAD TREASURER	12	41	34
RAILROAD UPS & DOWNS	03	43	43
RAILROAD VACATIONS	05	41	5
RAILROAD YMCA HOME AWAY FROM HOME	11	48	26
RAILROAD-WATERWAY COMPETITION	05	49	26
RAILROADING ACROSS NORWAY ON 4-8-0'S	11	54	48
RAILROADING FROM 1940-1975	11	75	ALL
RAILROADING IN AFRICA NAIROBI MORE GARRA	06	66	20
RAILROADING IN AFRICA ON THE ZAMBESI	05	66	44
RAILROADING IN ANGOLA STEAM LOVERS ONLY	04	72	40
RAILROADING IN BRAZIL	06	56	51
RAILROADING IN BRITAIN FREIGHTLINER/INTE	07	68	25
RAILROADING IN BRITAIN RAIL SPEEDSTERS	09	56	42
RAILROADING IN BRITAIN STEAMS STYLE	11	68	29
RAILROADING IN CENTRAL AMERICA HIBALL	05	64	40
RAILROADING IN CENTRAL AMERICA N GAUG SI	04	64	18
RAILROADING IN CHINA	12	49	44
RAILROADING IN CHINA MAO'S IRON HORSES	07	72	14
RAILROADING IN ENGLAND DIESELS	04	56	40
RAILROADING IN ENGLAND TRAINS TO THRONE	06	53	14
RAILROADING IN ENGLAND W-BARRE TO W VALL	09	74	40
RAILROADING IN FRANCE	11	53	14
RAILROADING IN FRANCE 141-R MEANS USA	07	66	42
RAILROADING IN FRANCE HOT RODS A VAPEUR	11	55	46
RAILROADING IN GUATEMALA 1	08	54	41
RAILROADING IN GUATEMALA BANANAS ROLLING	09	54	41
RAILROADING IN HAWAII SMOKE OVER HAWAII	12	63	42
RAILROADING IN INDIA FREE WORLDS LARGEST	03	68	20
RAILROADING IN INDIA STEAM OVER INDIA	11	70	30
RAILROADING IN JAMMAICA CANADIAN 4-8-0	05	75	48
RAILROADING IN JAPAN 66 YRS-GOING STRONG	10	63	38
RAILROADING IN JAPAN BALDWINS HOKKAIDO	09	63	42
RAILROADING IN JAPAN BULLET LINE	04	66	48
RAILROADING IN JAPAN FROM ASHES TO FAME	10	64	10
RAILROADING IN JAPAN RETURN OF STEAM	10	81	49
RAILROADING IN JAVA 2-8-8-0 IN 1971	10	71	25
RAILROADING IN MEXICO	10	53	24
RAILROADING IN MEXICO LUXURY TRAINS &MP	02	67	32
RAILROADING IN MOZAMBIQUE MOTIVE POWER	01	73	29
RAILROADING IN N KOREA WE NEVER STOPPED	07	56	16
RAILROADING IN NEW ZEALAND BY TANK ENGIN	02	72	23
RAILROADING IN NEW ZEALAND JA STEAM	05	70	20
RAILROADING IN NEW ZEALAND S PAC SALON	01	58	27
RAILROADING IN PERU SWITCHBACKS TO SKY	01	55	48
RAILROADING IN REP OF S AFRICA-STEAMTOWN	11	71	30
RAILROADING IN RHODESIA GARRATTS CRISIS	04	66	25
RAILROADING IN RUSSIA AS THEY SEE IT	06	57	28
RAILROADING IN RUSSIA REVISITED	07	62	40
RAILROADING IN RUSSIA RUSSIAN NOTEBOOK	12	59	27
RAILROADING IN RUSSIA STEAM IN SIBERIA	07	71	20
RAILROADING IN SOUTH AFRICA LONG LIVE ST	08	68	40
RAILROADING IN SPAIN UNCOMMON GARRATTS	08	66	32
RAILROADING IN SUMATRA RR TO THE CLOUDS	07	73	25
RAILROADING IN THAILAND	07	67	38
RAILROADING IN THE BALKANS	01	48	10
RAILROADING IN TURKEY OLD LAND YOUNG RR	04	70	20
RAILROADING IN VIETNAM COMPETITOUS WAR	04	69	37
RAILROADING IN VIETNAM CONVEYANCE BY FIR	03	69	20
RAILROADING IN WASHINGTON DC TODAY	08	77	27
RAILROADING LONDON TO PARIS	03	54	24
RAILROADING ON THE ISLE OF MANX	09	66	24
RAILROADING PRATT STREET BALTIMORE MD	11	51	42
RAILROADING SOUTH OF THE BORDER	07	74	40
RAILROADS AT THE FRONT	07	42	8
RAILROADS BE DAMNED DYKES PROTECT RAILS	03	49	24
RAILROADS OF AFRICA	12	43	12
RAILROADS OF AUSTRALIA 2461 MI W/STEAM	04	71	26
RAILROADS OF AUSTRALIA BIG NOT BUSY	08	57	23
RAILROADS OF AUSTRIA 2 IN 1 ENGINES	10	57	28
RAILROADS OF AUSTRIA ENCOUNTER W/4-8-0	03	64	53
RAILROADS OF BRAZIL	05	49	40
RAILROADS OF BRAZIL	10	56	15
RAILROADS OF BRAZIL LINK PIN & 2'6"	11	81	34
RAILROADS OF BRITAIN PHOTO ESSAY	03	60	42

GENERAL RAILROADING

	M	Y	P
RAILROADS OF BRITAIN GODS WONDERFUL RR	08	85	20
RAILROADS OF BRITAIN RR PARLMENT FORGOT	01	57	21
RAILROADS OF BULGARIA LONG LEGGED LOCOS	06	65	32
RAILROADS OF CANADA O CANADA-OH YES!	11	85	27
RAILROADS OF CENTRAL AMERICA	04	43	30
RAILROADS OF CHINA CHINA BY TRAIN	12	75	40
RAILROADS OF CHINA LOCO NAMED FOR MAO	11	72	38
RAILROADS OF CHINA TANGSHAN	02	77	48
RAILROADS OF CUBA PERPETUAL INTERURBANS	01	59	28
RAILROADS OF ETHEOPHIA SELASSIES I HORSE	11	69	34
RAILROADS OF EUROPE BEWARE OF TRAINS	03	57	52
RAILROADS OF FRANCE RR TIME PASSED BY	03	58	44
RAILROADS OF GREAT BRITAN	10	82	46
RAILROADS OF GREECE HUGE 2-10-2'S	06	64	18
RAILROADS OF GREECE METER GAUGE OLYMPIA	07	64	36
RAILROADS OF HAWAII	07	68	19
RAILROADS OF ITALY	05	44	20
RAILROADS OF ITALY SIDE RODS & OVERHEAD	11	62	42
RAILROADS OF JAPAN 140 MPH TARGET	03	62	32
RAILROADS OF JAPAN BALDWIN OF UPPER PIKE	10	59	26
RAILROADS OF JAPAN FAR EAST GETS DOME	01	59	25
RAILROADS OF JAPAN TRAIN RIDING	04	62	40
RAILROADS OF KOREA	01	52	6
RAILROADS OF KOREAN WAR STEWART SPECIAL	04	51	44
RAILROADS OF MALAYAN PENNINSULA 1	05	82	26
RAILROADS OF MALAYAN PENNINSULA 2	06	82	42
RAILROADS OF MARYLAND	05	44	28
RAILROADS OF MASSACHUSETTSS	03	44	14
RAILROADS OF MEXICO $4/ROOMETTE $.01/MIL	04	68	25
RAILROADS OF MEXICO 4-4-0'S OF YUCATAN	10	66	20
RAILROADS OF MEXICO BEEN THERE LATELY?	06	84	40
RAILROADS OF MEXICO MEXICANO!	05	61	15
RAILROADS OF MEXICO STEAM ON NDEM	12	60	38
RAILROADS OF NEVADA OUTLAW RR STATE	01	78	18
RAILROADS OF NEW SOUTH WALES	03	66	46
RAILROADS OF NEW ZEALAND 3'6" GAUGE	06	47	48
RAILROADS OF NEW ZEALAND NARROW GAUGE	05	77	28
RAILROADS OF OKLAHOMA	10	46	32
RAILROADS OF PAKISTAN THROUGH THE KHBER	01	65	46
RAILROADS OF PALESTINE	02	49	46
RAILROADS OF PENNSYLVANIA	10	42	12
RAILROADS OF RENO NV	01	78	48
RAILROADS OF REPUBLIC OF SOUTH AFRICA	02	66	50
RAILROADS OF ROCHESTER NH	12	51	20
RAILROADS OF ROCHESTER NY	06	47	40
RAILROADS OF RUSSIA HOW GOOD ARE THEY?	08	58	18
RAILROADS OF SCANDINAVIA LAPLAND EXPRESS	11	42	32
RAILROADS OF SPAIN 7 HRS TO SCHENECTADY	04	85	22
RAILROADS OF SPAIN EXPECT ANYTHING	07	58	50
RAILROADS OF SPAIN TALGOS NOT SIDETRACKE	09	58	22
RAILROADS OF SPAIN WHAT YOU SEE YOU GET	05	85	39
RAILROADS OF SWITZERLAND	10	43	21
RAILROADS OF TAIWAN NARROW GAUGE	02	78	42
RAILROADS OF TAIWAN SHAYS	02	78	48
RAILROADS OF THE AFRICAN SAHARA	11	52	24

	M	Y	P
RAILROADS OF THE DERBY CITY LOWSVILLE KY	05	49	16
RAILROADS OF TURKEY - ABOARD FOR ANKARA	12	61	34
RAILROADS OF UTAH OGDEN TODAY	10	60	36
RAILROADS OF UTAH PITTSBURGH MINUS PRR	09	60	27
RAILROADS OF WASHINGTON DC LITTLE LINES	08	51	18
RAILROADS OF WILMINGTON DELAWARE	09	49	18
RAILROADS OF WORCESTER MASS	07	50	41
RAILROADS OF YUGOSLAVIA	09	44	36
RAILROADS OF YUGOSLAVIA	09	62	42
RAILROADS ON CANVAS	05	60	48
RAILROADS RENOVATION OF PITTSBURGH PA	07	56	44
RAILROADS THAT STAYED OUT OF AMTRAK	10	74	32
RAILROADS TO GOLCONDA	09	45	20
RAILS 150TH ANNIVERSARY IN ENGLAND	10	76	22
RAILS ACROSS THE PACIFIC/MELBOURINE ELEC	08	43	6
RAILS VS RUBBER	08	54	18
RAILTRIP ON CP 2	09	42	35
RAILTRIP ON CP 3	10	42	34
RAILTRIP VACATIONS--ALL ABOARD	05	51	50
RAILWAY POSTER THAT BECAME A LEGEND	04	83	26
RAILWAYS OF BRAZIL RAILWAY OF THE DEAD	01	70	25
RAILWAYS OF BRITAIN NATIONALIZED	07	50	36
RDC PHOTO QUIZ	06	71	37
READINGS NEW BLUE PASSENGER FLEET	04	65	17
RELAYING RAILS STEEL MUSCLED RAIL GANG	02	56	14
REMOTE CONTROLLED DIESELS-WHY & WHEREFOR	02	83	34
RENT A STEAM RAILROAD	05	84	49
REPORTING MARKS OF RAILROAD	01	63	43
RERAILING ON THE RUN	03	65	28
RETURN OF FAST MAIL	02	85	2
REVOLUTION OF FRONT DIESEL CARS	07	81	48
RICHARD M NIXON: RAIL ROMANTIC	11	71	38
RIDE THE GEORGIA RD DEPTHS OF ENTHUSIUM	01	85	50
RIO GRANDE FAN TRIP	12	83	28
RIVER LINE B&M/CV/CP	01	82	35
ROADRAILER III	10	77	7
ROADRAILER RATIONALE	11	82	3
ROBERT R YOUNG REVISITED	04	68	22
ROGER LEWIS AMTRAK'S NEW ENGINEER	07	75	12
ROTARY PLOWS FIGHTING SNOW FOR PROFIT	03	76	22
ROUTE OF AMER FREEDOM TRAIN 1975-6 MAP	04	75	15
ROYAL HUDSON SPEED 98 MPH CP	12	64	37
RR BUILDER GEORGE WASHINGTON WHISTLER	04	48	14
RR BUILDER GRENVILLE DODGE UP	06	48	36
RR CONSOLIDATION - EASTERN TRUNK LINE	10	45	40
RR POINT OF LAW/GOOD PASSENGER CONDUCT	10	44	21
RR WONDERLAND SOUTHERN NEW YORK	06	42	38
RULES FOR BANKRUPT RAILS	05	80	28
RUN AN INTERURBAN EXCURSION W/OUT JUICE	07	59	40
RUNNING EXTRA-FAN TRIP	03	58	52
S/R 4-5-0-1 EXPERIMENTAL FOR AMTRAK	06	76	46
SAFETY JUST DOESN'T HAPPEN	03	42	10
SALT LAKE FILL SP	01	57	9
SAND FOR RAILS	08	46	18
SCENIC RAILWAYS SELL SOMETHING PEOP WANT	01	73	22

GENERAL RAILROADING

Title	M	Y	P
SCHENECTADY SKETCH 3 RR & LOCO WORKS	02	48	22
SCRAPPED-END OF LINE FOR WEARY STEAM	02	51	47
SEARCH FOR FINAL FT'S	03	76	48
SECONDHAND SHORTLINE STEAM PHOTO QUIZ	12	63	40
SHORT LINE RAILROAD PHOTO QUIZ	02	59	26
SHORT LINES A PHOTO HISTORY	03	44	32
SHOULD LOCOMOTIVE ENGINEERS BE LICENSED?	03	85	70
SHRINE SPECIAL 1952 CONVENTION TRAINS	10	53	54
SMOKE OVER PRAIRIES ALWAYS LOOK BACK	01	55	16
SMOKE OVER PRAIRIES BERKSHIRES ON MOVE	09	55	18
SMOKE OVER PRAIRIES C&IM OASIS DIESELDOM	08	55	22
SMOKE OVER PRAIRIES CURTAINS COAL FIELDS	10	55	25
SMOKE OVER PRAIRIES DIG THOSE DOMES	05	55	31
SMOKE OVER PRAIRIES ILLINOIS INCIDENTS	06	55	27
SMOKE OVER PRAIRIES PLUMBERS NIGHTMARE	02	55	42
SMOKE OVER PRAIRIES QUAINT & THE QUIET	07	55	24
SMOKE OVER PRAIRIES QUICK & DEAD	04	55	22
SMOKE OVER PRAIRIES SADDEST TRAIN OF ALL	01	56	14
SMOKE OVER PRAIRIES TAKING DOWN MARKERS	02	56	20
SMOKE OVER PRAIRIES TVA TO THE RESCUE	12	55	26
SMOKE OVER PRAIRIES YOUR TRAIN IS COMING	03	55	52
SNOW CLEARING BATTLE OF THE SNOWFLAKES	02	47	28
SNOW IS FOR FARMERS & ARTISTS NOT RRS	10	69	20
SNOW REMOVAL ON MILWAUKEE ROAD IN 1936	12	44	20
SO THIS IS RAILROADING --INSIDE STORY	12	53	20
SOMETHING ABOUT A DEPOT	11	62	39
SOUTHEASTERN JUNCTION HOTSPOT ON FRISCO	12	43	37
SOUTHERN IN STEAM PHOTO ESSAY	11	59	40
SPARK DEFLECTORS	02	46	48
SPECIAL TRAIN "COMBAT CANCER" 1968 S	05	70	27
SPEED & DOMES SPARK PASSENGER PROGRESS	12	52	8
SPEED REMEMBER WHEN BRITAIN ENVIED US?	06	79	35
SPRINGFIELD ILL SEASAW	06	75	14
ST THOMAS ONT 1906-7 PHOTO ESSAY	06	75	40
STANDARD ERA OF RAILROADING 1910-1930	09	54	22
STANDARD TIME HISTORY	02	42	38
STANDARDIZATION ON AMERICAN RAILROADS	01	45	16
STEAM 4-8-4 = 2 1/2 E8'S	06	77	22
STEAM ERA THE WAY IT WAS	07	77	44
STEAM IN EUROPE 1967	07	67	12
STEAM IND SUM 2 LIMAS FINEST IN TWILIGHT	07	56	50
STEAM IND SUM DIFFERENCE DRIVERS MAKE	01	57	47
STEAM IND SUM H FORD/4-6-0/BLISS/IGNORAN	11	56	48
STEAM IND SUM HOLLIDAYSBURG ORBISONIA	03	57	46
STEAM IND SUM LITTLE RAILROAD FAR AWAY	08	56	26
STEAM IND SUM LOOK UP BROTHER SHE'S STM	08	57	50
STEAM IND SUM MOHAWK REFUSES TO DIE	09	56	24
STEAM IND SUM QUARRIES & SAWMILLS	07	57	16
STEAM IND SUM ROANOKE	06	56	24
STEAM IND SUM SEA LEVEL & 6288 FT	06	57	22
STEAM IND SUM SHADES OF STEAM & SPEED	04	57	44
STEAM IND SUM SHORT LINES & 2-10-2	02	57	22
STEAM IND SUM SMALL ELDERLY ENGINES	12	56	26
STEAM IND SUM STEAM FARES IN FLATLAND	10	56	49
STEAM PICTURE IN AUSTRALASIA	09	64	9
STEAM RETREATS IN EUROPE	08	69	37
STEAM SAFARI D-I-E-S-E-L?	06	54	19
STEAM SAFARI EUREKA FOUND'EM	05	54	54
STEAM SAFARI IN CANADA	04	54	24
STEAM WORLD OF VICTOR HAND PHOTO ESSAY	07	68	31
STEAM-DIESEL-ELECT-TURBINE-ATOMIC LOCOS	03	53	12
STEAM-ELECTRIC TUG OF WAR	07	70	18
STEAM: WHERE TO FIND IT-1954	08	54	19
STRAIGHT THROUGH TO OREGON	08	78	50
STREAMLINER RAMP CHICAGO IL C&NW	06	51	48
STREAMLINERS OF THE UNITED STATES	07	48	45
STREAMLINERS TRAVEL WEST 1964	10	64	20
STRICKEN PRESIDENT GARFIELD TO SEASHORE	09	52	58
STYLE OF STEAM IN ITS BIRTHPLACE BRITAIN	11	68	29
SUPER RAILROADS POST-WAR	12	43	4
SUPERLINER SCORE CARD AMTRAK	06	82	15
SURVEY OF A NEW ROUTE SW	04	47	24
SWISS TOURIST RAILWAYS	04	44	16
SYSTEM MAP OF CONRAIL	06	76	14
TAKE YOUR VACATION BY RAIL	05	52	62
TARIFF PREPARATION	11	40	27
TARIFFS AND PRICING FOR THE FUTURE	02	63	38
TEHACHAPI	01	77	24
TEHACHAPI CA EARTHQUAKE 7-21-52	11	52	14
TERMINAL RAILROADS WHY WE HAVE THEM	01	49	28
TERRELL DICKEY'S WORLD OF TRAINS	07	83	32
TERRIBLY TOUGH PHOTO QUIZ	03	72	43
TEXAS TRAINS	06	43	5
THE 10:30 BUDD SELF-PROPELLED CAR RUNS	10	84	32
THE HUB BOSTON MASS	12	49	36
THIS SWIFT GIANT	07	79	28
THROUGH CHICAGO-PEOPLE AS WELL AS HOGS	04	72	28
TICKETS FOR LOCOMOTIVE FUEL	09	43	30
TIME TO RE-INVENT THE STEAM LOCOMOTIVE	06	82	66
TIMING TRAIN SPEED CHART	09	42	21
TIP TOP MOUNTAIN LINE RELOCATION MP	02	50	5
TOM BARNES' BALDWIN/LIMA #5207 4-6-2	07	84	49
TOMARROWS RAILROAD "BULLET LINE OF JAPAN	04	66	48
TONNAGE AND THE FLANGED WHEEL	10	45	32
TOPPING 100 WITH THE 100 MILW	05	68	20
TRA WTCHING ENGLEWOOD ON. STA CHI IL '40	12	80	28
TRACK DESTROYERS (MILITARY)	02	45	36
TRACK GANGS SOMETHING TO SING ABOUT	08	55	16
TRACK LAYING COST IN 1949	05	49	24
TRACK PANS WATER ON THE FLY MC	12	51	42
TRACK REDUCTION TO CUT MAINTENANCE NYC	03	65	20
TRACK RELOCATION IN FOUR HOURS MP	04	48	47
TRACKING TRAINS TEN-HUNDRED	04	85	20
TRACKS FOR RUNAWAYS ONLY S	08	49	39
TRACKS TO VICTORY	09	45	26
TRACTION TONNAGE PHOTO QUIZ	02	71	25
TRAIN DEMOLISHER 2 MILES OF TRESTLE	02	48	51
TRAIN DISPATCHER IT'S YOUR RAILROAD	01	53	20
TRAIN ORDER AT SUMMIT CA ATSF	09	74	38
TRAIN SCHEDULE FACTORS	03	46	22

GENERAL RAILROADING

Title	M	Y	P
TRAIN TALK HOW TO LISTEN IN	01	73	37
TRAIN THEY CALL SPRINT - TOFC	04	81	26
TRAIN TIME AT GRIZZLY FLATS BACKYARD RR	10	50	12
TRAIN TIME IN MARTHA'S VINEYARD	07	85	52
TRAIN TRAVEL 1943 A.D.	01	44	4
TRAIN TRAVEL FOR BASEBALL TEAMS	06	84	48
TRAIN TRIPS - 9 BEST VACATIONS EVER	05	42	28
TRAIN WATCHING IN WEEMS ALABAMA PH ESSAY	04	68	29
TRAIN X EXPERIMENTAL RUNS	07	52	6
TRAINS AMTRAK FORGOT PHOTO ESSAY	09	71	28
TRAINS DO MAKE MUSIC	12	54	48
TRAINS FOR THE THRIFTY BOSTON-ELLSWORTH	10	53	34
TRAINS FOR THE THRIFTY CHARLESTON-BUFFAL	10	53	33
TRAINS FOR THE THRIFTY CHICAGO-MIAMI	10	53	32
TRAINS FOR THE THRIFTY NEW ORLEANS-CHICA	10	53	35
TRAINS FOR TOMORROW BEST TRAINS FOR TRAK	07	77	28
TRAINS GOES ROUND WORLD AFRICA	03	61	30
TRAINS GOES ROUND WORLD AUSTRALIA	08	61	24
TRAINS GOES ROUND WORLD BRITAIN	02	61	28
TRAINS GOES ROUND WORLD EAST AFRICA	06	61	44
TRAINS GOES ROUND WORLD INDIA	07	61	46
TRAINS GOES ROUND WORLD JAPAN	10	61	28
TRAINS GOES ROUND WORLD JAPAN AGAIN	11	61	43
TRAINS GOES ROUND WORLD KENYA	05	61	36
TRAINS GOES ROUND WORLD NEW ZEALAND	09	61	34
TRAINS GOES ROUND WORLD SOUTH AFRICA	04	61	35
TRAINS HAVE PERSONALITIES	11	44	16
TRAINS IN FILMS "LEAP FROM WATER TOWER"	06	67	23
TRAINS ITINERARY CONSISTS	05	46	22
TRAINS OF TOMORROW ARTICULATED TOFC	08	77	44
TRAINS RIDES A CAMELBACK	03	56	26
TRAINS TAKES A TRAIN RAILFAN TRIP	10	59	36
TRAINS VS TRUCKS THE FEDS TAKE A LOOK	10	76	14
TRAINS WE REMEMBER 1933-53	06	53	20
TRANSCONTINENTAL RAIL TOUR	09	41	28
TRANSCONTINENTAL RAILROAD HISTORY	05	69	ALL
TRAVEL FAMILY STYLE	05	51	18
TRIP ON THE TRAIN - EXPERIENCE-OPPORTUN.	10	42	09
TRIPMASTER $50 1800 MILE MIDWEST TRIP	04	57	55
TRIPMASTER CLINCHFIELD OF THE WEST	08	57	48
TRIPMASTER NEW ENGLAND IN FEBRUARY	02	58	47
TRIPMASTER SCENERY, STREAMLINERS & STEAM	03	59	23
TRIPMASTER THROUGH THE MTS TO FLORDIA	12	56	49
TRIVIA NOTE ON GARRATTS IN IRAN	05	66	58
TROOP SLEEPER	11	43	36
TROUP TRAIN RIDER	08	43	28
TRUDEAU VS. CANADIAN TRAINS	03	82	2
TUNNEL CONSTRUCTION 1	09	64	36
TUNNEL CONSTRUCTION 2	10	64	40
TURBOTRAIN REVISITED	03	70	32
TWENTIES REVISTED PHOTO ESSAY	05	70	29
TWENTIETH CENTURY LIMITED CHRONICLE	08	62	16
TWILIGHT OF THE TROOP TRAIN	09	79	44
TWIN ZEPHYR SPEED CB&Q AMERICA'S FASTEST	11	64	28
TWO RAILROADS, ONE LOCOMOTIVE	09	72	34
UNION OF SOUTH AFRICA RAILROADS	09	46	34
UNION STATION ST LOUIS MO GATEWAY TO SW	07	48	13
UNIT TRAINS TRAINS FOR SURVIVAL	03	65	3
UNIT TRAINS- WHAT A RAILROAD DOES BEST	05	63	16
UNIVERSITY RESEARCH ON TRANSPORT PROBLEM	10	46	56
UP-ROCK ISLAND LITIGATION:LOST OPPORTUNI	06	81	24
US BY RAIL 1 1/2 CENTS PER MILE	05	52	22
US RAILROADS AND WARTIME TRAFFIC	07	44	6
US WORLDS FAIR 1939 RAILROAD EXHIBIT	09	77	36
VAGARIES OF VIA	11	83	36
VARNISH VIGNETTES	07	41	12
VAUGHN MS CASEY JONES WRECK 4-30-00 IC	05	65	20
VENANGO RIVER BOYS & THEIR ELECT TRAIN	07	85	16
VIEW FROM TOWER 55 FT WORTH TEXAS ATSF	02	85	36
WALK RIGHT IN VP & GENERAL MANAGER GW	02	54	27
WANING WAYCAR	01	83	4
WANT TO RENT A TRAIN? HARRISBURG SPECIAL	04	53	33
WAR TIME FREIGHT OPERATION ON THE CB&Q	03	43	20
WAR TIME UTILIZATION OF PASSENGER CARS	12	43	32
WARTIME BOMBING OF RAILROADS	09	43	3
WARTIME BOMBING OF RAILROADS	12	46	22
WARTIME RAIL FAN TRIP IN MICHIGAN	07	45	28
WARTIME RAIL RAMBLE TRIP	02	43	19
WASHINGTON DC RAIL YARDS	10	52	51
WASHINGTON DC RUNAWAY U STA 2-10-53 PRR	08	53	18
WASHINGTON'S EYE VIEW OF US RAIL MAPS	12	76	14
WATCHMAN FOR TODAY DELANSON, NY	06	49	28
WATER HOLES FOR IRON HORSES	06	44	18
WAY FREIGHT TRAINS	10	41	4
WEEKEND WITH STEAM RAILFAN TRIP	03	60	27
WELDED RAIL NO CLICKETY-CLACK	09	49	52
WEST OAKLAND YARD WEST OAKLAND CA SP	04	47	58
WEST TRENTON NJ 1938 PHOTO ESSAY	08	68	44
WESTINGHOUSE AIR BRAKE STORY	05	50	36
WHAT ARE WE STOPPING HERE FOR?	04	79	30
WHAT DID CHESSIE STEAM SPECIAL PROVE	03	79	29
WHAT DOES THE ICC COST YOU & ME?	06	78	28
WHAT IS A FREIGHT TRAIN? PHOTO ESSAY	09	53	39
WHAT IS A LIDGERWOOD?	01	45	40
WHAT IS A RAILROAD?	05	59	16
WHAT IS A STREAMLINER FOR?	04	53	10
WHAT IS THERE ABOUT A RAILROAD ?	11	52	21
WHAT MAKES THE WHEELS GO ROUND	09	71	22
WHAT PRICE LABOR PROTECTION?	06	82	47
WHAT SPERRY CARS LOOK FOR	02	83	23
WHAT THE SIGNALS SAY	09	43	13
WHAT'S NEW IN FREIGHT EQUIPMENT	08	52	62
WHAT'S RIGHT WITH AMERICAN RAILROADS	09	52	14
WHEN AMTRAK FLIES WHITE FLAGS	02	85	47
WHEN, WHERE & WHY RAILROADS SHARE TRACK	01	79	20
WHERE DID THE MILWAUKEE GO?	02	82	49
WHERE DIESELS FEAR TO TREAD	10	57	23
WHERE EAST MEETS WEST CHICAGO	08	48	18
WHERE STEAM RESIDES--1968	04	68	44
WHERE TO RIDE BEHIND STEAM 1961	06	61	15

STEPHANS' RAILROAD DIRECTORY

GENERAL RAILROADING

	M	Y	P
WHERE TO RIDE BEHIND STEAM SUMMER 1965	06	65	44
WHICH TRACK FOR JACK GOV REGULATION	02	61	20
WHISTLE SIGNAL MEANINGS	03	45	6
WHO INVENTED RAILROAD STANBYS? ETC.	05	78	44
WHO SAID RAILROADING LOST ITS ROMANCE?	10	55	46
WHO SAYS EVERYBODY'S FLYING?	06	58	16
WHO SHOT THE PASSENGER TRAIN?	04	59	14
WHY AMTRACK HAS TO BE A FIASCO	01	80	5
WHY DOORS ON CASCADE TUNNEL	05	68	32
WHY GIVE THE AIRWAYS MORE MAIL?	11	53	6
WHY I GREW UP WITH ELECTROLINERS	11	60	58
WHY NP OWENS AN AIRPLANE	09	56	49
WHY PRE-ELCTRONIC RAILROAD SURVIVES	05	74	20
WOMEN IN RAILROADING	04	82	20
WONDERFUL TRAINS OF THOMAS WOLFE	06	64	24
WORLD'S GREATEST JUNCTION CHICAGO ILL	08	48	40
WORLDS SMALLEST COMMON CARRIER	11	73	25
WORLDS WORST TRAIN WRECK BHAGMATI INDIA	01	82	51
WORLDWIDE HIGH SPEED TRAINS	11	69	40
WP WYE KEDDIE CALIFORNIA PHOTO	12	40	22
WRECK OF #1881 L&N	05	78	50
WRECKS & WARTIME RAIL ACTIVITIES	10	67	40
XPLORER TRAIN OF NYC	07	56	6
ZEPHYR DENVER TO CHICAGO SPEED '34 CB&Q	09	52	26
ZEPHYRS, SHORT ORDERS AND REALISM	04	83	25
ZOO JUNCTION PHILADELPHIA PA PRR	03	52	24

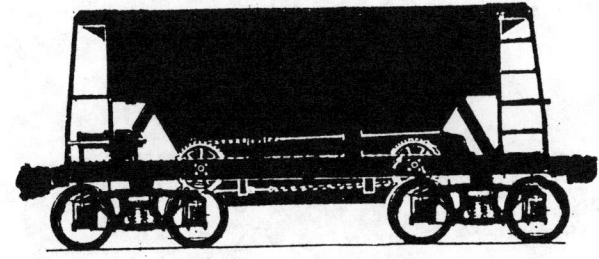

BILL OF LADING   APPENDIX A   (RAILROADS)

This appendix contains a listing of all RAILROADS that we have come across since we started our indexing project. All of the roads appearing in this directory appear in this appendix. However all of the entries in this appendix may NOT appear in this directory. These roads will appear in future volumes. There are two listings: one alphabetically by road followed by its assigned abbreviation and one alphabetical by abbreviation follwed by the road name. By knowing one you can find the other. It was felt that this section would be infrequently used so the small type was used to conserve space.

Don't count them -- We list 2445 roads. That number boggles our mind! The interesting fact is that we are still adding to the list. Don't forget this listing only covers roads sufficiently well known to have something published about them.

MANIFEST   APPENDIX A (RAILROADS)

	PAGE
APPENDIX A - ROADNAMES	350
ROADNAME-ABBREVIATION	351
ABBREVIATION-ROADNAME	362

APPENDIX A (RAILROADS)

ABERDEEN & ROCKFISH	A&R
ABILENE	ABI
ABILENE & SOUTHERN	A&SO
ABITIBI	ABIT
ADDISON	ADD
ADIRONDACK	ADIR
ADIRONDACK & ST LOUIS	AD&SL
AGRICO CHEMICAL (PIERCE PLANT)	AGR
AGUA PRIETA SONORA MEXICO PACIFIC RY	APSM
AHNAPEE & WESTERN	A&W
AKRON & BARBERTON BELT	A&BB
AKRON CANTON & YOUNGSTOWN	AC&Y
ALABAMA & FLORIDA	A&F
ALABAMA BY-PRODUCTS	AB-P
ALABAMA CENTRAL	ALC
ALABAMA DRYDOCK & SHIPBUILDING	AD&S
ALABAMA FLORIDA & ATLANTIC	AF&A
ALABAMA GREAT SOUTHERN	AGS
ALABAMA POWER COMPANY	APC
ALABAMA STATE DOCKS TERMINAL	ASDT
ALABAMA TENNESSEE & NORTHERN	AT&N
ALAMEDA BELT LINE	AB
ALANTIC STEEL	ATS
ALASKA RAILROAD	AL
ALBANY & NORTHERN	A&N
ALBANY PORT DISTRICT TERMINAL	APDT
ALBERTA RESOURCES	AR
ALBION MINES	AM
ALCAN	ALCA
ALCOA ORE COMPANY	AOC
ALCOA TERMINAL	AT
ALEXANDER	ALEX
ALGIERS WINSLOW & WESTSERN	AW&W
ALGOMA	ALG
ALGOMA CENTRAL	ALGC
ALGOMA CENTRAL & HUDSON BAY	AC&HB
ALHAMBRA & PASADENA	A&P
ALIQUIPPA & SOUTHERN	AL&S
ALLEGHENY & KINZUA	A&K
ALLEGHENY & SOUTH SIDE	A&SS
ALLEGHENY & WESTERN	AL&W
ALLEGHENY CENTRAL	AC
ALLEGHENY PORTAGE	AP
ALLENTOWN	ALLEN
ALLIED CHEMICAL (BRUNNER MOND)	ACBM
ALLIED CHEMICAL (SOLVAY)	ALL
ALMA & JONQUIERES	A&J
ALMANOR	ALM
ALTADENA	ALT
ALTON & SOUTHERN	A&S
ALTON RAILROAD (B&O)	ARR
ALTOONA & LOGAN VALLEY	A&LV
ALTUS WICHITA & HOLLIS	AW&H
ALUMINUM ORE COMPANY	AO
AMADOR CENTRAL	AMC
AMALGAMATED SUGAR	AMS
AMERICAN CAN COMPANY	ACC
AMERICAN CAST IRON PIPE	ACIP
AMERICAN COMMERCIAL BARGE LINES	ACBL
AMERICAN COMPRESSED STEEL	ACS
AMERICAN CYANAMID COMPANY	ACY
AMERICAN GRAINS	AG
AMERICAN PIPE & CONSTRUCTION	AP&C
AMERICAN REDWOOD LUMBER	AMRL
AMHERST & BELCHERTOWN	A&B
AMHERST INDUSTRIES	AI
AMOSKEAG MANUFACTURING COMPANY	AMO
AMTRAK	A
ANDROSCOGGIN	AND
ANDROSCOGGIN & KENNEBEC	AND&K
ANGEL'S FLIGHT RAILWAY	AF
ANGELINA & NECHES RIVER	A&NR
ANN ARBOR	AA
ANNA QUARRIES	AQ
ANNAPOLIS & ELK RIDGE	A&ER
ANNAPOLIS WASHINGTON & BALTIMORE	AW&B
ANTELOPE & WESTERN	AN&W
APACHE RAILWAY	APA
APALACHICOLA NORTHERN	AN
APPALACHIAN POWER	APO
APPOMATTOX	APP
ARCADE & ATTICA RAILROAD	A&A
ARCATA & MAD RIVER	A&MR
ARGENT LUMBER	ARL
ARGENTINE CENTRAL	ARC
ARIZONA & CALIFORNIA	A&C
ARIZONA & UTAH	A&U
ARIZONA CENTRAL RAILROAD	ARI
ARKANSAS & LOUISIANA	A&L
ARKANSAS & LOUISIANA MISSOURI	A&LM
ARKANSAS & OZARKS	A&O
ARKANSAS VALLEY INTERURBAN	AVI
ARKANSAS WESTERN	AW
ARMCO CHEMICAL COMPANY	ACH
ARMCO STEEL	AS
ARNAUD	ARN
AROOSTOOK VALLEY	AV
ARTEMUS-JELLICO	AJ
ASARCO MEXICANA	AME
ASBESTOS & DANVILLE	A&DA
ASHBURNAM	ASH
ASHLAND COAL & IRON	AC&I
ASHLEY DREW & NORTHERN	AD&N
ASSOCIATION OF AMERICAN RAILROADS	AAR
ATCHISON TOPEKA & SANTA FE	ATSF
ATL HIGHLANDS RED BANK & L BR ELEC	AHRB
ATLANTA & ST ANDREWS BAY	A&STAB
ATLANTA & WEST POINT	A&WP
ATLANTA BIRMINGHAM & COAST	AB&C
ATLANTA BIRMINGHAM & COAST.	AB&CO.
ATLANTA STONE MOUNTAIN & LITHONIA	ASM&L
ATLANTIC & DANVILLE	A&D
ATLANTIC & EAST CAROLINA RAILWAY	A&EC
ATLANTIC & GREAT WESTERN	A&GW
ATLANTIC & GULF	A&G
ATLANTIC & PACIFIC	A&PA
ATLANTIC & ST LAWRENCE	A&SL
ATLANTIC & WESTERN	A&WE
ATLANTIC CITY RAILROAD	ACRR
ATLANTIC CITY TRANSPORTATION	ACT
ATLANTIC COAST ELECTRIC	ACE
ATLANTIC COAST LINE	ACL
ATLANTIC COAST ST JOHNS & INDIAN RIV	ACJ&IR
ATLANTIC GULF & WEST INDIES TRANSIT	AG&WIT
ATLANTIC MISSISSIPPI & OHIO	AM&O
ATLANTIC NORTHERN	ATN
ATLANTIC SUWANEE RIVER & GULF	ASR&G
ATTICA & ALLEGHENY VALLEY	A&AV
ATTICA & FREEDOM	AT&F
AUBURN & SYRACUSE ELECTRIC	A&SE
AUBURN BRANCH	AUB
AUGUSTA	AU
AUGUSTA TRAMWAY & TRANSFER	AT&T
AURORA ELGIN & FOX RIVER ELECTRIC	AE&FRE
AURORA BRANCH	AUR
AURORA ELGIN & FOX RIVER	AE&FR
AUSTIN CITY RAILROAD (RAILWAY?)	ACR
AUTO TRAIN	ATR
AVONDALE SHIPYARDS	AVS
BABCOCK & WILCOX	B&WI
BALDWIN LOCOMOTIVE WORKS	BLW
BALTIMORE & ANNAPOLIS	B&AN
BALTIMORE & EASTERN	B&E
BALTIMORE & OHIO	B&O
BALTIMORE & OHIO CHICAGO TERMINAL	B&OCT
BALTIMORE CITY PASSENGER RAILWAY	BCPR
BALTIMORE TRANSIT	BALT
BAMBERGER	BAM
BAMBERGER ELECTRIC	BE
BANGOR & AROOSTOOK	B&AR
BANGOR & KATAHDIN IRON WORKS	B&K
BANGOR & PISCATAQUIS	B&PI
BANGOR OLD TOWN & MILFORD	BOT&M
BANGOR RAILWAY & ELECTRIC	BR&E
BARNES & TUCKER COAL COMPANY	B&T
BARRE & CHELSEA	B&CH
BARTLESVILLE INTERURBAN	BI
BARTLETT & ALBANY	B&AL
BASIC REFRACTORIES	BAS
BATH & HAMMONDSPORT	B&HA
BATH & HAMMONDSPORT.	BA&H.
BAUXITE & NORTHERN	B&N
BAY AREA RAPID TRANSIT	BART
BAY COLONY	BCO
BAY DE NOQUET & MARQUETTE	BDN&M
BAY STATE STREET RAILWAY	BSS
BEACH MOUNTAIN RAILROAD	BEEC
BEAUFORT & MOREHEAD	BE&M
BEAUMONT & GREAT NORTHERN	B&GN
BEAVER MEADE & ENGLEWOOD	BM&E
BEAVER MEADOW	BM
BECKER SAND & GRAVEL	BS&GR
BEECH CREEK	BC
BEECH CREEK CLEARFIELD & SOUTHWESTERN	BCC&S
BEECH MOUNTAIN RAILROAD	BEEC.
BELFAST & MOOSEHEAD LAKE	B&ML
BELLEFIELD BOILER PLANT	BBP
BELLEFONTAINE	BEL
BELLEFONTE CENTRAL	BEC
BELLEVUE & CASCADE	B&C
BELLINGHAM BAY & BRITISH COLUMBIA	BB&BC
BELMONT & BUFFALO	B&B
BELT RAILWAY OF CHICAGO	BRC
BELTON	BELT
BELVIDERE-DELAWARE RAILROAD	BD
BEMIS LUMBER COMPANY	BEM
BENNETSVILLE & CHERAW RAILROAD	BE&CH
BENNINGTON & GLASTENBURY	B&G
BENNINGTON & RUTLAND	B&R
BENSON	BEN
BESSEMER	BESS
BESSEMER & LAKE ERIE	B&LE
BETHLEHEM MINES	BETH
BEVIER & SOUTHERN	B&S
BIG HORN LUMBER COMPANY	BHL
BIG LEVEL & KINZUA	BL&K
BILLERICA & BEDFORD RAILROAD	BI&B
BILLMEYER & SMALL'S	BI&SM
BINGHAM & GARFIELD	B&GA
BINGHAMTON	BING
BIRMINGHAM & SOUTHEASTERN	BI&S
BIRMINGHAM COLUMBUS & ST ANDREWS	BC&SA
BIRMINGHAM ELECTRIC	BIR
BIRMINGHAM SLAG	BSL
BIRMINGHAM SOUTHERN	BIS
BIRMINGHAM TERMINAL	BIRM
BISMARCK WASHBURN & GREAT FALLS	BW&GF
BLACK HILLS & FORT PIERRE	BH&FP
BLACK HILLS CENTRAL	BHC
BLACK MESA & LAKE POWELL	BM&LP
BLACK MOUNTAIN RAILROAD	BMT
BLACK RIVER & WESTERN	BR&W
BLAIRSTOWN	BL
BLAIRSVILLE & INDIANA	B&I
BLATIMOR & HAMPDEN ELECTRIC	B&HE
BLAW-KNOX CORPORATION-UNION STEEL DIV	B-K
BLOOMSBURG & NORTHERN	BL&S
BLOOMSBURG & SULLIVAN	B&SU
BLUE RIDGE RAILWAY	BR
BLUE SPRINGS ORANGE CITY & ATLANTIC	BSOC&A
BOEING	BOE
BONHOMIE & HATTIESBURG SOUTHERN	B&HS
BOOTH KELLY LUMBER COMPANY	BKL
BORK COMPANY	BORK
BOSQUES DE CHIHUAHUA	BDC
BOSTON & ALBANY	B&A
BOSTON & LOWELL	B&L
BOSTON & MAINE	B&M
BOSTON & NEW YORK AIR LINE	B&NY
BOSTON & NORTHERN STREET RAILWAY	B&NSR
BOSTON & PROVIDENCE	B&P
BOSTON & WORCESTER	B&WO
BOSTON BARRE & GARDNER	BB&G
BOSTON CLINTON & FITCHBURG	BC&F

STEPHANS' RAILROAD DIRECTORY

APPENDIX A (RAILROADS)

Railroad	Abbr
BOSTON CONCORD & MONTREAL	BC&M
BOSTON ELEVATED LINES	BELL
BOSTON HOOSAC TUNNEL & WESTERN	BHT&W
BOSTON METALS COMPANY	BMC
BOSTON RAPID TRANSIT	BRT
BOSTON REVERE BEACH & LYNN	BRB&L
BOSTON SUBWAY	BS
BOWDON	BOW
BOYNE CITY	BOYN
BRADFORD & FOSTER BROOK	B&FB
BRADFORD & WESTERN PENNSYLVANIA	B&WP
BRADFORD BORDELL & KINZUA	BB&K
BRADFORD BORDELL & SMETHPORT	BB&S
BRADFORD ELDRED & CUBA	BE&C
BRADFORD RICHBURG & CUBA	BR&C
BRADFORD STEAM RAILROAD	BRAD
BRADSHAW MOUNTAIN	BRMT
BRAINERD & NORTHERN MINNESOTA	B&NM
BRANDYWINE TRANSIT	BWT
BRANFORD STEAM RAILROAD	BSRR
BRANTFORD WATERLOO & LAKE ERIE	BW&LE
BRASWELL SAND & GRAVEL	BS&G
BRATTLEBORO & WHITEHALL	B&W
BREWSTER PHOSPHATE	BP
BRIDGEPORT TRAMWAY	BRID
BRIDGETON & HARRISON RAILWAY	B&H
BRIDGTON & SACO RIVER RAILROAD	B&SR
BRIDGTON RAILROAD & DEVELOPMENT	BR&D
BRIGHT HOPE	BH
BRIMSTONE	BRI
BRISTOL TRACTION	BT
BRITISH COLUMBIA ELECTRIC	BCE
BRITISH COLUMBIA HYDRO & POWER AUTHOR	BCH&P
BRITISH COLUMBIA RAILWAY	BCRW
BRITISH RAILWAYS	BRW
BROCKINGS & PEACH ORCHARD	B&PO
BROCKVILLE & OTTAWA	B&OT
BRODERICK WOOD PRODUCTS	BWP
BROOKLYN & QUEENS	B&Q
BROOKLYN EASTERN DISTRICT TERMINAL	BEDT
BROOKLYN RAPID TRANSIT ELEVATED CO.	BRTE
BROOKLYN RAPID TRANSIT SUBWAY LINES	BRTS
BROOKSVILLE & HUDSON	BR&H
BROOKVILLE & MAHONING	B&MA
BROWARD COUNTY PORT AUTHORITY	BCPA
BROWN COUNTY	BRO
BROWNSTONE & MIDDLETOWN	BR&M
BUCK MOUNTAIN	BUCK
BUFFALO & LAKE HURON	B&LH
BUFFALO & ST MARYS	B&SM
BUFFALO & SUSQUEHANNA	B&SQ
BUFFALO ALLEGHENY & PITTSBURG	BA&PI
BUFFALO ATTICA & ARCADE	BA&A
BUFFALO BRADFORD & PITTSBURGH	BB&P
BUFFALO CORREY & PITTSBURGH	BC&P
BUFFALO CREEK	BCR
BUFFALO CREEK & GAULEY	BC&G
BUFFALO LOCKPORT & ROCHESTER	BL&R
BUFFALO ROCHESTER & PACIFIC	BR&PA
BUFFALO ROCHESTER & PITTSBURG RAILWAY	BR&P
BUFFALO ST MARYS & SOUTHWESTERN	BM&S
BUFFALO TERMINAL	BUT
BUFFALO UNION CAROLINA RAILROAD	BUC
BUICK	BUI
BULLFROG GOLDFIELD	BG
BUNKER HILL & SULLIVAN MINE & COAL CO	BH&SM&C
BURLINGTON	B
BURLINGTON & MISSOURI	B&MI
BURLINGTON & MISSOURI RIVER RAILROAD	B&MR
BURLINGTON CEDAR RAPIDS & NORTHERN	BCR&N
BURLINGTON NORTHERN	BN
BURNS BIGGS LUMBER COMPANY	BB
BUSH TERMINAL	BUSH
BUTTE ANACONDA & PACIFIC	BA&P
CADILLAC & LAKE CITY	C&LC
CADIZ	CAD
CAHUENGA VALLEY	CVA
CAIRO TRUMAN & SOUTHERN	CT&S
CALIFORNIA CENTRAL	CCE
CALIFORNIA EASTERN	CE
CALIFORNIA ELECTRIC RAILWAY	CER
CALIFORNIA MIDLAND	CAM
CALIFORNIA NORTHWESTERN	CNW
CALIFORNIA PACIFIC	CAPA
CALIFORNIA SOUTHERN	CAS
CALIFORNIA WESTERN NORTH	CWN
CALIFORNIA WESTERN RR & NAV CO	CW
CALTRANS	CAL
CALUMET & HECLA CONSOLIDATED COPPER	C&HC
CAMAS PRAIRIE RAILROAD	CAPR
CAMBRIA & INDIANA	C&I
CAMDEN & AMBOY	C&AM
CAMDEN & ATLANTIC	C&AT
CAMINO PLACERVILLE & LAKE TAHOE	CP&LT
CAMP MANUFACTURING	CMFG
CAMPBELL'S CREEK	CCR
CANADA & GULF TERMINAL	C&GT
CANADIAN COLLIERIES LIMITED	CAC
CANADIAN FOREST PRODUCTS	CFP
CANADIAN NATIONAL	CN
CANADIAN NORTHERN	CAN
CANADIAN PACIFIC	CP
CANADIAN PACIFIC GREAT WESTERN	CPGE
CANADIAN REFRACTORIES	CRE
CANADIAN SOUTHERN	CS
CANAJOHARIE & CATSKILL	C&CA
CANEY FORK & WESTERN	CF&W
CANTON	C
CANTON & CARTHAGE	C&C
CAPE BRETON TRAMWAYS	CBT
CAPE COD	CC
CAPE FEAR	CF
CAPE GIRARDEAU NORTHERN	CGN
CARBON COUNTY	CARB
CARGILL INCORPORATED	CAR
CARILLON & GRENVILLE	C&G
CARLTON & COAST	C&CO
CARLTON LOGGING COMPANY	CLC
CAROLINA & NORTHWESTERN	C&N
CAROLINA CLINCHFIELD & OHIO	CC&O
CAROLINA NITROGEN DIV OF GRACE CHEM	CND
CAROLINA POWER & LIGHT	CP&L
CAROLINA SOUTHERN	CARS
CAROLINA WESTERN	CAW
CARRABELLE TALLAHASSEE & GEORGIA	CT&G
CARROLLTON	CARR
CARSON & COLORADO RAILROAD	CA&C
CARSON & COLORADO SOUTHERN PACIFIC	C&CSP
CARTHAGE & ADIRONDACK	C&AD
CARTIAGE PAPER MAKERS	CPM
CARTIER RAILWAY	CART
CASCADE	CASC
CASPER SOUTH FORK & EASTERN	CSF&E
CASS SCENIC	CASS
CASSVILLE & EXETER	C&E
CATASAUQUA & FOGELSVILLE	C&F
CATAWISSA	CAT
CATSKILL MOUNTAINS	CMT
CAYUGA & SUSQUEHANNA	C&SU
CD JOHNSON LUMBER COMPANY	JL
CEDAR RAPIDS & IOWA CITY	CR&IC
CENTRAL APPALACHIAN COAL COMPANY	CACC
CENTRAL CALIFORNIA TRACTION COMPANY	CCT
CENTRAL FOUNDRY	CFO
CENTRAL INDIANA	CIN
CENTRAL IOWA TRANSPORTATION COOP	CITC
CENTRAL MASSACHUSETTS	CMA
CENTRAL MILITARY TRACT	CEMT
CENTRAL NEW ENGLAND	CNE
CENTRAL NEW ENGLAND & WESTERN	CNE&W
CENTRAL NEW YORK	CNY
CENTRAL NEW YORK & NORTHERN	CNY&N
CENTRAL NEW YORK & WESTERN	CNY&W
CENTRAL NEW YORK SOUTHERN	CNYS
CENTRAL OF GEORGIA	CGA
CENTRAL PACIFIC	CPA
CENTRAL RAILROAD OF LONG ISLAND	CRLI
CENTRAL RAILROAD OF NEW JERSEY	CNJ
CENTRAL RAILWAY OF PERU	CRMP
CENTRAL RR & BANKING CO OF GEORGIA	CRB
CENTRAL VALLEY	CEV
CENTRAL VERMONT (CN) RAILWAY	CV
CENTRAL WAREHOUSE COMPANY	CWC
CENTRAL WEST VIRGINIA & SOUTHERN	CWV&S
CENTRE & CLEARFIELD	CE&C
CHAMAS PRAIRIE RAILROAD	CHP
CHAMPION FIBRE	CFI
CHAMPLAIN & OGDENSBURG RAILROAD	C&OG
CHAMPLAIN & ST LAWRENCE	C&SL
CHARLES CITY WESTERN	CCW
CHARLESTON & WESTERN CAROLINA	C&WC
CHARLESTON CINCINNATI & CHICAGO	CC&CH
CHATAM IRON & METAL	CI&M
CHATHAM & LEBANON VALLEY	C&LV
CHATTAHOOCHEE INDUSTRIAL RAILROAD	CI
CHATTAHOOCHEE VALLEY	CHV
CHATTANOOGA TRACTION	CHTR
CHAUTAUQUA TRACTION	CHT
CHEHALIS WESTERN	CHW
CHERAW & COALFIELD	CH&C
CHERAW & DARLINGTON	CH&DA
CHERRY RIVER BOOM & LUMBER	CRB&L
CHESAPEAKE & OHIO RAILROAD	C&O
CHESAPEAKE & WESTERN RAILROAD	C&W
CHESAPEAKE BEACH	CBE
CHESHIRE	CHE
CHESSIE SYSTEM	CHESS
CHESTER PERRYVILLE & ST GENEVIEVE	CP&SG
CHESTERFIELD	CHES
CHESTNUT RIDGE	CRI
CHESUNCOOK CHAMBERLAIN	CCH
CHESWICK & HARMAR	C&H
CHICAGO & ALTON	C&A
CHICAGO & AURORA	C&AU
CHICAGO & EASTERN ILLINIOS	C&EI
CHICAGO & GRAND TRUNK	CH&GT
CHICAGO & ILLINIOS WESTERN	C&IW
CHICAGO & ILLINIOS MIDLAND	C&IM
CHICAGO & NORTH WESTERN	C&NW
CHICAGO & NORTHERN PACIFIC	C&NP
CHICAGO & NORTHERN RAILROAD	CH&N
CHICAGO & NORTHWESTERN BELT	C&NWB
CHICAGO & PACIFIC	CH&P
CHICAGO & SOUTH SIDE RAPID TRANSIT	C&SSRT
CHICAGO & WABASH VALLEY	C&WV
CHICAGO & WESTERN INDIANA	C&WI
CHICAGO AURORA & ELGIN	CA&E
CHICAGO BRIDGE & IRON	CB&I
CHICAGO BURLINGTON & QUINCY	CB&Q
CHICAGO CINCINNATI & LOUISVILLE	CC&L
CHICAGO FREIGHT CAR COMPANY	CFC
CHICAGO GRAVEL COMPANY	CG
CHICAGO GREAT WESTERN RAILWAY	CGW
CHICAGO HARLEM & BATAVIA	CH&B
CHICAGO HEIGHTS TERMINAL TRANSFER	CHTT
CHICAGO INDIANAPOLIS & LOUISVILLE	CI&L
CHICAGO JUNCTION	CJ
CHICAGO KALAMAZOO & SAGINAW	CK&SA
CHICAGO KANSAS & WESTERN	CK&W
CHICAGO LAKE SHORE & EASTERN	CLS&E
CHICAGO LOCOMOTIVE WORKS	CLW
CHICAGO MILWAUKEE & GARY	CM&G
CHICAGO MILWAUKEE & PUGET SOUND	CM&P
CHICAGO MILWAUKEE & ST PAUL	CMSP
CHICAGO MILWAUKEE ST PAUL & PACIFIC	MILW
CHICAGO NEW YORK ELECTRIC AIR LINE RR	CNYE
CHICAGO NORTH SHORE & MILWAUKEE	CNS&M
CHICAGO RAPID TRANSIT COMPANY	CRT
CHICAGO RIVER & INDIANA	CR&I
CHICAGO ROCK ISLAND & GULF	CRI&G
CHICAGO ROCK ISLAND & PACIFIC RR	RI
CHICAGO SANITARY DISTRICT	CHSD
CHICAGO SHORT LINE	CSL
CHICAGO SOUTH SHORE & SOUTH BEND	CSS&SB
CHICAGO ST LOUIS & WESTERN	CSL&W
CHICAGO ST PAUL & KANSAS CITY	CSP&KC
CHICAGO ST PAUL MINNEAPOLIS & OHIO	CSPM&O
CHICAGO ST PAUL MINNEAPOLIS & OMAHA	CPM&O
CHICAGO SUBWAYS	CSUB
CHICAGO SURFACE LINES	CSLS

352

STEPHANS RAILROAD DIRECTORY

APPENDIX A (RAILROADS)

CHICAGO TRANSIT AUTHORITY	CTA
CHICAGO TUNNEL	CT
CHICAGO UNION TRANSFER	CHUT
CHICAGO WEST PULLMAN & SOUTHERN	CWP&S
CHIHUAHUA-PACIFIC	C-P
CHIPPAWAH RIVER & MENOMONIE RAILWAY	CR&M
CHIPPEWA FALLS & WESTERN	CF&W.
CHOCTAW NEWCASTLE & WESTERN	CN&W
CHOCTAW OKLAHOMA & GULF RAILROAD	CO&G
CHUMBRES & TOLRIC SCENIC RAILROAD	C&T
CINCINNATI & LAKE ERIE	C&LE
CINCINNATI & NEW ORLEANS & TEXAS PAC.	CNO&TP
CINCINNATI GEORGETOWN & PORTSMOUTH	CG&P
CINCINNATI HAMILTON & DAYTON	CH&D
CINCINNATI LAWRENCE & AURORA	CL&A
CINCINNATI NORTHERN	CINO
CINCINNATI RAPID TRANSIT	CIRT
CINCINNATI UNION TERMINAL	CIUT
CITADEL CEMENT COMPANY	CIT
CITIES SERVICE COMPANY	CSC
CITIZENS TRACTIONS	CTR
CITY OF BALTIMORE	CBA
CITY OF PRINEVILLE	CPR
CITY POINT	CPT
CITY UTILITIES COMPANY	CU
CLAREDON & PITTSFORD	C&PI
CLAREMONT & CONCORD RAILROAD	CL&C
CLARION RIVER	CLA
CLEMENT LUMBER COMPANY	CLE
CLEVELAND COLUM CINCIN & INDIANAPOL	CCC&I
CLEVELAND CINCINNATI CHIC & ST LOUIS	CCC&SL
CLEVELAND ELECTRIC ILLUMINATING CO	CEI
CLEVELAND LORAIN & WHEELING RAILROAD	CL&W
CLEVELAND RAILWAYS	CRW
CLEVELAND RAPID TRANSIT	CLRT
CLEVELAND SOUTHWESTERN & COLUMBUS	CSCO
CLEVELAND UNION TERMINAL (NYC)	CUT
CLIFFSIDE RAILROAD	CLIF
CLINCHFIELD	CL
CLINCHFIELD COAL	CLI
CLINTON & OKLAHOMA WESTERN	C&OW
CLOVER HILL	CH
COAHUILA & ZACATECAS	C&Z
COAL & IRON	C&IR
COBOURG & PETERBOROUGH	C&P
COEUR D'ALENE RAILWAY & NAVIGATION	CDR&N
COLLINS & GLENNVILLE	C&GL
COLORADO & NORTHWESTERN	C&NWT
COLORADO & SOUTHERN	C&S
COLORADO & WYOMING	C&WY
COLORADO CENTRAL	COL
COLORADO COLUMBUS & MEXICAN RAILROAD	CC&M
COLORADO KANSAS & OKLAHOMA	CK&O
COLORADO MIDLAND	CMI
COLORADO SPRINGS & CRIPPLE CR DIST RY	CS&CC
COLUMBIA & COWLITZ	CO&C
COLUMBIA & MILLSTADT	C&MI
COLUMBIA NEWBERRY & LAURENS	CN&L
COLUMBIA PARK & SOUTHERN	CP&S
COLUMBIA PARK & SOUTHWESTSERN	CP&SW
COLUMBUS & GREENVILLE	C&GR
COLUMBUS DELAWARE & MARION	CD&M
COMMONWEALTH EDISON	CED
CONCORD & MONTREAL	C&MO
CONDON KINZUA & SOUTHERN	CK&S
CONEMAUGH & BLACK LICK	C&BL
CONNECTICUT & PASSUMPSIC RIVERS	C&PR
CONNECTICUT COMPANY	CONN
CONNECTICUT RAILROAD	CONNR
CONNECTICUT RIVER	COR
CONNECTICUT WESTERN	COW
CONNOR STEEL DIVISION	CSD
CONRAIL	CR
CONSOLIDATED CHICAGO ALTONA &SOUTHERN	CA&S
CONSOLIDATED KANSAS & SIDELL	CK&S
CONSOLIDATED ROCK PRODUCTS	CRP
CONSUMERS COMPANY	CONS
CONSUMERS POWER	CON
CONTINENTAL STEEL	CONT
CONWAY SCENIC	CONW
COOPERSTOWN & CHARLOTTE VALLEY	C&CV
COORS BREWERY	CB
COOS BAY LUMBER	CBL
COPPER RANGE	CRA
COPPER RIVER & NORTHWESTERN	CR&NW
CORAL GABLES RAPID TRANSIT	CGRT
CORINTH & COUNCE	CO&CO
CORNWALL & LEBANON RAILROAD	CO&L
CORNWALL RAILROAD	CORN
CORONADO	CO
CORTEZ MINES LIMITED	CML
COTTON BELT	CBELT
COUDERSPORT & PORT ALLEGHENY	C&PA
COWICHAN NARROW GAUGE	CNG
COWLITZ CHEHALIS & CASCADE	CC&C
CPPER RIVER & NORTHWESTERN	CR&N
CRAB ORCHARDS & EGYPTIAN	CO&E
CRAIG MOUNTAIN	CM
CROWN WILLAMETTE PAPER	CWP
CRYSTAL RIVER & SAN JUAN	CR&SJ
CUMBERLAND	CUM
CUMBERLAND & MANCHESTER	C&M
CUMBERLAND & PENNSYLVANIA	C&PE
CUMBERLAND & WESTERNPORT ELECTRIC	C&WE
CUMBERLAND VALLEY	CUMV
CUMBRES & TOLEC SCENIC RAILROAD	C&TS
CURRENT RIVER RAILROAD	CUR
CUSHING STONE	CUS
CUTLER & SAVIDGE	CU&S
CUYAHOGA VALLEY	CUY
DAN PATCH ELECTRIC	DPE
DANSVILLE & MT MORRIS	D&MM
DANVILLE & POTTSVILLE	D&P
DARDANELLE & RUSSELLVILLE	D&R
DARDANELLE OLA & SOUTHERN	DO&S
DAUPHIN & SUSQUEHANNA	D&SQ
DAVENPORT ROCK ISLAND & NORTHWESTERN	DRI&N
DAWES SILICA MINING	DSM
DEATH VALLEY	DV
DEEP CREEK	DC
DEITCH COMPANY	DEI
DELAWARE & BOUND BROOK	D&BB
DELAWARE & EASTERN	D&E
DELAWARE & HUDSON	D&H
DELAWARE & HUDSON GRAVITY	D&HG
DELAWARE & NORTHERN	D&N
DELAWARE LACKAWANNA & WESTERN	DL&W
DELAWARE OTSEGO SYSTEM	DO
DELAWARE RIVER PORT AUTHORITY	DRPA
DELAWARE SUSQUEHANNA & SCHUYLKILL	DS&S
DELMARVA POWER & LIGHT	DP&L
DELRAY CONNECTING	DE
DELRAY TERMINAL	DET
DELTA SOUTHERN	DES
DELTA VALLEY & SOUTHERN	DV&S
DENISON & WASHITA	D&W
DENVER & INTERMOUNTAIN	D&I
DENVER & RIO GRANDE RAILROAD	D&RG
DENVER & RIO GRANDE WESTERN	D&RGW
DENVER & SALT LAKE	D&SL
DENVER BOULDER & WESTERN	DB&W
DENVER COLORADO CANYON & PACIFIC	DCC&P
DENVER ENID & GULF	DE&G
DENVER PACIFIC RAILROAD COMPANY	DP
DENVER SOUTH PARK & PACIFIC	DSP&P
DEPARTMENT OF DEFENSE	DOD
DEQUEEN & EASTERN	DQ&E
DES MOINES & CENTRAL IOWA	DM&CI
DES MOINES & MINNESOTA	DM&MI
DES MOINES UNION	DMU
DESERET-WESTERN RAILWAY	DW
DETROIT & MACKINAC	D&M
DETROIT & TOLEDO SHORT (SHORE?) LINE	D&TSL
DETROIT CARO & SANDUSKY	DC&S
DETROIT DIESEL EDISON	DED
DETROIT GRAND HAVEN & MILWAUKEE	DGH&M
DETROIT MACKINAC & MARQUETTE	DM&M
DETROIT PONTIAC & MACKINAC	DP&M
DETROIT RIVER TUNNEL COMPANY	DRT
DETROIT STREET RAILWAY	DST
DETROIT TERMINAL	DT
DETROIT TOLEDO & IRONTON	DT&I
DEVCO	D
DEVILS LAKE & NORTHERN	DL&N
DIAMOND & CALDOR RAILROAD	D&CA
DIAMOND VALLEY	DIA
DIERKS FOREST INDUSTRIES	DFI
DISMAL SWAMP	DS
DIXIE SAND & GRAVEL	DS&G
DOMINION ATLANTIC	DA
DOMINION FOUNDRIES & STEEL	DF&S
DONORA SOUTHERN	DOS
DOWLING & CAMP	DO&C
DRY FORK	DF
DUKE POWER COMPANY	DPC
DULUTH & IRON RANGE	D&IR
DULUTH & NORTHEASTERN	D&NE
DULUTH & NORTHERN MINNESOTA	D&NM
DULUTH MISSABE & IRON RANGE	DM&IR
DULUTH MISSABE & NORTHERN	DM&N
DULUTH MISSABE & WESTERN	DM&W
DULUTH MISSISSIPPI RIVER & NORTHERN	DMR&N
DULUTH RAINY LAKE & WINNIPEG	DRL&W
DULUTH SOUTH SHORE & ATLANTIC	DSS&A
DULUTH UNION DEPOT & TRANSFER	DUD&T
DULUTH UNION DEPOT & TRANSFER.	DUP&T.
DULUTH VIRGINIA & RAINY LAKE	DV&RL
DULUTH WINNIPEG & PACIFIC	DW&P
DUNCANNON LANDISBURG & BROADTOP	DL&B
DURANGO & SILVERTON	D&SI
DURHAM & SOUTHERN	D&S
DUTCHESS & COLUMBIA	D&C
DUTCHESS COUNTY	DU
EAGLE LAKE & WEST BRANCH	EL&WB
EAGLE MOUNTAIN	EMT
EAST & WEST COAST	E&WC
EAST BARRE & CHELSEA	EB&C
EAST BRANCH & LINCOLN	EB&L
EAST BROAD TOP	EBT
EAST BROAD TOP RAILROAD & COAL CO	EBT&CC
EAST CAMDEN & HIGHLAND	EC&H
EAST ERIE COMMERCIAL	EEC
EAST FLORIDA	EF
EAST JERSEY RAILROAD & TERMINAL	EJR&T
EAST JORDAN & SOUTHERN	EJ&S
EAST LINE & RED RIVER	EL&RR
EAST MAHANOY	EMA
EAST PENNSYLVANIA	EP
EAST SHORE & SURBURBAN	ES&S
EAST ST LOUIS & CARONDELET	ESL&C
EAST ST LOUIS JUNCTION	ESLJ
EAST TENNESSEE & WESTERN N CAROLINA	ET&WNC
EAST TENNESSEE VIRGINIA & GULF	ETV&G
EAST WASHINGTON	EW
EASTERN MASSACHUSETTS STREET RY	EMSR
EASTERN OHIO TRACTION	EOT
EASTERN SHORE	ESH
EASTMAN KODAK COMPANY	EK
EBERLE TANNING	ET
EDAVILLE	ED
EDGMOOR & MANETTA	E&M
EDMODNTON TRANSIT	ETR
EDVAVILLE RAILROAD	ER
EL DORADO & WESSON	ED&W
EL PASO & SOUTHWESTERN	EP&S
EL PASO CITY LINES	EPCL
EL PASO SOUTHERN	EPS
ELECTRO-MOTIVE	E-M
ELGIN & BELVIDERE INTERURBAN	E&B
ELGIN JOLIET & EASTERN	EJ&E
ELI LILLY PHARMACEUTICAL	ELP
ELK & HIGHLAND	E&H
ELKHART & WESTERN	E&W
ELKHART METALS	EM
EMMITSBURG	EMM
EMPIRE DETROIT DIV OF CYCLOPS STEEL	E-D
EMPIRE SUGAR COMPANY	ESC
EMPORIUM & MT JEWITT	E&MJ
ENSLEY OPEN HEARTH	EOH
EPSOM SALTS MONORAIL	ES

353

APPENDIX A (RAILROADS)

ERIE	E
ERIE & KALAMAZOO	E&K
ERIE & ONTARIO	E&O
ERIE & WYOMING VALLEY	E&WV
ERIE LACKAWANNA	EL
ERIE MINING COMPANY	EMC
ESCANABA & LAKE SUPERIOR	E&LS
ESPEE	SP
ESQUIMALT & NANAIMO FAMILY LINES	E&N
ESSEX TERMINAL	ETE
ETHIOPIAN GOVERNMENT RAILWAYS	EG
ETNA & MONTROSE	E&MO
EUREKA & KALAMATH RIVER	E&KR
EUREKA & PALISADE RAILWAY	E&P
EUREKA NEVADA	EN
EUROPEAN & NORTH AMERICAN	E&NA
EUSTIS	EU
EVANSVILLE INDIANAPOLIS & TERRE HAUTE	EI&TH
EVERETT	EV
EVERETT PIPE & STEEL	EVP&S
EXCELSIOR BRICK	EB
EXPO '67 RAPID TRANSIT, MONTREAL	EXPO
FAIRBANKS MORSE	F-M
FAIRCHILD & NORTHEASTERN	F&N
FAIRFIELD WORKS TENNESSEE COAL & IRON	FWTC&I
FAIRMOUNT PARK TRANSIT	FPT
FAIRPORT PAINESVILLE & EASTERN	FP&E
FALCONBRIDGE NICKEL MINES	FNM
FALL BROOK	FB
FALL RIVER LINE	FRL
FAMILY LINES	FAM
FARMVILLE & POWHATAN	F&P
FEATHER RIVER	FR
FEDERAL BARGE LINES	FBL
FELICIANA EASTERN	FE
FERDINAND	FERD
FERNANDINA & AMELIA BEACH	F&AB
FERNANDINA & JACKSONVILLE	F&J
FERNWOOD COLUMBIA & GULF	FC&GU
FILTRATION PLANT	FPL
FITCHBURG RAILROAD	FI
FLAMBEAU PAPER	FP
FLEMINGSBURG & NORTHWESTERN	F&NW
FLORA LOGGING COMPANY	FLC
FLORENCE & CRIPPLE CREEK	F&CC
FLORIDA	F
FLORIDA ALABAMA & GEORGIA	FA&G
FLORIDA CENTRAL	FC
FLORIDA CENTRAL & GULF	FC&G
FLORIDA CENTRAL & PENINSULAR	FC&P
FLORIDA CENTRAL & WESTERN	FC&W
FLORIDA EAST COAST	FEC
FLORIDA MIDLAND	FM
FLORIDA RAILWAY & NAVIGATIONS	FR&N
FLORIDA SOUTHERN	FS
FLORIDA SOUTHWESTERN	FSW
FLORIDA TRANSIT	FT
FLORIDA TRANSIT & PENINSULAR	FT&P
FONDA JOHNSTOWN & GLOVERSVILLE	FJ&G
FOOTE MINERALS	FMIN
FORD MOTOR COMPANY	FMC
FORDYCE & PRINCETON	F&PR
FORE RIVER	FOR
FOREST GROVE TRANSPORTATION	FGT
FORT BRAGG & SOUTHEASTERN	FB&S
FORT DODGE DES MOINES & SOUTHERN	FDM&S
FORT EUSTIS MILITARY RAILROAD	FEM
FORT HOWARD PAPER COMPANY	FHP
FORT ORANGE PAPER COMPANY	FOP
FORT SMITH & VAN BUREN	FS&VB
FORT SMITH & WESTERN	FS&W
FORT SMITH SUBIACO & ROCK ISLAND	FSS&RI
FORT STREET UNION DEPOT	FSUD
FORT WORTH & DENVER	FW&D
FORT WORTH & DENVER CITY	FW&DC
FORT WORTH BELT	FWB
FRANKFORT & CINCINNATI	F&C
FRANKLIN & LEBANON TRACTION CO	F&L
FRANKLIN & MEGANTIC	F&M
FREEHOLD & JAMESBURG AGRICULTURAL	F&JA
FREEPORT	FRE
FREMONT ELKHORN & MISSOURI VALLEY RR	FE&MV
FRENCH RAILWAYS	FRW
FRIENDSHIP	FRI
FRISCO	FRIS
FRISCO MANDARIN	FRM
FULTON COUNTY NARROW GAUGE	FCN
GAINESVILLE & GULF	G&G
GAINESVILLE MIDLAND	GMI
GALENA & CHICAGO UNION	G&CU
GALESBURG & GREAT EASTERN	G&GE
GALLATIN VALLEY ELECTRIC	GVE
GALVESTON & WESTERN	G&W
GALVESTON HOUSTON & HENDERSON	GH&H
GALVESTON HOUSTON ELECTRIC RY	GHE
GALVESTON WHARVES TERMINAL	GCW
GARDEN CITY WESTERN	GAF
GENERAL ANILINE FILM	GCS
GENERAL CRUSHED STONE	GCS
GENERAL ELECTRIC	GE
GENERAL IRON WORKS	GIW
GENERAL LOGGING COMPANY	GLC
GENERAL MINING ASSN OF NOVA SCOTIA	GMA
GENERAL MOTORS	GM
GENESSE & WYOMING	G&Y
GEORGES CREEK & CUMBERLAND	GC&C
GEORGES VALLEY	GV
GEORGETOWN	GTN
GEORGETOWN BRECKENRIDGE & LEADVILLE	GB&L
GEORGETOWN STEEL	GTS
GEORGIA	G
GEORGIA & FLORIDA	G&F
GEORGIA & WEST POINT	G&WP
GEORGIA ASHBURN SYLVESTER & CAMILLA	GAS&C
GEORGIA MARBLE	GAM
GEORGIA MIDLAND & GULF	GM&G
GEORGIA NORTHERN	GNO
GEORGIA POWER COMPANY	GPC
GEORGIA SOUTHERN & FLORDIA	GS&F
GEORGIA SOUTHWESTERN & GULF	GS&G
GEORGIA-PACIFIC CORPORATION	G-P
GETTYSBURG & HARRISBURG	G&H
GETTYSBURG ELECTRIC	GET
GIFFORD-HILL	G-H
GILFORD TRANSPORTATION COMPANY	GIL
GILMORE & PITTSBURGH	G&P
GILMORE INDUSTRIAL CENTER	GIC
GILPIN	GI
GILPIN COUNTY TRAMWAY	GCT
GLENMORE DISTILLERIES	GDIS
GLENMORE DISTRIBUTORS	GD
GODCHAUX SUGAR	GS
GOLD COAST	GC
GOODPASTURE GRAIN	GG
GOVERNMENT OF ONTARIO TRANSIT	GOT
GRACE CHEMICAL	GCH
GRAFTON & UPTON	G&U
GRAHAM COUNTY	GCO
GRAND FALLS CENTRAL	GFC
GRAND RAPIDS & INDIANA	GR&I
GRAND RIVER	GR
GRAND TRUNK	GT
GRAND TRUNK OF CANADA	GTC
GRAND TRUNK PACIFIC	GTP
GRAND TRUNK WESTERN	GTW
GRANITE	GRA
GRANITE MOUNTAIN QUARRIES	GMQ
GRASSE RIVER	GRR
GRAYSONIA NASHVILLE & ASHDOWN	GN&A
GREAT CENTRAL	GCE
GREAT NORTHERN	GN
GREAT PLAINS	GP
GREAT SLAVE LAKE	GSL
GREAT SOUTHWEST	GSW
GREAT WESTERN	GW
GREAT WESTERN OF CANADA	GWC
GREAT WESTERN SUGAR	GWS
GREATER WINNIPEG WATER DISTRICT	GWWD
GREEN BAY & WESTERN	GB&W
GREEN COVE SPRINGS & MELROSE	GCS&M
GREEN MOUNTAIN	GMT
GREEN RIVER STEEL COMPANY	GRSC
GREENBRIER CHEAT & ELK	GC&E
GREENVILLE & NORTHERN	G&N
GREENVILLE STEEL CAR COMPANY	GSCC
GREENWICH & JOHNSONVILLE	G&J
GRIZZLY FLATS	GF.
GROVES COMPANY	GCOM
GUIGNARD BRICK	GB
GULF COLORADO & SANTA FE	GC&SF
GULF MOBILE & NORTHERN	GM&N
GULF MOBILE & OHIO	GM&O
GULFPORT & MISSISSIPPI COAST TRACTION	G&M
HACKENSACK & NEW YORK RAILROAD	H&NY
HAGERSTOWN & FREDERICK	H&F
HAMMOND LUMBER COMPANY	HLC
HAMPTON & BRANCHVILLE	H&B
HANNA NICKEL SMELTING	HNSM
HANNIBAL & ST JOSEPH	H&SJ
HANNIBAL CONNECTING	HANC
HARDWICK & WOODBURY	H&W
HARLEM TRANSFER COMPANY	HTR
HARRINGTON LUMBER COMPANY	HRLC
HARRISBURG PORSMOUTH MT JOY & LANCAST	HPM
HARRISBURG RYS	H
HARTFORD & CONNECTICUT VALLEY	H&CV
HARTFORD & CONNECTICUT WESTERN	H&CW
HARTFORD & NEW HAVEN	H&NH
HARTFORD & SLOCOMB	H&S
HARTWELL	HAR
HARVARD BRANCH	HB
HASSINGER	HAS
HAWAIIAN RAILROAD COMPANY	HRC
HAZELTON-SUGAR LOAF	HSL
HAZLETON	HA
HECLA & TORCH LAKE	H&TL
HELENA LIGHT & RAILWAY	HL&R
HELENA SOUTHERN	HESO
HELENA SOUTHWESTERN	HES
HELLENIC STATE RAILWAYS	HSR
HERCULES POWDER COMPANY	HPC

STEPHANS' RAILROAD DIRECTORY

APPENDIX A (RAILROADS)

HERSEY TRANSIT	HT
HERSHEY CUBAN	HC
HETCH HETCHY	HH
HIBISCUS & HELICONIA	H&H
HICKGAS COMPANY	HGC
HIGH POINT THOMASVILLE & DENTON	HPT&D
HILLCREST OSBORNE	HOS
HILLSBORO & NORTH EASTERN	H&NE
HILLSDALE COUNTY	HIL
HIMMTEBERG-HARRISON LUMBER CO	HHL
HINKLEY LOCOMOTIVE WORKS	HLW
HOBART SOUTHERN	HS
HOBOKEN MANUFACTURERS	HM
HOBOKEN SHORE	HSH
HOCKEN VALLEY SCENIC RAILWAY	HVS
HOCKING VALLEY	HV
HOERNER-WALDORF PAPER PRODUCTS	H-WPP
HOLLIS & EASTERN RAILROAD	H&E
HOLTEN INTERURBAN RAILWAY COMPANY	HI
HOOPPOLE YORKTOWN & TAMPOCO	HY&T
HOOSAC TUNNEL & WILLMINGTON RAILROAD	HT&W
HOOSAC VALLEY STREET RAILWAY	HVSR
HOPKINSVILLE & SOUTHERN	H&SO
HORNELLSVILLE & COHOCTON VALLEY	HV&CV
HORTON LUMBER & TIMBER	HL&T
HOT SPRINGS	HOTS
HOUGHTON & ONTONAGON	H&O
HOUSASTONIC	HO
HOUSE OF DAVID	HD
HOUSTON & BRAZOS VALLEY (MP)	H&BV
HOUSTON & TEXAS	H&T
HOUSTON & TEXAS CENTRAL	H&TC
HOUSTON BELT & TERMINAL RAILWAY CO.	HB&T
HOUSTON NORTH SHORE (MP)	HNS
HUDSON & BROAD TOP MOUNTAIN	H&BT
HUDSON & MANHATTAN SUBWAY	H&M
HUDSON RIVER RAILROAD	HRRR
HUNINGTON	HU
HUNINGTON & BROAD TOP	HU&BT
HUNTINGTON & BROAD TOP MOUNTAIN RR	H&BTM
HUNTSVILLE & LAKE OF BAYS	H&LB
HURON BAY & IRON RANGE	HB&IR
HUTCHINSON & NORTHERN RAILWAY COMPANY	H&N
ICE FULTON TRIANGLE	IFT
ILLINOIS CENTRAL	IC
ILLINOIS CENTRAL GULF	ICG
ILLINOIS MIDLAND RAILWAY	IM
ILLINOIS NORTHERN	IN
ILLINOIS RIVER PACKET CO	IRPC
ILLINOIS SLAG & BALLAST	IS&B
ILLINOIS TERMINAL	IT
ILLINOIS TRACTION RAILWAY	ITR
ILLINOIS VALLEY TRACTION	IVT
ILWACO RAILWAY & NAVIGATION COMPANY	IL
INDIAN HILL & IRON RANGE	IH&IR
INDIANA HARBOR BELT	IHB
INDIANA NORTHERN	INN
INDIANA RAILROAD	I
INDIANAPOLIS & CINCINATTI TRACTION CO	I&C
INDIANAPOLIS RAILWAYS	IRW
INDIANAPOLIS UNION	IU
INGALLS SHIPBUBILDING	IS
INGERSOLL RAND POWERED LOCOMOTIVES	IRP
INLAND EMPIRE SYSTEM	IES
INLAND LIME & STONE	IL&S
INSPERATION CONSOLIDATION COPPER CO	ICCO
INTER-URBAN RAILWAY	IUR
INTERCOLONIAL RAILWAY	ICO
INTERNATIONAL GREAT NORTHERN (MP)	I-GN
INTERNATIONAL MILLING	IMI
INTERNATIONAL MINERALS & CHEMICAL	IM&C
INTERNATIONAL RW OF CENTRAL AMERICA	IRCA
INTERSTATE	INTER
INTERSTATE PUBLIC SERV CO OF INDIANA	IPSI
INTERSTATE STREET RAILWAY	ISR
INTERURBAN RAILWAY & TERMINAL	IR&T
IOLA & NORTHERN	I&N
IOLA & ST JOSEPH CANAL & RAILROAD	I&JC
IOWA CENTRAL	IOWAC
IOWA POWER & LIGHT	IP&L
IOWA TERMINAL RAILROAD COMPANY	IOWA
IOWA TRANSFER	IOWAT
IRON MOUNTAIN	IMT
IRON ORE CO OF CANADA	IOCC
IRONTON	IR
ISLAND CREEK COAL	ICC
ISLAND TERMINAL COMPANY	ITC
ITHACA & OWEGO	I&O
JACKASS & WESTERN	J&W
JACKSON COUNTY GRAIN	JCG
JACKSONVILLE & SOUTHWESTERN	J&S
JACKSONVILLE BELT	JB
JACKSONVILLE GAINESVILLE & GULF	JG&G
JACKSONVILLE MAYPORT & PABLO RY & NAV	JM&P
JACKSONVILLE PENSACOLA & MOBILE	JP&M
JACKSONVILLE ST AUGUSTINE & HALIFAX R	JA&HR
JACKSONVILLE TAMPA & KEY WEST	JT&KW
JACKSONVILLE TERMINAL	JT
JAMESTOWN WESTFIELD & NORTHWESTERN	JW&N
JAPAN NATIONAL RAILWAY	JNR
JAPANESE NATIONAL RAILWAYS	JN
JAY STREET CONNECTING RAILROAD	JS
JEROME & SOUTHWESTERN	J&SW
JERSEY CENTRAL	JCE
JERSEYVILLE & EASTERN	J&E
JIM WALTER RESOURCES INC	JWR
JOHNSON LUMBER	JL
JOHNSONBURG	JO
JOHNSTOWN & STONY CREEK	J&SC
JOHNSTOWN TRACTION CO	JTC
JONES & LAUGHLIN STEEL	J&L
JUNCTION CITY-HORTON WOODEN RAILROAD	JC
KAHULUI	KA
KAISER BAUXITE	KB
KANAWHA & MICHIGAN	K&M
KANAWHA CENTRAL	KAC
KANE	K
KANE & ELK	K&E
KANSAS & OKLAHOMA	K&O
KANSAS CITY & PACIFIC	KC&P
KANSAS CITY & SOUTHERN RAILROAD	KC&S
KANSAS CITY CONNECTING	KCC
KANSAS CITY ELDORADO & SOUTHERN	KSE&S
KANSAS CITY KAW VALLEY	KCKV
KANSAS CITY KAW VALLEY & WESTERN	KCKV&W
KANSAS CITY MEXICO & ORIENT	KCM&O
KANSAS CITY PITTSBURGH & GULF	KCP&G
KANSAS CITY PUBLIC SERVICE	KSPS
KANSAS CITY SOUTHERN	KCS
KANSAS CITY TERMINAL	KCT
KANSAS OKLAHOMA & GULF RAILWAY	KO&G
KANSAS UTILITIES COMPANY	KUC
KATY NORTHWEST	KATY
KEATING & SMETHPORT	K&S
KEESEVILLE AUSABLE CHASM &L CHAMPLAIN	KAC&LC
KELLY'S CREEK (KELLEYS CREEK)	KC
KENDALL & ELDRED	K&EL
KENNEBEC CENTRAL	KCE
KENNECOTT	KE
KENTUCKY & INDIANA TERMINAL	K&IT
KENTUCKY & TENNESSEE RAILWAY	K&T
KENTUCKY TRACTION & TERMINAL	KT&T
KENTUCKY UTILITIES COMPANY	KTU
KERSEY	KER
KEWAUNEE GREEN BAY & WESTERN	KGB&W
KEY SYSTEM OF SAN FRANCISCO	KS
KEYSTONE	KEY
KINGFIELD & DEAD RIVER	K&DR
KINMOND BROTHERS MONTREAL	KBM
KINZUA	KI
KINZUA & TIONA	K&TI
KINZUA CREEK & KANE	KC&K
KINZUA HEMLOCK	KH
KINZUA VALLEY	KV
KIRBY LUMBER COMPANY	KLC
KISO FOREST JAPAN	KF
KITTY HAWK CENTRAL	KHC
KLICKITAT LOG & LUMBER	KL&L
KLIPNOCKIE	KLI
KNICKERBOCKER LIME	KL
KNOX	KN
KNOX & LINCOLN	K&L
KNOXVILLE POWER & LIGH	KP&L
KOPPERS COMPANY	KOP
KOSMOS TIMBER COMPANY	KTC
KUERT CONCRETE	KUCO
KUSHEQUA	KU
L&N SHOPS	L&NS
LA JUNTA INDUSTRIAL PARK	LJIP
LA SALLE & BUREAU COUNTY	LS&B
LACKAWANNA	LACK
LACKAWANNA & BLOOMSBURG	L&B
LACKAWANNA & PITTSBURG	L&P
LACKAWANNA & SOUTHWESTERN	L&SW
LACKAWANNA & WYOMING VALLEY	L&WV
LACKAWAXEN & STOURBRIDGE	LA&S
LACLEDE STEEL COMPANY	LSCO
LAKE CHAMPLAIN & MORIAH	LC&M
LAKE CHAMPLAIN & ST LAWRENCE JUNCTION	LC&LJ
LAKE ERIE & EASTERN	LE&E
LAKE ERIE & FORT WAYNE	LE&FW
LAKE ERIE & NORTHERN (CP)	LE&N
LAKE ERIE & PITTSBURGH RAILROAD	LE&P
LAKE ERIE BOWLING GREEN & NAPOLEON	LEBG&N
LAKE ERIE FRANKLIN & CLARION	LEF&C
LAKE SHORE & MICHIGAN SOUTHERN	LS&MC
LAKE SHORE ELECTRIC INTERURBAN	LSE
LAKE SUPERIOR & ISHPEMING	LS&I
LAKE SUPERIOR TERMINAL & TRANSFER	LST&T
LAKE TERMINAL	LT
LAKE WIMICO ST JOSEPH CANAL & RR CO	LW&JC
LAKELAND	L
LAKESIDE & MARBLEHEAD	L&MA
LAMAR QUEENS & NORTHERN	LQ&N
LANCASTER & CHESTER	L&C
LANCASTER & YORK FURNACE STREET RY	L&YF
LANCASTER LOCOMOTIVE WORKS	LLW
LANCASTER OXFORD & SOUTHERN	LO&S
LAONA & NORTHERN	L&NO
LARAMIE NORTH PARK & WESTERN	LNP&W
LAS VEGAS & TONOPAH	LV&T
LAUHOFF GRAIN	LG
LAUREL RIVER & HOT SPRINGS	LR&HS
LAURINBURG & SOUTHERN	LA&SO
LAWNDALE	LA
LAWTON RAILWAY & LIGHTING	LR&L
LEAVENWORTH KANSAS & WESTERN	LK&W
LEBANON SPRINGS	LS
LEE TIDEWATER CYPRESS	LTC
LEETONIA & CHERRY VALLEY	L&CV
LEHIGH & HUDSON RIVER	L&HR
LEHIGH & MAHANOY	L&M
LEHIGH & NEW ENGLAND	L&NE
LEHIGH & SUSQUEHANNA	L&SQ
LEHIGH LUZERNE	LL
LEHIGH NAVIGATION COAL COMPANY	LNCC
LEHIGH VALLEY	LV
LEHIGH VALLEY TRANSIT	LVT
LEIPER	LEI
LEONA HEIGHTS	LH
LEONARDS STORE	LST
LIGONIER VALLEY	LIG
LIMA HAMILTON CORPORATION	L-HC
LIMA LOCOMOTIVE WORKS	LILW
LIMA STONE COMPANY	LSC
LINCOLN STONE QUARRY	LSQ
LINWOOD STREET RAILWAY	LSR
LIPSETT STEEL COMPANY	LISC
LITCHFIELD & MADISON	LI&M
LITTLE EMMA SILVER MINE	LESM
LITTLE FALLS & DOLGEVILLE	LF&D
LITTLE RIVER RAILROAD	LITRI
LITTLE SCHUYLKILL NAV RR & COAL CO.	LSCH
LIVE OAK & GULF	LO&G
LIVE OAK PERRY & GULF	LOP&G
LIVE OAK TAMPA & HOWLAND'S BLUFF	LOT&HB
LIVE POULTRY TRANSPORT COPMPANY	LPT
LIVONIA AVON & LAKEVILLE	LA&L
LOCKS & CANALS COMPANY LOWELL MASS	L&CC
LODI	LODI

APPENDIX A (RAILROADS)

LONDON & PORT STANLEY	L&PS
LONE STAR STEEL COMPANY	LSSC
LONG BELL RAILROAD	LB
LONG ISLAND RAILROAD	LI
LONGVIEW PORTLAND & NORTHERN	LP&N
LORBERRY CREEK	LC
LORTON & OCCOQUAN	L&O
LOS ANGELES & EAGLE ROCK VALLEY	LA&ERV
LOS ANGELES & GLENDALE	LA&G
LOS ANGELES & LONG BEACH	LA&LB
LOS ANGELES & PACIFIC RR	LA&P
LOS ANGELES & REDONDO	LA&R
LOS ANGELES & SALT LAKE (UP)	LA&SL
LOS ANGELES & SAN DIEGO BEACH	LA&SDB
LOS ANGELES & SAN GABRIEL VALLEY	LA&SG
LOS ANGELES & SAN PEDRO	LA&SP
LOS ANGELES COUNTY	LAC
LOS ANGELES INDEPENDENT RAILROAD	LAIR
LOS ANGELES JUNCTION	LAJ
LOS ANGELES PASADENA & GLENDALE	LAP&G
LOS ANGELES RAILWAY	LAR
LOS ANGELES TERMINAL	LAT
LOS ANGELES TRANSIT	LATR
LOUISA	LOU
LOUISANA & ARKANSAS KANSAS CITY SOUTH	L&AKS
LOUISIANA & ARKANSAS RAILWAY COMPANY	L&A
LOUISIANA & NORTH WEST	L&NW
LOUISIANA & PINE BLUFF	L&PB
LOUISIANA CYPRESS LUMBER COMPANY	LCL
LOUISIANA EASTERN	LE
LOUISIANA MIDLAND	LM
LOUISIANA SOUTHERN	LOS
LOUISVILLE & FRANKFORT	L&F
LOUISVILLE & INTERURBAN	L&I
LOUISVILLE & NASHVILLE	L&N
LOUISVILLE HENDERSON & ST LOUIS	LH&SL
LOUISVILLE NEW ALBANY & CORYDON	LNA&C
LOWVILLE & BEAVER RIVER	L&BR
LOYAL	LO
LUDINGTON & NORTHERN	LU&N
LUDLOW & SOUTHERN	L&S
LUKENS STEEL	LUS
LYKENS VALLEY	LYK

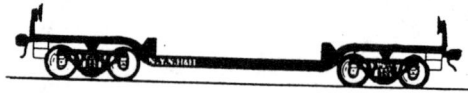

MACK TRUCK COMPANY	MTC
MACMILLAN BLOEDEL LIMITED	MBL
MACON & BIRMINGHAM	M&BI
MACON DUBLIN & SAVANNAH	MD&S
MAD RIVER & LAKE ERIE	MR&LE
MADEIRA-MAMORE RAILWAY (BRAZIL)	M-M
MADISON & INDIANAPOLIS	M&I
MADRID	MAD
MAGMA ARIZONA	MA
MAHANOY & SHAMOKIN	M&SH
MAINE CENTRAL	MC
MAINE CENTRAL SHOPS	MCS
MAMMOTH CAVE	MCA
MANAHAWKEN & LONG BEACH	M&LB

MANCHESTER & ONEIDA	M&ONE
MANCHESTER DORSET & GRANVILLE	MD&G
MANCHESTER LOCOMOTIVE WORKS	MLW
MANCHESTER STREET RAILWAY	MSRW
MANDEVILLE NORTHERN	MAN
MANHATTAN ELECTRIC	MAE
MANHATTEN ALMA & BURLINGAME	MA&B
MANILA RAILWAY (PHILIPPINES)	MRW
MANISTIQUE & LAKE SUPERIOR	M&LS
MANITOU & PIKE'S PEAK RAILWAY	M&PP
MANN'S CREEK RAILROAD	MCR
MANSFIELD COLDWATER & LAKE MICHIGAN	MC&LM
MANUFACTURERS	MFG
MANUFACTURERS JUNCTION	MJ
MARCELLUS & OTISCO LAKE	M&OL
MARENGO MILWAUKEE & NORTHERN	MM&N
MARIANNA & BLOUNTSTOWN	M&BL
MARIETTA & NORTH GEORGIA	M&NG
MARINETTE TOMAHAWK & WESTERN	MT&W
MARION POWER SHOVEL COMPANY	MPS
MARION RIVER CARRY	MRC
MARQUETTE & HURON MOUNTAIN	M&HM
MARQUETTE & ONTONAGON	M&ON
MARQUETTE & SOUTHEASTERN	M&SE
MARQUETTE & WESTERN	M&W
MARQUETTE CEMENT	MCEM
MARTHA'S VINEYARD	MV
MARYLAND & DELAWARE	M&D
MARYLAND & PENNSYLVANIA	MA&PA
MASON & OCEANA	M&OC
MASONITE CORPORATION	MCORP
MASSACHUSETTS BAY TRANSIT AUTHORITY	MBTA
MASSACHUSETTS CENTRAL	MASSC
MASSENA TERMINAL	MATE
MATERIAL SERVICE CORPORATION	MSCO
MATTAGAMI RAILROAD	MAT
MAUCH CHUNK	MCH
MAXTON ALMA & SOUTHBOUND	MA&S
MCCLOUD RIVER	MCRI
MCKEAN & BUFFALO	M&B
MCKEESPORT CONNECTING	MCKC
MEAD RUN	MR
MEADOW RIVER LUMBER	MRL
MEMPHIS EL PASO & PACIFIC	MEP&P
MEMPHIS UNION STATION	MUS
MERIDIAN & BIGBEE	M&BIG
MESABE SOUTHERN	MSO
METAL PROCESSING INC	MPI
METROPOLITAN TRANSIT AUTHORITY BOSTON	MTA
MEXICAN CENTRAL	MXC
MEXICAN SL & INDUST RR (VARIOUS)	MSL&IR
MEXICANO	MEX
MEXICO CITY STREETCARS	MCI
MEXICO CITY TRAMWAYS	MCT
MICH-CAL	MICH-CAL
MICHIGAN CENTRAL	MICHC
MICHIGAN LIMESTONE OPERATIONS	MLO
MICHIGAN NORTHERN	MN
MICHIGAN RAILWAY CO	MRR
MICHIGAN-CAILFORNIA LUMBER	M-CL
MIDDLE FORK RAILROAD	MF
MIDDLETOWN & NEW JERSEY	M&NJ
MIDDLETOWN & UNIONVILE	M&U
MIDLAND CONTINENTAL	MIDC
MIDLAND RAILROAD OF NEW JERSEY	MNJ
MIDLAND RAILWAY OF MANITOBA	MM
MIDLAND TERMINAL	MIT
MIDLAND VALLEY	MIV
MIDWAY	MID
MIDWEST CENTRAL RAILROAD	MWC
MILFORD MATAMORAS & NEW YORK	MM&NY
MILITARY RAILWAY SERVICE	MRS
MILL CREEK & MINE HILL NAV & RR CO	MC&MHN
MILL CREEK VALLEY	MCV
MILSTEAD	MIL
MILWAUKEE	MILW
MILWAUKEE & NORTHERN	M&N
MILWAUKEE ELECTRIC LINES SYSTEM	ME
MILWAUKEE ELECTRIC RAILWAY & LIGHT	MER&L
MILWAUKEE LAKE SHORE & WESTERN	MLS&W
MINARETS & WESTERN RAILWAY	MI&W
MINE HILL & SCHUYLKILL HAVEN	MH&SH
MINERAL ROCK TRAMWAY	MRT
MINERALES NACIONAL DE MEXICO	MNDM
MINNEAPOLIS & RAINY RIVER	M&RR
MINNEAPOLIS & ST LOUIS	M&SL
MINNEAPOLIS & ST PAUL	M&SP
MINNEAPOLIS ANOKA & CUYUNA RANGE	MA&CR
MINNEAPOLIS LYNDALE & MINNESOTA	ML&M
MINNEAPOLIS NORTHFIELD & SOUTHERN	MN&S
MINNEAPOLIS RED LAKE & MANITOBA	MRL&M
MINNEAPOLIS ST PAUL & SAULTE ST MARIE	SOO
MINNEAPOLIS ST PAUL ROCH & DUBUQUE E	MPR&DE
MINNESOTA & NORTH WISCONSIN	M&NW
MINNESOTA & NORTHWESTERN RAILROAD	MI&NW
MINNESOTA DAKOTA & WESTERN	MD&W
MINNESOTA TRANSFER	MITR
MINNESOTA WESTERN	MW
MISSISQUOI & CLYDE RIVERS	M&CR
MISSISSIPPI & SKUNA VALLEY	M&SV
MISSISSIPPI CENTRAL	MISSC
MISSISSIPPI EXPORT	MEXP
MISSISSIPPI RIVER & BONNE TERRE	MR&BT
MISSISSIPPIAN	MI
MISSOURI & ARKANSAS	M&A
MISSOURI & ILLINOIS BRIDGE & BELT	M&IB&B
MISSOURI & NORTH ARKANSAS	M&NA
MISSOURI KANSAS TEXAS	MKT
MISSOURI PACIFIC RAILWAY COMPANY	MP
MISSOURI PORTLAND CEMENT	MPCE
MISSOURI SOUTHERN	MS
MISSOURI-ILLINOIS	M-I
MOBILE & GULF	M&G
MOBILE & OHIO	M&O
MOBILE CHEMICAL	MOBCH
MOCTEZUMA BREWERY	MB
MODELTRONICS	MTR
MODESTO & EMPIRE TRACTION	M&ET
MOHAWK & HUDSON RIVER	M&HR
MOIRA & BOMBAY	M&BO

APPENDIX A (RAILROADS)

Railroad	Abbr
MOJAVE NORTHERN	MOJN
MOLINE TIMBER CO	MTI
MONMOUTH COUNTY ELECTRIC	MCE
MONOCACY VALLEY	MOV
MONOLITH PORTLAND CEMENT	MPC
MONON	M
MONONGAHELA	MON
MONONGAHELA CONNECTING	MCO
MONSON RAILROAD	MO
MONTAGUE STEEL COMPANY	MSC
MONTANA WESTERN	MOW
MONTCLAIR & GREENWOOD LAKE	M&GL
MONTEREY & SALINAS VALLEY	M&SVA
MONTOUR	MONT
MONTPELIER & BARRE	M&BA
MONTPELIER & WELLS RIVER RAILROAD	M&WR
MONTREAL & ATLANTA (CP)	M&AT
MONTREAL & CHAMPLAIN	M&C
MONTREAL & LACHINE	M&L
MONTREAL & PLATTSBURG	M&P
MONTREAL & SOREL	M&S
MONTREAL & SOUTHERN COUNTIES	M&SC
MONTREAL ICE RAILWAY	MIRW
MONTREAL PORTLAND & BOSTON	MP&B
MONTREAL TRANSIT	MT
MOPAC	MOP
MOREHEAD & NORTH FORK	M&NF
MORGON'S LOUISIANA & TEXAS RAILROAD	ML&T
MORRISTOWN & ERIE	M&E
MORSE & ORY	M&ORY
MOSCOW CAMDEN & ST AUGUSTINE	MC&SA
MOSHASSUCK VALLEY	MOVA
MOTLEY COUNTY RAILROAD	MCRR
MOUNT CARBON & PORT CARBON	MC&PC
MOUNT CARBON RAILWAY	MCRW
MOUNT GRETNA NARROW-GAUGE	MG
MOUNT HOOD	MH
MOUNT HOPE MINERAL	MHM
MOUNT JEWELL & SMETHPORT	MJ&S
MOUNT JEWETT CLERMONT & NORTHERN	MJC&N
MOUNT JEWETT KINZUA & RITERVILLE	MJK&R
MOUNT TAMALPAIS & MUIR WOODS	MT&MW
MOUNT WASHINGTON	MTW
MOUNT WASHINGTON COG	MWCOG
MOWER LUMBRE COMPANY	MLC
MUNCIE & WESTERN	M&WE
MUNICIPAL RAILWAY OF SAN FRANCISCO	MSF
MUNICIPAL DOCKS	MD
MUNISING	MU
MUNISING MARQUETTE & SOUTHEASTERN	MM&S
MUSKINGUM ELECTRIC RAILROAD	MEL
MUSKOGEE ELECTRIC TRACTION	MET
NACIONALES DE MEXICO	NDM
NAHMA & NORTHERN	N&N
NANTUCKET RAILROAD	NRR
NAPIERVILLE JUNCTION	NJ
NAPORANO IRON & METAL	NI&M
NARRAGANSETT PIER	NPIER
NASHUA & LOWELL	N&L
NASHVILLE CHATTANOOGA & ST LOUIS	NC&SL
NASHVILLE INTERURBAN RAILWAY	NIR
NATCHEZ URANIA & RUSTON	NU&R
NATIONAL CITY & OTAY	NC&O
NATIONAL IRON WORKS	NIW
NATIONAL PLATE GLASS CO	NPGC
NATIONAL RAILWAYS OF MEXICO	NRWM
NATIONALES DE MEXICOS	NDEM
NAUGATUCK	NAU
NAVEL ORDINANCE DEPOT	NOD
NEKOOSA PAPER COMPANY	NPCO
NELSON & ALBEMARLE	N&A
NELSON BC STREET RAILWAYS	NBCS
NESCOPEC	NES
NESQUEHONING	N
NEVADA & CALIFORNIA RAILROAD	N&CA
NEVADA CALIFORNIA OREGON	NCO
NEVADA CENTRAL	NC
NEVADA COPPER BELT	NCBT
NEVADA COUNTY NARROW-GAUGE	NCN
NEVADA COUNTY TRACTION	NCT
NEVADA NORTHERN	NN
NEW ALBANY & LOUISVILLE ELECTRIC	NA&LE
NEW BERLIN & WINFIELD	NB&W
NEW BRUNSWICK & CANADA	NB&C
NEW CANAAN	NCA
NEW CASTLE & FRENCHTOWN	NC&F
NEW CORNELIA BRANCH	NCB
NEW CORNELIA COPPER COMPANY	NCC
NEW ENGLAND LACKAWANNA & PITTSBURGH	NEL&P
NEW HAVEN	NH
NEW HAVEN & NORTHAMPTON	NH&NI
NEW HAVEN & SHORT LINE	NH&SL
NEW HOPE & IVYLAND	NH&I
NEW JERSEY & NEW YORK	NJ&NY
NEW JERSEY & PENNSYLVANIA	NJ&P
NEW JERSEY INDIANA & ILLINOIS	NJI&I
NEW JERSEY MIDLAND	NJM
NEW JERSEY RAILROAD & TRANSPORTATION	NJR&T
NEW JERSEY ZINC	NJZ
NEW MEXICO & SOUTHERN PACIFIC	NM&SP
NEW MEXICO LUMBER COMPANY	NMLC
NEW ORLEANS & CARROLLTON	NO&C
NEW ORLEANS & LOWER COAST	NO&LC
NEW ORLEANS & NORTHEASTERN	NO&N
NEW ORLEANS CITY & LAKE RAILROAD	NOC&L
NEW ORLEANS CITY RAILROAD	NOC
NEW ORLEANS PUBLIC BELT	NOPB
NEW ORLEANS PUBLIC SERVICE	NOPS
NEW ORLEANS TERMINAL	NOT
NEW ORLEANS TEXAS & MEXICO	NOT&M
NEW ORLEANS UNION PASSENGER TERMINAL	NOUPT
NEW SOUTH WALES GOVERNMENT RAILROAD	NSW
NEW SOUTH WALES GOVERNMENT RAILWAY	NSWG
NEW YORK & BROOKLYN BRIDGE	NY&BB
NEW YORK & ERIE	NY&E
NEW YORK & GREENWOOD LAKE	NY&GL
NEW YORK & HARLEM	NY&H
NEW YORK & LONG BRANCH	NY&LB
NEW YORK & NEW ENGLAND	NY&NE
NEW YORK & OSWEGO MIDLAND	NY&OM
NEW YORK & OTTAWA	NY&O
NEW YORK & PENNSYLVANIA	NY&P
NEW YORK & QUEENS COUNTY	NY&QC
NEW YORK AUBURN & LANSING	NYA&L
NEW YORK CENTRAL	NYC
NEW YORK CENTRAL & HUDSON RIVER	NYC&H
NEW YORK CENTRAL & NORTHERN	NYC&N
NEW YORK CHICAGO & ST LOUIS	NYC&SL
NEW YORK CITY & NORTHERN	NYC&N.
NEW YORK CITY ELEVATED RAILROAD	NYCE
NEW YORK CITY RAPID	NYCR
NEW YORK CITY SUBWAY-ELEVATED LINES	NYCS
NEW YORK CITY THIRD AVENUE ELEVATED	NYCTAE
NEW YORK DOCK	NYD
NEW YORK LAKE ERIE & WESTERN	NYLE&W
NEW YORK NEW HAVEN & HARTFORD RAIL RD	NYNH&H
NEW YORK ONTARIO & WESTERN	NYO&W
NEW YORK PITTSBURGH & CHICAGO	NYP&C
NEW YORK SUSQUEHANNA & WESTERN	NYS&W
NEW YORK WEST SHORE & BUFFALO	NYWS&B
NEW YORK WESTCHESTER & BOSTON	NYW&B
NEWARK SUBWAYS	NSUB
NEWBURGH & SOUTH SHORE	N&SS
NEWBURGH DUTCHESS & CONNECTICUT	ND&C
NEWFOUNDLAND	NF
NEWPORT & PROVIDENCE	N&P
NEWPORT & SHERMANS VALLEY	N&SV
NEZPERCE	NEZ
NIAGARA ESCARPMENT INCLINED PLANE	NEIP
NIAGARA JUNCTION	NJUN
NIAGARA PORTAGE INCLINE PLANE	NPIP
NIAGARA ST CATHERINES & TORONTO	NSC&T
NICHOLAS FAYETTE & GREENBRIAR	NF&G
NICHOLSON TERMINAL & DOCK	NT&D
NICKEL PLATE	NKP
NORANDA MINES	NM
NORFOLK & CAROLINA	N&C
NORFOLK & PORTSMOUTH BELT LINE	N&PBL
NORFOLK & VIRGINIA BEACH	N&VB
NORFOLK & WESTERN	N&W
NORFOLK CITY	NCI
NORFOLK FRANKLIN & DANVILLE	NF&D
NORFOLK SOUTHERN RAILWAY	NSO
NORTH AMERICAN COAL	NAC
NORTH AMERICAN DISPATCH	NAD
NORTH CAROLINA STATE PORTS AUTHORITY	NCSPA
NORTH COAST LINES	NCL
NORTH JERSEY RAPID TRANSIT	NJRT
NORTH LOUISANA & GULF	NL&G
NORTH PACIFIC COAST	NPC
NORTH PENNSYLVANIA	NPA
NORTH SHORE	NS
NORTH STAR STEEL COMPANY	NSSC
NORTH YAKIMA & VALLEY	NY&V
NORTH-WEST RAILROAD	N-W
NORTHAMPTON & BATH	N&B
NORTHEAST OKLAHOMA	NO
NORTHERN & NORTH WESTERN	N&NW
NORTHERN ALBERTA RAILWAY	NA
NORTHERN CENTRAL	NCE
NORTHERN CROSS	NCR
NORTHERN ELECTRIC	NE
NORTHERN INDIANA DOCK	NID
NORTHERN INDIANA RAILWAY COMPANY	NI
NORTHERN NEW BRUNSWICK & SEABOARD	NNB&S
NORTHERN NEW YORK	NNY
NORTHERN OHIO TRACTION & LIGHT	NOT&L
NORTHERN PACIFIC	NP
NORTHERN RAILWAY OF CANADA	NRC
NORTHWESTERN	NW
NORTHWESTERN OKLAHOMA	NWO
NORTHWESTERN PACIFIC RAILROAD	NWP
NORTHWESTERN PENNSYLVANIA RAILROAD	NPR
NORTHWESTERN STEEL & WIRE	NS&W
NORTHWOOD PULP & TIMBER	NP&T
NORWICH & WORCESTER	N&WO
NORWOOD & ST LAWRENCE	N&SL
NOVA SCOTIA	NSC
OAHU RAILWAY & LAND COMPANY	OR&LC
OAHU RAILWAY & TERMINAL WAREHOUSING	OR&TW
OAKLAND ANTLOCK & EASTERNY	OA&E
OAKLAND TERMINAL	OT
OCEAN CITY WESTERN	OCW
OCEAN SHORE RAILROAD	OS
OGDENSBURG & LAKE CHAMPLAIN	O&LC
OGDENSBURG & NORWOOD	O&N
OGDENSBURG BRIDGE & PORT AUTHORITY	OB&PA
OHIO & INDIANA STONE COMPANY	O&IS
OHIO & KENTUCKY	O&K
OHIO ELECTRIC RAILWAY	OER
OHIO MIDLAND	OM
OHIO POWER COMPANY	OPC
OHIO PUBLIC SERVICE COMPANY	OPS
OHIO RIVER	OR
OHIO RIVER & WESTERN	OR&W
OHIO SOUTHERN	OSO
OIL FIELDS SHORT LINES	OFSL
OKLAHOMA & ARKANSAS	O&A
OKLAHOMA & RICH MOUNTAIN	O&RM
OKLAHOMA CENTRAL	OC
OKLAHOMA CITY ADA-ATOKA	OCITY
OKLAHOMA RAILWAY	ORW
OKLAHOMA SOUTHWESTERN	OSW
OKMULGEE NORTHERN	ONO
OLD COLONY	OCO
OLEAN	O
OLEAN BRADFORD & WARREN	OB&W
OLIVER IRON MINING COMPANY	OIM
OMAHA LINCOLN & BEATRICE	OL&B
ONTARIO & QUEBEC RAILWAY	O&Q
ONTARIO NORTHLAND	ON
ONTARIO SIMCOE & HURON	OS&H
ORANGE BELT	OB
ORANGE MOUNTAIN TRACTION	OMT
OREGON & NAVIGATION COMPANY	OR&NC
OREGON & NORTHWESTERN	O&NW
OREGON AMERICAN	OA
OREGON CALIFORNIA & EASTERN	OC&E
OREGON ELECTRIC	OE
OREGON PACIFIC & EASTERN	OP&E

357

APPENDIX A (RAILROADS)

Railroad	Code
OREGON PORTAGE	OP
OREGON RAILWAYS & NAVIGATION COMPANY	URWO
OREGON SHORT LINE	OSL
OREGON STEAM NAVIGATION COMPANY	OSN
OREGON WASHINGTON RR & NAVIGATION CO	OWR&N
ORLEANS KENNER TRACTION	OKT
ORO DAM	ORO
OSAGE	OSA
OSHAWA	OSH
OSTRANDER RAILWAY & TIMBER CO	ORTC
OSTRICH FARM	OF
OTTAWA & PRESCOTT	O&P
OVERLAND DISPATCH	OD
PACIFIC COAST RAILWAY	PCOA
PACIFIC ELECTRIC	PE
PACIFIC GREAT EASTERN	PGE
PACIFIC LINES	PL
PACIFIC LUMBER COMPANY	PLC
PACIFIC MOBILE & OHIO	PM&O
PACIFIC RAILWAY OF MEXICO	PRWM
PACOLET MILLS MANUFACTURING	PMM
PANAMA RR	PAN
PARIS & DECATUR	P&D
PARIS & MOUNT PLEASANT	P&MP
PARK UTAH CONSOLIDATED MINES	PUCM
PARR TERMINAL	PARR
PARSONS & PACIFIC	P&P
PASADENA CITY	PCI
PASADENA RAILWAY	PARW
PATAPSCO & BACK RIVERS	P&BR
PATTEN & SHERMAN	P&SH
PATTERSON & HUDSON RIVER	P&HR
PATTERSON & WESTERN	P&WE
PEABODY COAL	PCOAL
PEABODY SHORT LINE	PSL
PEARL RIVER VALLEY	PRV
PECOS VALLEY & NORTHEASTERN	PV&N
PECOS VALLEY SOUTHERN	PVS
PEG LEG	PLEG
PENINSULA TERMINAL	PTER
PENN CENTRAL	PC
PENN ROAD SEA SHORE	PRSS
PENNSBORO & HARRISVILLE	P&H
PENNSYLVANIA & MARYLAND STREET RW	P&MSR
PENNSYLVANIA & NEW YORK	PA&NY
PENNSYLVANIA GLASS SAND COMPANY	PGS
PENNSYLVANIA POUGHKEEPSIE &BOSTON	PP&B
PENNSYLVANIA RAILROAD	PRR
PENNSYLVANIA READING SEASHORE LINES	PRSL
PENNSYLVANIA RR OF MARYLAND	PRRMD
PENOBSCOT & KENNEBEC	P&KE
PENSACOLA & ATLANTIC	P&A
PENSACOLA & GEORGIA	P&G
PENSACOLA & PERDIDO	P&PE
PENSACOLA ALABAMA & TENNESSEE	PA&T
PEORIA & EASTERN RAILWAY	P&EA
PEORIA & OQUQWKA	P&OQ
PEORIA & PEKIN UNION	P&PU
PEORIA DECATUR & EVANSVILLE	PD&E
PEORIA GATEWAY RAILROAD	PG
PEORIA TERMINAL	PETE
PERE MARQUETTE	PM
PERRY COUNTY	PECO
PETALUMA & SANTA ROSA	P&SR
PHILADELPHIA & COLUMBIA	P&C
PHILADELPHIA & READING	P&R
PHILADELPHIA & WESTERN RAILROAD	P&WR
PHILADELPHIA BETHLEHEM & NEW ENGLAND	PB&NE
PHILADELPHIA COKE COMAPNY	PCC
PHILADELPHIA GERMANTOWN & CHEST. HILL	PG&CH
PHILADELPHIA GERMANTOWN & NORRISTOWN	PG&N
PHILADELPHIA MARLTON & MEDFORD	PM&M
PHILADELPHIA NEWTON & NEW YORK	PN&NY
PHILADELPHIA RAPID TRANSIT	PRT
PHILADELPHIA READING & NEW ENGLAND	PR&NE
PHILADELPHIA SUBURBAN TRANS COMPANY	PSTC
PHILADELPHIA SUBWAYS	PSW
PHILADELPHIA TRANSPORTATION COMPANY	PTC
PHILADELPHIA WILMINGTON & BALTIMORE	PW&B
PHILLIPS & RANGELEY	P&RA
PICKENS RAILROAD	PI
PICKERING LUMBER	PLU
PIEDMONT & CUMBERLAND	P&CU
PIEDMONT & NORTHERN	P&N
PINAFORE PARK	PP
PINE CREEK	PCR
PIONEER & FAYETTE	P&F
PIRAEUS ATHENS PELOPONNESUS (GREECE)	PAPG
PITTSBURGH & BUTLER STREET RAILWAY	P&BS
PITTSBURGH & CASTLE SHANNON	P&CS
PITTSBURGH & LAKE ERIE	P&LE
PITTSBURGH & OHIO VALLEY	P&OV
PITTSBURGH & SHAWMUT RAILROAD	PI&SH
PITTSBURGH & SUSQUEHANNA	P&S
PITTSBURGH & WEST VIRGINIA	P&WV
PITTSBURGH ALLEGHENY & MCKEES ROCKS	PA&MR
PITTSBURGH BESSEMER & LAKE ERIE	PB&LE
PITTSBURGH CHARTIERS & YOUGHIOGHENY	PC&Y
PITTSBURGH COUNTY	PCO
PITTSBURGH FT WAYNE & CHICAGO	PFW&C
PITTSBURGH HARMONY BUTLER & N CASTLE	PHB&NC
PITTSBURGH LACKAWANNA & NORTHEASTERN	PL&N
PITTSBURGH LIBBON & WESTERN	PL&W
PITTSBURGH MCKEESPORT & YOUNGIOGHENY	PM&Y
PITTSBURGH RAILWAYS	PIT
PITTSBURGH SHAWMUT & NORTHERN	PS&N
PITTSBURGH SOUTHERN	PS
PITTSBURGH WESTMORELAND & SOMERSET	PW&S
PITTSBURGH YOUNGSTOWN & ASHTABULA	PY&A
POINT COMFORT & NORTHERN	PC&N
PONTIAC PACIFIC JUNCTION	PPJ
PORT ANGELES PACIFIC	PAP
PORT AUTHORITY TRANS HUDSON	PATH
PORT BIENVILLE	PB
PORT EVERGLADES	PEV
PORT HOPE LINDSAY & BEAVERTON	PHL&B
PORT HURON & DETROIT	PH&D
PORT JARVIS & MONTICELLO	PJ&M
PORT JERVIS MONTICELLO & NEW YORK	PJM&NY
PORT MANATEE	PMA
PORT OF TACOMA	POT
PORT OF TILLAMOOK BAY	POTB
PORT TOWNSEND	PTO
PORT UTILITIES COMMISSION RAILWAY	PUC
PORTAGE	PO
PORTAGE CREEK & RICH VALLEY	PC&RV
PORTER	POR
PORTERFIELD & ELLIS	P&EL
PORTLAND & KENNEBEC	P&K
PORTLAND & OGDENSBURG	P&O
PORTLAND & ROCHESTER	P&RO
PORTLAND & RUMFORD FALLS	P&RF
PORTLAND ELECTRIC POWER COMPANY	PEPC
PORTLAND LEWISTON RAILWAY	PLR
PORTLAND LOCOMOTIVE WORKS	PLW
PORTLAND PUBLIC DOCKS	PPD
PORTLAND RAILWAYS	P
PORTLAND TERMINAL COMPANY	PT
PORTLAND TRACTION	PTR
POTATO CREEK	POTCR
POTEAU & CAVANAL MOUNTAIN	P&CM
POTEAU VALLEY	PV
POTOMAC EDISON	PED
POTOMAC ELECTRIC POWER	PEP
POTOMIC REGION LINES	PRL
POUGHKEEPSIE & EASTERN	P&E
POUGHKEEPSIE BRIDGE COMPANY	PBC
POWDER RIVER RAILROAD	PRI
PRATTSBURGH	PR
PRECISION NATIONAL	PNA
PRESCOTT & EASTERN	PR&EA
PRESCOTT & NORTH WESTERN	P&NW
PRESTON	PRES
PRINCETON FAST LINE	PFL
PROFILE NORTHERN	PN
PROVIDENCE & SPRINGFIELD	P&SP
PROVIDENCE & WORCESTER	P&W
PUBLIC BELT ROAD	PBR
PUBLIC SERCICE OF COLORADO	PSC
PUBLIC SERVICE OF INDIANA	PSI
PUBLIC SERVICE OF NEW JERSEY	PSNJ
PUBLIC SERVICE RAILWAY CO UNION LINE	PSRW
PUEBLO & ARKANSAS VALLEY	P&AV
PURDUE UNIVERSITY	PU
QUAKAKE	QU
QUAKER OATS	QO
QUAKERTOWN & EASTERN	Q&E
QUANAH ACME & PACIFIC	QA&P
QUEBEC & GOSFORD WOODEN RAILWAY	Q&GW
QUEBEC CENTRAL	QC
QUEBEC CITADEL INCLINE PLANE	QCIP
QUEBEC IRON & TITANIUM	QI&T
QUEBEC MONTREAL & SOUTHERN	QM&S
QUEBEC NORTH SHORE & LABRADOR	QNS&L
QUEBEC RAILWAY LIGHT & POWER COMPANY	QRL&P
QUEENSBORO BRIDGE RAILWAY COMPANY	QBRW
QUINCY & TORCH LAKE (SAME AS QM)	Q&TL
QUINCY MINING COMPANY	QM
QUINCY RAILROAD	Q
QUINCY SOYBEAN COMPANY	QS
QUOCHITA & NORTH WESTERN	Q&NW
RAHWAY VALLEY RAILROAD	RV
RALEIGH & CHARLESTON	R&C
RAPID CITY BLACK HILLS & WESTERN	RCBH&W
RARITAN RIVER RAILROAD	RR
RAYONIER & NAVIGATION COMPANY	RAY
RAYONIER RAILWAY	RY
READER RAILROAD	RRR
READING & COLUMBIA	R&COL
READING RAILROAD	R
READING STREET RAILWAY	RSR
RED ARROW LINES	RAL
RED RIVER & GULF	RR&G
REDONDO	RE
REICHHOLD CHEMICAL	RC
REPUBLIC STEEL	RST
RESERVE MINING COMPANY	RMC
REW CITY & ELDRED	RC&E
RHINEBECK & CONNECTICUT	R&COL
RICHELIEU DRUMMOND & ATHABASKA	RD&A
RICHMOND & ALLEGHENY	R&A
RICHMOND & DANVILLE	R&D
RICHMOND FREDERICKSBURG & POTOMIC	RF&P
RICHMOND LOCOMOTIVE & MACHINE WORKS	RL&MW
RICHMOND TERMINAL	RT
RIDEAU CANAL TRAMWAY	RCT
RINGLING BROTHERS CIRCUS	RBC
RIO GRANDE	RG
RIO GRANDE & SOUTHWESTERN	RG&S
RIO GRANDE CITY	RGC
RIO GRANDE EASTERN	RGE
RIO GRANDE SOUTHERN	RGS
RIO GRANDE WESTERN	RGW
RIVER TERMINAL	RIVT
ROARING CAMP & BIG TREES RAILROAD	RC&BT
ROBERVAL & SAGUENAY	R&S
ROBY & NORTHERN	R&N
ROCHESTER & EASTERN	R&E
ROCHESTER & SODUS BAY	R&SB
ROCHESTER GAS & ELECTRIC	RG&E
ROCHESTER HORNELLSVILLE & LACKAWANNA	RH&L
ROCHESTER NEW YORK & PENNSYLVANIA	RNY&P
ROCHESTER NUNDA & PENNSYLANIA	RN&PA
ROCHESTER NUNDA & PITTSBURGH	RN&P
ROCHESTER SYRACUSE & EASTERN	RS&E
ROCHESTER TRANSIT CORPORATION	RTC
ROCHESTER TROLLEY LINES	RTL
ROCK ISLAND	RI
ROCK PORT LANGDON & NORTHERN	RPL&N
ROCKAWAY VALLEY	RVA
ROCKDALE SANDOW & SOUTHERN	RS&S
ROCKFORD & INTERURBAN RAILWAY	R&IR
ROCKPORT RAILROAD	ROC
ROCKTON & RION	R&R
ROME WATERTOWN & OGDENSBURG	RW&O
ROSCOE SNYDER & PACIFIC	RS&P
ROSECRANS	RO
ROWLAND SPRINGS RAILROAD	RS
ROY GREENE	ROY
ROYAL BLUE LINE	RBL
RUSSIAN DECAPODS	RD
RUTLAND RAILROAD	RU

358

APPENDIX A (RAILROADS)

SABDERSVILLE	SAB
SABINE RIVER & NORTHERN	SR&N
SACKETS HARBOR & ELLISBURG	SH&E
SACRAMENTO AUBURN & NORTHERN	SA&N
SACRAMENTO CITY LINES	SCLS
SACRAMENTO NORTHERN	SN
SACRAMENTO SOUTHERN	SSO
SACRAMENTO VALLEY	SAV
SAGIWAN LOGGING	SL
SALEM FALLS CITY & WESTERN	SFC&W
SALT LAKE GARFIELD & WESTERN	SLG&W
SAN ANTONIO PUBLIC SERVICE	SAPS
SAN ANTONIO SOUTHERN (MP)	SAS
SAN ANTONIO UVALDE & GULF	SAU&G
SAN BENITO & RIO GRANDE VALLEY	SB&RGV
SAN DIEGO & ARIZONA EASTERN	SD&AE
SAN DIEGO & CUYAMACA	SD&C
SAN DIEGO & SOUTHEASTERN	SD&S
SAN DIEGO CUYAMACA & EASTERN	SDC&E
SAN DIEGO ELECTRIC RAILWAY	SDE
SAN DIEGO OLD TOWN & PALM BEACH	SDOT&P
SAN DIEGO PACIFIC BEACH & LA JOLLA	SDPB&L
SAN DIEGO SOUTH EASTERN RAILWAY	SDS
SAN FRANCISCO & NORTH PACIFIC	SF&NP
SAN FRANCISCO & NORTHWESTERN	SF&N
SAN FRANCISCO & SAN JOAQUIN VALLEY	SF&SJV
SAN FRANCISCO & SAN JOSE	SF&SJ
SAN FRANCISCO & SAN MATEO	SF&SM
SAN FRANCISCO BELT LINE	SFB
SAN FRANCISCO MUNICIPAL	SFM
SAN GABRIEL VALLEY RAPID TRANSIT	SGV
SAN JOACHIN LUMBER	SJL
SAN JOAQUIN & EASTERN	SJ&E
SAN JUAN CENTRAL	SJC
SAN LUIS CENTRAL	SLC
SAN MANUEL ARIZONA	SMA
SAND SPRINGS	SSP
SANDERSVILLE	SAND
SANDUSKY & COLUMBUS SHORT LINE	S&CSL
SANDUSKY NORWALK & MANSFIELD	SN&M
SANDY RIVER & RANGELEY LAKES	SR&RL
SANFORD & ST PETERSBURG	S&SP
SANFORD TRACTION	SANT
SANTA BARBAR & SUBURBAN	B&S
SANTA BARBARA & SUBURBAN	SB&S
SANTA FE	SF
SANTA FE PRESCOTT & PHOENIX	SFP&P
SANTA MARIA VALLEY	SMV
SAPULPA UNION	SU
SAVAHHAN FLORIDA & WESTERN	SF&W
SAVANNAH & ATLANTA RAILWAY COMPANY	S&A
SAVANNAH STATE DOCKS	SSD
SAWYER RIVER	SAR
SCHENECTADY LOCOMOTIVE WORKS	SLW
SCHUYLKILL & SUSQUEHANNA	S&S
SCHUYLKILL VALLEY NAVIGATION & RR	SVN
SCIATO VALLEY SOUTHERN	SVS
SCIOTO VALLEY TRACTION	SVT
SCOTT & BEARSKIN LAKE	S&BL
SCRANTON & BINGHAMTON	S&B
SCRANTON DUNMORE & MOOSIC LAKE	SD&ML
SD WARREN PAPER COMPANY	SDW
SEABOARD	SEA
SEABOARD AIR LINE	SAL
SEABOARD AIR LINE.	SEA.
SEABOARD COAST LINE	SCL
SEATTLE & NORTH COAST	S&NC
SEATTLE COAL & TRANSPORTATION COMPANY	SC&T
SEATTLE LAKE SHORE & EASTERN	SLS&E
SEATTLE TACOMA INTERURBAN	STI
SEATTLE TERMINAL	SET
SEBASTICOOK & MOOSEHEAD LAKE	S&ML
SEEKONK	SEE
SEWARD PENINSULA	SPEN
SHAKER HEIGHTS RAPID TRANSIT	SHRT
SHAMOKIN & TREVERTON	S&T
SHAMOKIN SUNBURY & LEWISBURG	SS&L
SHAWMUT CONNECTING	SHAWC
SHAWNEE TECUMSEH TRACTION	STT
SHELBURNE FALLS & COLRAIN STREET RY	SF&CS
SHEPAUG LITCHFIELD & NORTHERN	SL&N
SHIP RAILWAY OF CHIGNECTO	SRC
SHORE LINE ELECTRIC	SLE
SIERRA PACIFIC	SIEP
SIERRA RAILROAD	SIE
SIERRA RAILROAD OF CALIFORNIA	SOC
SIERRA VALLEYS	SIEV
SILVER CITY PINOS ALTOS & MOGOLLON	SCPA
SILVER KING COALITION MINES COMPANY	SKM
SILVER PEAK	SILP
SILVER SPRINGS OCALA & GULF	SSO&G
SILVERTON	SILV
SILVERTON GLADSTONE & NORTHERLY	SG&N
SILVERTON NORTHERN	SNO
SIOUX CITY TERMINAL	SCT
SKAGIT RIVER RAILWAY	SR
SKANEATELES	SKA
SKANEATELES SHORT LINE	SSL
SMETHPORT	SMETH
SMETHPORT & OLEAN	S&OL
SMOKY MOUNTAIN	SMT
SOMERS LUMBER COMPANY	SLCO
SOMERSET	SOM
SONORA BAJA CALIFORNIA RAILWAY	SBC
SOO LINE	SOO
SOUTH ATLANTIC & OHIO	SA&O
SOUTH BRANCH	SB
SOUTH BROOKLYN	SBR
SOUTH BUFFALO	SBUF
SOUTH CAROLINA CANAL & RAILROAD	SCC&RR
SOUTH CAROLINA ELECTRIC & GAS	SCE&G
SOUTH EASTERN RAILWAY (CANADA)	SE
SOUTH FLORIDA	SOF
SOUTH GEORGIA	SG
SOUTH HOPKINS COAL COMPANY	SHC
SOUTH OMAHA TERMINAL	SOT
SOUTH PACIFIC COAST	SPC
SOUTH PARK	SOP
SOUTH PENNSYLVANIA RAILROAD	SPA
SOUTH SHORE	SS
SOUTH SHORE & SUTH BEND	SS&SB
SOUTH SIDE	SOS
SOUTH WESTERN RAILROAD	SW
SOUTHEAST OKLAHOMA INDUSTRIAL AUTHOR	SOIA
SOUTHERN CAMBRIA	SCA
SOUTHERN CEMENT COMPANY	SCC
SOUTHERN CENTRAL	SCE
SOUTHERN ELECTRIC GENERATING	SEG
SOUTHERN INDIANA	SIND
SOUTHERN INDUSTRIAL	SIN
SOUTHERN KANSAS	SK
SOUTHERN NEW YORK	SNY
SOUTHERN PACIFIC	SP
SOUTHERN PACIFIC LINES	SPL
SOUTHERN PACIFIC OF MEXICO	SPM
SOUTHERN RAILWAY	S
SOUTHERN SAN LUIS VALLEY	SSLV
SOUTHWEST FOREST INDUSTRIES	SFI
SOUTHWEST PORTLAND CEMENT	SWPC
SOUTHWEST RAILWAY CONSTRUCTION CO	SRCC
SOUTHWESTERN INTERURBAN	SWIU
SOUTHWESTERN SYSTEM (OHIO)	SWS
SPERRY RAIL SERVICE	SPS
SPOKANE & INLAND ELECTRIC RAILWAY	S&IE
SPOKANE & INLAND EMPIRE	S&IE.
SPOKANE INTERNATIONAL	SPI
SPOKANE PORTLAND & SEATTLE	SP&S
SPRINGFIELD ELECTRIC RAILWAY	SERY
SPRINGFIELD TERMINAL	ST
SQUAW CREEK COAL COMPANY	SCCC
ST AUGUSTINE & SOUTH BEACH	SA&SB
ST CLAIR TUNNEL CO	SCTC
ST CLOUD & SUGAR BELT	SC&SB
ST ELIZABETH HOSPITAL	SEH
ST JOHNS	SJ
ST JOHNS & INDIAN RIVER	SJ&IR
ST JOHNS & LAKE EUSTIS	SJ&LE
ST JOHNS RIVER TERMINAL	SJRT
ST JOHNSBURY & LAKE CHAMPLAIN RR	SJ&LC
ST JOHNSBURY & LAMOILLE COUNTY	SJ&LCO
ST JOSEPH & GRAND ISLAND (UP)	SJ&GI
ST JOSEPH & ST LOUIS	SJ&SL
ST JOSEPH BELT	SJB
ST JOSEPH TERMINAL	SJT
ST JOSEPH VALLEY RAILWAY	SJV
ST LAURENT & VILLAGE D'INDUSTRIE	SL&VD
ST LAWRENCE & ADIRONDACK	SL&AD
ST LAWRENCE & ATLANTIC	SL&A
ST LAWRENCE & INDUSTRIE VILLAGE	SL&IV
ST LAWRENCE INTERNATIONAL	SLI
ST LAWRENCE RAILROAD	STL
ST LOUIS & SOUTHWESTERN	CBELT
ST LOUIS BROWNSVILLE & MEXICO	SLB&M
ST LOUIS EL RENO & WESTERN	SLER&W
ST LOUIS IRON MOUNTAIN & SOUTHERN	SLIM&S
ST LOUIS KANSAS CITY & CHICAGO	SLKC&C
ST LOUIS KANSAS CITY SHORT LINE	SLKC
ST LOUIS MEMPHIS & SOUTHEATERN RR	SLM&S
ST LOUIS SAN FRANCISCO	FRIS
ST LOUIS VANDALIA & TERRE HAUTE	SLV&TH
ST MARYS	SM
ST MARYS & SOUTHWESTERN	SM&S
ST PAUL & PACIFIC	SP&P
ST PAUL UNION DEPOT	SPUD
STALEY SYSTEM OF ELECTRIFIED RW	SSE
STANDARD GRAVEL	STG
STANDARD STEEL DIV-BALDWIN LIMA HAMIL	STDS
STARK ELECTRIC RAILROAD	SERR
STARKE & SIMPSON CITY	S&SC
STATE BELT	SBELT
STATEN ISLAND	SI
STATEN ISLAND RAPID TRANSIT	SIRT
STAUFFER CHEMICAL	SCH
STEEL COMPANY OF CANADA	SCOC
STEELTON & HIGHSPIRE	S&H
STERLING IRON & RAILWAY	SI&R
STEWARTSTOWN	STEW
STOCKHAM VALVES & FITTINGS	SV&F
STOCKTON TERMINAL	STTER
STOCKTON TERMINAL & EASTERN	ST&E
STOCTON TERMINAL	STTE
STONE HARBOR RAILROAD	SH
STONE MOUNTAIN SCENECIC	SMS
STRASBURG RAILROAD	STRR
SUDBURY COPPER CLIFF ELECTRIC RAILWAY	SCCE
SUFFOLK TRACTION	SUFT
SUGAR LAND	SUGL
SUGAR PINE LUMBER COMPANY	SPLC
SUGAR RUN	SUGR
SULLIVAN COUNTY	SCO
SUMPTER VALLEY	SV
SUMTER & CHOCTAW	S&C
SUNBURY HAZELTON & WILLES BARRE	SH&WB
SUNCOOK VALLEY	SUNV
SUPERIOR STONE COMPANY	SSC
SURESTE RAILWAY (MEXICO)	SRM
SURRY SUSSEX & SOUTHHAMPTON	SS&S
SUSQUEHANNA	SES
SUSQUEHANNA & NEW YORK	S&NY
SUSQUEHANNA & WESTERN	S&W
SUSQUEHANNA CONNECTING	SUSC
SUSQUEHANNA RIVER & WESTERN	SR&W
SWAMP RABBIT	SWR
SWATARA & COLD SPRINGS	S&CS
SYDNEY & LOUISBURG	S&L
SYDNEY MINES	SMINE
SYLVANIA CENTRAL	SYC
SYRACUSE & CHENANGO VALLEY	S&CV
SYRACUSE & EASTERN	S&E
SYRACUSE & ONONDAGA	S&O
SYRACUSE & UTICA	S&U
TACOMA & COLUMBIA RIVER	T&CR
TACOMA MUNICIPAL BELT	TMB
TALBOTTON	TAL

APPENDIX A (RAILROADS)

TALLAHASEE	TALL
TALLULAH FALLS	TF
TAMA & TOLEDO	T&TO
TAMAQUA HAZLETON & NORTHERN	TH&N
TATUM LUMBER COMPANY	TL
TAUTON LOCOMOTIVE WORKS	TLW
TAVARES & GULF	T&GU
TAYLOR MOUNTAIN & BEAVER CREEK	TM&BC
TECOPA	TEC
TEMISCOUATA	TEM
TEMISKAMING & NORTHERN ONTARIO	T&NON
TENNESSEE	T
TENNESSEE & ALABAMA	T&A
TENNESSEE & COOSA	T&C
TENNESSEE ALABAMA & GEORGIA	TA&G
TENNESSEE CENTRAL	TENNC
TENNESSEE COAL & IRON	TC&I
TENNESSEE VALLEY AUTHORITY	TVA
TERMINAL RAILROAD ASSOC OF ST LOUIS	TRA
TERMINAL RAILROAD OF NEW ORLEANS	TRNO
TERRE HAUTE & INDIANAPOLIS	TH&I
TERRE HAUTE & LOGANSPORT	TH&L
TERRE HAUTE INDIANAPOLIS & EASTERN	THI&E
TEXAS & NEW ORLEANS	T&NO
TEXAS & NORTHERN	T&N
TEXAS & PACIFIC	T&P
TEXAS CENTRAL	TC
TEXAS CITY TERMINAL	TCT
TEXAS ELECTRIC	TE
TEXAS EXPORT	TEX
TEXAS MEXICAN	TMEX
TEXAS MIDLAND	TM
TEXAS OKLAHOMA & EASTERN	TO&E
TEXAS PACIFIC MISSOURI PAC TERM RR NO	TPMP
TEXAS SOUTH EASTERN	TSE
TEXAS STATE	TEXS
TEXAS TRANSPORTATION COMPANY	TTC
TEXAS WESTERN	TW
THAILAND RAILWAYS	TRW
THIRD AVENUE TRANSIT RAILROAD COMPANY	TAT
THUNDERBIRD COLLIERIES	THC
THURSO & NATION VALLEY	T&NV
TIDEWATER & WESTERN	T&W
TIDEWATER SOUTHERN	TS
TIMKEN ROLLER BEARING COMPANY	TRB
TIONESTA VALLEY	TIV
TOLEDO & OHIO CENTRAL	T&OC
TOLEDO ANGOLA & WESTERN	TA&W
TOLEDO BOWLING GREEN & SOUTHERN TRACT	TBG&ST
TOLEDO CLEVELAND LAKE SHORE ELECTRIC	TCLSE
TOLEDO EDISON	TED
TOLEDO PEORIA & WESTERN	TP&W
TOLEDO SAINT LOUIS & WESTERN	TSL&W
TOLEDO TERMINAL	TT
TOLEDO WABASH & WESTERN	TW&W
TONAWANDA GENESEE VALLEY & PINE CREEK	TGV&PC
TONAWANDA VALLEY	TV
TONAWANDA VALLEY & CUBA	TV&C
TONAWANDA VALLEY EXTENSION	TVE
TONAWANDA WISCOY & GENESEE VALLEY	TW&GV
TONOPAH & GOLDFIELD	T&GO
TONOPAH & TIDEWATER	T&T
TOOELE VALLEY	TOV
TORONTO GRAY & BRUCE RAILWAY	TG&B
TORONTO HAMILTON & BUFFALO	TH&B
TORONTO RAILWAY CO	TRCO
TORONTO RAPID TRANSIT	TRT
TORONTO TRANSIT COMMISSION	TTCO
TRAILER TRAIN	TTR
TRANS CAR SERVICES	TCS
TREASURE ISLAND	TI
TRENTON PRINCETON TRACTION	TPT
TRESCKOW	TR
TRI CITY TRACTION	TCTR
TRIAD CHEMICAL	TRC
TRONA	TRO
TROY & BOSTON	T&B
TROY & GREENFIELD	T&G
TUCKERTON	TUCK
TULIA GRAIN TERMINAL	TGT
TULSA SAPULPA UNION	TSU
TUSCALOOSA	TUS
TUSCON CORNELIA & GILA BEND	TC&GB
TUSKEGEE	TUSK
TWIN BRANCH	TB
TWIN MOUNTAIN & POTOMAC	TM&P
TWIN SEAMS MINING	TSM
TYRONE & CLEARFIELD	T&CL
UNADILLA VALLEY	UV
UNION CANAL	UCA
UNION CARBIDE	UNC
UNION ELECTRIC	UE
UNION FREIGHT	UF
UNION IRON WORKS	UIW
UNION PACIFIC	UP
UNION RAILROAD	URR
UNION RAILROAD OF OREGON	URO
UNION STREET RAILWAY	USR
UNION TERMINAL	UT
UNION TRACTION COMPANY	UTC
UNITAH RAILROAD	U
UNITED ELECTRIC COAL	UEC
UNITED RAILROADS OF SAN FRANCISCO	URSF
UNITED RAILWAY OF ST LOUIS	URSL
UNITED RAILWAYS & ELECTRIC	UR&E
UNITED RAILWAYS OF OREGON	URWO.
UNITED RAILWAYS OF YUCATAN	URY
UNITED RAILWAYS OF YUCATAN.	YU.
UNITED STATES ARMY	USA
UNITED STATES ATOMIC ENERGY COMMISSIO	USAEC
UNITED STATES MILITARY RAILROAD	USM
UNITED STATES NAVAL AMMUNITION DEPOT	USNAD
UNITED STATES NAVY	USN
UNITED STATES PIPE & FOUNDRY	USP&F
UNITED STATES RAILROAD ADMINISTRATION	USRA
UNITED STATES RAILWAY EQUIP MFG	USREM
UNITED STATES STEEL CORPORATION	USSC
UNITED STATES SUGAR	USS
UNITED STATES WAR DEPARTMENT	USWD
UNITED TRACTION STREET RAILWAY	UTSR
UNITY	UN
UNIVERSAL EXPLORATION COMPANY	UXL
UNIVERSITY OF MINNESOTA INTER-CAMPUS	UM
UPJOHN COMPANY	UJC
UPPER COOS & HEREFORD	UC&H
UPPER MERION & PLYMOUTH	UM&P
UTAH	UTAH
UTAH CENTRAL	UC
UTAH COAL ROUTE	UCR
UTAH COPPER DIV OF KENNECOTT COPPER C	UCKC
UTAH POWER & LIGHT	UP&L
UVALDE & NORTHERN	U&N
VALDOSTA SOUTHERN	VS
VALLEY	VAL
VALLEY & SILETZ	V&S
VANDALIA RAILROAD	VA
VENANGO RIVER RAILROAD	VR
VENTURA COUNTY	VCO
VERMONT	VER
VERMONT & MASSACHUETTS	V&M
VERMONT NORTHERN	VN
VERMONT VALLEY	VV
VICTORY PARK	VIP
VIET NAM RAILWAYS	VNR
VINELAND	VIN
VIRGINIA & MARYLAND	V&MA
VIRGINIA & RAINY LAKE	V&RL
VIRGINIA & TENNESSEE	V&TEN
VIRGINIA & TRUCKEE	V&T
VIRGINIA BLUE RIDGE	VBR
VIRGINIA CAROLINA	VAC
VIRGINIA CENTRAL	VC
VIRGINIA ELECTRIC & POWER COMPANY	VE&PC
VIRGINIA POCAHONTAS	VP
VIRGINIA TRANSIT	VT
VIRGINIAN RAILWAY	V
VISALIA ELECTRIC RAILROAD	VE
VULCAN DETINNING	VD
VULCAN MATERIALS	VM
WABASH	W
WABASH PITTSBURGH TERMINAL	WPT
WABASH ST LOUIS & PACIFIC RAILWAY	WSL&P
WABASH TERMINAL	WT
WACO BEAUMONT TRINITY & SABINE	WBT&S
WALLA WALLA VALLEY	WWV
WALLACE STONE	WAST
WALLKILL VALLEY	WAV
WARE SHOALS	WAS
WARNER SAND & GRAVEL	WS&G
WARREN & FARNSWORTH	W&F
WARREN & OUACHITA VALLEY	W&OV
WARREN & SALINE RIVER	W&SR
WARREN PAPER COMPANY	WPC
WARRENTON	WAR
WARWICK RAILROAD	WA
WASHINGTON & OLD DOMINION	W&OD
WASHINGTON ARLINGTON & FALLS CHURCH	WA&FC
WASHINGTON BALTIMORE & ANNAPOLIS ELEC	WB&AE
WASHINGTON BRANDYWINE & POINT LOOKOUT	WB&PL
WASHINGTON COUNTY	WCO
WASHINGTON IDAHO & MONTANA	WI&M
WASHINGTON TERMINAL	WASHT
WASHITA & SANTA FE	W&SF
WATERLOO	WLOO
WATERLOO CEDAR FALLS & NORTHERN	WCF&N
WATERVILLE	WAT
WATERVILLE FAIRFIELD & OAKLAND	WF&O
WAUPACA GREEN BAY	WGB
WAYNESBURG & WASHINGTON	W&WA
WAYNESBURG SOUTHERN	WS
WEATHERFORD MINERAL WELLS & NORTHWEST	WMW&N
WEBBER FALLS	WF
WEEMS ELECTRIC	WEL
WELLAND	WELL
WELLAND & PORT COLBORNE	W&PC
WELLSVILLE ADDISON & GALETON RAILROAD	WA&G
WELLSVILLE BOLIVAR & ELDRED	WB&EL
WEST FELICIANA	WFE
WEST JERSEY & SEASHORE	WJ&S
WEST PALM BEACH TERMINAL	WPBT
WEST PENN & PITTSBURG RAILWAY	WP&P
WEST PENN RAILWAY COMPANY	WPA
WEST PITTSTON EXETER	WPE
WEST POINT ROUTE	WPR
WEST RIVER	WR
WEST SIDE & YONKERS RAILWAY	WS&Y
WEST SIDE LUMBER	WSL
WEST VIRGINIA CENTRAL & PITTSBURGH RR	WVC&P
WEST VIRGINIA NORTHERN	WVN
WEST VIRGINIA PULP & PAPER COMPANY	WVPP
WESTCHESTER & WESTERN	WE&W
WESTERN & ATLANTIC	W&A
WESTERN BRICK COMPANY	WBC
WESTERN ENERGY COMPANY	WEC
WESTERN MARYLAND	WM
WESTERN NEW YORK & PENNSYLVANIA	WNY&P
WESTERN NORTH CAROLINA	WNC
WESTERN PACIFIC	WP
WESTERN PACIFIC & RIO GRANDE	WP&RG
WESTERN RAILROAD CORPORATION	WRC
WESTERN RAILROAD OF ALASKA	WRRA
WESTERN RAILWAY OF ALABAMA	WRA
WESTERN RAILWAY OF MASSACHUSETTS	WRM
WESTERN VERMONT	WV
WESTFIELD	WES
WESTFIELD PLANTAION	WPL
WESTINGHOUSE ELECTRIC	WE
WESTMINISTER	WEST
WESTMONT INCLINED PLANE	WIP
WESTON & BROOKER CRUSHED STONE CO	W&BCS
WEYERHAEUSER LUMBER COMPANY	WTC
WEYERHAEUSER TIMBER COMPANY.	WTC.
WHARTON & NORTHERN	W&NO
WHEELING & LAKE ERIE	W&LE
WHEELING PITTSBURGH STEEL	WPS
WHITE PASS & YUKON	WP&Y
WHITE TOP	WTP
WHITEHALL CEMENT	WHC
WHITMER & STEEL LUMBER COMPANY	W&SL
WHITNEYVILLE & MACHIASPORT	WV&M

APPENDIX A (RAILROADS)

Railroad	Reporting Mark
WICHITA & WESTERN	W&WE
WICHITA FALLS & NORTHWESTERN	WF&N
WICHITA FALLS & SOUTHERN	WF&S
WICHITA VALLEY	WIV
WILKES BARRE & EASTERN	WB&E
WILKES BARRE & HAZELTON	WB&H
WILLAMETTE IRON & STEEL COMPANY	WI&S
WILLIAM MASON	WMM
WILLIAMSPORT & NORTH BRANCH	W&NB
WILLIAMSTOWN	WI
WILLIAMSTOWN & REDFIELD	W&R
WILMINGTON & NORTHERN	W&N
WILMINGTON & WELDEN RAILWAY	W&NR
WILMINGTON & WESTERN	W&W
WINANS LOCOMOTIVES	WL
WINCHESTER & WESTERN	WI&W
WINFIELD	WINF
WINIFREDE	WINI
WINONA RAILROAD	WIN
WINSTON SALEM SOUTHBOUND	WSSB
WINSTON SALEM SOUTHERN	WSS
WISCASSET & QUEBEC	W&Q
WISCASSET WATERVILLE & FARMINGTON	WW&F
WISCONSIN & MICHIGAN	W&M
WISCONSIN & NORTHERN	WI&N
WISCONSIN CENTRAL	WC
WOBURN BRANCH	WB
WOOD RIVER BRANCH	WRB
WOODARD WALKER LUMBER COMPANY	WWL
WOODSTOCK	WO
WORCESTER NASHUS & ROCHESTER	WN&R
WRIGHTSVILLE & TENNILLE	W&T
WYANDOTTE SOUTHERN	WYS
WYANDOTTE TERMINAL	WYT
YAKIMA TRACTION COMPANY	YTC
YAKIMA VALLEY TRANSPORTATION	YVT
YAKIMA VALLEY TRANSPORTATION COMPANY	YAV
YAKUTAT & SOUTHERN	Y&SO
YAMPA VALLEY RAILROAD	YVA
YANCEY	Y
YANKEETOWN DOCK	YD
YAZOO & MISSISSIPPI VALLEY	Y&MV
YELLOW RIVER	YR
YORK PENNA. RAILWAYS	YP
YOSEMITE SHORT LINE	YSL
YOSEMITE VALLEY	YV
YOUNGSTOWN & NORTHERN	Y&N
YOUNGSTOWN & OHIO RIVER	Y&OR
YOUNGSTOWN & SOUTHERN	Y&S
YOUNGSTOWN & SUBURBAN	Y&SU
YOUNGSTOWN STEEL	YS
YREKA WESTERN	YW
YUCATAN RAILWAY	YU
ZALEV BROTHERS LIMITED	ZB
ZERBE VALLEY	ZV

ASAR	*AS
ALCOA	*ALC
AMERICAN REFRIGERATED TRANSIT	*ART
ARMOUR	*A
ARTIC OIL WORKS	*AOW
BABY RUTH	*BR
BAY SOL	*BS
BECCO	*B
BERKSHIRE BACON	*BEB
BLATZ	*BL
BLATZ OLD HEIDELBERG	*BOH
BOURK DONALDSON TAYLOR POTATOES	*BDTP
BUDLONG	*BDL
BULL FROG BEER	*BFB
CARNATION	*CAR
CHAREAU MARTIN WINE	*CMW
COLLEGE INN	*CI
COLUMBIA SOURS	*CS
COUNTRY CLUB BEER	*CCB
DAIRYMENS EXPRESS	*DE
DEEP ROCK	*DR
DOW CHEMICAL	*DC
DUBUQUE	*D
DUPONT (EI DUPONT)	*DU
FRUIT GROWERS EXPRESS	*FGE
GATX	*GA
GERBERS BABY FOOD	*GERB
GOODYEAR	*GY
GULF	*G
HAMS	*HAMS
HEINZ 57	*HZ
HUNTER PACKING COMPANY	*HPC
INLAND STEEL CO	*ISC
KAHN'S SONS' REFRIGERATION	*KSR
KINGAN RELIABLE HAM	*KRH
KOPPERS	*K
KRAFT	*KRA
KREY PACKING	*KP
LIBBY'S	*LIB
LIQUID CARBONIC DRY ICE	*LCDI
M.K.T.	*MKT
M.U.N.X.	*MUNX
MA BROWN	*MAB
MAINE POTATO	*MP
MATHIESON	*MAT
MERCHANTS BISCUITS	*MB
MERCHANTS DESPATCH	*MDT
MICHIGAN ALKALI	*MA
MINNESOTA MINING & MANUFACTURING	*3M
MOBILE GAS	*MG
MONARCH	*MOA
NATIONAL ALUMINATE COMPANY	*NAC
NORTH AMERICAN DESPATCH	*NAD
NORTHWESTERN REFRIGERATOR LINE	*NRL
OHIO SEAMLESS TUBE	*OST
OLD DUTCH CLEANSER	*ODC
OSCAR MEYER	*OM
PABST BEER	*PAB
PACIFIC FRUIT EXPRESS	*PFE
PACIFIC FRUIT GROWERS EXPRESS	*PFE
PAGE MILK	*PGM
PEERLESS BEER	*PB
PENNSYLVANIA MERCHANDISE	*PM
PETRO-TEX	*PT
PULLMAN COMPANY	*P
RAILWAY EXPRESS	*REA
RALSTON PURINA	*RP
RATH BLACK HAWK	*RBH
REINEGOLD	*RG
SCHLITZ BEER	*SCH
SCHWARGEHILD SULZBERGER	*S&S
SHELL OIL	*SHO
SHIPPERS CAR LINE	*SCL
SINCLAIR	*S
ST LOUIS REEFER EXPRESS	*SLRE
SUN OILS	*SO
SWIFT	*SW
TEXACO	*T
TIVOLI BEER	*TB
UNION CARBIDE	*UC
UNION REFRIGERATED TRANSIT	*URTX
UNION TANK LINE	*UTL
UTLX	*U
UWANTA EGG	*UE
WESTERN FRUIT EXPRESS	*WFE
WESTERN UNION TELEGRAPH CO	*WUT
WESTINGHOUSE	*WE
WESTVACO	*WV
WILSON	*W

APPENDIX A (RAILROADS)

A	AMTRAK
A&A	ARCADE & ATTICA RAILROAD
A&AV	ATTICA & ALLEGHENY VALLEY
A&B	AMHERST & BELCHERTOWN
A&BB	AKRON & BARBERTON BELT
A&C	ARIZONA & CALIFORNIA
A&D	ATLANTIC & DANVILLE
A&DA	ASBESTOS & DANVILLE
A&EC	ATLANTIC & EAST CAROLINA RAILWAY
A&ER	ANNAPOLIS & ELK RIDGE
A&F	ALABAMA & FLORIDA
A&G	ATLANTIC & GULF
A&GW	ATLANTIC & GREAT WESTERN
A&J	ALMA & JONQUIERES
A&K	ALLEGHENY & KINZUA
A&L	ARKANSAS & LOUISIANA
A&LM	ARKANSAS & LOUISIANA MISSOURI
A&LV	ALTOONA & LOGAN VALLEY
A&MR	ARCATA & MAD RIVER
A&N	ALBANY & NORTHERN
A&NR	ANGELINA & NECHES RIVER
A&O	ARKANSAS & OZARKS
A&P	ALHAMBRA & PASADENA
A&PA	ATLANTIC & PACIFIC
A&R	ABERDEEN & ROCKFISH
A&S	ALTON & SOUTHERN
A&SE	AUBURN & SYRACUSE ELECTRIC
A&SL	ATLANTIC & ST LAWRENCE
A&SO	ABILENE & SOUTHERN
A&SS	ALLEGHENY & SOUTH SIDE
A&STAB	ATLANTA & ST ANDREWS BAY
A&U	ARIZONA & UTAH
A&W	AHNAPEE & WESTERN
A&WE	ATLANTIC & WESTERN
A&WP	ATLANTA & WEST POINT
AA	ANN ARBOR
AAR	ASSOCIATION OF AMERICAN RAILROADS
AB	ALAMEDA BELT LINE
AB&C	ATLANTA BIRMINGHAM & COAST
AB&CO.	ATLANTA BIRMINGHAM & COAST.
AB-P	ALABAMA BY-PRODUCTS
ABI	ABILENE
ABIT	ABITIBI
AC	ALLEGHENY CENTRAL
AC&HB	ALGOMA CENTRAL & HUDSON BAY
AC&I	ASHLAND COAL & IRON
AC&Y	AKRON CANTON & YOUNGSTOWN
ACBL	AMERICAN COMMERCIAL BARGE LINES
ACBM	ALLIED CHEMICAL (BRUNNER MOND)
ACC	AMERICAN CAN COMPANY
ACE	ATLANTIC COAST ELECTRIC
ACH	ARMCO CHEMICAL COMPANY
ACIP	AMERICAN CAST IRON PIPE
ACJ&IR	ATLANTIC COAST ST JOHNS & INDIAN RIV
ACL	ATLANTIC COAST LINE
ACR	AUSTIN CITY RAILROAD (RAILWAY?)
ACRR	ATLANTIC CITY RAILROAD
ACS	AMERICAN COMPRESSED STEEL
ACT	ATLANTIC CITY TRANSPORTATION
ACY	AMERICAN CYANAMID COMPANY
AD&N	ASHLEY DREW & NORTHERN
AD&S	ALABAMA DRYDOCK & SHIPBUILDING
AD&SL	ADIRONDACK & ST LOUIS
ADD	ADDISON
ADIR	ADIRONDACK
AE&FR	AURORA ELGIN & FOX RIVER
AE&FRE	AURORA ELGIN & FOX RIVER ELECTRIC
AF	ANGEL'S FLIGHT RAILWAY
AF&A	ALABAMA FLORIDA & ATLANTIC
AG	AMERICAN GRAINS
AG&WIT	ATLANTIC GULF & WEST INDIES TRANSIT
AGS	ALABAMA GREAT SOUTHERN
AGR	AGRICO CHEMICAL (PIERCE PLANT)
AHRB	ATL HIGHLANDS RED BANK & L BR ELEC
AI	AMHERST INDUSTRIES
AJ	ARTEMUS-JELLICO
AL	ALASKA RAILROAD
AL&S	ALIQUIPPA & SOUTHERN
AL&W	ALLEGHENY & WESTERN
ALC	ALABAMA CENTRAL
ALCA	ALCAN
ALEX	ALEXANDER
ALG	ALGOMA
ALGC	ALGOMA CENTRAL
ALL	ALLIED CHEMICAL (SOLVAY)
ALLEN	ALLENTOWN
ALM	ALMANOR
ALT	ALTADENA
AM	ALBION MINES
AM&O	ATLANTIC MISSISSIPPI & OHIO
AMC	AMADOR CENTRAL
AME	ASARCO MEXICANA
AMO	AMOSKEAG MANUFACTURING COMPANY
AMRL	AMERICAN REDWOOD LUMBER
AMS	AMALGAMATED SUGAR
AN	APALACHICOLA NORTHERN
AN&W	ANTELOPE & WESTERN
AND	ANDROSCOGGIN
AND&K	ANDROSCOGGIN & KENNEBEC
AO	ALUMINUM ORE COMPANY
AOC	ALCOA ORE COMPANY
AP	ALLEGHENY PORTAGE
AP&C	AMERICAN PIPE & CONSTRUCTION
APA	APACHE RAILWAY
APC	ALABAMA POWER COMPANY
APDT	ALBANY PORT DISTRICT TERMINAL
APO	APPALACHIAN POWER
APP	APPOMATTOX
APSM	AGUA PRIETA SONORA MEXICO PACIFIC RY
AQ	ANNA QUARRIES
AR	ALBERTA RESOURCES
ARC	ARGENTINE CENTRAL
ARI	ARIZONA CENTRAL RAILROAD
ARL	ARGENT LUMBER
ARN	ARNAUD
ARR	ALTON RAILROAD (B&O)
AS	ARMCO STEEL
ASDT	ALABAMA STATE DOCKS TERMINAL
ASH	ASHBURNAM
ASM&L	ATLANTA STONE MOUNTAIN & LITHONIA
ASR&G	ATLANTIC SUWANEE RIVER & GULF
AT	ALCOA TERMINAL
AT&F	ATTICA & FREEDOM
AT&N	ALABAMA TENNESSEE & NORTHERN
AT&T	AUGUSTA TRAMWAY & TRANSFER
ATN	ATLANTIC NORTHERN
ATR	AUTO TRAIN
ATS	ALANTIC STEEL
ATSF	ATCHISON TOPEKA & SANTA FE
AU	AUGUSTA
AUB	AUBURN BRANCH
AUR	AURORA BRANCH
AV	AROOSTOOK VALLEY
AVI	ARKANSAS VALLEY INTERURBAN
AVS	AVONDALE SHIPYARDS
AW	ARKANSAS WESTERN
AW&B	ANNAPOLIS WASHINGTON & BALTIMORE
AW&H	ALTUS WICHITA & HOLLIS
AW&W	ALGIERS WINSLOW & WESTSERN
B	BURLINGTON
B&A	BOSTON & ALBANY
B&AL	BARTLETT & ALBANY
B&AN	BALTIMORE & ANNAPOLIS
B&AR	BANGOR & AROOSTOOK
B&B	BELMONT & BUFFALO
B&C	BELLEVUE & CASCADE
B&CH	BARRE & CHELSEA
B&E	BALTIMORE & EASTERN
B&FB	BRADFORD & FOSTER BROOK
B&G	BENNINGTON & GLASTENBURY
B&GA	BINGHAM & GARFIELD
B&GN	BEAUMONT & GREAT NORTHERN
B&H	BRIDGETON & HARRISON RAILWAY
B&HA	BATH & HAMMONDSPORT
B&HE	BLATIMOR & HAMPDEN ELECTRIC
B&HS	BONHOMIE & HATTIESBURG SOUTHERN
B&I	BLAIRSVILLE & INDIANA
B&K	BANGOR & KATAHDIN IRON WORKS
B&L	BOSTON & LOWELL
B&LE	BESSEMER & LAKE ERIE
B&LH	BUFFALO & LAKE HURON
B&M	BOSTON & MAINE
B&MA	BROOKVILLE & MAHONING
B&MI	BURLINGTON & MISSOURI
B&ML	BELFAST & MOOSEHEAD LAKE
B&MR	BURLINGTON & MISSOURI RIVER RAILROAD
B&N	BAUXITE & NORTHERN
B&NM	BRAINERD & NORTHERN MINNESOTA
B&NSR	BOSTON & NORTHERN STREET RAILWAY
B&NY	BOSTON & NEW YORK AIR LINE
B&O	BALTIMORE & OHIO
B&OCT	BALTIMORE & OHIO CHICAGO TERMINAL
B&OT	BROCKVILLE & OTTAWA
B&P	BOSTON & PROVIDENCE
B&PI	BANGOR & PISCATAQUIS
B&PO	BROCKINGS & PEACH ORCHARD
B&Q	BROOKLYN & QUEENS
B&R	BENNINGTON & RUTLAND
B&S	BEVIER & SOUTHERN
B&SM	BUFFALO & ST MARYS
B&SQ	BUFFALO & SUSQUEHANNA
B&SR	BRIDGTON & SACO RIVER RAILROAD
B&SU	BLOOMSBURG & SULLIVAN
B&T	BARNES & TUCKER COAL COMPANY
B&W	BRATTLEBORO & WHITEHALL
B&WI	BABCOCK & WILCOX
B&WO	BOSTON & WORCESTER
B&WP	BRADFORD & WESTERN PENNSYLVANIA
B-K	BLAW-KNOX CORPORATION-UNION STEEL DIV
BA&A	BUFFALO ATTICA & ARCADE
BA&H.	BATH & HAMMONDSPORT.
BA&P	BUTTE ANACONDA & PACIFIC
BA&PI	BUFFALO ALLEGHENY & PITTSBURG
BALT	BALTIMORE TRANSIT
BAM	BAMBERGER
BART	BAY AREA RAPID TRANSIT
BAS	BASIC REFRACTORIES
BB	BURNS BIGGS LUMBER COMPANY
BB&BC	BELLINGHAM BAY & BRITISH COLUMBIA
BB&G	BOSTON BARRE & GARDNER
BB&K	BRADFORD BORDELL & KINZUA
BB&P	BUFFALO BRADFORD & PITTSBURGH
BB&S	BRADFORD BORDELL & SMETHPORT
BBP	BELLEFIELD BOILER PLANT
BC	BEECH CREEK
BC&F	BOSTON CLINTON & FITCHBURG
BC&G	BUFFALO CREEK & GAULEY
BC&M	BOSTON CONCORD & MONTREAL
BC&P	BUFFALO CORREY & PITTSBURGH
BC&SA	BIRMINGHAM COLUMBUS & ST ANDREWS
BCC&S	BEECH CREEK CLEARFIELD & SOUTHWESTERN
BCE	BRITISH COLUMBIA ELECTRIC
BCH&P	BRITISH COLUMBIA HYDRO & POWER AUTHOR
BCO	BAY COLONY
BCPA	BROWARD COUNTY PORT AUTHORITY
BCPR	BALTIMORE CITY PASSENGER RAILWAY
BCR	BUFFALO CREEK
BCR&N	BURLINGTON CEDAR RAPIDS & NORTHERN
BCRW	BRITISH COLUMBIA RAILWAY
BD	BELVIDERE-DELAWARE RAILROAD
BDC	BOSQUES DE CHIHUAHUA
BDN&M	BAY DE NOQUET & MARQUETTE
BE	BAMBERGER ELECTRIC
BE&C	BRADFORD ELDRED & CUBA
BE&CH	BENNETSVILLE & CHERAM RAILROAD
BE&M	BEAUFORT & MOREHEAD
BEC	BELLEFONTE CENTRAL
BEDT	BROOKLYN EASTERN DISTRICT TERMINAL
BEEC	BEACH MOUNTAIN RAILROAD
BEEC.	BEECH MOUNTAIN RAILROAD
BEL	BELLEFONTAINE
BELL	BOSTON ELEVATED LINES
BELT	BELTON
BEM	BEMIS LUMBER COMPANY

APPENDIX A (RAILROADS)

BEN	BENSON
BESS	BESSEMER
BETH	BETHLEHEM MINES
BG	BULLFROG GOLDFIELD
BH	BRIGHT HOPE
BH&FP	BLACK HILLS & FORT PIERRE
BH&SM&C	BUNKER HILL & SULLIVAN MINE & COAL CO
BHC	BLACK HILLS CENTRAL
BHL	BIG HORN LUMBER COMPANY
BHT&W	BOSTON HOOSAC TUNNEL & WESTERN
BI	BARTLESVILLE INTERURBAN
BI&B	BILLERICA & BEDFORD RAILROAD
BI&S	BIRMINGHAM & SOUTHEASTERN
BI&SM	BILLMEYER & SMALL'S
BING	BINGHAMTON
BIR	BIRMINGHAM ELECTRIC
BIRM	BIRMINGHAM TERMINAL
BIS	BIRMINGHAM SOUTHERN
BKL	BOOTH KELLY LUMBER COMPANY
BL	BLAIRSTOWN
BL&K	BIG LEVEL & KINZUA
BL&R	BUFFALO LOCKPORT & ROCHESTER
BL&S	BLOOMSBURG & SOUTHERN
BLW	BALDWIN LOCOMOTIVE WORKS
BM	BEAVER MEADOW
BM&E	BEAVER MEADE & ENGLEWOOD
BM&LP	BLACK MESA & LAKE POWELL
BM&S	BUFFALO ST MARYS & SOUTHWESTERN
BMC	BOSTON METALS COMPANY
BMT	BLACK MOUNTAIN RAILROAD
BN	BURLINGTON NORTHERN
BOE	BOEING
BORK	BORK COMPANY
BOT&M	BANGOR OLD TOWN & MILFORD
BOW	BOWDON
BOYN	BOYNE CITY
BP	BREWSTER PHOSPHATE
BR	BLUE RIDGE RAILWAY
BR&C	BRADFORD RICHBURG & CUBA
BR&D	BRIDGTON RAILROAD & DEVELOPMENT
BR&E	BANGOR RAILWAY & ELECTRIC
BR&H	BROOKSVILLE & HUDSON
BR&M	BROWNSTONE & MIDDLETOWN
BR&P	BUFFALO ROCHESTER & PITTSBURG RAILWAY
BR&PA	BUFFALO ROCHESTER & PACIFIC
BR&W	BLACK RIVER & WESTERN
BRAD	BRADFORD STEAM RAILROAD
BRB&L	BOSTON REVERE BEACH & LYNN
BRC	BELT RAILWAY OF CHICAGO
BRI	BRIMSTONE
BRID	BRIDGEPORT TRAMWAY
BRMT	BRADSHAW MOUNTAIN
BRO	BROWN COUNTY
BRT	BOSTON RAPID TRANSIT
BRTE	BROOKLYN RAPID TRANSIT ELEVATED CO.
BRTS	BROOKLYN RAPID TRANSIT SUBWAY LINES
BRW	BRITISH RAILWAYS
BS	BOSTON SUBWAY
BS&G	BRASWELL SAND & GRAVEL
BS&GR	BECKER SAND & GRAVEL
BSL	BIRMINGHAM SLAG
BSOC&A	BLUE SPRINGS ORANGE CITY & ATLANTIC
BSRR	BRANFORD STEAM RAILROAD
BSS	BAY STATE STREET RAILWAY
BT	BRISTOL TRACTION
BUC	BUFFALO UNION CAROLINA RAILROAD
BUCK	BUCK MOUNTAIN
BUI	BUICK
BUSH	BUSH TERMINAL
BUT	BUFFALO TERMINAL
BW&GF	BISMARCK WASHBURN & GREAT FALLS
BW&LE	BRANTFORD WATERLOO & LAKE ERIE
BWP	BRODERICK WOOD PRODUCTS
BWT	BRANDYWINE TRANSIT
C	CANTON
C&A	CHICAGO & ALTON
C&AD	CARTHAGE & ADIRONDACK
C&AM	CAMDEN & AMBOY
C&AT	CAMDEN & ATLANTIC
C&AU	CHICAGO & AURORA
C&BL	CONEMAUGH & BLACK LICK
C&C	CANTON & CARTHAGE
C&CA	CANAJOHARIE & CATSKILL
C&CO	CARLTON & COAST
C&CSP	CARSON & COLORADO SOUTHERN PACIFIC
C&CV	COOPERSTOWN & CHARLOTTE VALLEY
C&E	CASSVILLE & EXETER
C&EI	CHICAGO & EASTERN ILLINOIS
C&F	CATASAUQUA & FOGELSVILLE
C&G	CARILLON & GRENVILLE
C&GL	COLLINS & GLENNVILLE
C&GR	COLUMBUS & GREENVILLE
C&GT	CANADA & GULF TERMINAL
C&H	CHESWICK & HARMAR
C&HC	CALUMET & HECLA CONSOLIDATED COPPER
C&I	CAMBRIA & INDIANA
C&IM	CHICAGO & ILLINOIS MIDLAND
C&IR	COAL & IRON
C&IW	CHICAGO & ILLINIOS WESTERN
C&LC	CADILLAC & LAKE CITY
C&LE	CINCINNATI & LAKE ERIE
C&LV	CHATHAM & LEBANON VALLEY
C&M	CUMBERLAND & MANCHESTER
C&MI	COLUMBIA & MILLSTADT
C&MO	CONCORD & MONTREAL
C&N	CAROLINA & NORTHWESTERN
C&NP	CHICAGO & NORTHERN PACIFIC
C&NW	CHICAGO & NORTH WESTERN
C&NWB	CHICAGO & NORTHWESTERN BELT
C&NWT	COLORADO & NORTHWESTERN
C&O	CHESAPEAKE & OHIO RAILROAD
C&OG	CHAMPLAIN & OGDENSBURG RAILROAD
C&OW	CLINTON & OKLAHOMA WESTERN
C&P	COBOURG & PETERBOROUGH
C&PA	COUDERSPORT & PORT ALLEGHENY
C&PE	CUMBERLAND & PENNSYLVANIA
C&PI	CLAREDON & PITTSFORD
C&PR	CONNECTICUT & PASSUMPSIC RIVERS
C&S	COLORADO & SOUTHERN
C&SL	CHAMPLAIN & ST LAWRENCE
C&SSRT	CHICAGO & SOUTH SIDE RAPID TRANSIT
C&SU	CAYUGA & SUSQUEHANNA
C&T	CHUMBRES & TOLRIC SCENIC RAILROAD
C&TS	CUMBRES & TOLEC SCENIC RAILROAD
C&W	CHESAPEAKE & WESTERN RAILROAD
C&WC	CHARLESTON & WESTERN CAROLINA
C&WE	CUMBERLAND & WESTERNPORT ELECTRIC
C&WI	CHICAGO & WESTERN INDIANA
C&WV	CHICAGO & WABASH VALLEY
C&WY	COLORADO & WYOMING
C&Z	COAHUILA & ZACATECAS
C-P	CHIHUAHUA-PACIFIC
CA&C	CARSON & COLORADO RAILROAD
CA&E	CHICAGO AURORA & ELGIN
CA&S	CONSOLIDATED CHICAGO ALTONA & SOUTHERN
CAC	CANADIAN COLLIERIES LIMITED
CACC	CENTRAL APPALACHIAN COAL COMPANY
CAD	CADIZ
CAL	CALTRANS
CAM	CALIFORNIA MIDLAND
CAN	CANADIAN NORTHERN
CAPA	CALIFORNIA PACIFIC
CAPR	CAMAS PRAIRIE RAILROAD
CAR	CARGILL INCORPORATED
CARB	CARBON COUNTY
CARR	CARROLLTON
CARS	CAROLINA SOUTHERN
CART	CARTIER RAILWAY
CAS	CALIFORNIA SOUTHERN
CASC	CASCADE
CASS	CASS SCENIC
CAT	CATAWISSA
CAW	CAROLINA WESTERN
CB	COORS BREWERY
CB&I	CHICAGO BRIDGE & IRON
CB&Q	CHICAGO BURLINGTON & QUINCY
CBA	CITY OF BALTIMORE
CBE	CHESAPEAKE BEACH
CBELT	COTTON BELT
CBL	COOS BAY LUMBER
CBT	CAPE BRETON TRAMWAYS
CC	CAPE COD
CC&C	COWLITZ CHEHALIS & CASCADE
CC&CH	CHARLESTON CINCINNATI & CHICAGO
CC&L	CHICAGO CINCINNATI & LOUISVILLE
CC&M	COLORADO COLUMBUS & MEXICAN RAILROAD
CC&O	CAROLINA CLINCHFIELD & OHIO
CCC&I	CLEVELAND COLUM CINCIN & INDIANAPOL
CCC&SL	CLEVELAND CINCINNATI CHIC & ST LOUIS
CCE	CALIFORNIA CENTRAL
CCH	CHESUNCOOK CHAMBERLAIN
CCR	CAMPBELL'S CREEK
CCT	CENTRAL CALIFORNIA TRACTION COMPANY
CCW	CHARLES CITY WESTERN
CD&M	COLUMBUS DELAWARE & MARION
CDR&N	COEUR D'ALENE RAILWAY & NAVIGATION
CE	CALIFORNIA EASTERN
CE&C	CENTRE & CLEARFIELD
CED	COMMONWEALTH EDISON
CEI	CLEVELAND ELECTRIC ILLUMINATING CO
CEMT	CENTRAL MILITARY TRACT
CER	CALIFORNIA ELECTRIC RAILWAY
CEV	CENTRAL VALLEY
CF	CAPE FEAR
CF&W	CANEY FORK & WESTERN
CF&W.	CHIPPEWA FALLS & WESTERN
CFC	CHICAGO FREIGHT CAR COMPANY
CFI	CHAMPION FIBRE
CFO	CENTRAL FOUNDRY
CFP	CANADIAN FOREST PRODUCTS
CG	CHICAGO GRAVEL COMPANY
CG&P	CINCINNATI GEORGETOWN & PORTSMOUTH
CGA	CENTRAL OF GEORGIA
CGN	CAPE GIRARDEAU NORTHERN
CGRT	CORAL GABLES RAPID TRANSIT
CGW	CHICAGO GREAT WESTERN RAILWAY
CH	CLOVER HILL
CH&B	CHICAGO HARLEM & BATAVIA
CH&C	CHERAW & COALFIELD
CH&D	CINCINNATI HAMILTON & DAYTON
CH&DA	CHERAW & DARLINGTON
CH&GT	CHICAGO & GRAND TRUNK
CH&N	CHICAGO & NORTHERN RAILROAD
CH&P	CHICAGO & PACIFIC
CHE	CHESHIRE
CHES	CHESTERFIELD
CHESS	CHESSIE SYSTEM
CHP	CHAMAS PRAIRIE RAILROAD
CHSD	CHICAGO SANITARY DISTRICT
CHT	CHAUTAUQUA TRACTION
CHTR	CHATTANOOGA TRACTION
CHTT	CHICAGO HEIGHTS TERMINAL TRANSFER
CHUT	CHICAGO UNION TRANSFER
CHV	CHATTAHOOCHEE VALLEY
CHW	CHEHALIS WESTERN
CI	CHATTAHOOCHEE INDUSTRIAL RAILROAD
CI&L	CHICAGO INDIANAPOLIS & LOUISVILLE
CI&M	CHATAM IRON & METAL
CIN	CENTRAL INDIANA
CINO	CINCINNATI NORTHERN
CIRT	CINCINNATI RAPID TRANSIT
CIT	CITADEL CEMENT COMPANY
CITC	CENTRAL IOWA TRANSPORTATION COOP
CIUT	CINCINNATI UNION TERMINAL
CJ	CHICAGO JUNCTION
CK&O	COLORADO KANSAS & OKLAHOMA
CK&S	CONDON KINZUA & SOUTHERN
CK&S	CONSOLIDATED KANSAS & SIDELL
CK&SA	CHICAGO KALAMAZOO & SAGINAW
CK&W	CHICAGO KANSAS & WESTERN
CL	CLINCHFIELD
CL&A	CINCINNATI LAWRENCE & AURORA
CL&C	CLAREMONT & CONCORD RAILROAD
CL&W	CLEVELAND LORAIN & WHEELING RAILROAD
CLA	CLARION RIVER
CLC	CARLTON LOGGING COMPANY
CLE	CLEMENT LUMBER COMPANY
CLI	CLINCHFIELD COAL
CLIF	CLIFFSIDE RAILROAD
CLRT	CLEVELAND RAPID TRANSIT

STEPHANS' RAILROAD DIRECTORY

363

APPENDIX A (RAILROADS)

CLS&E	CHICAGO LAKE SHORE & EASTERN
CLW	CHICAGO LOCOMOTIVE WORKS
CM	CRAIG MOUNTAIN
CM&G	CHICAGO MILWAUKEE & GARY
CM&P	CHICAGO MILWAUKEE & PUGET SOUND
CMA	CENTRAL MASSACHUSETTS
CMFG	CAMP MANUFACTURING
CMI	COLORADO MIDLAND
CML	CORTEZ MINES LIMITED
CMSP	CHICAGO MILWAUKEE & ST PAUL
CMT	CATSKILL MOUNTAINS
CN	CANADIAN NATIONAL
CN&L	COLUMBIA NEWBERRY & LAURENS
CN&W	CHOCTAW NEWCASTLE & WESTERN
CND	CAROLINA NITROGEN DIV OF GRACE CHEM
CNE	CENTRAL NEW ENGLAND
CNE&W	CENTRAL NEW ENGLAND & WESTERN
CNG	COWICHAN NARROW GAUGE
CNJ	CENTRAL RAILROAD OF NEW JERSEY
CNO&TP	CINCINNATI & NEW ORLEANS & TEXAS PAC.
CNS&M	CHICAGO NORTH SHORE & MILWAUKEE
CNW	CALIFORNIA NORTHWESTERN
CNY	CENTRAL NEW YORK
CNY&N	CENTRAL NEW YORK & NORTHERN
CNY&W	CENTRAL NEW YORK & WESTERN
CNYE	CHICAGO NEW YORK ELECTRIC AIR LINE RR
CNYS	CENTRAL NEW YORK SOUTHERN
CO	CORONADO
CO&C	COLUMBIA & COWLITZ
CO&CO	CORINTH & COUNCE
CO&E	CRAB ORCHARDS & EGYPTIAN
CO&G	CHOCTAW OKLAHOMA & GULF RAILROAD
CO&L	CORNWALL & LEBANON RAILROAD
COL	COLORADO CENTRAL
CON	CONSUMERS POWER
CONN	CONNECTICUT COMPANY
CONNR	CONNECTICUT RAILROAD
CONS	CONSUMERS COMPANY
CONT	CONTINENTAL STEEL
CONW	CONWAY SCENIC
COR	CONNECTICUT RIVER
CORN	CORNWALL RAILROAD
COW	CONNECTICUT WESTERN
CP	CANADIAN PACIFIC
CP&L	CAROLINA POWER & LIGHT
CP&LT	CAMINO PLACERVILLE & LAKE TAHOE
CP&S	COLUMBIA PARK & SOUTHERN
CP&SG	CHESTER PERRYVILLE & ST GENEVIEVE
CP&SW	COLUMBIA PARK & SOUTHWESTERN
CPA	CENTRAL PACIFIC
CPGE	CANADIAN PACIFIC GREAT WESTERN
CPM	CARTIAGE PAPER MAKERS
CPM&O	CHICAGO ST PAUL MINNEAPOLIS & OMAHA
CPR	CITY OF PRINEVILLE
CPT	CITY POINT
CR	CONRAIL
CR&I	CHICAGO RIVER & INDIANA
CR&IC	CEDAR RAPIDS & IOWA CITY
CR&M	CHIPPAWAH RIVER & MENOMONIE RAILWAY
CR&N	CPPER RIVER & NORTHWESTERN
CR&NW	COPPER RIVER & NORTHWESTERN
CR&SJ	CRYSTAL RIVER & SAN JUAN
CRA	COPPER RANGE
CRB	CENTRAL RR & BANKING CO OF GEORGIA
CRB&L	CHERRY RIVER BOOM & LUMBER
CRE	CANADIAN REFRACTORIES
CRI	CHESTNUT RIDGE
CRI&G	CHICAGO ROCK ISLAND & GULF
CRLI	CENTRAL RAILROAD OF LONG ISLAND
CRP	CONSOLIDATED ROCK PRODUCTS
CRT	CHICAGO RAPID TRANSIT COMPANY
CRW	CLEVELAND RAILWAYS
CRWP	CENTRAL RAILWAY OF PERU
CS	CANADIAN SOUTHERN
CS&CC	COLORADO SPRINGS & CRIPPLE CR DIST RY
CSC	CITIES SERVICE COMPANY
CSCO	CLEVELAND SOUTHWESTERN & COLUMBUS
CSD	CONNOR STEEL DIVISION
CSF&E	CASPER SOUTH FORK & EASTERN
CSL	CHICAGO SHORT LINE
CSL&W	CHICAGO ST LOUIS & WESTERN
CSLS	CHICAGO SURFACE LINES
CSP&KC	CHICAGO ST PAUL & KANSAS CITY
CSPM&O	CHICAGO ST PAUL MINNEAPOLIS & OHIO
CSS&SB	CHICAGO SOUTH SHORE & SOUTH BEND
CSUB	CHICAGO SUBWAYS
CT	CHICAGO TUNNEL
CT&G	CARRABELLE TALLAHASSEE & GEORGIA
CT&S	CAIRO TRUMAN & SOUTHERN
CTA	CHICAGO TRANSIT AUTHORITY
CTR	CITIZENS TRACTIONS
CU	CITY UTILITIES COMPANY
CU&S	CUTLER & SAVIDGE
CUM	CUMBERLAND
CUMV	CUMBERLAND VALLEY
CUR	CURRENT RIVER RAILROAD
CUS	CUSHING STONE
CUT	CLEVELAND UNION TERMINAL (NYC)
CUY	CUYAHOGA VALLEY
CV	CENTRAL VERMONT (CN) RAILWAY
CVA	CAHUENGA VALLEY
CW	CALIFORNIA WESTERN RR & NAV CO
CWC	CENTRAL WAREHOUSE COMPANY
CWN	CALIFORNIA WESTERN NORTH
CWP	CROWN WILLAMETTE PAPER
CWP&S	CHICAGO WEST PULLMAN & SOUTHERN
CWV&S	CENTRAL WEST VIRGINIA & SOUTHERN
D	DEVCO
D&BB	DELAWARE & BOUND BROOK
D&C	DUTCHESS & COLUMBIA
D&CA	DIAMOND & CALDOR RAILROAD
D&E	DELAWARE & EASTERN
D&H	DELAWARE & HUDSON
D&HG	DELAWARE & HUDSON GRAVITY
D&I	DENVER & INTERMOUNTAIN
D&IR	DULUTH & IRON RANGE
D&M	DETROIT & MACKINAC
D&MM	DANSVILLE & MT MORRIS
D&N	DELAWARE & NORTHERN
D&NE	DULUTH & NORTHEASTERN
D&NM	DULUTH & NORTHERN MINNESOTA
D&P	DANVILLE & POTTSVILLE
D&R	DARDANELLE & RUSSELLVILLE
D&RG	DENVER & RIO GRANDE RAILROAD
D&RGW	DENVER & RIO GRANDE WESTERN
D&S	DURHAM & SOUTHERN
D&SI	DURANGO & SILVERTON
D&SL	DENVER & SALT LAKE
D&SQ	DAUPHIN & SUSQUEHANNA
D&TSL	DETROIT & TOLEDO SHORT (SHORE?) LINE
D&W	DENISON & WASHITA
DA	DOMINION ATLANTIC
DB&W	DENVER BOULDER & WESTERN
DC	DEEP CREEK
DC&S	DETROIT CARO & SANDUSKY
DCC&P	DENVER COLORADO CANYON & PACIFIC
DE	DELRAY CONNECTING
DE&G	DENVER ENID & GULF
DED	DETROIT DIESEL EDISON
DEI	DEITCH COMPANY
DES	DELTA SOUTHERN
DET	DELRAY TERMINAL
DF	DRY FORK
DF&S	DOMINION FOUNDRIES & STEEL
DFI	DIERKS FOREST INDUSTRIES
DGH&M	DETROIT GRAND HAVEN & MILWAUKEE
DIA	DIAMOND VALLEY
DL&B	DUNCANNON LANDISBURG & BROADTOP
DL&N	DEVILS LAKE & NORTHERN
DL&W	DELAWARE LACKAWANNA & WESTERN
DM&CI	DES MOINES & CENTRAL IOWA
DM&IR	DULUTH MISSABE & IRON RANGE
DM&M	DETROIT MACKINAC & MARQUETTE
DM&MI	DES MOINES & MINNESOTA
DM&N	DULUTH MISSABE & NORTHERN
DM&W	DULUTH MISSABE & WESTERN
DMR&N	DULUTH MISSISSIPPI RIVER & NORTHERN
DMU	DES MOINES UNION
DO	DELAWARE OTSEGO SYSTEM
DO&C	DOWLING & CAMP
DO&S	DARDANELLE OLA & SOUTHERN
DOD	DEPARTMENT OF DEFENSE
DOS	DONORA SOUTHERN
DP	DENVER PACIFIC RAILROAD COMPANY
DP&L	DELMARVA POWER & LIGHT
DP&M	DETROIT PONTIAC & MACKINAC
DPC	DUKE POWER COMPANY
DPE	DAN PATCH ELECTRIC
DQ&E	DEQUEEN & EASTERN
DRI&N	DAVENPORT ROCK ISLAND & NORTHWESTERN
DRL&W	DULUTH RAINY LAKE & WINNIPEG
DRPA	DELAWARE RIVER PORT AUTHORITY
DRT	DETROIT RIVER TUNNEL COMPANY
DS	DISMAL SWAMP
DS&G	DIXIE SAND & GRAVEL
DS&S	DELAWARE SUSQUEHANNA & SCHUYLKILL
DSM	DAWES SILICA MINING
DSP&P	DENVER SOUTH PARK & PACIFIC
DSS&A	DULUTH SOUTH SHORE & ATLANTIC
DST	DETROIT STREET RAILWAY
DT	DETROIT TERMINAL
DT&I	DETROIT TOLEDO & IRONTON
DU	DUTCHESS COUNTY
DUD&T	DULUTH UNION DEPOT & TRANSFER
DUP&T.	DULUTH UNION DEPOT & TRANSFER.
DV	DEATH VALLEY
DV&RL	DULUTH VIRGINIA & RAINY LAKE
DV&S	DELTA VALLEY & SOUTHERN
DW	DESERET-WESTERN RAILWAY
DW&P	DULUTH WINNIPEG & PACIFIC
E	ERIE
E&B	ELGIN & BELVIDERE INTERURBAN
E&H	ELK & HIGHLAND
E&K	ERIE & KALAMAZOO
E&KR	EUREKA & KALAMATH RIVER
E&LS	ESCANABA & LAKE SUPERIOR
E&M	EDGMOOR & MANETTA
E&MJ	EMPORIUM & MT JEWITT
E&MO	ETNA & MONTROSE
E&N	ESQUIMALT & NANAIMO FAMILY LINES
E&NA	EUROPEAN & NORTH AMERICAN
E&O	ERIE & ONTARIO
E&P	EUREKA & PALISADE RAILWAY
E&W	ELKHART & WESTERN
E&WC	EAST & WEST COAST
E&WV	ERIE & WYOMING VALLEY
E-D	EMPIRE DETROIT DIV OF CYCLOPS STEEL
E-M	ELECTRO-MOTIVE
EB	EXCELSIOR BRICK
EB&C	EAST BARRE & CHELSEA
EB&L	EAST BRANCH & LINCOLN
EBT	EAST BROAD TOP
EBT&CC	EAST BROAD TOP RAILROAD & COAL CO
EC&H	EAST CAMDEN & HIGHLAND
ED	EDAVILLE
ED&W	EL DORADO & WESSON
EEC	EAST ERIE COMMERCIAL
EF	EAST FLORIDA
EG	ETHIOPIAN GOVERNMENT RAILWAYS
EI&TH	EVANSVILLE INDIANAPOLIS & TERRE HAUTE
EJ&E	ELGIN JOLIET & EASTERN
EJ&S	EAST JORDAN & SOUTHERN
EJR&T	EAST JERSY RAILROAD & TERMINAL
EK	EASTMAN KODAK COMPANY
EL	ERIE LACKAWANNA
EL&RR	EAST LINE & RED RIVER
EL&WB	EAGLE LAKE & WEST BRANCH
ELP	ELI LILLY PHARMACEUTICAL
EM	ELKHART METALS
EMA	EAST MAHANOY
EMC	ERIE MINING COMPANY
EMM	EMMITSBURG
EMSR	EASTERN MASSACHUSETTS STREET RY
EMT	EAGLE MOUNTAIN
EN	EUREKA NEVADA
EOH	ENSLEY OPEN HEARTH
EOT	EASTERN OHIO TRACTION
EP	EAST PENNSYLVANIA
EP&S	EL PASO & SOUTHWESTERN
EPCL	EL PASO CITY LINES

STEPHANS' RAILROAD DIRECTORY

APPENDIX A (RAILROADS)

EPS	EL PASO SOUTHERN
ER	EDVAVILLE RAILROAD
ES	EPSOM SALTS MONORAIL
ES&S	EAST SHORE & SURBURBAN
ESC	EMPIRE SUGAR COMPANY
ESH	EASTERN SHORE
ESL&C	EAST ST LOUIS & CARONDELET
ESLJ	EAST ST LOUIS JUNCTION
ET	EBERLE TANNING
ET&WNC	EAST TENNESSEE & WESTERN N CAROLINA
ETE	ESSEX TERMINAL
ETR	EDMODNTON TRANSIT
ETV&G	EAST TENNESSEE VIRGINIA & GULF
EU	EUSTIS
EV	EVERETT
EVP&S	EVERETT PIPE & STEEL
EW	EAST WASHINGTON
EXPO	EXPO '67 RAPID TRANSIT, MONTREAL
F	FLORIDA
F&AB	FERNANDINA & AMELIA BEACH
F&C	FRANKFORT & CINCINNATI
F&CC	FLORENCE & CRIPPLE CREEK
F&J	FERNANDINA & JACKSONVILLE
F&JA	FREEHOLD & JAMESBURG AGRICULTURAL
F&L	FRANKLIN & LEBANON TRACTION CO
F&M	FRANKLIN & MEGANTIC
F&N	FAIRCHILD & NORTHEASTERN
F&NW	FLEMINGSBURG & NORTHWESTERN
F&P	FARMVILLE & POWHATAN
F&PR	FORDYCE & PRINCETON
F-M	FAIRBANKS MORSE
FA&G	FLORIDA ALABAMA & GEORGIA
FAM	FAMILY LINES
FB	FALL BROOK
FB&S	FORT BRAGG & SOUTHEASTERN
FBL	FEDERAL BARGE LINES
FC	FLORIDA CENTRAL
FC&G	FLORIDA CENTRAL & GULF
FC&GU	FERNWOOD COLUMBIA & GULF
FC&P	FLORIDA CENTRAL & PENINSULAR
FC&W	FLORIDA CENTRAL & WESTERN
FCN	FULTON COUNTY NARROW GAUGE
FDM&S	FORT DODGE DES MOINES & SOUTHERN
FE	FELICIANA EASTERN
FE&MV	FREMONT ELKHORN & MISSOURI VALLEY RR
FEC	FLORIDA EAST COAST
FEM	FORT EUSTIS MILITARY RAILROAD
FERD	FERDINAND
FGT	FOREST GROVE TRANSPORTATION
FHP	FORT HOWARD PAPER COMPANY
FI	FITCHBURG RAILROAD
FJ&G	FONDA JOHNSTOWN & GLOVERSVILLE
FLC	FLORA LOGGING COMPANY
FM	FLORIDA MIDLAND
FMC	FORD MOTOR COMPANY
FMIN	FOOTE MINERALS
FNM	FALCONBRIDGE NICKEL MINES
FOP	FORT ORANGE PAPER COMPANY
FOR	FORE RIVER
FP	FLAMBEAU PAPER
FP&E	FAIRPORT PAINESVILLE & EASTERN
FPL	FILTRATION PLANT
FPT	FAIRMOUNT PARK TRANSIT
FR	FEATHER RIVER
FR&N	FLORIDA RAILWAY & NAVIGATIONS
FRE	FREEPORT
FRI	FRIENDSHIP
FRIS	FRISCO
FRL	FALL RIVER LINE
FRM	FRISCO MANDARIN
FRW	FRENCH RAILWAYS
FS	FLORIDA SOUTHERN
FS&VB	FORT SMITH & VAN BUREN
FS&W	FORT SMITH & WESTERN
FSS&RI	FORT SMITH SUBIACO & ROCK ISLAND
FSUD	FORT STREET UNION DEPOT
FSW	FLORIDA SOUTHWESTERN
FT	FLORIDA TRANSIT
FT&P	FLORIDA TRANSIT & PENINSULAR
FW&D	FORT WORTH & DENVER
FW&DC	FORT WORTH & DENVER CITY
FWB	FORT WORTH BELT
FWTC&I	FAIRFIELD WORKS TENNESSEE COAL & IRON
G	GEORGIA
G&CU	GALENA & CHICAGO UNION
G&F	GEORGIA & FLORIDA
G&G	GAINESVILLE & GULF
G&GE	GALESBURG & GREAT EASTERN
G&H	GETTYSBURG & HARRISBURG
G&J	GREENWICH & JOHNSONVILLE
G&M	GULFPORT & MISSISSIPPI COAST TRACTION
G&N	GREENVILLE & NORTHERN
G&P	GILMORE & PITTSBURGH
G&U	GRAFTON & UPTON
G&W	GALVESTON & WESTERN
G&WP	GEORGIA & WEST POINT
G&Y	GENESEE & WYOMING
G-H	GIFFORD-HILL
G-P	GEORGIA-PACIFIC CORPORATION
GAF	GENERAL ANILINE FILM
GAM	GEORGIA MARBLE
GAS&C	GEORGIA ASHBURN SYLVESTER & CAMILLA
GB	GUIGNARD BRICK
GB&L	GEORGETOWN BRECKENRIDGE & LEADVILLE
GB&W	GREEN BAY & WESTERN
GC	GOLD COAST
GC&C	GEORGES CREEK & CUMBERLAND
GC&E	GREENBRIER CHEAT & ELK
GC&SF	GULF COLORADO & SANTA FE
GCE	GREAT CENTRAL
GCH	GRACE CHEMICAL
GCO	GRAHAM COUNTY
GCOM	GROVES COMPANY
GCS	GENERAL CRUSHED STONE
GCS&M	GREEN COVE SPRINGS & MELROSE
GCT	GILPIN COUNTY TRAMWAY
GCW	GARDEN CITY WESTERN
GD	GLENMORE DISTRIBUTORS
GDIS	GLENMORE DISTILLERIES
GE	GENERAL ELECTRIC
GET	GETTYSBURG ELECTRIC
GF.	GRIZZLY FLATS.
GFC	GRAND FALLS CENTRAL
GG	GOODPASTURE GRAIN
GH&H	GALVESTON HOUSTON & HENDERSON
GHE	GALVESTON HOUSTON ELECTRIC RY
GI	GILPIN
GIC	GILMORE INDUSTRIAL CENTER
GIL	GILFORD TRANSPORTATION COMPANY
GIW	GENERAL IRON WORKS
GLC	GENERAL LOGGING COMPANY
GM	GENERAL MOTORS
GM&G	GEORGIA MIDLAND & GULF
GM&N	GULF MOBILE & NORTHERN
GM&O	GULF MOBILE & OHIO
GMA	GENERAL MINING ASSN OF NOVA SCOTIA
GMI	GAINESVILLE MIDLAND
GMQ	GRANITE MOUNTAIN QUARRIES
GMT	GREEN MOUNTAIN
GN	GREAT NORTHERN
GN&A	GRAYSONIA NASHVILLE & ASHDOWN
GNO	GEORGIA NORTHERN
GOT	GOVERNMENT OF ONTARIO TRANSIT
GP	GREAT PLAINS
GPC	GEORGIA POWER COMPANY
GR	GRAND RIVER
GR&I	GRAND RAPIDS & INDIANA
GRA	GRANITE
GRR	GRASSE RIVER
GRSC	GREEN RIVER STEEL COMPANY
GS	GODCHAUX SUGAR
GS&F	GEORGIA SOUTHERN & FLORDIA
GS&G	GEORGIA SOUTHWESTERN & GULF
GSCC	GREENVILLE STEEL CAR COMPANY
GSL	GREAT SLAVE LAKE
GSW	GREAT SOUTHWEST
GT	GRAND TRUNK
GTC	GRAND TRUNK OF CANADA
GTN	GEORGETOWN
GTP	GRAND TRUNK PACIFIC
GTS	GEORGETOWN STEEL
GTW	GRAND TRUNK WESTERN
GV	GEORGES VALLEY
GVE	GALLATIN VALLEY ELECTRIC
GW	GREAT WESTERN
GWC	GREAT WESTERN OF CANADA
GWH	GALVESTON WHARVES TERMINAL
GWS	GREAT WESTERN SUGAR
GWWD	GREATER WINNIPEG WATER DISTRICT
H	HARRISBURG RYS
H&B	HAMPTON & BRANCHVILLE
H&BT	HUDSON & BROAD TOP MOUNTAIN
H&BTM	HUNTINGTON & BROAD TOP MOUNTAIN RR
H&BV	HOUSTON & BRAZOS VALLEY (MP)
H&CV	HARTFORD & CONNECTICUT VALLEY
H&CW	HARTFORD & CONNECTICUT WESTERN
H&E	HOLLIS & EASTERN RAILROAD
H&F	HAGERSTOWN & FREDERICK
H&H	HIBISCUS & HELICONIA
H&LB	HUNTSVILLE & LAKE OF BAYS
H&M	HUDSON & MANHATTAN SUBWAY
H&N	HUTCHINSON & NORTHERN RAILWAY COMPANY
H&NE	HILLSBORO & NORTH EASTERN
H&NH	HARTFORD & NEW HAVEN
H&NY	HACKENSACK & NEW YORK RAILROAD
H&O	HOUGHTON & ONTONAGON
H&S	HARTFORD & SLOCOMB
H&SJ	HANNIBAL & ST JOSEPH
H&SO	HOPKINSVILLE & SOUTHERN
H&T	HOUSTON & TEXAS
H&TC	HOUSTON & TEXAS CENTRAL
H&TL	HECLA & TORCH LAKE
H&W	HARDWICK & WOODBURY
H-WPP	HOERNER-WALDORF PAPER PRODUCTS
HA	HAZLETON
HANC	HANNIBAL CONNECTING
HAR	HARTWELL

STEPHANS' RAILROAD DIRECTORY

APPENDIX A (RAILROADS)

HAS	HASSINGER
HB	HARVARD BRANCH
HB&IR	HURON BAY & IRON RANGE
HB&T	HOUSTON BELT & TERMINAL RAILWAY CO.
HC	HERSHEY CUBAN
HD	HOUSE OF DAVID
HES	HELENA SOUTHWESTERN
HESO	HELENA SOUTHERN
HGC	HICKGAS COMPANY
HH	HETCH HETCHY
HHL	HIMMTEBERG-HARRISON LUMBER CO
HI	HOLTEN INTERURBAN RAILWAY COMPANY
HIL	HILLSDALE COUNTY
HL&R	HELENA LIGHT & RAILWAY
HL&T	HORTON LUMBER & TIMBER
HLC	HAMMOND LUMBER COMPANY
HLW	HINKLEY LOCOMOTIVE WORKS
HM	HOBOKEN MANUFACTURERS
HNS	HOUSTON NORTH SHORE (MP)
HNSM	HANNA NICKEL SMELTING
HO	HOUSATONIC
HOS	HILLCREST OSBORNE
HOTS	HOT SPRINGS
HPC	HERCULES POWDER COMPANY
HPM	HARRISBURG PORSMOUTH MT JOY & LANCAST
HPT&D	HIGH POINT THOMASVILLE & DENTON
HRC	HAWAIIAN RAILROAD COMPANY
HRLC	HARRINGTON LUMBER COMPANY
HRRR	HUDSON RIVER RAILROAD
HS	HOBART SOUTHERN
HSH	HOBOKEN SHORE
HSL	HAZELTON-SUGAR LOAF
HSR	HELLENIC STATE RAILWAYS
HT	HERSEY TRANSIT
HT&W	HOOSAC TUNNEL & WILLMINGTON RAILROAD
HTR	HARLEM TRANSFER COMPANY
HU	HUNINGTON
HU&BT	HUNINGTON & BROAD TOP
HV	HOCKING VALLEY
HV&CV	HORNELLSVILLE & COHOCTON VALLEY
HVS	HOCKEN VALLEY SCENIC RAILWAY
HVSR	HOOSAC VALLEY STREET RAILWAY
HY&T	HOOPPOLE YORKTOWN & TAMPOCO
I	INDIANA RAILROAD
I&C	INDIANAPOLIS & CINCINATTI TRACTION CO
I&JC	IOLA & ST JOSEPH CANAL & RAILROAD
I&N	IOLA & NORTHERN
I&O	ITHACA & OWEGO
I-GN	INTERNATIONAL GREAT NORTHERN (MP)
IC	ILLINOIS CENTRAL
ICC	ISLAND CREEK COAL
ICCO	INSPERATION CONSOLIDATION COPPER CO
ICG	ILLINOIS CENTRAL GULF
ICO	INTERCOLONIAL RAILWAY
IES	INLAND EMPIRE SYSTEM
IFT	ICE FULTON TRIANGLE
IH&IR	INDIAN HILL & IRON RANGE
IHB	INDIANA HARBOR BELT
IL	ILWACO RAILWAY & NAVIGATION COMPANY
IL&S	INLAND LIME & STONE
IM	ILLINOIS MIDLAND RAILWAY
IM&C	INTERNATIONAL MINERALS & CHEMICAL
IMI	INTERNATIONAL MILLING
IMT	IRON MOUNTAIN
IN	ILLINOIS NORTHERN
INN	INDIANA NORTHERN
INTER	INTERSTATE
IOCC	IRON ORE CO OF CANADA
IOWA	IOWA TERMINAL RAILROAD COMPANY
IOWAC	IOWA CENTRAL
IOWAT	IOWA TRANSFER
IP&L	IOWA POWER & LIGHT
IPSI	INTERSTATE PUBLIC SERV CO OF INDIANA
IR	IRONTON
IR&T	INTERURBAN RAILWAY & TERMINAL
IRCA	INTERNATIONAL RW OF CENTRAL AMERICA
IRP	INGERSOLL RAND POWERED LOCOMOTIVES
IRPC	ILLINOIS RIVER PACKET CO
IRW	INDIANAPOLIS RAILWAYS
IS	INGALLS SHIPBUBILDING
IS&B	ILLINOIS SLAG & BALLAST
ISR	INTERSTATE STREET RAILWAY
IT	ILLINOIS TERMINAL
ITC	ISLAND TERMINAL COMPANY
ITR	ILLINOIS TRACTION RAILWAY
IU	INDIANAPOLIS UNION
IUR	INTER-URBAN RAILWAY
IVT	ILLINOIS VALLEY TRACTION
J&E	JERSEYVILLE & EASTERN
J&L	JONES & LAUGHLIN STEEL
J&S	JACKSONVILLE & SOUTHWESTERN
J&SC	JOHNSTOWN & STONY CREEK
J&SW	JEROME & SOUTHWESTERN
J&W	JACKASS & WESTERN
JA&HR	JACKSONVILLE ST AUGUSTINE & HALIFAX R
JB	JACKSONVILLE BELT
JC	JUNCTION CITY-HORTON WOODEN RAILROAD
JCE	JERSEY CENTRAL
JCG	JACKSON COUNTY GRAIN
JG&G	JACKSONVILLE GAINESVILLE & GULF
JL	JOHNSON LUMBER
JM&P	JACKSONVILLE MAYPORT & PABLO RY & NAV
JN	JAPANESE NATIONAL RAILWAYS
JNR	JAPAN NATIONAL RAILWAY
JO	JOHNSONBURG
JP&M	JACKSONVILLE PENSACOLA & MOBILE
JS	JAY STREET CONNECTING RAILROAD
JT	JACKSONVILLE TERMINAL
JT&KW	JACKSONVILLE TAMPA & KEY WEST
JTC	JOHNSTOWN TRACTION CO
JW&N	JAMESTOWN WESTFIELD & NORTHWESTERN
JWR	JIM WALTER RESOURCES INC
K	KANE
K&DR	KINGFIELD & DEAD RIVER
K&E	KANE & ELK
K&EL	KENDALL & ELDRED
K&IT	KENTUCKY & INDIANA TERMINAL
K&L	KNOX & LINCOLN
K&M	KANAWHA & MICHIGAN
K&O	KANSAS & OKLAHOMA
K&S	KEATING & SMETHPORT
K&T	KENTUCKY & TENNESSEE RAILWAY
K&TI	KINZUA & TIONA
KA	KAHULUI
KAC	KANAWHA CENTRAL
KAC&LC	KEESEVILLE AUSABLE CHASM &L CHAMPLAIN
KATY	KATY NORTHWEST
KB	KAISER BAUXITE
KBM	KINMOND BROTHERS MONTREAL
KC	KELLY'S CREEK (KELLEYS CREEK)
KC&K	KINZUA CREEK & KANE
KC&P	KANSAS CITY & PACIFIC
KC&S	KANSAS CITY & SOUTHERN RAILROAD
KCC	KANSAS CITY CONNECTING
KCE	KENNEBEC CENTRAL
KCKV&W	KANSAS CITY KAW VALLEY & WESTERN
KCKW	KANSAS CITY KAW VALLEY
KCM&O	KANSAS CITY MEXICO & ORIENT
KCP&G	KANSAS CITY PITTSBURGH & GULF
KCS	KANSAS CITY SOUTHERN
KCT	KANSAS CITY TERMINAL
KE	KENNECOTT
KER	KERSEY
KEY	KEYSTONE
KF	KISO FOREST JAPAN
KGB&W	KEWAUNEE GREEN BAY & WESTERN
KH	KINZUA HEMLOCK
KHC	KITTY HAWK CENTRAL
KI	KINZUA
KL	KNICKERBOCKER LIME
KL&L	KLICKITAT LOG & LUMBER
KLC	KIRBY LUMBER COMPANY
KLI	KLIPNOCKIE
KN	KNOX
KO&G	KANSAS OKLAHOMA & GULF RAILWAY
KOP	KOPPERS COMPANY
KP&L	KNOXVILLE POWER & LIGH
KS	KEY SYSTEM OF SAN FRANCISCO
KSE&S	KANSAS CITY ELDORADO & SOUTHERN
KSPS	KANSAS CITY PUBLIC SERVICE
KT&T	KENTUCKY TRACTION & TERMINAL
KTC	KOSMOS TIMBER COMPANY
KTU	KENTUCKY UTILITIES COMPANY
KU	KUSHEQUA
KUC	KANSAS UTILITIES COMPANY
KUCO	KUERT CONCRETE
KV	KINZUA VALLEY
L	LAKELAND
L&A	LOUISIANA & ARKANSAS RAILWAY COMPANY
L&AKS	LOUISIANA & ARKANSAS KANSAS CITY SOUTH
L&B	LACKAWANNA & BLOOMSBURG
L&BR	LOWVILLE & BEAVER RIVER
L&C	LANCASTER & CHESTER
L&CC	LOCKS & CANALS COMPANY LOWELL MASS
L&CV	LEETONIA & CHERRY VALLEY
L&F	LOUISVILLE & FRANKFORT
L&HR	LEHIGH & HUDSON RIVER
L&I	LOUISVILLE & INTERURBAN
L&M	LEHIGH & MAHANOY
L&MA	LAKESIDE & MARBLEHEAD
L&N	LOUISVILLE & NASHVILLE
L&NE	LEHIGH & NEW ENGLAND
L&NO	LAONA & NORTHERN
L&NS	L&N SHOPS
L&NW	LOUISIANA & NORTH WEST
L&O	LORTON & OCCOQUAN
L&P	LACKAWANNA & PITTSBURG
L&PB	LOUISIANA & PINE BLUFF
L&PS	LONDON & PORT STANLEY
L&S	LUDLOW & SOUTHERN
L&SQ	LEHIGH & SUSQUEHANNA
L&SW	LACKAWANNA & SOUTHWESTERN
L&WV	LACKAWANNA & WYOMING VALLEY
L&YF	LANCASTER & YORK FURNACE STREET RY
L-HC	LIMA HAMILTON CORPORATION
LA	LAWNDALE
LA&ERV	LOS ANGELES & EAGLE ROCK VALLEY
LA&G	LOS ANGELES & GLENDALE
LA&L	LIVONIA AVON & LAKEVILLE
LA&LB	LOS ANGELES & LONG BEACH
LA&P	LOS ANGELES & PACIFIC RR
LA&R	LOS ANGELES & REDONDO
LA&S	LACKAWAXEN & STOURBRIDGE
LA&SDB	LOS ANGELES & SAN DIEGO BEACH
LA&SG	LOS ANGELES & SAN GABRIEL VALLEY
LA&SL	LOS ANGELES & SALT LAKE (UP)
LA&SO	LAURINBURG & SOUTHERN
LA&SP	LOS ANGELES & SAN PEDRO
LAC	LOS ANGELES COUNTY
LACK	LACKAWANNA
LAIR	LOS ANGELES INDEPENDENT RAILROAD
LAJ	LOS ANGELES JUNCTION
LAP&G	LOS ANGELES PASADENA & GLENDALE
LAR	LOS ANGELES RAILWAY
LAT	LOS ANGELES TERMINAL
LATR	LOS ANGELES TRANSIT
LB	LONG BELL RAILROAD
LC	LORBERRY CREEK
LC&LJ	LAKE CHAMPLAIN & ST LAWRENCE JUNCTION
LC&M	LAKE CHAMPLAIN & MORIAH
LCL	LOUISIANA CYPRESS LUMBER COMPANY
LE	LOUISIANA EASTERN
LE&E	LAKE ERIE & EASTERN
LE&FW	LAKE ERIE & FORT WAYNE
LE&N	LAKE ERIE & NORTHERN (CP)
LE&P	LAKE ERIE & PITTSBURGH RAILROAD
LEBG&N	LAKE ERIE BOWLING GREEN & NAPOLEON
LEF&C	LAKE ERIE FRANKLIN & CLARION
LEI	LEIPER
LESM	LITTLE EMMA SILVER MINE
LF&D	LITTLE FALLS & DOLGEVILLE
LG	LAUHOFF GRAIN
LH	LEONA HEIGHTS
LH&SL	LOUISVILLE HENDERSON & ST LOUIS
LI	LONG ISLAND RAILROAD
LI&M	LITCHFIELD & MADISON
LIG	LIGONIER VALLEY
LILW	LIMA LOCOMOTIVE WORKS
LISC	LIPSETT STEEL COMPANY
LITRI	LITTLE RIVER RAILROAD

STEPHANS' RAILROAD DIRECTORY

APPENDIX A (RAILROADS)

LJIP	LA JUNTA INDUSTRIAL PARK
LK&W	LEAVENWORTH KANSAS & WESTERN
LL	LEHIGH LUZERNE
LLW	LANCASTER LOCOMOTIVE WORKS
LM	LOUISIANA MIDLAND
LNA&C	LOUISVILLE NEW ALBANY & CORYDON
LNCC	LEHIGH NAVIGATION COAL COMPANY
LNP&W	LARAMIE NORTH PARK & WESTERN
LO	LOYAL
LO&G	LIVE OAK & GULF
LO&S	LANCASTER OXFORD & SOUTHERN
LODI	LODI
LOP&G	LIVE OAK PERRY & GULF
LOS	LOUISIANA SOUTHERN
LOT&HB	LIVE OAK TAMPA & HOWLAND'S BLUFF
LOU	LOUISA
LP&N	LONGVIEW PORTLAND & NORTHERN
LPT	LIVE POULTRY TRANSPORT COMPANY
LQ&N	LAMAR QUEENS & NORTHERN
LR&HS	LAUREL RIVER & HOT SPRINGS
LR&L	LAWTON RAILWAY & LIGHTING
LS	LEBANON SPRINGS
LS&B	LA SALLE & BUREAU COUNTY
LS&I	LAKE SUPERIOR & ISHPEMING
LS&MC	LAKE SHORE & MICHIGAN SOUTHERN
LSC	LIMA STONE COMPANY
LSCH	LITTLE SCHUYLKILL NAV RR & COAL CO.
LSCO	LACLEDE STEEL COMPANY
LSE	LAKE SHORE ELECTRIC INTERURBAN
LSQ	LINCOLN STONE QUARRY
LSR	LINWOOD STREET RAILWAY
LSSC	LONE STAR STEEL COMPANY
LST	LEONARDS STORE
LST&T	LAKE SUPERIOR TERMINAL & TRANSFER
LT	LAKE TERMINAL
LTC	LEE TIDEWATER CYPRESS
LU&N	LUDINGTON & NORTHERN
LUS	LUKENS STEEL
LV	LEHIGH VALLEY
LV&T	LAS VEGAS & TONOPAH
LVT	LEHIGH VALLEY TRANSIT
LW&JC	LAKE WIMICO ST JOSEPH CANAL & RR CO
LYK	LYKENS VALLEY
M	MONON
M&A	MISSOURI & ARKANSAS
M&AT	MONTREAL & ATLANTA (CP)
M&B	MCKEAN & BUFFALO
M&BA	MONTPELIER & BARRE
M&BI	MACON & BIRMINGHAM
M&BIG	MERIDIAN & BIGBEE
M&BL	MARIANNA & BLOUNTSTOWN
M&BO	MOIRA & BOMBAY
M&C	MONTREAL & CHAMPLAIN
M&CR	MISSISQUOI & CLYDE RIVERS
M&D	MARYLAND & DELAWARE
M&E	MORRISTOWN & ERIE
M&ET	MODESTO & EMPIRE TRACTION
M&G	MOBILE & GULF
M&GL	MONTCLAIR & GREENWOOD LAKE
M&HM	MARQUETTE & HURON MOUNTAIN
M&HR	MOHAWK & HUDSON RIVER
M&I	MADISON & INDIANAPOLIS
M&IB&B	MISSOURI & ILLINOIS BRIDGE & BELT
M&L	MONTREAL & LACHINE
M&LB	MANAHAWKEN & LONG BEACH
M&LS	MANISTIQUE & LAKE SUPERIOR
M&N	MILWAUKEE & NORTHERN
M&NA	MISSOURI & NORTH ARKANSAS
M&NF	MOREHEAD & NORTH FORK
M&NG	MARIETTA & NORTH GEORGIA
M&NJ	MIDDLETOWN & NEW JERSEY
M&NW	MINNESOTA & NORTH WISCONSIN
M&O	MOBILE & OHIO
M&OC	MASON & OCEANA
M&OL	MARCELLUS & OTISCO LAKE
M&ON	MARQUETTE & ONTONAGON
M&ONE	MANCHESTER & ONEIDA
M&ORY	MORSE & ORY
M&P	MONTREAL & PLATTSBURG
M&PP	MANITOU & PIKE'S PEAK RAILWAY
M&RR	MINNEAPOLIS & RAINY RIVER
M&S	MONTREAL & SOREL
M&SC	MONTREAL & SOUTHERN COUNTIES
M&SE	MARQUETTE & SOUTHEASTERN
M&SH	MAHANOY & SHAMOKIN
M&SL	MINNEAPOLIS & ST LOUIS
M&SP	MINNEAPOLIS & ST PAUL
M&SV	MISSISSIPPI & SKUNA VALLEY
M&SVA	MONTEREY & SALINAS VALLEY
M&U	MIDDLETOWN & UNIONVILE
M&W	MARQUETTE & WESTERN
M&WE	MUNCIE & WESTERN
M&WR	MONTPELIER & WELLS RIVER RAILROAD
M-CL	MICHIGAN-CAILFORNIA LUMBER
M-I	MISSOURI-ILLINOIS
M-M	MADEIRA-MAMORE RAILWAY (BRAZIL)
MA	MAGMA ARIZONA
MA&B	MANHATTEN ALMA & BURLINGAME
MA&CR	MINNEAPOLIS ANOKA & CUYUNA RANGE
MA&PA	MARYLAND & PENNSYLVANIA
MA&S	MAXTON ALMA & SOUTHBOUND
MAD	MADRID
MAE	MANHATTAN ELECTRIC
MAN	MANDEVILLE NORTHERN
MASSC	MASSACHUSETTS CENTRAL
MAT	MATTAGAMI RAILROAD
MATE	MASSENA TERMINAL
MB	MOCTEZUMA BREWERY
MBL	MACMILLAN BLOEDEL LIMITED
MBTA	MASSACHUETTS BAY TRANSIT AUTHORITY
MC	MAINE CENTRAL
MC&LM	MANSFIELD COLDWATER & LAKE MICHIGAN
MC&MHN	MILL CREEK & MINE HILL NAV & RR CO
MC&PC	MOUNT CARBON & PORT CARBON
MC&SA	MOSCOW CAMDEN & ST AUGUSTINE
MCA	MAMMOTH CAVE
MCE	MONMOUTH COUNTY ELECTRIC
MCEM	MARQUETTE CEMENT
MCH	MAUCH CHUNK
MCI	MEXICO CITY STREETCARS
MCKC	MCKEESPORT CONNECTING
MCO	MONONGAHELA CONNECTING
MCORP	MASONITE CORPORATION
MCR	MANN'S CREEK RAILROAD
MCRI	MCCLOUD RIVER
MCRR	MOTLEY COUNTY RAILROAD
MCRW	MOUNT CARBON RAILWAY
MCS	MAINE CENTRAL SHOPS
MCT	MEXICO CITY TRAMWAYS
MCV	MILL CREEK VALLEY
MD	MUNICIPAL DOCKS
MD&G	MANCHESTER DORSET & GRANVILLE
MD&S	MACON DUBLIN & SAVANNAH
MD&W	MINNESOTA DAKOTA & WESTERN
ME	MILWAUKEE ELECTRIC LINES SYSTEM
MEL	MUSKINGUM ELECTRIC RAILROAD
MEP&P	MEMPHIS EL PASO & PACIFIC
MER&L	MILWAUKEE ELECTRIC RAILWAY & LIGHT
MET	MUSKOGEE ELECTRIC TRACTION
MEX	MEXICANO
MEXP	MISSISSIPPI EXPORT
MF	MIDDLE FORK RAILROAD
MFG	MANUFACTURERS
MG	MOUNT GRETNA NARROW-GAUGE
MH	MOUNT HOOD
MH&SH	MINE HILL & SCHUYLKILL HAVEN
MHM	MOUNT HOPE MINERAL
MI	MISSISSIPPIAN
MI&NW	MINNESOTA & NORTHWESTERN RAILROAD
MI&W	MINARETS & WESTERN RAILWAY
MICH-CAL	MICH-CAL
MICHC	MICHIGAN CENTRAL
MID	MIDWAY
MIDC	MIDLAND CONTINENTAL
MIL	MILSTEAD
MILW	MILWAUKEE
MIRW	MONTREAL ICE RAILWAY

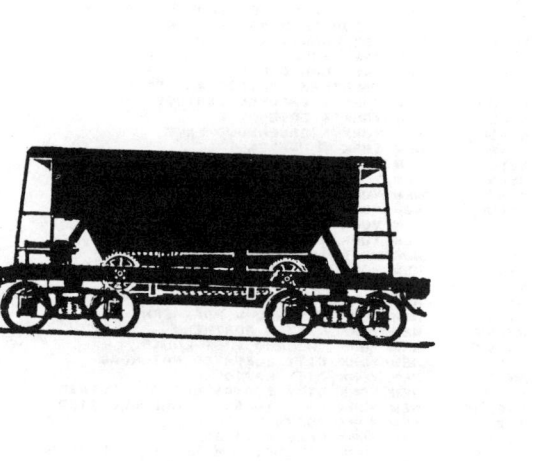

APPENDIX A (RAILROADS)

MISSC	MISSISSIPPI CENTRAL
MIT	MIDLAND TERMINAL
MITR	MINNESOTA TRANSFER
MIV	MIDLAND VALLEY
MJ	MANUFACTURERS JUNCTION
MJ&S	MOUNT JEWELL & SMETHPORT
MJC&N	MOUNT JEWETT CLERMONT & NORTHERN
MJK&R	MOUNT JEWETT KINZUA & RITERVILLE
MKT	MISSOURI KANSAS TEXAS
ML&M	MINNEAPOLIS LYNDALE & MINNESOTA
ML&T	MORGON'S LOUISIANA & TEXAS RAILROAD
MLC	MOWER LUMBRE COMPANY
MLO	MICHIGAN LIMESTONE OPERATIONS
MLS&W	MILWAUKEE LAKE SHORE & WESTERN
MLW	MANCHESTER LOCOMOTIVE WORKS
MM	MIDLAND RAILWAY OF MANITOBA
MM&N	MARENGO MILWAUKEE & NORTHERN
MM&NY	MILFORD MATAMORAS & NEW YORK
MM&S	MUNISING MARQUETTE & SOUTHEASTERN
MN	MICHIGAN NORTHERN
MN&S	MINNEAPOLIS NORTHFIELD & SOUTHERN
MNDM	MINERALES NACIONAL DE MEXICO
MNJ	MIDLAND RAILROAD OF NEW JERSEY
MO	MONSON RAILROAD
MOBCH	MOBILE CHEMICAL
MOJN	MOJAVE NORTHERN
MON	MONONGAHELA
MONT	MONTOUR
MOP	MOPAC
MOV	MONOCACY VALLEY
MOVA	MOSHASSUCK VALLEY
MOW	MONTANA WESTERN
MP	MISSOURI PACIFIC RAILWAY COMPANY
MP&B	MONTREAL PORTLAND & BOSTON
MPC	MONOLITH PORTLAND CEMENT
MPCE	MISSOURI PORTLAND CEMENT
MPI	METAL PROCESSING INC
MPR&DE	MINNEAPOLIS ST PAUL ROCH & DUBUQUE E
MPS	MARION POWER SHOVEL COMPANY
MR	MEAD RUN
MR&BT	MISSISSIPPI RIVER & BONNE TERRE
MR&LE	MAD RIVER & LAKE ERIE
MRC	MARION RIVER CARRY
MRL	MEADOW RIVER LUMBER
MRL&M	MINNEAPOLIS RED LAKE & MANITOBA
MRR	MICHIGAN RAILWAY CO
MRS	MILITARY RAILWAY SERVICE
MRT	MINERAL ROCK TRAMWAY
MRW	MANILA RAILWAY (PHILIPPINES)
MS	MISSOURI SOUTHERN
MSCO	MONTAGUE STEEL COMPANY
MSCO	MATERIAL SERVICE CORPORATION
MSF	MUNCIPAL RAILWAY OF SAN FRANCISCO
MSL&IR	MEXICAN SL & INDUST RR (VARIOUS)
MSO	MESABE SOUTHERN
MSRW	MANCHESTER STREET RAILWAY
MT	MONTREAL TRANSIT
MT&MW	MOUNT TAMALPAIS & MUIR WOODS
MT&W	MARINETTE TOMAHAWK & WESTERN
MTA	METROPOLITAN TRANSIT AUTHORITY BOSTON
MTC	MACK TRUCK COMPANY
MTI	MOLINE TIMBER CO
MTR	MODELTRONICS
MTW	MOUNT WASHINGTON
MU	MUNISING
MUS	MEMPHIS UNION STATION
MV	MARTHA'S VINEYARD
MW	MINNESOTA WESTERN
MWC	MIDWEST CENTRAL RAILROAD
MWCOG	MOUNT WASHINGTON COG
MXC	MEXICAN CENTRAL
N	NESQUEHONING
N&A	NELSON & ALBEMARLE
N&B	NORTHAMPTON & BATH
N&C	NORFOLK & CAROLINA
N&CA	NEVADA & CALIFORNIA RAILROAD
N&L	NASHUA & LOWELL
N&N	NAHMA & NORTHERN
N&NW	NORTHERN & NORTH WESTERN
N&P	NEWPORT & PROVIDENCE
N&PBL	NORFOLK & PORTSMOUTH BELT LINE
N&SL	NORWOOD & ST LAWRENCE
N&SS	NEWBURGH & SOUTH SHORE
N&SV	NEWPORT & SHERMANS VALLEY
N&VB	NORFOLK & VIRGINIA BEACH
N&W	NORFOLK & WESTERN
N&WO	NORWICH & WORCESTER
N-W	NORTH-WEST RAILROAD
NA	NORTHERN ALBERTA RAILWAY
NA&LE	NEW ALBANY & LOUISVILLE ELECTRIC
NAC	NORTH AMERICAN COAL
NAD	NORTH AMERICAN DISPATCH
NAU	NAUGATUCK
NB&C	NEW BRUNSWICK & CANADA
NB&W	NEW BERLIN & WINFIELD
NBCS	NELSON BC STREET RAILWAYS
NC	NEVADA CENTRAL
NC&F	NEW CASTLE & FRENCHTOWN
NC&O	NATIONAL CITY & OTAY
NC&SL	NASHVILLE CHATTANOOGA & ST LOUIS
NCA	NEW CANAAN
NCB	NEW CORNELIA BRANCH
NCBT	NEVADA COPPER BELT
NCC	NEW CORNELIA COPPER COMPANY
NCE	NORTHERN CENTRAL
NCI	NORFOLK CITY
NCL	NORTH COAST LINES
NCN	NEVADA COUNTY NARROW-GAUGE
NCO	NEVADA CALIFORNIA OREGON
NCR	NORTHERN CROSS
NCSPA	NORTH CAROLINA STATE PORTS AUTHORITY
NCT	NEVADA COUNTY TRACTION
ND&C	NEWBURGH DUTCHESS & CONNECTICUT
NDEM	NATIONALES DE MEXICOS
NDM	NACIONALES DE MEXICO
NE	NORTHERN ELECTRIC
NEIP	NIAGARA ESCARPMENT INCLINED PLANE
NEL&P	NEW ENGLAND LACKAWANNA & PITTSBURGH
NES	NESCOPEC
NEZ	NEZPERCE
NF	NEWFOUNDLAND
NF&D	NORFOLK FRANKLIN & DANVILLE
NF&G	NICHOLAS FAYETTE & GREENBRIAR
NH	NEW HAVEN
NH&I	NEW HOPE & IVYLAND
NH&NI	NEW HAVEN & NORTHAMPTON
NH&SL	NEW HAVEN & SHORT LINE
NI	NORTHERN INDIANA RAILWAY COMPANY
NI&M	NAPORANO IRON & METAL
NID	NORTHERN INDIANA DOCK
NIR	NASHVILLE INTERURBAN RAILWAY
NIW	NATIONAL IRON WORKS
NJ	NAPIERVILLE JUNCTION
NJ&NY	NEW JERSEY & NEW YORK
NJ&P	NEW JERSEY & PENNSYLVANIA
NJI&I	NEW JERSEY INDIANA & ILLINOIS
NJM	NEW JERSEY MIDLAND
NJR&T	NEW JERSEY RAILROAD & TRANSPORTATION
NJRT	NORTH JERSEY RAPID TRANSIT
NJUN	NIAGARA JUNCTION
NJZ	NEW JERSEY ZINC
NKP	NICKEL PLATE
NL&G	NORTH LOUISANA & GULF
NM	NORANDA MINES
NM&SP	NEW MEXICO & SOUTHERN PACIFIC
NMLC	NEW MEXICO LUMBER COMPANY
NN	NEVADA NORTHERN
NNB&S	NORTHERN NEW BRUNSWICK & SEABOARD
NNY	NORTHERN NEW YORK
NO	NORTHEAST OKLAHOMA
NO&C	NEW ORLEANS & CARROLLTON
NO&LC	NEW ORLEANS & LOWER COAST
NO&N	NEW ORLEANS & NORTHEASTERN
NOC	NEW ORLEANS CITY RAILROAD
NOC&L	NEW ORLEANS CITY & LAKE RAILROAD
NOD	NAVEL ORDINANCE DEPOT
NOPB	NEW ORLEANS PUBLIC BELT
NOPS	NEW ORLEANS PUBLIC SERVICE
NOT	NEW ORLEANS TERMINAL
NOT&L	NORTHERN OHIO TRACTION & LIGHT
NOT&M	NEW ORLEANS TEXAS & MEXICO
NOUPT	NEW ORLEANS UNION PASSENGER TERMINAL
NP	NORTHERN PACIFIC
NP&T	NORTHWOOD PULP & TIMBER
NPA	NORTH PENNSYLVANIA
NPC	NORTH PACIFIC COAST
NPCO	NEKOOSA PAPER COMPANY
NPGC	NATIONAL PLATE GLASS CO
NPIER	NARRAGANSETT PIER
NPIP	NIAGARA PORTAGE INCLINE PLANE
NPR	NORTHWESTERN PENNSYLVANIA RAILROAD
NRC	NORTHERN RAILWAY OF CANADA
NRR	NANTUCKET RAILROAD
NRWM	NATIONAL RAILWAYS OF MEXICO
NS	NORTH SHORE
NS&W	NORTHWESTERN STEEL & WIRE
NSC	NOVA SCOTIA
NSC&T	NIAGARA ST CATHERINES & TORONTO
NSO	NORFOLK SOUTHERN RAILWAY
NSSC	NORTH STAR STEEL COMPANY
NSUB	NEWARK SUBWAYS
NSW	NEW SOUTH WALES GOVERNMENT RAILROAD
NSWG	NEW SOUTH WALES GOVERNMENT RAILWAY
NT&D	NICHOLSON TERMINAL & DOCK
NU&R	NATCHEZ URANIA & RUSTON
NW	NORTHWESTERN
NWO	NORTHWESTERN OKLAHOMA
NWP	NORTHWESTERN PACIFIC RAILROAD
NY&BB	NEW YORK & BROOKLYN BRIDGE
NY&E	NEW YORK & ERIE
NY&GL	NEW YORK & GREENWOOD LAKE
NY&H	NEW YORK & HARLEM
NY&LB	NEW YORK & LONG BRANCH
NY&NE	NEW YORK & NEW ENGLAND
NY&O	NEW YORK & OTTAWA
NY&OM	NEW YORK & OSWEGO MIDLAND
NY&P	NEW YORK & PENNSYLVANIA
NY&QC	NEW YORK & QUEENS COUNTY
NY&V	NORTH YAKIMA & VALLEY
NYA&L	NEW YORK AUBURN & LANSING
NYC	NEW YORK CENTRAL
NYC&H	NEW YORK CENTRAL & HUDSON RIVER
NYC&N	NEW YORK CENTRAL & NORTHERN
NYC&N.	NEW YORK CITY & NORTHERN
NYC&SL	NEW YORK CHICAGO & ST LOUIS
NYCE	NEW YORK CITY ELEVATED RAILROAD
NYCR	NEW YORK CITY RAPID
NYCS	NEW YORK CITY SUBWAY-ELEVATED LINES
NYCTAE	NEW YORK CITY THIRD AVENUE ELEVATED
NYD	NEW YORK DOCK
NYLE&W	NEW YORK LAKE ERIE & WESTERN
NYNH&H	NEW YORK NEW HAVEN & HARTFORD RAIL RD
NYO&W	NEW YORK ONTARIO & WESTERN
NYP&C	NEW YORK PITTSBURGH & CHICAGO
NYS&W	NEW YORK SUSQUEHANNA & WESTERN
NYW&B	NEW YORK WESTCHESTER & BOSTON
NYWS&B	NEW YORK WEST SHORE & BUFFALO
O	OLEAN
O&A	OKLAHOMA & ARKANSAS
O&IS	OHIO & INDIANA STONE COMPANY
O&K	OHIO & KENTUCKY
O&LC	OGDENSBURG & LAKE CHAMPLAIN
O&N	OGDENSBURG & NORWOOD
O&NW	OREGON & NORTHWESTERN
O&P	OTTAWA & PRESCOTT
O&Q	ONTARIO & QUEBEC RAILWAY
O&RM	OKLAHOMA & RICH MOUNTAIN
OA	OREGON AMERICAN
OA&E	OAKLAND ANTLOCK & EASTERNY
OB	ORANGE BELT
OB&PA	OGDENSBURG BRIDGE & PORT AUTHORITY
OB&W	OLEAN BRADFORD & WARREN
OC	OKLAHOMA CENTRAL
OC&E	OREGON CALIFORNIA & EASTERN
OCITY	OKLAHOMA CITY ADA-ATOKA
OCO	OLD COLONY
OCW	OCEAN CITY WESTERN
OD	OVERLAND DISPATCH
OE	OREGON ELECTRIC
OER	OHIO ELECTRIC RAILWAY

APPENDIX A (RAILROADS)

OF	OSTRICH FARM
OFSL	OIL FIELDS SHORT LINES
OIM	OLIVER IRON MINING COMPANY
OKT	ORLEANS KENNER TRACTION
OL&B	OMAHA LINCOLN & BEATRICE
OM	OHIO MIDLAND
OMT	ORANGE MOUNTAIN TRACTION
ON	ONTARIO NORTHLAND
ONO	OKMULGEE NORTHERN
OP	OREGON PORTAGE
OP&E	OREGON PACIFIC & EASTERN
OPC	OHIO POWER COMPANY
OPS	OHIO PUBLIC SERVICE COMPANY
OR	OHIO RIVER
OR&LC	OAHU RAILWAY & LAND COMPANY
OR&NC	OREGON & NAVIGATION COMPANY
OR&TW	OAHU RAILWAY & TERMINAL WAREHOUSING
OR&W	OHIO RIVER & WESTERN
ORO	ORO DAM
ORTC	OSTRANDER RAILWAY & TIMBER CO
ORW	OKLAHOMA RAILWAY
OS	OCEAN SHORE RAILROAD
OS&H	ONTARIO SIMCOE & HURON
OSA	OSAGE
OSH	OSHAWA
OSL	OREGON SHORT LINE
OSN	OREGON STEAM NAVIGATION COMPANY
OSO	OHIO SOUTHERN
OSW	OKLAHOMA SOUTHWESTERN
OT	OAKLAND TERMINAL
OWR&N	OREGON WASHINGTON RR & NAVIGATION CO
P	PORTLAND RAILWAYS
P&A	PENSACOLA & ATLANTIC
P&AV	PUEBLO & ARKANSAS VALLEY
P&BR	PATAPSCO & BACK RIVERS
P&BS	PITTSBURGH & BUTLER STREET RAILWAY
P&C	PHILADELPHIA & COLUMBIA
P&CM	POTEAU & CAVANAL MOUNTAIN
P&CS	PITTSBURGH & CASTLE SHANNON
P&CU	PIEDMONT & CUMBERLAND
P&D	PARIS & DECATUR
P&E	POUGHKEEPSIE & EASTERN
P&EA	PEORIA & EASTERN RAILWAY
P&EL	PORTERFIELD & ELLIS
P&F	PIONEER & FAYETTE
P&G	PENSACOLA & GEORGIA
P&H	PENNSBORO & HARRISVILLE
P&HR	PATTERSON & HUDSON RIVER
P&K	PORTLAND & KENNEBEC
P&KE	PENOBSCOT & KENNEBEC
P&LE	PITTSBURGH & LAKE ERIE
P&MP	PARIS & MOUNT PLEASANT
P&MSR	PENNSYLVANIA & MARYLAND STREET RW
P&N	PIEDMONT & NORTHERN
P&NW	PRESCOTT & NORTH WESTERN
P&O	PORTLAND & OGDENSBURG
P&OQ	PEORIA & OQUAWKA
P&OV	PITTSBURGH & OHIO VALLEY
P&P	PARSONS & PACIFIC
P&PE	PENSACOLA & PERDIDO
P&PU	PEORIA & PEKIN UNION
P&R	PHILADELPHIA & READING
P&RA	PHILLIPS & RANGELEY
P&RF	PORTLAND & RUMFORD FALLS
P&RO	PORTLAND & ROCHESTER
P&S	PITTSBURGH & SUSQUEHANNA
P&SH	PATTEN & SHERMAN
P&SP	PROVIDENCE & SPRINGFIELD
P&SR	PETALUMA & SANTA ROSA
P&W	PROVIDENCE & WORCESTER
P&WE	PATTERSON & WESTERN
P&WR	PHILADELPHIA & WESTERN RAILROAD
P&WV	PITTSBURGH & WEST VIRGINIA
PA&MR	PITTSBURGH ALLEGHENY & MCKEES ROCKS
PA&NY	PENNSYLVANIA & NEW YORK
PA&T	PENSACOLA ALABAMA & TENNESSEE
PAN	PANAMA RR
PAP	PORT ANGELES PACIFIC
PAPG	PIRAEUS ATHENS PELOPONNESUS (GREECE)
PARR	PARR TERMINAL
PARW	PASADENA RAILWAY
PATH	PORT AUTHORITY TRANS HUDSON
PB	PORT BIENVILLE
PB&LE	PITTSBURGH BESSEMER & LAKE ERIE
PB&NE	PHILADELPHIA BETHLEHEM & NEW ENGLAND
PBC	POUGHKEEPSIE BRIDGE COMPANY
PBR	PUBLIC BELT ROAD
PC	PENN CENTRAL
PC&N	POINT COMFORT & NORTHERN
PC&RV	PORTAGE CREEK & RICH VALLEY
PC&Y	PITTSBURGH CHARTIERS & YOUGHIOGHENY
PCC	PHILADELPHIA COKE COMAPNY
PCI	PASADENA CITY
PCO	PITTSBURGH COUNTY
PCOA	PACIFIC COAST RAILWAY
PCOAL	PEABODY COAL
PCR	PINE CREEK
PD&E	PEORIA DECATUR & EVANSVILLE
PE	PACIFIC ELECTRIC
PECO	PERRY COUNTY
PED	POTOMAC EDISON
PEP	POTOMAC ELECTRIC POWER
PEPC	PORTLAND ELECTRIC POWER COMPANY
PETE	PEORIA TERMINAL
PEV	PORT EVERGLADES
PFL	PRINCETON FAST LINE
PFW&C	PITTSBURGH FT WAYNE & CHICAGO
PG	PEORIA GATEWAY RAILROAD
PG&CH	PHILADELPHIA GERMANTOWN & CHEST. HILL
PG&N	PHILADELPHIA GERMANTOWN & NORRISTOWN
PGE	PACIFIC GREAT EASTERN
PGS	PENNSYLVANIA GLASS SAND COMPANY
PH&D	PORT HURON & DETROIT
PHB&NC	PORT HARMONY BUTLER & N CASTLE
PHL&B	PORT HOPE LINDSAY & BEAVERTON
PI	PICKENS RAILROAD
PI&SH	PITTSBURGH & SHAWMUT RAILROAD
PIT	PITTSBURGH RAILWAYS
PJ&M	PORT JARVIS & MONTICELLO
PJM&NY	PORT JERVIS MONTICELLO & NEW YORK
PL	PACIFIC LINES
PL&N	PITTSBURGH LACKAWANNA & NORTHEASTERN
PL&W	PITTSBURGH LISBON & WESTERN
PLC	PACIFIC LUMBER COMPANY
PLEG	PEG LEG
PLR	PORTLAND LEWISTON RAILWAY
PLU	PICKERING LUMBER
PLW	PORTLAND LOCOMOTIVE WORKS
PM	PERE MARQUETTE
PM&M	PHILADELPHIA MARLTON & MEDFORD
PM&O	PACIFIC MOBILE & OHIO
PM&Y	PITTSBURGH MCKEESPORT & YOUNGIOGHENY
PMA	PORT MANATEE
PMM	PACOLET MILLS MANUFACTURING
PN	PROFILE NORTHERN
PN&NY	PHILADELPHIA NEWTON & NEW YORK
PNA	PRECISION NATIONAL
PO	PORTAGE
POR	PORTER
POT	PORT OF TACOMA
POTB	PORT OF TILLAMOOK BAY
POTCR	POTATO CREEK
PP	PINAFORE PARK
PP&B	PENNSYLVANIA POUGHKEEPSIE & BOSTON
PPD	PORTLAND PUBLIC DOCKS
PPJ	PONTIAC PACIFIC JUNCTION
PR	PRATTSBURGH
PR&EA	PRESCOTT & EASTERN
PR&NE	PHILADELPHIA READING & NEW ENGLAND
PRES	PRESTON
PRI	POWDER RIVER RAILROAD
PRL	POTOMIC REGION LINES
PRR	PENNSYLVANIA RAILROAD
PRRMD	PENNSYLVANIA RR OF MARYLAND
PRSL	PENNSYLVANIA READING SEASHORE LINES
PRSS	PENN ROAD SEA SHORE
PRT	PHILADELPHIA RAPID TRANSIT
PRV	PEARL RIVER VALLEY
PRWM	PACIFIC RAILWAY OF MEXICO
PS	PITTSBURGH SOUTHERN
PS&N	PITTSBURGH SHAWMUT & NORTHERN
PSC	PUBLIC SERCICE OF COLORADO
PSI	PUBLIC SERVICE OF INDIANA
PSL	PEABODY SHORT LINE
PSNJ	PUBLIC SERVICE OF NEW JERSEY
PSRW	PUBLIC SERVICE RAILWAY CO UNION LINE
PSTC	PHILADELPHIA SUBURBAN TRANS COMPANY
PSW	PHILADELPHIA SUBWAYS
PT	PORTLAND TERMINAL COMPANY
PTC	PHILADELPHIA TRANSPORTATION COMPANY
PTER	PENINSULA TERMINAL
PTO	PORT TOWNSEND
PTR	PORTLAND TRACTION
PU	PURDUE UNIVERSITY
PUC	PORT UTILITIES COMMISSION RAILWAY
PUCM	PARK UTAH CONSOLIDATED MINES
PV	POTEAU VALLEY
PV&N	PECOS VALLEY & NORTHEASTERN
PVS	PECOS VALLEY SOUTHERN
PW&B	PHILADELPHIA WILMINGTON & BALTIMORE
PW&S	PITTSBURGH WESTMORELAND & SOMERSET
PY&A	PITTSBURGH YOUNGSTOWN & ASHTABULA
Q	QUINCY RAILROAD
Q&E	QUAKERTOWN & EASTERN
Q&GW	QUEBEC & GOSFORD WOODEN RAILWAY
Q&NW	QUOCHITA & NORTH WESTERN
Q&TL	QUINCY & TORCH LAKE (SAME AS QM)
QA&P	QUANAH ACME & PACIFIC
QBRW	QUEENSBORO BRIDGE RAILWAY COMPANY
QC	QUEBEC CENTRAL
QCIP	QUEBEC CITADEL INCLINE PLANE
QI&T	QUEBEC IRON & TITANIUM
QM	QUINCY MINING COMPANY
QM&S	QUEBEC MONTREAL & SOUTHERN
QNS&L	QUEBEC NORTH SHORE & LABRADOR
QO	QUAKER OATS
QRL&P	QUEBEC RAILWAY LIGHT & POWER COMPANY
QS	QUINCY SOYBEAN COMPANY
QU	QUAKAKE
R	READING RAILROAD
R&A	RICHMOND & ALLEGHENY
R&C	RALEIGH & CHARLESTON
R&CO	RHINEBECK & CONNECTICUT
R&COL	READING & COLUMBIA
R&D	RICHMOND & DANVILLE
R&E	ROCHESTER & EASTERN
R&IR	ROCKFORD & INTERURBAN RAILWAY
R&N	ROBY & NORTHERN
R&R	ROCKTON & RION
R&S	ROBERVAL & SAGUENAY
R&SB	ROCHESTER & SODUS BAY
RAL	RED ARROW LINES
RAY	RAYONIER & NAVIGATION COMPANY
RBC	RINGLING BROTHERS CIRCUS
RBL	ROYAL BLUE LINE
RC	REICHHOLD CHEMICAL
RC&BT	ROARING CAMP & BIG TREES RAILROAD
RC&E	REW CITY & ELDRED
RCBH&W	RAPID CITY BLACK HILLS & WESTERN
RCT	RIDEAU CANAL TRAMWAY
RD	RUSSIAN DECAPODS
RD&A	RICHELIEU DRUMMOND & ATHABASKA
RE	REDONDO
RF&P	RICHMOND FREDERICKSBURG & POTOMIC
RG	RIO GRANDE
RG&E	ROCHESTER GAS & ELECTRIC
RG&S	RIO GRANDE & SOUTHWESTERN
RGC	RIO GRANDE CITY
RGE	RIO GRANDE EASTERN
RGS	RIO GRANDE SOUTHERN
RGW	RIO GRANDE WESTERN
RH&L	ROCHESTER HORNELLSVILLE & LACKAWANNA
RI	ROCK ISLAND
RIVT	RIVER TERMINAL
RL&MW	RICHMOND LOCOMOTIVE & MACHINE WORKS
RMC	RESERVE MINING COMPANY
RN&P	ROCHESTER NUNDA & PITTSBURGH
RN&PA	ROCHESTER NUNDA & PENNSYLVANIA
RNY&P	ROCHESTER NEW YORK & PENNSYLVANIA
RO	ROSECRANS

STEPHANS' RAILROAD DIRECTORY

APPENDIX A (RAILROADS)

ROC	ROCKPORT RAILROAD
ROY	ROY GREENE
RPL&N	ROCK PORT LANGDON & NORTHERN
RR	RARITAN RIVER RAILROAD
RR&G	RED RIVER & GULF
RRR	READER RAILROAD
RS	ROWLAND SPRINGS RAILROAD
RS&E	ROCHESTER SYRACUSE & EASTERN
RS&P	ROSCOE SNYDER & PACIFIC
RS&S	ROCKDALE SANDOW & SOUTHERN
RSR	READING STREET RAILWAY
RST	REPUBLIC STEEL
RT	RICHMOND TERMINAL
RTC	ROCHESTER TRANSIT CORPORATION
RTL	ROCHESTER TROLLEY LINES
RU	RUTLAND RAILROAD
RV	RAHWAY VALLEY RAILROAD
RVA	ROCKAWAY VALLEY
RW&O	ROME WATERTOWN & OGDENSBURG
RY	RAYONIER RAILWAY

S	SOUTHERN RAILWAY
S&A	SAVANNAH & ATLANTA RAILWAY COMPANY
S&B	SCRANTON & BINGHAMTON
S&BL	SCOTT & BEARSKIN LAKE
S&C	SUMTER & CHOCTAW
S&CS	SWATARA & COLD SPRINGS
S&CSL	SANDUSKY & COLUMBUS SHORT LINE
S&CV	SYRACUSE & CHENANGO VALLEY
S&E	SYRACUSE & EASTERN
S&H	STEELTON & HIGHSPIRE
S&IE	SPOKANE & INLAND ELECTRIC RAILWAY
S&IE.	SPOKANE & INLAND EMPIRE
S&L	SYDNEY & LOUISBURG
S&ML	SEBASTICOOK & MOOSEHEAD LAKE
S&NC	SEATTLE & NORTH COAST
S&NY	SUSQUEHANNA & NEW YORK
S&O	SYRACUSE & ONONDAGA
S&OL	SMETHPORT & OLEAN
S&S	SCHUYLKILL & SUSQUEHANNA
S&SC	STARKE & SIMPSON CITY
S&SP	SANFORD & ST PETERSBURG
S&T	SHAMOKIN & TREVERTON
S&U	SYRACUSE & UTICA
S&W	SUSQUEHANNA & WESTERN
SA&N	SACRAMENTO AUBURN & NORTHERN
SA&O	SOUTH ATLANTIC & OHIO
SA&SB	ST AUGUSTINE & SOUTH BEACH
SAB	SABDERSVILLE
SAL	SEABOARD AIR LINE
SAND	SANDERSVILLE
SANT	SANFORD TRACTION
SAPS	SAN ANTONIO PUBLIC SERVICE
SAR	SAWYER RIVER
SAS	SAN ANTONIO SOUTHERN (MP)
SAU&G	SAN ANTONIO UVALDE & GULF
SAV	SACRAMENTO VALLEY
SB	SOUTH BRANCH
SB&RGV	SAN BENITO & RIO GRANDE VALLEY
SB&S	SANTA BARBARA & SUBURBAN
SBC	SONORA BAJA CALIFORNIA RAILWAY
SBELT	STATE BELT
SBR	SOUTH BROOKLYN
SBUF	SOUTH BUFFALO
SC&SB	ST CLOUD & SUGAR BELT
SC&T	SEATTLE COAL & TRANSPORTATION COMPANY
SCA	SOUTHERN CAMBRIA
SCC	SOUTHERN CEMENT COMPANY
SCC&RR	SOUTH CAROLINA CANAL & RAILROAD
SCCC	SQUAW CREEK COAL COMPANY
SCCE	SUDBURY COPPER CLIFF ELECTRIC RAILWAY
SCE	SOUTHERN CENTRAL
SCE&G	SOUTH CAROLINA ELECTRIC & GAS
SCH	STAUFFER CHEMICAL
SCL	SEABOARD COAST LINE
SCLS	SACRAMENTO CITY LINES
SCO	SULLIVAN COUNTY
SCOC	STEEL COMPANY OF CANADA
SCPA	SILVER CITY PINOS ALTOS & MOGOLLON
SCT	SIOUX CITY TERMINAL
SCTC	ST CLAIR TUNNEL CO
SD&AE	SAN DIEGO & ARIZONA EASTERN
SD&C	SAN DIEGO & CUYAMACA
SD&ML	SCRANTON DUNMORE & MOOSIC LAKE
SD&S	SAN DIEGO & SOUTHEASTERN
SDC&E	SAN DIEGO CUYAMACA & EASTERN
SDE	SAN DIEGO ELECTRIC RAILWAY
SDOT&P	SAN DIEGO OLD TOWN & PALM BEACH
SDPB&L	SAN DIEGO PACIFIC BEACH & LA JOLLA
SDS	SAN DIEGO SOUTH EASTERN RAILWAY
SDW	SD WARREN PAPER COMPANY
SE	SOUTH EASTERN RAILWAY (CANADA)
SEA	SEABOARD
SEA.	SEABOARD AIR LINE.
SEE	SEEKONK
SEG	SOUTHERN ELECTRIC GENERATING
SEH	ST ELIZABETH HOSPITAL
SERR	STARK ELECTRIC RAILROAD
SERY	SPRINGFIELD ELECTRIC RAILWAY
SES	SUSQUEHANNA
SET	SEATTLE TERMINAL
SF	SANTA FE
SF&CS	SHELBURNE FALLS & COLRAIN STREET RY
SF&N	SAN FRANCISCO & NORTHWESTERN
SF&NP	SAN FRANCISCO & NORTH PACIFIC
SF&SJ	SAN FRANCISCO & SAN JOSE
SF&SJV	SAN FRANCISCO & SAN JOAQUIN VALLEY
SF&SM	SAN FRANCISCO & SAN MATEO
SF&W	SAVAHHAN FLORIDA & WESTERN
SFB	SAN FRANCISCO BELT LINE
SFC&W	SALEM FALLS CITY & WESTERN
SFI	SOUTHWEST FOREST INDUSTRIES
SFM	SAN FRANCISCO MUNICIPAL
SFP&P	SANTA FE PRESCOTT & PHOENIX
SG	SOUTH GEORGIA
SG&N	SILVERTON GLADSTONE & NORTHERLY
SGV	SAN GABRIEL VALLEY RAPID TRANSIT
SH	STONE HARBOR RAILROAD
SH&E	SACKETS HARBOR & ELLISBURG
SH&WB	SUNBURY HAZELTON & WILLES BARRE
SHAWC	SHAWMUT CONNECTING
SHC	SOUTH HOPKINS COAL COMPANY
SHRT	SHAKER HEIGHTS RAPID TRANSIT
SI	STATEN ISLAND
SI&R	STERLING IRON & RAILWAY
SIE	SIERRA RAILROAD
SIEP	SIERRA PACIFIC
SIEV	SIERRA VALLEYS
SILP	SILVER PEAK
SILV	SILVERTON
SIN	SOUTHERN INDUSTRIAL
SIND	SOUTHERN INDIANA
SIRT	STATEN ISLAND RAPID TRANSIT
SJ	ST JOHNS
SJ&E	SAN JOAQUIN & EASTERN

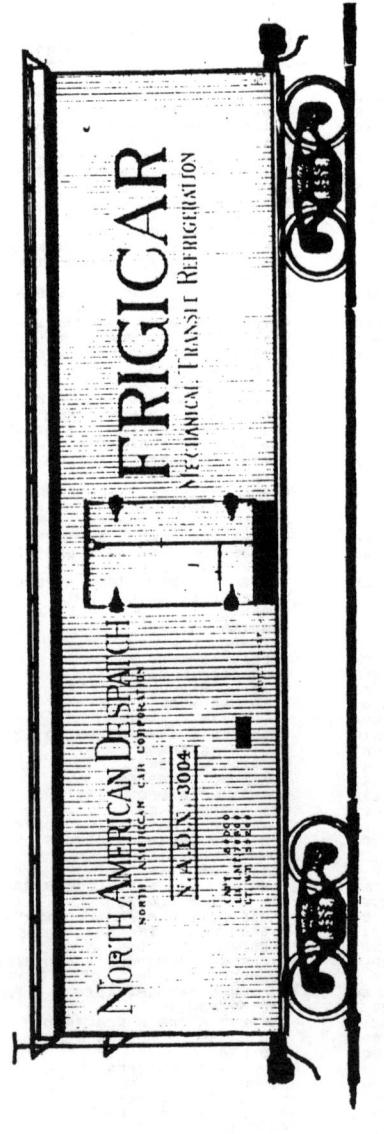

Stephans' Railroad Directory

APPENDIX A (RAILROADS)

SJ&GI	ST JOSEPH & GRAND ISLAND (UP)
SJ&IR	ST JOHNS & INDIAN RIVER
SJ&LC	ST JOHNSBURY & LAKE CHAMPLAIN RR
SJ&LCO	ST JOHNSBURY & LAMOILLE COUNTY
SJ&LE	ST JOHNS & LAKE EUSTIS
SJ&SL	ST JOHNS & ST LOUIS
SJB	ST JOSEPH BELT
SJC	SAN JUAN CENTRAL
SJL	SAN JOACHIN LUMBER
SJRT	ST JOHNS RIVER TERMINAL
SJT	ST JOSEPH TERMINAL
SJV	ST JOSEPH VALLEY RAILWAY
SK	SOUTHERN KANSAS
SKA	SKANEATELES
SKM	SILVER KING COALITION MINES COMPANY
SL	SAGIWAN LOGGING
SL&A	ST LAWRENCE & ATLANTIC
SL&AD	ST LAWRENCE & ADIRONDACK
SL&IV	ST LAWRENCE & INDUSTRIE VILLAGE
SL&N	SHEPAUG LITCHFIELD & NORTHERN
SL&VD	ST LAURENT & VILLAGE D'INDUSTRIE
SLB&M	ST LOUIS BROWNSVILLE & MEXICO
SLC	SAN LUIS CENTRAL
SLCO	SOMERS LUMBER COMPANY
SLE	SHORE LINE ELECTRIC
SLER&W	ST LOUIS EL RENO & WESTERN
SLG&W	SALT LAKE GARFIELD & WESTERN
SLI	ST LAWRENCE INTERNATIONAL
SLIM&S	ST LOUIS IRON MOUNTAIN & SOUTHERN
SLKC	ST LOUIS KANSAS CITY SHORT LINE
SLKC&C	ST LOUIS KANSAS CITY & CHICAGO
SLM&S	ST LOUIS MEMPHIS & SOUTHEASTERN RR
SLS&E	SEATTLE LAKE SHORE & EASTERN
SLV&TH	ST LOUIS VANDALIA & TERRE HAUTE
SLW	SCHENECTADY LOCOMOTIVE WORKS
SM	ST MARYS
SM&S	ST MARYS & SOUTHWESTERN
SMA	SAN MANUEL ARIZONA
SMETH	SMETHPORT
SMINE	SYDNEY MINES
SMS	STONE MOUNTAIN SCENECIC
SMT	SMOKY MOUNTAIN
SMV	SANTA MARIA VALLEY
SN	SACRAMENTO NORTHERN
SN&M	SANDUSKY NORWALK & MANSFIELD
SNO	SILVERTON NORTHERN
SNY	SOUTHERN NEW YORK
SOC	SIERRA RAILROAD OF CALIFORNIA
SOF	SOUTH FLORIDA
SOIA	SOUTHEAST OKLAHOMA INDUSTRIAL AUTHOR
SOM	SOMERSET
SOO	SOO LINE
SOP	SOUTH PARK
SOS	SOUTH SIDE
SOT	SOUTH OMAHA TERMINAL
SP	SOUTHERN PACIFIC
SP&P	ST PAUL & PACIFIC
SP&S	SPOKANE PORTLAND & SEATTLE
SPA	SOUTH PENNSYLVANIA RAILROAD
SPC	SOUTH PACIFIC COAST
SPEN	SEWARD PENINSULA
SPI	SPOKANE INTERNATIONAL
SPL	SOUTHERN PACIFIC LINES
SPLC	SUGAR PINE LUMBER COMPANY
SPM	SOUTHERN PACIFIC OF MEXICO
SPS	SPERRY RAIL SERVICE
SPUD	ST PAUL UNION DEPOT
SR	SKAGIT RIVER RAILWAY
SR&N	SABINE RIVER & NORTHERN
SR&RL	SANDY RIVER & RANGELEY LAKES
SR&W	SUSQUEHANNA RIVER & WESTERN
SRC	SHIP RAILWAY OF CHICNECTO
SRCC	SOUTHWEST RAILWAY CONSTRUCTION CO
SRM	SURESTE RAILWAY (MEXICO)
SS	SOUTH SHORE
SS&L	SHAMOKIN SUNBURY & LEWISBURG
SS&S	SURRY SUSSEX & SOUTHHAMPTON
SS&SB	SOUTH SHORE & SUTH BEND
SSC	SUPERIOR STONE COMPANY
SSD	SAVANNAH STATE DOCKS
SSE	STALEY SYSTEM OF ELECTRIFIED RW
SSL	SKANEATELES SHORT LINE
SSLV	SOUTHERN SAN LUIS VALLEY
SSO	SACRAMENTO SOUTHERN
SSO&G	SILVER SPRINGS OCALA & GULF
SSP	SAND SPRINGS
ST	SPRINGFIELD TERMINAL
ST&E	STOCKTON TERMINAL & EASTERN
STDS	STANDARD STEEL DIV-BALDWIN LIMA HAMIL
STEW	STEWARTSTOWN
STG	STANDARD GRAVEL
STI	SEATTLE TACOMA INTERURBAN
STL	ST LAWRENCE RAILROAD
STRR	STRASBURG RAILROAD
STT	SHAWNEE TECUMSEH TRACTION
STTE	STOCTON TERMINAL
STTER	STOCKTON TERMINAL
SU	SAPULPA UNION
SUFT	SUFFOLK TRACTION
SUGL	SUGAR LAND
SUGR	SUGAR RUN
SUNV	SUNCOOK VALLEY
SUSC	SUSQUEHANNA CONNECTING
SV	SUMPTER VALLEY
SV&F	STOCKHAM VALVES & FITTINGS
SVN	SCHUYLKILL VALLEY NAVIGATION & RR
SVS	SCIATO VALLEY SOUTHERN
SVT	SCIOTO VALLEY TRACTION
SW	SOUTH WESTERN RAILROAD
SWIU	SOUTHWESTERN INTERURBAN
SWPC	SOUTHWEST PORTLAND CEMENT
SWR	SWAMP RABBIT
SWS	SOUTHWESTERN SYSTEM (OHIO)
SYC	SYLVANIA CENTRAL
T	TENNESSEE
T&A	TENNESSEE & ALABAMA
T&B	TROY & BOSTON
T&C	TENNESSEE & COOSA
T&CL	TYRONE & CLEARFIELD
T&CR	TACOMA & COLUMBIA RIVER
T&G	TROY & GREENFIELD
T&GO	TONOPAH & GOLDFIELD
T&GU	TAVARES & GULF
T&N	TEXAS & NORTHERN
T&NO	TEXAS & NEW ORLEANS
T&NON	TEMISKAMING & NORTHERN ONTARIO
T&NV	THURSO & NATION VALLEY
T&OC	TOLEDO & OHIO CENTRAL
T&P	TEXAS & PACIFIC
T&T	TONOPAH & TIDEWATER
T&TO	TAMA & TOLEDO
T&W	TIDEWATER & WESTERN
TA&G	TENNESSEE ALABAMA & GEORGIA
TA&W	TOLEDO ANGOLA & WESTERN
TAL	TALBOTTON
TALL	TALLAHASEE
TAT	THIRD AVENUE TRANSIT RAILROAD COMPANY
TB	TWIN BRANCH
TBG&ST	TOLEDO BOWLING GREEN & SOUTHERN TRACT
TC	TEXAS CENTRAL
TC&GB	TUSCON CORNELIA & GILA BEND
TC&I	TENNESSEE COAL & IRON
TCLSE	TOLEDO CLEVELAND LAKE SHORE ELECTRIC
TCS	TRANS CAR SERVICES
TCT	TEXAS CITY TERMINAL
TCTR	TRI CITY TRACTION
TE	TEXAS ELECTRIC
TEC	TECOPA
TED	TOLEDO EDISON
TEM	TEMISCOUATA
TENNC	TENNESSEE CENTRAL
TEX	TEXAS EXPORT
TEXS	TEXAS STATE
TF	TALLULAH FALLS
TG&B	TORONTO GRAY & BRUCE RAILWAY
TGT	TULIA GRAIN TERMINAL
TGV&PC	TONAWANDA GENESEE VALLEY & PINE CREEK
TH&B	TORONTO HAMILTON & BUFFALO
TH&I	TERRE HAUTE & INDIANAPOLIS
TH&L	TERRE HAUTE & LOGANSPORT
TH&N	TAMAQUA HAZLETON & NORTHERN
THC	THUNDERBIRD COLLIERIES
THI&E	TERRE HAUTE INDIANAPOLIS & EASTERN
TI	TREASURE ISLAND
TIV	TIONESTA VALLEY
TL	TATUM LUMBER COMPANY
TLW	TAUTON LOCOMOTIVE WORKS
TM	TEXAS MIDLAND
TM&BC	TAYLOR MOUNTAIN & BEAVER CREEK
TM&P	TWIN MOUNTAIN & POTOMAC
TMB	TACOMA MUNICIPAL BELT
TMEX	TEXAS MEXICAN
TO&E	TEXAS OKLAHOMA & EASTERN
TOV	TOOELE VALLEY
TP&W	TOLEDO PEORIA & WESTERN
TPMP	TEXAS PACIFIC MISSOURI PAC TERM RR NO
TPT	TRENTON PRINCETON TRACTION
TR	TRESCKOW
TRA	TERMINAL RAILROAD ASSOC OF ST LOUIS
TRB	TIMKEN ROLLER BEARING COMPANY
TRC	TRIAD CHEMICAL
TRCO	TORONTO RAILWAY CO
TRNO	TERMINAL RAILROAD OF NEW ORLEANS
TRO	TRONA
TRT	TORONTO RAPID TRANSIT
TRW	THAILAND RAILWAYS
TS	TIDEWATER SOUTHERN
TSE	TEXAS SOUTH EASTERN
TSL&W	TOLEDO SAINT LOUIS & WESTERN
TSM	TWIN SEAMS MINING
TSU	TULSA SAPULPA UNION
TT	TOLEDO TERMINAL
TTC	TEXAS TRANSPORTATION COMPANY
TTCO	TORONTO TRANSIT COMMISSION
TTR	TRAILER TRAIN
TUCK	TUCKERTON
TUS	TUSCALOOSA
TUSK	TUSKEGEE
TV	TONAWANDA VALLEY
TV&C	TONAWANDA VALLEY & CUBA
TVA	TENNESSEE VALLEY AUTHORITY
TVE	TONAWANDA VALLEY EXTENSION
TW	TEXAS WESTERN
TW&GV	TONAWANDA WISCOY & GENESEE VALLEY
TW&W	TOLEDO WABASH & WESTERN
U	UNITAH RAILROAD
U&N	UVALDE & NORTHERN
UC	UTAH CENTRAL
UC&H	UPPER COOS & HEREFORD
UCA	UNION CANAL
UCKC	UTAH COPPER DIV OF KENNECOTT COPPER C
UCR	UTAH COAL ROUTE
UE	UNION ELECTRIC
UEC	UNITED ELECTRIC COAL
UF	UNION FREIGHT
UIW	UNION IRON WORKS
UJC	UPJOHN COMPANY
UM	UNIVERSITY OF MINNESOTA INTER-CAMPUS
UM&P	UPPER MERION & PLYMOUTH
UN	UNITY
UNC	UNION CARBIDE
UP	UNION PACIFIC
UP&L	UTAH POWER & LIGHT
UR&E	UNITED RAILWAYS & ELECTRIC
URO	UNION RAILROAD OF OREGON
URR	UNION RAILROAD
URSF	UNITED RAILROADS OF SAN FRANCISCO
URSL	UNITED RAILWAYS OF ST LOUIS
URWO	OREGON RAILWAY
URWO.	UNITED RAILWAYS OF OREGON
URY	UNITED RAILWAYS OF YUCATAN
USA	UNITED STATES ARMY
USAEC	UNITED STATES ATOMIC ENERGY COMMISSIO
USM	UNITED STATES MILITARY RAILROAD
USN	UNITED STATES NAVY
USNAD	UNITED STATES NAVAL AMMUNITION DEPOT
USP&F	UNITED STATES PIPE & FOUNDRY
USR	UNION STREET RAILWAY
USRA	UNITED STATES RAILROAD ADMINISTRATION
USREM	UNITED STATES RAILWAY EQUIP MFG

APPENDIX A (RAILROADS)

USS	UNITED STATES SUGAR
USSC	UNITED STATES STEEL CORPORATION
USWD	UNITED STATES WAR DEPARTMENT
UT	UNION TERMINAL
UTAH	UTAH
UTC	UNION TRACTION COMPANY
UTSR	UNITED TRACTION STREET RAILWAY
UV	UNADILLA VALLEY
UXL	UNIVERSAL EXPLORATION COMPANY
V	VIRGINIAN RAILWAY
V&M	VERMONT & MASSACHUETTS
V&MA	VIRGINIA & MARYLAND
V&RL	VIRGINIA & RAINY LAKE
V&S	VALLEY & SILETZ
V&T	VIRGINIA & TRUCKEE
V&TEN	VIRGINIA & TENNESSEE
VA	VANDALIA RAILROAD
VAC	VIRGINIA CAROLINA
VAL	VALLEY
VBR	VIRGINIA BLUE RIDGE
VC	VIRGINIA CENTRAL
VCO	VENTURA COUNTY
VD	VULCAN DETINNING
VE	VISALIA ELECTRIC RAILROAD
VE&PC	VIRGINIA ELECTRIC & POWER COMPANY
VER	VERMONT
VIN	VINELAND
VIP	VICTORY PARK
VM	VULCAN MATERIALS
VN	VERMONT NORTHERN
VNR	VIET NAM RAILWAYS
VP	VIRGINIA POCAHONTAS
VR	VENANGO RIVER RAILROAD
VS	VALDOSTA SOUTHERN
VT	VIRGINIA TRANSIT
VV	VERMONT VALLEY
W	WABASH
W&A	WESTERN & ATLANTIC
W&BCS	WESTON & BROOKER CRUSHED STONE CO
W&F	WARREN & FARNSWORTH
W&LE	WHEELING & LAKE ERIE
W&M	WISCONSIN & MICHIGAN
W&N	WILMINGTON & NORTHERN
W&NB	WILLIAMSPORT & NORTH BRANCH
W&NO	WHARTON & NORTHERN
W&NR	WILMINGTON & WELDEN RAILWAY
W&OD	WASHINGTON & OLD DOMINION
W&OV	WARREN & OUACHITA VALLEY
W&PC	WELLAND & PORT COLBORNE
W&Q	WISCASSET & QUEBEC
W&R	WILLIAMSTOWN & REDFIELD
W&SF	WASHITA & SANTA FE
W&SL	WHITMER & STEEL LUMBER COMPANY
W&SR	WARREN & SALINE RIVER
W&T	WRIGHTSVILLE & TENNILLE
W&W	WILMINGTON & WESTERN
W&WA	WAYNESBURG & WASHINGTON
W&WE	WICHITA & WESTERN
WA	WARWICK RAILROAD
WA&FC	WASHINGTON ARLINGTON & FALLS CHURCH
WA&G	WELLSVILLE ADDISON & GALETON RAILROAD
WAR	WARRENTON
WAS	WARE SHOALS
WASHT	WASHINGTON TERMINAL
WAST	WALLACE STONE
WAT	WATERVILLE
WAV	WALLKILL VALLEY
WB	WOBURN BRANCH
WB&AE	WASHINGTON BALTIMORE & ANNAPOLIS ELEC
WB&E	WILKES BARRE & EASTERN
WB&EL	WELLSVILLE BOLIVAR & ELDRED
WB&H	WILKES BARRE & HAZELTON
WB&PL	WASHINGTON BRANDYWINE & POINT LOOKOUT
WBC	WESTERN BRICK COMPANY
WBT&S	WACO BEAUMONT TRINITY & SABINE
WC	WISCONSIN CENTRAL
WCF&N	WATERLOO CEDAR FALLS & NORTHERN
WCO	WASHINGTON COUNTY
WE	WESTINGHOUSE ELECTRIC
WE&W	WESTCHESTER & WESTERN
WEC	WESTERN ENERGY COMPANY
WEL	WEEMS ELECTRIC
WELL	WELLAND
WES	WESTFIELD
WEST	WESTMINISTER
WF	WEBBER FALLS
WF&N	WICHITA FALLS & NORTHWESTERN
WF&O	WATERVILLE FAIRFIELD & OAKLAND
WF&S	WICHITA FALLS & SOUTHERN
WFE	WEST FELICIANA
WGB	WAUPACA GREEN BAY
WHC	WHITEHALL CEMENT
WI	WILLIAMSTOWN
WI&M	WASHINGTON IDAHO & MONTANA
WI&N	WISCONSIN & NORTHERN
WI&S	WILLAMETTE IRON & STEEL COMPANY
WI&W	WINCHESTER & WESTERN
WIN	WINONA RAILROAD
WINF	WINFIELD
WINI	WINIFREDE
WIP	WESTMONT INCLINED PLANE
WIV	WICHITA VALLEY
WJ&S	WEST JERSEY & SEASHORE
WL	WINANS LOCOMOTIVES
WLOO	WATERLOO
WM	WESTERN MARYLAND
WMM	WILLIAM MASON
WMW&N	WEATHERFORD MINERAL WELLS & NORTHWEST
WN&R	WORCESTER NASHUS & ROCHESTER
WNC	WESTERN NORTH CAROLINA
WNY&P	WESTERN NEW YORK & PENNSYLVANIA
WO	WOODSTOCK
WP	WESTERN PACIFIC
WP&P	WEST PENN & PITTSBURG RAILWAY
WP&RG	WESTERN PACIFIC & RIO GRANDE
WP&Y	WHITE PASS & YUKON
WPA	WEST PENN RAILWAY COMPANY
WPBT	WEST PALM BEACH TERMINAL
WPC	WARREN PAPER COMPANY
WPE	WEST PITTSTON EXETER
WPL	WESTFIELD PLANTAION
WPR	WEST POINT ROUTE
WPS	WHEELING PITTSBURGH STEEL
WPT	WABASH PITTSBURGH TERMINAL
WR	WEST RIVER
WRA	WESTERN RAILWAY OF ALABAMA
WRB	WOOD RIVER BRANCH
WRC	WESTERN RAILROAD CORPORATION
WRM	WESTERN RAILWAY OF MASSACHUSETTS
WRRA	WESTERN RAILROAD OF ALASKA
WS	WAYNESBURG SOUTHERN
WS&G	WARNER SAND & GRAVEL
WS&Y	WEST SIDE & YONKERS RAILWAY
WSL	WEST SIDE LUMBER
WSL&P	WABASH ST LOUIS & PACIFIC RAILWAY
WSS	WINSTON SALEM SOUTHERN
WSSB	WINSTON SALEM SOUTHBOUND
WT	WABASH TERMINAL
WTC	WEYERHAEUSER LUMBER COMPANY
WTC.	WEYERHAEUSER TIMBER COMPANY.
WTP	WHITE TOP
WV	WESTERN VERMONT
WV&M	WHITNEYVILLE & MACHIASPORT
WVC&P	WEST VIRGINIA CENTRAL & PITTSBURGH RR
WVN	WEST VIRGINIA NORTHERN
WVPP	WEST VIRGINIA PULP & PAPER COMPANY
WW&F	WISCASSET WATERVILLE & FARMINGTON
WWL	WOODARD WALKER LUMBER COMPANY
WWV	WALLA WALLA VALLEY
WYS	WYANDOTTE SOUTHERN
WYT	WYANDOTTE TERMINAL
Y	YANCEY
Y&MV	YAZOO & MISSISSIPPI VALLEY
Y&N	YOUNGSTOWN & NORTHERN
Y&OR	YOUNGSTOWN & OHIO RIVER
Y&S	YOUNGSTOWN & SOUTHERN
Y&SO	YAKUTAT & SOUTHERN
Y&SU	YOUNGSTOWN & SUBURBAN
YAV	YAKIMA VALLEY TRANSPORTATION COMPANY
YD	YANKEETOWN DOCK
YP	YORK PENNA. RAILWAYS
YR	YELLOW RIVER
YS	YOUNGSTOWN STEEL
YSL	YOSEMITE SHORT LINE
YTC	YAKIMA TRACTION COMPANY
YU	YUCATAN RAILWAY
YU.	UNITED RAILWAYS OF YUCATAN.
YV	YOSEMITE VALLEY
YVA	YAMPA VALLEY RAILROAD
YVT	YAKIMA VALLEY TRANSPORTATION
YW	YREKA WESTERN
ZB	ZALEV BROTHERS LIMITED
ZV	ZERBE VALLEY

STEPHANS' RAILROAD DIRECTORY

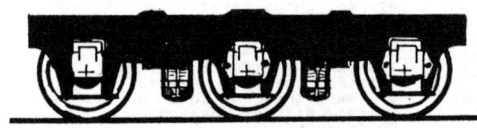

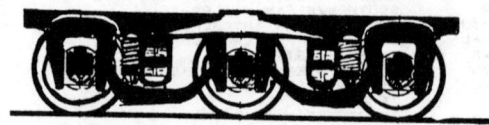

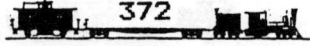

372

APPENDIX A (RAILROADS)

*3M	MINNESOTA MINING & MANUFACTURING
*A	ARMOUR
*AG	AGAR
*ALC	ALCOA
*AOW	ARTIC OIL WORKS
*ART	AMERICAN REFRIGERATED TRANSIT
*B	BECCO
*BDL	BUDLONG
*BDTP	BOURK DONALDSON TAYLOR POTATOES
*BEB	BERKSHIRE BACON
*BFB	BULL FROG BEER
*BL	BLATZ
*BOH	BLATZ OLD HEIDELBERG
*BR	BABY RUTH
*BS	BAY SOL
*CAR	CARNATION
*CCB	COUNTRY CLUB BEER
*CI	COLLEGE INN
*CMW	CHAREAU MARTIN WINE
*CS	COLUMBIA SOURS
*D	DUBUQUE
*DC	DOW CHEMICAL
*DE	DAIRYMENS EXPRESS
*DR	DEEP ROCK
*DU	DUPONT (EI DUPONT)
*FGE	FRUIT GROWERS EXPRESS
*G	GULF
*GA	GATX
*GERB	GERBERS BABY FOOD
*GY	GOODYEAR
*HAMS	HAMS
*HPC	HUNTER PACKING COMPANY
*HZ	HEINZ 57
*ISC	INLAND STEEL CO
*K	KOPPERS
*KP	KREY PACKING
*KRA	KRAFT
*KRH	KINGAN RELIABLE HAM
*KSR	KAHN'S SONS' REFRIGERATION
*LCDI	LIQUID CARBONIC DRY ICE
*LIB	LIBBY'S
*MA	MICHIGAN ALKALI
*MAB	MA BROWN
*MAT	MATHIESON
*MB	MERCHANTS BISCUITS
*MDT	MERCHANTS DESPATCH
*MG	MOBILE GAS
*MKT	M.K.T.
*MOA	MONARCH
*MP	MAINE POTATO
*MUNX	M.U.N.X.
*NAC	NATIONAL ALUMINATE COMPANY
*NAD	NORTH AMERICAN DESPATCH
*NRL	NORTHWESTERN REFRIGERATOR LINE
*ODC	OLD DUTCH CLEANSER
*OM	OSCAR MEYER
*OST	OHIO SEAMLESS TUBE
*P	PULLMAN COMPANY
*PAB	PABST BEER
*PB	PEERLESS BEER
*PFE	PACIFIC FRUIT EXPRESS
*PFE	PACIFIC FRUIT GROWERS EXPRESS
*PGM	PAGE MILK
*PM	PENNSYLVANIA MERCHANDISE
*PT	PETRO-TEX
*RBH	RATH BLACK HAWK
*REA	RAILWAY EXPRESS
*RG	REINEGOLD
*RP	RALSTON PURINA
*S	SINCLAIR
*S&S	SCHWARGEHILD SULZBERGER
*SCH	SCHLITZ BEER
*SCL	SHIPPERS CAR LINE
*SHO	SHELL OIL
*SLRE	ST LOUIS REEFER EXPRESS
*SO	SUN OILS
*SW	SWIFT
*T	TEXACO
*TB	TIVOLI BEER
*U	UTLX
*UC	UNION CARBIDE
*UE	UWANTA EGG
*URTX	UNION REFRIGERATED TRANSIT
*UTL	UNION TANK LINE
*W	WILSON
*WE	WESTINGHOUSE
*WFE	WESTERN FRUIT EXPRESS
*WUT	WESTERN UNION TELEGRAPH CO
*WV	WESTVACO

STEPHANS'_RAILROAD_DIRECTORY

BILL OF LADING — APPENDIX B (BUILDERS)

This appendix contains a listing of all BUILDERS that we have come across since we started our indexing project. A builder is defined as a company that built prototype equipment. All of the builders appearing in this directory appear in this appendix. However all of the entries in this appendix may NOT appear in this directory. These builders will appear in future volumes. There are two listings: one alphabetically by builder followed by its assigned abbreviation and one alphabetical by abbreviation followed by the builders name. By knowing one you can find the other. It was felt that this section would be infrequently used so the small type was used to conserve space.

MANIFEST — APPENDIX B (BUILDERS)

	PAGE
APPENDIX B - BUILDERS	374
BUILDER-ABBREVIATION	375
ABBREVIATION-BUILDER	376

APPENDIX B (BUILDERS)

BUILDERS	A
ALCO	ALCO
ALCO GE	AGE
ALLIS CHALMERS	AC
ALTONA (PRR) SHOPS	AS
ALWEG	AL
AMERICAN CAR & FOUNDRY	ACF
AMERICAN CAR COMPANY	ACC
AMERICAN GK LOCO WORKS	A
AMERICAN HOIST & DERRICK CO	AHD
AMERICAN LOCOMOTIVE COMPANY	ALCO.
AMERICAN RAILBOX CAR CO	ARCC
ASHLAND CAR WORKS	ACW
ATLAS INDUSTRIAL LOCOMOTIVES	AIL
ATSF SHOPS	ATSF
B&O SHOPS	B&O
BALDWIN	B
BALDWIN LIMA HAMILTON	BLH
BALDWIN-WESTINGHOUSE	BW
BARNEY & SMITH CO	BS
BETHLAHAM STEEL CO	BSC
BETTENDORF COMPANY, THE	BET
BEYER PEACOCK & COMPANY LTD.	BP
BILLMEYER & SMALLS	B&S
BILLMEYER & SMITH	B&SM
BIRNEY	BIRN
BLOOMSBURG CAR MFG COMPANY	BCC
BORDEN STD TANK CAR CO	BSTC
BRILL	BR
BROOKS LOCOMOTIVE WORKS	BLW
BUCYRUS-ERIE	BE
BUDD	BUDD
BURROW CRANE INC.	BCI
CALUMET IRON WORKS	CIW
CANADIAN LOCOMOTIVE COMPANY (WORKS)	CLC
CANADIAN NATIONAL SHOPS	CN
CARTER BROS CAR CO	CB
CATERPILLAR TRACTOR CO	CT
CB&Q SHOPS	CB&Q
CHARTER BROS CAR SHOPS	CBC
CHICAGO MOTOR BUILDERS	CLB
CINCINATTI CAR COMPANY	CCC
CN (CANADIAN NAT'L) SHOPS	CN.
CONNETICUT CAR CO	CTC
COOK LOCOMOTIVE & MACHINE WORKS	CLW
CP SHOPS	CP
CRAWFORD LOCO WORKS	CRLW
CUMMINS ENGINE COMAPNY	CE
D&H SHOPS	D&H
D&RGW SHOPS	D&RGW
DANFORTH COOKE & CO	DC&C
DANVILLE CAR CO	DCC
DAVENPORT LOCO WORKS	DLW
DAVIS & GARTNER	D&G
DICKSON	D
DIFFERETAIL CAR/STEEL CAR COMPANY	DC
DUCYRES ERIE	DE
EASWICK & HARRISON	E&H
ELECTROMOTIVE DIVISION OF GE	EMD
ENTERPRISE RR EQUIPMENT CO	EE
EVANS PRODUCTS CO.	EVANS
EVANS TRANSPORTATION GROUP	ETG
FAIRBANKS MORSE	FM
FAIRMONT RAILWAY MOTORS	FRM
FALLS CAR COMPANY	FCC
FGE SHOPS	FGE
FILER & STOWELL	F&S
FMC CORP	FMC
FRUEHAUF CORP	FC
G&B CAR COMPANY	G&B
GENERAL AMERICAN CAR COMPANY	GAC
GENERAL AMERICAN TRANSPORTATION CO	GAT
GENERAL ELECTRIC	GE
GILLINGHAM & WINANS	G&W
GLOVER MACHINE WORKS	GMW
GN SHOPS	GN
GRAND TRUNK SHOPS	GTS
GRANT LOCOMOTIVE WORKS	GLW
GREENVILLE CAR/STEEL CAR COMPANY	GSC
GUILFORD TRANSPORTATION CO	G
H&B CAR CO	H&B.
HACKWORTH	HACK
HALL SCOTT	HS
HARLAN & HOLLINGSWORTH	H&H
HARRISON & WINANS & EASTWICK	HW&E
HASKELL & BAKER CAR COMPANY	H&B
HAWKER SIDDELEY LIMITED	HSI
HEISLER	H
HOBARD (?) MILLS	HM
HOLMAN CAR COMPANY (HOLLMAN?)	HCC
IC SHOPS	IC
INDUSTRIAL HOIST	IH
INDUSTRIAL WORKS	IW
INGALLS SHIP BUILDING COMPANY	I
INGERSOLL RAND	IR
INTERNATIONAL CAR CO	ICC
INTERNATIONAL POWER CO	IP
IT SHOPS	IT
ITEL CORP	ITEL
J. BLAINE WORCHESTOR	JBW
JACKSON & SHARP	J&S
JAVWITH SHOPS	JS
JEWETT CAR COMPANY	J
JOHN STEPHENSON CO	JSC
KEITH CAR & MANUFACTURING COMPANY	KCM
KILBORNE & JACOBS	KJ
KRAUSS-MAFFEI	K-M
L&N SHOPS	L&N
LACONIA CAR COMPANY	LAC
LANCASTER LOCOMOTIVE WORKS	LLW
LENIOR CAR WORKS	LEN
LIBERTY CAR & EQUIPMENT COMPANY	LIB
LIMA	L
LIMA HAMILTON CORPORATION	LH
LIMA HAMILTON WESTINGHOUSE	LHW
LIMA MACHINE WORKS	LMW
LV SHOPS	LV
MACK	MACK
MABOR CAR COMPANY	MC
MARINE INDUSTRIES LTD	MI
MARION STEAM SHOVEL CO	MSS
MASON MACHINE WORKS	MMW
MCGUIRE CUMMINGS MFG COMPANY	MGC
MCKEEN	MCKEEN
MIDWEST FREIGHT CAR	MFC
MILWAUKEE LOCO MFG CO	MLMC
MILWAUKEE SHOPS	MS
MKT SHOPS	MKT
MONTREAL LOCOMOTIVE WORKS	MLW
MOUNT CLAIRE SHOPS	MCS
MP SHOPS	MP
MT VERNON CAR MFG COMPANY	MVC
N&O SHOPS	N&O
N&W ROANOKE SHOPS	N&W
N&W SHOPS	N&W.
NEW CASTLE	NC
NEW YORK LOCOMOTIVE WORKS	NYLW
NILES CAR & MFG. COMPANY	NILES
NJ LOCO & MACHINE COMPANY	NJ
NORRIS LOCOMOTIVE WORKS	NLW
NORTH AMERICAN CAR CO	NA
O.S. JORDAN CO	OSJ
OHIO FALLS CAR CO	OF
ORTNER CAR COMPANY	ORT
OSGOOD BRADLEY	OB
PAC CAR	PAC
PACIFIC CAR & FOUNDRY	PCF
PALACE AMERICAN CORP	PA
PHILADELPHIA & READING SHOPS	P&R
PHINEAS DAVIS	PD
PITTSBURGH CAR & LOCOMOTIVE WORKS	PCLW
PLASSER AMERICAN	PLA
PLYMOUTH LOCOMOTIVE WORKS	PLY
PORTER	POR
PORTLAND LOCO CO	PL
PRESSED STEEL CAR COMAPNY	PSC
PRR JUNIATA SHOPS	PRR
PRR SHOPS	PRR
PULLMAN BRADLEY	PB
PULLMAN CAR & MFG CORP CHICAGO	PLM
PULLMAN COMPANY	PLM.
PULLMAN STANDARD	PS
PULLMAN STEEL	PS
READING SHOPS	R
REEDER	RE
RGS SHOPS	RGS
RHODE ISLAND & RICHMOND LOCO WORKS	RIR
RHODE ISLAND LOCO WORKS	RI
RICHMOND LOCO WORKS	RLW
ROANOKE SHOPS	N&W..
ROGERS	ROG
ROME LOCO WORKS	RL
RUSSELL CAR & SNOW PLOW CO	RC&SP
SCHENECTADY LOCOMOTIVE WORKS	SLW
SEDALIA SHOPS	SS
SERVICE MOTOR TRUCK COMPANY	SMT
SHAY	SHAY
SHEFFIELD CAR CO	SHEF
SOO SHOPS	SOO
SOUTH BALTIMORE CAR CO	SBCC
SOUTHERN PACIFIC WORKS	SPW
SOUTHERN SHOPS	SS .
SP SHOPS	SP
SPERRY	SPER
SPOKANE PORTLAND & SEATTLE SHOPS	SP&S
ST CHARLES CAR COMPANY	SCC
ST LOUIS CAR COMPANY	SLC
STANDARD CAR COMPANY	SC
STANDARD STEEL CAR COMPANY	SSC
STANDARD TANK CAR COMPANY	STC
TAUNTON LOCOMOTIVE WORKS	TLW
THRALL CAR CO	THR
TOPEKA SHOPS	TS
TRA?ST EQUIPMENT COMPANY	TEC
UNION PALACE CAR CO	UPCC
UNITED STATES RAILWAY EQUIPMENT CO	USRE
UP SHOPS	UP
VULCAN IRON WORKS	V
W MILWAUKEE SHOPS	MILW
WASON CAR CO	WCC
WEST POINT FOUNDRIES	WPF
WESTERN WHEELED SCRAPER COMPANY	WWS
WESTINGHOUSE	W
WESTMINISTER IRON WORKS	WIW
WHITCOMB	WH
WHITEHEAD & KALES CO	W&K
WILLAMETTE IRON & STEEL	WIL
WINANS/WINAS?	WI
WT SNOW CONSTRUCTION CO	WT
YOUNGSTOWN STEEL DOOR CO	YSD

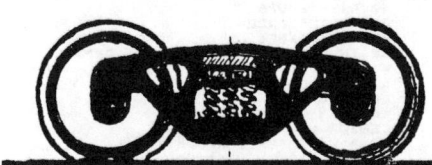

APPENDIX B (BUILDERS)

A	BUILDERS
A	AMERICAN BK LOCO WORKS
AC	ALLIS CHALMERS
ACC	AMERICAN CAR COMPANY
ACF	AMERICAN CAR & FOUNDRY
ACW	ASHLAND CAR WORKS
AGE	ALCO GE
AHD	AMERICAN HOIST & DERRICK CO
AIL	ATLAS INDUSTRIAL LOCOMOTIVES
AL	ALWEG
ALCO	ALCO
ALCO.	AMERICAN LOCOMOTIVE COMPANY
ARCC	AMERICAN RAILBOX CAR CO
AS	ALTONA (PRR) SHOPS
ATSF	ATSF SHOPS
B	BALDWIN
B&O	B&O SHOPS
B&S	BILLMEYER & SMALLS
B&SM	BILLMEYER & SMITH
BCC	BLOOMSBURG CAR MFG COMPANY
BCI	BURROW CRANE INC.
BE	BUCYRUS-ERIE
BET	BETTENDORF COMPANY, THE
BIRN	BIRNEY
BLH	BALDWIN LIMA HAMILTON
BLW	BROOKS LOCOMOTIVE WORKS
BP	BEYER PEACOCK & COMPANY LTD.
BR	BRILL
BS	BARNEY & SMITH CO
BSC	BETHLAHAM STEEL CO
BSTC	BORDEN STD TANK CAR CO
BUDD	BUDD
BW	BALDWIN-WESTINGHOUSE
CB	CARTER BROS CAR CO
CB&Q	CB&Q SHOPS
CBC	CHARTER BROS CAR SHOPS
CCC	CINCINATTI CAR COMPANY
CE	CUMMINS ENGINE COMAPNY
CIW	CALUMET IRON WORKS
CLB	CHICAGO MOTOR BUILDERS
CLC	CANADIAN LOCOMOTIVE COMPANY (WORKS)
CLW	COOK LOCOMOTIVE & MACHINE WORKS
CN	CANADIAN NATIONAL SHOPS
CN.	CN (CANADIAN NAT'L) SHOPS
CP	CP SHOPS
CRLW	CRAWFORD LOCO WORKS
CT	CATERPILLAR TRACTOR CO
CTC	CONNETICUT CAR CO
D	DICKSON
D&G	DAVIS & GARTNER
D&H	D&H SHOPS
D&RGW	D&RGW SHOPS
DC	DIFFERETAIL CAR/STEEL CAR COMPANY
DC&C	DANFORTH COOKE & CO
DCC	DANVILLE CAR CO
DE	DUCYRES ERIE
DLW	DAVENPORT LOCO WORKS
E&H	EASWICK & HARRISON
EE	ENTERPRISE RR EQUIPMENT CO
EMD	ELECTROMOTIVE DIVISION OF GE
ETG	EVANS TRANSPORTATION GROUP
EVANS	EVANS PRODUCTS CO.
F&S	FILER & STOWELL
FC	FRUEHAUF CORP
FCC	FALLS CAR COMPANY
FGE	FGE SHOPS
FM	FAIRBANKS MORSE
FMC	FMC CORP
FRM	FAIRMONT RAILWAY MOTORS
G	GUILFORD TRANSPORTATION CO
G&B	G&B CAR COMPANY
G&W	GILLINGHAM & WINANS
GAC	GENERAL AMERICAN CAR COMPANY
GAT	GENERAL AMERICAN TRANSPORTATION CO
GE	GENERAL ELECTRIC
GLW	GRANT LOCOMOTIVE WORKS
GMW	GLOVER MACHINE WORKS
GN	GN SHOPS
GSC	GREENVILLE CAR/STEEL CAR COMPANY
GTS	GRAND TRUNK SHOPS
H	HEISLER
H&B	HASKELL & BAKER CAR COMPANY
H&B.	H&B CAR CO
H&H	HARLAN & HOLLINGSWORTH
HACK	HACKWORTH
HCC	HOLMAN CAR COMPANY (HOLLMAN?)
HM	HOBARD (?) MILLS
HS	HALL SCOTT
HSI	HAWKER SIDDELEY LIMITED
HW&E	HARRISON & WINANS & EASTWICK
I	INGALLS SHIP BUILDING COMPANY
IC	IC SHOPS
ICC	INTERNATIONAL CAR CO
IH	INDUSTRIAL HOIST
IP	INTERNATIONAL POWER CO
IR	INGERSOLL RAND
IT	IT SHOPS
ITEL	ITEL CORP
IW	INDUSTRIAL WORKS
J	JEWETT CAR COMPANY
J&S	JACKSON & SHARP
JBW	J. BLAINE WORCHESTOR
JS	JAVWITH SHOPS
JSC	JOHN STEPHENSON CO
K-M	KRAUSS-MAFFEI
KCM	KEITH CAR & MANUFACTURING COMPANY
KJ	KILBORNE & JACOBS
L	LIMA
L&N	L&N SHOPS
LAC	LACONIA CAR COMPANY
LEN	LENIOR CAR WORKS
LH	LIMA HAMILTON CORPORATION
LHW	LIMA HAMILTON WESTINGHOUSE
LIB	LIBERTY CAR & EQUIPMENT COMPANY
LLW	LANCASTER LOCOMOTIVE WORKS
LMW	LIMA MACHINE WORKS
LV	LV SHOPS
MACK	MACK
MC	MAGOR CAR COMPANY
MCKEEN	MCKEEN
MCS	MOUNT CLAIRE SHOPS
MFC	MIDWEST FREIGHT CAR
MGC	MCGUIRE CUMMINGS MFG COMPANY
MI	MARINE INDUSTRIES LTD
MILW	W MILWAUKEE SHOPS
MKT	MKT SHOPS
MLMC	MILWAUKEE LOCO MFG CO
MLW	MONTREAL LOCOMOTIVE WORKS
MMW	MASON MACHINE WORKS
MP	MP SHOPS
MS	MILWAUKEE SHOPS
MSS	MARION STEAM SHOVEL CO
MVC	MT VERNON CAR MFG COMPANY
N&O	N&O SHOPS
N&W	N&W ROANOKE SHOPS
N&W.	N&W SHOPS
N&W..	ROANOKE SHOPS
NA	NORTH AMERICAN CAR CO
NC	NEW CASTLE
NILES	NILES CAR & MFG. COMPANY
NJ	NJ LOCO & MACHINE COMPANY
NLW	NORRIS LOCOMOTIVE WORKS
NYLW	NEW YORK LOCOMOTIVE WORKS
OB	OSGOOD BRADLEY
OF	OHIO FALLS CAR CO
ORT	ORTNER CAR COMPANY
OSJ	O.S. JORDAN CO
P&R	PHILADELPHIA & READING SHOPS
PA	PALACE AMERICAN CORP
PAC	PAC CAR
PB	PULLMAN BRADLEY
PCF	PACIFIC CAR & FOUNDRY
PCLW	PITTSBURGH CAR & LOCOMOTIVE WORKS
PD	PHINEAS DAVIS
PL	PORTLAND LOCO CO
PLA	PLASSER AMERICAN
PLM	PULLMAN CAR & MFG CORP CHICAGO
PLM.	PULLMAN COMPANY
PLY	PLYMOUTH LOCOMOTIVE WORKS
POR	PORTER
PRR	PRR JUNIATA SHOPS
PRR	PRR SHOPS
PS	PULLMAN STANDARD
PS	PULLMAN STEEL
PSC	PRESSED STEEL CAR COMAPNY
R	READING SHOPS
RC&SP	RUSSELL CAR & SNOW PLOW CO
RE	REEDER
RGS	RGS SHOPS
RI	RHODE ISLAND LOCO WORKS
RIR	RHODE ISLAND & RICHMOND LOCO WORKS
RL	ROME LOCO WORKS
RLW	RICHMOND LOCO WORKS
ROG	ROGERS
SBCC	SOUTH BALTIMORE CAR CO
SC	STANDARD CAR COMPANY
SCC	ST CHARLES CAR COMPANY
SHAY	SHAY
SHEF	SHEFFIELD CAR CO
SLC	ST LOUIS CAR COMPANY
SLW	SCHENECTADY LOCOMOTIVE WORKS
SMT	SERVICE MOTOR TRUCK COMPANY
SOO	SOO SHOPS
SP	SP SHOPS
SP&S	SPOKANE PORTLAND & SEATTLE SHOPS
SPER	SPERRY
SPW	SOUTHERN PACIFIC WORKS
SS	SEDALIA SHOPS
SS .	SOUTHERN SHOPS
SSC	STANDARD STEEL CAR COMPANY
STC	STANDARD TANK CAR COMPANY
TEC	TRA?ST EQUIPMENT COMPANY
THR	THRALL CAR CO
TLW	TAUNTON LOCOMOTIVE WORKS
TS	TOPEKA SHOPS
UP	UP SHOPS
UPCC	UNION PALACE CAR CO
USRE	UNITED STATES RAILWAY EQUIPMENT CO
V	VULCAN IRON WORKS
W	WESTINGHOUSE
W&K	WHITEHEAD & KALES CO
WCC	WASON CAR CO
WH	WHITCOMB
WI	WINANS/WINAS?
WIL	WILLAMETTE IRON & STEEL
WIW	WESTMINISTER IRON WORKS
WPF	WEST POINT FOUNDRIES
WT	WT SNOW CONSTRUCTION CO
WWS	WESTERN WHEELED SCRAPER COMPANY
YSD	YOUNGSTOWN STEEL DOOR CO

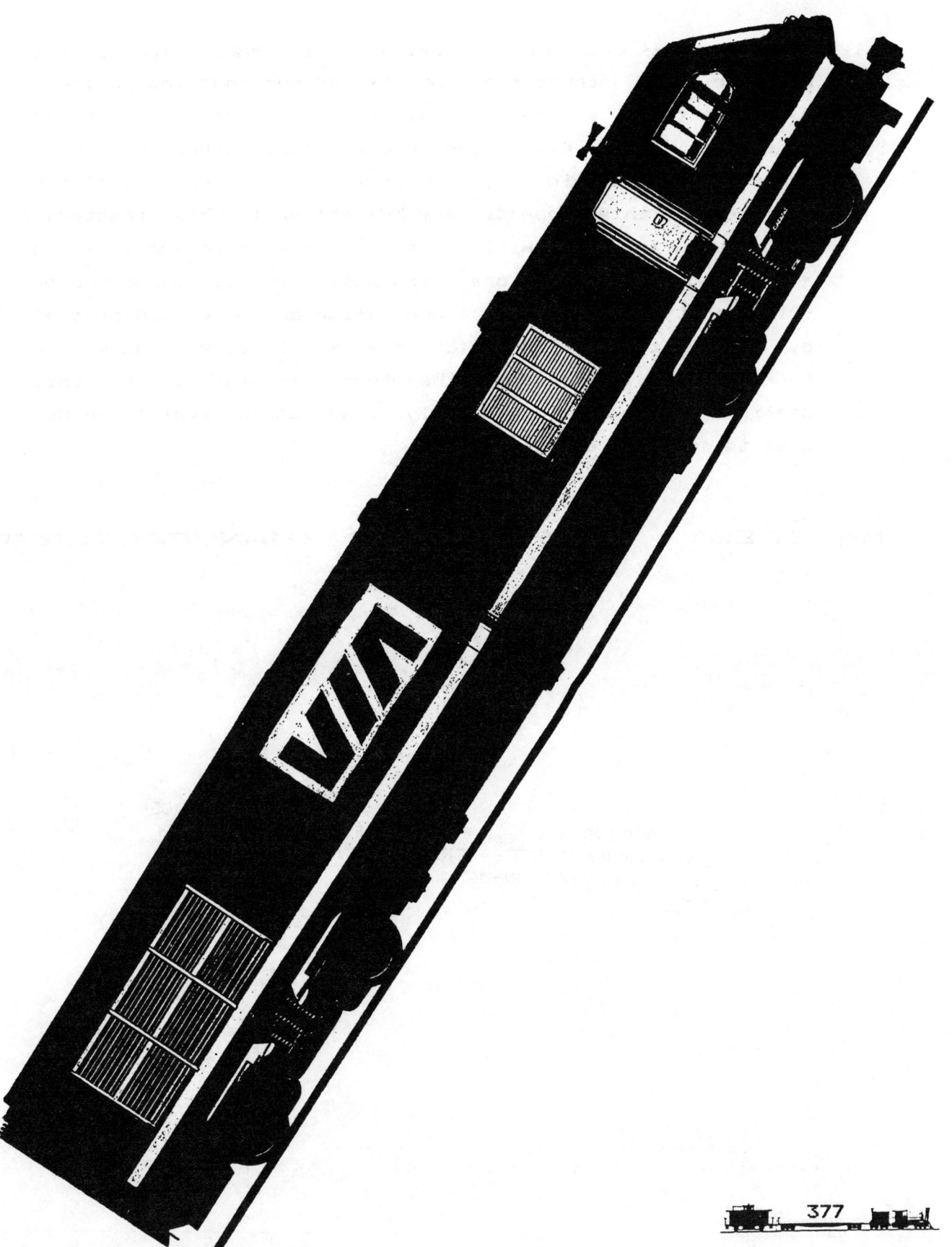

BILL OF LADING   APPENDIX C (MFG)

This appendix contains a listing of all MANUFACTURERS that we have come across since we started our indexing project. A manufacturer is defined as a company that manufactured model equipment. All of the manufacturers appearing in this directory appear in this appendix. However all of the entries in this appendix may NOT appear in this directory. These manufacturers will appear in future volumes. There are two listings: one alphabetically by manufacturer followed by its assigned abbreviation and one alphabetical by abbreviation followed by the manufacturers name. By knowing one you can find the other. It was felt that this section would be infrequently used so the small type was used to conserve space.

MANIFEST   APPENDIX C (MANUFACTURERS)

	PAGE
APPENDIX C - MANUFACTURERS	378
MANUFACTURER-ABBREVIATION	379
ABBREVIATION-MANUFACTURER	382

APPENDIX C (MANUFACTURERS)

MANUFACTURERS	A
101 PRODUCTIONS	101P
20TH CENTURY SALES	20C
A-WEST	AW
A. DEPIPPO	AD
A. MISENAR	AMIS
A.C. GILBERT	GIL
AB JAQUES	ABJ
AC MODEL	ACM
ACACIA SCALE MODELS	ACSM
ACE MODEL RR EQUIPMENT CO	A
ACI HOBBY	ACI
AHM	AHM.
AHM-AIRFIX	AHMA
AIM PRODUCTS	AIM
AIRFIX	AIRF
AKANE MODEL RAILROAD COMPANY	AK
ALAMOSA CAR SHOPS	ACS
ALCO ENGINEERING	ALCOE
ALCO MODELS	ALCO
ALEXANDER SCALE MODELS	ALEX
ALEXANDER SCALE MODELS.	ALEZ.
ALL-NATION HOBBY SHOP	AN
ALLOY FORMS	AL
AMBROID	AMB
AMERICAN "N" BRASS	ANB
AMERICAN BEAUTY LINES	ABL
AMERICAN FLYER	AF
AMERICAN GK LOCOMOTIVE WORKS	AGK
AMERICAN MODEL TOYS INC	AMER
AMERICAN MODELS INC	AMI
AMERICAN RR MODELS	ARR
AMERICAN STANDARD CAR CO	ASC
AMERICAN TRAIN & TRACK	ATT
APAG HOBBIES	APAG
ARBOUR MODELS	AM
ARDEN SCALE MODELS	ARD
ARGY SPECIALTIES	ARGY
ARISTO-CRAFT DISTINTIVE MINIATURES	ARISTO
ART FLEMING MODELS	AFM
ARVID ANDERSON	AA
ASHLAND CAR WORKS	ACW
ASSOCIATED HOBBY MANUFACTURERS	AHM
ASTER COMPANY	AST
ATA MODEL COMPANY	ATA
ATHEARN	ATH
ATLAS INDUSTRIES INC	UN
ATLAS TOOL COMPANY	AT
AURORA PLASTICS COMPANY	AUR
AYRES SCALE MODELS	ASM
B&W SPECIALTIES	B&W
B/T ENTERPRISES	B/T
BACHMANN INDUSTRIES	B
BACK SHOP	BS
BALBOA SCALE MODELS	BAL
BALDWIN MODEL LOCO WORKS	BM
BARR-NIXON PRODUCTS	BN
BART MODELS	BART
BAUMGARTEN MODEL RR EQUIP	BAU
BAY STATE MODELS	BSM
BEACH ISLAND MFG CO	BI
BEAVER CREEK MODELS	BCM
BELL MODEL SHOPS	BELL
BERG HOBBIES	BH
BINKLEY MODELS	BIN
BLACK HAWK LOCO WORKS	BHLW
BLUE LINE PRODUCTS	BL
BOB'S AIRCRAFT	BA
BOWSER	BOW
BOX CAR KEN	BCK
BOYDE MODELS	BOY
BRONSON	BR
BUILDERS IN SCALE	BSC
BUSCH	BU
C. BROMMER	CBRO
CADWELL INDUSTRIES	CI
CAL-SCALE	CAL
CAMBRON	CA
CAMINO SCALE MODELS	CAM
CAMPBELL	C
CANADIAN RAILWAY MODEL COMPANY	CRM
CANNON SCALE MODELS	CSM
CANNONBALL CAR SHOPS	CCS
CANNONBALL PRODUCTS	CAP
CAR PART INDUSTRIES	CPI
CAR SHOP	CS
CARY LOCOMOTIVE WORKS	CLW
CASCO ENCO CAR LINE	CECL
CASTOR PLASTICS	CAPL
CENTRAL LINES MFG CO	CL
CENTRAL LOCO WORKS	CLWO
CENTRAL VALLEY MODEL WORKS	CV
CHAMIS ENTERPRISES	CE
CHARLES DETTMANN	CD
CHAS C. MERZBACH COMAPNY	MER
CHOOCH ENTERPRISES	CHO
CHRIS MAHON INDUSTRIES	CHM
CHRISTOPH PRODUCTS COMPANY	CPC
CIBOLD CROSSING	CIC
CITY STREETS MODELS LTD	CSML
CJ ULRICH	U .
CLASSIC MINIATURES	CMI
CLEVELAND MODELS & SUPPLY CO	CMS
CLIFF LINE SCALE MODELS	CLIF
CM SHOPS	CM
COACH YARD	CY
COLLIER	CO
COLLINS	COL
COLORADO MODEL MASTERPIECES	CMM
COLUMBIA CAR & FOUNDRY	CCF
COLUMBIA VALLEY MODELS	CVM
COMET MODEL COMPANY	CMO
CON-COR COMPANY	CC
CONCORD CAR WORKS	CCW
CONOVER MINIATURE	COMI
CONRAD PRODUCTS	CPR
CONTINENTAL MODELS	CM
CONTINENTAL MONARCH MODEL CO	COMM
COOPER CRAFT	COC
COPETOWN CAR WORKS	COCW
CORNISA & SONS	C&S
CORONADO SCALE MODELS	COM
CRAFTSMAN KITS	CK
CRESCENT MODEL PRODUCTS	CMP
CROSSING GATE MODELS	CRGT
CRUMMY PRODUCTS	CP
CS RAFFING	CSR
CSC CORP	CSC
CUSTOM BRASS	CB
D.J. BAKER	DJB
DALE NEWTON COMPANY	DN
DALLAS MODEL CRAFT	DMC
DARR'S SCALE MODELS	DARR
DAVE'S MODEL TRAINS	DMT
DELAWARE VALLEY KITS	DVK
DENNIS	DE
DESIGNS OF TOMORROW	DT
DETAILS WEST	DW
DEVORT	DEV
DIA YONG MODELS COMPANY	DY
DIAMOND MODELS	DM
DIAMOND MOUNTAIN RAILROAD	DIM
DIAMOND SCALE CONSTRUCTION	DSC
DIMI-TRAINS	DIT
DMK REFINERY MODELS	DMK
DON FOWLER	DF
DONG JIN MODEL WORKS	DJ
DURANGO PRESS	DP
DYNA-MODEL PRODUCTS COMPANY	D
E SUYDAM & COMPANY	S
E&B VALLEY RAILROAD	EBV
E.H. BESSEY	EHB
EARL FRANCIS MINIATURE TRAINS	EFMT
EAST PENN MODELS	EPM
EASTERN CAR WORKS	ECW
ELECTRO-CRAFT APPLIANCES	ECA
ELECTRONIC SPECIALTY PRODUCTS	ESP
EMPIRE MIDLAND MODEL COMPANY	EMP
EMPIRE MODELS	EMM
ENGLISH	ENG
EP ALEXANDER	EPA
EUROTRAINS IMPORTERS	E
EVERETT SMITH	ES
EVERGREEN HILL DESIGNS	EHD
EVERGREEN SCALE MODELS	ESM
EXPRESS WAGON CONSTRUCTION	EW
F.A. SIMONS	FAS
FAIRFIELD MODELS	FA
FAIRFIELD TRACTION MODELS	FTM
FALLER	FAL
FAR EAST DISTRIBUTORS(NW SHORT LINES)	FED
FAR EAST IMPORTERS	FEI
FINDEX-SYSTEMS INC	FS
FINE SCALE MINIATURES	F
FISCHERS HOBBY SERVICE	FHS
FLEISCHMANN	FL
FLYING 200	F2
FOMART	FO
FORTY-NINTH STATE RR MODELS	FSM
FRANKLIN MODELS	FRM
FRED BRONNER	FB
FREDERICK MFG CO	FMC
FREW & GORDON LIMITED	F&G
FRONT RANGE PRODUCTS	FR
FRONTIER REPLICAS	FRR
FUJI MODELS	FM
FUJIYAMA KOGYO COMPANY LIMITED	FUJI
G.O. MODEL WORKS COMPANY LIMITED	GOTO
GAMCO PRODUCTS	GP
GANDY DANCER RR MODELS	GD
GAUGE ONE AMERICA	G1
GEIGER	GEI
GEM MODEL RAILWAYS	GEM
GEM MODELS (IMPORTERS)	G
GEM-TONE	GT
GENERAL MODELS CORP.	GM
GENESEE MODEL RR CO	GEMO
GEORGE STOCK	GS
GESCHA	GES
GHB INTERNATIONAL	GHB
GILBERT, A.C.	GIL
GLOBE MODELS	GLO
GOULD COMPANY	GC
GR SIGNALING	GRS
GRACELINE MODEL RAILROADS	GMR
GRANDT LINES	GL
GRANT LOCOMOTIVE WORKS	GLW
GREAT WESTERN MODEL LOCOS	GW
GREEN MAX	GMX
GSB RAIL ASSOCIATES	GSB
H-D SCALE MODELS	HDSM
H.P. PRODUCTS	HP
HALLMARK	H
HALLMARK KOREA MODELS	HK
HARRY GARRETT & COMPANY	HG
HARTLEY MODEL RAILROAD SUPPLY	HM
HAWK MODEL AEROPLANE CO	HA
HELJAN	HEL
HENNING SCALE MODELS	HSM
HENRY ZUHR INC	ZUHR
HERKIMER TOOL & MODEL WORKS	HERK
HERPA	HE
HETCH HETCHY SCALE MODELS	HHS
HEWAN	HEW
HI BALLER CORP	HIB
HI RAIL PRODUCTS	HR
HIGH QUALITY MODEL DISTRIBUTORS	HIQ
HINES LINES	HIL
HISTORICAL SCALE MINIATURES	HSM
HL WOODSON	WO
HO EITNER	HOE
HO RAILROAD & TROLLEY SUPPLY CO.	HORT
HO TRAIN COMPANY	HOT
HO WEST	HOW
HOBBIES INC	HI

379

APPENDIX C (MANUFACTURERS)

HOBBY BARN	HB
HOBBY HAVEN	HHA
HOBBY HOUSE INC	HH
HOBBY INDUSTRIES	HOI
HOBBY LINE	HL
HOBBY TECHNIQUES	HTE
HOBBYTOWN OF BOSTON	HOB
HOLGATE & REYNOLDS	H&R
HOUSE OF FOUR WINDS	HFW
HOUSE OF TRAINS	HT
HOWELL DAY	HD
HOWELL INDUSTRIES	HI.
HUNTINGTON MODEL WORKS	HUNT
ICKEN MODEL LOCO CO	IMC
IDEAL AEROPLANE & SUPPLY	IA
IDEAL MODELS	IM
IMAI MODELS COMPANY LIMITED	I
IMP/TAKARA	TAK
INDIANAPOLIS CAR COMPANY	IND
INDUSTRIAL MODEL WORKS	IMW
INLAND SCALE MODELS	ISM
INTERNATIONAL HOBBY CORP	IHC
INTERNATIONAL MODELS INC.	INT
IRON HORSE MODELS	IH
ISLE LABORATORIES	ISLE
J&J MODELS	J&J
J.C. MODELS	JC
J.C. ULRICH COMPANY INC.	U .
JACK COLLIER	CO .
JAMCO LIMITED	JAM
JANCO MODELS	JA
JEWEL MODELS	JM
JIM GRACES HOBBY CENTER	JGHC
JL MODELS	JL
JMC INTERNATIONAL	JMC
JOHN A. ENGLISH & COMPANY	JE
JOHN GRZYWNA	JG
JORDONS PRODUCTS	JP
JOUEF	J
JUNECO SCALE MODELS	JSM
K&L HOUSE OF WOOD	K&L
K&W SHOPS	K&W
K-VAL CARS	KVAL
KADEE CO.	KD
KALAMAZOO TOY TRAIN WORKS	KTTW
KARLINE	KL
KASINER HOBBIES	KAS
KATSUMI MOKEITEN COMPANY LIMITED	KATS
KAW VALLEY SCALE MODELS	KAW
KAWAI	KW
KEMTRON	KEM
KEN KIDDER RAILROAD MODELS	KK
KEY IMPORTERS/KEY IMPORTS LIMITED	KEY
KEYSTONE LOCOMOTIVE WORKS	KLW
KIBRI	KIB
KIMBALL-KRAFT	KIK
KING MODELS	KM
KINSMAN SCALE MODELS	KSC
KLE-WE	KLE
KOBRA MODELS	K
KODAMA SHISAKUSHO	KS
KOOK JEA MODELS	KJ
KOREA SCALE MODELS	KSM
KRIS MODEL TRAINS	KRIS
KUMATA MODELS (& CO LTD)	KUM
KURTZ-KRAFT	KKR
KWR INC	KWR
L.M. BLUM MODELS	LMB .
LA MAY INDUSTRIES	LM
LABELLE LOCOMOTIVE WORKS COMPANY	LA
LACONIA (BINKLEY) INDUSTRIES	LAC
LADD MODEL WORKS	LADD
LAMBERT ASSOCIATES	L
LANE JONES COMPANY	LJ
LANG CINCINNATTI CARS	LC
LAUNCH PAD DISTRIBUTORS	LPD
LAWRENCE LABORATORY	LLA
LCM BLOSS	LCM
LEETOWN	LEE
LEHIGH MODEL PRODUCTS	LMP
LEHIGH VALLEY MODELS	LV
LESLIE BROTHERS	LB
LESNEY	LES
LGB	LGB
LIBERTY MODELS INC	LI
LIFELIKE	LL
LIGHTNING HOBBIES	LH
LILIPUT	LIL
LIMA	LIMA
LIMITED EDITIONS	LE
LINDBERG	LIND
LINDSAY PRODUCTS INC	LIN
LIONEL	LIO
LITTLE MINI SHOPS	LMS
LMB MODELS	LMB
LOBAUGH	LOB
LOCOMOTIVE COMPANY, THE	LOC
LOCOMOTIVE WORKSHOP, THE	LW
LOGGERS SUPPLY	LOG
LOUIS MARX COMPANY INC.	MX
LOWRY	LOW
LS LOC LTD	LSL
LW MODELS	LWM
LYKENS VALLEY MODELS	LVM
LYTLER & LYTLER	L&L
M. DALE NEWTON COMPANY	DN .
M.B. AUSTIN	MBA
MAERKLIN	MKL .
MAGNUS	MAGN
MAGNUSON MODELS INC	MMD
MAIN LINE MODELS	MLI
MAINLINE VARNEY	VM
MANN-MADE PRODUCTS	MANN
MANTUA METAL PRODUCTS	M
MARION PRODUCTS COMPANY	MAP
MARKLIN	MKL
MASTER MODEL PRODUCTS	MMP
MAX GRAY	MG
MCKEAN MODELS	MKM
MEGROW	ME
MERKER-FISCHER	MFI
MERLE FABER	MF
MERZBACH COMPANY, CHAS. C.	MER
MICRO CAST MIZUNO	MCM
MICRO-SCALE MODEL PRODUCTS	MSMP
MIDGAGE MODELS	MIM
MIDWEST HOBBY SHOP	MHS
MIDWEST RAIL WORKS	MRW
MIDWEST TROLLEY MUSEUM INC	MTM
MIDWESTERN TRAIN HOBBY	MTH
MIL-SCALE PRODUCTS	MSP
MILESTONE MODELS	MISM
MILWAUKEE CAR WORKS DIV	MCW
MIN-SCALE MILL WORKS	MIN
MINI STRUCTURES	MIST
MINIATURE TOYS	MT
MINIKITS	MK
MINITRIX	MTX
MIYAZAWA MOKEI	MMO
MLR MANUFACTURING COMAPNY	MLR
MODEL BUILDERS SUPPLY	MBS
MODEL BUILDERS SUPPLY.	MDS.
MODEL CRAFT MFG CO	MC
MODEL DIE CAST	MDC
MODEL ENGINEERING WORKS	MEW
MODEL EXPRESS	MDX
MODEL HOBBIES	MH
MODEL MASTERPIECES MODEL	MM
MODEL POWER	MP
MODEL RAILROAD SHOP	MRS
MODEL RECITIFIER CORP	MRC
MODEL SHOP, THE	MOD
MODEL STRUCUTRES COMPANY	MS
MODEL TRAMWAY SYSTEMS	MTS
MODELTON MFG COMPANY	MO
MODELTRONICS	MT
MOUNTAIN AUTOMATION	MA
MOUNTAIN STATES MODEL WORKS	MSMW
MR WEATHER	MW
MUIR MODELS INC	MU
MULTIPLEX MFG CO	MULTI
N&G RAILWAY SIGNAL CO	N&G
N.A.P. COMPANY	NAP
N.J. INTERNATIONAL	NJI
NAKAMURA SEIMITSU COMPANY LIMITED	NAKA
NASON RAILWAYS	NR
NATIONAL CAR EAST	NCE
NICKEL PLATE PRODUCTS	NPP
NIXON MODELS	NM
NOCH & COMPANY	NOCH
NORTH JERSEY MODEL CAR CO	NJM
NORTHEASTERN SCALE MODELS	NSM
NORTHWEST SHORE LINE	NWSL
OHIO MODEL WORKS	OMW
OLDE HUFF 'N PUFF	OHP
OLYMPIA DISTRIBUTORS	OD
OLYMPIA PRECISION MODELS	OPM
OLYMPIC CASCADIAN	OC
OLYMPIC EXPRESS	OE
ORIENTAL LIMITED	OL
ORIGINAL WHISTLE STOP KIT CO	OWS
ORION MODELS	ORM
OVERLAND MODELS INC	OM
PACIFIC FAST MAIL	PFM
PACIFIC HO COMPANY	PHO
PACIFIC MODEL SUPPLIES	PMS
PACIFIC PIKE	PIKE
PACIFIC TRACTION	PT
PARAGON MODELS	PAR
PARK MODEL PRODUCTS	PMP
PARMELE & STURGES	PST
PB PRODUCTS	PBP
PEARCE TOOL	PTO
PEMCO INDUSTRIES INC	PCO
PENN LINE	PL
PENNSYLVANIA SCALE MODELS	PAM
PERFECT SCALE MODELS	PSM
PERIOD MINIATURES	PEM
PETER BUILT LOCOMOTIVE WORKS	PBLW
PETERSON MOTOR TRUCKS	PMT
PIEDMONT SOUTHEASTERN SHOPS	PSS
PIKE STUFF	PIS
PIONEER COMAPNY	PC
PITTMAN ELECTRICAL DEVELOPMENT CO.	PIT
PLACER NEVADA & EL DORADO RR CO.	PNED
POLA	POLA
POLK'S MODEL CRAFT	POLK
POTOMIC VALLEY GAUGE SUPPLY	PV
POWER SYSTEMS INC	PSI
PRECISION BRASS	PB
PRECISION MINIATURES	PM
PRECISION MODEL PRODUCTS	PMO
PRECISION MODELS OF CALIFORNIA	P
PRECISION SCALE COMPANY	PS
PREISEP	PR
PRITCHARD PATENT PRODUCE CO	PPP
PRO CUSTOM HOBBIES	PCH
PROTO POWER WEST	PPW
PROTOTYPE MODEL PRODUCTS	PMRR
PROTOTYPE MODLER INC	PMI
Q-CAR COMPANY	QCC
QUALITY CRAFT MODELS INC	QC
R ROBB LTD.	RRL
R&M INDUSTRY	R&M
R&T COMPANY	R&T
RABON RAILROAD	RAR
RAIL CHIEF PRODUCTS CO.	RCH
RAIL CRAFT MODELS	RC
RAIL LINE COMPANY	RL
RAIL MINIATURES	RMI
RAILHEAD	RH
RAILROAD EQUIP CO	RRE
RALPH TROXEL	RT
RAMAX	RAM
RAPIDO	RAP
RD DENISE	RDD
RED BALL	RED
REGAL KITS	REK
REMINGTON LOCOMOTIVE WORKS	RLW
RENWAL PRODUCTS	REN

380

APPENDIX C (MANUFACTURERS)

REVELL	RE
REX ENG & MFG CO	REX
REYNOLDS RAILROAD PRODUCTS	RRR
RHEOSTATE	RHE
RIB OF STIEHL	RS
RIBBONRAIL	RIB
RICHARD DATIN	RDA
RICHARD ORR	ORR
RICHARD-DENNIS MODELS	DE
RIOGRANDE MODELS	RGM
RIVAROSSI	RIV
ROBERT SLOAN	ROSL
ROBINS RAILS INC	RRI
ROCK LANE MODELS	RLM
ROCKY MOUNTAIN MODELS	RM
ROK-AM (REPUBLIC OF KOREA-AMERICAN)	RA
ROLLER BEARING MODELS	R
ROLLIN J LOBAUGH	LOB
ROLLINS HOUSE OF MINIATURES	RHM
ROSEBUD KITMASTER LTD.	RK
ROSEBUD PLASTICS CORP	RP
ROUNDHOUSE, THE	RD
ROWA	ROWA
ROYAL GEORGE SOUTHERN RAILROAD	RGSR
RTR INDUSTRIES	RTR
RUSSELL MOBI-MODELS	RMM
S SOHO & COMPANY	SOHO
S&P DISTRIBUTORS	S&P
S.E. DANCE	SED
S.K. INTERNATIONAL	SKI
SAGINAW PATTERN MFG CO	SPM
SAKURA-TAKENO	SAK
SAMHONGSA COMPANY LIMITED	SAM
SAMPSON MODEL COMPANY	SMP
SAN JUAN ENGINEERING	SJE
SANDY RIVER CAR SHOPS	SR
SATO MODELS	SAT
SCALE CRAFT ENGINEERING CO.	SCC
SCALE LOCOMOTIVE & SUPPLY	SLS
SCALE MODELERS INDUSTRIES	SMI
SCALE MODELS	SCMO
SCALE RAILWAY EQUIPMENT COMPANY	SRE
SCALE SCENICS DIVISION	SSD
SCALE STRUCTURES LIMITED	SSL
SCALE-RAIL MINIATURES	SRA
SCENERY PRODUCTS	SCP
SCENERY UNLIMITED	SU
SCOTIA SCALE MODELS	SCSM
SEIKO MODELS	SE
SELLEY INC	SEL
SEQUOIA SCALE MODELS	SSMO
SHERMAN DANCE	SD
SIERRA SOUTHERN PRODUCTS	SISP
SILVER LEAF RAPID TRANSIT MODELS	SLR
SILVER LEDGE MODELS	SLMO
SILVER STREAK	SS
SIMMONS SCALE MODELS INC	SISC
SIMPSON PRODUCT COMPANY	SIM
SLIM GAUGE PRODUCTIONS	SGP
SMALL SCALE PRODUCTS	SSP
SMOKE STACK HOBBY KITS CO	SSHK
SMOKEY VALLEY RAILROAD	SV
SOUTH PARK PRODUCTIONS	SPPR
SS LIMITED	SSL
STANDARD PRODUCTS	SP
STANDARD SCALE MODELS	STS
STAR CONTINENTAL KIT (MODELS)	SCK
STAR HOBBY PRODUCTS	SH
STAR LINE MODELS	SL
STAR MODELS	SMO
STATE LINE MODELS	SLM
STATE RAILROAD MODELS	SRM
STATE STREET MODELS	STST
STERLING MODELS	ST
STEWART HOBBIES INC	STEW
STROMBECK-BECKER MFG CO	SB
STRUCTURE COMPANY, THE	STC
SUGAR PINE MODELS	SUP
SUMMIT ENGINEERING	SEN
SUNCOAST MODELS	SC
SUNSET MODELS	SUN
SUNSHINE MODELS	SM
SUPER SCALE MODEL CORP.	SSM
SUPERIOR MODELS	SUM
SUPERQUICK	SQ
SUYDAM	S
SYCAMORE HOLLOW STATION	SHS
TAKARA/IMP	TAK
TAURUS PRODUCTS	TP
TENSHODO MODEL COMPANY	TEN
TETSUDO MOKEISHA	TMK
THOMAS A YORKE ENTERPRISES	TY
THOMAS INDUSTRIES	TH
THRALL MFG CO	THM
TIGER VALLEY MODELS	TVM
TIMBERLINE MODELS	TIM
TK MODELS	TK
TOBY MODEL COMPANY LIMITED	TOBY
TOHO MODELS	TOHO
TOMALCO	TOM
TOMHAR MFG CO	TOMH
TOWN CRAFTS MODELS	TCM
TOY & HOBBY HOUSE	THH
TP PRODUCTS	TPPR
TRACKSIDE INDUSTRIES	TRI
TRACTION MODELS	TRM
TRAIN CRAFT PRODUCTS	TC
TRAIN MINIATURE OF CALIF	TMC
TRAIN MINIATURE OF ILLINOIS	TMI
TRAIN MINIATURES	TM
TRAIN MODELS	TMO
TRAINS, INC.	TI
TRAINSTUFF	TRS
TRIX	TRIX
TROLLER	TR
TRU-SCALE MODELS	TSM
TRUXEL BROS ENTERPRISES	TBE
TSUBOMI	TS
TYCO INDUSTRIES	T
ULRICH	U
ULTRA SCALE	US
UNIVERSAL MODEL PRODUCTS	UMP
US AIRFIX	USAI
US HOBBIES	USH
UTAH SCALE MODEL COMPANY	USM
V LINE LOCOMOTIVES INC	VL
VALLAM ASSOCIATES	VAL
VALLEY CAR WORKS	VCM
VALLEY WORKS	VW
VAN HOBBIES	VAN
VANE JONES COMPANY	LJ
VARNEY	V
VARNEY MAINLINE	VM
VCM	VCM
VIRDEN	VI
VOLLMER	VOL
W&T MODELS	W&T
WABASH VALLEY LINE	WVL
WALKER MODEL SERVICE	WMS
WALLACE SCALE MODLES	WASM
WALTER S PARKS	WSP
WALTER SYRETT	WSY
WALTERS	WAL
WAYFREIGHT MODELS	WFM
WENTZCO PRECISION MODELS	WPM
WESTCHESTER MODEL CO	WMC
WESTERFIELD	WD
WESTERN MODELS	WM
WESTMORELAND CAR SUPPLY	WEC
WESTSIDE MODEL COMPANY	WSM
WESTWOOD	WEST
WHEEL WORKS	WW
WHITE GROUND MODEL WORKS	WGM
WIKING	WIK
WILLIAM BROTHERS	WB
WILLIAMS REPRODUCTIONS LTD	WRL
WINSTON MINIATURE ENGINEERING CO	W
WISONSIN CENTRAL SUPPLY	WCS
WOODLAND SCENICS	WS
WOODSON	WO
WR BROWN CORP	WRB
WRIGHT ENTERPRISES	WE
WS PARKS	WSP
YANK MODEL RESEARCH INC	YM
YE OLD HUFF 'N PUFF	YE
ZUHR	ZUHR

APPENDIX C (MANUFACTURERS)

Abbr.	Manufacturer
101P	101 PRODUCTIONS
20C	20TH CENTURY SALES
A	ACE MODEL RR EQUIPMENT CO
AA	ARVID ANDERSON
ABJ	AB JAQUES
ABL	AMERICAN BEAUTY LINES
ACI	ACI HOBBY
ACM	AC MODEL
ACS	ALAMOSA CAR SHOPS
ACSM	ACACIA SCALE MODELS
ACW	ASHLAND CAR WORKS
AD	A. DEPIPPO
AF	AMERICAN FLYER
AFM	ART FLEMING MODELS
AGK	AMERICAN GK LOCOMOTIVE WORKS
AHM	ASSOCIATED HOBBY MANUFACTURERS
AHM.	AHM
AHMA	AHM-AIRFIX
AIM	AIM PRODUCTS
AIRF	AIRFIX
AK	AKANE MODEL RAILROAD COMPANY
AL	ALLOY FORMS
ALCO	ALCO MODELS
ALCOE	ALCO ENGINEERING
ALEX	ALEXANDER SCALE MODELS
ALEZ.	ALEXANDER SCALE MODELS.
AM	ARBOUR MODELS
AMB	AMBROID
AMER	AMERICAN MODEL TOYS INC
AMI	AMERICAN MODELS INC
AMIS	A. MISENAR
AN	ALL-NATION HOBBY SHOP
ANB	AMERICAN "N" BRASS
APAG	APAG HOBBIES
ARD	ARDEN SCALE MODELS
ARGY	ARGY SPECIALTIES
ARISTO	ARISTO-CRAFT DISTINTIVE MINIATURES
ARR	AMERICAN RR MODELS
ASC	AMERICAN STANDARD CAR CO
ASM	AYRES SCALE MODELS
AST	ASTER COMPANY
AT	ATLAS TOOL COMPANY
ATA	ATA MODEL COMPANY
ATH	ATHEARN
ATT	AMERICAN TRAIN & TRACK
AUR	AURORA PLASTICS COMPANY
AW	A-WEST
B	BACHMANN INDUSTRIES
B&W	B&W SPECIALTIES
B/T	B/T ENTERPRISES
BA	BOB'S AIRCRAFT
BAL	BALBOA SCALE MODELS
BART	BART MODELS
BAU	BAUMGARTEN MODEL RR EQUIP
BCK	BOX CAR KEN
BCM	BEAVER CREEK MODELS
BELL	BELL MODEL SHOPS
BH	BERG HOBBIES
BHLW	BLACK HAWK LOCO WORKS
BI	BEACH ISLAND MFG CO
BIN	BINKLEY MODELS
BL	BLUE LINE MODELS
BM	BALDWIN MODEL LOCO WORKS
BN	BARR-NIXON PRODUCTS
BOW	BOWSER
BOY	BOYDE MODELS
BR	BRONSON
BS	BACK SHOP
BSC	BUILDERS IN SCALE
BSM	BAY STATE MODELS
BU	BUSCH
C	CAMPBELL
C&S	CORNISA & SONS
CA	CAMBRON
CAL	CAL-SCALE
CAM	CAMINO SCALE MODELS
CAP	CANNONBALL PRODUCTS
CAPL	CASTOR PLASTICS
CB	CUSTOM BRASS
CBRO	C. BROMMER
CC	CON-COR COMPANY
CCF	COLUMBIA CAR & FOUNDRY
CCS	CANNONBALL CAR SHOPS
CCW	CONCORD CAR WORKS
CD	CHARLES DETTMANN
CE	CHAMIS ENTERPRISES
CECL	CASCO ENCO CAR LINE
CHM	CHRIS MAHON INDUSTRIES
CHO	CHOOCH ENTERPRISES
CI	CADWELL INDUSTRIES
CIC	CIBOLD CROSSING
CK	CRAFTSMAN KITS
CL	CENTRAL LINES MFG CO
CLIF	CLIFF LINE SCALE MODELS
CLW	CARY LOCOMOTIVE WORKS
CLWO	CENTRAL LOCO WORKS
CM	CM SHOPS
CM	CONTINENTAL MODELS
CMI	CLASSIC MINIATURES
CMM	COLORADO MODEL MASTERPIECES
CMO	COMET MODEL COMPANY
CMP	CRESCENT MODEL PRODUCTS
CMS	CLEVELAND MODELS & SUPPLY CO
CO	COLLIER
CO	JACK COLLIER
COC	COOPER CRAFT
COCW	COPETOWN CAR WORKS
COL	COLLINS
COM	CORONADO SCALE MODELS
COMI	CONOVER MINIATURE
COMM	CONTINENTAL MONARCH MODEL CO
CP	CRUMMY PRODUCTS
CPC	CHRISTOPH PRODUCTS COMPANY
CPI	CAR PART INDUSTRIES
CPR	CONRAD PRODUCTS
CRGT	CROSSING GATE MODELS
CRM	CANADIAN RAILWAY MODEL COMPANY
CS	CAR SHOP
CSC	CSC CORP
CSM	CANNON SCALE MODELS
CSML	CITY STREETS MODELS LTD
CSR	CS RAFFING
CV	CENTRAL VALLEY MODEL WORKS
CVM	COLUMBIA VALLEY MODELS
CY	COACH YARD
D	DYNA-MODEL PRODUCTS COMPANY
DARR	DARR'S SCALE MODELS
DE	DENNIS
DE	RICHARD-DENNIS MODELS
DEV	DEVORT
DF	DON FOWLER
DIM	DIAMOND MOUNTAIN RAILROAD
DIT	DIMI-TRAINS
DJ	DONG JIN MODEL WORKS
DJB	D.J. BAKER
DM	DIAMOND MODELS
DMC	DALLAS MODEL CRAFT
DMK	DMK REFINERY MODELS
DMT	DAVE'S MODEL TRAINS
DN	DALE NEWTON COMPANY
DN	M. DALE NEWTON COMPANY
DP	DURANGO PRESS
DSC	DIAMOND SCALE CONSTRUCTION
DT	DESIGNS OF TOMORROW
DVK	DELAWARE VALLEY KITS
DW	DETAILS WEST
DY	DIA YONG MODELS COMPANY
E	EUROTRAINS IMPORTERS
EBV	E&B VALLEY RAILROAD
ECA	ELECTRO-CRAFT APPLIANCES
ECW	EASTERN CAR WORKS
EFMT	EARL FRANCIS MINIATURE TRAINS
EHB	E.H. BESSEY
EHD	EVERGREEN HILL DESIGNS
EMM	EMPIRE MODELS
EMP	EMPIRE MIDLAND MODEL COMPANY
ENG	ENGLISH
EPA	EP ALEXANDER
EPM	EAST PENN MODELS
ES	EVERETT SMITH
ESM	EVERGREEN SCALE MODELS
ESP	ELECTRONIC SPECIALTY PRODUCTS
EW	EXPRESS WAGON CONSTRUCTION
F	FINE SCALE MINIATURES
F&G	FREW & GORDON LIMITED
F2	FLYING 200
FA	FAIRFIELD MODELS
FAL	FALLER
FAS	F.A. SIMONS
FB	FRED BRONNER
FED	FAR EAST DISTRIBUTORS (NW SHORT LINES)
FEI	FAR EAST IMPORTERS
FHS	FISCHERS HOBBY SERVICE
FL	FLEISCHMANN
FM	FUJI MODELS
FMC	FREDERICK MFG CO
FO	FOMART
FR	FRONT RANGE PRODUCTS
FRM	FRANKLIN MODELS
FRR	FRONTIER REPLICAS
FS	FINDEX-SYSTEMS INC
FSM	FORTY-NINTH STATE RR MODELS
FTM	FAIRFIELD TRACTION MODELS
FUJI	FUJIYAMA KOGYO COMPANY LIMITED
G	GEM MODELS (IMPORTERS)
G1	GAUGE ONE AMERICA
GC	GOULD COMPANY
GD	GANDY DANCER RR MODELS
GEI	GEIGER
GEM	GEM MODEL RAILWAYS
GEMO	GENESEE MODEL RR CO
GES	GESCHA
GHB	GHB INTERNATIONAL
GIL	A.C. GILBERT
GIL	GILBERT, A.C.
GL	GRANDT LINES
GLO	GLOBE MODELS
GLW	GRANT LOCOMOTIVE WORKS
GM	GENERAL MODELS CORP.
GMR	GRACELINE MODEL RAILROADS
GMX	GREEN MAX
GOTO	G.O. MODEL WORKS COMPANY LIMITED
GP	GAMCO PRODUCTS
GRS	GR SIGNALING
GS	GEORGE STOCK
GSB	GSB RAIL ASSOCIATES
GT	GEM-TONE
GW	GREAT WESTERN MODEL LOCOS
H	HALLMARK
H&R	HOLGATE & REYNOLDS
HA	HAWK MODEL AEROPLANE CO
HB	HOBBY BARN
HD	HOWELL DAY
HDSM	H-D SCALE MODELS
HE	HERPA
HEL	HELJAN
HERK	HERKIMER TOOL & MODEL WORKS
HEW	HEWAN
HFW	HOUSE OF FOUR WINDS
HG	HARRY GARRETT & COMPANY
HH	HOBBY HOUSE INC
HHA	HOBBY HAVEN
HHS	HETCH HETCHY SCALE MODELS
HI	HOBBIES INC
HI.	HOWELL INDUSTRIES
HIB	HI BALLER CORP
HIL	HINES LINES
HIQ	HIGH QUALITY MODEL DISTRIBUTORS
HK	HALLMARK KOREA MODELS
HL	HOBBY LINE
HM	HARTLEY MODEL RAILROAD SUPPLY
HOB	HOBBYTOWN OF BOSTON
HOE	HO EITNER
HOI	HOBBY INDUSTRIES

APPENDIX C (MANUFACTURERS)

HORT	HO RAILROAD & TROLLEY SUPPLY CO.
HOT	HO TRAIN COMPANY
HOW	HO WEST
HP	H.P. PRODUCTS
HR	HI RAIL PRODUCTS
HSM	HENNING SCALE MODELS
HSM	HISTORICAL SCALE MINIATURES
HT	HOUSE OF TRAINS
HTE	HOBBY TECHNIQUES
HUNT	HUNTINGTON MODEL WORKS
I	IMAI MODELS COMPANY LIMITED
IA	IDEAL AEROPLANE & SUPPLY
IH	IRON HORSE MODELS
IHC	INTERNATIONAL HOBBY CORP
IM	IDEAL MODELS
IMC	ICKEN MODEL LOCO CO
IMW	INDUSTRIAL MODEL WORKS
IND	INDIANAPOLIS CAR COMPANY
INT	INTERNATIONAL MODELS INC.
ISLE	ISLE LABORATORIES
ISM	INLAND SCALE MODELS
J	JOUEF
J&J	J&J MODELS
JA	JANCO MODELS
JAM	JAMCO LIMITED
JC	J.C. MODELS
JE	JOHN A. ENGLISH & COMPANY
JG	JOHN GRZYWNA
JGHC	JIM GRACES HOBBY CENTER
JL	JL MODELS
JM	JEWEL MODELS
JMC	JMC INTERNATIONAL
JP	JORDONS PRODUCTS
JSM	JUNECO SCALE MODELS
K	KOBRA MODELS
K&L	K&L HOUSE OF WOOD
K&W	K&W SHOPS
KAS	KASINER HOBBIES
KATS	KATSUMI MOKEITEN COMPANY LIMITED
KAW	KAW VALLEY SCALE MODELS
KD	KADEE CO.
KEM	KEMTRON
KEY	KEY IMPORTERS/KEY IMPORTS LIMITED
KIB	KIBRI
KIK	KIMBALL-KRAFT
KJ	KOOK JEA MODELS
KK	KEN KIDDER RAILROAD MODELS
KKR	KURTZ-KRAFT
KL	KARLINE
KLE	KLE-WE
KLW	KEYSTONE LOCOMOTIVE WORKS
KM	KING MODELS
KRIS	KRIS MODEL TRAINS
KS	KODAMA SHISAKUSHO
KSC	KINSMAN SCALE MODELS
KSM	KOREA SCALE MODELS
KTTW	KALAMAZOO TOY TRAIN WORKS
KUM	KUMATA MODELS (& CO LTD)
KVAL	K-VAL CARS
KW	KAWAI
KWR	KWR INC
L	LAMBERT ASSOCIATES
L&L	LYTLER & LYTLER
LA	LABELLE LOCOMOTIVE WORKS COMPANY
LAC	LACONIA (BINKLEY) INDUSTRIES
LADD	LADD MODEL WORKS
LB	LESLIE BROTHERS
LC	LANG CINCINNATTI CARS
LCM	LCM BLOSS
LE	LIMITED EDITIONS
LEE	LEETOWN
LES	LESNEY
LGB	LGB
LH	LIGHTNING HOBBIES
LI	LIBERTY MODELS INC
LIL	LILIPUT
LIMA	LIMA
LIN	LINDSAY PRODUCTS INC
LIND	LINDBERG
LIO	LIONEL
LJ	LANE JONES COMPANY
LJ	VANE JONES COMPANY
LL	LIFELIKE
LLA	LAWRENCE LABORATORY
LM	LA MAY INDUSTRIES
LMB	LMB MODELS
LMB	L.M. BLUM MODELS
LMP	LEHIGH MODEL PRODUCTS
LMS	LITTLE MINI SHOPS
LOB	LOBAUGH
LOB	ROLLIN J LOBAUGH
LOC	LOCOMOTIVE COMPANY, THE
LOG	LOGGERS SUPPLY
LOW	LOWRY
LPD	LAUNCH PAD DISTRIBUTORS
LSL	LS LOC LTD
LV	LEHIGH VALLEY MODELS
LVM	LYKENS VALLEY MODELS
LW	LOCOMOTIVE WORKSHOP, THE
LWM	LW MODELS
M	MANTUA METAL PRODUCTS
MA	MOUNTAIN AUTOMATION
MAGN	MAGNUS
MANN	MANN-MADE PRODUCTS
MAP	MARION PRODUCTS COMPANY
MBA	M.B. AUSTIN
MBS	MODEL BUILDERS SUPPLY
MC	MODEL CRAFT MFG CO
MCM	MICRO CAST MIZUNO
MCW	MILWAUKEE CAR WORKS DIV
MDC	MODEL DIE CAST
MDS.	MODEL BUILDERS SUPPLY.
MDX	MODEL EXPRESS
ME	MEGROW
MER	CHAS C. MERZBACH COMAPNY
MER	MERZBACH COMPANY, CHAS. C.
MEW	MODEL ENGINEERING WORKS
MF	MERLE FABER
MFI	MERKER-FISCHER
MG	MAX GRAY
MH	MODEL HOBBIES
MHS	MIDWEST HOBBY SHOP
MIM	MIDGAGE MODELS
MIN	MIN-SCALE MILL WORKS
MISM	MILESTONE MODELS
MIST	MINI STRUCTURES
MK	MINIKITS
MKL	MARKLIN
MKL	MAERKLIN
MKM	MCKEAN MODELS
MLI	MAIN LINE MODELS
MLR	MLR MANUFACTURING COMAPNY
MM	MODEL MASTERPIECES MODEL
MMD	MAGNUSON MODELS INC
MMO	MIYAZAWA MOKEI
MMP	MASTER MODEL PRODUCTS
MO	MODELTON MFG COMPANY
MOD	MODEL SHOP, THE
MP	MODEL POWER
MRC	MODEL RECITIFIER CORP
MRS	MODEL RAILROAD SHOP
MRW	MIDWEST RAIL WORKS
MS	MODEL STRUCUTRES COMPANY
MSMP	MICRO-SCALE MODEL PRODUCTS
MSMW	MOUNTAIN STATES MODEL WORKS
MSP	MIL-SCALE PRODUCTS
MT	MINIATURE TOYS
MT	MODELTRONICS
MTH	MIDWESTERN TRAIN HOBBY
MTM	MIDWEST TROLLEY MUSEUM INC
MTS	MODEL TRAMWAY SYSTEMS
MTX	MINITRIX
MU	MUIR MODELS INC
MULTI	MULTIPLEX MFG CO
MW	MR WEATHER
MX	LOUIS MARX COMPANY INC.
N&S	N&S RAILWAY SIGNAL CO
NAKA	NAKAMURA SEIMITSU COMPANY LIMITED
NAP	N.A.P. COMPANY
NCE	NATIONAL CAR EAST
NJI	N.J. INTERNATIONAL
NJM	NORTH JERSEY MODEL CAR CO
NM	NIXON MODELS
NOCH	NOCH & COMPANY
NPP	NICKEL PLATE PRODUCTS
NR	NASON RAILWAYS
NSM	NORTHEASTERN SCALE MODELS
NWSL	NORTHWEST SHORE LINE
OC	OLYMPIC CASCADIAN
OD	OLYMPIA DISTRIBUTORS
OE	OLYMPIC EXPRESS
OHP	OLDE HUFF 'N PUFF
OL	ORIENTAL LIMITED
OM	OVERLAND MODELS INC
OMW	OHIO MODEL WORKS
OPM	OLYMPIA PRECISION MODELS
ORM	ORION MODELS
ORR	RICHARD ORR
OWS	ORIGINAL WHISTLE STOP KIT CO
P	PRECISION MODELS OF CALIFORNIA
PAM	PENNSYLVANIA SCALE MODELS
PAR	PARAGON MODELS
PB	PRECISION BRASS
PBLW	PETER BUILT LOCOMOTIVE WORKS
PBP	PB PRODUCTS
PC	PIONEER COMAPNY
PCH	PRO CUSTOM HOBBIES
PCO	PEMCO INDUSTRIES INC
PEM	PERIOD MINIATURES
PFM	PACIFIC FAST MAIL
PHO	PACIFIC HO COMPANY
PIKE	PACIFIC PIKE
PIS	PIKE STUFF
PIT	PITTMAN ELECTRICAL DEVELOPMENT CO.
PL	PENN LINE
PM	PRECISION MINIATURES
PMI	PROTOTYPE MODLER INC
PMO	PRECISION MODEL PRODUCTS
PMP	PARK MODEL PRODUCTS
PMRR	PROTOTYPE MODEL PRODUCTS
PMS	PACIFIC MODEL SUPPLIES
PMT	PETERSON MOTOR TRUCKS
PNED	PLACER NEVADA & EL DORRADO RR CO.
POLA	POLA
POLK	POLK'S MODEL CRAFT
PPP	PRITCHARD PATENT PRODUCE CO
PPW	PROTO POWER WEST
PR	PREISEP
PS	PRECISION SCALE COMPANY
PSI	POWER SYSTEMS INC
PSM	PERFECT SCALE MODELS
PSS	PIEDMONT SOUTHEASTERN SHOPS
PST	PARMELE & STURGES
PT	PACIFIC TRACTION
PTO	PEARCE TOOL
PV	POTOMIC VALLEY GAUGE SUPPLY
QC	QUALITY CRAFT MODELS INC
QCC	Q-CAR COMPANY
R	ROLLER BEARING MODELS
R&M	R&M INDUSTRY
R&T	R&T COMPANY
RA	ROK-AM (REPUBLIC OF KOREA-AMERICAN)
RAM	RAMAX
RAP	RAPIDO
RAR	RABON RAILROAD
RC	RAIL CRAFT MODELS
RCH	RAIL CHIEF PRODUCTS CO.
RD	ROUNDHOUSE, THE
RDA	RICHARD DATIN
RDD	RD DENISE
RE	REVELL
RED	RED BALL
REK	REGAL KITS
REN	RENWAL PRODUCTS
REX	REX ENG & MFG CO
RGM	RIOGRANDE MODELS
RGSR	ROYAL GEORGE SOUTHERN RAILROAD
RH	RAILHEAD
RHE	RHEOSTATE
RHM	ROLLINS HOUSE OF MINIATURES

APPENDIX C (MANUFACTURERS)

RIB	RIBBONRAIL
RIV	RIVAROSSI
RK	ROSEBUD KITMASTER LTD.
RL	RAIL LINE MODELS
RLM	ROCK LANE MODELS
RLW	REMINGTON LOCOMOTIVE WORKS
RM	ROCKY MOUNTAIN MODELS
RMI	RAIL MINIATURES
RMM	RUSSELL MOBI-MODELS
ROSL	ROBERT SLOAN
ROWA	ROWA
RP	ROSEBUD PLASTICS CORP
RRE	RAILROAD EQUIP CO
RRI	ROBINS RAILS INC
RRL	R ROBB LTD.
RRR	REYNOLDS RAILROAD PRODUCTS
RS	RIB OF STIEHL
RT	RALPH TROXEL
RTR	RTR INDUSTRIES
S	E SUYDAM & COMPANY
S .	SUYDAM
S&P	S&P DISTRIBUTORS
SAK	SAKURA-TAKENO
SAM	SAMHONGSA COMPANY LIMITED
SAT	SATO MODELS
SB	STROMBECK-BECKER MFG CO
SC	SUNCOAST MODELS
SCC	SCALE CRAFT ENGINEERING CO.
SCK	STAR CONTINENTAL KIT (MODELS)
SCMO	SCALE MODELS
SCP	SCENERY PRODUCTS
SCSM	SCOTIA SCALE MODELS
SD	SHERMAN DANCE
SE	SEIKO MODELS
SED	S.E. DANCE
SEL	SELLEY INC
SEN	SUMMIT ENGINEERING
SGP	SLIM GAUGE PRODUCTIONS
SH	STAR HOBBY MODELS
SHS	SYCAMORE HOLLOW STATION
SIM	SIMPSON PRODUCT COMPANY
SISC	SIMMONS SCALE MODELS INC
SISP	SIERRA SOUTHERN PRODUCTS
SJE	SAN JUAN ENGINEERING
SKI	S.K. INTERNATIONAL
SL	STAR LINE MODELS
SLM	STATE LINE MODELS
SLMO	SILVER LEDGE MODELS
SLR	SILVER LEAF RAPID TRANSIT MODELS
SLS	SCALE LOCOMOTIVE & SUPPLY
SM	SUNSHINE MODELS
SMI	SCALE MODELERS INDUSTRIES
SMO	STAR MODELS
SMP	SAMPSON MODEL COMPANY
SOHO	S SOHO & COMPANY
SP	STANDARD PRODUCTS
SPM	SAGINAW PATTERN MFG CO
SPPR	SOUTH PARK PRODUCTIONS
SQ	SUPERQUICK
SR	SANDY RIVER CAR SHOPS
SRA	SCALE-RAIL MINIATURES
SRE	SCALE RAILWAY EQUIPMENT COMPANY
SRM	STATE RAILROAD MODELS
SS	SILVER STREAK
SSD	SCALE SCENICS DIVISION
SSHK	SMOKE STACK HOBBY KITS CO
SSL	SCALE STRUCTURES LIMITED
SSL	SS LIMITED
SSM	SUPER SCALE MODEL CORP.
SSMO	SEQUOIA SCALE MODELS
SSP	SMALL SCALE PRODUCTS
ST	STERLING MODELS
STC	STRUCTURE COMPANY, THE
STEW	STEWART HOBBIES INC
STS	STANDARD SCALE MODELS
STST	STATE STREET MODELS
SU	SCENERY UNLIMITED
SUM	SUPERIOR MODELS
SUN	SUNSET MODELS
SUP	SUGAR PINE MODELS
SV	SMOKEY VALLEY RAILROAD
T	TYCO INDUSTRIES
TAK	IMP/TAKARA
TAK	TAKARA/IMP
TBE	TRUXEL BROS ENTERPRISES
TC	TRAIN CRAFT PRODUCTS
TCM	TOWN CRAFTS MODELS
TEN	TENSHODO MODEL COMPANY
TH	THOMAS INDUSTRIES
THH	TOY & HOBBY HOUSE
THM	THRALL MFG CO
TI	TRAINS, INC.
TIM	TIMBERLINE MODELS
TK	TK MODELS
TM	TRAIN MINIATURES
TMC	TRAIN MINIATURE OF CALIF
TMI	TRAIN MINIATURE OF ILLINOIS
TMK	TETSUDO MOKEISHA
TMO	TRAIN MODELS
TOBY	TOBY MODEL COMPANY LIMITED
TOHO	TOHO MODELS
TOM	TOMALCO
TOMH	TOMHAR MFG CO
TP	TAURUS PRODUCTS
TPPR	TP PRODUCTS
TR	TROLLER
TRI	TRACKSIDE INDUSTRIES
TRIX	TRIX
TRM	TRACTION MODELS
TRS	TRAINSTUFF
TS	TSUBOMI
TSM	TRU-SCALE MODELS
TVM	TIGER VALLEY MODELS
TY	THOMAS A YORKE ENTERPRISES
U	ULRICH
U	J.C. ULRICH COMPANY INC.
U .	CJ ULRICH
UMP	UNIVERSAL MODEL PRODUCTS
UN	ATLAS INDUSTRIES INC
US	ULTRA SCALE
USAI	US AIRFIX
USH	US HOBBIES
USM	UTAH SCALE MODEL COMPANY
V	VARNEY
VAL	VALLAM ASSOCIATES
VAN	VAN HOBBIES
VCM	VALLEY CAR WORKS
VCM	VCM
VI	VIRDEN
VL	V LINE LOCOMOTIVES INC
VM	MAINLINE VARNEY
VM	VARNEY MAINLINE
VOL	VOLLMER
VW	VALLEY WORKS
W	WINSTON MINIATURE ENGINEERING CO
W&T	W&T MODELS
WAL	WALTERS
WASM	WALLACE SCALE MODLES
WB	WILLIAM BROTHERS
WCS	WISONSIN CENTRAL SUPPLY
WD	WESTERFIELD
WE	WRIGHT ENTERPRISES
WEC	WESTMORELAND CAR SUPPLY
WEST	WESTWOOD
WFM	WAYFREIGHT MODELS
WGM	WHITE GROUND MODEL WORKS
WIK	WIKING
WM	WESTERN MODELS
WMC	WESTCHESTER MODEL CO
WMS	WALKER MODEL SERVICE
WO	WOODSON
WO	HL WOODSON
WPM	WENTZCO PRECISION MODELS
WRB	WR BROWN CORP
WRL	WILLIAMS REPRODUCTIONS LTD
WS	WOODLAND SCENICS
WSM	WESTSIDE MODEL COMPANY
WSP	WS PARKS
WSP	WALTER S PARKS
WSY	WALTER SYRETT
WVL	WABASH VALLEY LINE
WW	WHEEL WORKS
YE	YE OLD HUFF 'N PUFF
YM	YANK MODEL RESEARCH INC
ZUHR	ZUHR
ZUHR	HENRY ZUHR INC

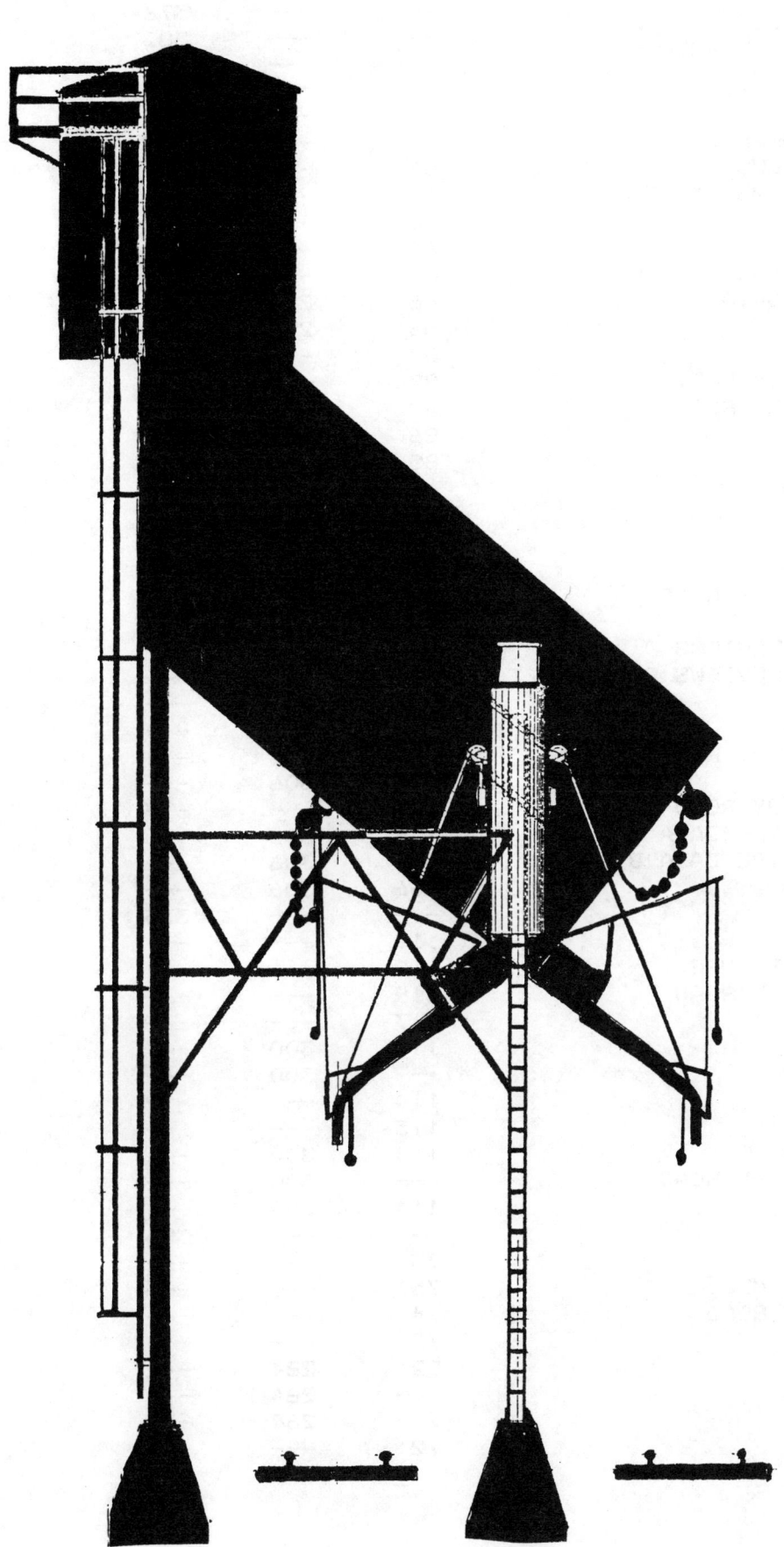

385

CATEGORY INDEX	1ST SEC MR	2ND SEC T	3RD SEC ADM
ABBREVIATION-BUILDER	---	---	376
ABBREVIATION-MANUFACTURER	---	---	382
ABBREVIATION-ROADNAME	---	---	362
APPENDIX A - ROADNAMES	---	---	350
APPENDIX B - BUILDERS	---	---	374
APPENDIX C - MANUFACTURERS	---	---	378
BAGGAGE CAR MODEL REVIEWS	66	---	---
BAGGAGE CAR MODEL REVIEWS BY MFG.	66	---	---
BAGGAGE CAR MODELS	66	---	---
BAGGAGE CAR PLANS	66	---	---
BAGGAGE CAR PLANS BY ROAD	66	---	---
BAGGAGE CAR PROTOTYPE DATA	66	284	---
BAGGAGE CARS	66	284	---
BOX CAR MODEL REVIEWS	87	---	---
BOX CAR MODEL REVIEWS BY MFG.	89	---	---
BOX CAR MODEL REVIEWS BY ROAD	89	---	---
BOX CAR MODELS	86	---	---
BOX CAR PHOTOS	85	294	---
BOX CAR PHOTOS BY ROAD	---	294	---
BOX CAR PLANS	84	---	---
BOX CAR PLANS BY ROAD	85	---	---
BOX CAR PROTOTYPE DATA	84	294	---
BOX CAR PROTOTYPE DATA BY ROAD	84	294	---
BOX CARS	84	294	---
BRIDGE & TUNNEL MODEL REVIEWS	138	---	---
BRIDGE & TUNNEL MODEL REVIEWS BY MFG	139	---	---
BRIDGE & TUNNEL MODELS	137	---	---
BRIDGE & TUNNEL PHOTOS	137	306	---
BRIDGE & TUNNEL PHOTOS BY ROAD	---	306	---
BRIDGE & TUNNEL PLANS	136	306	---
BRIDGE & TUNNEL PLANS BY ROAD	137	---	---
BRIDGE & TUNNEL PROTOTYPE DATA	136	306	---
BRIDGE & TUNNEL PROTOTYPE DATA BY ROAD	---	306	---
BRIDGES & TUNNELS	136	306	---
BUILDER-ABBREVIATION	---	---	375
CABOOSE MODEL REVIEWS	118	---	---
CABOOSE MODEL REVIEWS BY MFG.	119	---	---
CABOOSE MODEL REVIEWS BY ROAD	119	---	---
CABOOSE MODELS	117	---	---
CABOOSE PHOTOS	116	300	---
CABOOSE PHOTOS BY ROAD	---	300	---
CABOOSE PLANS	114	---	---
CABOOSE PLANS BY ROAD	115	---	---
CABOOSE PROTOTYPE DATA	114	300	---
CABOOSE PROTOTYPE DATA BY ROAD	---	300	---
CABOOSES	114	300	---
CATEGORY INDEX	---	---	386
COACH MODEL REVIEWS	73	---	---
COACH MODEL REVIEWS BY MFG.	75	---	---
COACH MODEL REVIEWS BY ROAD	74	---	---
COACH MODELS	73	---	---
COACH PHOTOS	72	284	---
COACH PHOTOS BY ROAD	---	284	---
COACH PLANS	71	284	---
COACH PLANS BY ROAD	72	---	---

CATEGORY INDEX	1ST SEC MR	2ND SEC T	3RD SEC ADM
COACH PROTOTYPE DATA	71	284	---
COACH PROTOTYPE DATA BY ROAD	---	284	---
COACHES	71	284	---
COMBINE MODEL REVIEWS	68	---	---
COMBINE MODEL REVIEWS BY MFG.	68	---	---
COMBINE MODELS	68	---	---
COMBINE PHOTOS	67	---	---
COMBINE PLANS	67	---	---
COMBINE PLANS BY ROAD	67	---	---
COMBINE PROTOTYPE DATA	67	---	---
COMBINES	67	---	---
COMMERCIAL BUILDING MODEL REV BY MFG.	148	---	---
COMMERCIAL BUILDING MODEL REVIEWS	145	---	---
COMMERCIAL BUILDING MODELS	143	---	---
COMMERCIAL BUILDING PHOTOS	142	306	---
COMMERCIAL BUILDING PLANS	141	---	---
COMMERCIAL BUILDING PLANS BY ROAD	142	---	---
COMMERCIAL BUILDING PROTOTYPE DATA	140	---	---
COMMERCIAL STRUCTURES	140	306	---
COMPUTERS	201	---	---
DEPOT MODEL REVIEWS	154	---	---
DEPOT MODEL REVIEWS BY MFG.	154	---	---
DEPOT MODELS	153	---	---
DEPOT PHOTOS	---	307	---
DEPOT PHOTOS BY ROAD	---	307	---
DEPOT PLANS	151	307	---
DEPOT PLANS BY ROAD	152	---	---
DEPOT PROTOTYPE DATA	150	307	---
DEPOT PROTOTYPE DATA BY ROAD	---	307	---
DEPOTS	150	307	---
DETAILED CONSIST	---	---	4
DIESEL LOCO MODEL REVIEWS BY MFG.	56	---	---
DIESEL LOCO MODEL REVIEWS BY ROAD	58	---	---
DIESEL LOCO PROTOTYPE DATA BY ROAD	47	268	---
DIESEL LOCOMOTIVE MODEL REVIEWS	54	---	---
DIESEL LOCOMOTIVE MODELS	51	---	---
DIESEL LOCOMOTIVE PHOTOS	48	269	---
DIESEL LOCOMOTIVE PHOTOS BY ROAD	---	274	---
DIESEL LOCOMOTIVE PLANS	48	278	---
DIESEL LOCOMOTIVE PLANS BY ROAD	49	278	---
DIESEL LOCOMOTIVE PROTOTYPE DATA	46	266	---
DIESEL LOCOMOTIVES	46	266	---
DINER MODEL REVIEWS	69	---	---
DINER MODEL REVIEWS BY MFG.	69	---	---
DINER MODELS	69	---	---
DINER PHOTOS	---	284	---
DINER PHOTOS BY ROAD	---	284	---
DINER PLANS	69	---	---
DINER PLANS BY ROAD	69	---	---
DINER PROTOTYPE DATA	69	284	---
DINER RECIPES	---	284	---
DINERS	69	284	---
DISPATCHERS REPORT	---	---	394
DOME CAR MODEL REVIEWS	76	---	---
DOME CAR MODEL REVIEWS BY MFG.	76	---	---

CATEGORY INDEX	1ST SEC MR	2ND SEC T	3RD SEC ADM
DOME CAR MODELS	76	---	---
DOME CAR PHOTOS	---	285	---
DOME CAR PHOTOS BY ROAD	---	285	---
DOME CAR PLANS	75	---	---
DOME CAR PLANS BY ROAD	75	---	---
DOME CAR PROTOTYPE DATA	75	285	---
DOME CAR PROTOTYPE DATA BY ROAD	---	285	---
DOME CARS	75	285	---
ELEC LOCO MODEL REVIEWS BY MFG.	61	---	---
ELEC LOCO MODEL REVIEWS BY ROAD	61	---	---
ELEC LOCO PROTOTYPE DATA BY ROAD	58	279	---
ELECTRIC LOCOMOTIVE MODEL REVIEWS	60	---	---
ELECTRIC LOCOMOTIVE MODELS	60	---	---
ELECTRIC LOCOMOTIVE PHOTOS	59	280	---
ELECTRIC LOCOMOTIVE PHOTOS BY ROAD	---	280	---
ELECTRIC LOCOMOTIVE PLANS	59	279	---
ELECTRIC LOCOMOTIVE PLANS BY ROAD	59	---	---
ELECTRIC LOCOMOTIVE PROTOTYPE DATA	58	278	---
ELECTRIC LOCOMOTIVES	58	278	---
ELECTRICAL & ELECTRONICS	200	---	---
EXPRESS CAR MODEL REVIEWS	69	---	---
EXPRESS CAR MODEL REVIEWS BY MFG.	69	---	---
EXPRESS CAR MODELS	68	---	---
EXPRESS CAR PLANS	68	---	---
EXPRESS CAR PLANS BY ROAD	68	---	---
EXPRESS CAR PROTOTYPE DATA	---	284	---
EXPRESS CARS	68	284	---
FLAT CAR MODEL REVIEWS	93	---	---
FLAT CAR MODEL REVIEWS BY MFG.	94	---	---
FLAT CAR MODEL REVIEWS BY ROAD	93	---	---
FLAT CAR MODELS	92	---	---
FLAT CAR PHOTOS	---	295	---
FLAT CAR PHOTOS BY ROAD	---	295	---
FLAT CAR PLANS	91	295	---
FLAT CAR PLANS BY ROAD	92	---	---
FLAT CAR PROTOTYPE DATA	91	294	---
FLAT CAR PROTOTYPE DATA BY ROAD	91	---	---
FLAT CARS	91	294	---
FREIGHT CARS	82	292	---
FREIGHT ORDERS	---	397	399
GENERAL RAILROADING	231	338	---
GENERAL ELECTRONICS	201	---	---
GENERAL FREIGHT CARS	109	297	---
GENERAL FREIGHT MODEL REVIEWS	110	---	---
GENERAL FREIGHT MODEL REVIEWS BY MFG.	111	---	---
GENERAL FREIGHT MODELS	110	---	---
GENERAL FREIGHT PLANS	109	---	---
GENERAL FREIGHT PROTOTYPE DATA	109	297	---
GENERAL FRT PROTOTYPE DATA BY ROAD	---	297	---
GENERAL LOCO PROTOTYPE DATA BY ROAD	---	281	---
GENERAL LOCOMOTIVE MODEL REVIEWS	63	---	---
GENERAL LOCOMOTIVE MODELING	62	---	---
GENERAL LOCOMOTIVE PROTOTYPE DATA	62	281	---
GENERAL LOCOMOTIVES	62	281	---
GENERAL PASS CAR MODEL REVIEWS BY MFG.	80	---	---

CATEGORY INDEX	1ST SEC MR	2ND SEC T	3RD SEC ADM
GENERAL PASS CAR PROTOTYPE DATA BY ROAD	---	289	---
GENERAL PASSENGER CAR MODEL REVIEWS	80	---	---
GENERAL PASSENGER CAR MODELS	79	---	---
GENERAL PASSENGER CAR PHOTOS	78	287	---
GENERAL PASSENGER CAR PHOTOS BY ROAD	---	287	---
GENERAL PASSENGER CAR PLANS	78	287	---
GENERAL PASSENGER CAR PLANS BY ROAD	78	---	---
GENERAL PASSENGER CAR PROTOTYPE DATA	78	287	---
GENERAL PASSENGER CARS	78	287	---
GENERAL RAILROADING	230	336	---
GENERAL RAILROADING FICTION	---	338	---
GENERAL RAILROADING NON-FICTION	---	337	---
GENERAL STRUCTURE MODEL REV BY MFG.	170	---	---
GENERAL STRUCTURE MODEL REVIEWS	170	---	---
GENERAL STRUCTURE MODELS	169	---	---
GENERAL STRUCTURE PLANS	168	---	---
GENERAL STRUCTURE PLANS BY ROAD	168	---	---
GENERAL STRUCTURE PROTOTYPE DATA	168	---	---
GENERAL STRUCTURES	168	---	---
GONDOLA MODEL REVIEWS	96	---	---
GONDOLA MODEL REVIEWS BY MFG.	97	---	---
GONDOLA MODEL REVIEWS BY ROAD	97	---	---
GONDOLA MODELS	96	---	---
GONDOLA PLANS	95	---	---
GONDOLA PLANS BY ROAD	95	---	---
GONDOLA PROTOTYPE DATA	94	295	---
GONDOLA PROTOTYPE DATA BY ROAD	94	295	---
GONDOLAS	94	295	---
HOPPER MODEL REVIEWS	101	---	---
HOPPER MODEL REVIEWS BY MFG.	102	---	---
HOPPER MODEL REVIEWS BY ROAD	101	---	---
HOPPER MODELS	100	---	---
HOPPER PHOTOS	99	295	---
HOPPER PHOTOS BY ROAD	---	296	---
HOPPER PLANS	98	---	---
HOPPER PLANS BY ROAD	99	---	---
HOPPER PROTOTYPE DATA	98	295	---
HOPPER PROTOTYPE DATA BY ROAD	98	295	---
HOPPERS	98	295	---
LAYOUT BUILDING	183	---	---
LAYOUT DESIGN	181	---	---
LAYOUT OPERATION	190	---	---
LAYOUT PLANS	182	---	---
LAYOUT VISITS	192	---	---
LOCOMOTIVES	16	242	---
MANUFACTURER-ABBREVIATION	---	---	379
MATERIALS	210	---	---
MODEL LAYOUTS	180	---	---
MODEL TRACKWORK	185	---	---
MODELING BOOKS	227	---	---
MODELING TECHNIQUES	213	---	---
MOW EQUIPMENT	120	300	---
MOW MODEL REVIEWS	122	---	---
MOW MODEL REVIEWS BY MFG.	123	---	---
MOW MODEL REVIEWS BY ROAD	123	---	---

CATEGORY INDEX	1ST SEC MR	2ND SEC T	3RD SEC ADM
MOW MODELS	121	---	---
MOW PHOTOS	121	301	---
MOW PHOTOS BY ROAD	---	301	---
MOW PLANS	120	---	---
MOW PLANS BY ROAD	121	---	---
MOW PROTOTYPE DATA	120	300	---
MOW PROTOTYPE DATA BY ROAD	---	300	---
NON-REVENUE EQUIPMENT	112	298	---
OBSERVATION CAR MODEL REVIEWS	76	---	---
OBSERVATION CAR MODEL REVIEWS BY MFG.	76	---	---
OBSERVATION CAR MODELS	76	---	---
OBSERVATION CAR PHOTOS	---	285	---
OBSERVATION CAR PHOTOS BY ROAD	---	286	---
OBSERVATION CAR PLANS	76	---	---
OBSERVATION CAR PLANS BY ROAD	76	---	---
OBSERVATION CAR PROTOTYPE DATA	76	285	---
OBSERVATION CARS	76	285	---
OPERATING INSTRUCTION UBRI-100	---	---	12
PAINTING TECHNIQUES	215	---	---
PASSENGER EQUIPMENT	64	282	---
PHOTOGRAPHY	216	311	---
PROTOTYPE BOOKS	221	329	---
PROTOTYPE EXAMPLES	176	311	---
PROTOTYPE MODELING IDEAS	174	310	---
PROTOTYPE SPEED	---	312	---
PROTOTYPE TRACKWORK	175	311	---
RAIL LITERATURE REVIEWS	220	328	---
RAIL ROSTERS	218	324	---
RAILCAR MODEL REVIEWS	77	---	---
RAILCAR MODEL REVIEWS BY MFG.	77	---	---
RAILCAR MODELS	77	---	---
RAILCAR PHOTOS	77	286	---
RAILCAR PHOTOS BY ROAD	---	287	---
RAILCAR PLANS	77	286	---
RAILCAR PLANS BY ROAD	77	---	---
RAILCAR PROTOTYPE DATA	77	286	---
RAILCAR PROTOTYPE DATA BY ROAD	---	286	---
RAILCARS	77	286	---
RAILROAD HISTORIES	178	314	---
RAILROAD STRUCTURE MODEL REV BY MFG.	164	---	---
RAILROAD STRUCTURE MODEL REV BY ROAD	165	---	---
RAILROAD STRUCTURE MODEL REVIEWS	162	---	---
RAILROAD STRUCTURE MODELS	159	---	---
RAILROAD STRUCTURE PHOTOS	---	308	---
RAILROAD STRUCTURE PHOTOS BY ROAD	---	308	---
RAILROAD STRUCTURE PLANS	156	---	---
RAILROAD STRUCTURE PLANS BY ROAD	158	---	---
RAILROAD STRUCTURE PROTOTYPE DATA	155	307	---
RAILROAD STRUCTURE PROTOTYPE DATA BY RD	---	308	---
RAILROAD STRUCTURES	155	307	---
RAILROADS YOU CAN MODEL	175	---	---
REFRIGERATOR CAR MODEL REVIEWS	104	---	---
REFRIGERATOR CAR MODELS	103	---	---
REFRIGERATOR CAR PHOTOS	103	296	---
REFRIGERATOR CAR PLANS	103	---	---

CATEGORY INDEX	1ST SEC MR	2ND SEC T	3RD SEC ADM
REFRIGERATOR CAR PROTOTYPE DATA	102	296	---
REFRIGERATOR CARS	102	296	---
REFRIGERATOR MODEL REVIEWS BY MFG.	105	---	---
REFRIGERATOR MODEL REVIEWS BY ROAD	104	---	---
REFRIGERATOR PLANS BY ROAD	103	---	---
REFRIGERATOR PROTOTYPE DATA BY ROAD	102	---	---
ROADNAME-ABBREVIATION	---	---	351
RPO CARS	70	284	---
RPO MODEL REVIEWS	70	---	---
RPO MODEL REVIEWS BY MFG.	70	---	---
RPO MODELS	70	---	---
RPO PHOTOS	---	284	---
RPO PLANS	70	---	---
RPO PLANS BY ROAD	70	---	---
RPO PROTOTYPE DATA	70	284	---
SCENERY	188	---	---
SIGNAL MODEL REVIEWS	167	---	---
SIGNAL MODEL REVIEWS BY MFG.	168	---	---
SIGNAL MODELS	167	---	---
SIGNAL PHOTOS	166	308	---
SIGNAL PHOTOS BY ROAD	---	308	---
SIGNAL PLANS	166	---	---
SIGNAL PLANS BY ROAD	166	---	---
SIGNAL PROTOTYPE DATA	166	308	---
SIGNAL PROTOTYPE DATA BY ROAD	---	308	---
SIGNALS	166	308	---
SLEEPER MODEL REVIEWS	71	---	---
SLEEPER MODEL REVIEWS BY MFG.	71	---	---
SLEEPER MODELS	71	---	---
SLEEPER PHOTOS	---	285	---
SLEEPER PHOTOS BY ROAD	---	285	---
SLEEPER PLANS	70	---	---
SLEEPER PLANS BY ROAD	70	---	---
SLEEPER PROTOTYPE DATA	70	285	---
SLEEPER PROTOTYPE DATA BY ROAD	---	285	---
SLEEPERS	70	285	---
SPECIAL TRAINS	---	312	---
STEAM LOCO MODEL REVIEWS BY MFG.	37	---	---
STEAM LOCO MODEL REVIEWS BY ROAD	41	---	---
STEAM LOCO PROTOTYPE DATA BY ROAD	20	250	---
STEAM LOCOMOTIVE MODEL REVIEWS	34	---	---
STEAM LOCOMOTIVE MODELS	28	---	---
STEAM LOCOMOTIVE PHOTOS	28	256	---
STEAM LOCOMOTIVE PHOTOS BY ROAD	---	261	---
STEAM LOCOMOTIVE PLANS	21	255	---
STEAM LOCOMOTIVE PLANS BY ROAD	24	255	---
STEAM LOCOMOTIVE PROTOTYPE DATA	18	244	---
STEAM LOCOMOTIVES	18	244	---
STOCK CAR MODEL REVIEWS	106	---	---
STOCK CAR MODEL REVIEWS BY MFG.	106	---	---
STOCK CAR MODEL REVIEWS BY ROAD	106	---	---
STOCK CAR MODELS	106	---	---
STOCK CAR PHOTOS	106	296	---
STOCK CAR PLANS	105	---	---
STOCK CAR PLANS BY ROAD	106	---	---

CATEGORY INDEX	1ST SEC MR	2ND SEC T	3RD SEC ADM
STOCK CAR PROTOTYPE DATA	105	---	---
STOCK CARS	105	296	---
STRUCTURES & SIGNALS	134	304	---
TANK CAR MODEL REVIEWS	108	---	---
TANK CAR MODEL REVIEWS BY MFG.	109	---	---
TANK CAR MODEL REVIEWS BY ROAD	108	---	---
TANK CAR MODELS	107	---	---
TANK CAR PHOTOS	107	296	---
TANK CAR PLANS	107	---	---
TANK CAR PLANS BY ROAD	107	---	---
TANK CAR PROTOTYPE DATA	107	296	---
TANK CAR PROTOTYPE DATA BY ROAD	---	296	---
TANK CARS	107	296	---
TECHNIQUES	212	---	---
TENDER MODEL REVIEWS	44	---	---
TENDER MODELS	44	---	---
TENDER PHOTOS	44	266	---
TENDER PHOTOS BY ROAD	---	266	---
TENDER PLANS	44	266	---
TENDER PLANS BY ROAD	44	---	---
TENDER PROTOTYPE DATA	44	266	---
TENDER PROTOTYPE DATA BY ROAD	---	266	---
TENDERS	44	266	---
THE OFFICIALS	---	---	396
THE SOURCE (HISTORY)	14	240	---
TOOLS	209	---	---
TOOLS & MATERIALS	208	---	---
TOY & TINPLATE TRAINS	218	---	---
TRACTION	126	302	---
TRACTION IN GENERAL	---	303	---
TRACTION MODEL REVIEWS	131	---	---
TRACTION MODEL REVIEWS BY MFG.	133	---	---
TRACTION MODEL REVIEWS BY ROAD	132	---	---
TRACTION MODELS	130	---	---
TRACTION PHOTOS	---	303	---
TRACTION PHOTOS BY ROAD	---	303	---
TRACTION PLANS	128	---	---
TRACTION PLANS BY ROAD	129	---	---
TRACTION PROTOTYPE DATA	128	303	---
TRACTION PROTOTYPE DATA BY ROAD	---	303	---
VEHICLE MODEL REVIEWS	173	---	---
VEHICLE MODELS	173	---	---
VEHICLE PHOTOS	---	311	---
VEHICLE PLANS	173	---	---
VEHICLES	172	---	---
VIDEOS	229	---	---
WEATHERING TECHNIQUES	216	---	---
WRECKS	---	311	---

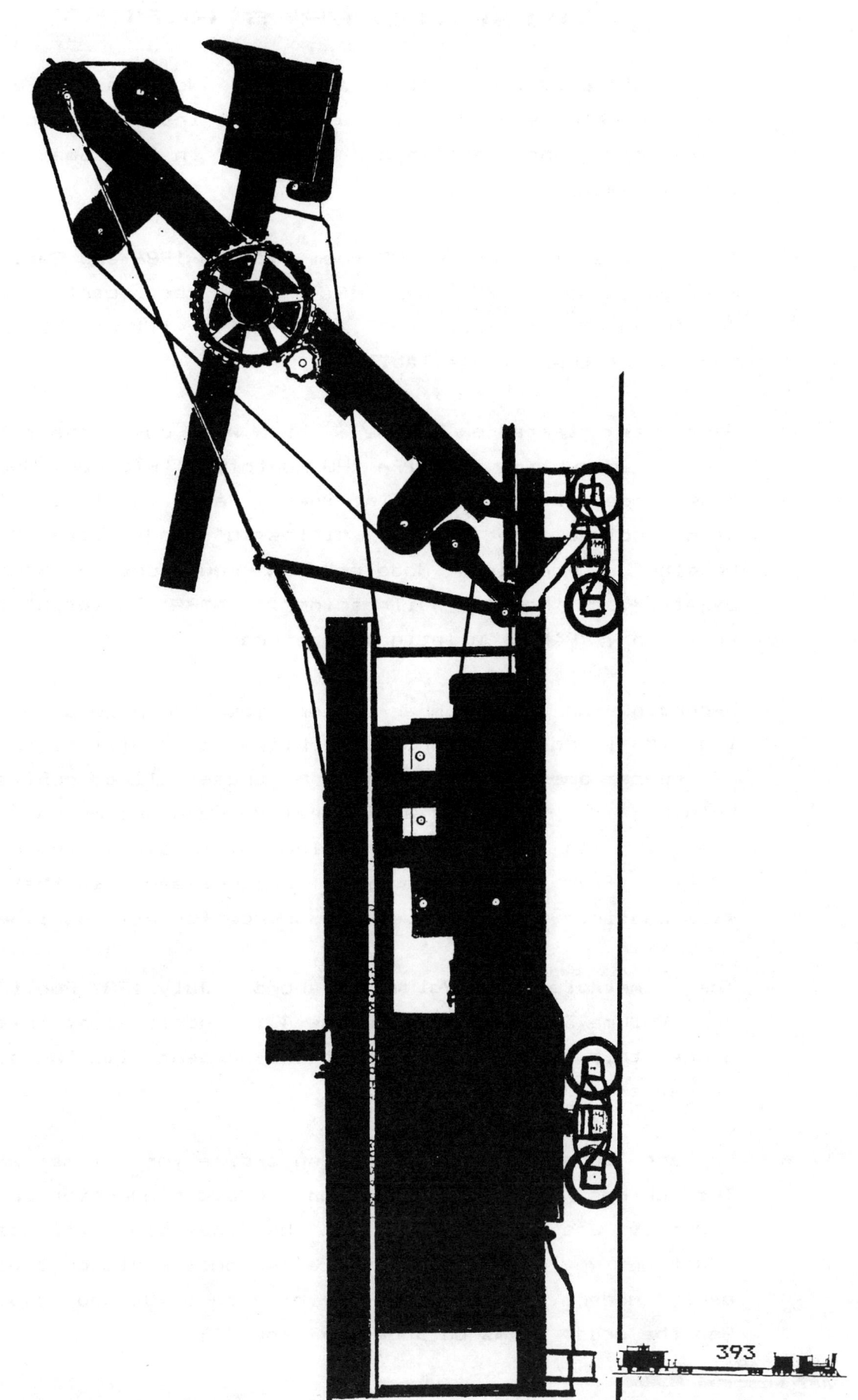

393

DISPATCHER'S REPORT

This volume is the first of a series. Work is well underway for the release of Volume 2 which will index "Railroad Model Craftsman" and "Railfan and Railroad" in the same format as this volume.

The volume will cover RMC from 1933 to 1986 and Railfan and Railroad from 1929 to 1986. The very early years of "Railroad Man's Magazine" (1900-1919) will not be included because of their unavailability.

Work has started on Volume 3 which will cover the titles no longer in publication like "HO Monthly", "Railroad Modeler", "The Model Builder", "Finelines", and the like. It will also include the smaller titles of today like "Mainline Modeler", "Prototype Modeler", "Narrow Gauge and Short Line Gazette", "Model Railroading", "NMRA Bulletin", "NRHS Bulletin", "R&LHS Bulletin", etcetera.

Depending on the number of entries, if space permits, the individual road historical publications will be included. If space does not permit, these will be published in Volume 4. Ideas for additional volumes are on the drawing boards. In addition each volume will release their second edition five years after its first release. In that way we will continue to have a current source for all magazines.

The timetable for Volume 2 shows a July 1987 Publication; for Volume 3 July 1988. Volume 4 is undefined at this time. Since this is an avocation at the present time the schedule is rather sluggish.

We are accepting pre-publishing orders for Volumes 2 and 3. The prices set are based on todays production costs and probably are less than what the final book will cost. In addition we will grant you a two dollar discount on these early orders. You will save a sure 10% and maybe more! See the order forms on pages 397 and 399.

THE OFFICIALS

This book is for Railroaders by Railroaders. Our staff consists of one and a half Railnuts like yourselfs. Earl Stephans provides the technical wisdom for categorizing. Karen Stephans through this project has learned the difference between a locomotive and a caboose. She provides the largest share of data entry and the administrative aspects of the endeaver.

Earl's interest in trains goes back to 1948 when the excitement at the grade crossing was "Will it be a diesel?". At that time watching a fathers "HO" layout starting to take shape helped. Over the years family moves, college, gainful employment, family creation, etc. worked at setting the train interests back. It was strong enough that it continually came back.

Currently he is still arm-chairing his railroad as THE DIRECTORY effort has stopped the pike at the bench level. He continues to accumulate the rolling stock and all the other "good stuff" needed for the super road. It is a shame that mundane things like working for a living get in the way of important things like trains "research and development".

By educational discipline Earl holds degrees in chemistry and chemical-physics. This makes him an engineer by definition. He works for a computer manufacturer and classifies himself as a "General Engineer" rather than a "Chemical Engineer". Twelve years as a manager as well as many diverse assignments have developed the attributes need to undertake this directory. The basic engineering concepts of his vocation plus the acquisition of a personal computer and the understanding and support of a new wife have made this directory possible.

Karen, an accountant, brings the business skills to the endeaver. She also developed an understanding to put up with wall to wall magazines and other railroad paraphernalia.

396

STEPHANS' RAILROAD DIRECTORY
ORDER FORM

	QTY	PRICE	
Directory Volume 1		X 19.95 +	
Directory Volume 2		X 19.95 +	
Directory Volume 3		X 19.95 +	
NYS Sales Tax		X 1.40 +	
Shipping & Handling VIA UPS (Insured)*		X 2.75 +	
	SUBTOTAL		
Pre-Publish Discount On Volumes 2 and 3		X 2.00 -	
	TOTAL ENCLOSED		

Please print your shipping address below. Remember we need a street adress for UPS Delivery.

NAME _____

ADDRESS _____

CITY _____

STATE _____ ZIP _____

* Shipping costs are our bugaboo. On multiple book orders excess shipping, if any, will be refunded with your order, so to save on shipping order 100 copies of each book!

Send your order today to:

Earl Stephans
Tioga Publications
101B N. Fenton Road
Chenango Forks, NY 13746

Quantity and Dealer discounts available. Send a Large Self-Addressed Stamped Envelope for details and terms.

STEPHANS' RAILROAD DIRECTORY
ORDER FORM

	QTY	PRICE	
Directory Volume 1		X 19.95 +	
Directory Volume 2		X 19.95 +	
Directory Volume 3		X 19.95 +	
NYS Sales Tax		X 1.40 +	
Shipping & Handling VIA UPS (Insured)*		X 2.75 +	
		SUBTOTAL	
Pre-Publish Discount On Volumes 2 and 3		X 2.00 −	
		TOTAL ENCLOSED	

Please print your shipping address below. Remember we need a street adress for UPS Delivery.

NAME _____

ADDRESS _____

CITY _____

STATE _____ ZIP _____

* Shipping costs are our bugaboo. On multiple book orders excess shipping, if any, will be refunded with your order, so to save on shipping order 100 copies of each book!

Send your order today to:

Earl Stephans
Tioga Publications
101B N. Fenton Road
Chenango Forks, NY 13746

Quantity and Dealer discounts available. Send a Large Self-Addressed Stamped Envelope for details and terms.

WE NEED YOUR HELP!!

The philosophy for the directory is that I must extract the article data directly from the source. As a result I need an example of every issue published for my review. I have most issues of most magazines but I am lacking a few. If you have any of the titles listed below for sale or if you would loan or rent me your personal issue you will be helping with future issues of the directory. Since the actual want list varies from week to week this list is by title only.

TITLES NEEDED
Send For Current List

Model Railroader	Jan 1937
RMC	1933 & 1934
Toy Trains	1954
PTJ	Prior to Jan 1979
Keystone	
Locomotive Quarterly	V5 #3 to Date
O&W Observer	
Slim Gauge News	Most
Short Line Railroader	(Youngs)
PC Railroading	
Rails Northeast	Pre 1977
Railroad	1906-1918, 1930
Traction & Models	1983 to Date
Traction Heritage	
Model Builder	
NRHS	Before 1962
R&LHS	Before #101
Western Railroader	Before #90
NYNH&H Shoreliner	
RR Enthusiast	
Other Historical Publications	

HAVE COMPLETE RUNS OF THE FOLLOWING:

Finelines	Railroad Modeler
Trains	HO Monthly
Mainline Modeling	X2200 South
Prototype Modeler	Railroading
SW Proto Modeler	Modeltec
S Proto Modeler	NMRA Bulletin
NW Proto Modeler	Lensman
Narrow Ga Gazette	The Short Line
Model Railroading	Pacific News